European Political Systems

EUROPEAN POLITICAL SYSTEMS

Edited by
Taylor Cole
DUKE UNIVERSITY

SECOND EDITION, REVISED

Alfred A. Knopf New York 1961

L. C. Catalog card number: 59–7366
© Alfred A. Knopf, Inc., 1959

THIS IS A BORZOI BOOK,
PUBLISHED BY ALFRED A. KNOPF, INC.

Published 1953. Reprinted once
Second Edition, Revised, Reset and Printed from New Plates, 1959
Reprinted 1961

Preface

Many significant political developments have been recorded in the six years that have elapsed since the original edition of *European Political Systems* was published in 1953. In Britain a national election was held in 1955 and a change in Conservative Prime Ministers occurred after the Suez crisis. The independent members of the "British" Commonwealth of Nations have grown in number, and its non-Christian and non-European elements have been augmented by the addition of Ghana and the Federation of Malaya. France has survived a steady succession of acute internal and external crises, which served to weaken her controls over the units composing the French Union. General de Gaulle, called to the prime ministership during one of these periods, succeeded in the fall of 1958 in securing the adoption of a new French constitution. The Fourth Republic thus gave way to the Fifth.

The Federal Republic in Western Germany re-elected a *Bundestag* in 1957 with a heavy majority supporting the "Old Man," Konrad Adenauer. His candidacy for the presidency of the Federal Republic in 1959 presages unpredictable changes in the future leadership. The problem of a united Germany continues to be a major, albeit a somewhat diminishing, concern of most Germans. It has become increasingly evident that "Bonn is not Weimar," to borrow from the title of a recent book. The national election of 1958 in Italy resulted in modest changes in the strength and alignments of the major parties in the two houses of the Italian parliament, and her governments thereafter have continued to find support in center coalitions in which the pendulum has moved first toward the left and then toward the right. Various provisions of the constitution of 1948, hitherto unused, have been implemented during the recent period.

Perhaps the most publicized changes have occurred in Soviet Russia since the death of Stalin in 1953. The rise of First Secretary Khrushchev to a position far above that of *"primus inter pares"* has been associated with an aggressive and highly flexible Soviet foreign policy. Internal political and economic reorganizations, affecting the power positions of the elite groups, have helped to add impetus to the speculation as to whether the future will see the emergence of a technocratic constitutionalism or a continuation of the essentials of Leninism-Stalinism. The satellite states in the Soviet orbit have been held in subjection by force of arms, as the events in Poland and Hungary have proved. In judging the present-day panorama it is obvious that the European political systems during the past six years have experienced rapid change and that the internal political developments cannot be isolated from the external ones.

The rapid development of thermonuclear weapons has added to the uncertainties of the future, and their wider availability in the years ahead may raise questions as to which European countries may be referred to as "major" ones. For the present, however, at least in terms of population and power potential, the European political systems of Soviet Russia, Great Britain, Western Germany, France, and Italy might be classed as the *major* European political systems. In any case, they have been so regarded in our selection.

Several changes have been made in this volume, as compared to the first edition. It will be noted that the order in which the countries are presented to the student differs from that in the earlier book. At that time the justification given for placing Soviet Russia and the satellite states first was that "in the short period of thirty-five years, Soviet Russia has emerged as one of the two major military powers of the world. She stands today as the chief example of a particular brand of totalitarianism and as the center of a new world empire. These facts, coupled with the inadequacy of the material available on Soviet Russia when considered *together* with her satellites, explain the focal position and attention given to the Soviet orbit in this volume." While attention to the Soviet orbit, in terms of available space, has not been reduced, it has been found desirable for teaching purposes to follow the more traditional arrangement of material and to introduce this volume with the section on "Great Britain and the Commonwealth." At the same time, the introductory chapters in this section have been largely rewritten and expanded in order to provide a more adequate discussion of the political process in Great Britain and the Commonwealth countries. New material in other sections of the present volume includes discussions of the constitution of the French Fifth Republic, the appraisal of Bonn's "First Decade," economic and social changes in Italy during the period from 1953–59, the analysis of Soviet internal reorganization and foreign policy, and recent developments that have taken place in the satellite states.

But, withal, the essential features and much of the basic material of the first edition have been incorporated in this volume. We have sought to prepare a textbook which would provide a historical setting and some examination of the "political culture and sub-cultures" of each political area, to borrow terms which have been popularized by Professor Gabriel Almond. Insights into the value systems of such political cultures may be found in the main writings in political theory, which provide us, not only with discussions of institutions, but also with certain of the criteria by which they have been evaluated. Accordingly, some attention has been devoted to the main currents in recent political thought of the countries under consideration. At the same time, the authors have sought to include the requisite amount of descriptive material on the existing political institutions and processes. This approach will also explain the emphasis placed upon political parties at the national level, and on the pressures and personalities which have influenced their role in the formulation of policy.

Such emphasis allows, within the limited space available, only a modest amount of attention to certain aspects of the governmental organization and administration, especially at the local governmental level.

Various classifications could be provided for the political systems discussed in this volume. However, we shall accept for our purposes the usual distinctions drawn between the democratic-constitutional political systems of Great Britain, France, Italy, and Western Germany, on the one hand, and the autocratic-totalitarian political systems of Nazi Germany, Soviet Russia, and the Soviet satellites, on the other hand. The major differences between the two types lie in the extent to which there exist recognizable and enforceable restraints on the exercise of arbitrary power and to which group competition for political control is unrestrained. Within the democratic-constitutional political systems further broad distinctions might be drawn between Great Britain, on the one side, and France, Italy, and Western Germany on the other. Britain possesses a more homogeneous and less fragmented political culture than the three continental states. One result is a higher degree of consensus, of fundamental agreement upon both means and ends, and of stability in Britain than in the continental countries. Indeed, one concern of the contributors to this volume has been to appraise the degree to which political consensus exists in the three continental countries of Western Europe and to which it finds reflection in the stability of their respective governments.

The traditional country-by-country approach, followed in *European Political Systems* and continued in this revision, has its merits in a textbook intended for undergraduates. Not the least of these is that, because every political system has its own unique features, there are advantages in studying it in the light of its own distinctive historical setting. This approach also provides an introduction either for more intensive work on one political system or for more serious efforts to examine the uniformities and differences among aspects of several political systems. However, while providing an essential background for the beginning student, this approach may have some limitations—particularly if it encourages "description for its own sake" or the belief that the study of "foreign" political systems necessarily implies comparison. We may, consequently, hope that this volume will encourage a continuing interest in the comparison of political systems, not only European but non-Western as well, and that it will promote an appreciation of the purposes of comparison, one of which is to probe for some greater degree of predictability in the future. In short, this volume is intended solely as an introductory study of European political systems, as its title indicates.

For reasons of space it was decided to omit an appendix for documents which may be found readily in source books or similar compilations. A selected bibliography appended at the end of each section has been included as of considerable usefulness to the student. Also, the use of references to main source materials in footnotes can be helpful in guiding the student in further reading and in providing him with some basis for evaluating the viewpoints of the authors. A few maps and charts have been selected, with an eye to their timeliness and non-availability in other convenient sources.

Most of the contributors to this volume have been recently engaged in field work abroad and have written extensively on the respective political systems with which they deal. As a consequence, each one of them is fully aware of the difficulties and limitations in the collection and presentation of his material, especially for the countries back of the Iron Curtain. Although differences in point of view are to be anticipated, and indeed have been encouraged, there will be found evidences of general agreement by the authors on their "inarticulate major premises."

Following is a list of the contributors to this second edition of *European Political Systems,* and a recent publication by each: Cyril E. Black, professor of history at Princeton University, and editor and co-author of *Rewriting Russian History* (1956); Alexander Brady, professor of political economy at the University of Toronto, and author of *Democracy in the Dominions* (3rd ed., 1958); Randolph L. Braham, a member of the Department of Social Science at Fairleigh Dickinson University, and co-author of *The People's Democracies of Eastern Europe* (1958); David R. Deener, professor of political science at Tulane University, and author of *United States Attorneys General and International Law* (1957); Gerard J. Mangone, professor of political science at the Maxwell Graduate School, Syracuse University, and author of *Short History of International Organization* (1954); Sigmund Neumann, professor of political science at Wesleyan University, and editor and co-author of *Modern Political Parties* (1956); Julian Towster, professor of political science at the University of California (Berkeley), and author of *Political Power in the U.S.S.R., 1917–1947* (1948); and Gordon Wright, professor of history at Stanford University, and author of *The Reshaping of French Democracy* (1948).

Taylor Cole

DUKE UNIVERSITY

Contents

I GREAT BRITAIN AND THE COMMONWEALTH, *by Taylor Cole, David R. Deener, and Alexander Brady*

1	BRITISH CONSTITUTIONALISM	3
2	POLITICAL PARTIES	29
3	PARLIAMENT	56
4	THE EXECUTIVE	83
5	COURTS AND LOCAL AUTHORITIES	106
6	BRITAIN AND THE WELFARE STATE	125
7	THE BRITISH COMMONWEALTH	151
	SELECTED BIBLIOGRAPHY	180

II FRANCE, *by Gordon Wright*

8	THE HERITAGE OF CONTEMPORARY FRANCE	189
9	THE POLITICAL STRUCTURE OF THE FOURTH REPUBLIC	213
10	THE SUBSTRUCTURE OF FRENCH POLITICS	252
11	FROM FOURTH TO FIFTH REPUBLIC	293
12	THE INTERNATIONAL POSITION OF FRANCE	307
	SELECTED BIBLIOGRAPHY	314

III GERMANY, *by Sigmund Neumann*

13	INTRODUCING A PEOPLE OF TENSIONS	323
14	THE BISMARCKIAN EMPIRE	341
15	THE WEIMAR REPUBLIC	357
16	THE THIRD REICH	375
17	BASES OF THE SECOND REPUBLIC	395
18	BONN: THE FIRST DECADE	416
	SELECTED BIBLIOGRAPHY	442

IV ITALY, *by Gerard J. Mangone*
   19 THE ITALIAN HERITAGE   455
   20 ITALIAN LIFE: CRUCIBLE OF POLITICS   482
   21 THE GOVERNMENT OF THE ITALIAN REPUBLIC 504
   22 ITALY ON THE INTERNATIONAL HORIZON 528
   SELECTED BIBLIOGRAPHY   533

V THE SOVIET ORBIT: UNION OF SOVIET SOCIALIST RE-
  PUBLICS, *by Julian Towster*
   23 THE CONDITIONING FACTORS   541
   24 THE SOCIAL ORDER   566
   25 THE POLITICAL STRUCTURE: THE COMMUNIST
      PARTY   606
   26 THE POLITICAL STRUCTURE: THE SOVIET
      GOVERNMENT   632
   27 ORGANS OF ENFORCEMENT AND DEFENSE 662
   28 THE PLANNED ECONOMY   676
   29 SOVIET FOREIGN POLICY   693
   SELECTED BIBLIOGRAPHY   722

VI THE SOVIET ORBIT: THE PEOPLE'S DEMOCRACIES OF
  EASTERN EUROPE, *by C. E. Black and R. L. Braham*
   30 STRUCTURE OF EASTERN EUROPEAN POLITICS 741
   31 POLITICAL PROGRAMS AND PARTIES   753
   32 COMMUNIST POLICIES IN EASTERN EUROPE 768
   33 THE PEOPLE'S REPUBLICS   789
   34 ECONOMIC AND SOCIAL STRUCTURE   806
   SELECTED BIBLIOGRAPHY   822

  INDEX   *follows page* 837

Maps

BY GUY FLEMING

The British Commonwealth and Empire 1959   6–7

The French Community of Nations 1959   192–3

Federal Republic of Germany   326

The Italian Republic   458

The Soviet Union and Communist Satellites 1959   716–17

PART ONE

GREAT BRITAIN &
THE COMMONWEALTH

———◆———

by Taylor Cole
David R. Deener
and Alexander Brady

1

BRITISH CONSTITUTIONALISM

1. INTRODUCTION

Britain's contributions to the art of self-government are many. England provides, of course, the classic example of the parliamentary system of government. English common law and legal procedure, and the political ideas of British philosophers, also have taken root in alien climates and different political cultures. Indeed, the widespread diffusion of political principles and practices associated with the "Mother of Parliaments" suggests, as students of politics from the time of the ancient Greeks have argued, that governments have many things in common.

Yet governments also differ. It has proved easier to adopt English parliamentary forms than to make them work in the English manner. Even in countries that share the heritage of Britain, such as the Commonwealth nations of Canada and Australia, parliamentary government does not operate exactly like the English model. And although the name is the same, the parliament at Paris, just across the narrow English Channel, functions very differently from its counterpart at Westminster. In other words, as Sir Stafford Cripps put the matter, methods of government are not simply commodities of international commerce.[1]

The British political system provides, then, a good introduction to two of the major tasks faced by the student of comparative government. The first is that of gaining an appreciation of the unique aspects, the individuality, that each system of government possesses. The second task is the search for the universal and general, as well as the variant, elements of politics, in order to find the bases on which to make comparisons of political systems.

Some of the unique and distinctive features of British government are readily apparent. The pageantry of an opening of Parliament, the ceremony of a coronation of a queen, the ritual of the changing of the guard—all these through the media of the newsreel and television have

[1] *God in Our Work* (1949), p. 77. Cripps was a prominent member of the postwar Labour government.

3

been witnessed by millions throughout the world. But a caution is in order, for, as Sir Winston Churchill has observed, in Britain pomp has become separated from power. Much of the ceremony and formality attendant upon the conduct of government in Britain bears only a remote and indirect relation to the actual decisions that alter and shape the daily way of life of England. British government will thus introduce another problem encountered in the study of politics, namely, that of distinguishing between formal and effective power, between the things that really count and those that do not.

Public pageantry and ritual are, of course, to be found in government everywhere, and their universality suggests that formalities deserve some attention. Especially is such attention necessary in Britain. The outward forms of British institutions as well as many archaic details of procedure reincarnate in the twentieth century ways of doing things that originated centuries ago. The formal side of British government serves to emphasize how deeply British parliamentary government is rooted in tradition and history. Parliamentary democracy and constitutional government in Britain are the result of long and continuous historical development. In a sense history and experience have demonstrated to the Englishman what logic cannot prove: that his parliamentary institutions stand to provide liberty under law through the alternative of counting heads instead of breaking them. Hence the British approach to problems of politics is marked by a respect for the traditional ways of getting things done. Experience is the known guide; innovation is unsure; adaptation is better. And British history reveals a mastery in adapting old political forms and methods to new situations.

The stubborn persistence of time-tested forms and methods in Britain suggests another point. Institutions, it is true, evolve through man's efforts to solve his spiritual and material problems, but institutions also affect his solutions, by limiting or predisposing the choices made in working out man's aims and aspirations. Some institutions have proved effective in channeling the forces that impel men to love and hate into constitutional pathways; others have directed them toward tyranny and despotism. Nevertheless, whether constitutional government is conceived in Professor Friedrich's[2] terms as regularized and enforceable restraints on the exercise of arbitrary power or more simply as liberty under law, it seems impossible of realization without political institutions. For the purpose of illustrating the general role of institutions in translating the ideal of constitutional government into reality, no government is more appropriate for study than that of Great Britain.

There is a last point. British institutions are the product of centuries-long historical evolution, and their analysis will underscore the importance of the study of history to the study of politics. Responsible government in Britain is the resultant of the historical interaction between many factors—economic classes and interests, geography, national culture characteristics, legal and political philosophies, religious beliefs and schisms, technological change, personalities, and just plain historical

[2] See Carl J. Friedrich. *Constitutional Government and Democracy* (rev. ed., 1950), pp. 123–26.

accident. To put these factors into some sort of preliminary focus, Professor Friedrich's concept of constitutionalism, mentioned above, will prove useful. Accordingly, attention will first center on the constitutional principles governing the exercise of power and the imposition of restraints in the British system. Then, the historical growth of a central locus of power, the Crown—without which effective government could hardly develop—will receive brief consideration. Next, the development of a source of effective restraints centering in Parliament—without which constitutionalism would likely have failed—will be sketched. Finally, the historical stream of British political thought will be surveyed. Admittedly, the role of words, ideas, and theories in politics is a controversial question. But, whatever stand may be taken on this question, without the word there is no memory of the deed; without the idea the act is devoid of significance.

2. CONSTITUTIONAL PRINCIPLES

Britain, it is commonly said, has an "unwritten" constitution. What is meant, of course, is that in Britain there is no legal document conveniently labeled "the constitution" and acknowledged to be superior to ordinary law. An ordinary act of legislation can amend or repeal any of the great landmarks of British democracy, from the Magna Carta to the Bill of Rights. Thus, to say that the English constitution is unwritten is to state in one way the principle of parliamentary sovereignty, the legal keystone of British constitutionalism.

The classic exposition of the principle of the legal sovereignty of Parliament is that given by Professor A. V. Dicey in the late nineteenth century.[3] The principle means that Parliament has the power "to make or unmake any law whatever," and that no other body or person has authority to set aside an act of Parliament. Or, stated differently, the principle means that British courts will enforce an act of Parliament without questioning its "constitutionality," and, conversely, will refuse to enforce any rules contravening parliamentary statutes.

The principle of parliamentary sovereignty obviously vests legal absolutism in Parliament. To the American student who is familiar with the idea that Congress must conform to the Constitution or the Supreme Court will declare its laws unconstitutional, this principle is likely to raise an immediate question. How is it possible to square a principle that admits of legal absolutism with the notion of constitutionalism? The two seem clearly incompatible.

British history, however, suggests that conflict between the principle and the ideal of constitutionalism may be more a paradox of logic than an inexorable result of actual experience. Certainly, the principle of parliamentary sovereignty has not produced despotism in modern British

---

[3] *Introduction to the Study of the Law of the Constitution* (5th ed., 1897), pp. 37–38. Dicey defined Parliament as the queen, the House of Lords, and the House of Commons acting together.

THE BRITISH COMMONWEALTH AND EMPIRE 1959

Forms of Government

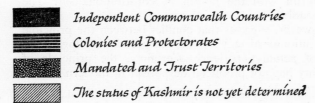

Independent Commonwealth Countries

Colonies and Protectorates

Mandated and Trust Territories

The status of Kashmir is not yet determined

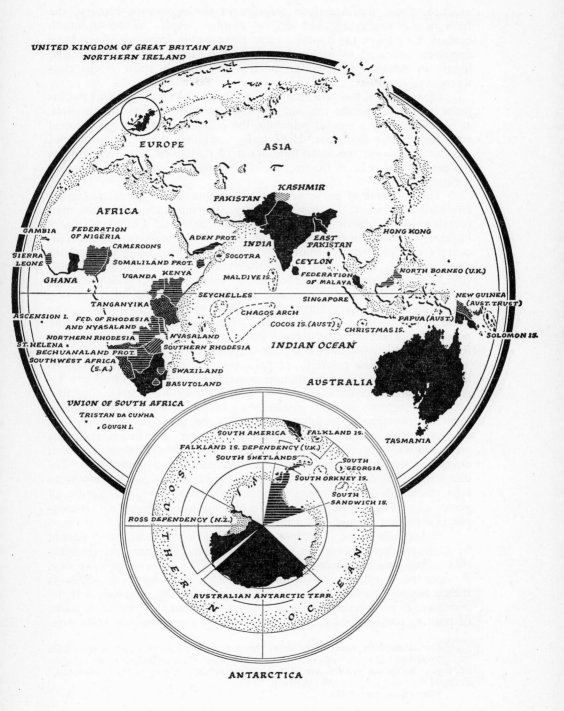

UNITED KINGDOM OF GREAT BRITAIN AND
NORTHERN IRELAND

EUROPE

ASIA

AFRICA

KASHMIR

PAKISTAN

GAMBIA

FEDERATION
OF NIGERIA

CAMEROONS

ADEN PROT.

INDIA

EAST
PAKISTAN

HONG KONG

SIERRA
LEONE

SOMALILAND PROT.

Socotra

CEYLON

GHANA

UGANDA KENYA

MALDIVE IS.

FEDERATION
OF MALAYA

NORTH BORNEO (U.K.)

SEYCHELLES

SINGAPORE

NEW GUINEA
(AUST. TRUST)

TANGANYIKA

ASCENSION I.

FED. OF RHODESIA
AND NYASALAND

CHAGOS ARCH

COCOS IS. (AUST)

PAPUA (AUST.)

ST. HELENA

NORTHERN RHODESIA

NYASALAND

CHRISTMAS IS.

SOLOMON IS.

BECHUANALAND PROT.

SOUTHERN RHODESIA

INDIAN OCEAN

SOUTHWEST AFRICA
(S.A.)

SWAZILAND

AUSTRALIA

BASUTOLAND

UNION OF SOUTH AFRICA

TRISTAN DA CUNHA

GOUGH I.

SOUTH AMERICA

FALKLAND IS.

TASMANIA

FALKLAND IS. DEPENDENCY (U.K.)

SOUTH SHETLANDS

SOUTH
GEORGIA

SOUTH ORKNEY IS.

SOUTH
SANDWICH IS.

ROSS DEPENDENCY (N.Z.)

SOUTHERN OCEAN

AUSTRALIAN ANTARCTIC TERR.

ANTARCTICA

practice. True, the American colonies in the eighteenth century, the
Irish in the nineteenth, and various empire peoples in the twentieth
century have taken the opposite view. Even within England groups have
appeared prepared to argue the point. But, in any reasonable view,
liberty in Britain has been far more secure than in most places elsewhere.

Clearly, then, the principle that ascribes legal sovereignty to Parliament does not describe the whole of modern English constitutionalism.
It is balanced by a second principle, the practical one that the political
sovereign is the electorate. Historically speaking, these two principles
did not develop at the same time. That of parliamentary sovereignty is
the earlier, and it bears the impress of the historical conditions in which
it emerged.

The principle of parliamentary sovereignty is the product of crisis
conditions in society. It derives basically from one answer Western man
found to the problem of civil order when medieval Christian society
began to crumble. In the terrible disorders of sixteenth- and seventeenth-
century Europe, Western man searched for a way to bring peace again
upon the land. There must be a power somewhere to cure civil chaos.
Bodin, the sixteenth-century Frenchman, gave the answer: Sovereignty,
the highest power over citizens and subjects *unlimited by law*.[4] Hobbes,
the seventeenth-century Englishman, called forth the *Leviathan*.[5] The
brute sword, so these men maintained, is the instrument for keeping the
peace. But who holds the sword? Parliament, was the answer England
found through civil war in the seventeenth century.

In a sense the principle of parliamentary sovereignty attempts to
name the possessor of that ultimate power necessary to hold society together in time of crisis. Civil chaos is not, however, the normal condition
of life in England, and the unsheathed sword is not the normal instrument of government. In day-to-day affairs the ultimate sword remains
safely sheathed under the restraints of the English constitution, restraints
grounded in the principle of the sovereignty of the electorate that
developed as English government became democratic government. Today it is expected that full exercise of parliamentary sovereignty is to
take place only in extremities. For normal times, then, the pattern of
power alone is deceptive; the pattern of restraints is necessary to complete the picture of English constitutionalism.

Nevertheless, the principle of parliamentary sovereignty cannot
be neglected, for it serves an essential function. It permits the constitution to be described in legal terms, especially in terms of positive law.
Positive law—in the classic definition given by John Austin in 1832—is
the command of a superior to an inferior followed by punishment if the
command is not heeded. To describe any constitutional system in terms
of positive law obviously requires postulating a superior who can com-

[4] Some modern interpreters stress the general limitations imposed by Bodin
on sovereign power as necessary to the understanding of his definition of sovereignty
as "legally unlimited power." See Max A. Shepard, "Sovereignty at the Crossroads,"
Political Science Quarterly, 45 (1930), p. 580.

[5] See below, pp. 23–24.

mand, and in England this legal superior is Parliament. Theoretically (and emphasis needs to be placed on the term) the fact that a parliamentary statute is supreme simplifies legal analysis of the constitution.

Law and the legal system describe only a part of political behavior, however. To state this proposition negatively: people every day break the law for such things as love or money. And, to state it positively, such intangibles as honor, moral ideals, sense of responsibility, even simple habit, impel men to efforts that no law could evoke. These non-legal factors are especially important in the British political system because the principle of popular sovereignty is not wholly or even mainly expressed in legal terms. The operation of the principle of the sovereignty of the electorate is to be found largely in the body of "constitutional conventions." Constitutional conventions or customs are habitual and expected modes of behavior in certain types of political situations. In England, for example, the queen is expected to appoint as prime minister the leader of the party having a majority of seats in the House of Commons, but there is no law compelling her so to act.

Hence, in the broad view, it is proper to conceive of Britain's unwritten constitution as the body of legal and non-legal rules followed by Parliament and officers of the Crown in exercising control over the lives and property of British subjects. In legal theory there are no limitations on what Parliament can do. In political practice, however, the principle of popular sovereignty ensures that, whatever Parliament does, it must ultimately meet with the consent of the British people or be undone.

A simplified and schematic presentation of the manner in which political authority is exercised in Britain may serve to illustrate how the principles and conventions of the English constitution operate as effective restraints on power. To begin with, the officials who exercise authority over lives and property can do so only because they are servants of Her Majesty. As private individuals these persons have no authority at all, and when they take action as public officials, it is by order of the queen. But "the queen can do no wrong." This means two things. One, the queen cannot issue an illegal order, but only those orders that under customary law or statute she has authority to issue. Second, the queen takes no action (with one or two possible exceptions) on her own initiative. She acts only on the advice of her ministers. Consequently her ministers bear responsibility for all action taken in the name of Her Majesty. The ministers are not responsible to the queen alone, however. They are also responsible to the House of Commons and to the electorate. The ministers can advise the queen only as long as they enjoy the confidence of the House, which means as long as a majority of the members of the House support them. Finally, the House of Commons is elective, and the majority that supports the minister sooner or later must face the people in a general election. Thus, the act of a lowly civil servant can set in motion a chain of accountability that runs via Her Majesty's ministers to the cabinet and the monarch, thence to the House of Commons, and in the end to the British electorate.

Where do the restraints come in? At several points along the chain described above there is opportunity to ask, Why?; and if a satisfactory

answer is not forthcoming, remedial action is possible. At the very outset
an individual arrested by a police official, for example, can apply to a
court for a writ of habeas corpus. If the arrest is not authorized by law,
the individual will be set free. Again, a regulation issued by a minister
must be authorized by law; otherwise an affected individual may carry a
protest to the courts against its enforcement. Even if authorized, individuals may protest through political channels and bring the matter to
the attention of members of Parliament. The queen, of course, bears
no responsibility for the issuance of the regulation, but her ministers
may very well be questioned in the House of Commons about it. If the
ministers cannot provide a satisfactory answer, the House could refuse
to support them. In any event, at election time members of the House
who have supported the ministers must persuade the voters to re-elect
them rather than other candidates who will undoubtedly be criticizing
the ministers.

The above description of the British constitutional process is admittedly elementary and simplified. Indeed, it so greatly ignores certain
factors, the political party for one, that it is more of a caricature than
anything else. Nevertheless, it suggests how the body of constitutional
rules hedge in the legal sovereignty vested in Parliament.[6]

What guarantee is there, however, that the rules will be followed?
In some instances departures from the rules run directly into legal
barriers. An illegal order, as already seen, will not be enforced by the
courts. In other cases departures bring into play indirect legal barriers.
Thus the queen's ministers might refuse to resign even though the House
of Commons failed to support them. Such action could result in impeachment, or the House might simply refuse to vote money for the
carrying on of government. And it is always possible that a flouting of
a "constitutional convention," although neither illegal nor criminal in itself, will result in the enactment of laws making a similar flouting in
the future impossible. When the House of Lords in 1909 defied convention by rejecting the budget passed by the House of Commons, the
result was the Parliament Act of 1911. This act stripped, for practical
purposes, the upper house of any powers over money bills and, for
good measure, reduced its powers over general legislation.

By and large, individual departures from the rules have not proved
overly troublesome. Change in the rules themselves, however, is another
matter.

With respect to change in constitutional conventions there is not
much that can be said, except to emphasize its importance. Indeed, the
whole structure of cabinet government and ministerial responsibility to
Commons is very largely the product of evolving constitutional convention. Constitutional change through parliamentary enactment deserves
some attention in view of the fact that in legal form it is indistinguishable
from routine legislation. Constitutional statutes, so-called, receive during
passage far different political treatment than ordinary measures. Parlia-

[6] The student, it is trusted, will accept this brief account of the patterns of
power and restraints in the British constitution for what it is: nothing more than an
introductory picture of the subtleties that make up Britain's constitution.

ment, especially that portion hostile to the ministers proposing the change, is quick to recognize matters of constitutional import, and the whole tone of debate reflects this awareness. On a few occasions in the past the extraordinary device of threatening to "pack" the House of Lords was used to obtain passage of important measures.[7] There have also been times when a government majority, although having the legal power to act, has chosen to get a mandate from the people before carrying out far-reaching changes.[8]

Constitutional change in the modern British system has really not been an insuperable problem. As might be expected, there are some who will argue that a given change should have happened much sooner, and there are others who will argue that it should not have taken place at all. Generally speaking, however, constitutional change has come about when necessary.

There remains, then, "unconstitutional" change, that is, change that observes the proper forms but is designed to subvert the constitution. Legally speaking, a dictatorially minded person having a majority of the House of Commons behind him could in effect abolish the British constitution. One answer, and one likely to be given by the Englishman, lies in history: since Cromwell there has been no successful attempt to subvert the constitution. This answer suggests that the English have an abiding faith in their political institutions and the pattern of power and restraints evolved through the centuries of English history. And, before dismissing that faith lightly, it would be well to consider the historical experience upon which it rests.

3. GROWTH OF SOVEREIGN POWER

England, along with France and Spain, was among the first of the Western nations to achieve the form of the nation-state and to develop institutions through which central power could be effectively exercised. The consolidation of royal authority was the first historical stage in the evolution of constitutionalism in Britain. It produced effective governmental power, which is just as necessary to constitutional government as enforceable restraints. The central monarchy in England antedates by several centuries those institutions—Parliament and the courts of law— that later were to serve as instruments of restraint. Indeed, as Sir Ernest Barker points out, the British monarchy is the oldest existing institution in Europe save one, and that one is the Papacy.

The historical steps by which the Crown became the focal point of sovereign power are exceedingly complex. The factors that aided the triumph of royal power over the pretensions of feudal and local magnates are many, and the proper weight to be assigned to particular factors is

[7] The threat to "pack" the Lords was a decisive factor in ensuring passage of the Reform Act of 1832 and the Parliament Act of 1911.

[8] The election of 1923 was called by Baldwin in order to obtain a mandate to abandon Britain's historic free-trade policy.

still a controversial question. There is, for example, a significant difference of opinion as to the influence of Anglo-Saxon institutions existing at
the time of the Norman Conquest in 1066 on developments thereafter.
It will not be feasible to attempt here any detailed account of historical
events from the time of the later Anglo-Saxon kings to the reign of the
Stuarts in the seventeenth century. Instead several broad developments
illustrating the growth of royal powers will be discussed.

A basis for centralized royal power was already in existence at the
time of the Norman Conquest. In form, if not in fact, the Anglo-Saxon
kingship to which William the Conqueror succeeded represented a unified
realm.[9] In addition the Norman kings manipulated the powers and
prerogatives of the Anglo-Saxon kingship to enhance royal power. For
example, the Danegeld, originally a levy on land imposed for the purpose
of buying off the Danes, was revived by William as a source of revenue.[1]
Again, the Anglo-Saxon duty, obligatory on all freemen, of bearing arms
in the fyrd, a sort of national militia, was not allowed to disappear. The
Norman kings found the military services of the fyrd very valuable in
their struggles with refractory feudal barons.

In general, William and his successors managed to combat the
divisive and separatist tendencies seemingly inherent in the nature of
feudal monarchy. Despite the strength shown by the barons from time
to time, and periods when monarchical power was notably weak, feudal
domains did not in the end achieve the status of politically independent
principalities and duchies. It is true that the nobility as a class sought, and
often successfully, to resist royal encroachments upon what it considered
to be its rights. What resulted, however, were checks like the Magna
Carta (1215) on the exercise of royal power, rather than a successful
challenge to the existence of the unified realm.[2]

The success of the medieval English kings in holding their own
and more against the powerful magnates is attributed to many factors.
For one thing, the feudal system itself apparently never developed in
England the tenacious roots that characterized the system on large parts
of the European Continent. Also, in the Oath of Salisbury (1086),
William the Conqueror severed in part the feudal bond between the
lesser men of the realm and their feudal lords. Under the Oath the
fealty and homage due the lord did not require the vassal to take up
arms against the king. Perhaps most important of all, however, was the
growth of central administrative machinery, modest, of course, in comparison with the modern bureaucracy, but with a significance beyond its
size because it was the king's own.

This central administration had simple origins.[3] It grew out of the
king's household by a slow and essentially pragmatic process. In time
this process led to the dissociation of certain activities—particularly

[9] There were as many as ten kingdoms in the sixth century. Final unification
was carried out under Cnut (1017–35).

[1] The Danegeld was not levied after 1162.

[2] For earlier documents see Charter of Liberties of Henry I (1100) and First
Charter of Stephen (1135).

[3] For a detailed account of this process see S. B. Chrimes, *An Introduction to
the Administrative History of Medieval England* (1952), Chapters I and II.

money-getting and spending, corresponding, the hearing of appeals—from the mass of business conducted by and for the king, and to the establishment of more or less public routines for the carrying out of these particular functions. During the reign of Henry I (1100–35), for example, the Treasury apparently became separated from the household. Well before the end of the twelfth century, as the *Dialogus de Scaccario* (*ca.* 1175) reveals, an elaborate system of finance and accounting had evolved. Then, too, the Norman kings retained holdings in France and were frequently absent from England. To act as viceroy during such absences, a justiciar was appointed by William I. Under William II (1087–1100) the office became permanent and its incumbent acted as chief executive officer of the king. During the age of the justiciars[4] the central administration clearly demonstrated a capacity to carry on the king's government even in periods of prolonged royal absence. This central executive machinery was never seriously shaken, although from time to time it required strengthening and rejuvenation.

Vitality in central administration meant, of course, less dependence upon the baronage in day-to-day matters of governance. In addition royal influence was extended into local areas through the medium of local officers representative of the king. Until the fifteenth century the sheriff was the most important functionary in this respect. When the sheriffs proved susceptible to corruption, the Tudors created the lords lieutenant to oversee the keeping of the peace in the shire and devolved upon the justices of the peace the major burdens of local government and administration. The royal judiciary also played a big part in effecting greater central rule over local jurisdictions. Through the royal judges both civil and criminal justice throughout most of England became the king's affair. And from the twelfth century on Justices in Eyre were sent into the counties with powers to hold inquests concerning almost any sort of local governmental business.

There were also external threats to the position of the English monarchy to be countered. England's insular position lessened the dangers of foreign military invasion and probably contributed, indirectly at least, to the success of the English monarchs in their struggles with the Papacy. Until the reign of Henry VIII (1509–47) the church in England was formally part of the universal Roman Catholic Church. For the first two centuries after the Conquest, relations between the king and the pope did not lead to an open break. In the fourteenth century, however, statutory restrictions were imposed upon appointments to higher church offices in England, and appeals from ecclesiastical courts to the papal Curia were forbidden in those cases in which the Crown had an interest.[5] Finally, in the 1530's, a number of parliamentary enactments extinguished papal authority in England. The Act of Supremacy (1534) declared the king to be "the only Supreme Head on earth of the Church of England."

[4] The dismissal of Hubert de Burgh in 1232 marks the end of the age of the justiciars.
[5] See the Statute of Provisors of Benefices (1351) and the Second Statute of Praemunire (1393), respectively.

The Tudor period (1485–1603) saw the culmination of the ascendancy of the Crown over the feudal aristocracy, internally, and over the powers of the papacy, externally. Yet even the Tudor kings did not hold absolute power, for they ruled through Parliament rather than without it. They used Parliament for their own ends, to be sure, but they enabled it to grow.

In sum, the English kings never succeeded in throwing off the form of the feudal monarchy. The feudal king was under the law and he governed through his counsels. Some kings of England felt the yoke of law less than others, and some dispensed in large measure with counsel, but none completely. Indeed, in the course of their struggles against the powers of the feudal baronage and the Roman Church, the monarchs had helped, unwittingly perhaps, to infuse life into the very institution, Parliament, which would finally see to it that no king could pretend for long to be above the law and to rule his subjects in disdain of their counsel.

4. RISE OF PARLIAMENT

On January 30, 1649, the head of Charles Stuart, King of England, rolled beneath the swing of the executioner's ax. History may never settle whether the execution of Charles I was justified or was simply murder. But the bloody blow of the headsman demonstrated one thing. Thenceforth, there could be little doubt that Parliament could restrain a headstrong king.

Some of the quarrels between Parliament and the Stuarts may appear to a later age to have concerned matters of little moment. But this merely illustrates the English habit, to use a phrase of Bishop Creighton, "of fighting great principles over outward trifles." For there was a grand constitutional issue involved in the controversy. It was whether the king would break out of the form of the feudal monarchy.

The system of feudal monarchy—and Lord Acton insists that constitutionalism in Britain stems from "consistent, uninventive, stupid fidelity" to it—contained, as we have seen, two essentials. The king was under the law and he governed through his counsels. Indeed, in strict theory, action of the king took place almost exclusively with the assent of the feudal council composed of the great lay and clerical magnates of the realm, the king's tenants-in-chief. But, as already indicated, William the Conqueror and his successors laid claim to independent powers, prerogative powers so-called, and also built up central government administration.

Still, for various reasons, including the royal need for money, the medieval English kings could not dispense with the feudal council. Nor, on the other hand, did the great lords succeed in making the council an instrument of permanent baronial control of the monarch. The council did not disappear, however. It became transformed—into Parliament.

The term "Parliament" appears in usage only during the middle of the thirteenth century. Its appearance is coincidental with demands of the barons that they should meet more frequently to discuss "the business of the king and the kingdom." An equally significant coincidence was the change in composition of the periodically summoned *concilium*. By the end of the thirteenth century Parliament had become more of a *national* assembly than a feudal council. "What touches all, shall be approved by all," declared Edward I in summoning the Model Parliament of 1295.

The elements imparting a national character to the Model Parliament were representatives from the counties and the towns, knights of the shires and burgesses of the boroughs. The change in complexion of Parliament from a feudal body to a truly representative body has received much emphasis. And rightly so, for in the long run the representative character of Parliament provided the foundation for its lasting vitality as a political institution. Yet the beginning of territorial representation in Parliament was merely a by-product of events in thirteenth-century England. Certainly the knights and burgesses were not then clamoring for a voice among the king's counsels. They received summons principally because the monarchs wanted money.

The important role of the pence and farthing in English constitutional development derived from the nature of the finances of medieval kingship. The king had certain revenues, from royal demesne lands, various fines and fees, and customs, which were more or less considered to be his personal income. But the expenses of royal government were also considered to be the king's personal expenses. The king's personal income should pay for the ordinary expenses of government, or, as it was put in medieval times, "the king should live of his own."

The personal nature of royal government probably facilitated the building up of the royal administration. However, the expenses of ordinary government eventually outstripped the king's personal revenues. In the early 1300's the king's hereditary revenues were amounting to about £28,000 annually, but he was borrowing at the rate of £20 per day to meet ordinary expenses.[6] And wars were not included among the ordinary expenses, even though they were practically ordinary occurrences.

To meet the growing cost of royal government and, above all, the costs of military ventures, the king had no general power of taxation. He relied upon grants and aids from his subjects. But these had first to be asked for and then given. When the monarchs began to summon the knights and burgesses in order to get them to grant subsidies, Commons, as the phrase goes, had arrived.

It is easy to see in retrospect how the royal need for money placed Parliament, and the Commons particularly, in a strategic position *vis-à-vis* the king. Before the middle of the fourteenth century Commons had hit upon the practice of tying in grants with petitions for redress of grievances, and had managed to get enacted into statute the principle that no tax should be levied without the consent of Parliament.[7] Com-

[6] These figures are taken from William A. Morris and Joseph R. Strayer, *The English Government at Work, 1327–1336,* Vol. II, *Fiscal Administration* (1947).

[7] In 1340; see K. R. Mackenzie, *The English Parliament* (1950), pp. 64–65.

mons also gained a share in legislation. But Parliament under the leadership of Commons moved only to the threshold of constitutional government. After the fifteenth century Parliament seemed to retreat, or at any
rate found itself eclipsed by the strong, even despotic, personal government of the Tudors. Strangely enough, it was in the Tudor period that
the Commons was able to lay the foundation of parliamentary privileges,
such as freedom of debate and freedom from arrest. Probably the Tudors were not disposed to quarrel too much over privileges with the
House that proved so useful in their struggles with the aristocracy and
the Roman Church.

To the great Tudor, Henry VIII, England was a body politic "knit
together." The three great elements of English government—Crown,
Parliament, and the common law—were blended, in a juridical sense,
into the "commonwealth," with no clear legal precedence acknowledged
to any one over the others. This "organic" fabric of the English state
was to suffer a violent rending in the seventeenth century, with the
accession of the house of Stuart.

It began with the death of the Virgin Queen, Elizabeth I (1558–
1603). There were, of course, no direct heirs, and the right of James,
who was king of Scotland, to the English throne rested upon natural
inheritance. Arguments were advanced against James's right and they
were answered by asserting the divine right of inheritance. The next
step was the fatal one—if possession of the throne rested upon divine
right, then exercise of its powers must rest upon divine right also. And
James I (1603–25) took that step in expounding upon the "absolute
prerogative" and the "mystical reverence that belongs unto them that
sit in the throne of God." He openly claimed the power "to exalt low
things, and abase high things, and to make of [his] subjects like men at
the Chesse." [8]

Such royal pretensions evoked protests not only from Parliament
but from the common lawyers as well. Under the leadership of Chief
Justice Coke the judges declared that "the King hath no prerogative but
that which the law of the land allows." [9] When James I argued that it
was treason to affirm that the king was under the law, Coke replied by
quoting the medieval lawyer Bracton: the king should be under no man,
but under God—and law.[1]

James I could dismiss powerful opponents from among the judges
on his own law benches, as he did in the case of Coke. Parliament was
another matter. James I discovered that, when he summoned Parliament,
he could not prevent it from debating royal policy or from attempting
impeachment of his ministers. In the domain of finance James I received some relief by the favorable decision in *Bate's Case* (1606)
which concerned the imposition of customs duties by prerogative. But
James got entangled in the religious controversy concerning reform of

[8] For an account of the intermingling of the doctrine of divine right with the
great constitutional questions see J. R. Tanner, *English Constitutional Conflicts of
the Seventeenth Century 1603–1689* (1948), pp. 1–50.
    [9] 12 Coke 76 (1610).
    [1] 12 Coke 65 (1607).

the Church of England. He stood by the Anglican hierarchy and thus found himself in opposition to the tide of Puritanism. When the Puritans failed to obtain reforms by appeal to James as supreme head of the Church, they moved to act through Parliament, only to run into the King James version of the royal prerogative.

With the accession of Charles I the issues tightened. In general, Parliament coupled its power to refuse financial aid with its right to petition for redress of grievances, and added to both the tactic of impeachment of the king's ministers. The royal answer was the dissolution of Parliament and dependence on prerogative revenues plus exaction of loans from reluctant subjects. Some measure of reconcilation might have been possible but for the flaring up of the religious question. In the spring of 1629 the Commons began to pass resolutions hostile to the king's High Church religious policy and to debate his financial maneuvers. Charles I commanded an immediate adjournment, but the Commons passed their resolutions of protest while the speaker was forcibly constrained in his chair. Thereafter Charles I summoned no more Parliaments for eleven years.

During this decade Charles I managed to rule without Parliament. Subsequently his High Church policy aroused revolt among the Scots. To meet the invasions from the north, the king was forced to summon Parliament. Once again Crown and Parliament clashed. Once again the religious issue proved decisive. In November, 1641, the Grand Remonstrance, a Puritan document, passed the Commons by a narrow margin. Charles attempted in person to arrest five members of the Commons within the House itself. The attempt failed. Charles fled from the capital, and England plunged into civil war.

In the next two decades violent hands sullied England's ancient constitution. Parliament assumed executive and sole legislative powers. Charles I lost his head. The monarchy and the House of Lords were abolished. Finally Cromwell established a military dictatorship. Then Cromwell died. For a short while Cromwell "ruled England from his urn," [2] but the edifice he had erected crumbled. In 1660 the son of Charles Stuart was called to the throne, with Parliament itself voting that "according to the ancient and fundamental laws of this kingdom, the government is and ought to be by King, Lords, and Commons."

Partly because of the adroitness of Charles II the effects of the civil conflict on the ancient constitution were not immediately visible. It also took time for the revolutionary forces let loose in the civil war to right themselves and find their true direction. Most serious and radical criticisms of the social and economic order had found expression alongside the constitutional and religious questions of the period. The protests were submerged, first, by the dictatorship, later, by the Restoration. A more moderate, but nonetheless powerful, revolution prevailed, namely, the liberal revolution.

The liberal revolution might have been delayed had it not been for the Catholicism of James II, the successor and brother of Charles II.

[2] This is the phrase of G. P. Gooch, *English Democratic Ideas in the Seventeenth Century* (1898), p. 283.

Opposition to popery from both Whigs and Tories was strong enough to secure co-operation in setting a Protestant monarch on the throne and to ensure that all future rulers would be Protestant. After the Convention Parliament of 1689 and the Act of Settlement of 1701, title to the Crown depended no longer on divine right but upon parliamentary enactment, into which the liberal principle of social contract had been subtly woven.[3] Civil war and dictatorship had bequeathed, so it seems, a sobering remembrance. Destruction of monarchical power left a void, and tyranny, as the Greek philosophers had foretold, hastened to fill it. The price for departing from the ancient forms came high. Parliament, then, did not attempt to supplant the restored Crown nor to obliterate executive powers. Instead, it sought more effective means of restraint. By statutory enactment Crown powers were selectively clipped. The Habeas Corpus Act (1679), the Mutiny Act (1689), and the Bill of Rights (1689) guaranteed that basic individual rights could not be overridden by the Crown acting alone but only in concert with Parliament. The royal judges were made secure from royal dismissal.[4] In short, the doctrine of parliamentary supremacy gained firm entrenchment in the constitution. How to reconcile this doctrine with the ancient form whereby the king ruled through his advisers remained to be worked out. The solution was, of course, cabinet government, which made possible the adaptation of the ideal of feudal constitutionalism to modern times.

5. ROLE OF POLITICAL THEORY

The story thus far told of British constitutionalism is largely one of men and their deeds, of the constitutional forms they have created, of the history they have made. It is now time to turn from men to ideas. Accompanying the growth of royal power and the refinement of techniques for restraining it is a stream of political thought and theory dealing with the age-old conflict between freedom and authority. This body of theory reflects, perhaps more clearly than anything else, the factors that guided government in England along constitutional and democratic pathways rather than along the road to dictatorship and authoritarianism.

Temporal and Spiritual Powers. Not long after the Christian Church gained official acceptance from the Roman state the basic principle to govern the organization of Christian society in the West appeared. This principle was the "two-swords doctrine" given authoritative expression by Pope Gelasius in the fifth century. Founded on the words of Christ, "Render therefore unto Caesar the things that are Caesar's; and unto God the things that are God's," the doctrine held man to be subject

[3] A resolution of the Convention Parliament spoke of James II's "breaking the original contract between the king and the people."

[4] Act of Settlement (1701), Sec. 3. However, no such general distrust of executive power as has marked French practice since 1871 prevailed.

to two powers: the temporal power (*imperium*) and the spiritual power (*sacerdotium*). Both *imperium* and *sacerdotium*, the two swords, were ordained of God. Secular authorities wielded the first, the church held the second. The two powers were co-ordinate with a single purpose: to maintain Christian society.

For several centuries the two-swords doctrine served its purpose. Then in the late eleventh century the investiture conflict between Pope Gregory VII and Emperor Henry IV signified the beginning of the breakdown of the doctrine. At the beginning of the twelfth century the investiture question extended into England and resulted in a controversy between Anselm and Henry I. These early conflicts were not between church and state; the state, in the modern sense of the word, did not exist. Nor was the conflict concerned with the source of political authority. That both swords, *sacerdotium* and *imperium*, were ordained of God was an unquestioned proposition. The argument concerned the proper demarcation between the two spheres of authority. Later the question of which power was superior arose. Eventually, when the controversy and its consequences had run the course of five centuries, the universal Christian society lay shattered both in fact and theory. The modern era of the nation-state had arrived.

An early writing appearing in England, the *York Tracts* (*ca.* 1100), advanced a claim for the superiority of the temporal power over the spiritual. The author of the *Tracts* denied the superiority of a bishop over a king, and also of the pope over a bishop, and he further declared it to be just that kings should have power and rule over priests. Even so, the author recognized a difference between a king and a tyrant, asserting that the latter ruled not through the grace of God but in the spirit of evil. The views expressed in the *York Tracts* were undoubtedly exceptional for the twelfth century,[5] and they did not go unopposed. Thomas à Becket stated the opposite position very simply. Kings, he wrote to Henry II (1154–89), receive their power from the Church, but the Church receives its power from Christ, and not from kings. The exile of Thomas and his eventual murder and martyrdom underscored his stand.

John of Salisbury in the *Policraticus* (1159) carried the papal argument a step farther. He deemed the temporal sword to be lower than the spiritual sword, because the former partook of the "character of the executioner." More significantly, John claimed that both swords belonged ultimately to the Church, although the Church did not actually wield the temporal sword. The prince, while he wielded the temporal sword, had merely the right to use it; he acted as the minister of the priestly office. And if a king abused his powers and became a tyrant, then John declared: "He who usurps the sword is worthy to die by the sword."

At first the investiture conflict was one between two powers within the unity of Christendom. As the conflict continued, arguments led to a questioning of the universal Christian society itself. Drawing upon Ro-

[5] There was even in the *Tracts* a suggestion that the Church could claim only the right to preach, a position taken by Marsiglio of Padua in *Defensor pacis* (1324).

man law precepts and later upon Aristotelian principles, kings and
princes sought to justify their wielding of temporal power (itself becoming more broadly defined) within their own realms without interference from Rome. At the same time the organization and hierarchy
of the Church came under attack.

During the thirteenth century the popes began to claim a *plenitudo
potestatis* (absolute power) in both temporal and spiritual affairs. In
the fourteenth century William of Occam denied that the pope had a
plenitude of power. In brief Occam asserted that the pope could not
deprive any man of rights not held from the pope, that is, rights held
from God, from nature, or from another man. Temporal matters were,
therefore, the province of secular authority and the layman. Moreover,
Occam's thought, summarized in *De imperatorum et pontificium pote-
state* (*ca.* 1347), contained the suggestion that temporal authority is
derived not from God himself but rather from the order of nature
established by God. This distinction was systematized by John Wyclif
in the doctrine of *dominium. Dominium* was the relationship between
inferior and superior in the order established by the Creator. As Wyclif
interpreted this order, the king was the vicar of God in temporal matters,
the priest in spiritual matters. The two powers were separate, but the
king might aid the Church by correcting abuses when the clergy failed
in its duties. Wyclif further declared that England was not subject to the
Holy Roman Emperor and was independent of outside temporal or
spiritual powers. But Wyclif did not envisage an absolute monarch. The
relation of *dominium* between king and subject required the king to
protect his subjects in their rights and to institute and administer wise
and just laws.[6]

By the close of the fourteenth century English thought had moved
to the point where the conflict between the temporal and spiritual powers
of Christendom was being transformed into one between papal authority
and the power of the king within his own realm. In the early sixteenth
century, as has been seen, Henry VIII applied the Roman law maxim,
Rex est imperator in regno suo (the king is emperor in his own realm)
and severed spiritual bonds with Rome. Thereafter the religious aspects
of political authority were to receive examination in a church-state
context. Ultimately the divine source of political authority was to be
questioned.

Laws and Customs of England.   England shared with northern
Europe the Germanic conception, so-called, of law as folkright. Folkright—a broad synonym would be tribal custom—had a fundamental
and immutable quality. Although rules of law evolved from the ways of
the folk, the notion that the folk could change the law at will was alien
to the Germanic concept. Folkright in this sense was law that was
"found," not law that was "made." Also, the conception of law as folkright suggests the idea that political authority derives from the people
and not from a divine source.

[6] See especially *Tractatus de officio regis* (1378–79).

In England as in Europe the Germanic concept blended with Christian and Roman law ideas. In England this medieval mixture developed into the common law. In the evolution of English common law certain Roman law concepts that remained strong on the continent gradually disappeared. Glanvil's legal writings of the late twelfth century are, according to Maitland, in some respects almost wholly Roman, but Bracton's treatise of less than a century later is primarily English.[7] Bracton, moreover, interpreted Justinian's *Institutes* so as to harmonize the precept "What pleases the prince has the force of law" with the proposition that the king is under the law in England. "Thus if the king should be without a bridle," Bracton asserted, "that is, without the law, they ought to put a bridle on him." [8] In the next century Wyclif was to claim that the laws of England were better than Roman law. Finally, in *De laudibus legum Angliae* (*ca.* 1470), Fortescue had his chancellor lecture the prince:

> For you have already heard how among the civil laws there is a famous sentence, maxim or rule which runs: *Quod principi placuit legis habet vigorem* [What pleases the prince has the force of law]. The laws of England do not sanction any such maxim, since the king of that land rules his people not only regally but also politically, and so he is bound by oath at his coronation to the observance of his law.[9]

To rule according to the civil law principle, Fortescue explained, was to be able to change the laws of the realm; but in England the king rules politically and cannot change the laws without the assent of his subjects.

The common law, then, denied legality to the mere whim of the king. Instead it bestowed upon ancient custom and long-standing right the quality of public law (as distinguished from private law). Of course the immutability of the common law eventually yielded to the principle of parliamentary sovereignty. Nevertheless, there was for several centuries (and still is to some extent) a body of legal rules that were not made by any legislature yet were enforceable in the English courts. And, as already seen, the common lawyers argued that the king's prerogatives depended upon the common law, the law of the land.

English legal thought up to the civil war of the seventeenth century emphasized two propositions relative to the nature and use of political authority. A prime source of political authority lay in ancient custom and historical right. But custom and historical right also served as restraints on authority, for the king was under and not above the law of the land.

---

[7] F. W. Maitland and F. C. Montague, *A Sketch of English Legal History* (1915), pp. 43–45.

[8] *De legibus et consuetudinibus Angliae* (*ca.* 1256). On the distortion of the *Institutes* by Bracton, see C. H. McIlwain, *The Growth of Political Thought in the West* (1932), pp. 195–97.

[9] Chapter 34.

Commonwealth and Reformation.   Henry VIII, as mentioned earlier, referred to England as a body politic "knit together." In theory
the three great powers of the realm—king, Parliament and common
law—held an essentially co-ordinate relation one to another. An expression of this view of the commonwealth appeared in Sir Thomas Smith's
De republica Anglorum (1565). Smith distinguished between "authority" and "power." Authority was vested in the king, and by virtue of
this authority the king could take many actions on his own. However,
some actions required the participation of Parliament. Moreover, Smith
declared Parliament to be the highest power in the realm. But it seems
that Smith did not conceive of Parliament as a lawmaking body with
supreme powers over all, but rather as the highest court whose decisions
interpreting the law and custom of the realm could not be overruled by
any other body.

Religion, however, was the burning question of the times. The
Catholic position was exemplified in Sir Thomas More's answer at his
trial in 1535 to the query whether or not an act of Parliament should
decide the election of the pope in the event Parliament decided to pass
such an act. More refused to be trapped into denying the binding force
of an act of Parliament by asking his questioner: "Suppose Parliament
would make a law that God should not be God, would then you, Master
Rich, say God were not God?"

Of more importance was the opposition of various Protestant sects
to royal supremacy in the Anglican Church. Very influential among
the English Protestants were the Puritan Independents, or Congregationalists. Desirous of reforms looking toward less control over religious
matters by the established Church hierarchy, the Independents at first
would have used political authority to obtain their ends. Failing to gain
the support of political authority, the Independents, as suggested by the
title of Robert Browne's *A Treatise of Reformation without Tarrying
for Anie* (1582), finally advocated reform from completely "within" the
Church. In order to escape the control of established authorities they
held the Church to be simply a free association of like-minded persons
in faith, which as a body could regulate its worship and religious offices
without ordination from any outside secular or religious power. In
England the Independents' minority position led them to arguments
stressing the dissociation of political authority from religion.[1]

Naturally there were those to support the established church and to
deny that there could be separation between church and state. In this
vein is Richard Hooker's *The Laws of Ecclesiastical Polity* (1594).
Hooker affirmed with Aristotle that political society arises naturally
through the needs of sociability. Government, although a necessity, is
formed through consent and political authority rests upon common consent. In a true Christian society the nation is at once both church and
state. By the Protestant credo of every man his own priest, however,
there is no reason why a national church should be accepted any more
than the Roman Church. To this difficulty, vividly real in the form of

---

[1] In colonial Massachusetts, however, the Puritans did not hesitate to use
political authority to reinforce the claims of the Puritan Church.

Puritanism, Hooker presented a twofold reply. First, he suggested that reason is something more than the transient cogitations of the daily multitude. "That which all men have at all times learned, nature herself must needs have taught," was Hooker's way of expressing the sign of true reason and also of subtly implying that dissent has the greater burden of proof thrust upon itself. Second, in the English commonwealth, ecclesiatical law, not being contrary to reason or Christian faith, was binding on all Englishmen just as was the rest of English law. Disobedience to the ecclesiastical law resulted in the undermining of the entire social order and hence negated the natural purposes of society, as well as the consent on which the commonwealth rested.

Divine Right of Kings. In one sense the theory of divine right of kings is an aberration in the stream of English political thought. The great constitutional and political questions involved in the civil war of the seventeenth century—the relative positions of the king, Parliament, and the common law; the religious issues; the growing power of the commercial classes—had begun to arise before James I came to the throne. The theory of divine right was, then, in no sense the origin of these great questions. Rather the theory became attached to a pattern of events already in motion.

In his *Trew Law of Free Monarchies* (1598) James I maintained that kings were not only God's lieutenants on earth but were by God himself called gods. Further, kings were the authors and makers of laws, not laws of kings. Such views when applied to the royal prerogative in England received, as already discussed, rather emphatic rejection at the hands of Parliament and the common law judges. This rejection betokened the passing of the doctrine that political authority is ordained of God. Henceforth the search for the source and basis of political authority would run along different lines.

Social Contract and Natural Law. One path taken in the search for a non-divine source of political authority led, along lines suggested by Hooker, to common consent or social contract and natural law. In the seventeenth century both Thomas Hobbes in the *Leviathan* (1651) and John Locke in the *Second Treatise of Civil Government* (1690) chose this path. It is unfortunate that Locke and Hobbes used the same terminology, for beyond semantic similarities there is little in common between the two men. In fact Locke wrote with a view to refuting Hobbes.

Both men premised political authority on an act of consent in the form of social contract. The contracts each had in mind differed markedly. Locke's contract was between the governed and the governor, and it placed limits on the powers of the governor. Should the governor exceed those limits, the people had a right of revolution. Hobbes, however, conceived of each man contracting with every other man to submit to a practically absolute sovereign. The ruler in Hobbes' theory was not a party to the contract and hence could not be bound by it. Thus, in Locke, contract leads to limited political authority with stress on individual rights. In Hobbes, contract results in limitless authority with virtually no recognition of individual rights.[2]

Both Locke and Hobbes believed in the need for government. They arrived at such opposite conceptions of government because each held different views regarding the nature of man and the state of non-government or the state of nature. To Hobbes man was a thoroughgoing egoist, so concerned with his own interests that in the state of nature he would have to make war on his neighbor before his neighbor devoured him. Nothing was secure except under an absolute power that could checkrein individual appetites and impose order. To Locke man was a reasonable creature, endowed with conscience, who would get along tolerably well with his fellow man in the state of nature. Government could be highly advantageous, but it also could become so unbearable as to warrant revolution and a return to the natural state. It follows almost as a matter of course that natural law differs for each. For Locke the law of nature is reason. For Hobbes the law of nature appears to be nothing more than the instinct of self-preservation.

There is another consideration. The two men were attacking different questions. Hobbes grappled with the problem of government versus non-government, of order versus chaos. When Locke wrote, the civil war was past. His concern was essentially with disaffection with government, and his solution met the needs of the rising commercial classes. Although Locke's view of natural law and the social contract was later to come in for serious criticism, his proposition that political authority rests upon consent of the people has remained dominant in English thought.

Tradition and Custom. Edmund Burke (1729–97) restated the case for tradition and custom as the source for political authority. The doctrine of tradition is not inconsistent with the theory of consent. Both had found a place in Hooker's philosophy. As Burke saw it, however, tradition was not merely a matter of emphasis in relation to the theory of consent. It was a major modification.

Society, Burke affirmed, is indeed a contract, but a contract not only between the living but also with the dead and the yet-to-be-born.[3] The English constitution was, as Burke termed it, a prescriptive constitution. Prescription was the most solid title of all to government.[4] In some respects Burke's language recalls the old Germanic conception of folkright, but without the dead dependence on the past sometimes connected with folkways and customs. After all, Burke acknowledged the coming generations. Burke's proposition that political authority derives from tradition has continued to carry great weight in English thought.

---

[2] Hobbes did acknowledge that the contract might be voided in one circumstance—whenever the sovereign failed to maintain order, the purpose for which the contract was entered into. *Leviathan* (Everyman's Library ed., 1914), p. 116. Nor did Hobbes insist that the sovereign must be a monarch.

[3] "Reflections on the Revolution in France," *The Works of Edmund Burke* (1896), Vol. II.

[4] "Reform of Representation in the House of Commons," ibid., Vol. VI.

Nature's Laws of Political Power.   Another approach in English thought has tended to treat the problem of political authority as if it were a problem of natural science or one of logic. Authority or power is an empirical fact, so this approach seems to hold, and the object is to discover the laws that regulate its existence and use.

An early example of this approach is James Harrington's *Oceana* (1656). Harrington posited that political authority was the outgrowth of the economic order; more specifically, that political power follows economic power. Harrington's theory was novel, not so much because of his awareness of the interrelationships between economics and politics (for Aristotle had been thoroughly aware of the connection between these forces), but because of the time when he emphasized this inter-relationship. In Harrington's own day wealth and poverty were burning questions with the Levellers[5] and the Diggers.[6] Harrington, however, thought not so much in terms of individual wealth and poverty as in terms of impersonal economic forces. He held that economic forces determined the distribution of political power among the classes of the nation. Although not primarily derived from Harrington, the emphasis placed by Adam Smith[7] and the laissez-faire school on the free-enterprise and market economy was of undoubted significance in British politics of the nineteenth century, and it still has some advocates.

Other variations of the idea that the political order evolves out of some greater order of nature have appeared since the seventeenth century. Some writings have stressed the economic order as fundamental. Others have attempted to apply Darwin's biological findings to politics.[8] Indeed, Marxism accepts the premise of the primacy of an immanent order of history that is greater than man, but Marxism has played a relatively minor role in British politics.

Utilitarianism and Positive Law.   One of the most influential of modern English attempts to deal with the problem of political authority was utilitarianism. The utilitarians directed attention to the reverse side of the problem of authority, that is, why men obey political authority. The utilitarians discarded such explanations as the social contract and natural law. They emphasized the role of habit as a basis for obedience.

The utilitarians had, however, a deep interest and concern in political change and reform. And they developed a set of criteria—the pain-pleasure calculus—by which the uses of political authority might be judged.

As stated by Jeremy Bentham in his *Introduction to the Principles of Morals and Legislation* (1789), the calculus of pain-pleasure begins

[5] Leaders of the Levellers were John Lilburne and Richard Overton. Leveller literature is collected in W. Haller and G. Davies, eds., *The Leveller Tracts, 1647–1653* (1944), and D. M. Wolfe, *Leveller Manifestoes in the Puritan Revolution* (1944).

[6] Gerrard Winstanley's *Law of Freedom* (1652) is a major writing of the Diggers.

[7] Particularly in his *Wealth of Nations* (1776).

[8] See especially Herbert Spencer's *Social Statics* (1850), *First Principles* (1864), and *Man Versus the State* (1884).

with the assumption that men will avoid pain as something bad and welcome pleasure as something good. A given action will produce in a given individual either a preponderance of pleasures or pains. Political action could also be evaluated by the calculus. All that was necessary was to count off on one side the individuals who would receive pain as a result of the action, and, on the other side, count off those who would receive pleasure. If the greater number of individuals received pleasure from the action, then it was good for the community as a whole. This is the principle of the greatest happiness or greatest good for the greatest number.

The pain-pleasure calculus proved not so attractive in the longer run. John Stuart Mill (1806–73) began to have doubts that one man's pleasure should cancel out another man's pain. There were, perhaps, differences in kind between pleasures as well as differences in the capacities of particular men to enjoy particular pleasures. Significantly, Mill raised his voice to speak for the liberty of the individual to do certain things regardless of whether or not the greatest number thought that it was for the greatest good.[9]

There was also an important relation between utilitarian theory and the school of positive law. The seeds of the doctrine of positive law were present in Bentham's *A Fragment on Government* (1776). Here Bentham defined political society as one in which the subjects were in the habit of paying obedience to the will of a governor or governors. John Austin (1790–1859) went a step farther and asserted that only positive law—which he defined as a command of a political superior to persons in a state of subjection—created legal obligation.[1] The principle of parliamentary sovereignty, the legal cornerstone of the modern British constitution, is, as already mentioned, the result of Professor Dicey's application of Austin's definition of positive law to the constitution.

The gross difficulty with utilitarian theory lies in its possible consequences. Given a pleasure-bent majority, there is nothing explicit in the theory to set bounds on what may or may not be done by law. However, in England, the theory has not been pushed to its logical extremes, despite its undoubted influence.

Idealism and the "New" Liberalism. Late in the nineteenth century the currents of idealism, found on the Continent most prominently in the thought of Kant and Hegel, reached England through the works of T. H. Green (1836–82). Green dealt explicitly with both the problems of obedience and of authority, and argued that will, rather than force, was the basis of the state. Obedience resulted from the control that a "universal rational will" exercised over the inclinations of men. This will had its source in social relations of men "interested in each other" and "acting together for common ends."[2] As to the source of political authority Green affirmed that it resided in the state. Unlike

---

[9] See his *Representative Government* (1861) and *On Liberty* (1859).
[1] See his *Province of Jurisprudence Determined* (1832) and his *Lectures on Jurisprudence* (1861–63).
[2] *Lectures on the Principles of Political Obligation* (1941 edition), p. 103.

Kant he did not posit an idealized original contract as the source from which the state derived political authority. Nor did he follow Hegel in regarding authority as the result of the state being the chosen instrument for the historical march of God in the world. Green is, as Sir Ernest Barker says, more Kantian and Aristotelian than Hegelian and Platonic. The state is the best society because it has an ethical end or purpose. The source of political authority is found really in the end and purpose of the state.

The thinking reflected in Green's philosophy had a heavy impact on liberal thought. By insisting that state and society rather than the individual were the arbiters of freedom and by asserting that the measure of individual rights is social utility, Green aided in the transition from the liberal "police" state to the liberal "social welfare" state.

Socialism. Modern British socialism is closely connected with the social protest that arose during the nineteenth century against the effects of industrialism upon the British laboring classes. But socialist and social-protest writings had appeared much earlier; they can be found in the utopias of Sir Thomas More and Francis Bacon.[3] And men like Winstanley in the seventeenth century and Godwin in the eighteenth had raised frank questions concerning private property and its relation to political freedom.[4]

In the early nineteenth century came the work and ideas of Robert Owen.[5] Although Owen eventually advocated the abolition of private property and the profit system, he did not base his position on the premise of class warfare. Owen contributed heavily to the idea that man's nature and character are made for him by his environment. This proposition lends itself to the argument that the capitalist's character can be altered and the errors of his way corrected, and also that the common man can be taught the necessary virtues by means of suitable education and proper environment. This is reformism in the broadest sense and is today a basis of the main current of British socialist thought. Owen also initiated the use of co-operatives and provided great impetus to trade unionism in the first half of the nineteenth century. Both co-operation and trade unionism remain cardinal tenets of British socialism and Labour Party doctrine.

During the last half of the nineteenth century socialist thought in Britain received a number of accretions. Non-Marxist critiques of contemporary society appeared in the Christian Socialist writings of F. D. Maurice and Charles Kingsley, in the utopian socialism of William Morris, and in the artist's revolt against a material civilization of John Ruskin.[6] Marxism reached England through Henry M. Hyndman and

[3] Sir Thomas More, *Utopia* (1516); Francis Bacon, *New Atlantis* (1627).
[4] Gerrard Winstanley, *Law of Freedom* (1652); William Godwin, *Enquiry Concerning Political Justice* (1793).
[5] Writings of Owen include *A New View of Society* (1813), and *Letters to the Human Race on the Coming Universal Revolution* (1850).
[6] Writings of this group include: Maurice, *Tracts on Christian Socialism* (1850); Kingsley, *Alton Locke* (1850); Morris, *News from Nowhere* (1891); and Ruskin, *Unto This Last* (1860), and *Time and Tide* (1867).

the Social Democratic Federation, founded in 1881, but the main stream of British socialism has remained non-Marxist. Most important of all was the establishment of the Fabian Society in 1884. The Fabians were frankly socialist, dedicated to the abolition of a system in which the means of production were in private hands. The Fabians remained, however, devoted to constitutional methods. The Fabian Society has numbered among its members such important personages as Sidney and Beatrice Webb, George Bernard Shaw, Ramsay MacDonald, G. D. H. Cole, Harold Laski, R. H. Tawney, and Clement Attlee.

Twentieth-century British socialist thought contains, as might be expected, many side roads. On the whole, however, it has held that its aims can be achieved through orthodox democratic methods. British socialism frankly looks forward to changes in the system of private ownership of capital. It has emphasized equality of men rather than individual liberty, and has come to stress the role of co-operation as opposed to authority in the future "society in which free and independent men and women work together as equals."

Summary: Thought and Action. British political thought has maintained a rough pace with historical events. The sources of political authority and its uses and abuses were among the main concerns of political inquiry up to the seventeenth century. Parliament's triumph, the Glorious Revolution, brought in its train the doctrine of popular consent. More recent theory reflects the diversity of ideas that must arise wherever democratic government thrives.

Above all, British thought lends support to the constitutional system evolved through historical experience. There is in Britain wide intellectual acceptance of the basic propositions of the constitution: that political authority derives from popular consent, that sovereign power is legally unlimited, that authority should serve the general good. British thought provides moderating forces on the working of the constitution through its emphasis on tradition, order, and individual rights. Alongside these conservative and moderating elements is a critical element, widely diffused through most sectors of British thinking as a result of the impact of utilitarianism, one that serves to quicken the adaptation of constitutional forms to new social and political needs. And whatever else it may or may not do, the body of English political theory saves English constitutional history from being a "great, buzzing confusion" or a series of highly unlikely but lucky events. The Englishman trusts his institutions because they work, but British thought suggests that there may be reasons for this and, consequently, that the Englishman's trust in history and experience is not simply a faith in miracles.

C H A P T E R

2

POLITICAL PARTIES

1. GROWTH OF DEMOCRATIC SUFFRAGE

"Our Parliamentary institutions express themselves through party government, at any rate in times of peace." These words, spoken by Winston Churchill when he returned as prime minister in 1951, underscore the importance of political parties in modern British government. But party government is something relatively new in Great Britain. As it is understood today, party government is largely a development of the last four decades of the nineteenth century. There is a good reason for this late appearance of government by party in Britain. The modern British party had to await the growth of a broad, democratic franchise. And democratization of British suffrage did not begin until 1832.

Mere figures scarcely indicate the importance and effect of the Reform Act of 1832. Prior to 1832 approximately 500,000 persons held the parliamentary suffrage. The immediate effect of the measure was to add only about 200,000 voters to the electorate, although within a short time the number of voters more than doubled.

Despite the small numerical addition to the electorate resulting from the Reform Act some historians have characterized its passage as a "bloodless revolution," for the act enfranchised the British middle classes. With respect to suffrage requirements the act of 1832 left virtually intact the forty-shilling freehold, the basis for county suffrage since 1430. But to the forty-shilling freehold it added a number of franchises based upon either ownership or occupation of property. In the boroughs the Reform Act abolished a "curious medley" of customary voting rights, and placed the borough franchise on a property-occupation basis, the £ 10 "rate payer" franchise.

Equally important with franchise alterations were the provisions of the Reform Act relating to borough constituencies, in particular the "rotten" boroughs. Some fifty rotten boroughs lost their representation

29

and others had their representation reduced.[1] All in all, approximately one hundred and forty seats (more than one fifth of the seats in Commons) were redistributed. Thirteen of the seats made available went to Scotland and Ireland, the English counties received sixty-five additional seats, and some forty boroughs obtained representation from the remainder.

The Reform Act of 1832 did not long stifle further demands for a less restricted electorate. Chartism, a movement for parliamentary reform, sprang up in the late 1830's and flamed intermittently for twenty years. Among the reforms proposed by the Chartists was universal manhood suffrage.[2] The Chartist movement spent itself before additional enlargement of the electorate occurred, but there seems little doubt that it helped to awaken the political consciousness of the disfranchised classes.

At any rate another reform measure became law in 1867.[3] This act resulted primarily in the enfranchisement of the town artisans or the urban working class. The Reform Act of 1867 made several changes in both borough and county voting qualifications, but its major innovation was the £10 lodger and householder franchise in boroughs. Although the act did redistribute some fifty borough seats, it did not increase borough representation in Commons. Thus the urban electorate had increased, but not its representation. In fact the passage of the act occasioned much concern about the political behavior of the newly enfranchised workingman. Whether the workingman would continue to accept government by his "betters" was a question asked by many public figures in Britain. As events turned out, the effects of the act were more immediately evident on the party level than in Parliament. Not until the Parliament of 1906 was there a striking shift in the complexion of Commons as measured by the economic interests and social backgrounds of its members.

The Reform Act of 1867 added slightly more than a million voters to the electorate. Within twenty years another electoral measure added another two million. The Representation of the People Act of 1884 enfranchised two important groups, the agricultural workers and the miners. This resulted from extending to the counties the franchise requirements applied to the boroughs in 1867. Coupled with the representation act of 1884 was the redistribution act of the following year. In general the act of 1885 marked an attempt to apply to both counties and boroughs alike the single-member district principle, with districts more or less in proportion to population. Mr. Gladstone thought that the one-member district principle of the act of 1885 would go "a very long way towards what is roughly termed the representation of minorities." Of course, to

---

[1] An estimate made in the 1790's indicated that fifty-one Welsh and English borough constituencies with a total of fifteen hundred voters returned one hundred members to the House of Commons.

[2] Other reforms advocated by the Chartists were: the secret ballot, equal electoral districts, abolition of property qualifications for members of Commons, payment of salaries to members of Commons, and annual elections. Except for the last all were eventually adopted.

[3] By a quirk of parliamentary politics the measure went through under the Conservatives.

advocates of proportional representation, the act had no such effect. Indeed Professor Smellie has interpreted the act of 1885 as having replaced the conservative principle of representation of communities with the radical-liberal principle of representation of majorities.[4]

At the close of the nineteenth century British suffrage was fairly broad but far from universal. Major criticisms concerned the disfranchisement of women in parliamentary (but not local) elections, the retention of property qualifications, and the practice of plural voting. Also, the large quota of Irish seats was felt to be disproportionate, especially by the Conservatives.[5] The most persistent advocates of electoral reform in the first decades of the twentieth century were the suffragettes. When appeals and petitions failed to bring results, the suffragettes turned to direct action. In order to attract attention to their cause, the ladies indulged in such maneuvers as pouring sticky syrup into mailboxes, breaking windows, and going on hunger strikes when taken into custody.

Hostile action in the House of Lords and the outbreak of World War I postponed action on reform proposals introduced by the Liberal government. In 1916 a parliamentary committee presided over by the speaker of the House of Commons began study of the suffrage situation. Its recommendations formed the basis of the Representation of the People Act of 1918.

The act of 1918 swept away property qualifications for males. With the principal exceptions of "peers, lunatics and criminals" men twenty-one years of age or older could exercise the franchise subject only to residence and registration requirements. The problem of woman suffrage was awkward because women would outnumber men for some time after the conclusion of the war. A compromise resulted. Women thirty years of age or older received the parliamentary franchise if they or their husbands could qualify as local electors. The act of 1918 continued plural voting, however. It retained the "business premises" franchise and increased the number of university constituencies. Thus it was possible for a man (or woman) to qualify for several franchises on the basis of residence in one constituency, business premises in another, and eligibility to vote as a member of a university constituency. The act did limit plural voting to a single vote in two constituencies only. Another feature of the 1918 act was a redistribution of seats. All in all, the act of 1918 added more than 13,000,000 voters to the existing electorate of 8,500,000.

During the 1920's the problem of Irish seats in Commons disappeared with the creation of the Irish Free State. Commons decreased in size from 707 seats to 615. In 1928 the "Flapper Act" placed woman suffrage on the same basis as the male suffrage. Further steps occurred after World War II. Prior to the Labour victory in 1945 four boundary commissions were appointed to examine the problem of apportionment. A scheme was thereafter adopted for continuing redistribution of seats at ten- to fifteen-year intervals, to be based on the recommendations of

[4] K. B. Smellie, *A Hundred Years of English Government* (1937), p. 192.
[5] As a result of Liberal support for Irish home rule a large number of Irish Nationalists usually supported the Liberals.

parliamentary boundary commissions. The proposals of these commissions made in 1954 resulted in a House of 630 seats for the 1955 general election. The Representation of the People Act of 1948 finally established the principle of one man, one vote. This act abolished the "business premises" franchise and the university constituencies[6] and instituted facilities for mail voting.

Thus, in not much more than a century, British suffrage has attained a broad, democratic character, with citizenship, age, residence, and registration as the positive requirements for voting. While provisions for disqualification remain, they are for the most part of a personal nature and do not include a literacy requirement as found in many American states. One has but to compare the few hundred thousand voters of 1832 with 34,855,907 registered in 1955 to get a small idea of the impact of democratization of the franchise on British political parties.[7]

2. DEVELOPMENT OF PARTY SYSTEM

Party before 1832.   Many writers trace the origins of British political parties to the civil war of the seventeenth century. Decided differences of opinion with regard to the extent of the royal prerogative and the authority of the established church divided Royalist from Parliamentarian, Cavalier from Roundhead, Petitioner from Abhorrer. Then, in 1680 or thereabouts, the term "Tory" appeared as a mark of derision applied to those who stood by Charles II in his opposition to the Exclusion Bill, which sought to exclude Charles's brother, James, from the throne on account of the latter's Catholicism. "Whig" was the epithet hurled at supporters of this measure.

The terms Whig and Tory stuck. They reflected at the beginning the two broad divisions of opinion among the aristocracy and the upper classes on certain political questions. The Tory generally favored the established church and a strong monarchy. The Whig stood for a limited monarchy and for tolerance with respect to religious dissent. There were also fundamental points of agreement between Whig and Tory. Both opposed Roman Catholicism. Both accepted the monarchy. Both, as already mentioned, were of the upper classes, but here, again, there was a difference. The Tories came mainly from the landed gentry, the country squires, and the rural clergy of the established church. The Whigs included some noblemen plus the wealthy business interests of the larger cities.

[6] At the time 12 seats were distributed among the following universities: Oxford, 2; Cambridge, 2; London, 1; Scottish universities, 3; English provincial universities, 2; University of Wales, 1; Universty of Belfast, 1. The practice of degree holders of universities returning members to Commons dated back to James I, who granted seats to Oxford and Cambridge. The Conservative Party included in its 1951 election program a proposal to reinstitute the university constituencies, but nothing came of it.

[7] The population of the United Kingdom (England, Wales, Scotland, Northern Ireland) in 1951 was 50,212,000. Somewhat less than 70 per cent of the population was registered.

For a century after the Restoration the Whigs and Tories operated more like permanent factions than anything else. There was a repugnance, more or less general, to the idea of partisan groupings in Parliament. Party groups were frequently identified with "connexions," "factions," and "interests." Their presence seemed to disrupt the harmony and unity of the kingdom. Then, in 1769, Edmund Burke pointed out in his *Observations . . . on the Present State of the Nation* that "Party divisions, whether on the whole operating for good or evil, are things inseparable from free government." A year later Burke pronounced the classic definition of the political party: "Party is a body of men united, for promoting by their joint endeavors the national interest, upon some particular principle in which they are all agreed." Yet Burke's ideas on party did not find ready acceptance. His friend, Oliver Goldsmith, gently chided Burke as one

> Who, born for the universe, narrowed his mind,
> And to party gave up what was meant for mankind.

It is clear that the concept of party emerged in the period from the Restoration to the Reform Act of 1832. But most of the features that are now associated with the modern party system were still lacking. The Whigs and Tories were not mass, popular organizations. There was virtually no national political campaign. Indeed, there was no mass electorate. Only a few hundred thousand persons could vote, and many votes were either controlled or up for purchase.[8] Nor did either group exhibit in Parliament the close-knit cohesiveness that marks the party in Parliament today. True, Commons had begun to exert controls over the king's ministers. But the real link between party and government, the cabinet system, was still in its formative stages.

Yet the period cannot be written off, as far as party development is concerned. For out of the depths of the civil war had come Milton's classic defense of freedom of speech and expression, his *Areopagitica* (1644). At the same time the Levellers were advancing the argument that opposition to government policy was not necessarily treason.[9] Finally, before the end of the seventeenth century, John Locke would present the case for toleration in matters of faith. The foundations had arisen for that climate of opinion essential to the growth of democratic parties. Then, in the half century between Burke and the Reform Act of 1832, the first offspring of the industrial revolution, the middle class, grew strong enough to demand a voice in the running of things.

Party in the Nineteenth Century.   The Reform Act of 1832, by enfranchising the middle classes, provided the basis for realignment of

[8] It is estimated that at the beginning of the nineteenth century only one third of Commons was actually chosen by the electorate. In England and Wales, 218 seats were controlled by 87 peers, and 137 seats by other persons. As a matter of fact, for some years after the Reform Act of 1832, it was not unusual for two thirds or more of the seats to be filled in unopposed elections. In 1841, for example, only 170 seats were contested in Great Britain.

[9] See William Haller and G. Davies, eds., *The Leveller Tracts, 1647–1653* (1944), p. 36.

Whig and Tory into Liberal and Conservative. The "shopocracy," with its eyes turned toward the capitalistic future, was to work this transformation. The beginning of the change is evident in the cleavage over the Reform Act itself. Opposed to the measure were the Church, the legal profession, the military services, the universities, many banking houses, and the great majority of farmers and country squires. Support for the measure came from Nonconformists, merchants and manufacturers, professional classes other than law, town tradesmen and artisans, and the Whig aristocracy.

The Liberal and Conservative parties did not spring up full born immediately after passage of the Reform Act. Although the act expanded the electorate, it certainly did not extend the franchise to the masses. Still, one provision of the act—that making registration a requirement for voting—operated directly to bring parties in closer contact with the voter. Within a few years central party organs, the Carlton Club (Conservative) and the Reform Club (Liberal), became active along with local party associations in supervising electoral rolls.[1] Then Conservative ranks broke over repeal of the Corn Laws in 1846. Thereafter the Liberal Party came to stand more or less for laissez-faire economic policies domestically, and for free trade and anti-imperialism in the realm of foreign affairs. The Conservatives adopted, under the leadership of Disraeli, an attitude of paternalism toward the laboring classes and later turned to empire.

Meanwhile, the basic links between the cabinet and the party majority in the House of Commons were forged. As late as 1841 Macaulay was to argue before Commons that a ministry was not bound to resign because it could not carry legislation through the House. Since then, however, there has been little doubt that a government is not to remain in office without the support of a majority in Commons. The reverse proposition—the right of the prime minister to obtain a dissolution and appeal to the electorate in the event his majority deserts him— established itself a little later. In 1858 Disraeli complained: "The House of Commons is broken into sections which, although they have no unity of purpose or policy, can always combine to overthrow the Queen's Government however formed." But in the same year Lord Derby took office with advance assurance that the queen would grant a dissolution if his government failed to receive support.

Impetus for large-scale party organization among the people came from the Reform Act of 1867. This act increased the electorate in significant proportion by extending the franchise to the urban working classes. It was not long after this act, in 1877 to be exact, when Joseph Chamberlain announced his plans for the Birmingham Caucus. The caucus was to be a kind of party legislature outside of Parliament, and it was to formulate party policy and control party members in Parliament. Chamberlain's plan met with opposition from leaders in both parties and did not succeed. Nevertheless, constituency party organization has continued to be a feature of the British party system.

From 1868 until World War I the Liberal-Conservative alignment

[1] Secret balloting was introduced in 1872.

dominated the political scene. In 1868, 1880, 1885, and 1892 the Liberals were successful at the polls. In 1874, 1886, and 1895 the Conservatives emerged victorious. Beginning in 1895, the Conservatives enjoyed ten years of office, followed by ten years of Liberal rule ending in the coalition govenments of World War I.

During this period events occurred that served to weaken the Liberal Party. Gladstone's ill-fated Home Rule Bill of 1886 for Ireland drove a number of so-called Liberal Unionists into the Conservative ranks. Of course the Home Rule Bill insured for the Liberals the support of the Irish Nationalist Party. Then in 1906 the Labour Party appeared. Its strength was small but persistent (twenty-nine seats in 1906, forty-odd seats in the elections of 1910).

The situation in which the Liberal Party found itself is illustrated in the two elections of 1910. In the first election the distribution of seats in Commons was as follows: Liberals 275, Conservatives 273, Irish Nationalists 82, Labour 40. The second election produced virtually no change in party strengths. The Liberals could remain in office only with the support of minor parties.

Parties since World War I. After World War I competition ensued between the Liberal Party and the Labour Party for the place of second party in a two-party system. Labour emerged the winner. First of all, the Liberal Party split into factions headed by Lloyd George and Asquith. Although attempts at reunion took place, they never were successful for long. But, split or united, the Liberals never again received the seals of office.[2] Labour, on the other hand, twice took office in the interwar period (1923 and 1929), although both times as a minority government dependent upon Liberal support. Meanwhile, the Conservatives were doing quite well. They won majorities in 1922 and in 1924. In 1931 and 1935 a National Coalition, so-called, received tremendous majorities at the polls, but in both instances Conservatives formed the great bulk of the coalition.[3]

World War II brought a halt to partisan politics. Winston Churchill, with the backing of Labour, succeeded the discredited Neville Chamberlain in 1940. In 1945 party politics began again. Labour swept into office by a landslide, capturing 393 seats in Commons as compared with 198 for the Conservatives and 12 for the Liberals.[4] In 1950 Prime Minister Attlee's party managed to maintain a slim hold on office. Labour won 315 seats to the Conservatives' 298 and the Liberals' 9. Moreover, Labour's popular strength declined to only 46.4 per cent of the votes cast, which was less than the combined Conservative (43.5 per cent) and Liberal (9.1 per cent) popular vote.

[2] In 1931 the Lloyd George wing of the party was reduced to Lloyd George himself, his daughter, his son, and his son's brother-in-law.

[3] In 1931 the Conservatives held 470 of the Coalition's 556 seats. Ramsay MacDonald, who had headed the two Labour governments of 1923 and 1929, remained as prime minister until 1935, when Stanley Baldwin assumed the office. In 1935 the Conservatives accounted for 387 of the Coalition's 431 seats.

[4] The percentage vote for the three major parties was: Labour, 48; Conservative, 39.9; Liberal, 9.

In the fall of 1951, after a split between Prime Minister Attlee and Aneurin Bevan, the Conservatives came back into power. They and their allies won 321 seats, Labour captured 295 seats and the Liberals held 6.[5] Curiously, Labour polled the largest number of votes ever cast for a single party in Britain and, at the same time, showed a slight popular advantage over the Conservatives. In 1955, Prime Minister Churchill put aside the burdens of office. His successor, Anthony Eden, chose to call a general election. Eden's decision proved sound from the Conservative point of view. His party increased its margin in Commons by winning 345 seats, while Labour fell off to 277 seats and the Liberals kept 6 seats.[6]

Since World War I the British two-party system has realigned itself along a Conservative-Labour balance. The decline of the Liberal Party seems permanent. Indeed, the election of 1951 has been aptly described as a fight between Labour and Conservative for the "corpse" of the Liberal Party. Contributing to the decline of the Liberals are many factors. The split in the party was aggravated by the single-member district system, which "threw away," figuratively speaking, hundreds of thousands of Liberal votes.[7] Liberalism as a political faith lost strength not only in Britain but elsewhere. The economic situation since World War I has called, generally speaking, for increasing state activity. Both the Conservative and Labour parties have been prepared to advocate state activity, although of different kinds and for different purposes. The Liberal Party remained plagued by its historic antipathy to state intervention in the economic realm, despite its willingness to embark upon social welfare programs such as those initiated by Lloyd George and the Asquith government in the first decade of the twentieth century. But the small entrepreneur is becoming (comparatively speaking) a vanishing race in England. The Labour Party has argued that it is the natural vehicle to carry out programs on behalf of the working masses. The Conservatives have appeared as the natural guardians of private property. The Liberal Party saw its economic and class foundations crumble.

The Labour-Conservative balance centers on economic questions and factors, although the dividing line between the two parties has become less distinct. The parties draw their popular support on a group and class basis that reflects a division of economic interests, but this division is by no means rigid. The working-class vote, more particularly the trade-union vote, forms the core of Labour Party support, yet an indispensable fraction of support regularly comes from the middle class

[5] The percentage vote for the three major parties was: Labour, 48.7; Conservative, 48; Liberal, 2.5.

[6] The percentage vote for the three major parties was: Conservative, 49.8; Labour, 46.3; Liberal, 2.7. The 1955 election was the first since 1832 in which no member was returned unopposed.

[7] In 1950, Liberal popular strength would have produced about 56 seats under a system of proportional representation. Instead the Liberals won 9 seats.

In the spring of 1958, Liberal Party candidate Mark Bonham Carter won the first Liberal victory in a by-election in twenty-nine years in Torrington, Devonshire. This victory and other developments touched off talk of a Liberal revival and plans for the party to run about 150 candidates in the next general election.

and professional people.[8] The Conservative Party finds its roots among the propertied classes, the farmers and landowners in the country, and the business, trade, financial, and industrial groups in the cities, yet it receives a small but significant share of the working-class vote. Some observers argue that the balance wheel between the two parties is the "floating" vote. The "floating" vote is made up of middle-class and lower-middle-class voters, especially in the cities and large towns, who have not permanently committed themselves to either party. In terms of party policies and programs the place of private property and the role of the state still provide questions on which the parties disagree. But even here disagreement is not in terms of black and white. The Conservative Party has accepted in the main the social security aspects of the welfare state and has continued to support some nationalization of industry. And Labour on its part has become less doctrinaire on the point of nationalization. Differences on grounds of economic principle remain between the two parties, but in practice these oftentimes appear to reduce to differences of degree, especially when concrete solutions to problems are concerned. Indeed, Mr. Jo Grimond, leader of the Liberal Party has recently charged in a party pamphlet, "The New Liberal Democracy," that the "Conservative Party has in fact been conserving Socialism for the last eight years."

3. PARTY ORGANIZATION

"I would vote for a pig if [my] party put one up."[9] This declaration of faith pledged by a Midland voter in 1951 pungently testifies to the impact of party on the British electorate. Even stronger has been the impact on the politician, for, as one writer has recently put it, outside the party "there is no salvation." [1] In other words, the independent candidate in British politics is finding the going extremely tough. Not a single independent succeeded in winning a seat in 1951. Virtually the same result occurred in 1955. Of the 1,409 candidates who entered the 1955 polling only a dozen could be called real "independents," and none of these was successful.[2] Clearly, party has profoundly affected the political role of the individual Britisher, whether voter or politician. And party organization has played a leading part in the process.

A fundamental issue of principle with respect to party organization arose almost as soon as large-scale organization began. Joseph Chamberlain's Birmingham Caucus plan brought the issue to a head very

[8] Labour Party membership in 1953 was 6,107,569, of which 5,071,935 represented affiliated trade-union members. The total Labour vote in 1955 was over 12,400,000.

[9] As quoted in D. E. Butler, *The British General Election of 1951* (1952), p. 173.

[1] R. T. McKenzie, *British Political Parties* (1955), p. 4.

[2] In addition, the Sinn Fein put up 12 candidates in Northern Ireland and 2 were elected. Both declared that they would not sit in the Imperial Parliament; both happened to be in the Belfast prison serving jail sentences for felony-treason.

quickly. Was the party organization *outside* Parliament to dictate to the party *inside* Parliament? Broadly speaking, this proposition received a negative answer. As a result the party inside Parliament not only preserved its independence but also maintained its autonomy and prerogatives with respect to policy formulation.

Conservative Party. Since the resignation of Lord Salisbury in 1902 the leader of the Conservative Party has come from the House of Commons. Formally, the leader is elected by the Conservative Party meeting, composed of Conservative members of Commons and the House of Lords, prospective Conservative candidates, and the executive committee of the National Union of Conservative and Unionist Associations, the Conservative organization outside Parliament. The meeting merely ratifies, however, a choice made elsewhere, as is illustrated by the change in leadership from Sir Anthony Eden to Harold Macmillan in January 1957. As prime minister Eden had led England to the use of armed force in Egypt during the Suez crisis of 1956, and his policy came under heavy attack. The situation was complicated by Eden's illness, but finally, in early January 1957, Sir Anthony resigned as prime minister. Speculation arose as to his successor as prime minister, with R. A. Butler, leader of the party in the House of Commons, and Macmillan, chancellor of the Exchequer, being mentioned as the top contenders. In naming the new prime minister Queen Elizabeth was advised, not only by Sir Anthony, but also by Sir Winston Churchill and Lord Salisbury. These advisers preferred Macmillan over Butler, for reasons that went back to Butler's identification with the appeasement policy followed at Munich in 1938. In addition some thirty members of the Conservative Party referred to as the "Suez group" had publicly let it be known that they would not be satisfied with Butler. Queen Elizabeth called Mr. Macmillan to be prime minister. Sir Anthony Eden did not resign as party leader until two weeks later, at which time the Conservative Party meeting unanimously elected Mr. Macmillan to head the party. Some Labour spokesmen charged that this procedure had put the queen in politics, arguing that the queen's designation of Mr. Macmillan as prime minister had in effect made him party leader. But this charge did not get very far. As a matter of fact, the procedure followed in 1957 had been used consistently by the Conservatives. Since the election of Bonar Law in 1923 the post of Conservative Party leader has changed hands when the party has been in office and the party leader also has been prime minister. The outgoing leader has resigned first as prime minister, and the person called by the king or queen (acting upon advice, of course) to be the new prime minister has always later been accepted as party leader by the Conservative meeting. Once in office, the leader does not submit to re-election. He stays as leader until he retires, although four Conservative leaders since 1900 have in effect been forced to resign.[3]

[3] Balfour in 1911, Austen Chamberlain in 1922, Neville Chamberlain in 1940, and Sir Anthony Eden in 1957. Strictly speaking, Austen Chamberlain was leader of the party only in the House of Commons.

The Conservative leader has a free hand in selecting his circle of close advisers: the cabinet when the party is in power; the "Shadow Cabinet" when the party is out of power. The leader also appoints the chief whip and his deputies as well as a number of party officials outside Parliament. Of this last group the most important is the chairman of the party organization, who directs the Conservative central office.

Not all party organization within Parliament comes under the direct control of the Conservative leader. There is a body of party apparatus that is primarily the backbenchers' organization. An important organ falling in this category is the Conservative (Private) Members Committee, or the 1922 Committee, as it is popularly called. The 1922 Committee meets regularly under the chairmanship of a backbencher. It does not formulate policy, but it does discuss policy. When the party is in power, the discussions of the 1922 Committee provide a sounding board for backbench sentiment on the path being pursued by the party leader, who is then, of course, the prime minister.[4]

There is also a number (usually fewer than twenty) of functional party committees. Each of these deals with a particular governmental activity such as agriculture and food, Commonwealth relations, defense, foreign affairs, etc. When the party is in power, the functional committees are chaired by backbenchers.[5] The precise role of the functional committees is not clear. Individual committees have brought criticism against particular ministers. Too much activity on the part of these committees stands, on the other hand, to conflict with the policy-making prerogatives of the leader and his cabinet.[6]

As mentioned earlier, the Conservative Party leader appoints the chairman of the party organization, who directs the central office.[7] The functions of the central office are to co-ordinate party activities throughout the country, to advise and assist constituency and regional party organizations, and to provide various services in connection with campaigning and electioneering. These last include: raising money; screening potential candidates; providing handbooks, party literature, and national publicity; training party agents; directing organizational activity among labor and youth; and undertaking co-ordination tasks in local elections.

The National Union of Conservative and Unionist Associations, the party outside Parliament, dates from 1867. The National Union is federal in form, made up in 1955 of some 540 constituency associations in

[4] The whips attend meetings of the committee and report to the party leader. The chairman of the committee has direct access to the party leader. When the party is out of power, each Conservative M.P. is a private member and can attend meetings of the committee. The party leader normally does so only on important occasions.

[5] When the party is in opposition, these committees are usually chaired by front-bench party members.

[6] There also arises the constitutional question of how far a minister can go in revealing to these committees matters that have not yet been placed before the House.

[7] The party leader appoints a number of other important party headquarters officials, including the chairman of the Conservative research department. The central "civil service" of the party at the central office numbered about two hundred in 1952.

England and Wales with a membership of over 2,800,000.[8] Constituency associations are also federated on a regional basis.[9] The governing body of the National Union is the central council. It is a large body with a potential size of about 3,600, composed of all members of the party inside Parliament, officials of the central office, prospective Conservative candidates, and representatives from the National Union, the constituency associations, and various advisory committees. The Conservative annual conference is even larger (about 5,600 potentially), as it is made up of the central council plus additional representatives from the constituency associations. There is also the executive committee of the National Union, which meets periodically, and a general purposes subcommittee, which meets monthly as a rule.[1]

Two series of advisory committees and boards complete the broad outline of Conservative Party structure. One series reports to and advises the executive committee of the National Union.[2] Another group, although containing representatives from the National Union, is responsible, not to the National Union, but either directly or indirectly to the leader of the party. And this last group includes the highly important committees on policy, party finance, and parliamentary candidates.[3]

Labour Party. The Labour Party inside Parliament is known as the Parliamentary Labour Party. When Labour is in opposition, the parliamentary party, consisting of Labour members of Commons and Lords, annually elects one person to serve as chairman and leader. Once elected, the party chairman and leader is normally re-elected as a matter of course.[4] When the party comes into power, the chairman and leader can be expected to receive the call to office as prime minister.[5]

[8] Separate party organizations exist for Scotland and Northern Ireland.

[9] England and Wales are divided into 12 regional areas; the system of regional organization dates from 1886.

[1] The executive committee numbers about 150; the subcommittee about 56. Both bodies contain members from the party inside Parliament.

[2] Among others these include the Women's National Advisory Committee, the Trade Unionist National Advisory Committee, and the National Advisory Committee on Political Education.

[3] Included in this group are the examination board for agents and organizers and the superannuation fund.

[4] The only real exception to this practice was the resignation of George Lansbury in 1935. Lansbury held pacifist views, and, after the Labour annual conference carried a resolution supporting sanctions against Italy, Lansbury resigned. Curiously, the parliamentary party at first declined to accept his resignation. Ramsay MacDonald's exodus in 1931 was more a case of the leader leaving the party.

[5] Attlee was confirmed as leader in special meetings of the parliamentary party after he became prime minister in 1945 and 1951. He had been elected leader in 1935 and had held the post continuously since then. The post of leader of the Labour Party has never fallen vacant while the party was in office.

Mr. Attlee resigned as leader of the Labour Party in December 1955 and accepted a peerage. In the ensuing election of a new leader the parliamentary party chose Hugh Gaitskell. Mr. Gaitskell received 140 votes to Aneurin Bevan's 70 and Herbert Morrison's 40. Gaitskell is a comparative newcomer to the party, having entered Commons in 1945. He rose rapidly to ministerial rank, however. He was minister of Fuel and Power in 1947–50 and chancellor of the Exchequer in 1950–51. He is considered to be right-wing in the party.

The post of party chairman and leader then divides. A backbencher is annually elected as party chairman. But the Labour prime minister remains the party leader and he does not submit to annual re-election as leader as long as he continues as prime minister. When, as in 1951, the Labour Party goes out of office, the former prime minister becomes once more chairman and leader of the party and, of course, submits to annual re-election.

As prime minister the Labour Party leader selects his own cabinet much as the Conservative Party leader does in the same circumstances. When the party is out of office, the leader (and chairman) is a member of the parliamentary committee. This committee is the executive body of the Parliamentary Labour Party when in opposition. It numbers eighteen members, most of whom are elected by the Labour members of Commons. The parliamentary committee was superseded by a much smaller liaison committee of six (later seven) members during the period of Labour power from 1945 to 1951.

The Parliamentary Labour Party also uses "subject groups," which are similar to the "functional committees" of the Conservative Party.[6] Backbenchers chaired these groups during the period 1945–51, but several of the groups came under the chairmanship of former ministers after 1951. These groups pose essentially the same problems for the policy-making prerogatives of the Labour prime minister and his cabinet as those discussed in connection with the Conservative functional committees.

The organization of the Labour Party outside Parliament is, like the Conservative, federal in form. According to the party constitution, "the work of the Party shall be under the direction and control" of the annual conference. The conference has a potential size of about 2,500. Members ex officio are: members of the Parliamentary Labour Party; prospective Labour candidates; members of the national executive committee; the secretary of the party; and representatives of the Labour League of Youth. Ex-officio members of the annual conference do not as such have the right to vote or to be nominated for office. Delegates to the annual conference are sent by affiliated national trade unions, affiliated socialist and co-operative societies, and constituency parties (of which there are several kinds). The trade unions and constituency parties provide the great bulk of representation at the annual conference. Indeed, the constituency parties send in practice as many or more delegates as do the trade unions,[7] but when balloting is "by card," the trade unions cast about five sixths of the votes.

The national executive committee is the "Administrative Authority of the Party," working under the control and direction of the annual conference. It is chosen annually, and in 1957 consisted of twenty-seven members. The party leader is an ex-officio member. The affiliated trade unions elect twelve members; the various constituency parties elect seven;

[6] There is also a Trade Union group composed of members whose candidatures are sponsored by trade unions. Recently "area groups" have also been set up.

[7] Trade unions are entitled to more delegates, but constituency parties send almost their full complement, while trade unions do not.

and the affiliated socialist and co-operative societies elect a single member. The annual conference elects five women members and the party treasurer. The national executive committee appoints a number of subcommittees to deal with matters such as finance, policy and publicity, elections, etc. The party leader and deputy leader are ex-officio members of the most important of these subcommittees. Primarily under impetus supplied by the national executive committee the Labour Party has established since 1938 eleven regional councils covering England, Wales, and Scotland.

The Labour head office (Transport House) corresponds to the Conservative central office. The head office is not under the direction of the party leader, however; it is under the direction of the national executive committee. With a smaller staff than the Conservative central office Transport House apparently does a good job. At any rate Transport House drew from its Conservative opponents the concession that it was a "magnificent political machine."

Leadership and Discipline. On the surface the Conservative Party leader appears to be a much more powerful figure than his Labour counterpart. The Conservative leader does not submit to annual re-election; he has wide appointing powers to party posts; and he controls the party's central office and the funds at the disposal of the central organization. The Conservative leader is acknowledged to be the oracle of party policy: "Endorsement and pronouncements on Party policy are the prerogative and responsibility of the Leader." [8] It is recognized that resolutions of the Conservative annual conference do not bind the party leader. On the other hand, the leader of the Labour Party submits to annual re-election when the party is in opposition; he has little appointing power; and the national executive committee has control of the party's head office. Furthermore, party literature emphasizes the point that Labour Party policy is made democratically by party members: "The Parliamentary Party carries through its duties within the framework of policy laid down by the Annual Party Conference to which it reports each year." [9]

In practice the Conservative Party leader is far from being an absolute dictator. Proceedings of the Conservative annual conference are not necessarily ignored simply because they do not bind the leader. Conservative cabinet ministers have appeared before the conference to urge loyalty to the leader. Resolutions of the conference have received acceptance from the leader, sometimes, perhaps, with misgivings. Finally, party rank and file both inside and outside Parliament can bring strong pressure to bear on party leadership, as the forced departures of Balfour, Austen Chamberlain, Neville Chamberlain, and Anthony Eden attest.

[8] *Interim and Final Reports of the Committee on Party Organization 1948 and 1949* (1949), p. 36.

[9] *The Rise of the Labour Party* (1948), p. 14. Former Prime Minister Attlee himself has written that the annual conference "lays down the policy of the Party and issues instructions which must be carried out by" the party's representatives in Parliament. *The Labour Party in Perspective* (1937), p. 93.

And the Labour Party leader is far from being a puppet. Attlee, on becoming prime minister, formed his government without *formally* consulting any party organ.[1] Furthermore, he made it clear that responsibility for conduct of the government lay with the cabinet and not with the annual conference or the national executive committee. A prime factor contributing to the success of the Labour Party leader in maintaining a strong position is the interlocking of personnel between the parliamentary party and the national executive committee. During the first postwar Labour government (1945–50), sixteen of the twenty-seven members of the committee were members of Parliament, and of these nine or more were ministers.[2] Equally important is the "alliance" between the parliamentary leaders and the trade-union leaders.[3] As long as this alliance persists, the party leader can expect support from the annual conference since the trade unions cast, as we have seen, about five sixths of the votes in the conference.[4]

In marked contrast to American practice the British national parties exercise strong control over party candidates. There is no provision for a direct primary in Britain.[5] Local constituency parties adopt candidates.[6] Both the Labour and Conservative national parties reserve the right to withhold the party label from a candidate even though he might be adopted by a local party.[7] An individual or even a local party candidate who does not have the endorsement of the national party can expect little success against one who has. In some instances national party leaders have prevailed upon local parties not to run a candidate at all

[1] In so doing Attlee ignored a decision of the 1933 party conference that a Labour prime minister should form his government with the advice of three members of the parliamentary party specially elected for the purpose.

[2] See R. T. McKenzie, *British Political Parties* (1955), pp. 421–23.

[3] Ibid., pp. 506–7.

[4] When voting by card, unions and constituency parties normally cast their vote *en bloc*. Trade unions also sponsor candidates, and these form a sizable bloc in the Parliamentary Labour Party (96 in 1955).

[5] Nomination is a simple process in Britain. The candidate files papers bearing the signatures of ten persons and deposits £150, which sum he forfeits if he does not poll at least one eighth of the votes cast.

[6] The procedure used for adoption of candidates is substantially as follows: A small committee of the local party gathers together a list of nominations. Included in this list will usually be names suggested by national party headquarters, and all names must have been screened by a national party committee, the standing advisory committee on candidates (Conservatives), the national executive committee (Labour). The small committee cuts the list of nominations to three or four persons. These then appear before the executive body of the local party to give a short talk and answer questions. The executive bodies of the local parties are, it should be noted, fairly representative, containing delegates from ward committees and organizations (such as youth and labor) affiliated with the local party. In the Labour Party the choice of the candidate is made by the executive body, subject to final endorsement by the national executive committee. In the Conservative Party the choice of the executive council is submitted to a general meeting of the constituency party, but the meeting almost invariably accepts the council's selection. Occasionally a defeated nominee will enter the poll, but he has little chance of success against the adopted nominee who will have the endorsement of the national party.

[7] In an extreme case the national party can "disaffiliate" the local party, but it should be stressed that the national parties prefer not to run roughshod over the constituency parties in such matters.

but to give support to a candidate of an allied party.[8] Also, in Britain, neither law nor custom requires a candidate to reside in the constituency that elects him. As a consequence the national parties are generally able to take care of a prominent frontbencher who runs into difficulties in a particular constituency by finding a relatively safe constituency for his candidature.[9]

In another contrast with American parties British national parties can exercise strong discipline over individual party members in the House of Commons.[1] Both the major parliamentary parties can "withdraw the whip" from a recalcitrant member. Withdrawal of the whip itself simply means that the member is excluded from the parliamentary party's proceedings. But it very likely will also mean refusal to endorse the recalcitrant one in the next parliamentary election and could even result in expulsion from the party as a whole.

The net effect of party organization and discipline in Britain is to maintain a remarkable long-run continuity of personnel in the House of Commons. In the election of 1955 candidates running for the first time numbered 494. Only 26 of these were successful. Over two thirds of the 630 members elected in 1955 had made their first candidature in 1945 or earlier, and over one third in 1935 or earlier.[2] In this respect the Labour Party exhibited a greater tendency toward continuity of personnel than the Conservative. Approximately 84 per cent of Labour members had made their first candidature in 1945 or earlier; the corresponding proportion for the Conservatives and their allies was only 60 per cent. However, in the Eden cabinet of 1955, thirteen of the fourteen Commoners had first been elected to the House in 1945 or earlier, nine in 1935 or earlier, and five before 1925.

A final observation concerns the effect of the British parliamentary system on the organization of parties. The Conservative Party outside Parliament was created by the party inside Parliament to be a "handmaid" to the parliamentary group. The Parliamentary Labour Party, on the other hand, was the creature of various groups outside Parliament that combined to form the Labour movement. Some of the leaders of the Labour movement frankly intended that the parliamentary party should be under the control and direction of the party outside Parliament. But the leaders of the Parliamentary Labour Party found it easier and perhaps preferable to conform to the principles and practices of British parliamentary government. By so doing they and their members succeeded in gaining a good deal of independence from and influence in the party outside Parliament.

Yet, despite their tight organization and discipline, British parties

[8] In 1955 the Conservative Party allowed five of the six sitting Liberal members to run without Conservative opposition. In 1951 Conservatives supported Liberals in seven constituencies.

[9] In the revision of constituencies in 1955 the seat of Dr. Edith Summerskill, chairman of the Labour Party, disappeared. She finally found a constituency, but only after twice failing to be adopted by local parties.

[1] See James M. Burns, "The Parliamentary Labour Party in Great Britain," *American Political Science Review*, 44 (1950), pp. 855–71.

[2] See D. E. Butler, *The British General Election of 1955* (1955), pp. 38–39.

are by no means impervious to sectional, social, and economic group pressures. Indeed, the history of group organizations for the specific purpose of bringing pressure to bear on Parliament dates at least from the latter half of the eighteenth century, or the same period in which the notion of the political party itself emerged. But British party organization leads pressure-group politics into somewhat different forms than these activities take in the United States. The cabinet system places power in the hands of a relatively small group of ministers rather than in the hands of individual members of Parliament. In addition special or private legislation is handled in a manner that permits local groups ready access to Parliament; otherwise parliamentary committees are not the point of contact between interest groups and the legislature. Pressure seeks the holders of power. Thus pressure organizations in Britain are more likely to put their cases before the responsible ministers or the functional committees of the parliamentary parties. Also, groups in Britain are more openly represented in the parliamentary parties. The trade unions now regularly sponsor about a hundred members of Commons, and other groups have acknowledged spokesmen in the House. Widespread use of advisory councils further permits consultation between government and private interests. And with regard to sectionalism the major parties exhibit an increasing awareness of the regional aspirations of Scotland and Wales.[3]

4. PARTY PRINCIPLES

Liberalism. The Liberal Party has declined, indeed almost vanished, as a political force in modern Britain. Nevertheless liberalism, variously interpreted, has been the keystone in the pattern of modern British political thought. Liberalism was the ideological bridge between the absolutist-minded state of the Tudors and the parliamentary state of the seventeenth century. Both British conservatism and socialism represent reactions to liberal doctrine. Conservatism began as a recoiling against the extremes of political liberalism as demonstrated in the French Revolution. Socialism emerged as a protest against the social evils that flowed in the wake of economic liberalism in the nineteenth century.

Early liberal theory found classic expression in the thought of John Locke. Locke's theory contains several basic conceptions and premises. Man is by nature a rational creature, endowed with conscience, on the whole good-minded, and, by nature, free, equal, and independent. There is a law of nature, "and reason, which is that law," teaches that "No one ought to harm another in his life, health, liberty or possessions." Man enters into political society only by his own consent, and only the

[3] See Samuel H. Beer, "Pressure Groups and Parties in Britain," *American Political Science Review,* 50 (1956), pp. 1–23; also S. E. Finer, "Interest Groups and the Political Process in Great Britain," in Henry W. Ehrmann, ed., *Interest Groups on Four Continents* (1958). For discussion of parliamentary committees see below, pp. 69–70; for discussion of regionalism, pp. 122–24.

"better to preserve himself, his liberty and property." In agreeing to
unite into one community men (unless they specifically conclude otherwise) agree to be bound by the decision of the majority. The majority
then establishes the legislative power, the "supreme power of the commonwealth, but sacred and unalterable in the hands where the community have once placed it." But the "obligations of the law of nature
cease not in society"; they stand as "an eternal rule to all men, legislators
as well as others." The legislative power, therefore, is only a "fiduciary
power to act for certain ends," and the people retain the power to alter
or remove the legislative power if it betrays its trust. In the extreme the
people have a right to revolution against tyrannical government.

As time went by, first one and then another of Locke's concepts
and premises underwent severe criticism or reinterpretation. For example,
Locke's theory of contract was objected to by many later liberal writers.
Both Bentham and T. H. Green denied the validity of the social-contract theory on historical and logical grounds. The theory of natural law
and individual rights received varying treatment. Bentham dismissed the
theory as nonsense and insisted that no rights exist as against the state.
The positive lawyers emphatically held that all rights are legal rights, to
be given or taken away by law. At the other extreme were men like
Adam Smith, John Stuart Mill, and Herbert Spencer. Smith and the
laissez-faire school generally identified natural rights with the profit motive and natural law with the "invisible hand," a *deus ex machina* of
competitive capitalism. The younger Mill equated natural rights with individual liberty and freedom of action. Spencer, building upon the natural laws of biological evolution, stressed natural law as the equal right
of unequal men to develop unequally. A common feature in the thought
of Smith, Mill, and Spencer is the insistence that the individual has
specific, concrete rights that cannot be invaded by the state. A middle
ground is that of T. H. Green. Green denied that rights exist independently of the state and society; at the same time he insisted that it is the
duty of the state to sustain rights arising from other forms of community
relations. Green, anxious to avoid the stultifying effects of natural rights
as interpreted by the extreme individualists, seems willing to concede
only the abstract right to the good life. Further, he argues that the
jurisdiction to define in particular of what the good life consists belongs
to society and the state, not to the individual.

Locke's views on the rationality of man—his trust in human reason
—also underwent transformation. First, Hume demonstrated that there
was no necessary connection between experiential fact and logical reason.
No comparison of ideas, Hume insisted, can prove a matter of fact;
cause and effect in the realm of fact mean nothing more than the observed fact that two phenomena are found to occur together, not that
one causes the other. In the realm of human conduct Hume argued
that "reason is and ought to be the slave of passions." After Hume, Bentham built his calculus not upon reason but upon emotion and feeling,
the greatest happiness for the greatest number. Finally, Hobhouse came
to the conclusion that it is useless to appeal to the man in the street in
terms of reason. The new "public opinion of the streets and the tramcars

. . . has not time to put the two ends of an argument together; it has hardly patience to receive a single idea, much less to hold two in the mind and compare them."

Liberal thought at last reached an impasse. In order to cope with the forces let loose by modern industrialism and nationalism, Liberals found themselves in danger of rejecting the fundamental tenets of their creed: individualism and natural law. The British Liberal Party[4] chose on the whole to remain true to liberalism's basic premises. In its 1955 election manifesto, *Crisis Unresolved,* the party declared:

> We exist as a party to defend the rights of the individual, his liberty to live his own life subject to respect for the rights of others, to hold and express his own views, to associate with others of his own choice, to be granted all possible freedom of opportunity, and to be subject to no penalty or discrimination by reason of his colour, race, or creed.

On economic matters the party urged reduction and eventual abolition of tariffs, restriction of monopolies, re-examination of the place and function of trade unions, and co-ownership schemes in industry. In the international field it endorsed the general aims of present British foreign policy. But the party did suggest restriction of the veto in the Security Council of the United Nations, membership for Red China in the United Nations, and closer association with movements for European unification.

These proposals fell, as we have seen, on deaf ears. And the reason is apparent in the Liberal manifesto itself. The party appealed to the "independent mind, the small man. and the consumer," who were, as Mill had feared almost a century before, being ground to pieces in a "struggle between two class parties." But there were far too few "independent minds" left.

Still, the legacy of liberalism to British constitutionalism is great indeed. Government by consent, majority rule, political equality, respect for human dignity, Lord Beveridge's "cradle-to-the-grave plan"—these stand as integral parts of present-day political life in the British Isles.

Conservatism. British conservatism grew out of the reaction to the excesses of the French Revolution, which, rightly or wrongly, were attributed to the effects of liberalism. Appropriately enough, it was Edmund Burke, a member of the Whig Party, who voiced the principles of conservatism. As Burke saw them, these principles were merely a reaffirmation of the principles of 1688, the selfsame principles that Locke essayed to vindicate. British conservatism, then, accepted England's political revolution, a fact that distinguishes it from conservatism in many

---

[4] There is also a National Liberal Party, which was formed in 1931. It has aligned itself with the Conservative Party because, as its 1955 election statement, *Freedom for the Future,* said, "even a united Liberal Party could not defeat Socialism and make Liberalism effective, alone."

other countries. It is doubtful, for example, whether French conservatism really accepts the implications of the revolution of 1789.

Burke seldom rejected liberal premises *in toto;* instead he insisted that the liberals failed to take into account other factors. He conceded the existence of natural rights apart from government and "in total independence of it." But he drew a distinction between the rights of man in the abstract and those he is able to enjoy as a member of any particular society. Burke objected to the reliance that liberalism during the Enlightenment placed upon the individual and his abstract reason. He held that experience and tradition, the collected reason of the ages, ought to be given weight. The ruling majority should not be an "individual momentary aggregation," with its shifting whims and false moods. To be sure, society was a contract, but the state was something more than an "agreement in a trade of pepper and coffee, calico or tobacco." It was a vast partnership "between those who are living, those who are dead, and those who are to be born." Man had a duty, not simply to his own individual desires, but to his ancestors and progeny, to the society in which he found himself, and to God, the "Master, Author, and Founder of society."

As the nineteenth century progressed, serious misgivings regarding the tenets of individualism were voiced by spokesmen of both liberalism and conservatism, for example, by Walter Bagehot on psychological grounds in *Physics and Politics* (1873) and by Sir Henry Sumner Maine on historical grounds in *Popular Government* (1885). The Conservative was generally skeptical of the conception of man that stressed his inherent goodness and the susceptibility of his nature to change by environmental manipulation. Yet the Conservative did not embrace state authoritarianism, one obvious antidote for the defects of man's nature. For one thing, Conservatives like Sir James Stephen in his *Liberty, Equality, Fraternity* (1873) argued strenuously that government must have a moral and religious basis. The conservative view that morals and religion exist as standards for the conduct of government helps to account for the reluctance of British conservatism to receive with open arms the Hegelian idealism of F. H. Bradley[5] and Bernard Bosanquet.[6] And writers like the lawyer, F. W. Maitland,[7] and the church scholar, J. N. Figgis,[8] re-emphasized the personality of the group and its claim to an independent place in society.

In Disraeli the Conservative Party found a spokesman who was able to translate the Conservative creed into workable principles for political action. Tory democracy, according to Disraeli, had three major purposes: "to maintain the institutions of the country," "to uphold the Empire of England," and "to elevate the conditions of the people." These principles remain broadly valid today. Sir Anthony Eden, who succeeded Churchill as prime minister and party leader, restated them after World War II as follows:

[5] *Ethical Studies* (1876).
[6] *The Philosophical Theory of the State* (1899).
[7] *Political Theories of the Middle Age* (1900), Introduction.
[8] *Churches in the Modern State* (1913).

. . . We believe in the British tradition. We take pride in the history of our race and Empire. We believe there is a vast deal of good in this structure of the British way of life that has been built up over so many centuries by patience and far-seeing effort. We believe in using all that is good in our existing institutions, in our law, in our way of life, in our economy, as the only sound and sure basis for future progress.

. . . We must have regard for the whole man. We recognize that man cannot develop as a moral being unless his material life is properly ordered. But at the same time we recognize that the excessive ordering and regulation of his material life may in the end destroy his moral and intellectual freedom.[9]

Conservative principles may seem vague and ill-defined, especially to political opponents. Labour spokesmen sometimes dismiss conservatism as anything the Conservative Party leader says or does and gets away with. The Conservative is apt to reply: "Other parties have come and gone, as they will come and go again. Conservatism will remain because it is based on certain fundamental principles, and not on a rigid formula applicable only to a single generation." [1] There is a good deal of political truth in this answer.

For whatever else Conservative principles may be, they are flexible and adaptable. While they permit strong stands on particular issues, they do not demand the Conservative to continue fighting a hopeless battle, once the issue is lost. On the contrary, they allow the Conservative to accept the verdict, grudgingly and partially perhaps, and then to find new vantage points from which to continue the party struggle. Thus the Conservatives fought Labour bitterly in 1945, and continued to raise loud protests as Labour put into effect its measures for partial nationalization and greater planning in the economy. Yet, in the end, the Conservatives did not insist that everything Labour did must be undone. The Conservatives argued for *less* nationalization, *less* government controls, and *less* taxation. When the Conservatives returned to power in 1951, there was no wholesale reversal of Labour policies at all. Instead the Conservatives undertook a careful pruning of the postwar socialist garden.

Also, Conservative principles do not require a negative approach to government. On economic matters Conservatives do not regard themselves as "the children of the laissez-faire school." An illustration is postwar housing. New housing in Britain was a difficult problem after the war, and almost by accident the party in 1950 endorsed a program for building three hundred thousand new homes per year. After it took office in 1951, the party realized this goal. Naturally, its 1955 election manifesto *United for Peace and Progress* made much of this feat, and then went on to announce intentions for large-scale slum clearance and school building.

[9] From a speech to his constituency association in 1946, contained in *Days for Decision* (1950), pp. 4–9.
[1] From a speech of Sir Anthony Eden to the Conservative party conference in 1947, ibid., p. 120.

Another characteristic of British conservatism is its strong empirical and pragmatic tinge. The Conservative can pose as the stout defender of private property and private enterprise and stand for a "property-owning democracy" and "proper rewards for extra skill, effort and responsibility." But the Conservative does not define his objectives in terms of doctrinaire logic purely. Private property and free enterprise are also empirically defined, and inevitable changes in property rights and necessary restrictions on enterprise become after a while accepted as a part of the Conservative's definition of his objectives. The same process takes place in the realm of foreign affairs. The British Empire can turn before his very eyes into a Commonwealth, and the Conservative soon is defending the Commonwealth with the same ardor that Disraeli preached empire. Thus British conservatism is resistant to change but is not necessarily reactionary. Its Labour opponents have well summed up the role of conservatism in the British party struggle: the Conservative Party is the guardian of tradition and acts as "democracy's brake on social change." [2]

Conservative thought in Britain has taken issue with liberalism primarily over individualism; it argues that liberalism sacrifices order for freedom. On the other hand, British conservatism takes issue with socialism primarily over equality; it argues that socialism sacrifices freedom for order. Yet conservative thought is ductile enough to find areas of agreement with both of its opponents. As Harold Macmillan said upon the occasion of his election as Conservative Party leader in 1957:

I hear a lot of silly talk about the left and the right. To the broad stream of our philosophy there are many tributaries. Indeed, we are always adding to this flow as the parties of the left break up into a kind of delta of confusion. And so our great river flows on triumphantly to the sea.

To use Disraeli's phrase, we must be conservative to conserve all that is good and radical to uproot all that is bad.

We believe that men and women have both rights and duties —rights for themselves and their families, duties to the Crown and to their fellow-subjects. This philosophy governs our views about social problems. . . . What distinguishes both [the conservative and liberal] points of view from the socialist is this: we believe that unless we give opportunities to the strong and able we shall never have the means to provide real protection to the weak and old.

British Socialism. The origins of British socialism do not, as already emphasized, spring from Marxism. In fact, when the Labour Representation Committee (predecessor of the Labour Party) was formed in 1900, the non-Marxist character of British socialism was reaffirmed. A resolution sponsored by the Social Democratic Federation, calling for a party that would represent the working-class movement and recognize the doctrine of class warfare, was voted down. The Labour Party

[2] See R. H. S. Crossman *et al., New Fabian Essays* (1952), p. 3.

became dedicated to "promoting legislation in the direct interest of labour," and held itself ready to co-operate with other parties to attain that end. In 1918 the socialist objectives of the party were made explicit. The constitution of 1918, framed by Sidney Webb, declared one of the party's aims to be: "To secure for the producers by hand or by brain the full fruits of their industry, and the most equitable distribution thereof that may be possible, upon the basis of the common ownership of the means of production, and the best obtainable system of popular administration and control of each industry or service."

The main stream of British socialist thought and practice has proceeded on the premise that socialism can be obtained by orthodox democratic methods. The Labour Bournemouth Declaration of Policy in 1940 embraced "reconstruction in Socialist terms," to be obtained by "necessary social changes upon the basis of Democracy and Justice," with all confidence "that the historic forms of Parliamentary Democracy provide a highroad along which the nation can pass peacefully from an acquisitive to a Socialist society."

Not all British socialists at all times have expressed confidence that the British constitution would provide the "highroad" for peaceful transition from capitalism to the new order. During the 1930's, when socialist movements on the Continent were being submerged by fascist and nazi advances, some British socialists like Harold Laski became doubtful about the democratic method in achieving the ends of socialism. Laski at this time indicated a measure of reserve with respect to the feasibility of "revolution by consent." Claiming that "the logic of revolution excludes the possibility of compromise," Laski voiced fears that the capitalistic state will ultimately be driven to use extreme means to protect capitalistic values and that the Labour Party might consequently be driven to use undemocratic methods.[3] Earlier some British socialists had argued that their objectives would not be served by the presently existing parliamentary state. Speculation on the various alternatives produced the early guild socialism of G. D. H. Cole and early pluralistic ideas of the Webbs and Laski, but these ideas were on the wane by the decade of the 1930's.

Nevertheless, many British socialists thought (and many non-socialists feared) that "reconstruction in Socialist terms" would result in massive change. Indeed, Laski at one time had prophesied the day when "a Labour majority in the House of Commons seeks, as it will have to seek, to revise the foundations of the state." The day of Labour's power came in 1945, and it came in a democratic way. Yet, when the day passed in 1951, the "Labour majority in the House of Commons" had not by any means revised "the foundations of the state." In fact Labour hardly touched the fabric of the British constitution; the party reduced the already drastically curtailed powers of the House of Lords and eliminated plural voting, but otherwise made few changes of real constitutional consequence. In the economic field Labour nationalized only the basic sector of industry, leaving 80 per cent in private hands.

[3] *The State in Theory and Practice* (1935), pp. 253, 254, 263.

Controls and planning were features of the Labour regime, but these were directed at least as much toward curing the postwar economic problem as toward instituting a socialist society. Social services were increased, but some increase in services would have come under any postwar government. Even before the party had left office, some of its theorists were admitting that the Labour government had lost its impetus and drive. And since passing into opposition the party has not regained full momentum. Its 1955 election manifesto, *Forward with Labour,* did not propose much beyond replacing those items of its 1945 plan extirpated by the Conservatives during the period 1951–55. The party did call for additional nationalization in the chemical and machine-tool industries and for restoration of a free health service. However, in its program, "Industry and Society," adopted in 1957, the party called only for renationalization of the iron and steel and the long-range road-haulage industries. Beyond that, emphasis was placed upon "public ownership" (instead of "nationalization") by acquisition of shares in companies rather than outright government take-over, and on increasing the accountability of major industrial concerns to the government.

The basic factor in Labour's loss of thrust is that selfsame strain of empiricism and pragmatism that acts as a leavening in the Conservative approach. From almost its very inception British socialism was empirically rather than theoretically defined. It took its form from the society it desired to reform. Now that reform is substantially under way, it is becoming difficult to tell which is the mold and which is the clay.

5. THE PARTY BATTLE CONTINUES

As the Parliament elected in 1955 passed the midpoint of its statutory life of five years, the parties in Britain began to gird in earnest for the general election drawing inevitably nearer. Just when the event would occur, no one could say for certain. The decision to dissolve Parliament lies with the prime minister and his advisers. Whether Mr. Macmillan would call for an election in the spring of 1959 or later, the major parties—Conservative, Labour and Liberal[4]—had to reckon with the possibility that their party conferences to be held in the fall of 1958 might be the last before they went to the electorate. Consequently, the party conclaves of 1958 devoted their energies to putting their organizations, principles, and programs into shape in the event they would be called to face the British voter.

[4] There are other parties present on the British scene, but their significance in terms of electoral strength is not very great. In addition to Liberal and National Liberal candidates, Communist, Independent Labour, Co-operative, Welsh Nationalist, Scottish Nationalist, Sinn Fein, and various Independent candidates entered the 1955 election. In the 1955 British election the Communist Party ran 17 candidates (15 lost their deposits) and received a total of 33,144 votes.

It should be emphasized that political parties in Britain are treated in the main like other voluntary associations; they are subject to few special legal regulations. This contrasts with the situation in the United States, where legislation increasingly regulates party affairs and organization.

The Labour Party conference met during the first week of October in Scarborough. At the outset, steps were taken to indicate unity among the top leaders. Aneurin Bevan, longtime spokesman for the dissident left in the party, announced that he was not an aspirant for the post of party leader, and in return was hailed as the next Foreign Secretary. Then, Mr. Gaitskell, party leader, thumpingly proclaimed that "Labour's task" had not ended with the welfare state. But when it came to specific questions of policy, it was obvious to the leadership that Labour would have to sell itself to the voter at the political center if the party were to have any hopes of victory at all.

The Labour conference did not alter the party's stand on renationalization of iron, steel, and the long-distance road haulage industries as set forth in "Industry and Society" (1957). But the party leadership disputed the view that "Industry and Society" was a mandate for the party, if elected, to "Transfer to public ownership by compulsory sale, and as quickly as possible, all the equity shares of about 600 giant companies." This view was termed a "wild threat" and a "discredit" to the party. Again, the policy statement "Homes of the Future" (1956) proposed that local authorities be empowered to buy up certain types of rental housing; but the leadership denied that this meant a wholesale "municipalisation" of some 5,000,000 rented homes as the Conservatives have charged. On the other hand, "Learning to Live" (1958) advocates a system of "comprehensive" secondary education, a policy certainly aimed at lessening the influence of "grammar" (privately operated) schools in the scheme of British education. Indeed, a resolution pledging the party to abolish "fee-paying in any school" was only narrowly defeated at the conference by a vote of 3,544,000 to 3,067,000. In the area of foreign policy, several resolutions indicative of discontent within the party were offered. One advocated that Britain should "cease unilaterally to manufacture and test nuclear weapons"; it was defeated by a vote of 5,611,000 to 890,000. Another expressed hostility to rocket missile bases in Britain; it went down by a vote of 5,349,000 to 1,026,000.

Matters of party program were not the only items on the agenda of the Labour conference. Steps, designed to rejuvenate the party's political organization, were announced. A goal was set for an election fund of £725,000, ten times the amount spent in 1955, with indications that special efforts would be made to "stimulate" party organization in some 200 marginal constituencies. When the "tumult and shouting" was over, many observers went away feeling that the conference had attained "unity through compromise" but at the expense perhaps of dampening enthusiasm within some sections of the party's own ranks.

The Conservative conference met about a week later in Blackpool. The mood of the meeting was described as one of "aggressive confidence," despite such disquieting factors as increasing unemployment and some fall-off in by-election polls. Enthusiasm for Mr. Macmillan's leadership ran high, although he did receive some heckling from the Empire Loyalists. Conference proceedings suggested that the Conservatives would continue to attack the Labour program as one of "socialism, socialism, and more socialism" on the one hand, and "unprincipled office seeking" on the other. Indeed, the Conservatives exulted openly that a third defeat of Labour in the coming election would spell the final destruction of socialism."

Yet it was clear, as more than one observer said, that welfare state ideas are still broadly accepted by the Conservative Party. The Conservative government has introduced many new changes into the national health service program, but at the same time has built a number of new service hospitals. The national insurance tax has been increased by the Conservative government, but so have benefit payments. In fact, the Conservative government has presented a plan for graduated pensions so that persons earning above a set minimum would contribute more but would also receive higher pension payments. (This plan must be regarded in the light of Labour's proposal for "national superannuation," which would pay both a flat pension plus an additional payment, so that retirement on half-pay might be expected.) On the other hand, the Conservatives point to their record in housing (650,000 new houses for owner-occupation in six years) and defend the results of such actions as the Rent Act, 1957.

Mention may also be made of the Liberal Party conference held in September, 1958, especially since Liberal gains in the spring by-elections had revived Liberal spirits. The conference revealed some confusion among Liberal sympathizers as to what Liberal policy was or ought to be. In fact, the *Manchester Guardian* asked whether the proceedings of the conference might not lead an uncommitted voter to conclude that the party was "dominated by cranks." Nevertheless, the party leader, Mr. Jo Grimond, has attempted to set forth a program in such pamphlets as "The New Liberalism" and "The New Liberal Democracy."

The Liberals advocate, of course, some sort of proportional representation, preferably the single transferable vote, since the party is at a disadvantage under the present single-member district system. Mr. Grimond has stressed the notion of a three-party system, in which Liberals should aim for a contingent in Commons sufficiently large to prevent either Conservatives or Labour to hold power alone. In such a situation, the Liberal contingent, possibly as large as 40 members, would be in a position to affect governmental policy decisions. On questions of policy, however, the party is somewhat vague. Mr. Grimond attacks the Conservative and Labour parties for the "socialism" in both their programs. He wants to "bring the Welfare Society up to date" by reducing taxation, reforming the nationalized industries, reducing tariffs, and recasting the unemployment insurance system so as "to relieve real need and poverty." In the realm of foreign policy, the Liberals accept the fact that Britain's security lies in co-operation with the Commonwealth and NATO, but also stress the need for an "international approach" rather than a "national approach" in such matters as control of atomic energy and disarmament.

As events turned out, the party conferences of 1958 did prove to be the last before the general election. Mr. Macmillan obtained a dissolution of Parliament on September 18, 1959, and the election took place on October 8. Many factors enter into an election that party conferences can do little about. Unemployment, industrial unrest, bad farming weather, unexpected developments in foreign affairs, and fluctuation in the import-export balance are some of these. It is expected that the party in power will select a date for the general election when such factors seem likely to operate to its best advantage. Mr. Macmillan could never be accused of faulty timing in this respect, for the Conservatives scored a smashing victory at the polls.

The Conservatives and their allies won 364 seats in Commons, a gain of 23. Labour garnered 258 seats, a loss of 23. The Liberals won 6 seats, the same number held in the previous House. In terms of popular vote, the results were: Conservatives and allies, 13,750,935; Labour, 12,216,-166; and Liberal, 1,640,761. The Communist party received 30,897 votes, and other candidates received a total of 223,949.

Naturally, Conservative leadership was exultant over the results for it was the first time since the Reform Act of 1832 that a party had won three consecutive general elections. Naturally, too, neither the Labour nor the Liberal party found much solace in the balloting. Mr. Gaitskell managed to beat down attacks on his leadership of the Labour party, but only at the price of open disagreement with important persons in his party, Mr. Crossman for example. In addition, Labour suffered a distinct loss in the death of Aneurin Bevan in 1960. The Liberals under the leadership of Mr. Jo Grimond did double their popular vote over 1955, but fell far short of obtaining any significant strength in Commons. There has been some speculation that a revived form of the "Lib-Lab" alliance of pre-World War II days might be formed, but whether this will happen, is for the future.

Meanwhile, the Conservative party continues to demonstrate its historic adaptability and flexibility of program. The task of the Labour and Liberal parties in the decade of the 1960s is to find the drive that will enable one of them to offer serious competition to the Conservatives for managership of Britain's welfare state.

CHAPTER
3

PARLIAMENT

British legislative, executive, and judicial institutions, according to A. F. Pollard, "descended from a single ancestor," and this common ancestor was "a sort of constitutional protoplasm" consisting of the governmental activities carried on by and through the courts and councils of the medieval English kings.[1] Traces of this common ancestry remain in the formal participation of the sovereign in Britain's basic political processes. The queen-in-Parliament enacts legislation; the queen-in-Council takes important executive decisions; and the queen's courts dispense justice.

It is with the queen-in-Parliament, or more simply Parliament, that this chapter is concerned. The first section will trace the historical evolution of Parliament and the development of parliamentary government. Next the Houses of Parliament will be taken up, primarily from the point of view of their composition. A brief discussion of parliamentary organization and procedure will follow. Attention will then turn to the practice of cabinet government, the particular type of parliamentary government resulting from English political experience. The last portion of the chapter deals with Parliament as a representative institution, with emphasis on the theoretical as well as the practical relationships of Parliament and its individual members to the British people.

1. EVOLUTION OF PARLIAMENT

Parliament is not an institution designed by blueprint; it is an institution developed by evolution. Many of its characteristics originated before the rise of political parties and the cabinet system, indeed even before its

[1] *The Evolution of Parliament* (2nd ed. rev., 1934), p. 25. Some writers stress Anglo-Saxon institutions in tracing the ancestry of Parliament. Reference is made particularly to the council of the Anglo-Saxon kings, the witenagemot. See E. A. Freeman, *The Growth of the English Constitution* (1894).

supremacy was acknowledged. The debt that the Parliament of the twentieth century owes to centuries of precedent and practice is great, and no less great is the British knack for adapting ancient ways to modern uses revealed in historical evolution of the institution of Parliament.

Origin and Development of Parliament. The historical details of the emergence of Parliament as a separate institution are not entirely clear. As mentioned in Chapter 1, the name "Parliament" itself did not appear in usage until the middle of the thirteenth century. Prior to the appearance of Parliament in that period the locus of central authority lay in the *curia regis,* or the king's court. But on various occasions before the thirteenth century the English kings had assembled the notables of the realm in what was called the *magnum concilium* or *commune concilium.* Whether the great council or common council originally was considered as being distinct from the *curia regis* or simply an enlarged version of it is difficult to say. However, C. H. McIlwain has argued that the functions of the earlier *curia* and councils were primarily judicial and that the first Parliaments were essentially judicial bodies and hence represented a continuation of the earlier royal institutions.[2]

The appearance of the first Parliaments did, however, signify some important innovations. To the Model Parliament of 1295 and earlier to Simon de Montfort's Parliament of 1265 were summoned the knights of the shire and the burgesses of the boroughs. These groups constituted new elements in the composition of the king's councils, which hitherto had been drawn mainly from the feudal nobility. The knights and burgesses formed, of course, the basis upon which the House of Commons was erected.

The Model Parliament of 1295 contained several distinct groups: the temporal lords, the spiritual lords, representatives of the lower clergy, the knights of the shires, and representatives from the boroughs. The lower clergy did not, however, relish being summoned to Parliament, and by 1332 succeeded in withdrawing.[3] By the end of the fourteenth century the knights and the burgesses were acting together as Commons, although for a while there was a possibility that the knights would keep separate. Even so, it would be premature to speak of "Houses" of Parliament much before the end of the fifteenth century. The term House as applied to Commons appeared in 1450, and the term "House of Lords" came even later.

Meanwhile, precedents that later were to buttress Commons' claims to powers and privileges were being established. The knights and burgesses had received the royal summons in order to assent to taxes, and, almost from the first, the representatives from the shires and boroughs had begun to couple petitions of various kinds with their money grants.[4]

---

[2] See *The High Court of Parliament and Its Supremacy* (1910).

[3] After their withdrawal the lower clergy taxed themselves in convocation. After 1664 the clergy submitted to taxation in the same measure as the laity.

[4] At first petitions were made by the knights and burgesses individually. The first petition clearly endorsed by Commons as a body—the first public bill originating in Commons—dates from 1327.

Eventually the process of requesting redress of grievances through petitions became converted into the method of initiating legislation by bill,
which is, of course, the method followed today. Commons also made
progress toward gaining a position of primacy in matters of supply, and
in 1407 Henry IV acknowledged that the initiative in making money
grants belonged to Commons. An important step in connection with procedure was the selection in 1376 of a member—the first "speaker"—to
report on Commons' deliberations to the king. The early speaker was far
from being the impartial and independent presiding officer he is today;
in fact the king was soon successfully nominating his own choice for the
position and it was not until after the Restoration that the practice
ceased.[5] Not many decades after the selection of the first speaker Commons began to assert the right to freedom of debate. This freedom was
generally upheld during the Tudor period and was finally given statutory
sanction in the Bill of Rights of 1689. Also, the privilege of freedom from
arrest was clearly established by the end of the sixteenth century.[6]

By the time the Stuarts assumed the English throne, the House of
Commons had become a real source of power in the realm.[7] But it is
worth while to remember that Commons was called into existence by the
medieval monarchs, and nurtured by the Tudors in the course of their
battles with the Roman church and the feudal aristocracy. When the last
of the Tudors had passed, the House of Commons found itself in possession of a reservoir of precedent and historical right with which to
buttress its claims of powers and privileges as against the Stuarts.

Development of Parliamentary Government. After the revolutionary events of the seventeenth century had run their course, Parliament occupied the position of ultimate supremacy in the English constitution. But Parliament did not immediately attain the pre-eminent
place in day-to-day government it later came to enjoy.

Parliament's rise to eminence is associated with the subjection of
king and Crown to parliamentary control. In the nature of the means
by which this control was perfected and conditioned lie the essentials of
the British system of parliamentary government. Parliament abandoned
attempts to control the executive by strictly legal means, and instead
developed effective political and conventional methods of holding the
executive accountable.

One method of legal control—impeachment of the king's ministers
—was important during the seventeenth century. However, impeachment is no longer of importance in relations with the executive, even

[5] Even after 1679—the date when Commons asserted its right to make a free
choice—royal influence continued to play a part in the selection of the speaker.

[6] Parliamentary procedure had also become formalized by the end of the sixteenth century, when the first treatise on procedure in the House of Commons appeared.

[7] The size of Commons steadily increased. In the fifteenth century it stood at
about 300; at the end of Tudor period it was 460, and it reached 513 in the reign of
Charles II. After the unions with Scotland and Ireland additional seats were added,
and Commons contained over 700 members prior to the creation of the Irish Free
State.

though the power still resides in Parliament. Another method of control, that of placing statutory restrictions on executive powers, has been used on many occasions. Despite recent concern with the extent of executive powers,[8] statutory restrictions remain secondary, at least in so far as normal functioning of the constitution is concerned.

The various principles and practices involved in parliamentary control of the executive developed continuously and to some degree simultaneously. During the eighteenth and early nineteenth centuries major developments were, first, the gradual transfer of legal and political powers from the king to his ministers, and second, the forging of non-legal parliamentary controls over the ministers. After the Glorious Revolution of 1688 the monarchs did not withdraw from politics. But the kings found that they had to retain as ministers persons who enjoyed the confidence of or who could manage the House of Commons. True, the monarchs were able to ease the path of their ministers by the practice of "purchasing" seats in the rotten boroughs. Even so, the king sometimes had to modify his views on policy and his preferences as to ministers in order to obtain a ministry Parliament would support.[9]

With the transfer of powers from king to ministers the relationship of the ministers to Parliament underwent a change. At first Parliament resisted one essential element of cabinet government, that is, membership in Commons of ministers. Indeed, a short-lived provision of the Act of Settlement (1701) went so far as to prevent a minister from sitting in the lower House. Less than fifty years later, however, Sir Robert Walpole, frequently called the first prime minister, resigned when defeated in a committee of the House on the matter of an election petition. Despite the implication of Walpole's resignation the role of Commons in determining the government during this period should not be overemphasized. Actually, prior to 1832, only two other prime ministers after Walpole resigned because of defeats in the House of Commons. The patronage powers of the king and Crown plus the presence of a "court" faction in Commons usually made it possible for a ministry enjoying the confidence of the king to obtain support in Commons. After the death of George III (1760–1820), however, the kings ceased to take an active hand in parliamentary elections and gradually began to reign instead of to rule.

The period from 1832 to 1867 appears as the "classic" era in so far as dependence of the government of the day on Commons is concerned. The influence of the monarch in Commons had waned, and political parties, with their methods for organizing their delegations in Commons, had not yet fully arisen. Generally speaking, a ministry was usually overthrown through defeat in Commons on a "vital issue." But, even as Commons was enjoying its heyday, developments that would radically change the nature of a ministry's dependence upon the lower House were taking place.

One of these developments was the acknowledgment that the prime minister has the right to advise and to obtain a dissolution. The prime

[8] For discussion of the problem of executive powers see Chapter 4, pp. 95–105.
[9] For example, in 1746 and 1757 the king was forced to appoint the elder Pitt to office.

minister gained thereby a choice of alternatives whenever his government lost the confidence of the House of Commons. He might accede to the wishes of the Commons and resign, or he might advise a dissolution, to be followed by an election in which his opponents (or his friends) might be defeated. Perhaps even more significant were the growth of mass parties after 1867 and the emergence of the prime minister as a strong party leader. These developments did not alter the requirement that a government must maintain the confidence of a majority in the lower House, but they did go far to ensure that the majority would be a disciplined party (on occasion, a party coalition) majority. As a consequence the fall of a government, especially of a non-coalition government, because of a defeat in Commons has become increasingly rare. Thus cabinet government arrived, but further consideration of its practical working will be deferred until the Houses of Parliament and their organization and procedure have been reviewed.

2. THE HOUSES OF PARLIAMENT

The political role of Parliament through the centuries has not remained constant. Nor have the relative positions of the two Houses, Lords and Commons, vis-à-vis each other. Their composition and their respective powers are the results of evolution and continual adaptation, and that these processes are still at work becomes evident from the experience of the upper House since 1900.

House of Lords. Legislative enactments of the twentieth century have greatly reduced the powers of the House of Lords and altered its composition. As Lord Bryce observed in the 1920's, the questions of the powers and of the composition of the upper House are "closely interconnected." Yet it was not found politically possible to attack the two questions together. Reduction of powers came first, in the Parliament Acts of 1911 and 1949. Change in the composition of the upper House did not result until passage of the Life Peerages Act in 1958. Opponents of the bill charge (and many proponents would probably admit) that the measure did not get at the heart of the matter, and it is unlikely that its passage will settle the question of "Reform of the House of Lords." As a background for further discussion of that important constitutional question, it will be useful to begin with the composition of the upper House as it stood a few years before the passage of the 1958 Life Peerages Act.

The membership of the House of Lords in 1955 was as follows:

Royal Peers	4
Archbishops	2
Dukes	21
Marquesses	27
Earls	133

Viscounts	103
Bishops	24
Barons	538
Scottish Representative Peers	16
Irish Representative Peers	5
TOTAL	873 [1]

The archbishops and bishops, twenty-six in all, constitute the lords spiritual. The remaining peers are known as the lords temporal.

Most members of the House of Lords sit as a matter of hereditary right, and the Life Peerages Act of 1958 was not calculated to change the upper House in this respect. Those who do not sit by right of heredity are: the archbishops and bishops, the Scottish representative peers, the Irish representative peers, and the "law lords," nine lords of appeal in ordinary who are appointed to life baronages under legislation of 1876; to this list will be added life peers appointed under the legislation of 1958. The Archbishops of Canterbury and York, the Bishops of London, Durham, and Winchester, and the twenty-one senior bishops of the Church of England comprise the lords spiritual.[2] The law lords are distinguished lawyers who are appointed to carry out the judicial duties of the upper House. The presence of the Scottish and Irish representative peers is the result of the acts of union with those countries. Prior to the union with Scotland in 1707 there were separate peerages for England, Scotland, and Ireland, but only English peers sat in the House of Lords. Under the Act of Union of 1707 the Scottish peers elect sixteen of their number to serve for a Parliament. Under the Act of Union of Great Britain and Ireland, 1800, the Irish peers elected twenty-eight of their number to serve for life. Since the creation of the Irish Free State, there have been no elections to fill the Irish vacancies, and the Irish peers are, as was said in 1948, a "gradually dying race." [3]

For the most part hereditary peerages descend to the eldest male heir, and only the holder of a peerage is, strictly speaking, of the nobility. Other members of the family including the wife of a peer and an heir before he actually inherits are commoners.[4] Some twenty peerages, "baronies by writ" so-called, may descend through female heirs. After

[1] By 1958 the total number had increased to 887. Of this number, some 20 peers were minors and not yet entitled to a seat in the House. Of the five ranks of the nobility, that of earl is the oldest, dating from Anglo-Saxon times. The title of baron was given to the tenants-in-chief of the Norman kings. Duke, the highest rank, was created in 1373, and marquess in 1386. The title of viscount dates from Henry IV's reign.

[2] During debate in the House of Lords on the Life Peerages Bill the suggestion was made that leaders of churches other than the Church of England might be made life peers. The lord chancellor stated that further consideration would be given to the suggestion.

[3] By 1958 the number of Irish representative peers had been reduced to three.

[4] Thus the wife of a peer may sit in the House of Commons; also an heir before he comes into the title. An heir may use a courtesy title, and the wives of peers are customarily addressed as duchess, marchioness, etc., as appropriate. Members of the Irish peerage who are not members of the House of Lords may sit in the House of Commons, but Scottish peers may not.

enactment of the Sex Disqualification (Removal) Act in 1919, Viscountess Rhondda led an attempt by "peeresses in their own right" to
gain admittance to the House of Lords, but failed. However, under the
1958 legislation life peerages were conferred on four ladies in July, 1958.
On October 21, 1958, the Baroness of Swansborough became the first
lady ever to sit in the House of Lords. A few weeks later, the Baroness
Elliott became the first lady ever to speak in the upper chamber. As she
rose to speak in the chamber that had been eulogized as the last stronghold of the male, she recited a couplet from Matthew Pryor:

> Be to her frailties very kind,
> Be to her faults a little blind.

Hereditary peerages are created by exercise of the royal prerogative,
and new peerages are usually announced at the New Year or on the
monarch's birthday.[5] A person to whom a hereditary peerage is offered
may decline,[6] but, once accepted, the peerage cannot be refused by an
eligible heir. Indeed, some heirs who have been active in the House of
Commons have tried, unsuccessfully, it may be added, to refuse, since
inheritance of a peerage disqualified them from sitting in Commons. The
grant of a peerage is a mark of honor, and it has become customary to
grant peerages without partisan distinction to men who have been
prominent in the life of the nation.[7] In the 1920's charges arose that
peerages were being sold, but a royal commission appointed to investigate
the matter found no corruption, although it did recommend that certain
safeguards be erected in connection with the bestowal of titles.

Members of the House of Lords enjoy the same parliamentary
privileges and immunities in respect to arrest and freedom of speech as do
members of the House of Commons.[8] They also suffer certain disadvantages. They are not paid for their services in the House, although
since 1946 lords (with a few exceptions, like the lord chancellor) have
been entitled to traveling expenses if they attend regularly, and since
1957 to claim expenses in attending sittings up to a maximum of three
guineas a day. They cannot sit in Commons or vote in parliamentary
elections.[9] And a lord nowadays has little chance of becoming prime
minister.

[5] Since 1800 creation of peers has been in the peerage of the United Kingdom,
and well over 600 of the existing titles have been created since that time. In fact,
over 400 of the present titles date from 1900 or later.

[6] Winston Churchill, for example, declined a peerage upon his retirement as
prime minister; Clement Attlee, on the other hand, accepted an earldom when he
resigned as leader of the Labour Party.

[7] Some peerages are created necessarily for political reasons. During the period
of Labour power, 1945–51, it was necessary for the party to have a contingent in the
upper House. Even so, only 35 of the 109 peerages created in this period were bestowed on persons active in the Labour Party.

[8] A lord still has the privilege of access to the sovereign. Formerly a lord was
entitled to be tried by the upper House on criminal charges, but this was curtailed by
statute in 1948.

[9] Peers may vote in local elections.

Reform of the Upper House. As mentioned earlier, reform of the House of Lords has centered mainly on the questions of composition and powers. During the nineteenth century a shortage of lords with appropriate judicial experience developed, and, to remedy this situation, a life peerage was conferred on Lord Wensleydale in 1856. The Lords, however, refused to consider him as entitled to sit and vote in the House. Later, in 1876, a statutory measure made possible the granting of life peerages with the right to sit to lords of appeal in ordinary, the so-called "law lords." The question of life peerages continued to arise, but events of the years 1909–11 turned attention to the problem of the powers of the upper House.

In 1909 the Lords rejected a Liberal government budget measure passed by the House of Commons, an action conformable with strict law but contrary to constitutional convention and practice. After two dissolutions of Parliament and a promise by the king to create if necessary a sufficient number of peers willing to support the Liberals, the Liberal Asquith government pushed through the Parliament Act of 1911. This legislation cast the primacy of Commons into statutory form. It stripped the upper chamber of any real powers over money bills, and in addition reduced its powers over general legislation upon which Commons insisted to a delaying period of a minimum of two years.

The position of a second chamber in a cabinet system raises difficult problems, for it is hard for a cabinet to be responsible to two masters. And in the case of the House of Lords its representative characteristics certainly contributed to the decline in its powers. The Lords, being a hereditary body, came to speak for an increasingly small segment of the British people. Indeed, after 1886, the Lords became for practical purposes an appendage of the Conservative Party. The Commons, meanwhile, preserved through election some contact with popular aspirations. And with the progressive broadening of the suffrage after 1832, Commons could with reason claim the right to express the will of the people. The relationship between the powers and the composition of the upper House was recognized in the Parliament Act of 1911, even though it dealt only with the question of powers. The preamble of the act declared that "it is intended to substitute for the House of Lords as it at present exists a Second Chamber constituted on a popular instead of a hereditary basis, but such substitution cannot be immediately brought into operation."

Efforts to find a substitute were not abandoned. In 1918 a commission headed by Lord Bryce proposed an upper House of 327 members with twelve-year terms. Eighty-one of these members were to be selected from the hereditary peerage by a standing committee of both Houses of Parliament. The remaining 246 members were to be elected by district electoral colleges. Thirteen such colleges were proposed, to be composed of members of Parliament from the areas represented by the districts. The Bryce proposals did not gain much support, however.

Between the world wars the Labour Party voiced insistent demands for reform. In 1935 the party went on record for complete abolition of the upper House, calling it an unrepresentative and undemocratic carry-over from the Middle Ages.

On coming to power in 1945 the Labour Party again warned: "We give clear warning that we will tolerate no obstruction to the people's will by the House of Lords." After the upper House threatened to remain sitting when the lower House was not in session and to hold up urgent legislation delegating wide powers to deal with the foreign-exchange crisis of August 1947, the Labour government announced that it would introduce legislation to amend the Parliament Act of 1911. There is little doubt, however, that the most crucial consideration bearing on this decision was the desire to complete the passage of the iron and steel nationalization program before the expiration of the five years of the Parliament elected in 1945. The Lords had announced their intention to veto the steel bill, and the Labour government feared that the two-year delay thus interposed would make passage of the measure impossible before new elections were required in 1950. Thus, to ensure passage before then, the Parliament Act of 1949 reduced the suspensive veto power of the Lords to one year.[1]

Meanwhile, additional efforts were put forth to find a solution for this controversial question of the composition and powers of the House of Lords. A conference of party leaders in February 1948 made the most promising progress. Their report included nine recommendations: (1) that the second chamber should be complementary to, and not a rival of, the Commons; (2) that it should contain no permanent majority from any one party; (3) that the right to attend and vote should not be based upon heredity; (4) that the "Lords of Parliament" should be appointed for distinction in public service from hereditary peers or from common-ers who had been created life peers; (5) that women should have equal rights with men; (6) that membership should include descendants of the sovereign, the lords spiritual, and the law lords; (7) that adequate remuneration should be provided; (8) that other hereditary peers should be able to stand for a seat in Commons; (9) that there be a continuous check on the "Lords of Parliament" to prevent neglect of their duties or to compel resignation from the House. But the Conservative and Labour parties could not agree on the length of the delaying power of the upper House, and the proposals went for naught. The Labour government then, as has been seen, continued with passage of the Parliament Act of 1949.

The latest episode concerning reform, passage of the Life Peerages Act in 1958, has already been mentioned. Sponsored by the Conservative government, this measure provides for life peerages for either men or women, with no specific limit set on the number of appointments. The Labour party opposed the bill, which certainly did not deal with the overall problem of the representative nature of the upper chamber. It seems likely, therefore, that interest in further reform of the House of Lords will continue. In fact the chamber is in the process of taking steps

[1]Under the act of 1949 the House of Commons must pass the measure in two successive sessions, and one year must elapse between the second reading in first session and the final passage in the second session.

to implement some of the conclusions offered by the Select Committee on the Powers of the House in Relation to the Attendance of Its Members in its report of 1956. Specifically, procedure was suggested whereby a "known working body of peers" would be established through granting leaves of absence to peers not desiring to attend sittings of the chamber.

House of Commons. As noted earlier, the size of the House of Commons has varied. For the election of 1955 the House consisted of 630 seats, each representing a single-member constituency. The geographical distribution of seats was as follows:

England (511)	
London	42
Counties	222
Boroughs	247
Wales (36)	
Counties	26
Boroughs	10
Scotland (71)	
Counties	39
Burghs	32
Northern Ireland	12

As the figure for London suggests, there is some concentration of seats in the big cities. Besides the 42 seats in London, Glasgow has 15, Birmingham 13, Liverpool and Manchester 9 apiece, Edinburgh 7, and Bristol, Leeds, and Sheffield 6 seats each.

There is considerable variation in the size of constituencies. In making the redistribution of seats for 1955 the Boundary Commission for England aimed at a mean electoral quota of 55,670. Actually the constituencies finally adopted ranged from 40,000 electors to 80,000, although the bulk of the English constituencies fell in the 50,000 to 60,000 bracket. The average Scottish constituency is, it may be noted, about 48,000, while constituencies in Northern Ireland average over 70,000.[2]

Members of Commons now receive £1,000 per year and may also claim relief from income tax for expenses resulting from parliamentary duties. In addition members may draw an allowance of £2 per day for every day (except Friday) when the House of Commons sits.

What kinds of persons are elected to Commons? The median age of the House elected in 1955 was 51; the median for Conservative members was 49; for Labour it was 54. A significant number of members had had local government experience: 29 per cent of the Conservative members

[2] In the redistribution of 1955 major revisions were made in ninety-two constituencies then held by the Labour Party and in seventy-nine constituencies held by the Conservatives. Aneurin Bevan charged during the campaign of 1955 that the revision worked to the advantage of the Conservative Party, but his charge does not appear to have been borne out by election results; see D. E. Butler, *The British General Election of 1955* (1955), p. 157.

and 56 per cent of Labour members. With respect to education 218 Conservatives out of 344 had been to a university, while 110 of the 277
Labour members had a university background. There were some significant differences in the occupational background of Conservative and
Labour members, as is seen in the following table.

FIG. I

OCCUPATIONAL BACKGROUND IN THE HOUSE OF COMMONS IN 1955

OCCUPATION	CONSERVATIVE	LABOUR
Law	77	36
Armed Services	47	3
Teaching	4	39
Company Directors and Managers	78	6
Journalists	19	27
Workers	1	97
Farmers	31	5
Private Means	11	0

(Adopted from D. E. Butler, *The British General Election of 1955*, p. 43)

The above figures (which obviously do not include all members of
the 1955 House) indicate that Commons is not representative in any
proportional sense of the British population. On the other hand, in a
composite view, Commons does draw from many walks of British life.

Elections.   Under the Parliament Act of 1911 the maximum duration of a Parliament is five years. This period may be extended by statute,
as was done in both World War I and II. In normal times Parliaments
usually do not last out the five-year term, although there is a tendency
for a government with a good majority to hold off elections until late in
the statutory life of Parliament. At any rate, the election process begins
with a royal proclamation dissolving the old Parliament and ordering
the writs of election to be issued.

The election period in England is very brief compared to campaigns
in the United States.[3] Eight days after the writs of election are issued,
nominations are made to the constituency-returning officers. If more
than one nomination is made, an election follows nine days later.

As mentioned in Chapter 2, nomination procedure in England is
simple. A candidate files a petition signed by two sponsors and eight
assenters, plus a deposit of £150. This deposit becomes forfeited if the
candidate does not poll at least one eighth of the total votes cast. The
purpose of the deposit is to discourage "freak" candidatures, but it also
presents a hazard to candidates of the established parties. In the 1955
election, for example, 60 of the 110 Liberal candidates forfeited their
deposits.

It is almost true to say that anyone who is eligible to vote is also

[3] In 1955, Prime Minister Eden announced on April 15 that Parliament would
be dissolved on May 6, followed by elections on May 26, with the new Parliament
to meet on June 7. Actual campaigning did not begin until after May 1.

eligible for a seat in Commons. In general terms various classes of persons may be said to be ineligible: aliens, lunatics, infants, peers, bankrupts, felons, those convicted of corrupt practices at elections (for a limited period), and persons holding an office or place of profit under the Crown. This last category raises many questions, not only because doubts have arisen as to whether a particular office or place was one of profit, but also because doubts have arisen as to whether certain offices ought to work disqualification even though they fell within the technical definition. To clarify this last category, the government brought in a bill in 1955 which became law as the House of Commons Disqualification Act, 1957.

This measure sets forth the following as disqualified: holders of specified judicial offices; civil servants; members of the regular armed forces; members of public forces maintained by police authorities; holders of a wide variety of specified executive, administrative, and other offices; and members of the legislature of any country or territory outside the Commonwealth. An important set of disqualifications removed by the act were those imposed in 1931 on persons holding pensions and contracts from the Crown. The act preserves, of course, the ability of ministers up to seventy in number to sit in the House. It does not affect the other classes of ineligibles mentioned above.

Money spent in a general election in Britain is very much less than amounts expended in the United States. In the 1955 election the total sum spent by all candidates was in the neighborhood of £903,000, but this sum does not reflect the money spent by parties and prospective candidates before and after the actual election period. Statute regulates the maximum amount that a candidate may expend. For borough constituencies the sum is £450 plus 1½ d. for each elector; for county constituencies it is £450 plus 2 d. for each elector. The total amount allowable thus varies from constituency to constituency; for an average-size borough constituency it was about £800 in 1955.[4] As a rule candidates do not spend the maximum. The average Conservative candidate spent £735 in 1955, or 88 per cent of the allowed maximum; Labour candidates spent £611 on the average or 73 per cent of the maximum.[5]

The use of radio and television in campaigns involves some special problems, because these means of mass communication are government-operated. Political parties receive an allotment of a specified number of broadcasts for the campaign period. In 1955 the Conservative and Labour parties had four twenty-minute radio broadcasts apiece, and the Liberals one. For television the Conservative and Labour parties had

[4] In Britain campaign expenditures are channeled through the party agent in the constituency. This arrangement facilitates the accounting for money spent in elections.

[5] Statutes bar corrupt and illegal practices such as false registration, deliberate miscounting of ballots, etc. Charges of illegal or corrupt practices are investigated by two judges of the Queen's Bench Division of the High Court of Justice, and their report to the House of Commons determines whether or not the charges are upheld. It is generally acknowledged that the restriction on the use of automobiles to carry voters to the polls was not well observed in the 1955 elections, but few charges resulted.

two broadcasts of fifteen minutes plus one of half an hour, and the Liberals had one of fifteen minutes.[6] The three parties also used part of their yearly broadcast allotments during the campaign.[7] But, even so, in the three to four weeks of the campaign only twenty-four party broadcasts bombarded the British electorate.

British law authorizes mail or proxy ballots for those who are absent because of occupational reasons, who are physically incapacitated, or who have recently moved. The mail vote fell from 757,000 in 1951 to 527,000 in 1955. The significance of the mail ballot seems to be greater than its size (2 to 3 per cent of the total votes cast) would suggest. The mail vote apparently aids the Conservatives more than Labour. Only estimates are available as to the effect of the mail vote, but informed estimates suggest that the Conservatives may owe six to ten seats to the mail ballot.

Under British practice ballots are brought to a central place in the constituency for counting. The candidate with the greatest number of votes is the victor, and in the event of a tie the contest is decided by lot.

During the life of a Parliament seats in Commons will fall vacant owing to deaths and resignations. When this occurs, a by-election is held. The by-elections receive keen attention, as seats occasionally change hands from one party to another, usually from government to opposition when there is a change. In 1953 the Conservatives won a seat from Labour in South Sunderland, and this was the first time the government had wrested a seat from the opposition in a by-election since 1924. The by-elections also afford a basis (sometimes not completely reliable) for comparing the government's popularity after it has been in office for a time with its strength when it took office. For example, by-elections during 1954 and 1955 showed the Conservatives falling off, in comparison with 1951, in only six of the twenty-two constituencies involved. The ability of the Conservative Party to maintain its strength could have been taken as a favorable portent of success in the general election of 1955. However, in using by-elections as political barometers, it must be remembered that the issues presented in a by-election may be quite different from those important in a general election.

3. PARLIAMENTARY ORGANIZATION AND PROCEDURE

As indicated in the first section of this chapter, much of the organization and procedure of Parliament developed before the change in the parlia-

[6] Any other party that ran fifty or more candidates was entitled to one broadcast, but no other party qualified.

[7] For the year April, 1955–March, 1956 the Conservative Party was given six radio and two television broadcasts, the Labour Party five radio and two television broadcasts, and the Liberals one broadcast, which could be either radio or TV or both simultaneously. The budget happened to be presented on April 19, 1955, and the parties also had their traditional opportunity to state their views on the budget via radio and TV during the campaign period.

mentary system of government brought about by the rise of mass political parties and the cabinet system. Yet organization and procedure have been adapted to this change, and are geared so as to permit the numerical majority in the Houses to prevail. This numerical majority is, in the normal situation, a party majority, and parliamentary processes vest effective direction and control over the party majority in the cabinet, which is, of course, composed of the party leaders. For the most part, then, parliamentary processes operate to get done what the government of the day wants to be done. As suggested, there are some qualifications to this general rule. The right of the opposition party to criticize and to question is carefully safeguarded; cabinet and party controls are relaxed in the case of measures affecting local areas and individuals only; and individual members retain the right to question ministers directly and to propose legislation. But, to repeat, the machinery of Parliament runs at the behest of the government of the day.

Officers and Committees. The principal officer of the House of Commons is the "speaker," who has come to be an impartial presiding officer of the chamber. Though elected by the House, he is chosen by the government majority when the office falls vacant. Once elected, a speaker is by convention re-elected at the beginning of each Parliament even though a new party majority may have come into power. Thus Mr. Douglas Clifton Brown, who was first put in office by the Conservatice majority in 1943, continued under Labour after 1945. The speaker after his election divorces himself from party politics; he does not even campaign for re-election in his constituency.[8] He receives a salary of £5,000 per year and other perquisites, and upon his retirement is granted a pension and offered the honor of a peerage.

The speaker's task is a delicate one. He guides the House, making sure that, while the opposition has ample opportunity to criticize, the government's program is not bogged down by sheer obstructionist tactics. His rulings on matters carry great authority. On certain points, for example the certification of money bills, his certificate has been made final and conclusive by statute. Other officers include the clerk and his assistants and the sergeant-at-arms and his deputies. They are appointed for life by the Crown. The chairman and deputy chairman of committees are elected by the House and change with the party majority.

Much of the business of the House takes place in committee of the whole. In committee of the whole the speaker leaves his chair and the chairman or deputy chairman presides. Financial measures and matters of high constitutional importance are usually considered in committee of the whole.

There are four other types of committees used in the House. Sessional committees, as the name implies, are constituted for a single session of Parliament. There are ten or so of these, including the Committee on Selection (which selects the members for most other committees),

---

[8] Until recent decades the speaker was not opposed for re-election in his constituency. In 1935, 1945, and 1955, the Labour Party contested the re-election of a Conservative speaker, but without success.

the Committee on Standing Orders, the Committee on Public Accounts, and that on Statutory Instruments. Select committees, of which twenty or more may be established in a session, are appointed to study a particular matter and report to the House. A third kind of committee, those on private bills, will be discussed below. There remain the standing committees. These are designated as A, B, C, D, and E and the Scottish Committee, the last composed of Scottish members, which handles legislation dealing with Scottish affairs. The other standing committees are not specialized. Whenever a bill is referred to them, their normal membership of fifteen to twenty is augmented by an additional thirty or forty members. Included among these additional members will normally be persons who have specialized knowledge of the particular bill referred to the committee. Commons committees are chosen in proportion to party strength in Commons.[9]

The committee system in Commons is not so highly organized as that in the American Congress, nor do British committees have the powers over the content of legislation that committees of the Congress exercise. Under British practice bills do not go to committee until after second reading by the House. If a bill passes second reading, it means that the House of Commons has approved the principles of the measure. Consequently committee handling of a bill is limited to details and minor alterations. The reason for the relative lack of power of British committees is not difficult to appreciate. The British system of cabinet responsibility does not permit legislative committees to become rivals of the government of the day.

Party organization in the House centers about the leader of the House of Commons, on the government side, and the leader of the opposition. Assisting the leader of the House are the government whips. The chief whip and several others hold ministerial posts in the Treasury for which they receive compensation. The leader of the opposition receives a salary of £2,000 per year, but opposition whips receive no pay except their parliamentary salaries.

The presiding officer of the upper House is the lord chancellor, who customarily holds cabinet rank in the government of the day. This official could be a commoner, but invariably he is a peer. Organization and procedure in the House of Lords is much less rigid than in Commons. The House itself, rather than the lord chancellor, rules on procedural matters. There is party organization in the House, centering about party leaders and their whips, but party discipline is less strict than in Commons.

The committee system in the upper chamber is also simpler than that of Commons. Some proceedings take place in commitee of the whole, and when this occurs the lord chairman of committees, a supporter of the government, presides. The only standing committee is one on textual revision, which handles bills passed in Committee of the Whole House. Select and sessional committees are sometimes appointed to consider particular pieces of legislation and to obtain information

---

[9] Chairmen of standing committees are not necessarily from the majority party. They are chosen from a panel nominated by the speaker.

relevant to pending measures. Committees on private bills also function in the House of Lords.

Parliamentary Procedure.   There are four main kinds of bills introduced into Parliament. A public bill is usually drafted by a minister and his departmental advisers and has the support of the cabinet; it will alter or add to the general law. A private member's bill also affects the general law, but it is introduced by a member in his private capacity and not as a member of the government. A private bill concerns the interests of a particular locality, individual, or corporation only. A money bill relates to taxation and supply. Parliamentary procedure varies for each of these types of bills.

Most public bills of importance originate in the House of Commons, although they could be first introduced in the House of Lords. Introduction is by leave or notice. The first reading is by title only, after which the bill is printed and circulated. On second reading the principles of the measure are debated. After second reading the bill goes to either the committee of the whole or one of the standing committees. In committee the individual provisions of the bill are examined, and amendments, if any, are made. The committee then reports to Commons. The House may amend at the report stage, but eventually it either recommits the measure or accepts the report. The bill then has a third reading, during which stage only verbal amendments are permitted. After passage on third reading the bill goes to the Lords for their concurrence. In the House of Lords the bill must also pass through three readings. The Lords may amend the bill. If this occurs, the House must agree or a compromise be worked out, unless, of course, the government wishes to invoke the Parliament Act.[1] The royal assent converts a bill passed by Parliament into law.

The procedure used for public bills gives Parliament ample opportunity to amend these measures introduced by the government. But amendments proposed in Commons must be accepted by the government, otherwise a question of confidence would arise. Actually amendments may prove acceptable to the government for a variety of reasons: better language, curing of difficulties unforeseen by the departmental experts, even concessions to opinions strongly held in the House. Also, a government may wish to get a piece of legislation enacted in short order and consequently agree to changes. This last point—the desire to avoid delay —sometimes puts in the hand of the Lords a powerful lever; the fact that amendments made by the Lords can be overridden does not mean that they always are.

During and immediately after World War II it was not possible to give time to private members' bills, but in 1949 time once again was set aside for bills introduced by private members. Today the first twenty Fridays of each session are given over to private members' bills and motions. In addition, on Tuesdays and Wednesdays a member may introduce a bill after the question period under the ten-minute rule. That

[1] The procedure of the Parliament Act is not invoked as frequently as might be thought. Only three public bills were passed under the Parliament Act of 1911.

is, one ten-minute speech proposing and one opposing are allowed, after which the House of Commons decides whether to grant leave to bring the bill in.

Even though a private member may introduce a bill (which is easily done through notice), he has no assurance that it will ever reach second reading. Actually lots are drawn to see which private members' bills will be considered on the Fridays set aside for this purpose. Normally only twenty or so bills receive consideration in a session. Also, if the government opposes a private member's bill, it has virtually no chance of getting through the second reading. And after second reading there remain the committee stage, third reading, and the other House.[2]

Despite the difficulties faced by private members' bills some notable pieces of legislation have reached the statute books in this manner. Some examples are Samuel Plimsoll's Merchant Shipping Act of 1876; Sir A. P. Herbert's Matrimonial Causes Act of 1937; and Miss Irene Ward's Rights of Entry (Gas and Electricity Boards) Bill of 1954. More recently, in 1956, a private member's motion calling for the abolition of capital punishment passed and resulted in the introduction of a bill for this purpose. Opposition to complete abolition of the death sentence arose, however, being particularly vocal in the House of Lords. The final legislation, the Homicide Act, 1957, consequently did not go as far as the abolitionists wanted but much farther than some persons in Britain felt desirable. The act left untouched the death sentence for high treason and piracy, but abolished it for murders generally, except for a limited number of specified murders, such as those in furtherance of theft, those caused by shooting or explosion, etc.

Money bills have a special status under the Parliament Act of 1911. A money bill, when certified by the speaker of the House and sent up to the House of Lords at least one month before the end of the session, will receive the royal assent regardless of what the Lords do about it.

Money bills grow out of the budget, which is presented by the chancellor of the Exchequer in the spring of the year.[3] The opening of the budget and the consideration of the supply and tax measures provide an annual occasion for debate and criticism of the worthiness of the government of the day.[4]

The procedure used for private bills is virtually divorced from the normal partisan procedure of Parliament. The proposer of a private bill must submit a petition to the examiner of petitions for private bills of either the House of Commons or the House of Lords. This petition contains the proposed legislation and any costs involved. In addition the sponsor must notify the government department that would be most concerned with the proposal and all affected private interests.

[2] The private member introducing a bill is responsible for steering it through. This is a time-consuming task that is shouldered by the whips in the case of government bills. Also, when the government is in need of more time for consideration of its business, the temptation to trench upon the Fridays set aside for private members' bills is great. In the period 1951–58, eighty private members' bills were passed.

[3] Under a standing order of Commons dating from 1706 no measure for expenditure will be considered unless it is submitted by the government.

When the examiner certifies that these requirements have been satisfied, the private bill may be introduced. Each House receives about half the private bills introduced in a session.

Unopposed private bills proceed routinely through Parliament, although they receive consideration by a small committee. For opposed private bills the committee (composed of four members in Commons) holds hearings. The proponents and opponents appear with counsel and experts to present their cases. After this quasi-judicial hearing the committee decides whether to report the bill favorably, possibly with amendments, or unfavorably. The report of the committee almost always determines the fate of the private bill. A private bill passed in one House seldom is opposed in the other.[5]

Question Time.   One of the most effective ways of throwing a "searchlight upon every corner of the public service" is the question period. In the House of Commons question time begins immediately after opening on the first four days of the week and lasts for about forty-five minutes. Private members may ask up to three questions a day,[6] by handing them in to the clerk two days in advance. Questions are directed to the ministers and pertain to almost every conceivable phase of the government. The most interesting ones are those to which an oral reply is given. The reply of the minister is, of course, drafted by departmental experts, but members may ask supplementary questions and then the minister is on his own. The minister may refuse to answer on grounds of public interest, but this stand is usually avoided if possible. If a member is not satisfied with the minister's reply, he may by giving notice bring the matter up again on the motion for adjournment.

The question period is only one of the means by which Parliament can bring criticism to bear on the ministers. As mentioned earlier, the

[4] The national budget for the year 1955–56 was as follows (£ million):

REVENUE		EXPENDITURES	
Personal income taxes	1,317	Defense	1,557
Companies taxes	901	National debt	636
Death duties	185	Health service	462
Tobacco	660	Education	343
Alcohol	388	Agriculture and food subsidies	311
Purchase tax	368	Pensions, family allowances, etc.	414
Oil and motor duties	400	Assistance to local authorities,	
Entertainment and betting	70	housing, roads, etc.	265
Import and stamp duties	197	General governmental services	574
Broadcast licenses, etc.	224	Surplus	148
	4,710		4,710

[5] The procedure for private bills saves Parliament from devoting its attention to matters of limited interest, and there is much to commend in the judicial approach to opposed private bills. The use of delegated legislation has lessened the need for private bills in connection with local government affairs. Central government departments can issue the appropriate orders at the request of local authorities, or approve schemes relating to education, public health, etc., submitted by them, subject to final approval or disapproval by Parliament.

[6] Questions may be asked by any member except ministers, the chair, and the leader of the opposition.

debate on the budget is another annual occasion, as is the debate on the reply to the queen's speech. Other times when the government generally comes under attack are on the days set aside for debate of foreign policy. Of course, during the passage of any public bill, the opposition has numerous opportunities to voice criticism.[7]

4. CABINET GOVERNMENT

The essential functions of parties in a democracy are, according to Professor A. Lawrence Lowell, to bring public opinion to a focus and to frame issues for popular verdict. The British party system performs these functions, but its chief function is that of establishing the government of the day. Under the British two-party system an election results in a mandate for a party to take over the reins of government. Through the institutions of parliamentary government party leaders are installed as the queen's ministers and party policies carried out by state action.

The government of the day, the cabinet, is able to carry out its program largely because of the effective control the party exercises over its members in the House of Commons. Party orthodoxy enforced through the whips is strong; effective party irregularity is rare. The position of the party regarding the member's freedom to vote in Commons is straightforward. The member is elected on the basis of his standing for the party's program and is consequently expected to support the program in Commons. However much a member dissents from the policy decisions of the party majority, he is expected to go along with them in Commons. The alternatives to support of the party majority and its leadership are drastic, involving in some instances either voluntary withdrawal or involuntary excommunication from the party.[8] In the extreme case party irregularity could, although nowadays it rarely does, lead to defeat of the cabinet and a dissolution of Parliament. As a result there is strong pressure to resolve dissent through informal channels rather than through the formal methods of voting against the cabinet or party majority on the floor of Commons.[9]

The British party system also imposes a thoroughgoing discipline over the electorate. There are usually more than two sides to any political question, but the British two-party system generally limits the voter's choice to only two effective alternative solutions to political problems,

[7] Also, important executive policy decisions—such as a decision to devalue the pound—frequently provoke debate when announced in Commons.

[8] In some instances a dissident group within a party may be so large that it cannot be drastically disciplined; such appears to have been the case for the Bevanites within the Labour Party. When only an individual is involved, the party may "withdraw the whip" and eventually refuse to adopt the individual as a candidate when election time comes.

[9] For discussion of the general problems involved see James MacGregor Burns, "The Parliamentary Labor Party in Great Britain," *America Political Science Review,* 44 (1950), pp. 855–71; Leon D. Epstein, "Cohesion of British Parliamentary Parties," ibid., 50 (1956), pp. 360–77.

that is, to either the program of the government or that of the opposition.
It is possible, of course, for third and fourth parties to enter the electoral
arena and even to garner a respectable number of votes. Their strength is
usually dissipated, however, by the effects of the single-member district
system.[1] The failure of this system to afford representation commensu-
rate with the popular strength of third parties is one of the strongest
arguments used by the proponents of proportional representation. On the
other hand, most Englishmen seem to prefer a party and electoral system
that provides strong cabinet leadership to one that would permit a more
accurate reflection in Commons of the various political groups, but at
the expense of cabinet leadership.

In yet another way does the working of the two-party system influence parties. The two major parties, in order to gain a parliamentary
majority, attempt to appeal to a majority of the electorate. Under present
conditions both major parties slant their programs toward the "floating"
vote, the lower middle class. Thus major party programs are directed
more toward the center than the left and right axes of the class and
economic-interest support of the Labour and Conservative parties would
at first indicate. Extremists in both parties, rabid Socialists and high
Tories, quite naturally dislike this middle-of-the-road aspect of the party
system. But as long as the parliamentary and two-party systems continue
to function as they do, extremists will find it difficult to obtain an effective outlet for their views.

Both the British party system and the parliamentary system reflect
a basic tenet of the British concept of democracy, namely, majority rule.
The operation of the party system stresses the formation of a governing
majority by popular vote. The popularly endorsed majority then becomes
the legislative majority. In the French Third and Fourth Republics the
cabinet was not formed by the party system outside the legislature or by
the express endorsement of the electorate. The French Parliament, through
shifts in alignment of its party *groupements,* actually formed the government. From one point of view, then, the British party system performs a
function that is left to the legislature in many other countries. From another point of view the British party system gives the electorate a much
greater voice in the formation of governing majorities than do other
systems, except in some of the Commonwealth countries. But the party
system in Britain limits the voter's range of effective choice, a factor that
tends to produce majorities that are both disciplined and tempered.

As is easily seen, the leadership position of the British cabinet is

[1] Conversely, the system inflates the strength of the two major parties; in each
of the elections from 1945 to 1955 one party managed to gain an absolute majority
of seats in Commons, but in none of these elections did a party get as much as 50
per cent of the popular vote. It has been suggested that the present system gives the
Conservative Party a 1- to 2-per-cent advantage over Labour, that is, the Labour
Party has to get 1 or 2 per cent more of the popular vote than the Conservatives to
win an equal number of seats. The mathematically minded student may wish to test
the "cube law," which has also been propounded in connection with British elections.
The "cube law" holds that, if the popular vote of the two major parties is divided in
the ratio A:B, then the parties will divide their seats in Commons in the ratio
$A^3:B^3$.

exceedingly strong, and there is some justification for characterizing the relation between the executive and Parliament as one in which the cabinet controls Parliament, rather than vice versa. Indeed, Sir Ivor Jennings suggests that the combination of the powers of a party leader and those of a prime minister could result in a cabinet dictatorship lasting for five years, with Parliament exercising in fact only the power to criticize. The combination of powers envisaged is a delicate one, for few prime ministers have been able (even if they had wished to, which is doubtful) to run roughshod over the feelings of the party rank and file in Commons. And there are other circumstances that make it difficult to push cabinet leadership to its logical limits. Obviously, under conditions of coalition government, the prime minister cannot depend upon party discipline unfailingly to produce government majorities in Commons. Even under conditions of one-party cabinets, there are situations in which cabinets cannot dictate. A cabinet with a small and precarious majority may find it prudent to bend a sympathetic ear to the wishes of Commons. And divisions of opinion within a party—such as those that prevailed within Labour after the election of 1950—may make it impossible for a cabinet to embark upon certain programs without arousing opposition within its own ranks.

In other words, British experience with cabinet government has produced a principle that acts as a self-imposed brake upon cabinet power, namely, the principle of cabinet unity. Although the opposite has been attempted (for example, the coalition cabinet of MacDonald, composed of free traders and protectionists, agreed to differ in 1932), cabinets have been found to hold together best when all members are agreed upon policy. Seldom, if ever, has a prime minister been in position to place in his cabinet only persons in perfect accord with his and every other member's views. As a result cabinet agreement is normally reached through compromise. If compromise fails, cabinet unity is destroyed, and one or more cabinet officers may feel impelled or be asked to resign. The agreement to differ reached in the MacDonald cabinet lasted nine months, after which several free traders withdrew when the government adopted a program of imperial preference. Sometimes a cabinet may weather the withdrawal of a particular member, but again it may not, as was the case when Bevan left the Labour government in 1951. Thus, although cabinet decisions will generally be supported in Commons, the necessity for cabinet unity limits cabinet discretion in arriving at decisions.

A consideration of the relationship of the executive to Parliament would be incomplete without mention of Her Majesty's Loyal Opposition. Much can be said regarding the role of the Loyal Opposition in criticizing government measures, in interposing delay in the passage of government bills, and in subjecting the performance of the government of the day to pitiless, albeit partisan, scrutiny. Now, in any democratic parliament or legislature, the government and its policies will be subjected to partisan opposition. What differentiates the British Parliament from so many other legislatures is that the Loyal Opposition is a responsible opposition. In many legislative bodies a great deal of criticism and opposition is essentially negative and irresponsible. Those who offer opposition frequently do so only in order to defeat and frustrate government measures or to advance their own personal political ambitions, with little thought and less hope of forming a government or of attempting to do better. The Loyal Opposition, however, represents not merely the right to criticize and harass but also a standing offer to take over the reins of government.

From another point of view the existence of the Loyal Opposition attests the belief of the British people that democracy is government by discussion. Of course the opposition and the government do not engage in parliamentary debate with the expectation that they will alter the opinions or votes of members of Commons. But they do expect, and rightly so, that the opinions and votes of the electorate may be affected by what is said in Parliament. Historically British regard for the values of free discussion is deep-seated, a classic defense of freedom of speech having been given as early as the seventeenth century by Milton in his *Areopagitica* (1644). It may be mere coincidence, but the seeds of the idea for the Loyal Opposition may be found in the Leveller tracts of the same period during which Milton wrote. Opposition to established government was not necessarily treasonable, the Levellers argued, and today one of the first acts of treason against democratic government is recognized to be the stamping out of opposition.

The successful blending of the two-party system with the historic institutions of parliamentary government is certainly one of the noteworthy achievements of British democracy. One question that arises, however, is why the English voter and member of Commons continue to accept the strictures imposed by the cabinet and two-party systems. Unfortunately there is no single answer to this question. As Professor Jennings points out, the major party leaders are interested in maintaining the system; the constitution is geared to operate best on a two-party basis; and the English voter apparently would rather cast his ballot for an imperfect but potential winner than for an ideally perfect but lost cause. Also, some of the forces making for separate parties on the Continent—class divisions in the Marxist sense and a large Catholic population—are relatively absent from the British scene. Historical circumstance undoubtedly played its part in the development of cabinet government, too. And another factor is the British concept of representation, which in both theory and practice has left its impress upon parliamentary institutions.

5. REPRESENTATION AND PARLIAMENT

Modern democratic theory makes a sharp distinction between state and society, a distinction that affects the concept of the representative legislature in modern constitutions. The legislature is frequently conceived of as an organ of the state, quite distinct from the people. It becomes an organ through which the people exercise their sovereignty. Before the modern distinction between state and society developed, the British Parliament had assumed many of its basic characteristics and the tradition of Parliament contains elements that counteract the modern insistence upon a separation of the national representative body from the people.

The infusion of the element of representation into the English Parliament occurred, as mentioned earlier, in the thirteenth century.[2] In Parliament were found the three great estates of medieval society: the lords temporal, the lords spiritual, and Commons; and Parliament became closely identified with the realm of England itself. In the late fifteenth century Sir John Fortescue quite naturally equated the "assent of the whole realm" with the "assent of commons and nobles of the realm" given in Parliament.[3] In the sixteenth century Sir Thomas Smith wrote of Parliament: "For every Englishman is intended to be there present, either in person or by procuration and attorneys." In the middle of the seventeenth century Edward Coke spoke of the king and the three estates as "the great corporation or body politick of the kingdome." [4] And in the middle of the next century Blackstone declared that Parliaments were "coeval with the kingdom itself."[5]

Of course the identification of Parliament with the realm has not completely survived into modern times. Nevertheless, not all vestiges of the earlier notion have disappeared. There is still acceptance of the idea that the will and reason of Parliament are the will and reason of the people, not merely the will of a transient majority or the desires of an invidious combination of groups and interests. Conversely, a fundamental British constitutional principle is one that calls for a dissolution of Parliament whenever it appears that the popular will is no longer truly represented. The mechanics of this constitutional principle found, it may be noted, a place in the constitutions of both the Third and Fourth French republics, but French practice failed to give primacy to the idea that the standing Parliament ought to represent the will of the people even if it means dissolution.

In general, there lingers about the British Parliament some residue of the medieval notion of the "organic" state, in which the judgment of Parliament was reckoned to be co-ordinate with the judgment of the realm. True, the mechanistic theory of state and society and individualism have affected the concept of Parliament. The presumption persists, nonetheless, of a basic accord between Parliament and the people rather than of a probable, if not fundamental, antagonism. As Edmund Burke declared, Parliament is a *"deliberative* assembly of *one* nation, with *one*

---

[2] Representative institutions appeared not only in England at this time; as a matter of fact, they appeared earlier in Southern France and Northern Spain; see E. M. Sait, *Political Institutions, A Preface* (1938). Other theories on the origins of representation stress the practices of the Germanic tribes: see Charles A. Beard, "Teutonic Origins of Representative Government," *American Political Science Review*, 26 (1932), pp. 28–44; the English jury system and the practices of the Dominican Order: see James Hogan, *Election and Representation* (1945), and Ernest Barker, *The Dominican Order and Convocation* (1913).

[3] *De laudibus legum Angliae,* Chapter 18.

[4] *Institutes,* 2.

[5] *Commentaries,* Book I, Chapter 2.

interest, that of the whole." [6] Much doubt has been expressed that Parliament is any longer a "deliberative" assembly, but less doubt has been voiced that Parliament is, or, what is equally important, can be, representative of one nation with one interest, when the occasion so requires.

Theories of Representation. Underlying the Englishman's high regard for Parliament is a body of thought and theory concerning the nature of representation. The major political forces of modern Britain—conservatism, liberalism, and socialism—agree that representative government is the best form, and not merely a necessary substitute for direct democracy. On some of the main points involved in the practice of representation, however, there is variation among the views held by the major forces, and, for that matter, variation within particular bodies of thought.

The outstanding spokesman for the conservative view is Edmund Burke. In Burke's thought the individualistic premise of liberalism is rejected. To Burke the "nation is not only an idea of local extent, and individual momentary aggregation; but it is an idea of continuity, which extends in time as well as in numbers and in space." The notion of mere numerical majority rule was utterly repugnant to Burke, yet he believed in popular government. But popular government to him took into account the experience of the ages as well as the general good. He felt that the element of election was essential in representation, but he did not advocate a universal franchise. Virtual representation, he held to be "in many cases, even better than actual." Virtual representation was a "communion of interests, and a sympathy in feelings and desires, between those who act in the name of any description of people, and the people in whose name they act, though the trustees are not actually chosen by them." Perhaps the most renowned pronouncement of Burke on the subject of representation is his repudiation of the idea of the restricted mandate before his Bristol constituency.

> Your representative owes you, not his industry only but his judgment, and he betrays, instead of serving you, if he sacrifices it to your opinion. You choose a member, but when you have chosen him, he is not a member of Bristol, but he is a Member of Parliament. If the local constituent should have an interest, or should form a hasty opinion, evidently opposite to the real good of the rest of the community, the member for that place ought to be as far as any other from any endeavour to give it effect. . . .

The representative's "unbiased opinion, his mature judgment, his enlightened conscience," Burke maintained, "he ought not to sacrifice to you, to any man, or to any set of men living." Representation signified to Burke deliberation, not the counting of individual wills. And the representative had many obligations, not to his constituents alone, but to the nation and to his own conscience as well.

[6] *Works* (Bohn edition, 1896), Vol. I, p. 447.

Liberal theory finds illustration in the thought of John Locke and John Stuart Mill. Locke accepted the territorial principle. The constituency was first of all a geographic place, but population was not the sole criterion of the right of a place to be distinctly represented. Wealth, as well as the number of inhabitants, was a measure of representation. The number of members from a constituency ought to be "in proportion to the assistance which it affords the public." Locke did not deal directly with the question of whether the representative operated under a strict mandate from his constituency. Instead he placed limits on the powers of the representative assembly, the legislative power "being only a fiduciary power to act for certain ends." The ends were decreed by natural law, and to Locke consisted of the individual's right to life, liberty, and property. Within these limits Locke asserted that the mode of action was majority action or majority rule.

The individual emerges as the unit of representation more definitely in the thought of John Stuart Mill. Mill enthusiastically endorsed the proportional-representation scheme set forth by Thomas Hare in 1859. Significantly, however, Mill termed it "personal representation." In his *Representative Government* (1861) Mill held that it was not enough that every individual citizen have the franchise, but that each vote must count equally with every other vote. Accordingly, Mill rejected the territorial principle. Any group of electors, however dispersed throughout the land, should be capable of combining to return representatives as their combined numbers warranted. Despite his insistence that as many individual interests as possible ought to be represented, Mill did not advocate the restricted mandate, nor did he repudiate majority rule. However, as an individualist, Mill recognized the possible conflict between individual liberty and majority rule. His endorsement of proportional representation and his proposals for plural votes indicate his concern with the dangers of majority rule. Although the idea of proportional representation has gained some support, it has not been accepted as a substitute for the single-member district system. As mentioned earlier, whatever its theoretical advantages may be, opponents of proportional representation feel that its adoption would lead to a weak and unstable cabinet system.

British socialist thought on representation reflects many theories. Early socialist writings, for example, G. D. H. Cole, *Guild Socialism* (1920), and Beatrice and Sidney Webb, *A Constitution for the Socialist Commonwealth of Great Britain* (1920), proposed radical changes in the existing system of representation. Mr. Cole's thesis in *Guild Socialism* may be used as one illustration of these early proposals. Cole maintained that "will" and not "consent" holds society together. The individual is "fundamentally incapable of being represented." To attempt to represent an individual "in all aspects of citizenship" is really to substitute the will of one man (the representative) for the wills of many men (the represented). All that can be represented is the common view held by a group of men toward a particular purpose or function; in relation to another purpose or function this same group very likely will not have a common view. Hence Cole advocated functional representation, that is, separate representative institutions for various social and economic activities.

The dominant trend, at least so far, in the Labour Party has not followed the ideas advanced in these early socialist writings. Sir Stafford Cripps, in *Democracy Up-to-Date* (1939), proposed to measure the representative character of Commons "by the degree with which the electoral system throws up true representatives of the majority view of the electors in each constituency." The reforms that he felt were necessary to guarantee the representative character of Commons are significant. The removal of the influence of money from elections was the most important among them. Abolition of plural votes, redistribution of seats, and the elimination of "stunt" elections would also be desirable. Although Cripps wanted a Commons that "truly reflects the opinion of the country," this was to be obtained by having "a straight fight between the Government and the party or group of parties which represent the practical alternative Government in which two rival programmes only need be voted upon." Cripps disavowed the utility of proportional representation but was partial to the idea of compulsory voting in national elections.

Synthesis of Theory and Practice.   Modern British representation is a synthesis of theory and practice. Practice, extending far back into medieval times, initiated and then confirmed the territorial principle. To practice and to the social-contract theory of the state, particularly as advanced by Locke, may be attributed the acceptance of the majority principle. Conservatism and Edmund Burke contributed to the rejection of the idea of the restricted mandate,[7] and also tempered the rigor of majority rule by emphasizing the importance of experience and tradition as against the desires of the temporary majority. Socialist theory contains many striking suggestions, but the Labour Party in practice has on the whole accepted the system of representation that stresses the single-member district and a two-party fight.

The British conception of the representative legislature stresses its deliberative function (although modern practice may not) and its character of representing individuals as complete persons, as they are conditioned by the community in which they live and are affected by the practical choices they have to make. The conception rejects the primacy of local interests as such and emphasizes the representative purpose as that of the good of the whole. One illustration of this is the rule that a member of Commons need not reside in the constituency he represents.

Modern political theory admits of many conceptions of the legislature. It may be regarded as an instrument for inflecting a Rousseau-

[7] Whether or not the medieval representative in Commons was bound by his constituents or instead had full power to bind his constituency is a pertinent question. The medieval king insisted that the knights and burgesses have power to assent to proposals laid before Parliament; on the other hand, members of Commons apparently felt some obligation to present petitions on behalf of their constituencies. In the *Osborne Case* (1910) the House of Lords accepted the interpretation that Parliament was summoned to advise the king freely, a fact that implied the absence of restrictions on the powers of the representative in Commons. Of course members of Parliament do take actions for the benefit of their local constituents, but their obligation to their party normally has primacy.

istic "general will" or as a means for transmuting a Hegelian will of the idealized state or simply as a channel for reflecting a babel of special interests. The historical roots of the British Parliament, however, reach back into an earlier age and another climate of thought. They reach to the common lawyer Coke and to his declaration that, when Parliament was "assembled and joyned together," there resulted the "highest wisdom" (*ultimum sapientiae*) of the realm. And at the very beginning of the representative Parliament there stand the words of Edward I when he summoned the Model Parliament: "what touches all, shall be approved by all." The role of the British Parliament has not been untouched by modern theory, but Parliament is still thought of as a body for ascertaining the highest judgment and general consent of the land.

CHAPTER

4

THE EXECUTIVE

In the British system the Crown is the repository of the variety of powers and functions associated with the executive branch in Western constitutional government. As Sir William Anson has said: "In treating of the executive of this country we must always bear in mind that the Crown, acting directly or remotely through ministers or officials, is the executive."[1]

As the executive, however, the Crown is not a single entity;[2] rather it consists of several institutional components functioning together. Three of these components are easy to identify and the manner in which they function together is governed by settled constitutional principle. These three components are: the sovereign or monarch, who is the formal executive; the cabinet and ministry, which have become the political executive; and the permanent civil service, which may be termed the working or administrative executive. The principle governing their relationship is that of cabinet and ministerial responsibility. The cabinet, as political executive, is responsible for advising the sovereign on matters of governmental policy. Under the conventions of the constitution such advice is accepted. And then the ministers as heads of the various administrative departments and agencies become responsible for implementation of governmental policy. Of course the workaday tasks involved in administering policy are not expected to be performed personally by the ministers. These tasks fall to the civil service. But if any political responsibility arises from the activities of a civil servant, it is the minister and not the civil servant who assumes that responsibility and who must answer to Parliament.

There are other components of the British executive, whose importance has continually increased during the twentieth century. Public

---

[1] *The Law and Custom of the Constitution.* Part II. *The Crown.* (2nd ed., 1896), Introduction.

[2] The term "Crown" is used in various ways. For example, it may signify the monarchy as such; again, it is used to represent the legal personality of the state, as in such phrases as Crown property, servants of the Crown, etc.

corporations, especially after the nationalization program of the post-
World War II Labour government, have come to dominate vital sectors
of the British economy, particularly transportation, communications, and
power.[3] As the activities of the state have increased, machinery to adjust
and adjudicate the rights of individuals affected has become necessary.
In Britain no organized system of administrative courts such as exists in
France, Germany, and other Continental countries has developed. On
the other hand, there has been an unwillingness to vest in the ordinary
courts full jurisdiction to determine cases involving individual property
rights and administrative implementation of statutory policy. The result
has been a welter of boards and other adjudicatory machinery more or
less attached to the various administrative agencies. The relationships of
the public corporations and this adjudicatory machinery to the political
executive, the cabinet and ministers, and to Parliament have involved
concrete problems not easily resolved by a straightforward application
of the principle of ministerial responsibility. These problems will be the
subject of the last portion of this chapter, and will follow separate discussion of the monarchy, the cabinet, and the civil service.

1. THE MONARCHY

It was Edmund Burke who said: "People will not look forward to poster-
ity who never look backward to their ancestors." In their monarchy the
British people have a constant reminder of their long historical past. The
British trace their monarchy back some eleven centuries to the year 829
when Egbert, a Saxon king, united England for a brief period before
the Danish invasions began. Since then the monarchy has continued,
unbroken but for the years of Cromwell and the Commonwealth,
1649–60.

The term "British monarchy" is today perhaps somewhat of a
misnomer, for the monarchy has become an international institution. Although Australia, Canada, New Zealand, and South Africa are free and
independent nations, Elizabeth II is queen of them all, as well as of the
United Kingdom and the dependent empire. Even the republican members of the Commonwealth of Nations, India and Pakistan, accept the
queen as "Head of the Commonwealth." This status of the monarchy
is reflected in the royal title in the United Kingdom: "Elizabeth the
Second, by the Grace of God of the United Kingdom of Great Britain
and Northern Ireland and of Her other Realms and Territories Queen,
Head of the Commonwealth, Defender of the Faith."

Succession to the throne is by inheritance. Sons of the sovereign
and their descendants enjoy precedence over daughters.[4] Daughters and
their descendants take precedence over lateral heirs. Parliament has,

---

[3] See below, Chapter 6, pp. 131–34.
[4] The wife of a king has the rank of queen; the husband of a queen has no
special rank or style. The husband of Queen Elizabeth II is Prince Philip, Duke of
Edinburgh.

however, altered and restricted the natural path of succession, most notably in the Act of Settlement, 1701. The act placed the present House of Windsor[5] on the throne and also excluded Catholics from the succession. The line of succession can still be altered, but under a convention embodied in the Preamble of the Statute of Westminster, 1931, only with the common consent of those members of the Commonwealth owing allegiance to the Crown.

When the death or abdication of one sovereign occurs, his successor is immediately proclaimed. This is done at an accession council to which all privy councilors are summoned and other notables invited. The actual coronation takes place later. In the event the new heir should be under eighteen, a regency is provided. Under the Regency Act, 1953, the Duke of Edinburgh, given the title and style of Prince Philip in 1957, is the first potential regent followed by those in line of succession who are of age. A regency also would function in case of total incapacity of the sovereign. In event of partial incapacity or absence abroad, counselors of state are appointed to perform necessary royal functions.

Royal Functions. As Walter Bagehot pointed out, the legal powers of the queen are formidable. She is commander-in-chief of the armed forces, temporal head of the Church of England, the "fountain of justice," and the "fountain of honour." She concludes treaties, makes war, creates peers, appoints and dismisses officials of state. It is through the queen's speech from the throne that the legislative program and general policy of the government of the day are formally presented to Parliament. And no bill of Parliament can become law without her assent.

But, of course, the queen does none of these things on her own. She reigns, as the phrase goes, but does not rule. She acts on the advice of her ministers. Yet there remain a few functions wherein the action of the sovereign is personal as well as formal, where it is recognized that a situation could develop in which the sovereign might be required by circumstances to exercise a choice. An example of the exercise of the queen's personal prerogative was the naming of her son Prince Charles as Prince of Wales in the summer of 1958.

It is in the sovereign function of giving continuity to the political life of the state, of effecting the transition from one government to another, that an opportunity of exercising a choice may arise. The prerogatives of the queen include the designation of a prime minister and dissolution of Parliament. Normally the designation of a prime minister is determined by the party situation in the House of Commons and the queen has no choice. At times the situation may not be clear, as in 1923 when the Conservative Party found itself without a leader after the resignation of Bonar Law. King George V chose Stanley Baldwin over Lord Curzon, but only after obtaining advice from several prominent Conservative Party members. Another situation that may result in the opportunity for choice is when no party commands a majority in Com-

[5] The name Windsor was adopted during World War I; the original name was Hanover.

mons. But even here the possibility of exercising royal discretion may be restricted. After the Conservative Party failed to receive the confidence of the country in 1924, there was hardly any alternative but to call the leader of the Labour Party, for Labour had been the official opposition to the previous Conservative government and was the second party in parliamentary seats. Much the same circumstances prevailed in 1929, only this time the Labour Party was first in parliamentary strength. In assessing the significance of the queen's power to choose in cases where the parliamentary situation is unclear there is one basic condition to be remembered. Whoever may be designated prime minister must still be able to form a government that Commons will support.

Whether the queen retains any degree of personal prerogative with regard to dissolution is questionable. Some opinion continues to appear to the effect that there may occur some highly unusual circumstances in which the queen might refuse a dissolution or, conversely, might insist on one.[6] In so far as normal functioning of the constitution is concerned, however, the prerogative of dissolution is exercised on the advice of the prime minister.[7]

In the exercise of all her formal powers the queen is expected to follow the path of impartiality as between parties. What is done for one party must likewise be done for another in like circumstances. Any departure from this rule would mean a departure from the practice of constitutional monarchy.

Royal Influence. A wise queen, Walter Bagehot once wrote, would want no other rights than those she already has—"the right to be consulted, the right to encourage, and the right to warn." The queen is kept advised of all important state matters and sees a vast amount of state papers. After a while the queen is in position to have an unmatched view of the course of state affairs. Men who have held the post of prime minister have acknowledged the fund of experience that lies in the monarch. To what extent a sovereign's experience and views based on that experience will influence his advisers is, on the other hand, difficult to say. About the best that can be said is that the possibility of influence exists and instances do come to light in which royal views exerted influence.

There is another aspect of royal influence that comes in for criticism from certain quarters. It involves the perpetuation of class divisions, of aristocratic pretension, of snobbishness, to which royalty is said to lend itself. As against this there seems to be increasing appreciation of the monarchy as a symbol of English unity and aspiration, and of the value

---

[6] See S. B. Chrimes, *English Constitutional History* (1947), pp. 85ff.; W. Ivor Jennings, *The British Constitution* (3rd ed., 1950), pp. 113–14. The queen certainly would have the right to caution against a proposed dissolution. Jennings also comments, p. 112, that the monarch has sometimes made inquiries concerning matters coming before him as king-in-council and that action sometimes has been postponed as a result of his inquiry.

[7] It is pointed out that the sovereign could reject advice to dissolve, provided that he could find a minister who would advise against dissolution. But the new minister would have to be supported by the House of Commons.

of the monarchy and its pageantry in bringing the "littlest he" in all England in close communion with his nation.[8]

2. CABINET AND MINISTRY

In the British system political responsibility falls to the cabinet and ministry. The cabinet has direct responsibility for the formulation of policy. It is not, however, an executant or administrative body in itself. As stated in the *Report of the Machinery of Government Committee* (1918) the functions of the cabinet are: (1) final determination of policy to be submitted to Parliament, (2) control of the national executive in accordance with policy laid down by Parliament, and (3) co-ordination and delimitation of the authority of the various government departments.

Execution of policy is the function of the individual departments and the responsibility of the ministers who head them. Yet the cabinet cannot completely avoid the question of responsibility in regard to administration. Some administrative decisions are of such political importance that cabinet sanction will be sought in advance. Furthermore, if the conduct of a department comes under severe parliamentary criticism, the cabinet is faced with the choice of disowning the minister and letting him fall alone or of making the matter one of confidence in the government.

Cabinet Organization. The British cabinet is the creature of convention and usage. In 1937 the Ministers of the Crown Act gave legal recognition to the existence of the cabinet and the prime minister. Even so, the composition of the cabinet is not specified by law. The prime minister determines what officials shall be included in the cabinet, although many posts are customarily given cabinet rank.

The size of the cabinet varies, running as a rule between fifteen and twenty-five. The cabinet of Prime Minister Eden after the election of 1955 numbered eighteen; in 1957 his successor, Prime Minister Macmillan, increased the cabinet to nineteen posts, as follows:

Prime Minister, First Lord of the Treasury
Secretary of State for Foreign Affairs
Lord President of the Council
Lord Chancellor
Home Secretary and Minister for Welsh Affairs
Chancellor of the Exchequer
Chancellor of the Duchy of Lancaster

---

[8] The cost of the monarchy is a point sometimes raised. Parliament in the "civil list" makes an annual tax-free grant for maintenance of the queen and grants annuities to other members of the royal family. The civil list for Elizabeth II is £ 475,000. In return for the civil list the queen surrenders her hereditary revenues, which well exceed the amount granted in the civil list.

Lord Privy Seal
Minister of Defence
Secretary of State for Commonwealth Relations
Secretary of State for the Colonies
Secretary of State for Scotland
Minister of Labour and National Service
Minister of Housing and Local Government
President of the Board of Trade
Minister of Agriculture, Fisheries, and Food
Minister of Education
Minister of Pensions and National Insurance
Paymaster General

As can be seen from the above, many cabinet posts consist of the heads of important government departments. But there are more departments than cabinet posts usually, and equally important departments consequently are denied cabinet rank.[9] Several cabinet posts do not have onerous administrative duties connected with them; this is the case for the Lord President of the Council, Chancellor of the Duchy of Lancaster, and the Lord Privy Seal. These cabinet members find increasing use in co-ordination of top-level executive business and in planning. When the Paymaster General was added to the Macmillan cabinet in 1957, he was given responsibility for co-ordinating planning in connection with Britain's relations to the then-proposed European free-trade area. To be noted is a principle of the Ministers of the Crown Act of 1937. By limiting the number of persons who can sit in the House of Commons and draw salaries as ministers at the same time, this act ensured for a normal-sized cabinet that some members will be from the House of Lords.[1] This principle was continued in the House of Commons Disqualification Act, 1957, although the number of senior ministers permitted to sit in the House was increased to twenty-seven.

Cabinet working methods have become more formalized since World War I. Although cabinet meetings (usually twice a week when Parliament is in session) are held in private, there is now a cabinet secretariat, which handles agenda, records of discussions and decisions. The secretariat also conveys relevant cabinet decisions to departments concerned, provides information to ministers, and in general operates to co-ordinate policy at the top level. Also attached to the cabinet is the Central Statistical Office, which is concerned with the gathering and publication of statistics, particularly those relating to the national economy.

There are a number of standing and *ad hoc* cabinet committees.

[9] For a list of the more important ministers not in the Macmillan cabinet (as of the fall of 1957) see below, p. 89.

[1] Under the 1937 act the prime minister drew £10,000 per year and most cabinet-rank ministers £5,000. When the Churchill government of 1951 took office, it was announced that cabinet members would draw less than the amounts mentioned above. The Ministerial Salaries Act, 1957, provided for increases up to £1,000 where the salary was less than £3,000, and for increases up to £750 for salaries above that figure.

Principal standing committees that have functioned in the postwar period are the Legislation Committee, the Defence Committee, the Economic Policy Committee, the Production Committee, and the Lord President's Committee. *Ad hoc* committees, which may number between one and two dozen at any given time, deal with special problems as they arise. Membership on cabinet committees may include ministers who are not in the cabinet proper.

Ministry. Broadly speaking, the term "ministry" refers to the group of officials responsible to Parliament for the formulation and execution of policy. Hence, the ministry is considerably larger than the cabinet (which may be regarded as an "inner circle" of the ministry), since, as has been seen, many important department heads are not of cabinet rank. Ministerial posts are political positions and, whenever the party majority in the House of Commons changes, ministerial posts also change hands from the outgoing to the incoming party. Important department heads and other officers not included in the Macmillan cabinet after changes made in September, 1957, were as follows:

Minister of Supply
Minister of Fuel and Power
Minister of Transport and Civil Aviation
Minister of Works
Minister of Health
Postmaster General
First Lord of the Admiralty
Secretary of State for War
Secretary of State for Air
Attorney General
Solicitor General
Solicitor General for Scotland
Lord Advocate

Also included in the ministry are the parliamentary secretaries and undersecretaries, the lords commissioners of the Treasury, and ministers of state for foreign affairs, Scotland, colonial affairs, and the Board of Trade, and certain officers of Her Majesty's household. The House of Commons Disqualification Act, 1957, limits to seventy the number of persons who can sit in the House and also hold ministerial posts. Since a number of lords will usually be included in the ministry, the size of the ministry will normally approach ninety or a hundred.[2]

The ministry as such never meets together. But ministers not in the cabinet are included in cabinet committees, and they are entitled, of course, to place matters before the prime minister and the cabinet. An example of one way in which cabinet members and non-cabinet min-

[2] The size of the ministry gives some idea of the few positions that change hands when a government changes in Britain. Although there are some other changes in personnel, there is simply no comparison with the turnover in Washington when the administration changes.

isters are brought together through cabinet committees is the Defence Committee. As announced in a White Paper of 1958 (Cmd. 476), this committee includes the Prime Minister as chairman, and the Home Secretary, Foreign Secretary, Chancellor of the Exchequer, Commonwealth Secretary, Colonial Secretary, Minister of Defence, Minister of Labour and National Service, First Lord of the Admiralty, Secretary of State for War, Secretary of State for Air, and Minister of Supply. Several members of the committee, e.g., the First Lord of the Admiralty and the Secretaries for War and Air, are not members of the cabinet, and many cabinet members are, obviously, not members of the committee. In addition, the prime minister may invite other ministers to committee meetings at which matters affecting their departments are to be discussed. Also to be noted is the point that the chiefs of staff of the military services will be in attendance at meetings of the Defence Committee.

Privy Council. The Privy Council is today a relic of times when the monarch was a powerful force in British government. Today its functions are largely formal. Proclamations and orders-in-council are issued by the queen by and with the advice of the Privy Council. These instruments are of undoubted legal importance, but the policy decisions behind them are made elsewhere, primarily in the cabinet.

The Privy Council consists of about three hundred members. Councilors are appointed by the queen upon the advice of the prime minister and they serve for life. Appointments go to cabinet members, other important ministers, judges, ambassadors, and various official figures, including, it should be noted, some Commonwealth prime ministers and high judges. It is as privy councilors that cabinet members take the oath required of the chief advisers of the queen. Men prominent in other aspects of public life, in letters or science, for example, may also receive the honor of appointment as a councilor.

The lord president of the Council presides over its meetings. The Council has several committees, some prerogative and some statutory, dealing with a variety of subjects: medical, scientific, and agricultural research; grants of charters to municipal corporations; and Oxford, Cambridge, and the Scottish universities. One committee, the Judicial Committee, has a special significance in connection with appeals from the courts of the dependent empire and certain Commonwealth countries.[3]

3. THE CIVIL SERVICE

The modern British civil service enjoys a high reputation, not only at home, but abroad as well. Yet, not much more than a century ago, it was the object of criticism and derision. John Bright referred to it as "the outdoor relief department of the British aristocracy." Reform of the service began with the East India Company, culminating in 1853 in Lord Macaulay's successful effort to introduce competitive selection for posts in the Indian service. The Trevelyan-Northcote Report, submitted to

[3] For discussion of the Judicial Committee's activities see below, pp. 112–13.

Parliament in 1854, recommended recruitment by open competition in the home service. In 1855 the Civil Service Commission was established to examine and certify candidates nominated for junior positions by the departments. In 1859 a parliamentary enactment limited, with some exceptions, retirement benefits to persons appointed after certification by the Commission. Then, in 1870, the government by order-in-council made open competition the method of recruitment for practically all administrative and clerical positions. Since 1870 the principle of merit recruitment has prevailed.

By and large the British civil service rests upon orders-in-council and executive regulations rather than statute. Parliament has remained content to leave management of the service, even including the setting up of pay scales, to the executive. Moreover, the British civil servant does not have any statutory right to tenure and retirement benefits. Nevertheless he enjoys, as a matter of established practice, thorough protection in these vital aspects of a career service.

Organization. Recruitment of permanent civil servants rests with the Civil Service Commission. Control falls within the province of the Treasury, which contains an Establishments Department to deal with management of the service. The permanent secretary of the Treasury is officially recognized as "Head of the Civil Service."

Although considerable progress toward integration of the branches of the service has been made since World War I, complete integration has not taken place. Distinction is still maintained between the Home Civil Service, the Foreign Service, and the Overseas Civil Service. More important is the distinction between "industrial" employees and "non-industrial" employees. Even though the number of industrial employees is large, over 400,000, the term "civil service" is generally applied to the body of non-industrial servants, which totaled 636,000 in 1955.

The non-industrial civil servants are largely organized into several service-wide classes. The Treasury classes, so called, comprise the administrative and clerical personnel. The *administrative class* is the top level of the service. Its members are in closest contact with the ministers, hold the highest departmental posts, and play an important role in policy formulation. It is relatively small, numbering about 3,430 in 1955. Next is the *executive class*. It is responsible for the actual operations of government within the framework of established policy. The executive class also contains specialists such as auditors and statisticians. It totaled about 68,000 in 1955. Then come the *clerical classes*. These perform the mass of detailed work of government, corresponding, account-keeping, etc. In 1955 these classes numbered some 186,000. The *typing class* numbers about 27,000.

Outside of the Treasury classes are several other groups. Of special significance are the *professional, scientific, and technical classes,* made up of lawyers, engineers, doctors, scientists, etc. The number of specialists employed has steadily increased and they number over 100,000. The *manipulative classes* form the largest group in the service, totaling over 236,000 in 1955. These classes consist of postal and telegraph workers, messengers, office cleaners, and the like. Then there are some *departmental classes,* which, as the name implies, are not service-wide. They include the inspectors of the Board of Inland Revenue, factory inspectors of the Ministry of Labour and National Service. The number in the departmental classes is small, about 2,700.

Recruitment. As noted earlier, the Civil Service Commission handles recruitment of permanent civil servants.[4] The principles evolved for recruitment of the Treasury classes emphasize entrance into the service by open competition, attraction of persons desiring to make the service their career, and selection on the basis of general intellectual capacity rather than on the basis of specialized knowledge and skills.

In accordance with these principles recruitment policies were designed in the light of Britain's educational system. Entrance ages to the Treasury classes (except typist) were set so as to coincide with the age at which persons would normally have received the level of education deemed necessary for the duties of the particular class.[5] Examinations are general in nature, rather than specialized. In the case of the administrative class particularly, there has been criticism of the recruitment policies. The nature of the examination in the past seemed to stress the kind of education obtained at Oxford and Cambridge, and graduates of these two universities provided the great bulk of those successful in entering the class. This criticism led to modification of recruitment methods for the class and seems to have cut down on the proportion of successful candidates coming from Oxford and Cambridge and also from the public schools.[6]

Problems of Bureaucracy. As the criticism of the recruitment policies for the administrative class indicates, Britain has by no means solved all the problems of modern bureaucracy. In addition to technical matters, such as pay scales for women,[7] promotion procedures, and in-service

[4] The Commission consists of six members, including part-time members, appointed on the recommendation of the prime minister, who is advised by the head of the civil service. They are not political appointees.

[5] The entrance ages for the administrative class are 20½–24; the executive class 17½–19, 20½–24; the clerical class 16–18. For persons already in the civil service or who have served in the armed forces the entrance ages are higher. It seems, however, that this gearing of entrance ages to the educational system is breaking down. In 1954 only 18 per cent of the openings in the executive class were filled through the traditional eighteen-year-old examination, while 61 per cent of the openings were filled through promotions. Slightly more than 30 per cent of recruits in the clerical class in 1954 entered through the sixteen-year-old examination. See W. J. M. Mackenzie, "The Royal Commission on the Civil Service," *The Political Quarterly,* 27 (1956), pp. 135–38.

[6] The modifications consisted of increasing the range of special subjects for written examinations and, more important, of providing an alternative method (known as Method II), which stresses the interview techniques developed for selection of army officers. Method II, as originally adopted, was to provide 25 per cent of entrants through open competition and was to be reviewed after a ten-year period ending in 1957.

[7] Women are paid on the average from 75 to 80 per cent of the amount paid men in the same grade and class. Women make up about one third of the nonindustrial civil servants.

training, problems relating to unionization, political rights, and security measures have arisen.

With respect to unionization approximately 80 per cent of the non-industrial employees belong to service unions or associations. After the general strike of 1926 legislation was enacted that required service associations to break any affiliation with outside unions. The Labour government that came into office in 1945 removed the ban on affiliation. The right to strike has not been officially forbidden, but neither has it been affirmed.

Political rights were reviewed by a Treasury committee appointed in 1949. At the time the general rule was that non-industrial servants could not participate actively in politics, but that industrial employees could. The Treasury committee recommended that the Treasury classes and the professional, scientific, and technical classes refrain as in the past from active politics, but that the industrial employees and the manipulative classes be allowed to engage in political activity as long as it did not interfere with their duties. This recommendation as finally implemented by the government will permit slightly more than 60 per cent of the civil servants to stand for Parliament. Those in the groups permitted to stand may obtain one month's leave for candidature. They must resign if elected to Parliament, but are entitled to reinstatement under certain conditions. Of those remaining over half are free, subject to the need for discretion, to take part in national politics except for candidature; the rest are barred from active participation in national politics.

The problem of security has centered about communism. The position of the government, as stated by Prime Minister Attlee in 1948, was that the state had no concern with the political views, *per se,* of its servants. On the other hand, the only "prudent course" was "to ensure that no one who is known to be a member of the Communist party, or to be associated with it in such a way as to raise legitimate doubts" about his reliability should be connected with work "vital to the security" of the state. Civil servants about whom there were legitimate doubts were to be transferred to alternative jobs if at all possible. Procedures were established for investigation of those working at sensitive posts, with an advisory board to advise the minister on decisive actions. Relatively few cases reached the stage of official action. Up to January, 1954, there were 148 cases, of which 69 were transferred and 42 were discharged or resigned.[8] In 1957 security regulations were tightened, by adding as grounds for a ruling by the minister (subject to appeal) "reasonable doubts" raised by the manner in which the servant has been or is "sympathetic" to communism.

A variation of the problem of loyalty to the state is loyalty to the government of the day. The British solution has depended upon a strong tradition of neutrality toward party politics, especially on the part of the higher civil service. Those critics who have argued that British recruitment policies for the administrative class draw in the top level of the

[8] See H. H. Wilson and Harvey Glickman, *The Problem of Internal Security in Great Britain, 1948–1953* (1954). The same proceedings applied to fascists.

bureaucracy almost exclusively from a few universities maintain that the top civil servants stand to form a group devoted to the "middle class" state. They may be neutral with respect to the policies of the "middle class" parties, that is, the Liberal and Conservative. But would they be neutral toward the Labour Party? J. D. Kingsley, for one, speculated that the top civil servants might well sabotage the programs of the Labour Party if and when the party took office and power. However, the experience of the Labour government after World War II did not bear out such fears, for it appears that the bureaucracy attempted to implement Labour's programs with all conscientiousness and efficiency. Certainly the Labour government did not feel impelled to inaugurate any purge of anti-Labour elements in the civil service. This in itself, however, does not answer the basic problem of whether the bureaucracy ought to be representative of the society in which it functions.[9]

Another problem concerns the *expertise* of the bureaucracy and the dependence of the ministers upon it. Critics like Ramsay Muir[1] emphasize that skilled politicians are as a rule amateur administrators. A minister cannot know all the intricate details involved in the workings of a department; only the permanent civil servant may have such information. Consequently the civil servant is in a position to prove with his expertness why certain items require certain procedures. Moreover, when the minister is called upon to defend his policies and actions before Commons, he falls back upon the civil servant to provide the information and data on which the ministerial defense will be based. Finally, the bureaucracy has indirectly invaded the field of legislation. Much legislation emanates from the departments, not from the cabinet or party, and this legislation embodies the views of the bureaucracy as to what is and is not desirable. In short, the argument holds that the bureaucracy impresses its views upon the cabinet, and the cabinet then forces these views upon Parliament. Even if overstressed, the problem is nonetheless real. Unfortunately the solution is not readily at hand. Muir, for example, argued for changes in the two-party system to be effected through the adoption of proportional representation. Presumably, under proportional representation, cabinets would have to depend upon coalitions between parties to provide parliamentary majorities, and hence would not be able to dictate to Commons. Under these circumstances, it is argued, cabinets would accede more to the wishes of Commons and succumb less to the blandishments of the bureaucracy. Whether, on the other hand, weak

[9] For Mr. Kingsley's views see his *Representative Bureaucracy* (1945). There have been some shifts in the social origins of the administrative class. With reference to the highest posts, in 1929, only 7 per cent were filled by persons coming from a manual-worker or domestic-servant family background; in 1950 the figure was 17 per cent. In 1950 about 25 per cent of the posts were held by persons with a family background in the skilled occupations; in 1929 the figure was 12 per cent. However, in 1950 the skilled, partly skilled, and unskilled classes, which comprise almost 80 per cent of Britain's population, provided less than 30 per cent of the holders of the highest posts. See also R. K. Kelsall, "The Social Background of the Higher Civil Service," *The Political Quarterly*, 25 (1954), pp. 385–86.

[1] *How Britain Is Governed* (1930).

coalition cabinets would not be more dependent on the stable bureaucracy is an unknown element in the argument.

Of special concern in Britain is the matter of "Treasury control." This concern stems from the role of the Chancellor of the Exchequer and the Treasury in British government. As the House of Commons Select Committee on Estimates said in its Sixth Report (1958): "Parliament especially relies on the Chancellor of the Exchequer, as the Minister responsible for raising the revenue and, nowadays, for managing the national economy, to exercise the major control (within the executive) over the total of Government expenditure." This statement suggests that the powers of the Treasury are broad and pervasive, and indeed they are, extending to budget making, planning, approval of projects in some instances, and above all to the personnel policies of the civil service itself.

It is not surprising then that concern and even alarm is voiced regarding the uses of Treasury powers. One source of anxiety stems from the proposition expressed by the Haldane Committee in 1918 that "experience seems to show that the interests of the tax-payer cannot be left to the spending Departments," and looks to Treasury control for protection of the tax payer. Others, however, see in Treasury control a means whereby financial considerations may unduly influence policy decisions. The Select Committee on Estimates did not regard Treasury control of policy decisions as necessarily nefarious; indeed the committee felt that spending departments "should be forced to face the financial implications from the inception of the proposed policy." Nevertheless, the committee expressed concern over Treasury control of policy on three counts: the practice of scrutinizing new policy closely while allowing old policy "to carry on without modification"; a tendency to underestimate the costs of new policy and projects; and the tendency to concentrate too much on the "coming financial year with too little regard to the commitments and consequences for future years."

As to the system of Treasury control as a whole, which the Select Committee described as a "complex of administrative practice that has grown up like a tree over the centuries, natural rather than planned, empiric rather than theoretical," the conclusion was that it worked "reasonably well." But the Select Committee did recommend that a "small independent committee, which should have access to Cabinet papers, be appointed to report upon the theory and practice of Treasury control of expenditure."

4. EXECUTIVE POWERS

Historically the question of executive powers has always occupied a large place in British politics. In modern times royal powers as such are no longer a matter of prime concern. But twentieth-century life, with its increasing complexity and its periods of wars and internal crises, has resulted in the vesting of more and more discretionary power in ministers and other executive officials. In Britain, as elsewhere, the extent of executive authority over the individual's liberty and property promises to remain an ever-recurring problem, and the search for appropriate controls a constant quest. Consideration of these problems posed by the burgeoning powers of the executive in Britain may appropriately begin with a few remarks on the legal nature of Crown powers, to be followed by more extended discussion of the problems raised by crisis situations, delegated powers, and the public corporations.

Powers of the Crown. The many powers exercised by the Crown come from two sources, the royal prerogative and parliamentary statutes. Prerogative powers are those which the queen or her servants may exercise without authority of an act of Parliament; they are, in Dicey's frequently quoted words, "the residue of discretionary or arbitrary authority which at any time is legally left in the hands of the crown." As Dicey's definition suggests, prerogative powers may be altered or taken away by parliamentary statute. And Parliament has acted to restrict the prerogative on many occasions. Still, the body of prerogative remaining is considerable, and it concerns in the main the fundamental operations of the government (such as appointment and dismissal of high state officers and the dissolution of Parliament), the preservation of the peace of the realm (although martial-law powers have in fact seldom been invoked), and the conduct of foreign relations (making of treaties, sending and receiving of ambassadors, declaring war and concluding peace). Even in the exercise of prerogative powers the Crown may find itself dependent eventually upon legislation. Thus the Crown may declare war, but the money and the mass of legislation necessary to fight a war must still come from Parliament. Again, the Crown may conclude treaties, but most treaties (the main exception being those affecting belligerent rights) in order to be judicially enforced in English courts require executory legislation on the part of Parliament. Actually, since World War I, the growing practice is for the more important treaties to be laid before Parliament prior to ratification as a measure of precaution.

It would leave a wrong impression to speak of parliamentary statutes only in relation to limitations on the prerogative. As a matter of fact, statutes have been the means whereby the powers of the Crown have been increased enormously, and especially in the last century. And it is this practice of delegating by statute extensive legislative and judicial powers to the Crown that has led to the problems to be discussed separately below.

With respect to the position of the Crown as party litigant in the British courts, a notable piece of clarifying legislation, the Crown Proceedings Act, was enacted in 1947. Prior to this act the individual had no general statutory means for legal recourse against the state, either in contract or tort, although in cases of contract the Crown might, by granting a petition of right, consent to suit, and in some instances particular administrative bodies were suable under the statutes constituting them. With respect to tort actions the legal maxim "The queen can do no wrong" permitted suit against a Crown servant acting *ultra vires* (that is, in excess of his legal powers), but the Crown itself was not answerable. The Crown Proceedings Act made the government legally responsible for negligence, wrongful acts, or default of its agents, as well as for malfeasance in certain specified cases. It abolished archaic procedures used in Crown proceedings, and enabled civil actions against the Crown to begin in the county courts. The only exceptions to the act are matters pertaining to the defense of the realm, to the administration of the armed forces, and to the suppression of disorder. Indeed, the great historic significance of the act lies in its virtual abolition of the legal immunity of the Crown.

Crisis Government. Twice in the first half of the twentieth century Britain has faced grave danger in the form of external war. Ever since Cincinnatus left his plow to aid the Roman Republic, it has been more or less axiomatic that constitutional government must depart from its usual ways in time of crisis. The British constitution contains no explicit directions detailing the procedure to be followed whenever the state becomes involved in a crisis situation. Yet there is a good deal of similarity in the steps taken by British leaders of World War I and World War II to adapt British government to the necessities of wartime.

In both war periods the outbreak of hostilities came very late in the statutory five-year life of the Parliament in session. Nevertheless, in each case, the decision was to prolong the life of Parliament from year to year by statute and to postpone general parliamentary elections until the end of major hostilities. Also, at the beginning of both conflicts, leaders concluded party truces designed to permit the government to focus its efforts on winning the war with as little partisan distraction as possible.

A second parallel step was the formation of coalition cabinets. Coalition governments did not immediately arise in either war but were formed within a year after the outbreak of hostilities. Pressure on the part of opposition parties seems to have been a greater factor in bringing about the coalition in 1915 than it was in 1940. At any rate Labour and Liberal leaders resisted overtures to enter the cabinet in World War II until Winston Churchill became prime minister.

Professor Brogan has observed that, when disaster comes to the English, they do not begin a search for a scapegoat. Instead they start to look for a new leader.[2] The early years of both World War I and World War II were periods of disappointment to the British. Despite the brakes placed on parliamentary politics at the beginning of each war the English political system contained enough vitality to replace the leaders who took Britain into war with leaders who gave more promise of carrying Britain through her difficulties. David Lloyd George replaced Asquith in 1916 and Winston Churchill succeeded Chamberlain in 1940.

While the replacement of Asquith and Chamberlain suggests that war conditions may not lead to personal dictatorship, it is nonetheless true that executive powers and activities increased enormously in both

[2] *The English People* (1943), p. 18.

war periods. New ministries sprang up, especially in World War II, to handle the direction and co-ordination of a total war effort. At the same time concentration of leadership took place, evidenced by the appearance of small, "inner" war cabinets. But, as Professor Chase points out, the war cabinets in both wars were concerned primarily with civilian affairs. The direction of the war itself rested largely with the prime minister.[3] The expansion of the legal powers of the executive came about by means of statutory delegation rather than through the exercise of martial-law powers or latent constitutional war powers. The Defence of the Realm Acts (D.O.R.A.) of World War I gave the Crown extensive authority to control both production and manpower by means of orders and regulations and to take against individuals administrative action that under normal circumstances would have required the use of the courts. A series of Emergency Powers (Defence) Acts of World War II conferred upon the Crown even greater powers than those granted during World War I. Sir Ivor Jennings comments that the legislation of World War II specifically bestowed upon the executive almost every power which the courts had held that D.O.R.A. failed to delegate. The acts of World War II apparently empowered the king-in-council to do anything except acquire land, levy taxes, or borrow money.[4]

Of course there were differences in the steps taken in the two war periods. Military conscription, for example, was not introduced in World War I until 1916, but a form of conscription was in effect when World War II broke out. Moreover, in World War II, women of specific categories were for the first time subject to conscription for industrial and military non-lethal service. Again, World War II resulted in a much greater decentralization and deconcentration of central government services and offices than occurred in World War I. As might be expected, the role of Parliament in both wars was eclipsed by the activities of the executive. In World War I the House of Lords functioned as a more useful chamber of criticism and exchange of views than it did in World War II. By way of contrast, the House of Commons was more effective after 1939 as an organ of criticism than it had been in World War I or even during the late interwar years. Even so, the practice of secret sessions of Commons, although used in both wars, was criticized during World War II. All in all, World War II was a much deadlier conflict than the war of 1914–18, and the necessity of opposing Hitler was more readily accepted than was the decision to go to war against the kaiser. These factors help to account for the extremely rigorous imposition of executive control and direction in World War II and for public acquiescence in the stringencies of crisis government.

Despite concentration of effort on the prosecution of the war British leaders of 1914–18 and 1939–45 did not neglect the postwar

[3] Eugene P. Chase, "The Government of England in Wartime," in Harold Zink and Taylor Cole, eds., *Government in Wartime Europe and Japan* (rev. ed., 1942), p. 11.

[4] W. Ivor Jennings, "The Rule of Law in Total War," *Yale Law Journal*, 50 (1941), pp. 365–86.

future. In both periods planning committees were established that made important recommendations for government postwar policy. For example, land-planning policy and the comprehensive program of social insurance were the fruits of advisory committees set up during World War II.

This attention to the future proved fortunate on the whole, since postwar elections revealed that both periods of wartime government had produced an acceleration of economic and sociological trends that were to affect the course of British politics. For example, elections after World War I indicated that liberalism had lost much of its strength as a political force. Also, the activity of women in the mobilization program of World War I did much to hasten the elevation of their status in society. One significant revelation of the election of 1945 was the strong hold achieved by British labour socialism on large segments of the population. In the economic field World War II brought about a rapid liquidation of British overseas assets, hastening a trend that was apparent in the 1930's.

In the formal sense wartime government in Britain did not produce marked permanent change in the British constitution. Crisis government did leave some political residues, however. The formalization of cabinet working methods that took place during the wars was carried over into peacetime government. The cabinet secretariat received its start in World War I, and World War II gave impetus to the use of cabinet committees. In the field of planning World War II developments were especially important. Much of Britain's postwar planning machinery originated in the total mobilization of the nation against Hitler and the Axis. There was, of course, a sharp wartime increase in the size of the civil service, leaving particularly after World War II a much-enlarged bureaucracy. However, the basic characteristics of the service, even taking into account such reforms as those initiated by Eden after 1943, were not altered in a substantial way. Finally, despite all desires to do away with the restrictions and controls imposed in wartime, both periods of war government left a legacy of increased executive powers. For example, at the end of World War II, the over-all economic situation of Britain required the retention of powers vested in the wartime government for the regulation and control of prices and supplies. To continue many wartime executive powers, the Labour government passed the Supplies and Services (Transitional Powers) Bill through Parliament in October, 1945. The powers continued by this act proved useful in steps toward nationalization taken later by the Labour government.

The guiding principle in both war crises was or came to be coalition government, which meant that the major parties and their leaders undertook joint support of a prime minister who became the driving force in the war effort. The coalition device has also appeared in times of domestic crisis. A notable instance was the National Coalition of the 1930's, but in this case the Labour Party refused to join. It may be easier to make the coalition principle work in time of war. In periods of domestic crisis political parties may well differ regarding the proper cures for internal difficulties.

Delegated Powers.   The delegation of powers to the executive by means of statute is not a practice limited to crisis conditions.[5] As Herbert Morrison, then home secretary, remarked in 1944, "Parliament must be prepared to leave to the executive the task of working out the details, within the policy Parliament has approved." The fact must be faced, Mr. Morrison continued, that "we may have to accept in peace-time rather more use of delegated legislation than we had before the war." His forecast proved correct, for 1,707 administrative rules and orders were registered in 1945, and 2,287 more during the following year. There were 2,918 such rules and orders in 1947, when three volumes and 4,397 pages of delegated legislation could be compared with two volumes and 2,000 pages of parliamentary statutes.

As early as World War I vigorous protests had arisen against the practice of delegation. In the abstract, delegated legislation appears to be based on a sound division of function: Parliament lays down broad policy in outline, the executive merely fills in the details. Under this division, however, the legal decisions affecting individual rights are really made by ministers or in the name of the minister. Indeed, critics point out that ministers seldom have the time and often do not possess the qualifications personally to issue regulations or make orders on the complicated subjects dealt with by means of delegated legislation. Consequently the work falls to the permanent civil servants, although in theory the ministers retain control over their subordinates. But the suspicion persists that the ministers exercise little effective control over the bureaucrats.

Furthermore, as argued by Lord Hewart in *The New Despotism* (1929), many statutes, in delegating powers, confer such great discretion upon the minister that the ordinary courts are precluded from ascertaining whether rules and regulations are in conformity with the original statute. In some instances the conditions on the exercise of delegated power are extremely broad; for example, executive action may be authorized "whenever the Minister is satisfied" that the action is proper. Such a grant of power obviously limits the basis for judicial review.[6] This whole general situation Lord Hewart denounced as "administrative lawlessness." His remedy was to allow greater review of administrative action by the ordinary courts, but Parliament was not ready to adopt this course.

The problem has not been ignored, however. In 1929 a Select Committee (Donoughmore) began an investigation of the subject. In its *Report . . . on Ministers' Powers* (1932) the committeee did not condemn the practice of administrative legislation, but it did recommend

----

[5] Indeed, statutes delegating to the king-in-council authority to make rules having the "virtue and strength of parliament" appeared in the fourteenth century; the phrase quoted is from a law of 1385 empowering the king-in-council to regulate markets.

[6] Some enabling statutes have provided that rules "shall have effect as if enacted in this act," but in *Ex parte Yaffe* (1930) it was held that this language did not preclude judicial inquiry into the conformity of rules with the basic statute.

that Parliament exercise greater oversight with respect to the vast number of administrative rules and orders promulgated every year. One specific proposal of the committee was to establish a standing committee in each House of Parliament for the purpose of scrutinizing both the bills delegating legislative powers and the rules and regulations issued under these powers. Little was done, however, until 1944, when the climax of wartime dissatisfaction against the flood of statutory regulations, coupled with constant criticism by a small group of parliamentary backbenchers, forced the government to accept a restricted version of the 1932 proposal. In June, 1944, the House of Commons ordered the appointment of the Select Committee on Statutory Rules and Orders to review without regard to the merits of policy all rules, orders, or drafts upon which proceedings might be taken in either House. This committee, now known as the Select Committee on Statutory Instruments, is to direct Parliament's attention to a statutory instrument (1) if it imposes a fiscal charge, (2) if it excludes challenge in the courts, (3) if it has retrospective effect, (4) if there appears to have been an unjustifiable delay in its publication or in laying it before Parliament, (5) if it shows some unusual or unexpected use of powers, or (6) if, for any special reason, it calls for elucidation as to form or purport.

Two later pieces of legislation, the Statutory Orders Act of 1945 and the Statutory Instruments Act of 1946, aided the work of the Select Committee by attempting to bring some sort of system out of the welter and variety of improvised rules, orders, bylaws, and orders-in-council that had grown up over the centuries. At present, statutory instruments, as most pieces of administrative legislation are now designated, fall into one of three categories depending upon the basic statute under which they are made. Some statutory instruments are not required to be submitted to Parliament at all. Others are submitted and can be annulled by a resolution passed within forty days of the date of submission by either House.[7] Another type does not become effective, or remain effective, unless both Houses (in some instances the House of Commons alone) affirmatively approve by resolution.[8]

Establishment of the Select Committee on Statutory Instruments has not solved every problem relating to delegated legislation. For one thing, the mass of statutory instruments is large, averaging well over a thousand a year, and this number places a heavy burden on the Select Committee. Furthermore, only a very few instruments are reported to the House; for example, between 1944 and 1948 only fifty-two were reported. Nor does a report guarantee action on the part of Commons. The government is naturally disposed to defend its own actions, and when the government's majority is large, it may not feel compelled to yield to a challenge. On the other hand, knowledge that statutory instruments will have to run the gantlet of informed criticism by the Select Commit-

---

[7] This is known as "negative resolution procedure." The forty-day period does not include time during which Parliament is dissolved or prorogued or during which both Houses are adjourned for more than four days.

[8] This is known as "affirmative resolution procedure."

tee apparently has resulted in more careful preparation and draftman-
ship.[9]

In addition to the Select Committee another device for controlling
the exercise of delegated legislative powers and for maintaining a channel of responsibility through which public opinion may operate appeared
in the National Insurance Act of 1946. The minister of national insurance is required to appoint an advisory committee, to which he must
submit preliminary drafts of all instruments. This committee publicly
announces receipt of the drafts and fixes a period during which individuals may raise objections. The minister need not accept the committee's report, but he must explain to Parliament his failure to do so. This
type of advisory committee, it may be noted, concerns itself with the
merits of orders and directives, whereas the Select Committee does not.

An increase in delegated judicial powers has accompanied the
growth of delegated legislative powers. In recent years administrative
tribunals not only have increased in number, but their jurisdiction has
also widened, particularly as a result of such legislation as the Education
Act (1944), the Town and Country Planning Acts, the National Insurance Act (1946), and the Agriculture Act (1947). As a consequence
many matters of deep concern to the individual, such as rents or compensation claims, are now decided initially by administrative agencies
rather than in the courts. Furthermore, in many instances, appeals to
the courts from administrative decisions have been severely limited, as
for example in connection with the agricultural land tribunals. At the
same time attempts to provide adequate administrative machinery for
appeals have been made. Under the National Insurance scheme some
three hundred local tribunals hear appeals from the insurance officer's
decisions, and in some cases a further right to appeal to the National
Insurance Commissioner exists. The significant feature about this appellate machinery is that it is entirely independent of the Ministry of
Pensions and National Insurance.

There are potent arguments to support this expansion of administrative tribunals. Not the least potent are the high costs and snail's pace
of the ordinary courts, and the need for technical and specialized knowledge of the subjects involved. Nevertheless voices continued to sound
warnings. Professor Schwartz, for one, wrote: "However justified may
be the initial conferring of judicial power of this nature upon agencies
other than the ordinary courts, the grant to them of immunity from any
judicial control is surely inconsistent with the rule of law." [1] Then, a

[9] See K. C. Wheare, "Controlling Delegated Legislation, A British Experi-
ment," *Journal of Politics,* 11 (1949), pp. 748–68; the chapter by W. A. Robson,
"Administrative Law in England, 1919–1948," *British Government since 1918;* and
Bernard Schwartz, *The Law and Executive in Britain* (1949).

[1] *The Law and Executive in Britain,* p. 101; cf. Sir Alfred Denning, *Freedom
under the Law* (1949). The Crown Proceedings Act (1947), discussed above,
pp. 96–97, facilitates individual legal action against the government, but the traditional legal remedies of suits in tort and contract have only a very limited application
to the general situations resulting from extensive delegation of legislative and judicial powers.

quarter of a century after the Donoughmore Committee, the Committee on Administrative Tribunals and Enquiries was appointed, under the chairmanship of Sir Oliver Franks. It submitted its report in 1957.[2] The Committee reiterated the view that administrative tribunals are properly kept distinct from the ordinary courts, but it also went a step further. It concluded that administrative tribunals "should properly be regarded as machinery provided by Parliament for adjudication rather than as part of the machinery of administration." It made ninety-five specific recommendations of which the government accepted seventy-nine in whole or in part. Some of the more important of these included: principles of procedure based on the standards of openness, fairness, and impartiality; creation of a Lord Chancellor's Council on Administrative Tribunals, which among other things is to be consulted by ministers on the appointment of members of tribunals; removal of the appointment of chairmen of tribunals (who are to be lawyers as a rule) from the hands of the ministers; and less secrecy regarding public inquiries. The committee also recommended that appeals be allowed to a higher administrative tribunal, and to the courts on questions of law only. This recommendation was reserved for further consideration by the government. However, the Tribunals and Inquiries Act, 1958, based on the recommendations of the Franks Committee, does make provision for appeal on a point of law to the High Court from a certain number of designated tribunals, including various boards and referees adjudicating compensation claims for loss of office or employment, and pensions. In addition, and subject to limitations, the act extends the supervisory powers of the High Court over executive and administrative orders and determinations, and requires tribunals and ministers to give reasons for decisions.

The Government Corporation. The Government corporation is nothing new in Britain, but its widespread use in the nationalization of various industries after World War II has served to focus attention on the problems of executive powers posed by the corporate form. Government corporations are similar in many respects to private corporations. They are capable of suing and of being sued in contract and tort, and they are subject to taxation. They are not bound by civil service regulations with regard to employees.[3]

The fundamental question raised by the government corporation does not involve its legal status, however. The problem is a constitutional difficulty centering around the extent of ministerial and parliamentary control to which these entities ought to be subjected. On the one hand, need for flexibility and co-ordination, for freedom from continuous criticism in the House of Commons, and for independence of management within the limits permitted by ultimate ministerial direction were among

[2] Cmd. 218 (1957).

[3] A few of these public corporations may be noted by name; they include: the National Coal Board, British Transport Commission, British Electricity Council, the Gas Council, British Overseas Airways Corporation, British European Airways, and the Bank of England. For further references see below, Chapter 6.

the reasons for use of the corporate form. On the other hand, the public corporations could not be too independent in their operations without vitiating the principle of ministerial responsibility to Parliament.

A partial solution to this dilemma was found in two conventions that had developed prior to 1945. The first was that, although ministers were responsible for appointment and removal of the members of the corporation board, the board, and not the minister, was responsible for the detailed handling of the corporation's affairs. The second was that the minister would not be answerable to Parliament for details of the corporation's activities, but only for general directions given in the national interest and on those matters on which he had specific powers. The second convention has continued (although a knotty problem remains as to the questions concerning day-to-day corporate activities the minister should answer before Commons), but the original degree of immunity of the corporation from ministerial direction has been reduced. In nearly all of the postwar nationalized industries the minister who appoints the members of the corporation has been given general but ill-defined powers of control. In addition corporations make various reports to Parliament through the minister, and ministerial consent in some instances is required for certain fiscal operations.

In March, 1955, Parliament took additional steps with respect to the nationalized industries. The House of Commons appointed a thirteen-member Select Committee on Nationalized Industries (Reports and Accounts) to examine the reports and accounts of industries for which boards are appointed by ministers and that do not operate primarily on funds provided by Parliament or the Exchequer. The Select Committee also is to obtain information regarding current policy and practices but is *not* to inquire into matters (1) that are decided by or engage the responsibility of ministers, (2) that concern wages and other matters usually decided through collective bargaining, (3) that would be considered through formal machinery established by statute, and (4) that are matters of day-to-day administration.

The Select Committee on Nationalized Industries made its first report in late 1957. It dealt in general terms with the extent to which the finances of nationalized industries are controlled by the departments and specifically with the reports and accounts of the Coal Board, the South of Scotland Electricity Board, and the North of Scotland Hydro-Electric Board. When the North of Scotland Board came under consideration by the committee, several Scots, Members of Parliament, appeared to criticize. The chairman of the Select Committee announced: "We would like to say that we are not going to make ourselves a receptacle for complaints from Members of Parliament about individual instances in their constituencies. That would obviously tie us down day and night *ad infinitum.*" This remark illustrates a basic difficulty facing the committee. Its terms of reference are vague and it must of necessity determine what matters it will and will not attempt to do. The committee's first report indicates that it is prepared to inquire into criticism involving policy and general operations, but also that it will stand ready to help the boards of the nationalized industries "in their relations with the House of Commons."

Another broad approach to the problem of control of nationalized industry is the use of advisory committees and councils. Most of the postwar nationalization statutes made provision for consultative bodies designed to represent the interests of the consumer, and emphasis has also been placed on joint consultation between labor and management in the nationalized industries. Underlying the advisory-committee device are apparently two broad principles. The first is representation of the interests directly affected by the operations of a nationalized industry. The second is widespread consultation between the groups and interests concerned. Both principles have found application in other phases of British government, and they may prove useful also in attacking the problems of executive powers resulting from the new position of the state as owner of vast industrial properties.[4]

[4] For further discussion of labor-management problems in the welfare state see below, Chapter 6, pp. 139–42.

COURTS AND LOCAL AUTHORITIES

1. JUDICIAL SYSTEM

England is the birthplace of one of the principal legal systems of the modern world. Britain's legal system—the common-law system—has followed the reach of Britain's empire. It is to be found today, with modifications, in the United States and the Commonwealth countries of Australia, Canada, and New Zealand. Many of its features have become integral parts of judicial practice in nations with cultural and religious backgrounds vastly dissimilar from Britain's; India, Pakistan, and Ceylon are good examples. What are the distinctive elements of the common-law system, which, like the parliamentary system, has been diffused so widely over the face of the earth? Before taking up the details of judicial organization and procedure in Britain itself it may be well to inquire briefly into the common law as a legal system.

The Common-Law System. Common law is, first of all, judge-made law, and in this respect common law contrasts with statutory law or laws enacted by Parliament. A third kind of law applied by British courts is equity. Equity, like the common law, is not the product of parliamentary enactment. It originated in petitions to the king to do justice in cases where it was alleged that the common law did not afford justice. These petitions came to be acted upon by the lord chancellor, who in medieval times was usually an ecclesiastic. The guide for the chancellor was "conscience" rather than rigid rule, but equity itself eventually became a systematized body of rules. Today perhaps the most convenient distinction between the common law and equity lies in the nature of the remedy afforded by each. In civil proceedings the common law affords a money compensation (damages) for wrongs (torts) suffered. Equity, on the other hand, provides means to prevent torts.[1] Thus

---

[1] Equitable remedies are discretionary, that is, in principle the judge may in his discretion grant or refuse the remedy requested. Under the common law damages are a matter of right; they must be given if a right has been infringed. The amount of damages awarded, however, may vary with the circumstances of the case.

equity and common law have come to complement rather than to compete with each other.

Another feature of the common-law system is the nature of the trial. By and large trials in the common-law system are not conducted on an inquisitorial basis; that is, the judge does not himself inquire into the charges leveled at the defendant.[2] Associated with the accusatorial or contest nature of the common-law trial is the jury, which in those instances where it is used has the function of finding the facts in issue in a given case.

Also considered to be part of the common-law system is the principle of "the rule of law." The rule of law emphasizes the doctrine that the individual can do anything not forbidden by law. Further, it insists that alleged infractions of the law are to be determined by the ordinary courts and not by special tribunals. The rule of law acts also as a restraint on arbitrary action by executive officials and as a consequence operates to protect civil liberties in England.

Perhaps the essential feature of the common-law system is its conception of the judicial office. The judiciary in the common-law conception is one of the high organs of the state, co-ordinate with the legislature and the executive. The judge in common-law countries is not a minor civil servant or part of the executive bureaucracy. He enjoys thorough independence. Decisions of the common-law judge are precedents, and through operation of the doctrine of *stare decisis* become integral parts of the body of law applied by the courts. In Great Britain the judiciary does not exercise the power of judicial review. Nevertheless, when the House of Lords places a construction on the meaning of a statute, there is virtually no way of altering that construction, although Parliament can alter or amend the statute in question. In practice, then, the common-law judge is an authoritative expounder of what the law actually is.

Hierarchy of Courts. The British court system as it exists today is largely the product of the past century. Prior to the Judicature Acts, 1873–75, British courts presented a complex and confusing pattern. Over a half-dozen major courts had original jurisdiction in civil matters, and appellate procedure was characterized by its intricacies. In the criminal field it was an "astonishing fact," in the words of one authority, that until 1907 there was no machinery for appeals from jury verdicts, although appeals on points of law were possible. Reorganization and reform have resulted in a simpler court structure, which in the case of England and Wales follows the outline below.

The system in Figure II does not apply to Northern Ireland or Scotland.[3] These regions have separate court systems, although the House of Lords is the highest appellate court in both civil and criminal cases for Northern Ireland and in civil cases for Scotland.

[2] English civil proceedings have been classed, however, as inquisitorial; see R. M. Jackson, *The Machinery of Justice in England* (2nd ed., 1953), pp. 60–62.

[3] Also not shown is the Judicial Committee of the Privy Council, which is dealt with below, pp. 112–13. The High Court of Justice and the Court of Appeal comprise the Supreme Court of Judicature.

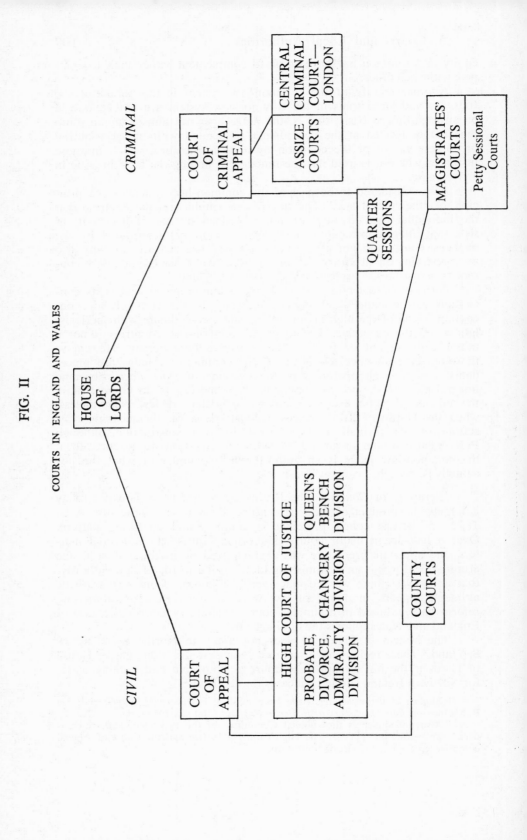

FIG. II

COURTS IN ENGLAND AND WALES

Even in the case of England and Wales the outline presented in Figure II must be used with caution. There still exist some special local courts exercising civil jurisdiction, and the paths of appeal shown in the outline do not indicate the restrictions involved in appellate action. Furthermore, a fairly sizable number of administrative tribunals have appeared in recent decades. And these do not fit into the pattern of two hierarchies of courts, one civil and one criminal. However, as indicated in Chapter 4, the Tribunals and Inquiries Act, 1958, has effected a closer relationship between certain administrative tribunals and the ordinary courts through provisions for appeals.

Civil Courts. A basic principle underlying the establishment of the county courts in 1846 was to have a tribunal for small civil cases within a reasonable distance of every part of the county. Today there are more than four hundred county courts in England and Wales. The county courts are arranged in circuits. In the large metropolitan districts a circuit consists of one court; in some country areas a circuit may embrace a dozen or more courts.

For handling the work of the county courts there are sixty-five judges.[4] They are appointed on the recommendation of the lord chancellor,[5] who may also remove on grounds of misbehavior or inability to perform the duties of the office. Attached to the county court is a registrar, also appointed and removed by the lord chancellor. Both the county-court judge and the registrar are legally trained. The judge is a barrister of at least seven years' standing; the registrar is a solicitor.

The jurisdiction of the county court is limited. With certain exceptions it may hear actions in tort and contract involving not more than £200, but if the sum is more than £100, the defendant may move for trial in the High Court of Justice. The county court also has restricted jurisdiction in equity, admiralty, bankruptcy, land recovery, and in actions arising out of social legislation dealing with adoption, rent regulations, etc. Appeals, usually on points of law, lie to the Court of Appeal.[6]

The number of actions entered in the county courts is large. In 1950 over 496,000 were commenced. Of these 193,000 were stricken or withdrawn and another 268,000 were disposed of without hearing or in the defendant's absence. Only 28,000 actions were actually heard,[7] but in not a single one of these was a jury used.

The High Court of Justice has original jurisdiction over almost any

[4] Under the High Court and County Court Judges Act, 1950.

[5] Except in the Duchy of Lancaster, where appointments are on the recommendation of the chancellor of the duchy.

[6] In Scotland, the sheriff court corresponds to the county court, although its jurisdiction is unlimited by the amount in controversy. As mentioned in the text, there are many special local courts still existing, although most are defunct. Some of these remaining active have a wider jurisdiction than the county court; for examples, the Bristol Tolzey Court, the Liverpool Court of Passage, the Salford Hundred Court, and the Mayor's and City of London Court.

[7] In matters involving very small sums the registrar may hear the case, and between one fourth and one third of all hearings are usually before the registrar.

kind of civil action triable in the ordinary courts.[8] The High Court is organized into three divisions, which provide specialization for the various classes of actions coming before the court. The Chancery Division handles equity cases. The Probate, Divorce, and Admiralty Division is sometimes referred to as the court of "wrecks"; wrecks of wills, marriages, and ships. The Queen's Bench Division is basically a common-law court,[9] although it has some appellate and criminal functions.

On points of law, appeal from the High Court lies to the Court of Appeal, which can reverse or modify the judgment of the lower court. If the appeal is against a verdict, then the Court of Appeal may direct a retrial.

The Court of Appeal consists of eight lords justices of appeal plus the master of the rolls and other ex-officio members. Appeals are heard by a bench of three justices. Appeal on points of law to the House of Lords is possible, but it requires leave of either the Court of Appeal or the House itself.

Technically, and in form, the whole House of Lords hears appeals. Actually the judicial business of the House is carried on by the lord chancellor, the lords of appeal in ordinary, and any other member of the House who has held high judicial office. Since 1948 an appellate committee (which can sit separately while the House is in session) usually hears the arguments of a case. The final decision is taken, however, by the law lords sitting as the House of Lords, and it is done by a formal vote after the law lords have given their individual judgments in the form of speeches to the House.[1]

Criminal Courts. Courts exercising original criminal jurisdiction are the magistrates' courts, courts of quarter sessions, and the assize courts.[2] The magistrates' courts are courts of summary jurisdiction, that is, they try cases without a jury. Trials at quarter sessions or assizes are with a jury. For the more serious crimes jury trial is mandatory, and for petty offenses (those carrying three months' or less imprisonment as a penalty) summary trial is mandatory. There are, however, three other divisions of offenses in which either summary or jury trial may result, depending upon the option of the defendant, the discretion of the judge, and the length of the sentence.

Magistrates' courts in London and certain other cities are staffed

[8] Some actions founded on various social-welfare statutes must begin in the county courts.

[9] In 1950 over 60,000 proceedings were entered in this division, but only 978 went to trial. Only 39 of these were before a jury. The decline of the jury in civil cases is due not so much to legal restrictions on their use as to the desire to obtain speedy and economical justice.

[1] The supreme civil court in Scotland is the Court of Session. It is divided into two Houses, the Inner and Outer. The former is mainly an appeal court; the latter one of first instance. Appeal from the Inner House to the House of Lords is possible.

[2] In Scotland, there are justice of the peace courts and magistrates' courts which hear petty offenses. The sheriff court handles most criminal cases. Serious crimes are tried in the High Court of Justiciary, which also takes appeals from the inferior criminal courts. There is no appeal from the High Court of Justiciary to the House of Lords.

by stipendiary magistrates, who receive pay. Elsewhere these courts are known as "petty sessions" and are made up of lay justices of the peace who are unpaid.[3] The great majority of trials are held before two or more justices of the peace or one paid magistrate. From the magistrates' courts there are two paths of appeal. By a method known as "case stated" a point of law can be taken directly to a Divisional Court of Queen's Bench Division. Appeal also lies to the court of quarter sessions[4] and it is not restricted to points of law but may also involve fact and the sentence imposed. From quarter sessions the appeal may go by the "case stated" process to Queen's Bench. Both the prosecution and the defense can appeal, using the "case stated" process, but a prosecutor as a rule cannot appeal an acquittal to quarter sessions. In connection with appeals to quarter sessions by a convicted defendant there is one very important point to consider—the higher court can *increase* as well as decrease sentences.

The court of quarter sessions tries indictable offenses that do not carry the death penalty or imprisonment for life on the first conviction.[5] In the counties the court of quarter sessions consists of a maximum of nine justices of the peace. In the boroughs it consists only of the recorder, who is a paid official, appointed from barristers of five years' standing. As mentioned earlier, trial at quarter sessions is by jury. There is no appeal against an acquittal. A convicted defendant may appeal on a point of law to the Court of Criminal Appeal. With leave of the trial judge or of the Court of Criminal Appeal, appeal on fact or law is possible. Appeal against the sentence is permissible with leave of the Court of Criminal Appeal.

Assize courts try the most serious offenses. In London the Central Criminal Court, Old Bailey, functions as the assize court. Elsewhere a Queen's Bench judge (or a commissioner) on circuit holds assizes. Appeals from assizes are similar to those from quarter sessions.

The Court of Criminal Appeal consists of the lord chief justice and members of the Queen's Bench Division. The court must have an uneven number of judges when hearing an appeal; three is the minimum and also the usual number. The powers of the court are broad, including increase of sentence when it is appealed. It can substitute conviction for another offense instead of that found, but it has no power to order a new trial. Appeals from the Court of Criminal Appeal to the House of Lords are restricted to points of law, and then only if the attorney general gives a certificate that the point is of exceptional public importance. Appeals are not numerous.

There are several features of English criminal procedure that merit attention. First of all, indictment by grand jury has been abolished.

[3] Justices of the peace are appointed by the Crown on the recommendation of the lord chancellor (or in the Duchy of Lancaster by the chancellor of the duchy). A justice of the peace or a stipendiary magistrate may also act as a committing magistrate, that is, decide whether to hold over a person for indictment.

[4] Appeals are heard by an appeal committee.

[5] Burglary is an exception. The jurisdiction of quarter sessions varies, depending on whether it operates with a legally trained or a lay chairman.

Indictment now is by the process of information.[6] Secondly, there exists in England no counterpart of the district attorney, a familiar figure in American politics and government. There is a director of public prosecutions, but he prosecutes only in a relatively few important cases.[7] The great bulk of prosecutions is handled by local police officials, who may employ professional advocates in the magistrates' courts. In all assize courts and in most quarter sessions courts prosecution must be by a barrister. In addition any private person may prosecute, and prosecutions by private individuals, using professional advocates when required or desirable, are not uncommon. Another feature is the coroner's court. If a coroner's inquest results in a verdict of homicide against a person, then that person must be committed for trial.[8] The power of appeal courts to raise sentences under certain conditions has already been mentioned. Finally, the magistrates' courts, although basically criminal courts, have important jurisdiction in matrimonial and bastardy cases. Juvenile courts are magistrates' courts, but are governed by principles different from those applied in ordinary criminal proceedings.

With all its intricacies, however, the English criminal court seems to work well, at least by comparison. Several factors are commonly cited as contributing to the high quality of English criminal justice. For one thing, rules of procedure are made, not by Parliament, but by committees consisting of judges and practicing lawyers acting under powers delegated by Parliament. These committees function under the cognizance of the lord chancellor, and rules when made must be laid before Parliament. There is also less stress placed on technicalities of procedure, and appeals on matters of technical errors are infrequent. Compared to an American judge, the English judge exercises greater control over the course of trials. Of course, all English judges are appointed, while state judges in the United States are often elected. All in all, there seems to be less opportunity for abuse of procedure in English criminal justice, and it is a matter of frequent comment that criminal trials in England proceed with far more dispatch than in the United States and that justice is done more swiftly and surely.

Judicial Committee of the Privy Council. Lord Haldane once declared that the Judicial Committee is "no more an English body than an Indian body, or a Canadian body, or a South African body." The committee sits, he continued, "as an Imperial court which represents the Empire, and not any particular part of it."

Times have changed since 1926, when Lord Haldane made his

[6] The grand jury was abolished by the Administration of Justice (Miscellaneous Provisions) Act, 1933.

[7] Out of 18,779 persons tried on indictment in 1950 the director of public prosecutions prosecuted 1,026. The director's role is essentially one of co-ordination and supervision of the decentralized system of prosecution. He is appointed from barristers or solicitors of ten years' standing by the home secretary.

[8] There is dissatisfaction with the coroner's jury. In 1953 a coroner's inquest resulted in a verdict of manslaughter against a bus driver who was consequently committed to assizes for trial. Before the trial he was charged in a magistrates' court but was discharged. Nevertheless he was tried at assizes, but the Crown offered no evidence; see F. T. Giles, *The Criminal Law* (1954), p. 83.

observation, but it remains true that the Judicial Committee is not solely an English body. This can be seen from its jurisdiction. In England it is the final court of appeal from the ecclesiastical courts of the Church of England. In time of war the committee hears appeals from the Admiralty Division in prize cases. It is the final court of appeal from courts in the Channel Islands, the Isle of Man, colonies, protectorates, and trust territories. With respect to the Commonwealth nations, Canada, South Africa, India, and Pakistan have abolished appeals to the Committee. Appeals still lie from Ceylon and New Zealand, and in some cases from Australia, as well as from Ghana and the Federation of Malaya.[9]

To be eligible to sit on the Judicial Committee, a person must be a privy councilor. The working strength of the committee is supplied for the most part by the law lords of the House of Lords. Other high judicial officers in England are eligible, as well as certain high judges from the colonies and the Commonwealth countries.[1]

The Legal Profession. The legal profession in England is divided into solicitors and barristers. Solicitors are primarily legal advisers; an individual seeking legal advice would consult a solicitor. Barristers are advocates; they argue cases before the courts. This division is not rigidly maintained, however. Some courts give solicitors the right of audience, and where this is so solicitors may act as advocates. Barristers may give legal advice, although not as a rule to lay clients.

The distinction between barristers and solicitors is important in connection with judicial appointments. Superior judges, that is, judges of the High Court, the Court of Appeal, and the law lords, are appointed from the ranks of the barristers. The lord chancellor nominates most judges of the High Court. The prime minister nominates the other superior judges with, it is generally assumed, the advice of the lord chancellor.[2] Salaries paid judges are high when compared to salaries

---

[9] Appeal to the committee is by petition and leave, except for those instances where a right exists under statute or order-in-council. In practice it seems that civil appeals are allowed more frequently than criminal.

[1] Appeals are heard by boards of three or five members who are invited to sit by the lord chancellor. A judgment of the committee is in the form of advice to the Crown, since the appeal is technically a petition to the queen-in-council to do justice. Also, since advice rendered to the Crown must be unanimous, there are no dissenting opinions emanating from the committee.

[2] Puisne or ordinary judges of the High Court are appointed from barristers of ten years' standing. Lords justices of appeal must be barristers of fifteen years' standing or a High Court judge. Law lords are appointed from barristers of fifteen years' standing or those who have held high judicial office for two years. In practice there is no regular promotion of judges. There is some feeling that a system of promotion might create undesirable pressures, and as salaries are now set there is not a great deal to be gained financially by promotion. The extent to which party politics influences judicial appointments is an important factor. Figures collected for the period 1832 to 1906 indicate that out of 139 appointments 80 were made to members of Parliament, and, of these, 63 to those whose party was in office. But there are signs to suggest that appointments as a reward for party services have diminished in recent years; see R. M. Jackson, *The Machinery of Justice in England* (2nd ed., 1953), pp. 226–28.

in the public service generally, but they do not approach the income of the successful barrister in the prime of his practice.[3]

Since judgeships from the county courts up are staffed from the ranks of barristers, the legal training of the bar obviously has an important bearing on the quality and characteristics of the English judiciary. The training of the barrister is in the hands of the Inns of Court,[4] and the training required is sometimes criticized because of its emphasis on preparing students for private practice. This emphasis leads, so it is contended, to a narrowness of outlook that is not altogether appropriate when transferred to the judicial office.[5]

2. THE RULE OF LAW

Modern British government is founded on the legal principle of parliamentary sovereignty or legislative omnipotence. Devices that an American student usually associates with civil liberties and individual rights are not to be found in Britain. England has no written constitution. English courts do not exercise the power to declare statutes unconstitutional. Nevertheless, in few countries have individual liberties been more secure than in Great Britain.

One explanation of the security of individual liberties in England is Dicey's classic exposition of the rule of law. To Dicey the rule of law meant that no man could be punished except for a breach of law established before the ordinary courts, and, further, that no man was above the law and everyone regardless of rank was amenable to the jurisdiction of the ordinary courts.[6] The principles of the rule of law, coupled with statutory charters like the Habeas Corpus Act and the Bill of Rights, do afford protection against arbitrary executive action. Executive action not sanctioned by law can be resisted in the courts. The individual has remedies against arbitrary arrest, including the writ of habeas corpus as well as civil suit for false arrest.

[3] The salary scale in 1955 was:

Lord chancellor	£ 10,000
Lord chief justice	£ 8,000
Lords of appeal in ordinary and master of the rolls	£ 6,000
Lords justices of appeal and other superior judges	£ 5,000

[4] The Inns of Court are ancient institutions dating back to medieval times. The training of solicitors is governed through their Law Society.

[5] There are some broadening trends apparent. Since 1922 a person must attend a law school for one year before taking the solicitor's final examination. During and since World War II increased funds have been available for research in social studies, and this research has stimulated a broader approach to problems of law by the teachers in the law schools. Also, for many positions in the public service, legal training is advantageous, and a growing number of university law students are interested in public service rather than in private practice.

[6] See A. V. Dicey, *Introduction to the Study of the Law of the Constitution* (8th ed., 1920), Chapter 4. A third point emphasized by Dicey was that the English constitution was "not the source but the consequence of the rights of individuals, as defined and enforced by the Courts." In many other countries, Dicey maintained, individual liberties depended upon principles embodied in the formal constitution.

But the principle of the rule of law affords no direct legal protection against legislative action. In fact on the statute books are laws dealing with sedition and unlawful assembly under which a wide variety of acts could be prosecuted. In practice, however, prosecutions are seldom brought under these laws by executive or police officials. In wartime Parliament has severely curtailed individual liberties. Furthermore, the growing body of social-welfare legislation has changed the individual's rights with respect to private property and its economic uses, and in many cases this newer legislation has directed the individual to administrative tribunals rather than to the ordinary courts for adjudication of his rights, at least in the first instance. Again, however, the provisions of the Tribunals and Inquiries Act, 1958, allowing appeals from certain tribunals, merit mention.

There is no denying, of course, that economic and social legislation of the twentieth century has altered the Englishman's relations with his family, his neighbors, his employer, and the community at large. This legislation has not, however, made serious inroads on personal and political liberties. Freedom from arbitrary arrest, privacy of the home, freedom of religion, the right to vote, to express one's political beliefs, to criticize the government—these remain secure.[7] The rule of law acts as a legal restraint on the executive and the police. For restraints on Parliament the Englishman looks to the electoral process and the political party. And underlying the effectiveness of both the legal and political restraints of the British constitution is a legacy of political thought in which the dignity of man is firmly imbedded.

3. LOCAL AUTHORITIES

Governmental Units. Although some local governmental areas and some local officers trace back to medieval and even pre-Conquest times, the present structure of English local government dates from the nineteenth century. The Municipal Corporations Act of 1835 initiated the use of elective councils in borough government. In 1888 the "historic" county was abandoned as an instrument for general local government. The Local Government Act of that year established the administrative county and the county borough, both with an elective council as the governing body. The Local Government Act of 1894 established the urban district, rural district, and parish councils. The legislation mentioned above created or reorganized six different local units—county boroughs, administrative counties, non-county boroughs, rural districts, urban districts, and parishes. These remain as the basic units of English local government,[8] but the Local Government Act, 1958, looks toward some

[7] It is well to remember that some discriminations were still in effect a hundred years ago. For example, it was not until 1866 that persons of any religious faith could sit in Parliament.

[8] The wartime coalition government issued a white paper on *Local Government in England and Wales during the Period of Reconstruction,* and a Local Gov-

possible far-reaching changes in the pattern of local authorities in England and Wales. Local government commissions established under the act will review counties and county boroughs, with power to recommend changes in boundaries and status or creation of new units. The Minister of Local Government can implement recommended changes by order subject to approval by Parliament. After the local government commissions have completed their task the county councils will review the areas and boundaries of the county districts and parishes. Subject to ministerial order, the county councils can effect amalgamations and other structural changes. A royal commission, appointed in 1957, has begun review of the Greater London area, and other "conurbations" are scheduled for study.

In England and Wales the numbers of local authorities are as follows: administrative counties, 61; county boroughs, 83; non-county boroughs, 312; urban district councils, 568; rural district councils, 476; parish councils and meetings, over 11,000. London presents a special case. For the City of London proper (an area about one mile square) there is the Corporation of the City of London. The county of London covers some 117 square miles. It has its own county council and is divided into 28 metropolitan boroughs, each with its own council. The Metropolitan Police District covers some 692 square miles with a population of 8,500,000; this is the London that appears in census figures.

Powers and Services. The important distinctions among these several units of local government lie in their powers or, to phrase it in another way, in the services they provide.[9] The county borough itself provides the full range of local government services; it is distinct from the administrative county. The non-county borough, the urban district, and the rural districts are parts of the administrative county, and to each of these units is allotted a certain number of services. Thus a person living in an urban district finds that his local government services are provided in part by the county and in part by the district.[1]

The distribution of local government functions between the administrative county and its subdivisions varies according to the category of services involved. In the police and protective category of functions the county is the authority for police and fire services, while the non-county borough and the urban and rural districts are responsible for enforcement of the Shops Acts, control of nuisances under the Public Health Act, and enforcement of disease regulations. With respect to communal and environmental functions the county is responsible for town and country planning, maintenance of main roads other than truck routes, and for primary and secondary education; the subdivisions

---

ernment Boundary Commission was created. The commission issued reports in 1947 and 1948, proposing a general revision of local government areas and functions. However, Parliament abolished the commission in 1949.

[9] There is little uniformity in population. County boroughs range from less than 70,000 to more than 200,000; administrative counties from 18,000 to 4,500,000; non-county boroughs from less than 2,500 to over 100,000; urban districts from under 5,000 to over 100,000.

[1] In rural districts the parish continues to provide a limited number of services. Urban parishes now serve mainly as areas for registration of births, deaths, etc.

are responsible for building regulation, sewerage and refuse disposal, street lighting, street cleaning, and cemeteries. There is also an overlap in some instances, for example, library services, parks, and pleasure grounds. In the area of social services the county is responsible for the provision of the wide variety of public health and social-welfare services that are locally provided. However, all local units are housing authorities. There still exist some municipal trading services, despite postwar nationalization of utilities; with some exceptions the county subdivisions carry on these services.[2]

The distribution of services indicated above is, of course, given in general terms; there are many exceptions and in some cases the use of joint authorities is permitted. Two further points regarding the distribution of local services deserve emphasis. For the most part the distribution is made by act of Parliament. Hence the county subdivisions are not subordinate to the county; their status and powers are derived from parliamentary statute, which is the source of all local government powers in England. Since World War II, however, Parliament has transferred a number of functions from the subdivisions to the county; the functions involved were police, fire, and certain aspects of public education and public health. The second point is the marked trend, especially since 1930, to transfer functions from local authorities to central authorities.[3] This has been very noticeable in the field of public utilities, which is one of the areas where large-scale nationalization took place after World War II.

The trend toward greater central responsibilities has been offset to some extent. As Aneurin Bevan, then speaking for the Labour government, said in 1946: "If it happens that local government loses functions because they have to be carried out by different instruments, additional functions must be given to it to maintain its vitality and importance in the state." The care of underprivileged children may be mentioned as one of these new local government services. In 1947 the Civic Restaurants Act empowered local authorities to compete with private enterprise by establishing restaurants. Additional powers were granted to local authorities over rent control, housing, and parks. And under the Local Government Act of 1948 encouragement has been given to local authorities to provide public entertainment and leisure-time facilities.[4]

Internal Organization. With one exception the governing body in all local units is an elective council. The exception is found in about one third (3,800) of the rural parishes where a meeting of the qualified electors is the governing authority. All councils are elected for three-

[2] Municipal trading services cover a variety of activities, such as civic restaurants, municipal markets, water supply, and public transportation. Prior to the nationalization of the electricity and gas industries, local governments frequently provided such utility services.

[3] The National Assistance Act of 1948, which replaced the old poor law, transferred to central authorities primary responsibilities for care of the destitute.

[4] For developments in local government see Winston Crouch, "Local Government under the British Labour Government," *Journal of Politics,* 12 (1950), pp. 232–59; J. H. Warren, "Local Government," in *British Government Since 1918* (1950), p. 193.

year terms, but in boroughs, and rural and urban districts, terms of councilors are staggered, with one third retiring each year.[5] The local government franchise is practically the same as the parliamentary franchise.[6] In the case of boroughs and counties a part of the council is indirectly elected. Approximately one fourth of the council consists of aldermen, and these are elected for six-year terms by the council itself, with approximately one half of the aldermen retiring every three years. The council chooses its own chairman for a term of one year. In the boroughs the chairman is known as the mayor.[7] The mayor has by law no special administrative responsibilities, but by custom and tradition he acts as the town's civic leader.

A typical county borough (and most large cities are county boroughs) will have over a dozen departments. General supervision of the departments is carried out by committees of the local council. The principal administrative officers of departments are appointed by the local council upon the recommendation of the supervising committee. By statute most local councils must appoint a clerk,[8] a treasurer, a surveyor, a medical officer of health, and a sanitary inspector. In some instances consent of the appropriate central minister is necessary for appointment or dismissal. As a rule dismissals except for cause are not common, and higher local officers enjoy tenure as a matter of practice.

Local units employed in 1954 over 1,400,000 persons in all.[9] There has been and still is diversity in the personnel practices of the many local units. Pressure toward uniformity has increased in recent years, coming from both the top and the bottom. National standards of pay and qualifications have been established in the case of teachers, policemen, and firemen. And local government employees have sought to better conditions of service through their own labor union, the National Association of Local Government Officers. In 1945 a National Joint Council (Whitley Council) for the Administrative, Professional, and Technical Staffs of Local Authorities was established. The National Council has formulated a general personnel program, called the "Scheme of Service." This Scheme has gained adoption by the great majority of local authorities, and, without the rigidity of an official set of centrally promulgated civil service rules, it has constituted a workable basis for achievement of greater uniformity. Since legislation requires local authorities to provide pension plans, since standards for recruitment are in effect, and since arbitrary dismissals are rare, it is safe to regard English local government as operating on a career service basis.[1]

[5] Urban and rural districts may adopt under certain conditions the system of *en bloc* retirement.

[6] Residence and registration are the main requirements for voting, but nonresidents may qualify on the basis of property owning or occupation.

[7] In those boroughs styled as cities he is the lord mayor.

[8] The town clerk is generally regarded as the most important local administrative officer.

[9] This total includes teachers; employees classified as in public administration numbered about 750,000.

[1] It is not unusual for a higher official of one unit to move to a larger unit which can offer higher pay. Pension rights, it may be noted, are transferable.

Finance. Local government revenue derives from three main sources: rates (local taxes), grants from the central government, and loans. To these are added a variety of miscellaneous incomes. For the year 1951–52 rates provided £318,000,000, loans £398,000,000, grants £359,000,000, and miscellaneous sources £347,000,000. The principal objects of expenditure are education, individual and public health, housing, fire and police, roads and bridges, and local welfare services.

As can be readily seen from the figures above, local taxes (rates) provide less than one fourth of the total amount of local revenue. Rates are the English version of the real-property tax. The basis for rating is not, however, the value of the real property, but rather its rental value, specifically the annual rent a property could reasonably expect to command.[2] Rates are levied for the most part on the occupier and not the owner unless he is also the occupier. In the past the appropriate local units valued property for rates, but by the Local Government Act of 1948 valuation was transferred to the central Board of Inland Revenue.

Grants from the central government are of various types. One is the equalization grant designed to aid those units where ratable property values fall below the national average. Another kind is the percentage grant, in which the central government pays a specific proportion of the cost of a local government service. Percentage grants are used in connection with fire, police, education, health and children's services. Unit grants are used in the housing field. Here a specific sum per unit is paid, regardless of the cost of the unit to the local authority. Special grants are also paid from time to time. There are also a number of national taxes the revenues of which are assigned to local units. Examples are license fees for game and guns.

Local government loans are raised for purposes of capital expenditure. The approval of the central department concerned with the service for which capital funds are sought is required. During the period 1945–52 local units could borrow only from a public agency, the Public Works Loan Board. In 1953 local authorities were again permitted to borrow on the open market if they so desired.

In the group of miscellaneous revenues one may be mentioned briefly. Income from trading activities yielded in 1951–52 approximately one third of the total miscellaneous revenues. However, municipal trading activities are not designed to return a profit in the business sense, and trading revenues just about balance expenditures made for these activities.

Central Government Control. A principal feature of English local government, one authority points out, is the comparative absence of a centrally appointed or approved official (common in many European countries) with broad powers to oversee and supervise the work of local

---

[2] The rent a property actually brings in may be less or more than the ratable value. Agricultural land is exempt, and certain other types of property are partially exempt. County councils do not levy rates directly; their rates are collected by the county subdivisions.

authorities.[3] But the absence of a prefect or his counterpart should not give a false impression. There is a great deal of central control over local government operations.

Central control and supervision appear in many ways: rules and regulations, audits, inspections, approval of appointments, approval of local planning for education and other services, and approval of local loans. Central controls are, however, not centralized; that is, one central department, the Ministry of Health, exercises oversight in connection with public health services, while another, the Home Office, is the responsible agency in connection with fire and police, and so on.

In view of the importance of central grants to local finance it is not surprising that the purse string is used as an effective instrument of control. In the police services, for example, the home secretary may withhold all or a part of the 50-per-cent grant if he is not satisfied with the efficiency and administration of police forces of a local authority. The minister of health may reduce the equalization grant if he is not satisfied with the efficiency of a local authority's public health services. However, financial reforms proposed under the Local Government Act, 1958, will abolish many specific grants and substitute general grants with no "strings" attached. It is expected that such general grants will account for two thirds of all grant income to local authorities instead of only one eighth as at present.

Some measure of uniformity is desirable in local government and the services it provides. Central oversight appears to be the most feasible way to achieve this end. Still, it is not difficult to appreciate the concern sometimes expressed over central supervision. There is a danger that central control will lessen the vitality and initiative of the local authorities.

4. TOWN AND COUNTRY PLANNING

Official concern with problems of land use in Britain began as early as 1909, when the Housing and Town Planning . . . Act gave local authorities limited powers in the field of land development. In the period between the world wars several pieces of legislation added to the planning functions and responsibilities of local authorities. The Town and Country Planning Act of 1932, for example, broadened the scope of planning to built-up areas as well as to land to be developed or in the course of development. The results achieved were not especially noteworthy. The approach to planning was essentially local; large areas of land were not subject to plan either because of lack of legal power or failure to develop plans; the method of enforcing compliance was cumbrous; and, finally, no workable solution was found to the problem of

[3] W. Eric Jackson, *The Structure of Local Government in England and Wales* (1949), p. 147.

compensation for land or land values taken in the interests of planned development.[4]

Considerable impetus to further steps resulted from the reports of official bodies established in 1937 and 1940. These reports, the Barlow and the Scott and Uthwatt reports, by dealing with problems such as redevelopment of congested areas, provision of industrial employment throughout the country, and urban encroachment upon agricultural land, stressed the national aspects of land planning. All three reports urged the creation of a central planning authority. The destruction of World War II underscored the general conclusions of these committees.

In 1943 the office of minister of town and country planning was created by act of Parliament. In the same year interim planning legislation was enacted. A white paper issued in 1944, *The Control of Land Use,* was followed by the Town and Country Planning Act of 1944. In 1947 another Town and Country Planning Act reached the statute books. This act, together with portions of the earlier laws and amendments of 1953 and 1954, and related legislation, such as the New Towns Act of 1946 and the Distribution of Industry Act of 1945, provide a comprehensive basis for land planning and development.

In England and Wales county councils and county borough councils are the local planning authorities. Joint boards may also be established.[5] Each local planning authority must survey its own area and submit a proposed plan to the Ministry of Housing and Local Government.[6] The minister hears local objections to a proposed plan. Once the plan has been approved at the ministerial level, it cannot be challenged on its merits.[7] Resurveys are required every five years, but amendments to a plan may be made at any time. County boroughs and county districts may themselves acquire land for development purposes.[8] For the most part permission of the local planning authority is required before any development can be undertaken. If development proceeds without permission, the local authority can require the land to be restored to its original condition.

The postwar legislation attempted to solve the problem of finance by transferring the development value of all land to the state. Land developers were required in essence to buy back the development value from the state, and a fund was established to compensate anyone who could show that his interest in land had been materially depreciated in

[4] Under this legislation a person did not have to get permission to build a project. If he did not get permission and the project were later found to conflict with the plan, he could be required to tear down the project at his own expense.

[5] In addition county subdivisions have planning functions delegated to them by the county.

[6] The planning functions originally vested in the Ministry of Town and Country Planning were transferred in 1951 to the Ministry of Housing and Local Government.

[7] A plan may be challenged on the grounds that it goes beyond the powers granted in planning legislation or that the requirements of the law have not been fulfilled.

[8] A county council may also acquire land if specially authorized by the minister.

value as a result of planning. This system ran into difficulties and it was abandoned by amendments enacted in 1953–54. Under these amendments betterment charges have been discontinued, and owners of land receive compensation for compulsory acquisition or refusal of planning permission on the basis of the existing use value of the land in question.[9]

Some achievements have been realized in all the various phases of planning. As of late 1954 almost all of the local planning authorities in England and Wales had submitted development plans for ministerial approval. Work in rebuilding war-damaged cities did not commence until 1949. In a few provincial cities reconstruction of devastated centers has been completed, and varying progress has been made in other cases. In England and Wales eight national parks and nineteen nature reserves have been designated and approved. In Scotland five national parks have been proposed. In England and Wales twelve new towns have been established as well as two in Scotland. The total population of the new towns in England and Wales is designed to be 545,000. As of late 1954 their population was 216,000.

Planning in Britain, because of its comprehensive nature, involves a number of government departments and agencies besides the Ministry of Housing and Local Government. These include the Board of Trade, the Ministry of Agriculture and Fisheries, the Ministry of Transport and Civil Aviation, the Ministry of Works, the armed services, and the Development Corporations of new towns.

5. REGIONALISM AND DEVOLUTION

In legal form the United Kingdom is a unitary state. During the past fifty years, however, there have appeared proposals for devolution of some of Parliament's work upon special regional bodies. At the conclusion of World War I sentiment for regional devolution was especially strong. The House of Commons in 1919 expressed itself in favor of the creation of "subordinate" legislatures within the United Kingdom, and further requested the appointment of a parliamentary commission to study the matter. A speaker's conference in its report, *Conference on Devolution* (1920), agreed on the principle of subordinate legislatures in England, Scotland, and Wales, and also on the powers to be exercised by them. There were differences with respect to the form of the proposed regional bodies. The majority plan envisaged for each region a council of commons, consisting of members of the House of Commons from the constituencies within the region, and a council of peers, consisting of members of the House of Lords selected by a committee

---

[9] Established claims for depreciation of value under the previous arrangement were not abolished. Where land had been compulsorily acquired or subjected to planning restrictions, immediate payment was made out of the fund of £300,000,000 originally set aside for this purpose. In other cases the claims remain as future credits, to be paid if the owner suffers financially as a result of planning restrictions.

of the upper House of Parliament. The minority plan advocated separately elected regional legislatures.

The proposals of the speaker's conference did not lead to action, but the postwar Irish settlement resulted in the creation of a Parliament for the six counties of Northern Ireland. The Northern Ireland Parliament is bicameral, with a Senate and a House of Commons. With certain exceptions it has the power to make laws for peace, order, and good government in domestic matters. Laws passed by the Northern Ireland Parliament must not conflict with legislation of the United Kingdom Parliament extending to Northern Ireland. Some of the matters reserved for the United Kingdom Parliament include the postal services, the judiciary, custom and excise duties, and income and profits taxes.[1]

Scotland was united with England by the Act of Union in 1707, but the Scots retain their own educational system, their own system of law, which differs from English common law, and their own established church. No local legislature exists for Scotland. However, with respect to matters that pertain to Scotland, the Scottish Committee in Commons operates much in the manner of a legislative body for Scotland. Even in cases of legislative policy designed to affect the entire United Kingdom it has become common practice to enact separate acts to apply to Scotland alone. Administration in Scotland is also separate from that in England and Wales. There is a secretary of state for Scotland, and he is the responsible minister for the execution of parliamentary statutes in Scotland. Under the secretary of state for Scotland are four major departments—the Scottish Home Department, the Department of Health for Scotland, the Scottish Education Department, and the Department of Agriculture for Scotland. These departments have their main offices in Edinburgh. World War II and its aftermath have witnessed an increased demand by the Scots for greater control of their domestic affairs. The Scottish secretary tried to revive the Scottish Privy Council and to organize a Scottish bloc vote in Parliament. By 1948 the Labour government felt constrained to issue a white paper on the subject. The question cuts across party lines, and sentiment has been strong enough to gain an increasing measure of home rule for Scotland.

Welsh nationalism, too, has revived. The postwar Churchill government recognized this when it appointed an undersecretary for Welsh affairs in the Home Office. In the election of 1955 the three major party manifestoes all supported in varying degrees the Welsh cause. The Liberals called for separate parliamentary institutions in Wales (and Scotland); Labour promised to safeguard the "distinct national cultures" of Wales and the other regions; and the Conservatives proposed to continue the "steady policy of administrative devolution" for Wales. In 1957 a new minister of state for Welsh affairs, whose office is located in Wales, was appointed. This office does not supplant the post of Minister of Welsh Affairs, now held by the Minister of Housing. This arrangement provides for a Welsh minister at cabinet level in London, and another who is active in Wales.

[1] There are also local legislative bodies of ancient lineage in the Channel Isles and the Isle of Man.

Whither regional sentiment will eventually carry is difficult to say. But it would be in keeping with the British way to evolve a larger degree of regional autonomy without disturbing the fundamental forms of the constitution.

6

BRITAIN AND THE WELFARE STATE

Post-World War II Britain has become almost synonymous with the "welfare state." But Britain's welfare state did not spring like a Pallas Athene, fully armed, from the split brow of a Socialist Zeus. As Harold Macmillan remarked in 1957: "There are some people in this country who are persuaded that social reform began in 1945 with the Socialists. That is not true. Our structure of social services has been built up by centuries of conservative thought and action." Mr. Macmillan might have added that Labour Party thought and action had also contributed to the structure of social services developed before 1945. Nevertheless his general point is sound. While the postwar Labour government was the chief architect of the "welfare state," it did not build from scratch or design in a vacuum. For Britain's preoccupation with her economy and social services long antedates World War II. Indeed, speaking in 1930, Winston Churchill concluded that the British had in the main the political system they wanted. The British "nation is not interested in politics," he declared, "it is interested in economics."

1. ECONOMIC BACKGROUND

The economic problems that have become the major concern of British politics stem largely from the effects of the Industrial Revolution on British life and society. Although the beginning of the Industrial Revolution may be dated as around 1750, important changes had been taking place in English economic life for several centuries. As a result of the inclosures movement and the land speculation following the dissolution of the monasteries in Henry VIII's reign, much landholding had been placed on a commercial basis, either for rents or for the profits from wool raising. Trade, particularly foreign trade, was consuming a great deal of the energies of English seaport towns. Manufacturing of woolens and iron was established, although on a small scale.

The decline of the feudal system in agriculture brought with it a change in the concept of and attitude toward private property. The medieval Christian concept of private property as wealth held in trust for the public good and the medieval attitude against profit taking lost strength. A new attitude gradually took shape, culminating, to use Professor Tawney's phrase, in the "triumph of the economic virtues." Money-making, to many English minds of seventeenth century, "could be, and ought to be carried on for the greater glory of God." Linked with individualism, the newer attitude toward property led to Adam Smith's thesis that the good of all is best served when men are left free to follow their own economic interests. Much of the philosophical basis of the Industrial Revolution had been laid before the movement itself began to rework English economy and social life.

The Industrial Revolution.   The first phase of the Industrial Revolution, lasting roughly until the middle of the nineteenth century, accompanied the political rise of the British middle classes. The figure below presents some general indices of the physical growth of British industry during the first phase. The industrial expansion depicted in Fig. III not only produced the thriving middle classes of nineteenth-century Britain; it also created the wage-earning laboring classes, whose problems and aspirations have profoundly affected modern politics. Estimates of the English class structure in 1688 and 1812 indicate that the proportion of English society comprising the artisan classes and below rose from 60 per cent to 70 per cent. By 1867 another estimate indicated that 78 per cent of all persons in England and Wales with individual incomes were to be found in the laboring classes.[1] Further industrial movement emphasized the development of English society in the direction of a numerically preponderant wage-earning proletariat.

FIG. III

THE RISE OF INDUSTRY IN THE UNITED KINGDOM *

YEAR	RAW COTTON IMPORTS (TONS)	PIG IRON OUTPUT (TONS)	COAL OUTPUT (TONS)	POPULATION (MILLIONS)
1760	1,700	——	6,000,000 (1770)	8.0
1800	28,000	250,000	——	10.5
1830	125,000	1,000,000 (1835)	23,000,000	16.5
1850	——	2,000,000	65,000,000	21.0
1870	630,000	6,000,000 (1875)	110,000,000	26.0

* Figures are for comparison and are therefore approximate.

[1] See G. D. H. Cole and Raymond Postgate. *The British People, 1746–1946* (2nd ed., 1947), pp. 62–63, 299.

During the middle of the nineteenth century British politics reflected the rise of the middle classes, which after 1832 shared political power with the aristocracy and upper classes. In the period from 1840 to 1880 the laissez-faire economic liberalism of the middle classes became an important factor in English politics. However much the philosophy of laissez faire may have suited the needs of an expanding industrialism, its hostile attitude toward state activity in the economic realm severely hampered the adoption of constructive political measures to alleviate the social distress of the working masses who were crowding into the new factory towns and cities. Nevertheless, despite the views of extreme laissez-faire liberals, some intervention of state authority occurred. A series of Factory Acts beginning in 1802 gradually regulated the conditions of employment of women and children and placed restrictions upon working hours in a number of enterprises. Other limited social and welfare measures included the revised Poor Law of 1834, the establishment of the Board of Health in 1848, public grants for education, and in 1870 the beginning of public elementary education.

Although unenfranchised until 1867 the working classes were far from passive. The tactics of the Luddites, which aimed at preserving the status of the home artisan by physical destruction of the machine, were an early and unsuccessful reaction to the new industrialism. Later, after the Combination Acts were repealed in 1824, trade unions were legally permitted to organize. Both trade unionism and the co-operative movement took permanent roots in the middle portion of the nineteenth century. By the 1870's substantial legal sanction had been given to the rights of trade unions in collective bargaining.

By the time the franchise was extended to large numbers of urban workers in 1867, the British economy had begun to take on new characteristics. Corporate enterprise began to assume greater importance in economic development after the Companies Acts of 1844 and 1855, the latter giving limited liability to joint stock companies upon registration. Previously, general limited liability could be obtained only through incorporation by means of a special act of Parliament, or after 1837 by charter issued by the Crown. Until the legislation of the 1850's corporate enterprise was found mainly in the fields of transportation and public utilities. Economic activities other than manufacturing gained in importance. For example, British railroad trackage doubled from 1853 to 1873. British shipping tonnage trebled in the period 1853–1913 from 4,000,000 tons to 12,000,000 tons.

Trends of the Early Twentieth Century. After 1880 internal and external developments occurred that contributed to the decline of the liberal creed. The liberal ideal of a "little England" was swept away by what Sir Ernest Barker calls "exclusive nationalism," which brought about the addition of vast territories in Africa and Asia to the British Empire. The existence of the Empire and later the Commonwealth has been a factor in the economic thinking of all British political parties to the present day. Then, at the turn of the nineteenth century, Britain's position as a producer for the world market was challenged by the emergence of other industrial nations, especially the United States and Germany.

The effects of an altered international trade situation were not felt in terms of unemployment until after World War I. In the decade before 1914 there were signs that the British economy was reacting to international competition. There was a small but significant shift in the nature of British exports. The exports of consumers' goods, particularly cottons and woolens, fell off, and the export of coal and machines rose. At the same time British investments abroad increased rapidly. British overseas investment doubled from £2,000,000,000 in 1900 to £4,000-000,000 in 1914. Finally, although the period from 1900 to 1914 was one of favorable export balance, the real wages of the laboring classes declined. From 1850 to 1900 real wages steadily increased (reaching an index figure of 180 based on 1850 levels), but by 1913 they had fallen off by 10 per cent from their high level at the end of the nineteenth century.

A major internal political development was the appearance of the Labour Party in 1906. This "Union of Socialism and Trade Unionism in the political field" augured that in the future the working of the economy would be judged more and more on new criteria, such as the wage rate, the unemployment rate, and the distribution of wealth. In short, the Labour Party would insist that the benefits of industrialism should flow in proportionate share to the laboring classes.

After the Liberal victory in 1906 several types of social services appeared. In some localities corrective health treatment for school children began as early as 1907. Old-age pensions administered on a means test commenced in 1908. A contributory unemployment-insurance program covering limited groups was introduced in 1911. In 1912 a contributory health-insurance plan was introduced, with limited coverage and with administration through approved private insurance companies. The first of a series of workmen's compensation acts had been passed earlier, in 1897.

Interwar Economic Developments. World War I and its aftermath witnessed additional economic problems. First of all, the interdependence of the British economy and world trade was brought home vividly. Unemployment statistics and export figures, even before the world depression, show a striking correspondence between high unemployment and low exports.[2] Economic distress in the cotton trades mounted as the Japanese and Indian cotton industry expanded. Coal mining suffered by the shift from solid to liquid fuels in industry and transport. Yet maintenance of domestic consumption and industrial levels required substantial imports, for Britain was importing four fifths of her wheat and flour, three fifths of her meat, all of her raw cotton, one third of her iron ore, and over nine tenths of her wool and timber.

During the interwar period British economy was beginning to face a basic problem. In order to sustain the standard of living that the

[2] See Pauline Gregg, *A Social and Economic History of Britain, 1760–1950* (1950), p. 420.

British masses were politically strong enough to demand, Britain had to import. But her industrial machine was not able to compete internationally, at least not in a world where only Britain practiced free trade, in order to use exports as payment for needed imports. For political reasons it was difficult to fall back on the classical economic solution of depression of wage rates and unemployment. There was a movement toward "rationalization" (general over-all efficiency in order to minimize production costs) in industry during the late twenties. The major casualty of the interwar period was Britain's free-trade policy. Baldwin's Conservative government failed to obtain a mandate in 1923 to abandon free trade, but in the early thirties Britain adopted the policy of empire preference. Nevertheless the import imbalance remained and it was made up largely by revenues from international economic services such as shipping and insurance and from repatriation of British overseas investment at a rate of between £50,000,000 and £60,000,000 a year during the late thirties.

Internally the interwar period saw increased state activity in the economic sphere. Agriculture had been a neglected area in the period from the repeal of the Corn Laws in 1846 to World War I. In 1889 the problem of disease in animals led to the creation of the Board of Agriculture, which in 1919 became a ministry. The depression period of 1931–33 resulted in the Agricultural Marketing Acts and the establishment of marketing boards. Designed to protect farmers from depressed prices in times of plenty and to encourage efficiency in production and marketing, these boards (elected by farmers under plans approved by Parliament) had statutory powers of discipline over participating farmers. In the public-utilities field considerable state intervention occurred. In 1919 the Electricity Commission was established to draw up plans for a national "grid," a transmission system linking the principal generating stations and supplying the bulk output to certain statutory distributors. The system was set up in 1926 and operated by a public corporation, the Central Electricity Board. Distribution remained in the hands of local power distributors, two thirds of which were the great municipalities. A somewhat similar situation existed in the gas industry, much of which was municipally owned and all of which was subject to considerable public regulation. In transportation the Port of London Authority, created in 1908, had jurisdiction over London's dock and harbor facilities. The subways, busses, and streetcars of metropolitan London came under the London Passenger Transport Board in 1933. Prior to World War II, British railroad lines had been merged into four great area systems, and the government operated these during the war. The Imperial Airways and a number of overseas airlines were receiving subsidies prior to 1939, and in that year a public corporation, the British Overseas Airways Corporation, assumed jurisdiction over all British overseas air schedules. Radio broadcasting was a monopoly under the British Broadcasting Corporation, chartered in 1927. Two so-called "sick" industries received special attention. Under the provisions of the Coal Act of 1930 the independently owned and financed coal-producing units managed to create co-operative bodies for regulating quotas and joint sales. A Coal Mines Reorganization Commission attempted to encourage amalgamations among the independent units for the sake of efficiency and sales, but did not accomplish very much. However, with penalties for overproduction, and bonuses for underproduction, with minimum prices fixed and the entire organization subject to the approval of the Board of Trade, free competition among the collieries ceased. In the cotton industry Parliament attempted to stimulate modernization and reorganization. Under the Cotton Spinning Industry Act of 1936 a program for compensating owners who scrapped surplus spindles began. In 1939 the Cotton Industry Board was established to co-ordinate the branches of the cotton textile industry and to effect reorganization of the trade.

Further extension of the social services also occurred in the interwar period. The Blind Persons Act of 1920 introduced pensions for the blind. Contributory pensions for widows and orphans began in 1925, and the next year saw the introduction of contributory old-age pensions. In 1931 the national government undertook support of the more or less permanently unemployed. Between 1919 and 1939 various housing acts provided subsidies to local authorities for the construction of rental housing, and some 1,367,000 houses were erected by the local authorities in the interwar period. Land use had been recognized as a major problem in Britain even before World War I. After World War I the national government assumed the initiative in planning. The Town and Country Planning Act of 1932 consolidated earlier legislation and extended planning powers. The measure also emphasized the role of local councils in the planning process. This legislation admittedly achieved only limited success. A royal commission appointed in 1937 and two committees appointed in 1940 made a series of recommendations that were embodied in comprehensive planning legislation enacted during and after World War II.[3]

World War II accelerated certain adverse economic trends and brought new problems as well. During World War II, Britain's overseas investments were practically liquidated.[4] In fact, by the end of the war, Britain had become a debtor of some of her former colonies, some of which later became independent states. War damage in Britain was, of course, great; for example, enemy action destroyed or damaged approximately one third of Britain's houses.[5] Still, Britain did not enter the postwar period on a note of panic. During the war the coalition government had sponsored study committees on various subjects, and there was a broad area of minimal agreement on necessary changes in the economic and social fields regardless of the party that would take office at the end of the war.

---

[3] The report of the 1937 royal commission is popularly known as the Barlow Report; the reports of the later committees are known as the Uthwatt and Scott Reports.

[4] Over £1,000,000,000 in overseas investments were liquidated and new debts of £3,000,000,000 were incurred.

[5] Total war damage to British domestic capital is estimated at £3,000,000,000.

2. WELFARE STATE IN PRACTICE

The welfare state has resulted in a greater degree of governmental intervention in daily life than modern Britain has ever witnessed, except in time of war. But welfare state activities have not embraced the whole of life by any means. Governmental intervention in postwar Britain has been concentrated on nationalization of industry, economic planning and controls, and the social services. And even in these specific fields of activity, practice of the British welfare state exhibits a strong continuity with policies of the past.

Nationalization of Industry. The 1945 election manifesto of the Labour Party, *Let Us Face the Future,* did not propose wholesale socialization of British industry. The sector of the economy marked off for nationalization was the so-called basic sector, comprising in the main the public utilities, transportation, coal, iron, and steel. Indeed, as announced by Herbert Morrison in 1948, the private sector of the economy remaining after Labour's nationalization program was carried out would include about 80 per cent of all industry.

Nor was the Labour Party alone in recognizing the need for a greater amount of state enterprise in the postwar era. In 1943 Prime Minister Churchill had declared that in "projects for the future employment of the people," it would be necessary to make sure "that private enterprise and state enterprise are both able to play their parts to the utmost." Indeed, Mr. Churchill went on to say: "There is a broadening field for state ownership, especially in relation to monopolies of all kinds." Even in the Liberal Party, where the "Quintillians of individualism" remained strongest, there was some recognition of the necessity for a measure of governmental enterprise and planning. Lord Beveridge, for example, saw in the formula "state enterprise and free enterprise both serve the national interest" a possibility that the way "to the practical end of ordered opportunity for all will be found along a middle course between conflicting ideologies." [6] Of course the Labour Party was willing to go farther along the road to socialism than the other parties, but there was much agreement among Englishmen in 1945 that additional encroachments on private enterprise would have to be made.

One of the first steps taken by the Labour government was the acquisition of the share capital of the Bank of England in 1946.[7] Nationalization did not change the essential role of the bank, which had already assumed the position of a central bank and had very close ties

[6] *The Pillars of Security* (1943), pp. 189–90.

[7] The Bank of England was established by act of Parliament in 1694. It has the sole right in England and Wales to issue bank notes, which are legal tender throughout the United Kingdom. Private commercial banks handle the bulk of domestic banking in the United Kingdom. In 1955 twenty-seven banks controlled 12,500 branches with total assets of over £8,000,000,000. The Post Office Savings Bank had nearly 23,000,000 accounts with deposits totaling £1,735,000,000 in 1955.

with the government. Rather, in the words of Hugh Dalton, then chancellor of the Exchequer, the purpose of the Bank of England act was "to bring the law into relation with the facts as they have gradually evolved over the years." Even certain financial circles of "The City" approved, at least in principle, the changes that put the Bank of England in a relationship with the government similar to that existing in certain other countries.

As previously noted, a step toward greater state intervention in the field of commercial aviation occurred in 1939 when the British Overseas Airways Corporation was established. In 1946 the Civil Aviation Act placed all scheduled air services under three government corporations (British Overseas Airways Corporation, British European Airways, British South American Airways Corporation) and their associates. In 1949 the British South American Airways Corporation was merged into the British Overseas Airways Corporation by the Air Corporations Act. Not all British air services are nationalized. Independent air companies provide most charter services and also some scheduled services as associates of the two public airways corporations.

As in most European countries British electronic communications systems have long been under government operation. Private telegraph systems, for example, came under the control of the postmaster general in 1870, and radio broadcasting has been a monopoly of the British Broadcasting Corporation since 1927. In 1947, Cable and Wireless, Ltd., which operated a large overseas telegraph network and radio facilities, was nationalized. Then, in 1954, the Conservative government introduced a system of commercial television services, to be in addition to and independent from those offered by the British Broadcasting Corporation. The Television Act established the Independent Television Authority as the controlling agency for these new services. The Authority receives a limited subsidy from the public treasury, but also derives revenues from sale of television time to "program contractors." The Authority lays down general policy for programs, but the actual programs are produced by the program companies. These contractors in turn may sell advertising time during the intervals of their programs to firms and businesses. Proponents of the system argue that the programs offered are thereby not controlled by the advertisers. This innovation in the television field is to continue for an initial period of ten years, although Parliament may extend the period if the experiment proves successful. Independent television was controversial from the beginning. Arguments against it stressed that independent programs would be "popular" if not vulgar, and in general depart from the presumably high standards of the BBC. Certainly, independent television has proven popular; it reached in 1958 some five and a half million British homes and its friends assert that, where a choice between independent and BBC programs is possible, the new services are preferred 65–75 per cent of the time.

In the field of inland transportation the Transport Act of 1947 placed British railways, railway-owned steamships, hotels, docks and road transport lines, the bulk of the country's canals, and London's transportation system under the British Transport Commission, a public corporation. The Transport Commission also had the task of acquiring privately owned long-distance road-haulage companies. The Transport Act of 1953, passed by the Conservative government, made significant changes in the plan set up under the act of 1947. The Transport Commission was directed to return long-distance road haulage to private enterprise and to decentralize the administration of the nationalized railways. The decentralization arrangements established six area boards, which are responsible for railway management in their respective areas, but over-all financial control remains with the Transport Commission.

The gas and electricity industries (which already were subject to a large measure of public control and ownership) were nationalized under the Electricity Act of 1947 and the Gas Act of 1948. The Electricity Act established the British Electricity Authority and over a dozen area boards. The Electricity Authority was responsible for generation of power; the area boards handled distribution and sale of electric power. The Electricity Act, 1957, reorganized the industry. The central Electricity Authority was abolished. An advisory Electricity Council was given supervisory functions over the industry; a new Central Electricity Generating Board took over the function of generating power. The area boards were given greater autonomy and are expected individually to pay their own way. The Gas Act vested the assets of all gas undertakings (some of which were already operated by local authorities) in twelve area boards, which became responsible for the manufacture and distribution of fuel gas. A national Gas Council was created to advise the minister of fuel and power on matters pertaining to the gas industry. Atomic energy research and development, it may be noted, is now the responsibility of a public corporation, the United Kingdom Atomic Energy Authority, under the Atomic Energy Act of 1954. Plans announced in 1955 and revised in 1957 call for twelve nuclear power stations designed to produce one fourth of Britain's electricity by 1966.

At the end of World War II the coal industry (already under rigid controls and heavily subsidized) was in such a state that it was estimated that £150,000,000 over a period of five years would be necessary for required modernization. The colliery companies proved unwilling or unable to undertake the task, and only the resources of the state could furnish the large capital investment involved. The Coal Industry Nationalization Act of 1946 put the entire coal-mining industry (which employed some 750,000 men with an annual production of over 200,000,000 tons) under the National Coal Board. In 1950 the Coal Board announced a long-term development plan, calling for capital investment of £635,000,000, which would eventually result in four fifths of British coal production coming from new mines. Even though the Coal Board's structure has undergone reorganization and considerable effort and study have been given to the problems of the coal industry, no really satisfactory solution is in sight.

By far the most controversial of the postwar nationalization projects was that for the iron and steel industry. The industry itself was a vigorous, articulate, closely knit organization with its own plans for reconstruction and development. But the Labour government was convinced that it could not reach its goal of "planned economy" without the assured support of the iron and steel interests. The bill to nationalize the industry was slow taking shape and, anticipating difficulties in the House of Lords, the Labour government, as noted previously, pushed through the Parliament Act of 1949. Nationalization finally occurred in February, 1951, under the terms of the Iron and Steel Act of 1949. The Conservative Party did not approve of this action and proposed in its election campaign of 1951 to denationalize the industry. Denationalization has been largely carried out under the Iron and Steel Act of 1953, which repealed the earlier law.

The Labour government made moves to nationalize other industries, such as chemicals, sugar, and cement, but these did not materialize. Thus, even at the peak of postwar nationalization, the bulk of British industry remained in private hands. The private-industry sector included the greater part of manufacturing, shipbuilding, wholesale and retail trading, commercial banking, publishing, insurance, and certain types of business. An estimate made in 1950 (before iron and steel nationalization) put 22.5 per cent of persons in civil employment in the public sector of the economy, a proportion that represented a 50-per-cent increase over 1945.[8] This division probably has not changed significantly since 1950.

Nationalization Methods.   As Professor Friedrich points out, there is a distinction between socialization and nationalization. Nationalization is but one kind of socialization, involving in particular transfer of title to property to the state. Other types of socialization might involve transfer of title to various other entities, such as municipalities or cooperatives.[9]

Broadly speaking, the Labour government program emphasized nationalization rather than other types of socialization, for it instituted ultimate proprietary control by the national government over those enterprises marked off for public ownership. Still, the postwar socialization plans did not result in nationalization in the strictest sense. Title to the socialized property was not transferred specifically to the state, but to public corporations created by statute. However, these public corporations are not independent of the national government. True, they have neither shares nor shareholders, but, in the words of Professor Friedmann, the public corporation's "shareholder, in a symbolic sense, is the nation represented through government and Parliament."[1]

The transfer of property to the public corporations was carried out in two different ways under the postwar nationalizations. In some instances the property transferred consisted of the physical (real and per-

[8] Members of the armed forces are not included in the term "civil employment." The public sector includes all those employed by governmental bodies, national and local. Of those in the public sector the nationalized industries employ over 2,000,000, or about 10 per cent of all those in civil employment.

[9] See *Constitutional Government and Democracy* (rev. ed., 1950), p. 492.

[1] W. Friedmann, "The Legal Status and Organization of the Public Corporation," *Law and Contemporary Problems,* 16 (1951), p. 578.

sonal) properties of the private enterprises concerned. This direct method was used for coal, transport, electricity, and gas. In other cases the property transferred was the controlling interest in the shares of the particular enterprises to be nationalized. This indirect method was used in the case of the Bank of England, Cable and Wireless, Ltd., and the iron and steel program.

Regardless of the method of nationalization used the owners of the expropriated property received compensation, a feature that distinguished British nationalization from similar programs in certain other countries.[2] Where the direct method was followed, compensation for the physical assets expropriated was paid to the companies that formerly owned the properties. These companies through their shareholders then decided what to do with the compensation stock issued to them. Some decided to liquidate; others continued their corporate existence as finance and investment companies; and others converted to businesses still open to private enterprise. Where the indirect method was used, compensation was paid directly to the shareholders whose shares were acquired by the public corporation.

The compensation paid to former owners consisted for the most part of interest-bearing government stocks, although in some specified instances money payments were authorized. To determine the amount of compensation to be paid necessitated the establishment of intricate procedures and standards, which varied from enterprise to enterprise. Generally speaking, the postwar nationalizations compensated only for the capital value of the assets expropriated, and one criticism made by the Conservative Party was that the income deriving from the capital investment ought to have been given consideration. In the case of the Bank of England income was a criterion. The owners of bank stock received compensation in government stock so that the interest therefrom equaled the average annual dividend paid during a twenty-year period ending in 1945. The bank had averaged 12 per cent annually during this term, and since government stock paid only 3 per cent, the amount of compensation stock issued was four times greater than the face value of the bank stock acquired. On the other hand, owners of stock in other enterprises claimed that compensation based on stock-market quotations did not result in adequate compensation for their equity in the value of the entire enterprise. The question of whether the former owners were over- or undercompensated is difficult to determine. At any rate the total amount of compensation liability assumed by the nationalized enterprises was large, amounting to more than £2,500,000,000, and it contributed to the financial problems of the newly formed state enterprises.

As mentioned earlier, the Conservative government that took office in 1951 denationalized the iron and steel and the long-distance road-haulage industries. This process also met with problems. From the very beginning the Labour Party announced its intention of renationalizing

[2] On the expropriation phase of British postwar nationalizations see Mary Bell Cairns, "Some Legal Aspects of Compensation for Nationalized Assets," *Law and Contemporary Problems,* 16 (1951), pp. 594–619.

these industries when they should be returned to power. In its program, "Industry and Society," adopted in October, 1957, the Labour Party remains pledged to renationalize the iron and steel industry and long-range road haulage, even though for other sectors it has placed emphasis on acquisition of shares in companies rather than outright nationalization. Also, Labour spokesmen have declared "that under no circumstances will the total compensation already paid out be increased," when renationalization occurs.[3] The threat of renationalization complicated the transfer of the state enterprises to private ownership, particularly in the case of iron and steel. Nationalization of iron and steel had been accomplished through acquisition by a public corporation, the Iron and Steel Corporation, of the shares of ninety-two private companies. The companies nationalized were retained as individual units, under their former names. The Iron and Steel Act of 1953 established the Iron and Steel Holding and Realization Agency to dispose of the stock holdings of the Iron and Steel Corporation. Two types of resale were made. In private sales many of the smaller nationalized companies were resold to their former owners, often on a no-profit-no-loss basis. For the larger firms public sale of shares was the rule. In the public sales former shareholders received priority in repurchase, but limitations were imposed on all sales so as to "spread out" ownership by preventing initial large block purchases. At first public sales did not go so well. Even though promised yield on the stocks was high (over 7 per cent), issues were undersubscribed and shares sold at discounts. By early 1955 (when approximately three fifths of the industry had been returned) market conditions were much more favorable. Issues were being oversubscribed, the promised yield had dropped below 6.5 per cent, and the Realization Agency was taking a profit on the resale transactions.

Despite the eventual success of the return of iron and steel to private ownership, a fundamental problem remains. The Conservative Party did not return the industry to a condition of uncontrolled free enterprise. On the contrary, the act of 1953 set up the Iron and Steel Board with general powers of supervision over the industry and specific powers with regard to development plans, raw-materials procurement, and the fixing of maximum prices. Yet Labour, as again evidenced in 1958, remains firm in its stand to renationalize this and the long-range haulage industry. But it hardly seems possible to keep a basic industry like steel swinging back and forth from private to public ownership with the election returns.

Social Welfare Services.   In the half century prior to World War II, Britain developed a broad but unco-ordinated program of social services. During the war the report of an interdepartmental committee, the now-famous Beveridge Report, called for a comprehensive social insurance system covering the entire population from "birth to burial." The National Insurance Act of 1946 and the National Insurance (Industrial

---

[3] The securities of the Iron and Steel Corporation to be resold carried a book value of £246,100,000; the book value of the assets of the nationalized long-distance truck industry was computed at £45,600,000.

Injuries) Act of the same year implemented the Beveridge Report by establishing a comprehensive national insurance plan on a contributory, compulsory, and actuarial basis. This national insurance system became operative in July, 1948.

Under the basic national insurance legislation, as amended, and allied legislation, the following benefits are available: maternity, family allowance, sickness, unemployment, guardian's, widow's, retirement, and death grants; industrial injury, disablement and death benefits; and national assistance for those who do not, for one reason or another, come under the insurance programs. As mentioned above, the national insurance scheme is contributory and the great bulk of persons contributing (21,500,000 out of 23,500,000) is employed wage earners. Under an increased schedule of rates, effective in 1958, an employed male over eighteen contributes 9s. 5d. per week, his employer 8s. 1d., and the national exchequer supplements these with a small grant. Rates are lower in the case of males under eighteen and for women generally; rates also vary in the case of self-employed contributors and non-employed contributors. Persons with a small income, £104 a year or less, can apply for exemption. The amounts paid recipients vary according to the type of benefit and other circumstances,[4] but a few illustrative payments may be noted. Under the family allowance program (1958 rates) 8s. per week is paid to the mother for the second child below the school-leaving age and 10s. for every child after the second. The standard rate for sickness, unemployment, and retirement benefits was raised in 1958 to 50s. per week for a single person and to 80s. for a married couple. Married women, unless employed, qualify for widow's, maternity, and retirement benefits on their husband's insurance. Some idea of the cost and advantages of the national insurance program to the individual may be had by comparing the contribution and benefit rates with the average weekly industrial wage in Britain, which in 1956 was about £12.[5]

Probably the most widely publicized aspect of Britain's welfare state is the National Health Service, which went into operation in 1948. The health program falls into three parts: general-practitioner and dental services, hospital and specialist service, and local health-authority services. The National Health Service is voluntary in basis. Individuals

[4] As a rule a minimum number of contributions must have been made before benefits are payable, and a higher number of contributions paid before maximum benefits are payable.

[5] For the year April, 1951–March, 1952 gross expenditures from the national insurance fund totaled £389,000,000, distributed as follows:

	(millions)
Unemployment	15
Sickness	63
Maternity	8
Widow's and Guardian's	24
Retirement	275
Death	3

For the year 1956–57 expenditures under the National Insurance plans were estimated at £715,200,000, but this figure includes sums for administration and other items not given in the above table.

do not have to use the service at all, nor do doctors, dentists, etc., have to join it.[6] There is considerable freedom within the service. For example, the individual is free to choose or to change his family doctor, and the doctor in turn does not have to accept any given individual as his standing patient. Further, a doctor in the service can attend private paying patients if he wishes.

Despite objections to the idea of "socialized" medicine and criticisms of the operation of the National Health Service, the vast majority of Britons, both doctors and laymen, have joined. About 95 per cent of the fifty million people in the United Kingdom, 90 to 95 per cent of the general practitioners, the great majority of the specialists, over 90 per cent of the dentists, and practically all of the druggists are taking part in the public health and medical program. Over 3,000 hospitals are in the service, and the 250 hospitals and homes remaining outside are operated for the most part by religious orders.

For the individual, enrollment in the service did not at first depend upon any contribution, but in the spring of 1957 the Macmillan government announced intentions to establish a separate contribution by users of the service. This contribution was increased in July, 1958 to 2s. per week for women and 1s. 10d. per week for men. For employed persons the employer contributes part of the weekly charge. The national exchequer aimed to assume about four fifths of the total cost (the objective was to keep the charge on the exchequer at £400,000,000 annually, but costs have steadily risen, and in 1957–58 the cost to the exchequer will be about £550,000,000); the remainder comes from the transfers from the national insurance fund, charges and contributions, and from certain other miscellaneous sources. At first the health services were virtually free. The National Health Service (Amendment) Act of 1949, however, empowered the minister of health to introduce charges for drug prescriptions, and in 1952 a charge of one shilling per prescription became effective. Under the National Health Service Act of 1951 charges to meet part of the cost of dentures and spectacles began. In 1952 a charge of £1 per dental treatment was introduced (or the full cost if the treatment is less than £1). At the same time charges were introduced for medicines, dressings, and appliances supplied to hospital outpatients. For persons taking part in the health plan there is no charge for treatment or normal maintenance in the service hospitals.

The method for remuneration of doctors and others providing services in the national health plan varies. In the case of family medical service the doctor receives a set yearly payment for each person registered as his patient.[7] The number of patients registered is limited to

[6] When the plan went into effect, doctors joining could continue to practice in their established areas. To obtain a better distribution of medical services, doctors entering the service after 1948 must apply to the Medical Practices Committee to begin practice in an area. In addition various payments are made to doctors taking up practice in rural areas, and initial practices allowances are paid to those entering areas designated as in need of doctors.

[7] The rate is 17s. per year per patient on the doctor's list, with 10s. additional for each patient from 501 to 1,500 on the list. Dentists and druggists are normally paid on a prescribed scale of fees for the particular treatment or prescription in-

3,500; the average doctor's list is 2,400. Dissatisfaction with remuneration led to the appointment of a Royal Commission in 1957. In its *Report* of 1960 (Cmnd. 939), the Commission recommended general increases, with family doctors to receive an average income of £2,425 from official sources.

Only a broad outline and few details of the National Health Service appear above. The stated objective of the service is to provide the necessary medical and health services as every citizen's right. Although some charges were instituted under the Labour government, the Labour Party now proposes to abolish charges on glasses, prescriptions, and dental work. But even with some services carrying a fee, the program goes a long way toward achieving its purpose and, despite criticisms, stands to remain a permanent feature of British life.[8]

Labor Relations. The welfare state has produced remarkably little change in the pattern of labor relations in Great Britain. Beginning in the 1870's, trade unions have acquired a legal status that gives them substantial immunity from suit with respect to collective-bargaining activities, and also the right of registering so as to obtain certain additional legal privileges and obligations. Trade unions may set up political funds subject to conditions. The fund must be approved by a majority of members, and members must be allowed to "contract out," that is, to give written notice that they do not desire to pay into the fund.[9]

Trade-union membership in Britain has reached all-time highs since World War II. In 1952 it was 9,524,000, distributed among some 690

---

volved.

[8] The over-all estimated cost of the National Health Service for the United Kingdom was £526,800,000 in the year 1952–53. The largest items of this total were (millions):

Hospital, specialist, etc., services	310.9
General medical services	89.3
Pharmaceutical services	42.5
General dental services	21.0
Grants to local health authorities	21.5

[9] After the general strike of 1926 the Conservative government then in office enacted the Trade Disputes and Trade Unions Act of 1927, under which union members did not contribute to the political fund unless they "contracted in," i.e., agreed specifically to pay into the fund. After passage of this act trade-union membership of the Labour Party fell from 3,300,000 to 2,000,000. The act was repealed in 1946, after which trade-union membership of the Labour Party rose from 2,600,000 to 4,400,000.

The figures on trade-union membership may be compared with Britain's total manpower force of 23,875,000 as of June, 1955. Of this total 22,896,000 (including 7,734,000 women) were in civil employment. The larger industrial groups of workers were as follows (thousands):

Metals, engineering, vehicles	4,569
Professional, financial, etc.	4,092
Distributive trades	2,793
Transport and communications	1,714
Textiles, clothing	1,639
Building and contracting	1,466
Public administration	1,215
Agriculture and fishing	1,052

separate unions. Most of these unions are small; some 390 have fewer than 1,000 members each and account as a group for only 1 per cent of total trade-union membership. At the other extreme 17 unions, each with a membership of 100,000 or more, contain two thirds of all trade-union members.

The basis for union organization varies. Some, like the National Union of Mineworkers (with membership in the neighborhood of 700,000), are organized on an industry basis. Others, like the Amalgamated Society of Woodworkers (with approximately 200,000 members), follow a craft or occupation basis for organization. The two largest unions are general unions, covering members of various industries and occupations. These two are the Transport and General Workers' Union (membership about 1,300,000) and the National Union of Municipal and General Workers (membership approximately 800,000).

The vast majority of trade-union members, 8,000,000, or more, are affiliated to the Trades Union Congress.[1] The Congress meets annually and is composed of delegates from the affiliated unions. A union is entitled to one delegate for every 5,000 members or fraction thereof, and one vote for every 1,000 members or fraction when voting is by card. Resolutions and deliberations of the annual Congress do not bind affiliated unions, but they have played an important part in framing the general policy of the trade-union movement. The Congress annually elects a general council of thirty-five members. The general council represents the trade-union movement on a number of advisory councils and other bodies, and also performs educational and co-ordination functions. The general council sends eight representatives to the twenty-four member National Council of Labour, a body that provides co-ordination of policy between the Trades Union Congress and the Labour Party.[2]

Generally speaking, wages and hours in Britain are determined through the process of voluntary collective bargaining. Working conditions (safety, health, etc.) are, on the other hand, laid down by statute.[3] To the rule of voluntary bargaining respecting wages and hours there are some exceptions. Wage councils and wage boards have been established by law for agriculture, catering, and several other specific industries.[4] These councils make proposals, regarding minimum wages, that become legally effective by order of the minister of labour. About three million workers fall within the groups subject to these statutory provisions. In

[1] There is also a Scottish T.U.C. with an affiliated membership of about 700,000.

[2] In addition to the eight representatives from the general council, the National Council includes four members from the Parliamentary Labour Party, four members from the national executive committee of the Labour Party, and eight from the Co-operative Union.

[3] Legislation affecting working conditions dates from the beginning of the nineteenth century. The major pieces of protective legislation are: Factories Acts, 1937 and 1948; various Mines and Quarries Acts and Public Health Acts; Children and Young Persons Act, 1933; Employment of Women, Young Persons and Children Act, 1920; Young Persons Employment Act, 1938; Shops Act, 1950.

[4] The principal acts are the Wages Councils Acts, 1945 to 1948; the Catering Wages Act, 1943; the Agricultural Wages Act, 1948; and the Dock Workers Regulation of Employment Act, 1946.

voluntary collective bargaining, practice in Britain emphasizes negotiations at the national level between employer associations and the national union involved, but local variations from the terms of national agreements do occur.[5] In World War II the practice began of placing in collective agreements and wage orders a guarantee of a minimum weekly wage regardless of the hours worked. These guarantees, usually for two thirds or three fourths of the normal weekly wage, at present cover some eight to nine million workers.

Various types of machinery exist in Britain for conciliation, arbitration, and joint consultation. Conciliation services provided by the Ministry of Labour and National Service date from the Conciliation Act of 1896. The Industrial Courts Act of 1919 established a permanent Industrial Court to which disputes may be referred by joint agreement. The same act empowered the minister of labour to appoint courts of inquiry in cases of disputes of major importance and wide industrial significance. The report of these courts is not binding, but their findings and recommendations have proved useful in settling disputes. Trade unions and employers by mutual agreement may refer their differences to *ad hoc* arbitration, but decisions reached in this manner are not legally enforceable.

In 1940 the Conditions of Employment and National Arbitration Order introduced compulsory arbitration and placed a ban on strikes and lockouts for the purpose of preventing interruption of war production. Under this order a dispute not settled by existing machinery was reported to the minister of labour and national service, who in turn referred it to the National Arbitration Tribunal. The award of the National Arbitration Tribunal was binding. The Industrial Disputes Order of 1951 replaced the wartime order of 1940. It removed the ban on strikes and lockouts and replaced the earlier tribunal with an Industrial Disputes Tribunal. At the same time the type of dispute referable to the Disputes Tribunal was more narrowly defined.[6] In November, 1958, an order was laid before Parliament to abolish the Industrial Disputes Tribunal, to be effective March, 1959.

Joint consultation between employer and employee received emphasis in the report of the Whitley Committee of 1917, and some limited advances in the establishment of joint consultative machinery were made in the period between the wars. In 1947 the National Joint Advisory Council (composed of representatives from the Trades Union Congress and the British Employers' Confederation) recommended the establishment on a voluntary basis of advisory joint consultation committees where none existed. A 1950 survey estimated that over 50 per cent of the employees in each of the main industries were represented in arrangements

[5] Negotiating machinery varies widely from industry to industry. National Joint Industrial Councils, as recommended by the Whitley Committee in 1917, provide the negotiating machinery for about one half of all workers covered by voluntary agreements.

[6] Strikes were also banned during the period 1915–18. In neither period did the ban prevent strikes; see H. A. Clegg, "Strikes," *The Political Quarterly*, 27 (1956), pp. 31–43.

for joint consultation at the factory level. The setting up of consultation machinery has not solved, however, the major difficulties involved. The fundamental question is the extent of employee participation in (and responsibility for) those decisions affecting management of the enterprise, and on this question there remain wide differences of opinion.

As noted previously, approximately two million persons are employed in Britain's nationalized industries. The relationship of the employee and the trade union with the public corporation presents some special difficulties. Here, of course, the "boss" is not the traditional stereotyped exploiting capitalist; indeed, he may very well be one of the leaders of labor's own party. And the employee cannot escape completely from being considered a public servant. To the larger problems involved, such as strikes in nationalized industries, no definitive solution has been found. Negotiating machinery for questions affecting wages and conditions of employment follows the general pattern of a joint negotiating committee, composed of members appointed by the board of the public corporation and by the national union or unions involved. In all nationalized industries there is some form of joint consultation between union and corporation representatives. The possible areas for consultation include those of general policy, production planning, workers' welfare, workers' training and education, promotion, recruitment, and discipline. The least controversial and probably the most progressive results of joint consultation thus far in the nationalized industries concern the training and education of workers.[7]

Economic Planning. "We must plan our civilization or we must perish." This warning by Harold Laski suggests the emphasis placed upon planning in British socialist thought. The necessity for economic planning in postwar Britain springs, however, from many sources besides socialist ideology. Indeed, as Professor Milne points out, "British planning machinery is not particularly 'Socialist' but largely the product of external forces acting on the traditional framework of government." [8]

At the top of British planning machinery is the cabinet, which must take the major decisions involved in planning and also accept the political responsibility for results. Beneath the cabinet are a number of ministerial committees. Some are relatively permanent standing cabinet committees; others are formed on an *ad hoc* basis. Membership on these committees falls primarily to those ministers concerned with the "economic" departments, but one department, the Treasury, has assumed major responsibilities in the field of economic planning. The principal staff planning group, the Central Economic Planning Staff, is now located in the Treasury. Other agencies supplying technical and statistical data for planning purposes are the Central Statistical Office and the Economic Section of the Cabinet Office.

British planning machinery is not rigidly centralized, however. In certain areas, town and country planning, for one example, particular

---

[7] See Hugh Clegg, *Labour in Nationalized Industry* (1950).
[8] "Britain's Economic Planning Machinery," *American Political Science Review,* 44 (1952), pp. 406–21.

ministries retain special planning and control functions. For another example, under the Agriculture Act of 1947, the Ministry of Agriculture, Fisheries and Food, acting in conjunction with county agricultural executive committees, assumed wide powers over farm production. On the one hand, the government, on the basis of an annual review of agricultural conditions, made price guarantees for certain farm products; on the other, it required a minimum level of farm efficiency. In order to achieve this efficiency, agricultural and estate lands could be placed under supervision and, if this measure proved insufficient, dispossession of a tenant farmer or compulsory purchase of land could follow. The Agriculture Act, 1958, however, repealed the powers of farm supervision and dispossession, although the Agriculture Act, 1957, continued provisions to guarantee farm prices. British post-war agricultural policy has resulted in a noticeable increase in domestic food production, but Britain must still import between 30 and 40 per cent of its food supplies.[9] Although food rationing ended in July, 1954, food subsidies continue to be a heavy charge on the national exchequer. For the year 1953–54 total subsidy payments amounted to £334,000,000, and £337,300,000 was estimated for 1954–55.

There is close contact between British industry and government. In most instances a particular government department acts as a "production department" for a particular industry or industries. Thus the Ministry of Works is the production department for building, civil engineering, and building materials; again, the Ministry of Supply is the production department for iron and steel and all alloys, vehicles, explosives, and various types of engineering (aeronautical, electrical, and radio). With most wartime and postwar controls now relaxed the production departments operate to promote increased industrial output and efficiency. But some general controls remain. Treasury consent is necessary for outlay of large amounts of capital and for purchase of foreign currency. The Board of Trade (which also acts as a "catchall" production department) must approve the import and export of certain items and, in addition, has statutory powers to influence the location of industry.[1] For interchange of policy views between government, employers, and workers, several consultative bodies exist. One of these is the National Joint Advisory Council (N.J.A.C.), mentioned previously; another is the National Production Advisory Council on Industry (N.P.A.C.I.).[2]

The over-all role of British government in management of the

[9] In 1953 imports of food, drink, and tobacco amounted to £1,319,000 or approximately 40 per cent of all imports; in 1954 they made up 39 per cent.

[1] Under the Distribution of Industry Act of 1945 the Board of Trade may designate areas in danger of unemployment as "development areas." The Board, through Industrial Estate Companies, may construct factories in these areas for leasing to private companies. Approximately 38 per cent of new factory space added in the period 1945–54 was in the various "development areas."

[2] The N.J.A.C. consists of representatives of the British Employers' Confederation, the Trades Union Congress, and the managements of nationalized industries, meeting under the chairmanship of the minister of labour and national service. The N.P.A.C.I. consists of representatives from government, labor, and employers, and is under the chairmanship of the chancellor of the Exchequer.

economy has become very large. Britain's gross national product in 1954 was over £15,700,000,000. Of this amount approximately 40 per cent (£5,900,000,000) passed through the hands of public authorities. This high proportion of public to total expenditures illustrates that the state in Britain is in position to attempt to maintain the high levels of investment, consumption, and employment that the economic analysis of Keynes suggests are necessary for a continued rise in the standard of living. British public finance policy has resulted in the use of the public budget as a means for limited *redistribution* of wealth. Of the total sum of £5,900,000,000 noted above approximately £1,900,000,000 represented payments of pensions and subsidies to individuals and the costs of social services. Not all of this £1,900,000,000 represented a redistribution of wealth, since the national insurance schemes are basically contributory and indirect taxation provides a sizable portion of governmental income, but one estimate for 1954 placed 7 per cent of total *personal* income in Britain as deriving from public pensions, grants, and social services. To be noted is the fact that Britain's gross national product is rising; in 1959 it was slightly above £20,800,000,000. As a result of this growth and limited tax reductions, the percentage passing through governmental authorities has fallen. The Conservative government claims that the *national* budget now accounts for one quarter of national income, whereas the proportion was one third in 1951.

As already suggested, the role of British government in management of the economy is not so much the result of socialist or any other doctrine as the cumulative response to "felt needs." Before World War II a high population density dictated governmental intervention in land-use planning, and "sick" industries such as coal and cotton required a degree of direction and co-ordination not likely obtainable under conditions of free economic competition. During World War II over-all government control of the economy became essential under conditions of full mobilization of the human and material resources of the nation. Need for planning and controls continued after the defeat of Hitler and the Axis. Britain's world economic situation was such that much production had to be channeled to the export market, while imports and domestic consumption required drastic controls. Nor could replacement of war-damaged and worn-out capital equipment proceed haphazardly in view of Britain's exceedingly tight international trade position. Finally, rearmament in the face of the "cold war" opened a still-controversial question regarding the amount of resources to be diverted to military ends.

The circumstances under which British planning machinery developed explain in large part its improvised structure and informality of methods. These same circumstances also suggest a reason why planning in Britain, contrary to the expectations of some Labour theorists, did not become the vehicle for carrying out socialist doctrine. For the most part the problems came first, and planning came later as an effort to find ways and means to meet specific difficulties.

3. FUTURE OF BRITAIN'S WELFARE STATE

During the British election of 1955 a seasoned campaign worker remarked that there were no "issues" involved, that the election was simply a "national census to see who's Labour and who's Conservative."[3] This remark expresses in another way a possibility mentioned in an earlier chapter, namely, that the party struggle in Britain might settle down to a contest between Labour and Conservative for managership of the welfare state. Whether England has entered the era of an "Elizabethan compromise" similar to "the Victorian compromise" is a question to which a categorical answer is not possible. Too much depends upon the nature of internal and external problems that Britain's welfare state seems to face.

Internal Political Problems. If the operation of British political institutions were the only consideration, the picture of Britain's prospects might be painted with a fairly confident brush. Post-World War II political developments certainly seem to bear out Winston Churchill's observation that the British people have the political system they want. They also seem to have vindicated the Labour Party's confidence in the "historic forms of Parliamentary Democracy." Indeed, the events of the postwar period may even have given the lie to Laski's dictum that the "logic of revolution excludes the possibility of compromise." At any rate such a socialist theorist as John Strachey has concluded that popular forces acting under favorable conditions and through effective democratic institutions can turn capitalism out of its ordinary path of development.[4]

Even though there is no substantial dissatisfaction with the institutions or principles of the British constitution, there are many areas in which unsolved or only partially solved problems remain. With respect to particular institutions the House of Lords still presents the same problem in regard to its composition as it did when the Parliament Act of 1911 was passed. In the vital field of executive powers there exist knotty questions concerning administrative justice and parliamentary controls over the exercise of ministers' powers. Demands for greater autonomy from Scotland and now Wales raise the matter of devolution. Indeed, a list of particular political problems could be extended to some length, as is indicated by further mention of such matters as ministerial and parliamentary supervision over the public corporations, central government controls over the local authorities, and recruitment of the higher civil service.

Most, if not all, of Britain's internal political problems appear capable of resolution within the forms of the historic British constitution. But the British constitution as it works today depends heavily upon the

[3] See D. E. Butler, *The British General Election of 1955* (1955), p. 164.

[4] "Tasks and Achievements of British Labour," in *New Fabian Essays* (1952), pp. 188–89.

two-party system. And the question of whether the welfare state can provide a suitable climate for continuance of the two-party system leads to economics, the field that Churchill said a quarter of a century ago had become of prime interest to the British people.

Economic Problems of the Welfare State. At least since the time when Edmund Burke became its spokesman, British conservatism has managed to adapt itself to economic change. And the Conservative Party at mid-twentieth century seems to have accepted, grudgingly perhaps, the welfare state. Thus, if history is any guide, major discontent with the economy of the welfare state will likely come from the party of the left, the Labour Party.

As a matter of fact, some Labour theorists have already taken pains to demonstrate that the welfare state falls considerably short of the socialist ideal. Illustrative of this segment of thought within the ranks of Labour are the views contained in the *New Fabian Essays* (1952), authored by several younger members of the party.[5] R. H. S. Crossman, for example, maintains that the welfare state falls short of socialism in the following ways. First, the concentration of capital and economic privilege remains as it was under capitalism, even though there is now a more equal distribution of national income. Second, wages and profits are still determined by the methods of laissez-faire capitalism rather than by standards of national interest or social justice. Third, even though private industry is under increased governmental control and some industries have been nationalized, real power lies with a small managerial and civil service elite.[6]

The other side of the picture—how far the welfare state has moved from laissez-faire capitalism—is discussed by another new Fabian, C. A. R. Crosland. Of course private property has not been abolished in Britain. But, according to Mr. Crosland's argument, economic and political power no longer depends primarily on individual private property rights. The corporate form has come to dominate industry and business, and "passive shareholding" has replaced "active ownership." The passive shareholder has yielded control of economic enterprise to the managers. While the managers are not a totally different breed from the classical entrepreneur, they are not ruled completely by the profit motive. Consequently managerial decisions are not always based on the desire for higher profits and dividends. At the same time the state has assumed a dominant position in economic life. By means of direct ownership of productive capital, by legal controls, and by means of taxing and spending powers, government in the welfare state can and does determine the utilization of a considerable part of the nation's productive capital. Under laissez-faire capitalism this would be a function of the economy

---

[5] The *Essays* do not represent the official position of the Labour Party, of course. Indeed, former Prime Minister Attlee in his preface to the *Essays* made a point of commenting on the fact that only one of the several authors had had any ministerial experience.

[6] "Towards a Philosophy of Socialism," *New Fabian Essays,* pp. 26–27.

acting autonomously through the market. In Britain government intervention in economic affairs has resulted in a high level of social services from which the name "welfare state" springs. In addition government in the welfare state must work to maintain a high level of employment and an upward trend of production. Indeed, popular discontent with the depression-unemployment-low-production cycles of capitalism is responsible in large measure for the political developments that led to the welfare state. The welfare state has also produced some class changes in society. Society has become more rather than less striated in terms of economic classes. To the proletariat and bourgeoisie of the Marxist analysis are now added sizable professional, technical, and managerial groups whose relationship to the means of production is quite different from that of either the owner or factory worker. Moreover, modern society has created a great demand for services (as opposed to goods) and a significant portion of the population is engaged in supplying these services rather than in production, strictly speaking. Ideological changes, too, have appeared. There is greater emphasis on economic security and on the duties of the state, Mr. Crosland concludes, instead of on such ideals as private initiative, competition, and private property.[7]

Whatever sort of hybrid economic system the welfare state represents, it did, according to John Strachey, another of the new Fabian essayists, cure certain "morbid" symptoms of pre-World War II capitalism. These symptoms were: (1) mass unemployment, (2) low investment levels, (3) inadequate export markets, and (4) a stagnant agricultural economy.[8] As a consequence, in Britain's postwar welfare state, there has been a real and increasing rise in the standard of living for the bulk of the British people.[9] And this rise in living standards was not

[7] "The Transition from Capitalism," ibid., pp. 38–42. With respect to the intermediate classes stressed by Mr. Crosland, it may be well to mention that, as of June, 1953, over a third of all persons employed in Britain were engaged in distribution, public administration, or various professional or other services; also see table, Footnote 9, p. 139. The 1951 sample census showed that less than one third of all men workers and less than one fourth of all women workers were actually "production" workers. The figures in the table of Footnote 9, p. 139, include administrative and clerical workers in the industries mentioned.

[8] "Tasks and Achievements of British Labour," *New Fabian Essays*, pp. 182–85.

[9] As Mr. Strachey points out, there was also a marked rise in productivity in the United States during the same period. He concludes, therefore, that the particular reforms of the postwar Labour government were not wholly responsible for the rise in Britain.

It is appropriate to mention that the development of the welfare state has occasioned a critical re-evaluation of some basic socialist tenets. The Marxist notion that socialism would inevitably follow capitalism is one of these tenets. As Mr. Crosland writes, events of the twentieth century suggest that there are several possible successors to a declining system of laissez-faire capitalism. The welfare state is one of these, but so also are fascism and communism. On a somewhat broader scale Mr. Crossman questions the idea of inevitable progress, pointing out that the tools and techniques of modern civilization can be used to enslave people as well as to provide for the better life. Mr. Crossman, incidentally, argues that the time has come for British socialism to throw off its pragmatic and empirical habit, and to adopt a theoretical basis for its practical political programs.

reversed under the Conservative government returned to power in 1951. In fact Hugh Gaitskell, the leader of the Labour Party, attributed Labour's defeat in 1955 to the fact that full employment and general economic well-being had continued under the Conservatives.[1]

The ability of the welfare state to continue to provide minimal mass economic security for all and a rising standard of living for most cannot be taken for granted, however, despite its success so far. The economic betterment of the British masses achieved under the welfare state appears to be the product of two main factors: redistribution of the national income with a greater share going to wages and salaries, and expanding economic production.[2] Of these two factors increased economic production may well be the most important, especially in the long run.

It is not so much that cries for further redistribution will cease. In fact the most vocal dissent within the Labour Party today—the Bevanite dissent on the issue of military spending versus expanded social services—revolves on a question of allocation of the nation's stock of goods. Rather, the problem is how much more in terms of the general standard of living could be obtained by further redistribution of income, even granted the political feasibility of steps in that direction. As Roy Jenkins, writing in the *New Fabian Essays* points out, the working classes themselves are already paying in large measure for the program of social services. And a 100 per cent tax on all net personal incomes over £2,000 per year would hardly yield enough to pay for a sixth or a seventh of the cost of the National Health Service alone.[3] Redistribution of wealth (as opposed to income) is another possibility. In this respect Labour's program at present proposes some further limited redistribution of capital wealth in the form of renationalization of steel, etc. But any substantial move toward drastic elimination of private capital would certainly strain, if not shatter, the political consensus that underlies the welfare state.[4]

Nevertheless, if the British economy should begin to slump, pressure for further redistribution may well increase. Unfortunately the productivity of the British economy is not a matter solely dependent upon domestic factors. On the contrary, it is heavily dependent upon external factors. Britain's economic machine consists of a skilled labor force,

[1] See D. E. Butler, *The British General Election of 1955,* p. 162.

[2] The degree of redistribution may be illustrated in various ways. Before World War II the share of the national income going to wages was a little more than a third; by 1950 it had risen to almost a half. Conversely, the share going to rents, interest, and profits fell from a little over a third to a quarter. The redistribution had begun earlier, however. In 1929 the highest 5 per cent of incomes accounted for 34 per cent of total personal income; in 1946 the top 5 per cent accounted for only 18 per cent. With respect to expanding production, estimates have British production increasing at rates of from 3 to 5 per cent per year in the postwar period.

[3] "Equality," *New Fabian Essays,* pp. 75–76.

[4] Another problem of welfare-state economy in addition to those stressed in the text is that of inflation. It is related to redistribution of income in that, as long as a given distribution as between wages and profits obtains, a rise in wages appears to be matched by a rise in prices.

industrial techniques, and capital equipment, plus hard fuel.[5] In order to keep this economic machine running Britain must import a sizable portion of its foodstuffs and virtually all of its raw materials. And, to sustain the flow of vital imports, Britain must export.

In a very real sense, then, the overseas market contains the key to Britain's future. The overseas market is not simply a matter of economics, however. It is part of the realm of foreign relations, an area in which no nation today has complete control over its political destiny.

Problems of External Relations. In few cases are external factors more important than in Britain's. Former Prime Minister Attlee put the situation somewhat mildly when he complained that members of his own party sometimes fell into the error of assuming that a British foreign minister has more freedom to act than he really does.[6]

Britain's freedom of action in the international field is limited, first of all, by her postwar political commitments. In the split between East and West, Britain must take into account her position as a leading member of the Western bloc. Her military commitments as part of the North Atlantic Treaty Organization have already become a matter of domestic political controversy. Her position in the Western group also affects overseas trade. Certain patterns of trade are not wholly compatible with this position, as is illustrated by Britain's dealings with Red China. Great Britain also played a leading role in fostering European unity. Yet Britain has been unwilling to participate in the European unity movement as fully as some nations on the continent would desire. British reluctance to plunge fully into the European movement becomes a little more understandable when her relations with a third circle of countries is considered. This circle is the Commonwealth, the empire, and the sterling bloc. The sterling bloc is now the most important area for British overseas trade, accounting in 1954 for 44 per cent of imports and 49 per cent of exports.

The Commonwealth, empire, and sterling areas seem to hold an especial importance for the future of British international trade. British trade figures reveal a significant shift toward export of durable consumer goods and capital equipment.[7] Coincident with this shift is the movement in the vast underdeveloped countries of the world toward industrialization. Industrialization of the underdeveloped countries will require huge amounts of capital and industrial machinery. If Britain, through the Commonwealth and sterling bloc, can become a major supplier of capital goods for the underdeveloped areas, the outlook for the future of the British economy is good. But there are difficulties here, too. Britain faces

[5] The development of atomic energy for industrial uses is a possibility that should not be overlooked, especially in view of Britain's almost total dependence upon imports for oil.

[6] See his preface to the *New Fabian Essays.*

[7] In 1938 metals and engineering products made up 37 per cent (by value) of British exports; in 1953 they made up 51 per cent. Textiles and clothing fell from 21 to 15 per cent over the same period, and raw materials from 12 to 5 per cent.

competition from other industrial nations, including resurgent Japan. The rise of nationalism in the underdeveloped countries also complicates matters, as the Iranian oil crisis, the Cyprus situation, and the Suez Canal controversy have given evidence in the recent past.

A balancing of the external forces affecting Britain's welfare state will not be an easy task, and it may tax very heavily the British spirit of compromise. The British people have found that agreement on the essentials of common existence and toleration for the other person's point of view make for a durable constitution and a free way of life. To get other peoples to respect and reciprocate that spirit is the task of British diplomacy, now that Britain is no longer mistress of the seas.

7

THE BRITISH COMMONWEALTH

1. THE NEW COMMONWEALTH

The inclusion of a chapter on the British Commonwealth in a book on European political systems needs little apology. The self-governing nations freely associated with Britain to constitute the Commonwealth are scattered over the globe, and, apart from Britain, contain more than 480,000,000 people of varied races, religions and cultures. But they have in common one fundamental feature: they seek to live politically in greater or less degree by an inheritance from Europe, or more specifically an inheritance of ideas and institutions from Britain. They adapt to their own needs and circumstances certain essential elements in the British system. They succeed in maintaining a commonwealth based on free association mainly because of common political conceptions.

Commonwealth and Empire. Since it first came into use during World War I, the term "British Commonwealth" has been applied either broadly as a substitute for the older term "British Empire," embracing all territories under the Crown, or, narrowly, in reference only to communities fully autonomous and freely associated within the empire.[1] The broader usage, now favored by many writers in Britain, has some warrant in the fact that the seminal idea of local self-government, which characterized the institutions of the dominions, has become active everywhere throughout the colonial lands and is in process of development there. The ethos of the modern empire has been the achievement of local responsibility, and with it has gone the enfranchisement of the queen's subjects at a pace related to the circumstances of the area. In the territories dependent on Britain there is no uniform social development, and hence no uniform political advance. But an increased reliance is placed upon local bodies responsible for enacting local law. Never was

[1] In the Queen's titles, as recommended by the Commonwealth prime ministers in December, 1952, the simple term "Commonwealth" received explicit sanction. Obvious, however, is the value of the prefix "British."

this fact more true than in the years after World War II, as new constitutions for colonies, especially in Africa, followed one another in rapid
succession. Although in colonial rule the supreme direction continues
to be exerted through a bureaucratic elite drawn from Britain and supervised by the Colonial Office, the inhabitant on the spot, whatever his race
and color, is increasingly utilized in the tasks of administration. Even in
1939 fewer than 66,000 officials among the 250,000 in the sixty territories of the British Empire were drawn from the United Kingdom. What
the dominions in the plenitude of their freedom have long reflected,
colonial communities in Africa and elsewhere are preparing to reflect.
Common and dynamic ideas operate at different stages in both. The
dominions express them in their maturity, the colonies in their rudiments.

Postwar Developments. The significance of developments in the
Commonwealth since the end of World War II is profound. These developments are the fruit of ideas that for nearly a century had quietly
germinated and grown, especially the ideas of self-government and liberal
nationalism. They illustrate another fact. In 1939 the free and autonomous members of the British Commonwealth were Canada, Australia,
New Zealand, and South Africa, countries colonized mainly from the
British Isles or Western Europe by immigrants who had common elements of culture. Linguistic and other diversities existed, particularly
in Canada and South Africa, which were introduced by peoples not
derived from the British stock, and with different traditions shaped by
their own struggle for cultural survival. But all these peoples shared, at
any rate, an inheritance from Western Europe, albeit modified by local
environment, and on this cultural bedrock a commonwealth of free nations was built.

By contrast, after the war, the new member states of India, Pakistan, Ceylon, and most recently (in 1957) the Federation of Malaya have
ancient and indigenous cultures and classes, very unlike those of the
older members, such as Canada and Australia. What they share in common is certain British political conceptions, legal ideas, and administrative techniques. In an Asian milieu their leaders seek to operate institutions that originated in Westminster and also to preserve the mutual
discussion and flexible consultation that Britain and the older dominions
had formerly established. Similar to these Asian states is Ghana in West
Africa, which became a full member of the Commonwealth in 1957.

These new states, however, introduced signal changes. The most
notable was the formal declaration, after the Prime Ministers' Conference of April, 1949, that India, as a sovereign republic, would retain
full membership in the Commonwealth but would accept the king simply
as a symbol of the free association of its members and, as such, its head.
Monarchies and republics (for Pakistan later followed India's example
in becoming a republic) were thus joined together in an experiment of
combining East and West on a basis of liberal association; they attempt
to bridge great cleavages of outlook among regions, races, religions, and
cultures. General Smuts once extolled for his fellow South Africans the
ideal of the Commonwealth as "full sovereign status, freedom to the

utmost without limit, but always in the group of comrades and friends with whom we have marched hitherto in our history." Into this unique fellowship the new states were incorporated. The complex problems of this incorporation hardly need emphasis. Neither do its possibilities. Its future success is likely to depend upon world circumstances and upon the enduring will of all these states to be guided in their relations by the liberal-democratic spirit. There is, however, little doubt that the postwar developments have resulted in a Commonwealth less close-knit and cohesive, less able to reach unanimous agreement on world policy, less capable of marshaling immediate power to support policy, and hence inevitably less weighty in world counsels. Comprehensiveness and variety in composition are bought at a price, and the price for the adhesion of the new states is an increased difficulty in pursuing common ends. But partly a balance to that fact is the imponderable moral influence of the Commonwealth and its ideals among the Asian members, which is not to be written off as slight. In a critical period it might decisively determine the course of events. If we assume the necessity for Western democracies to compete with Soviet Russia in the Far East, not in mere terms of power but of ideas, then the Commonwealth and its bonds of association constitute a potent form of such competition.

2. INSTITUTIONS OF DEMOCRACY

The British Heritage. In the older and original dominions institutions are rooted in a long development and are directly derived from Britain and shaped by British political thought.[2] Here are present, although often modified by local environment, the symbolism of monarchy, the characteristic bicameral system, the supremacy of the first chamber, the relative impotence of the second, the intimate bonds between legislative and executive powers, the close control of national expenditure by the executive, the recognition of an opposition as little less important than the government, the independence and anonymity of civil servants, and the rule of law in the British sense.

These countries inherited the main constitutional achievements of seventeenth-century England and the more gradual developments of the eighteenth and nineteenth centuries, including that which is perhaps the peculiar secret of British parliamentary strength—effective rules of procedure, backed by centuries of experience. "The parliament at Westminster," wrote Sir Courtenay Ilbert, "is not only a busy workshop; it is a museum of antiquities." Many of its antiquities, as well as its useful instruments, have been imported by the parliaments across the sea, and to them its rules of procedure and its temper of mind introduced dignity and efficiency. It influenced colonial legislatures in the nineteenth century because for them it was always the supreme model, although admittedly, in many instances, the model was not faithfully followed or was followed

[2] Throughout this brief survey the author has relied heavily upon his *Democracy in the Dominions* (3rd ed., 1958).

merely in the letter rather than in the spirit. In no dominion parliament does the speakership resemble exactly the institution of that name in the British House of Commons, for in none is the speaker free from the trammels of party. In none is the question period utilized so skilfully as at Westminster. Canada and Australia in the twentieth century have failed to follow closely the British precedent of an effective public accounts committee, sedulously pursuing its task session after session. The British system of treasury control has influenced all these countries, but in none has it worked precisely as in Britain. In the dominions civil liberties are on the whole less scrupulously respected than in the British Isles.

Other departures from the British model are evident. The historical reasons for them are many, but perhaps the most important has been the absence of critical electorates that appreciated all the significant features of the British parliamentary system. When local politicians thought that some of these features were inconvenient, they simply ignored them without being held to account. The social environment of frontier countries nurtured indifference if not hostility to the subtleties of parliamentary rule. It was difficult to persuade communities excessively confident about the abundance of their resources and the splendor of their future to adopt the rigorous financial controls that Gladstone established at Westminster. A careless, almost profligate, attitude toward public spending was endemic, and was fostered by the facts of frontier and colonial life, especially by the necessity for numerous public works that would stimulate the exploitation of natural resources.

Significant in their political thought is the fact that the dominions had no revolution and no revolutionary tradition. They have reflected the characteristic British political temper, with its zeal for pruning the branch but sparing the root. The achievement of self-government in the nineteenth century was for them the decisive turning point in development, and, except in Upper and Lower Canada, it came with little strain. It was the product of democratic persuasion and repeated argument. It involved no drastic change in the fabric of government, but merely an alteration in its conventions and procedures to ensure that the executive was always responsible to the legislature. In the words of Lord Durham it was simply "administering the government on those principles which have been found perfectly efficacious in Great Britain." Its colonial champions indeed argued that they were asking only for the constitutional liberties that belonged to Englishmen. With parliamentary institutions went their democratic accompaniments of free labor organizations, voluntary associations, social services, and compulsory education for the masses. Important was the abundant activity of religious bodies that in the nineteenth century migrated from Britain and flourished under colonial conditions. Such institutions and associations in the older portion of the Commonwealth constitute the foundations of political life and create its moral unity.

The British idea of parliamentary government in these states is too firmly held to permit any wide acceptance of the procedures of direct democracy, which in the United States appealed so strongly in the last century. In ordinary lawmaking the referendum has seldom been used except to ascertain the popular opinion on the sale of alcoholic liquor and the methods of such sale. In municipal affairs it is also sometimes resorted to in consulting electors on questions of local improvements. The view has prevailed that the only proper appeal to the electorate is made by a government that submits its whole fate to the popular verdict. Australia, which in some respects was more receptive to American political ideas than any of the other dominions, uses the referendum in amending the constitution of the Commonwealth, but otherwise in the making of law is devoted to the supremacy of parliament. Similarly these democracies set their face against the direct election of administrative and judicial officers. All such officials are servants of the Crown, and in general enjoy a permanent tenure.

Environment and Other Influences. In the older dominions, as suggested above, local environment and history have exerted their power and modified the original inheritance. In all these countries there has been the leveling influence of the frontier, breaking down the peculiar class distinctions of the old land, stimulating an egalitarian spirit (notably in Australia and New Zealand), and creating a type of collectivism concerned not merely with social welfare but with railroad construction and other public utilities related directly to the development of natural resources. With such collectivism have gone protective and neomercantilist policies for the rapid creation of national economies. The substance of politics, therefore, was different at the outset from that in the British Isles because the social experience of the people was novel. The American, claimed Crèvecœur in the eighteenth century, was "a new man." New men and a new society also emerged in the British colonies of the subsequent century and exhibited abundant political energy. This fact was notably illustrated early in the twentieth century in the reputation won by Australia and New Zealand as social laboratories. "New Zealand democracy," wrote the American liberal Henry Demarest Lloyd, "is the talk of the world today. It has made itself the policeman and partner of industry to an extent unknown elsewhere." In the same period a more critical observer, André Siegfried, was no less impressed by the social experiments of New Zealand and Australia, and upon them passed a similar judgment.[3] Here he found the forces of conservatism weak, and those of innovation strong.

Canada won less acclaim for precocious political experiment than its sister nations in the Antipodes because its geography and society, in which the interest of a small farmer class was early potent, gave more scope for individual enterprise and less scope for welfare collectivism. The complicated relations of French and English also doubtless made it less disposed to pursue social innovation, although, like the other dominions, it relied much upon government to assist in the development of natural resources. In the twentieth century, however, especially in the western provinces, a bolder political spirit has often been evident. In 1944 the Cooperative Commonwealth Federation, a zealous social demo-

[3] Henry Demarest Lloyd, *Newest England* (1901); André Siegfried, *Democracy in New Zealand* (1914). Siegfried visited New Zealand in 1904.

cratic party, came to power in the province of Saskatchewan and pursued policies that were sometimes described as those of agrarian socialism.[4] Earlier still (in 1935) the Social Credit movement won a provincial election in Alberta and remains still in office at the time of writing. But since the leaders of this movement did not have the constitutional power in Alberta to establish what they regarded as social credit, they reverted to policies that in most respects are scarcely distinguishable from those of the more orthodox parties. Some of their political methods, however, have diverged from the main British parliamentary tradition.

South Africa has a singular position among the older states of the Commonwealth. Basic to every other aspect of its political life is the fact that its people of European descent represent little more than one fifth of the population. The remainder consists of the Bantu peoples (approximately 68 per cent of the whole), the Coloureds, a mixed race, and the East Indians, who are mainly the descendants of laborers imported in the last century to the sugar plantations of Natal. Only the Europeans have full political rights. The others live under a rule that they cannot effectively influence or control through the procedures of parliamentary institutions. The Bantu in their tribal areas possess elements of local government, but a large proportion now reside outside these tribal lands and under a network of administrative regulations. In a state where democratic rights are thus confined to a minority the atmosphere of politics is at times saturated with passion. The democratic state here tends to be impaired by its failure to embrace as full citizens all adults within its boundaries; it must unfortunately be organized to assert a domination of a minority over a majority.

State Services and Social Democracy.   At the outset the drive for state services in the dominions was created by the necessities of the frontier, rather than by the pressures of industrialism so influential in Europe. But in these countries industrialism also advanced with the flow of capital from the money markets of London, and with it came the agitations of opinion that characterized society in Britain and the United States. Trade unions in Australia, favored by peculiar circumstances, became well established by the turn of the century, and created labor parties, which, in the twentieth century, began to extol the goals of a liberal socialism. In these actions the Australians were not responding to a political thought original with them. The conceptions current in their progressive movements came primarily from Great Britain, and to some extent from the United States. Henry George's *Progress and Poverty,* Bellamy's *Looking Backward,* the books of William Morris, Robert Blatchford's *Merrie England,* the Fabian tracts—these and other writings from across the sea helped to stir the social conscience in the Antipodes. But if their ideas were not original, Australians at least had a favorable opportunity to implement them. Keir Hardie's concept of an Independent Labour Party, for example, readily appealed to workers in Sydney and

4 See S. M. Lipset, *Agrarian Socialism: The Cooperative Commonwealth Federation in Saskatchewan* (1950).

Melbourne, and with them achieved earlier and more impressive successes than among the toilers of Tyneside and London.

In the twentieth century the pressures in Britain for social democracy became stronger, and the lead of the older dominions in forms of collectivism was overtaken, a development that Sir Charles Dilke in the nineties had shrewdly forecast. The gradual supersession of the traditional ruling class brought democracy in the British Isles closer in character to that in the dominions. The road, for example, pursued by the Australian colonies was that followed by Britain herself when the labor movement attained sufficient strength. All the advanced communities in the Commonwealth now responded to like stimuli: they became increasingly absorbed in developing social services, regulating public utilities, and providing more amenities for the ordinary people. Under the influences of modern industrialism and the social conscience, they acquired a more uniform character than they had possessed in the nineteenth century. The moving frontiers of settlement, which hitherto had differentiated the dominions from the motherland, signify much less today. More important are the common forces of an industrial civilization, which rapidly demolish the distinctions of the past and create a similarity of problems. The dominions, like Britain herself, are involved in the difficult search for a satisfactory equilibrium between public and private enterprise. All seek a balanced economy and full employment. All are engaged in siphoning off income from the few who are wealthy to benefit the many who are poor.

3. FEDERAL SYSTEMS

A conspicuous aspect of democracy in the Commonwealth is the successful combination of federalism with parliamentary government. This federal experience began with the establishment of the Canadian state in 1867, and assumes a new and larger phase with the emergence of federations in India, Pakistan, the African territories of Rhodesia and Nyasaland, Nigeria, and the West Indies. The three major federal regimes in the Commonwealth deserve comment, however brief, for each illustrates an attempt to adapt the federal idea to special circumstances and history.

Canada. The dominion of Canada at the outset had four provinces and today has ten. The original confederation resulted from economic and other forces similar in some respects to those which created American union eighty years before, or Australian union thirty years later, but naturally in Canada these forces had a distinct complexion. The federation might be viewed as a long-delayed by-product of the American Revolution, a consolidation of those northern territories which had remained within the empire alongside the republic and which must become united in order to survive and grow. The fathers of the federation were alternately attracted and repelled by the example of the American union:

attracted by its grand design and repelled by its defective details. They grappled with the contentious points of their own constitution (in 1864) when the American Civil War was still pursuing its grim course, and for them this tragic struggle seemed to teach a lesson. They were resolved to escape if possible, or at any rate to minimize, the frustrations and dangers of a dual sovereignty. Hence they were halfhearted and tentative in adopting the federal idea and determined on political strength at the center. They endeavored to divide the legislative power of provinces and nation in such a way that the residue would clearly dwell with the national parliament. They endowed the national executive with the power to nominate for life the members of the senate in Ottawa, which for any government is obviously a fat patronage plum. Likewise to the national executive they gave an authority to appoint the provincial lieutenant governors and to disallow acts of the provincial legislatures. Here was a striking departure from American precedents. If the disallowance power were to be used extensively, it could cripple the autonomy of the provinces and reduce to a fiction the federality of the constitution.

Significantly, with time the Canadian system actually grew, not less federal, but more. This result came in great part from the decisions of the courts, for a federal constitution is necessarily what the courts decide. They have so interpreted the original distribution of legislative power as to enlarge that of the provinces beyond anything envisaged by the architects and builders of the federation. Likewise, although in the first thirty-odd years of union, the national executive disallowed as many as sixty-five provincial acts, the use of such power has now become relatively infrequent, although by no means obsolete. The number of acts disallowed in the last sixty years is considerably less than in the preceding thirty, although in the interval the volume of provincial legislation has rapidly grown.

The reasons for the enduring strength of Canadian federalism are clear: in the long run a constitution in a liberal state, whatever its terms, must bend to social and economic facts. Canada began and remains a country of dual cultures and dual languages, indeed almost a country of two nations within a nation. The French constitute some 30 per cent of the population. In the province of Quebec they have deep and ancient roots, and are ever mindful that they must employ provincial autonomy in the struggle to preserve their culture on a continent where Anglo-Saxon ways of life prevail. As a powerful and vigilant minority they can be relied upon to emphasize constantly the federal idea, whoever else may desert it. There is another salient fact. Contemporary Canada contains ten provinces in a state larger than the United States. Some of these provinces are immense regions. Ontario is bigger than France and West Germany combined, and Quebec is bigger still. The natural resources of such extensive lands have become very important, and, as the custodians of these resources, the provincial governments must of necessity shoulder enhanced responsibilities. Municipal government and education, matters originally left to the provinces, produce with the growth of population a recurrent crop of new problems. In a century of total war and the effects of war there are counteracting forces that stress the need for concentrated power at the center, and the essence of the federal problem has always been to strike a workable balance between the claims of province and nation. The balance, however, must often change in response to the currents of economic and social need.

Canada's experience demonstrates that federalism, while invaluable for free government in a continental state, demands for efficiency constant and fresh thinking about procedures and methods. It does not flourish in neglect; it places a premium on political alertness. It demands also that which in the long run is imperative for any democracy, an active spirit of give and take, a readiness in the majority not to impose insufferable decisions on the minority. Without a tolerant acceptance of cultural differences between French and English the Canadian federation would resemble a house on shifting sand. Granted tolerance, however, a relatively secure national structure can be built. Out of differences a workable, if not an ideal, unity can be created, and that is the main achievement of Canada.

Australia. The Australian federation was born and nurtured under different circumstances, and hence has different features. It came to birth in 1901 after a prolonged debate in the six colonies that now constitute its member states. Its political leaders had little reason to see in the American system elements to shun, and least of all the notion of a strict dual sovereignty. The Civil War and its unhappy incidents had passed into history, and what in the late nineties the Australians perceived in the United States was a great and affluent republic confidently launched on a remarkable career of expansion. They were much impressed by what they found in James Bryce's *American Commonwealth,* and the name of their new state, the "Commonwealth of Australia," was suggested by this famous book. The democratic federalism that Bryce described appealed to their minds and suited their moods, whereas in Canada, as one of them confessed, it was impossible to believe "that the essence of federation exists." [5] Hence they devised federal arrangements closer to those in the constitution of the United States than to those in the constitution of Canada. They rejected any provision for a federal disallowance of state law; endeavored to place the residuum of power with the state legislatures; gave to each state an equal representation in the senate; and required senators to be elected directly by the people for six years and not, as in Canada, appointed by the national government for life. They also left to the states their own systems of courts and the power to appoint their own judges, in contrast to the Canadian system whereby the judges presiding in the provincial courts were appointed by the government in Ottawa. Finally the Australians, unlike the Canadians, provided for the amendment of their system by a method deemed to be both simple and democratic: an amending bill, after being passed by the two houses of

[5] In August, 1899, G. B. Barton, a brother of Sir Edmund Barton, first prime minister of the Commonwealth, wrote to Goldwin Smith in Toronto that the Canadian model "never received a moment's serious consideration, either in the Conventions or out of them." Doubtless his view was an exaggeration, but it indicated the prevalent attitudes of his associates.

the national parliament, becomes law when submitted to and approved by a majority of electors in four of the six states and in the Commonwealth electorate as a whole. But while this method may be simple, it has not been easy in the last half century to persuade the electors to sanction amendments. Out of twenty-four proposals submitted to popular decision by referendum only four have received the requisite majorities.

In its operation the Australian federation has had experiences in some respects similar to and in others different from those of Canada. Important is the greater ease with which agreement and co-operation among the several states is achieved, and the reason is doubtless found in the greater social and cultural cohesion of the Australian people. Before World War II, 88 per cent of the population were of British descent, and no troublesome bi-cultural and bilingual problems were present. There are, of course, the plural and contending interests usually associated with the regional divisions of a continental community, but they are generally more placable than those of Canada. On the whole, despite the initial bias in favor of the states, there is a stronger unifying trend manifest in Australia, for, where there is more substantial unity among the people, the federal idea is less able to resist the centralizing forces, economic and political, that operate in the modern state.

Yet in most matters these federations differ only in degree. In both, thanks to the wealth of their resources, industrialism grows rapidly, and results inevitably in special concentrations of wealth and population in certain areas. In both the national government performs tasks that now become ever more important, and it is endowed with an unlimited right to raise revenue by any means in contrast to the limited rights of the provinces and states. This fact tends to exalt its position. Financial power commands other power, even without a reallocation of legislative jurisdiction in the federation. It has been well illustrated that the power to tax is the power to destroy. But it also implies the power to create. In both federations the national authority must provide for defense and hence for all the varied activities and heavy expenditures directly or indirectly associated with this responsibility. In both the appetites of the democracy for policies of social welfare are avid and grow more avid, and can be satisfied only by direct national services, or by funds contributed in part or whole from the national treasuries. Democratic politics is always the art of compromise; federal politics is especially so. Hence the federal system operates best when masters of this art are present and active. Here are facts fruitful in consequences for the federal regimes of both countries.

India. It seemed natural that when in 1947 the independence of India and Pakistan was established both states should assume a federal form. Their size and cultural diversities suggested it, and in any case their leaders were familiar with the idea, for the British before World War II had projected for a united India a large federation. This British plan, contained in the Government of India Act of 1935, remained the basis of rule until India and Pakistan should each create a new framework of government. For various reasons Pakistan did not complete its task until March, 1956, but India was relatively prompt. In January, 1950, its federal constitution came into operation.[6]

It is premature to assess confidently the effectiveness in operation of India's Union of States, for it is still young. But the constitution is a document of singular interest and an invaluable index to Indian political thinking. It well illustrates the depth of inheritance from Great Britain in particular and the Western world in general. It is also one of the longest and most complex constitutions on record, a fact explained by the country's social environment and checkered history. As a land of 360,-000,000 people India has a remarkable diversity of cultures, races, languages, and religions. Thirteen languages are mentioned in the constitution, and hundreds of dialects exist. In the past the British naturally thought that such a country when granted independence might be violently torn apart by strife, unless its different communities received communal guarantees. The Indian leaders, however, fired by an intense devotion to the concept of a liberal nationalism, were determined to emphasize at any cost India's oneness. For them the supreme goal was a single nation. They argued that the cultural diversities would not prove fatal, if the constitution secured an ample protection for the fundamental liberties of individual citizens, and this they were resolved to accomplish. They provided, not merely for a declaration of Fundamental Rights in twenty-four lengthy articles, but also for Directive Principles of State Policy. Such general declarations had not hitherto, except in Eire, been put in constitutions within the British Commonwealth, but the circumstances of India had no real precedent.

The declaration of Fundamental Rights enumerates in detail the rights to equality, personal freedom, protection against exploitation, religious freedom, education, property, and constitutional remedies. The ultimate effect on the federation of this elaborate attempt to protect the individual is difficult to predict, but inevitably it must lead to constitutional complexity and the abundant employment in the future of constitutional lawyers.[7] Many of the fundamental rights are likely to restrict executive and legislative power, a fact already illustrated during the short interval in which the constitution has operated. Judges have sometimes given more weight to the rights of an individual than to the needs of a government. The draftsmen of the constitution intended that the supremacy of the law should ensure the common good no less than the individual good, but the latter is often more concrete and discernible than the former.

The declaration on the Directive Principles of State Policy has no equivalent in the constitutions of the older dominions, although probably suggested by Eire's constitution of 1937, which in turn was influenced by that of republican Spain. The enumerated principles are not intended to be enforceable in the courts; they are merely a guide to legislatures as to the course they should take. They are aspirations, not law. They

---

[6] The principal articles of the constitution are printed in Sir Ivor Jennings and C. M. Young, *Constitutional Laws of the Commonwealth* (1952), pp. 480–515.

[7] See remarks of Sir Ivor Jennings, *Some Characteristics of the Indian Constitution* (1953), p. 50.

might not unfairly be described as the goals that the Congress Party in 1950 regarded as so important that for emphasis they placed them in the constitution. Mr. Nehru and his colleagues sought not merely a unified but a reformed India. An old civilization must undergo change in the interests of social progress and national security. The principles in themselves are on the whole emanations from British liberal and Fabian thought. They range from the humanitarian declaration that citizens, men and women, have a right to an adequate means of livelihood, to the concrete prescription that "the state shall endeavour to organize agriculture and animal husbandry on modern and scientific lines and shall, in particular, take steps for preserving and improving breeds, and prohibiting the slaughter, of cows and calves and other milch and draught cattle."

The two sets of declarations apply to the national parliament and to the state legislatures. The distribution of power between these bodies is the crucial feature of a federal system. In the Indian Union it is clearly intended to place the predominant power with the national parliament, which consists of two houses, the elected House of the People and the Council of States, whose members are mainly elected by the state legislatures for six years. The leaders of India, like those of Canada in the sixties of the last century, were compelled by circumstances to build a federal state, but were determined that within it the national interest must be paramount. They began with a bias for centralization. The fact is amply illustrated in the very detailed distribution of powers, provided in a Union list, a concurrent list, and a state list. The Union list is an impressive enumeration of ninety-seven subjects, and under Article 248 the residuary power is left to the national parliament. Whenever the use of the concurrent powers produces conflicts in law, the legislation of the Union parliament is ordinarily to prevail.

The scheme of government for the states is prescribed in the constitution, and can be amended only by an act of the Union parliament. Moreover this parliament is empowered to admit new states to the Union or form new states by altering the boundaries of the old. Thus in law the Indian states are virtually the creatures of the national parliament, with a status inferior to that of the provinces in Canada or the states in Australia. Under Article 249 a resolution of the upper house passed by a two-thirds majority may enable the national parliament to legislate on any matter in the state list for a specified period. Under the next article a like power may be exercised in an emergency. In order to implement a treaty the national authority can similarly encroach upon state jurisdiction.

In view of these facts it is little wonder that a distinguished Indian lawyer should describe the Union's constitution as that of "a quasi-federation." [8] At the outset the same remark might have been made of the Canadian, although in operation and spirit it has since become federal. Whether the Indian will similarly develop remains to be seen, but at any rate in terms of existing law extensive powers are left with the national government and parliament. An amendment of these is unlikely

[8] M. Ramasswamy, *The Constitution of the Indian Republic* (1950), p. 5.

to be easy. As noted before, the national parliament may by ordinary statute change the structure of government for the states and in most other subjects may effect changes in the same way. But under Article 368 amendments require (1) a majority of the total membership in each house of the national parliament; and (2) a majority of not less than two thirds of the members present and voting in each house. The amendment of certain clauses of the constitution also requires ratification by a specified number of the states.

India is a republic, whose head is a president, elected for five years by an electoral college, consisting of the elected members of the Union and state legislatures. But, despite this republican status, the British system of a parliamentary and responsible ministry, with its attendant and unwritten conventions, is preserved. The president is actually intended to be the equivalent of the British constitutional monarch, endowed with wide executive powers, which he is expected to exercise on the advice of his prime minister and ministers, sitting in and responsible to parliament. The governor of each state is appointed by the president and can withhold his assent to a bill of the state legislature and refer it to the president. The British principles of responsible government govern the executives in the states as well as in the Union.

4. PARTIES AND POLITICAL IDEAS

General Characteristics of Parties. The significant political forces in the dominions are all admirably illustrated and brought to a focus in the life of the parties. In few aspects of political behavior is the interaction of environment and inheritance more clearly evident. In Canada, Australia, and in New Zealand particularly, the character of parties from the outset was shaped by the precedents set by the British parties, especially by the cleavage into Whigs and Tories that developed into one between Liberals and Conservatives. The Liberal parties reflected the ideas of British liberalism, and in the nineteenth century sought to achieve and extend responsible government, to establish the framework of political democracy, to further the corpus of British civil rights, to promote religious liberty, to enlarge the freedom of commerce, and to exalt the tactics of gradual reform. Herbert Asquith, Sir Wilfrid Laurier, Alfred Deakin, and Richard Seddon, however much in their respective countries they might differ in details of policy, were inspired by elements of the same liberal philosophy, much like their predecessors earlier in the nineteenth century. It was Laurier, a Frenchman from the heart of Quebec, who described himself as a liberal of the school of Gladstone. It was another Frenchman, a more passionate French nationalist than Laurier, Henri Bourassa, who declared in 1900 that "I am a Liberal of the English school. I am a disciple of Burke, of Fox, of Bright, of Gladstone, and of all those Little Englanders who have made England and the Empire what they are today." The philosophy of British liberalism in its different phases was the central dynamic in the self-governing countries of the empire; it became expressed, not merely in their liberal democracy, but in their liberal nationalism, and hence helped to transform the empire into the Commonwealth.

The parties that assumed the label of Conservative, once the issue of responsible government had been settled and the office-holding oligarchies destroyed, bore little resemblance to the party of that name in the British Isles because the chief loyalties of British conservatism to the Throne, the House of Lords, the aristocratic principle, the established church, and the imperial idea were less relevant in communities absorbed in the prosaic affairs of colonization and subject to the leveling influences of the frontier. It was not by accident, but by design, that early in the twentieth century the term "conservative" had virtually disappeared from the party politics of Australia and New Zealand. Such a term in these lands had associations that seemed inappropriate. The issue of tradition versus change was present, but once colonial society had embarked on rapid material development, it became difficult to make this issue a principal basis of political struggle. It certainly proved difficult to foster a cult of tradition. All parties were glad on occasion to make political capital out of innovation. All competed in fostering material progress by one means or another, with little concern for the legacies of the past. Yet all, with some exceptions to be mentioned, have tended to uphold the general ideas of liberal economics tempered by the type of collectivism that was forced on these countries by their peculiar necessities.

Although Sir John Macdonald, as the leader of a Conservative Party in Canada for some twenty-five years after federal union and for many years before, greatly admired Disraeli, he obviously could not in his policies follow closely on those of his British contemporary; the economic and social circumstances of Canada were too different from those of Britain. But in one significant respect he resembled Disraeli: he was governed by a general expediency, and rarely was disposed to make his party the symbol of excessively rigid principles or of a too formal traditionalism. He distrusted enthusiasms for democracy in the form of wide popular control. In devising the Canadian Senate, he sought, much as John Adams would have done, a chamber whose members were beyond recall by the people and represented, not mere numbers, but wealth and social position. "The rights of the minority," he remarked, must be protected, "and the rich are always fewer than the poor." Yet he was not an inflexible upholder of vested interests or the opponent of every reform, for, like Disraeli, he himself introduced liberal legislation that facilitated the development of trade unions and on many other matters was no less progressive than his Liberal opponents.

Indeed, the principal political parties in the dominions resemble modern British parties in avoiding any hard doctrinaire attitude for or against change. At all times they are inclined to emphasize the assemblage of free and equal individuals, but in the final analysis they recognize that social claims must prevail and that the freedom of the individual in itself is simply the best means to a general welfare. They tend to eschew a dogmatic and purely rational approach to politics; seldom will they push an abstract theory into a debate on material issues. They are guided ultimately by an empirical attitude, with a peculiar concern for the particular and the concrete. The binding force in their thought is the principle of utility. In these respects they are all, whatever their names, liberal parties in the broader British tradition of liberalism. In the Conservative Party of Canada it has been difficult to determine in the last generation what it has been seeking to conserve, unless it is the liberal inheritance of the nineteenth century. Its adoption of the name "Progressive Conservative" in 1942 aptly reflects the ambiguous feelings of its membership. Significantly, in Australia today, the party to the right is called Liberal. Its proclaimed aim is to preserve the essentials of a liberal economy and society against the complete domination of both by the state.

The national parties in these countries commonly are separated more by subtleties of emphasis and gradations of feeling than by clear-cut distinctions of doctrine. It was characteristic of Arthur Meighen, when prime minister and leader of the Conservative Party, to say that "no one is prouder than I to be a British subject, no one more thrilled by the splendid history and heritage that is ours as a member of the great British Commonwealth." [9] Mackenzie King, in the same period, may have experienced similar sentiments, but as a Liberal leader he would not have declared the fact in such terms, for in his party certain elements would have expected him to emphasize more the claims of Canadian nationality. Yet it would be misleading to assume that the Conservatives are unresponsive to national sentiments and the Liberals indifferent to imperial feeling. These are potent emotions that the two national parties cannot ignore; to them each party pays tribute in its own way and with its own emphasis.

Special Phases of Party Life. The preceding paragraphs are general in scope, but in order to complete the picture some special phases of party life in these countries need mention, because to some extent they modify the generalizations above. The first of these is the existence in Australia and New Zealand of Labour parties, which in Australia, even before World War I, had already held office in the Commonwealth and some states. Since that war the Australian Labour Party has exercised power in the Commonwealth between 1929–31 and again between 1941–49. The New Zealand Labour Party first won office in 1935 and controlled the administration for the next fourteen years. In 1957 it again returned to power.

Three traits in particular distinguish these Labour parties. They make a greater pretense than their opponents of a firm attachment to a program and principles, including a program of socialization; they require from representatives of the party pledges of fidelity to platforms; and they set much store on an organization designed to ensure a control over the leadership by the rank and file. Thus a caucus, which embraces all their members in parliament, persistently seeks to assert supremacy over the leaders. This type of democracy has a long tradition in the Aus-

[9] The remark appears in a speech of 1920. See Arthur Meighen, *Unrevised and Unrepented: Debating Speeches and Others* (1949), p. 102.

tralian party, where by majority vote the caucus selects, not merely the national leader, but other cabinet members, and leaves with him only the allocation of offices among his colleagues. This practice, it may be observed, is in contrast with that of British Labour at Westminster.[1] Another marked feature of these parties is an intimate dependence upon the trade unions for financial sustenance and electoral aid. In Australia especially it has been the powerful movement of industrial labor, a special product of the country's economic and social conditions, that made the victories of the party possible. This fact in turn helps to explain the anti-intellectualism that tends to prevail in the party. The leaders most esteemed by the rank and file are usually practical men, disciplined in the hard school of trade-union politics, and destitute of much interest in intellectual explorations and debate. This emphasis on a disciplined movement in the interests of a social class does not, of course, characterize the opponents of Labour.

Yet one must not exaggerate distinctions. These Labour parties also respond to the principle of expediency. They also inherit the British liberal tradition, with its concern for reasonableness and a broad social utility. Hence they are ever anxious to effect a balance between extreme views. Despite their name and their primary concern with the welfare of the workingman, they do not exalt any doctrinaire concept of a social class. The sentiment of class consciousness is tempered by liberalism and also by religion. "Labour," declared John Curtin, one of the most successful of its national leaders, "is not a class movement; the Party belongs to the whole people." Despite the theoretical attachment of Labour to socialization, it has never in either Australia or New Zealand pressed rigorously toward anything like full socialization within the state. It has shown neither an anxiety to move much ahead of current public opinion nor a wish to discard the Fabian belief in the inevitability of gradualness. In the early years of the present century Alfred Deakin, as a Liberal leader, fought Australian Labour on the grounds of a distinction that he drew between supervisory controls in industry and state socialism; and in political debate forty years later his Liberal successors were concerned with similar distinctions. But in actual practice the Labour Party itself does not act in harmony with any such clear dividing lines. Whatever its theoreticians may write, it also recognizes a grand expediency, and is fully committed to slow transformations by progressive opinion.

In Canada and South Africa, Labour parties also appeared, but in neither country have they played the significant role of those in Australia and New Zealand. The Cooperative Commonwealth Federation in Canada is a counterpart of the Labour parties of the Antipodes in its general socialist aims, in its aspirations to be democratic in procedure, and in the anxiety of its rank and file to control leadership. It seeks to be single-

---

[1] At intervals some members of the British party would have imitated the Australian practice. See R. J. McKenzie, *British Political Parties* (1955), pp. 315–16. For detailed discussions of Australian Labour politics see Louise Overacker, *The Australian Party System* (1952), and L. F. Crisp, *The Australian Federal Labour Party, 1901–1951* (1955).

minded in its policies and pure in its motives, traits that it easily enough exhibits as long as it has not achieved major rank in national politics. The dominance of democratic philosophy among its leadership and adherents makes it certain that when and if it becomes the official opposition at Ottawa, or assumes there the reins of office, it also will act the part of conciliator among many diverse interests, regional, economic, and social; it no less will be forced to recognize that the heart of democracy in the British political tradition is compromise.

In the Union of South Africa the most distinctive feature in party life is an element that often severely strains democratic compromise, namely, the ideals and sentiments of Afrikaans nationalism, especially in its more revolutionary forms. In no other dominion has there been such intense preoccupation with the ideas and issues of nationalism. In Afrikaner thought there are broadly two schools. The first is represented in the liberal-nationalist concept of the late General Smuts and, before his death in 1919, of General Botha. It emphasizes that the Afrikaners should preserve their distinct culture, language, and traditions, but at the same time intimately collaborate with the English-speaking people in order to create a united South Africa. The analogy that seems most often to govern the thinking of the associates of General Smuts is the coming together of the English and the Scots, united in one state and, to the outer world at any rate, in one spirit. Like other concepts of nationality this one inevitably implies an attitude toward history: the things that divided the two peoples in the last century should be less emphasized than the things that unite them in the present. "Let us not mope over the past" was the characteristic injunction of General Smuts to his countrymen. With this liberal concept of nationality, so much akin to that in other countries of the Commonwealth, goes a devotion to British constitutionalism and democratic technique, combined with a zeal to assist in creating an international system.

The other school of nationalist thought is concerned with emphasizing the necessity for keeping the Afrikaners distinct from the British, with a cultural cohesion, undiminished by anglicization and undisturbed by the alien currents of life in the English-speaking world. Such a view has had many and diverse exponents; some are moderate and some extreme; some cling to British parliamentarism, and others reject it. Chief among the moderates in the past generation was General Hertzog, who enunciated what he called the two-stream policy, whereby he would leave both peoples to pursue their separate lives, while at the same time they collaborated to the extent imperative for the maintenance of a common state. At some distant time in the future, he thought, the two peoples might coalesce to constitute a single South African nation, but such coalescence must be regarded as only a remote event. He differed from the school of Botha and Smuts in believing that no precipitate efforts must be made to quicken the process; haste in seeking that goal would outrage the deep national feelings of the Afrikaners. In this nationalist sentiment there is present an element of sturdy liberalism, expressed in willingness— evident in General Hertzog's career—to achieve some accommodation and tolerance between the Afrikaners and the British South Africans.

But the exponents of ultra-Afrikaans nationalism, whose ideas are often colored by Calvinist religion, reject liberalism as a social philosophy alien to the survival of the nation. A few regard it as a British import, which like other things British is viewed with suspicion. "We are going to postulate," wrote one ardent exponent, "the flashes of truth in National Socialism. We cannot but do all these things, because our national danger number one today is liberalism, and our greatest distress at the moment is our sinking nation." [2] The writer regarded liberalism as the principal enemy because it implied compromises between the Afrikaans ideas and culture and those of the English in South Africa, and any compromise was a likely sacrifice of the national faith; it interfered with that distinct mission to which God had called the nation.

In 1948 the Nationalist Party under Dr. D. F. Malan defeated the United Party of General Smuts and assumed power. This event marked a watershed in the history of South African politics. For the first time since the establishment of the Union in 1910 a government composed exclusively of Afrikaners and devoted to Afrikaans nationalist aspirations was constituted. Yet the electoral decision of 1948 turned less on the issue of nationalism than on that of racialism. The demands for labor during World War II brought a larger flow of natives to the towns and industry than ever before. Hence the battle cry of the Nationalists then and since has been the menace to European society of native competition, and their proposed solution is *"apartheid,"* or a firm policy of achieving an economic and social segregation of natives from Europeans. The racial and nationalist issues, however, are related, for they both involve the question of the Afrikaner's cultural survival, threatened on the one hand by the natives and on the other by the British. The most serious threat obviously now comes from the natives, and on it D. F. Malan and his successors, J. G. Strydom and H. F. Verwoerd, concentrated the major energies of their party. Issues of race and nationality arouse deep emotions, and in an atmosphere of emotion South African politics at present follows its course.

Parties in New Asian Dominions. In this brief survey no adequate attempt can be made to discuss the parties and political thought in the new Asian dominions, for in all of them the independent national state is only at the beginning of its evolution. What tomorrow will bring is almost certain to be different from what we have today. The whole political situation is provisional. Behind the present political structure mighty cultural and social forces are in active operation. No one can yet say that a final equilibrium or synthesis has been reached in the impact of the West upon the cultures of Hinduism and Islam, and in the long run the character of government will be affected by what transpires in the sphere of cultural concepts concerning the individual, society, and the universe. The men who achieved freedom are no less attached to the British party idea than to other aspects of the inheritance, and they appear anxious to pursue the path of liberal democracy. But in these

[2] Quoted by M. Roberts and A. E. G. Trollip, *The South African Opposition, 1939–1945* (1947), p. 156.

countries the domestic situation—political, economic, and social—will not render easy the task of creating normal, competitive political groups, whatever the aspirations of individuals may be. In India, Congress was an instrument used by Gandhi and an elite of intellectuals to achieve national liberation. It was dedicated to one supreme end, and Gandhi made allegiance to it a revolutionary religion that embraced in one faith men of many social categories, from Brahmins to Untouchables, from millionaire mill owners to zealous Communists, although the middle class and peasants were the elements that gave it the most reliable support. It aspired to be the one party of the nation, more a movement than a party, but in any case the monopolist of political action on behalf of the nation. This character assumed by Congress was doubtless inevitable in the struggle for independence, but under constitutional democracy there can be no single party that in this fashion embraces the whole nation, for the play of competitive opinion among diverse parties would thereby have no scope, except such restricted scope as it found within the party conclaves.

Thus, in the strict theory of British parliamentarism, Congress should break into at least two parties. Such development to some extent has taken place with the secession of Socialists and Communists and is encouraged by the adoption of a constitution for Congress, wherein it recognizes itself as purely a political party. But there is a strong and understandable feeling among many that Congress must continue to be the chief agent of national unity in a country where the fissiparous elements are powerful, where large numbers of the people feed excessively upon religious and other prejudices that descend from the past, and where the explosion point for mass emotion is singularly low. In this land the shadows of divisions might readily develop into cloudbursts. Symbolic of the intensity of current emotions was the assassination of Gandhi in 1948. He lost his life by the hand of a Hindu because he stood for a democratic and secular state without religious discrimination in opposition to the views of an extreme and inflexible Hinduism.

Moreover, as long as large masses live in dire poverty, the menace of communism as a threat to liberal democracy can be real, for communism, as well as liberalism, has come from the West. The writings of Marx and Lenin have been read, as well as those of Macaulay and Mill. In Bombay, particularly, men between the two world wars studied Lenin's philosophy and methods to discover what they had to teach the revolutionaries of India, and out of their speculations has come the Indian Communist Party. Some Hindu minds believe that the most effective counter to this threat is an intense patriotism linked to reform, of which Congress has hitherto been the vehicle. They would make Congress the agency of social amelioration, and are responsible for including in its constitution the objective of "a Cooperative Commonwealth based on equality of opportunity and of political, economic, and social rights." It remains to be seen during the next decade whether the loyalty that Congress is able to win will hamper unduly the development of healthy, competitive party life.

India has thus embarked on a remarkable experiment. Its political leaders, an elite drawn in the main from a professional middle class, seek to transform an old society by the procedures of liberal democracy. Their conduct of the general election in the midwinter of 1951–52 was a triumph. The electorate was then 176,000,000, of whom perhaps 85 per cent were illiterate. Yet the election was carried through in an orderly manner, even if malpractices and corruption were not absent. Shrewd observers thought that some sense of the issues was conveyed to the millions in the countryside, although their understanding of the constitutional system must be hazy. Yet despite initial victories the members of the political elite are conscious of their heavy responsibility for the future success of the experiment, and conscious no less that India is now an alternative model to China for other countries of Asia to follow. China and India have similar material problems to solve, especially the colossal problem of poverty and want. In setting out to solve them by the methods of parliamentary democracy India is attempting the more difficult task, for these methods imply, not merely intellectual and moral qualities in the leadership, but also sober qualities in the people; they imply a popular understanding and a code of public ethics that cannot be acquired quickly. If the parliamentary regime does not produce the results that the awakening masses desire, it will no doubt be swept away by a revolt from below, directed by other eager intellectuals to the right or the left. The discerning members of Congress from Mr. Nehru down appreciate this danger, and for them it accentuates the urgency of social reform and public education.

Similar difficulties beset the development of parliamentary parties in Pakistan, as in India, with the added difficulty that the middle class is relatively smaller and hence more handicapped in maintaining a liberal democratic system. Here the Muslim League played a role like that of Congress, except that it regarded itself as the special agent of Islam, dominated and directed by adherents of one faith. Pakistan itself, unlike India, is not a truly secularized state, but one dedicated to the ends of a religion. The leading politicians and the Muslim League have been emphatic that this circumstance does not in any way limit the freedom of religious minorities and non-believers, because, as a religion, Islam stands for the essential elements of freedom and democracy, not merely for its own adherents, but for all men. "When we use the word democracy in the Islamic sense," remarked Liaquat Ali in 1949, "it pervades all aspects of our life; it relates to our system of Government and to our society with equal validity, because one of the greatest contributions of Islam has been the idea of the equality of all men." To the idealistic leaders of the Muslim League, Islam has in its Shariat, or canon law, the secret for solving the crucial problems of the age; it is regarded as providing a way of life superior to that of either capitalism or communism. Its principles can become the guide for sweeping changes.

Despite these elements in Islamic thought, parliamentary democracy up to the present has dismally failed to work. In October, 1958, Major-General Iskander Mirza, backed by the army, revoked the constitution. The obvious reason for this failure is that the politicians, unrestrained by their immature parties, did not respect the necessary rules and ethics of parliamentary government. In fighting for personal power they ignored or misapplied the rules. Hence political practice did not conform with the democratic ideal, although to that ideal most educated Pakistanis still apparently cling.

Thus, within the countries of the Commonwealth, there is a wide variety of parties and doctrines. In this diversity the one important factor is the attempt to achieve government through competitive parties dependent upon the free choice of electors and the free play of persuasion. The tolerant acceptance of an opposition and its liberty to convince the electorate that it should control both executive and legislature is the essence of the British parliamentary tradition, and this tradition, with the modifications and insecurities mentioned, survives. But the arts of an opposition are no less difficult, as they are no less important, than those of a government. One would be unduly sanguine to conclude that the new states of the Commonwealth, such as India and Pakistan, have fully mastered them. They have yet to develop dual and disciplined parties, with a keen sense of responsibility whether in or out of office. In these lands acute social divisions and tensions make difficult the growth of a pervasive liberal spirit, so imperative for parliamentary parties. Yet the survival of their democracy depends upon such growth and in turn determines the special role that the Commonwealth can play in Asia.

5. THE COMMONWEALTH AND INTERNATIONAL SOCIETY

General Considerations. The Commonwealth, although not a diplomatic unit with a single policy, is significant in international society as an intimate group of nations subscribing to liberal-democratic ideals. This description is apt, granted that its many members have not yet perhaps perfected all the arts, or cherished all the ethics, of democracy, and that the cultures of the Asian and non-Asian members are different. The Commonwealth's scale of political values is important to itself and to the world. Its spirit and procedures, for example, are antithetic to those of communist states, and its members view any spread of revolutionary communism throughout the globe as a menace to the stability of their own institutions. Their association ensures a defense of the democratic idea.

The Commonwealth, as a type of international democracy living by free discussion, provides for its independent members a special status and a distinctive mode of co-operation. At every stage in its modern evolution the position of its free members is reflected, not simply in law, but in conventions and understandings no less potent than law. In discussing their status we are concerned indeed less with statutes than with a living complex of relationships, rooted in opinions, sentiments, and traditions. The Commonwealth in certain respects resembles a family: both are knit together by moral intangibles. Such intangibles may often be obscure and puzzling to the outside observer because they are also often unmentionables, rarely discussed and analyzed in public. Seldom do the members of a family examine and proclaim the basis of their common loyalty, either among themselves or among their neighbors. They regard such action as difficult, embarrassing, and perhaps even indecent.

A landmark in the attempt to define the Commonwealth and the basis of its association was the pronouncement of the Inter-Imperial Relations Committee of the Imperial Conference of 1926. It emphasized the free and equal status of its members, their community of ideals and interests, and their voluntary determination to co-operate on all matters of fundamental importance. For decades before 1926 there had been a gradual evolution of the self-governing colonies or dominions to the rank of national states, recognized and accepted in their own right by international society. This evolution had been quickened by their active participation and heavy sacrifices in World War I. They had contributed significantly to victory, and hence other nations were now more ready to recognize their stature. Thus in its famous declarations the Imperial Conference did no more than describe a relationship that already existed and was the product of growth. But thereby it clarified this relationship to people in the Commonwealth and the outside world. The Statute of Westminster of 1931 supported these formal declarations by eliminating legal anomalies inconsistent with the root principle of equality, especially by removing the rule whereby dominion laws were void when repugnant to British statutes, by recognizing the extraterritorial effect of such laws, and by translating into legal form a long-standing convention that the British Parliament legislated for the dominions only at their request and with their consent.[3] The principal terms of the Statute of Westminster were embodied in the Independence Acts of 1947, which constituted, as self-governing nations, India, Pakistan, and Ceylon. The title of these acts is itself revealing. Membership in the Commonwealth imposes no legal limit whatever on autonomy.

Certainly the freedom of the dominions in terms of law and fact is that of independent states. They are free to make treaties with other powers, free in international conferences to align with other powers for common ends, free in disputes with fellow members to appeal to an outside and international tribunal, and free to decide the issues of peace and war. The essential elements of their status are still aptly described in the words of General Hertzog at the Imperial Conference of 1926: "In principle unrestrained freedom of action to each individual member . . . in practice consultation with a view to cooperative action wherever possible." In the United Nations, as formerly in the League of Nations, they do not constitute a bloc, bound always to vote and act together. They consult with one another, exchange abundant information, but freely vote as their own governments decide. Although no legal restraint is imposed on their independence, they enjoy in the imperial preferential tariffs the special fiscal and economic privileges of membership, privileges

[3] A standard book on this subject is K. C. Wheare, *The Statute of Westminster and Dominion Status* (5th ed., 1953). Illuminating also on the development of the Commonwealth before World War II is Nicholas Mansergh, *Survey of British Commonwealth Affairs, 1931–1939* (1952).

recognized by international law. But, as members of a voluntary body, they have moral obligations nowhere expressed on paper and rarely even alluded to in public debate. The Imperial Conference of 1926 declared their freedom and equality but shrank from indicating, and no other conference has ever indicated, the requisite sense of moral claim that should accompany this common freedom. Yet, we may assume, such obligations are real. When they are no longer real, the Commonwealth will cease to be anything more than a frail skeleton and will disintegrate under the first rude shock from without.

What are these obligations? The chief obligation is an interest in preserving the group and its political way of life. Each is expected to consult fully with the others to promote this end, deal with others as associates, and, despite a complete freedom of action in law, abstain from an alliance with a power that menaces the others. It is questionable, as General Smuts long ago argued, whether a neutrality that endangers the existence of fellow associates would be consonant with the spirit of the Commonwealth. Eire's neutrality in World War II seemed for an interval to imperil Britain and hence the whole war effort of the Commonwealth. Although she still remained nominally a member, the moral bonds undoubtedly wore thin, and her own declaration of independence in 1949 was a logical outcome. A member may, of course, make a pact or pacts with other powers. Canada has a defense agreement with the United States, and with that country operates a Permanent Joint Board on Defense. In company with Great Britain she has signed the North Atlantic Treaty, although sister dominions outside the Atlantic basin are not signatories. But these arrangements, far from being a threat to other members of the Commonwealth, are regarded by most of them as imperative for security. To them the Pax Atlantica is crucial.

However frequently the members may differ, as they do differ, in the strategy and tactics of policy, and however often they may vote against one another in international conferences, a decisive menace to world peace would probably close their ranks, for on the need of world peace they agree. Their foreign policies to this extent move on converging lines. They all desire global peace on terms that will ensure their national freedom. They recognize common purposes and participate in "an unwritten treaty of mutual guarantee," because as scattered communities throughout the globe they are vulnerable to violence and are moved by common political beliefs that have shaped their internal life: the beliefs in gradual change, in peaceful solutions, in parliamentary systems, and in the settlement of differences by discussion. They seek to protect a civilization in which such beliefs can flourish.

Although equality of status is the central feature of the Commonwealth, equality in function is still not achieved, as the predominant role of Britain well illustrates. Britain internationally still assumes a lead, for she has the richest political experience and the sinews of a great power, with important interests in almost every sector of the world. Her leadership is solicited by states in the troubled area of Western Europe, and even despite her diminished economic resources since 1939 she has intimate links with many countries beyond Europe and outside the

Commonwealth. Hence, from London and through the Commonwealth Relations Office, much illuminating information on foreign affairs is sent to the dominion capitals. The British Foreign Office, with its scattered agencies and its established *expertise,* in this way provides an invaluable service for dominion governments, while in turn they give what data they can. This exchange makes possible a careful discussion on issues of policy. Cables and dispatches are bilateral as well as multilateral; the range of the relationship between Britain and a dominion determines the volume of transmissions and the intimacy of consultation.

In this matter geography has much relevance. In certain contemporary methods of consultation, for example, Canada is favored over the other dominions by her geographic propinquity to Britain, which with modern facilities of air travel makes Ottawa in war or in peace an accessible point in a triangle embracing London and Washington. During World War II cabinet ministers and officials moved readily from one capital to another, and since 1945 such movement in reduced volume has continued. British leaders and officials on visits to Washington can with little delay call in at Ottawa, and peculiarly valuable is the consultation carried out in person by cabinet ministers and top civil servants. Similarly, Canadians have an advantage in the informal discussions that take place among the Commonwealth delegations to the United Nations in New York, since they are more immediately in touch with their home base in Ottawa. In all these respects Australia is at a disadvantage as compared with Canada.

A significant development during and after World War II was the exchange of high commissioners, who opened larger channels of official communication among the countries of the Commonwealth, and hence provided more opportunity than hitherto for reciprocal consultation and discussion. The necessities of war similarly speeded the emergence of regional co-operation. The Canberra Agreement of 1944, for example, was negotiated by representatives of Australia and New Zealand to achieve a closer collaboration in postwar policies, involving alternate meetings of ministers in the two capitals, a regional zone of defense, a military co-ordination to the highest degree possible, the promotion of a South Seas Regional Commission, and generally the achievement of common policies on issues affecting both countries. The whole system of intra-Commonwealth consultation has become what Mackenzie King extolled, "a continuing conference of cabinets." There is constant exchange of views between leaders responsible to parliaments, and under their direction between civil servants.

British Dependence. Although her leadership in the Commonwealth remains paramount, never before has Britain been so dependent upon her fellow members, especially in economics. After the triumph of free trade in the nineteenth century she created a great commercial and investment empire outside the territories under the British Crown. But owing to many adverse circumstances in the present century, especially the severe strains before, during, and after World War II, her external economic empire has relatively contracted, and her reliance upon the countries of the Commonwealth increased. The figures of her import trade during a period of twenty years partly illustrate this shifting emphasis. In 1929, 30 per cent of her imported merchandise came from countries of the empire; by 1938 this figure had increased to 40 per cent. It rose still higher in the forties, and in 1949 stood at 49 per cent. Since the end of World War II the trade with the sterling countries notably expanded while that with the non-sterling Canada contracted, although even despite currency difficulties the proportion of total British imports purchased from Canada in 1949 was as high as in 1938.

Britain's political reliance upon the Commonwealth, which was evident before World War I, increased in the interwar period, and continues to be pronounced, although hidden by her maneuvers and action as a great power. It is now normal that before taking any fresh and major step in foreign policy Britain would seek assurance that it did not contravene dominion interests and better still that it received dominion sanction. The Suez incident in 1956 is a notable exception, which had disturbing effects on Commonwealth relationships. Yet, increasingly, Britain's bonds with the Commonwealth, combined with her closer relations with the United States, affect her action within and beyond the confines of Europe. She cannot summarily reject her past; nor indeed could she brighten her future by doing so. However genuinely British leaders wish to foster intimate political ties with the countries of Western Europe, they hesitate to purchase them at the price of Commonwealth links, for they are not forgetful of the prompt aid that came from the dominions in the grim days of the early forties. But in any case they are influenced by more than memory. Crucial is the growing economic nexus to which reference has been made, and weighty is the strategic consideration that, should Western Europe go down in a future struggle, help might still be found from across the sea. In all this there is instinct as much as calculation.

Common Institutions and Bonds. Although the Commonwealth dwells essentially in the unique relations between Britain and her associates rather than in a rigid legal structure, it still possesses some common institutions and formal bonds, albeit they become less significant. Its principal institutional symbol is the common sovereign, who, except in the states of Malaya, India, and Pakistan, is the sovereign of each as well as of all. The allegiance to the sovereign still expresses a common personal status in countries where he or she is the formal head and a distinct part of the constitution, and between these states such allegiance is a logical link. Less clear is the logic of this regal bond in a state like India, which accepts the sovereign, not as its own head or as a part of its legislature and executive, but only as the symbol of its free association with the member nations of the Commonwealth. Admittedly the words "symbol of association" are elusive. Yet British constitutionalism has always been remarkably successful in absorbing, and even in utilizing, ambiguous terminology, and will doubtless do so here. As Bagehot long ago urged, we need to look upon political anomalies with a little tenderness and a little interest. What counts is not the tidiness of the formula but the reality of the association and the flexibility of its procedures, and time will test the extent of both.

Allegiance to the sovereign in the past gave the status of British subject to people born in the Commonwealth or naturalized therein, but the special rights of citizenship were matters of local law. Thus, before 1946, except in Eire, British subjects had an identical status throughout the Commonwealth in harmony with the ancient doctrine that the lieges of the king had equal rights and duties wherever they might live, subject to regulation by local statutes; and the growth of dominion nationhood consequently made local statutes on immigration and public rights increasingly important.

Significant, however, is the postwar trend of legislation, which emphasizes more sharply the distinct citizenship of each member state as an underpinning for British nationality in the Commonwealth. The source of nationality, indeed, is no longer in allegiance but in the statutory definition of citizenship. Canada set a pattern in its act of 1946, which provides for a citizenship enjoyed by native Canadians as their birthright, but not automatically granted to British subjects, wherever born, unless specific residential and other qualifications are met. Aliens are subjected to more exacting requirements. Although under the act a British subject is not necessarily a Canadian citizen, a Canadian citizen is a British subject. In other words Canadian citizenship is precedent to, but clearly implies, British subjecthood or nationality, and hence preserves an invaluable link with the Commonwealth. A corollary provision is that a person with the status of a British subject, acquired by birth or naturalization elsewhere in the Commonwealth, shall have such status recognized by Canada.

Similar legislation has been enacted in Britain, Australia, and New Zealand, writing out the fact that in each of these countries people possess, as citizens of their own land, a special status that is basic to their common status as members of the wider community of the Commonwealth. The gateway to British nationality or subjecthood is through citizenship in a member state, and the nature of that gateway, broad or narrow, is determined by the parliamentary enactment of the member state. Such is even the case in Britain itself. To give a true symmetry to the law prevalent in the Commonwealth, the Parliament at Westminster created in the Nationality Act of 1948 a citizenship of the United Kingdom and the colonies, and the road to the common status is via this citizenship. The British act, incidentally, provides that the term "Commonwealth citizen" can be used as equivalent to "British subject," in order to satisfy those who dislike to be described as British subjects. More notable than the practical implications of this legislation is its political symbolism. Like the Statute of Westminster and much else in the last thirty years, it reflects the drift of sentiment and opinion that emphasizes the Commonwealth as consisting of equal nations freely and genuinely associated. It seeks to bring law into harmony with the two principles of national freedom and common association.

Effects of Dominion Nationalism.   Where the currents of an exclusive nationalism are strong, however, as in South Africa, the Commonwealth status is least generously recognized or not recognized at all. The South African Citizenship Act of 1949 drastically changed a former situation, whereby British subjects automatically acquired South African nationality after two years' domicile in the country. A British subject can now obtain citizenship only by registration after five years' residence with a formal application to the minister of the interior, who exercises a discretion and satisfies himself that certain other requirements are fulfilled. An alien proceeds to citizenship through naturalization after six years' residence and the fulfillment of somewhat similar requirements. The South African Act differs from all other Commonwealth legislation in not explicitly recognizing a Commonwealth status, although it does require from those seeking citizenship by registration and naturalization an oath of allegiance to the queen. In the debates on the bill the minister of the interior made the claim that a common status no longer existed after the declaration of the prime ministers in April 1949. Significant also in the South African situation is the direct linking of the franchise with citizenship, which forces British immigrants to wait at least five years to acquire voting rights that in Canada and Australia they can normally acquire after a year's residence. Here clearly is a separatist influence in the internal relations of the Commonwealth. The whole emphasis is upon national convenience, with a very minimum regard for the common association and virtually no regard for the common status designed to express that association.

Another traditional and legal bond with Britain that has undergone change is appeals to the Privy Council. Before the establishment of the modern Judicial Committee by the imperial acts of 1833 and 1844, appeals had been carried in virtue of the royal prerogative from colonial courts to the king-in-council, and even in the twentieth century it was still assumed that cases before the Privy Council were brought to the foot of the Throne. The sovereign was the ultimate fountain of justice, and the Judicial Committee was regarded, not as an ordinary court, but as a group of selected men advising the sovereign.[4]

Since courts of any kind are significant instruments of internal government, the growth of nationality and the widening of autonomy inevitably brought restrictions upon appeals to an outside tribunal. To the nationalist self-government is commonly incomplete as long as such appeals exist; and in any case there are practical issues involved, such as the burdensome costs of carrying litigation overseas, which in time weigh heavily in favor of making the appellate courts in the dominions supreme. At the turn of the century the draftsmen of the Australian constitution limited appeals to the Privy Council in cases affecting the rights *inter se* of the Commonwealth and of the states. They were influenced by the impulses of nationalism and by the conviction that a constitution can be better interpreted by jurists who live under it and daily witness its operations. Earlier still, in 1875, the Canadian Parliament sought to abolish all appeals from the Supreme Court to London

<hr />

[4] A useful account of the Judicial Committee in the early part of the century is contained in Norman Bentwich, *The Practice of the Privy Council in Judicial Matters* (1926).

and was prevented from doing so only by the constitutional ambiguity of such action and by the evident opposition of the contemporary British government. What Parliament failed to do in 1875 it accomplished in 1949, all doubt of its power to do so having been removed by the Statute of Westminster. Canada's elimination of appeals to an external body owes something to the growth of centralizing drives, stimulated by economic and social forces and concerned with strengthening for national purposes the apparatus of government in Ottawa. Defenders of such appeals in the past have often been provincialists, fearful, rightly or wrongly, that the Supreme Court would be insufficiently sympathetic to the claims of the provinces. But they have retreated before the insistent pressures of a growing nationalism, whose exponents are confident that in the future the Supreme Court is likely to provide a salutary corrective to provincial ambitions. It may be added that India abolished appeals to the Privy Council in 1949, Pakistan in 1950, and South Africa in 1950.

Hitherto the appeals to the Privy Council have been important in strengthening the common-law traditions throughout the countries of the Commonwealth, enriching thereby their local systems of jurisprudence, even in communities where Roman Dutch law or the French codes prevail. It need not be assumed that the reduction or discontinuance of appeals, now evident in all these states except New Zealand, will involve a sharp break in the common-law inheritance. Courts in Britain and the dominions are disposed to be influenced by one another's decisions and to respect one another's interpretations. This mutual interplay of legal thought will doubtless continue to exert a subtle and unifying influence.

Conclusion. In conclusion it may be emphasized that the older institutional bonds derived from the imperial past increasingly become less significant in the Commonwealth than the new bonds now being forged through consultation among the member states, a consultation more informal and intimate than is customary in diplomatic relationships. No longer is the cardinal issue that of communities freeing themselves from British control and evolving to a national status; rather it is that of states utilizing the most effective basis for collaboration and achieving common ends, even though in some cases they are separated by race and culture. The institutional roots in the past will mean little if the substance of real collaboration among the member states on the critical issues of the modern world is absent or inadequate.

The difficulty of such collaboration dwells in the diversity of these nations in outlook and interest, a diversity sharpened by the accession of the new Asian dominions, which tend to view the world differently. It has been indicated earlier that the members possess in common a parliamentary heritage. But the furtherance of their common purposes raises questions of policy on concrete matters, such as economics, defense, strategy, and foreign policy. The Asian dominions, backward in capital equipment and technical skills, confront the problems of raising the standards of life among the depressed millions who constitute the bulk of their populations, and the other dominions are no less profoundly concerned with the difficult issues of stability and development in the advanced economies of the West. A collaboration with deep meaning for all must bear directly upon these situations and produce results.

Notable in view of these facts is the broad scheme of economic co-operation known as the Colombo Plan. Its leading principles were accepted at a conference of Commonwealth foreign ministers at Colombo in January, 1950, which incidentally was the first Commonwealth conference of its kind held in Asia. The plan was designed to concentrate an attack upon two major ills in the economic situation of South and Southeast Asia: the immense poverty and the presence of undeveloped resources. The substance of the attack has been to bring into the area more capital and technical skills and make more effective the use of whatever is there. This is achieved through carefully planned mutual aid among the Commonwealth members, directed by a Consultative Committee. Not the least interesting feature of the plan has been the invitation extended to non-Commonwealth countries in the region to participate in the projects undertaken, while the aid of other countries outside the region, notably the United States, has likewise been solicited. Thus under the aegis of the Commonwealth a great regional scheme of mutual assistance has been launched to raise the standards of life among populations that total close to 600,000,000. No venture perhaps can better demonstrate the value of the association, and none can constitute a more fruitful collaboration between the Asian and Western members of the Commonwealth.

SELECTED BIBLIOGRAPHY

I. GREAT BRITAIN

The enormous amount of published materials on British government precludes any but a most highly selective bibliography. The following short list of titles hardly constitutes an introduction to the wealth of writing on Britain. Among the conspicuous omissions in this bibliographical note are the lives, memoirs, studies, and polemical writings of those who have played and are playing their roles in British public life; nor is the copious literature found in periodicals and journals included. The text contains citations to some writings in the scholarly journals, and for further guidance to current articles the indexes mentioned at the end of this note may be consulted.

Primary Source Materials. There are many source books and collections of basic British documents, of which the following may be mentioned: G. B. Adams and H. M. Stephens, *Select Documents of English Constitutional History* (New York, 1901); D. O. Dykes, *Source Book of Constitutional History from 1660* (London, 1930); J. R. Tanner, *Constitutional Documents of the Reign of James I* (Cambridge, 1930) and also *Tudor Constitutional Documents, A.D. 1485–1603* (Cambridge, 1922); S. R. Gardiner, *The Constitutional Documents of the Puritan Revolution, 1625–1660* (2nd ed., Oxford, 1899); R. K. Gooch, *Source Book on the Government of England* (New York, 1939); D. J. Medley, *Original Illustrations of English Constitutional History* (2nd ed., London, 1926); Sir George Prothero, *Select Statutes and Other Constitutional Documents Illustrative of the Reigns of Elizabeth and James I* (4th ed., Oxford, 1913); C. Stephenson and F. G. Marcham, *Sources of English Constitutional History; A Selection of Documents from A.D. 600 to the Present* (New York, 1937); W. Stubbs, *Select Charters and Other Illustrations of English Constitutional History from the Earliest Times to the Reign of Edward the First* (9th ed., Oxford, 1913); *English Historical Documents,* D. C. Douglas, gen. ed. (Oxford, 1953–   ); and E. M. Violette, *English Constitutional Documents since 1832* (New York, 1936).

Debates of the House of Commons and the House of Lords will be found in the appropriate series of *Parliamentary Debates (Hansard).* Statutory materials for the period 1235–1920 may be found in *The Statutes Revised* (2nd ed.), and in *Public General Acts* (1921 and after). A cumulative publication entitled *Statutory Rules and Orders . . . in Force on December 31, 1903* was published by H.M.S.O. (His Majesty's Stationery Office) in 1904, and annual volumes have been issued since then. Decisions of English courts are to be found in a wide variety of *Reports,* a convenient guide to which is contained in F. C. Hicks, *Materials and Methods of Legal Research* (3rd ed. rev., Rochester, 1942), pp. 114–29, with a list of separate *Reports* at pp. 432–52. Statistical materials may be obtained from *Monthly Digest of Statistics, Annual Abstract of Statistics* and the earlier series, *Statistical Abstract for the United Kingdom.* For further guidance to the mass of British governmental documents the following may be consulted: *Government Publications Monthly List* (H.M.S.O.); *Catalogue of Papers Printed by Order of the House of Commons, 1731–1800* (H.M.S.O., 1953); *Consolidated Index to Government Publications, 1951–1955* (H.M.S.O., 1958); *Hansard's Catalogue and Breviate of Parliamentary Papers: 1696–1834* (repr., Oxford, 1953); C. T. Carr, *Delegated Legislation* (Cambridge, 1921); P. and G. Ford, *Select List of British Parliamentary Papers, 1833–1899* (Oxford, 1953), *A Breviate of Parliamentary Papers, 1900–1916* (London, 1957), and *A Breviate of Parliamentary Papers, 1917–1939* (Oxford, 1951); and H. B. Lees-Smith, *A Guide to Parliamentary and Official Papers* (London, 1924).

Historical Works.   Among the many works on English constitutional history the following may be mentioned: G. B. Adams, *Constitutional History of England* (rev. ed., New York, 1934); S. B. Chrimes, *English Constitutional History* (2nd ed., London, 1953); H. Hallam, *The Constitutional History of England from the Accession of Henry VII to the Death of George II* (rep., New York, 1930); Sir David L. Keir, *The Constitutional History of Modern Britain, 1485–1950* (5th ed., London, 1953); A. Berriedale Keith, *The Constitution of England, from Queen Victoria to George VI* (London, 1940), 2 vols.; F. W. Maitland, *The Constitutional History of England* (Cambridge, 1908); T. E. May, *The Constitutional History of England since the Accession of George the Third* (Holland ed., London, 1912), 3 vols.; D. J. Medley, *A Student's Manual of English Constitutional History* (3rd ed., Oxford, 1902); Sir Lewis B. Namier, *The Structure of Politics at the Accession of George III* (2nd ed., London, 1957); and W. Stubbs, *The Constitutional History of England in Its Origin and Development* (4th and 5th eds., Oxford, 1891–96), 3 vols.

An introduction and further references to modern economic and political development can be obtained from Thomas S. Ashton, *An Economic History of England: The 18th Century* (London, 1955) and *The Industrial Revolution, 1760–1830* (London, 1949); J. H. Clapham, *An Economic History of Modern Britain* (Cambridge, 1926–38), 3 vols.; G. D. H. Cole and Raymond Postgate, *The British People, 1746–1946* (2nd ed., New York, 1947); W. H. B. Court, *A Concise Economic History of Britain, from 1750 to Recent Times* (Cambridge, 1954); C. R. Fay, *Great Britain from Adam Smith to the Present Day: an Economic and Social Survey* (London, 1928); G. P. Jones and A. G. Pool, *A Hundred Years of Economic Development in Great Britain, 1840–1940* (repr., London, 1948); K. B. Smellie, *A Hundred Years of English Government* (2nd ed., London, 1950); A. P. Usher, *An Introduction to the Industrial History of England* (New York, 1920).

Constitution and Government.   There are many outstanding works on the constitution, especially L. S. Amery, *Thoughts on the Constitution* (2nd ed., Oxford, 1953); W. R. Anson, *The Law and Custom of the Constitution* (5th ed., Oxford, 1922), Vol. I, (4th ed., Oxford, 1935), Vol. II; Walter Bagehot, *The English Constitution* (World Classics ed., London, 1933); A. V. Dicey, *Introduction to the Study of the Law of the Constitution* (9th ed., London, 1939); C. S. Emden, *The People and the Constitution* (Oxford, 1933); Sir Ivor Jennings, *The British Constitution* (3rd ed., Cambridge, 1950) and *The Law and the Constitution* (2nd ed., London, 1938); H. J. Laski, *Reflections on the Constitution* (New York, 1951); Sidney Low, *The Governance of England* (new ed., London, 1915); and Ramsay Muir, *How Britain Is Governed* (4th ed., London, 1940).

Useful general volumes on British government are A. L. Lowell, *The Government of England* (new ed., New York, 1912), 2 vols.; R. K. Gooch, *The Government of England* (New York, 1937); H. M. Stout, *British Government* (New York, 1953); and L. W. White and W. D. Hussey, *Government in Great Britain, the Empire and the Commonwealth* (New York, 1957). Recent developments are treated in Lord Campion *et al., British Government since 1918* (London, 1950).

A handy reference is *Britain: An Official Handbook* (H.M.S.O.). This annual appeared in 1954; it is revised each year and contains a short bibliography.

Parties and Elections.   Works on the development of parties and the party system include Sydney D. Bailey, ed., *Political Parties and the Party System in Britain: A Symposium* (New York, 1952); Ivor Bulmer-Thomas, *The Party System in Great Britain* (London, 1953); Frank Bealey and Henry Pelling, *Labour and Politics 1900–1906* (London, 1958); G. D. H. Cole, *A History of the Labour Party from 1914* (London, 1948); G. W. Cooke, *The History of Party; from the Rise of the Whig and Tory Factions, in the Reign of Charles II, to the Passing of the Reform Bill* (London, 1836–37), 3 vols.; K. Feiling, *A History of the Tory Party, 1640–1714* (Oxford, 1924) and *The Second Tory Party, 1714–1832* (London, 1938); F. J. C. Hearnshaw, *Conservatism in England* (London, 1933); R. T. McKenzie, *British Political Parties: The Distribution of Power within the Conservative and Labour Parties* (New York, 1955); H. M. Pelling, *The Origins of the Labour Party, 1880–1900* (London, 1954); Sir H. Slesser, *A History of the Liberal Party* (London,

1944); Herbert Tracey, *The British Labour Party: Its History, Growth, Policy, and Leaders* (London, 1948), 3 vols.; F. Williams, *Fifty Years' March: The Rise of the Labour Party* (London, 1949); and Maurice Woods, *A History of the Tory Party* (London, 1924). To be mentioned also is J. D. Stewart, *British Pressure Groups* (Oxford, 1958).

With respect to party policies and principles the following may be consulted: C. R. Attlee, *The Labour Party in Perspective—and Twelve Years Later* (London, 1949); Alan Bullock and M. Shock, eds., *The Liberal Tradition: From Fox to Keynes* (New York, 1957); C. A. R. Crosland, *The Future of Socialism* (London, 1956); R. H. S. Crossman *et al., New Fabian Essays* (New York, 1952); L. T. Hobhouse, *Liberalism* (New York, 1911); Q. Hogg, *The Case for Conservatism* (Harmondsworth, 1947); S. MacCoby, ed., *The English Radical Tradition, 1763–1914* (London, 1952); E. R. Pike, *Political Parties and Policies* (3rd ed., London, 1948); R. J. White, ed., *The Conservative Tradition* (London, 1950); and Elaine Windrich, *British Labour's Foreign Policy* (Stanford, 1952); also Hugh Gaitskell, *The Challenge of Coexistence* (Cambridge, 1957); H. M. Pelling, *America and the British Left: from Bright to Bevan* (New York, 1957); and Richard W. Lyman, *The First Labour Government, 1924* (London, 1958).

The electoral system and recent elections are treated in D. E. Butler, *The Electoral System in Britain, 1918–1951* (London, 1951); R. B. MacCallum and A. Readman, *The British General Election of 1945* (London, 1947); H. G. Nicholas, *The British General Election of 1950* (London, 1951); D. E. Butler, *The British General Election of 1951* (London, 1952) and *The British General Election of 1955* (London, 1955). Very useful in connection with the results of general elections is *The Times House of Commons* (London), which contains such information as lists of candidates, results by constituencies, etc.

Parliament and Cabinet.   Much has been written about the British Parliament and cabinet system, of which the following titles afford a small sampling: Sydney D. Bailey, ed., *The Future of the House of Lords* (London, 1954); P. A. Bromhead, *The House of Lords and Contemporary Politics, 1911–1957* (London, 1958); Lord Campion, ed., *Parliament: A Survey* (London, 1952); Byrum C. Carter, *The Office of Prime Minister* (Princeton, 1956); A. H. Dodd, *The Growth of Responsible Government from James I to Victoria* (London, 1956); Strathern Gordon, *The British Parliament* (4th ed., New York, 1952); Sir Courtenay Ilbert, *Parliament: Its History, Constitution and Practice* (3rd ed. rev., by Sir Cecil Carr, London, 1950); Sir Ivor Jennings, *Cabinet Government* (3rd ed., Cambridge, 1959) and *Parliament* (2nd ed., Cambridge, 1957); A. B. Keith, *The British Cabinet System* (2nd ed., by H. N. Gibbs, London, 1952); Betty Kemp, *King and Commons, 1660–1832* (London, 1957); Harold J. Laski, *Parliamentary Government in England* (New York, 1938); K. R. Mackenzie, *The English Parliament* (Harmondsworth, 1950); Sir Thomas Erskine May, *Treatise on the Law, Privileges, Procedure and Usage of Parliament* (16th ed., London, 1957); C. H. McIlwain, *The High Court of Parliament and Its Supremacy* (New Haven, 1910); Herbert Morrison, *Government and Parliament: A Survey from the Inside* (London, 1954); A. F. Pollard, *The Evolution of Parliament* (2nd ed., London, 1926); Edward Porritt, *The Unreformed House of Commons; Parliamentary Representation before 1832* (Cambridge, 1903); Eric Taylor, *The House of Commons at Work* (Harmondsworth, 1951); and Kenneth C. Wheare, *Government by Committee* (Oxford, 1955). See also Christopher Hollis, *The British Statute Book* (London, 1957).

Administration and Civil Service.   To the increasing number of studies of early English administration the following few titles will provide an introduction and further references: S. B. Chrimes, *An Introduction to the Administrative History of Medieval England* (Oxford, 1952); the series published by the Medieval Academy of America, *The English Government at Work;* and T. F. Tout, *Chapters in the Administrative History of Medieval England* (Manchester, 1920–33), 6 vols. A volume meeting a long-felt need is D. N. Chester, ed., *The Organization of British Central Government, 1914–1956* (London, 1957); see also W. J. M. Mackenzie and J. W. Grove, *Central Administration in Britain* (London, 1957). Sir Frank Newsam,

The Home Office (London, 1954); Sir David Milne, *The Scottish Office* (Oxford, 1958); Lord Strang, *The Foreign Office* (London, 1955); Sir Charles Jeffries, *The Colonial Office* (London, 1956); and Sir Harold Emmerson, *The Ministry of Works* (London, 1957) are volumes of the New Whitehall Series. Works on the civil service include: Sir Edward Bridges, *Portrait of a Profession: The Civil Service Tradition* (Cambridge, 1950) and *Treasury Control* (London, 1950); T. A. Critchley, *The Civil Service Today* (London, 1951); Herman Finer, *The British Civil Service* (rev. ed., London, 1937); E. N. Gladden, *The Civil Service: Its Problems and Future* (2nd ed., London, 1948); R. K. Kelsall, *Higher Civil Servants in Britain: from 1870 to the Present Day* (London, 1955); Bosworth Monck, *How the Civil Service Works* (London, 1952); and W. A. Robson, ed., *The Civil Service in Britain and France* (New York, 1956). Increasing executive power has raised many legal questions that are treated in Gordon Hewart, *The New Despotism* (new ed., London, 1945); W. A. Robson, *Justice and Administrative Law* (3rd ed., London, 1951); and B. Schwartz, *Law and the Executive in Britain* (New York, 1949). Of recent investigations, special mention should be made of *Report of the Committee on Administrative Tribunals and Enquiries* (Cmd. 218, July, 1957).

Law and Justice. English legal history is thoroughly treated in W. S. Holdsworth, *A History of English Law* (London, 1903–38), 12 vols.; and F. Pollock and F. W. Maitland, *The History of English Law before the Time of Edward I* (2nd ed., repr., Cambridge, 1923), 2 vols.; to be mentioned also is Edward Jenks, *A Short History of English Law* (5th ed., London, 1938). Legal problems and recent developments are discussed in W. Friedmann, *Law and Social Change in Contemporary Britain* (London, 1951); Lord MacDermott, *Protection from Power under English Law* (London, 1957). Judicial procedure and organization are dealt with in F. T. Giles, *The Criminal Law* (Harmondsworth, 1954); H. G. Hanbury, *English Courts of Law* (2nd ed., New York, 1953); R. M. Jackson, *The Machinery of Justice in England* (2nd ed., New York, 1953); and C. Perry Patterson, *The Administration of Justice in Great Britain* (Austin, 1936).

Local Government. In addition to the historical work of Sidney and Beatrice Webb, *English Local Government* (London, 1906–29), 9 vols., the following may be mentioned: C. Barratt, *Your Local Authority* (2nd ed., London, 1949); G. D. H. Cole, *Local and Regional Government* (London, 1947); Herman Finer, *English Local Government* (4th ed. rev., London, 1950); E. L. Hasluck, *Local Government in England* (2nd ed., Cambridge, 1948); W. E. Jackson, *The Structure of Local Government in England and Wales* (London, 1949); P. G. Richards, *Delegation in Local Government: County to District Councils* (London, 1956); W. A. Robson, *The Development of Local Government* (3rd ed., London, 1954); K. B. Smellie, *A History of Local Government* (London, 1946); J. H. Warren, *The English Local Government System* (3rd ed., London, 1953).

The "Welfare State." The following short list of titles will provide an introduction to the many aspects of Britain's welfare state: Samuel H. Beer, *Treasury Control: The Co-ordination of Financial and Economic Policy in Great Britain* (New York, 1956); Robert A. Brady, *Crisis in Britain* (Berkeley, 1950); D. N. Chester, *The Nationalised Industries* (2nd ed. rev., London, 1951); Hugh Clegg, *Labour in Nationalised Industry* (London, 1950); G. D. H. Cole, *An Introduction to Trade Unionism* (London, 1953); S. J. Curtis, *History of Education in Great Britain* (3rd ed., London, 1953); J. E. Gerald, *The British Press under Government Economic Controls* (Minneapolis, 1956); Charles M. Haar, *Land Planning in a Free Society. A Study of the British Town and Country Planning Act* (Cambridge, 1951); William W. Haynes, *Nationalization in Practice: The British Coal Industry* (Boston, 1953); Ben W. Lewis, *British Planning and Nationalization* (New York, 1952); David C. Marsh, *National Insurance and Assistance in Great Britain* (London, 1951); J. P. Martin, *The Social Aspects of Prescribing* (London, 1957); Barton Paulu, *British Broadcasting* (Minneapolis, 1956); H. E. Raynes, *Social Security in Britain: A History* (London, 1957); W. A. Robson, ed., *Problems of Nationalised Industry* (New York, 1952); A. A. Rogow, *The Labour Government and British*

Industry, 1945–51 (Oxford, 1955); Sir James Stirling Ross, *The National Health Service in Great Britain* (Oxford, 1952); George Watson, ed., *The Unservile State* (New York, 1957); and Francis Williams, *Socialist Britain* (New York, 1949). Also to be mentioned are H. A. Clegg and T. E. Chester, *Wage Policy and the Health Service* (Oxford, 1957); Harry H. Eckstein, *The English Health Service* (Cambridge, 1938); and R. Kelf-Cohen, *Nationalisation in Britain* (New York, 1958).

Political Thought. The contributions of English philosophers to political thought and theory are, of course, treated in general works on political theory. A short list of volumes dealing with various phases of English political thought would include the following: J. W. Allen, *English Political Thought, 1603–1660* (London, 1938); Sir Ernest Barker, *Political Thought in England, 1848 to 1914* (2nd ed. rev., London, 1947); Max Beer, *A History of British Socialism* (London, 1919–20), 2 vols.; Crane Brinton, *English Political Thought in the Nineteenth Century* (London, 1933); Ivor Brown, *English Political Theory* (London, 1920); G. P. Gooch, *English Democratic Ideas in the Seventeenth Century* (2nd ed., Cambridge, 1927); G. P. Gooch, *Political Thought in England from Bacon to Halifax* (London, 1937); H. J. Laski, *Political Thought in England from Locke to Bentham* (London, 1920); Sir Leslie Stephen, *History of English Thought in the Eighteenth Century* (2nd ed., London, 1881), 2 vols.

Newspapers and Periodicals. Useful newspapers are *The Times* (independent conservative), *Manchester Guardian* (liberal), *Daily Herald* (labour) and the Sunday *Observer* (independent). Among British periodicals the *Economist, Contemporary Review, New Statesman and Nation,* and *Spectator* may be mentioned. Scholarly journals include the *Political Quarterly, Political Studies, Parliamentary Affairs, Public Administration, Public Law,* and *International Affairs.* There are several indexes that will serve as guides to the rich periodical literature on British government; these include the *International Index to Periodicals, Bulletin of the Public Affairs Information Service, Readers' Guide to Periodical Literature,* the bibliographical section of the *American Political Science Review,* the *United Nations Monthly List of Selected Articles,* and the *Index to Legal Periodicals.*

II. THE BRITISH COMMONWEALTH

From the extensive literature on this subject only a small number of works is here selected. Brief and acute interpretations written from somewhat different points of view and published since the conclusion of World War II are Nicholas Mansergh, *The Commonwealth and the Nations* (London, 1948); H. V. Hodson, *Twentieth Century Empire* (London, 1948); Frank H. Underhill, *The British Commonwealth, An Experiment in Co-operation among Nations* (Durham, N.C., 1956). Important is K. C. Wheare, *The Statute of Westminster and Dominion Status* (5th ed., Oxford, 1953). Invaluable are the three volumes by Professor W. K. Hancock: *Survey of British Commonwealth Affairs*—Vol. I, *Problems of Nationality, 1918–1936* (London, 1937); Vol. II, Part 1, *Problems of Economic Policy, 1918–1939* (London, 1940); Vol. II, Part 2, *Problems of Economic Policy, 1918–1939* (London, 1942). Equally valuable is Nicholas Mansergh, *Survey of British Commonwealth Affairs, Problems of External Policy, 1931–1939* (London, 1952), and *Documents and Speeches on British Commonwealth Affairs, 1931–1952* (London, 1953), 2 vols. Studies on the history of constitutional law in the Commonwealth are the many volumes by the late Professor Berriedale Keith, published within the three decades 1909–39. The latest is *Dominions as Sovereign States* (London, 1938). Useful for introduction and documents is R. M. Dawson, ed., *The Development of Dominion Status* (London, 1937). Also of note is Gwendolen Carter, *The British Commonwealth and International Security, 1919–39* (Toronto, 1947). A work published during World War II has some sections of interest, W. Y. Elliott and H. D. Hall, eds., *The British Commonwealth at War* (New York, 1943). A brief but interesting essay is that by Sir Ernest Barker, *Ideas and Ideals of the British Empire* (Cambridge, 1941), and a companion essay, less comprehensive, is C. E. Carrington, *An Exposition of Empire* (Cambridge, 1947). Very useful for the constitutional documents is W. I. Jennings and C. M. Young, *Constitutional Laws of the Commonwealth* (2nd ed., Oxford, 1952).

A comparative study of political institutions in the dominions, with special reference to the interplay of history and geography and with a select bibliography is Alexander Brady, *Democracy in the Dominions* (3rd ed., Toronto, 1958). A recent volume worthy of mention is J. D. Miller, *The Commonwealth in the World* (Cambridge, Mass., 1958). Significant studies on political life in the individual dominions are: R. M. Dawson, *The Government of Canada* (2nd ed., Toronto, 1954); C. Hartley Grattan, ed., *Australia* (Berkeley, 1947); L. F. Crisp, *The Parliamentary Government of the Commonwealth of Australia* (New York, 1949), and *The Australian Federal Labour Party, 1901–1951* (New York, 1955); W. K. Hancock, *Australia* (London, 1930); J. L. Robson, ed., *New Zealand* (London, 1954); Leslie Lipson, *The Politics of Equality: New Zealand's Adventures in Democracy* (Chicago, 1948); Horace Belshaw, ed., *New Zealand* (Berkeley, 1947); Jan H. Hofmeyr, *South Africa* (rev. ed., London, 1952); Michael Roberts and A. E. G. Trollip, *The South African Opposition, 1939–45* (London, 1947); Ellen Hellmann, ed., *Handbook on Race Relations in South Africa* (London, 1949); Gwendolyn M. Carter, *The Politics of Inequality: South Africa Since 1948* (New York, 1958); and R. F. A. Hoernlé, *South African Native Policy and the Liberal Spirit* (Cape Town, 1939). The last-mentioned volume is perhaps the most penetrating and provocative study among the many on South Africa's racial issues. Some studies have appeared on the institutions and politics of the new Asian states, among which may be cited: Percival Spear, *India, Pakistan, and the West* (London, 1949); L. S. S. O'Malley, ed., *Modern India and the West* (London, 1941); W. H. Morris-Jones, *Parliament in India* (London, 1957); Keith Callard, *Pakistan* (London, 1957). Of special interest are the writings of Sir Ivor Jennings: *The Commonwealth in Asia* (Oxford, 1951), *The Constitution of Ceylon* (2nd ed., Oxford, 1951) and *Some Characteristics of the Indian Constitution* (London, 1953). K. C. Wheare, *Federal Government* (3rd ed., London, 1953), provides a useful general survey.

Selected Bibliography

PART TWO

FRANCE

———◆———

by Gordon Wright

CHAPTER

8

THE HERITAGE OF
CONTEMPORARY FRANCE

1. THE DEMOCRATIC TRADITION

Ideals and Institutions.   For almost a century past the public buildings of France have borne on their façades the motto "Liberty, Equality, Fraternity." No triad could summarize more succinctly the ideals held by a majority of Frenchmen. The democratic tradition is both old and deep in France; it goes beyond forms into the realm of spirit. Most Frenchmen are proud that their forebears were among the pioneers of democratic theory; they are proud of the world-wide impact of their revolution of 1789, with its principles enshrined in the classic Declaration of the Rights of Man. There exists a profound and firm conviction—a democratic conviction, in its better sense—that the ideals and interests of Frenchmen can never conflict with the true ideals and interests of humanity as a whole.

In such a nation it might seem that the problem of government would be relatively simple, and that the institutional forms of democracy would be both efficient and stable. Yet modern France has gained an almost legendary reputation for political instability and ineffectiveness. The reasons for this incongruous situation are extremely complex and controversial, but they must be examined if the character of the contemporary political system is to be understood.

Antidemocratic Forces.   One obvious determining factor is that some Frenchmen have never accepted the democratic tradition. From 1789 to the present day a minority has steadily denied the validity of the revolutionary principles and has sought to return to the principles and institutions of the old regime. This antidemocratic minority has never formed a solid monolithic bloc, except in the negative sense that all antidemocrats have rejected government by the people. In fact one powerful strain within the French antidemocratic tradition is the pseudodemocratic

189

Bonapartist strain, which claims to rest its support upon the plebiscitary will of the whole people and which takes the position that no body such as a parliament can stand between the people and the man who somehow embodies their will. This theory, especially as it was applied by Napoleon III, has been described as "authoritarian democracy." It would seem more accurate, however, to classify Bonapartism as a kind of protofascism with a peculiarly French flavor.

The persistence of this antidemocratic current has led many observers to describe modern French history as a simple struggle between two irreconcilable groups—authoritarian France versus democratic France, with first one and then the other in control. This thesis would suggest that every dispute France has known in the last two centuries is fundamentally the same dispute. It is buttressed by studies of electoral behavior in selected districts, tending to show that from 1848 to the present the percentages of votes cast for candidates of the right and candidates of the left have been almost constant. But the thesis is an oversimplification, whose partial truth obscures the more complex whole truth. At critical moments all Frenchmen of antidemocratic persuasion have not always stood together, and even less have all Frenchmen in the democratic tradition formed a solid phalanx. At most one can say that the existence of the antidemocratic minority has constantly complicated the problem of operating democratic institutions. But that minority would have been impotent if the partisans of liberty, equality, and fraternity had been united as to the precise meaning of their ideals or the manner of translating them into practice.

Inside Democracy. One is led, therefore, to a closer examination of the democratic tradition in France, with a view to analyzing its content and its internal weaknesses. A modern scholar has remarked that, if democratic government is to flourish, two prior conditions must be fulfilled. The first condition is psychological in character: there must be a widely held popular vision of the most desirable type of society, which will give the greatest degree of freedom and happiness to its citizens. The second condition is sociological in character: there must be a certain balance between the forces of cohesion and the forces of individualism in the society concerned. On both these counts French democracy has fallen somewhat short of success. The sociological aspect will be discussed in a later chapter; the psychological aspect may properly be considered here.

The aims of French democrats in the eighteenth century were, like those of virtually all early democratic theorists, individualistic. They were agreed in their antagonism to arbitrary or oligarchical government and they wished to substitute government by the people. But their very slogan—"Liberty, Equality, Fraternity"—contained an almost irreconcilable contradiction which they either failed to recognize or sought to by-pass. Once in power, should democrats aim at liberty or at equality as the fundamental good? If liberty were to be the main end of government, then the central purpose of democrats should be to set limits upon governmental authority, to make government negative or weak. But if equality were to be the highest value, then positive governmental action

might be essential as a leveling force to keep certain individuals or groups
from oppressing weaker individuals.

Liberty versus Equality Since 1789.   This split was already present
at the time of the great revolution and was reflected in the contradictory
doctrines of Montesquieu and Rousseau. For Montesquieu and his
followers liberty could be assured only by dissipating governmental
authority through a separation of powers, a system of checks and
balances, a considerable grant of local self-government. For the disciples
of Rousseau power could not be dissipated in such fashion but must rest
uninhibited in the sovereign majority. The partisans of liberty aimed to
"render government as nearly powerless as is compatible with the most
urgent dictates of associated activity," even at the risk of permitting such
evils as social inequality or injustice. The partisans of equality aimed to
wipe out social (and perhaps economic) inequality, even if they had to
ride roughshod over the rights and desires of minority groups.

Throughout the nineteenth century this dichotomy within the democratic tradition became more intense. Political thinkers like Benjamin
Constant and Alexis de Tocqueville carried on the liberal tradition.
De Tocqueville, reflecting on the American experience with democracy,
remarked: "Men desired to be free in order to be able to make themselves equal, and, in proportion as equality established itself with the aid
of liberty, it made liberty more difficult of attainment." In De Tocqueville's thinking there was, perhaps, an anticipatory fear of one perverted
offshoot of democracy, twentieth-century totalitarianism. On the other
hand, many French democrats were impatient with De Tocqueville's fears
and argued that government ought to be made a positive agency through
which the majority might achieve its urgent needs. On occasion the split
became so critical as to produce bloodshed—for example, during the
June Days of 1848.

Libertarian Predominance.   It was the partisans of liberty who
dominated the democratic current almost constantly from 1789 through
the nineteenth century. Their greatest manifesto was the Declaration of
the Rights of Man, which stated in classic phraseology the rights of the
individual against an arbitrary, despotic state. The later declaration of
rights of 1793, which incorporated some of Rousseau's equalitarian ideas,
was quickly forgotten after the fall of Robespierre. During the nineteenth
century economic factors helped to keep the libertarians more powerful
than the disciples of Rousseau, for their leadership came in considerable
part from the well-to-do bourgeoisie. Besides, they could depend on a
kind of passive support from the peasantry. Perhaps the liberal position
also harmonized with popular mores and especially with the spirit of
individualism that is so widespread among modern Frenchmen. Why that
spirit should be peculiarly strong in France is difficult to explain, but
its prevalence is beyond doubt. From the great revolution onward individualism took on, in the phrase of one Frenchman, an "aggressive and
doctrinaire" quality. The effect was to make Frenchmen less governable
animals than their more compliant and conformist English neighbors and

THE FRENCH COMMUNITY OF NATIONS 1959

New African Republics in the Community
Created by Acceptance of the New Constitution
in the Referendum of September 28, 1958 (opposite)

Areas voting for independence and membership in the Community

Areas approaching self-government

Guinea was the only area electing independence outside the Community

FRANCE

CORSICA

ASIA

AFRICA
(See insert below)

COMORO IS.

INDIAN OCEAN

RÉUNION I.

AUSTRALIA

MOROCCO

TUNISIA

ALGERIA
(METROPOLITAN
FRANCE)

LIBYA

EGYPT

RIO DE ORO

ISLAMIC
REPUBLIC OF
MAURITANIA

SOUDANESE
REPUBLIC

NIGER
REPUBLIC

CHAD
REPUBLIC

SUDAN

FRENCH SOMALILAND

BRITISH SOMALILAND

REP. OF
SENEGAL

GAMBIA
PORT. GUINEA

GUINEA

VOLTAIC
REP.

NIGERIA

SIERRA
LEONE

LIBERIA

IVORY COAST
REPUBLIC

GHANA
TOGO
DAHOMEY REP.
SPANISH GUINEA

GABONESE REPUBLIC

REPUBLIC OF CONGO

CAMER-
OON

CENTRAL
AFRICAN
REPUBLIC

ETHIOPIA

SOMALIA

UGANDA
KENYA

BELGIAN
CONGO

TANGAN
YIKA

ZANZIBAR

ANGOLA
(PORT)

FED. OF RHODESIA
AND
NYASALAND

MOZAMBIQUE
(PORT)

SOUTH WEST
AFRICA

BECHUANA
-LAND

MALGACHE
REPUBLIC
(MADAGASCAR)

SOUTH
AFRICA

SWAZILAND

BASUTOLAND

to encourage that *incivisme,* or lack of civic spirit, that so many contemporary Frenchmen deplore. This libertarian individualism was perhaps best exemplified in the formula of the philosopher Alain: "Obey, but resist—there is the whole secret. Anything which destroys obedience is anarchy, anything which destroys resistance is tyranny." Or again, in Alain's comment on the white wall posters that are reserved for official use: "One must die for what is inscribed on the white posters; but beyond that, one owes them absolutely nothing." With the libertarian ideal dominant, equality continued to receive lip service but not much more. As Alain ironically remarked, the French were willing to let inequality exist, provided that the principle of equality be loudly proclaimed.

Equalitarian Persistence. Nevertheless the equalitarian faction made steady gains in size and strength during the first half of the nineteenth century, until by 1848 the doctrines of Rousseau tended to be equated with the idea of a republican form of government. The libertarians, on the other hand, usually preferred the institutions of constitutional monarchy. But the revolutionary year 1848 complicated matters. The equalitarians, beaten by both votes and violence, were pushed into the background once more. On top of that defeat came the experience of Napoleon III's authoritarian regime, which exerted a deep influence on the French democratic tradition. The emperor crushed liberty but insisted that he loved equality; by a kind of emotional reaction many French democrats swung more strongly than ever to the libertarian ideal as the highest good. This reaction helped to shape the character of the Third Republic and to make it an essentially negative instrument of government. Not until the twentieth century did the equalitarian ideal again threaten libertarian dominance within the democratic current. And by that time the conflict was made far more complex by the impact of two new factors: industrialization and Marxian ideology.

New Complications. The French Marxists became the principal heirs of the equalitarian tradition of Rousseau and Robespierre, with its corollary that the state machinery should be a positive instrument in the hands of the sovereign majority. But French Marxists then proceeded to split down the middle over how that positive instrument should be won and in what spirit it should be used. Many of them hesitated to carry their doctrine to its logical extreme, which might have involved a kind of totalitarian despotism by the majority over all minority groups; they preferred to seek a compromise between liberty and equality. They hesitated, too, to accept the Leninist view that a faction claiming to represent the majority may properly perpetuate itself in power by any methods. As the split within Marxism became deeper, even the meaning of the term "democratic" itself showed signs of becoming more controversial than ever before.

To make matters still more complex, the heirs of the libertarian tradition became divided and confused by the impact of industrialism, with all of its socioeconomic problems. Some of them still clung to their nineteenth-century ideal that the freedom of the individual was the supreme good, and that government should be so checked and balanced that no man or group could infringe upon that freedom. But others, disturbed at the way their institutions failed to come to grips with twentieth-century problems, began to seek some kind of positive state action that would not involve a threat to the rights of minorities or individuals. Their inclination was to favor strengthening the executive, which they sincerely believed to be a step toward positive government; yet they could not quite break away from the libertarian safeguard furnished by the separation-of-powers principle. Surrounded by a whole series of real or potential dangers—inefficient government, authoritarian rule, the tyranny of a majority—they groped for a middle solution without being quite sure that such a solution was possible.

Democracy, for What?   Few great nations possess so strong a democratic tradition as France; yet few nations have found it so difficult to solve the eternal problems of politics—to reconcile authority with liberty, the rule of law with individual freedom, efficiency with popular control. It would seem that the cause lies not so much in democracy's enemies in France as in democracy's internal conflicts. What kind of democracy? In what spirit? To what ends? Perhaps that issue is a universal one, but that it underlies the problem of government in contemporary France can hardly be doubted.

2. THE REPUBLICAN EXPERIENCE (1875–1940)

Present and Past.   When France emerged from World War II, almost every Frenchman took for granted that the republic ought to be restored. The character of that republic was, however, open to dispute, for France had already known three different regimes by that name. Any nation that possesses so rich a store of experience with various kinds of republican institutions will naturally try to profit by its experience. In constructing the Fourth Republic, French politicians were deeply influenced by the character of the system they had known before 1940 and that had served their fathers and grandfathers as well. By a curious irony they sought to sweep the Third Republic completely into the discard, yet they ended by establishing a regime strongly reminiscent of the old one.

Dual Heritage.   Someone has said that the Third Republic possessed two constitutions—one parliamentary, the other Napoleonic. Beneath the formal constitutional structure of 1875 there persisted the elaborate administrative mechanism which Napoleon I had built and bequeathed to the regimes that followed him. When the Third Republic was founded, neither of these "constitutions" seemed to be in harmony with republican ideals or traditional republican institutions. Before 1875 the world had never seen a parliamentary republic, nor had there ever been a republic with so highly centralized an administrative machine as that which the Third Republic inherited. Yet the republicans gradually

adapted themselves to both the parliamentary structure and the Napoleonic administration; and in 1946 they perpetuated both aspects in the
Fourth Republic.

Administrative Structure.   Napoleon's system was a reversion to
the centralizing trend that had marked the growth of the old monarchy in
France. The revolutionary leaders of 1789 had temporarily reversed
that trend by introducing a considerable degree of local self-government.
Their policy was inspired mainly by the libertarian desire to check the
government by scattering authority. However, they feared to hand over
these new local powers to the old provinces, with their tradition of
particularism; the result might be the disintegration of the nation or a
strengthening of the feudal element in French society. As a safeguard,
therefore, they redrew the political map of France. In place of the
historic provinces, such as Normandy or Anjou, they constructed an
artificial scheme of eighty-odd "departments" of roughly equal size, sub-
divided in turn into *arrondissements,* cantons, and communes. Within
each unit a locally elected council was granted extensive powers.
    Napoleon accepted the system of departments, but he brought them
under his direct control by assigning a centrally appointed prefect to
each one, with a subprefect in each *arrondissement.* Local self-government was virtually extinguished. This administrative system endured
with only minor changes through the various upheavals of the nineteenth century and emerged intact in the Third Republic. During the
first decade after 1875 republicans introduced a whole series of proposals for returning to the decentralized policy of 1789; but in the end
they limited themselves to granting to the communes the right to elect
their own mayors. Some minor governmental functions were also turned
over to the locally elected councils of the communes and the departments, although the prefect's authority continued to be overshadowing.
Thus Napoleon's administrative centralization became "republicanized."

Parliamentary System.   Meanwhile the parliamentary system was
also taking root. Before 1875 that system had been the ideal of constitutional monarchists. A quasi-parliamentary system had already existed in France during the period 1814–48, although, technically speaking, the cabinet had never come to be responsible to Parliament during
those years. British experience, too, encouraged French monarchists to
favor a parliamentary regime. It was precisely because such a regime
was monarchical in flavor that the assembly of 1875 adopted it. The
monarchists in the assembly were joined by a small group of conservative republican deputies who belonged to the libertarian school of
thought and who felt that the constitution of 1875 distributed power
sufficiently to check any kind of tyranny, whether of a man or of a
majority. True, the separation-of-powers principle was not specifically
written into the constitution, but the existence of a strong, indirectly
elected upper house and of a potentially influential presidency satisfied
these exponents of negative government. The conservative republicans

then swung into alliance with the left wing of the assembly to attach the republican label to the new regime.

Most French republicans accepted the parliamentary system only with a view to getting control of it in order to abolish it. They clung to the tradition of the First Republic, which had to some degree institutionalized the equalitarian concepts of Rousseau. Both in 1793 and in 1848 republicans had sought to concentrate power in a one-house legislature, selected directly by universal suffrage. In 1848, however, the system had been "falsified" against their will by the establishment of a powerful presidency, chosen by direct election for a fixed term. This extreme form of separation of powers had been resisted by most republicans in 1848; and its consequence—dictatorship through a *coup d'état* in 1851—reinforced their convictions. A single chamber, with an executive committee or cabinet subject to its constant control, was the republican goal in 1875. The republicans' immediate aim, therefore, was to abolish both the Senate and the presidency.

Process of Adaptation.   In the process of winning control of the Third Republic, however, a majority of republicans became reconciled to the system as it stood. Their conversion was partly due to modifications in the functioning of the regime between 1875 and 1884. The chief mechanical change was a weakening of the executive and a relative strengthening of the legislative branch, which brought the system more into line with republican tradition. This change was brought about by President MacMahon's ill-considered decision, in May, 1877, to dissolve the Chamber of Deputies (with the consent of the compliant, monarchist-dominated Senate). MacMahon's monarchist supporters were defeated in the election that followed, and shortly afterward the disgruntled president resigned his office, remarking that he had "had enough toads to swallow." The republicans promptly took over the presidency, and their representative, Jules Grévy, took care to establish all possible precedents to make the office weak. But the principal long-term result of the MacMahon incident was to deprive the French executive of its power to dissolve the Chamber of Deputies. That power remained in the constitution, but no cabinet dared ask a president to use it for fear of being called antirepublican, or for fear that the Senate would refuse to authorize dissolution. The Senate, meanwhile, was gradually taken over by the republicans, who changed its electoral system in 1884 in order to consolidate their control. With that amendment the last antirepublican stronghold in the government was destroyed.

But it was not only these mechanical changes that reconciled republicans to the parliamentary regime. Their conversion was psychological as well. In 1875 many of them had been strongly attracted—at least in theory—by the equalitarian tradition of Rousseau. During the next decade the libertarian ideal tended gradually to push equalitarianism into the background. Most of the republican leaders of that epoch represented bourgeois or peasant interests, and neither group had any practical reason to desire a strong, untrammeled mechanism of government. On the contrary, they had material interests they wished to protect, and the libertarian ideal was attractive to such men, provided that the government gave them a minimum of protection. The negative character of the Third Republic, its distribution of power through an undeclared system of checks and balances, suited them well enough. After 1880 one segment of republican leaders, labeling themselves Opportunists (and, later, Moderates), rallied openly to the Third Republic as it stood. The other segment, whose members came to be called Radicals, still clung to the old ideal and fulminated against the presidency and the Senate, but their complaints became increasingly *pro forma* in nature. Most republicans gave little more than lip service to equalitarianism. Their attitude is perhaps best characterized by a legendary anecdote about President Grévy. On his official visit to the annual art show Grévy was allegedly told: "No extraordinary paintings this year, but a good average." "A good average!" cried the president. "That's just what a democracy ought to have." It was the newborn socialist movement that took over the equalitarian tradition of powerful, positive government in the hands of the majority.

Nineteenth-Century Achievements. Within this negative framework of the Third Republic, Frenchmen gradually worked out some of the more serious problems of the nineteenth century. In 1882 they struck at church influence in education by establishing a whole hierarchy of public schools completely divorced from religious teaching or control. This measure was the first victory of the anticlerical sentiment that pervaded republican thought in France. Church schools continued to exist and to attract a considerable proportion of French children; but the nationwide hostility between clericals and anticlericals reached a climax of intensity, with the primary-school teachers—"the black hussars of the republic"—leading the anticlerical forces. After the bloodless civil war called the Dreyfus Affair, in which many church officials were unnecessarily active, the republicans proceeded to expel certain religious congregations from the country, and finally, in 1905, to break the tie between church and state by destroying the Concordat of 1801. Thereafter the clerical issue gradually ceased to dominate French thinking, and by 1940 it began to seem a mere emotional remnant of a bygone era.

While the republicans were pushing the church out of its special position in the state, they were also engaged in taking over control of the higher levels of the army and the bureaucracy, both of which were heavily staffed by monarchists for some years after 1875. Long before 1914 the conversion was accomplished, although some Frenchmen complained that the change was never complete in the army, and that the higher civil service posts had fallen to a new elite drawn from a very narrow social stratum, the upper bourgeoisie.

Another change was to give the press a new status of unprecedented freedom by a law of 1881. So powerful did the newspapers become during subsequent decades that the essayist Robert de Jouvenel ironically called the press the fourth branch of the government, on a par with the executive, legislative, and judicial branches. But power and freedom did not produce in the French press any adequate sense of public responsibility. Its tone was scurrilous in the extreme, so lax were the libel laws. Furthermore, its character was both corrupt and strongly slanted; almost every newspaper sought to persuade rather than to inform its readers. That subsidies were accepted and even solicited from private interests, from foreign embassies, and from the French government itself was generally known. De Jouvenel wrote bitterly: "Newspapers are called 'governmental' when they are servile; they are called 'oppositionist' when they are flirting with the authorities. As soon as the opinions of a newspaper begin to count for something, that newspaper ceases to have any opinions." Yet so strong was the libertarian ideal that little effort was made to clean up these evils. Even a socialist like Léon Blum wrote in 1934: "Liberty above all! I would rather have a perverted press than a press in chains." Blum's Popular Front cabinet in 1936 did push through the Chamber a bill designed to control libel and corruption in the press, but it was buried in the Senate. Thus the problem was passed on to the new Fourth Republic.

Still another achievement of the Third Republic was the rebuilding of a colonial empire. France already possessed a few tiny remnants of its seventeenth-century empire, plus Algeria and Cochin China, which were added between 1815 and 1870. From 1880 onward, under the leadership of the republican politician Jules Ferry, and through the agency of bored army officers looking for excitement, France entered the imperialist race in earnest, gathering in by 1914 the second-largest empire of any power. Few parts of the empire, however, were suitable for colonization, and few Frenchmen were attracted by the prospect of pioneering in the tropics or the desert. Most of the colonies were primitive areas that required heavy investment for both social services and economic development. But only a small fraction of France's available investment capital went into the empire; before 1914 far more was poured into Russia alone, and after 1918 the capital resources of France were simply inadequate. Some halting steps were taken after 1930 under the new slogan *mise en valeur* (i.e., economic development), but, all in all, progress to 1940 was meager. Commercially the colonies were bound closely to the mother country; they were either completely or partially assimilated into the French tariff system. Politically few of the colonies possessed any appreciable degree of self-government; centralization was the rule here, as in trade policy. Culturally the normal ideal was to "assimilate" the overseas natives, or at least a selected elite overseas, and to convert them, through proper education, into Frenchmen. Here again the Third Republic bequeathed to its successor a whole complex of problems it had not even recognized very clearly.

Problem of Instability.   It is evident that in a number of ways the Third Republic muddled along in a generally creative and constructive direction. Above all it survived, which was more than any preceding regime during the past century had been able to do. Its negative character, in the circumstances of the late nineteenth century, was perhaps a virtue, for European and world conditions in that era were such as to allow a fair degree of stability, prosperity, and expansion without government intervention. By virtue of its negative character it served also as the regime that divided Frenchmen least and that therefore survived by sufferance of all parties. It was only after the turn of the century, and still more after 1918, that the rise of new economic and social issues presented the state with a new kind of challenge—a challenge which, in the opinion of a growing number of Frenchmen, could not be met through a negative instrument of government.

But even before this challenge began to force itself on French minds, some French republicans had become dissatisfied with certain aspects of their regime. Well before 1900 they had begun to criticize the instability of a system that allowed cabinets to last only an average of ten months. This "waltz of cabinets" made any continuity of policy difficult; moreover, it impaired popular respect for the republican regime both at home and abroad. Some republicans were so eager for a stronger and more stable executive that they backed General Boulanger in his ambitious scheme to take power and revise the constitution. But the Boulanger campaign collapsed in melodramatic fashion in 1889, and Frenchmen soon learned that "the brave general" had been collaborating secretly with the monarchists and the Bonapartists. The episode intensified the existing fear that a strong executive implied a threat to the republic. The memory of Boulanger, in addition to that of the two Napoleons, reinforced the libertarian ideal of weak government. After Boulanger the most daring suggestion in republican ranks was that the president of the republic ought to dust off and use his proper constitutional powers, notably the power to dissolve the Chamber with the Senate's consent. Even that change, however, was viewed with suspicion by most republicans. No president dared risk such an experiment, not even Raymond Poincaré or Alexandre Millerand, who were the only first-rank statesmen ever to serve as presidents of the Third Republic.

Significance of Dissolution. Beyond much doubt the atrophy of the dissolution power was a major cause of executive weakness and cabinet instability. Its loss left the cabinet with no effective weapon to discipline the Chamber. The threat of dissolution might have had a sobering effect on impulsive deputies if the fall of the cabinet had involved the possible loss of their own seats. But with four-year terms assured deputies were free to let their prejudices and ambitions guide them in votes of confidence or non-confidence.

The decay of the dissolution power had a second significant effect which likewise contributed to cabinet weakness. It helped to produce a curious party system of variegated, undisciplined, amorphous party groups. The multiparty system would no doubt have existed in some form even if dissolution had survived, for it reflected the individualistic temper of the French, their intense concern for political principles, their indifference to the Anglo-Saxon principle of constructive compromise, and their complex history. Besides, a multiplicity of parties has been the normal state of affairs in continental countries. What was unique in France was the high degree of indiscipline within most parties, the shifting nature of the groups, the practice of jumping party lines. In the last Chamber of Deputies of the Third Republic there were some twenty different groups, and all of those groups except the two Marxian parties and the tiny Popular Democratic fraction regularly split on every important vote. If dissolution had remained a usable weapon in the hands of the executive, party leaders might have been able to keep their followers in line, and the total number of parties might have been reduced somewhat. Even at best the multiparty system weakened the cabinet by making it an uneasy coalition of incompatible groups, any one of which might upset the cabinet by withdrawing from it. But party indiscipline made matters still worse, for even when party leaders wanted to hold a cabinet together some of their followers were apt to bolt in votes of confidence, or desert to the ranks of a rival party, or found a new one of their own.

Electoral Reform Issue. Because the revival of the dissolution power was rejected by most republicans, the problem of party discipline seemed insoluble unless some change could be made in the electoral law. The system that was used throughout the Third Republic (except in 1885, 1919, and 1924) encouraged indiscipline, since it made electoral success depend upon the candidate's personal influence in his district rather than upon his national party label. The *arrondissement* served as the normal electoral district, and one deputy was chosen from each. A politician shrewd enough to keep his fences mended could soon turn his district into an electoral "fief," from which he could scarcely be dislodged even if he ignored party instructions or programs. Candidates almost never could be elected unless they had strong personal connections in the locality; no party could force an outsider on the voters.

Of equal importance was the fact that the system required a runoff election whenever no candidate gained a clear majority in the first day's voting. This arrangement gave middle-of-the-road candidates a noticeable advantage over those of extreme right or left, for the process of horse-trading between the first and second ballots put the center candidate in a favored position. It was this electoral system that contributed much to the rise of the Radical-Socialist Party to a leading position from about 1900 to 1936; and the Radical Party was so undisciplined and decentralized that someone described it as no party at all, but only a state of mind.

Critics of this electoral procedure began to grow more vocal after 1900, with the appearance of the idea of proportional representation. "P.R." was designed by its inventors to give proper representation to minority groups, whose votes were allegedly wasted in a system of majority or plurality election. Most of the exponents of this reform were to be found on the extreme left or right wings. Political self-interest naturally inspired the demand, for the extremist parties were sure to suffer as long as the runoff ballot gave center candidates their peculiar advantage. But the proportionalist scheme also drew support on grounds of principle: first, that justice required representation for minority groups; and second, that party discipline and governmental stability would be strengthened through use of the proportionalist system. These virtues, its sponsors believed, would far offset the two chief drawbacks of proportionalism. These drawbacks were: 1) that it would perpetuate and even perhaps increase the multiplicity of parties; and 2) that it might make viable coalitions more difficult to form because extremist groups would gain strength at the expense of the center. The proportionalist campaign continued sporadically for forty years before it achieved success. In 1939 the Chamber of Deputies voted to adopt proportional representation, but the outbreak of war temporarily robbed the proportionalists of the fruits of their victory. In the Fourth Republic, however, the idea was to reappear more strongly than ever.

Twentieth-Century Challenge. By 1914 the Third Republic was about to enter a new and critical phase. The older issues of the nineteenth century had been for the most part either abandoned or resolved. The regime, however negative and colorless, had outlasted any of its predecessors and had managed better than any other to reconcile the divergent currents in French society and ideology. But new issues were beginning to press themselves upon every industrial nation, and there were many who doubted that these issues could be resolved through a negative-state apparatus. These critics noted that, although Germany and Great Britain were adopting extensive programs of social legislation, France remained a relative paradise of *laissez faire* (except with respect to tariff policy). The old equalitarian tradition of positive state action gained rapidly in the years before 1914, but these issues of domestic policy were suddenly shunted aside by World War I. The war not only postponed a great many problems but intensified those problems by its drain on manpower, its material destruction, and its disastrous effect on the stability of the franc. After the elation of victory had worn off somewhat, Frenchmen began to question the virtues of the Third Republic more seriously than they had ever done in the past.

The collective impact of the old and new problems of the interwar period produced a sharp increase in cabinet instability. Whereas cabinets before 1918 had averaged ten months in duration, those after 1918 lasted only half as long. This instability stemmed in part from the increased fragmentation of party groups in the Chamber and in part from the deepening split between libertarians and equalitarians in the face of pressing socioeconomic issues. As the equalitarian, positive-state ideal spread from the extreme left into the left-center of the political spectrum, the center groups became far more incompatible than ever before, and coalitions became increasingly precarious.

Question of Constitutional Reform. With successive governments bogging down in semi-impotence, the enemies of the parliamentary system grew more vigorous and more vocal. On the right wing authoritarian and fascist groups appeared; on the left the Communists urged the conversion of the republic to a Soviet form. Both right and left claimed to represent true democracy in the sense of unrestricted majority rule over dissident minorities. Between these extremes the libertarian right-center and the equalitarian left-center sought to preserve the parliamentary republic by altering the balance of executive-legislative relations. They differed, however, in diagnosing the republic's ills. By and large the right-center felt that the legislative branch had encroached too much on the powers of the executive, so that the latter possessed merely the shadow of authority. Its aim was to redress the balance in order to strengthen and stabilize the cabinet. Its method was to revive the power of dissolution or to create some mechanical device to limit the Chamber's right to bring down cabinets. In appearance the right-center's desire was vigorous, positive government, but in fact it clung to the libertarian ideal of separation of powers.

The left-center took the opposite position and rejected the doctrine that the executive ought to be free from legislative control. "Ministry and parliament," wrote Léon Blum in 1934, "are in no way two autonomous machines . . . They are two cogs in the same machine whose coordinated movements, whose joint operation, whose isochronal pulsations must work together toward the same end." In fact the left-center contended that the real trouble was the encroachment of the executive upon the legislative branch through the new procedure of decree laws. This procedure, they claimed, falsified democratic processes by transferring legislative decisions to an executive body that acted without public debate. The decree-law expedient was first used in 1926, and again repeatedly from 1930 to 1936, in an effort to cope with the economic-financial crisis. Cabinets were authorized by the Chamber to legislate by decree for a limited period on certain specified matters, with the reservation that the Chamber might later repudiate any such decree laws. On each occasion the grant of authority tended to become somewhat broader and the ex-post-facto control of the Chamber more lax. This was particularly true in 1935, when the Laval cabinet was in office; hundreds of decrees of widely varied character were issued in that period. By resorting to this procedure the Chamber seemed to be confessing its inability to meet the problems of the epoch; a fundamental change in the operation of the parliamentary system was in the making unless the trend were checked.

The left-center, along with its hostility toward decree laws, showed a growing tendency to blame the Senate for the ills of the Third Republic. It alleged that the Senate, elected by a system of indirect suffrage that gave rural areas a heavy advantage, had set itself up as a barrier against vigorous reform measures sponsored by the people's representatives in the lower house. The Senate's frequent practice of burying bills adopted by the Chamber won it the label, "graveyard of laws." In addition the Senate had arrogated to itself the power to overthrow cabinets on rare but critical occasions by rejecting measures the cabinet considered indispensable. The left-center, therefore, insisted that the Senate's wings be clipped in order to allow positive governmental action by the representatives of the majority in the Chamber.

Reform Stalemated. It was the right-center element that came closest to attaining its reform aims. The Stavisky scandal early in 1934 produced a crisis that was resolved only by the appointment of a National Union cabinet under the venerable former president, Gaston Doumergue. Doumergue concluded that it was his mission to shift the balance of authority toward the executive branch, and he proposed to achieve this goal by empowering the premier to dissolve the Chamber freely at any time except during the first year after a general election.

Several lesser infringements upon the Chamber's powers were also included in Doumergue's program, but the whole scheme collapsed when some of his ministers, suspicious of Doumergue's alleged contacts with semi-fascist agitators, resigned. Not long afterward the left-center (Radicals and Socialists) and the extreme left (Communists) joined forces for the first time in a Popular Front coalition, which took power in 1936 and effectively scotched the hopes of the right-center. On the other hand, the Popular Front was neither strong enough nor homogeneous enough to carry through the reform program of the left-center. It was able only to adopt a series of significant social reform measures that were at least a decade overdue and that possibly prevented civil war in France, so intense had social strife become. But the economic reforms that ought to have accompanied these social measures were blocked by the Senate, and the Popular Front shortly disintegrated. When World War II began, the framework and spirit of the Third Republic remained more or less what they had been two decades earlier. Within that framework the balance of social forces and of political power had shifted considerably since 1918. But the prospect of a fundamental change in French political institutions seemed more distant in 1939 than it had for a decade past.

3. THE DESTRUCTION AND RECONSTRUCTION OF THE REPUBLIC (1940–46)

Collapse of 1940. Political systems, whatever their intrinsic merits, rarely survive a military disaster. The Third Republic, a curious blend of merits and demerits, was not the sort of regime to endure when others collapse. The crushing blow struck by the Nazis in May–June, 1940, left Frenchmen dazed and bewildered, but in the midst of that bewilderment they felt almost instinctively that their political regime had been found wanting. When the new premier, Marshal Pétain, called Parliament into session at Vichy on July 9, most of the deputies and senators were ready to accept sweeping constitutional changes. None of them had a precise program of reform, but their inclination was to favor a stronger executive, greater stability, and a curbing of the excessive political maneuvering that had characterized the prewar system.

There were some parliamentarians, however, who hoped to salvage the name as well as part of the framework of the Third Republic. They proposed to suspend the constitution for the duration of the war and to leave the question of reform in abeyance until calmer thinking could prevail. But the machinations of Pierre Laval in the lobbies of Parliament at Vichy brought a more drastic decision to destroy the republic at once. Parliament, in accord with Laval's urging, authorized Pétain to draft a new constitution, with the sole reservation that it be submitted to popular ratification. That act of suicide marked the end of the Third Republic.

Vichy Interlude.   As events turned out, Pétain's constitution was never drafted. The Vichy interlude from 1940 to 1944 contributed little to French governmental ideals or practices; its effect on the founders of the Fourth Republic was mainly negative in that they were inclined to reverse everything Vichy had tried to do. Vichy's barrenness resulted in part from its faulty fundamental premise that Germany would win the war. Once that premise became doubtful, Vichy turned into a phantom rather than the framework for a new order in France. But Vichy was barren also because it represented such a hodgepodge of ideologies. One follower of Pétain later remarked that Vichy had reminded him of a café which bore the sign *"Aux Anciens Romains et aux Nouveaux Cyclistes."* Some of Pétain's advisers, like the monarchist Charles Maurras, leaned toward a French traditionalism that smacked of the *ancien régime.* They sponsored a type of regionalism through a return to the old pre-1789 provinces. Other Vichyites favored varying forms of the modern fascist corporative state. Steps in this direction were the creation of the Peasant Corporation and of a single, state-sponsored Labor Front. To make matters worse, Vichy was an incongruous combination of unscrupulous opportunists and well-meaning idealists. Out of this mélange there never did crystallize any firm ideology or formal governmental structure. Toward the end Pétain and Laval even considered an attempt to resuscitate the Third Republic by calling the parliament of 1940 into session once more.

Aims of the Underground.   Meanwhile an anti-Vichy opposition was gradually appearing, both underground in France and overseas in London. Its ideas on government developed slowly and fitfully over a four-year period and were still somewhat amorphous at the time of the liberation. General Charles de Gaulle, leader of the Free French movement in exile, at first took the cautious line that the constitution of the Third Republic had been destroyed illegally and was therefore still valid. His own personal sympathies, however, certainly did not lie with such a feeble, politician-ridden regime as the Third Republic must have appeared to a man of his authoritarian temper. He was doubtless glad to discover that the underground in France was completely disillusioned with the prewar regime and insisted on the creation of a new, purified republic. In 1942 an informal pact was made between De Gaulle and representatives of the underground; the general was accepted as leader of the entire anti-Vichy movement, in return for which he promised free elections after the liberation to determine the character of the future regime. From that time forward De Gaulle's public statements contained the phrase "Fourth Republic."

As the tide of Allied victory rose steadily, various individuals and groups within the underground began to consider the nature of their future regime. The collapse of 1940 had produced a general revulsion against the "parliamentary excesses" of prewar days, together with an intense desire for more authority and integrity in government. There was even some revival of interest in the American presidential system among young intellectuals in the underground. For the first time since Boulanger the doctrine of a strong executive won converts in left-wing circles; men of the equalitarian tradition were tempted to believe that a powerful president or premier might provide the kind of positive, vigorous state action they had always desired. Well before the liberation, however, most of the leftists had veered away from this dangerous heresy. Rejecting the separation-of-powers principle, they returned to their old ideal of concentrating authority in a one-house legislature. The idea of greater independence for the executive or of a "balance" between cabinet and legislature once more became the special property of center and right-center libertarians.

Communist Program. Early in 1944 the Communist Party brusquely entered this clandestine debate. Its views were sure to carry special weight, for no other party had played so active a role in the underground movement. The bravery and intransigence of its members had almost succeeded in making other Frenchmen forget the party's curious record of "revolutionary defeatism" during the period of Nazi-Soviet collaboration. The Communists were disturbed at the circulation of various draft schemes filled with devices to strengthen the executive, and they asserted that these schemes rested on a false premise. The fault of the Third Republic, they declared, had not been executive weakness and legislative encroachment but exactly the opposite. The Chamber had abdicated its authority through the decree-law procedure, thus permitting unrepresentative cabinets to run the country virtually unchecked. The proper goal, they concluded, would be a constitution vesting all power in a one-house assembly. That assembly would effectively control the cabinet, and the deputies in turn would be constantly controlled by their electors, who should be empowered to recall them at any time if they should neglect their duty or violate a campaign promise. By this statement of policy the Communists seemed to be placing themselves squarely in the equalitarian-democratic tradition of Rousseau and Robespierre.

The Communists' manifesto created a mild sensation in underground circles. For one thing, the party had never before expressed any views on the structure of a bourgeois republic. In prewar days Communists had insisted that their only goal was a Soviet-type democracy and that they were indifferent to the superficial variations in bourgeois political institutions. Furthermore, the Communist attitude blasted the plans of certain center and right-center resistance groups which had hoped that the whole underground might agree on the structure of the future republic. The best that the underground could do was to draw up a general manifesto containing broad political, economic, and social demands, the so-called National Resistance Council Program.

Gaullist Plans.   Meanwhile, in 1943, De Gaulle had moved his headquarters to Algiers, where he prepared plans for the postliberation period. The ordinance that he finally issued provided for a lengthy period of provisional government, during which his own position would approach that of a presidential executive. Only after a year or two of this semi-presidential regime would Frenchmen elect an assembly to draw up a constitution. The Communists openly voiced suspicion that De Gaulle's aim was to implant an American-type presidential system in France. They charged that the general expected the country to grow accustomed to a strong executive and to perpetuate it in the constitution. A few Radical-Socialist politicians, on the other hand, recovered their voices sufficiently to complain that De Gaulle was acting illegally by discarding the Third Republic. Between these two groups of critics De Gaulle moved straight ahead as his conscience dictated. When the liberation was finally complete, he reduced the provisional period of semi-presidential rule to the shortest possible time—little more than a year, in fact. And when the moment for elections arrived, he put the question of a return to the Third Republic squarely up to the voters. Whatever the general's failings, his procedure in restoring republican rule to France was thoroughly democratic.

Gaullist Achievements.   During the interim period from the liberation of Paris (August, 1944) to the election of a Constituent Assembly (October, 1945) France was governed by what was essentially a dictatorship by tacit consent. De Gaulle was a combined president-premier; the cabinet was chosen by him and responsible to him. The only semi-representative organs were the National Resistance Council (a kind of board of directors of the federated underground groups) and the Consultative Assembly (nominated by various resistance groups and party organizations). It was the nearest approach to presidential government that republican France had known since 1848. Had the system proved highly successful in tackling the critical problems of the moment, many Frenchmen might have been inclined to perpetuate some aspects of it in the new constitution. But the problems were far too serious for any man or group of men to solve. Besides, De Gaulle had no real understanding of certain issues, notably the economic ones; his brilliant success as a symbol before 1944 could not be repeated as an active executive official after 1944. Furthermore De Gaulle's scruples or uncertainties led him to postpone as many problems as possible until a responsible government could be chosen.

Yet some decisions had to be taken during that interim year, and their consequences were to be felt well after the De Gaulle period. Wages were raised in an effort to bring them into line with rising price levels; the social-security system was broadened and co-ordinated into a unified whole; elective works councils were set up in all large factories to give labor some voice in the management and control of industry. Cautious steps were taken toward the nationalization of key industries and monopolies, which had figured large in the National Resistance Council's underground program. But De Gaulle's inclination was to move slowly in all these spheres; for example, to nationalize few enterprises except those whose owners had clearly collaborated with the Germans. The general problem of what and how to nationalize he preferred to leave until after elections could be held. Likewise, he moved cautiously with respect to the problem of inflation, avoiding the kinds of measures that Belgium and the Netherlands had adopted to convert their old currency and to restrict excess buying power in a time of scarcity. His hesitation bequeathed to succeeding governments an inflationary condition that weighed heavily on the political institutions of the Fourth Republic and that might have been somewhat alleviated had vigorous measures been taken in 1944.

De Gaulle refrained also from any attempt to shape the character of the Fourth Republic's party system. He refused to lead or sponsor any party himself, as some of his backers had hoped that he might. In fact his policy toward the underground while in exile had encouraged the revival of most of the parties of the Third Republic. Some of these groups, however, had been badly shattered, and their prospects in the new Fourth Republic looked dim. This was notably true of the right-wing groups, such as the Republican Federation and the Democratic Alliance, and of the great left-center party, the Radical-Socialists, which had been the fulcrum of republican politics for forty years. On the left, however, the Communists and Socialists were better organized and were ready to resume operations from the moment of the liberation. Some underground leaders hoped to convert their resistance groups into political parties with a broad center appeal, but the only effective steps in this direction were taken by a group of young Catholics who, in the autumn of 1944, announced the formation of the Popular Republican Movement (*Mouvement Républicain Populaire,* or M.R.P.).

Constitutional Programs.   The leaders of all these parties were so busy with organizational problems that they had little time for the question of France's future political institutions. Only the Communist program was clear-cut and detailed; it demanded that all power be concentrated in a one-house assembly whose members would be subject to recall by the voters. It flatly rejected any system of separation of powers, any effort to give the cabinet some independence of the assembly, any scattering of power through an expansion of local self-government. The Communist program was thoroughly consistent and remained so; it fitted perfectly into the equalitarian tradition of positive majority rule. The M.R.P., on the other hand, took the libertarian line. It sought a balance between the legislative and executive branches through the use of the dissolution power; it favored a distribution of power through the establishment of a two-house legislature and through a sharp expansion of local self-government. Many of the M.R.P. leaders even advocated the creation of an American-type supreme court, with the right to invalidate laws. They also stressed a novel arrangement called a party statute, designed to regulate the organization and ensure the integrity of political parties. Sponsors of the scheme argued that since parties had come to be such vital and direct organs of government they could no longer be treated as ordinary private associations of citizens. The constitution, therefore, should set up safeguards to prevent any party from falling under the control of undemocratic forces or leaders.

The Socialists stood somewhere between their two neighbors, leaning first toward one side, then toward the other. On most fundamental issues their program harmonized with that of the Communists, and placed them in the equalitarian tradition, where they had always been. They insisted on a one-house legislature and held that the executive ought to be an agency closely integrated with the legislative majority rather than an organ balanced against it. Yet they were inclined to favor some of the M.R.P.'s ideas: the party statute, for example, and an expansion of local self-government to bring democracy close to the people. They were even prepared to accept a curious form of dissolution, which André Philip, their leading constitutional expert, called "automatic dissolution." By this device the legislature might overthrow a cabinet at will, but the legislature would be automatically dissolved so that the voters might decide the issues involved. The Socialists did not see dissolution as a club to be wielded by the executive in order to give itself greater authority. Rather, it would be a safety valve to get rid of a legislature that could not agree on a stable coalition government.

Little was heard from the feeble remnants of the Radical and right-wing parties, which took the line that the safest course would be to salvage as much as possible of the prewar regime. Such a policy, they felt, might block the threat of tyranny by a triumphant leftist majority. Men like Édouard Herriot hoped that they might persuade De Gaulle to restore the old constitution and to provide for its revision in due time. In the end De Gaulle agreed only to let the people choose by referendum at the same time they elected a Constituent Assembly in October, 1945. The popular decision was overwhelming; more than 96 per cent of the voters chose to discard the Third Republic and to move toward a new and presumably better regime.

First Constituent Assembly. The Constituent Assembly of 1945 was more heavily weighted toward the left than any other elected body in French history. The Communists and Socialists together won a slight but clear majority, and the new M.R.P., led by progressive Catholics, captured another quarter of the seats. The outcome was in part the consequence of the left's resistance record; in part the outgrowth of the right's political incoherence and lack of leadership; and in part the result of De Gaulle's adoption of proportional representation. All of the victorious parties had urged him to accept proportionalism, whereas the Radicals and right had favored the prewar electoral law. The system finally accepted by De Gaulle was a modified form of proportionalism, roughly comparable to that used in Belgium. It applied the proportional principle within each electoral district (usually the department) rather than on a nationwide scale. Therefore some minority votes in each district were wasted, yet the system came closer to ensuring electoral justice than any system the French had ever tried. Its effect was to enhance the chances of a few large nationally or regionally organized parties without producing either a two-bloc system on the one hand or a heterogeneous collection of splinter parties on the other.

The distribution of power in the assembly made it clear that neither of the two largest parties—the Communists or the M.R.P.—could write its principles into the new constitution without the aid of the third-place Socialists. During the initial weeks the Socialists zigzagged between their two neighbors. On some fundamental issues, such as unicameralism, they agreed with the Communists; on a number of more secondary points, like the "party statute," they supported the M.R.P.; and on still other problems, such as dissolution and decentralization, they offered a kind of compromise. Perhaps a middle ground might have been found if there had been good will on all sides, although the issue of libertarian versus equalitarian represented a profound divergence. But the Communists were determined not to water down their ideal of concentrated power in a one-house assembly, and they saw an opportunity to achieve it almost completely. They undertook an intense propaganda campaign, in which they accused the Socialists of selling their Marxian birthright by collaborating with the bourgeois clericals of the M.R.P. Many Socialists were deeply sensitive to such a charge, and before long the Communist allegations led the Socialists to shift ground toward the left on several constitutional points. The M.R.P. was left to fight a rear-guard action in an effort to regain Socialist confidence or to secure a minimum of concessions from the Communists. A few minor concessions they did gain, but the draft which was finally completed in April, 1946, represented a clear margin of victory for Communist-sponsored principles, and the M.R.P. naturally voted against it along with the Radicals and the right.

The Socialists' decision to concentrate power in a one-house assembly, rather than to distribute it as the M.R.P. desired, had also produced the brusque resignation of President de Gaulle in January, 1946. De Gaulle had never publicly outlined his own constitutional ideas, but it was obvious that he favored a strong executive to balance a popular assembly. A public controversy that occurred between De Gaulle and the Socialist André Philip, in the Constituent Assembly on January 1, sharpened the issue of executive *versus* legislative authority. Most Frenchmen, however, were astounded when De Gaulle suddenly resigned, and for some months his prestige dropped to an all-time low. He was still in self-imposed retirement in May, when the people were asked to vote by referendum on the first constitutional draft.

Rejection of the First Draft.   Even without De Gaulle's active aid, however, opponents of the draft were able to have it rejected by a 53 per cent majority. The fight was led by the M.R.P., whose spokesmen alleged that the draft provided no adequate barriers against totalitarian rule by the Communists should they ever gain a clear majority in the country. They also claimed that the Declaration of Rights in the draft was dangerously lax, since it did not flatly guarantee such liberties as freedom of the press and of education (i.e., the right to operate church schools), and since it defined property rights as something less than sacred. These charges disturbed a great many Frenchmen who were not prepared to accept equality if it meant sacrificing liberty. The Communists bolstered these fears by a strategic error; in the midst of the campaign they revived their old battle cry, *"Thorez au pouvoir!"* and thus implied a connection between the constitutional draft and their hopes for control of the state.

Second Constituent Assembly. The outcome of the referendum weighed heavily upon the election of the second Constituent Assembly only four weeks later. The M.R.P. gained a million votes to oust the Communists as "France's first party," and the clear Communist-Socialist majority was wiped out. But the proportionalist electoral system prevented any violent shift in the make-up of the assembly. This time no two parties combined were strong enough to adopt a constitution. The only two possibilities were, first, a compromise that would satisfy all three of the big parties, or, second, a Socialist-M.R.P. draft that would win the adherence of the Radicals or the right. Neither alternative offered the prospect of a coherent, homogeneous set of institutions for the Fourth Republic.

The assembly's problem was made even more difficult when General de Gaulle suddenly entered the constitutional debate just after it convened, and again toward the end of its labors. For the first time De Gaulle, in a speech at Bayeux, sketched a cloudy outline of his constitutional ideas. He demanded a strengthening of executive authority, a bicameral legislature, and a tightening of the bonds of empire (which the first Constituent Assembly had been inclined to relax). Radical and right-wing politicians at once rallied to the Gaullist program as a possible vehicle for ensuring a separation of powers and for hoisting their respective parties back to political prominence. Many M.R.P. deputies were tempted to do the same, for the party had always proclaimed itself to be deeply Gaullist in its loyalties. But the M.R.P. leadership, for reasons of principle as well as strategy, preferred to try for a compromise agreement with the leftist parties. Such an agreement, they thought, would permit the Fourth Republic to be built on the broadest possible popular base. Besides, it would keep the M.R.P. facing toward the left in its general policies and it would keep the party from sliding into the abyss of sheer conservatism, where it might become totally dependent upon the prestige and the whims of De Gaulle.

The M.R.P.'s conciliatory attitude encouraged the Socialists to meet it halfway; the two parties together proceeded to revise the defeated constitutional draft on a limited number of points. They added an upper house of Parliament but made sure that its powers would be mainly advisory. They strengthened the office of president of the republic slightly and gave the upper house of Parliament a share in electing him. They agreed that the premier should be nominated by the president. They tightened the bonds between the overseas colonies and France somewhat and dropped from the Declaration of Rights some of the more controversial passages. A few minor governmental organs were added or altered, though without great effect on the whole pattern. Not one of these changes was of major significance; even taken all together they did not modify the April draft very much. In fact they were so limited that the Communists, after long and loud protests at these "antidemocratic" revisions, came in the end to support the second draft. Only the minor parties and General de Gaulle continued hostile.

Adoption of the Second Draft.   The second referendum, in October, 1946, was essentially a two-way battle between the three major parties on the one hand and De Gaulle on the other. The general's public appearances were few, but his prestige was clearly reviving. The success of his campaign depended on his ability to divert the supporters of the big parties, most notably those of the M.R.P. When the returns came in, De Gaulle could claim with some validity that he had won a moral victory. Only slightly more than one third of the voters approved the new constitution, another third voted against it, and the remainder stayed away from the polls in uncertainty or disgust. It was scarcely an auspicious beginning for the constitutional phase of the Fourth Republic. True, the Third Republic at its origin had been greeted with no more enthusiasm; it too was a minority regime at first. But the Third Republic was lucky enough to be born in an era of prosperity, and good times tend to dissipate political bitterness. The dominant atmosphere by the end of 1946 was, on the contrary, one of pessimism, cynicism, and frustration. One may properly doubt whether any of the previous regimes in French history ever got under way in the face of so many unfavorable omens. But at least the republic existed and possessed a formal framework. In a nation so deeply democratic yet so deeply split that alone was perhaps a notable accomplishment.

9

THE POLITICAL STRUCTURE
OF THE FOURTH REPUBLIC

1. ORGANS OF PARLIAMENTARY RULE

Character of the Regime. In October, 1945, the French electorate voted almost unanimously to move on from the decrepit Third Republic to a new governmental system. Exactly a year later the electorate accepted a regime that differed little from the Third Republic in most important structural respects. It is true that the new constitution altered the governmental machinery here and there and introduced several new devices, but none of these mechanical changes seriously affected the fundamental nature of the old system. Furthermore, after 1946 the forces of tradition and habit tended to push the politicians back into the old grooves. In 1954 a series of minor constitutional amendments stripped away some of the novel "gadgets" and gave the system an even stronger resemblance to its predecessor. Parisians had long since been heard to remark ironically that the Fourth Republic was already dead and had been replaced by the Third.

It might be concluded that the citizens of France who voted *en masse* for a new deal were cheated by the politicians who drafted and applied the constitution. Such a conclusion, however, would be unjust. In the minds of the voters in 1945 there were vague aspirations but no precise outlines of reform. Many of them supported parties that favored a stronger executive; many others backed parties that demanded an omnipotent legislature. Between these two conflicting groups there was no middle ground except the ground on which the Third Republic had been built. It was not so much by choice as by force of circumstance that the founders of the Fourth Republic found themselves back there once more.

Besides, it is possible to exaggerate the degree to which the Fourth Republic came to resemble the Third. The structural and functional similarity may be striking, but it would be improper to say that the new

213

system was merely a carbon copy of the old. Beneath the apparent and obvious similarities there were significant changes: in the character and alignment of the parties, in the nation's social texture, and in the mental outlook of Frenchmen. No political system can long resist the effect of such basic changes in the substructure upon which it rests.

Parliamentary System. France after 1946 once again became a parliamentary republic—provided that the parliamentary system is defined as one in which the majority in a popularly elected legislature can choose and change the executive at will. Some French exponents of the separation-of-powers principle have sought to deny its parliamentary character by arguing that a true parliamentary regime cannot exist unless the cabinet possesses some independent power (such as the weapon of dissolution) to balance the power of the legislature. Their label for the Fourth Republic was "government by assembly." This problem of definitions may be left for academicians to debate; what mattered was that the cabinet was an emanation of the Assembly's majority and could be overthrown at the latter's pleasure. A president of the republic did exist, but in contrast to the American president he was merely a formal executive.

In the precise character of the relationship between cabinet and legislature lay the key to an understanding of the system. This relationship, in practice, did not fully conform to the theory of the constitution makers. Their purpose was to place the cabinet under the Assembly's constant supervision, yet at the same time to make cabinets more stable than in the past. They intended also to strengthen the authority of the premier, yet at the same time to protect the legislature against the use of undue pressure by the premier.[1] This complex and somewhat contradictory set of aims was probably beyond human ability to achieve. It is not surprising that practice diverged somewhat from theory.

Formation of a Cabinet. Just as in prewar days the Fourth Republic's premier was nominated by the president of the republic and had then to be approved by the lower house of Parliament (renamed the National Assembly). From 1946 to 1954 each new premier had to run the parliamentary gantlet twice. First, his own appointment had to be ratified, and that by an absolute majority of the total membership; then, a few days later, his whole cabinet and projected program had to get the Assembly's sanction. This cumbersome scheme failed to achieve its two main purposes, which were to give the premier greater personal authority and to increase the Assembly's control over the process of cabinet-making. The real result was to make the formation of a new cabinet a long and complex task, so that ministerial crises sometimes lasted several weeks. In 1954, therefore, Parliament restored the simpler prewar system. A premier appeared before the Assembly with his list of ministers and his program, and, to take office, needed only a simple majority of the votes actually cast.

[1] For the sake of convenience and clarity the term "premier" will be used instead of the title "president of the Council of Ministers," which is technically correct.

Legislative Control.   Once a cabinet was constituted, it became collectively responsible to the National Assembly and might be over- thrown by a vote of non-confidence or a vote of censure. There were only two restrictions on this fundamental legislative right. First, when the premier demanded that the vote on a given issue be made a ques- tion of confidence, on which the cabinet would stand or fall, a "cooling- off" period of one full day had to intervene before the voting occurred. Second, a vote of non-confidence required an absolute majority of the Assembly's total membership, and not merely a majority of those voting. These two devices were designed to reduce the turnover of cabinets by preventing those spur-of-the-moment cabinet crises that sometimes oc- curred during the Third Republic.

In practice these limitations seem to have had little effect. Possibly cabinet crises would have been even more frequent if the new con- stitutional safeguards had not existed, but that seems doubtful. Most of the Fourth Republic's cabinets, as a matter of fact, fell without a formal majority vote of non-confidence. Some of them disintegrated when one party withdrew its ministers from the cabinet. Others disappeared when the premier chose to avoid the test of a confidence vote and preferred to resign without a fight. The politicians were often inclined to arrange for cabinet disintegration or resignation without a vote in order to avert the possibility of dissolution of the National Assembly. During the life of the Fourth Republic only six out of twenty-one cabinets were forced out by formal votes of non-confidence.[2] Cabinets averaged almost ex- actly six months in duration—scarcely more than the average during the later years of the Third Republic. By 1958 it was clear that con- stitutional devices designed to restrain the assembly from impulsive action—short of effective dissolution power, at least—could not produce cabinet stability in France. The only way to achieve such stability within the framework of the Fourth Republic would have been to create somehow a really homogeneous majority in the National Assembly. That task proved to be far too difficult for the politicians of the era.

Question of Confidence.   In another way practice gradually altered the intentions of those who drew up the constitution. Sponsors of the draft in 1946 promised the Constituent Assembly that premiers would no longer be able to "abuse" the question-of-confidence procedure as they had done before 1940. Certain premiers in the past had been inclined to push bills through the Chamber by making the vote on each important article a question of confidence. Deputies resented the practice (which denied them the chance to introduce amendments), but they usually gave grudging assent rather than bring the cabinet down on a

[2] There are different ways to calculate the number of cabinets in the Fourth Republic, and the total will depend on the method used. Some authorities regard a reshuffled cabinet under the same premier as an entirely new cabinet. Some also count premiers who were defeated at their first appearance before the National Assembly.

In addition to the six cabinets that were overthrown by formal votes of non- confidence (i.e., by an absolute majority) several others chose to resign after votes that went against the cabinet but fell short of the absolute majority.

secondary issue. The Fourth Republic's premiers quickly found it necessary to renew this practice. Edgar Faure, for example, demanded twenty votes of confidence in one day during a budgetary debate in 1952. Premiers also resorted to a more informal kind of pressure. They sometimes refrained from invoking the formal question-of-confidence procedure, which required on each occasion a cabinet deliberation, a one-day suspension of parliamentary business, and a roll-call vote. Instead the premier simply let it be known that, if a certain bill or part of a bill was rejected or altered by the Assembly, he would turn in the cabinet's resignation. The effect was to force the Assembly to choose between producing a cascade of cabinet crises or knuckling under to cabinet demands for legislative action. Exponents of the doctrine that the Assembly should possess unrestricted power resented this emerging practice, but it appeared to be normal and inevitable if the cabinet were to get any positive program through the fragmented legislature.

Dissolution Procedure.   In a parliamentary system the most important power for the executive is the right to dissolve the legislature and order new elections. Article 51 of the 1946 constitution contained a complex arrangement (representing a compromise between the M.R.P. and the Communist viewpoints) that vested this power in the cabinet, which could request the president of the republic to issue the dissolution decree. The right of dissolution, however, was narrowly restricted. It could not be exercised during the first eighteen months after a general election, and even then it could not be used unless two cabinets had been overthrown by formal votes of non-confidence during a consecutive eighteen-month period. Since cabinets rarely fell because of formal non-confidence votes, the dissolution power became in fact almost unusable. The only use of the executive's dissolution power occurred in December, 1955, when the Assembly's five-year term was almost over. Premier Edgar Faure's decision to ask for dissolution (for the first time since 1877) caused such violent criticism, and the outcome of the subsequent elections was so disappointing to Faure and his friends, that subsequent premiers were even more reluctant to resort to this weapon. Many French politicians and political scientists concluded that the republic was doomed to perpetual instability unless some sort of effective dissolution power (possibly automatic in character) could be introduced.

Decree Laws.   Another changing aspect of executive-legislative relations was the *sub rosa* revival of the decree-law procedure. After 1940 it was widely and loosely alleged that the use and abuse of decree laws had contributed to the downfall of the Third Republic. The constitution makers in 1946 forebade the practice, at least by implication; Article 13 declared that the National Assembly might not delegate to anyone else its power to make laws. Only the right-wing spokesman Paul Reynaud in the Constituent Assembly rose to defend the decree-law procedure, contending that the complexity of modern society requires the legislature to transfer some lawmaking power to the executive branch. In spite of Article 13 the Assembly in 1948 granted a cabinet the right to issue decrees in certain spheres with a view to bringing about financial stabilization, and in subsequent years similar delegations of power were made repeatedly. The phrase "decree law" was carefully avoided, but it was plain that the prewar practice had crept back through a technical loophole. Indeed, there seemed to be no way to avoid it as long as the deputies were inclined to evade such painful responsibilities as increasing taxes or reducing expenditures.

Sphere of Legislative Action.   Underlying this whole issue was the problem of legislative *versus* executive action in the modern state. Both the Third and the Fourth republics weighted the balance in favor of the legislative branch. The contrast with the Anglo-Saxon countries is striking. Whereas the powers of the United States Congress have been said to consist largely of "complaint, investigation, and veto," and whereas the British Parliament acts mainly on the initiative of the cabinet, the French Assembly dominated and monopolized the legislative process. The cabinet did, of course, propose bills, but an Assembly committee normally made drastic changes in such bills before they came up for floor debate, and the debate revolved around the committee's version. Furthermore, the cabinet could not force the Assembly to begin debate on a measure until the Assembly and the appropriate committee were ready. The possibilities of obstruction and delay were great, as were the opportunities for avoiding responsibility for such delay. The government, remarked one keen critic, was paralyzed by this dilution of responsibility; Parliament continued to be organized as it was under the July monarchy, when its problems were far more simple. Many Frenchmen, disillusioned by such a state of affairs, were driven to the conclusion that democratic processes must inevitably be ineffective and negative in character.

French political experts and leaders admitted that the Fourth Republic's National Assembly was overloaded, and that it could not legislate carefully, wisely, or rapidly on all the detailed problems that demanded action. Its agenda was often cluttered with such items as the question of permitting third-class rail passengers to ride second-class on crowded trains, and the determination of the number of stallions to be kept on the national stud farms. Obviously the cabinet could have acted more efficiently by decree, but many legislators feared to transfer any of their power to the executive branch on the ground that an aggressive cabinet might keep asking for more. They pointed out too that legislation by the cabinet would make effective popular control more difficult, for it would permit no public debate on the measures taken. Some of them argued that it might favor obscure but powerful pressure groups or that it might produce a kind of bureaucratic dictatorship. Others replied that the bureaucrats were already running France, for the very reason that the Assembly spent its time on petty details instead of laying down the broad outlines of policy and controlling the officials who executed it.

Among the many solutions that were discussed in postwar France some reform in legislative methods seemed to find most favor. One proposal was to provide an easier procedure for getting non-controversial bills adopted without floor debate. Another was to authorize parliamentary committees to take final action in certain spheres on behalf of the Assembly. Some experts urged the Assembly to confine itself to adopting *lois-cadres,* or measures establishing general principles, leaving the details to be filled in by administrative action. There was also a revival of support for open resort to the old decree-law procedure, especially among certain planners who were impatient with Parliament's delays. All this criticism of legislative inefficiency contributed much to French disaffection toward the Fourth Republic.

Premier. In turning now from the nature of executive-legislative relations in the Fourth Republic, some attention must be given to each of the executive and legislative organs in turn. In doing so one is struck by the apparent similarity between the Third and the Fourth republics, yet analysis shows that some significant changes in organization and in the location of authority did take place.

One of the principal authors of the new constitution told the Constituent Assembly in 1946: "We have aimed to institute a real head of the government, a prime minister in the English sense of the term." In practice it would be virtually impossible for an English-type prime minister to emerge so long as a multiparty system exists, but it is true that the French premier did become the real head of government in the Fourth Republic. Many of the powers that had been vested formally in the president of the Third Republic were transferred to the premier. He was given the right to initiate legislation; his signature formally validated almost all decrees; he appointed the most important civil and military officials. He was the co-ordinator of all cabinet activities and the director of the armed forces; he supervised the entire structure of public administration and the planning of the national economy. Attached to his office were agencies of the most varied sort, among them, for example, the official broadcasting agency, Radiodiffusion Française; the information and counterespionage service; and the High Commission on Atomic Energy.

This list of functions makes it plain that the premier was by far the most important figure in the Fourth Republic. So he was in the Third as well, but then he had risen to power in extraconstitutional fashion, and not by formal dictum of the constitution. The Fourth Republic's premier was assisted by one or more "secretaries of state," who ranked just below full cabinet status. He was also assisted by a staff of career civil servants called the General Secretariat (Secrétariat-Général du Gouvernement), which was the outgrowth of an agency set up by De Gaulle at London in 1940. The secretary-general and his staff performed two functions: 1) they acted as technical co-ordinators of the cabinet's activity, and 2) they maintained liaison between the cabinet and Parliament. The secretary-general prepared the agenda for cabinet meetings (which he attended as well); he drew up an official record of those meetings; he was responsible for drafting an accurate text of decrees adopted by the cabinet; and he acted as official custodian of those decrees. Thanks to the General Secretariat the premier's office at last began to operate efficiently from the administrative point of view. Its creation corrected one of the worst administrative flaws of the Third Republic.

The political organization of the premier's office, however, was much less satisfactory. French critics suggested that both too many agencies and too few were attached directly to it. Many nondescript functions might better have been transferred to other supervision. On the other hand, certain key services, such as the Budget Office (now located in the Ministry of Finance) and the office that supervises prefects (now in the Ministry of Interior), should have been placed directly under the premier. It was suggested also that he should have been given a staff of inspectors with supervisory powers over all branches of the bureaucracy, and that one or two full-scale cabinet ministers might have been assigned to the premier's office to help carry the burden of cabinet co-ordination and legislative liaison. Such changes would have freed the premier from many of the routine tasks that continued to sap his energy and divert his mind from the shaping of general policy. *Gouverner, c'est prévoir,* the French like to say. But the premier could scarcely be farsighted as long as his eyes had to be fixed too constantly on day-to-day details.

President of the Republic.   The similarity between the Third and Fourth republics was nowhere clearer than in the role of the formal executive, the president of the republic. In point of law his prerogatives were considerably narrower than they had once been, for the new constitution transferred many of his former powers to the premier. In point of fact, however, the president's role was not materially altered. In the Third Republic all of his acts had to be countersigned by a responsible cabinet minister; therefore, he could never act independently but could only exercise what has been called a magistracy of influence. That continued to be his situation in the Fourth Republic.

Elected for a seven-year term by the two houses of Parliament sitting jointly, the president presided over cabinet meetings[3] and over a whole series of specialized bodies set up by the constitution (the Constitutional Committee, the High Council of the Judiciary, the National Defense Committee, and the High Council of National Defense).[4] His most striking function, however, was the right to nominate a new premier when a cabinet fell, a prerogative that led some prewar critics to de-

[3] As in prewar days the cabinet could meet either in *conseil des ministres* (with the president in the chair, according to Article 32 of the constitution) or in *conseil de cabinet* (with the president absent). In practice the latter procedure was infrequently used.

[4] The National Defense Committee is made up of those cabinet ministers whose duties are connected with military affairs, either directly or indirectly. The High Council of National Defense is a technical advisory and planning body composed of cabinet ministers, military officers, and technicians. There is also a Permanent Military Staff (*État-Major Permanent*), attached to the premier's office. This small group of civilians and soldiers has the task of co-ordinating and preparing all aspects of national defense. Strictly military planning is entrusted to a combined-chiefs-of-staff committee under the chairmanship of the minister of national defense.

scribe the president as a kind of pin boy in the parliamentary bowling alley, assigned to pick up cabinets as the Chamber knocked them down. The president's freedom of choice continued to be markedly greater than is the king's in the British two-party system, but it was probably less great after 1946 than it was in the prewar era of shifting, undisciplined party groups. A skillful president could, however, do much to resolve a cabinet crisis by acting as a kind of mediator among the party leaders of a potential coalition. Vincent Auriol, the Fourth Republic's first president (1947–54), succeeded admirably in this respect.

Another presidential prerogative was a kind of suspensive veto over laws adopted by Parliament. He might return such bills to the National Assembly and request a second deliberation. This power, however, went virtually unused during the Fourth Republic. When President Auriol did resort to it, he did so only on grounds of faulty drafting, and not because of the content of the legislation. In fact, when trade-union officials appealed to him to send back one bill because they found its content objectionable, the president flatly refused on the ground that such an act would exceed his authority.

One new aspect of the president's position was his ex-officio post as president of the French Union, as well as president of the republic. It was intended that he should serve as formal head of the new colonial commonwealth, thus furnishing a symbolic unity like that embodied in the British Crown. In fact, this added role proved to be of meager importance. The colonial empire disintegrated too rapidly to permit its effective reorganization either as a federation or as a multinational republic.

The president's role has been well described as "the highest moral magistracy of the regime." Much of his time had to be devoted to purely formal functions, such as receiving ambassadors or presiding at public ceremonies. But behind the scenes he could be the discreet adviser of the cabinet and could exert real influence upon important decisions. Indeed, some authorities argued that Article 32 of the constitution, which authorized the president to act as presiding officer and keeper of the records at cabinet meetings, gave him a new role of real significance. On the whole, however, the influence of the presidency continued to vary according to the strength and personal authority of the man who held the office. Such had been the long tradition of the Third Republic as well.

National Assembly. The real center of authority in the Fourth Republic was to be found, not among its executive organs, but rather in the lower house of the legislature. The National Assembly, elected for a five-year term by direct universal suffrage, represented the popular will more clearly than did any other agency of the regime. Its dominance over the upper house was far greater than it had been during the Third Republic. Its power to control the executive was not really diminished, despite the new constitutional devices designed to reduce cabinet crises. Deputies preserved the traditional right to "interpellate," i.e., to call for a formal debate on the policy of a minister or of the cabinet as a whole. Any deputy or party group might introduce bills (called *prop-*

ositions de loi to distinguish them from cabinet-sponsored *projets de loi*). Debate on the annual budget put every public expenditure more or less directly under the Assembly's control. However, deputies might no longer propose any increase in public expenditure during the discussion of the budget.[5] This provision was placed in the constitution in an effort to reduce costly demagoguery and "log-rolling," but the Communist deputies especially have been ingenious in finding ways to evade it.

In organization and procedure the National Assembly strongly resembled the prewar Chamber of Deputies. The president of the Assembly was potentially more important than his predecessor, since in certain circumstances he might serve as interim substitute for either the premier or the president of the republic. A "committee of presidents," made up of the Assembly's annually elected officers, heads of committees, and heads of party groups, served as a steering committee to plan the agenda.

A more important heritage from the Third Republic was the parliamentary committee system. Each of the nineteen standing committees, chosen on the basis of proportional representation of party groups, was a kind of small edition of the whole Assembly. Each one examined and reported on bills in a particular subject category, e.g., agriculture or finance. Committee members might thus become experts on matters within their special competence, but they sometimes tended also to become jealous and presumptuous, especially toward the cabinet minister who was supposed to establish policy for their particular area of specialization.

Committees often buried bills or reported them out with such drastic revisions that they scarcely resembled the author's or the cabinet's draft. They appointed a special *rapporteur* for each bill to shepherd it through public debate in the Assembly and to present the viewpoint of the committee's majority. Furthermore, committees commonly went beyond the work of legislation; they sought to supervise the activities of the cabinet as well. They were empowered to summon a minister or

[5] Budgetary reform remains a serious unfulfilled need in France. Article 16 of the 1946 constitution authorized such reform, but no organic law on budgetary procedure has yet been adopted. As in prewar France the annual budget debate has developed into a series of catchall sessions in which the deputies discuss any subject that may be of electoral value or that they have been unable to introduce during the year. Often the budget is not voted until several months after the fiscal year has begun; the 1948 budget, for example, was nine months late. The government meanwhile limps along with monthly grants of provisional credits. Some postwar cabinets have gotten a skeleton budget through on time by including in it only the maximum amount each government department may spend. But a series of laws must subsequently be adopted to define more precisely how each department is to spend its allotment, and this process takes many months.

Until recently it was common for several "extraordinary budgets" to be set up outside the regular budget, and, adding still more to the chaos, a number of "special treasury accounts" concerning such public services as the nationalized railways were extra-budgetary. Some progress is now being made toward unifying the budget and bringing the special accounts under more effective parliamentary control.

For a more extended discussion of budgetary problems see Philip Williams, *Politics in Post-War France* (1954), pp. 252–66.

even the premier to appear before them to furnish an explanation of his past, present, or future activities. (In accordance with Article 53 of the constitution ministers were given the right to appear.) The Committee on Foreign Affairs, which had few bills to consider, devoted most of its time to such supervisory action.

This committee system had often been criticized during the Third Republic. Many Frenchmen felt that the mother-in-law behavior of the committees hampered effective action by the executive, burdened the ministers with long-winded and nerve-racking hearings, and contributed much to the instability of cabinets. Some critics thought that the evil could be corrected only by abandoning the system of specialized standing committees and substituting an *ad hoc* committee for each bill. These complaints, however, had no effect when the time came for the National Assembly to draw up its rules of order. The deputies in 1946 returned almost automatically to the old system, presumably on the ground that its virtues (specialized knowledge and constant democratic control over the executive) outweighed its faults. The critics shortly renewed their attacks, using the same arguments as in prewar days. And defenders of the system continued to answer that, if the committees interfered with the cabinet's work, they did so only because the cabinet failed to do its job with proper vigor and authority.

Council of the Republic.   The most significant novelty in the legislative pattern of the Fourth Republic was the reduced role of the upper house. Both the Communists and the Socialists in 1946 were strongly opposed to any upper house at all, and finally accepted one only with the proviso that it should not be "a younger brother of the [prewar] Senate." Even the M.R.P. felt that the powers of the two houses should not be equal, although the party wanted to vest some real authority in the upper house and would have liked to make it semi-corporative in composition.

Members of the Council of the Republic were elected for six-year terms, with half of the terms expiring every three years. From 1946 to 1948, when the Council was elected by proportional representation, it was virtually a carbon copy of the lower house in its political composition. After 1948 the center of gravity was pushed farther to the right through the adoption of an electoral system much like the one used for the old Senate (except that the special advantage enjoyed by rural areas was somewhat reduced). Elections were indirect, with the choice in each department being made by an electoral college composed of the deputies of that department, the members of the department's general council, and delegates of the various municipal councils. The effect of this system was to favor candidates possessing local prestige, whatever their national party connections.

The constitution specifically denied to the Council of the Republic all of the most important powers possessed by the old Senate. The Council was not authorized to overthrow cabinets; it might not permanently block or bury bills sent up from the Assembly; and until the 1954 constitutional amendment it was not permitted to consider any bill until the lower house had completed action on such bill. The Council's chief prerogatives were: 1) to share in electing the president of the republic, 2) to elect some members of bodies like the Assembly of the French Union and the Constitutional Committee, 3) to initiate the new procedure designed to test the constitutionality of laws, and 4) to exercise a limited power of amendment or suspensive veto over legislation.

From the outset most councilors of the republic resented their state of gilded impotence, and their complaints grew louder with the revival of the right-wing parties, which had always favored bicameralism. After the 1948 elections, when left-wing strength in the Council was cut back sharply, the councilors embarked on a vigorous campaign to regain both prestige and power. As a kind of symbolic gesture they voted to revive the title "Senator"; they managed to restore a kind of interpellation power by calling ministers before them under a procedure called "oral question with debate"; and they pushed hard for a constitutional amendment that would broaden the Council's prerogatives.

This drive for authority had somewhat contradictory effects. On the one hand the Council's influence did experience a slow but real growth: the lower house began to accept more of its legislative amendments, and premiers began to appoint some councilors to ministerial posts in almost every new cabinet. On the other hand the Council antagonized the left-wing parties (and the National Assembly in general) by its refusal to accept its constitutional role as a mere *chambre de réflexion,* and by its tendency to spend more time in complaining and regretting the past than in constructive activity. In 1950 the National Assembly finally agreed to amend those constitutional articles that defined the Council's powers, but it took four more years of parliamentary haggling to get the amendment adopted. Furthermore, the reforms fell far short of the hopes nursed by the councilors and the exponents of bicameralism.

Two principal changes were introduced by the 1954 amendment. First, bills might now be debated and adopted by the upper house before transmittal to the lower house for action.[6] This change added nothing to the Council's power, but it enabled the Council to spread its work load over a whole session instead of tackling a huge pile of bills at the very end. Second, the Council was given the right to hold up a bill for one hundred days (or fifteen days in the case of bills labeled "urgent" by the lower house), during which time it might repeatedly propose amendments to the National Assembly's version.[7] This procedure restored, within sharply restricted limits, the prewar practice known as the *navette,*

---

[6] Money bills and those involving the ratification of treaties were exceptions to this rule.

[7] Before 1954 the Council had only one opportunity to examine and amend each bill, and the National Assembly could (and often did) brusquely ignore all the proposed amendments by readopting its own original version. Unintentionally, however, the constitution makers did give the upper house a curious kind of potential veto power: if the Council rejected or amended a bill by an absolute majority, the Assembly could not readopt the measure except by an absolute majority. On some controversial issues no such majority could be found in the lower house, so that legislation might be stalled. In 1954 the Council agreed to accept the elimination of this veto power, in return for which the Assembly approved the hundred-day rule.

or the shuttling of bills between the two houses in order to reach agreement on them. At the end of the hundred-day (or fifteen-day) period, however, the National Assembly still retained the right to insist on its own version of a bill. Thus the change gave the Council a device by which to exert greater influence in the shaping of legislation, yet it still left the Council a *chambre de réflexion* rather than the second chamber in a truly bicameral system. If it is true that the Senate, with its peculiar composition and powers, was in certain ways the key institution in the Third Republic, then in one important respect the Fourth Republic was clearly different from the Third.

Economic Council. One of the new quasi-parliamentary agencies established in 1946 was the Economic Council. Unlike its shadowy predecessor in the later years of the Third Republic it was attached to Parliament, and summaries of its debates were published in a supplement to the *Journal Officiel.* Its members possessed many of the prerogatives of members of Parliament. The Economic Council's role, however, was purely advisory. The constitution empowered it to examine all proposed bills of an economic or social nature (except the budget) and to initiate resolutions to be submitted to the National Assembly. In addition, a law of 1951 required it to make an annual report on the progress of all national economic plans, to report twice yearly on the general economic situation in France, and to make periodic evaluations of the national income.

In an era when social and economic problems dominate politics a body like the Economic Council ought to be of inestimable value to an overloaded Parliament whose members are often not very literate in economics. The Economic Council gradually worked its way toward such a solid and respected status in the regime, but its progress was slow and jerky. Perhaps the trouble lay in the fact that the Council was a child of compromise. The left-wing parties in 1946 insisted that it should be nothing more than a body of technical advisers to be consulted only when the cabinet or the Assembly so desired. The M.R.P., on the other hand, wanted to give it a major role as a semi-corporative chamber just short of full parliamentary status. They proposed to include representatives of a great many economic and social interest groups, plus regional and overseas representatives. Through such a body, argued the M.R.P., all of the economic forces in France could be made to participate effectively in the life of the state. The compromise that finally emerged has been described as "bastard and imprecise," and the Council's role was therefore somewhat ambiguous.

Most of the 169 members of the Council were chosen by such nationwide organizations as the various trade-union federations, the farmers' syndicate, and employers' groups. It met in plenary session only once or twice a month, for half of its members lived outside Paris, and most of them held full-time jobs of some sort. The council's work was done in its nine major committees, which were chosen according to proportional representation of party groups, and not according to technical competence. Thus the committee on agriculture might contain only a minority of farmers or farm specialists. Some excellent reports were produced, but the Council's work tended to be spotty; its resolutions were sometimes based on superficial study and might be the outcome of political compromises or log-rolling among the big interest groups. "The Economic Council is undeniably a forum for pressure groups," remarked one observer, "but it is one where they are obliged to operate in the open instead of in the dark." [8] There is much to be said for the existence of such a forum, provided that the public interest and the consumers' interest get an adequate hearing along with the special interests.

In its first years the Economic Council got scant notice from either the cabinet or the National Assembly; it was rarely consulted, and its reports were ignored. Even during the second term of the Council (1951–54), the cabinet asked its opinion only four times, and the Assembly five. But the Council continued to initiate numerous studies on its own responsibility; during its second term 105 reports were drafted and examined, and twenty-six of its opinions led to some action by the appropriate authorities. Several of its best reports won a wide audience in Parliament and through the press, and the Council's prestige rose accordingly. Although the Economic Council's role in the Fourth Republic remained somewhat ambiguous, the utility of such a body in one form or another came to be generally recognized.

Constitutional Committee. The French parliamentary system leaves no place for the kind of judicial review of legislation that has grown up in the United States. Even Frenchmen of the libertarian school have long regarded such review as a violation of the separation-of-powers principle rather than a consequence of that principle, as Americans tend to regard it. However, a few of the constitution makers in 1946 did favor the idea of an American-type supreme court, in an effort to distribute power through checks and balances. What they finally achieved was only a pale shadow of their hopes, an agency labeled the Constitutional Committee.

This thirteen-man watchdog committee was made up of experts in constitutional law who either sat ex officio or were elected by the National Assembly (seven members) and the Council of the Republic (three members). Its task was to examine new laws when jointly requested to do so by the president of the Republic and the Council of the Republic, and to rule on the compatibility of such laws with the constitution. But the committee could not invalidate a law in American supreme-court fashion; it could only request the National Assembly to amend the law to make it conform to the constitution, or to amend the constitution to make it conform to the new law.[9]

[8] Philip Williams, *Politics in Post-War France* (1954), p. 300.

[9] The process of constitutional amendment was slow and cumbersome. Proposals to amend could be initiated only by an absolute majority of the National Assembly. A three-month waiting period followed, unless the upper house also approved the proposal to amend by an absolute majority. The National Assembly next drafted and adopted the amendment in precise form and submitted it to popular referendum. The referendum might be omitted if the amendment had carried by a sufficient margin in Parliament (two thirds in the lower house, or three fifths in both

The chief limitation on the Committee's power was the proviso that it might not question laws on the ground that they violated the preamble of the constitution. The preamble incorporated the Declaration of Rights of 1789, with all of its guarantees of individual liberties. The left-wing parties in 1946 feared that, if the Committee were allowed to invoke these general principles, it might obstruct future economic and social reforms. Obsessed by the memory of Roosevelt's struggle with the Supreme Court, they saw to it that the Constitutional Committee could not set itself up as protector of the individual's rights against the state.

In consequence the Committee was one of the most quiescent organs of the Fourth Republic. It functioned only once, and the issue involved was not the constitutionality of a law but a procedural dispute between the two houses of Parliament. The Council of the Republic complained in 1948 that the National Assembly was infringing the rights of the upper house by labeling too many bills "urgent," thus depriving the Council of adequate time for serious debate on such bills. Technically, therefore, it was not the constitution but the Assembly's rules of procedure that were at issue. The Constitutional Committee accepted jurisdiction in spite of some protests and, in effect, acted as conciliator between the two houses. In the end the Assembly yielded and modified its rules. After that initial but minor success the Committee was not again called upon to function, despite several abortive attempts by minorities in the Council of the Republic to get controversial bills referred to it.

2. PROCESSES OF ADMINISTRATION AND JUSTICE

Policy and Execution. For purposes of analysis the modern state may be artificially dissected into two main parts: the organs of political power and the organs of administrative action. In general, the former make policy, the latter execute it. Since the line between them is not always clear, no great effort need be made to draw it with scientific accuracy.

At the top of the administrative structure in the French republican system is the cabinet itself. Cabinet organization has varied considerably in the postwar period; the total number of ministerial departments fluctuates, titles change, functions are shifted from one department to another as political considerations seem to require. Even though the cabinet has grown too large and unwieldy to function effectively as a unit, the number of posts has tended to grow rather than to diminish. When a new coalition cabinet is being formed, it is always easier to balance the demands of the component parties by adding rather than subtracting. Frequent proposals have been made to fix and limit the

houses). In the only successful constitutional amendment to date (November, 1954) no referendum was needed because the Assembly's vote was 412 to 141. However, four full years had elapsed since the first step in the procedure—the Assembly's general proposal to amend—had been accomplished.

number of cabinet posts by law or even by constitutional amendment, but the realities of the political game have kept those proposals in the academic realm. Occasionally a premier has risked a break with tradition; Guy Mollet in 1956 cut down the number of ministers in his cabinet to the unprecedented figure of twelve. Not much was gained, however, for Mollet had to increase the number of quasi-ministerial posts (secretaries and undersecretaries of state) to twenty-three. In 1957 Premier Bourgès-Maunoury broke all records by forming a cabinet that included forty-six ministers and undersecretaries.

Ministers in the Third and Fourth Republics were not always experts in the fields to which they were assigned, and they rarely remained in the same post long enough to become so. Although they made policy and were responsible for it, they had to lean heavily on the career civil servants who staffed the administration. The essayist Robert de Jouvenel cynically remarked about fifty years ago that French cabinet ministers quickly become prisoners of the bureaucrats, and that the minister's function is "to appoint officials about whom he knows nothing to posts about which he knows nothing." Actually a minister in the Fourth Republic had few appointments to make. He brought into office with him only a handful of political appointees (his private staff or *cabinet*), who normally left the practical job of administration to the career technicians. There have been times, however, when jealousies and personal ambitions have created considerable friction between the two groups. High civil servants in the Fourth Republic complained that the minister's appointees showed a growing tendency to usurp the decision-making powers of the career men.

Administrative Personnel.   The importance of the civil service in any modern state is too obvious to need much stress. In France, a centralized country with a long tradition of "statism" and a steady expansion of governmental services, that importance is particularly clear. The French bureaucracy, which numbers more than one million, not including the employees of the nationalized industries, has some of the virtues and many of the faults of any bureaucratic body. It is presently in a state of transition, from which it is not likely to emerge for several years to come.

The builders of the Fourth Republic could not ignore the widespread criticism that had been leveled at the bureaucracy of the prewar regime. Perhaps the most glaring evil was the compartmentalization of the civil service. Each ministerial department set up its own standards, devised its own examinations, chose its own personnel, and paid and promoted them according to its own scale. There was no equivalent of the United States Civil Service Commission to co-ordinate or standardize these separate rules and practices. Government departments therefore remained isolated from one another both in function and in mentality, and educational preparation for civil service examinations came to be narrowly specialized as well as excessively theoretical. A further weakness was the failure to distinguish clearly between the higher levels and the routine posts in most ministries. Frustration was widespread because of outdated methods, an excessively bureaucratic spirit in many quarters, and the general lack of a rational promotion system. Another flaw was the monopolization of the most desirable posts (in the Diplomatic Corps, the Treasury, and the Council of State) by the upper bourgeoisie, whose sons could afford to attend the law schools and the École Libre des Sciences Politiques, which virtually controlled entrance into those positions. Furthermore, there were too many civil service jobs and not enough adequate salaries. The result was widespread inefficiency, indifference, and petty graft.

Civil Service Reform.   To tackle all of these problems in the confused post-liberation period required vigor and vision. It is to the credit of the Fourth Republic's founders that they made an effective start toward reform. In 1945 the De Gaulle government created the Direction of the Public Service, a central agency attached to the premier's office, with responsibility for supervising the recruitment of civil servants, setting up rules for discipline and promotion, and standardizing administrative methods. A uniform classification system was established, with two professional categories (the "civil administrators," or policy formulators, and the "secretaries of administration," or technicians), plus two lower categories of employees to handle the routine work. In 1946 a civil servants' statute codified the rights and privileges of career personnel, and two years later a general reclassification of jobs according to new wage scales was undertaken. An elaborate series of consultative councils (resembling the British Whitley Councils) has also been created to give civil service employees a voice in administrative and personnel matters.

A more unusual experiment is the new educational structure set up to train candidates for high government posts. The keystone in this structure is the National School of Administration. Students are selected by examination for its three-year course, and they are placed on the government payroll as soon as they enter. Most candidates for the National School prepare either in the law schools or in the new institutes of political studies set up within various universities. The National School of Administration provides an intensive course of academic training along with internship experience in various government departments. Another novel institution is the postgraduate Center of Advanced Administrative Studies. This center enrolls a small, highly select group of career civil servants who desire a broad refresher program of intensive study that will take them beyond their narrow specialties. The center is designed to prepare top-notch men for the highest civil service grades.

Effect of Reform Program.   It is not easy to measure the total impact of all these reforms, some of which may take a full generation to work themselves out. Roger Grégoire, the first Director of the Public Service, believes that enough has been done to call the postwar decade a major turning point in French civil service history, but he admits that some reforms have fallen far short of their purpose.[1] The Direction of the

[1] See R. Grégoire, *La fonction publique* (1954), for the most complete and authoritative discussion of these problems.

Public Service remains a tiny co-ordinating agency with a staff of only about thirty officials; it has little in common with the American Civil Service Commission. Its most important achievement has been to simplify professional recruitment procedures. Instead of the old multiple entrance examinations given by separate agencies a single recruitment channel now exists through the National School of Administration. On the other hand the attempt to create a uniform classification system cutting across government departments has not been very effective; each department remains autonomous both in practice and in mentality. The examination system, according to M. Grégoire, is still too narrowly academic in spirit, and provides no way to test a candidate's over-all fitness for the public service. Salary levels have fallen sharply below those in equivalent private employment, despite the abortive salary reclassification of 1948. Finally, M. Grégoire laments the decline in the bureaucracy's sense of public service. The old *esprit de corps,* he believes, has given way to a kind of trade-union mentality, a narrow corporatism concerned mainly with the protection of vested interests. Such flaws as these will not be easily corrected, but at least French experts are willing to admit that they exist and to consider possible methods for correcting them.

Council of State. Several of the central administrative organs of the republic—those which the French call *les grands corps de l'État*—deserve some special mention. At the head of the list stands the Council of State, an almost unique body in many ways. The Council of State, though an agency by that name existed in prerevolutionary days, actually dates from its establishment by Napoleon in 1799. It has survived every governmental change since that time. As the capstone of the system of administrative courts more will be said of it later. It also constitutes an elite corps of top-level civil servants whose members may be "drafted" from time to time for special technical tasks in France or abroad. In addition it advises the cabinet on legislation and other matters. Since 1945, when the role of the Council of State was redefined by law, the cabinet is required to secure the Council's opinion on any government-sponsored bill before it can introduce such a bill into the National Assembly. The Council of State possessed this power during the Third Republic, but in permissive rather than mandatory form. In fact the cabinet rarely consulted the Council before 1940. The reason was in part an old heritage of republican suspicion toward the Council. Authoritarian regimes like those of the two Napoleons had used it to substitute for, or to weaken, the elected assemblies. In recent decades, however, this suspicion has been completely dissipated; the only complaint about the Council of State has been that its membership is too narrowly bourgeois and conservative in character. The advantages of having a body of administrative and legal experts examine bills before adoption are generally recognized today. The cabinet, of course, is not bound to accept the Council's opinion.

Another old prerogative that has been revived since 1945 is the right of the Council of State to give an opinion on any question presented to it by the cabinet or by a minister, even if no projected legislation is involved. During the early years of the Fourth Republic the Council was repeatedly consulted with respect to what might be called the constitutionality of acts contemplated by the cabinet. Furthermore, the Council now has a certain limited initiative; it may draw the attention of the cabinet to any reforms it considers to be in the general interest. Its contemporary prestige is clearly greater than it had been for almost a century.

Inspectorate General of Finances.   Also a Napoleonic re-creation, although the title has changed somewhat through the years, are the inspectors of finance, the highest officials in the French Treasury. An elite corps numbering approximately one hundred officials, the inspectors enjoy a prestige comparable to that of the councilors of state. Like the councilors, however, they have been criticized for their narrowly upperbourgeois spirit, the result, in part, of the system of co-optation used in selecting personnel until 1936. Another complaint during the Third Republic was that many inspectors used their posts as springboards from which to attain more lucrative positions in private banking or industry. The Fourth Republic made an effort to correct both of these abuses. All new appointments to the Inspectorate now are made from the ranks of the National School of Administration, and all students in that school must pledge themselves to remain in government service for at least twelve years after graduation.

The traditional function of the inspectors of finance has been to examine the accounts and the accounting methods of all state agencies that handle government funds. During the last few decades the scope of their duties has expanded so rapidly that the Inspectorate can no longer verify accounts in detail. General supervision at irregular intervals is the best that can be achieved. In addition, individual inspectors can be "drafted" by the cabinet for a variety of special tasks, in much the same fashion as councilors of state.

The career of an inspector of finance is by no means so drab as his function might seem to suggest. One veteran member of the corps writes:

> As a young beginner, he may pass the night pursuing smugglers in the mountains, then turn to counting the stamps in a post office or the casks of a wine wholesaler . . . Later on in his career, one day may be spent with the warden of a prison, the next at a race track, whence he may return home in the evening to be informed that he alone is qualified to carry out the financial integration of certain ex-Italian villages into the French state. At any moment he must be ready to depart, whether it be for Versailles or for the island of Réunion. . . . Men who accept this life are likely to develop a sense of humor, a certain aptitude to observe and understand, a certain skepticism perhaps—and an intense love for France in all its

Court of Accounts.   The Court of Accounts is another agency of Napoleonic creation, but with some roots that go back into the Middle Ages. A quasi-judicial body of some hundred and fifty officials, its function for more than a century past has been to post-audit the accounts of the various administrative agencies and to submit an annual report to Parliament that never attracted public attention and was politely buried in the parliamentary archives. However, the widespread belief that the Court was usually a decade or two in arrears in its reports is pure legend.

The constitution of 1946 lifted the Court of Accounts out of its obscurity by making specific mention of its power to assist the National Assembly in "regulating the nation's accounts." Early in 1949 the Court was suddenly catapulted into the limelight when it presented its report for the biennium 1946–47. The report spared no one; it severely criticized certain ministers and officials for irregularities and wastefulness. In 1952 the Court tackled another explosive issue in its first report on the controversial social security system. Although some politicians dislike this "meddling," it is clear that the Court of Accounts is taking its new role seriously and that it is making a valuable contribution to efficiency and honesty in government.

One problem, however, has only been sharpened by the court's exposés: how can the National Assembly punish officials for mistakes long since committed? French practice provides little control of public expenditure at the time the money is spent; the Budget Office in the Ministry of Finance merely makes sure that the spending agency has adequate funds available. If the money is spent improperly, a post-audit system can do little except throw the light of publicity on the irregularity. The problem of control has become even more serious since the state has taken over such huge enterprises as the coal and electricity industries. Here too the post-audit system is being used, with a number of judges from the Court of Accounts serving on the new "verification commission" set up in 1948.

Prefectoral Corps.   Probably no other group of officials is so distinctively French as the prefectoral corps, which is another Napoleonic agency that survived the emperor's downfall. France is the world's most centralized republic, and the prefects play a unique role in its administrative structure. In each department the prefect is the official representative of the central government. Under him serve several subprefects— normally one in each *arrondissement.* On behalf of the cabinet the prefect acts as chief administrative officer for national services, and coordinates the work of all centrally appointed officials assigned to his area. He also serves ex officio as the departmental chief executive, carrying out the instructions of the department's elected general council. A third function grows out of the prefect's power of "tutelage" over all municipalities in his area. This means that he (or a subprefect in the smaller communes) is required to approve certain acts of a municipality in order to make them valid, and that he may nullify other acts on the ground that the municipality has exceeded its powers. In a sense, therefore, the prefect operates on three levels: national, departmental, and municipal. It is not surprising that the prefecture has been described as "the hub of local affairs" in France.

Prefects are rarely, if ever, run-of-the-mill bureaucrats. Their functions are not merely administrative in nature; they are at least quasi-political as well, and their role corresponds in some ways to that of a professional diplomat in a provincial rather than a foreign post. Like diplomats most of them now rise through the hierarchy of their own career service, but prefects may also be appointed freely from outside the career ranks, and they may be transferred or demoted at will. Through most of the nineteenth century the prefects were the political "hatchet men" of successive governments, influencing public opinion and shaping the outcome of elections through various kinds of persuasion and pressure. In more recent times their political role has come to be a more restrained and subtle one, and there is now less likelihood of a wholesale dismissal or transfer of prefects when the political majority in Paris changes. Nevertheless they occupy a sensitive position at the point of convergence of many pressures, so that agility and diplomacy are sometimes more useful qualities than the toughness of nineteenth-century prefects. Partly because of this change modern prefects can less often point to a record of really constructive achievement at the end of their service in a department.

"Super-Prefects." The Fourth Republic's most important innovation in the prefectoral system was the creation of the so-called "super-prefects." Eight of these new officials, technically labeled "inspectors general on special mission," were named by cabinet decree in 1948, at a time when a Communist-inspired strike wave was seriously threatening public order. The cabinet's immediate purpose was to ensure speed and efficiency in shifting the state police force across departmental boundaries. To this end each inspector general was assigned an area that coincided with one of France's eight military regions, and was given emergency powers to be used in moments of crisis.

The strike wave has long since subsided, but the "super-prefects" remain. Their continuance on a permanent basis may modify the relationship between the prefects and the Ministry of Interior in Paris if (as seems to be the case) the super-prefects gradually gain supervisory and co-ordinating authority over the prefects in their respective regions. It does not appear that any powers will be taken away from the prefects, but rather that certain powers of the Ministry of Interior may devolve upon the "super-prefects." In other words, a process of "deconcentration" of the central government's authority from Paris to the provinces seems to be under way, and this deconcentration may be combined with the growth of a kind of regionalism.[2]

---

[2] Regionalism, which has long been advocated by some Frenchmen, suffered a serious setback when Pétain in 1940 adopted the idea of a return to the pre-1789 provinces. The postwar revulsion against everything Vichyite swept aside Pétain's "regional prefects" and the whole regionalist idea, despite De Gaulle's attempt to retain the regional prefects under another name.

Exponents of regionalism argue that too much authority has been concentrated

Deconcentration. The idea of shifting more power from Paris to the prefects appealed to the constitution makers in 1946. Every Frenchman could cite ridiculous examples of excessive centralization, such as the rural school building with the broken wall through which rain and snow poured for weeks while full documentation on the case made its way to Paris and back again. Lamennais a century ago remarked that the system produced "apoplexy at the center and paralysis at the extremities." The 1946 constitution (Articles 88 and 89) made provision for deconcentration, but in general terms only; the details were left to be filled in by legislation.

In fact no such legislation has yet been enacted. Indeed, for some years after 1946, there actually seemed to be a decline in the powers of the prefects, as various ministries in Paris expanded their regional services and managed to establish their right to control these services directly. In 1953, however, this trend was not only checked but reversed. A governmental decree ordered a return to prewar practice and thus re-established the prefect's right to supervise and co-ordinate all services of the central government in his department. This was not a very long step toward deconcentration, but it does seem to indicate a trend toward an increase in prefectoral authority.

Decentralization. The constitution makers also adopted in 1946 the principle of decentralization: i.e., the transfer of certain powers from the national administration to the elected units of local government. Before analyzing the consequences of this decision it will be necessary to explain the general nature of French local government.

France's long tradition of centralization, broken only for a few years after 1789, has kept local government in a state of chronic anemia. During the Third Republic elected councils did exist in each commune, *arrondissement*,[3] and department, and each of these councils had the right to elect its mayor or its president. Furthermore, a number of local functions were entrusted to these agencies. The municipal authorities possessed police power and operated municipal services, such as public transportation; the departmental councils administered certain public welfare services, minor highways, and the like. In practice, however, their autonomy was narrowly circumscribed, both through the prefect's power of tutelage over the communes and through financial penury.

In point of fact penury proved to be the more important of these limiting factors. Most public tax receipts go to the central government; only a trickle finds its way into the local treasuries. Fifty years ago that disproportion was not serious, but since 1914 the local burden of public

---

in Paris, but that the departments are too small to serve as efficient administrative units in our era. A kind of "creeping regionalism" has been developing in recent decades; several of the Paris ministries have set up their provincial services on a regional rather than a departmental basis. Unfortunately, few of these regional schemes coincide geographically. "Creeping regionalism" has produced some confusion, for a prefect finds it hard to co-ordinate the work of ministerial departments whose local officials are organized in regions that overlap his jurisdiction.

[3] The *arrondissement* councils were dissolved by the Vichy Government and have never been revived. Their importance was always meager.

services has steadily expanded. In recent years most communes have kept solvent only through heavy subsidies from the central government; and subsidy usually means control. The departments are not much better off financially, except that they have fewer functions of their own to perform. There are in fact no important departmental services, but only national services organized within the departmental cadre.

The constitution makers in 1946 not only stated the principle of decentralization, but specified some of the things they wanted to achieve. For one thing, the elected president of the departmental general council was to replace the prefect as the department's chief executive officer, and, by implication at least, the prefect's tutelage power was to be reduced. But the details and extent of decentralization were left for future definition in an organic law, and until that law could be adopted the old relationship between prefect and local units of government was to be maintained without much change.

These plans of the constitution makers soon evaporated almost without trace. No law defining the extent of the new local freedoms was ever adopted, and probably the whole issue is now dead. Almost nobody any longer wants the reform that was promised, though no one is tactless enough to say so publicly. Matters have therefore reverted to their prewar state, with the prefect administering departmental affairs and acting as counselor and censor to the municipalities. Anglo-Saxons may lament the missed opportunity to create a more virile kind of local government, which in theory ought to develop in Frenchmen a higher sense of civic responsibility. But to embark on such an experiment in times like ours, when many painful decisions have to be made and when political rivalries are intense, might carry serious risks. Perhaps a period of peace and stability would be a better time to try to inject new vigor into French local democracy.[4]

Judicial System. "Judicial organization in France," notes an official governmental release, "is exceptionally complex. It is the product of successive contributions from centuries of our history, and in it, tradition continues to play a very important role." Yet beneath this complexity can be detected a certain logic in the French judicial system—a logic that goes back to the reforms of Napoleon. No fundamental changes have occurred since Napoleon's advisers worked out their law codes and their centralized court hierarchy, although a variety of exceptional courts have been added by a process of accretion, and some relatively minor changes have been made under the Fourth Republic.

The French courts are divided into two more or less symmetrical pyramids: the courts that handle civil and criminal cases and those that function in the sphere of administrative law. A Tribunal of Conflicts at the top assigns disputed cases to one set of courts or the other. At the bottom of the system of civil-criminal courts are the justices of the peace, normally one to each canton. They are semi-administrative, semi-judi-

[4] For a full-scale analysis of French local government and administration see two monographs by Brian Chapman: *Introduction to French Local Government* (1953) and *The Prefects and Provincial France* (1955).

cial officials who handle minor offenses and petty civil disputes. On the next higher level are the *arrondissement* tribunals, each of which is divided into two sections for civil and criminal cases. They handle appeals from the justices of the peace, but also possess primary jurisdiction over a large number of cases, such as those involving theft, the illegal practice of medicine, or violations of the press laws.

From the *arrondissement* tribunals civil cases may be appealed to a regional appeals court, and criminal cases to an assize court. The assize courts also have primary jurisdiction over serious criminal cases, such as those involving murder charges. Finally, cases may be carried upward from either the appeals courts or the assize courts to the highest regular tribunal, the Court of Cassation in Paris. Its function is strictly limited in character; it decides whether the lower court has properly applied the law. The court rules on the decision rendered, not on the content of the case. Its role is to standardize French jurisprudence by maintaining a certain uniformity in the interpretation and the application of the law. If the court overrules a lower court's judgment, the case must be retried before another tribunal at the same level, where the views of the Court of Cassation usually prevail.

Judicial Practices.   Several special aspects of French judicial organization and practice call for some comment. One such aspect is the custom of using a panel of judges rather than a single judge for each case. This system is used at every level from the *arrondissement* courts upward. For some decades this "collegiate" principle has been criticized as wasteful and unnecessary, and in 1945, at a time when the courts were desperately shorthanded, the De Gaulle government ordered the adoption of the single-judge system. But the old arrangement had deeper roots than the reformers realized; the new plan was badly received both by the judges and by the citizens. In 1948 the National Assembly brusquely abrogated the reform and returned to the collegiate principle.

A second peculiarity is the meager use made of the jury system by the French. French opinion has always been suspicious of juries on the grounds that they are too much inclined to be swayed by emotional appeals and that they are inconsistent in their decisions. As a result the jury has been used only in the assize courts; even there it was empowered only to deliberate on the facts of a case and to render a majority decision, after which the judges deliberated on the legal aspects and fixed the penalty. Sporadic criticism of the system finally led the Vichy government in 1941 to decree that jury and judges in the assize courts should henceforth deliberate together both on the facts and on the law. This change has been perpetuated in the Fourth Republic in the hope that judicial guidance during the deliberation may correct the weaknesses that the French believe are inherent in the jury system.

French dissatisfaction with their system of justice focuses mainly on the civil courts. In recent years they have been desperately overloaded; the Court of Cassation in 1953 had a backlog of twenty-four thousand cases. Experts agree that court procedures are unnecessarily complicated and archaic, and that the profession is understaffed for the expanded duties it now faces. Justice can be had in France, but only if the citizen has time and patience.

Judicial Personnel. The character of judicial personnel also requires some mention. French judges do not arrive at their positions via the American route (from lawyer to judge); rather they are civil servants who are normally chosen by examination and enter the magistrates' corps at the beginning of their careers. They are usually assigned first to a provincial court at the lowest level or to the corps of prosecutors (which is a separate branch of the magistracy), and they proceed to work their way up by ability, luck, and personal connections. One French critic has remarked that the judicial corps is "more respectable than respected." To the extent that his comment is just it rests on two factors: the inadequacy of judicial salaries and the dependence of magistrates on political favors to gain advancement. Judges are protected against arbitrary dismissal, but not against what might be called premature burial in some obscure provincial town. Although their impressive judicial robes lend them distinction, they must be content to see the lawyers who plead before them draw incomes many times greater than their own. One result is that recruitment of able personnel has grown more difficult in recent years. What is more surprising is that the honesty of the judges as a group has remained above serious reproach.

The constitution of the Fourth Republic contained one innovation designed to ensure the judges greater independence of political influence. This novelty was the High Council of the Judiciary, a fourteen-man body chosen in part by the National Assembly and in part by the judges themselves, with the right to supervise judicial administration and the appointment, promotion, and disciplining of judges. The council also advised the president of the republic on pardons. The membership of this council represented a compromise between those constitution makers who feared that the National Assembly might try to make it a political agency and those who feared that the professional judges might turn it into a clannish corporative organ. In practice the equal division of membership seems to have worked smoothly, although many judges are still suspicious of a High Council half filled with men chosen by the politicians.

The precise effect of this new body on the judiciary is still not fully clear, partly because the High Council's powers were stated rather vaguely in the constitution and remain to be defined in an organic law. Successive ministers of justice have been inclined to interpret the High Council's role narrowly, in order to keep in their own hands the right to appoint, promote, and discipline judges. They have argued that the council ought only to supervise the minister's administrative actions from a relatively Olympian height, whereas the council holds that it was meant to be the active administrative agency rather than a mere board of overseers. Even if the High Council were eventually to win its point, it could probably not restore the full prestige of the magistracy as long as salaries are so low and the number of courts in obscure provincial centers is so great.

Special Courts.   Apart from the regular court hierarchy many special courts of various types have been created during recent decades. For example, there are tribunals of commerce in a number of cities, composed of businessmen who are elected by their own members. *Conseils de prud'hommes* (industrial disputes councils), which are elected by employers and workers, act as arbitral tribunals in certain labor controversies. Special courts were set up in rural regions in 1946 to handle disputes over the new law that protects farm tenants and share croppers. In the penal sphere there are the juvenile, military, and maritime courts.

Administrative Courts.   France has long been the classic land of administrative courts, i.e., special courts that concern themselves with the claims of citizens against agents of the state acting in the discharge of their official duties. In the Anglo-Saxon countries claims against government officials have traditionally been brought in the regular courts; these countries have prided themselves on "the same justice for all." The French are fully convinced that their system of separate administrative tribunals is far superior. They point out that to sue a state agent on such a charge as having exceeded his legal power is difficult in the Anglo-Saxon countries, whereas the French made regular provision for such cases. In a centralized country with a tradition of statism, as in France, some machinery for the protection of the citizen is certainly necessary, and, in general, the French system has provided an adequate mechanism. The effect has been, not to protect bureaucrats when they abuse their power, but rather to provide citizens with means for redress.

The hierarchy of administrative courts is much less complex than the pyramid of civil-criminal courts. There are only two levels: the regional administrative tribunals (one in each of twenty-three regions) and the Council of State in Paris. In the past the regional tribunals handled only complaints against local officials, but a decree in 1953 broadened their authority considerably. The Council of State hears appeals from the regional tribunals and retains original jurisdiction in important or delicate cases.

Jurisdiction of Administrative Courts.   Most of the cases brought before the administrative courts are concerned with what is called *excès de pouvoir,* that is, administrative acts that are performed by the wrong official, in the wrong manner, or in the wrong spirit. Any citizen or professional association may, on behalf of one of its members, bring action against a specific act of a public official, using a simple and inexpensive procedure. The administrative tribunals are empowered to annul acts if they find that such acts were improperly performed. This power of annulment may even extend to certain types of decrees issued by the cabinet, if the Council of State finds that the decree does not conform to the law on which it is based. Another function of the Council is to receive and act on petitions from civil servants against improper acts (such as transfer or dismissal orders) committed by their superiors in the bureaucracy.

As presently organized the 149 officials of the Council of State are distributed among five sections, one of which (*section du contentieux*) handles all administrative law cases, while the other four examine the cabinet's requests for advisory opinions on legislation or other matters.[5] Since 1946 most members of the Council have been recruited from the National School of Administration. They must work up from the entering rank of "auditor" through "master of petitions" to full status as councilors of state.

The prestige of the Council of State is exceptionally high, but many of its members have been disturbed about the possible loss of that prestige through sheer inability to cope with the flood of work forced upon the Council in recent years. With the broadening role of government in economic and social affairs the chances of curtailing the citizen's rights become steadily greater. The practice of issuing decree laws after 1930, notably with respect to direct taxes, gave the Council the task of protecting the taxpayer against arbitrary acts. The collapse of Vichy and the confusion of the post-liberation period left the Council with a heritage of thorny issues. As a result the backlog of cases rose from three thousand in 1939 to twenty-six thousand in 1954, and the Council's peak "production record" has been only about five thousand cases in one year. Added to all this judicial labor is the Council's time-consuming new duty of advising the cabinet on all projected legislation. In the single year 1947 the number of bills and decrees examined totaled 403, with more than half of these labeled "urgent" by the cabinet.

This critical state of affairs led to the 1953 reform, which shifted a large share of the judicial burden to the regional tribunals. It is still too early to say whether these heretofore-obscure agencies are capable of handling the flood of cases that will now come their way. Probably a gradual but thorough revamping of their personnel will be needed, involving higher salaries and more rigorous selection standards. Without such improvement citizens may get a lower grade of justice, but at least they will get it much more quickly than in the past. And the fact that they can appeal to the Council of State is a pretty effective guarantee of justice, since the Council is jealous of its reputation for providing citizens with full protection against abuses by the bureaucratic state.

3. FROM LAISSEZ FAIRE TO SEMI-SOCIALISM

Role of the State.   Not so many years ago the role of the state was confined primarily to the task of governing men. In our era it also possesses a second and more complex function—the administration of things. This revolutionary change in the scope of government has led some theorists to argue that both the old state machinery and its underlying principles are outmoded and that they should undergo the same drastic revision. Certainly the problem of adaptation has been a difficult one in France, for the negative machinery of the Third Republic, with its undeclared system of checks and balances, was not well fitted to the

[5] See above, pp. 229–30.

kind of positive action that the state's new economic duties required. No doubt that is why the institutions of the Third Republic functioned less successfully after 1918 than they had in earlier years.

The Fourth Republic faced a much greater positive challenge than did the Third. Not only has the over-all planning of the national economy come to be its business, but the state has also become outright owner and operator of a large segment of that economy, amounting to between one fourth and one third of the nation's productive capacity. Although most of the so-called public sector of the economy has been created since 1945, state ownership does have a long ancestry in France. The Sèvres and Gobelins factories (which produce porcelain and tapestries respectively) have been government enterprises since the time of Colbert. The production and sale of tobacco, matches, and gunpowder have been state monopolies for many decades. Victory over Germany in 1918 brought the Alsatian potash mines into government hands.

Mixed Corporations. After 1930 "mixed corporations" began to appear in increasing numbers, with the state owning an interest that ranged from 4 per cent to 99 per cent of the stock. Sometimes the state's intervention grew out of the financial difficulties of a private enterprise —as in the cases of the principal transatlantic shipping companies and the railroad lines. The latter were reorganized in 1937 under the name S.N.C.F. (French National Railroad Corporation), with the government holding 51 per cent of the stock. The S.N.C.F. is still the largest of the mixed corporations. Another motive for state intervention was a desire to control the activities of certain enterprises that impinged upon French foreign or economic policy. Thus in 1936, after a violent public campaign against the iniquities of the munitions makers, the Popular Front government turned the aircraft plants into mixed corporations. The government rarely, if ever, acquired a share in these enterprises with a view to profit or to raising the level of production. Once established, however, the mixed corporations were supposed to operate as any private capitalistic enterprise, under private law and with profit as the goal. By 1940 the number of enterprises owned or controlled by the state totaled about two dozen.

Pressure for State Ownership. All through the interwar period a more aggressive policy of nationalization was sponsored by the Socialist Party and by organized labor, but their campaign brought no result until the early months of the Fourth Republic. The collapse of 1940 and the Vichy experience produced a powerful emotional surge in favor of state ownership. Every member of the National Resistance Council—including right-wing members—signed the famous underground manifesto of 1944 that called for "the eviction of the great economic and financial feudalities from control of the economy" and "the return to the nation of the great monopolized means of production," including power, minerals, insurance, and the principal banks.

The motives and arguments for this trend toward nationalization were curiously mixed. It was seen as a remedy for past economic decadence, as retribution for the Vichyite proclivities of many big business-men, and as the path to a future social-economic utopia. The private monopolists were widely held to have been poor enterprisers as well as poor patriots, and there was considerable evidence to support both contentions. French exponents of public ownership often quoted Herbert Morrison's phrase: "To nationalize is not to struggle against private enterprise, but against private non-enterprise." About the whole issue there hung an aura of emotionalism that gave the term "nationalization" a kind of mystic value.

De Gaulle and Nationalization. De Gaulle bent before this storm of opinion, yet he moved cautiously after the liberation. He declared that "the state should keep the levers of control in its own hands," but that outright state ownership should be confined to a few monopolies. Most of the enterprises that were nationalized by De Gaulle in 1944–45 were confiscated because their owners had allegedly aided the Germans. The government took over such plants as the Renault automobile works and the Gnome-et-Rhône aircraft-motor factory, as well as a large number of newspaper-publishing plants and offices. The number of mixed corporations also jumped since the government took over many industrial shares that had been confiscated by the Germans. Thus the state acquired a heavy interest in the advertising agency Havas-Publicité and in the dye combine Francolor. The commercial air line Air-France was also nationalized, as were the coal mines of the northern basin. Toward the end of his period in power De Gaulle took a more striking step: he carried through the nationalization of the Bank of France (the bank of issue) and the four largest deposit banks, which together handled 55 per cent of the nation's deposits. The law also established a new National Credit Council under the minister of finance, with broad advisory powers concerning all aspects of banking and credit. The only vocal critics of this bank-nationalization measure were the left-wing parties, which felt that it should have been broadened to cover other powerful banks as well. The Communists also opposed any grant of compensation to the expropriated shareholders, but they were overruled by all other parties.

Climax of Nationalization. De Gaulle's resignation early in 1946 opened the way for the left-wing majority in the first Constituent Assembly to push through an extensive program of nationalization. Within four months the state had taken over the coal industry, the gas- and electricity-producing and distributing systems, and the thirty-seven largest insurance companies. The Communists also proposed to nationalize the steel industry, but no action was taken on their bill. This period proved to be the high point of the wave of nationalization. In succeeding assemblies the balance of power shifted away from the left, and the center and right-wing groups were able to block further additions to the list. They even reversed the trend slightly by voting in 1948 that Air-France should be organized as a mixed corporation, partially owned by private shareholders, and not as a "public enterprise" like coal and electricity. The dye combine Francolor was also returned to private hands in 1951 by court order.

The merits or defects of state operation of industry have been a subject of continuing debate ever since the Fourth Republic moved into that field. Enemies of nationalization have been aided by the fact that most of the new state enterprises operated at a loss for several years after 1946 and that some mixed corporations (notably the railways) have suffered from chronic financial difficulties that have heavily burdened the taxpayer. The critics were aided too by clear evidence that the Communists for a time managed to turn some of the nationalized enterprises into economic empires dominated by the party's high command. Defenders of nationalization have replied that there are valid economic reasons why certain state-owned enterprises have lost money, and they add that public service may be a higher motive than profit when the state runs a vital branch of the economy. They admit that the Communists did get an initial strangle hold on nationalized coal, gas, and electricity, but they point out that this grip was broken as early as 1947. They agree that it is not easy to ensure efficient state operation and adequate control, but they argue that these problems are less serious than the abuses chargeable against the "feudal interests" that were formerly in control.

Structure of Public Enterprises.   Over the past decade French politicians and experts have been debating the proper organizational structure for state-run enterprises. There are three major schools of thought: a) statist, b) syndicalist, and c) autonomist. Elements of all three systems can be found in French nationalized industry as it has functioned in the Fourth Republic.

Statist Formula.   Partisans of the statist formula believe that state enterprises ought to be run directly by government officials, functioning as regular civil servants under the rules of administrative law. Prewar France offers numerous precedents for this formula; it has long been used in the tobacco monopoly, as well as in the so-called *offices* (such as the state-owned Office Nationale de l'Azote, set up in 1924 to manufacture industrial nitrates). In the Fourth Republic it was applied from the outset in the Renault automotive plant, where the director-general is named by cabinet decree and is not controlled but is only advised by a board of directors representing the employees and the consumers. The system has worked well in the Renault plant, perhaps because it perpetuates an organizational structure of one-man management that was efficient when the plant was privately run. Exponents of statism contend that direct state operation is both most efficient and most likely to be concerned with the general interest, for career officials of the state presumably represent the interests of all citizens, whereas the representatives of employees or of large consumers are inclined to look out for their special interests.

Syndicalist Formula. The syndicalist plan has long been favored by organized labor, and for a time after 1946 it was widely used in the new state enterprises—notably in coal, gas, and electricity. This formula places control of an enterprise in a tripartite board of directors, one third of whom represent the employees, one third the large consumers, and one third the government. It gives the state's representatives only a minority position in directing an enterprise that the state itself owns.

Proponents of the system contend that it is more democratic than the statist solution and that it will turn the employees into enthusiastic participants in the enterprise. Its critics reply that there has been no evidence yet of such a psychological transformation of the workers. They point out, too, that the tripartite boards sometimes resort to "log-rolling" tactics at the expense of the state. On the coal board, for example, the principal consumers of coal (heavy industry and the railroads) some years ago approved higher wages for the miners on condition that the workers' representatives would agree to keep coal prices low. The state (i.e., the taxpayer) was left to worry about the resulting deficit.

In 1953 the government tacitly abolished the syndicalist experiment by decreeing a reorganization of the boards of directors for coal, gas, and electricity. The decree provided that the representatives of the large consumers would be replaced by men chosen by the government for their technical competence. Thus the state has promoted itself from a minority to a majority position on the boards of directors.

Autonomist Formula. Partisans of autonomy for state enterprises look to British nationalized industry and the American TVA for their model. They would like to adopt the British system of vesting broad authority in a non-political board of experts named by the government for their technical competence alone. They are aware, however, that French political tradition and mentality would not permit the creation of such boards. Their organizational plan is more modest, therefore; it calls for a quadripartite board of directors, with a category of "technicians" added to the three groups included in the syndicalist formula. Something like this arrangement may be found in the nationalized insurance companies and the nationalized banks, but in both cases the size of the technicians' group and the amount of autonomy enjoyed by the enterprise fall far short of the autonomists' ideal.

Problems of Control. Perhaps the most difficult practical problem created by the state's venture into business is that of combining operational efficiency with governmental control. One possible method is direct advance control, with the appropriate cabinet minister or his agent required to give prior approval to any important decision by the management. Another method is ex-post-facto control through an auditing of the accounts. Parliament moved in this latter direction in 1948 when it set up a special Verification Commission, whose members were mostly judges from the Court of Accounts. The Commission has functioned effectively and its reports have been heard with respect, but there is still no easy way to fix responsibility for past errors in judgment or to decide on proper punishment for such errors.

More recently the government has shifted sharply in the direction of tighter direct controls. By a decree of 1953 the minister of industry assigns a commissioner to each enterprise to serve as the government's technical watchdog and spokesman. He attends all board of directors meetings and possesses a suspensive veto over any board action pending review by the minister. The 1953 decree also authorizes the minister of finance to set up a supervisory committee for each enterprise; its chairman is a full-time control officer and can suspend any current decision until his minister has examined it. Each year the supervisory committee is required to present a detailed report to the minister of finance.

The effect of these changes is to introduce something very much like statism into the major public enterprises. Many French experts believe that the process has been carried much too far. Management is confined in a virtual strait jacket by the complex network of controls, so that efficient operation may be seriously hampered. The result, warns the expert Maurice Byé, can be "immobility, which is the very worst form of statism." Pressure for a retreat from statism comes from three different quarters. A turn toward the autonomist solution is urged especially by the M.R.P., which has long been pushing a bill designed to systematize all public enterprises and to broaden managerial powers. The Communists, on the other hand, have been preaching a return to organized labor's old ideal, the syndicalist formula. Finally, right-wing politicians contend that the best solution would be to transform all public enterprises into mixed corporations, with private capital allowed to participate.

Which of these various paths the French Republic will follow no one can safely say. At any rate the experiment in a mixed economy, with public and private sectors coexisting side by side, seems to be generally accepted by Frenchmen after a decade of trial. Certainly the emotional surge of 1940–46 that held nationalization to be a panacea has been pretty well dissipated, and skepticism has replaced conviction in many French minds. Neither the fears nor the hopes of the liberation era have been fulfilled, yet the return of the public sector to private hands seems most unlikely. The problem is to make this mixed economy work efficiently within the democratic framework. The success or failure of the experiment will have broad implications for the French republican system and for Western democracy in general.

4. FROM EMPIRE TO QUASI-COMMONWEALTH

Nature of the French Union.   The problem of government in contemporary France would be complex enough if it were confined to the nation's home territory alone. It becomes immensely more difficult when the task of transmuting a large and diverse colonial empire into a com-

monwealth of peoples is added to the purely domestic issues. The two
constituent assemblies spent a disproportionate share of their time in debating the character of what they chose to call the French Union, yet
when they had finished even the drafters themselves were not quite sure
what the new Union would be like or how best to go about building it.
Worse still, the colonial upheaval that has marked the years since 1946
has made a difficult task almost impossible. It is not easy to convert an
old structure into an experimental new one when part of the building is
on fire.

Both in structure and in spirit the new commonwealth created by
the constitution of 1946 was full of anomalies and ambiguities. Most
curious of all was the fact that, although the French Republic was declared to be only one component part of the French Union, the constitution of the Union was merely a subsection of the republic's constitution
(Section VIII). Structurally, federal organs were set up in Paris, but
they were scarcely more than appendages to the organs of continental
France. A complex duality of citizenship was created: citizens of France
(or of an "associated state" like the Republic of Viet-Nam) were at the
same time citizens of the French Union. But the rights and privileges
attached to such citizenship in the overseas areas remained juridically
obscure. The contradictions reflected not only the extreme complexity
of the empire but also the variety of concepts that had to be reconciled
in the Constituent Assembly in order to secure the establishment of the
Union.

Background of the Problem. The idea of a colonial commonwealth is of recent growth in France. Before 1940 it was taken for
granted that the center of imperial gravity ought to remain in Paris.
This view was held by Frenchmen of the traditional "assimilation" school,
which maintained that the proper goal of colonial policy was to turn the
overseas populations into Frenchmen both culturally and politically. It
was also held by those French leftists who produced the rival doctrine
of "association." The latter group aimed to assimilate only a small
colonial elite who would then share with Frenchmen the task of administering the empire. Almost no one conceived of a true federation of
peoples under French guidance, with broad powers of self-government
in the various federated units. The example of the British Commonwealth had little appeal; it was too alien to the French colonial tradition, and it seemed ill adapted to an empire populated mainly by
varied and often primitive indigenous groups rather than by French emigrants.

The events of World War II accelerated changes in the attitude of
the overseas peoples and in the thinking of Frenchmen, changes that
might normally have taken a generation to develop. Well before the
liberation it was clear that some kind of reform program would be
necessary to calm the nationalist agitation of certain overseas groups. In
addition the Free French felt a sense of obligation to the colonial peoples for the support they had given against Vichy. Early in 1944, De
Gaulle called a conference of French colonial administrators at Brazza-

ville (French Congo) to study projected reforms. An impressive list of changes was approved, but it was noted that no representatives of the colonized areas were invited to attend the conference and that the delegates began by ruling out "any idea of autonomy, any possibility of evolution outside the French imperial bloc." When De Gaulle returned to France, he brought no plan for a structural reform of the empire. Neither did the reviving parties in France have such a program. Only the Communists had taken an open stand; they urged full citizenship and political rights for the overseas peoples but added that French sovereignty must not be infringed.

Most Frenchmen, however, were much more receptive to a fundamental change than they would have been ten years earlier. Therefore, there was general approval when De Gaulle announced that the overseas peoples would be given a share in drafting the Fourth Republic's constitution. During the Third Republic a few of the "old colonies" like Senegal and Martinique (which had long since been culturally assimilated) had already begun to send deputies and senators to Paris. But De Gaulle broadened the prerogative to include all parts of the empire except Indo-China, which was still in a chaotic state in 1945. He set up safeguards, however, against the potential power of the vast indigenous vote. Only certain limited categories of the local populations were given the suffrage, and the French colonist minority was assured of representation by being allowed to vote in a separate electoral college.

Almost no one recognized the long-range significance of this decision. Once granted, representation for the overseas peoples could scarcely be rescinded in any future elected bodies, unless the French were to decide to decentralize the empire by granting real power to local assemblies in Africa and Asia. Pressure for a colonial New Deal was sure to be constant all through the sessions of the Constituent Assembly, and that pressure might push the Assembly further and faster than it wanted to go. Besides, the presence of a large colonial bloc in this and future assemblies might decide the fate of purely domestic French issues if the colonials should happen to hold the balance of power.

Constituent Period. Out of the foggy debates of the first Constituent Assembly three different concepts of the French Union gradually emerged. The first was proposed by the sixty-four deputies who represented overseas constituencies. Their draft plan would have created a full-blown federal structure at once, with a powerful federal assembly, a federal cabinet responsible to it, and a broad grant of local self-government in each part of the new commonwealth. But no party in France was ready to try what seemed to be so explosive an experiment. Even the Communists and Socialists, who professed to favor federalism as the ultimate goal, felt that it could be achieved only on the installment plan. They proposed to begin by setting up territorial assemblies throughout the empire, and then to expand the powers of these bodies as the local populations developed a capacity for self-government. Pending the arrival of full-scale federalism, the overseas peoples would be given French citizenship plus some representation in the Paris Parliament. Still a third concept was that of the center and right groups, including the M.R.P. They preferred a somewhat modified version of the old prewar associationist ideal, with some concessions to the overseas peoples but with centralized control remaining in Paris.

The draft plan worked out by the first Constituent Assembly was a nebulous compromise that leaned in the direction of the Communist-Socialist thesis. It even provided that membership in the French Union would be a matter of "free consent"—which implied the right to secede at any time. In a haze of good will and brotherly love all parties in the Assembly gave their approval to this section of the constitution. But brief reflection led the center and right groups to regret their impulsiveness, and when the voters turned down the first constitutional draft, these parties decided that the bonds of empire must be tightened. Their revised plan, sponsored by the M.R.P., superficially appeared to go even further and faster toward federalism than did the leftists' project. It proposed not only the establishment of local assemblies overseas but also the immediate creation of a set of federal organs in Paris. The key aspect of the plan, however, was the M.R.P.'s insistence that these new organs should be granted only such powers as Frenchmen might choose to give them and that any future structural changes must also originate in Paris.

The struggle between these two viewpoints—that of the left and the overseas deputies, on the one hand, versus that of the right and the M.R.P. on the other—almost wrecked the second Constituent Assembly. At the last minute the left gave in on most of the points at issue. It was agreed that several quasi-federal organs would be set up in Paris at once, that the authority of the overseas assemblies would be narrowly restricted, and that the possibility of secession would be ruled out. The M.R.P. in turn agreed to grant the overseas populations French citizenship, as the left insisted. This compromise was grudgingly accepted by the overseas deputies in the Assembly, although it fell far short of their somewhat utopian dreams.

Structure of the French Union. The constitution defined the French Union as a group of "nations and peoples who pool or co-ordinate their resources and their efforts to develop their respective civilizations. . . . Faithful to her traditional mission, France proposes to lead the peoples of whom she has assumed charge to a state of freedom in which they administer themselves and conduct their own affairs democratically." The preamble guaranteed to all overseas citizens "equal access to the public service, and the individual or collective exercise of the rights and liberties" that were vested in citizens of continental France.

Structurally the Union was divided into two main segments. The first of these was the French Republic, which included not only a) continental France and Algeria, but also b) those "old colonies" that were assimilated as French departments in 1946 (Martinique, Guadeloupe, Guiana, and Réunion); c) the "overseas territories" (West Africa, Equatorial Africa, Somaliland, Madagascar, the Comores Islands, New

Caledonia, and Saint Pierre-Miquelon); and d) the "associated territories" (the two former mandates of Togoland and the Cameroons, which are now trusteeship areas under the United Nations). French nationals in all parts of the French Republic were advanced to the status of French citizens, and, in theory at least, there remained no distinction in rights between a white Frenchman in Paris and a black Frenchman in Brazzaville.

The second main subdivision consisted of the so-called associated states, which might be loosely compared to the British Dominions. This category was set up to cover former protectorates like Morocco, Tunisia, and various segments of Indo-China, each of which technically possessed its own ruler and its own sovereignty. In each case the new relationship between the French Republic and the associated state was to be determined by a bilateral treaty. Nationals of these states were to retain their own citizenship rather than French citizenship, but were to be brought under the French umbrella by being made "citizens of the French Union" as well. The juridical significance of the latter status remained somewhat obscure.

This whole experiment in dominion status was disrupted at the very outset by the war that broke out in Indo-China in December, 1946, and by the explosion of nationalist sentiment in postwar North Africa. At the end of a decade all of Indo-China had been lost. Northern Viet-Nam won its de-facto independence by war; Cambodia followed when its parliament voted in 1955 to secede from the French Union. Treaties with both the Republic of Viet-Nam (or southern Viet-Nam) and the little kingdom of Laos asserted the continuing membership of those states in the French Union, but in fact the tie henceforth had little meaning. As for Morocco and Tunisia, growing violence there forced the French in 1955 to abandon all but the shadow of control. France agreed to convert the two protectorates into independent states, which by treaty would be "united to France by the permanent ties of an interdependence freely accepted and defined." This ambiguous face-saving formula could not conceal the fact that Tunisia and Morocco were unlikely ever to assume the role of associated states in the constitutional sense. Thus by the end of the Fourth Republic the new experiment had withered away almost completely.

Federal Organs. The French Union possessed three new quasi-federal organs designed to represent all of its parts. The first of these was the presidency of the French Union, a post held ex officio by the president of the republic. Overseas representatives had some voice in electing him, since more than one hundred of them sat in the two houses of the Fourth Republic's Parliament. The second organ, the High Council of States, bore some slight resemblance to the Conference of Prime Ministers of the British Commonwealth. It was made up of selected cabinet ministers of the French Republic and of the associated states, and its functions were purely consultative. Although the High Council met annually in Paris from 1951, its role remained insignificant because the list of associated states was so short. The third federal organ, the Assembly of the French Union, enjoyed a kind of subparliamentary status. Half of its members represented continental France, while the other half sat for the overseas territories and departments and the associated states. The overseas members were selected by the various territorial assemblies; those from France proper were named by the two houses of Parliament on the basis of proportional representation of parties.

Assembly of the French Union.   Of all the federal organs the Assembly of the French Union had the greatest potential importance, but its life proved too brief to permit this potential to be realized. Its powers were purely advisory, although the constitution did require the cabinet to ask its opinion on certain types of laws and decrees that were to be applied overseas. The Assembly might also be consulted by the National Assembly or by the governments of the associated states, but such consultation was in fact rare. The bulk of the Union Assembly's work was self-generated, in the form of resolutions transmitted to the cabinet or the National Assembly. This power to emit resolutions was utilized freely; indeed, the Union Assembly stretched that power somewhat by proposing detailed and lengthy legislation. Furthermore, it argued for a loose construction of the constitution, which would allow it to send investigating committees overseas and to discuss problems of the whole French Union rather than those of the overseas territories alone.

Unfortunately for the assembly, it could not force either the cabinet or Parliament to consider its resolutions, so that most of its labor was expended in vain. After a pompous and exotic opening session in the palace at Versailles the new body dropped into almost total obscurity. It bombarded the authorities at Paris with hundreds of resolutions, few of which had any effect; it protested angrily at reports that some prominent men considered the Union Assembly a waste of money, and at one journalist's description of the assemblymen as "political eunuchs." Its presiding officer called for "an end to the sumptuous and glacial exile which has deported us to this palace of Versailles." This last protest did finally bring results in 1955, when a public building in the heart of Paris was assigned to the Union Assembly as its new permanent home.

The proper role of the Union Assembly was bound to remain ambiguous as long as the character of the French Union itself was not clearly defined. Some of its critics argued that it ought to be merged with the upper house of Parliament. Others complained that in a commonwealth so varied as the French Union there could be no common legislative matter to be considered, just as there could be few representatives technically competent to study the problems of all parts of the Union. These critics concluded either that the Union Assembly should be broken up into sections, each of which would deal with a geographic segment of the Union, or that the powers of the Assembly should be transferred to the territorial legislatures overseas. Despite its shortcomings the Assembly did serve as a sounding board for overseas opinion. It was not without significance that the republic provided a forum wherein complaints and suggestions could be (and were) vigorously aired.

Role of Parliament in French Union Affairs. Since the French Union never got beyond the stage of quasi-federation, and since its new central organs were mainly a façade, it followed that real authority remained in the French National Assembly and in the cabinet responsible to it. Overseas France, though it was underrepresented in the Parliament of the Fourth Republic, was certainly not unrepresented there. In the National Assembly there were eighty-three overseas deputies, of whom the largest bloc—thirty deputies—represented Algeria. In the Council of the Republic the proportion was even more impressive: 74 of the 320 senators represented overseas constituencies.

If these representatives had found enough common interests to bind them into a single bloc in Parliament, distinct from the parties of continental France, they could often have held the balance of power at critical moments, and they might have extorted important concessions for the overseas areas. Such a bloc, however, never crystallized. Some of the overseas deputies adhered to the major French parties, while others organized small parliamentary groups like the Overseas Independents or the Algerian Movement for the Triumph of Democratic Liberties. Repeated efforts to form a single nationalist party to represent all of Black Africa foundered on the twin rocks of personal and regional rivalries. By 1958, however, after a bewildering series of fissions and mergers, there had emerged two dominant movements in Black Africa: the *Rassemblement Démocratique Africain* (R.D.A.) and the *Parti de Regroupement Africain* (P.R.A.). In some respects there were more differences within each of these parties than between them, for they reflected the views of rival leaders rather than rival doctrines. In the R.D.A., Félix Houphouet-Boigny of the Ivory Coast and Sékou Touré of French Guinea were the dominating figures; in the P.R.A. it was Léopold Senghor and Lamine-Gueye, both of Senegal.

Despite this failure of the overseas deputies to achieve unity, their influence in a fragmented National Assembly proved to be out of proportion to their strength. Often ten or fifteen votes meant the difference between survival or overthrow of a cabinet, and the Black African representatives especially soon proved themselves most adept at the parliamentary game. During the later years of the Fourth Republic few cabinets did not invite at least one overseas deputy to serve as minister or undersecretary. The Gaillard cabinet in 1957 included five African undersecretaries or secretaries of state as well as one African minister—M. Houphouet-Boigny. The key post of minister for overseas France, however, was always reserved for a metropolitan Frenchman.

Growth of Local Autonomy Overseas. A truly federal commonwealth would require not only federal organs at the center but also a devolution of power to regional and local elected bodies overseas. The constitution of 1946 did provide for the creation of such assemblies in every overseas territory and department. In addition huge areas like French West Africa and French Equatorial Africa (which are in themselves federations of several territories) were given federal assemblies, and Algeria (consisting then of three departments) got a new Algerian Assembly. The establishment of these bodies was called at the time "the most revolutionary act of the Constituent Assembly," on the ground that they represented a fundamental commitment to real federalism and local autonomy.

During the first decade of the Fourth Republic this initial commitment seemed to lack much real meaning. The overseas assemblies were granted very limited powers, the authority of the various governors remained predominant, and all key administrative posts were still held by Frenchmen. Furthermore, the continuing use of a two-college electoral system ensured at least equal representation to the French colonist minority, even though that minority might total (as in Upper Volta) only four thousand people in a total population of three and a half million. There was also evidence that in Algeria heavy administrative pressure falsified the election results. Frenchmen justified the system by pointing out that the great bulk of indigenous citizens were illiterate and indifferent to politics, and that the alternative to this restricted autonomy was not real democratic self-government but oligarchic rule by a tiny educated elite.

The loss of Indo-China in 1954 and the outbreak of rebellion in Algeria a few months later convinced many French leaders that most of overseas France would be lost if they continued to follow a reform policy of too little and too late. The problem of finding an Algerian solution acceptable to both the Algerian Moslems and the large French colonist group proved to be virtually insoluble, and the war rendered it steadily more hopeless. But in Black Africa and Madagascar the French at last sought to act before it was too late. In 1956 Parliament adopted a sweeping *loi-cadre* designed to speed the growth of real self-government in French Africa south of the Sahara. This law abolished the double electoral college outright and authorized the cabinet to carry out by decree a whole series of political, administrative, and economic reforms.

The altered system went into operation in 1957, with promising initial results. Territorial assemblies were elected by universal suffrage in each segment of West Africa and Equatorial Africa; these assemblies in turn chose representatives to reorganized federal assemblies in Dakar and Brazzaville. In each territory a kind of cabinet was established, with the governor as its presiding officer but with a chosen representative of the assembly as its vice-president. These new executive organs received much-broadened powers over domestic affairs, although such services as foreign relations, foreign trade, and justice remained in French hands. A similar system also went into operation in Madagascar, while in one of the two trusteeship territories, Togoland, the French went even further by proclaiming an autonomous republic with its own premier. The white colonist minority south of the Sahara, unlike that of Algeria, accepted the new state of affairs, and a number of whites won election to the territorial assemblies in 1957 on joint tickets with African candidates. The *Rassemblement Démocratique Africain* emerged as the most powerful political movement in Black Africa.

Whether the French at last had gotten ahead of history in their African possessions remained an open question. Many observers believed that they had granted the Africans as much self-government as these populations could intelligently use without further education and training. It was also clear that Black Africa would continue to need the economic aid that France had been providing on a sizable scale. Yet the impulse for still broader autonomy and even for outright independence was reinforced by the grants already made by France. Some African leaders were ready to settle for an interim stage during which the African elites could gain some experience in self-government, but others were determined to strike out on their own at once. Regional and personal rivalries further divided the Africans. Should Black Africa be "Balkanized," or consolidated into large federal units? If federalized, should leadership come from Senegal, Ivory Coast, or Guinea? These and many other issues left the fate of the French Union's largest remaining sector clouded with uncertainty as the Fourth Republic gave way to the Fifth.

THE SUBSTRUCTURE OF FRENCH POLITICS

1. PARTY PATTERN

Conditioning Factors. Textbooks sometimes leave the misleading impression that political systems function in a vacuum, and that the mechanical details are all that matter. Yet it should be obvious that the success of a system of government depends far less upon its structure than upon the influence of a whole series of conditioning factors. Tradition—the cultural and psychological heritage of the nation—is one such factor, much too complex to measure, but much too real to ignore. Of equal importance are the social and economic factors that make for national strength or weakness, for flexibility or rigidity, for cohesion or disintegration. These characteristics, too, are exceptionally difficult to analyze and weigh, yet they cannot be bypassed by any student of contemporary political systems.

French Party Alignment. Between the structure of government and the social forces that underlie it the party system serves as a kind of connecting link. To be sure, parties never reflect social forces accurately; perhaps it would be regrettable if they did. The influences of ideology, tradition, and leadership in any democratic country tend to cut across what are loosely called class lines. Still, a multiparty system like that of France better reflects the diverse interests and ideas of its citizens than does any two-party or one-party system. As agencies for channeling the wishes of individuals or groups their importance is so great that some of the Fourth Republic's founders wanted to set up special constitutional controls designed to keep them democratic in organization and leadership.[1]

After the collapse of 1940 most Frenchmen were determined never to allow a return to the party system of the Third Republic, with its loose and shifting groups. The old parties, except the Communists, disintegrated with the Republic, and it seemed that perhaps the moment had come to

[1] See above, p. 209.

252

sweep away the debris in favor of a wholly new system. From 1940 to 1944 speculation among underground leaders and French republicans in exile tended to center around the idea of a two- or three-party alignment, along left-right or left-center-right lines. Another theory, more utopian or perhaps more authoritarian in nature, suggested the creation of one broad Gaullist party or *rassemblement* that would range from right-center to left-center and would possess a monopoly of political power through sheer size. Its sponsors felt that the wartime experience of common resistance to the Germans had produced a new sense of unity that blunted old differences, and they believed that Charles de Gaulle was a figure capable of serving as both symbol and active chief.

On both counts these speculations were groundless. Underground unity was never more than superficial, and De Gaulle was temperamentally unsuited for such a herculean task. As a matter of fact De Gaulle's agents in France did much to resuscitate the prewar multiparty system. They encouraged the old party groups to reorganize and to enter the National Resistance Council in an effort to offset the charge that De Gaulle's aim was a one-party fascist system. Even after the liberation De Gaulle chose to assume a position above party conflicts and to let political currents swirl and eddy far beneath him. Without his active leadership no broad *rassemblement* was possible. A few reformers still hoped that they might persuade him to adopt an electoral law that, they believed, might produce a two-party system in France. Their scheme called for relatively large electoral districts, with a mere plurality required to elect an entire ticket in each district. Its effect would presumably have been to force all parties to coalesce into two rival blocs, which might have developed gradually from electoral coalitions into genuine parties. But De Gaulle chose instead to adopt proportional representation in a form that encouraged the growth of several large, nationally organized parties, and at the same time discouraged the survival of small splinter groups or independent candidacies.[2]

Proportional Representation at Work. This electoral system survived (with some notable modifications) as long as the Fourth Republic, and did much to shape the party system of postwar France. It blocked any trend toward a two-party alignment, although such a trend in a coun-

[2] As an example of how the French electoral system operated in 1945–46, the elections of November 10, 1946, in the department of the Corrèze may be cited. In competition for the department's four seats in the National Assembly the parties polled the following totals:

Communists	52,864
M.R.P.	29,978
Left Republican Rally	26,082
Socialists	23,615

The first seat was assigned to the Communists, whose total vote was then divided by two, giving a figure of 26,432. Since the M.R.P. total was greater than this figure, seat number two went to the M.R.P. The third seat went again to the Communists, for their total divided by two was greater than the total of the Left Republicans or Socialists. The fourth seat went to the Left Republicans; the entire Socialist vote was wasted as far as representation was concerned.

try like France was most unlikely. It placed more power in the hands of party leaders, who could punish rebellious deputies by shunting them down the list of candidates at the next election. It increased the importance of party labels and programs and reduced the influence of individual deputies, who found it harder to build electoral "fiefs" now that the small electoral districts of prewar days were gone. It made the boundaries between parties more rigid and impermeable, since each party ran its own list of candidates and stressed the differences that separated it from its closest neighbors. The general result was to produce a somewhat more rigid and disciplined multiparty structure than in the past and, by that very fact, to make cabinet coalitions among the parties more difficult to form.

Thus both the new electoral system and the post-liberation mood seemed at first to guarantee a party system markedly different from that of the execrated Third Republic. Instead the years of the Fourth Republic brought an undeniable (though not complete) return to the pattern of the past. French tradition, psychology, and sheer habit reasserted themselves to offset many of the changes caused by proportionalism, and to produce a party alignment that was a blend of old and new. The number of parties increased slightly, and the number of parliamentary groups markedly, between 1946 and 1958; discipline within many of the parties became somewhat more lax; some deputies chose to remain independent or, more frequently, to join a loosely articulated group that would allow them wide freedom; a few deputies resumed the habit of "shopping around" in search of personal advantage.[3] Yet alongside these familiar traits from the Third Republic there persisted certain new factors introduced by the Fourth and maintained by the system of proportional representation. Of these new factors the most notable was the emergence of powerful disciplined parties not only on the left but also in the center (the Catholic *Mouvement Républicain Populaire,* or M.R.P.) and even on the right (the Gaullist *Rassemblement Populaire Français,* or R.P.F. and Pierre Poujade's *Union de Défense des Commerçants et Artisans* [U.D.C.A.]). Alongside them the older, more individualistic parties made a notable comeback, but even these groups were driven to a higher degree of discipline by the competition of their great "monolithic" or centralized rivals.

Issue of Electoral Reform. In general the more highly disciplined parties clung to proportional representation, while the older and looser groups urged a return to the prewar electoral system of small single-member districts. Many Gaullists favored still a third plan: a kind of plurality system resembling those of Britain and the United States, but with large multimember districts. This device was designed to force all

[3] In the later years of the Fourth Republic the number of parties of major importance in the country and in Parliament became stabilized at six, but the number of parliamentary groups grew steadily until it reached fifteen. In an effort to reduce this fragmentation the National Assembly late in 1957 voted to require that groups have 28 rather than 14 members in order to qualify for representation on committees.

the parties into two voting blocs, thus producing in France at least the appearance of a two-party system. But the advocates of electoral change were so divided among themselves, and the defenders of proportionalism (mainly the Communists and the M.R.P.) so tenacious, that "P.R." continued in force throughout the Fourth Republic.

Just before the 1951 general elections the system was modified somewhat by attaching to proportionalism a curious scheme authorizing coalitions or alliances of party lists (*apparentements*). This device, designed to cut down the number of Communist and Gaullist deputies, enabled two or more major parties to negotiate electoral agreements loosely linking their separate lists of candidates in a given district. If the allied parties could poll more than half the total vote cast, they would then share all of the Assembly seats for that district.[4] The device was bitterly denounced as complicated and unjust, but it did achieve its purpose by cutting back the extreme parties and ensuring a center majority in the Assembly of 1951–55. Vigorous efforts to achieve a more sweeping electoral reform before the 1956 elections canceled themselves out; a majority in Parliament wanted a change but could not agree on what change. As a result the same complex system used in 1951 was applied again in 1956. This time, however, it worked much differently. The center parties were so badly split that they failed to organize many electoral alliances capable of winning half the votes in a district. In only seven departments did the *apparentement* system operate when the votes were counted; everywhere else the straight proportional system had to be applied, so that the extreme left and right parties made notable gains.

Distribution of Power in Parliament. The political center of gravity was noticeably different in each of the three National Assemblies elected in the course of the Fourth Republic. The balance in the first Assembly (1946–51) lay slightly to the left of center. Governing France during most of this period was the so-called Third Force coalition, composed of such center and left-center groups as the Socialists, the M.R.P., and the Radicals. The major opposition group was the Communist Party, the largest single group in the Assembly; the right-wing opposition, on the other hand, was still small and divided. Gaullist strength in Parliament was meager, for De Gaulle's party was not organized until after the 1946 elections.

[4] The election in the Dordogne Department offers a good example of how the 1951 system operated. Six lists competed for the department's five seats. The four center lists were allied; the Communists and the R.P.F. ran alone. The outcome was as follows:

Radicals and near-Radicals	40,889	(2 seats)
Socialists	36,102	(2 seats)
M.R.P.	14,114	(1 seat)
Independents and Peasants	13,883	—
	104,988	
Communists	61,479	—
R.P.F.	25,078	—

The allied lists, having polled a clear majority of the total vote, shared all five seats on a proportional basis.

In the second National Assembly (1951–55) the fulcrum moved to the right of center. On the left Communist and crypto-Communist representation fell from 182 to 103 seats, while on the far right a powerful Gaullist Party (the R.P.F.) won 121 seats to emerge as the largest single group in the Assembly. The old-fashioned libertarian parties of the right-center also made important gains: notably the Radicals, the Independent Republicans, and the new Peasant Party. The Third Force coalition lost control, and even the label itself disappeared. In its place a series of right-center coalition cabinets governed France, with the M.R.P., the Radicals, and the Independents furnishing most of the leadership. The Socialists went into the opposition, refusing to participate in coalitions that were oriented toward conservatism. They would have liked to take this step much earlier, but dared not do so until the right-center groups got a clear majority and could keep the republic afloat without Socialist help.

This swing to the right in 1951, combined with the tempting prospect that cabinet posts might be the reward of collaboration, soon split the Gaullist group in Parliament. A large segment refused to stay in the opposition despite the general's maledictions; they contributed ministers to successive cabinets and soon became almost indistinguishable from the right-center Independent Republicans. The conversion of these Gaullists from enemies to supporters of the regime assured the right-center of a narrow but workable parliamentary majority throughout the second National Assembly. But the disintegration of the Gaullist threat seemed to mean that the republic was safe, so that the center parties could risk squabbling among themselves. By 1955 a deep rift had developed within the Radical Party, with Pierre Mendès-France and Edgar Faure leading hostile factions and advocating rival policies. Mendès-France became the symbol of the left-center parties' hopes, while Faure headed a loose alliance of the right-center. Out of this conflict came Premier Faure's decision in December, 1955 to dissolve the National Assembly. It was the first use of the dissolution power in France since 1877, and it aroused a storm of criticism on the ground that Faure's motivation was selfishly political. Faure presumably believed that the Mendès-France forces would be put at a disadvantage by hasty elections, and that the right-center coalition would emerge stronger than ever.

If this was Faure's calculation, it boomeranged badly. The third National Assembly, elected in January, 1956, was unlike either of its predecessors in political composition. The rift between *Mendèsistes* and *Fauristes* had prevented the formation of effective electoral coalitions of the center, and opened the way to gains by both the extreme right and the extreme left. The Communists, despite a slight drop in their percentage of the popular vote, climbed to 151 seats, while the new Poujadist anti-tax movement on the opposite wing elected 51 deputies. Most of the parties of both right-center and left-center lost a few seats: the "pure" Gaullists (i.e., those who had remained loyal to the general) were almost wiped out.[5]

[5] The following table indicates the distribution of groups in the National Assembly in January, 1958. It will be noted that there were more parliamentary groups

As usual no party or leader could command anything like a dependable majority in the new Assembly, and the Mendès-versus-Faure feud rendered difficult even the shaky coalition arrangements to which Frenchmen had become accustomed. Some observers predicted that the new Assembly would be ungovernable, since no center coalition could now get a majority without including both the Socialists on the left and the Independents on the right, and since those two parties seemed irreconcilable on a great many issues. This forbidding prospect fed the Communists' hope that they might soon return to power by tempting the left-center groups into a new Popular Front coalition like that of 1935. Instead the left-center parties decided to risk the formation of what was essentially a minority government of Socialists and Mendès-France Radicals, dependent for its creation and survival on the support of the right-center groups. The Socialist leader Guy Mollet became premier.

This shaky experiment, by what seemed a kind of miracle, lasted sixteen months, and thus broke the Fourth Republic's longevity record for governments. The Mollet cabinet's durability, however, was traceable, not to any special virtues it possessed, but simply to the fact that the parties backing it saw no workable alternative. The right-center supported Premier Mollet because he accepted a tough policy in repressing the Algerian rebellion, and because he postponed economic and social reforms demanded by his own Socialist Party; the right-center abandoned him in May, 1957 when he finally began to press for social reforms. With great difficulty the politicians managed to patch up a flimsy new coalition headed by a Radical named Bourgès-Maunoury, with its center of gravity

---

than national parties, and that group labels were not always identical with party labels. Groups whose names are indented in the list below were affiliated, for purposes of committee representation, with the group just preceding in the list. Groups are listed as they sat from left to right.

During the two years since the Assembly was elected in January, 1956 a number of changes had occurred. Some groups adopted new names; some divided, amoeba-like; some suffered a severe drop in membership. The Poujadists were hardest hit, falling from 51 at election time to 31 two years later, partly through defections and partly through the invalidation of elections. The 30 Algerian seats were still vacant; elections could not be held there in 1956 because of the rebellion.

Communists	143
Progressives	6
Socialists	97
African Socialist Movement	4
Radical Socialists	43
U.D.S.R. and African Democratic Rally	21
Left Republican Rally (R.G.R.)	13
Dissident Radicals	14
M.R.P.	75
African Convention	7
Social Republicans (Gaullists)	21
Independents	92
Peasants for Social Action	6
U.F.F. (Poujadists)	31
Peasant Party	12
Unaffiliated	10
Vacant seats	31
	626

farther to the right. When that cabinet in turn collapsed four months later, the republic approached complete deadlock. The crisis of September, 1957 lasted thirty-six days, breaking all previous records, and it ended with another Radical-led cabinet under Félix Gaillard, scarcely different in personnel or policy from the one that had just been overthrown. Thus the record of the third National Assembly underlined once again the disadvantages of France's multiparty structure and of the electoral system that helped to perpetuate it.

With this general background a brief analysis of the organization and character of each major group will fill in the remaining details of the Fourth Republic's party pattern.

Communists. The existence of a powerful and highly disciplined Communist party was perhaps the most important factor that distinguished the Fourth Republic from the Third. It also distinguishes France (and Italy) from all other countries in the non-Communist world. In every election from 1945–56 the Communists polled between 25 and 28 per cent of the French national vote, thereby establishing themselves as the largest and most solid mass party in modern French history. They have almost doubled their strength over prewar days, and they have notably broadened their geographical and sociological base. The party's stronghold is the urban proletariat, more than half of which votes Communist by a kind of automatic reflex. Communist domination of the principal labor organization, the *Confédération Générale du Travail* (C.G.T.), solidifies the party's hold over the workers. But there is no social category without an important nucleus of Communist militants and followers, and there is no electoral district in France that has not been penetrated by Communist activity. Before the war most of the Communist deputies came from the "red belt" surrounding Paris; now they represent every section of France.

It is commonplace to say that communism thrives on misery and appeals to the downtrodden. Certainly much of the party's support comes from people in the lowest income bracket, but the Communist appeal is clearly more varied and deeper than mere economic protest. Its best militants often come from among the better-paid workers and from other social categories that are far from miserable. For many Frenchmen there is an undeniable appeal in a movement that prides itself on being something more than an ordinary party—that demands of its followers a total commitment, offers them a rational explanation of their world, and gives them a quasi-religious faith. "We are not the party of the poor," proclaimed one high French Communist; "we are the party that is always right." Perhaps this sense of conviction explains the party's hold on intellectuals and young people; in 1952, 42 per cent of the Communist voters were below thirty-five years of age. The persistence of the old equalitarian ideal also works to the benefit of the Communists, and they profit too by the widespread habit in southern France of voting as far left as possible.

The tightly-knit organizational pattern of the Communist Party concentrates power in a small group of leaders, with Secretary-General

Maurice Thorez at the pyramid's apex. These policy-making officials are presumably responsible to the central committee, which in turn is elected at the biennial party congress of delegates from all local units. In practice, however, decisions are made at the top and instructions go downward through the hierarchy to the fourteen thousand factory, local, and rural cells.

In spite of frequent rumors of factionalism in the upper reaches of the party there has been no serious defection since the war. Even the anti-Stalin campaign in the Soviet Union and the impact of the Hungarian rebellion in 1956 failed to shatter the party's unity. A few high-ranking leaders have been purged or severely disciplined in recent years, apparently because of a combination of personal rivalries and policy conflicts. Some of the victims (notably André Marty and Charles Tillon) had been exponents of tougher revolutionary tactics than those sponsored by Thorez; others, like Auguste Lecoeur, were accused of scheming to get a personal strangle hold on the party; still others, like the young intellectual Pierre Hervé, publicly advocated a softer party line just before the 1956 Soviet party congress gave its blessing to such a change. But none of these deviates from party discipline has been able to pull a segment of the apparatus away from the regular leadership. Large-scale "Titoism" remains improbable, for the Titoist heresy grows best in a country where Communism has already arrived in power.

The Communists have always been frank about their ultimate goal— the establishment of a Soviet-type republic in France. Their strategy and tactics in attaining that goal, however, have been remarkably flexible. For more than two years after the liberation their line was ultrapatriotic. They collaborated with the "bourgeois" parties in successive cabinets, preached political and social democracy in the Rousseau tradition, and discouraged overt evidences of labor discontent. Apparently the Communist high command aimed at a gradual unresisted conquest of France via the ballot box. Or, failing that, they could hope to get so strong a foothold in the government and the armed forces that they could carry out a sudden *coup d'état* on the Czechoslovak model. By 1947, however, cold-war conditions had undermined this strategy. The Communist ministers were pushed out of the cabinet, and the party's attempt to wreck the new center coalition by sponsoring nationwide strikes in 1947 and 1948 did not succeed. The center politicians fought back more stubbornly than the Communists had expected, and the party hestitated to push matters to the point of open civil war. Several years of voluntary political isolation followed. Then, in the mid-1950s, the Communists reverted to an older line: they unfurled the banner of the Popular Front and sought to get back into power by tempting the parties of the democratic left into a "progressive" coalition.

The decade since 1947 has brought some evidence of Communist decline. Dues-paying membership fell off from a peak of almost a million to 400,000; a number of party newspapers had to suspend publication; the workers showed increased apathy when called upon to demonstrate; and a segment of the C.G.T. broke away to form a new anti-Communist labor confederation called C.G.T.F.O. (*Force Ouvrière,* or Workers'

Strength). Between the 1946 and the 1951 elections the Communist share of the popular vote cast fell from 28 per cent to 26.4 per cent, and in 1956 it dropped further to 25.5 per cent. The party showed some concern too over signs of aging among its active militants: delegates to a recent party congress were warned that, among the dues-paying members, those over fifty years of age outnumber those under twenty-five years by a ratio of three to one. But the party's losses in size and momentum have been remarkably small when one considers the effect of their political isolation, and when one recalls that this was a decade of economic prosperity and expansion. In the 1956 elections the party was still far and away the largest one in France, polling a total of 5.5 million votes and keeping a firm grip on its principal strongholds.

A distinction is often made between the mass of Communist voters and the hard nucleus of perhaps fifty thousand fanatically devoted militants. That difference is real enough, but its implications are open to dispute. It would not be safe to conclude that the voting mass can be easily pried loose from its leaders through propaganda and enlightenment. French Communist leaders have managed to stake out an exclusive claim on the revolutionary tradition, and this claim gives them an automatic hold on many voters. They have also been astute enough to analyze the grievances of all groups, and to center their agitation around these grievances. The party's highly developed organizational structure and dynamic leadership give it still another advantage over its rivals. No doubt it is true that the bulk of Communist voters resemble British Laborites of the Aneurin Bevan wing more than they resemble their own fanatically devoted leaders. Their primary interest is not the strengthening of the Soviet Union or the arrival of the Communist era in France; rather it is the immediate improvement of their own economic and social status and the preservation of peace. Yet they remain convinced that only the Communist leadership, with all of its blind devotion to Moscow, has their interests at heart and really intends to do something for them. This link between militants and masses gives the party much of its strength. Some observers fear that communism, although not strong enough to take power itself, may be able not only to delay but actually to prevent the effective solution of France's social and economic problems through democratic procedures. Whether or not this gloomy forecast is valid, the strength of communism has been and continues to be the most important political factor conditioning the future of free government in France.

Socialists. The Socialist Party, although theoretically bound together by Marxian dogma, has never managed to achieve such unity as the Communists can boast. By long tradition it is much more democratic and decentralized; in the Third Republic the party's branch unit in each department chose its own policy line and sought to impose that line on the party's leadership. Even more important, the party's prewar statutes recognized the existence of intraparty factions, and these various "tendencies," as they were called, were given a kind of proportional representation in the high councils of the party. This condition was a source of weakness that Socialist leaders hoped to eliminate after 1944, and to this end the party statutes were revised. Representation of "tendencies" was ruled out, and it was agreed that the majority's wishes in the annual congress should be binding on all party members. In practice, however, it has been impossible to tighten the screws of discipline very much. Many militant Socialists are too individualistic in spirit to accept the kind of regimentation that marks the Communist Party.

During the early months of the Fourth Republic it seemed that the Socialist Party might become the strongest political force in the new France. Its program of drastic social and economic reform within the democratic framework had a wide appeal in that era of rejuvenation. In the first general election of 1945, however, it ran only third among the parties, and its popular vote declined steadily thereafter until in 1951 it had lost almost 40 per cent of its postwar electoral support. Party membership, too, steadily evaporated from a high of 355,000 members to 110,000. From about 1953, however, the membership figure leveled off and remained stable; and in the 1956 elections the Socialists made their first gain in popular support since the liberation. The rise was modest— from 14.2 per cent to 14.8 per cent of the votes cast—but at least it checked and reversed a trend that had begun to seem unstoppable.

The Socialists' disappointing record is often traced to weak leadership, an excessively doctrinaire outlook, and an inability to choose between alternative courses of action. The party has been accused of talking revolution without meaning it, and of mouthing proletarian slogans when it has actually lost all proletarian support. These harsh charges are somewhat excessive. True, there has been a doctrinal (or, better, a temperamental) split within the party for many years. Some Socialists are hard-shelled doctrinaires, clinging to a narrowly dogmatic Marxism that is antibourgeois and anticlerical in spirit. Others are moderates, in the tradition of Jean Jaurès and Léon Blum; they preach "humanistic" socialism and would like to replace the phrase "class conflict" by the softer phrase "class action." The proletarian bias of the doctrinaire wing produces still another division. Some doctrinaires are constantly tempted by the idea of proletarian unity, or common action with the Communists. Others demand that the party devote all its efforts to competing with the Communists for the working-class vote. Both segments of the doctrinaire wing look with suspicion on the humanists' willingness to co-operate with "bourgeois" parties and on the humanists' desire to convert the party into a non-class movement like British Labor.[6]

No doubt these internal differences have hampered the party's action, but the problems faced by the Socialists have not been entirely of their own making. At bottom they have had to face the critical tactical problem of how best to contain and combat Communist power, and they have been forced to choose between postponing their own reform demands or

[6] Over the last decade at least a dozen attempts have been made to found a party that would sit between the Communists and the Socialists, and that would somehow re-create proletarian unity by attracting the followers of both left-wing parties to its banner. Late in 1957 several of these splinter movements coalesced to form a new *union de la gauche socialiste*—the most serious effort to date to create a "new left."

seeing the democratic republic destroyed by their enemies. These choices have naturally created severe internal tension and have left the party open to charges of weakness and hypocrisy. The Socialists' participation in Third Force cabinets before 1951 probably contributed to their decline, but it also contributed to the republic's survival. The internal stresses were much reduced when the party went into opposition after 1951, and this greater unity and toughness may explain why the Socialists made an electoral comeback in 1956.

Whether or not the Socialists are ready to admit it, their party is no longer mainly proletarian either at the top or at the bottom. An analysis of the party's official cadres in 1952 showed that 80 per cent of those who held offices in the party were white-collar workers, civil servants, or small business or professional men, while only 13.5 per cent were laborers. The Socialists win more votes in the small and middle-sized towns than in the large cities; they are slightly stronger in the agricultural south than in the industrial north. In competing for the votes of urban laborers they are handicapped by a certain lack of dynamism and by inadequate organization. As one Frenchman has ironically remarked, "herbivorous Marxians" like the Socialists are inevitably at a disadvantage when faced by "carnivorous Marxians" like the Communists. Nevertheless it is an exaggeration to conclude that the party has been totally abandoned by the working class. The Socialists retain an important foothold in some industrial areas (notably in the northeastern departments adjoining Belgium), and they are particularly strong in the public service industries.

Radical Socialists.   The Radical Socialist Party, whose history almost coincided with that of the Third Republic, seemed in 1945 to be as dead as the prewar regime. Its recovery since that low point has been steady rather than spectacular, and after 1951 it had a key role in most cabinets. The party's loose organizational structure and its libertarian doctrines still appeal strongly to certain petty-bourgeois elements, especially in the provincial towns and the small-farming areas of the southwest. Part of its influence has come from the personal prestige of some of its elder statesmen like the late Édouard Herriot. Indeed, its appeal is clearly stronger among older voters than among young people. No other party has so small a proportion of voters in the below-thirty-five age bracket, and no other has so few women voters, either.

The Radicals enjoy a strategic middle position in the political spectrum. They straddle the center: their traditional anticlericalism inclines them to the left, while their social and economic doctrines (which are generally *laissez faire* in nature) put them on the right. Thus they are well placed to join coalition cabinets of any kind. Discipline is almost unknown in the party; frequently its deputies split three ways in voting on important issues—some for, some against, and some abstaining. Party organization is rudimentary, consisting of little more than a congeries of local electoral committees with an annual congress devoid of real power to impose the will of the majority. The party has been described, with some justice, as nothing more than "an electoral co-operative society."

Despite the unrivaled flexibility of its organization the Radical

Party has been torn apart by internal dissension during the last few years. In 1954 Pierre Mendès-France, a Radical deputy who had long been preaching the need for drastic economic reforms in France, became premier. Although his stay in power was brief, his dynamic leadership inspired a wave of enthusiasm both within the party and outside it; young Frenchmen especially rallied to his banner. This impetus enabled Mendès-France to gain control of the party machinery in 1955 and to expel his leading rival, Edgar Faure. Mendès-France then set out to convert this loose and individualistic collection of politicians into a more disciplined party, with a common set of goals and a crusading spirit. The effect of his campaign was contradictory; while reinvigorating the party he also split it badly. Soon after Faure and his followers were expelled a second crisis led to the secession of another segment of the party, led by such old-time Radicals as Henri Queuille. Furthermore, within the regular Radical organization that remained, growing factionalism led Mendès-France in 1957 to resign the party leadership. The failure of the Mendès-France experiment indicates a return to the undisciplined, flexible Radicalism of the past.

Near-Radical Groups. The *Union Démocratique et Socialiste de la Résistance* (U.D.S.R.) represents almost the only direct political survival of the wartime underground groups. Its founders, mostly newcomers to politics, hoped to create a broad left-center party that might hold together the non-Communist resistance forces and become the fulcrum of politics in the Fourth Republic. Instead it developed into a splinter party not much different from the Radicals except for its more neutral attitude toward the church and its freedom from a weighty tradition. Some of its leaders, notably René Pleven and François Mitterrand, have frequently held cabinet posts, for the U.D.S.R.'s few votes in the assembly were often vital for the survival of a ministry. Its strength, however, progressively declined, until in 1956 it was able to win only six assembly seats in continental France plus several others overseas.

The *Rassemblement des Gauches Républicaines* (R.G.R.) was formed early in the Fourth Republic as a loose electoral coalition of Radicals, U.D.S.R., and fractional center groups. Some politicians hoped to convert it into a great centrist party that would swallow up its constituent elements, but the Radicals preferred to retain their autonomy and name. When the Radical rivalry between Mendès-France and Faure erupted in 1955, it led to an open break between Radicals and R.G.R. Faure and his ex-Radical supporters took over the R.G.R. and converted it into a small right-center party, loosely linked with the U.D.S.R. in Parliament. Like similar strategically-located splinter groups in prewar days the R.G.R. managed to get more than its share of ministers in coalition cabinets. This remained its only real *raison d'être.*

M.R.P. The most important and most durable new party in the Fourth Republic was the *Mouvement Républicain Populaire.* Its meteoric rise in 1945–46 was followed by such a sharp decline that some Frenchmen predicted its early extinction. But the decline was checked after the party had lost more than half its support, and it has remained a stable and significant force in French politics.

In at least two respects this new Catholic-inspired movement has been unique in modern French history. First, its founders sought to give it a rigid organizational structure such as no French party except those of the far left had ever possessed. They even borrowed several features from Communist practice, such as the use of training schools to indoctrinate party workers and the use of mass propaganda media. In practice, however, their movement has come to resemble the Socialist much more than the Communist party, both in structure and in spirit. But they have attempted to build the first disciplined bourgeois party that Frenchmen had ever known.

The second unique aim of its founders was to drag the mass of conservative voters into a working alliance with the left-center groups in order to create a democratic collectivist state. In the Third Republic no center party had been large or dynamic enough to make such an attempt; the M.R.P.'s forerunners, the prewar Popular Democrats, constituted only a tiny fraction with about a dozen deputies. The founders of the M.R.P. not only possessed the requisite dynamism but also profited by the fact that the mass of right-wing voters was drifting almost leaderless for the first two years after the liberation. Inevitably, however, these unwilling converts to Christian socialism were bound to seek and to find new leaders more to their liking. The appearance of organized Gaullism and the revival of the "classic right" soon reduced the M.R.P. to its true proportions.

Like the Radical party the M.R.P. straddles the center. Its aim, in the words of ex-Premier Georges Bidault, is to "govern in the center with right-wing methods to attain left-wing ends." In the social and economic sphere the M.R.P.'s program is not far removed from that of the Socialists. Politically the party's ideal is "pluralism," with a touch of corporative doctrine attached. By pluralism the M.R.P. means the preservation and encouragement of certain groups like the family, the local community, and the profession, which, it believes, are better able to resist the despotism of the state than can a collection of "atomized" individuals. These groups, the M.R.P. holds, should be given a special status and a certain autonomy within the state. They might also be used as a base for representation in the upper house of Parliament and in the Economic Council. These M.R.P. doctrines are derived from the papal encyclicals rather than from such corrupters of corporativism as Mussolini. Nevertheless the anticlerical Socialists are sharply critical of such ideas, and the M.R.P. has prudently pigeonholed the issue of pluralism since the constitutional debates of 1946.

But the clerical problem was bound eventually to produce a clash between Socialists and M.R.P. and to drive the latter party toward the right. The issue of state subsidies to church schools remained dormant for some years after the liberation, and most M.R.P. leaders might have preferred to keep it that way. About 1950, however, the reviving right-wing parties threw it into the political arena, and the M.R.P. had to support a subsidy bill that was adopted in 1951. A deep wedge was thus driven between the Socialists and the M.R.P., and the latter party soon found itself the prisoner of the right. Some M.R.P. politicians are quite at home on the right, but most of the party's founders have regretted this evolution and have hoped that somehow the movement might be brought back to its left-wing origins. In theory, and even in practice, the M.R.P. continues to be more genuinely leftist than any other Christian democratic party in Europe.

The M.R.P. has a more varied sociological than geographic base. Its strength since 1951 has been heavily concentrated in the strongly Catholic eastern and western frontier areas (Alsace, Flanders, and Brittany), and in scattered rural regions south of the Loire. It has retained significant working-class support in areas where the Catholic Labor Confederation (C.F.T.C.) has deep roots, but a larger share of its clientele comes from the small-town and rural populations in the less prosperous and less dynamic parts of France. Like the Socialists, the M.R.P. is pulled two ways by its voters, some of whom want drastic social and economic change, while others fear that change will come at their expense. One healthy sign is the M.R.P.'s appeal to young voters; only the Communists outdo them in this respect. Even though the M.R.P. has tended to become a kind of regional party, it seems destined to remain an influential and vigorous force in French politics.

The "Classic Right."   Two varieties of right-wing party existed in the Third Republic: those that were antiparliamentary or quasi-fascist, and those that accepted the parliamentary republic. The latter variety was commonly labeled the "classic right," and its members were called "moderates." None of these prewar groups survived the Vichy experience, which tainted so many of their leaders. But both varieties have gradually revived under new names, and with a somewhat different spirit.

The first postwar attempt to resuscitate the "classic right" came in 1945 with the founding of the *Parti Républicain de la Liberté* (P.R.L.). But the P.R.L. never quite managed to catch on; many rightist deputies like Paul Reynaud preferred to go their own way as independents, and the rise of an organized Gaullist party still further undermined the experiment. In 1951 the P.R.L. quietly disbanded; half of its leaders went over to De Gaulle, while the rest turned independent.

Meanwhile, however, the independents were gradually converting themselves into an organized movement that belied their label. At first they had virtually no party structure at all; they joined together as "Independent Republicans" to get representation on assembly committees and to help one another in election campaigns. But the advantages of tighter organization were soon borne in upon them, and the little independent faction of 1946 evolved into the powerful Independent-Peasant group of almost a hundred members in the 1956 Assembly. This fusion of 1956 marks the first time in modern French history that all the "moderates" have joined forces in a single parliamentary faction.

At the outset the Independent group was only a partial merger of several small parties—Independent Republicans, Peasants, ex-Gaullists— each of which retained its identity. Time has brought a somewhat greater cohesion, although the Independents still do not form a solid monolithic bloc. Party discipline is not much greater than it is among the Radicals. Some of the Independent deputies (notably those who cling to the label "Peasant") get their support from rural and small-town voters, especially in the less dynamic parts of France; others appeal mainly to the urban bourgeoisie. Taken as a whole, however, the Independent-Peasant coalition draws from the same social groups and geographical areas that were faithful to the "classic right" in prewar days. Its representatives stand for the old libertarian ideal: *laissez faire* in economic policy, reduced taxes and government expenditure, the encouragement of private enterprise, a strengthening of the upper house of Parliament, and opposition to "dangerous" experiments designed to shift the distribution of income or to modify the social structure. There is room within it for both ex-Vichyites and ex-resisters; for both a Paul Reynaud, the exponent of American-type industrial competition, and an Antoine Pinay, the archetype of small family enterpriser. Real unity or discipline can hardly be expected in such a group.

De Gaulle's R.P.F.   The rapid rise and still more rapid decline of the organized Gaullist movement (the *Rassemblement du Peuple Français*) in the years 1947–53 is of primarily historical interest now. Still, a brief account of its aims and of its failure are essential if the Fourth Republic is to be seen in full perspective.

De Gaulle's return to politics came in 1947, after more than a year spent in self-chosen obscurity. He declared that his new movement would be above parties; its purpose was not only to revise the constitution but to rid France of the party system itself. All power, De Gaulle declared, had come to be concentrated in the central offices of a few political cliques, so that the voter had little freedom and the state little authority. The evil done by party government was that it stressed those factors that divide Frenchmen; the aim of the R.P.F. would be to stress those factors that unite them.

It soon became plain that De Gaulle intended his movement to be almost as monolithic as the Communist Party, and almost as authoritarian as well. In practice no important decision could be taken without the general's personal approval. The selection of officials was made from the top down. A program of drastic reforms gradually crystallized out of the mists of De Gaulle's pronouncements. Among the essential points were a strengthening of the executive power, a tightening of the bonds of empire, the voluntary establishment of a profit-sharing scheme in industry, and enough state intervention in economic life to ensure the rapid modernization of the whole French economy. Many of De Gaulle's enemies set up a cry of "fascism!" and dark references to Boulanger and to Napoleon III were heard. That De Gaulle was not really comparable to either of those alleged predecessors should have been quite clear, but certainly his program did appeal to some of the heirs of those Frenchmen who had backed earlier aspirants to dictatorship. On the whole, however, the R.P.F. was made up of a curious blend of discontent and high idealism, mixed in roughly equal parts.

The first impact of De Gaulle's action was felt by the M.R.P., whose popular support was quickly cut in two. The second result was the formation of the Third Force coalition, which managed to steer between the Communist and the Gaullist threats for several years. The third outcome was a modification of the electoral law in 1951, in an effort to limit the gains of the two extreme parties. The R.P.F. nevertheless emerged as the largest party in the second National Assembly, but it fell far short of the majority or near-majority that its more sanguine leaders had predicted. De Gaulle ordered his 121 deputies to adopt a line of intransigent opposition, with a view to undermining the shaky center coalition. Instead, it was Gaullism that was quickly undermined. A fair share of the new Gaullist deputies were really old-style conservatives at heart, and as soon as that old-style conservative Antoine Pinay came to power, they were powerfully tempted to give him their support. Only a few months after the elections about thirty of these political hitchhikers rebelled against the general, seceded to form their own parliamentary group, and offered their support to Premier Pinay.

As evidence came in that a great many R.P.F. voters felt the same way about the Pinay government, the remaining R.P.F. deputies grew restless too, and some of them began to back the cabinet on important votes. It was even argued that the Gaullists ought to consider entering the next coalition. By 1953, De Gaulle lost patience; he brutally repudiated his parliamentary group, set its members free to vote as they wished, and declared that henceforth the R.P.F. would be only a kind of patriotic organization unsullied by any participation in politics. The Gaullist deputies, though deprived of their R.P.F. label, continued to protest their allegiance to the general and his program, but their *raison d'être* had pretty much disappeared. In the 1956 elections they were almost wiped out; only 22 "Social Republicans" loyal to De Gaulle managed to win re-election.

The rise and fall of the R.P.F. indicates that despite persistent and widespread dissatisfaction with the functioning of the Fourth Republic, this discontent was often vague and diffuse, and much of it was easy to divert by politicians who offered clear-cut policies and vigorous leadership within the parliamentary framework. First Pinay was able to capture the conservative wing of De Gaulle's movement, after which Mendès-France in 1954 captured part of the progressive wing. These facts would suggest that much of the Fourth Republic's protest vote on the far right (and probably much of it on the extreme left as well) did not represent real antirepublican or antiparliamentary sentiment so much as a vague desire for some kind of new deal.

The remnant of the Gaullist political movement that survived after 1953 under the new label "Social Republicans" adopted a somewhat anomalous position. While its deputies continued to sit on the right, their program took on more leftist overtones. In 1956 the Social Republicans were the only right-wing group to participate in Guy Mollet's left-center cabinet. They continued to advocate constitutional changes and the reinforcement of the nation's prestige and power, but they stressed also the need for drastic modernization of the nation's economy and for social reforms that would reintegrate the working class with the rest of the nation. It may be worth noting that, according to some calculations (based primarily on public opinion polls), the R.P.F. in 1951 received more workers' votes than any other party except the Communist. Some observers thought they detected here the growth of a new, more dynamic, and more social variety of conservatism in one segment of the French right. Others recalled that a blend of social reform, economic dynamism, and authoritarian efficiency had been the hallmark of the Bonapartist tradition in France.

Poujadism. The withering away of Gaullism as a mass movement was promptly offset by the emergence of a much more raucous and more demagogic right-wing party founded by a village stationer from the rural southwest. In part Pierre Poujade's Union for the Defense of Shopkeepers and Artisans (U.D.C.A.) served as a rallying point for those antiparliamentary Frenchmen who had hoped for a time that De Gaulle would overthrow the regime. But Poujade's meteoric rise cannot be explained merely by his appeal to the rather small quasi-fascist element or by his conversion of dissatisfied Gaullists. The bulk of his followers came from the petty bourgeoisie—the small shopkeepers, the marginal farmers, the artisans and white-collar workers, who barely manage to make ends meet and who fear the growing influence of economic planners and tax reformers. Their almost instinctive reflex of desperate self-defense was combined with the deep-rooted suspicion and hostility of provincial France toward Paris and toward politicians in general.

Poujade's activity began in 1953 when he formed a non-political association of small businessmen to block the activities of the government's new special squads of tax investigators. He frankly admitted that most of his followers indulged in some tax-dodging, but he insisted that few of them could stay in business except through this time-honored practice. There was a fair amount of truth in this generalization; and Poujade profited also from the fact that the tax collector has always been an especially unpopular figure in France. By 1955 his little association had mushroomed into a nationwide mass movement, with surprisingly large funds at its disposal and with a series of affiliated groups added to propagandize the peasants, the workers, and Frenchmen in general. In 1956, Poujadist candidates ran for the Assembly in almost every district; their supporters spent as much time heckling and roughing up opposition candidates as listening to the oratory of their own. Their success startled almost every Frenchman. Not only did they poll more than two million votes and win over fifty seats, but they managed to deprive the center coalition of a clear majority in many districts, thus assuring about fifty additional seats to the Communists.

Despite its dramatic victory Poujadism soon proved itself to be an even less effective opposition force than was Gaullism. Its electoral program was vague and incoherent, and Poujade himself (who remained outside Parliament) failed to give his followers any clear lead. The Poujadist tactic of sheer obstructionism in the Assembly produced no result except to irritate the politicians and the country. Several of the

U.D.C.A. deputies were unseated at the very outset on charges of electoral irregularities, and over the next two years another dozen resigned in order to join various right-wing parties. By 1958 the parliamentary group retained little more than half its original strength, and several disastrous failures in by-elections indicated that the movement had lost its momentum. Poujade sought to check the trend by seizing on an emotional issue (e.g., the all-out defense of French rights in Algeria) or by forging alliances with dissatisfied politicians and demagogic peasant agitators. It was clear, however, that Poujadism had neither the leadership nor the program to crystallize all of the nation's discontent or to offer a substitute for the parliamentary republic.

General Character of the French Party System. Critics of the Fourth Republic's party pattern find it easy to point out its theoretical and practical disadvantages. Any multiparty system, even where the major parties are comparatively well disciplined, is likely to produce more unstable government than a two-party pattern can do. Postwar experience has tended to show that greater party discipline in such a system may actually increase political instability by reducing the flexibility of political combinations. The loose and shifting groups of prewar days were more amenable to compromise, so that coalition cabinets were easier to form. Some critics also argue that increased party discipline reduces the individual deputy to an automaton or a cipher, leaving real decisions to be made by small cliques of party leaders who are often co-opted rather than elected and controlled by the voters.

Still another set of critics complains that French parties are enslaved to outmoded theories and slogans, that each one ought to be firmly rooted in one social group and devoted to the practical interests of that group, instead of chasing after ideological phantoms. Finally, it has been argued that only a two-party system can create the proper atmosphere for party co-operation. In such a system both parties are competing for the same large pool of undecided voters in the middle, and both must stress what the two parties have in common if they want to win this floating vote. The multiparty system, on the other hand, permits no such central pool of voters, but forces neighboring parties to compete virulently with each other for narrow and sharply defined segments of the electorate.

Defenders of the French party pattern argue that it is better to have several parties with clear doctrines than two large amorphous ones split into internal factions, and they add that a two-party system (even if it were imported into France) might be disastrous as long as communism remains powerful. They contend also that it is more important for the voter to express his confidence in a given party with a known program than in a given candidate who may be committed to nothing except personal success. Many judicious Frenchmen feel that the stronger party discipline of the postwar years is more to be praised than condemned. A series of "monoliths" as rigid as the Communist Party would of course be disastrous for democracy, but French tradition and habits of thought rule out any such prospect. Perhaps the problem is really more psychological and moral than mechanical. Any kind of party pattern is likely to be satisfactory if the principal leaders can develop a spirit of constructive compromise, a spirit that is pragmatic rather than doctrinaire; and if they can put the interests of the nation higher than those of party or class.

2. SOCIAL TEXTURE

Social Forces in Politics. Among the factors that underlie the structure of government in any modern state the character and cohesion of society rank high in importance. The problem of government is not solved by getting the executive, legislative, and judicial branches into proper equilibrium. Rather it is the principal social forces that must be brought into some kind of harmonious interrelationship. No democratic system is likely to function successfully if any broad sector of society nurses a continuing sense of injustice—whether that injustice be fiscal or social. Obviously the state would not be able to ensure perfect social justice even if it could define that slippery term. At best statesmen can only aspire to such an ideal.

The task of keeping all segments of society reasonably contented becomes more difficult as social crystallization increases. Groups tend to solidify, to form broad organizations that will represent their interests, and to clash with each other in their quest for relative advantage. France, as much or more than other major nations, has experienced such a trend toward crystallization throughout recent decades. Labor has its three great union federations, one Communist-controlled, one Catholic, and one near-Socialist; employers are represented by the National Council of French Employers (Conseil National du Patronat Français—C.N.P.F.); the peasants have been brought together in the new General Confederation of Agriculture (Confédération Générale d'Agriculture); and small enterprisers are grouped in the Small Businessmen's Confederation (Confédération des Petites et Moyennes Entreprises—C.P.M.E.). This trend is so marked that a kind of corporative society seems to be replacing the old individualistic system. To maintain some harmony among these powerful factions is one of the most difficult and most critical tasks of French statesmen.

Agrarian France. The social structure of France has been changing steadily during the past fifty years, but at a slower rate than in most other industrialized Western countries. The drain of population from country to city has lagged well behind the parallel urbanization of Great Britain, Germany, or the United States. According to the most recent census, 44 per cent of the population is still rural, in the French definition of this term.[7] True, not all of these are farmers, but 26 per cent of the active population still earns its entire income from agriculture.

[7] In France a commune (and its whole population) is classified as rural if it has no town with 2000 inhabitants. Obviously such a classification can sometimes be misleading. But it is significant that a heavy majority of the 38,000 communes in France are rural by this definition, and that more than 23,000 communes have a total population of fewer than 500 inhabitants each.

Since 1789, France has been commonly regarded as a paradise of small peasant owners. The truth about agrarian France is far more complex. Probably no other social category is so heterogeneous, so difficult to organize, so divided against itself as the farmers. Many large estates survived the revolution intact, and in recent decades large farms have come to dominate most of the region between Paris and the Belgian frontier. The number of small farms, which increased gradually from 1800 to about 1890, has been declining ever since that time and has now fallen below two million. Meanwhile the number of middle-sized farms (25 to 125 acres) has been rising, and at present there are almost a million of them. Large farms (over 125 acres) total just over a hundred thousand.

Not only is the proportion of small peasants falling, but their share of the total farm acreage is meager. Only about 20 per cent of the land is in their hands; the middle farmers operate 50 per cent, and the large farmers 30 per cent. These figures suggest a slow but steady trend toward concentration in agriculture, with the marginal smallholders gradually disappearing in favor of the middle farmers. The figures also reflect the subsistence nature of most small farming in France. Some specialized small farmers do well, but a majority of the two million little peasants can do little more than scratch out a meager living by about the same methods their ancestors used. They remain pretty much in a precapitalist stage of development, whereas many of the middle and large farmers have adapted themselves to modern methods of operation and commercialization. The contrast between these two sectors of French agriculture—backward and modernized—has been growing in the last few years.

Still another complicating factor in agrarian France is the presence of about a million landless farm laborers, and the persistence of tenancy and sharecropping alongside peasant ownership. Of the 2,000,000 small farmers, only about 1,200,000 are owners; the rest are either sharecroppers called *métayers* (20,000), or tenants who pay cash rents (600,000). Many of the well-to-do operators of middle- or large-scale modernized farms are also tenants rather than owners. Thus tenancy does not always mean poverty in France, nor does ownership equal prosperity. In the main, however, the sharecroppers, small tenants, and farm laborers are more susceptible to radical propaganda than are the owner-operators.

Political Role of the Peasantry.   The diversity of the rural population makes generalizations dangerous. Yet it is obvious that France contains a larger bloc of small and middle peasants than almost any other Western country, and that this bloc exerts a constant influence on the French political system. Whether that influence is for good or ill is sharply debated. Some Frenchmen hold that the peasantry constitutes a reservoir of the best French virtues. A noted sociologist, for example, calls the farmer "the greatest supporter of the French Republic and of democracy," and bemoans the rural exodus as a source of political and social instability. A dissenting school condemns the peasantry for its "passive and negative" domination of French political life. As one British critic puts it, "The continuing influence of the peasantry is the chief reason why the so-called Fourth Republic cannot escape from the Third, and remains petrified in the past." Some exponents of this latter thesis believe that the bulk of the marginal peasants will have to disappear if the nation is to be made dynamic; that France contains, as one of them puts it, "a million too many peasants."

This debate grows out of two conflicting social doctrines. One concept sees stability as the major virtue; the other fears that stability is likely to mean stagnation, especially in a world in dynamic change. It seems clear that during the Third Republic the political influence of the unorganized peasant mass was directed mainly toward three negative ends: peace at almost any price, protection against foreign competition, and taxation at the lowest possible rate. This negative attitude, exerted primarily through the Senate, lay like a wet blanket upon the sporadic efforts of French cabinets to follow a vigorous foreign policy or to experiment with daring but costly social reforms. The problem in postwar France is to know whether such a peasantry is capable of the kind of mental transformation needed to make it a constructive and civic-minded force in politics. Some optimists believe that the process of change is already under way; many pessimists consider this view the worst kind of wishful thinking.

Critics of the peasantry place great stress on the issue of tax evasion, a traditional French pastime in which the farmers have long excelled. Their defenders reply, with much justice, that the great majority of peasants barely subsist even with the aid of tax evasion. Indeed, most of the evasion they practice is a legalized variety, consisting of outright exemption from the income tax by act of Parliament. The effect is to keep many uneconomic farms operating, and to ensure special advantages to other, more prosperous farmers who share the advantages of the broad income-tax exemption. It is true that the peasants do pay other taxes (notably a property tax and indirect levies on the goods they buy), but their chronic discontent cannot conceal the fact that their fiscal burden is lighter than that of most other Frenchmen. In 1952, for example, farmers contributed only 4 per cent of the direct taxes received by the Treasury, although their share of the national income was roughly 15 per cent.

Over the past generation this imbalance has helped to weaken the nation's financial structure; it has shifted an unjust portion of the tax burden to the wage-earning and salaried classes; and it has delayed the adoption of costly social services demanded by urban and rural workers. Social tensions have been increased by the resentment of the workers and by the answering resentment of the peasants, most of whom are quite sincerely convinced that the farmer is worse off than the city laborer. Yet the adoption of a more rigid and modern tax system is almost impossible by the very nature of France's social structure. Fiscal justice is not easy to attain when so many of the peasants (and small tradesmen as well) keep no books and subsist on a marginal living standard.

In postwar France peasant influence in politics probably continues to be more negative than positive, but it is more effectively organized than ever before, and there is a greater sense of class or corporative consciousness. More than half of the farmers are enrolled in some branch of the new agricultural confederation, the C.G.A. Its most sizable subdivision, the Federation of Farmers' Unions, acts as a pressure group and represents agricultural interests in many government commissions. The Federation has been actively engaged in politics since the 1951 elections, not by nominating its own slate of candidates, but by giving its seal of approval to selected individuals. It has rebuffed advances by Paul Antier's Peasant Party, which sought to get itself recognized as the Federation's official arm in politics. Local or national office in the Federation has come to be a useful springboard from which aspiring politicians can launch careers.

In recent years the Farmers' Federation has taken on a predominantly right-center hue. Left-wing sentiment does continue to exist, however, especially in other branches of the C.G.A. The Socialists and Radicals dominate the farmers' co-operative movement, and the M.R.P. is influential in mutual-aid societies and youth groups. A Communist attempt to "colonize" the C.G.A. in its early years was a failure; they have now been dislodged from all positions of power. Nevertheless the Communists retain a considerable following among the southern smallholders, tenants, and share croppers, and they dominate the national farm laborers' organization. The farm vote is scattered more widely than that of any other social category; from Poujadism to Communism, no party is without a good-sized rural following. The great bulk of the peasants, however, continues to support the republican center groups—especially those just to the right of center. A larger segment of the urban and industrial population, in contrast, seems inclined to swing to the extremes of either right or left. In this respect the peasantry acts as a factor of political stability—or perhaps stagnation.

Urban Workers. The only segment of French society that outweighs the peasantry in sheer size is the urban working class.[8] However,

---

[8] The National Statistical Institute recently prepared these figures on the socio-professional structure of the French electorate. They are based on the 1954 census:

	Number of eligible voters
Farmers	3,442,100
Farm workers	829,000
Manufacturers and businessmen	2,164,000
Liberal professions and higher cadres	534,400
Middle cadres	1,075,300
White-collar workers (*employés*)	1,791,100
Industrial workers (*ouvriers*)	5,134,800
Service workers	755,400
Miscellaneous (artists, clergy, military)	453,200
No professional activity	11,414,700
	27,594,000

80 per cent of the last category above is made up of women, most of whom are presumably housewives.

a comparison between labor's political power and that of the farmers is not easy to make. The workers are probably better organized and more vigorously led; they are also more vocally class conscious. But much of their potential influence in the state is sterilized by the self-chosen isolation of more than half the workers in the Communist Party. Another obvious weakness is labor's lack of unity. During most of the Third Republic, and again since 1947, organized labor has been split into three separate unions—one Communist, one Catholic, and one with unofficial Socialist connections. Another shortcoming of the French labor movement is the tendency of many workers to flood into the unions in moments of enthusiasm (e.g., 1936–38 and 1944–46) and to drop out again when things begin to go badly. Union membership hit an all-time high in 1946, when almost seven million workers were enrolled; since then the decline has been drastic, and current estimates vary from two to three million. The biggest union of all, French labor leaders remark ruefully, is "the union of the unorganized."

The structure of the French working class has changed markedly over the past generation. Before 1914 the dominant element consisted of skilled laborers, many of whom worked in small shops. But the impact of World War I and of postwar industrial modernization created a new mass of machine operators, semi-skilled at best, which now makes up two thirds of the entire labor force. This element has been more resistant to unionization, but it can also be more malleable in the hands of leaders who get themselves accepted as spokesmen for the "gray mass." Another change since World War II grows out of the trend toward government ownership; many thousands of workers are now employed by the state rather than by private enterprisers. On the whole they enjoy better wages and union rights than most workers in private industry, yet their mental outlook and their political behavior seem to have changed little. In the state-owned Renault automobile plant, for example, where wages and conditions are well above average, the Communist-controlled C.G.T. continues to be the dominant union, and the Communist party the dominant political movement. As one official in a coal miners' union puts it, "We have a boss today as yesterday: he has changed his name, that's all."

Labor's Postwar Gains.   Many overripe social issues, the product of urbanization and industrialization, were inherited by the Fourth Republic at its inception. Such problems as social security, public health, and housing had been only partially solved before 1940, and long postponement, together with the effects of wartime property destruction, made them more intense. The Vichy experience made matters even worse, for Pétain's wage-freeze policy reduced labor's share of the national income.

For a time after the liberation there was real progress toward social reform. A current of rejuvenation was strong in the country, and the retarding influence of peasants and employer groups was temporarily weakened. Besides, the voice of organized labor had never been stronger; labor had played an active role in the underground movement and had managed to achieve something like unity. Until 1947, 90 per cent of the organized workers were concentrated in the General Labor Confederation (C.G.T.), which co-operated harmoniously with the Catholics' smaller French Confederation of Christian Workers (C.F.T.C.). The post-liberation government ordered wage increases that restored labor's approximate prewar share of the national income. They fused into one broad social security system the somewhat heterogeneous prewar laws; they increased benefits and set up new machinery placing social security in the hands of the trade unions. Another old demand of labor was granted when the government ordered the establishment of joint management-labor works committees in all plants employing more than fifty workers, and when the 1946 constitution underwrote this experiment by guaranteeing labor's right to participate in the management of enterprises.

The bright promise of the liberation epoch, however, faded somewhat in subsequent years. The immediate effect of the social security laws was not to increase labor's total income but to redistribute income *within* the working class in favor of the underprivileged and large-family elements at the expense of skilled labor and workers without children. Money wages in many cases remained below the prewar level, and it was not till 1951 that take-home pay plus social security benefits regained their combined real level of 1938. Even when the great boom of 1952–57 raised French industrial production by 50 per cent and boosted the over-all standard of living by about 4.5 per cent a year, many French workers remained convinced that they were getting less than their fair share of these gains. The new works committees and the social security boards have also lost much of their glamour. Their operation has often been distorted by political controversies. Works committees have withered away in more than half the factories, and where they survive their role is confined mainly to managing services like the canteen or endorsing Communist-proposed propaganda resolutions. A sense of apathy and cynicism has become widespread among the workers. Yet there were signs midway through the 1950's of the gradual *embourgeoisement* of at least part of the working class, as rising income enabled them to break old habits by buying household appliances, motor scooters, or even cars.

One of the most pressing social problems (for the rural as well as the urban population) is that of housing. Prewar neglect plus wartime destruction have condemned a heavy proportion of Frenchmen to live in antiquated apartment buildings or cottages that lack adequate sanitary or heating facilities and are often near outright collapse. In the Paris region alone 350,000 families in 1957 were classed as *"non-logées"* because they were forced to live with relatives or in hotel rooms without housekeeping facilities. Public investment in housing has been limited, and private investment has been hampered by excessively tight rent controls that date from World War I. It has been estimated that France would need to build 240,000 new units annually for thirty years to catch up with the nation's needs. For the first few years the Fourth Republic fell far short of that figure, but after a decade it began to seem attainable at last, with 274,000 units actually completed in 1957. Construction is still much too slow, however, and the number of low-rent units too limited.

In public health, as in housing, France has lagged behind other Western European countries. Medical services and hospital facilities have not been adequate, so that infant mortality rates and the incidence of certain communicable diseases remain relatively high. The effect is revealed not only in the lowered physical vigor of the urban population but also in reduced labor productivity and in weakened allegiance to a political regime that has not been able to assure higher standards. It might be noted, however, that gradual progress is being made in the field of public health. Infant mortality, for example, has reached the lowest level in French history, although it is still twice as high as in neighboring Switzerland.

All of the foregoing shortcomings contribute to the workers' sense of injustice and help to explain why about half of the urban proletariat, despite its apathy and cynicism, steadily votes Communist. Never before in France has so big a segment of any social category been so strongly marshaled behind a single party. Repeated efforts have been made to dislodge them by creating a new party between the Communists and the Socialists, but all have failed dismally. Only the well-established left-center parties remain as potential threats to the Communists' paralyzing grip on the working class. The difficulty is that as these parties come to depend more and more on peasant and middle-class support, they find it harder to back those working-class demands that clash with the short-term interests of their more faithful voters.

The Urban Middle Classes.   There is no easy way to delimit that social category which the French call the bourgeoisie. No real definition or delimitation will be attempted here; the phrase will be used arbitrarily to cover all urban groups above the level of wage earner, including even some white-collar workers who think of themselves as bourgeois rather than proletarian. In this loose connotation the plural form "middle classes" has some advantages, for it can be stretched to cover everyone from the business tycoon to the corner grocer, and from the highly trained technician to the bank clerk.

It was the bourgeoisie that put its stamp most clearly on the Third Republic. Smaller in numbers today than either the working class or the peasantry, the French middle classes nevertheless continue to be larger than those of many industrialized countries, and they still possess great influence in the French political system. Private enterprise still owns and operates about three quarters of the nation's productive plant, and private banking survives alongside the public sector. The bulk of the middle classes, however, is engaged in trade, the professions, or the civil service. France is unique in the number of small factories and shops that have managed to survive alongside big business; their persistence tends to conceal the near-monopoly position that has been attained by a handful of producers or distributors in many spheres of the economy.

Lower Bourgeoisie. The lower levels of the bourgeoisie continue to furnish a disproportionate share of France's politicians. Traditionally, the lower middle classes have been a main bulwark of the Radical Party, but a trend toward the Socialists was already taking place before 1940. The economic fluctuations of the past two decades have tended to "proletarianize" some segments of the petty bourgeoisie. The effect has been most serious on those who live wholly or in part on fixed incomes like salaries, pensions, or rents. But many shopkeepers have suffered too: 1,400,000 shops now share a total turnover not much greater than that which only 1,000,000 shared in 1938. These pressures have driven some elements of the lower bourgeoisie to the extremes of left or right—to Communism, Gaullism, or Poujadism. But most members of the lower middle classes remain faithful to the republican center parties; many small businessmen favor the Radicals or the Independents, while the civil servants, the white-collar employees, and many professional men lean toward the Socialists. Their most effective pressure groups have been the civil servants' unions and the Small Businessmen's Confederation (C.P.M.E.).

Upper Bourgeoisie. The status of the upper bourgeoisie (industrialists, bankers, and certain professional, managerial, and technical elements) is even more difficult to analyze. In the early years of the Fourth Republic its prestige and power were severely reduced, but since then it seems to have made a complete recovery. Its political influence has always been exercised in rather devious fashion; few members of the upper bourgeoisie enter active politics, and there is no single party devoted to the interests of big business. For a time De Gaulle's R.P.F. appealed to a segment of the business community (and even more to the managerial and technical elements). With the R.P.F.'s decline businessmen turned for the most part to the Independent bloc, which now represents a combination of large and small private enterprise, both urban and rural.

The upper bourgeoisie's most effective pressure group is the National Council of French Employers (C.N.P.F.). It allegedly maintains a good-sized slush fund that is judiciously doled out to friendly politicians and journalists; and its lobbyists are among the most active in the corridors of parliament. Whether these devices can give big business a degree of political power equal to that of millions of peasants or working-class voters is an open question. The prewar slogans of the left concerning "the 200 families who rule France" are no longer heard, but the Communists continue to pound away on the theme of *"les trusts,"* and to stress the complex personal interrelationships that can be found in big business, banking, and politics.

Whatever may be the kernel of truth in these charges, it is clear that the French upper bourgeoisie has a long record of shortsightedness and narrow-minded class selfishness to live down. It bears a heavy responsibility for the long postponement of social reforms between the wars—a postponement that exacerbated class conflict and made the workers more unreasonable in their demands. Its lack of dynamism contributed to the nation's economic stagnation and destroyed the kind of confidence in private enterprise that American or Swiss workers possess. Its record in labor relations could scarcely have been worse. There have been, and there are now, honorable exceptions, especially in the ranks of younger Catholic industrialists and businessmen. But the strength and influence of this progressive element is a matter of sharp controversy among French and foreign observers. Such signs of change as can be seen in the postwar years suggest a growing interest in economic modernization rather than an improved social consciousness or even a hardheaded concern for better labor relations. Yet, unless this latter type of change occurs, there is not much chance for greater social cohesion in France.

Distribution of Wealth and Income.   A clearer idea of the nature of any society might be gained by examining statistics on the distribution of wealth and income and on the incidence of the tax burden. Unfortunately, French statistics on these subjects are hard to come by, and are not very reliable when they are found. There is a common popular belief that wealth is spread more evenly in France than in most countries and that this relative lack of concentration tends to give French society a better balance and greater cohesion. It is unquestionably true that France has proportionately fewer multimillionaires than the United States and fewer cases of abject poverty than Spain or Italy. Yet scattered studies of such evidence as inheritance tax returns suggests a relatively high concentration of wealth—great enough to keep consumer buying power low, to keep the French domestic market limited, and to foster resentment among the underprivileged or the marginal groups.

A recent study made by economists in the Ministry of Finance lists the following average family incomes in 1952:

FIG. IV

AVERAGE FAMILY INCOMES IN 1952

	AVE. NO. OF PERSONS IN FAMILY	AVE. INCOME IN FRANCS	APPROX. DOLLAR EQUIVALENT
Wage earners	3.0	640,000	$1830
Farmers	3.8	670,000	$1915
Other independent workers	3.1	1,000,000	$2860
Retired persons	1.9	290,000	$ 830

Such averages of course conceal great inequities within each social group. For example, it has been estimated that 10 per cent of the farmers receive about half the total farm income; thus many peasant families must receive less than $1000 a year. Other studies indicate that the average per-capita income for the agricultural population (including home consumption of foodstuffs) is 160,000 francs ($457), while the average for the non-agricultural population is 250,000 francs ($714). Such statistics throw light on both the backwardness and the discontent of much of the rural population, as well as on the generally low income level of most Frenchmen.

Distribution of Tax Burden. Most experts agree that the total tax burden in France is both heavy and unfairly distributed. One left-wing Frenchman has gone so far as to call the tax system "more iniquitous than that which provoked the French Revolution." The inequities result in part from tax evasion, in part from legal loopholes in the tax laws, and in part from the generally regressive character of the system as a whole.

Tax evasion would produce no great inequity if all classes were equally able to dodge payment. In fact, however, the system benefits independent enterprises (farmers, shopkeepers, and professional men) at the expense of wage and salary earners, whose incomes are subject to withholding. Large corporations also find it more difficult to evade taxes. Legal loopholes also benefit the independent operator; for political reasons whole segments of the small farmer and small tradesman groups receive a blanket exemption from the income tax.[9] According to one recent estimate, wage earners pay about one third of the total received by the state in income tax, while industrial and commercial enterprises pay about 40 per cent and farmers only 1.2 per cent.

An equally serious flaw is the regressive nature of the French tax system. In 1953 the graduated income tax produced only 26 per cent of the central government's total receipts, while 64 per cent came from indirect taxes and 10 per cent from miscellaneous sources. The largest single source of government income is a kind of turnover tax, the burden of which is carried by the consumer. According to one recent estimate,

[9] One American study of tax evasion in France estimates that small enterprises and the professional classes conceal about 40 per cent of their real income from the tax authorities; that large corporations conceal about 10 per cent; that 80 per cent of all farmers are legally exempt from the income tax; and that small shopkeepers evade about 40 per cent of the indirect taxes due on their sales. Such evasion, incidentally, is not uniquely French.

One type of quasi-legal tax evasion grows out of the *forfait* system used to determine the taxable income of most farmers and small tradesmen. These citizens are not required to keep books or to report annual profits. The *forfait* (estimate of taxable income) is automatically fixed according to a complex scale set up by a national tax commission. For political reasons the figures have normally been set far below the real incomes of these taxpayers. The *forfait* for most professional men is fixed by direct negotiation between the taxpayer and the tax collector, often without reference to the taxpayer's records of income. One Paris doctor admitted privately some years ago that his *forfait* had been set at one tenth of his real income.

Efforts by the Ministry of Finance to plug some of these gaps have always had severe political repercussions; the Poujadist agitation, for example, had its origin there. Some French economists doubt that a "modernized" tax system like that of the United States, with its heavy dependence on a graduated income tax, would be either workable or fair in a nation with an economic and social structure like that of France. The experience of Italy, which modernized its tax system some years ago, may test the validity of this viewpoint.

at least two thirds of the government's total budgetary receipts are levied on the great mass of consumers without much reference to differences in individual incomes. Probably no nation is free of fiscal injustice, yet so great a degree of it over so long a period can do serious injury to the fabric of society.

Other Social Problems.   There remain several problems that transcend the separate segments of French society and apply to the nation as a whole. These items include population and immigration, the role of the Church, and the mass-communications media.

The Demographic Question.   The population problem has long been a subject of serious concern to many Frenchmen, who have regarded their declining birth rate as a threat to the nation's security, prosperity, and self-respect. By 1936 the birth rate had actually fallen below the death rate, so that France faced an absolute decline in population. One of De Gaulle's first appeals to French patriots after the liberation was for *"deux million beaux bébés."* Some Frenchmen trace the decline to the "desertion of the countryside" in favor of urban living, a contention that contains some truth. But France is not highly urbanized, and besides many of the rural areas have a low birth rate. Birth control and a relatively high infant mortality appear to be more responsible.

Some serious problems have arisen from the changing structure of the French population, with its growing proportion of aged people to be cared for and its declining proportion of men and women fit for productive labor. The prospect is particularly serious in a country that has suffered from a labor shortage most of the time since World War I and has shown signs of economic decadence for a generation. Concern over this situation led the French to invent the system of family allowances during the interwar period. Since its origin on a voluntary basis, about 1930, the family allowance system has grown to be the very core of the whole French social security structure, much as unemployment insurance became the core of the British structure. The allowances, which are attached to the worker's base wage, are not large enough to compensate fully for the cost of maintaining a child, but they do make the financial burden of a family bearable for the French worker.

One of the most striking changes brought by the Fourth Republic has been a sharp reversal in this century-old population trend. From 1943 the birth rate began to climb, until in 1948 the annual excess of births over deaths broke all modern French records. The rise has slackened off somewhat since 1950, yet there seems to be no sign of a return to the prewar trend. One major factor contributing to this change is the expanded system of family allowances and social insurance. The effect is to give France a population growth rate about like that of Switzerland, and actually higher than that of some Western countries. Nevertheless, the nation's demographic position is still unfavorable, for it will take decades rather than years to correct the results of a population-aging process that began so long ago. The ratio of non-productive persons remains high, the active labor force low, and the potential consumers' market relatively static. The new trend will have to continue for at least a generation or two if France is to reach what some planners call the optimum population (fifty to seventy-five millions) for the exploitation of France's resources.

Immigration. One corrective device used after World War I was immigration, with a view to solving the labor problem in the mines and on the farms. By 1940, France had a larger immigrant population than any other country in Europe. The manpower losses suffered during World War II gave new impetus to the idea; officials estimated in 1945 that France needed 700,000 additional workers. But Frenchmen hesitated to admit an uncontrolled flood of immigrants who might be difficult to assimilate; they preferred to select them on the basis of economic status and ethnic background. The policy quickly broke down, for even when the proper kinds of immigrants were found to be available (notably in Italy), such practical problems as inadequate housing turned the potential flow into a mere trickle.

The only immigrant group that has arrived in great numbers has actually created far more problems than it has solved. Algerians, who are subject to no immigration controls, poured into France after the war and crowded into the slums of Paris or other large cities. Unofficial estimates put their number at about a third of a million—most of them single men, or men who have had to leave their families behind. Only the poorest jobs have been open to them, so they have sunk to a kind of subproletarian status. The sudden mushrooming of Algerian nationalism has made their presence an even more serious threat for the French.

"Paris and the French Desert." Still another aspect of France's demographic problem is the high concentration of population around Paris and a few other centers, and the marked depopulation of many regions. Two thirds of the departments in France have decreased in population since the late nineteenth century—some of them by as much as 50 per cent. Some French demographers and economists contend that Paris has drained those regions of their best talent and has stultified them economically. One journalist dramatizes the problem by entitling his book on the subject *Paris and the French Desert*. These critics advocate a program of building up various regional centers and of scattering industries more widely throughout France. Such a program takes high priority among those planners who follow the lead of Mendès-France; it would be accomplished by means of subsidies together with a restrictive policy of building permits.

The Church. One of the most influential forces in French society continues to be the Catholic Church. Since 1905 it has no longer been the established church of France, but most Frenchmen are still nominally Catholic. Nine out of ten are baptized, though the ratio of practicing Catholics is far lower than that. According to the Church's

best statistician, only 29 per cent of all adults attend Mass at Easter.[1]
The figures on religious practice vary widely from region to region.
Some whole areas are virtually dechristianized and have been un-
officially labeled "missionary areas" by the Church. Other regions, such
as Brittany and Alsace, are still fervently Catholic; most of the population there attends Mass regularly, and the children go to parochial
schools. The working-class quarters in the cities are most completely
dechristianized, but there are also vast rural regions (notably south of
the Loire) in the same category.

The Church emerged from the Vichy experience with a somewhat
equivocal record. Some members of the hierarchy had been violently
pro-Pétain, although others had opposed Vichy and had even been
active in the underground. The courage of many Catholic laymen, including the principal leaders of the M.R.P., served to offset the effect
of the Church's Vichyite aberrations. Although the Catholic hierarchy
has never taken a public stand in favor of any political party, most of
its influence was thrown to the M.R.P. for a time after the liberation.
Conservative Catholic elements soon deserted to Gaullism or to the
various right-wing groups. There has never been a single Catholic party
in France, nor is there likely to be one. Perhaps the deep-rooted Gallican
tradition is in part responsible for this fact. At any rate, there is much
truth in the remark of one Catholic journalist that "French Catholics
have never been more divided politically than they are today." Within
the priesthood and among Catholic laymen there is almost every shade
of opinion from right to left. No party could possibly reconcile all these
views.

The only religious issue to impinge seriously upon politics during
the Fourth Republic has been the problem of state aid to church schools.
Prior to 1940, Catholic and public schools existed side by side, with
about one fifth of the primary students and two fifths of the secondary
students enrolled in Catholic schools. Pétain, by granting state subsidies
to the church schools, upset this peaceful compromise. After the liberation Catholics hoped that the subsidies might continue, but leftist parties
rejected the idea of subsidies and tried to write their old ideal of a state
monopoly of education into the new constitution. They charged that
the existence of Catholic schools is socially divisive and that such schools
are "mental incubators" designed to inculcate a precise set of dogmas
while the child is still at an impressionable age. The Catholics countered
with a demand that "freedom of education" be guaranteed in the constitution. The parent, they held, should be free to choose any kind of
education for his child. They argued that a single school system would
smack of totalitarianism and that the "Godless" schools were by no
means so objective and neutral as the leftists claimed. In the end the
prewar compromise was re-established. But the issue boiled up again
as soon as the right-wing groups began to regain strength, and after the
1951 elections the so-called Barangé law was adopted granting subsidies

[1] Abbé Boulard, in the Catholic daily *La Croix,* quoted in *Le Monde,* January
8, 1953. There is also a small but vigorous Protestant minority in Alsace, in the
south, and in Paris.

to parents whose children attend parochial schools. The controversy has seriously hampered co-operation among the center parties, and has been used repeatedly as a divisive weapon by the extreme right and left.

The Church's most effective work in recent years has been the organization of Catholic youth groups among workers (*Jeunesse Ouvrière Chrétienne*), farmers (*Jeunesse Agricole Chrétienne*), and so on. Only the Communists have shown an equal interest in young people and an equal vigor in organizing them. The Catholic groups have been active in studying social issues and the problem of economic modernization; their educational impact in these spheres is considerable. More and more ex-JOCists and ex-JACists are entering politics or are assuming leadership roles in trade unions, farm organizations, and social security boards.

The Church has also experimented with sending specially trained "missionaries" into the dechristianized rural and urban areas. After the war about a hundred "worker-priests" took factory jobs and lived in proletarian quarters in an effort to reconvert their fellow workmen. However, the Vatican concluded that the experiment was endangering the Church more than it undermined Communism, and in 1953 the worker-priest movement was virtually suppressed.

The Press. Any healthy democratic system depends heavily upon the media of mass communication to keep its citizens informed on current issues. In the field of radio and television the government has maintained a monopoly from the outset. The newspapers, however, are far more important than broadcasting in France. Leaders of the Fourth Republic, well aware that the nation had been ill served by a corrupt and scandal-mongering press in past years, took early and drastic purification measures. Most newspapers that had continued to publish during the German occupation were permanently suppressed, and many of their plants were confiscated by the government, which set up a state agency called the *Société Nationale des Entreprises de Presse* to manage them. These properties were leased to newspapers founded clandestinely during the war or established after the occupation. In addition, the old quasi-monopoly of the two Havas agencies in news-gathering and advertising was partially broken. The state's share in the ownership of Havas was increased, and a new state-owned news-gathering agency, the *Agence France-Presse,* was created.

The years since 1944, however, have brought a steady retrogression toward old habits. The reform campaign soon lost its impetus, and a proposed press statute designed to tighten the libel laws, to force newspapers to publish the sources of their funds, and to keep the press out of the grip of the "financial and industrial oligarchies" never managed to reach the floor of Parliament. In 1954 the idea of such state control was quietly buried when the National Assembly adopted a press law providing for the sale of government-owned printing plants and newspaper offices to their current occupants. The law contained no provisions designed to clean up press abuses and placed no restrictions on ownership or source of funds. Even before 1954 some of the prewar owners had managed to regain partial or complete control of their newspapers, and powerful economic groups both old and new had bought controlling interests in some leading organs.

The 1954 law confirmed the fact that the Fourth Republic intended to treat the press as a purely commercial enterprise rather than as a kind of quasi-public service. The effect is likely to be a continuing trend toward concentration, with the weaker dailies disappearing in favor of a few mass-circulation papers or organs that enjoy large private subsidies. This trend has already reduced the number of daily papers by half over the past decade, and those that have gone under or have been bought out include virtually all of the new organs that sought to inject a new spirit into French journalism. Declining circulation, caused in part by public apathy, has speeded the process, and the meager use of advertising by French businessmen leaves private subsidies an almost unavoidable necessity. Any hope of a renovated and rejuvenated press in the foreseeable future seems to be dead.

Character of French Society. An earlier chapter pointed out that any successful democracy requires a balance between the forces of individualism and the forces of cohesion in society. Opinions differ as to whether the proper balance exists in contemporary France, for social forces are amorphous things to handle, and they almost defy analysis and measurement. The best conclusion seems to be that there are elements of both significant strength and serious weakness in the texture of French society. There do exist social tensions and animosities that are strong enough to instill revolutionary ideas in some French minds. Latent discontent is even more common. "Since 1945 all social groups, even the most privileged, have considered themselves unfortunate," remarks one observer. Public-opinion polls show that each social category is inclined to be critical and envious of most other categories. Another probable source of weakness is the relatively low level of mobility in French society. The chance to rise in the social scale does exist, but the number of Frenchmen who manage to do so is much smaller than is the case in a more "open" society.

Nevertheless, the fabric of French society is too old and tough to disintegrate easily. Its strength and cohesion seem to be great enough to support a democratic political system in relatively quiet and prosperous times. Its weaknesses, on the other hand, are serious enough to endanger the republic in a period of intense or prolonged crisis.

3. ECONOMIC FRAMEWORK

Character of the French Economy. Still another factor that conditions the success of any political system is the strength and vitality of the national economy. Marxists regard the organization of economic forces as the real substructure underlying the complex superstructure of social forces, of parties, political concepts, and form of government itself.

One need not be a Marxist, however, to recognize the direct and crucial significance of economic factors in the modern state. The question is not primarily one of government-versus-private ownership of the nation's productive system; rather it involves the basic soundness of the economy, whether collectively or individually owned. Some effort must be made to go beyond the immediate economic problems that face contemporary France and to analyze the endemic qualities of weakness or strength in the economy as a whole.

Frenchmen in the past have often pointed proudly to the balanced and harmonious nature of their economic structure. Alongside a notable development of industry, agriculture has preserved an almost equal position. Great industrial and commercial enterprises exist, yet small producers and traders have managed to survive in large numbers. National self-sufficiency has been more nearly achieved in France than in any other Western European country. Here, it seemed, was a brilliant example of the golden mean.

Since 1940, Frenchmen have been much less certain that harmony and balance are unadulterated virtues. The years of crisis have forced them to do some hard thinking about their economic and political structure, and to ask whether their democratic system can long endure without some basic changes. In the early postwar years Frenchmen seemed almost unanimously agreed that such changes were necessary. Proof of this unanimity may be found in the spontaneous approval given to the recommendations of the Monnet Commission in 1946. Since that time, however, the pendulum has swung back part way. The revival of the right and right-center reflects the continuing strength of the old libertarian current in economic as well as political thinking. These elements fear that attempts to alter the economic structure may lead to revolution or dictatorship; they condemn the planners as "sorcerers' apprentices." They also oppose any drastic change in the present distribution of the national income. These issues caused serious dissension within the coalition governments of the Fourth Republic.

Prewar Stagnancy. The exponents of economic reform in France stress the irrefutable fact that the nation's economy was stagnant before it was struck by the war. The national income, which had risen steadily before World War I, was still at about the 1913 level in 1939. Capital investment dried up almost completely during the depression decade; in 1938 only about 2 per cent of the national income was used to maintain or expand France's productive plant. In direct contrast to the Soviet experiment productive power was sacrificed on the altar of consumption, but the net effect was to keep the consumption level static. In spite of this stagnancy there was a continual rise in public expenditures, which resulted in a serious strain on the French financial structure. Social gains, although inadequate and retarded when compared to those of more progressive countries, outran the economic progress on which they ought normally to be based. Unbalanced budgets became the general rule; inflation drained off four fifths of the value of the franc, which before 1914 had been one of Europe's most solid currencies.

The reasons for this condition are controversial, but to some degree they are tied up with that very characteristic of which Frenchmen were so proud: the harmonious balance between industry and agriculture, between big and small enterprise. The widespread persistence of small farming, small artisanry, and multiple retail shops may have contributed to social stability, but it tended to foster economic sluggishness as well. The French economy, far from keeping pace with its competitors, fell into a condition that some economists describe as "archaism." This condition, to paraphrase the Monnet report, was not only a state of things but also a state of mind. It involved a clinging to old methods, to outdated machinery, to an ultracautious and narrow mentality that discouraged experimentation with new methods.

Role of Monopoly. The tendency to archaism, however, was by no means confined to the small man. Large-scale enterprise in France (with some notable exceptions) also showed a less vigorous pioneering spirit than did big business in some other countries. The prewar doctrine of French business has sometimes been described as "economic malthusianism." Its general aim was to produce for a limited, protected market in France and in the empire, without much concern for expanding that market or adding new outlets abroad. "Small deals, but good deals" might have been the businessman's slogan. This policy was made feasible by the Third Republic's program of high tariff protection for both industrial and agricultural products. Protectionism stimulated the growth of industrial and commercial quasi-monopolies in many fields (e.g., steel, coal, chemicals, electricity, cement, flour-milling) and assured those groups of a regular home market. Protectionism also enabled traditional French agriculture to survive the impact of overseas competition, which, after 1880, forced other Western European states either to revolutionize their agricultural production (as in Denmark) or to cut it back drastically (as in Great Britain). Both the persistence of "unreconstructed" agriculture and the lack of a really competitive system in industry contributed to the archaistic tendency in the French economy.

It is true that on the face of things monopoly seemed far less advanced in pre-1940 France than it was in other industrialized countries. For one thing, the actual concentration of industry was not so great. Big business was big, but rarely gigantic. Furthermore, the persistence of small business and trade tended to conceal the degree of monopolization that existed.[2] But behind this screen the major producers controlled most of the limited internal market and kept their productive methods adjusted to that market. The existence of many small producers

[2] The proliferation of small retail outlets that marked the Third Republic became even more pronounced in the Fourth. In 1938 there were 1,000,000 commercial establishments, not including cafés and restaurants; in 1950 the figure had risen to 1,450,000. Since 1950, however, a decline has set in, and the number of retail shops has been decreasing annually. According to one estimate, an average of 800 shops per month went out of business in 1954 and 1955. Meanwhile, the degree of concentration in industry and commerce has grown. In 1954 the Ministry of Finance estimated that 0.14 per cent of the enterprises in France accounted for 40 per cent of the total business turnover.

and traders was tolerated by their larger and more efficient rivals because it was thought to guarantee social stability, and also because it kept prices high enough to ensure a comfortable profit margin for large-scale operators. Most of the big producers preferred peaceful coexistence to vigorous competition with rival firms; price-fixing and market-sharing agreements were common. In these circumstances it is not surprising that French enterprise failed to keep up with rival countries and even began to fail to keep up with its own past record. From 1929 to 1939 there was a net disinvestment in France; the nation's productive power suffered not merely a relative but an absolute decline.

Other Sources of Weakness. Not even the most severe critics, however, can successfully blame French business leadership alone for France's lack of economic vitality in recent decades. Perhaps no section of French society was entirely free of responsibility for this decadence. Certainly the peasants were essentially negative in their outlook, and, as for the working class, Léon Blum has attested that it lacked far-sightedness during the critical decade before 1940. The political leaders of the period, too, were on the whole inadequate to meet such a deep and long-range crisis. Not a single cabinet of the depression decade struck out on a vigorous and well-planned campaign to change the trend. For that matter, it is doubtful whether the nature of the Third Republic's political system and the precarious distribution of political power would have permitted any statesman to embark on such a positive program at that time.

Along with these political handicaps certain natural shortcomings hampered the French economy, especially the nation's inadequate supply of several essential raw materials. Two world wars brought widespread destruction and the liquidation of most of France's overseas investments. Ten per cent of the national income between the wars had to be spent on reconstruction, war pensions, and national defense, thus diverting those sums from new capital investment. Finally, it should be pointed out that France has not been alone in experiencing a tendency to economic regression. That tendency has been shared in greater or lesser degree by all of the former great powers as the center of economic gravity shifted away from Western Europe and as the United States gradually developed what has been described as a case of "economic elephantiasis." Even with the best will in the world, and the most states-manlike leadership besides, France and its neighbors would still have been forced to fight an uphill battle to retain their economic positions. After all of these reservations have been made, however, the fact remains that the signs of debility before 1940 were sharper in France than in any other major country. In consequence, the Fourth Republic was faced by greater initial handicaps that had to be overcome if it was to survive.

Modernization or Decay? The foregoing signs of regression contributed much to the widespread demand after 1940 that the great "economic feudalities" be pushed out of their position of power. The same considerations intensified the long-standing French concern over population decline, which seemed to be one contributing factor in economic decadence. Finally, they inspired one of the Fourth Republic's first cabinets in 1946 to establish a new planning agency in an effort to guide the nation out of its economic rut.

This *Commissariat-général du plan* (formerly called the Monnet Commission after its first head, Jean Monnet) shortly proved itself to be one of the most remarkable agencies of the new regime. It immediately undertook what has been called "the first attempt in postwar Europe to take stock of a nation and to draw up an over-all program for the future." As an educational device the experts drew into their work more than a thousand managers, technicians, and workers from all branches of the economy. Subcommissions tackled special aspects of the problem, but all groups were urged to focus their attention on the national economy as a whole.

At the end of a year of study the commission produced a report that not only laid out a blueprint for the future but searched deep into the nature of France's crisis. Without trying to apportion responsibility for the nation's stagnancy the commission presented to the people a blunt choice: "modernization or decay." No citizen who studied its conclusions could retain any illusions about automatic recovery. The all-party approval that greeted the report was some measure of French willingness to face the facts, but it was also a measure of the commission's success in surmounting political issues to get at the facts. Even such issues as private-versus-public ownership were bypassed by the commission in order to get at more fundamental problems.

The original Monnet blueprint projected an initial four-year program of heavy capital investment in six key branches of the economy: coal, electricity, steel, cement, transportation, and agricultural machinery. After channeling investment into these pace-setting sectors for four years the planners proposed to broaden the investment current into less vital sectors. Their long-term goals were increased labor productivity through better methods and machines, lower production costs to permit France to compete in world markets, and higher living standards for the whole population.

National Planning in Operation. Not all Frenchmen were persuaded at first that a national economic plan could be implemented within the democratic framework. The Planning Commission, after all, had no authority to impose its recommendations, and successive cabinets had to depend on the National Assembly to underwrite the plan. Skeptics felt that only a dictatorship could force through the kind of unpopular measures that would be required, and could challenge the special interests of powerful pressure groups.

Perhaps a decade of experience is not enough to prove these doubters wrong, yet it does seem fair to say that the experiment has been at least a partial success. It is true that the first four-year plan had to be drastically revised midway through the planning period, and that it eventually had to be stretched out over an additional year. But when the first plan officially ended late in 1952, the Planning Commission was able to point out that target figures in five of the six chosen sectors of the economy had been met, and that the nation's over-all industrial production had surpassed the prewar (1938) level by 45 per cent.

The commission had already begun to blueprint a second four-year plan, whose emphasis was shifted more strongly toward consumer industries, housing, and agriculture. It was accompanied by one of the most remarkable periods of industrial expansion in French history. Industrial output rose by about 10 per cent annually after 1952, while per-capita productivity reached one of the highest levels in Western Europe. For a time the chronic gap between exports and imports was reduced, and prices tended to stabilize for the first time since the war. But by the time the third plan (1957–61) was put into operation, there were renewed signs of serious economic difficulties that threatened to undermine the remarkable achievements of a planning era that had given France a modern and efficient productive base.

Overseas Planning. Brief mention should also be made of the Fourth Republic's efforts to develop the overseas territories. Even before the Monnet Commission was created, an Overseas Modernization Commission was established, and in 1946 the government added a special investment fund to finance development in the French dependencies. Inevitably overseas planning came to be interlinked with planning for France proper, but this is not to say that the interests of the overseas peoples have been overlooked in favor of French interests. It is true that the overseas populations have not been given much voice in the planning that affects them, yet they have certainly benefited immensely from it.

The first four-year plan stressed the building up of the "infrastructure," i.e., transportation and communication facilities. The second plan, coinciding in duration with that of France proper, shifted the emphasis to expanding production; the largest sums have been going to industrial and hydroelectric projects and to improving the rural economy. Considerable amounts have also been spent for schools, hospitals, and other social services. The Fourth Republic's policy contrasted strikingly with the Third Republic's habitual neglect of the colonies. Only small driblets of public funds went to the empire before 1940, but during the postwar decade the French invested more than 2 per cent of their total national income in the overseas territories.

The greatest handicap to overseas development is sheer penury; France simply cannot afford to pour into these underdeveloped areas the vast sums needed to make them modern and prosperous. The cost of military operations, first in Indo-China and then in North Africa, has also been a serious diversion. The French have given some attention to private foreign investment as a way to supplement their own capital resources, but they are too suspicious of foreign motives to open the door very far.

New Problems and Persisting Uncertainties. Midway through the 1950's the promising growth and stabilization of the French economy began to be undermined. The most serious new source of trouble was the outbreak of the Algerian rebellion, for the repression of which the government diverted more than 400,000 troops and large sums of money. The operation proved even more expensive than the long drain of the war in Indo-China, and it threatened to drag on in the same fashion. In addition the French industrial boom required a rising level of raw material imports to feed the industrial machine and brought a rising level of domestic consumption. Successive French cabinets feared to introduce austerity measures, and preferred to keep the boom going through deficit financing. All these factors conspired to reverse the earlier trend toward a balance of foreign payments and a stable franc. By 1958 France was once again facing the chronic problems of inflation and a large foreign-trade deficit.

Some observers concluded that the Algerian crisis had undone most of the gains of the preceding decade, and that the Fourth Republic itself was seriously threatened. Other critics, however, have been more inclined to believe that Algeria merely exposed the graver weaknesses in the French economy that had been concealed by the surface improvements of the postwar years. Some of them contend that the Monnet Plan has done nothing more than prevent France from slipping backward into total decadence. The real problem, asserts the noted demographer Alfred Sauvy, is that most Frenchmen still cling to their "ideal of painless immobility." Protectionism, says an American observer, has become so deeply embedded in economic life that privileges have come to be regarded as rights; France has become a country "dedicated to the survival of the unfit." Feeble governments, declares the political scientist Maurice Duverger, have found it impossible to introduce basic reforms; instead they have appeased the right by protecting the most outmoded sectors of the economy, and have placated the left by distributing pensions and bonuses. "France," says the Swiss journalist Herbert Luethy, "has everything needed to be a country of unlimited possibilities," but, he asks despairingly, "how can stagnation overcome itself?"

Static versus Dynamic France. This gloomy viewpoint is rooted in a growing awareness that a basic dichotomy exists within the French nation. As the political scientist François Goguel puts it, there are in fact two Frances—one "static," the other "dynamic." The former consists of great areas and segments of the population that cling to traditional ways of working and thinking: the small peasants, the artisans, the shopkeepers, and owners of little family firms. But superimposed upon this static sector is a dynamic sector made up of modernized factories, large mechanized agriculture, and some small but efficient and highly specialized firms and farms. There is no clear-cut geographical boundary between the two sectors, but in general the dynamic sector is concentrated in the northeastern quarter of the country, from Paris to the Belgian frontier. The journalist Georges Boris has dramatized the situation by suggesting that, if this northeastern quarter were independent, it might rival any nation in Europe in productive levels, living standards, and general economic vigor. But "static France," essentially underdeveloped and stagnant, acts as a constant drag on the progressive part of the nation and manages to keep a dominant voice in politics through its slightly greater population total.

One might suppose that Frenchmen of the static sector would be the chief exponents of a vigorous drive toward modernization. The difficulty has been that many of them are attracted to the idea yet fear it at the same time, for how can they be sure of survival in a dynamic economy? Most of them, therefore, have fallen back on an essentially defensive position that they improperly describe as economic liberalism because it opposes any vigorous state action for change. In fact, what static France has sought (and attained, in large part) is a return to the prewar system of governmental and private controls, which assures it of survival at about the level of subsistence. This network of controls, such as tariffs and quotas, anti-chain-store laws, domestic price-fixing agreements, and special legislation to shelter certain rickety sections of the economy, constitutes a kind of barbed-wire entanglement protecting static France. Behind that barrier, as Herbert Luethy puts it with some exaggeration, thousands of Frenchmen "languish and decay in a nation that is growing poorer and poorer"; their fears have produced a state of "ossified equilibrium," a "guild economy vegetating in a well-protected hothouse." In political life a serious dilemma results. The dynamic sector tends to breed extremists of left or right whose impatient demands for change frighten the traditionalists; while the static sector breeds standpatters whose stolid resistance further infuriates the proponents of reform.

Future Perspectives. The next decade or two should show whether there can be a peaceful solution to this dilemma. If the exponents of dynamic change were not so deeply split over the Communist issue, the chance of success would be much greater, but the Communists' strength and unscrupulous demagogy tend to sterilize the efforts of the reformers. On the favorable side is the fact that Frenchmen have never before been so widely aware of the flaws in the substructure of their state. Many French political leaders, unlike their prewar predecessors, have spoken out as frankly as they dare, and have even taken some action in the direction of healthy change. If cabinets during the Fourth Republic still fell as frequently as those of the Third, this was in part because some politicians were trying to face up to their painful responsibilities. Some cabinets were overthrown, not because they failed to act, but because they really intended to carry out some fundamental change.

Not all French political leaders agree on how to attack the problem, or on just how fast it is safe to move. Some of them (notably Paul Reynaud) advocate a policy of true *laissez faire* in order to encourage the growth of dynamic capitalism on the American model. Others (notably Pierre Mendès-France) have been crusading for a greater degree of planning and public investment in order to put France's limited resources where they will do the most good. The *Mendèsistes* would like to reduce France's military expenditures and overseas commitments in order to devote every possible franc to modernizing the static sector. Still others favor a more gradual evolution in the same general direction, with greater stress on encouraging and channeling private investment.

Discussion of these issues at the top has begun to affect the thinking of the mass of Frenchmen, and perhaps the best hope is that this gradual educational process may eventually give the reformers a solid base on which to stand. A generation of peace and relative stability would probably bring a gradual expansion of dynamic France, and would give the dynamic elements control of the political machinery. In any event the success or failure of French efforts in the economic sphere will go far to determine the durability of the republic as a political system.

11

FROM FOURTH TO FIFTH REPUBLIC

1. THE ALGIERS REVOLUTION

The Fourth Republic in 1958, despite its record of real accomplishments since the end of World War II, was showing serious signs of strain. The regime had survived for eleven years, yet it had never really rooted itself in the nation. One major source of its weakness was the fact that since its inception the republic had been almost constantly at war: first in Indochina from 1946 to 1954, then in Algeria from 1954 onward. The struggle had been costly in both men and money, and it weighed heavily on the nation's morale. The conviction grew that somehow a way out of the impasse must be found, yet few prominent Frenchmen dared say so publicly, for there had already been a whole series of retreats.

Premier Guy Mollet, when he took office early in 1956, made an abortive effort to pave the way for a negotiated settlement in Algeria, but abandoned it in the face of violent protests by the French settlers (*colons*) there. Mollet turned instead to a policy of military repression. Robert Lacoste, a tough Socialist trade union leader and deputy, was sent to Algiers as resident minister, and the bulk of the French army (more than 400,000 troops) was transferred there to crush the rebellion. During the next two years, Lacoste repeatedly announced that the task was on the verge of completion—that the rebellion was entering "its last quarter of an hour," in his unfortunate phrase. Cynics began to remark that this was the longest quarter of an hour in history. Worse still, hostilities threatened to spread to Tunisia as well.

Although there were ominous rumblings of discontent in both France and Algeria, and some open predictions of major crisis, few Frenchmen guessed that the situation would shortly lead to the utter collapse of the Fourth Republic. The regime might lack popularity, but it was hard to conceive of an alternative to the Fourth Republic that would produce greater consensus rather than exacerbated division. Yet the deadlock in Algeria, with its repercussions on the French

economy and on French morale, cast a dangerous shadow over the
regime. One leading politician allegedly remarked in conversation that
only one thing was lacking in France for a fascist seizure of power,
namely, someone willing to take the risk of seizing it.

There were signs, however, that a new factor was coming into play
in France's domestic power balance. That factor was the army, which
by long tradition had remained aloof from politics and had loyally
served each established regime. Almost imperceptibly, a new mood had
been penetrating the officer corps. Many French officers had been almost constantly in action since 1939, and had lived for most of that
time outside France—mainly in Indochina and North Africa. To a considerable degree, they had lost touch with opinion at home. Even more,
they had lost confidence in the civilian politicians who, they felt, had
assigned them a series of hopeless tasks and had failed to support them
adequately in their heroic fight against odds. A sense of bitter humilia-
tion had developed, combined with a conviction that "Paris" had somehow betrayed both the army and the nation. Here for the first time was
a potential striking force that might, in certain circumstances, challenge
the republic.

The occasion arrived somewhat unexpectedly. In April, 1958, the
Gaillard cabinet was overthrown, and the usual protracted crisis ensued
before a new premier managed to get a confidence vote. That new
premier, approved by the National Assembly on May 13, was the
M.R.P. leader Pierre Pflimlin, a prominent member of the outgoing
cabinet. Pflimlin's nomination crystallized the discontent of two influential groups in Algeria: the diehard extremists among the French
colons, and the army officers who had lost patience with the flabby
republic. On May 13 they staged a huge demonstration in Algiers; the
mob sacked the government offices, and a group of civilian and military
leaders organized what they called a Committee of Public Safety. General Raoul Salan assumed control of Algeria on the Committee's behalf,
and virtually repudiated the authority of Paris. The insurrectionists'
excuse was the assumption that Pflimlin intended to try—however
cautiously—to extricate France from Algeria by negotiations with the
rebels. In fact, the *coup* was not entirely a spur-of-the-moment affair.
For several months a small group of officers, *colons,* and obscure right-
wing politicians who had arrived from France had been plotting such a
coup as soon as the opportunity might arise. On May 17, Jacques
Soustelle, leader of the Gaullist group in the National Assembly and
former governor-general of Algeria, evaded police surveillance in Paris
and flew to Algiers to join the rebels. In various French cities, rightist
groups began to organize affiliated Committees of Public Safety, and it
was widely believed that army units, demobilized paratroopers, and
elements of the mobile police would join them if the government chose
to make a stand. On May 24 a *coup* in Corsica put that island into the
control of the insurrectionists, and seemed to suggest that the rebellion
was crossing the Mediterranean to France itself.

For a week or two, the Fourth Republic's leaders sought to resist
this flagrant though still bloodless rebellion. Pflimlin broadened his

cabinet to include most of the major parties, and received a huge vote of confidence from the Assembly when he promised to defend the integrity of the regime. But his support was already beginning to disintegrate. Some of the moderate rightists in his cabinet, and even some leftists as well, were reluctant to face the prospect of civil war. They turned instead to what seemed to be the only middle way between violence and capitulation: the political resurrection of General Charles de Gaulle.

Since the disintegration of his political movement, the R.P.F., in 1953, De Gaulle had been living in provincial obscurity and completing his memoirs. His name had been advanced by the Algiers insurrectionists almost from the start, for they could produce no well-known charismatic leader from their own ranks. Apparently De Gaulle was not entirely ignorant of the scheming in Algiers that had preceded the *coup* of May 13, but he had taken no active role in preparing that *coup,* nor had he committed himself to collaborate with its perpetrators. On May 15, De Gaulle let it be known that he would respond if called by the nation; and during the critical days that followed, he issued a series of rather cryptic statements that revealed little more than his willingness to return to power on his own terms. On May 27 President René Coty, convinced that France faced civil war, persuaded Premier Pflimlin to resign in spite of a new vote of confidence by the Assembly, and on the 29th Coty nominated De Gaulle as Pflimlin's successor. Three days later the Assembly ratified the choice by a vote of 329 to 224, against the sharp opposition of the Communists, half of the Socialists, and the Mendès-France wing of the Radical group.

2. THE GAULLIST INTERLUDE

Technically, Charles de Gaulle became the last premier of the Fourth Republic. In fact, the regime went into a kind of suspended animation on that day, and was doomed to disappear as soon as a new governmental system could be worked out. Just what kind of regime would succeed it remained uncertain for a time, for the nature and strength of De Gaulle's support were still not fully clear, and the general's own purposes were obscure. It was obvious, however, that a regime which had abdicated before the threat of civil war was not likely to be resurrected. In somewhat similar fashion (though in much different circumstances), the Third Republic also had committed suicide.

De Gaulle demanded and received a vote of special powers limited in duration to six months, but limited in scope hardly at all. Parliament was adjourned, and its functions absorbed by the cabinet. The government was authorized to prepare a new constitution for submission to the voters by referendum, subject to the proviso that a committee of parliamentarians and experts might first examine the draft and suggest amendments.

De Gaulle's first act was to fly to Algeria in order to affirm his authority over the rebels of May 13. They could scarcely repudiate the man whose accession to power they had been demanding; yet not all of them were pleased with the general's moderate and conciliatory behavior. The extremists had hoped that he would sweep away the republic and the party system, and proclaim a frankly authoritarian regime. Instead, his cabinet included a number of the Fourth Republic's leading figures, among them both Pierre Pflimlin and Guy Mollet. The insurrectionists were disappointed too at his rather cryptic remarks about the future of Algeria, which both *colons* and army were determined to hold by force and to integrate completely with the homeland. De Gaulle's prestige was sufficient, nevertheless, to win over most of the army leaders, and his influence thus divided and undermined the cabal of officers and *colons* that had carried out the May 13 *coup*. The Committees of Public Safety in Algeria and France, some of whose members had hoped to play key roles in the new regime, were gradually pushed into the background, and many were dissolved.

De Gaulle and his ministers—a curious combination of technicians, personal henchmen, and republican politicians—moved promptly to tackle the nation's pressing problems. He established a small committee of experts under Minister of Justice Michel Debré (one of De Gaulle's oldest and most faithful supporters) with authority to draft a new constitution. Late in July this draft was presented to a consultative committee composed in large part of members of the moribund parliament, and representing all major parties except the Communists. This body, under the chairmanship of Paul Reynaud, studied the draft for two weeks and returned it with the approval of thirty of the thirty-nine members. The committee proposed, however, a large number of minor changes, and a half-dozen major amendments designed to soften the somewhat authoritarian appearance of the document and to bring it closer to the parliamentary tradition. Significant changes were also suggested with respect to the overseas territories, in an effort to provide a more supple framework to replace the French Union. The cabinet accepted most of these amendments in whole or in part, though on a few key issues De Gaulle refused to retreat. After a final check by the Council of State, the draft was adopted by the cabinet on September 3.

3. THE REFERENDUM

France was called to vote on the constitution on September 28, and the campaign began without delay. Indeed, De Gaulle had already begun campaigning in August, when he undertook a dramatic speaking tour through the major capitals of French Africa. In the course of this journey, he made the startling announcement that any territory might peacefully secede from the new French "Community" if it chose to vote against the constitution. He warned, however, that such action would mean an immediate severance of all ties with France, and an end to financial and administrative aid so essential to most of the African territories. His promise of independence to those who wanted it carefully skirted the problem of Algeria, the only area where the issue had reached the explosive stage.

As various political leaders and groups took formal positions on the referendum, it became obvious that approval was a foregone conclusion, and that the only question would be the size of the majority. Every party of right and center campaigned for a "yes" vote, although Pierre Poujade ended by advocating "no" against the wishes of the great bulk of his shopkeeper followers. The Radicals and the Socialists, both deeply divided ever since the May crisis, held party congresses in September that voted by clear majorities to support the new constitution. A number of eminent Socialists, however, continued to campaign for a "no" vote, as did the Mendès-France faction in the Radical party. Only the Communist party stood solidly against the new system, alleging (as it had done ever since May) that De Gaulle was either the prisoner or the spokesman of fascist elements in France.

The outcome of the voting on September 28 astounded even De Gaulle himself. He had hoped for a majority of seventy per cent; he got instead almost eighty per cent of the heavy vote cast in continental France, and an even more overwhelming margin in almost every part of French Africa. Only French Guinea, in response to the appeal of its favorite son Sékou Touré, ran counter to the current by voting itself overwhelmingly out of the French Community. Elsewhere, leading African politicians recommended a "yes" vote on the ground that French aid was still essential and that De Gaulle had guaranteed them the right to choose independence whenever they might want it in the future. The most startling result of all was that in Algeria, where 97 per cent of the Moslem and settler votes combined favored the constitution, and where 83 per cent of the registered electorate turned out to vote in spite of the Algerian nationalist leaders' appeal for a boycott. Whether this result reflected the thirst of the Algerian masses for compromise and peace remained a highly controversial question; many Algerians doubtless hesitated to risk displeasing the army, which campaigned vigorously for a "yes" vote and hauled voters to the polls in army trucks. It represented, nevertheless, a notable victory for the army in Algeria, and strengthened the determination of the diehards to keep Algeria French at any cost.

In France itself, it was the Communist party that suffered the most obvious defeat. Many Frenchmen who had consistently voted Communist since 1945 had obviously rejected the party's guidance in this instance; the total "no" vote (which included a fair number of non-Communists) fell markedly below the usual Communist share. In some departments, the drop was more than fifty per cent when compared with the 1956 elections. Even in the "red belt" around Paris, only one of eighty suburbs came up with a negative majority. Those Socialists and Radicals who had campaigned against the constitution also suffered severe defeats; not one of them could even carry his own home town.

The full significance of this landslide was more difficult to assess. Opinion polls made it clear that few voters had read the new constitution, or had much of an idea what changes it might introduce. A "yes" vote meant different things in different cases—indeed, diametrically opposite things in some instances. A good many moderate leftists ended by voting for the constitution simply because they feared that the only alternative would be an authoritarian army-backed regime, and because they believed that De Gaulle alone could keep the men of May 13 in check. Some Frenchmen voted "yes" in the hope that De Gaulle might be strong enough to keep Algeria; others because they thought he might be strong enough to get France out of Algeria. Many rightists wanted stabler government in France but disliked the liberal provisions of the constitution with respect to Black Africa; many leftists reacted in just the opposite fashion. But underlying this heterogeneity, two things could be detected clearly: a general revulsion against the Fourth Republic as a system, and a revived admiration for, and confidence in, De Gaulle as leader. The general's conduct since May had converted many doubters; he had displayed not only nobility and disinterestedness, but a degree of vigor and of flexibility that had been far less evident in his earlier political career. After the haggling and bickering of previous political campaigns, the lofty tone set by De Gaulle in this one came as a welcome relief. Thirst for change, hope of a real new deal, were clearly revealed by the electoral results, even when they were accompanied by a persistent strain of skepticism and by the nagging uncertainty: "After De Gaulle, what?"

4. THE NEW POLITICAL SYSTEM

On October 5, 1958, the Fifth Republic officially came into existence when the new constitution was proclaimed as the basic law of the land. Its full operation, however, was postponed for four months in the case of France proper, and six months in the case of the new overseas Community. During that transitional period, the authority of De Gaulle's government was prolonged in almost unrestricted form. It was authorized to draft and proclaim a new electoral law, and to arrange for the election of the Fifth Republic's first National Assembly and first president.

Frenchmen who examined their new constitution found some difficulty in characterizing the system and in predicting how it was likely to operate in practice. Some of them found it strongly reminiscent of the quasi-presidential system sketched out by De Gaulle many years earlier in his Bayeux speech of 1946, during the debate on the previous constitution. Others pointed out that the final draft had been significantly altered in the direction of the traditional parliamentary system, which would thus be preserved and improved. Still others contended that the new basic law was tailored to De Gaulle's personal measure, that it embodied a kind of system of limited and non-hereditary monarchy, and that it bore a curious resemblance to the Orleanist system of 1830–48. There was general agreement on only two points: that the constitution represented a compromise once again, and that its functioning would be shaped more by events than by texts.

Although many of the Fourth Republic's institutions carry over into the Fifth, the constitution provides for extensive changes in both structure and function. Most important, perhaps, is the attempt to strengthen and stabilize the executive at the expense of the legislative branch. The old constitution began with a section on Parliament; the new one, with a section on the president of the republic. The president is now chosen for a seven-year term not by the members of Parliament, but by a much-broadened electoral college totalling some 80,000 persons. It includes the deputies and senators and all members of the departmental general councils and overseas assemblies, but these electors are heavily outnumbered by representatives of the municipal councils in France's 38,000 communes. Such a voting body is weighted heavily in favor of the rural areas, for 31,000 of the French communes have fewer than 1000 inhabitants each, and 23,000 have fewer than 500 each. Presidents of the Fifth Republic will thus be chosen by the country mayors of France, and not by the professional politicians as in the past. Since the bulk of the rural mayors are moderate conservatives, they are likely to favor candidates of similar views.

The heart of the new system is the altered three-way relationship between president, premier, and parliament. The president appoints the premier, who takes office at once without being required to secure a prior vote of confidence from the National Assembly. The premier and his cabinet are, nevertheless, still collectively responsible to the National Assembly. But the overthrow of the cabinet by the Assembly has been made more difficult by requiring a formal motion of censure, introduced by at least one tenth of the Assembly's members and approved by an absolute majority of the total membership. There are limitations, too, on the number of motions of censure that may be brought in by the same group during a legislative session. The dissolution power has also been strengthened, and the decision to use it has been transferred from the premier to the president. That power is now hedged by only two restrictions: the president must first consult the premier and the presidents of both houses of parliament, and he may not order a dissolution during the first year of the Assembly's life.

One novelty introduced by De Gaulle over the protests of Paul Reynaud's consultative committee is the provision that no cabinet member may simultaneously hold any other national office, whether in politics, in the public service, or in a business, professional, or labor organization. By long tradition, ministers in France have almost always been drawn from Parliament, and have resumed their seats when cabinets fell. De Gaulle was determined to break this link between executive and legislative, and to produce a more clear-cut separation of powers. Henceforth any deputy or senator who is named a minister must resign his seat. The purpose of this change is to end the scramble for portfolios by reducing the deputies' temptation to overthrow a cabinet in the hope of being included in the new one. However, the change may exclude from cabinet office many able political figures, and may tend to create a class of professional cabinet ministers. Whether such a trend is compatible with a parliamentary system remains to be seen.

The real nature of the new executive-legislative relationship will emerge in practice. Presumably cabinets will last longer and will be less subject to parliamentary influence; yet the Assembly's right to overthrow the cabinet seems to preserve the essence of the parliamentary system. The new and uncertain factor here is the expanded role of the president. His freedom to choose among potential premiers is clearly greater than it used to be, though he cannot safely ignore the reactions of the National Assembly. His personal influence over the premier is likely to be noticeably increased by the fact that the premier is his personal choice. His sphere of autonomous action has also been broadened in a number of ways by the constitution; he is no longer forced to stand in the premier's shadow on all except formal occasions. More significant still, his moral authority is likely to be enhanced by the broadened base of his election, so that he may sometimes feel justified in challenging Parliament and using his prestige to influence important decisions. Clashes between president and National Assembly would seem to be more likely, therefore, than conflicts between premier and Assembly. In some ways, the presidency will resemble that of the Third Republic in 1875, before it was undermined by MacMahon's rash action in 1877.

In the process of shifting the balance between executive and legislative branches, the drafters of the new constitution also took care to cut back somewhat the formerly extensive powers of the National Assembly. The length of its annual sessions has been reduced to five and one half months, and its power to delay action on the budget and to bury or maim government bills in committee has been restricted. The constitution reduces the number of standing committees in the Assembly to six; and the cabinet may require that government bills be referred to special *ad hoc* committees rather than to one of the more powerful standing committees. The authority of the upper house has also been increased as a counterbalance to the Assembly. The old name "Senate" has been restored to the upper house, and it is to function once again as a real second chamber in a bicameral system. Its power, however, will fall somewhat short of that of the Third Republic's Senate, which could overthrow cabinets and could permanently block bills sent up from the lower house. The Senate's right to delay and amend has been increased, but in case of complete deadlock between the two houses, the will of an absolute majority of the National Assembly will prevail.[1]

In an early draft of the De Gaulle constitution, the Assembly's area of legislative competence was sharply reduced, and the cabinet was authorized to legislate by ordinance in all unspecified domains. Paul Reynaud's consultative committee protested vigorously against this arrangement, and in the final draft the Assembly's sphere of action was defined in much broader terms. However, the constitution once more legalizes the pre-war practice of cabinet legislation by decree (now called "ordinance"), provided that the Assembly grants a specific authorization and is given the right to ratify all ordinances *ex post facto*. Thus the Fifth Republic has openly recognized what the Fourth had to admit in fact: that the decree-

[1] See esp. Articles 45 and 46 of the constitution.

law procedure is virtually unavoidable in a system like France's parliamentary republic.

Taken together, all these restrictions reduce the dominant role of the National Assembly without destroying the parliamentary principle. Other constitutional changes are likely to be even more important in shifting power from the legislative to the executive branch: notably the president's strengthened dissolution power, the new limitations on the overthrow of cabinets, the ineligibility of deputies to cabinet posts, and the right assigned to De Gaulle's interim government to draft a new electoral law.

Several other changes in the governmental machinery have been made by the new constitution. The High Council of the Judiciary, formerly chosen in majority by the National Assembly and by the professional magistrates, will now be appointed by the president of the republic. The Economic Council has been renamed, and reduced somewhat in status. It is now called the Economic and Social Council, and is attached to the cabinet rather than to the National Assembly. Thus it no longer enjoys quasi-parliamentary status, but becomes once again a consultative body, much like its earlier predecessor in the Third Republic. The cabinet is required to ask its opinion on any planning measure of an economic or social nature; other matters will be referred to it only at the cabinet's discretion. The Constitutional Council, on the other hand, seems to have been elevated in status when compared to the old Constitutional Committee. This nine-member body will now be appointed by the president of the republic (three members) and the presidents of the two legislative houses (three members each). Ex-presidents of the republic will also be lifetime members of the Council. It will rule on the regularity of presidential and legislative elections, and on the constitutionality of laws. Its decisions on constitutionality will be final. The Council must also be consulted by the president of the republic before the latter may invoke Article 16 to declare a state of national emergency.

This national emergency clause is one of the few novelties introduced into the constitution at the personal insistence of De Gaulle, and retained in the final draft in spite of many protests. Article 16 authorizes the president to assume exceptional and virtually unlimited powers whenever the institutions of the republic or the nation's independence or territorial integrity are gravely threatened. To assuage the fears of the critics, De Gaulle agreed to make the exercise of this power contingent on the president's prior consultation with the premier, the presidents of both houses, and the Constitutional Council. He further agreed to rule out any dissolution of the National Assembly during the exercise of exceptional powers. De Gaulle's chief constitutional aide Michel Debré, questioned by the press on the purpose of this article, declared bluntly that it was designed for use in only one circumstance—the outbreak of an atomic war. De Gaulle's insistence upon it reflects his personal experience in the crisis of 1940.

Another sharply-disputed novelty in the constitution was introduced at the request of the consultative committee headed by Paul Reynaud. It is the provision in Article 4 that "political parties . . . must respect the principles of national sovereignty and democracy." This clause is a faint echo of the "party statute" advocated by the M.R.P. in 1946. Its vagueness opens the way to a variety of interpretations; some Frenchmen believe that a future government may try to use it to outlaw the Communist party as well as right-wing antirepublican groups. Their fear is that the suppression of any party, no matter how undemocratic in spirit, may be the prelude to the destruction of all dissenting opinion.

Still another change simplifies somewhat the procedure for constitutional amendment. The initiative may be taken either by the president, on the proposal of the premier, or by any member of Parliament. Two paths to amendment are provided: (1) approval by both houses of Parliament, followed by a popular referendum; (2) approval by three fifths of the votes cast in a joint session of Parliament convoked by the president of the republic.

Perhaps the most elaborate and extensive set of changes is that contained in Section XII, which converts the old French Union into "the Community." During the drafting of the constitution, a deadlock developed between partisans of "federation" and exponents of "confederation"—rival principles that reflected sharply different attitudes toward the structure of the refurbished Union. Out of this deadlock there finally emerged the compromise term "Community," which was ambiguous enough to cover a possible evolution toward either a federal union centered in Paris or a loose decentralized confederation of sovereign equals. The flexibility provided by this happy compromise, and the manner in which De Gaulle proceeded to interpret it during the referendum campaign, did much to swing the French African voters behind the new constitution.

Section XII opened three alternative paths to the overseas peoples who might choose to stay within the French Community. They were authorized to retain their existing status as partially self-governing Overseas Territories; or to become Overseas Departments of the French Republic, like Martinique and Guiana; or to be transformed into full member states of the Community, with domestic autonomy and a kind of incipient sovereignty. A fourth alternative—outright withdrawal from the Community—will also be permanently open. This latter choice was made by Guinea, whose independence was formally recognized by France in January, 1959. All of the other territories in French West Africa and French Equatorial Africa, along with Madagascar, promptly chose to become autonomous republics within the Community. The smaller and more isolated French possessions (the Comoro Islands, French Polynesia, New Caledonia, French Somaliland, and St. Pierre-Miquelon) decided to retain their old status as Overseas Territories, which gives them representation in the French parliament.

Section XII establishes a somewhat refurbished set of federal institutions for the Community, which will possess jurisdiction over such matters as foreign policy, defense, and economic and financial policy. The president of the republic will serve *ex officio* as president of the

Community, and will preside over the Community's Executive Council (which replaces the old High Council of States). This Council will be made up of the heads of government of each of the member states, together with those cabinet ministers who deal with Community affairs. A new body, the Senate of the Community, will replace the defunct Assembly of the French Union. The Senate's members will be chosen by the French parliament and the various overseas assemblies; it will meet twice annually, and will discuss the Community's economic and financial problems. A third new organ is the Community's Court of Arbitration, which will function in case of conflicts among member states. The old and awkward system of dual citizenship—of France and of the French Union—is abolished in favor of a single citizenship of the Community.

Despite the variety and flexibility that mark the new system, its character is more precise and coherent than was the case with the ill-conceived and ambiguous section on the French Union in the 1946 constitution. The various alternatives have now been clearly defined, and the chances for harmonious evolution are correspondingly increased. The guaranteed right of future peaceful secession has relieved most of the nationalist pressure that had begun to threaten France's relations with Black Africa. Almost no one among the founders of the Fourth Republic could have foreseen how far their successors would feel compelled to go only twelve years later. The change in outlook over so short a time is impressive evidence of flexibility in Paris.

5. THE NEW MACHINERY IN OPERATION

By the end of 1958, most of the important institutions of the remodelled system were ready to function. On November 23–30, a new National Assembly was elected; on December 21 the presidential electors met in various provincial cities and chose Charles de Gaulle as first president of the Fifth Republic; on January 8, 1959, De Gaulle appointed Michel Debré premier. The National Assembly convened a few days later to hear Debré's statement of policy, and voted its approval by a margin of 453 to 56. Pending the election of the new Senate in April, the old Council of the Republic continued to sit as the upper house.

The clearest indication of change was given not by any structural alterations but by the composition of the new National Assembly. Three quarters of the Fourth Republic's political personnel were swept into the discard in the 1958 elections, and the left-wing parties were almost wiped out as an effective parliamentary force.

De Gaulle's interim government, in drafting the new electoral law, had considered two plans to replace proportional representation: (1) a system of large districts with list-voting, or (2) a system of small single-member districts, with a run-off ballot where no candidate won a majority on the first day. Many of De Gaulle's advisers urged the former plan, on the ground that only thus could a workable majority be secured in parliament. De Gaulle chose instead the single-member district system so closely identified with the Third Republic. De Gaulle evidently hoped to avert a landslide victory for a right-wing coalition that might seek to profit by Gaullist slogans to win pluralities almost everywhere. He apparently believed that the single-member district might produce a more balanced Assembly containing alternative majorities of left-center and right-center. In an effort to further this purpose, he denied to any party the right to call itself Gaullist or to claim his benediction.

These safeguards did not suffice to prevent ambitious politicians from seizing De Gaulle's coattails, nor did it avert the landslide. A voting trend toward the right was supplemented by electoral rivalries among the left groups that completed the latter's rout. Two right-wing parties that managed to cooperate in most districts emerged far ahead of all rivals. One was a well-established party: the Independent Republicans, led by Pinay, Reynaud, and Duchet. The other had been organized barely in time for the elections: it was called the Union for the New Republic (U.N.R.), and was led by Jacques Soustelle. The U.N.R., with 26.4% of the popular vote in continental France and 189 seats, led all the rest; the Independents followed with 23.6% and 132 seats. On the left, the Communists (with 20.7%) were cut back to 10 seats, and the Socialists (with 13.8%) to 40 seats. In the center, the Radicals fell to 13 seats, while the M.R.P. and Bidault's dissident Christian Democratic group managed to salvage 57. The returns from Algeria pushed the fulcrum still farther to the right. Moderate and left-wing candidates in Algeria refused to run, leaving the field largely to the ultraconservative *colon* element and its "tame Moslem" allies.[2]

Although the electoral outcome again reflected the nation's extraordinary confidence in De Gaulle, it threatened to complicate his task by packing parliament with diehard nationalists determined to hold Algeria by force, and by leaving the French working class almost unrepresented. It threatened also to force De Gaulle's hand in choosing a premier, since Jacques Soustelle had been catapulted into a position of almost unrivaled prominence in the new parliament. Although Soustelle was a longtime and fervent Gaullist, there had been some signs of strain between the two men, and their political "styles" seemed to be diverging. Besides, the U.N.R. was an unknown quantity. A jerry-built coalition that had almost fallen apart on the eve of the elections, it was too new and too disparate to enable anyone to estimate its future character and program.

De Gaulle's choice of Michel Debré rather than Soustelle as premier indicated his determination not to become the prisoner of the new majority in the Assembly. Debré, during the election campaign, had sought to keep the U.N.R. from entering into a tight and exclusive coalition with right-wing groups, and preferred De Gaulle's policy of giving the cabinet a broader base. His new cabinet was in the main a revised edition of De Gaulle's interim government, save for the fact that the Socialists chose to withdraw their ministers and embark on a policy of

2 In Algeria the electoral system provided for large multimember districts, and required each list of candidates to include a specified number of Algerian Moslems.

constructive opposition. Of the 27 ministers and secretaries of state, ten were non-political "technicians" and five were senators; only twelve had been elected deputies in November and had to resign their parliamentary seats.[3]

Just before Debré took over the premiership, De Gaulle's temporary government adopted a final series of emergency measures strongly affecting the policies of the new government. In the economic sphere, the franc was devalued and a new "heavy franc" created; rather severe austerity measures were proclaimed in an effort to check inflation, reinvigorate the economy, and clear away some of the undergrowth of protective controls, restrictions, and subsidies. De Gaulle also passed on to his successor the outlines of a long-term plan for economic and social reform in Algeria, designed to create a healthier base on which to build the peaceful coexistence of *colons* and native Algerians. But this program, even if the French could bear its enormous cost, seemed unlikely to contribute to an early settlement of the dragging Algerian war. And the austerity program at home, however praiseworthy its purposes, threatened to undermine the government's popular support, since its impact on the living standard of ordinary Frenchmen would be severe.

6. THE PROSPECT FOR THE FIFTH REPUBLIC

France's new system has been launched on a remarkable wave of euphoria, with a breadth of support never approached by the Fourth Republic during its whole existence. Public opinion polls indicate near-unanimity with respect to De Gaulle's statesmanship. Parliament, for the first time in recent French history, contains a massive and fairly coherent majority. The government, for the time being at least, has been relieved of the problem of Communist obstructionism in the Assembly. Perhaps the opportunity is at last at hand for a vigorous executive to carry out effective long-term policies, and to give Frenchmen a taste for positive rather than negative government.

The Fifth Republic's prospects, however, depend on a whole series of potential shaping factors. One of these is the outcome of the Algerian conflict. If the costly rebellion with its attendant terrorism drags on indefinitely, France will have gained little by altering its political institutions. The Fourth Republic died of its overseas wars; the same ailment could kill its successor. A second factor will be the government's ability to pursue effective economic and social policies without splitting the nation. Vigorous attempts to check inflation and expand productivity may be risky at a time when the working class sees itself unrepresented in politics, and when it may conclude that it is being victimized because of its loss of political influence. The drastic shift of power to the right might end by producing a compensatory shift toward the extreme left. Still another shaping factor will be the eventual issue of the succession

[3] The 1958 electoral law required each candidate to name a substitute who would automatically replace him in the Assembly if he were named to a cabinet post.

to De Gaulle, whose unique role as a stabilizing influence cannot be duplicated.

The eminent commentator Raymond Aron, a supporter of the new system, has nevertheless described the 1958 constitution as "incontestably reactionary in spirit," in the sense that it runs counter to the general trend in the Western world. It rests, says Aron, on the theory that majority government is impossible in France, since there exists no coherent majority or common will. Universal suffrage, if this is true, can only produce deadlock, so that the normal parliamentary system and the normal presidential system are both unworkable. De Gaulle's attempted solution is to create an executive capable of making choices in a country that is irremediably divided, and capable of imposing those choices on a fragmented parliament. For the moment, Aron argues, the political class has accepted the system because its members fear a worse alternative. But, he concludes, "the struggle for revision will begin as soon as the state of urgency comes to an end." At that point, contradictory pressures will tend to push the system toward either a more traditional parliamentarianism or a more rigorous authoritarianism.

Reformers, like revolutionaries, rarely arrive at the precise goal toward which they had charted their course. The Fifth Republic, with all its uncertainties, is unlikely to disprove this theorem of history.

12

THE INTERNATIONAL POSITION OF FRANCE

1. RESIDUE OF GREAT-POWER STATUS

Past and Present. "For a nation which has known greatness and glory, there is no middle ground between the maintenance of its old prestige and complete impotence." So wrote the noted French liberal Prévost-Paradol in 1868. At the time there seemed to be no good reason to suppose that France would ever cease to enjoy greatness and glory. Bismarck reflected the views of his contemporaries when he remarked early in his career that, if he were the French chief of staff, he would permit no gun to go off in Europe without his permission. The pre-eminence that France had possessed on the continent for centuries was taken almost for granted. The military defeat of 1870–71 shook French prestige for a time, but after 1918 France once again emerged as the leading nation of the continent. French statesmen of the interwar era, to compensate for their nation's demographic and economic debility, wove a network of alliances with the new states of Eastern Europe. True, France gradually abdicated that position of leadership after 1930, but Frenchmen remained almost universally convinced until the collapse of 1940 that France could not conceivably be anything less than a great power.

It is not easy for any nation to change old mental habits, even under the shock of national disaster. Some Frenchmen still hold, as Prévost-Paradol did, that France has only two alternatives, and that the sole choice lies between "power and slavery." Such patriots are fond of recalling that France in the past has been often down but never out. The proud motto of Paris, *Fluctuat nec mergitur* ("She is battered by the waves but does not founder"), has a symbolic value to many Frenchmen. A deep feeling persists that, because the nation has climbed back from disaster before, there must be something automatic and inevitable about the process. The illusion is strengthened by the fact that modern history offers so few examples of once-great powers that have been pushed down permanently into the ranks of intermediate states.

Spain is the exception, but Frenchmen find it hard to believe that their nation could ever be another Spain. No doubt this tendency to look backward at France's past greatness reflects the Frenchman's ingrained habit of historical thinking. French statesmen, unlike the more pragmatic Anglo-Saxons, have always shown an intense concern for what they call "the verdict of history." And this consciousness of history becomes abnormally acute at moments of French weakness.

Prestige Politics.   Among contemporary French statesmen Charles de Gaulle has represented most clearly this determination that France can and must be nothing less than a great power. There was general approval of his crusading during the war years, for French morale had been badly shattered by the 1940 collapse. His attitude became more controversial after the liberation, when the nation had to face more pressing issues than the restoration of national prestige. Not only foreigners but a great many Frenchmen looked askance at De Gaulle's *"politique de grandeur,"* as reflected in the general's attempt to seize bits of Italian territory on the Alpine frontier in 1944, in his desire to rebuild the armed forces and to hold all parts of the empire at any cost, and in his attitude of haughty resentment when France was not treated as a full partner at Yalta and Potsdam.

The doubters have steadily outnumbered the partisans of "prestige politics" in postwar France. A few of these skeptics have swung over to the opposite extreme of defeatism. Overwhelmed by the decline of France, they are frankly prepared to accept the role of satellite in either the Soviet or the Western sphere.[1] But far more Frenchmen hope to steer a middle course between the extremes of "power" and "slavery." They sense that France must seek its proper place among the nations in a new kind of world—one that is dominated, at least for the time, by two super-powers. They realize that France's present position results from something deeper than the crushing impact of two world wars, that it derives also from the relative decline of Western Europe as a whole in the twentieth century. Some of them even suggest that an unrealistic policy of prestige during the decades before 1940 is partly responsible for France's present plight. They believe that the Third Republic burdened itself with a set of military and imperial obligations it could no longer afford, and that it wasted additional capital in loans to potential allies for military purposes. The resulting fiscal charges weighted down the nation's economy and impeded the modernization or expansion of France's productive plant.

This middle ground in foreign policy reflected the thinking of most of the Fourth Republic's leaders. Naturally, there have been nuances of opinion on foreign as well as on domestic issues. Some Frenchmen still believe that with luck and skill the nation can once more maneuver its way to a kind of marginal great-power status. They stress the advantages that France still possesses—strategic location, diplomatic experience, cultural influence, important overseas possessions. Some of

---

[1] A somewhat similar defeatist sentiment before 1940 probably inspired certain Frenchmen, like Pierre Laval, to favor collaboration with Nazi Germany.

them also believe that the first and essential step is to merge France into a larger Western European entity, within which and through which the nation's voice would have far more resonance. Their motives are less idealistic than realistic; they hope that unity may allow a weakened Western Europe to keep some of the power of decision that might otherwise be transferred to Washington. But beneath all the variations of emphasis and detail there is considerable agreement among the leaders of the principal center parties. So far, time has worked in their favor. In spite of the disaster of 1940 and the nation's persistent internal weaknesses, France has already regained an international role of real importance. It would be hard to conceive of an effective Western coalition—whether in the diplomatic, economic, or military sphere— without the participation of France as one of the leading members. Perhaps history (toward which Frenchmen show such deference) has played an unkind trick on the nation by loading it with such responsibility after the trials of the last two decades.

2. FRANCE IN THE COLD-WAR ERA

Between East and West. The initial phase of the Fourth Republic's foreign policy lasted from the liberation until the spring of 1947. During that period the major aim of French leadership was to keep the nation neutral in the rising tension between Soviet Russia and the Western powers. France's hope, as De Gaulle and his ministers saw it, was to rebuild its influence by serving as a bridge or a balance wheel between the two super-powers of the postwar world, to mediate between them, and to construct a bloc of neutralist states under French leadership. One of De Gaulle's first acts after his return to France was to sign a Franco-Soviet treaty of alliance and mutual aid. The corollary to the Russian pact, a treaty with Great Britain, was delayed for a time by Franco-British friction in the Near East, but it was finally consummated in 1947.

By that time, however, the bankruptcy of the "bridge" policy had become too obvious to ignore. Stalin's condescending attitude toward the French at international conferences caused resentment, and the Soviet refusal in 1947 to back French claims to the Saar virtually completed the rupture in Franco-Soviet friendship. The inauguration of the Marshall Plan shortly after, and Moscow's pronouncement of anathema against American aid, left the French with no real choice. In retrospect it seems at least possible that the Soviet leaders missed an invaluable opportunity to shape France's destiny. A more flexible Soviet policy in the years after 1945 might have kept France either neutralist or so completely divided as to cancel out France's value to the Western bloc. It is true, however, that most of France's centrist leaders were pulled toward the West by their ideological preferences, and this factor, together with the pressing need for Marshall aid, might have been enough to offset even the most astute Soviet blandishments.

The German Question. In most respects French interests ran parallel to the interests and policies of the other Western powers. One partial exception was the problem of Germany—an issue closely tied up with the emotions of every Frenchman. In French minds World War II was a tragic vindication of their insistence on a harsh policy toward the Germans after 1918. They felt that the other Western powers had learned something by the experience, but they continued to fear that the Americans and British might once again lapse into a soft and generous attitude. Frenchmen in 1945 generally favored the political decentralization or even the dismemberment of Germany. All parties, with varying emphasis, backed De Gaulle in his insistence that the Saar basin be absorbed into the French economic system, and that the whole Rhineland-Ruhr industrial area be detached from Germany and placed under international supervision.

When France abandoned its attempt to preserve neutrality between East and West, French leaders recognized that they would have to make concessions on Germany. Such a change of attitude not only ran counter to French prejudices but also violated France's traditional foreign policy, which had been based on French collaboration with either Russia or a bloc of Eastern European states to checkmate German power. Yet the change was carried through without producing a major upheaval in France, which suggests that most Frenchmen had come to regard the Soviet Union as a more immediate threat than Germany. Step by step, and without much enthusiasm, successive cabinets jettisoned the policy of severe repression. By 1950 it was clear that Western Germany was once more on the way to a position of great economic and political power in Europe.

Plans for Containing German Power. French policy makers, in an effort to harness and utilize this resurgent power, then struck out in a new direction. The cabinet proposed the so-called Schuman Plan, designed to integrate the steel and coal industries of all Western Europe under a supranational authority. Through this mechanism, the French believed, Germany's industrial power might be kept within bounds, and Germany's future freedom of political maneuver might be limited. With surprising speed and ease the Plan was written into a treaty, and the new Coal and Steel Community went into operation in 1952. The Community chose the Frenchman Jean Monnet as its first president and set out to stimulate expansion and rationalization of industry as well as to encourage a freer flow of products throughout Western Europe. So far neither the hopes nor the fears aroused by the Schuman Plan seem to have been justified by the rather cautious activity of the Steel Community. Perhaps, as Jean Monnet has argued, it can never grow out of the embryo stage unless it can be expanded far beyond the area of coal and steel alone.

While the Coal and Steel Community was still in the making, a new complication had been introduced by the American Government, which began after Korea to press for the partial rearmament of Western Germany without delay. The French cabinet, frightened and irritated by this pressure but unable to ignore it, countered with a hastily drafted plan to merge the German forces into a Western European army. But German rearmament in any form aroused great antagonism in France, and the integrated-army scheme was doubly unpopular because it would mean that the French Army too would be merged into something supra-national. French cabinets backed and filled over the issue until, by 1954, a curious and embarrassing dead end had been reached: the plan had been accepted by every prospective member state except France, which had first proposed it. The denouement came when the National Assem-bly voted to reject the treaty that embodied the plan, thus strangling the integrated army before it was born. But the French recognized that they could no longer delay German rearmament, and they reluctantly agreed to the revival of an independent German force under rather sketchy controls. A further blow to French pride came in 1955 when the citizens of the Saar, which had been under French control for a decade, voted into power a set of leaders committed to the Saar's return to Germany.

So it was that, only a decade after the utter destruction of German power, the French saw their neighbor once more strong, prosperous, and about to take up arms. Only the division of Germany into eastern and western halves ensured France a shaky superiority, and even that su-periority was threatened. To some Frenchmen this outcome was proof of the blindness of their Western allies and the weakness of their own leaders. To others, however, it was evidence of the nation's remarkable realism and ability to face unpleasant facts. After all, the French might have chosen a policy of blind resistance to any sort of German revival. Such a policy, understandable enough in the circumstances, could have led to nothing more than utter failure and frustration. What the French got after ten years of strategic retreats may have appeared to be no better, but in fact something valuable did remain. At least the possibility of friendly collaboration with a reformed Germany remained open.[2] And if the future were to prove that this possibility rested on a false premise, the French could expect greater understanding and support from the British and the Americans than they got in the years between the wars.

Western European Integration.   Few nations have gone so far as postwar France in advocating supranational institutions. In the 1946 constitution the founders of the Fourth Republic bound France to accept such limitations on her sovereignty as might be "necessary for the or-ganization and defense of peace." All of the center parties have pledged themselves to the ideal of European federation in one or another form. The M.R.P. has taken the lead, but many Socialists and some Radicals are not far behind. The French were the chief exponents of the Council of Europe, established at Strasbourg in 1949, and except for British

---

[2] According to a public opinion poll in 1957, a heavy majority of Frenchmen have come to favor a *rapprochement* with Germany, despite some continuing doubts. Seventy per cent approved an attitude of "confidence combined with prudence" to-ward the Germans.

reluctance they would have made it much more than a mere forum for debate. It was a Frenchman who conceived the idea of the Coal and Steel Community; and other Frenchmen have worked vigorously for the creation of the new atomic-energy pool and the European common market, both of which were approved by the French Parliament in 1957.

Not all Frenchmen, however, are convinced of the virtues of these supranational schemes. The Communists bitterly oppose them; so did the Gaullist R.P.F. and the Poujadist movement during their respective heydays. Even within the major parties of the center, some politicians are lukewarm at best and the popular appeal of federation among the voters has lost much of its strength with the passing of time. Some years ago "integration" was a kind of magic word that seemed to imply some sort of automatic solution to France's ills. Now many of the same young idealists who crusaded for federation are more inclined to follow the lead of Mendès-France, who contends that integration might be disastrous for France unless the nation first puts its own economic house in order. Furthermore, the reluctance of the British to merge their destinies with those of Western Europe makes many Frenchmen hesitate. For only if the British are full partners will the French feel safe in a closer union with Germany. And perhaps British partnership alone will make France feel that she can be a real associate rather than a satellite of the United States.

The Appeal of Neutralism. During the early years of the cold-war era a small but vocal group of French left-wing intellectuals coined the term "neutralism" and sought to get it accepted as the nation's official policy. Their thesis was that the United States and the Soviet Union were not only equally barbarous but were also equally responsible for the cold war, and that a well-armed but uncommitted France might be able to sit out a third world war in Swiss fashion. Many of these intellectuals were inclined to prefer Soviet communism to American capitalism, though they disliked the means used by the Soviet Government to attain its ends. In the 1951 elections a number of them ran for the National Assembly on a neutralist ticket, but all were overwhelmingly defeated. It soon became clear, however, that these meager electoral results did not adequately reflect the depth and strength of neutralism's emotional appeal. France's geographical position as a potential battleground between the super-powers, combined with the memory of recent invasion, induces a sense of impotence either to prevent war or to survive it if it comes. Even those Frenchmen who vote Communist have shown themselves strongly susceptible to the neutralist idea. An opinion poll in 1952 indicated that 65 per cent of the Communist voters would like to see France stay out of a future Soviet-American war if that could be managed. Latent neutralism exists all the way across the political spectrum from left to right, and as the cold-war era drags on, it may develop from the latent to the active stage. The Soviet Union's post-Stalin line is well designed to encourage it; so is the successful balancing act of Marshal Tito; and French resentment at American criticisms of French policy in Algeria may further cool France's relations with the West.

Although France is still a loyal member of the Western bloc, and although most Frenchmen remain devoted to the democratic ideal, there is at least some possibility that a third phase in postwar France's foreign policy is in the making, and that the nation may someday seek escape from the weight of its international responsibilities through the easy trap door of neutralism.

Destiny of the Republic. The French Republic's greatest weakness in international affairs derives not from France's relative decline among the powers but rather from its internal division. No state is likely to play an effective role in the world unless the bulk of its citizens is united on certain fundamentals of foreign policy. Contemporary France is unfortunate enough to live in a deeply divided world, and to see that division reflected among its own citizens. As long as a powerful Communist Party exists in France, with its decisions linked to those of Moscow, there is little chance of a foreign policy based on unified public sentiment. Yet as long as certain fundamental weaknesses exist in the social texture and the economic structure of France, the Communist Party is likely to remain powerful. The Republic cannot escape this dilemma. The basic question is whether it can contribute to dissipating the dilemma and can survive the long and difficult period that must elapse before a broader and more fundamental unity of Frenchmen becomes an attainable goal.

SELECTED BIBLIOGRAPHY

The past few years have brought a freshet of books on contemporary France, many of them excellent. Among the best of the general works on the subject are these: F. Goguel, *France under the Fourth Republic* (Ithaca, 1952), and the same author's *Le régime politique français* (Paris, 1955); H. Luethy, *France against Herself* (New York, 1955); D. Pickles, *French Politics; the First Years of the Fourth Republic* (London, 1953); M. Duverger, *The French Political System* (Chicago, 1958); and P. Williams, *Politics in Post-War France* (2nd ed., London, 1958). Monographs on particular aspects of the French system will be listed below under appropriate headings.

Bibliographical Guides. The standard bibliographical aid is A. Grandin, *Bibliographie générale des sciences juridiques, politiques, économiques et sociales* (Paris, 1926, with annual supplements). For periodical items there is also the excellent *Bulletin analytique de documentation politique, économique, et sociale contemporaine,* published bimonthly since 1946 by the National Political Science Foundation in Paris.

Primary Sources and Government Publications. The text of the 1946 constitution may be most conveniently found in Williams (op. cit.) or in G. Berlia *et al., Les constitutions et les principales lois politiques de la France depuis 1789* (7th ed., Paris, 1952). The process of drafting the Fourth Republic's constitution may be studied in two volumes published by the constituent assemblies of 1945–46, entitled *Séances de la commission de la constitution* (Paris, 1946). The text of the Fifth Republic's constitution has been published in pamphlet form by the Press and Information Service of the French Embassy in New York City.

The French legislative records are contained in the *Journal officiel de la république française,* published in several series (laws and decrees, parliamentary documents, and administrative annexes).

Current statistical information is most readily available in the *Bulletin de la statistique générale de la France* (monthly, with a quarterly supplement containing valuable special studies). The Ministry of Finance has twice (1946 and 1949) published an *Inventaire de la situation financière,* covering the years 1913–49; a succeeding volume is entitled *Rapport sur les comptes de la nation 1949–1955.* The National Statistical Institute in 1957 produced a volume entitled *Mouvement économique en France de 1944 à 1957.* A useful monthly organ called *Études et conjoncture* is published by the Ministry of Finance.

The Planning Commission has issued annual progress reports since 1947, and from time to time it surveys a broader span (e.g., *Rapport sur la réalisation du plan de modernisation et d'équipement de l'Union Française: année 1952* [Paris, 1953]).

Other useful government publications are the Council of State's annual reports called *Études et documents* (1947–), and its *Livre jubilaire* commemorating its 150th anniversary (Paris, 1952); the annual reports of the Court of Accounts (published in the *Journal officiel*); the Economic Council's brief self survey entitled *Activité du Conseil Économique (1951–1954)* (Paris, 1955); and many of the pamphlets in the series *Notes documentaires et études,* produced by the government's information office.

Reference Works. A committee headed by André Siegfried has been publishing annually since 1946 an invaluable yearbook entitled *L'Année politique.* Complete electoral statistics for the general elections of 1945–46 were published in two

314

volumes by R. Husson: *Elections et référendums* (Paris, 1946 and 1947). The government's information office took over this task for the 1951 and 1956 elections: *Les élections législatives de 1951* (Paris, 1952); *Les élections législatives du 2 janvier 1956* (Paris, 1957).

General Background: Third Republic. The most enlightening recent attempts to re-examine the Third Republic are those by D. Thomson, *Democracy in France* (3rd ed., London, 1958); F. Goguel, *La Politique des partis sous la IIIe république* (Paris, 1946); and A. Siegfried, *De la IIIe à la IVe république* (Paris, 1956). Good prewar studies include W. R. Sharp, *The Government of the Third Republic* (New York, 1938); W. L. Middleton, *The French Political System* (New York, 1933); D. Pickles, *The French Political Scene* (London, 1938); J. Barthélemy, *Le Gouvernement de la France* (3rd ed., Paris, 1939); and P. Maillaud, *France* (London, 1943). A. Werth's *The Twilight of France, 1933–1940* (New York, 1942) is a remarkable though somewhat slanted journalistic study of the prewar decade. The best general historical accounts are D. W. Brogan, *France under the Republic* (New York, 1940), and J. P. T. Bury, *France, 1814–1940* (3rd ed., London, 1954). A notable recent textbook is J.-J. Chevallier, *Histoire des institutions politiques françaises de 1789 à nos jours* (Paris, 1952). There are some useful chapters on prewar France in E. M. Earle, ed., *Modern France* (Princeton, 1951).

Four prewar essays on French politics have become semi-classics: R. de Jouvenel, *La République des camarades* (Paris, 1914); "Alain," *Éléments d'une doctrine radicale* (Paris, 1925); A. Siegfried, *France: a Study in Nationality* (New Haven, 1930); and A. Thibaudet, *Les idées politiques de la France* (Paris, 1932).

French scholars in the past have been inclined to stress the juridical aspect of government. Among the standard works on constitutional law are these: A. Esmein and H. Nézard, *Éléments de droit constitutionnel français et comparé* (8th ed., Paris, 1927–28); L. Duguit, *Traité de droit constitutionnel* (3rd ed., Paris, 1927–30); and E. Pierre, *Traité de droit politique, électoral et parlementaire* (5th ed., Paris, 1924).

From Third to Fourth Republic. The Vichy interlude has recently been the subject of several studies, notably these: A. Cobban, "Vichy France," in A. Toynbee, ed., *Survey of International Affairs 1939–46: Hitler's Europe* (London, 1954); R. Aron, *Histoire de Vichy, 1940–1944* (Paris, 1954); A. Mallet, *Pierre Laval* (Paris, 1954); P. Farmer, *Vichy: Political Dilemma* (New York, 1955); D. Thomson, *Two Frenchmen: Laval and de Gaulle* (London, 1950); S. Hoffmann, "Aspects du régime de Vichy," *Revue Française de Science Politique*, 6 (1956), pp. 44–69. H. Michel's *Histoire de la résistance* (Paris, 1950) is brief but very good; Michel together with B. Mirkine-Guetzévitch has edited a documentary collection entitled *Les idées politiques de la résistance* (Paris, 1954). Memoirs by Vichy leaders and prominent resistance figures have appeared in profusion over the past decade. The most notable is Charles de Gaulle's *Mémoires de guerre* (2 vols., Paris, 1954–56).

Fourth Republic: General. Along with the books listed at the beginning of this bibliography the following general works are useful: D. C. McKay, *France and the United States* (Cambridge, Mass., 1951); S. Padover et al., *French Institutions: Values and Politics* (Stanford, 1954); R. Matthews, *The Death of the Fourth Republic* (New York, 1954); C. Gavin, *Liberated France* (New York, 1955); A. Werth, *France 1940–1955* (New York, 1956); E. Berl, *La France irréelle* (Paris, 1957); J. Fauvet, *La France déchirée* (Paris, 1957); D. Schoenbrun, *As France Goes* (New York, 1957).

The only full-length study of the making of the 1946 constitution is G. Wright, *The Reshaping of French Democracy* (New York, 1948); a brief account may be found in the anonymous brochure *A Constitution for the Fourth Republic* (Washington, 1947). On the early post-liberation months see J. E. Sawyer, "The Reestablishment of the Republic in France," *Political Science Quarterly*, 62 (1947), pp. 354–67.

Several dozen specialists have contributed chapters to the following symposia or special issues of periodicals: M. Guernier, ed., *Encyclopédie politique de la France et du monde* (Paris, 1950); E. M. Earle, ed., *Modern France* (Princeton,

1951); *La Nef,* April-May 1951 ("Tableau Politique de la France"); *Yale French Studies,* No. 15, 1955 ("Social and Political France"); *Occidente,* No. 5, 1955 ("The Crisis of France"); *Esprit,* Dec. 1957 ("La France des Français").

Recent French manuals on government, constitutional law, or administrative law include the following: J. Théry, *Le gouvernement de la 4e république* (Paris, 1949); J. Laferrière, *Manuel de droit constitutionnel* (Paris, 1947); M. Duverger, *Manuel de droit constitutionnel* (Paris, 1948); M. Prélot, *Précis de droit constitutionnel* (Paris, 1952); R. Pinto, *Éléments de droit constitutionnel* (Paris, 1952); L. Trotabas, *Manuel de droit public et administratif* (Paris, 1950); M. Waline, *Traité élémentaire de droit administratif* (Paris, 1951); P. Duez and G. Debeyre, *Traité de droit administratif* (Paris, 1952); and A. de Labaudère, *Traité élémentaire de droit administratif* (Paris, 1953). The foregoing list reflects a variety of schools of interpretation.

Several French periodicals are indispensable for their articles on current political and administrative problems: notably the *Revue Française de Science Politique, Revue du Droit Public et des Sciences Politiques, Revue Administrative, Droit Social,* and *Politique Étrangère.* Of more sporadic interest are such periodicals as *La Revue Socialiste* and *Les Cahiers du Communisme* (both of which are official party organs); *Esprit* (left-wing Catholic); *Christianisme Social* (Protestant); *Revue de l'Action Populaire* (Catholic); *Revue Politique et Parlementaire* (right-center); *L'Express* (the organ of Mendès-France); and *La Nef.* The results of public-opinion polls are published in the review *Sondages.* One Paris daily newspaper, *Le Monde,* is of special value for its broad coverage of current politics and its frequent background articles.

Specialized Aspects of Government. On the legislative branch see especially D. W. S. Lidderdale, *The Parliament of France* (London, 1951); also R. K. Gooch, *The French Parliamentary Committee System* (New York, 1935); A. Soulier, *L'instabilité ministérielle sous la troisième république* (Paris, 1939); M. Debré, *La Mort de l'état républicain* (Paris, 1947), *La République et ses problèmes* (Paris, 1952), *Ces princes qui nous gouvernent* (Paris, 1957); E. G. Lewis, "The Operation of the French Economic Council," *American Political Science Review,* 49 (1955), pp. 161–72; L. Noel, *Notre dernière chance* (Paris, 1956); P. Bromhead, "Some Notes on the Standing Committees of the French National Assembly," *Political Studies,* 5 (1957), pp. 140–57; P. Williams, "Compromise and Crisis in French Politics," *Political Science Quarterly,* 72 (1957), pp. 321–39; C. Melnik and N. Leites, *The House Without Windows: France Selects a President* (Evanston, Ill., 1958); N. Leites, *On the Game of Politics in France* (Stanford, 1959).

On the constitutional revision of 1954: C. Poutier, *La réforme de la constitution* (Paris, 1955); F. Goguel in *Revue Française de Science Politique,* 5 (1955), pp. 485–502; R. Pierce in *Journal of Politics,* 17 (1955), pp. 221–47.

On the judiciary and the court system: R. C. K. Ensor, *Courts and Judges in France, Germany, and England* (London, 1933); R. Charles, *La Justice en France* (Paris, 1953); B. Schwartz, *French Administrative Law and the Common-Law World* (New York, 1954); M. Letourneur and J. Méric, *Conseil d'Etat et juridictions administratives* (Paris, 1955); G. Langrod, "The French Council of State," *American Political Science Review,* 49 (1955), pp. 673–92.

On administrative problems: E. Bonnefous, *La réforme administrative* (Paris, 1958).

On the civil service: see especially R. Grégoire, *La Fonction publique* (Paris, 1954); also T. Feyzioglu, "The Reform of the French Higher Civil Service," *Public Administration,* 33 (1955), pp. 69–93, 173–90; W. A. Robson, *The Civil Service in Britain and France* (London, 1956); A. Sauvy, *La Bureaucratie* (Paris, 1956); R. Jumper, "Recruitment Problems of the French Higher Civil Service," *Western Political Quarterly,* 10 (1957), pp. 38–48. An older monograph still useful for background purposes is W. R. Sharp, *The French Civil Service* (New York, 1931).

On the Court of Accounts: A. P. de Mirimonde, *La Cour des comptes* (Paris, 1947).

On the police: B. Chapman, "The Organization of the French Police," *Public Administration,* 29 (1949), pp. 67–75.

On the army: J. Planchet, *Le Malaise de l'armée* (Paris, 1957); E. L. Katzenbach, "The French Army," *Yale Review,* 45 (1956), pp. 498–513.

On local government: see especially two remarkable books by B. Chapman, *Introduction to French Local Government* (London, 1953), and *The Prefects and Provincial France* (London, 1955). Also, R. K. Gooch, *Regionalism in France* (New York, 1931); P. Doueil, *L'administration locale à l'épreuve de la guerre* (Paris, 1950); F. Hermens, "Local Autonomy in France and Italy," in A. J. Zurcher, ed., *Constitutions and Constitutional Trends since World War II* (2nd ed., New York, 1955).

On taxation: L. Formery, *Les Impôts en France* (Paris, 1946); M. Duverger, *Les Finances publiques* (Paris, 1950); L. Trotabas, *Les Finances publiques et les impôts de la France* (Paris, 1953); J. Houghteling in C. J. Friedrich and J. K. Galbraith, eds., *Public Policy,* V (Cambridge, Mass., 1954); M. Lauré, *Traité de politique fiscale* (Paris, 1956).

On nationalized industry: see especially M. Einaudi, M. Byé, and E. Rossi, *Nationalization in France and Italy* (Ithaca, 1955); also L. Julliot de la Morandière and M. Byé, *Les Nationalisations en France* (Paris, 1948); J. Rivéro, *Le Régime des nationalisations* (Paris, 1949); C. A. Colliard *et al., Le fonctionnement des entreprises nationalisées en France* (Paris, 1956); B. Chenot, *Les entreprises nationalisées* (Paris, 1956); J. Meynaud, *Études politiques* (Paris, 1957).

On electoral problems and political behavior: P. Campbell, *French Electoral Systems and Elections 1789–1957* (London, 1958); M. Duverger *et al., L'Influence des systèmes électoraux sur la vie politique* (Paris, 1950); C. Morazé *et al., Études de sociologie électorale* (Paris, 1947); G. Dupeux and F. Goguel, *Sociologie électorale* (Paris, 1951); F. Goguel, *Géographie des élections françaises 1870–1951* (Paris, 1951); F. Goguel *et al., Nouvelles études de sociologie électorale* (Paris, 1955); M. Dogan and J. Narbonne, *Les Françaises face à la politique* (Paris, 1955); M. Duroselle *et al., Les élections du 2 janvier 1956* (Paris, 1957); H. G. Nicholas *et al.,* "The French Elections," *Political Studies,* 4 (1956), pp. 139–282.

On the French party system: J. Fauvet, *Les Forces politiques en France* (Paris, 1950); M. Duverger, *Les Partis politiques dans l'état contemporaine* (Paris, 1951); G. Lavau, *Partis politiques et réalités sociales* (Paris, 1953); C. A. Micaud, "French Political Parties: Ideological Myths and Social Realities," in S. Neumann, ed., *Modern Political Parties* (Chicago, 1955); P. Williams, *Politics in Post-War France* (2nd edition, London, 1958), "The French Party System," *Occidente,* 10 (1954), pp. 158–83; F. Goguel, "Political Instability in France," *Foreign Affairs,* 33 (1954), pp. 111–22; R. Aron, "Electeurs, partis, et élus," *Revue Française de Science Politique,* 5 (1955), pp. 245–66; M. Duverger, ed., *Partis politiques et classes sociales* (Paris, 1955); P. Campbell, "French Party Congresses," *Parliamentary Affairs,* 10 (1957), pp. 412–23.

On specific parties: M. Einaudi *et al., Communism in Western Europe* (Ithaca, 1951); A. Brayance, *Anatomie du parti communiste français* (Paris, 1952); G. Almond *et al., The Appeals of Communism* (Princeton, 1954); C. A. Micaud, "Organization and Leadership of the French Communist Party," *World Politics,* 4 (1952), pp. 318–55, "The Bases of Communist Strength in France," *Western Political Quarterly,* 8 (1955), pp. 354–66, "The 'New Left' in France," *World Politics,* 10 (1958), pp. 537–59; E. D. Godfrey, "The Communist Presence in France," *American Political Science Review,* 50 (1956), pp. 321–38, *The Fate of the French Non-Communist Left* (New York, 1955); J. Colton, "The French Socialist Party," *Yale Review,* 43 (1954), pp. 402–13; C. A. Micaud, "Social Democracy in France," *World Politics,* 7 (1955), pp. 532–45; P. Rimbert, "L'avenir du parti socialiste," *Revue socialiste* (1952), pp. 122–32, 288–97; M. Einaudi and F. Goguel, *Christian Democracy in Italy and France* (Notre Dame, 1952); E. P. Noether, "Political Catholicism in France and Italy," *Yale Review,* 44 (1955), pp. 569–83; W. R. Yates, "Power, Principle, and the Doctrine of the *Mouvement Républicain Populaire,*" *American Political Science Review,* 52 (1958), pp. 419–36; C. Nicolet, *Le Radicalisme* (Paris, 1957); R. Pierce, "De Gaulle and the RPF—a Post-Mortem," *Journal of Politics,* 16 (1954), pp. 96–119; S. Hoffmann, *Le mouvement Poujade* (Paris, 1956); G. Wright, "The Resurgence of the Right in France," *Yale French Studies,* No. 15 (1955), pp. 3–11; R. Rémond, *La Droite en France de 1815 à nos jours*

(Paris, 1954); P. Sérant, *Où va la droite?* (Paris, 1958); E. Weber, *"La Fièvre de la raison:* Nationalism and the French Right," *World Politics,* 10 (1958), pp. 560–78.

On the role of public opinion: A. Sauvy, *Le Pouvoir et l'opinion* (Paris, 1949); J. M. Domenach, *La Propagande politique* (Paris, 1950).

On pressure-groups: J. Meynaud, *Les Groupes de pression en France* (Paris, 1958); B. E. Brown, "Pressure Politics in France," *Journal of Politics,* 18 (1956), pp. 702–19; H. W. Ehrmann, *Organized Business in France* (Princeton, 1957); V. Lorwin, *The French Labor Movement* (Cambridge, Mass., 1954); G. Lavau, "Note sur un 'pressure-group' français: la Confédération générale des petites et moyennes entreprises," *Revue Française de Science Politique,* 5 (1955), pp. 370–83; G. Wright, "Agrarian Syndicalism in Postwar France," *American Political Science Review,* 47 (1953), pp. 402–16; J. Fauvet and H. Mendras, *Les Paysans et la politique dans la France contemporaine* (Paris, 1958).

On the press: G. Boris, "The French Press," *Foreign Affairs,* 13 (1935), pp. 319–27; R. Manévy, *La presse de la IIIe république* (Paris, 1955); J. Mottin, *Histoire politique de la presse, 1944–49* (Paris, 1949); J. Park *et al., The Culture of France in Our Time* (Ithaca, 1954). A Communist exposé of ownership of the press may be found in *Economie et Politique,* Nos. 5–6 (1954).

On the French Union: M. Devèze, *La France d'outre-mer* (Paris, 1948); D. Boisdon *et al., Les Institutions de l'union française* (Paris, 1949); C. A. Julien, *L'Afrique du Nord en marche* (Paris, 1952); P. Mus, *Le Destin de l'Union française* (Paris, 1954); K. Robinson, *The Public Law of Overseas France since the War* (Oxford, n. d.); E. Hammer, *The Struggle for Indo-China* (Stanford, 1954); R. Aron, *La Tragédie algérienne* (Paris, 1957); G. Tillion, *L'Algérie en 1957* (Paris, 1957); P. Moussa, *Les Chances économiques de la communauté franco-africaine* (Paris, 1957); A. Blanchet, *L'Itineraire des partis africains depuis Bamako* (Paris, 1958); K. Robinson, "Constitutional Reform in French Tropical Africa," *Political Studies,* 6 (1958), pp. 45–69; V. Thompson and R. Adloff, *French West Africa* (Stanford, 1958).

Social and Economic Aspects. The social and economic substructure of French politics is at last becoming the subject of careful analysis, although much remains to be done. The following items represent a sampling of the material available.

General analyses of social structure: P. Frédérix, *Etat des forces en France* (Paris, 1935); G. Gurvitch, "Social Structure of Pre-War France," *American Journal of Sociology,* 48 (1943), pp. 535–54; A. Siegfried *et al., Aspects de la société française* (Paris, 1954); R. Aron, "Social Structure and the Ruling Class," in R. Bendix and S. Lipset, *Class, Status, and Power* (Glencoe, Ill., 1953); C. Morazé, *Les Français et la république* (Paris, 1956).

On economic structure and the problem of economic development: see especially W. C. Baum, *The French Economy and the State* (Princeton, 1958); also A. Sauvy, *Chances de l'économie française* (Paris, 1946); J. Fourastié and H. Montet, *L'économie française dans le monde* (Paris, 1946); C. Bettelheim, *Bilan de l'économie française 1919–1946* (Paris, 1947); J. Sawyer, "The Entrepreneur and the Social Order: France and the United States," in W. Miller, ed., *Men in Business* (Cambridge, Mass., 1952); P. Mendès-France, *Gouverner, c'est choisir* (Paris, 1953); M. Lauré, *Révolution: dernière chance de la France* (Paris, 1954); J. F. Gravier, *Décentralisation et progrès techniques* (Paris, 1954); G. Boris, "Les Problèmes du développement économique de la France et leurs origines," *Politique Étrangère,* 19 (1954), pp. 123–42; United Nations, Economic Commission for Europe, *Economic Survey of Europe in 1954* (Geneva, 1955); D. Landes, "Observations on France: Economy, Society, and Polity," *World Politics,* 9 (1957), pp. 329–50; W. C. Peterson, "Planning and Economic Progress in France," *World Politics,* 9 (1957), pp. 351–82; S. B. Clough, "Economic Planning in a Capitalist Society—France from Monnet to Hirsh," *Political Science Quarterly,* 71 (1956), pp. 539–52.

On social security: B. Rodgers, "Social Security in France," *Public Administration,* 31 (1953), pp. 377–98; H. C. Galant, *Histoire politique de la sécurité sociale française* (Paris, 1955); P. Laroque, ed., *Les Institutions sociales de la France* (Paris, 1955).

On demographic problems: L. Chevalier, *Démographie générale* (Paris, 1951); A. Sauvy, *Théorie générale de la population* (Paris, 1952). See also the quarterly journal *Population,* published by the French Demographic Institute.

On labor: see especially V. Lorwin, *The French Labor Movement* (Cambridge, Mass., 1954); also H. W. Ehrmann, *French Labor from Popular Front to Liberation* (New York, 1947); M. Collinet, *Essai sur la condition ouvrière 1900–1950* (Paris, 1951); A. Tiano et al., *Expériences françaises d'action syndicale ouvrier* (Paris, 1956).

On the peasantry: see especially J. Fauvet and H. Mendras, *Les Paysans et la politique dans la France contemporaine* (Paris, 1958); also N. Hunter, *Peasantry and Crisis in France* (London, 1938); L. Chevalier, *Les Paysans* (Paris, 1947); M. Augé-Laribé, *La Politique agricole de la France de 1880 à 1940* (Paris, 1950), *La Révolution agricole* (Paris, 1955); G. Friedmann, ed., *Villes et campagnes* (Paris, 1953); H. Ehrmann, "The French Peasant and Communism," *American Political Science Review,* 45 (1952), pp. 19–33; G. Wright, "Four Red Villages in France," *Yale Review,* 41 (1952), pp. 361–72, "Peasant Politics in the Third French Republic," *Political Science Quarterly,* 70 (1955), pp. 75–87.

On the middle classes: C. Morazé, *La France bourgeoise* (Paris, 1947); E. Beau de Loménie, *Les Responsabilités des dynasties bourgeoises* (Paris, 1943–54); D. Landes, "French Business and the Businessman," in E. M. Earle, *Modern France* (Princeton, 1951), pp. 334–53; P. Bleton, *Les Hommes des temps qui viennent-essai sur les classes moyennes* (Paris, 1956); and the remarkable monograph of H. W. Ehrmann, *Organized Business in France* (Princeton, 1957). A special issue of the Communist periodical *Economie et Politique* (Nos. 5–6, 1954), entitled "La France et les Trusts," contains some interesting though sharply slanted information on big business.

On the churches: F. Boulard, *Essor ou déclin du clergé français?* (Paris, 1950), *Premiers itinéraires en sociologie religieuse* (Paris, 1954); A. Latreille and A. Siegfried, *Les forces religieuses et la politique* (Paris, 1951); J. N. Moody et al., *Church and Society* (New York, 1953); E. Léonard, *Le Protestant français* (Paris, 1953); S. Schram, *Protestantism and Politics in France* (Alençon, 1954); G. Wright, "Catholics and Peasantry in France," *Political Science Quarterly,* 68 (1953), pp. 526–51; R. F. Byrnes, "The French Priest-Workers," *Foreign Affairs,* 33 (1955), pp. 327–31; A. Dansette, *Destin du catholicisme français, 1926–1956* (Paris, 1957). See also a special issue of *La Nef* (No. 5, 1954) on "Problèmes du catholicisme français."

International Role of France. J. B. Duroselle, ed., *La Politique étrangère et ses fondements* (Paris, 1954), "L'élaboration de la politique étrangère française," *Revue Française de Science Politique,* 6 (1956), pp. 508–24; A. Outrey, *L'administration française des affaires étrangères* (Paris, 1954); J. E. Howard, *Parliament and Foreign Policy in France* (London, 1948); E. S. Furniss, *France: Keystone of Western Defense* (New York, 1954), *Weaknesses in French Foreign Policy-Making* (Princeton, 1954), "The Twilight of French Foreign Policy," *Yale Review,* 44 (1954), pp. 64–80; J. T. Marcus, "Neutralism in France," *Review of Politics,* 17 (1955), pp. 295–328; A. Philip, *L'Europe unie* (Paris, 1953); M. E. Naegelen, *Grandeur et solitude de la France* (Paris, 1956); D. Lerner and R. Aron, *France Defeats EDC* (New York, 1957). A representative sampling of current French views on France's European and world role may be found in the files of the periodicals *Politique Étrangère* (Paris) and *Foreign Affairs* (New York) over the past decade.

Beginnings of the Fifth Republic. A. de Sérigny, *La Révolution du 13 mai* (Paris, 1958); R. Dronne, *La Révolution d'Alger* (Paris, 1958); "Sirius" [H. Beuve-Méry], *Le Suicide de la IVe république* (Paris, 1958); R. Aron, *L'Algérie et la république* (Paris, 1958); M. Duverger, *Demain la république* (Paris, 1958); P. H. Simon, *La France à la fièvre* (Paris, 1958); R. Massigli, *Sur quelques maladies de l'état* (Paris, 1958); R. Triboulet, *Des vessies pour des lanternes* (Paris, 1958); M. Bloch-Masquart, *La Prochaine république sera-t-elle républicaine?* (Paris, 1958); P. Gérin, *L'Algérie du 13 mai* (Paris, 1958); J. Ferniot, *Les Ides de mai* (Paris, 1958); A. Fabre-Luce, *Gaulle deux* (Paris, 1958); M. Debré, *Refaire une démocratie, un état, un pouvoir* (Paris, 1958).

PART THREE

GERMANY

———————◆———————

by Sigmund Neumann

13

INTRODUCING A PEOPLE OF TENSIONS

1. CRISIS GOVERNMENT

Introduction. In a comparative study of political systems, Germany differs from other major nations in that she does not offer a persistent or definite political pattern that can be taken as a measure of her contribution to political society. On the contrary, she offers the ideal case study of crisis government in our times. She has challenged our fundamental concepts, international, national, and personal. She has experimented with most divergent forms of government until at present she has again arrived at a turning point and a new beginning with which her history seems to be so plagued.

Situated at the crossroads of Europe, her unrest has spelled anxiety to the whole continent and to the world. Twice within one generation she has taken arms against the international order and has aspired to establish a New Order of her own. Both attempts were marked failures.

On the national plane, Germany has experimented with several governmental systems which have reflected most of the crisis elements of modern society. The dynamics of social classes and their effects on the constitutional developments, together with their impact on international relations, are clearly illustrated in German history.

The clash of these elementary forces reaches down to the individual. Nowhere in the Western world has man more radically seized upon the fundamental issues of human existence; nowhere else has he been more systematically enslaved. Germany has become simultaneously the home of great political philosophers, reaching for the stars, and the example of the total state denying the right of expression to the individual. The whole depth of modern man's crisis has been epitomized by this unhappy people.

For these reasons a study of Germany's political dynamics represents a challenging task for the political scientist. Such a study will definitely not unfold a well-integrated system of government, but rather one of crisis government *par excellence.*

Social Dynamics. This very instability of crisis government indicates another important and unique feature of the German political scene. The time-honored British government may suggest concentration on a well-balanced system of interrelated institutions; even the less stable French political structure is balanced by the consistency of popularly accepted standards and formulated documents that may serve as a key toward understanding its national constitution. Germany possesses neither Britain's solid institutions nor the French rational belief in the codification of political action, national or international.

For better or worse, Germany's constitution is neither a set of clearly defined institutions nor a written document. It must be conceived above all as a shifting correlation of social and political forces that always assert themselves in the changing pattern of politics. This is the "real" constitution, as Ferdinand Lassalle phrased it in a classic address almost a century ago, in the midst of the historical conflict over the Prussian constitution.[1] An analysis of Germany's constitutional system is thus essentially a study in political sociology. The society's continuous shifts and strains spell out the real constitution of this nation.

Between East and West—Clashes in Space. Geography is at the base of Germany's political tensions. Situated between Eastern and Western Europe and without natural barriers, the *Land der Mitte* was always open to the dynamic forces that spilled across the northern plains of Europe. Frontierless, formless, insecure, open to any outside influence and attack, Germany became bridgehead or battlefield, balance or buffer of the great pendulum moves that defined the western world's momentous history.

The great wave of "barbarian invasions" that meant the end of the ancient world was followed in the Middle Ages by the eastern colonization that extended Europe's frontiers, geographic and spiritual. And while these waves have not yet exhausted themselves, the East has again reasserted itself since the middle of the nineteenth century. Bolshevism is only the latest expression of this new westward move. "The problem child of Europe" always carries the brunt, absorbing, yet not quite assimilating, the shocks of the ever renewed influxes. Such a fate explains to a large extent the deep insecurity of the nation. So different from the British Isles and their thousand years' protection from foreign invasions, Germany could not crystallize and mature her national form.

Geography goes far in explaining the autocratic tradition and militant aggressiveness of a people that, continuously threatened from without, has tried to overcome and overcompensate its insecurity by a persistent drive for power and prowess. It has given the military an essential function and therewith a preferred position. It has made the army the "ideal-type" of the people's aspirations. The army's prestige was not even broken by the defeats of Emperor William II or Hitler; their failure was explained by a "stab-in-the-back" theory. If for no other reason, the people swallowed this deception because it relieved every "good national" citizen from responsibility and from the need for political re-

[1] Ferdinand Lassalle, *Über Verfassungswesen* (1862) and *Was nun? Zweiter Vortrag über Verfassungswesen* (1863).

orientation. He could still adore his fallen gods. They had been betrayed, but they had never accepted defeat.

Insecurity has permeated the whole social fabric. A chaotic nation has always highly prized order and discipline—a fact which might explain the frequent use of the word *Ordnung* in German speech. A fondness for titles and the insistence upon proper respect for status are other characteristics of a nation that is "formless with emphasis," as Oswald Spengler once said. The unruly at heart submits to the strict formalism of the omnipresent police and the orderly bureaucrat, knowing that the slightest deviation from the set rules of an outside power might throw him back into the chaos of his inner uncertainties. He has to surround himself with *Verboten* signs. He needs a rule for everything. Even his revolutions have to be orderly and lawful and, as long as they seemingly follow regular procedure, they are acceptable to the law-abiding citizen. Discipline and order are the marks of Germany's Prussian legacy.

History in Flux. To the heritage of Prussia and Potsdam, one must add the ideals represented by "Weimar," that other pole in the set of values that characterize Germany. But these are not the only images by which the Reich lives. There are at least ten different concepts of Germany competing with each other, pulling in different directions, creating divided loyalties and causing that unhappy nation a kind of cultural indigestion.

It has often been remarked that the Germans even today cannot make up their minds what the true Germany ought to be. Is it the tribal Germany, pugnacious and parochial, of Tacitus' days? Is it the universal Holy Roman Empire or the provincialism of the medieval territorial princes? Are the dreams of a humanitarian *Kulturnation* of Herder, Schiller, and Goethe more real than the ardent desire of a belated nationalism? Who has more right to represent the Reich: Catholic Hapsburg or Bismarck's Protestant Prussia? How deeply did the short-lived Weimar Republic, reaching out toward the West, affect Germany's imagination? How much has the Nazi rejection of Europe awakened the real ambitions of the people? Which ideals will finally prevail nobody knows. Yet the past is very much present in the Germany of today.

Each major period has left a sediment of institutional remnants and lasting problems which must be digested in days to come. Like a volcano that sends up its disruptive forces from time to time, the convulsive lava of Germany's past may suddenly break through to the present-day surface and cause havoc to its political landscape. To understand the Germany of our times means to unearth its underlying, deeper strata. Surely, for the student of German affairs history is no mere memory or monument of past events; it is also the present and future, wrapped in one. It is within this continuum of historic forces that the political scientist must approach the German constitutional development.

It is dangerous to streamline history from a present-day vantage point into a single pattern and to see in the whole of German history

FEDERAL REPUBLIC OF GERMANY

SCALE OF MILES
0   50   100

SOVIET SATELLITES

BALTIC SEA

SCHLESWIG-
HOLSTEIN

NORTH SEA

BAY OF POMERANIA

Kiel

KIEL CANAL

Lübeck

Rostock

Hamburg

FRISIAN IS.

Bremerhaven

POLAND

Wilhelmshaven

Groningen

Oldenburg

Bremen

GERMAN
DEMOCRATIC
REPUBLIC

LOWER

SAXONY

ALLER R.

IJSEL
MEER

NETHERLANDS

Osnabrück

Hannover

BERLIN

Potsdam

Münster

WESER R.

Braunschweig

Magdeburg

Arnhem

NORTH - RHINE -

Dortmund

ELBE R.

Essen

WESTPHALIA

Leipzig

Dresden

Düsseldorf

Kassel

Aachen

Köln (Cologne)

Weimar

Chemnitz

Bonn

RHINE R.

HESSE

Plauen

BELGIUM

Koblenz

Wiesbaden

RHINELAND

Mainz

Frankfurt

Schweinfurt

Praha (Prague)

LUX.

Trier

PALATINATE

MAIN R.

Würzburg

CZECHOSLOVAKIA

SAAR

Mannheim

Saarbrücken

Heidelberg

Fürth ●● Nürnberg

Metz

Karlsruhe

Regensburg

FRANCE

Stuttgart

DANUBE R.

Nancy

RHINE R.

BADEN

Ulm

BAVARIA

ISAR R.

WÜRTTEMBERG

Augsburg

UPPER AUSTRIA

Freiburg

München (Munich)

Salzburg

Basel

Berlin and Environs

SCALE OF MILES
0   5   10   25

FR. SECTOR

Brandenburg

Spandau

SOVIET
SECTOR

ELBE R.

Genthin

HAVEL R.

BRIT. SECTOR

Potsdam

Burg

BERLIN CORRIDOR (AUTOBAHN)

U.S. SECTOR

Magdeburg

━━━ AUTOBAHN   ┼┼┼ RAILROADS

─·─ MAJOR ROADS   ╫╫ CANALS

nothing but a drive towards world conquest, climaxing in Hitler's pretentious Thousand Years' Reich. Such an approach makes history seemingly more conclusive and inevitable. Actually, history at any time is polyform, full of divergent trends. German history, above all, has been characterized by a deep antagonism between opposing forces. To detect in their intertwining web lasting dilemmas may give a key to a better understanding of the German people and may forewarn of oversimplified answers. The tragic difficulties are not of yesterday; they will not be resolved tomorrow. We may have to live with them for a long time to come.

Here are a few of those conflicting and recurrent themes that spell out Germany's stresses and strains. They may provide the leitmotivs for the past and for today's challenge.

2. UNIVERSALISM VERSUS PARTICULARISM

Ever since the days when the "barbarians of the North" encountered the Roman Empire, the problem of universalism and particularism has constituted a major split in the German lands. The clash—first in frontier fighting and then in renewed major invasions—established the predominance of the German tribes. Their eventual absorption of the decaying Empire, even their acceptance of the Roman law and classical civilization, was not sufficient to uproot the traits peculiar to the Germanic peoples. Throughout history, the German provinces preserved their specific character and mustered continuous resistance against centralized authority despite their subsequent change from ephemeral tribal existence to more stable territorial principalities. Early German history is the story of the failure of central authority to impose its rule upon the resisting tribes.

Unlike French and British monarchs, the weak and frequently absentee emperors of the High Middle Ages allowed feudal lords and territorial princes (*Landesfürsten*) to assume the real power of the medieval Reich. It often seemed that unity, if attained for a short time, was only forced on the people from without, by the Frankish kings from Clovis to Charlemagne, by the long line of German emperors, by Napoleon (empire builder for the glory of France, and at the same time, awakener of European nationalism), by Bismarck, and by Hitler.

Pride of independence made variety, rather than uniformity, a German characteristic. "The liberty of the Germans is a deadlier foe than the tyranny of the King of Parthia." This dictum of Tacitus' *Germania* (A.D. 98), the classic study of the character, customs, and geography of a people, pointed at the centrifugal tendencies in its history.

This tendency toward variety is one of the reasons why it is difficult to detect fundamental traits common to all Germans. The Germans have differed from one era of history to another; the individualism of regional groups and social classes even today is evident in the conflicts among the various peoples thrown together in the pulverized cities of the present Western Germany.

And yet, nowhere has the conception of empire struck deeper roots than in Germany. This was the potent attraction Rome held for the barbarian leaders, Theodoric, Alaric, and Odoaker. The Empire's memory, kept alive by the Roman Catholic Church, was revived by Charlemagne in the epoch-making coronation on Christmas Day of the year 800. The Holy Roman Empire of the German nations became the heir to and the champion of the classical Christian world. It was not the emperor's complicated institutions, which did not wield much power in the far-flung Reich, so much as the empire's claim to universalism that created a lasting effect on German history.[2]

The glory that was Rome drew into its circle emperors, pilgrims, and scholars through the ages. The drive for universal order was more than a romantic's dream; it became the people's yardstick for the validity of all political plans. It has been abused again and again by ambitious schemers of world empires; yet the myth of the Reich has always fascinated large masses. In our day and age of rising super-powers and a shrinking planet, it has gained an added urgency; and the idea of parochial, self-sufficient provinces has lost meaning and political strength.

One could easily show that German constitutional development has taken cognizance of this trend toward greater units and, step by step, has weakened the separate states (Länder) economically, politically, and emotionally. These tendencies hardly justify the hopes raised since 1945 among the Western Powers that Germany would develop a decentralized federal state. Even the "Federal German Republic" of Bonn recognizes that the signs of the time point toward unity. Moreover, present-day plans for Western union offer such an appeal to many Germans, not the least because they feed this urge for a restoration of empire.

The unending struggle for a working compromise between uniformity and diversity reflects a permanent theme in German history and is still of significance to Germany today.[3]

3. THE RELIGIOUS SCHISM

The same discord can be seen in the other great split that has characterized German history for four centuries—the religious schism. The church had played a major part in the establishment of the medieval empire that united the two "divinely appointed authorities," the Church and

---

[2] In fact one could agree that the creation of a unified Germany without the help of the supranational forces of the church would have been difficult, although the universal aspirations of Otto the Great (A.D. 936–73) and his successors were not easily harmonized with the national interests and, indeed, were severely criticized by numerous German historians. For a balanced and concise historical analysis see Hajo Holborn, "Germany," Encyclopaedia Americana, Vol. XII (1952), pp. 508–32.

[3] For the federalist view, see Wilhelm Röpke, The Solution of the German Problem (1947); H. H. Leonhardt, Der Weg preussischer Vorherrschaft und das unsichtbare Reich der Welfen (1949).

State. The feudal estate, the social institution and military arm of the decentralized Reich, had taken on its *universal* mission as the champion of Christendom against the infidels. Literally and symbolically, the Gothic cathedral, overtowering the modest houses of the hemmed-in city, dominated the noisy market place; it rang the curfew for its busy burghers, and gave them peace of mind and a place in the procession of a Christian society. The traditions and institutions of the age were centered around the church. Its hierarchy and its monasteries, its sacraments and colorful rituals held together a society not too far removed from barbarism. The Western world had become *res publica Christiana*. The emperor, defender of the faith, after a long struggle with the pope, had to concede supremacy to the strengthened church.

Then came the Reformation, which reflected the changing spirit of the times all over the Western world. An awakening middle class, proud and self-conscious, revolted against the church—against its failure to institute reforms; against its whole sacramental system, and its other-worldliness.[4] The territorial princes saw in this popular movement a chance to free themselves from the bonds of Rome. In England, Sweden, and the Netherlands, this separation from Rome was instrumental in the rapid development of the national state.

The cradle of Protestantism, however, experienced an altogether different fate. Although Luther with his German translation of the Bible contributed greatly to an awakening German national consciousness, the lasting effect of the Reformation was the division of the Reich into two warring camps. Its whole destroyed, Germany's territorial parts reasserted themselves in the sovereign principalities.

Moreover, the ensuing religious wars, marked by the sovereigns' shifting alliances with foreign powers, completely destroyed the weak ties of the Reich and made it an easy prey of external forces, which left it a ruined battlefield in the wake of the Thirty Years' War. A burgeoning middle-class society was set back for centuries. With cities ruined, trade disrupted, and ambitions for political representation and power broken, the once proud burgher became an obedient servant to the dominant territorial princes. The rising absolutism, greatly accelerated by the religious wars, left no active field for personal initiative or for wider political responsibility. The much-lamented failure of a political middle class in modern Germany may well have had its roots in this seventeenth-century tragedy.

Some historians even see in the Reformation and its aftermath the mainspring of the contemporary crisis. Since Luther's destruction of the universal church, so they claim, Germany has been in peril.[5] In any case,

[4] In retrospect one should, however, recognize the significance of the medieval church as a forerunner of modern institutions—of *Amt* and *Beruf*—in state, bureaucracy, and economics. Cf. Karl Dunkmann, *Lehre vom Beruf* (1922); Ernst Troeltsch, *The Social Teaching of the Christian Churches* (1931), Vol. I, pp. 118ff., 246ff.; Max Weber, *Gesammelte Aufsätze zur Religionssoziologie* (1922), Vol. I, pp. 63ff., 93ff., 163ff., 207ff.; and Joachim Wach, *Sociology of Religion* (1944).

[5] Erich Meissner, *Germany in Peril* (1942): "The religious dissensions paved the way for all evils to come, for the unity of Christendom, which is the basis of our civilization, became precarious, and disruptive forces found less resistance."

the tension between the Protestant majority and the Catholic minority led to deep conflicts within Germany. The Reformation did not conquer the whole of the Reich; neither did the Counter Reformation regain the lost provinces. The split cut across the nation. Finally, following the formula of the Peace of Augsburg (1555)—*cuius regio, eius religio*—the religious partition followed strictly dynastic divisions. Although Austria remained the chosen daughter of the Catholic church, Prussia became the spearhead of Protestantism in Germany, and the historic dualism between the two contending powers was thus re-emphasized by the religious conflict.

Even in the unified Second Empire of Bismarck (1871), directed by Protestant Prussia, the issue remained crucial. A well-organized Catholic minority, under the able leadership of men like Windhorst, succeeded in gaining a position of power. Although this Catholic Center Party, growing up under the impact of Bismarck's unfortunate *Kulturkampf*,[6] never regarded itself as being responsible for the Second Empire, it won a key position in the Wilhelminic era. As far as the Reich called for parliamentary support, no administration could govern for long without the Center Party's approval. This strategic position permitted a shrewd leadership to remain the balancer, and at the same time to command an uncommitted power in respect to the German Empire and its fate.

The position of Prussian Protestantism was very different. The traditional alliance between Throne and Altar made the Prussian monarch a ruler *"von Gottes Gnaden."* It bound Protestantism to the fate of the monarchy.[7] This very fact explains also the precarious plight of Protestantism under the Weimar Republic. The Protestant parish house had been the center of nationalist education. It quickly lined up behind those forces that seemed to restore a nineteenth-century nationalism. Only at a late hour, and too late for a rehabilitation of independent Protestantism, did it realize that its alliance with the rising National Socialists meant the loss of religious independence in the total state. The voice of Pastor Niemöller (himself an ardent Nazi until this crucial conflict) was a weak and lonely one.

Catholicism, on the other hand, remained much more independent, even under the Third Reich. It was a leading power of the Weimar coalition, and it succeeded in retaining considerable discretion within

---

[6] The fundamental tensions and unreconcilable concepts of state underlying the conflict are well brought out in Heinrich Bornkamm, *Die Staatsidee im Kulturkampf* (1951).

[7] The far-reaching political effect of Lutheranism, with its stress on the pure inwardness of religious experience, and its consequent submission to the powerful state, is pointedly described by the contemporary German historian Fritz Fischer: "In the Western concept man sins by the abuse of power, in the German Lutheran concept, man sins by revolting against power": "Der Deutsche Protestantismus und die Politik im 19ten Jahrhundert," *Historische Zeitschrift*, 171 (May, 1951), p. 475. For a comprehensive analysis, see Ernst Troeltsch, *The Social Teaching of the Christian Churches* (1931), especially Vol. II, pp. 569ff.; cf. Gerhard Ritter, *Luther, Gestalt und Symbol* (1925).

the republic by adroitly using its left and right wing at appropriate times. No doubt the very fact that the supreme authority of Catholicism was outside Germany had made this religious power suspect to the political rulers of Germany since the days when Bismarck branded the Catholic church the Ultramontane International. Yet this extraterritorial position gave Catholicism a much better chance for survival in the Third Reich. (The protective walls of the Holy See literally saved a great number of leading Catholics throughout the terror period.) Moreover, Catholicism had a great attraction for many Germans, who found in its all-embracing creed a refuge against totalitarianism. At the end of Hitler's regime, Catholicism emerged a much stronger power, numerically and spiritually, than divided Protestantism, which to some extent at least had been branded by "collaboration."

In the amputated and partitioned Germany, the weight of the Catholic church is increasingly felt, especially in Western Germany where it now represents the majority of the population. Even though the newly established Christian Democratic Party claimed to be nonconfessional (it includes, in fact, a large percentage of Protestants), it soon permitted Catholicism to reassert itself and to attain a position of power under the chancellorship of Dr. Konrad Adenauer. It is understandable why unification of East and West Germany, with a population overwhelmingly Protestant, is fought for with great fervor by Protestant leaders. Unification would re-establish the balance, if not the predominance, of Protestantism in a united Germany.

In the meantime, both the Catholic and Protestant churches have acquired a renewed prestige, at least for a brief period, as the strongest integrating forces of social cohesion and tradition in a disjointed society. A common front against paganism, with which national socialism was identified, may even give promise to a united church as the spearhead for the regeneration of human dignity and European traditions and as a rallying point against materialistic communism. Whether this recovery represents a true religious revival or a mere escape from chaos and despair will depend on the genuine strength mustered by the churches. In Germany today, as in the past, they are, however, weakened by the persistent confessional division.

4. CONFLICT BETWEEN AUSTRIA AND PRUSSIA

Another more recent conflict, and one with a lasting effect on German politics, was that between Austria and Prussia which found its dramatic expression in their historic struggle for predominance. Even the final victory of the Hohenzollern over the Hapsburgs did not remove this perpetual tension from the German political landscape.

Through the ages Austria represented Europe *par excellence*— Roman traditions, the Christian church, feudal conceptions, the absolute monarchy, the ideas of the Enlightenment, the great music of Haydn,

Mozart, and Strauss, and the middle-class world of the *Bieder-Meier* and *Alt-Wien*. Austria's mission in Europe was to act as spearhead and defense, the missionary force and bridge to a non-European world.

Three times in modern history Austria was repulsed. The year 1806 marked the end of the Holy Roman Empire; 1866 saw Austria excluded from the unfolding Reich; and 1918 witnessed the final destruction of the Austrian Empire. Yet, the political situation in the divided world of the twentieth century made it the more necessary to have a people who could build a bridge from nation to nation. The Austrian, living among different nationalities, had learned to think and sympathize with others. He had become a man who knew human affairs and the human soul, a true psychologist, tolerant, urbane, and international in his outlook.

It was Prussia, under the leadership of its efficient monarchs, that finally won the crown of a new empire. The Prussian tradition, nurtured in the meager environment of the Mark, the Holy Roman Empire's "sandshaker" (*Streusandbüchse*), is militaristic indeed. Militarism, however, is not what many honest but confused lovers of peace believe it to be. It is not primarily measured in terms of arms and military preparedness. A nation with the biggest standing army, such as France during the greater part of modern history, may not be a militaristic nation at all.[8] Militarism is a political system under whose influence and overpowering weight other elements of national life grow weak. Militarism permeates all institutions—schools, factories, family. Prussia was militaristic; Rome was not.

The cause of militarism is often fear. In Prussia, it was dictated by the pathology of the frontier. Prussia, and under her leadership Germany, was the *Land der Mitte,* between east and west and without natural barriers. With her possessions spread across Central Europe, Prussia participated in all the battles of the German tribes and soon made herself their spokesman everywhere. The "people in arms" became the slogan of Prussia.

Contrary to the common conception, Prussian militarism was more than the power and prowess of an army. It was a curious mixture of the soldier and the monk. It was the tradition of the Teutonic Order. It was militarism with a mission. The strange intermarriage between Prussianism and romanticism has given the idea strength, appeal, and articulation. It has made it one of the most powerful and most disquieting forces in modern history.[9]

[8] The percentage of army to population in France rose from 1.25 per cent to 1.87 per cent from 1875 to 1914; the German army comprised from 1.05 per cent to 1.17 per cent during the same period. See Bernadotte E. Schmitt, *Triple Alliance and Triple Entente* (1934) pp. 117–19.

[9] In view of prevailing stereotyped concepts, two recent publications may be singled out to illustrate the complex character of historic Prussia: Otto Heinrich v.d. Gablentz, *Die Tragik des Preussentums* (1948), a Christian criticism of the Bismarckian Prussia; and Hans Joachim Schoeps, *Die Ehre Preussens* (1951), a defense of the "other" Prussia. See also, Sigmund Neumann, *Die Stufen des Preussischen Konservatismus* (1930), and Armin Mohler, *Die Konservative Revolution in Deutschland* (1950).

5. *MACHT UND GEIST*

The victory of Prussianism is partly accounted for by the failure of the German intelligentsia. Before this intelligentsia became the ready servant of the governmental powers, it had weakened its position by its early retreat from politics. This resignation was largely due to the existence of the hundreds of small German states, which did not inspire a sense of national pride or mission. Was it not natural to escape into the loftier realms of the spirit and to prescribe to the German the proud role of a *Kulturnation* that knew no boundaries and therefore possessed the world? This was the Germany of Lessing and Herder, of the young Romantics Schlegel and Novalis, of Goethe and Schiller. The original claim of the French Revolution of an all-embracing order and Napoleon's call for a United States of Europe found ardent admirers among Germany's greatest minds. Beethoven originally dedicated his "Eroica" to the great Corsican, and it was only Bonaparte's change to a world conqueror that made adamant foes of his ertswhile admirers and awakened among his victims in central Europe the strong patriotism which led to the Battle of Leipzig in 1813.

For a short while, this nascent German nationalism seemed to be promoted by the cultural elite. The academic youth became the standard-bearers of liberalism and unification, and the "political professors" the spokesmen of the people's ambitions. This early trend presaged an intellectual leadership where spirit and power would join forces. Yet the fate of Germany's intelligentsia did not follow these promises. On the contrary, with the defeat of 1848 and Bismarck's ascendancy, the contrast between *Macht* and *Geist* was sealed.

The conflict went deep. It reflected the very split which has often been simplified as a cleavage of the two Germanies by the Elbe River. Geography, however, cannot circumscribe the conflict. It went through Germany, if not through every German. The *Limes Germanicus* that once separated the Roman Empire and the barbarians of the north (at that time roughly running from Bonn on the Rhine to Regensburg on the Danube) moved back and forth through history. In reality, it was an invisible dividing line that marked the varying degrees of Europeanization of the different parts of Germany.

The Eastern provinces, even if they were drawn belatedly into the European family, were touched only superficially, but Southern and Western Germany were always European to the core. The latter areas had a large share in the nation's great cultural legacy. From the adoption of Christianity and Greco-Roman traditions, through the Middle Ages, the Renaissance and Reformation, and finally to the Industrial Revolution and the victory of middle-class civilization, Western Germany had played an outstanding part. Its proud cities, its monuments and cathedrals, its great poets and thinkers testified to its lasting contributions.

Yet, the German intelligentsia, recognized though it was as the symbol of this spiritual Europe, lived essentially separated from the

German people. The tragic isolation of these intellectuals, so different
from the position of the French *hommes des lettres,* was partly due to
the deep antagonism that has prevailed between the politically powerful
and the cultural elite throughout German history. This tension was
heightened by the success-ridden Bismarckian Empire and the pseudo-
civilization of the Wilhelminic era with its noisy union of Mars, Mam-
mon, and the masses. There was a retreat into esoteric literary circles
and the ivory towers of the universities; and those who rebelled openly
(as did some middle-class youth in the *Jugendbewegung*) remained utterly ineffective against the robust power of the state. Not until after the
revolution of 1918 was there a full-fledged attempt to eliminate the antagonism between *Macht* and *Geist,* and in this effort the short-lived
Weimar Republic failed.

National socialism in a way was the most radical revolt against
Western civilization and against all that historic Europe represented. By
no mere accident did the Third Reich concentrate its attack on the intellectuals who by fate and tradition were the prototype of this Europe.
Different from its older brother, Mussolini's fascism, Hitler's national
socialism could appeal to pre-Roman pagan traditions, which were still
alive in the north under the thin-veiled cover of an accepted Western
code. Count Evola's *Imperialismo Pagano,* which made no impression
when originally published in Italy, created quite a vogue in Nazi Germany.

The breakdown of the unscrupulous power state of the Third Reich
has posed once more the problem of *Macht und Geist.*[1]

6. THE LATE ARRIVAL

One cause of this traditional discrepancy between a popular megalo-
mania of power and a personal retreat from political responsibility may
be found in another tragic anomaly in German history—its late arrival
among the major powers. It was not before the mid-nineteenth century
that the unification of Germany was attained; ever since that time, the
Reich, suffering from a sense of inferiority, has tried to make up for
missed opportunities and to find, at last, a "place in the sun."

It is strange to hear thoughtful Germans, even today, who complain about their nation's historic inability to attain democratic self-rule

[1] This persistent conflict as an expression of the fundamental tension between
Germany and the Western world is the central theme of the thought-provoking
essays by Benedetto Croce, *Germany and Europe: a Spiritual Dissension* (1944).
The present day discussion among German academicians gives testimony and prom-
ise of a serious re-evalution of the nation's past by its intelligentsia. To mention
only a few recent publications, there are Friedrich Meinecke, *The German Catastro-
phe* (1950); Gerhard Ritter, *Die Dämonie der Macht* (1948); Alfred von Martin,
Geistige Wegbereiter des Deutschen Zusammenbruchs (1948); Ludwig Dehio,
Gleichgewicht oder Hegemonie (1948); and Alfred Weber, *Farewell to European
History* (1948). For an over-all view, see also Hajo Holborn, "Irrwege in unserer
Geschichte," *Der Monat,* No. 17 (February, 1950); and Hans Kohn, "Rethinking
Recent German History," *Review of Politics,* 14 (July, 1952), pp. 325–45.

and who nevertheless demand the controlling position in a future co-
operative United States of Europe. It is not too farfetched to recognize
in this behavior pattern attitudes of a politically adolescent people. By
no mere accident have the Middle Ages always enchanted the German
people.

> All experience had yet, to the mind of man, the directness and
> absoluteness of the pleasure and pain of child life. All things
> presenting themselves to the mind in violent contrasts and im-
> pressive forms lent a tone of excitement and of passion to every-
> day life and tended to produce that perpetual oscillation be-
> tween despair and distracted joy, between cruelty and pious
> tenderness, which characterized life in the Middle Ages.

These masterful lines from Johan Huizinga's *Waning of the Middle
Ages* reflect the spiritual climate of a romantic nation that has carried
the same "violent tenure of life" into our own days.

If, following the Epicurean definition, happiness is a state of tran-
quility, the Germans have never been a happy nation, never at peace
with themselves nor with the outside world. Such a nation has little or
no consideration for the people around it, but it nurtures a continuous
complaint, with a good measure of self-pity, against the cold outer world
that neither appreciates nor understands it. In truth, no one understands
it except the Infinite. This may be the design for a nation of great
thinkers and poets, but it does not make for pragmatic politics or for
compromise.

Western philosophy and life have recognized an area of social existence that permits a natural and fruitful balance between a well-
integrated personality and a free society. It is the strength of self-con-
tained individuality to recognize in its own particularity the right of
everyone to differ from everyone else. This recognition makes for
moderation, open-mindedness, restraint, and tolerance. Anarchic man,
in contrast, cannot establish this balance and knows only complete submission when he turns toward the world. The utter loneliness of the
frustrated is complemented by the impatient desire to be submerged in
the great community. This explains the riddle of a nation of proverbial
individualists submitting to the unconditional control of modern dictatorship.

In view of the long and persistent history of this adolescent nation,
still not grown to full maturity, one may wonder whether Germany is
not fated to be a perennial adolescent. The Third Reich in its all-consuming drive for world power, was the latest, the most arrogant attempt
at limitless undertakings. Does its downfall presage a new beginning?

7. THE SOCIAL QUESTION

Failure of the Middle Class.   The German failure in politics, heretofore, can partly be ascribed to the frustrations of the rising middle

class, that crucial stratum in the modern democratic process. The German middle class met its test in the nineteenth century. Why did it weaken when Western Europe established the definite rule of a proud bourgeoisie? What were the reasons for the lasting discrepancies in the nation's social structure?

There was, first of all, the feudal tradition which, unlike the case in other countries, remained strong throughout German history, almost up to the present. In other parts of Western Europe, by contrast, the middle class soon attained a position of power and even succeeded in assimilating the old aristocratic ruling class.

Wherever he succeeded, the modern burgher had to fight to gain and hold his place. Indeed, his was a fighting class, at least when it was young. By fighting feudal society and its rigid class system, it became the champion of free enterprise and religious freedom, of property rights and individual independence.

Why did the German burgher fall short of his aim? Was it Germany's belated entrance into Western civilization? Was it the delayed unification? Was it the Thirty Years' War with its lasting destruction of the flourishing cities of bourgeois pride? Was it the weakness of the world-embracing Hapsburg monarchy? Or was it the militarism of provincial Hohenzollern Prussia that did not allow an independent middle class to grow? All these factors contributed to the character of the German middle class that entered the critical nineteenth century in a weakened position, unprepared for the great battle of control that culminated in the revolution of 1848.

The Revolution of 1848.   The revolution of 1848, as is so often the case with lost causes in history, was misjudged and minimized in its spirit and performance, especially in Germany where it failed utterly.[2] As in every revolutionary upheaval, the driving forces of 1848 were rooted in the failure of the preceding order. The basis of unrest in the 1840's was the coincidence of the long-lasting repression that characterized the Metternich era and the irrepressible march of the Industrial Revolution, which in its infancy could not yet make the necessary adjustments. The plight of the old handicraft society and of the new proletariat was desperate everywhere, especially in Germany. Years of famine and unrest—the Weavers' Revolt in Silesia (1844) and the Berlin *"Kartoffelkrawalle"* (1847)—reflected the instability of the "hungry forties."

The February revolt of 1848 in France, the sparkplug of similar movements in other countries, set the pattern. Though the revolutions in 1848 lacked the conscious planning and extended premeditations of their twentieth-century successors, these upheavals revealed three definite stages. Starting originally from a wide, liberal, and popular base, they took a proletarian turn and subsequently ended in reaction. The revolutionary failure was largely because of the split among the original

[2] For a most recent German evaluation, see Karl Griewant, "Ursachen und Folgen des Scheiterns der Deutschen Revolution von 1848," *Historische Zeitschrift,* 170 (October, 1950), pp. 495–523.

allies of different classes. Wherever this division did not occur, as in Switzerland, the revolution was successful. In the leading countries, however, the fight for national liberation, for constitutional guarantees, and for social change soon turned those revolutionary forces whose aims were fulfilled into staunch defenders of their newly gained status. Thus the united front was dissolved. Such disappointments made ardent foes of former friends.

The 1848 movements, even in Germany, were no mere *coup d'état*. They had political aims and they tried to establish a social basis; yet the weakness of this social basis was obvious. In Central Europe, to be sure, the crucial middle class was just beginning to emerge. Economically unstable and inexperienced politically, it soon resigned from its revolutionary role. The German Constituent National Assembly of 1848, with its arguments over generalities, was symbolic of the state of mind in which the newly rising classes found themselves and because of which they were unable to exploit the "revolutionary situation." True, it is not fair to ridicule this "professors' convention," as is usually done in the literature on 1848. The assembly debates in the Frankfurt *Paulskirche* laid the groundwork of constitutional deliberations, e.g., its bill of rights discussion, that left a deep impact on the Weimar constitution and on other twentieth-century documents. Although the Frankfurt Assembly thus represented an impressive articulation of the liberal and national desires of the German middle class, it was not strong enough to force the Prussian monarch and his princely confreres to accept the revolution. Political control soon passed into the experienced hands of the old masters.

One reason for the failure of the middle class was the apathy of the people. Their indifference was felt everywhere in Europe's capitals, broken only by a short flurry of revolutionary holiday spirit. The people soon settled down with the forces of "law and order." Only for a few days were the fighting students of Berlin the celebrated heroes of the middle class. It soon sighed with relief when the liberal banker, Ludolf Camphausen, and the Rhenish merchant, David Hansemann, became their spokesmen and assured them that the revolution was ended. Even their authority was not to last for many months, and the reaction soon undid what a half-hearted revolution had attempted.

Another weakness, if not the greatest one, within the crucial middle class was its fear of the "Red" danger, real and imagined. It influenced the rise of Napoleon III in France and brought about reaction in Prussia and Austria. In Germany, furthermore, the accustomed obedience to authority and parochial traditionalism soon reasserted itself. Compliance and docility again became the "first duty of the loyal citizen." Under the Prussian Eagle, the bourgeoisie, big and small, settled down to work and to mind its own small business—in the often-quoted words of the Berlin tailor: "Under your protective wings I can safely press my things"—and the revolution died down.[3]

---

[3] The history of the revolution of 1848, its recent centennial celebrations notwithstanding, must still be written. If its social basis is actually studied, one may well discover as a clue to its rise and fall the crucial political position of the *Hand-*

Seen in the greater framework of history, the real issue of the 1848 revolution, as of the whole nineteenth century, was the conflict between state and society, the adjustment of an old power system to the new social forces. The failure to strike a proper balance in Prussia-Germany was of serious consequence. It foreshadowed the frustrations of Weimar.

Stages of Conservative Rule. Since 1848, the German attempt at a solution of this deep antagonism between state and society, different from the straight middle-class victory in Western Europe, followed three stages—romantic, liberal, and realistic—which were reflected in the subsequent responses of the old ruling class.

Romantic conservatism did not want to recognize the new forces at all. King Frederick William IV, the "Romanticist on the Throne" (r. 1840–61), tried, after a short and unhappy bow to the revolution, to turn the clock back. The reactionary government of General Manteuffel, although it was accepted for a time by the frightened middle class, was still no answer for Prussia-Germany, if it were to attain a position of power in society. Yet the *Junkers* were adamant in their rejection of any reform, a position they held even in the late days of Weimar. It was no coincidence that the republic's gravedigger, von Papen, chancellor of 1932's "Midsummer Night's Dream," unearthed Manteuffel's speeches and used them practically verbatim in his governmental declarations when pathfinding for Hitler's twentieth-century autocracy.

The tragedy of the old German ruling class was that it did not recognize the dynamics of modern society. True, throughout the nineteenth and twentieth centuries some open-minded conservatives made themselves the vanguard of the rising social forces; but this group always remained a small elite at the periphery of events. Tory "democracy," although it was accepted by British conservatism, which rejuvenated itself by absorbing newly emerging strata of society, could never reach the core of German conservatism, which isolated itself from the progressive forces and thus became sterile. The liberals among the aristocracy were few. From the great reformers under Freiherrn vom Stein and Generals Boyen, Scharnhorst, and Gneisenau in the age of the War of Liberation, to the *Wochenblattpartei* of von Bethmann and Joseph Maria von Radowitz (hapless advisor to his stubborn royal friend, Frederick William) in the days of 1848, to the *Freikonservative* in the Second Empire and the *Volkskonservative* of the Weimar Republic, to the rightist opposition against national socialism which ended with the futile attempt on Hitler's life in 1944—this was a continuous line, in-

---

werk. The craftsmen, a much-neglected group in political literature (and naturally so, since it represented a declining class in a rising industrial society), actually furnished the mass basis for the revolution. It manned the barricades, but was defeated in the Frankfurt Assembly, where the intelligentsia of an emerging society led the fight for legislation in *Gewerbefreiheit.* It is this disappointed, small handicraft group that soon turned its back on the revolution, and instead, was received as a welcome ally by the reactionary regime. The restoration of the *Zunftszwang* was of vital importance for the survival of the independent handicraft. From then on, it became a bulwark of conservatism, and despite its disappointments with the ruling clique, it remained loyal to the rightist parties.

volving largely the same families who tried to bring a New Deal to Germany. Only a few fleeting moments in German history indicated what they might have meant to a liberal Germany.

The new era of 1858–62, which ushered in the rule of Prince William (later king of Prussia, first emperor of the Second Empire, then serving as regent for his insane brother, Frederick William), brought to the fore the liberal-minded conservatives, but not for long. They soon found that their plea for a new economic society did not attract the old ruling class.

This short interlude was interrupted by the Prussian constitutional conflict in 1862, when King William finally called Bismarck to power. The argument between the Crown and the Prussian parliament spelled the second defeat of the German middle class and its parliamentary majority. Not only did the Chancellor completely disregard the parliament's persistent rejection of the budget but he broke its resistance by "blood and iron" in his victories in the Danish War (1864), the Prussian-Austrian conflict (1866), and the Franco-Prussian War (1870–71), the crowning event of unification. It was a bad omen for the politics of the German bourgeoisie. Although Bismarck in an astute gesture bowed to the parliamentary majority after his victory over Austria by introducing the law of indemnity (*Indemnitätsvorlage*), which exonerated him for his unconstitutional action, it was in reality the middle class that acquiesced.

The Feudalized Society. This was the Bismarckian compromise of a realistic conservatism. In contrast to Britain, where the middle class forced the aristocracy to accept new standards of society, in Germany it was the bourgeoisie that became feudalized. In a division of labor Bismarck forced it to accept the political rule of the *Junkers,* although he left the middle class in control of economic life. This realistic conservatism, in short, neither accepted the Romantic rejection of the Industrial Revolution nor followed the liberal claim of a Tory democracy for leadership of this new society. Bismarck realized that the young capitalism was needed in the power struggle of the new nationalism and thus he pledged to the middle class the government's full support.

The burgher, in return for the promise of protective tariffs, colonial expansion, and of assurances against the proletarian threat, surrendered his political birthrights to the feudal guarantors of "law and order." The German *Rechtsstaat* indeed endeared itself to the middle class, which under the protection of law and order could grow rich and smug.

This was a high price to pay. It meant the political abdication of a proud middle class and its degradation to the condition of an irresponsible bourgeoisie. The group now had no recourse except to go to "Father State" and ask for help—for colonial markets, for economic monopolies, for factory controls—without regard for the social, domestic, and international consequences of these policies. It was only after the breakdown of the Second Empire that the serious effects of such a political surrender became evident.

On first sight, the Bismarckian compromise appeared a feasible

solution. The forces of a modern industrial society were put to work for
the mighty state and helped to bring about economic prosperity,
national unity, efficient adminstration—in short, the fulfillment of the
burgher's dreams. However, assent to the continuous rule of the established caste meant more than acquiescence, in its political dictates; it
soon led to acceptance of the values and images of this caste as well.

This deep penetration of "feudal yardsticks" is fully reflected in the
popular writings of the times. The emperor, the royal court, the army,
the higher bureaucracy, and, above all, the aristocracy, collectively became the unquestioned ideal of the "little man." And the very fact that
this ideal was beyond his reach, gave it the nimbus of a symbolic and
powerful myth. There was the "Student Prince" who mixed with the
simple folk—of course, in disguise—but once he revealed his station,
he had to return to his duties at the feudal manor or in the king's
army, to follow his dying father's pursuits or his commander's call for a
supreme sacrifice on the field of honor. The strict code of a caste
society could not be overruled; the fairyland of princesses and palaces
remained.

The feudal society was not only passively accepted and admired
by the loyal *Kleinbürger;* it was actively courted by the upper middle
classes in many ways. Although they could never hope to become
genuine members of the nobility, they tried hard to imitate it by a
pseudo-aristocratic life in expensive castles and through the acquisition
of titles by intermarriage. Aristocracy by association naturally became
profoundly feudal, and a duchess by matrimony could be unbearably
"patrician."

The eventual breakdown of Bismarck's order should not mislead
us into underestimating its hold on the people. Although this power was
primarily based on its success in international affairs, it had also penetrated the fiber of the nation. True, Bismarck was not so fortunate in
handling domestic politics as he was in his astute manipulation of
Germany's limited influence in the international balance-of-power game.
His failure to assay correctly the strength of Catholicism and socialism
led him to two great internal defeats involving his anti-Catholic *Kultur-
Kampf* (1871–79) and his anti-Socialist *Socialistengesetzgebung* (1878–
90). They foreshadowed the final disintegration of the Second Empire.
Yet Bismarck was not completely blind to the explosive forces within
the nation. His social insurance policy was part of his crucial attack
against insecurity in order to defeat effectively the "Red" danger, which
was fed by the system's inability to meet the needs of the masses. In
this sense Bismarck's legislation was a forerunner of the progressive
policies of the western nations half a century later.

Bismarck's answer to the inner tensions, however, did not create a
stable governmental basis in a new mass age. It only temporized with
the real challenge of the time because he did not call in these new forces
as partners in a new political society. His solution remained basically
a personal formula, and his powerful personality overshadowed the
flaws of his system. This personal factor became most obvious in the
constitutional structure of the Second Empire. He was its sole architect.

14

THE BISMARCKIAN EMPIRE

The constitution of the Second Empire—an extension of the North German constitution of 1867, which had been written by the Iron Chancellor—lent itself particularly well to both the gigantic stature of Bismarck's personality and that of modest Emperor William I, the soldier king. In a sense it reflected a most personal government, which presupposed for its proper functioning close co-operation between kaiser and chancellor. As long as the partnership of the founders lasted, the delicate system of interlocking human relations seemed to work. But it was an instrument with flaws that became increasingly obvious when the capricious young emperor, William II, and a succession of weak chancellors were unable to maintain the difficult balance.

1. HISTORICAL BACKGROUND

The constitution was the result of more than half a century of political experimentation that had seen crucial attempts at a solution of the German question, each step adding a peculiar feature to the final edifice.

In the sweep of the French Revolution and the Napoleonic conquest, the outdated cluster of innumerable little German states collapsed; so did their equally meaningless imperial bond. The thousand-year-old Holy Roman Empire, the so-called First German Empire, was officially buried in 1806, long after it had ceased to exist as a political entity. For a short while the vacuum in Central Europe was filled by the *Rheinbund* (Confederation of the Rhine), which soon included all Germanic states except Austria, Prussia, and the German possessions of Sweden and Denmark.

The Confederation of the Rhine was obviously a French satellite, and as such, a forerunner of those established by Hitler and Stalin in their empire building. It introduced into the German lands progressive administration and legal procedure, and liberal-democratic thinking. These innovations were to affect deeply Southern and Western Germany,

341

and through them, the whole Reich. The Confederation of the Rhine also constituted a first consolidation of the German states under the principle of federalism that played a unique part in the constitutional development of the Second Empire.

The peculiar features of this confederation of independent states became obvious in the *Deutsche Bund* (German Confederation), which was established, after the defeat of the Napoleonic Empire, within the frame of the Vienna settlement of 1815. It was a compact between sovereign princes, a defense treaty against the foes from without and within. As such it represented an integral part of the Holy Alliance, Austrian Chancellor Metternich's instrument to suppress French hegemonic ambitions and the ideas of 1789. No doubt, Metternich's world meant order and stability, much desired after an era of war and revolution; but it was a return to past principles of legitimacy and a bitter reaction against the popular movements encouraged by the French Revolution. This was no way to absorb the dynamic forces of the century or to direct them into constructive channels. Its historic origin spelled the later doom of the German Confederation, as well as tragic consequences for the Second Empire. The peculiar unification from above conflicted with an aspiring nationalism among the rising middle classes, whose most articulate spokesmen, the academic youth, were the first victims of a reactionary persecution under Metternich's rule.

Moreover, the German Confederation was hopelessly split by the continuous conflict between its two major powers, Austria and Prussia. Indeed it was stalemated by the complicated organization and procedure of the Frankfurt Assembly, which, by its strict states (*Länder*) representation, by its continuous instruction from the state authorities, and by the necessity of statewide passage of all federal statutes and decisions, left the forty-odd member states with uncontested freedom of action.

The contribution of the German Confederation to the national problem was primarily negative, proving that unification would come only if one of the two predominant rivals were eliminated, if the integrity of the princely rulers were guaranteed, and if the people's role were minimized to a mere acclamation of unification from above.

The solution finally arrived at was certainly an anachronism in a democratic age. If it were at all constitutional and acceptable to the masses, this was only because the monarchy seemed to fulfill the national aspirations and economic needs of a new bourgeoisie. Prussia's fight for a German tariff union put her in the vanguard of the move for political unification. If proof were needed of the people's eventual acquiescence in a federation of princes instead of a popular national government, the pathetic revolution of 1848 furnished it.

The king of Prussia, to whom the imperial crown was finally offered by the people's parliament, could simply reject it, as it was not presented to him "by the grace of God" and the German princes. The dynastic principle was thus officially declared a prerequisite of unification.

The following two decades of reaction added another element to the peculiar German solution, namely, that of militarism. Its champion was Prussia, which had not only easily overcome the revolutionary challenge of the mid-century but had also weathered the constitutional storm over military organization during 1862–66, when the army—its reforms, expansion, and budget—became the king's prerogative. The minister president's military budget had been persistently rejected by an obstinate parliamentary majority, which knew that "control of the purse" was crucial. In turn, Bismarck's was a policy of *fait accompli,* of success on an ever-increasing scale. He started the Danish War (which did not break a staunch liberal opposition) and continued with the ten-weeks blitzkrieg against Austria to arouse national feeling. Both these actions were undertaken without the consent of a parliamentary majority, which consequently had to bow to the victorious army. Thus the hegemony of militant Prussia was definitely established and instituted in the North German Federation. This adroitly executed maneuver of Bismarck found its crowning sequel in his third military undertaking, the Franco-Prussian War, which appealed to the people's national aspirations and attracted the Southern German states as allies against the traditional archenemy, France.

On the basis of this comradeship in arms, the "proper" foundation was laid for the proclamation of the Second German Empire. Amid the thunder of cannons bombarding Paris, Bavaria's King Ludwig offered the crown to the Prussian monarch in the same Hall of Mirrors of Versailles that half a century later was to see the breakdown of this imperial regime. It was not a strong government; but while it lasted, it permitted a delicate balance of the traditional forces that were Germany.

2. UNDERLYING PRINCIPLES

The constitution of the Second Empire represented a peculiar balance among the emperor, the dynasties, and the people. Its center of political gravity was to rest with the Crown, which retained the position of supreme leadership in accordance with the theory of *monarchical prerogatives* proposed by the Prussian conservative, Friedrich Julius Stahl. Such a power could be easily turned by an autocratically inclined ruler into a personal government. *Suprema lex regis voluntas esto* ("Let the sovereign's will be the highest law"): this autograph of William II in the Golden Book of Senators in Munich was the epitaph to a troubled regime.

The monarch in Bismarck's constitution was no mere figurehead; nor was he supposed to be an absolute ruler. He was a constitutional emperor who possessed considerable powers. He had the right to make peace and to declare "defensive" war. He was the commander in chief of the army, and, backed by popular traditions of military glory and by freshly won victory over parliament, he assumed complete control of the nation's key power.

The emperor appointed the Reich officials of the diplomatic corps, the judicial and civil administration, and above all, the chancellor, chief figure of the Second Empire. The latter was the kaiser's confidant and could not be compelled to resign by even the most obstinate parliament.

The principal legislation was prepared by the Federal Council and the cabinet, members of which were chosen by the chancellor and were responsible solely to the sovereign. The only legislative power left to parliament was in reality a veto. There was finally a provision recognizing *Notverordnungsrecht,* the power of the emperor to rule by decree, without parliament, in case of an emergency. This article was taken from the Prussian constitution of 1850 and later reappeared in the ominous Article 48 of the Weimar constitution.

The strength of the constitutional monarch, however, lay in his dual role of hereditary German emperor and king of Prussia. This duality of office was repeated in the lower echelons, from the post of Reich chancellor and Prussian minister president down to significant civil service positions. Behind the Reich stood Prussia with her well-established feudal traditions. The real power of the kaiser did not derive so much from his position as the emperor of the federation as from his status as sovereign of the strongest member of the *Deutsche Bund.*

The Hohenzollern Empire was an "eternal alliance" between the states, a union of dynastic rulers. Bismarck had been careful not only to preserve the rights of the dynasties but also to curb their "selfishness." By allowing the Bavarian monarch to offer the imperial crown to the Prussian king and by granting the southern states "reserved rights" over military and postal affairs, direct taxation, and cultural matters—the control over foreign affairs, economic legislation, and indirect taxation was vested in the Reich—the semblance of a free association of independent states was preserved. These arrangements, however, did not check the general trend toward unification. In fact, Bismarck did not hesitate to use the popular support for national unity against the resisting princes. The granting of universal suffrage for elections to the imperial *Reichstag,* conceded by the Prussian *Junker,* can be partly explained as a weapon in the fight against the centrifugal forces.[1]

Still, next to the monarchy and the chancellorship, the most important agency of the Reich was the *Bundesrat* (Federal Council). The composition and competence of the *Bundesrat* gives a good illustration of the interplay of forces on the federal level. Composed of delegates from

---

[1] The very fact that the Second Empire, in its first two decades, was truly personified in Bismarck makes a full appraisal of his personality and his influence a prerequisite for a proper understanding of that period.

It is interesting to note that the present re-evaluation of Germany's past centers around a reinterpretation of the Iron Chancellor and his great influence on the Reich's tragic course. In addition to publications previously mentioned, see Gerhard Ritter, "Das Bismarckproblem," *Der Merkur,* 4 (1950), pp. 657–76, and "Grossdeutsch und Kleindeutsch im 19. Jahrhundert," in Kaehler Festschrift, *Schicksalswege deutscher Vergangenheit* (1950); cf. also Franz Schnabel, "Das Problem Bismarck," *Hochland,* 42 (1949), pp. 1–27, and his "Bismarck und die Nationen," in *Europa und der Nationalismus* (1950), pp. 91–108; Heinrich Ritter Von Srbik, "Die Bismarck Kontroverse," *Wort und Wahrheit* (1950), pp. 918–31; Eduard Hemmerle, *Der Weg in die Katastrophe* (1949); and Hans Rothfels, "Problems of a Bismarck Biography," *Review of Politics,* 9 (1947), pp. 362–80. See also Leonhart von Muralt, *Bismarck's Verantwortlichkeit* (1955), emphasizing the Christian foundations of the Chancellor's policies; for a contrasting view among recent English studies, cf. the fresh biography by A. J. P. Taylor, *Bismarck: The Man and the Statesman* (1955).

the states, it was so delicately balanced that both Prussia and the combination of the middle powers, namely, the southern states, possessed an effective veto power within it. Its members were comprised of seventeen governmental representatives from Prussia, six from Bavaria, three from Saxony and Württemberg, two from Mecklenburg-Schwerin, two from Brunswick, and one from each of the remaining member states. Here in secret sessions the federal legislation was often initiated, and always agreed upon, before it went to the *Reichstag* for approval or possible rejection. Under Bismarck, who showed it extreme consideration and courtesy, the *Bundesrat* was probably the key institution of the Second Empire. Certainly it guaranteed the federal character of the Reich.

The *Reichstag* was the fifth wheel in the imperial machinery, which was run by the emperor, the chancellor, the cabinet, and the *Bundesrat*. The lower house of the parliament represented above all a negative, veto power. Its main strength rested in its power to pass on the budget and federal loans, but even this crucial function was curtailed by the *Septennat*, which excluded the military expenses from the yearly scrutiny. Moreover, Bismarck's notorious theory of the constitutional gap (*Lückentheorie*) enabled him to circumvent parliamentary control over the budget in case of disagreement between monarch and chamber and to spend at his discretion in "the interest of the state." True, the empire's freedom of speech was a strong, though indirect, weapon of the parliament, and some of its best representatives, like Progressive leader Eugen Richter, showed courage and ingenuity that won increasing admiration among the educated classes. In the eyes of the great majority, however, the parliament was little more than a hollow "debating gallery," and political action was concentrated in extraparliamentary agencies.

At the same time, this popularly elected chamber had truly democratic possibilities, though not in a way anticipated by Bismarck. For one thing, the electoral system provided for direct, secret, universal suffrage for every male citizen over twenty-five; in fact, the suffrage was more democratic than that of the United States or Great Britain. One should add, however, that certain aspects of the system favored the ruling conservative elements, i.e., the unaltered distribution of the 397 seats based on the census figure of 1869 (without consideration of the far-reaching population shift toward the urban centers of political radicalism that occurred in the following decades). Moreover, the single-member constituencies necessitated a run-off election when no clear majority was attained, and in this second ballot the right and center parties, through coalitions, were definitely favored.

Theoretically, the chancellor, although appointed by the emperor, had to retain parliamentary support in order to stay in power. Yet while the monarch had the constitutional choice of dismissing the chancellor or dissolving the parliament in case of conflict, even a militant majority of the *Reichstag* could not overthrow the chancellor, despite a clear-cut vote of nonconfidence (as the historic Zabern affair of 1913 proved). By 1907 a majority of the voters (6.2 out of 11.3 million) had cast their ballots against the government, though the representation still showed a majority of 219 to 178 seats in the government's favor. The newly elected *Reichstag* of 1912 had a definite antigovernment majority; yet a persistent indifference to the people's verdict was possible because of the play of extraparliamentary forces, or what might properly be called the unwritten and real constitution of the Reich.

3. EXTRAPARLIAMENTARY FORCES

Junker Camarilla. There was close to the monarch an irresponsible court of military advisers, the so-called camarilla, whose influence became at times paramount, especially during the reign of William II. Important decisions, particularly in international affairs, were often made by this personal military cabinet in complete contradiction to the advice of the appointed officials. Flatterers and sycophants had the ear of the self-centered, romantic monarch. Byzantinism flourished at court. Yet more important than the much-discussed revelations of corruption among the kaiser's clique, which appeared in Maximilian Harden's *Zukunft,* was the thoroughly reactionary outlook characteristic of the ruling caste as a whole. It isolated the impressionable monarch from the progressive trend of the times.

The basis of the Second Empire was still the rule of a semi-feudal society. It completely controlled the dominant Prussian government. The upper house (*Herrenhaus*) was composed exclusively of representatives of the hereditary landed aristocracy (*Junkers*). Representation in the popular chamber (*Landtag*) also favored the old ruling classes through the notorious three-class electoral law, which divided the electorate into three classes of equal tax assessment, each of which possessed the same number of electors. The result was a most undemocratic overrepresentation of large property holders. The much-demanded reform of this reactionary voting system did not materialize until the end of World War I, and by that time, the government's concession came too late to prevent the complete collapse of the empire.

While the empire lasted, the feudal forces reinforced themselves within and without the government, despite, or because of, the threat to their position in an increasingly industrialized society. In 1893 the aggressive Agrarian League (*Landbund*) had been established as an arm of the embattled landed aristocracy, and it continued to exert its pressures most vigorously on government and parliament throughout the following decades. What was even more important, the feudal aristocracy, with the help of the government, entrenched itself in the key positions of the Reich. The army and the bureaucracy, main pillars of the modern state, underwent radical reforms that strengthened their reactionary character and left a lasting effect beyond the Second Empire.

Army. The Prussian army from its beginning had been a feudal institution, and its officers' corps an aristocratic domain, although later it did not escape the influence of the rising middle class. Frederick the Great in his day spoke with contempt of the bourgeoisie, but the shock of defeat by the revolutionary armies of the French *levée-en-masse* raised questions about the feudal organization of Prussia's military forces. In fact, Generals Boyen, Scharnhorst, and Gneisenau supported movements for a people's army, but their reform of 1812 was soon submerged by the rising tide of reaction in nineteenth-century Prussia.[2] By the time Bismarck came to power, Generals von Manteuffel and von Roon had purged the Prussian army of popular influences.

There still remained the fundamental issue of recruiting a reliable officers' corps from the thinning ranks of the aristocracy, especially in view of the ever-increasing duties of an army greatly expanded by general conscription from a rapidly growing population. The solution finally arrived at was the institution of the reserve officer, a type of position permitting a notorious exploitation of the burgher's yearning for the noble life. The king's army was undoubtedly in need of officers. The higher ranks had to remain a feudal privilege, but the lower echelons could safely be entrusted to eager bourgeois lieutenants (not really ranking officers, to be sure, but mere "officers in reserve") who would be loyal to the system that graciously had admitted them as second-class aristocrats. They proved highly reliable.

Bureaucracy. The administration also proved loyal, especially after Robert von Puttkamer, Prussian minister of the interior (1881–88), had purged the bureaucracy of all "untrustworthy" elements. By then, the conservative character of the higher civil service was fully established and could be counted upon in public administration as well as in national elections. Civil servants were carefully screened; they could be trusted to serve unswervingly those in power. Such unquestioning, dutiful performance had become bureaucratic tradition. It explained the tragic failure of the "neutral" public servant who could obey any master, including Hitler, so long as he preserved formal adherence to the letter of the law and due respect for the administrative expert.

The bureaucracy, with its formal beginnings in Brandenburg-Prussia in the early part of the seventeenth century, had once been hailed by the middle class as a safeguard against arbitrary government, and justifiably so, because of its principles of competence, strict accountability, and regulated procedure. Now it became the instrument of a closed caste system; and an idealistic school, resting on the teachings of Hegel and his enthusiastic academic admirers of the omnipotent state, glorified the bureaucracy as the guarantor of transcendental order against the anarchy of Western democratic ideas.

The universities, once the centers of the fight for freedom, were transformed into guardians of proper training for leadership in important public offices, the judiciary, the bureaucracy, and the teaching profession. In performing this crucial function, the academicians could allow themselves the privilege of "freedom of research," especially in the less dan-

[2] Many of the leading "reformers," incidentally, were not native Prussians. Gneisenau came from Austria; Scharnhorst came from Hannover, as did the Prussian prime minister, Prince Hardenberg, who succeeded Baron vom Stein, son of an Imperial Knight from Nassau.

gerous fields of philosophy and art. Even a professor of economics was permitted to utter some radical thoughts, for the Second Empire was not totalitarian. It did allow for certain aberrations, if only as a safety valve, as long as they did not disturb the political order.

These were the mainstays of the Second Empire: the landed aristocracy, the army, the bureaucracy. Yet these three pillars could not have held the seemingly impressive edifice of the Reich, had they not been reinforced by the substantial stratum of the new industrial society.

Industrial Society. German manufacturers received their full awards in the tremendous industrial and colonial expansion; these came in the form of favorable fiscal legislation (especially under Miquel's tenure as Prussian minister of finance, 1890–1901), in extended tariff protection of the infant industries, in an ambitious naval program, and in the acquisition of a world market. In fact, the bourgeoisie became the loudest champion of Germany's imperialistic drives and soon played a dominant part in molding the Reich's foreign policy. The barons of the factory chimneys (*Schlotbarone*), the Krupps, von Stumms, and Thyssens, commanded at times a more powerful influence than the east Elbian *Junker,* Baron von Heydebrand, although the latter was often called "the uncrowned king of Prussia."

The Pan-German League, which was organized in 1890 and which served together with Admiral von Tirpitz' Naval Society and the Colonial League as the popular base for imperialist drives, found its strongest backing among the young, imperious, self-made men of the middle class. The bourgeoisie demonstrated the chauvinism of political amateurs, the bumptiousness of parvenus, and the insatiable demands of irresponsible interest groups.

At first, the Bismarckian compromise reconciling the old conservative aristocracy with the new liberal industrial society seemed to pay dividends. Yet the fate of the Reich spelled out a different story. The fundamental shortcomings of the Bismarck formula became fully recognizable in the politics of the Second Empire. If Bismarck really wanted such genuine collaboration between the two key groups of the Reich, his attempt failed.

It is difficult to outline clearly the balance of political forces. Not only were they shifting continuously but their interplay did not always operate in the open. There was much shadowboxing in a constitutional system that did not allow for a fully responsible government, and hence for the development of statesmanship in parliamentary party leaders. Yet political parties represent a nation's political lifeline, frayed though it may be.

4. PSEUDO–PARTIES AND UNPRINCIPLED POLITICS

The German party system impresses the casual observer as an impenetrable labyrinth of constantly shifting political organizations with unpronounceable names and undefinable aims—in short, a multiparty agglomeration which defies all classification. In reality, however, one of the most surprising features of the German parties is their relative stability in program, membership, and problems, particularly if one ignores the insignificant splinter groups and concentrates on the major political forces.[3] Once their fundamental character is recognized, the changing nomenclature and temporary reshuffle of fronts will not deceive the student of German politics. At the same time, viewed in the historical setting of its party development, the persistent crisis of the political system that has beset Germany during the last century will become clear.

The German party system has been characterized by two major features: emphasis on *Weltanschauung* (philosophy of life) and strict class alignments. Both factors have been evident since the birth of the parties, and indeed are rooted in their peculiar origin. Furthermore, the German party system, originating in an atmosphere that did not permit responsible participation in the monarchical autocracy of Prussia-Germany, has not yet fully recovered from these fatal beginnings.[4]

The year 1848 marked the official beginning of the German parties. The revolution seemed to promise popular participation in a unified nation; thus it aroused the desire to continue political organizations. During the Restoration, budding formations had already developed in the southern German monarchies, which under the impact of neighboring France had granted a quasi-parliamentary regime "by the grace of the Crown." Limited in power though these bodies were, they gave the people some political participation in contrast to the situation in Northern Germany. This earlier political experience may even explain a note of greater realism and deeper rooted attachment to popular government, which might be observed in the southern and western wings of the German parties down to the present time. Because of its greater proximity, Western thinking had permeated the society of Hesse, Baden, Württemberg, and the Rhineland.

[3] The percentage of popular votes in *Reichstag* Elections from 1871 to 1912 are as follows:

	1871	1874	1877	1878	1881	1884	1887	1890	1893	1898	1903	1907	1912
Conservative Parties *Konservative Freikonservative*	23.0	14.1	17.7	26.6	23.7	22.0	25.0	19.1	19.2	15.4	13.5	13.6	12.2
National Liberals *Nationalliberale*	30.0	29.7	27.2	23.1	14.6	17.6	22.3	16.3	13.0	12.5	13.9	14.4	13.7
Center Party *Zentrum*	18.6	27.8	24.8	23.1	23.2	22.6	22.1	18.6	19.0	18.9	19.7	19.4	16.4
Progressive Groups *Liberale Liberale Vgg. Fortschrittspartei Deutsche Volkspartei*	16.5	10.0	10.0	10.5	23.1	19.3	14.1	18.0	14.8	11.1	9.3	10.9	12.3
Social Democrats *Sozialdemokraten*	3.2	6.8	9.1	7.5	6.1	9.7	7.1	19.7	23.3	27.2	31.7	29.0	34.8

[4] For an overall discussion of the German party system, particularly its specific features as compared with the developments in other major nations, see Sigmund Neumann, ed., *Modern Political Parties* (1956), esp. "Germany: Changing Patterns and Lasting Problems," pp. 354–92.

The ideas of the French Revolution, in fact, had increasingly affected the whole of Germany long before they influenced organized political parties. In the fight for and against the principles of the revolution, the cleavage of opinion crystallized in the ideological camps of liberalism and conservatism.

The liberals could trace their proud ancestry from the Age of Enlightenment and could point to Lessing, Kant, and Humboldt as their spokesmen. Conservatism, though slightly younger in its intellectual articulation, was rooted still more deeply in German history. A compound of elements drawn from the legitimistic ideas of restoration, pietism, and the historical school, conservative theory found a formulation in the writings of Adam Müller, Karl Ludwig von Haller, and Friedrich Julius Stahl.[5] In short, the predominant political movements commanded a fully developed theory long before they entered the area of decision making.

Party followers prided themselves on an almost religious adherence to a fundamental program; it made them deride Anglo-American party systems, with their loose and often noncommittal party platforms. This rigidity of political fronts in the name of well-defined ideologies has remained the main feature of German politics. It has consequently been difficult, if not impossible, to accept compromise as the appropriate technique for adjusting the divergent aims of the political contestants.

These difficulties of the German *Weltanschauungsparteien* were accentuated by a second characteristic—namely, their close connection with definite social classes. In a complex society, such as that of late nineteenth-century Germany, class affiliations of inflexible political groups encouraged the development of a multiparty system, which represented another stumbling block for responsible government based on majority-party coalitions.

The revolution of 1848 at first seemed to establish a simple two-party arrangement with the emergence of a liberal opposition from the bourgeoisie to challenge the ruling social groups, which, in response, called on the conservative forces to defend the *status quo*. This conservative party behind the Crown naturally comprised the feudal aristocracy, the main utilizer of the absolute state, and therefore its most reliable mainstay in the army and bureaucracy.

Soon, however, the opposition revealed a schism between the moderate liberal constitutionalists and the more radical democratic parliamentarians. Although the failure of the 1848 revolution and the reaction in the following decade apparently reunited the antagonists, their inner splits were cleverly exploited by Bismarck during the crucial period of constitutional conflict.

The National Liberals, as they finally emerged, saw in the Iron Chancellor's empire the fulfillment of their aims of unification and con-

---

[5] For a detailed analysis, consult Sigmund Neumann, *Die Stufen des Preussischen Konservatismus* (1930), and *Die Deutschen Parteien* (1932); for background study, see Fritz Valjavec, *Die Entstehung der Politischen Strömungen in Deutschland 1770–1815* (1951).

stitutionalism,[6] and the unreconciled among the leftist Progressives were quickly stamped as enemies of the nation. In fact, Bismarck succeeded in splitting the middle class permanently and thus prevented it from making its full political weight felt in the Reich. Though Bismarck later turned his back on the National Liberals, the Liberals and Progressives remained separated largely because they recruited their members from different social strata. An industrial middle class looked for its natural representation within the National Liberal group, but commerce and banking found their political home among the Progressives. Divergent economic interests, which became increasingly decisive in political alignments, accentuated the contrasts as the years went by. Soon the National Liberals were unmistakably a rightist party, and the Progressives could definitely be counted as part of the leftist opposition.

In the meantime the Social Democrats had established themselves as a fourth party and as the leading leftist group. The Communist Manifesto of 1848 had laid the ideological and programmatic basis for the movement, which in the economic prosperity of the 1860's found its social backing in a rapidly increasing and self-confident proletariat. It was watched with fear by a still politically immature middle class. Ferdinand Lassalle's General Association of German Workers, founded in 1863, and Liebknecht-Bebel's International Workers' Association, founded in 1869, were united in the German Social Democratic Party in 1875. By 1912 the Social Democrats, supported by a third of the electorate, had become the strongest party in the *Reichstag.*

In contrast to these parties, which were circumscribed by class alignments, the *Zentrum* (Center Party) of the Catholic minority attracted members from different social strata who had most divergent ideological leanings. In consequence, it had to resolve conflicts within its own ranks, and thus became a school of politics par excellence. It is no wonder that the Center Party, especially after Bismarck's futile attempt to break its power in his *Kulturkampf,* established itself as the strategic center between rightist and leftist parties. "Nothing happens that the *Zentrum* does not want," was the dictum that also held true in the Wilhelminic era, at least until the short-lived anti-Catholic coalition of Chancellor von Bülow.

The existence of a multiparty system allowed Bismarck to break with the National Liberals in 1878 and to turn for a time to a new coalition of the Center Party and the Conservatives, who, after their initial period of opposition to the centralist Reich, finally acquiesced in its rule, especially when their demands for agrarian tariffs were satisfied.

These shifts in political support on the part of the chancellor reflected not only an adroit utilization of conflicting interest groups in the Reich but also a fundamental contempt for political parties and professional politicians (*Berufspolitiker*), whose competition he feared. The prevailing motto of the authoritarian state, "The government above the party," was based on the mistaken idea that, to borrow Bismarck's words,

[6] Significantly, they were re-enforced by the ardent imperial supporters from those provinces newly acquired by Prussia, such as the Hanoverian liberals von Bennigsen and Miquel.

"in moments of decision, the masses will always stand by the king, no matter whether he rules in a more liberal or more conservative manner." For that very reason, the chancellor had introduced universal suffrage, which would "raise the king high upon a rock that the waters of revolution would never touch." History disproved such a prediction. Yet, so long as Bismarck ruled, his attitude of unprincipled opportunism retarded genuine parliamentarian development.

Hopes were raised among the progressive forces that the succession of Crown Prince Frederick, whose definite liberal leanings as the son-in-law of Britain's Queen Victoria were common knowledge, would usher in a truly new era. However, fate gave Frederick III a reign of only ninety-nine days. When this son of William I died, a whole generation was lost and history denied liberalism its chance in Germany.[7] William II assumed the throne in 1888, the year that marked the succession of three German emperors and the beginning of the decline of the Bismarckian Reich.

5. WILLIAM II AND THE DEMISE OF THE BISMARCKIAN EMPIRE

Tolerance had been the fundamental principle of Frederick's life—*Audiatur et altera pars* ("Let the other side also be heard"). His son moved in the opposite direction. William II was the last proponent of a medieval divine-right-of-kings theory. But different from his great-uncle Frederick William IV, the young monarch was possessed of an untiring energy and a dangerous capacity for rash and epigrammatic articulation. His father had warned Bismarck against the eldest son's judgment in politics; his mentor, Professor Gneist, had complained that the prince imagined he knew everything without having learned anything; and even his staunchest supporter, Count Alfred Waldersee, stated in his diary that the emperor was bored by sustained and serious work. Immature, unstable, vain, and inflated by the flattery from the officers of his Potsdam Guard, he took Bismarck's myth of the emperor as the real policy-maker at face value. Where William I had ruled in silence, constraint, and dignity as the first servant of the empire, his braggart and bombastic grandson revealed to an anxious world the dangerously fickle power of autocracy.

From the dismissal of the Iron Chancellor in 1890 to the ascendancy in 1916 of another viceroy, General Ludendorff, the emperor seemed to possess unlimited personal power, and in fact, presided over the chaotic liquidation of an incoherent Reich. That the empire lasted for almost three decades beyond the passing of Bismarck was largely because of the absence of major conflicts without and of the enthusiastic support of a hero-worshipping people within. Still excited by the 1871 victory, the young nation felt need for a symbolic expression of its newly won unity. The emperor posed as the exponent of national sentiment, the coarseness and vulgarity of which was offensive to an increasingly articulate and refined intelligentsia and to an ever-broadening opposition within the

[7] See Werner Richter, *Kaiser Friedrich III* (1938).

middle class and the proletariat. Nietzsche, Gerhard Hauptmann, Max Liebermann, among others, protested against the self-satisfied and success-ridden society that had fallen prey to an unprincipled regime.

How different was the emperor's position from that of the British king! That the British monarch could play his role was due to the fact that the Glorious Revolution of 1688 had clearly assigned him a limited constitutional position, one above partisan struggle. The British king's functions eventually became "the right to be consulted, the right to encourage, the right to warn," [8] and thus to serve as a much-desired stabilizing force of the constitution, without interfering with the controls of parliamentary government.

6. A ROAD TO PARLIAMENTARISM

There were, no doubt, certain tendencies visible even within the Wilhelminic Empire that suggested possibilities of a parliamentary development. Apart from the growing popular demand for constitutional change, as expressed in the consistent electoral gains of the parliamentary parties, and therewith, a growing popular distrust of the autocratic regime, its continuous blunders led to numerous crucial incidents that shook the system to its foundations. In time it might well have crumbled, even without war and defeat.

A few major events stood out among the domestic developments under the rule of William II, presenting opportunities for reform and, indeed, indicating undeniable shifts in the constitutional balance. There was, first of all, Bismarck's dismissal. This episode was more than a personal conflict; it involved more than a clash of generations between the aging chancellor and the monarch, then hardly thirty years old. There were fundamental disagreements over domestic and foreign policies that led to the *neue Kurs*. William II might have flattered himself in being *le roi des gueux* (king of the beggars), or as the executor of Lorenz von Stein's idea of the social kingdom, the *Volkskaiser*. Despite his sincerity and early sympathy with the working man, he was naïve, to say the least, if he believed that he could settle the conflicts of industrial society by royal decree and that he could bribe a class-conscious proletariat by social reforms from above. All that he succeeded in doing was to raise doubts in the minds of the politically and economically powerful, on whose secure support the stability of an absolute monarchy depended.

William II was personally the least suited to establish a working balance between the Prussian military aristocracy and the new forces of society, in line with Bismarck's original intentions. The political equilibrium shifted slowly but visibly. Although the chancellors were the emperor's choice—from General Caprivi (1890–94), to Prince Hohenlohe (1894–1900), to Count von Bülow (1900–09), and to Theobald von Bethmann-Hollweg (1909–17)—it became increasingly evident that they could not stay in power without parliamentary support. Yet Bis-

[8] Walter Bagehot, *The English Constitution* (1898), p. 143.

marck's strategy of shifting majorities in the *Reichstag,* even more
clumsily followed by his successors, led neither to a reliable parliamentary
leadership nor to a responsible opposition.

At the same time, one should emphasize that a spirit of public re-
sponsiveness and self-confidence steadily evolved through the contributions of an efficient civil administration, a comprehensive system of social
legislation, and a vigorous municipal government that held promises for
an eventual democratic turn.

Even in national politics some brighter prospects seemed to arise
with the von Bülow bloc government. Ranging from the Conservatives
to the liberal left, it attempted to broaden the political base of the empire,
to revitalize domestic forces, and to create stable parliamentary support of
governmental policies. Its efforts ended in failure. Its actual position was
tested by the ill-fated *Daily Telegraph* affair in 1909. This imperial interview, for which the kaiser was fully responsible (and Chancellor von
Bülow, at least, by his negligence in checking the text), contained shock-
ing and embarrassing pronouncements on foreign affairs, which were in
no way shared by public opinion. The storm of protest from the whole
nation and from all parties forced the emperor to an official declaration
that in the future he would "insure the stability of imperial policy by
respecting his constitutional obligations." This crisis could have led to
radical reform, taking foreign politics out of the kaiser's prerogatives and
placing it under parliamentary control. It was, in fact, the last great chance
for the ruling circles to bring about a fundamental, peaceful, transformation before war and revolution destroyed the empire. The Conservatives,
however, resisted the increase of parliamentary role until it was too late.
When in 1909, with the help of the Center Party, they overthrew the von
Bülow bloc cabinet, the emperor unjustifiably interpreted this step as an
indirect vote of confidence in his self-rule to counter the chancellor who
had embarrassed him. The appointment of the acquiescent bureaucrat,
von Bethmann-Hollweg, to the chancellorship testified to this view.

The ruling clique did not recognize the signs of the time. Even the
1912 elections, which illustrated drastically the estrangement between
government and people, were of no avail. A clear-cut parliamentary
majority introduced, through a reform of the *Reichstag's* standing orders,
the institution of a vote of lack of confidence in the cabinet. In the one
instance when such a vote was taken (the symbolic Zabern incident of
1913) and the government was censored by an overwhelming vote of 293
to 54 for high-handed treatment of civilians by the military caste, the action was merely ignored by the chancellor.

Foreign affairs, to be sure, remained in imperial hands. The emperor,
influenced by von Bülow and von Holstein of the foreign office, was responsible for the refusal to renew the Reinsurance Treaty with Russia,
which destroyed Bismarck's balance of European powers; furthermore,
to him goes the responsibility for the rejection of a British alliance at
the turn of the century, and the ensuing naval armaments race, the
blocking of French colonial ambitions in Africa, leading to the Morocco
incident in 1905 and the Agadir crisis in 1911, and the support of the
Dual Monarchy in the Balkans (as in Austria's annexation of Bosnia-

Herzogovina in 1908). All these steps helped forge the Triple Entente. It is a significant illustration of the empire's pseudo-parliamentary façade that the *Reichstag* was completely uninformed about the international situation and negotiations when war finally came in 1914.

7. WAR GOVERNMENT—FORETASTE OF DICTATORSHIP

Parliamentary self-assertion was stifled, and domestic forces in conflict with the irresponsible monarch were once more stymied by the call for unity in "national self-defense." Social Democratic internationalists, who only a few days before the outbreak of hostilities had demonstrated in huge mass meetings for peace and world brotherhood, fell into military cadres to fight for "home and hearth" against the barbarian invasion from the east. And the emperor, who had recently called the Socialists "vagabonds without a fatherland," solemnly declared: "From now on I recognize no factions; I recognize only the united German people."

This was to be a people's war on the twentieth-century pattern. Encircled by the enemy, *Festung* Germany immediately declared its *Burgfrieden*. The war lasted four long years and finally destroyed all vestiges of civilian control. The *Reichstag* itself, in a patriotic mood, voted on August 4, 1914, for a sweeping delegation of power to the Federal Council for the "regulation of the economic life."

War centralization and military authorities soon undermined the weak fabric of the complex federal structure and subjected the country to a complete military dictatorship. No doubt, such a conversion was easily made against the background of the Second Empire's brittle constitutionalism. And although Clemenceau and Lloyd George, strengthened by the traditions of national institutions, successfully resisted the wartime trend toward complete military control in France and Britain, General Ludendorff took over the reins of government in Germany. Constitutional limitations did not bother him; they were simply ignored. It was an additional misfortune for the Reich that the general, who demanded unqualified obedience to the supreme military commander in all political and military matters, was possessed of a mediocre mind and a reactionary outlook and had no understanding of economic and social dynamics. Forerunner of Hitler though he was, his was merely an efficient bureaucratic dictatorship.

It might be worth remembering that Ludendorff did not belong to the ruling aristocracy. In a sense, he was a social upstart who certainly destroyed the established constitutional balances. Under his rule, the emperor and his military cabinet were bypassed and chancellors and ministers were dismissed.

Even the *Reichstag* became a puppet of the German high command. One illustration may be cited. The renowned resolution of July, 1917, sponsored by the Center, the Progressive, and the Social Democratic parties (the future Weimar coalition) demanded "peace without annexations." The parliamentary overthrow of Bethmann-Hollweg, who was regarded as a hindrance to peace and parliamentarism, turned out to be only a paper victory. The succeeding chancellor, Michaelis, declared ambiguously that he accepted the resolution "the way he understood it," and soon afterward Ludendorff completely deflated the German peace offensive by the harsh treaties of Brest-Litovsk and Bucharest. These test cases evidenced the hollow sincerity of the intentions of Germany's rulers and the limited strength of the peace parties. Only when the Reich was threatened by defeat did the *ancien régime* promise a democratic over-hauling of the German political system. Such a move, in October, 1918, came too late.

15

THE WEIMAR REPUBLIC

The Weimar Republic is more than a historic phase in the unhappy sequence of German constitutional experimentation. What made it possible for this exemplary democratic constitution to end in the worst autocratic regime, one which could use Weimar as a legal basis for the seizure of power? Were any factors inherent in the system that lent themselves to such a dismal sequel? What steps should be taken to prevent a similar fate for the "Second German Republic"? Is there any fundamental cause for such democratic self-destruction?

A warning may be appropriate at the outset. Attractive and popular though it may seem in an age longing for clear and positive directives, there is no simple answer to questions involving the complex problem of a nation's constitutional balance. Neither proportional representation nor Article 48 of the Weimar constitution, neither presidential usurpation nor ministerial apathy, neither the reactionary bureaucracy nor military intrigues, neither the high treason of industrial barons nor the fratricidal fight between labor parties, neither Versailles nor Moscow are the sole causes of the breakdown. Nor is national character, that last refuge of baffled historians, the open sesame to an explanation of Germany's democratic failure. All these factors contributed in a measure to the downfall of the republic. Woven together with a whole nexus of interrelated forces, some of them accidental, they brought about the fateful outcome.

In the history of the rise and fall of the Weimar Republic, each step seemed to make the next one inevitable; yet almost to the end, avenues were left open for any determined and courageous leadership to find a way out of the labyrinth of political dilemmas. This lack of leadership may well have been the root of the republic's difficulties.

1. REVOLUTION FOR DEMOCRACY?

The failure of the old ruling clique was undoubtedly the primary cause of the 1918 revolution. The Bismarckian Empire was born in military

357

victory; it went down in military debacle, even if a "stab-in-the-back" theory soon served to divert responsibility. Its ruling class failed at its own calling, and its supreme commander, nominal though his rule had become by this time, took the symbolic step of abandoning the nation by his ignominious flight to Holland. Such was the November revolution, and Germany experienced little else by way of internal upheaval at that time.

There was certainly no resolute new elite ready to conquer the state. The revolution was unprepared, undirected, unwanted. It was received by default. Could there be a more legal transfer of power than the solemn request of the last imperial chancellor, Prince Max von Baden, to the leader of the major opposition party to take over his legacy? And Friedrich Ebert, the sober, lifelong Socialist, deeply touched by this confidence, promised to keep the trust.

Was Ebert's action high treason to the cause of the socialist revolution? The core of German social democracy was not revolutionary. There was no Danton, no Marat, no Robespierre among its leaders. It did not dream of the militant *élan* of Sorel's Napoleonic battles. It prided itself on orderly organization and discipline of daily performance. Next to the army and bureaucracy, the S.P.D. was probably the most Prussian institution. The S.P.D. had always been a deeply national movement, a party of patriots, however, that had not been permitted to play the role of his majesty's loyal opposition in the empire. In this hour of defeat, it became the victim of its national conscience, without having been apprenticed in the art of statesmanship. It could never rid itself fully of a sense of inferiority toward the experienced army and civil servants, especially as it had to call on them for help.

Monarchists at heart continued to man the machinery of the state, paying mere lip service to its inexperienced new masters. Indebtedness to the expert servants, mixed with justified suspicion of their loyalty, made for an uneasy beginning of the Weimar Republic.

Born out of defeat and apparent dictation by the enemy, the new regime had to carry the stigma of the old regime's failures. Versailles, though it followed the harsher and conveniently "forgotten peace" of Brest-Litovsk, was soon identified in the people's mind with Weimar.[1] A heavy mortgage was imposed on the young republic by the victorious powers. After the treaty's acceptance by the National Assembly, Germany's outstanding social scientist, Max Weber, prophetically exclaimed: "In ten years we shall all be nationalists." Yet it would be misleading to believe the Paris peace settlement accountable for Hitler's rise to power. His movement was not simply the natural reaction of a proud people against a humiliating defeat and grievous treaty dictation. The "shame of Versailles" was neither the preoccupation of every German nor the real driving force behind the Nazis during the twenties. A decade later, however, the legend was used as a powerful weapon by the unscrupulous Third Reich. It broke the moral defense lines of the *status quo* powers,

[1] Cf. John W. Wheeler-Bennett, *The Forgotten Peace: Brest-Litovsk 1918* (1939).

allowed the unilateral demolition of the planks of the peace system one by one, and buried under the impact of easy victories in foreign affairs the republic that had accepted a "policy of fulfillment." From its outset, the Weimar Republic was marked by the dilemmas imposed upon it by the legacy of the defeated empire and by the Versailles dictate.

Considering these insurmountable handicaps, it was surprising how much was accomplished on short notice by the new regime. Three major tasks were foremost on the agenda of the provisional government: demobilization, economic rehabilitation, and the creation of a stable political order. The first two assignments were completed with the co-operation of both the old and new leaders. The von Hindenburg-Ebert agreement made possible the safe return of millions of the defeated army; the Legien-Stinnes understanding between trade unions and industrial organizations facilitated the relatively smooth transition from war to peace economy. Thus, chaos and civil war were prevented, though nobody thanked the "November Criminals" for what they had accomplished.

The third and decisive step in the establishment of a democratic regime presupposed a clear renunciation by the provisional government, the Council of the People's Commissioners, of revolutionary policies, as instigated by the Soviet Union's dictatorship of the proletariat.[2] This crucial decision was made at the dramatic National Congress of the Councils of Workers, Peasants, and Soldiers, when on December 16, 1918, an overwhelming majority accepted the early election of the National Assembly. Having dismally failed at the opening conference, the small but determined group of Communists, the so-called Spartacists, then tried to conquer the weak state by force in the streets of Berlin. In this desperate plight, Ebert and Noske, the Socialist commissioner of the armed forces, called on veteran "volunteers" of the old regime to suppress the revolt. The republic was saved by the very forces that were instrumental in its eventual breakdown.

This tragic choice shockingly revealed the government's fundamental failure to establish a people's army, a truly democratic administration, and a new political elite. Was the republic doomed and betrayed before it had even established its constitution?

2. FRAMING OF THE WEIMAR CONSTITUTION

The meeting of Weimar, that provincial Thuringian town off the beaten path of world events, signified not merely an escape from the influence of the metropolitan mob but also a symbolic turn toward the West. In choosing this cultural center, the new Germany took a stand against militant Potsdam and for the humanist Western traditions of Goethe and Schiller. It was the republic's misfortune that at this very moment,

[2] This decision led to the resignation of the radical Independent Socialists (U.S.P.) from the Council. Originally it was composed of six members, three from the S.P.D. and three from the U.S.P.

for a time at least, Germany lost her westernmost provinces, the Rhineland and the Saar Basin, and that she did not succeed in incorporating Austria, that great European citadel.

The Weimar constitution, no doubt, represents an impressive document evidencing earnest effort, legal logic, and exacting comprehension. It dealt more realistically with the complex problems of the modern state and society than had the 1848 *Paulskirche* parliament, whose spiritual heritage it received. Yet, although the Weimar Republic was clearly oriented to the principal concepts of popular democracy, social welfare, and a strongly emphasized national centralism, the different parts of the constitution attest to the quite divergent aims of the men who formed the Weimar coalition.

And yet, the often contradictory roles of the partners could be clearly recognized throughout the document. The German Democratic Party (D.D.P.), represented by the constitution's chief draftsman, Professor Hugo Preuss, was primarily interested in the democratic framework, with special emphasis on the articles affecting fundamental rights, national unity, and popular participation. The nation's general acceptance of these principles, though only in a most formal manner, may well be one reason for the decreasing attraction of the party to the electorate after the republic was established. In the days of the Weimar Republic, however, the leaders of the D.D.P. played a most important role as "honest brokers," very similar to that played three decades later by Theodor Heuss at Bonn, in getting difficult partners to work together.

The Social Democrats (S.P.D.) concentrated on the socio-economic aspects and thus introduced certain elements into the constitution that gave it a unique twentieth-century character. Such an extension added new dynamics to the fundamental order with their attendant and lasting tensions.

The Center Party, by its very tradition, saw its major function in the safeguarding of religious and cultural minority rights, in the clear-cut separation of church and state, and supported by the closely allied Bavarian People's party, in the preservation of states' rights.

With these often contradictory approaches to the framing of the constitution, it is no wonder that many crucial issues had to be left undecided. The frequently vague formulation of significant constitutional articles was not accidental. The best illustration of the sometimes ingenious and more often tortuously phrased "elastic" clauses in the basic law of the republic was Article 146, which dealt with the delicate problem of the school system. There were irreconcilable conflicts between the three major parties on this issue. The Democrats were champions of a humanistic approach; the Catholic Center Party, on the other hand, was adamant about an autonomous sphere for parochial education; and the Social Democrats were primarily interested in making free and equal education available to the lower classes. In return for the vague promise of "ideological schools," the Social Democrats acquiesced in the Catholic demand for confessional schools. The final document contained so many ambiguities that only a special law could have clarified the actual policies. This detailed school legislation, although seriously considered four times, was never passed during the lifetime of the republic. In the meantime, numerous and conflicting interpretations brought about educational practices most confusing for a democratic society.

The same difficulty was encountered in other matters. Basic issues, on which the majority parties disagreed, included the jurisdiction of state and federal authorities (Arts. 5–19); the definition of, and restrictions on, private property, together with the hotly debated issue of socialization (Arts. 26 and 153); and the scope and function of economic representation and economic democracy (Art. 165).[3]

3. THEORY AND PRACTICE

The interpretation, and in fact the whole future of the nation's "real constitution," depended on the actual balance of forces at the moment when crucial steps were taken. The basic law could be enacted only by the majority's agreement on a temporary postponement of decisions that were beyond compromise at Weimar. Parenthetical expressions and qualifying statements gave each faction the consoling thought of eventual triumph through "proper reading" of the text. That these divergent interpretations were written into the constitution at all may reflect a German peculiarity. The weighty German document of 181 articles did not make for a flexible application of the nation's supreme directive to unforeseeable circumstances; such a document could not offer promise of a long life. At a later date the Bonn lawmakers, adopting a basic law of 146 articles, followed a similar pattern.

Apart from the ambiguous formulations of the constitutional text, its salient features reflected fundamental conceptual discrepancies. First of all, it was an eclectic document, with contradictory and unreconciled ideas entering into the making of the final draft. The French, American, and Swiss constitutions had served as models; and, as the popular saying goes, "Too many cooks spoil the broth." Masterly though the Weimar Constitution was as a legal document, it was an intellectual construction. Moreover, it left out some ingredients that might be regarded as customary elements, deeply imbedded in German traditions. This omission was its second liability.

President or Monarch?   One might start at the beginning and question the very first article of the constitution: "The German Reich is a republic." Even Ebert did so at the hour of its birth when Scheidemann announced it from the Chancellory's window to forestall Karl Liebknecht, who, so rumor had it, was about to proclaim a Soviet republic at the nearby Wilhelmplatz. The excited holiday crowd milling around Wilhelmstrasse expected something spectacular; thus Scheidemann spoke on the spur of the moment. It was a proud, brief moment. A regency under

[3] Cf. H. Herrfahrdt, *Das Problem der berufsständischen Vertretung* (1921); E. Tatarin-Tarnheyden, *Die Berufsstände* (1922); and G. Bernhard, *Wirtschaftsparlamente: Von den Revolutionsräten zum Reichswirtschaftsrat* (1923).

liberal Prince Max von Baden might have been more appropriate. Ebert had seriously considered it. In the final stage of the republic, even the S.P.D. thought about the reintroduction of the monarchy to stem the rising tide of national socialism. But it was too obvious a maneuver to succeed at that late hour. Besides, von Hindenburg, the monarchist in presidential robes, was too ill to act upon such a crucial decision.

Would it have been possible to introduce a parliamentary monarchy at the outset in 1918? Would the Allies, who pressed for the abdication of the kaiser, have permitted it? Was Germany ready to accept a new emperor? The Hohenzollern dynasty, especially its last incumbent, William II, certainly had undermined the reputation of the monarchical institution and had identified it with reactionary practices. Nevertheless, a monarchy might have provided stability and continuity, particularly in a revolutionary situation. Embodying the abstract idea of the state, a monarchy, at this crucial period, might have transformed law and order into images that the German people could understand.

Institutional symbolism is felt, even by adroit dictators of the twentieth century, to give much-needed traditional support by transmitting loyalties usually concentrated in offices to the controlling party.[4] No doubt, one of the fundamental weaknesses of the Weimar Republic was its lack of symbolism. Not only might deep-seated traditions of the German people have been satisfied by a hereditary monarchy, but the role of the cabinet system amid the complexities of modern government might also have been strengthened by the preservation of such a *rocher de bronce,* the French republican experience notwithstanding.

The French political system, in fact, was regarded by the Weimar lawmakers as an outstanding example of legislative control over executive power. Certain superficial parallels—a multiparty system, desired checks on a traditionally powerful bureaucracy, and a republican form of government—seemed to suggest the applicability of France's experiences. At the same time, the obvious difficulty of the French chief executive to establish a meaningful balance in national policies was largely due to the indirect method used by the National Assembly to select the president. This procedure frequently led to a choice between weak candidates. The Weimar Republic, therefore, introduced the popular election of the chief executive, borrowing from the United States' constitutional arsenal. This popular basis gave the German president an independent status and a direct mandate from the nation.

The carefully conceived balance of power was even further complicated by the double position of the chancellor and his cabinet, who were selected on the president's initiative (Art. 53), but who had to secure the majority support of parliament (Art. 54). Serving two masters put the government under great strain. With the aggravation of the economic

---

[4] This was the reason why the "republican" Mussolini made a last-minute switch before his "March on Rome" (October 28, 1922) and preserved King Victor Emmanuel's throne behind the power of *Il Duce*. This was the same reason why Hitler bowed to von Hindenburg at Potsdam in March, 1933, and why he retained the institution of the Reich presidency, as long as the "Venerable" Marshal held office.

crisis and with dwindling parliamentary support it was not surprising that the presidential cabinet system asserted itself. Under the doubtful constitutional practice of separating Articles 53 and 54, which was followed by heated debate among the experts, the Weimar cabinet soon adjusted itself to the past monarchical tradition of functioning without clear parliamentary support. "Governments above the parties" became the increasing practice after 1926.

In a way, this tenuous situation only proved that the discordant political elements of the Weimar constitution had not been synthesized. Chaos was the result. Within a short time, eager constitutional "reinterpreters" proclaimed the president to be the only "guardian" of the constitution.[5] It did not take him long to destroy parliamentary democracy altogether and to deliver the nation over to the dictator.

The Plebiscite. One avenue that opened the way for the demagogue was provided by an institution which, praised as a most democratic device, had been borrowed from the political systems of neighboring states. The popular initiative and referendum had indeed successfully served in Switzerland and elsewhere as a valuable device for direct democratic participation. Yet these institutions worked differently when taken out of the limited context of municipal and cantonal governments and transferred to great industrialized states with their amorphous masses ready to follow the modern Pied Piper. Contrary to theoretical expectations, the experience of the referendum in modern governments does not suggest that it is especially helpful to democracy. Under dictatorship, the people's ballot becomes a useful weapon to make the masses want what the leader wants.[6]

Long before Nazi dictatorship could exploit the institution of the plebiscite, the Weimar Republic's use of it revealed its dangers. At first, the popular referendum seemed to be of minor significance, as none of the three German plebiscites ever attained the majority that would have forced legislative measures.[7] The Young Plan plebiscite of 1930, although polling less than 14 per cent of the electorate, was in fact the prelude to the mobilization of popular mass support. It laid the groundwork for the so-called National Harzburg Front, the cabinet of national concentration of January, 1933, and the establishment of the "ennobled" democracy of the Hitler regime.

[5] Cf. Carl Schmitt, *Der Hüter der Verfassung* (1931).
[6] On direct legislation in Germany, see H. Finer, *The Theory and Practice of Modern Government* (rev. ed., 1949), pp. 564ff.; R. Thoma, "The Referendum in Germany," *Journal of Comparative Legislation and International Law,* 10 (February, 1928), pp. 55–73; C. J. Friedrich, *Constitutional Government and Democracy* (rev. ed., 1950), pp. 546–71. For German commentaries, note F. Poetzsch-Heffter, *Gesetz über den Volksentscheid;* G. Kaisenberg, *Volkentscheid und Volksbegehren* (2nd ed., 1926); Carl Schmitt, *Volksentscheid und Volksbegehren* (1927).
[7] Social Democratic-Communist plebiscite against compensation to former ruling houses (*Fürstenabfindung,* June 20, 1926); Communist initiative against the building of battleships (October 16, 1928); and Nationalists' plebiscite against the Young Plan (December 22, 1930).

Cabinet Instability. The rise of the Nazi dictatorship through constitutional channels, after its failure at direct action in the amateurish Munich beer hall *Putsch* in 1923, was facilitated by another constitutional anomaly—parliamentary overthrow of the cabinet by a simple vote of nonconfidence, without any commitments on the part of the victorious majority to accept governmental responsibilities. The dangers inherent in such a democratic impasse were obviously much greater in a multiparty system than in a well-established two-party state. They became paramount in the later days of the republic, when the extremist parties, the Nazis and Communists, could simultaneously fight each other in violent street battles and combine forces in parliament. With the continuous shrinking of the moderate center bloc, they were eventually able to mobilize an opposition majority, without the slightest intention of subsequent positive co-operation.[8]

Reich and Länder. The formation of an effective central regime was further handicapped by the traditional conflict between the Reich and Prussia, a conflict which the Weimar government could not resolve.

This tension created an additional element of unrest in Germany. The constitutional provisions dealing with the federal structure of the republic, as compared with those in the Bismarckian constitution of 1871, indicated a considerable step toward a unitary state. Though the states were still granted wide powers, no special prerogatives were reserved for any of them, and any state legislation not compatible with Reich legislation was automatically invalid.[9] Moreover, the *Reichsrat* (Federal Council), successor of the imperial *Bundesrat,* had lost its major political influence and had instead become primarily an effective organ of Reich administration. With the help of Article 48, it was even possible to enforce federal supremacy by direct intervention, going beyond the far-reaching powers of supervision of the *Land* authorities (Arts. 14 and 15). The *Reichswehr,* the only official military arm (under the exclusive command of the Reich president) could be used in the interests of unified democratic action. Although one may dispute the political astuteness of Ebert's interference, the legitimacy of his moves in Saxony, Thuringia, and Bavaria in the early days of the republic cannot be questioned. The situation was far different when von Papen engineered his coup in Prussia in 1932.

Leaving aside smaller incidents, the greatest difficulties in the Weimar days arose in connection with the conflict between the federal government and Prussia. These strains were not lessened by the geographic proximity of their respective governmental agencies, facing each other on opposite sides of the Wilhelmstrasse in Berlin. In contrast to the Bismarckian Empire, where the identity of the Prussian king and German Emperor combined the two governments, and in fact, guaranteed the predominance of the Prussian rule, the republic was torn by the persistent dualism in

[8] The Bonn Basic Law tried to avoid this constitutional flaw by introducing its much-disputed Art. 67: "The Bundestag may express its lack of confidence in the federal chancellor only by electing a successor with the majority of its members."

[9] Art. 13: *"Reichsrecht bricht Landesrecht."*

the heart of the capital. It led to duplications in centralized machinery and to conflicts in administrative practice.

There had been attempts to reform the federal structure and thereby completely eliminate this dualism. They were promoted by nonpartisan movements and finally taken up by a national committee of Reich and *Länder*. In May, 1930, an overwhelming majority of this body agreed to proposals for a merger of the Reich and Prussian governments. Prussia's premier, Otto Braun, spearheaded the move; presiding chancellor Brüning accepted it. The chances for a constitutional amendment were bright. However, crucial economic and international issues resulted in postponement of the solution of "the Prussian question." [1] If Otto Braun had been able to join the Reich cabinet in these crucial years, it might have meant the survival of the republic.

Prussia at this time was no longer the last citadel of reaction. On the contrary, it had become the center of social democracy. Under the able leadership of Otto Braun, the "Red Czar," it was governed by a stable coalition of Socialists and Centrists for twelve years and actually became the last major center of resistance to Germany's steady move toward the political right.

The tension between the two governments increased until it led to an open break, whereupon von Papen, via Article 48, seized the Prussian government in July, 1932. This was the first attempt at *Gleichschaltung* (co-ordination), most clumsily and arrogantly administered; finally, in a roundabout way, it was even rejected by the Supreme Court. In a decision worthy of Solomon, the court preserved the *de jure* legitimacy of the Prussian government and the *de facto* existence of the von Papen regime in Prussia. The decision was a farce. Hair-splitting differentiations between legality and legitimacy had their heyday,[2] but they had lost their significance by that time.

Proportional Representation.   Conflicts between theory and practice, however, were not limited to the last days of the republic. The constitution stipulated that "the members of the *Reichstag* are representatives of the whole people. They are subject only to their conscience and not bound by instructions" (Art. 21). Coupled with the introduction of equal, direct and secret ballot for men and women over twenty years of age (Art. 22), application of the principles of proportional representation in elections seemed to promise genuine democracy. In reality, the outcome was quite different.

Hailed by the Weimar lawmakers as the most democratic procedure, in which every vote would count, proportional representation was truly the "Trojan horse of democracy."[3] Although it cannot justifiably be con-

[1] It was finally solved by decree of the Allied Military Government. For the text of this historical event, see E. Huber, "Die Auflösung des Staates Preussen," *Quellen zum Staatsrecht der Neuzeit* (1951), Vol. II, p. 648.

[2] Cf. Carl Schmitt, *Legalität und Legitimität* (1932).

[3] Proportional representation has been presented as the "Trojan horse" of democracy, and the Weimar Republic as providing the clearest case study in F. A. Hermens, *Democracy or Anarchy?* (1941), and "Proportional Representation and the Breakdown of German Democracy," *Social Research*, 4 (1936), pp. 379–423. For a

sidered the only factor responsible for the breakdown of the Weimar Republic, proportional representation re-emphasized the dangers of the German political system. It operated as a rigid list system, the so-called Baden system, throughout the thirty-five constituencies into which the Reich was divided. For every 60,000 votes a candidate was elected from a straight party ticket. The remainders were pooled and utilized, subject to certain restrictions on district and national lists so that few votes were lost. This elaborate system was "heaven for statisticians, but hell for statesmen."

Indeed, the assumptions upon which proportional representation rests may be fundamentally questioned. If the function of elections is to mirror public opinion as accurately as possible, then proportional representation no doubt gives a truer reflection than does the majority or plurality system. Yet elections are supposed to provide the avenue and foundation for an effective majority government. In order to accomplish this task, the voter is forced to make crucial policy decisions, to choose between alternatives, and to strike a workable compromise. Under proportional representation, these essential functions of responsible politics are taken out of the hands of the electorate and left for the legislature. The voter, therefore, can indulge in an irresponsible demonstration of his fundamental, uncompromising convictions without any thought of the penalties such action may incur for the nation. Certainly, such an electoral system has fostered political disintegration, constitutional deadlocks, and therewith, the breakdown of democratic institutions. The dangers are especially noticeable among peoples with the integrating experiences of equity, common law, and community. With its traditionally irresponsible parties, ideological stalemates, and strategic power position in the heart of Europe, which demanded a national solidarity and a capacity for clear-cut policy decisions, Germany presented the leading exhibit against proportional representation.

The negative effects of proportional representation in Germany were equally serious in respect to the character of political parties, their organization and leadership. Although it was not responsible for the origin of a multiparty system, which can also be explained in terms of social, religious, and regional differences, proportional representation undoubtedly encouraged splinter parties and made the creation of new parties much easier than was possible under a single-member constituency and plurality system.[4] It intensified cleavages, solidified political fronts,

---

differing view, see R. Aris, "Proportional Representation," *Politica,* 2 (1937), pp. 433–45. The effect of the electoral reforms is analyzed in a collection of essays: J. Schauff, ed., *Neues Wahlrecht* (1929). For a comprehensive collection, see Karl Braunias, *Das Parlamentarische Wahlrecht* (1932), 2 vols. See also, Auguste Soulier, "Le mode de scrutin sous la République de Weimar," in Maurice Duverger, *L'Influence des systèmes électoraux sur la vie politique* (1950).

[4] Johannes Schauff, *op. cit.,* fully proved that the National Assembly in 1919 would have had a Social Democratic majority under a plurality system. On the basis of distribution of 400 mandates in single-member constituencies, the S.P.D. would have secured 225 seats with the 37.9 per cent of the votes cast for the party. Such a hypothetical result might easily have led to the consolidation of the opposition parties.

created political creeds and irreconcilable opposition; in short, it fostered ideological war between competing parties, instead of co-operation.

Moreover, the natural ties between voter and representative were completely severed. A candidate had to depend on the party machine for nomination, election, aid in his parliamentary career, and tenure of office. This made for an all-powerful party machine, highly bureaucratized and inflexible, and not for the development of young, enterprising parliamentarians, responsible only to the "whole people and their conscience," as the constitution had promised.

The warnings of Weimar did not prevent the architects of the second German republic from again incorporating proportional representation into the Bonn constitution. Whether its hybrid system, whereby 50 per cent of the representatives are elected by majority vote and the remaining 50 per cent by proportional representation, will salvage the positive features of proportional representation or create even greater complications, only the future can tell.

4. POLITICS OF THE REPUBLIC

Serious and numerous though the structural flaws of the Weimar constitution were, they might have been eliminated, given sufficient time, proper historical climate, and an adequate social basis. These conditions, unfortunately, were absent.

Party Politics. The brief fourteen-year history of the Weimar Republic was divided into three fairly distinct phases, of which only the middle span (1924–29) presented a testing ground of its stability. These middle years were preceded by a five years' aftermath of war and defeat, which in turn was followed by another period of mounting crisis.[5] Versailles, civil strife, and inflation marked the hour of its birth; its demise was ushered in by economic depression, international unrest, and finally, political revolution. The short interval of the Locarno period, personified in Stresemann, brought stabilization and reconstruction at home and Germany's readmission into the "society of nations." True, peace and prosperity proved to be only a boom on credit during the brief interlude. And yet, despite present-day debunking, Locarno held promise for a generation that believed in the League of Nations and democracy. If time had permitted his development, a political burgher might finally have arisen.

It was the tragedy of Germany that the belated awakening of the middle class occurred just when its property and security were being largely erased by the inflation of 1923. Five short years of seeming recovery could not restore its capital, its confidence, or its strength. For a while it seemed to the casual traveler in the late twenties that Berlin had become the real capital of Europe, with its spreading industry, outstanding

[5] For a fuller analysis of Weimar Germany within the framework of the interwar period, see Sigmund Neumann, *The Future in Perspective* (1946).

theater, and busy populace. But the great depression shortly revealed the brittle economic basis of Weimar Germany.

The growth of the radical parties was evidence of the social disintegration of the German Republic. By the early 1920's, the Weimar coalition had lost considerable strength, and it became necessary to include the German People's Party, which only reluctantly accepted the republic, in order to establish a working majority in a "great coalition."

Moreover, the parties themselves changed in their political outlook. Especially was this true of the crucial Center Party, which, originally leftist under the leadership of Matthias Erzberger and Dr. Wirth, moved steadily toward the right until it had virtually accepted an authoritarian regime. The genuinely republican Democratic party had disappeared for all practical purposes by the end of the twenties, and the German People's Party, before experiencing a similar fate, stiffened in its anti-leftist attitudes, especially after Stresemann's influence had vanished. This change made co-operation with the moderate Social Democrats increasingly difficult.

It took four weeks of painful political maneuvering in May, 1928, before the Müller cabinet could be constituted. This was the last government to be established that functioned within the normal framework of the constitution. For two years it lived through a continuous crisis. The Brüning cabinet of 1930, a creation of President von Hindenburg's administration, commanded a slim and shifting majority composed of parties, which at times, only tolerated him as less dangerous than the threatening alternative of national socialism. Besides, the spectacular elections of September, 1930 gave the National Socialists and Communists such numerical strength that their close tactical collaboration as a negative opposition frustrated the normal functioning of the *Reichstag*.[6]

[6] The percentage of popular votes in *Reichstag* Elections from 1919 to 1933 is as follows:

	JAN. 1919	JAN. 1920	MAY 1924	DEC. 1924	MAY 1928	SEPT. 1930	JULY 1932	NOV. 1932	MAR. 1933
National Socialists (N.S.D.A.P.)			6.6	3.0	2.6	18.3	37.1	33.0	44.2
German Nationalists (D.N.V.P.)	10.3	14.9	19.4	20.4	14.3	7.1	6.0	8.4	7.9
Conservative Groups (K.V., L.V., C.S.V.)			2.0	1.7	4.5	5.1			
Business Party (W.P.)	0.9	0.8	2.4	3.3	4.5	4.0	0.4	0.4	
German Democratic Party (D.D.P.)	18.6	8.3	5.8	6.3	4.9	3.7	1.1	0.8	0.8
Center Party (Zentrum)	19.7	18.1	16.7	17.5	15.2	14.8	15.7	15.0	14.0
German People's Party (D.V.P.)	4.4	13.9	9.2	9.9	8.7	4.6	1.1	2.0	1.0
Social Democrats (S.P.D.)	37.8	21.7	20.4	26.0	29.7	24.6	21.6	20.3	18.4
Independent Socialists (U.S.P.D.)	7.6	17.9	0.7	0.3					
Communists (K.P.D.)		2.1	12.6	8.9	10.7	13.1	14.3	17.0	12.2

By this time, the regime had ceased to be a parliamentary democracy and had become at best a "constitutional dictatorship" that made maximum use of the ill-famed Article 48. This emergency legislation still necessitated parliamentary control and permitted appeal.[7] Yet, confronted with almost insurmountable economic difficulties and political intransigencies, parliament, by 1930, had practically abdicated, even to the point of giving up control of the budget. Enabling legislation, delegated legislation, and emergency legislation had slipped more and more power into the hands of the executive.

Extraparliamentary Forces. The complete collapse of the republic's social and political basis was evident in the role and activities of important extraparliamentary forces: the functional organizations of industry and agriculture, the bureaucracy, and the army. Despite the trappings of parliamentary democracy, they represented the "real constitution" of the nation by that time. Whether the republic was to blame for such complete failure in co-ordinating or destroying its declared foes, whether it was the negligence of the democratic leaders or the political immaturity of the German citizen or the entrenched power of the reactionary forces, these groups had, after the short disturbance caused by defeat and revolution, re-established their traditional positions and influence. These same extraparliamentary forces were to provide the gravediggers of the Weimar Republic.

There were, first, the powerful industrial organizations, the leading Federal Union of German Industry, and even more important, the regional associations, such as the *Langnamverein,* the most effective pressure group of heavy industry in Western Germany. In general, the policies of German industrialists toward the Weimar Republic were dictated by opportunism. Though traditionally nationalistic, under the slogan "economics is destiny," they were, at the beginning of the republic, ready to collaborate with the unions and to seek investors or markets, notwithstanding the language their customers spoke. Peace was their best business, they declared during the prevailing economic recovery of the mid-twenties.

With the rising depression of the late twenties, however, the traditional rightist views became predominant again. Industrial society lost confidence in democratic processes and in international co-operation;

[7] According to Art. 48, the Reich president could "if the public safety and order in the German Reich are considerably disturbed or in danger, take such measures as are necessary to restore public safety and order"; yet, it added: "The Reich president shall inform the Reichstag without delay of all measures taken under this Article. On demand by the Reichstag, the measure shall be repealed." Moreover, the parliament was empowered by the same Art. 48 to regulate further details by simple majority (which it never did). These constitutional safeguards, and in addition, those provided by the popular election of the president and the required counter-signature of the chancellor, proved to be insufficient when the crisis of the constitution arose. Although Brüning himself tried to keep up at least its legal substance, the president misinterpreted his constitutional duties altogether. With the chancellor's abrupt dismissal by von Hindenburg in May, 1932, after he had fought valiantly for the president's re-election, the last remnants of constitutional procedure disappeared.

they came to accept the promises of autocratic control and imperialistic expansion as the solution to the mounting crisis. The notorious speech made by Hitler before a representative group of western industrialists in 1931 was the beginning of their increasing shift toward national socialism. The profitable rearmament race was proceeding full speed. Although only a small group of industrialists had officially joined the party before 1931, many of them were already sympathetic to its cause.

In agriculture the big landowners were even more consistently opposed to the republic, though their strategy shifted from a policy of passive resistance to one of infiltration and indirect control (especially when von Hindenburg became president), and finally to one of active opposition. Even then their uncompromising enmity toward the republic did not hinder them from profiting extensively from financial aid through the government *Osthilfe*. Its obvious favoritism toward the *Junkers* caused a major political scandal in the late days of the republic, involving even von Hindenburg and his ancestral manor Neudeck, which had been presented to him by the eastern *Junkers* and paid for by western industrialists.

Most important, the republic never made a serious effort to liquidate the big eastern estates, irreconcilable bulwarks of reaction though they were. When finally in 1932 the Brüning cabinet, and later the Schleicher government, suggested the foreclosure of about two thousand of the hopelessly bankrupt estates, von Hindenburg's good neighbor, von Oldenburg-Januschau, and others of the camarilla round the president blocked the move and caused the downfall of these "agrarian Bolsheviks." They were also instrumental in bringing together the industrial baron, Alfred Hugenberg, the semi-*Junker* von Papen, and Hitler in the fateful coalition of January, 1933. They helped kill a republic that did not have the courage to destroy such conspirators.

The Civil Service.   There were other powerful forces at work, especially in the established services, that helped to undermine the republic. Some attacked it openly. The judiciary, for example, soon became the focus of the counterrevolution. The shameful record of political trials gives a rich illustration of such bias, doubly demoralizing in view of the popular respect for the law. Others opposed the parliamentary regime more indirectly, under the cloak of official "neutrality." And the power of the "neutral services" increased, while the political forces obliterated each other.

The civil service, traditionally conservative, extended its power as the only stable factor in the process of continuous ministerial change. The inexperienced political minister was often unable to control his professional executive officers. The influence of these officers increased under the continuous expansion of governmental activities and emergency legislation until they really enjoyed a controlling position in the state. There was an almost religious respect for the trained specialist in Germany; and the more confusing and insecure social and political life became, the readier were the perplexed voter and his elected representative to hand over responsibility to the self-styled experts.

By 1932, the parliamentary machinery was a sham; the bureaucrats soon delivered the state into the hands of the activists. These followed each other in quick succession: von Papen, Schleicher, Hitler—the reactionary, the military leader, the demagogue.

Von Papen and Schleicher. Chancellor von Papen's "cabinet of barons," personally chosen by von Hindenburg, possessed not a shred of legality. A renegade from the strategic Center party, von Papen represented an amazing selection. If the presidential "guardian of the constitution" were at all interested in the support of parliament, von Papen was of little value, for the smashing defeat in the elections of July, 1932, clearly demonstrated that this personal cabinet had no backing in the country. Von Papen's regime showed the definite failure of prewar conservatism. It was a last amateurish attempt to re-establish a patriarchal order of the old ruling classes by making illegal use of Article 48. With no grasp of the nation's political forces, von Papen's only accomplishment during this historical interlude of six months was the coup in Prussia in July, 1932, when he ousted the legally established coalition government of Otto Braun. The last defense line of the republic went down without a fight. This surprising capitulation of German social democracy might be explained in the words of one of its best representatives, Friedrich Sollmann, who said: "The free labor movement with highly civilized methods, humanitarian and nonviolent, could not be expected to change its character in a day in the face of rising barbarism."

General Schleicher, for years the mystery man of German politics, succeeded von Papen in the chancellery and in a mere two months was put to the test openly. Schleicher had some understanding of the prevailing social forces, possibly because of his experience as the Reichswehr's political liaison officer from the early days of the republic. He knew that a strong social basis was imperative for modern government, if for nothing else but the army. Whether he could have revitalized a dying German democracy by creating new political fronts and welding together the army, the trade unions, and other functional organizations may well be doubted. Such a grandiose strategy assumed the disintegration of the major parties, above all, of the Nazis.

November, 1932 Election. By way of a short respite, the November election of 1932 showed a considerable decline of the Nazi vote. There is little doubt that this decline was partly due to the confusion of the average voter, who could no longer understand the increasing complexity of modern politics. Four times he participated in national elections, to say nothing of the numerous state and municipal elections, during 1932, the critical year preceding the National Socialists' seizure of power. The major reason for the decline, however, seemed to be a sort of law of diminishing returns for a mass party that had been nothing but a destructive force over an extended period.

Despite the premature confidence of its opponents, the Nazi decline proved only temporary; the dynamic forces that had been brought to the fore by the movement could not be stopped. Germany was at the brink of a revolution, and revolutions cannot readily be controlled. At the outset they may be checked; but as they gain momentum, only courageous leadership and a sound people, only rational thinking and the planned mobilization of all intellectual and institutional reserves may turn the tide. By this time, however, a nation usually has lost its resilience. Its institutions shattered, its loyalties dissipated, its social and economic girders crumbled, its self-confidence exhausted, the country is ready to receive the "liberator" and to surrender to him its liberties in return for ardently desired security. This is exactly what happened in Germany during the early thirties.

The destruction of the republic, to be sure, was due to a number of circumstances, among them, personal failure and intrigue. Yet crucial as the *histoire scandaleuse* of the von Hindenburg camarilla was, it did not reveal the driving forces that directed the breakdown. The political machinery of the republic had failed. The nation's spiritual reserves were worn thin; the established classes had lost confidence in themselves, and bottomless despair had seized the mass of society. The stage was set for the demagogue.

5. CRISIS OF DEMOCRATIC SOCIETY

These last stages of the Weimar regime clearly indicated that the crisis of the first German Republic was more fundamental than constitutional weaknesses and political maneuvers might indicate. It reached the very core of European society, undermining its established agencies and challenging the whole of Western civilization. Germany again represented the most advanced stage of total upheaval. It had been a slow erosion covering more than half a century, and though especially accelerated in Germany by World War I and typified by the later garrison state of Naziism, it was not a phenomenon confined to Germany.

Crisis Strata. European society had experienced a fundamental change under the impacts of concentration of capital, monetary inflation, the great depression, and the wholesale destruction of men and material in war. These developments made any return to normalcy difficult. This was particularly true of the newly emerging crisis strata: the frustrated middle class of inflation days, including the salaried employee, the restless and rootless unemployed of the great depression, and the young soldiers of fortune who were the sordid legacy of World War I. These constituted the raw emotional material for modern totalitarianism.

The great majority of salaried employees, who provided the strongest mass support for the Nazis, did not join the labor unions; nor did they accept a socialist theory that labeled the white-collar reaction a false class consciousness. On the contrary, they embraced a pseudo-aristocratic view that reserved for the group a special position of responsibility and social esteem. This new middle class, sandwiched between capital and labor, was antiproletarian and anticapitalistic at the same time. It considered itself the last guardian of personal values in a mechanized world of superorganization. It revolted against the world of rationalization and depersonalization. Always in danger of being crushed by capital and labor, the two anonymous forces of modern society, the salaried employee had become the frustrated class of industrial society. No wonder that a surprising number among them held vague longings for a return to a handicraft society where the artisan possessed a professional status, with a secure livelihood and a well-defined place in society. It was, in fact, this romantic idealization of a much less harmonious sustenance economy of the Middle Ages that caused the salaried employee to accept fascism's notoriously vague theories of a corporate state.

The frustrated *Kleinburgher's* entrance into politics was nothing but an escape from a petty, private existence to a large, collective experience. National socialism found ardent recruits among the forlorn people of the big cities, who entered its mass assemblies as though they were revivalist meetings. The party slogan—"Germany Awake!"—reflected the reaction of the thwarted little man, who regarded the reality of his position as merely a bad dream from which he could be aroused by the master's voice.

National socialism advanced a simple solution to all the ills that had befallen the nation: world conquest by the master race. Such a formula seemed natural to the German bourgeoisie. The nation would give the fuller life to the little man, hopelessly lost in his personal plight. When the nation won its predominant position of world power, it would lift the small shop assistant to the heights of lordship over huge provinces of trembling slaves. It was a mad dream, but by a strange turn of history it came true in the short-lived New Order.

The unemployed served as another major source for recruitment. By 1932, unemployment had reached 6 million, or more than 20 per cent of the working population. The statistics of Germany's radical parties in the early thirties show that these unemployed had become the political driftwood of the revolution. Although they represented a great danger to society, they also threatened the revolution itself. Their radicalism was not genuine; it was not deep-rooted because the unemployed were rooted in nothing. They became the raw material of a nihilistic revolution; but they did not possess the strength nor the direction to launch a revolution.

The frustrated middle class and the rootless unemployed needed leadership that would articulate their vague desires. This position was seized by the irregulars, the small but decided band of young soldiers of World War I who had never found their way home from the battlefields and who led their countrymen straight into World War II.

The Irregulars. It is no mere accident that almost every National Socialist leader was born between 1890 and 1900, including Goering, Hess, Goebbels, Himmler, Bormann, Gregor Strasser, Ribbentrop, Funk, Ley, Amann, Otto Dietrich, Darré, and Alfred Rosenberg. War had become their formative experience in their most impressive years. Fighting became the only craft they really knew, the military society the only group they recognized, the sword the only law they obeyed. Thus to them might became right, and brutality an accustomed and effective weapon in their strategy of terror. Human life had little value. Politics was no longer an instrument to establish order or to prevent war, but a part of warfare, actual and potential. All that counted was obedience, success, and more conquest—perpetual motion for those who were never at peace with themselves or with the world. These men had entered their adult life under the impact of the great war, and when it was over they carried on as militant irregulars in fighting leagues, in the Black *Reichswehr,* and finally in the N.S.D.A.P. They repudiated civil society and dedicated themselves to permanent revolution.

The formulation of the Third Reich policies was to rest in the hands of this capricious group. Although they represented only a small segment of the young generation, they constituted the daring and unscrupulous among them. But the very fact that they could find "respectable experts" of an older generation, such as Hugenberg, Schacht, and von Papen, to support them made their movement successful in Germany. Moreover, they could mobilize and organize the dissatisfied middle class, the unemployed, and others who harbored grievances against state and society. The old nationalists could never have made an effective appeal to them; the "popular" movement of dynamic national socialism did.

Hitler became their spokesman because he was the personification of the irregulars. He was the marginal man of the marginal groups of the crisis strata of modern society. The breakdown of the Weimar Republic must be seen above all as an expression of fundamental social crisis.

16

THE THIRD REICH

1. CHANGING INTERPRETATIONS

The Third Reich came into power against the background of a total revolution. Italian fascism, in comparison to national socialism, was a mere prelude to revolution, as it never destroyed Italy's social fabric or the roots of its Western existence. It never matured into a full-fledged modern dictatorship. National socialism, however, the younger and more vigorous movement to the north, became the prototype and pattern of contemporary totalitarianism.

National socialism in its early days was viewed by some uninitiated as "one-man rule." To them Hitlerism, like Leninism, Mussolinism, Kamalism, and Stalinism, seemed to be the exciting story of an unknown soldier rising to world position. Soon after national socialism had come to power with its ever-increasing challenge to the Western world, it was presented as the natural reaction of a proud people to the "shame of Versailles." A rising Third Reich forged a potent weapon from Western feelings of guilt and concessions extorted from the "decadent democracies," such as the return of the Saar (1935), the remilitarization of Germany (1935), and the liberation of the Rhineland (1936). Then came the theory of fascism as "the last stage of capitalism." This interpretation, stemming originally from Marxist sources,[1] was quickly accepted in a special version by rightist industrialists, and Nazi Germany was regarded in these circles as a "bulwark against the Soviet Union." [2] Probably no theory has caused more harm than this mistaken simplification that underestimated the radical dynamics of the movement. It perverted political fronts, led the Communists to a convenient toleration of the rising Nazis as essential forerunners of the "real" revolution, and blinded conservatives of Western Europe to the consequences of the equally fatal

---

[1] Note John Strachey, *The Coming Struggle for Power* (1933).

[2] Marquess of Londonderry, *Ourselves and Germany* (1938), and G. Ward Price, *I Knew These Dictators* (1938); for further literature see Sigmund Neumann, "Europe before and after Munich," *Review of Politics,* 1 (1939), pp. 212–28.

strategy of appeasement. The breakdown of Hitler's empire, its quick disintegration under the blows of the united Allied forces, destroyed the myths created by Goebbels' propaganda and introduced the theory that national socialism was merely the typical expression of German national character—schizophrenic, paranoiac, and incurable.[3] In the aftermath of the Allied victory, it became a natural but unsound practice to define totalitarianism as a mere German disease.

There was, however, some truth in each of these interpretations. The *Führer* was important as a crystallizing force; the plight of Germany after World War I created convenient scapegoats of distraction; continuous economic crises recruited a mass basis; astute propaganda techniques softened and organized the diffused people; and personal insecurity readied many for the demagogical appeal. Each interpretation articulated fundamental grievances regarding political leadership, international position, economic power relations, public opinion control, and personal plight that were deeply felt in both state and society.

The Nazi regime deliberately exploited all these national perplexities and adapted its program and policy accordingly. This very ambiguity was the secret of its success. It promised to fulfill everybody's expectations: law and order to the frightened burgher; the "nights of the long knives" to the activist stormtroopers; the end of the trade unions and big business control to Thyssen and other industrial barons in the Rhineland; job security, higher wages, and respected positions to the proletariat; national autarchy and high prices to the peasants; the "good old times" to nostalgic conservatives; and radical reforms to disappointed left-wingers. The Third Reich was reactionary or revolutionary, nationalist or socialist, whatever the hour or class demanded. Eager to fight for any cause as long as it delivered a mass following, and equally ready to relinquish the struggle as soon as the source of support outlived its usefulness, national socialism exemplified unscrupulous opportunism.

What held the movement together was its promise of action and booty to both leaders and followers. Once on the march, it had to continue its conquest until the entire European continent was in its power. National socialism lived on continuous dynamics. Its nonstop drive could never be satisfied, appeased, or halted until it overreached itself and collapsed. If any formula could express the essence of this regime, it was permanent revolution.

2. PERMANENT REVOLUTION: FUNDAMENTAL TRAITS

What must still be remembered of the ruined Third Reich is neither the nightmare of its ignominious deeds nor the detail of its complicated machinery, the seeming efficiency of which only yesterday filled the naïve onlooker with awe and admiration, until the breakdown revealed its basic flaws. The myth and the glamour of national socialism are gone. What is imperative now, however, is a clear understanding of dictatorship's fun-

[3] Richard M. Brickner, *Is Germany Incurable?* (1943).

damental principles. These can best be defined by contrast to democracy, which they defy.

Four basic traits characterize present-day dictatorship and distinguish it from its nominal antecedents. Modern autocracies, as exemplified in the Third Reich, are totalitarian, institutionalized, demagogic, and expansionist without limit.

Totalitarianism. The all-embracing revolution is fundamentally *totalitarian.* Unlike its classic forerunner, the extraordinary magistrate in the Roman commonwealth, who was called in for a six months' period only when a major emergency of war, sedition, or constitutional deadlock arose, the modern dictator makes his emergency rule the lasting law of the nation. He extends it into all activities of life, including politics, economics, education, the family, and even the most personal sphere of religious confession and conscience. This marks the end of privacy, all fundamental and inalienable rights, and individuality. The enforcement of conformity replaces the free interplay of competing parties and spontaneous social agencies, the life stream of democratic society. The individual becomes a mere functionary of the community, and the dictator alone can express, and therefore must dictate, the will of the whole. Once in power, the one-party state does not recognize majority rule or the even more significant democratic respect for minority rights. It does not allow for peaceful change or for a "revolution by consent." It is total power. A revolution from within is well-nigh impossible. The new masters play for permanent power even if this calls for continuous purges and eternal vigilance.

Institutionalization. A second characteristic is that of *institutionalization.* To perpetuate the revolutionary regime beyond the lifetime of the dictatorial founder, a complex organizational pyramid is established. It reaches from the leader and his lieutenants through the party in an all-inclusive net of mass organizations down to the lowest level of society. Nothing is left to chance. Paradoxical though it seems for a movement that originally set out to destroy institutions by establishing personal rule, the conscious creation of an apparatus is the most significant political feature of modern totalitarian revolutions. It is exactly this fact that distinguishes the present-day autocracy from earlier despotic rule. Symbols of the awakened nation though they may be, it is not the leaders—the Hitlers, Mussolinis, and Stalins—but their lieutenants and the party apparatus who represent the daily life of permanent revolution.

Through such a complete pyramid, modern totalitarianism poses a system of government opposed to democracy. Even if the terminology is the same, their institutions are worlds apart. It is misleading and unfortunate that an insufficient nomenclature bestows the same labels on most divergent phenomena. There are leaders and followers in both systems, diametrically opposed to each other on each stratum of the hierarchy. In democracies, leaders always remain representatives of institutions. The rise and acceptance of the dictator, on the other hand, reflects personal leadership. The cry for a leader is the result of the weakness or nonexistence of political institutions, of a ruling class, of an accepted code of values. Wherever these institutions and their governing elements are strong enough not only to preserve but also to adjust a society in its evolutionary development, the danger of personal dictatorship does not arise. In contrast, the dictator is a substitute for institutions in the age of mass society. A law unto himself, his is not government by law but by decree, not constitutional but arbitrary. The leadership principle satisfies the human yearning for worship. Modern dictatorship assumes the place of religion for people who have lost their faith in transcendental power. This explains the subsequent and deadly conflict of totalitarianism with religious authority.

Rule of the Demagogue. Modern postdemocratic dictatorship, despite popular misconceptions, cannot afford to neglect the masses. An awakened people can no longer be forced into an unpopular autocracy. It may deceive them, but it cannot ignore them. A dictatorship consequently becomes the *rule of the demagogue.* Its "leader" knows that he must counteract the democratic memory wherever possible. He seizes power "legally" by adroit use of democratic institutions, thus reinforcing himself with the help of the prevailing myth. After he has won control and while he debunks "democracy's decadent deeds," he attempts to establish an ennobled democracy of his own through the pretense of plebiscitary elections and constant appeal to the nation's acclaim. Formation of a mass basis and continuous popular participation are a primary concern of twentieth-century revolutionary regimes.

Participation of the masses is assured through institutions, through violence, and through propaganda. A comprehensive net of institutional controls reaches down to the citizens everywhere: in politics through the monolithic party, at work through the omnipresent Labor Front, at home through the reliable block warden, and even at play through the "Strength through Joy" movement usurping man's leisure time. There is little escape from this active, though not always voluntary, participation.

In addition, there is also a negative, enforced participation through a system of interlocking fears. The rule of terror and the concentration camps, so inhuman dictatorships have discovered, break man's physical resistance and moral personality and make him "conform." Himmler's Gestapo has deservedly become the symbol of modern totalitarianism. Properly applied to a mere portion of society, their weapons force a whole people into line.

Even with the highly developed controls, the Nazis realized that "one can do almost anything with bayonets, but one cannot sit on them." Thus an elaborate propaganda becomes the third line of attack, and probably the most powerful one. "Bread and circuses" are the bait used to capture the people's favor. Yet it is perilous to discount the demagogues' effective appeal. They rise to power by capitalizing on the failures of rational and democratic leadership and its inability to satisfy and integrate large segments of society. A dictatorship's propaganda derives its success from the grievances of society and from the promises it extends. The demagogue mobilizes the irrational instincts of the masses, their spiritual hungers, their desire to belong, their frustrations, their hatreds, and channels them into aggression against the enemy, first within and then beyond the state.

Expansionism. Continuous dynamics, reaching a climax in unlimited *expansion,* make up the fourth characteristic of modern totalitarian rule. In fact, this is the feature of permanent revolution that decides war and peace in the international society. "The proletarian among nations" finds in international adventure a most suitable safety valve against internal upheaval. The dictatorship becomes the exploiter of the world revolution and continuous conflict.

A constant state of war is the natural climate for the modern dictatorship. Dictatorial regimes are governments at war, originating in war, aiming at war, thriving on war. The idea of the totalitarian state was born in Germany during World War I, which was the beginning of total conflict.[4] The claim to absolute control by the German dictatorial parties during the interwar period was justified in the name of a real or presumed danger from abroad. And certainly the essential beliefs of their leaders and followers, their racial ideologies, their economic policies of *Wehrwirtschaft,* their rearmament, their plans in foreign affairs, and their actual attacks show that they were set on expansion. War was inseparable from the meaning of national socialism; belligerence in world affairs denotes a major element, if not the crucial one, of its definition.

3. STAGES OF TOTALITARIAN GROWTH

These fundamental characteristics were visible long before national socialism came into power. A careful analysis of the inner-party activities would have revealed the revolutionary character of the movement. Even during the time of parliamentary respectability, the ruthless oppression of opposition within the party was evident. Party purges were continuously going on. The repudiation of Drexler, founder of the National Socialist party, of Gottfried Feder, father of the Twenty-Five Point Program, of SA leader Stennes, of the Strasser brothers, chieftains in the party council, and the notorious June purge of 1934, when SA chief, Captain Roehm and his lieutenants were assassinated, were all telling examples of Hitler's strategy to mold the party into a reliable weapon.[5]

This strategy exhibited the typical twofold technique of separate treatment for the insider and the outsider. Although the party at this point was dictatorial within its own ranks, it still made conciliatory gestures in its relations to possible allies in the outside world. But even in these early days there was ample warning in the treatment meted out by the Nazis to their declared internal enemies, the Communists and the Jews. Anti-

[4] Ernst Jünger, *Die totale Mobilmachung* (1931); see also Hans Speier, "Ludendorff: the German Concept of Total War," in E. M. Earle, ed., *Makers of Modern Strategy* (1943).

[5] See Konrad Heiden, *Der Führer: Hitler's Rise to Power* (1944).

Semitism was not only a key to the origins of totalitarianism; it was even more a telling indication of things to come.[6] Persecution of the Jews, especially in its legalized practice, was a general rehearsal of basic policies toward minorities, a systematic training in the use of violence, and a practice drill "at peace" for the *Herrenvolk's* conquest of the "Fortress Europe" under the New Order. The first Nazi outrages of 1933 momentarily shocked the world. German conservatives, however, convinced themselves that the intemperate young Nazis would mature into responsible moderate citizens under the guidance of older, more experienced politicians. In fact, Hitler's first gestures supported this opinion of the naïve and self-assured rightists.

National socialism came to power as a coalition government, as had bolshevism and fascism. This National Front of January 30, 1933, which was made up of Hugenberg's Nationalist Party, Seldte's *Stahlhelm,* and the National Socialists, was initially only a weak coalition that appeased President von Hindenburg and a legal-minded populace. It took Hitler more than a year to eliminate the last remnants of a multiparty system and to complete the party's absolute monopoly.

The Third Reich was fully established with Hitler's seizure of the Reich presidency after von Hindenburg's death. Theoretically at least, the *Führer* was only the appointee of his superior; and although Hitler had been accepted by the aging marshal, another president might have undone the Nazi revolution, especially if supported by the still independent and powerful *Reichswehr.* To prevent this, the June purge of 1934 was staged. By degrading the Nazi Stormtroopers (who in a way had fought and won the revolution for him) to a "philosophical debating society," Hitler seemingly acquiesced in the demands of the *Reichswehr.* The army's military monopoly was clearly recognized, at least so it seemed. Yet, contrary to contemporary conservative estimates, the blood purge was not a turn of national socialism toward stability and respectability; it was a step calculated to secure the permanence of Hitler's arbitrary rule. He became the unchallenged master over his party's factions and, in his own words of defense, "the supreme tribunal of the German nation."

The purge was only a preparatory move. Between the seemingly quiet and stable years of 1934 and 1938, national socialism entrenched itself until it had really become the total state, absorbing all institutions. One agency after another fell under the systematic assault of the Third Reich: the bureaucracy, the courts, the press, the radio, the motion-picture industry, the schools and youth organizations, the churches, and other social and economic agencies. If some semblance of independence were granted them, it was only in order to employ their traditional loyalties and experiences in the service of the Third Reich. But even the need for experts did not prevent the party from carrying through its relentless nazification of all services and from dismissing the specialists when subservient party men could take their place (Hjalmar Schacht's replacement by Funk being a case in point). This whole process of infiltration and co-ordination took years.

[6] Hannah Arendt, *The Origins of Totalitarianism* (1951).

Finally, the two most stubborn agencies, the foreign office and the army, were conquered. Hitler's personal confidant, von Ribbentrop, succeeded career diplomat von Neurath; Generals von Blomberg and von Fritsch were replaced by von Brauchitsch and von Keitel, who although not officially affiliated with the Nazis, accepted orders from the party as "good experts should." With this completion of totalitarian control by spring, 1938, the Third Reich was ready for the final step—world conquest.

4. NATIONAL SOCIALISM AND THE FORCES OF REGIMENTATION

With the complete records of the Third Reich at hand, it is now possible to appraise with some conclusiveness the structure and strategy of the revolution; the strength of its institutions; and the response and reaction, the resilience and resistance, the exposure and vulnerability of the nation's social forces.

What constituted the Third Reich at work? It certainly was not embodied in a written document. As a matter of fact, the Weimar constitution was never formally abrogated. It was allowed to carry on a convenient existence of legal fiction, although its substance was superseded by governmental decrees and "organic statutes." The opening Emergency Ordinance of February 28, 1933, the day after the Nazi-fabricated *Reichstag* fire, proclaimed the end of the constitution's most important fundamental rights. It was followed by the Enabling Act (*Ermächtigungsgesetz*) of March 24, 1933, which was passed by an intimidated *Reichstag* to relieve "the distress of nation and Reich," and which by virtue of two extensions remained the fundamental law of totalitarianism. It replaced the constitutional separation of legislative and executive domains with the concentration of all power in the executive.

The *Reichstag* was streamlined into a "spontaneous" acclaiming machine of yes-men, "freely" elected from an appointed one-party list; the Federal Council and the Reich Economic Council were abolished in 1934; and the office of Reich president was merged with that of Reich chancellor on August 2, 1934. Power was fused in the office of the *Führer,* declared to be the pinnacle of the pyramid. According to the new *Führerprinzip,* each subordinate leader was responsible not to those below him but only to those above him; he was, therefore, finally accountable only to the supreme *Führer,* who was responsible to nobody but "to God and the nation." Hermann Goering, Hitler's "truest Palladin," once stated: "We National Socialists believe that in political affairs Adolf Hitler is infallible, just as the Roman Catholic believes that in religious matters the pope is infallible. His will is my law."

This was secularized theology, garbed in German romanticism of Wagnerian vintage. The dictator became a superman, a demigod. He epitomized the system: *Ein Volk, Ein Reich, Ein Führer.* He was the demagogic leader of the people and the absolute master of the party machine.

Guide and model of his people though he was, he still remained a stranger to them, a marginal man, nationally, socially, psychologically.

The Allocation of Authority. Supreme though the power of the leader was, the actual Nazi dictatorship did not depend on his active participation. He could and did retire to his remote mountain castle on the Obersalzberg; in fact, he was more important and useful as a myth than as the capricious, intuitive *deus ex machina* that he often was. The quasi-religious, apostolic character of the *Führer* made it necessary that the real work, not only of execution but of governing, be done by his lieutenants. These constituted the power and driving force of Nazi rule, the backbone of its institutions. They were the guarantors of the system and of its survival beyond the life of Hitler. The *Führer's* constant glorification notwithstanding, they reflected the essence of national socialism.

The role of these lieutenants in Nazi Germany furnish some contrasts to Fascist Italy. Unlike *Il Duce's* sudden rise to power, German national socialism underwent a long period of preparation before its spectacular breakthrough. Its slow development and numerous setbacks created a stronger comradeship among its early followers. Moreover, the complex German social structure demanded a concerted effort and varied appeals to win a near majority for the movement. Pompous Goering addressed himself to the powerful among the army, bureaucracy, and industry; rabble-rouser Goebbels appealed to the urban proletarian masses and the unemployed; romantic Darré to the peasants; reactionary Prince Auwi (son of the late Emperor William II) to the monarchists, and revolutionary Captain Roehm to the perennial soldiers of the Free Corps and the Black *Reichswehr*. Like vassals-in-chief of their overlord, they brought their following and their patronage into the movement, and in return they expected a share of the spoils. Powerful in their own right, these tried and true subleaders could not be removed as easily as Mussolini had "changed his guards." They could only be purged.

This elite exhibited several marked characteristics; it was bureaucratic, feudal, demagogic, and militant. The efficient lieutenants of the full-grown revolution were above all reliable staff officers of the organization. This was true of Goering, Hess, Himmler, and Bormann. But some of the most powerful were unknown to a wide public. Anonymity is the mark of the bureaucratic leader. This holds true today of Moscow's Presidium; it was equally so with some of the key men of the Nazi Directorate (*Oberste Reichsleitung*), like press president Max Amann, business manager Philipp Bouhler, chief of the supreme party court Walter Buch, and party treasurer Franz Schwarz.[7]

They were bureaucrats in all save one important respect: their specific power and function did not derive from specialized training or tested experience, but was subject to the daily, shifting confidence of the *Führer*. All subleaders stood in a feudal relation to Hitler, symbolized

[7] For suggestive material on the dictatorial elite, see the *Hoover Institute Studies,* especially George K. Schueller, *The Politburo* (1951), and Daniel Lerner, *The Nazi Elite* (1951).

by their oath to the leader, in whom exclusive sovereignty rested. There were members of the inner circle, who were entrusted with powerful positions as personal confidants of the *Führer:* comrades-in-arms of early and trying conspiracies, of the Beer Hall *Putsch* and of the Landsberg prison days (Hess); bodyguards of the leader (Schreck, Brückner, Schaub, Himmler); his superiors of the past (his wartime sergeant, Max Amann, and his captain, Carl Wiedemann); and mere parvenus of the party who appealed to him (von Ribbentrop). Even social charmers and mystery women took part in this return to the camarilla policy of uncontrollable court intrigue. They all were satellites whose power was dependent on the grace of the supreme leader, who in return distributed spoils and positions to his protégés.

At the same time, the veil of Hitler's sham democracy concealed his absolute power. He was a man of the people, rising from the dark as an unknown soldier. So were his henchmen. The nobility were suspect and rarely reached a powerful position. The community of leaders and followers was played up in the party's elaborate propaganda, in the street collections for voluntary winter help, in the shared monthly one-dish meal, in the rigid frugality (with Goering a conspicuous exception). Debasing Nietzsche and Pareto, the dictator's councilmen divided the nation into a two-caste society, the superhuman elite and the all-too-human masses. These leaders, rationally directing the irrational stream of the helpless masses, revealed the system's arrogance and unmasked its seeming democracy.

The contrast between the leaders and the led became evident in the most significant feature of naziism, its militancy. The subleaders were, above all, lieutenants because the system was belligerent. Politics was nothing but continuous warfare. In the *Führerstaat,* civic democracy was superseded by militant authoritarianism and subordination. The holy war of the creed made every partisan aggressive. Advocates of violence ranked high in the *Führer's* council (e.g., Roehm and Heydrich). Yet it was not the army's discipline, its hard and fast rules, to which Hitler's lieutenants conformed; they frowned upon the methodical, rational, and well-regulated services. They were amateurs, soldiers of fortune, viewed with increasing alarm by the professional military, who finally defied them and lost.

Despite significant tensions among the lieutenants, the hatred between the party bureaucrats and the perennial revolutionaries, the experts and the demagogues, the old guard and the parvenu, a revolution from within was well-nigh impossible. It was the *Führer's* power and privilege to compromise their differences and to play up the competing factions. As the high priest of the political religion and the unchallenged master of the machine, he could always force them into the undisputable party line.

One-Party Rule. The National Socialist Reich was a *one-party state*. The monolithic party, a misnomer though it was, was vital to the system. Its functions were fivefold. Originally the esoteric "nucleus of the coming New Order," and at all times the "training school for the ruling class," it concentrated, after the seizure of power, on the "control and education of the masses" and on the "maintenance of communication between state and society." Only by assuming all these functions could it hope to fulfill its most important task, "the preservation of the dictatorial status quo."

The efficiency of the one-party state depended on its strikingly novel organizational elements. These were not all Hitler's invention; indeed, he borrowed heavily from the church, from the army, from business,[8] and not least of all, from his declared archenemy, the U.S.S.R. Three features of the Nazi Party were outstanding: hierarchical order, close-knit organization, and military structure.

Lenin's concept at the turn of the century of a small, centralized, and revolutionary Bolshevik elite, as opposed to the Menshevik idea of a loose democratic mass organization, was taken up by Hitler when he joined the band of political bohemians as member number seven and when, in numerous intra-party struggles, he forced his discipline on the growing party. The political hierarchy, firmly maintained in a central directorate at the summit, was reflected in a whole set of regional and local groups. This system necessarily created a troublesome dualism between party and state. The two parallel pyramids of party officers and state bureaucracy led to confusing overlapping of responsibilities, constant interference, and tensions in the administrative process. Though the legal monopoly of the party was formally established in the early single-party law of July 14, 1933, and the law of safeguarding the unity of party and state of December 1, 1933, a real equilibrium was never attained. The top-heavy mechanism, however, established a close-knit organization that reached through a web of associations down to the smallest groups similar to the early Bolshevik cells, controlling the members in their day-by-day pursuits and often even penetrating the opposition's conspiracies.

The active core of the movement was held together by the integral groups of the party, such as the Storm Troops, the Elite Guards, the National Socialist Motor Corps, Hitler Youth, National Socialist Student Association, and National Socialist Women's Organization. The affiliated associations enlarged the circle to include professional groups; the German Labor Front, with its enforced membership, finally numbered close to 30 millions.

The outstanding and most alarming feature of the N.S.D.A.P. was its military structure. Presumed to be "defense organizations" to protect "peaceful" National Socialist meetings and "to free the streets for the Brown battalions," the semimilitary SA and SS became a threat to the state. Weimar's vacillating policy, first outlawing the SA in 1932 and then, under extra-parliamentary pressure, restoring this competitive military arm, was a decisive factor in the breakdown of the republic. The N.S.D.A.P. from the outset was not a parliamentary party but a militant

[8] Consult R. A. Brady, *The Spirit and Structure of German Fascism* (1937), and *Business As a System of Power* (1943); Franz L. Neumann, *Behemoth* (rev. ed., 1944).

order.[9] As a fighting league, it was able to win easy victories against an unarmed foe in notorious *Saalschlachten,* to frighten a confused populace into acquiescence, if not submission, and finally to wrest political control from a feeble government.

Dual State. To become an effective regime, however, national socialism needed the support of the established organs of state and society. The civil service was first in line. Without its help the Third Reich could never have functioned, especially as the Nazi movement was lacking in administrative talents (with the notable exception of Albert Speer, who succeeded Fritz Todt as minister of armaments and munitions in February, 1942). Whether through cowardice, call of duty, or naïve expectation that the bureaucracy could destroy any revolution, the traditional services continued to operate after they were purged of all those politically and racially "incompatible" with the New Order. The designation of this "cleansing process" as the restoration of the professional civil service (law of April 7, 1933, and later codification in the public officials act of January 26, 1937) was mere lip service to the neutral bureaucrats.[1]

The co-ordination of party and government was facilitated by the strange legal fiction of a dual state, allowing for the coexistence of the "prerogative state" (*Massnahmen Staat*) and the "normative state." Although the latter represented an administrative body endowed with elaborate powers for safeguarding legal order as expressed in statutes, court decisions, and activities of the administrative agencies, the former stood for that governmental system which exercised unlimited arbitrariness and violence unchecked by any legal guarantees.[2]

This combination of "arbitrariness and efficiency based on order" was the essence of the Nazi state. It accounted for the enduring power of its rule, as well as for its deep contradictions and its inner duplicity. The separation between party and state became a useful device for a novel division of labor—the one part free from official handicaps, expressing the "boiling soul of the people," the other not responsible for its outbursts. Such procedures could both legalize revolutionary upheavals and appease a nation accustomed to law and order. Thus the pogrom of April 1, 1933, and the burning of the synagogues on November 10, 1938, could be legalized through formal legislation, although the systematic purging of the judiciary and the introduction of special Nazi courts, such as the dreaded People's Court (*Volksgerichtshof*), soon made it absurd to resort to such legal fictions.

Industrial Leaders and Nazi Economics. The industrial ruling

[9] Gottfried Neesse, *Partei und Staat* (1935), and H. P. Ipsen, "Vom Begriff der Partei," *Zeitschrift für die Gesamte Staatswissenschaft,* 100 (1940), pp. 309–36, 447–510; on the concept of the totalitarian party, see also, Sigmund Neumann, *Permanent Revolution* (1942), especially pp. 126ff.

[1] The political inclination of the traditional civil servants under Weimar was illustrated by the fact that, of its members in 1930, more than one million were enrolled in the politically "neutral" *Deutscher Beamtenbund* and only 175,000 in the Social Democratic *Allgemeiner Deutscher Beamtenbund.*

[2] Ernst Fraenkel, *The Dual State* (1941).

classes were inextricably involved. Hitler, whom they had tried to hire as a political manager, came to control them completely. Nazi economics was above all *Wehrwirtschaft*. Oriented at war preparedness, the economic organization of the garrison state proclaimed the supremacy of politics. Its measures could disregard rules concerning gold reserves, general fiscal policies, and a balanced agricultural and industrial production, as long as the essential aims of effective military striking power were served. The Third Reich could afford a top-heavy economy, an ever-expanding bureaucracy, a wasteful utilization of national resources, provided that this economic mobilization would finally bear fruit in total victory, territorial conquest, and the exploitation of other economies. Under the Nazis, the war economy evolved from one of emergency into one of normalcy, as did the political rule.

This does not mean that German industry failed to profit handsomely from its collaboration. Initially, at least, the Nazis were vitally concerned about the preservation of the skill and services of the authoritative German industrialists. The future of the Third Reich and its plans for world conquest depended on them. They in return held many key positions, even when they were not genuine members of the party, e.g., Hugenberg, Seldte, Dr. Kurt Schmitt, Schwerin-Krosigk, and their ministerial bureaucracies. The account of the rise and fall of Hjalmar Schacht, economic czar of these early years, indicates the initial range of power enjoyed by these men and their contribution to the stabilization of the Third Reich. Schacht's early success rested largely on the shrewd combination of the objectives of rearmament and recovery. But the central and consistent aim of national socialism was preparation for war. For its sake any ideological commitment had to be shelved, such as the idea of the corporate state, highly regarded by early Nazi romantics. Neither ideologies nor sound economics mattered to the political adventurers. And when the more conservative Schacht criticized their expansionist plans, he too had to go.

With Goering's appointment as general plenipotentiary for the Four-year Plan in October, 1936, the second stage of Nazi economics began. From then on the experts were subordinated to the party's incompetent policy planners like Funk, Wilhelm Keppler, Joseph Wagner, Koehler, Paul Koerner. The party extended its sway by engaging in the direct operation of giant combines such as the Hermann Goering works, the Wilhelm Gustloff foundation, the German Labor Front enterprises, the Franz Eher publishing house. The army also participated in the economic planning, increasingly so with the coming of war. Although Hitler's war economy thus changed the direction and strategy of control, and often the recipients of its profits, it accelerated the process of concentration and deeply committed the captains of industry to Germany's fate. This period serves to illustrate the utter inability of the Nazis to establish the economic basis and organization necessary for their unlimited ambitions of conquest.

Even when competent Albert Speer took over the disorganized, inefficient economic apparatus in 1942, naziism had already overreached itself. With the destruction of the Third Reich, the "neutral" profiteers of its economic empire also disappeared, at least for the time being.

Peasantry. Of all classes under totalitarianism, the peasantry, on the whole, seemed to fare best. Its early alignment with naziism was based on cold opportunism. National socialism served as a Pandora's box. It awakened and revolutionized the hitherto dormant agrarian groups in Germany (as it did in the German satellite states of south-eastern Europe). But the majority of the peasants, although tradition-ally opposed to the democratic society, was neither impressed by the Nazi slogans of "Blood and Soil" nor by their chief farm legislation, the Hereditary Estate Law and the Food Estate Law. The small peasant elite of hereditary farmers almost doubled its average landholdings from 1933 to 1939, attained an unchallenged leadership in the overall Nazi organization of the Reich Food Estate as Peasant leaders (*Bauern-führer*), and was often rewarded with giant estates in the occupied eastern territories during the war; but even so, the fundamental structure of German agriculture was not changed. The contrast between the large estates of the landed aristocracy, which remained intact, and the hold-ings of the small farmers, which furnished only a meager existence, con-tinued. Both groups became increasingly articulate in their hostility to rigid regimentation and attempted collectivization by the Third Reich. Despite restrictions, controls, and requisitions under the New Order, which the farmers naturally resisted in accordance with their individual-istic and conservative traditions, the peasants, nevertheless, seemed to be the only class to succeed in collecting spoils from the permanent revolutionaries. Certainly, this class did not suffer as much as the urban classes from the bombing attacks and economic dislocations of total war; it emerged at the end as a crucial power. Self-sufficient individualists that they were, the peasants were neither conquered nor broken by naziism.

Proletariat. The fate of the proletariat under the Third Reich was a less happy one, especially so far as its participation in policy making was concerned. The Labor Front originally succeeded the dissolved trade unions, but it soon included all working people, employers and employees, and became an economic complement to the party. At best, it represented the party and governmental bureaucracy, but never labor itself. The Nazi regime left no room for the working class, notwithstand-ing the advertised slogans of the "dignity of work." This status was partly self-imposed, for the proletariat remained the social class that most consistently associated itself with democracy in Germany. Even throughout the Nazi period, many of the workers kept their sociopolitical loyalties to their party and trade unions, went underground, and thus gave promise for a new democracy.

However a large part of the population—the crisis strata of the dispossessed middle class, the rootless unemployed, and the perennial warriors of the preceding conflict—accepted national socialism and its expanding range of empire. The little man counted on profiting from its conquest of the globe and remained a devoted fighter for the cause, as long as success seemed to be assured. Aggrandizement became the trademark of totalitarianism.

Monolithic Structure in a Pluralistic Society. In sum, national socialism was possessed of a monolithic structure; still, its inner workings revealed a great complexity of pluralistic elements. In order to acquire and maintain control, the party had to call upon the heterogeneous elites: the civil service, the captains of industry, the agrarian leadership, the armed forces. It was pluralism without the necessary safeguards of parliamentary control, of open competition among the oligarchical groups, of freely formed public opinion. The longer the system lasted, the more its inherent contradictions hindered its performance. Hitler, utterly incapable of performing the daily tasks of governing, increasingly depended on appointed plenipotentiaries; yet even communication among these top men broke down. Cabinet meetings were discontinued after 1937. Communication by memoranda replaced personal discussion of conflicting policies. Hitler never exchanged views; he always addressed his lieutenants as if they were a public assembly. Key men of the system, including his secretary of state, Karl-Heinrich Lammers, found it difficult even to see the *Führer.* Interviews were granted only to confidants, who were often sycophants. Thus, Hitler became the prisoner of his own propaganda. The *Führerstaat,* particularly in its late stages, was a feudal empire with all its weaknesses paramount, among which was the breakdown of communications.

5. HITLER AND THE GENERALS

Dictatorship geared for war had to make its peace with the armed forces. This "marriage of convenience" between the National Socialist party and the German army was, however, a stormy relationship from the outset. Its record is of more than historic interest at a moment when German remilitarization has become a major issue of policy decisions, when the future of the second German republic and of Europe as a whole may depend on the "political reliability" of the German armed forces, and when another "stab-in-the-back" theory is in the making.

This time a double-edged myth, designed for all eventualities, is being built around the generals. If national socialism should really be dead, the image of the courageous generals under and against Hitler is certainly being revived, as a daily increasing literature attests.[3] The

[3] There is the widely read, devastating pamphlet, "Hitler als Feldherr" (1949) by General Halder, chief of the general staff from 1938 to 1942, and the Rommel eulogy, written by his gifted chief of staff, General Hans Speidel, *Invasion, ein Beitrag zu Rommels und des Deutschen Reiches Schicksal* (1949), which was received with enthusiasm even in Great Britain; mention might also be made of British Brigadier Desmond Young's *Rommel: The Desert Fox* (1951), and Liddell Hart's *The Other Side of the Hill* (1948).

generals present themselves again, as in the days of Seeckt and von Hindenburg and Schleicher, as leaders above politics and above reproach. The recently established *Brüderschaft* of former commanding *Reichswehr* officers is only a forerunner.

At the same time, there is still a way open for the very different view of a victorious Third Reich, one betrayed by those "scheming, cowardly, reactionary" *Junkers* among the military chieftains, should renewed Nazi ideology require a "stab-in-the-back" theory. Its most outspoken representative so far was probably General Remer, who saved the day for Hitler as the commander of Berlin on the tragic July 20, 1944, and who came to the fore after World War II as the leader of the neo-fascist Socialist Reich party.

It is one thing to defend the German soldier against unjust criticism, as has been done with dignity by the Federal Republic's president, Theodor Heuss; it is another matter to free the army leadership of any major responsibility. It was army leadership that forced out of office the minister of war Groener, the only general who dared to disband the Storm Troops in 1932 and who openly resisted their overt attack on the "neutral" state; it was the army that played with the rising Nazis, just as it had with the conservatives, naïvely hoping to control them; it was the army's supreme commander, President von Hindenburg, who formally delivered the nation to Hitler. It was the leading military journal, the *Militärwochenblatt,* that cordially welcomed the coming of the Third Reich;[4] it was the army that capitulated in face of the murder of Generals von Schleicher and von Bredow and acquiesced in the stabilization of a regime making frank preparations for war.[5]

There was reason, though no excuse, for the army's misjudgment of Hitler's national socialism. The military leaders, deeply concerned about a social mass basis in the age of total war, looked upon Hitler as a valuable force, the demagogue who could win over the masses from what they considered an unsoldierly republic. They were seduced by his promises of a restored and expanded army and by the expectations of speedy promotion. True, they never trusted Hitler. He was always the leader of the *Landsknechte.* The Nazis were irregulars, even in the military sense. They did not fit into the hard and fast rules of army discipline. They were difficult and daring, irrational, and irresponsible.

The modern army is a highly rational institution. This truism holds for Prussia-Germany, despite its feudal basis. Indeed, there was a characteristic tension in the German army between middle-class rationality and the feudal idea of personal loyalty (reflected during the critical Nazi years in the oath given the supreme commander by the officers, who nonetheless hated his system). This conflict remained latent only because the middle class in Germany did not succeed in winning

[4] To quote: "the *Wehrmacht* is no foreign body as it was after the November revolt of 1918. Today it is a part of the organic community and shares in the common distribution of the nation's task; and it follows Adolf Hitler as the Führer of the people with full confidence and with devotion to its great national task."

[5] Walter Goerlitz, "Wallensteins Lager 1920–1938, Das Verhältnis der deutschen Generalität zur Republik und zum National-Sozialismus," *Frankfurter Hefte,* (May–June, 1948; March, 1949).

political control or sufficient social prestige to challenge the contradictory Prussian formula. Certainly, only a very small number of the old
army joined the National Socialists, and in fact, the army was often
regarded as neutral ground during the early years of the new regime.
People jokingly referred to the possibility of "emigrating into the army."
Nevertheless, the party triumphed, especially in the most spectacular
units of the militarized Third Reich: the newly created air force, the
Panzer divisions, and the paratroops. And the army accepted the new
political leadership.

Was it typically military *Kadavergehorsam*, political naïveté, moral
blindness of the technical expert, or a vague realization that the old
army leadership had lost out in the new world of mechanized total war
that made them surrender to the Third Reich? Whatever the answer,
the capitulation certainly pointed up the great dilemma of the military
in modern dictatorship.

These ever-present strains inherent in the system did not mean that
the long-predicted break between Hitler and his generals was always
imminent. A defection could certainly not materialize so long as the
nation enthusiastically followed the leader and so long as the success of
his conquest continued.

6. WAR ON THE WORLD

Conquest began as a modest undercover expansion through bilateral treaties and unilateral piecemeal changes. Thus anxious neighbors, including
the archenemy Poland, were appeased by treaties of nonaggression before
they realized that these friendship pacts were a cover for attack and absorption. Through this policy of erosion, the whole World War I treaty system
was undermined before responsible Western statesmen were ready to recognize the fundamental shift in the balance of power. This was diplomatic
warfare, the first stage of total war.

The second stage of economic warfare supported the diplomatic
pressure. By 1938, Schacht's ingenious barter treaties had brought southeastern Europe under Nazi control. If national socialism had let this
invisible invasion take its course, the whole Danube basin for all practical
purposes would have become its prize possession without moving a German soldier. Nazi psychology, fortunately, did not run along these lines
of patient waiting. Lovers of the spectacular, they had to goose-step across
Europe to awaken their own people. They might have even forced their
sleepy foe into action, had it not been for their third weapon, psychological warfare against the Red peril. Fear of bolshevism and the strategy
of terror broke the West's spirit and made it ripe for surrender, at least
temporarily, to the power of the anti-Comintern crusaders. The Western
democracies were neutralized in the Italo-Ethiopian War, in the Spanish
Civil War, and finally in Hitler's conquest of the Danube basin.

Austria and the Sudetenland were conquered with the help of an
additional ideological weapon taken directly from the arsenals of the vic-

torious democracies, national self-determination. Claiming all Germans beyond the nation's frontiers in the name of Greater Germany, *Anschluss* was enforced, the Sudetenland was "liberated," and one "last territorial claim" after another was demanded. Munich, the historic mark of the dictator's appeasement, was praised by the semi-official *Deutsche Diplomatische Korrespondenz* as a belated victory for Wilson's Fourteen Points and the League Covenant's Article 19, which promised peaceful change. But Munich was not "peace in our time," as Neville Chamberlain's weak vindication of his surrender claimed; it was not even prolonged armistice to give the Western Powers a belated chance to catch up. It was preparation for assault, as definitely pronounced by Hitler at his notorious secret council meeting on November 7, 1937.

Munich was primarily conceived in terms of military strategy. With Austria a part of Greater Germany, Czechoslovakia was caught in a pincers; with the Sudeten Mountains under control of the *Reichswehr,* the Bohemian basin, and with it thirty-five divisions of the Czech army, fell to Germany. "The master of Bohemia is veritably the master of Europe," Bismarck had said. That was the main reason why Hitler moved to destroy "the outpost of bolshevism in central Europe"; it was not for the "protection of those fellow Germans who live beyond our frontiers."

In January, 1939, Hitler warned the world that Germany could not be deprived by the other great powers of much-needed "living space" (*Lebensraum*). This was the fanfare for a new campaign. In fact, on the very day that Greater Germany had been fully established, Hitler seized upon new ideas that promised further expansion. This was the hour of *Geopolitik,* the rule of the Herrenvolk, and the beginning of the New Order. Only a short while earlier, Hitler had proudly declared that he did not want to incorporate "a single Czech" into the Reich. Now he borrowed General Haushofer's expedient formula of "the natural right of the capable peoples to living space as against that of the possessors of territory who are unable to develop it." The concept of *Lebensraum* opened perpetual possibilities to a power-ridden people. Moreover, the right to *Lebensraum* was an exclusive possession of the master race and therefore not applicable to adjacent Poland, despite its higher birth rate. The complete absence of any sense of reciprocity was a characteristic of National Socialist thinking. *Lebensraum* was granted or denied to nations in the court of geopolitical potentates. If the British Empire cooperated with the "renovating powers," she might keep a sphere of interest of her own. If not, the "declining empire" would have to disappear. This obvious claim for world control was carried one step further in the even more flexible concept of *Befehlsraum,* the area in which Germany was to give orders. The evolution of Greater Germany's demands from *Lebensraum* to *Befehlsraum* indicated Hitler's design for world control.

The blueprints of the geopoliticians, in the meantime, were converted into an explosive force by union with the Nazi concept of the master race. The idea of racial superiority was not the expression of a strong and pure people; it was a definite sign of inferiority. It found acceptance among the frustrated *Kleinbürger* and furnished an escape valve for the high-pitched emotions in defeated postwar Germany. For national socialism it became a militant symbol distinguishing friend from enemy. Anti-Semitism unified an otherwise diversified Nazi society. It also was an excellent article for export to the traditionally anti-Semitic Danubian countries. Above all it was preparation for the New Order.

The New Order's first practice drill came with the seizure of Czechoslovakia. The "organic law of the Czech protectorate" of March 16, 1939, furnished a preview of the complete pattern. It brought into being that fantastic Nazi caste system of nations, wherein the *Volkdeutsche* were the Brahmins. Germany was to become the unchallenged ruler of Europe politically and militarily, and, in a strict division of labor, the industrial heart of the Eurasian *Grossraumwirtschaft*. She was to be supported by her vassals-in-chief—the "Nordic nations" of Scandinavia, Flanders, and the Netherlands; the Italians ("Nordics of the South"), the Japanese ("the Aryans of the East"), and Laval's Vichy France. At the bottom of the pyramid were the outright colonies of eastern Europe—Czechoslovakia, Poland, the Balkans, and Russia. This New Order was to win the war and to perpetuate the power of the Third Reich; and in case of defeat, it was to prepare the resurrection of naziism out of the vacuum left by its decay. This was a part of the Nazi dream world.

7. RESISTANCE TO THE TOTAL STATE

What institutions, what social groups, what traditions stood their ground against the Third Reich? The spectacular though futile attempt of July 20, 1944, brought them together and highlighted for a short moment the five major resistance forces: those in the army, the churches, the conservatives, the labor movement, and the German youth.

Army. It was the tragedy of the resistance that the army, the only agency capable of bringing about a revolutionary upheaval within the police state, was institutionally deaf and dumb to politics. By tradition it expected the watchword to come from the political powers in control, whoever they were. Its leaders lacked judgment and courage. "The generals who want to overthrow a government refuse to act without its orders," Ambassador von Hassell bitterly commented on their failure to fight the tyrant.

The easy optimism of the early years had changed into profound defeatism among the old ruling classes, and opportunism—corruption by money, special favors, and increased prestige—ate deeply into the moral fiber of the traditionally disciplined army. True, courageous generals like Hammerstein, Fritsch, Beck, Oster, and the mysterious chief of the *Abwehr,* Admiral Canaris, stood up against Hitler; but even where they gave military counsel of prudence, it was discredited again and again by the world appeasers' acquiescence in Hitler's daring moves. Although these resisting generals were proved to be right in the end, their patriotism and deep concern for the future of Germany became an overwhelming deterrent to open rebellion. With the Allied demand for unconditional surrender, their chance for an alternative German government disap-

peared. The failure on July 20 may have resulted partly from the demoral-
ization and fatal resignation of tired and disillusioned commanders who
had been defeated, within and without, and who had lost direction and
faith.

Churches.   The importance of the churches in the resistance movement should not be measured by their active role, though some religious
leaders, such as Catholic Cardinal Faulhaber of Munich and Protestant
Bishop Wurm of Würtemberg, took a courageous stand at early dates in
open declarations and continued sermons. "We Christians do not make
a revolution. Against the enemy at home there is but one weapon: to hold
out with vigor and toughness. We are at this moment not hammer but
anvil. The anvil cannot and need not hit back; it must only be firm and
hard." These words of Bishop Galen on July 20, 1941, summed up the
persistent, though cautious attitude of the churches. Tactical moves, such
as the Holy See's early Concordat with the Third Reich on July 20, 1933,
must be viewed in their long-range aspect. This holds equally true for the
numerous warnings in the latent warfare between the two powers, climaxing in the papal encyclical, *With Burning Sorrow* (1937).

Catholicism and Protestantism naturally were in different positions,
the latter being more vulnerable to attacks by the Nazis, who unscru-
pulously played off the religious factions against each other. The Nazi
attempt to create a unified German Christian Church, or even a romantic
neopagan movement, proved, however, to be a complete fiasco. It marked
totalitarianism's first major defeat. Strategic considerations at times forced
national socialism to adopt a conciliatory attitude, especially when the
Lord's help was needed. Still, no compromise was possible.

The churches represented a supreme challenge to the dictator's
"political religion." They defied this modern tribalism and called upon
moral standards, individual responsibility, and the recognition of a transcendental power. As a system of values beyond human reach, the Church
established a bulwark against human absolutism. It is no wonder that the
deepest roots of resistance against the monolithic state were found in the
religious circles of the confessional fronts.

Conservatives.   This religious appeal was significantly instrumental
in bringing an increasing number among the "substantial classes" into the
opposition camp. Ulrich von Hassell, the refined German diplomat, appeared as their tragic prototype. He hated the National Socialist barbarians for their treason to the Western heritage of religious values, of
law and order, of respect for human personality. He represented the old
aristocracy at its best. A cultured European and knight of a bygone era,
he increasingly realized with rare insight that a turn to reaction would
affect the nation adversely. He sharply criticized "outmoded" Dr. Goerdeler, who was slated to be the political head of the conspiracy in 1944;
and yet von Hassell himself could not find the bridge to the common
man. Throughout modern history, this has been the tragedy of Germany's
enlightened conservatives until they lost their last battle and the best of
their stock in resistance against Hitler.

Labor. The ties of the moderate conservatives with the leftist forces were indeed weak. Still, some of the most significant early leaders of July 20, like Leuschner, Leber, Reichwein, and Haubach, came from the Social Democratic ranks. Moreover, the labor resistance, throughout the whole period, reached down to the roots of trade unions and party organization. And although it never exhibited a marked militancy, and in fact, had given up hope by 1937–38 for an internal overthrow, labor presented a nucleus of post-Nazi leadership for a "new beginning." [6]

Youth. No doubt some of the outstanding and most thoughtful members of the July, 1944, conspiracy belonged to the younger generation. The *Kreisau* Circle around young Counts Helmut von Moltke and Yorck von Wartenburg, in many ways the intellectual sparkplug of the resistance movement, appealed to a new intelligentsia.[7] A number of student incidents, most spectacular among them the Munich demonstrations of Hans and Sophie Scholl and their academic friends, revealed the increasing unrest among German youth. The Nazi defeat at Stalingrad crystallized and helped spread this resistance.

But it was not merely the recognition of pending defeat that converted erstwhile believers into opponents, waiting for the appropriate time to make their convictions known. A progressive disintegration of the total regime had preceded its final breakdown under the concerted Allied attack on the constantly shrinking *Festung Europa.* Hitler's Reich depended a good deal on the acquiescence of the many who had wishfully read into national socialism their own divergent aims and purposes and the many more who simply accepted its all-inclusive institutions, its organized system of interlocking fears, and its ever-pervasive propaganda. The slow recognition of the total state's real character—its infinite cruelties, its fundamental inefficiencies, its flagrant failure to bring promised security, order, and peace—undermined loyalties that were widely given to a functioning system.[8]

Even Goebbels' belated appeal to sacrifice and suffering could not regain the magician's touch over people who, in the hour of Nazi success, had swallowed his propaganda. The failing dictatorship's strategy of terror could caution the resistance; it could not extinguish it. And when in the last stage Hitler abandoned his super-race altogether and decreed a fantastic campaign of self-destruction, his orders were simply ignored, even by some of his lieutenants, such as Speer. Although they may thus have prevented the nation's utter annihilation, the regime had still eaten deeply into the substance of the people, killed its youth, destroyed its cities, pulverized its society, and left in its wake a great void.

[6] *Neubeginnen* was one of its most active left-wing groups.

[7] Note especially, Hans Rothfels, *The German Opposition to Hitler* (1948).

[8] Possibly the best description of this metamorphosis within the articulate intelligentsia is vividly and truthfully described in Bruno E. Werner, *Die Galeere* (1949). An English translation has been published under the title, *The Slave Ship* (1951). This book shows the daily life under the dictator and the step-by-step shift from naïve unawareness of the rising peril through acquiescence in the successful system, sporadic resistance, heroic and hopeless nevertheless, apathetic acceptance, and finally, to the complete emptiness of a burned-out existence.

CHAPTER

17

BASES OF THE SECOND REPUBLIC

1. HEIR TO DICTATORSHIP

The legacy of totalitarianism is a vacuum—political, economic, spiritual. The Second Republic is the heir to dictatorship and defeat. With the surrender on May 8, 1945, the German government ceased to exist and sovereign rights were transferred to the Allied military authorities, whose divided rule spelled the doom of an empire's dream. Berlin, the quartered city, was soon to serve as a telling symbol of this breakdown. Although a new Germany has by now emerged, it still is divided, and the fundamental East-West conflict remains. Germany's political status is a transitional one as far as its frontiers, its leaders, its parties, and its loyalties are concerned.

No doubt this second aftermath of defeat for Germany in this century was altogether different from that of 1918. There was, first, the overwhelming physical destruction. The centers of all major German cities were destroyed beyond recognition, and in many cases, beyond repair, although there has been amazing recovery and reconstruction in recent years. The political disintegration was also an obvious fact. The Versailles peace had left German unity intact. The establishment of the Western German government and the Eastern Peoples' Republic did not restore the power of the erstwhile Reich; rather their creation evidenced the far-reaching dependence of the European balance on the role of the two peripheral superpowers.[1]

In some respects the consequences of World War II do not seem to have fulfilled expectations. First of all, there were many who believed in 1945 that the omnipresent ruins would suffice as a constant warning against the fatal fallacies of war and dictatorship. On the contrary, the ruins have become to many Germans a reminder of the victor's "wrongdoings," and thus, an easy vindication of the vanquished nation's guilt.

---

[1] For a comment on this fundamental transformation of Germany's position and that of Europe as a whole, see Hajo Holborn, *The Political Collapse of Europe* (1951) and W. T. R. Fox, *The Superpowers* (1944).

Even the memory of air raids has produced a certain nostalgia. To the very young those were exciting days—life out of the ordinary, excitement and noise, and a liberating equalization with adults, whose world of security was smashed before their very eyes. Even to the older people, hateful though the whole war atmosphere was to them, without privacy and possessions, the years of destruction have attained a heroic color. That wretched life in the bunkers has been elevated to a cherished memory of great ordeals, to a new "socialism of the trenches."

The human destruction of World War II will have a more lasting effect than the physical leveling of Germany's big cities. In all walks of life, the absence of a missing generation is felt—in politics and economics, as well as in the field of education. An over-aged group, whose crucial experiences date back to the early Weimar days or even to the Wilhelminic era, has assumed control of the key positions. At best, they can be only place-holders. Neither German politics nor its educational system can be built up with men in their seventies and eighties. If there is any hope at all, it lies with the younger generation. This crucial group is still waiting and watching. The youth remains largely outside of the political arena of the present.

One might, however, recognize some promising signs. There is, primarily, the rediscovery of freedom of conversation. This new freedom is especially recognized because of the Soviet dictatorship next door. Were it not for such proximity, liberty would not be so highly prized. But the art of compromise, democracy's fundamental virtue, is often still missing.

Yet an understanding observer may recognize, behind the surface of a confused and complicated jargon (another reminder of dictatorial days and the need for verbal camouflage), a new realism among the young that is very different from the heritage of World War I. They are suspicious of big words because they have become "propaganda-wise." *Nüchternheit* (soberness) has become a popular catchword for the German people, which is not surprising after their sobering experiences.[2] This attitude is a positive legacy of dictatorship. They are critical of, and almost cynical toward, everything, especially toward ideologies. They tend to be skeptical of the present German party system. It is not that they are opposed to politics *per se* or that they are apolitical, but as a young German put it: "I am neither Christian enough to be a Christian Democrat nor Socialist enough to be a Social Democrat." It is a sober and experienced generation, grown old on the battlefields of Russia and in the grim realities of prison camps. It is a pragmatic generation, and as such, it constitutes something really new in German history.

2. BALANCE SHEET OF MILITARY GOVERNMENT

To the historical liabilities of German political development, the existence of military government added a further complication for the future of

[2] Cf. Arnold Wolfers, "West Germany—Protectorate or Ally?" *Yale Review,* 40 (Winter, 1951), pp. 223–24.

German democracy. The transition from military government to civilian authority, and the substitution for the Occupation Statute of a carefully prepared contractual agreement recognizing full domestic sovereignty for the West German Federal Republic marked the end of an era. Now might be a proper time to take account of the results of this military control.[3]

The purposes of the four occupying powers in their respective zones were different and often conflicting after 1945. After the first phase of military control—designed to permit the most effective pursuit of military warfare—was concluded by total victory in all areas, military government still had a twofold task: "The effective elimination of Germany's ability to wage modern war and the reconstruction of German and European life on a democratic basis." The tug-of-war between the

[3] This removal of restrictions on German sovereignty proceeded in a step-by-step development. Although the Allied Control Council and the four zonal governments originally possessed complete authority over Germany (June 5, 1945), the American Military Government from the outset encouraged German political participation on the local and regional (Kreis) level, to be followed by an early recreation of state (Länder) governments, and their coordination on a zone-wide basis through the institution of the Laenderrat (November 6, 1945). See Occupation of Germany, Department of State Publication, No. 2783, pp. 181ff.; Heinz Guradze, "The Laenderrat: Landmark of German Reconstruction," Western Political Quarterly, 2 (June, 1950), pp. 190–213; Harold Zink, The United States in Germany, 1944–1955 (1957).

In similar fashion, the British Zonenbeirat was established; and in the Soviet zone, the Zentral-Verwaltung was set up, although the Soviet Military Administration (S.M.A.) granted this agency merely administrative functions.

The next step was the establishment of the bizonal economic administration of the United States and British zones under the agreement of June, 1948, at the London Conference of the Western Allies. The bizonal arrangement was converted into a trizonal one, and the establishment of the West German Federal Republic followed at a later date. Its creation was accompanied by the proclamation of an Occupation Statute, as agreed on by the three Western foreign ministers at a Washington Conference (April 8, 1949). The subsequent transformation was prepared by the promulgation, on March 7, 1951, of the "First Instrument of Revision of the Occupation Statute." Consult H.I.C.O.G. "The Federal Government Assumes Wider Powers," Report on Germany, 6th Quarterly (January–March, 1951), pp. 35–36; the pertinent documents are included on pp. 128–44.

Pursuant to these decisions, important Allied controls over internal matters were relinquished, and the West German government was authorized to establish a ministry of foreign affairs. On March 13, 1951, Dr. Adenauer, by official act of the Federal Cabinet, was appointed to head the new foreign ministry. See H.I.C.O.G. "The Federal Foreign Office," Report on Germany, 7th Quarterly (April–June, 1951), pp. 22ff.

On May 26, 1952, the federal chancellor and the foreign ministers of the three Western Powers signed the Bonn "Contractual Agreement" which included the Federal Republic as an equal member in the military, economic, and political system of the Western Powers, giving this greater part of Germany an almost absolute sovereignty.

The final "Protocol on the Termination of the Occupation Regime in the Federal Republic of Germany," was signed at Paris, October 23, 1954, and came into force on May 5, 1955, thereby making the German Federal Republic a sovereign state. Though somewhat different from the intentions of the original Bonn Convention (owing to the failure to set up the E.D.C.), the agreements provided the extension of the Federal Republic in the Western European Union and NATO. On these complex problems of Bonn's political integration into Western Europe, see discussion below, pp. 437ff.

objectives of security and democratization constantly created conflicts
that were evidenced in the fluctuating policies, contradictory statements,
and frustrating actions of the military authorities.

Among other directives, the Potsdam Agreement in August, 1945,
instructed the military authorities of the signatory powers to take steps
toward the disarmament, dismantling, de-Nazification, and democratization of Germany. In carrying out these directives, the occupying powers
placed from the very beginning a different emphasis, if not an altogether
different interpretation, on these four aims, depending on the respective
national interests of the powers involved.

To the French, security was naturally the main, if not the exclusive,
concern. All occupation policies were predicated on this objective. Centralization was strictly opposed; the principle of federalism, if not separatism, was strongly supported, for a politically weak and divided Germany
gave promise of greater French security. Living off the land seemed
equally justified for the victorious power that, twice invaded by Germany
in a generation, was deathly afraid of this potentially stronger neighbor.
The integration of the Saar Basin into the French economy, with the
possible prospect of an eventual political absorption, was systematically
pursued. This rich prize, fought over in the past and again in our time,
would certainly have enhanced France's economic potential. The outcome of the Saar elections of 1955 minimized these chances, if it did not
destroy them altogether.

In the meantime, even the positive policies of the French occupational forces, including their notable educational and cultural work, could
be seen as an attempt to reestablish eighteenth-century Germany, which
was divided into territorial principalities and did not constitute a danger
to French security. Whatever the motives, the French occupational policies in cultural matters were not altogether without success, although it is
still doubtful that they have lessened the deep-seated suspicion and
resentment of the Germans.

The Russians followed an equally clear line. The immediate purpose of the Soviet government was to secure reparations for the tremendous losses suffered as the result of Nazi aggression. Dismantling, therefore, was the foremost Russian concern, even if it meant stripping the
German economy and removing capital equipment in violation of the
Potsdam Agreement. Such action did not make the Russians popular
with the German people or with the Western Powers, who for the most
part had to pay with their own contributions for the surrender of reparations taken from Western zones.

The other obvious aim of Russia's policy, and soon the predominant
one, was the establishment of a regime "friendly to the Soviet Union."
Democratization meant to the Russians the establishment of a satellite
regime, and all political forces that resisted such an enforced conformity
were quickly labeled fascist. With the support of bayonets, the Russians
successfully suppressed all oppositional forces within their own zone.
Even though their broader aim to extend their sway over all Germany
failed, at least temporarily, the Soviet Union quickly changed the social
structure of its zone by dividing the big estates and by nationalizing an

ever-increasing segment of German industry. Such a radical transformation, according to Soviet definition, guaranteed the destruction of the true basis of fascism. It certainly crippled the middle class in the Eastern zone.

The British had none of these far-reaching plans. One might even suspect that they originally approached military government as merely another problem in colonial administration, in which they were experienced. A considerable part of the personnel of the British occupation forces was drawn from their far-flung empire, and even the advent of the Labour government in 1945 did not bring about any basic change in the composition of the early occupational echelons. This policy, different from that followed by the United States, possibly made for greater continuity and efficiency of personnel in the British zone. De-Nazification and democratization were played down in the name of a well-functioning administration. Right-wing forces had an opportunity to reassert themselves, and even the former military leaders were not silenced. Dismantling seemed to be the main restrictive policy in the British zone, and here German public opinion quickly suspected fear of future competition in a world market as a main motive of such action. Although this assumption may not be justified, the strict enforcement of dismantling certainly did not enhance British prestige.

The Americans reluctantly entered military government without any expectation of economic gain, and, for this reason, commanded the greatest respect in the beginning from the German populace. Disillusionment could easily follow from exaggerated expectations; in any case, sharp criticism was eventually directed by many Germans against the American Military Government. Having no immediate stake in security or reparations—in contrast to France and the U.S.S.R.—the United States concentrated on the loftier aims of democratization. Although these plans for a "reeducation of Germany" were obviously naïve (if democratization is possible, it can never be enforced from without but only developed from within), it was not mere primitive proselyting ardor that brought about the ambitious policies of "reorientation." Whatever its attainments, American policy was based on the correct realization that dictatorship is not destroyed on the battlefield but must be eradicated from the minds of the conquered.

The German problem was soon complicated by another paramount issue, the East-West split that manifested itself in the Greek Civil War in March, 1947, and in the Czech coup in February, 1948, and was openly declared with the Berlin blockade in June, 1948. From this point on, Germany was dealt with not primarily as a separate problem to be settled on its own merits but as a major factor in the cold war. The split affected, and often frustrated, all measures of de-Nazification and democratization, as well as of disarmament and dismantling. By establishing false fronts and artificial alliances, it gave the Germans the opportunity to play one occupation power against the other. The two-front war against an antidemocratic Germany and a Communist dictatorship, which could easily take advantage of traditional authoritarian instincts in the Reich, demanded flexible finesse and profound knowledge, which even the best among the occupational authorities rarely possessed.

If one draws the balance today, one might single out the United States policy of de-Nazification as having been the greatest failure. This difficult task would have been simplified if it had been initially directed at a clearly defined and rigidly limited group of responsible Nazis and if the process itself had been accelerated. But these steps were not taken. The extraordinary number of persons charged and the inordinate time required for processing their cases led to a general skepticism. Such procedures were not favorable to a democratic reorientation and could, in fact, lead to the reconstitution of the party by creating a large group of former Nazis.[4] Moreover, the formula of a collective German guilt created, unfortunately, a sense of social solidarity that rallied many Germans against de-Nazification. It even led to a widespread feeling of self-justification, according to which Naziism was regarded merely as a political error, or even as a good idea, badly administered, to be blamed only for its failure, not for its immorality. And with the transfer of de-Nazification to German authorities, there was an expected return of many former Nazis of various "gradations" to positions of influence.

In the final analysis, the chances for Nazi revival, still discussed abroad, will depend on the German people's reaction when the foreign military forces are withdrawn altogether. Then the real test of German democracy's positive appeal will come, and the deeper effects of the military government experiment will be fully weighed. In the meantime the invisible and informal influences of the occupation should not be underestimated. The daily encounter with a sincere, democratic force and the possible extension of a well-planned international exchange program might, in the long run, have a lasting effect in instilling democratic procedures and habits and in rewakening respect for civil liberties, for the rule of law, and for constitutional safeguards.

The Occupation Statute for the German Federal Republic still reserved some important controls for the High Commission, composed of representatives of the United States, Britain, and France. The extensive discussion in preparation for an agreement on the basis of equal partnership between the Western Powers and the German Federal Republic had raised the issue of these controls to a new level and tied it up with the security of the whole of Western Europe and the Atlantic community. Yet even this contractual agreement (Convention on Relations with the Federal Republic of Germany), signed together with the European defense treaty (Protocol to the North Atlantic Treaty), by the

[4] The "Law for Liberation from National Socialism and Militarism" (March 5, 1946) was designed, in fact, to counteract this danger. It required the registration and classification of every adult in the American zone in accordance with the minutely worked out questionnaire listing five categories ("Major Offender," "Offender," "Lesser Offender," "Follower," "Exonerated"). Yet, under its stipulation, as many as 27 per cent of the adult population were affected by the trial tribunals. Even after a series of amnesties, some 800,000 persons were made subject to penalties, although only 24,000 were classified in the first two categories as being permanently ineligible to hold public office and to vote. Cf. H.I.C.O.G., *Report on Germany,* 5th Quarterly (October–December, 1950), pp. 46ff. A clever, though utterly cynical, use was made of the "questionnaire" in the best-seller novel by nationalist Ernst von Salomon, *Der Fragebogen* (1951).

foreign ministers of the United States, Britain, France, and the Federal Republic on May 26, 1952, foresaw not only an integration of German armed forces into the NATO but also large non-German contingents stationed on German territory. The function of these latter forces, however, has changed from that of an army of occupation to a protective agency against aggression and to "a contribution to the common defense of Europe and the free world." This change did not come about only because of radical shifts of the international power constellation but also because of the inner recovery of German sovereignty, which found its first full articulation in the approval of the Bonn constitution.

3. THE BONN CONSTITUTION: FORM AND ESSENCE

The basic law for the Federal republic adopted by the German Parliamentary Council at Bonn on May 8, 1949—four years to the day after the unconditional surrender of the Third Reich—marked the end of an interregnum and a new beginning for Germany. A careful analysis of the evolution of this basic law must be made in the light of the military government's waning control and the increasing self-assertion of a political Germany, as molded by new integrating and centrifugal forces.

The Bonn constitution can be traced back to instructions of the military governors to the minister presidents of the western zones on July 1, 1948, "to convene a Constitutional Assembly." This directive reflected the failure of the conferences of Potsdam (July 17–August 2, 1945), of Moscow (March 10–April 24, 1947), and of London (November 26–December 16, 1947), to reach an Allied agreement on unified action. The constitution was to provide a partner for Western European integration; it was to guarantee democratic rule, limited executive and federal powers, strict separation of legislation and civil service, judicial review and an independent judiciary, and the freedom and rights of the individual. Despite successive Allied reservations, letters of advice, memoranda, and daily liaison, the pressures of military government had a very limited effect on the final document.

General Features. The German lawmakers, from the preliminary Chiemsee meeting of experts during August 10–23, 1948, through the protracted sessions of the Bonn Parliamentary Council between September, 1948, and May, 1949, made the basic law their own product. The final document—intricate, complicated, and reminiscent of earlier German constitutions—showed professional skill, seriousness of purpose, democratic resolution, and resistance to all outside interference. It was meant to be only a "provisional" constitution that would not preclude the possibility of a future reunited Reich; yet it had definite character. Above all, it was antitotalitarian (and therefore also decidedly anti-Communist); it was antipagan (and in this sense genuinely Christian, European, and conservative); it was antistatist (and thus deeply concerned with personal freedom and a free enterprise society).[5] However, it did provide for a strong, stable, and efficient government, because it was the handiwork of a generation of seasoned Weimar politicians who wanted to protect the Second Republic against both the failures of the first one and the dangers of a revived national socialism.

Bonn's basic law, like many social documents, was written as a protest against the last usurper. Will it protect Germany against the next aggressor? The answer depends on the nature of the "real" constitution, which will have to prove itself in the future. Within the short period since its promulgation, political developments have resulted in major modifications in the original intentions of the framers of this "draftsman's delight."

Federalism. Especially affected were the provisions outlining the republic's "federal structure," which was imposed upon Bonn by the Western Allies and which was championed by the Christian Democrats (C.D.U., and especially the C.S.U.); but as soon as the elections to the federal Diet gave their leader, Dr. Adenauer, a secure majority in a coalition, the first chancellor of the republic did not hesitate to assert the central government's actual authority, through his almost invulnerable prestige.

The state governments, on the other hand, motivated by their unequal social and financial needs, especially where hard-pressed by a large refugee population and an unbalanced economy, live only by the "sufferance of the federation" and a complicated federal law on the "equalization of financial burdens." [6] The progressive political and administrative centralization of the preceding systems seems to be effective again. True, the Federal Council (*Bundesrat*) is in a somewhat more powerful position than the Weimar *Reichsrat,* but apart from certain financial laws (Arts. 105–115) and emergency legislation (Arts. 80–1), its power is primarily reserved to the introduction of bills (Art. 76), a delaying veto (Arts. 77–78), and participation in the amending process and in the technical aspects of legislation. Despite the fact that the Federal Council has thus regained a stronger position than the Weimar *Reichsrat,* coming somewhat closer to Bismarck's *Bundesrat,* it does not re-establish a genuine bicameral system; with its delegates bound by instructions and selected from their respective state governments, the

[5] The special character of the Bonn constitution was partly due to the different expectations of the major parties. The Christian Democrats tried to make use of their strategically powerful position by anchoring their particular cultural and educational philosophy securely in the "fundamental rights" of the basic law. The Social Democrats, on the other hand, hoping for a stronger representation in the future (and especially in a reunified Germany), wanted to postpone most substantive decisions on social and economic issues. For this reason, the omission of basic social rights, which were explicitly elaborated in the Weimar constitution, might not be construed as a departure from the social-welfare-state concept of the First Republic. See H. P. Ipsen, *Über das Grundgesetz* (1950).

[6] This so-called *Finanzausgleich,* promulgated on March 16, 1951, after protracted negotiations, resulted in an intricate system of tax division between the Federal Republic and the *Länder,* adjusting the differential taxing power of the states through an equalization fund to be used in support of the weaker members.

upper house is essentially a bureaucratic chamber. Each of the ten *Länder* appoints at least three representatives (Saar, Bremen, Hamburg); those with over 2 million inhabitants select four members (Hesse, Rhineland-Palatinate, Schleswig-Holstein); and *Länder* with more than 6 million have five members (Bavaria, Lower Saxony, North Rhine-Westphalia, Baden-Württemberg).

The *Bundesrat* originally included forty-three full members from eleven states. After the consolidation of Baden, Württemberg-Hohenzollern, and Württemberg-Baden in one Southwest State (Baden-Württemberg) and the incorporation of the Saar with its three members, it is now composed of forty-one members, excluding West Berlin's four representatives who attend only in an advisory capacity as "observers."

The president of the *Bundesrat* is elected for one year, chosen successively from the *Länder* prime ministers. The fact that these prime ministers are regular participants in the sessions has given the *Bundesrat* added political prestige. Moreover, the very fact that the composition of the *Bundesrat* is dependent on the prevailing political constellations of the *Länder* governments, which in turn are decided by the *Länder* elections, gives the changing *Länder* coalitions an increasing impact on the stability of the federal government and influence on its legislative program. The shifting fate and sometimes precarious position of the Adenauer regime during the lifetime of the Second *Bundestag,* which in the national elections of September 6, 1953, had returned a safe majority for the chancellor, was largely caused by these political changes in *Länder* governments. The government of the Third *Reichstag* could experience similar shocks, if *Länder* elections in 1957–58 are indicative, and if future *Länder* elections follow past patterns. In this sense, the *Bundesrat* has become a powerful barometer of public opinion between national elections. And yet the upper house, in composition and activities, is not primarily the mouthpiece of popular views but the spokesman of the *Länder* administrations.

The predominance of the ministerial bureaucracy may become even more marked through the office of the chancellor. In fact, he presides over his chosen cabinet of seventeen appointees and their well-trained (and probably over-staffed) administration.[7] Whatever implication this renewed emphasis on the traditionally conservative civil service in a "government by bureaucracy" may have for the future of German democracy,

---

[7] The members of the Cabinet (as of January 1, 1959) were Dr. Konrad Adenauer, Chancellor (C.D.U.); Dr. Ludwig Erhard, Vice-Chancellor and Economic Affairs (C.D.U.); Dr. Heinrich von Brentano, Foreign Affairs (C.D.U.); Dr. Gerhard Schröder, Interior (C.D.U.); Franz-Josef Strauss, Defense (C.S.U.); Franz Etzel, Finance (C.D.U.); Fritz Schäffer, Justice (C.S.U.); Dr. Hermann Lindrath, State-Owned Enterprise (C.D.U.); Dr. Heinrich Lübke, Food and Agriculture (C.D.U.); Theodore Blank, Labor and Social Security (C.D.U.); Dr. Hans-Christoph Seebohm, Transport (D.P.); Paul Lücke, Housing (C.D.U.); Ernst Lemmer, All-German Affairs (C.D.U.); Dr. Hans-Joachim von Merkatz, Bundesrat and State Affairs (D.P.); Richard Stücklen, Post and Telecommunications (C.S.U.); Dr. Theodor Oberländer, Expellees and War Victims (C.D.U.); Dr. Franz-Josef Wuermeling, Family and Youth Affairs (C.D.U.); Dr. Siegfried Balke, Atomic Energy and Water Supply (C.S.U.). *Political Handbook of the World, 1959* (1959), p. 76.

the motivation for the strengthening of the cabinet was the desire for stable government lacking during the period of the Weimar Republic.[8]

Chancellor. The chancellor emerges as the foremost power. His position is reminiscent of that held by Bismarck, though it is possibly even potentially stronger, as the chancellor today is not confronted by a constitutionally powerful and capricious monarch, but by a relatively powerless president. Here again, the basic law tried to counteract a fundamental weakness of the Weimar Republic, namely, the dualism between a popularly elected president and a cabinet responsible to parliament. The fact that the Bonn president is chosen by a federal convention (*Bundesversammlung*), consisting of the members of the Federal Diet (*Bundestag*) and of an equal number of members chosen by the *Länder* parliaments, limits the role of the president and excludes the possibility of a plebiscitary Caesarian democracy. Even though the first incumbent, Theodor Heuss (elected on September 12, 1949 and reelected for a second five-year term on June 17, 1954), may give the office prestige, it still cannot compete in the extent of its power with the Chancellery. It will be interesting to watch the further development of the Presidency, especially if Theodor Heuss should be succeeded by Konrad Adenauer, who might try to give the office a greater political significance.

The federal chancellor (*Bundeskanzler*), on the proposal of the federal president, must be elected by the *Bundestag* (Art. 63); yet he can be overthrown by its motion of censure only after a forty-eight hour interval and only by the election of a successor (Art. 67). Such a requirement of a positive vote of nonconfidence is designed to protect the government against a combination of irresponsible radical parties of the right and left, which had constituted a continuous threat to Weimar's stability. At the same time, this procedure may well permit the chancellor to remain in power, even without parliamentary backing, until he chooses to ask the president for the dissolution of the Federal Diet (Art. 68). In this respect, he has the power to time the elections. Moreover, should the *Bundestag* not be dissolved, the chancellor can, with the approval of the *Bundesrat,* ask the president to declare a state of legislative emergency (Art. 81). Thus the *Bundestag* may be excluded altogether from the exercise of its legislative power—though only for a six-month period during a chancellor's term. There are, no doubt, dangers in such a qualified democracy, with a government once removed from the people and without a directly elected president or the popular initiative (much discredited by its role in the breakdown of the Weimar Republic).

The Second Republic's stability will depend on the working relation-

---

[8] The political role of the civil service is further illustrated by the fact that some 14.5 per cent of the members of the first *Bundestag* had at one time or another been *Beamte*. The corresponding number for the *Landtage* reaches up to 30–40 per cent. Arnold Brecht, "What is Becoming of the German Civil Service," *Public Personnel Review,* 12 (April, 1951), pp. 83–89.

In 1950, federal officials and employees comprised 765,000 persons, i.e., more than 5 per cent of West Germany's total labor force. See Taylor Cole, "The Democratization of the German Civil Service," *Journal of Politics,* 14 (February, 1952), pp. 3–18.

For an astute analysis of the political views and attitudes of the West German civil service, see John H. Herz, "German Officialdom Revisited," *World Politics,* VII (October, 1954), pp. 63–83.

FIG. V

ORGANIZATION OF THE GERMAN FEDERAL REPUBLIC

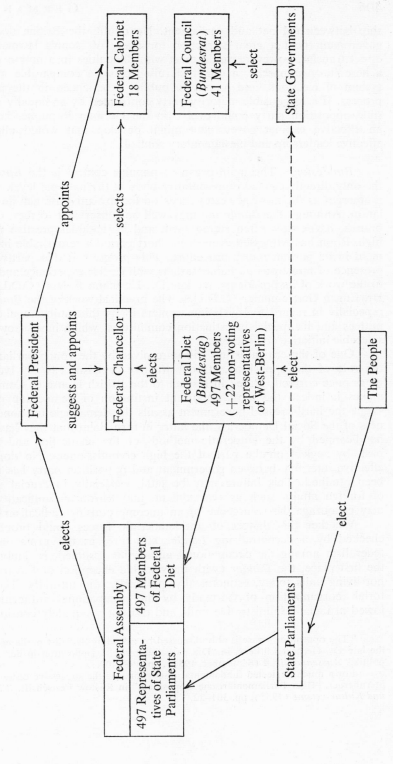

ship between cabinet and parliament. No doubt, the British system of government held a great attraction for many of Bonn's lawmakers; a direct transfer, however, would meet with difficulties in a nation without a hereditary monarchy, a qualified ruling class, a comparable majority system of elections, and a mature public, experienced in the political process. If a responsible majority party confronted by an equally responsible opposition party could evolve in the German Republic, however, an effective cabinet government might develop that would allow for effective leadership and parliamentary control.

Bundestag. The main organ of popular control is the *Bundestag,* the only directly elected representative body at the national level. In fact, it emerges as the most powerful check on the executive branch and legislation. Although the *Bundestag* may well be subservient to the executive branch, its debates often stereotyped, and its national prestige not too high, Bonn has witnessed even in its short period a remarkable improvement in its parliamentary procedure. This progress is due partly to the presence of numerous parliamentarians with earlier experience and partly to the work of its presidents, the late Dr. Hermann Ehlers (C.D.U.) and Dr. Eugen Gerstenmaier (C.D.U.). The practical work of the *Bundestag,* especially in regard to legislation, centers in its thirty-nine regular committees and its special investigation committees, which have shown considerable initiative and success.

One of the critical issues still unresolved by the young parliament is the role of the opposition. Its constructive criticism (as W. Ivor Jennings once correctly stated in respect to the British House of Commons) makes it indeed the most important institution of democratic control. While the hard-pressed government assails the demagogic uncooperativeness of the Social Democrats, the latter in turn claim that they have been handicapped by the autocratic methods of the chancellor and, in the past, by neglect on the part of the high commissioners. No doubt, an effective interplay between government and opposition party has not yet been attained. This failure may be fatal, especially in crucial matters of foreign affairs such as rearmament, and European unification, and may encourage the resurgence of an uncompromising radicalism.[9]

Whether this danger of antidemocratic forces could properly be checked by a decentralizing *Länder* structure, as the protagonists of federalism among the occupational authorities assumed, is doubtful. In the first place, the *Länder* (with the possible exception of Bavaria) are not living units today, economically, politically, or culturally. The territorial reorganization of Germany by the occupational authorities followed artificial administrative units and did not adequately consider cul-

---

[9] The opposition's case is ably discussed by a leading Socialist parliamentarian, the late Dr. Gerhart Lütkens, in "Die parlamentarische Opposition in der Aussenpolitik," *Aussenpolitik,* 2 (September, 1951), pp. 398–407.

For a much neglected fundamental discussion, see the suggestive essay of Dolf Sternberger, "Über Parlamentarische Opposition," in Rüstow Festschrift, *Wirtschaft und Kultursysteme* (1955), pp. 301–22.

tural and historical boundaries and economic problems. It was a temporary structure and clearly recognized as provisional. The Bonn constitution established a complicated procedure of revision, involving the only remaining use of a referendum (Art. 29). The highly controversial and intricate issue of the Southwest State, however, certainly did not produce the expected balancing and revitalization of genuine regional forces.[1]

Moreover, careful students of German constitutional development have shown that in a nation, without the restraining experiences of the western democracies, popular government is not guaranteed by a decentralization of political responsibilities or by a basic emphasis at the local level. If the "grass-root" cells are not genuinely democratic, as is the case in some *Länder,* the strengthening of local and regional forces may open an easy avenue to power for new antidemocratic elements and vested interests.

Political Parties and Democracy. The real test of Germany's democratic future rests with the national parties and their development. During the short history of German parliamentarism, truly democratic parties occasionally mustered strong support and often represented a majority of the electorate; yet it was always an uneasy majority, faced by an articulate and powerful opposition.[2]

The current parliamentary strength of the national parties in Germany may well be deceptive. The political parties, the vital stream of any genuine democracy, still live a shadow existence, reaching only a small percentage of the population. Re-created since the war, the parties are already mortgaged by a past. At first they tended to reflect zonal differ-

[1] Some German advocates of federalism have been deeply concerned about the *Kleinstaaterei* and the economic waste of its present-day forms, and have sought to save German federalism from its own federalists. The governments of the West German states have already amassed 106 ministers, as compared with eighty-seven under the much larger Weimar Republic. See Werner Weber, *Spannungen und Kräfte im Westdeutschen Verfassungssystem* (1951), especially pp. 65ff. For general treatments, see the historical analysis by Walther Vogel, *Deutsche Reichsgliederung und Reichsreform in Vergangenheit und Gegenwart* (1932); the symposium by the Institut zur Förderung Öffentlicher Angelegenheiten, *Die Bundesländer, Beiträge zur Neugliederung der Bundesrepublik* (1950); and H. Peters, *Deutscher Föderalismus* (1947).

On the specific issue of the Southwest State, see HICOG, *Report on Germany,* 7th Quarterly (April–June, 1951), pp. 70ff., and the informative insights in the pamphlet, *Baden 1945–1951; was nicht in der Zeitung steht* (1951).

On December 9, 1951, the electorate in a plebiscite voted overwhelmingly (1,748,136 to 758,518) to consolidate the three southwest German states, Wuerttemberg-Baden, Baden, and Wuerttemberg-Hohenzollern, into one bigger unit. Significantly, Catholic South-Baden voted against the merger, suggesting that the religious schism played an important part in this complex conflict.

[2] For an overall analysis of the history of the German party system, see Sigmund Neumann, ed., *Modern Political Parties* (1956), pp. 354–92. On the Weimar Republic, consult Arnold Brecht's incisive *Prelude to Silence* (1944), pp. 7–14; for a comparison between the last "normal" election of the First Republic in 1928 with the first *Bundestag* election in August, 1949, see the excellent paper, "Analysis and Effects of the Elections in Western Germany," by Otto Kirchheimer and Arnold H. Price, in Department of State *Bulletin,* 21 (October 17, 1949), pp. 563–73.

ences and the coloring of their respective occupational authorities. Since the establishment of the Federal Republic and the coming to office of the coalition led by Dr. Adenauer's Christian Democratic Union, the zonal differences between the three former Western occupation areas have become blurred. Whatever differentiations still exist are based largely on diverse regional social structures of long standing.

One fact impresses even the casual observer of the German party system. It does not reach down to the people. It only represents a thin layer of political activity, superimposed on a country where most of the people still avoid political participation, yet at the same time resent increasingly their exclusion from the counsel of the decision makers. A deep-seated skepticism and a lack of political self-confidence have stifled interest.

Originally, the fear of becoming, or being called, Quislings made the truly politically-minded hesitant to enter fully into party life which, in 1945, looked too much like a controlled experiment under military government. For this and other reasons, there was a return of the old programs and old leaders, who had failed before 1933 and had been eliminated by Hitler. Certainly there was a rejuvenation of the septuagenarians and octogenarians. At the outset, the party system thus resembled that of the Weimar Republic.

Some of the young new leaders who might have emerged were broken, spiritually and physically, in Hitler's concentration camps. Others were lost in futile revolts against the all-powerful dictatorship, the most promising ones being killed after the unsuccessful July, 1944, attempt on Hitler's life. A few young and enterprising politicians appeared in the parliament at Bonn, in regional party headquarters throughout the country, in newspaper offices, and even in sleepy university towns. But a good number among these have already been worn out by the ever-increasing duties and responsibilities necessarily placed upon them. Thus, while Germany waits for a gap of nearly two generations to be filled, the country still remains heavily dependent on the leadership of its elders.

In view of these almost fatal handicaps in the beginning, it is surprising how many new faces, how many new ideals, and how many new movements have appeared in the party arena since 1945, and especially during the most recent period. Perhaps Bonn is not Weimar after all!

Before the amazing story of the first decade of the Federal Republic can be told one must, however, take account of a new and most disturbing phenomenon: the German partition. In fact, one major reason why the Second Republic cannot simply repeat the past pattern is given by this present-day existence of the German Democratic Republic.

4. GERMAN DEMOCRATIC REPUBLIC, EASTERN VERSION

One may easily criticize the German Democratic Republic (D.D.R.) as being neither German nor democratic nor republican, but one must also remember that it includes almost 18 million people,[3] a third of the former German territory and much of the original agricultural and industrial potential. And while it does not offer any challenging "constitutional" features, its monolithic control over the eastern provinces constitutes a power factor which may decide Germany's future. As such it represents a reservoir of Communist strength, and its impact on Western Germany should not be underestimated.

True, the intimate contact with the realities of Soviet overlordship in the eastern zone has created more opposition to the revolutionary myth than may be found in either France or Italy. At the same time, the very proximity of the Soviet fatherland commands respect, if not fear, this side of the Iron Curtain. To some German youth, accustomed to discipline and direction, Communist totalitarianism may even seem to provide renewed certainty, devotion, sacrifice, and community spirit. The German Democratic Republic has also become a not-so-silent, though indirect, partner in the functioning party system of Bonn; each failure of the western republic to solve its persistent problems of unemployment, refugees, military security, and, above all, national unity gives the eastern German administration opportunity to appeal through open "peace" propaganda and clandestine terror techniques to dissatisfied masses.

The political structure of the eastern zone does not warrant much discussion. It is definitely not described by its constitution. The constitution of the D.D.R. was initiated by the Socialist Unity Party (S.E.D.), and a hand-picked conference of delegates (the *Deutsche Volkskongress*, December 6–12, 1947), was prepared by its elected executive committee (the *Deutsche Volksrat*), was submitted to a newly elected second *Volkskongress* (its plebiscite of May 15, 1949, recorded a surprising number of 6.7 per cent invalid votes and an explicit opposition vote of 33.9 per cent), and was approved by a vote of 2,087 to 1 (May 30, 1949). Although it pretended a constitutional continuity by a close textual adaptation of the Weimar constitution, the meaning of the constitution was completely revamped according to the "principles" of the satellites' *Volksdemokratie*. In contrast to the western "formal" political democracy, the eastern state claimed to establish an immediately effective legal order of a "real" social democracy.[4]

In reality the political process reflects the established dictatorial techniques of appealing to the people's democratic memories by formal adherence to popular sham elections, parties, and institutions—gestures that are doubly important in view of the Soviet aim to win over Western Germany.

The election to the People's Chamber (*Volkskammer*) of October

[3] The population estimate for 1954 was 17,830,000 (including East Berlin). This figure represented a decline of almost one million within the last half-decade. The population of the Federal Republic had increased by more than two million to 52 million during the same period, an increase largely due to the continuous stream of refugees from the eastern zone.

[4] See K. Polak, *Marxismus und Staatslehre* (1947); Karl Steinhoff, *Die Verfassung der Deutschen Demokratischen Republik* (1950); and W. Abendroth, "Zwiespältiges Verfassungsrecht in Deutschland," *Archiv des öffentlichen Rechts*, 76 (1950), pp. 1ff.

15, 1950, brought out 98.5 per cent of the eligible citizens, with 99.3 per
cent of these voting for the Unity list of the so-called National Front
(thus even outdoing the Nazi-organized plebiscite of 1936 with its mere
98.8 per cent support). Its pretense of non-party national unity was
illustrated by its complex composition. Apart from the S.E.D. representatives, the coalition included members of the "co-ordinated" middle-class
parties, the eastern C.D.U. and Liberal Democratic party (L.D.P.), the
Communist-created National Democratic party (N.D.P.) and the Democratic Farmers' party (D.B.P.), the last of which tries to activate the
peasants and the "little Nazis." In addition to these party groups—and
as painful reminders of the Third Reich's totalitarian control and penetration—auxiliary mass organizations, such as the Free German Trade
Union League (with more than 5 million members), The Free German
Youth (claiming 3 million members), and the Democratic Women's
Union held 30 per cent of the new Chamber's 400 seats. According
to the constitution, all parties must participate in the government, i.e.,
must be subservient to the S.E.D. The election to the People's Chamber
(October 17, 1954) showed the same predictable results as the first
parliamentary plebiscite. Out of a registered electorate of 12,085,380,
some 11,892,849 votes were cast, comprising 11,828,877 for the National
Front and 63,972 invalid ballots.

The declared supremacy of the People's Chamber in a system that emphasizes the rejection of the Western concept of "separation of powers"
becomes a farce in view of the actuality of complete control by the
executive over all other branches of government. Equally illusory is the
much-advertised *block system,* which, by doing away with the "outmoded
bourgeois and undemocratic" idea of competing political parties, is supposed to guarantee full responsibility and adequate participation of the
opposition. In fact it creates a complete conformity of parliament with
government—a *Gleichschaltung*—frighteningly reminiscent of Goebbels'
"ennobled democracy." [5]

The long-range objective of Soviet control over the whole of Germany, however, does not delay the Communists' immediate plan to consolidate their complete command over the eastern zone. Comprehensive
centralization is the password of the regime. It has not only degraded the
ministries to mere administrative organs,[6] but has also sapped the foundations of the five *Länder* of the Democratic Republic, despite the early
institution of an upper chamber (*Länderkammer*) alongside the People's
Chamber. In July, 1952, these traditional *Länder* (Brandenburg, Meck-
lemburg, Saxony, Saxony-Anhalt, and Thuringia) were dissolved and their

[5] For an official analysis, see Alfons Steiniger, *Das Blocksystem* (1949), and
Karl Polak "Staatsform und Verfassungsstruktur der Volksdemokratie," in *Neue
Justiz* (1950), pp. 291, 327.
[6] In fact, the cabinet comprises so many ministries (with numerous sub-
branches especially in the economic departments) that it never meets as a whole and
only serves as a technical agent. The actual policy decisions are in the hands of
"Co-ordinators" of an inner-cabinet, officially under the leadership of Minister President Otto Grotewohl, in reality under the thumb of the all-powerful first deputy
president Walter Ulbricht. Especially appointed independent agencies exercise additional party control over government and administration.

respective governments and parliaments abolished. These steps, together with the elimination of the provincial committees of the East German political parties, point to a further centralizing of party administration. A new monolithic authoritarianism has been established.

The control pattern and techniques are similar to those applied in other Eastern European satellite states, with modifications appropriate to the special case, yet always in line with the foreboding fluctuations of Soviet world strategy. Here, as elsewhere, the main agent of Sovietization is the Communist Party. Although it calls itself the Socialist Unity Party (S.E.D.),[7] after the forced merger of eastern Socialists and Communists in April, 1946, it quickly abandoned the rule of parity, eliminated former Socialist leaders, and put trustworthy, Moscow-trained functionaries into key positions. Continuous and ruthless purges of its restive members are designed to enforce party discipline.[8]

A Politburo presides over the one-party state, and Secretary-General Walter Ulbricht is the undisputed boss in the Soviet zone, despite the titular government positions of aged State President Wilhelm Pieck and Prime Minister Otto Grotewohl, a former Social Democratic leader. Until now, at least, Ulbricht seems to have weathered some most precarious

[7] For a reliable collection of materials, see Carola Stern, *Die SED. Ein Handbuch über Aufbau, Organisation and Funktion des Parteiapparates* (1954) and her more recent *Porträt einer Bolschewistischen Partei* (1957).

[8] A recent purge (February, 1958) affected the following key men of the system: Fritz Selbmann, Minister of Heavy Industry; Ernst Wollweber, dreaded master of the State Security System; Karl Schirdewan and Fred Oelssner, members of the powerful "Politburo." The official membership statistics of the S.E.D. show the following changes:

April, 1946		
(at the time of merger)	K.P.D.	619,256
	S.P.D.	679,159
		1,298,415
June, 1948	S.E.D.	2,000,000
April, 1954	S.E.D.	1,413,313

The decline is largely due to the purging and/or resignation of former S.P.D. partisans. Many of the members obviously joined and stayed in the party for opportunistic reasons only.

Interesting is the shifting social composition. The percentage of industrial workers declined during 1947–1954 from 47.9 per cent to 39.1 per cent. This figure should be adjusted downwards even further, as the official party classification registers its members in terms of "occupational training," thus covering up the large percentage of governmental and party officials who were once workers.

The changing per cent in the age pyramid is equally revealing:

	Under 21	21–30	31–40	41–50	over 50
1947	6.8	13.6	23.7	27.3	29.2
1950	8.8	11.0	18.7	27.6	33.9

Cf. Carola Stern, *Porträt,* p. 284.

On the persistent difficulties of the S.E.D. in the recruitment, organization, and purging of a tight inner core of party functionaries who direct a loosely-knit outer ring of followers, see Joachim Schultz, *Der Funktionär in der Einheitspartei: Kaderpolitik und Bürokratisierung in der Sozialistischen Einheitspartei Deutschlands* (1956).

phases in a ruthless power struggle by carefully adjusting the changing policies to the shifts in the Communist party line.[9]

Even the German popular rising of June 17, 1953, and its aftermath were linked with the internal Soviet struggle leading to Beria's fall. This critical revolt, without precedent in a totalitarian state, was planned in the belief that the Russians were ready to sacrifice Ulbricht and his followers. When instead the Soviet troops intervened to "restore order," the bankrupt S.E.D. internally and the D.D.R. internationally received new leases on life. The tragic events of Berlin foreshadowed the later Soviet moves in the even bloodier Hungarian revolt.[1]

This East German system has in fact become a replica of the Third Reich, including its dreaded concentration camps. The law for the protection of peace, promulgated on December 15, 1950, is a good illustration of the new terroristic devices for the enforcement of conformity.

It is in this context, and not as a mere response to Western rearmament, that the militarization of the former Eastern "zone" must be evaluated. A paramilitary police force of 110,000 men, reenforced by 10,000 air police, 9,000 naval police, and about 40,000 transport and frontier police; the S.E.D. fighting groups, organized since the June revolt and numbering perhaps 100,000; and hundreds of thousands of young men and women, given military training through the Society for Sports and Technology—all these forces add up to a military potential by far outnumbering the much-publicized army of the Federal Republic which has not developed much beyond its initial skeleton formations.[2] Moreover, the Eastern troops, in contrast to the stress in the Federal Republic, significantly pride themselves in the restoration of the traditional military uniforms, organizations, and personnel. Such a calculated recall and transfer of past glory may not be without effect on the impressionable populace. The May Day parade of 1956 in Berlin gave a

[9] These continuous policy reversals are visible in the changing composition of the Politbüro. See the writings of Carola Stern, cited in Footnotes 7 and 8, p. 411.

[1] For an accurate report of the June rising, see Stefan Brant, *The East German Uprising* (1955); also see the sensitive account, "Der Aufstand im Juni," *Der Monat* (September, 1953), pp. 596–624 and (October, 1953), pp. 45–66.

[2] See Carl G. Anthon, "East Germany," *Current History,* 30 (April, 1956), pp. 231–37. These figures, as of 1956, are the latest available. They are higher at this time. We must also remember that in consequence (or independent) of the Federal Republic's inclusion in the Western defense system, the D.D.R. has been increasingly tied to the East-European satellite system, as witness her attendance at the Moscow conference on the "Safeguarding of Peace and Security in Europe" (December, 1954), her formal agreement to the Warsaw Pact together with the U.S.S.R. and the Eastern satellites (May 14, 1955), and the official union of all armed forces (January, 1956) with the D.D.R. defense minister Willy Stoph serving as Deputy Commander of the Warsaw Pact forces.

Added to these "security measures" must be mentioned the "temporary stationing" of an estimated 400,000 Soviet troops in East Germany, whose presence is regulated by a treaty between the U.S.S.R. and the D.D.R. of March, 1957, which allows the Soviet army to intervene "in case of a threat to Soviet Armed forces" (Article 18). For these crucial military aspects and for a judicious overall evaluation, see Melvin Croan and Carl J. Friedrich, "The East German Regime and Soviet Policy in Germany," *Journal of Politics,* 20 (February, 1958), pp. 44–63.

foretaste of a reconstituted army at the service of an unscrupulous and determined regime.

Although these aggressive institutions are the most disturbing features of the system, the revolutionary Sovietization of industry and agriculture may be of even more lasting importance. This transformation, especially in the industrial field, has led to a far-reaching socialization that has whittled down the "capitalist" sector to less than 15 per cent of the total East German population, according to Ulbricht's statement, before the third Party Conference.[3]

The Soviet Zone's plans (the Two-Year Plan from 1949–50, the First Five-Year Plan from 1951–56, and the Second Five-Year Plan after 1956) are transforming the former Eastern German provinces to such a degree that unification with the West will become increasingly difficult. At the same time the decision of the S.E.D. in July, 1952 to "build the foundations of socialism" and to reject any special German form of socialism, as advocated by old Communists like Anton Ackermann and Franz Dahlem (both ousted from party positions in the aftermath of the June, 1953 uprising), has led the East German economy to a chaotic situation marked by overplanning and bureaucratic complexities. The results have been continuous dissatisfaction and unrest among the working population, occasioned in part by shortages of meat, potatoes, and vegetables in this former breadbasket of the nation.

All these difficulties should, however, not mislead the careful observer into assuming that the East German economy has remained stagnant. On the contrary, at least according to official statistics, the production, both industrial and agricultural, at the end of 1953 was 77 per cent above that of 1936; crude steel production by 1954 was double that of 1936 (and approximately 12 per cent of Germany's total production in 1954, in contrast to around 7.7 per cent in 1938); foreign trade has tripled since 1950 and, while 75 per cent of this trade is going to the U.S.S.R., vigorous and not entirely unsuccessful efforts have been made to expand the western markets, as reflected in the amazing development

[3] See *Neues Deutschland,* March 26, 1957; cf. also Walter Möbius, "Die Stellung der privatkapitalistischen Betriebe in unserer anti-faschistisch-demokratischen Ordnung," *Die Arbeit* (July, 1951); on labor, trade unions, wage structure, labor compulsion, see O.I.R., Department of State, "The Status of Labor in Eastern Germany," Intelligence Report, No. 546 (October, 1951).

On recent experimental plans for state participation in the financing of the remaining private enterprise, cf. Helmut Sandig, "Zur Problematik der staatlichen Beteiligung an privatkapitalistischen Betrieben," *Einheit,* (March, 1957).

The changes within the agrarian structure were even more far-reaching. Above all, they spelled the end of the *Junkers,* whose large estates, as well as all other holdings over 100 hectares were expropriated and redistributed among tenant farmers, workers, and expellees, bringing the average farm size down to 7–9 hectares. Cf. H. O. Lewis, *New Constitutions in Occupied Germany* (1948); see also Hartmut Zimmermann, "Die Wirtschaft der Sowjetzone zu Beginn des Zweiten Fünfjahrplanes," *Die Neue Gesellschaft,* 3 (March–April, 1956), pp. 110–15.

For a comprehensive picture of the planned attempt at reshaping the East German regime in the image of the U.S.S.R., cf. J. P. Nettl, *The Eastern Zone and Soviet Policy in Germany 1945–1950* (1951) and the more recent Horst Duhnke, *Stalinismus in Deutschland; Die Geschichte der Sowjetischen Besatzungszone* (1955).

of shipping from such Baltic ports as Wismar and Rostock. Disregarding the methods applied and the price paid, these achievements are impressive, and especially in view of the fact that the U.S.S.R. had through dismantling reduced the area's total industrial capacity by at least one half during the early years after 1945.

It is in comparison to the economic revival of the Federal Republic that the East Zone economy shows up poorly. But comparisons of daily experiences in the East, with the abundance and freedom of the West, are not permitted behind this part of the "Iron Curtain." The D.D.R. is trying to narrow this gap between eastern and western economic standards, in order to provide a stronger material foundation for what is already a politically militant regime.[4]

Berlin remains the island and the proving ground. The mere existence of West Berlin as a bastion of democratic life and its stubborn refusal to capitulate is a persistent threat to the Eastern regime. Efforts at absorption by the D.D.R. have by no means ceased, even after the dismal failure of the Berlin blockade in 1948. The isolated city is incessantly attacked through a type of "creeping blockade," which presents a continuous threat to it. All these attempts were pushed with renewed vigor after "sovereignty" was bestowed on the D.D.R. by Soviet Russia in March, 1954, and after the Moscow conference of September, 1955 (itself a sequel to Adenauer's visit to the Kremlin) when the Soviet commandant declared the Four Power Control in Berlin at an end. Khrushchev's threat, late in 1958, to turn over to the D.D.R. the Soviet-controlled communication lines from the Federal Republic to Berlin provoked the most serious crisis to date.

Yet, even after this formal acknowledgment of its independence by the U.S.S.R., the German Democratic Republic has remained a creature of the Soviet Military Adminstration (S.M.A.), its civil successor after June, 1950, the Soviet Control Commission, and of the German Communist Politburo. It has not been recognized by the Federal Republic and the Western powers. It will last as long as the Soviet occupation forces protect it; it could not stand the test of a free election and may not even be sure of its own functionaries, as numerous defections attest. If the Soviet Union expected to win over the people of Eastern Germany, it has failed. Yet this present record does not imply that Communist rule may not have a lasting impact.

In a totalitarian system it is not necessary to have a large popular following. The backing of about 20 per cent of the populace may

---

[4] For an appraisal of the zonal economy, seen as a transitional period to socialism over a long period, note Fred Oelssner, *Die Übergangsperiode vom Kapitalismus zum Sozialismus in der deutschen Demokratischen Republik* (1955). For a critical view of these reformist critics see also Anton Ackermann, "Gibt es einen besonderen deutschen Weg zum Sozialismus?" in *Einheit*, 1 (1946), p. 22ff.

A comprehensive study of the structural changes in the zonal society is presented in Otto Stammer, "Sozialstruktur und System der Werthaltungen der sowjetischen Besatzungszone Deutschlands," *Schmollers Jahrbuch für Gesetzgebung, Verwaltung u. Volkswirtschaft*. See the entire March, 1957, issue of *Einheit*, which deals with these changes, and especially the article "Zur Ökonomischen Theorie and Politik in der Übergangsperiode."

suffice to smash all opposition. The Soviet Union may have built up such support in Eastern Germany, especially among the susceptible youth. Certainly, no efforts are being spared to bolster this support.[5] And, given a sufficient period of enforced insulation from the outside world, continuous improvement of living standards within the zone, and a complete economic coordination under the aegis of the Council for Mutual Economic Assistance (the so-called Molotov Plan, instituted on September 29, 1950 as a counter to the Marshall Plan), the German Democratic Republic may permanently be incorporated into the Soviet satellite system. In the meantime a highly developed propaganda from the East is directed with some measure of success against the government of West Germany; in the guise of a ceaseless campaign for German unification and world peace, it denounces the Bonn Republic as a force of reaction, remilitarization, and neo-fascism.

[5] For the tremendous efforts to indoctrinate young Germans, see the comprehensive studies by M. G. Lange, *Totalitäre Erziehung: Das Erziehungssystem der Sowjetzone Deutschlands* (1954) and *Wissenschaft im Totalitären Staat: Die Wissenschaft der Sowjetischen Besatzungszone auf dem Weg zum "Stalinismus"* (1955); also the revealing autobiography of Wolfgang Leonard, *Die Revolution entlässt ihre Kinder* (1955), translated under the title of *Child of the Revolution* (1958).

For the continuous unrest among the academic youth, especially in the period of the "Great Thaw" in the follow-up of the Twentieth Congress of the Communist Party of the U.S.S.R., and the measures to combat its effects, see Gerd Böttger, "Die politische Situation an den Hochschulen," *SBZ-Archiv,* June 25, 1957, pp. 178–83. A good analysis of the systematic mass manipulation and a penetrating examination of the state apparatus in the Soviet zone can be found in Ernst Richert, *Agitation und Propaganda* (1958) and *Macht ohne Mandat* (1958).

18

BONN: THE FIRST DECADE

1. EXECUTIVE LEADERSHIP

The past ten years seem to have telescoped several generations into one in this fast moving century. For Germany, they have witnessed an amazing recovery from total defeat and a return to a position as a world power. To interpret finally the direction of this whirlwind development is impossible. This miracle of Germany's startling revival leaves the interpreter hopelessly uncertain in his analysis and in deep doubt about the nature and strength of the underlying forces responsible for this mushroom growth. It is still too early to give an exacting account of what has already happened, and even more impossible to predict with any finality the future trends in Germany. At best, this can only be an exploratory and tentative inquiry.

There is the question of Germany's sovereignty. The *Bundesrepublik* has been a fully independent state since 1955, with all its appropriate institutions for law-making and law enforcement, for the exercise of the treaty-power, and for international representation. However, the enforced partition of the Reich makes the real meaning of this sovereignty unclear.

No doubt the very existence of the D.D.R. serves to frustrate the aspirations for a reunited Germany and thereby provides a constant element of unrest. At the same time, whatever those long-range chances for reunification may be, the present international constellations call for an accommodation of the German people within a divided Reich. This situation creates divided loyalties, if not a split personality. Surface reaction and underlying response may not always be identical or the difference between them clearly discernible to the responsible observer, who is left with doubt and uneasiness as to the future of the Reich.

One element of stability (though possibly of immobility as well) is provided by the continuation of experienced leadership in Bonn, as personified in that fruitfully complementary combination of Theodor Heuss and Konrad Adenauer. Both have exercised a considerable, if

416

not decisive, influence on the daily decisions during the decade, and they have thus helped stabilize the major institutions of the young republic.

Theodor Heuss, President of the German Federal Republic, did not seek the presidency, but, having been elected twice to the presidency (in 1949 and 1954), gave the office meaning and dignity. Its prominence is dimmed by the power of the chancellor whose position has priority resulting not only from his constitutional powers but even more so from the practices of the Second Republic.

Heuss is the best that German liberalism can offer. He has fought for German democracy since his youth, when he was a disciple of Friedrich Naumann, the outstanding ethical reformer at the turn of the century. A leader of the Democratic Party in the days of the Weimar Republic, he represents most that is worth saving of the traditions of that era. Further, he is a gifted publicist, a historian, and a teacher, having served as the first Director of the pre-1933 *Deutsche Hochschule für Politik*. He returned to the academic life after 1945, but he was soon active as a leader of the newly founded Free Democratic Party. After his election to the presidency in 1949, he not only resigned from his other public offices (in accordance with the regulations of the basic law), but he also terminated his membership in the Free Democratic Party. This voluntary act gave him in the German political scene a unique position, indeed one most appropriate to his personality.

He has always been a sincere broker and a great balancer, and he played these roles particularly well during the struggles to draft the Bonn constitution. His characterization of his position as minister of education in Wurttemberg in the early postwar years—"I give no directives, I give atmosphere"—applies equally well to him as President of the Republic. He has made this office a vital symbol of stability and national unity, an end not realized by his predecessors of Weimar days. The myth of the monarchy has been killed. "Father" Heuss has filled the void. He has become the proven moderator of daily conflicts within a tense society, within a strained government coalition, and within a divided world. He has softened political antagonisms and humanized institutional tools with the disarming directness of a genuine Swabian liberal, and he has helped restore respect for Germany abroad.[1]

If the president sets the tone of the Second Republic, the chancellor articulates its themes. Towering over the mediocrities at Bonn, Konrad Adenauer neither looks nor acts his age. In fact, this octogenarian's fixed face seems to be as impenetrable as his life.

[1] The unique and representative position of the first *Bundespräsident,* Theodor Heuss, has been well appraised in Hans Bott, ed., *Begegnungen mit Theodor Heuss* (1954); and Margaret Boveri, *Theodor Heuss: Die literarische Gestalt* (1954); see also H. H. Welchert, *Theodor Heuss: Ein Lebensbild* (1953). Of Heuss's numerous publications, the following may be most revealing as to his personality: *Vorspiele des Lebens: Jugenderinnerungen* (1953); *Friedrich Naumann* (2nd. ed., 1949); *Deutsche Gestalten: Studien zum 19. Jahrhundert* (1949); *1848; Werk und Erbe* (1948); *Verfassungsrecht und Verfassungspolitik vom monarchischen Konstitutionalismus zum demokratischen Parlamentarismus* (1950); and his selection of speeches and writings 1949–1955, *Würdigungen* (1955).

Adenauer is one of the great statesmen of the twentieth century, whom one must characterize by the use of such contrasts as astute and arrogant, committed and cynical, indefatigable and decent, stubborn and sensitive, autocratic and humane, austere and impatient. It is impossible to reduce the "Old Man" to a simple formula. He has tremendous will-power and strictly disciplined ambitions. Moreover, he has an unblemished record as a courageous, though cautious, fighter for democracy. His political foes accuse him of being an autocrat, and even his close collaborators complain at times about his authoritarian attitudes. In fact, his leadership may be best described as a type of paternalism. It is a product of both his personal experiences and of the historical setting, and has been accepted by a society ready for it at this time.[2]

Cologne and Catholicism are at the basis of Adenauer's political world. The proud Rhineland traditions of independence and individualism, of industry and pious serenity, found their best expression in the man who as Lord-Mayor from 1917–1933 turned old Cologne into a model city. He was one of many German public servants (including Luther, Jarres, Koch-Weser, Gessler, Sahm, Goerdeler) whose first political experiences were in municipal and provincial administration. This type of laboratory was a cradle of conservative democrats. Whatever be the nature of the final popular controls, the concepts of democratic leadership of the men nurtured in this tradition were, no doubt, colored by their daily experiences in making frequent decisions on their own initiative. When at the age of seventy Adenauer started his career at the national and international levels, it was certainly shaped in terms of his impressive experiences as a pragmatic, down-to-earth administrator, one who was ready to assume responsibilities and who had a deep disdain for the demagogue and for vague, irresponsible criticism. For this reason, he has found it hard to understand the crucial function of Her Majesty's Opposition and even more difficult to picture himself as the leader of such opposition—a position which he might easily have occupied after each past *Bundestag* election. Adenauer's bureaucratic background of pre-Hitler days may have closed the door to a full appreciation of this aspect of a democratic-parliamentary political system.

This is not to say that the chancellor of Bonn did not play a significant role on the national scene during the Weimar era. As permanent president of Prussia's second chamber, his influence was considerable

[2] For a most suggestive interpretation along these lines, see Edgar Alexander, *Adenauer and the New Germany* (1957). This first significant attempt at placing this complex personality into such a historical setting opens the door for other interpretations of the past, present, and future of Germany. Apart from this introductory study, which is to be followed by a comprehensive two-volume study, Adenauer's life and work have not received much attention. For a factual and, in places, fascinating account, cf. Paul Weymar, *Konrad Adenauer* (1955). The paternalistic democracy of this "autocrat of the breakfast table" is strikingly illustrated by a half humorous remark of his oldest daughter, Frau Ria Reiners: "Since my childhood days the democratic maxim prevailed in our home: the children have complete freedom to want everything that father wishes." Ibid., p. 257.

and his advice widely sought. In fact, he almost became German chancellor in 1926, a possibility which—considering him as an alternative to Brüning—allows for intriguing conjectures as to lost opportunities during the First Republic.[3]

This contrast between the defeated Chancellor Brüning and the "chancellor of the defeated" suggests another aspect of Adenauer's political personality. Christian statesman though he be, he is a declared foe of the political clericalism and the narrow confessionalism of numerous leaders of the old Catholic Center. His purpose in helping create a united front of Protestants and Catholics in the founding of the C.D.U. was to fill the spiritual vacuum left by the Nazis through stress on the ethical principles of natural law and of human dignity, basic to Western Christian civilization. The realization of this aim within his own heterogeneous party and, even more, within a divided governmental coalition demands effective strategy. But this veteran of the political game sees the jealousies and weaknesses of his opponents and, as a past master of political realism (and of a well-organized party machine), knows how to utilize them.

Adenauer also recognizes the basic dilemmas of his own people. In quiet conversation, he will confess some concern about the political future of his people, who lack two fundamental qualities for a working democracy: a sense of fair play and compromise and an ability to recognize the attributes of responsible leadership. A half-century of experience in public affairs gives him justified concern about his country's strength to resist the rise of another demagogue. In the meantime, he holds the reins with a strong hand, and serves as the successful spokesman for political stability, ethical conservatism, and economic recovery.

While in Germany he has thrice won electoral victories with increased majorities in each instance, Adenauer wishes also to be a European statesman. In fact, it may well be in the international field that he will make his lasting reputation.

The political future of Germany will depend heavily on the critical issue of succession. To be sure, there is no new Adenauer in sight to follow the present chancellor, but, after all, Adenauer's has been a unique role for a special period. His primary task of mastering the chaos inherited from the Hitler debacle called for trustworthy leadership to lend a strong and sympathetic hand to democratic growth. Adenauer's paternalistic guidance provided this. Much has been said recently about the prevailing father image in political leadership of present-day America. There seemed to be a more pressing need for this quality of leadership during the transitional period of post-dictatorial Germany. However, the supreme test of Bonn's maturity will only be passed when the chief feature of western democracy, a functioning party system, has been effectively achieved.

[3] On the implications of this incident as a revealing case study on perplexing problems of the Weimar regime, see the informative essay of Fritz Stern, "Adenauer and a Crisis in Weimar Democracy," *Political Science Quarterly*, 73 (March, 1958), pp. 1–27.

2. THE PARTY SYSTEM

The demise of the monarchical myth and the successful assertion of
executive leadership are landmarks of Bonn's new political scene. Even
more distinctive have been the transformations in the process of legislation and in the functioning of the political parties.[4] Indeed, the changes
in the party pattern amount to a silent revolution in German politics. Out
of the seemingly persistent multi-party groupings, a clear concentration
around two major blocks appears to be evolving, evidencing ever-
increasing similarities to the Anglo-American two-party system. The
combined strength of the two major parties (C.D.U. and S.P.D.) comprised 60.2 per cent of the total vote cast in 1949; 74 per cent in 1953;
and 82 per cent in 1957. At the same time extremist parties, which
had undermined and finally destroyed the Weimar Republic, have for
all practical purposes disappeared in the Second Republic. These developments, which augur well for the future, have occurred within the
short span of a decade. They are the more surprising as, in the beginning,
the Bonn party system looked very much like an older and weaker
edition of that of the First Republic.

There was nothing but chaos in 1945 when the "Thousand Years'
Reich" collapsed, after only twelve years of the total yoke. Gone were
Hitler and his lieutenants and the one-party state. The law of the land
was that of the occupying powers, and they decreed the early restoration
of German political parties. Though one might argue about the wisdom
of this decision (which in a way was forced on the Western powers by
the early provision for political institutions in the Soviet Zone), it
definitely gave a direction to the re-established parties. Their early,
possibly premature, revival naturally encouraged the restoration of the
pre-Nazi system. The old leaders, programs, and some of the membership reappeared almost as they were when they had gone underground
with the coming of the one-party state twelve years earlier. This was a
bad omen for a fresh start. In view of this almost fatal handicap, it was
surprising how many new faces, how many new ideas, and, in fact, how
many new trends could be noticed in the party arena after a very short
time.

In the beginning, of course, the military government placed heavy
restraints on the developing parties; in fact, there was a danger that the
pseudo-parliamentarism of the Bismarck Empire, with its political irresponsibility, might recur. As the final word in crucial policy decisions was given by the Allied military governments, the party leaders

---

[4] It is obviously too early to expect an analysis of Bonn's party system; for
preliminary, yet substantial, case studies, see the publications of the Berlin Institut
für Politische Wissenschaft, especially *Die Parteien in der Bundesrepublik* (1955)
and Wolfgang Hirsch-Weber *et al., Wähler und Gewählte* (1957). See also the incisive essay of F. R. Allemann, "Das Deutsche Parteiensystem," *Der Monat*, 52
(1953), pp. 365–88, and the informative compendium of Ludwig Bergsträsser, *Geschichte der Politischen Parteien in Deutschland* (9th ed., 1955), and F. A. von der
Heydte and K. Sacherl, *Soziologie der deutschen Parteien* (1955).

FIG. VI

BUNDESTAG ELECTIONS, 1949–1957
(DEPUTIES, EXCLUDING BERLIN DELEGATES)

	POSITION IN THE SECOND BUNDESTAG	VOTES RECEIVED 1957	PERCENTAGE OF VALID VOTES			THIRD BUNDESTAG	SECOND BUNDESTAG		FIRST* BUNDESTAG
			1957	1953	1949		AT START	AT END	
C.D.U./C.S.U.	Govt.	15,008,399	50.2	45.2	31	270	244	255	139
S.P.D.	Opp.	9,495,571	31.8	28.8	29.2	169	151	153	131
F.D.P.	Opp.	2,307,135	7.7	9.5	11.9	41	48	36	52
G.B./B.H.E.	Opp.	1,374,066	4.6	5.9	—	—	27	19	—
D.P. (D.P./F.V.P.)	Govt.	1,007,282	3.4	3.3	4	17	15	33	12
Deutsche Reichspartei	Not rep.	308,564	1.0	1.1	—	—	—	—	—
Föderalistische Union	Opp.	254,322	0.85	2.5	—	—	2	1	—
Bund der Deutschen	Not rep.	58,725	0.19	—	—	—	—	—	—
Deutscher Mittelstand	Not rep.	36,362	0.12	—	—	—	—	—	—
Südschleswigscher Wählerbund	Not rep.	32,262	0.10	0.2	—	—	—	—	—
Deutsche Gemeinschaft	Not rep.	17,490	0.05	—	—	—	—	—	—
Vaterländische Union	Not rep.	5,020	0.01	—	—	—	—	—	—

* The following parties were represented only in the First Bundestag (seats and percentage of valid votes):

Kommunistische Partei	15 — 5.7%	
Bayernpartei	17 — 4.2%	
Zentrum	10 — 3.1%	
Wirtschaftliche Aufbau-Vereinigung	12 — 2.9%	
Splinter parties	9 — 8%	

were relieved of the full weight of responsibility. Any failure could easily be blamed on foreign authorities, and political demands could be raised without consideration of the consequences, just as had been done during the Second Empire. More important, the people's attitude toward political parties was again one of playful non-commitment, allowing for irresponsible criticism and preposterous demands on the political spokesmen who, through a kind of schizophrenia, were regarded both as puppets of foreign powers and as responsible decision-makers. Thus, political parties did not possess a popular base, the prerequisite for any functioning democratic party system.

And there were good reasons for the popular reaction. The persistent memories of the all-embracing total state and its controls of communications had made the people alert to propaganda, suspicious of public authority, and desirous of privacy. True, there have been notable shifts in recent years, due partly to an improved economic situation in which the fight for mere survival is no longer the only thing that matters. The high and increasing voting percentages in the national elections of 1949 (78.5 per cent of those eligible), 1953 (86 per cent) and 1957 (88.2 per cent) showed a revived popular interest in a nation awakening from the stupor of defeat.

For the time being, however, this newly aroused public opinion in this era of the "economic wonder" has channeled itself in interest group activities, as the effective mass organizations of employers' associations and trade unions bear witness,[5] while skepticism of the political parties is deep-seated. The party direction is largely left to a small group of the former professionals. The people—skeptical, uncertain, restless—still avoid politics and in a crisis period may not be immune to the appeals of another demagogue who promises them desired solutions to problems and especially security.

Such uncertainties notwithstanding, one can by now clearly see the main outlines of the German party panorama. The number of parties has shrunk, from ten represented by members in the First *Bundestag* to only four in the Third *Bundestag*. This amazing shrinkage has no doubt been due in part to the electoral law of 1956, which, together with the preceding law of 1953, reflects the hard lessons learned from the experiences of the First Republic. Proportional representation, often called by its ardent critics "the Trojan Horse of Democracy," had certainly been a contributing factor in the splintering process of Weimar's political scene. The revived, yet refined, proportional representation put forth by the Bonn government was designed to avoid the emergence of many small splinter parties. For this reason, the significant "five per cent clause," discussed below, plays an important role in deterring the creation and continuation of splinter parties.

[5] Among numerous studies on interest groups in Germany, the following merit special mention: Rupert Breitling, *Die Verbände in der Bundesrepublik* (1955); Joseph Kaiser, *Die Repräsentation Organisierter Interessen* (1956); Theodor Eschenburg, *Herrschaft der Verbände?* (1955), and *Staat und Gesellschaft in Deutschland* (1956).

Under the electoral law each voter has two votes. The first vote is cast directly by name for a candidate of his constituency. The "second vote" is cast for the so-called party *"Land* list" which is composed of a number of candidates whom the party has selected and who in turn are assigned seats in the *Bundestag* according to the D'Hondt system, in direct ratio to the strength of the vote cast for them. Since a party may occupy only the number of seats to which it is entitled by the proportionate strength of the votes received, its directly elected "first vote" candidates must be included in the number of seats won under the "second vote." Any party which does not obtain a majority of "first votes" for its candidate in at least three constituencies or a minimum of 5 per cent of all valid votes cast in the entire Federal area can not be represented in the *Bundestag*. It is this prerequisite which has removed a number of parties from the national scene. Such was the fate of the Communist Party.[6] Largely in consequence thereof, the character of the German parties has changed. In place of the traditionally rigid political grouping, characterized by its ideology and/or special interest affiliations, the Bonn system shows increasingly a broadly-based coalition party, with little internal cohesion, yet held together by strong leadership.

The C.D.U./C.S.U. The Christian Democratic Union of Chancellor Adenauer may well be the best illustration of the type of coalition party of the Second Republic. The old *Zentrum,* by cutting across social class lines and combining diverse political groups under the banner of Catholicism, had foreshadowed this later development. The C.D.U., however, is not simply the revival and continuation of the old Catholic Center but the product of a purposeful attempt to create an interconfessional Christian party by attracting the former followers of the Protestant *Christlichsoziale Volksdienst* and the German National People's Party, as well as the Catholic Center. The need to heal the religious schism that had caused much harm throughout Germany's history was uppermost in the minds of the founders of the C.D.U. in 1945 when they insisted on a rough parity of Catholic and Protestant representation in the party councils. One may question the success of the C.D.U./C.S.U. in attaining their objective, and critics will point not only to the unchallenged position of Catholic Dr. Adenauer but also to the disturbing practice of distributing party patronage on the local level according to confessional affiliation. Yet, the party can refer to numerous Protestant leaders among its key men, such as the late speaker of the *Bundestag,* Dr. Hermann Ehlers, and his successor, Dr. Eugen Gerstenmaier, or to the Chancellor's young minister of interior Dr. Gerhard

[6] One way of escaping such an elimination is an agreement with a stronger party to vote for the candidates of the stronger party in return for various degrees of support in the next parliament. Some numerical differences might be observed in the party distribution of the two votes. Personal and local preferences may play a part in the casting of the first vote, and the opposition party may get some second ballot votes even from its opponents in order to prevent a "threatened dictatorship" of the majority party.

Schröder, and Vice-Chancellor Dr. Ludwig Erhard, the masterful minister of economics.[7]

More important yet is the party's insistence, to quote Dr. Ehlers' programmatic declaration at the C.D.U.'s congress of 1954, that "We are a political party, not an ecclesiastical institution . . . The C.D.U. is not the Church and the Church is not the C.D.U." This position has often been reiterated by Chancellor Adenauer, whose traditional differences with former Chancellor Brüning and his *Zentrum* leadership largely rested on conflicting interpretations of the interrelations of religion and politics.

While the churches, which provided much of the original support for the movement, tended to minimize the need for a centralized party apparatus, an effective party machine has been developed under the able leadership of Dr. Bruno Heck and his associates. Their effective election campaign, borrowing liberally from American techniques, is in part responsible for Adenauer's amazing victory in 1957.

The party undoubtedly shows the imprint of the chancellor's durable leadership. At the same time, it illustrates the historical danger of a governmental party. If there is any trend toward petrification within the C.D.U., it does not arise so much from the nature of the inner party organization as from its official power position. Such a peril should not be minimized, especially after the overwhelming electoral success in 1957. The party may misinterpret its mandate (as probably its sister organization in Italy did after its electoral victories since 1948) and try to exploit its unique position of vantage. It may then neglect its traditional role of protector of minority rights—a failure which in the long run has always been fatal to a political movement.

Such a policy above all would violate some basic tenets of the party, founded as it was on a genuine and continuously renewed compromise between the groups and forces within its own ranks and on a pragmatic approach to the social and political problems within the nation as a whole. And, indeed, the C.D.U. has succeeded better than any other party movement in creating a people's party which has united a variety of groups without permitting any one of them to become dominant. While Adenauer has often been more identified with the conservative big industry of the Rhineland than with the liberals or Christian Socialists led by the late Dr. Karl Arnold (former prime minister of North Rhine Westphalia), he has always been regarded as providing the cement to bind divergent forces.

During the past decade Adenauer has formulated with precision and directed with firm purpose his nation's policies, domestic and foreign. The heavy vote of confidence for the C.D.U. in 1957 was in reality a vote for the "Old Man." True, his unquestioned leadership

---

[7] Significant, in this connection, is the consistently high percentage of Protestants among representatives in the *Bundestag*. Thirty-eight per cent of the C.D.U./ C.S.U. members in the *Bundestag* of 1953 were Protestants (94 out of 244), and the fusion with the predominantly Protestant F.V.P. may have increased this percentage in 1957.

points also to future uncertainties for the C.D.U. In the meantime, the party can identify itself with the nation's spectacular economic revival and the restoration of its world position while denouncing the risks of experimentation. In this sense, it offers a "new look" in the German party scene; and its present position indicates that it has obtained wide support in the land which has lost interest in nuances and ideologies.

The S.P.D. By contrast with the C.D.U., the Social Democratic Party is the "traditional" party *par excellence;* in fact, on close examination it appears to be the only one. This is its advantage and also its liability. Miraculously the S.P.D. survived the Nazi impact; and memories of common suffering as well as a pride in its past have created a unique loyalty which gives the party its lasting foundation.

This strength has understandably resulted in a certain conservatism. Just as some *Zentrum* circles of the Second Empire argued that "they did not want to be too definitely known as a party of the Church," so the Social Democrats of today are critical of the characterization of the S.P.D. as a purely class party, which in fact it never was. If "the opposition" ever expects to secure the votes of a majority, it must reach outside its traditional 30 per cent of the national electorate and win new followers from non-traditional strata.

This necessity was recognized by the late Dr. Kurt Schumacher, the dynamic reorganizer of the party after the collapse of the Third Reich, when he concentrated on broadening the social base of the party's rank and file. He correctly realized that such an aim would require a programmatic shift from doctrinaire Marxism. Schumacher's persistent drive for the middle class vote helps explain his strident appeals to nationalist sentiment. True, these appeals rested on more than pure opportunism, and they were rooted in the historical role played by the S.P.D. In fact, nationalism had been both a vital force and a liability in the party since early days, and for the latter it paid a heavy price when the party assumed political responsibility during the uneasy beginning of the Weimar Republic.[8]

Schumacher merely wanted to free and to recapture from a usurping "rightist" radicalism a national sentiment that after all had stemmed from a Jacobin "leftist" tradition. While one should not doubt the sincerity of Schumacher's responsible nationalism, one could seriously question his capacity to feel the popular pulse. Might it be that nationalism had lost some of its appeal after the outrages that had been committed in its name by National Socialism? Could it be that a desire for a supra-national order—that original aim of the traditional Marxist —would a century later hold greater attraction for a new generation?

In any case, one is forced to the conclusion, after Schumacher's death, that he had failed in his task. The party had not recruited any appreciable number of new voters, as the bitter experience of the last

[8] How deeply these ideas represented the fundamental attitude of Dr. Schumacher may be illustrated by his Ph.D. thesis written in the early 1920's and entitled *Der Kampf um den deutschen Staatsgedanken in der deutschen Sozialdemokratie.*

elections proved. Nor has the shock and disappointment over the results of these elections pushed programmatic reforms beyond a rather fruitless debating stage.

One reason for this failure derives from another Social Democratic misjudgment, namely that the free enterprise economy in defeated Germany was doomed and could only lead, as it did in the First Republic, to mass unemployment and to an economic and political crisis. Thus a reassertion of the socialist tenet of a democratic planned economy seemed to be a proper antidote. The unquestionable success of Dr. Erhard's free market economy (to be sure, not without help of the United States military government and American economic support) raised basic questions for the German S.P.D. and, indeed, for socialism. It has given added impetus to the movement to adapt its program to the new circumstances, particularly as they are affected by the personality of Adenauer.[9]

The S.P.D. is presently passing through a critical stage, which the C.D.U. may eventually also face, of seeking a successor to a charismatic leader, such as it had not possessed since Lasalle's day. It was difficult, if not altogether impossible, for this successor to grow up in the leader's shadow. Moreover, Schumacher did not fit himself or his party into the role of a "responsible opposition" (nor was Adenauer always helpful in allowing his political foes to play this role). Schumacher's moral stamina, political intelligence, and sincere integrity were beyond question. But he was also stubborn, tough, and uncompromising. His oratory was unequalled in present-day Germany. He had the courage, background, and zeal of a martyr; he had lost one arm in World War I and had spent ten years in a Nazi concentration camp, emerging a physical wreck. His hatreds reflected his experiences during this period. Although he had antagonized many of his subordinates, he remained until his death the unchallenged leader of the Social Democratic masses.

Erich Ollenhauer—Schumacher's closest collaborator and supporter—did not become the master of the party machine by accident. He followed in the order of succession, as is typical of the hierarchy in modern mass movements, and was generally accepted by the rank and file of the S.P.D. From the beginning the rigid organization of social democracy has been an element of both strength and weakness. The fight against the *Bonze,* as the typical party functionary was described with increasing frequency, was pushed by the party's powerful foes and was reflected in the critical analysis of the oligarchical tendencies in the modern party by one of the original sons of German social democracy, Robert Michels. Today, the S.P.D. faces fundamentally the same basic problems as its pre-Nazi predecessor. The rapidity of its

[9] The power of personal appeal was well described during the 1957 election campaign by an astute observer: "Ollenhauer went around the country, patiently reciting facts and figures which told the story of how the party's Bundestag deputies had fought to push through social reforms, and often his speeches got dull. Adenauer was too vague to stick to the same figures in any two speeches, and too austere to descend to the facts. He calls himself a 'simplificator'—which is another way of saying that he knows intuitively the campaign art of reducing the complex and tortured web of actuality to a few over-sharp issues and a few over-glib slogans . . ." Max Lerner, "After the Miracle—What?," *Midstream,* 3 (Autumn, 1957), p. 16.

organizational growth and centralization of its party apparatus are illustrated by the large number of paid secretaries (probably constituting
not less than 20 per cent of the leadership group). This dominance of
the machine, demanding continued and loyal services from any aspirants to office, has long made it difficult for ambitious young men to
rise quickly to leading positions.

Nevertheless, the S.P.D. has succeeded in recruiting some new
leaders. While the "number one" man of the S.P.D. may be no match
for the C.D.U.'s chieftain, one must add that the party can count in its
high councils on an impressive group of experts. To mention only a
few, Professor Carlo Schmid, who entered politics in 1945, soon became
the party's recognized parliamentary leader. Among the younger *Bundestag* members are the defense and foreign policy spokesman, Fritz Erler;
the legal expert, Adolf Arndt; and the economic expert, Heinrich
Deist. In the *Länder* governments, where the party has played a significant role, personalities who have come to the front include Friedrich
August Zinn of Hesse, Wilhelm Hoegner, long-time minister-president
of Bavaria, and Waldemar von Knoeringen, the dynamic party leader
who, with influence far beyond his Bavarian bailiwick, was recently
elected deputy chairman of the party. High on this leadership list would
be the triumvirate of Burgomasters, veterans Wilhelm Kaisen of Bremen and Theodor Brauer of Hamburg, and the youthful Karl Brandt
of West Berlin. These and other highly qualified men have been attempting to reshape the old Social Democratic Party, with its rather rigid
Marxism, into a party resembling somewhat the less doctrinaire British
Labor Party.[1]

Political parties must face the possibility of ideological obsolescence.
But why do the socialists seem to be especially concerned with this
problem? For one reason, the socialist movement in Western Europe is
today a historical party with its heritage of program, personalities, and
organization. It does not have the advantage of new parties, which, even
where operating under the old names, can claim to represent "the wave
of the future." In addition, modern capitalism has not acted according
to socialist rules. Since 1848, when the electrifying, revolutionary *Communist Manifesto* was issued, the European economy has developed in
such a way as to vitiate the somber, "scientific," Marx-Engels predictions
of the growing impoverishment of ever-increasing proletarian masses.
Furthermore, the initial demands of the socialist movement have found
at least a partial satisfaction through legislative and administrative measures in the Western societies. The welfare state has completely changed
the social and political climate of Europe and has eliminated much of the
substance from the traditional socialist appeal.

For the socialist, the real question is this one of goals.[2] Is the goal

---

[1] Note the programmatic paper presented at the S.P.D. Congress in 1950 by
Carlo Schmid, *Die Sozaldemokratische Partei Deutschlands vor der geistigen Situ-
ation dieser Zeit* (1950); also the significant speech of Waldemar von Knoeringen on
"Culture and Politics" at the May, 1958, convention of the S.P.D.

[2] The most extensive and articulate discussion of these problems has been in
Britain; see the Labor Party's new policy statements, *Public Enterprise* and *Industry*

further nationalization of the means of production, distribution, and exchange? Is it co-determination and cooperation in the industrial sphere? Or are there other issues which challenge outside the economic field? Socialist spokesmen, at least in Britain, are becoming increasingly concerned about human freedom in the welfare state, emphasizing the possibilities of individual initiative (Gaitskell), more group involvement of the local level within the society (Martin), and the development of personality and the spread of culture (Crosland). Any idea of class warfare seems to have been totally abandoned, for the party now seeks majority support in national elections.

Similarly, the German Social Democrats also emphasized in the election campaign of 1957 that the vital problems of the German people could be solved only through the co-operation of all groups, including the opposition Christian Democrats. The Social Democratic program is characteristically vague on economic matters. Nationalization is barely mentioned. Co-determination in industry, which only a few years back seemed to take a central position in socialism's fight for true industrial democracy, has lost much of its appeal, in part because the Adenauer government has accepted some of its tenets. What remains is a vague demand that coal mines and atomic industries be "placed under democratic control as the foundation of prosperity for all." Its other economic aims—"unimpeded economic development," extension of social security, and enlarged public health programs—are probably accepted by proponents of economics minister Ludwig Erhard's "social market economy." Such a program, whatever its popularity, hardly encourages a change in governmental stewardship.

What is surprising is that the Social Democrats have not seized upon more pressing and timely economic issues, such as productivity, inflation, and automation. Is the neglect due to the fact that these burning problems do not carry any vote-getting appeal? Is it because such problems are not relevant to the traditional conflict between capitalism and socialism? Or is it because the socialist thinkers have so far been unable to reach any agreement on them? In any case, this failure to find constructive answers to vital internal problems can prove fatal to this or to any other major party.

The Social Democratic leaders have under these circumstances focused most of their attention on foreign affairs. The shift of emphasis to the world scene may well be indicative of a general trend in party developments. Certainly, the Socialists could make out a good case for a "social security" which in this global, atomic age might be attainable only through new adjustments at the international level. Hugh Gaitskell, British Labor's party leader, to borrow the title of his most recent volume, considers the question of *The Challenge of Coexistence;*[3] and the German Social Democratic Party leaders have concentrated their

---

and Society; Hugh Gaitskell, *Socialism and Nationalization* (1956); Kingsley Martin, *Socialism and the Welfare State* (1952); and, above all, C. A. R. Crosland, *The Future of Socialism* (1956). Cf. Sigmund Neumann, "The Socialists' Dilemma," *Challenge,* 6 (November, 1957), pp. 29ff.

[3] (1957).

attacks almost exclusively on Adenauer's foreign policies and the international issues of German reunification and rearmament. In the future, world affairs may well provide the main stage for the European political parties.

The F.D.P.   In 1956, divergent views on foreign policies provided the grounds for the withdrawal of the Free Democratic Party from Adenauer's coalition. The Free Democrats thought a reunited Germany ought not to be committed in advance to the international agreements of the West German government and felt that the Adenauer regime had not been vigorous and resourceful enough in its efforts to bring about reunification. In addition, they accused the chancellor of fostering a single-party dictatorship (even when they were in the coalition). The Free Democrats apparently regarded this separation from the coalition as a necessary consequence of the steps to force an "unnatural" two-party system on Germany's political landscape.

The need for a "third party," to serve as a balancing force and cushion between the two major parties, has been the chief argument for the continued existence of the F.D.P. Such essential counterweights were considered by the F.D.P. to be by no means automatic in the operation of the West German Republic with its bitterly antagonistic major parties. Its founder and most illustrious spokesman, Theodor Heuss (until elected to the highest national office), certainly held this view, and, no doubt, during the early days of the struggling Bonn Republic helped support the party's claim that "those countries which can afford a two-party system had time to develop a system of constitutional and parliamentary checks and safeguards against the domination of one party holding an absolute majority over the other." This conception of the role of the F.D.P. as counterweight has become more questionable since the 1957 elections which gave Adenauer's C.D.U. an absolute majority in the Bundestag.

One might also question the F.D.P.'s further claim of being the only really independent party, "because it is free from the ideologies which shape the policies of the S.P.D. and C.D.U. . . . Independent thinking demands not only freedom from external control but also freedom from the internal bonds of ideology." True, the original appeal of the F.D.P.—being anti-Marxist, anticlerical, antiauthoritarian—was to that large segment of the population, which, in the words of one of its early adherents, was "neither socialist enough to vote for the S.P.D. nor religious enough to vote for the C.D.U."

This type of appeal made for divergent factions and bitter intraparty feuds. These tensions within the party are reminiscent of those within Weimar's *Deutsche Volkspartei*,[4] from which the original leadership of the F.D.P. was largely recruited. The traditional liberal forces, emphasizing above all else a strong stand for freedom, have been clashing with vigorous and self-confident industrialists who, with pride in the amazing

[4] The two parties formerly flanking the *Deutsche Volkspartei*, the German Democratic Party and the German National People's Party, also provided some of the leadership.

economic recovery, have increasingly dominated the party congresses and policy-making bodies. If there be any bond between such diverse types of membership, it is in a liberalism which stresses an undogmatic view of politics and accepts a variegated type of party membership. This seemingly vague and negative bond must be understood as the natural heritage of the totalitarian Nazi past and the Soviet present. The authoritarian milieu has provoked a strong reassertion of the demand for individualism and privacy in almost all walks of life.

This demand has been in evidence in all German Democratic parties, and its wide acceptance may well be one reason for the F.D.P.'s decreasing voter appeal. In fact, the more realistic and flexible, the more heterogeneous and undogmatic the major parties became (not by accident did the strongest group call itself a "union" and not a "party"), the less could the F.D.P. uphold its claim of uniqueness. Whatever influence the F.D.P. may eventually command in an increasingly polarized party system, it certainly has given to the German political scene colorful leaders and powerful personalities. Such, for example, are statesmanlike Reinhold Maier, since 1957 its chairman and minister-president of Baden-Wuerttemberg (that cradle of German liberalism); fighting parliamentarians Dr. Dehler and Dr. Erich Mende; dignified octogenarian Marie-Elizabeth Lueders; and youthful campaign manager Wolfgang Doering. Their voices carry weight in the political forums as a third force.

Splinter Parties. More doubtful is the influence of the remaining parties, including the fourth and only other parliamentary fraction, the German Party (D.P./F.V.P.). It owes its survival in the election slaughter of the smaller parties in 1957 almost entirely to its regional appeal and to its campaign coalition and close working relationships with the C.D.U. Its continuous participation in the Adenauer cabinets and its leadership in Lower Saxony give it greater weight than its electoral vote might suggest. It was further strengthened by its merger with the governmental Free People's Party (F.V.P.), consisting of the minority which seceded from the F.D.P. when that party withdrew from the Adenauer government. Yet, while its leaders succeeded in their early aim to create the *Land* of Lower Saxony, the fate of this party, similar to that of other regional parties such as the Bavarian Party, seems to be sealed after a short life span.

The rise and fall of other minor parties is illustrated by the history of the Bloc of Expellees and Dispossessed, the All-German Bloc (B.H.E./G.B.). For a short while it looked as if this newcomer among the German parties, appealing particularly to the millions of expellees from the East, would introduce a disturbing force into German politics by attracting this rootless new citizenship group, which, with little to lose and with limited encouragement from the old residents (*Besitzbuerger*), would be open to demagogical enticements to return to the "promised land" beyond the Oder-Neisse line. Instead, the party became increasingly conservative in its program and finally, after the 1953 election, entered the Adenauer government as a member of the coalition.

During its short parliamentary history the party was not without influence in improving the status of the expellee social groups. Yet the more successful the B.H.E. has been in integrating the expellees into a new German society and in securing their economic rehabilitation, the more it has hastened its own self-liquidation. It may be doubted whether the B.H.E. can ever succeed in reaching out beyond the expellees themselves (of whom only an estimated 20 to 25 per cent voted for the party even at its height) and organize politically a wider segment of society. Even more doubtful is the claim of a few of its intellectual spokesmen that the movement represents a new ideology, emanating from the dynamic new crisis stratum of irregulars comprising a true fifth estate, who are heralds of a new society. After a promising beginning the B.H.E. seems, especially in the light of *Land* elections in 1958, to have lost its momentum and its place in German politics.

The Bonn regime, in contrast to its Republican predecessor, has reached a degree of political stabilization which does not, to outward appearances, leave any room for the rise of splintering radical movements. Today, there appears to be no appreciable antidemocratic force in the main body of the electorate. The neo-Nazi Socialist Reich Party (S.R.P.), which attracted as much as 11 per cent of the votes in the *Land* elections of Lower Saxony in 1951, was declared to be unconstitutional in the summer of 1952.[5] The Communist Party (K.P.D.), which failed to win a seat in the *Bundestag* elections of 1953, having polled only 2.2 per cent of the votes, was also outlawed by the Federal Constitutional Court in a decision of August 17, 1956.[6]

Important though the judicious attitude of the courts and the awakened responsibility of the administrators may be, what will count in the end will be the prevailing political climate within the nation. The outer contours of the party system may not be indicative of the tensions of the inner core. As of this time, it is too early to tell whether a genuine democratic spirit has permeated Germany. The most alarming possibility, in the inner political scene of Western Germany, is not so much the actual or prospective increase of radical wing parties themselves as the results which they can produce through continuous pressure on the moderate parties. Eager to counteract their rivals and to compete with them for public support, these majority parties might even become the prisoners of a revived radical nationalist fervor. In short, the final picture

[5] It should be marked to the credit of the Bonn lawmakers that they tackled the delicate issue of the "limits of intolerance against tolerance," an issue which had been seriously neglected by the Weimar Republic. "Whoever abuses freedom of expression of opinion . . . in order to attack the free democratic basic order . . . shall forfeit these basic rights." Thus reads Art. 18 of the Bonn Basic Law, and Art. 21 adds that parties "which, according to their aims and the behavior of their members, seek to impair or abolish the free and democratic basic order . . . shall be unconstitutional." Under this stipulation the S.R.P. was outlawed in 1952 by the Federal Constitutional Court.

[6] For a verbatim translation of the Court decision, see Wolfgang P. von Schmertzing, *Outlawing the Communist Party, A Case Study* (1957). For an overall examination of the role and decisions of the *Bundesverfassungsgericht*, see the comprehensive study by Taylor Cole, "The West German Federal Constitutional Court," *Journal of Politics*, 20 (1958), pp. 278–307; note the bibliography contained therein.

of the Western German party system will depend on the stability of the Bonn Republic itself.

3. "THE ECONOMIC MIRACLE"

Great indeed has been the success in producing a stable political system within this first decade of the Second Republic. Final victory of democracy, however, will be assured only when the political institutions have proven their strength after the end of the period of Adenauer's personal leadership. Moreover, the durability of the young republic will be spelled out largely in terms of the genuine social and economic viability of the young nation. Such viability could prevent the return of those crisis strata which once before wrecked the democratic party system.

Stabilization and Social Market Economy. No doubt, unbelievable progress has been made since the hopeless days immediately following World War II, when a pulverized society lost its remaining ethical standards and when black markets demoralized the daily life of the nation. The turning point came with the currency reform of June 20, 1948. Like the monetary stabilization of 1923, which checked the runaway inflation following World War I, the introduction of the new mark in West Germany in 1948 produced an overnight shift which allowed the economy to pull itself together. Today, the recovery of Germany outstrips that of all other European nations. The wave of prosperity has reduced unemployment to extremely low levels, and has raised the workers' real wages 60 per cent in the past eight years. It has more than doubled the industrial production index of 1936, and has helped Germany to accumulate reserves of over 5.5 billion dollars in gold and foreign currencies.

What has brought about this amazing recovery? Is it simply that proverbial German efficiency or some mysterious miracle? Certainly, there has been no miracle, if this means some type of black magic. The economic recovery can be explained, though it is not traceable to any single cause. Germany's economic and human geography have something to do with it. Hard work, labor discipline, good management, and a favorable trade route location have played an important part. In addition, there are also specific historical events such as the momentous East-West split and the Korean war and its aftermath which have fortuitously furthered Germany's development. And, finally, the actual economic policies, initiated and stimulated by the Allied Military Government and later developed by the Federal Republic, have given the German economy direction, drive, and substance.

On the tenth anniversary of the adoption of the new German economic policy one must indeed give special recognition to the efforts of Dr. Ludwig Erhard, the architect of the controversial but highly successful "Social Market Economy." Contrary to the predictions of many circumspect experts among his political opponents in the S.P.D., and even among many military government advisers, the triumph of free enterprise, heralded by Dr. Erhard, has probably done more to stabilize Germany than all the political measures of the Second Republic. In fact, the greatest difference between Weimar and Bonn lies in this successful attainment of Bonn's economic prosperity, in contrast to the First Republic's experience with the disastrous depression at the end of its first decade.

When the foundation of the currency reform was laid, ending the inflation which had accompanied price-fixing and which had been characterized by rationing and the black market, Erhard proceeded where possible to remove all controls over prices, production, materials, and trade. This strict adherence to an almost classic concept of economics (widely regarded as antiquated in an age of a directed economy) was at the very base of the Social Market Economy.

It should be stated that Erhard's thesis of "prosperity through competition" did not mean a simple return to laissez faire. The instruments for enforcing policies which are available to the German minister of economics and are energetically used by him are considerable and indeed involve controls which are more extensive than those of the United States. Erhard's consistent fight against inflation through a manipulated monetary and credit policy has resulted in restraints on wages and prices which have helped keep the German currency and the price level more stable than those of most other European countries. His determined arguments for anti-cartel legislation, finally enacted in amended form in 1957 as the "law against restrictions of competition," certainly come close to embodying the prevailing American philosophy on cartel regulation.

Erhard carried his fight for "liberation for productive competition" into the international field too. In fact, he has been an ardent advocate of greater freedom of foreign trade for Germany, and here his stand was as revolutionary as his fight against a trust policy which had deep roots in German history. While he is a staunch supporter of the European Economic Community, he has at the same time forewarned his people against an economic integration through the European Common Market, if it is to isolate and insulate the six-nation community (in the guise of protectionism) against the rest of the Free World. What he is pleading for is a free trade area, larger than the original six nations, including the United States and Latin America. And while he recognizes the co-existence of the two contrasting social systems of our times, he wishes to see an expansion of economic trade even beyond the Western World, and thus to restrict the conflict between the two worlds to the area of spiritual forces.[7]

However great the role of Dr. Erhard, the German postwar economic revival is by no means the work of a single man. But, next to the chancellor, Erhard undoubtedly enjoys the greatest popular esteem

[7] A presentation of Dr. Erhard's economic policies may be found in his *Prosperity Through Competition* (1958), and his essay, "Germany's Economic Goals," *Foreign Affairs,* 36 (July, 1958), pp. 611–17; for a judicious overall analysis, consult Henry C. Wallich, *Mainsprings of the German Revival* (1955); also Miriam Camps, *The European Common Market and Free Trade Area* (1957).

as the creator of an unexpected prosperity, and for this reason he has well earned the position of vice-chancellor.

Impressive as this economic improvement is, a great number of problems remain. Several of these call for special mention.

Industrial Leadership. Has the leadership of Germany's economy undergone any fundamental change since the breakdown of the Third Reich? Alliances between authoritarian political forces and the monster economic combines that control German industry helped weaken the young Weimar Republic and contributed to its surrender to Naziism. As previously pointed out, Hitler changed the direction of the German economy, strengthened the system of controls, and altered the priority list of those receiving the major economic rewards. But one main result of this "new order" was greater economic concentration, deeply involving industrialists in the totalitarian, power-mad state.

Recognizing that the prospects for peace and democracy in Germany would be related to social and economic reorganization, the United States military directives were aimed at the dissolution of gigantic combines such as the I.G. Farben Chemical Trust and the establishment of an international Ruhr authority. But the decartelization program, which in a way represented the transfer of American antitrust legislation to Germany, faced great obstacles. Among these were the need for industrial efficiency and productivity, which called for the return of "seasoned experts," and resistance to outside interference. The sequel of the story indicates that many of the old leaders of industry have once more assumed their former positions, despite Dr. Erhard's persistent fight against cartelization. The amazing revival of the Krupp empire may be an indication of such restored power. Still, just as the renowned munitions maker has channeled his production toward peaceful industrial purposes, so other industrialists under the lasting impact of the Nazi experience may have become more cautious. But have they become more attached to the democratic way of life?

Organized Labor. One may well ask whether the forces for a democratic change can be found within the ranks of labor, traditionally the champion of democracy in Germany. The working class is not politically strong today. Unemployment and fear of inflation have weakened its bargaining power. And while wages and real income have continuously risen during the last years, labor's share of the national income is still, on a percentage basis, lower than it was before the war.

The re-established German Confederation of Trade Unions (D.G.B.), with its impressive membership of 6.5 million, deserves credit for its part in the economic recovery of Western Germany.[8] Yet its members are politically handicapped by the fact that they are organized into a

8 M. A. Kelly, "The Reconstitution of the German Trade Union Movement," *Political Science Quarterly*, 64 (March, 1949), pp. 24–49; Sidney Lens, "Social Democracy and Labor in Germany," *Foreign Policy Reports* (November 15, 1950); and the overall view by Taylor Cole, "Post War Labor Relations in the German Federal Republic," in E. H. Litchfield, ed., *Governing Post War Germany* (1953).

single federation (in contrast to the pre-Hitler pattern when there were three leading organizations) and by the necessity to adhere at least outwardly to a policy of virtual neutrality in party politics. There are, however, noticeable trends toward renewed, separatist tendencies among groups in the D.G.B. and toward political alignments. These sentiments have become increasingly more outspoken since the death of Hans Boeckler, the effective leader at the time of federation.

The trade unions are continuing to seek co-determination in industry, a voice for labor in the economic decisions from which it was excluded under the Third Reich.[9] Labor's intensified demand for codetermination reflects the drives of the Weimar days for "economic democracy."[1] This program, which has met with some success, has been considered one keystone of trade union policy. But the government-sponsored codetermination law of July 19, 1952, extending in a modified form the previously enacted legislation on codetermination in coal, steel, and iron plants to industry generally, and subsequent codetermination legislation has found declining support from the trade unions.

At this point, the D.G.B.'s program of action does not seem to indicate a radical socialist turn by Western Germany's organized labor. Although there has been of late a growing tension in industrial relations (marked by a number of strikes in crucial industries) and an increasing agitation among the leadership and rank-and-file members of unions for a more determined political and economic role, the emergent labor relations system in the Bonn Republic represents on the whole one of the most encouraging landmarks on Germany's social economic scene.[2]

Such a development may result in labor's sober and responsible participation. But will it effectively mobilize the constructive spirit of this great potential force for a dynamic democracy?

Economic Problems. In the economic sector, other key questions still remain unanswered, such as the proper distribution of goods and earnings, the renewal of capital accumulation, and the full reestablishment of international markets.

Prewar Germany was not self-sufficient and had to import from 15 to 30 per cent of its essential food. Because of the loss of Eastern farm lands, Western Germany may in the future have to import up to 45 per cent of its food, paying for these imports with extensive heavy industry exports. The revival of East-West trade, obviously attractive on historical grounds, is advocated by the East bloc for political reasons and is sought by certain ambitious West German power groups. And while it

[9] For a comparative analysis of the history, ideology, and politics of co-determination, see the excellent study by Herbert J. Spiro, *The Politics of German Codetermination* (1958); cf. also *Das Mitbestimmungsgespraech* (1955); Clark Kerr, "The Trade Union Movement and the Redistribution of Power in Post War Germany," *Quarterly Journal of Economics,* 68 (November, 1954), pp. 535–64; and Werner M. Blumenthal, *Co-determination in the German Steel Industry* (1956).

[1] Fritz Naphtali, ed., *Wirtschaftsdemokratie* (1928), and Karl Landauer, *Planwirtschaft und Verkehrswirtschaft* (1931).

[2] See Taylor Cole, "The Role of Labor Courts in Western Germany," *Journal of Politics,* 18 (1956), pp. 479–98.

finds increasing support among some segments of the population, it may not be the natural or cheapest international trade route, as a number of experts emphasize.[3]

The alternative markets to the potential Eastern ones, especially those outside of Continental Europe, still have to be fully developed. While the promises of the European common market may in time compensate for the low level of Eastern European trade, larger overseas outlets in the long run are likely to be more important. The need for markets is an increasingly vital one. It is bound up with Germany's desire for *Lebensraum*, an appeal which was used effectively by the last dictator and which might be used again with more valid statistical evidence.[4]

In the meantime there are other warning signs for the economy of the Bonn Republic. Although Western Germany has a substantial head start over the Soviet zone, Eastern Germany's rate of recovery should not be underestimated in the battle for popular allegiance, particularly in view of its emphasis on full employment. To be sure, Western Germany is presently in a very favorable position. The unemployed represent only the hard core of unemployables or temporarily unemployed people. Yet the influx of the comparatively large war generation into a saturated labor market and the continued immigration of refugees into Western Germany, especially in view of world market fluctuations, offer some somber prospects. In case of an economic downturn, one might be again forewarned about another "political reserve army" similar to the one that brought Hitler to power in 1933. It could be recruited from these ranks of the unemployed.

Expellees. The partition of Germany has created a new crisis stratum in Western Germany, the expellees. They comprise primarily those people who were forceably evacuated in consequence of pre-treaty arrangements: those of German descent from Czechoslovakia's *Sudetenland,* Rumania, and Hungary, and the *Reichsdeutsche* from the East provinces that were taken over by the Polish government. A conservative estimate puts the number at more than 7.5 million in the Western zones alone. One must add another million interzonal refugees from the Soviet zone and evacuees from bombed areas who still number more than 1.5 million. In sum, this new "fifth estate" of former outcasts easily represents 10 million people, i.e., 20 per cent of the population of Western Germany. Although an increasing number of these recent citizens have been absorbed and integrated into the Western German society, bringing new skills and other contributions to the

[3] See Theodore H. Schultz, "Effects of Trade and Industrial Output of Western Germany Upon Agriculture," *American Economic Review, Papers and Proceedings,* 40 (March, 1950), pp. 522–30; cf. Theodore Zotschew, "Die Strukturwandlungen im deutschen Aussenhandel und deren Folgen fuer die Westeuropaeische Wirtschaft," *Weltwirtschaftliches Archiv,* 66 (1951), pp. 293–328; and William Diebold, *Trade and Payments in Western Europe* (1952), a study in economic co-operation between 1887 and 1951.

[4] In 1956 the population density per square Km. in West Germany was 206 and in East Germany 155, as compared with 78 per square Km. in France.

Bonn Republic, an appreciable percentage of them are still "pariahs," uprooted from their traditional homesteads, their jobs, and their accustomed ways of life. Thrown into a society which some of these new citizens feel does not want them, and does not properly care for them, these stepchildren of Germany could become a decisive group in the political future of the Bonn Republic, if it should experience another economic setback. Up to the present, however, the Second Republic has fared well with its stepchildren and any deep concern for their future seems to be out of place.

To absorb permanently the millions of expellees and refugees, to integrate insecure groups into society and, above all, to gain the confidence of Germany's youth, the Republic's leaders must find new images and goals worth seeking. There is reasonable hope for such a development, but it is one which awaits a definition of Germany's proper place in the world of nations.

4. GERMANY AMONG THE NATIONS

What is the place of Germany in the world of nations? Is it battlefield, buffer, bastion or bridge? Obviously one cannot continue to regard it as a power vacuum in a world split by the East-West conflict, for this is no longer true. Yet will it become another Korea, with Berlin to serve as Europe's 38th parallel? This is the all-consuming fear of many Germans. What avenues will be open to them to escape such a fate? Should Germany tie its future to the Atlantic community or give in to the might of the continental colossus of the Soviet Empire? Or is there a chance to "play the game"? It may be tempting for clever schemers to use this tug-of-war as a weapon to gain power, to play off Russia against the Western powers, thus gaining advantage from both sides. To Germany, again Europe's strongest nation in population, industrial potential, and organization—this strategy would not be an unfamiliar one. The former allies, wooing yesterday's foe, presently invite such a policy. An atmosphere of intrigue easily creates strange alliances in the name of sober *Realpolitik*.

The German politicians who today favor an Eastern orientation are not necessarily, in fact, they are rarely, close to the communist camp. The Eastern school knows no class or party lines as the aftermath of World War I has proved all too well. The turn toward Russia at that time was made not only by ardent communists but also by industrialists, intellectuals, diplomats, and, above all, by military leaders.[5] Yet the present power constellations are far different from those of earlier days. In this age of ideological civil war, it is more dangerous to play

[5] These included General Hans von Seeckt, the founder of the Reichswehr; Count Brockdorff-Rantzau, Germany's spokesman at Versailles and its first ambassador to the Kremlin; Walter Rathenau, foreign minister and architect of the German-Soviet Rapallo Treaty of 1922; and literary men such as Moeller van den Bruck and Karl Haushofer.

the game of strategic alliances of which the men of the Kremlin are master manipulators. The experience of the Soviet satellite countries should forewarn industrialists and intellectuals alike against working for Germany's unification and liberation on Moscow's terms.

And still it must be recognized that the drive for unity has a tremendous appeal. Few Germans can acquiesce in the fatal split of their fatherland. An astute Soviet propaganda has always tried to put the exclusive blame for this unfortunate state of affairs on the Western allies. The Kremlin may even be holding in reserve another Polish partition which would return some of the Eastern territories to a "friendly" German nation and thereby undo the Potsdam lines of demarcation, despite the fact that the Eastern German government "voluntarily" accepted it in an agreement with Poland in June, 1950.

Since the days of Potsdam, the relations between Eastern and Western powers, focusing on Germany, have continuously deteriorated until both camps are now courting Germany as a much-sought-after military ally. Such alternatives have to be kept in mind, even though Western Germany is presently closely tied up with the Western world.

The dramatic battle of Berlin in 1948–49 was won by the resolute perseverance of General Lucius B. Clay and the men of the airlift, aided by the faithful co-operation and stamina of the Berliners. This episode, however, was only the first round. The glamor of heroic resistance has faded into the boredom of daily routine. And while the economic situation of Berlin has increasingly improved, the strategy of the Russians and the East-German satellite government works relentlessly, alternating between vague insinuations of Western unreliability, steps to interfere with the Berlin economy, and open threats of retaliation "when the day comes" and the Americans are thousands of miles away.

The Germans may well prefer to decline either an East or West orientation. They might be attracted by the prospects of neutralization (or "disengagement," as it has been called by George Kennan in his B.B.C. lectures on "Russia, the Atom and the West" which have been widely discussed in Germany), of taking Germany out of the conflict altogether and making it a buffer, a greater Switzerland. Yet such an artificial vacuum could be preserved only if neighboring nations permit it. As long as no genuine East-West agreement seems possible, withdrawal of occupying forces in the West will only expose the country to attack by the Soviet Union. Neutralization, in other words, would mean above all else a neutralization of United States forces. It certainly could not restore Germany to the position of a balancer, of a third force in a two-power world.

Actually, the realities of today do not suggest a neutralization of Germany, taking the Federal Republic altogether out of the present power balance, but rather a restoration of the nation to a stable economic and political position, an independent status which does not threaten the peace of its neighbors. Western policy has sought to provide the conditions necessary for lasting peace. The inclusion of Western Germany in the Marshall and Schuman Plans were first steps toward closer integration with the whole Western economy. This movement was strengthened by Germany's full membership in NATO since May, 1955. By 1957 the German government had continued its active co-operation in the European movement by the approval of the creation of the European Economic Community (Common Market) and the European Atomic Energy Community (Euratom).

Despite heated debates concerning Germany's international position, the Bonn Republic is clearly committed to a Western orientation. And yet this decision, accepted *de facto* by all political parties, will not necessarily ease international tensions. On the contrary, it has not only resulted in expected threats from the U.S.S.R. but has also brought to the fore an increasing demand in Germany for a recognition of her importance as a "powerful equal." With this demand, one might anticipate the revival of nationalist sentiment in Germany, which in part would be a natural consequence of the new freedoms given, after defeat and years of occupation, to a proud and still somewhat provincial people. And this fact must be recognized by the Western allies before insisting upon the acceptance by this sensitive nation of policies which might be foreign to its traditions and will.

Whatever the final historical judgment may be on the Adenauer era, the chancellor's fundamentally European orientation has helped in finding the solution for difficult international disputes. The Saar issue is an illustration in point. On October 27, 1956, the French and German foreign ministers signed a treaty implementing and superseding the Saar statute of October 23, 1954. This statute had envisaged the creation of a semi-autonomous territory in the Western European Union, contingent on the approval of the Saar people. The referendum taken on October 23, 1955, resulted in a two-thirds majority against the Europeanization of the Saar. The final treaty, agreed upon by the French and West German governments, led to the political integration of the Saar with Western Germany on January 1, 1957. But, at the same time, it provided for close economic co-operation with France, at least during the period of transition. The new Saar treaty not only settled the major controversial issue in French-German relations but opened the way for a closer and more active co-operation in European affairs. What had thus been for long a barrier to improved relationships between the two great neighbors can now possibly furnish an added impetus for a new regional European approach.

If one were to appraise the ideological trends in present-day Western Germany, he would particularly note the lasting strength of the sentiment toward unity. In fact, the characteristic obsession with the issue may blind many Germans, as it has throughout modern history, to the perplexities of the international situation. The prospect for unification—in view of the *fait accompli* of German partition, the growing rigidity of the world power blocs, and the economic price necessary to be paid for an eventual reintegration of the two parts—seems to become increasingly remote, even though the clamor for its attainment remains a dominant cry in German politics. This dilemma has created an atmosphere of unreality in German politics which may have serious implications for the future.

The two major alternatives offered to attain unity are reflected in the positions of the present German government and of its S.P.D. opposition. Adenauer (whose views are almost identical with those of the United States) publicly assures his people that the Western integration of the Bonn Republic will in the end create such a situation of strength, economically and politically, that the sheer weight of the resulting accomplishment will automatically pull the Eastern zone into a unified democratic Reich. Thus Adenauer's plank is integration before unification. After the experience of one decade, despite Bonn's resumption of diplomatic relations with Moscow in 1955, one may question the certainty of this road to Germany's unity.

In contrast to this confident view, the Social Democratic Party insists that Bonn's close ties—economical, political, and military—within the Western European framework may destroy all chances for the German unification. Its achievement, the Socialists maintain, can only be secured by direct four-power negotiations. Any Soviet gesture for negotiation therefore is welcomed. In such a stand the Social Democrats have wide support, albeit for somewhat divergent reasons, among the trade unions, protestant church circles, and war-weary people. In effect, the S.P.D. finds itself aligned with forces of disengagement, despite the fact that since the days of the late Schumacher the S.P.D. has always shown a realistic appraisal of and a traditional enmity to the totalitarian dictatorship of the East. For this very reason, even the opposition party has factually accepted the Second Republic's political and military integration into the Western camp. And the continuing Berlin crisis, especially as it reached its acute stage in early 1959, has not been encouraging, even in the eyes of the S.P.D., for the early attainment of German unification.

Despite such differences as to the means to secure unification, and despite continuing pressures and blandishments from the East, Western Germany is definitely a part of the Atlantic Community. Her Western neighbors, notwithstanding prevailing misgivings of a rearmed Germany, seemingly acquiesce in Germany's rearmament as involving a lesser risk than a power vacuum. And the German people, regardless of bitter and lasting experiences of war and dictatorship (and the consequent fears of renewed international involvement, of a reassertion of the military-caste spirit, and of a shifting political balance of domestic forces within the young democracy), have accepted the re-establishment of Germany's military forces under NATO command. The *Land* elections in 1958 have indicated, as well, a strong support of the government's policy of atomic rearmament.

Such new power arrangements, however, do not answer conclusively the crucial question: *Can* Western Germany be defended? *Will* it be defended? Can the military potential of the West give promise of protection against a Soviet attack or against the prospect of Germany's becoming a battlefield in a nuclear conflict of the two contending super powers? Only NATO's successful establishment of a wall of security, which will prevent another world conflagration, can dispel the doubts and fears raised by these questions.

And even given such security, there would still remain a most fundamental question in the minds of the Germans, especially the young ones, as to their place in the world. Beyond economics and strategy, a spiritual vacuum must be filled. A United States of Europe represents a clarion call that might rally this present generation to a new beginning, eclipsing the appeal of a Third International. The historic rivals for European domination might finally line up in a common front for its preservation. Indeed, the idea of European unification is favored by an increasing number of persons. With the launching of the Schuman Plan, the creation of the Council of Europe, and the development of the European Economic Community, a stage of policy-making has been reached. But these integrating steps are only preliminary ones, for difficult questions still remain to be properly answered. Will France and Germany at last provide a complementary balance in the great community? What are the chances for a reunification of Germany in such a Western bloc? And if attainable, would this reunification again lead to German predominance? Can the smaller nations trust their neighbors enough to accept added limits on their own preciously guarded sovereignty? Will Britain pool its forces with Western Europe? How far will the United States support a united Europe? And what will be the final reaction of the U.S.S.R.?

Century-old conflicts between the European nations must be overcome, accustomed patterns of thought abandoned, and new loyalties created. The adjustment of diverse modes and levels of living will demand many patient, practical steps. All these developments will take time, and time may be lacking. One may already detect a slackening in the enthusiasm for the much-delayed European union. Western Europe today will need the ingenuity of abler men than Briand and Stresemann; and it will require a more constructive and more lasting formula than that of Locarno. The German problem is only a small part, though a crucial one, of this worldwide issue.

The Western German government by joining the European Community, made its choice, and an overwhelming majority of the nation is ready to follow the road to European integration. However, for survival's sake, German policies must guard the nation against once more becoming the battlefield. She cannot retreat into the no-man's land of a buffer state; history and geography have made her the bastion and border of Western civilization. Faced with this great responsibility, Germany may yet participate in a genuine revival of Europe and may truly become the bridge between East and West—the *Land der Mitte.*

SELECTED BIBLIOGRAPHY

There is an abundance of literature appearing continuously on the complex, crucial, and highly controversial topic of Germany's political systems. A bibliography, if it is to be a manageable and useful guide at all, must be selective and incomplete. Selections have been made on the basis of authenticity, suggestiveness, and readability. Although the study itself is based primarily on firsthand sources, the bibliography concentrates on easily available English publications. Reference to German material is made only where unique material and fresh interpretations are offered, or where no translations of the original studies have been published. The same yardstick is applied to writings on Germany in other foreign languages.

In keeping with the broad approach to politics, basic to this study, the bibliography emphasizes—in addition to the literature on the constitutional and institutional developments—representative works dealing with the underlying social forces operative in Germany, past, present, and future.

I. BACKGROUND STUDIES

For a proper evaluation of Germany's political systems, it is essential to view them within their constantly shifting historical setting. Unfortunately, no adequate short history is available in either English or German. For general orientation the following books may be found most useful: Geoffrey Barraclough, *Factors in German History* (New York, 1946), and *The Origins of Modern Germany* (New York, 1946); E. F. Henderson, *A Short History of Germany* (New York, 1902), 2 vols., (New York, 1928), 1 vol.; Henri Lichtenberger, *Germany and Its Evolution in Modern Times* (New York, 1913); Erich Meissner, *Germany in Peril* (London, 1942), and *Confusion of Faces* (London, 1946), describing the struggle between religion and secularism in Europe; Roy Pascal, *The Growth of Modern Germany* (London, 1946); Hermann Pinnow, *History of Germany* (New York, 1933); S. H. Steinberg, *A Short History of Germany* (New York, 1945); Veit Valentin, *The German People* (New York, 1946); Edmond Vermeil, *Germany's Three Reichs* (London, 1944), analyzing the Holy Roman Empire, the Bismarckian Empire, and the Hitler Reich; Sir Adolphus W. Ward, *Germany, 1815–1890* (Cambridge, 1916–18), 3 vols.; the authoritative work by Hajo Holborn, *A History of Modern Germany: The Reformation* (New York, 1959); and the comprehensive study of James K. Pollock and Homer Thomas, *Germany in Power and Eclipse: the Background of Germany's Development* (New York, 1952).

Specific periods and aspects of lasting significance for a fuller interpretation are well analyzed in: James Bryce, *The Holy Roman Empire* (London, 1919); J. W. Thompson, *Feudal Germany* (Chicago, 1928); Ernst Kantorowicz, *Frederick the Second, 1194–1250* (New York, 1931); Heinrich Mitteis, *Der Staat des Hohen Mittelalters* (Weimar, 1944); Sidney B. Fay, *The Rise of Brandenburg Prussia to 1786* (New York, 1937); Gustav F. von Schmoller, *The Mercantile System and Its Historical Significance* (New York, 1896); W. H. Bruford, *Germany in the 18th Century* (Cambridge, 1935); Walter L. Dorn, *Competition for Empire, 1740–1763* (New York, 1940); G. P. Gooch, *Germany and the French Revolution* (London, 1920); C. T. Atkinson, *A History of Germany 1715–1815* (London, 1908); W. O. Henderson, *The Zollverein* (Cambridge, 1939); Sir John H. Clapham, *The Economic Development of France and Germany, 1815–1914* (Cambridge, 1936); J. G.

442

Legge, *Rhyme and Revolution in Germany, 1813–1850* (London, 1918); Heinrich von Sybel, *The Founding of the German Empire by William I* (Eng. ed., New York 1890–8); Heinrich von Treitschke, *History of Germany in 19th Century* (Eng. ed., 1915–19), 7 vols.; Friedrich Meinecke, *Weltbürgertum und Nationalstaat* (7th ed., Berlin, 1928); Franz Schnabel, *Deutsche Geschichte im 19ten Jahrhundert* (Freiburg, 1929–37), 4 vols.; Herbert Marcuse, *Reason and Revolution: Hegel and the Rise of Social Theory* (London, 1941); Heinrich von Srbik, *Deutsche Einheit; Idee und Wirklichkeit vom Heiligen Reich bis Königgrätz* (Munich, 1935–42), 4 vols.; A. J. P. Taylor, *The Hapsburg Monarchy, 1809–1918* (London, 1948); Heinrich Friedjung, *The Struggle for Supremacy in Germany, 1859–1866* (London, 1935), a condensed translation of an Austrian historian's study, published in 1897; Leonard Krieger, *The German Idea of Freedom* (Beacon Press, 1957); Prince Hubertus zu Loewenstein, *The Germans in History* (New York, 1945); Koppel S. Pinson, *Modern Germany* (New York, 1954); Gordon A. Craig, *The Politics of the Prussian Army, 1640–1945* (Oxford, 1955); Henry C. Meyer, *Mitteleuropa in German Thought and Action, 1815–1945* (The Hague, 1955).

On 1848 and especially the impact of its failure on Germany society and political attitudes, see Ernst Kohn-Branstedt, *Aristocracy and the Middle Classes in Germany; Social Types in German Literature, 1830–1900* (London, 1937); Lewis Namier, *1848: the Revolution of the Intellectuals* (London, 1944); Veit Valentin, *1848: Chapters of German History* (London, 1940), an abridged edition of a larger study in German. See, also, Sigmund Neumann, "The Structure and Strategy of Revolution: 1848 and 1948," *Journal of Politics*, 11 (1948), pp. 532–44; Friedrich Meinecke, "The Year 1848 in German History: Reflections on a Centenary," *Review of Politics*, 10 (1948), pp. 475–92; Ricarda Huch, *Alte und Neue Götter* (Berlin, 1930); Wilhelm Mommsen, *Grösse und Versagen des deutschen Bürgertums* (Stuttgart, 1949); and Rudolf Stadelmann, *Sociale und politische Geschichte der Revolution von 1848* (Munich, 1948).

For an account of the constitution of the Paulskirche, consult J. A. Hawgood, *Modern Constitutions since 1787* (London, 1939). A German text will be found in F. Marschall von Bieberstein, *Verfassungsrechtliche Reichsgesetze und wichtige Verordnungen* (Mannheim, 1929), pp. 85–118.

The classical, comprehensive bibliography of Dahlmann-Waitz, ed., *Quellenkunde der Deutschen Geschichte* (9th ed., Leipzig, 1931) has recently had a short and useful up-to-date successor in Günther Franz, *Bücherkunde zur Deutschen Geschichte* (Munich, 1951).

II. THE BISMARCK EMPIRE

For a general appraisal of the period, see C. G. Robertson, *Bismarck* (London, 1918); Erich Eyck, *Bismarck and the German Empire* (London, 1950); Friedrich Darmstaedter, *Bismarck and the Creation of the Second Reich* (London, 1948); B. E. Howard, *The German Empire* (New York, 1906); Fritz-Konrad Krueger, *Government and Politics of Germany* (Yonkers, 1915); R. H. Fife, *The German Empire Between Two Wars* (New York, 1916); A. L. Lowell, *Governments and Parties in Continental Europe* (Boston, 1896), 2 vols.; William H. Dawson, *The German Empire, 1867–1914* (London, 1919), 2 vols.; and Johannes Ziekursch, *Politische Geschichte des neuen deutschen Kaiserreiches* (Frankfurt a. M., 1925–30), 3 vols.

The text of the Bismarck constitution may be found in W. F. Dodd, *Modern Constitutions* (Chicago, 1909), Vol. I, pp. 325–51; B. E. Howard, *The German Empire* (New York, 1906). For the best German collection of the fundamental constitutions, see Karl Binding, *Deutsche Staatsgrundgesetze in diplomatisch genauem Abdrucke* (Leipzig, 1915); especially valuable are its comparative analyses of the North German Confederation constitutions (1867) and the German Empire (1871).

The outstanding German treatise on the imperial constitution is Paul Laband, *Das Staatsrecht des deutschen Reiches* (5th ed., Tübingen, 1911–14), 4 vols., later published in a one-volume edition (Tübingen, 1909). See, also, Heinrich Triepel, *Quellensammlung zum deutschen Reichsstaatsrecht* (5th ed., Tübingen, 1931). An excellent analysis of the writings of the jurists of the Empire and of the early Weimar Republic is Rupert Emerson, *State and Sovereignty in Modern Germany* (New Haven, 1928).

On the interrelations between foreign affairs and international political forces during this period, see Raymond J. Sontag, *Germany and England; Background of Conflict, 1848–1894* (New York, 1938); E. M. Carroll, *Germany and the Great Powers, 1866–1914: a Study in Public Opinion and Foreign Policy* (New York, 1938); Pauline R. Anderson, *The Background of Anti-English Feeling in Germany, 1890–1902* (Washington, 1939); Erich Brandenburg, *From Bismarck to the World War* (Eng. ed., London, 1927); and, for an overall analysis, William Langer, *European Alliances and Alignments, 1871–1890* (New York, 1931), and *The Diplomacy of Imperialism, 1890–1902* (2nd ed., New York, 1951). Note, also, on military affairs: Alfred Vagts, *A History of Militarism* (New York, 1937); E. M. Earle, ed., *Makers of Modern Strategy* (Princeton, 1943).

An insight into the sociopolitical tensions within the Second Empire, especially under William II, can be gained from Thorstein Veblen, *Imperial Germany and the Industrial Revolution* (New York, 1939); W. F. Bruck, *Social and Economic History of Germany from William II to Hitler, 1888–1938* (London, 1938); H. Levy, *Industrial Germany; a Study of Its Monopoly Organizations and Their Control by the State* (Cambridge, 1935); Lysbeth W. Muncy, *The Junker in the Prussian Administration under William II, 1888–1914* (Providence, 1944); Alexander Gerschenkron, *Bread and Democracy in Germany* (Berkeley, 1943); Mildred Wertheimer, *The Pan-German League* (New York, 1924); F. Lilje, *The Abuse of Learning; the Failure of the German University* (New York, 1948); Theodor Wolff, *The Eve of 1914* (New York, 1936); and above all, Arthur Rosenberg, *The Birth of the German Republic, 1871–1918* (New York, 1931).

For poignant, critical analyses in German, see Max Weber, "Parlament und Regierung im neugeordneten Deutschland," *Gesammelte Politische Schriften* (Munich, 1921), pp. 126–260, and *Gesammelte Aufsätze zur Soziologie und Sozialpolitik* (Tübingen, 1924), pp. 323–93. See, also, the studies of Eckart Kehr, *Schlachtflottenbau und Parteipolitik, 1894–1901* (Berlin, 1930); "Zur Genesis des Kgl. preussischen Reserveoffiziers," *Die Gesellschaft*, 2 (1928), pp. 492 ff., and "Das soziale System in Preussen unter dem Minister Puttkamer," *Die Gesellschaft*, 2 (1929), pp. 253 ff.; Carl Brinkmann, "Die Aristokratie im Kapitalistischen Zeitalter," *Grundriss der Sozialökonomik*, 9 (1923), pp. 22–34; F. C. Endres, "Soziologische Struktur und ihr entsprechende Ideologien des deutschen Offizierkorps vor dem Weltkriege," *Archiv für Sozialwissenschaft und Sozialpolitik*, 58 (1927), pp. 282 ff.; Theodor Heuss, *Friedrich Naumann* (2nd ed., Stuttgart, 1949), a superb biography by the present president of the German Federal Republic, which deals with the outstanding German Liberal of the Wilhelminic era, who personified an uneasy compromise of freedom and power.

For the critical von Bülow period, consult, apart from his more comprehensive *Denkwürdigkeiten* (Berlin, 1931), Bernhard von Bülow, *Imperial Germany* (New York, 1914); Theodor Eschenburg, *Das Kaiserreich am Scheidewege* (Berlin, 1929); Walter Koch, *Volk und Staatsführung vor dem Weltkriege* (Stuttgart, 1935).

Among the recent monographs on the Empire, special mention should be made of the following, not only for their substantive contents but also for their methodological contributions to the field. Carl Schorske, *German Social Democracy* (Cambridge, 1955); William O. Shanahan, *German Protestants Face the Social Question* (Notre Dame, 1954); Annelise Thimme, *Hans Delbrück als Kritiker der Wilhelminischen Epoche*, edited by the Kommission für Geschichte des Parlamentarismus und der politischen Parteien (Düsseldorf, 1955); Peter Gay, *The Dilemma of Democratic Socialism* (New York, 1952). For World War I and the transition period, see A. J. Berlau, *The German Social Democratic Party, 1914–1921* (New York, 1949); and E. Prager, *Geschichte der U.S.P.D.* (2nd ed., Berlin, 1932).

The war government, its character, effect, and breakdown are discussed in J. W. Wheeler-Bennett, *Wooden Titan: Hindenburg in Twenty Years of German History, 1914–1934* (New York, 1936); Karl Tschuppik, *Ludendorff; the Tragedy of a Military Mind* (Boston, 1932); Hans Speier, "Ludendorff," in E. M. Earle, ed., *Makers of Modern Strategy* (Princeton, 1943); A Mendelssohn-Bartholdy, *The War and German Society* (New Haven, 1937); R. H. Lutz, *Fall of the German Empire, 1904–1918* (Stanford, Cal., 1932); and for a collection of principal documents, Harry Rudin, *Armistice, 1918* (New Haven, 1944); and Prince Maximilian of Baden, *Memoirs* (London, 1928), 2 vols.

III. THE WEIMAR REPUBLIC

English translations of the Weimar constitution may be found in: H. L. McBain and L. Rogers, *The New Constitutions of Europe* (Garden City, 1922), pp. 176–212; H. Kraus, *The Crisis of German Democracy* (Princeton, 1932), pp. 179–216; F. Blachly and M. Oatman, *The Government and Administration of Germany* (Baltimore, 1928), pp. 642 ff.

Among the outstanding commentaries, the following German studies may be mentioned: Gerhard Anschütz, *Die Verfassung des deutschen Reichs* (14th ed., Berlin, 1933), and, also, his short essay, *Drei Leitgedanken der Weimarer Reichsverfassung* (Tübingen, 1923); W. Apelt, *Geschichte der Weimarer Verfassung* (Munich, 1946); Johannes V. Bredt, *Der Geist der Deutschen Reichsverfassung* (Berlin, 1924); Friedrich Glum, *Das parlamentarische Regierungssystem in Deutschland, Grossbritannien und Frankreich* (Munich, 1950); H. C. Nipperdey, ed., *Die Grundrechte und Grundpflichten der Reichsverfassung* (Berlin, 1929–30), 3 vols.; Hugo Preuss, *Deutschlands republikanische Reichsverfassung* (2nd ed., Berlin, 1923), *Staat, Recht und Freiheit* (Tübingen, 1926), and *Reich und Länder* (Berlin, 1928); Rudolf Smend, *Verfassung und Verfassungsrecht* (Munich, 1928).

For illuminating analyses of the origin and development of the constitution, consult Walter Jellinek, "Revolution und Reichsverfassung," *Jahrbuch des öffentlichen Rechts der Gegenwart,* 19 (1920), pp. 1–128; Fritz Poetzsch-Heffter, "Vom Staatsleben unter der Weimar Verfassung," ibid., 13 (1925), pp. 1–248, and 17 (1929), pp. 1–141; Ernst Wolgast, *Zum deutschen Parlamentarismus: Der Kampf um Artikel 54 der deutschen Reichsverfassung* (Berlin, 1929).

The best German sources for reference purposes are: Cuno Horkenbach, ed., *Das Deutsche Reich von 1918 bis Heute* (Berlin, 1931); M. Müller-Jabusch, *Handbuch des öffentlichen Lebens* (6th ed., Leipzig, 1931); Bernhard Harms, ed., *Volk und Reich der Deutschen* (Berlin, 1929), 3 vols., and *Recht und Staat im neuen Deutschland* (Berlin, 1929), 2 vols. For a systematic collection of all the relevant constitutional documents, see E. R. Huber, *Deutsche Verfassungsdokumente der Gegenwart, 1919–1951* (Tübingen, 1951).

Among the innumerable treatises in English, the following deserve special consideration: Herman Finer, *The Theory and Practice of Modern Government* (rev. ed., New York, 1949); H. J. Heneman, *The Growth of Executive Power in Germany; a Study of the German Presidency* (Minneapolis, 1934); Hajo Holborn, "The Influence of the American Constitution on the Weimar Constitution," in Conyers Read, ed., *The Constitution Reconsidered* (New York, 1938), pp. 285–96; Karl Loewenstein, "Government and Politics in Germany," in James T. Shotwell, ed., *Governments of Continental Europe* (rev. ed., New York, 1952); Johannes Mattern, *Principles of Constitutional Jurisprudence of the German National Republic* (Baltimore, 1928); Nathan Reich, *Labor Relations in Republican Germany* (New York, 1938); Lindsay Rogers et al., "Aspects of German Political Institutions," *Political Science Quarterly,* 47 (1932), pp. 321–51, 576–601; A. J. Zurcher, *The Experiment with Democracy in Central Europe* (New York, 1933). See, also, the studies from the pen of the outstanding French specialist, Edmond Vermeil, *La Constitution de Weimar et le principe de la démocratie allemande* (Strassbourg, 1923), and *L'Allemagne contemporaine, 1919–24* (Paris, 1925).

No adequate study is yet available in English on the German parties. For certain party developments during the Weimar Republic, see Sydney L. W. Mellen, "The German People and the Post-War World," *American Political Science Review,* 37

(1943), pp. 601–25; Rudolf Heberle, *From Democracy to Nazism* (Baton Rouge, 1945), a regional case study on Schleswig-Holstein; James K. Pollock, "An Area Study of the German Electorate, 1930–33," *American Political Science Review,* 38 (1944), pp. 89–95, and *German Election Administration* (New York, 1934); F. A. Hermens, *Democracy or Anarchy? A Study of Proportional Representation* (Notre Dame, 1941).

Among German studies, the following should be consulted: Ludwig Bergsträsser, *Geschichte der politischen Parteien in Deutschland* (9th ed., Munich, 1955); and Sigmund Neumann, *Die Deutschen Parteien* (2nd ed., Berlin, 1932), which includes a detailed bibliography. See also, for a short English resume, the author's article, "Parties, Political: German," *Encyclopedia of the Social Sciences,* Vol. XI, pp. 615–19; Heinrich Striefler, *Deutsche Wahlen in Bildern und Zahlen* (Düsseldorf, 1946).

On the history and politics of the republic, consult James W. Angell, *The Recovery of Germany* (New Haven, 1929); Otto Braun, *Von Weimar zu Hitler* (New York, 1940); Arnold Brecht, *Federalism and Regionalism in Germany* (New York, 1945); Robert T. Clark, *The Fall of the German Republic* (London, 1935); William S. Halperin, *Germany Tried Democracy* (New York, 1946); John B. Holt, *German Agricultural Policy, 1918–1934* (Chapel Hill, 1945); E. K. Poole, *German Financial Policies, 1932–1939* (Cambridge, Mass., 1939); Hugh Quigley and R. T. Clark, *Republican Germany* (New York, 1928); Godfrey Scheele, *The Weimar Republic, Overture to the Third Reich* (London, 1946); Eric Sutton, ed., *Gustav Stresemann: His Diaries, Letters and Papers* (New York, 1935–40), 3 vols.; Antonina Vallentin, *Stresemann* (New York, 1931); Frieda Wunderlich, *Labor under German Democracy, Arbitration, 1918–1933* (New York, 1940). For the last stages of Weimar, note especially: Arnold Brecht, *Prelude to Silence, the End of the German Republic* (New York, 1944); F. M. Watkins, *The Failure of Constitutional Emergency Powers under the German Republic* (Cambridge, Mass., 1939); J. W. Wheeler-Bennett, *Wooden Titan: Hindenburg in Twenty Years of German History, 1914–1934* (New York, 1936). On the earlier period, see the recent study of Klaus Epstein, *Matthias Erzberger and the Dilemma of German Democracy* (1959).

On the crisis of democratic society, see C. Bresciani-Turroni, *The Economics of Inflation* (Eng. ed., London, 1937); Erich Fromm, *Escape from Freedom* (New York, 1941); Theodor Geiger, *Die soziale Schichtung des deutschen Volkes* (Stuttgart, 1932); Alfred Whitney Griswold, "The Junkers: Hostages to the Past," *Virginia Quarterly Review,* 19 (1943), pp. 362–77; Paul Kosok, *Modern Germany: a Study of Conflicting Loyalties* (Chicago, 1933); H. D. Lasswell, *World Politics and Personal Insecurity* (New York, 1935); Heinz Marr, "Die Grossstadt als politische Lebensform," in *Grossstadt und Volkstum* (Hamburg, 1927); Sigmund Neumann, "Germany, Battlefield of the Middle Classes," *Foreign Affairs,* 13 (1935), pp. 271–83; Herbert Rosinski, *The German Army* (London, 1939); Hans Speier, "The Salaried Employee in Modern Society," *Social Research,* 1 (1934), pp. 111–33; A. F. Sturmthal, *The Tragedy of European Labor, 1918–1939* (New York, 1943); Pierre Vienot, *Incertitudes allemandes* (Paris, 1931); Frieda Wunderlich, "New Aspects of Unemployment in Germany," *Social Research,* 1 (1934), pp. 97–110.

Recent books on the Weimar Republic, which have been published in Germany, include: Karl Dietrich Bracher, *Die Auflösung der Weimarer Republik* (Stuttgart, 1955); Erich Eyck, *Gechichte der Weimarer Republik* (Stuttgart, 1954); and Theodor Eschenburg, *Die Improvisierte Demokratie der Weimarer Republik* (Schloss Laupheim, 1955). Mention might also be made of Hans Kohn, ed., *German History, Some New German Views* (London, 1954).

IV. THE THIRD REICH

The concept of modern dictatorship as exemplified in national socialism is systematically analyzed in Sigmund Neumann, *Permanent Revolution* (New York, 1942), including on pp. 313–75 an extensive bibliography on all aspects of totalitarianism. See also, Alfred Cobban, *Dictatorship, Its History and Theory* (New

York, 1939); Elie Halévy, "The Age of Tyrannies," *Economica*, N.S., 8 (1941), pp. 77–93; C. J. Friedrich, *Constitutional Government and Democracy* (rev. ed., Boston, 1950), especially his definitions for contrast. The classic formulation of the fundamental conflict between democracy and dictatorship will still be found in F. Dostoevskii, "The Grand Inquisitor," *The Brothers Karamazov* (New York, 1936).

The significant documents of the Third Reich are easily available in English translations, among others in James K. Pollock and H. J. Heneman, *The Hitler Decrees* (Ann Arbor, 1934); W. E. Rappard *et al., Source Book on European Governments* (New York, 1937), Pt. IV, pp. 1–202. For a systematic collection of Nazi legislation, consult Werner Hoche, *Die Gesetzgebung Adolf Hitlers* (Berlin, 1933 ff.). An almost inexhaustible source of information can be found in the rich documentation of the Nuremberg War Crimes Trials: *Nazi Conspiracy and Aggression* (Washington, 1946–48), 10 vols., and *The Trials of the Major War Criminals before the International Military Tribunal* (Nuremburg, 1947–49), 42 vols. See, also, Telford Taylor, *Nuremberg Trials, War Crimes and International Law* (New York, 1949).

The Nazis' rise to power is well analyzed in Konrad Heiden, *Der Führer* (Boston, 1944); C. B. Hoover, *Germany Enters the Third Reich* (New York, 1933); F. L. Schuman, *The Nazi Dictatorship: a Study in Social Pathology and the Politics of Fascism* (New York, 1935). A good bibliography covering recent writings may be found in John L. Snell, ed., *The Nazi Revolution* (Boston, 1959), pp. 94–97.

On the ideological background, in addition to Hitler's *Mein Kampf* and the "court philosopher" Alfred Rosenberg's *Der Mythus des 20. Jahrhunderts* (Munich, 1934), see Arthur Moeller van den Bruck, *Germany's Third Empire* (London, 1934), by an intellectual pathfinder though not a follower of Nazism. For critical studies see Hannah Arendt, *The Origins of Totalitarianism* (New York, 1951); R. D'O. Butler, *The Roots of National Socialism, 1783–1933* (London, 1941); A. Kolnai, *The War Against the West* (London, 1938); H. D. Lasswell, "The Psychology of Hitlerism," *Political Quarterly,* 4 (1933), pp. 373–84; H. Mankiewicz, *Le National-socialisme allemande, ses doctrines et leures realisations* (Paris, 1937); Edmond Vermeil, *Doctrinaires de la revolution allemande* (Paris, 1939); Maurice Baumont *et al., The Third Reich* (New York, 1955).

Among the numerous studies on the Third Reich in its concrete manifestations, the following may be selected as outstanding contributions: Franz L. Neumann, *Behemoth* (new ed., New York, 1944); Karl Loewenstein, *Hitler's Germany* (New York, 1940); R. A. Brady, *The Spirit and Structure of German Fascism* (New York, 1937); S. H. Roberts, *The House that Hitler Built* (London, 1939).

National socialism and its institutional aspects are specifically discussed in A. V. Boerner, "The Position of the NSDAP in the German Constitutional Order," *American Political Science Review,* 32 (1938), pp. 1059–81; Hans Gerth, "The Nazi Party: Its Leadership and Composition," *American Journal of Sociology,* 45 (1940), pp. 517–41; Fritz Brennecke, ed., *The Nazi Primer. Official Handbook for Schooling the Hitler Youth* (Eng. ed., New York, 1938); E. Y. Hartshorne, *The German Universities and National Socialism* (Cambridge, Mass., 1937); James K. Pollock and A. V. Boerner, *The German Civil Service Act* (Chicago, 1938); Ernst Fraenkel, *The Dual State* (New York, 1941); Karl Loewenstein, "Law in the Third Reich," *Yale Law Journal,* 45 (1936), pp. 779–815, and "Dictatorship and the German Constitution," *University of Chicago Law Review,* 4 (1937), pp. 537–74; L. Preuss, "Germanic Law versus Roman Law in National Socialist Legal Theory," *Journal of Comparative Legislation and International Law,* 16 (1934), pp. 260–80; John B. Mason, "The Judicial System of the Nazi Party," *American Political Science Review,* 38 (1944), pp. 96–103; Otto Kirchheimer, "Criminal Law in National Socialist Germany," *Studies in Philosophy and Social Science,* 8 (1939), pp. 444–63; H. J. Heneman, "German Social Honor Courts," *Michigan Law Review,* 37 (1939), pp. 725–44; C. W. Guillebaud, *The Social Policy of Nazi Germany* (Cambridge, 1941), and *The Economic Recovery of Germany* (London, 1939); Taylor Cole, "The Evolution of the German Labor Front," *Political Science Quarterly,* 52 (1937), pp. 532–58; Otto Nathan, *The Nazi Economic System: Germany's Mobilization for War* (Durham, 1944); Guenter Reimann, *The Vampire Economy* (New York, 1939); George N. Shuster, *Like a Mighty Army: Hitler versus Established Religion* (New York, 1935); Waldemar Gurian, *Hitler and the Christians* (New York, 1936); Edmond Taylor, *The Strategy of Terror* (Boston, 1940); Eugen Kogon, *The Theory and Practice of Hell* (New York, 1950); Ernst Kris and Hans Speier, *German Radio Propaganda* (New York, 1944); Derrick Sington and Arthur Weidenfeld, *The Goebbels Experiment: a Study of the Nazi Propaganda Machine* (New Haven, 1943); Alfred Vagts, *Hitler's Second Army* (Washington, 1943), a description of the movement's semimilitary organizations; and the elaborate, apologetic, but revealing story of Otto Meissner, *Staatssekretär unter Ebert, Hindenberg, Hitler* (Hamburg, 1950). On Hitler's plans and policies in respect to the destruction of European Jewry, see the comprehensive study of Gerald Reitlinger, *Die Endlösung* (Berlin, 1956).

On the complex relations between the Reichswehr and the Third Reich, consult H. E. Fried, *The Guilt of the German Army* (New York, 1942); Felix Gilbert, ed., *Hitler Directs His War* (New York, 1950), a selection of stenographic records of Hitler's daily military conferences; Adolf Heusinger, *Befehl im Widerstreit* (Tübingen, 1950); Friedrich Hossbach, *Zwischen Wehrmacht und Hitler, 1934–1938* (Wolfenbüttel, 1949); Peter Kleist, *Zwischen Hitler und Stalin, 1939–1945* (Bonn, 1950); Walter Görlitz, *Der Deutsche Generalstab* (Frankfurt a.M., 1950); Siegfried Westphal, *Heer in Feeseln, Aus den Papieren des Stabschefs von Rommel, Kesselring und Rundstedt* (Bonn, 1950); and Telford Taylor, *Sword and Swastika; Generals and Nazis in the Third Reich* (New York, 1952). A recent volume that throws light on the political role of the German army is J. W. Wheeler-Bennett, *The Nemesis of Power* (New York, 1953).

World affairs under the impact of National Socialism are analyzed in W. M. Jordan, *Great Britain, France and the German Problem, 1919–1939* (London, 1943); J. W. Wheeler-Bennett, *Munich: Prologue to Tragedy* (London, 1948); L. B. Namier, *Europe in Decay: A Study in Disintegration, 1936–1940* (London, 1950); Sigmund Neumann, *The Future in Perspective* (New York, 1946); E. Wiskemann, *The Rome-Berlin Axis* (New York, 1949); A. Rossi, *Deux ans d'alliance Germano-Sovietique* (Paris, 1949); Erich Kordt, *Wahn und Wirklichkeit* (Stuttgart, 1948), and *Nicht aus den Akten* (Stuttgart, 1950); Paul Schmidt, *Statist auf Diplomatischer Bühne* (Bonn, 1949). For the most important documentary background of World War II, see R. J. Sontag *et al., Documents on German Foreign Policy, 1918–1945* (Washington, 1949 ff.). Cf., also, Boris Celovsky, *Das Münchener Abkommen von 1938* (Stuttgart, 1958).

Recent German writings on foreign policy during the Nazi period are carefully reviewed in E. M. Carroll, "Recent German Publications and German Foreign Policy, 1933–1945," *American Political Science Review,* 46 (1952), pp. 525–51.

On the resistance against the Third Reich, consult: A. W. Dulles, *Germany's Underground* (New York, 1947); H. R. Trevor-Roper, *The Last Days of Hitler* (New York, 1947); Hans Rothfels, *The German Opposition to Hitler* (Hillsdale, 1948); H. B. Gisevius, *To the Bitter End* (Boston, 1947); Ulrich von Hassell, *The von Hassell Diaries, 1938–1944* (Garden City, 1947); G. A. Almond, ed., *The Struggle for Democracy in Germany* (Chapel Hill, 1949); F. Ford, "The Twentieth of July in the History of the German Resistance," *American Historical Review,* 51 (1946), pp. 609–26; Annedore Leber, *Das Gewissen steht auf. 64 Lebensbilder aus dem deutschen Widerstand* (Berlin, 1956); see also Bernhard Vollmer, *Volksopposition im Polizeistaat* (Stuttgart, 1957).

V. THE SECOND REPUBLIC

On the aftermath of war and dictatorship, see United States Strategic Bombing reports: *The Effects of Strategic Bombing on the German War Economy* (Washington, 1945); also Leonard Krieger, "The Interregnum in Germany," *Political Science Quarterly,* 6 (1949), pp. 507–32; Hoyt Price and Carl E. Schorske, *The Problem of Germany* (New York, 1947); and Sigmund Neumann, *Germany: Promise and Perils* (New York, 1950).

Rich material on the Allied Military Government can be drawn from Hajo Holborn, *American Military Government, Its Organization and Policies* (Washington, 1947); C. J. Friedrich *et al., American Experience in Military Government in World War II* (New York, 1948); Wolfgang Friedmann, *The Allied Military Government of Germany* (London, 1947); James K. Pollock and J. H. Meisel, *Germany under Occupation: Illustrative Materials and Documents* (rev. ed., Ann Arbor, 1949); Lucius D. Clay, *Decision in Germany* (Garden City, 1950); R. E. Elder, "Quadripartite Military Government Organization and Operations in Germany," *American Journal of International Law*, 41 (1947), pp. 650–55. See, also, the critical essays of John H. Herz, "The Fiasco of Denazification in Germany," *Political Science Quarterly*, 63 (1948), pp. 569–94, and the "Symposium on Military Government in Germany," *Annals of the American Academy of Political and Social Science*, 267 (1950); Harold Zink, *American Military Government in Germany* (New York, 1947); Karl Loewenstein, "Law and the Legislative Process in Occupied Germany," *Yale Law Journal*, 57 (1948), pp. 724–60, 994–1022. Among the official United States publications, past and present, the following are imperative for current information: Department of State *Bulletin* (Washington, D.C.); *Information Bulletin*, monthly magazine of the Office of United States High Commissioner for Germany (Frankfurt a.M.), and *Report on Germany*, also a publication by H.I.C.O.G.; for the eastern zone and world communism, see *Ost-Probleme* (Information Services Division, H.I.C.O.G., Bad Nauheim). Among the German contributions, the following are worth considering: Wilhelm Grewe, *Ein Besatzungsstatut für Deutschland* (Stuttgart, 1948), and Erich Kaufmann, *Deutschlands Rechtslage unter der Besatzung* (Stuttgart, 1948). Harold Zink, *The United States in Germany 1944–55* (New York, 1957), provides the most complete account of the American occupation.

For the background of the Bonn constitutional development, consult: *Bericht über den Verfassungskonvent auf Herrenchiemsee Aug. 10–23, 1948* (Munich, 1948); also *Documents on the Creation of the German Federal Constitution*, and *Constitutions of the German Länder* (Berlin, 1947–9), prepared by the Civil Administration Division, O.M.G.U.S. An English translation of "The Basic Law for the Federal Republic of Germany" is available through the United States Government Printing Office, *The Bonn Constitution* (Washington, 1949). Among the notable analyses may be listed Arnold Brecht, "The New German Constitution," *Social Research*, 16 (1949), pp. 425–73; C. J. Friedrich, "Rebuilding the German Constitution," *American Political Science Review*, 43 (1949), pp. 461–82, 704–20; Hans Simons, "The Bonn Constitution and Its Government," in Hans Morgenthau, ed., *Germany and the Future of Europe* (Chicago, 1951).

For a German text of the Bonn document, the Länder constitutions, and the occupational statutes, see E. R. Huber, *Quellen zum Staatsrecht der Neuzeit* (Tübingen, 1951), Vol. II, pp. 154–621. Among the German commentaries, the following should be consulted: Hermann von Mangoldt and Friedrich Klein, *Das Bonner Grungesetz* (2nd ed., Berlin, Frankfurt a.M., 1957), Vol. I; Theodor Maunz, *Deutsches Staatsrecht* (Munich, 1951); and the rich collection of essays in *Festgabe für Erich Kaufmann* (Stuttgart, 1950). See, also, Theodor Eschenburg, *Staat und Gesellschaft in Deutschland* (Stuttgart, 1956).

Among the numerous evaluations of Bonn's first decade, the following studies stand out: Richard Hiscocks, *Democracy in Western Germany* (London, 1957); Alfred Grosser, *The Colossus Again* (Praeger, 1955); Hans Speier and W. Phillips Davison, ed., *Western German Leadership and Foreign Policy* (Evanston, 1957); Hans Speier, *German Rearmament and Atomic War* (Evanston, 1957); and James B. Conant, *Germany and Freedom: a Personal Appraisal* (Cambridge, 1958). A comprehensive bibliography may be found in John Brown Mason, "Government, Administration, and Politics in West Germany: a Selected Bibliography," *American Political Science Review*, 52 (1958), pp. 513–30.

Representative monographs evidencing promising field research are Rudolf Wildenmann, *Partei und Fraktion: Ein Beitrag zur Analyse der politischen Willensbildung und des Parteiensystems in der Bundesrepublik* (Meisenheim, 1954); Hans Georg Wieck, *Die Entstehung der CDU und die Wiedergründung des Zentrums im Jahre 1945* (Düsseldorf, 1953); Stephanie Munke, *Wahlkampf und Machtverschiebung: Geschichte und Analyse der Berliner Wahlen, 1950* (Berlin, 1952); H. Hund, *Der BHE in Koalition und Opposition* (Heidelberg, 1953); Götz Roth, *Fraktion und Regierungsbildung: Eine monographische Darstellung der Regierungsbildung in*

Nierdersachsen (Meisenheim, 1954); Heinz Markmann, *Das Abstimnungsverhalten der Parteifraktionen in deutschen Parlamenten* (Meisenheim, 1954); Wolfgang Hirsch-Weber *et al., Wähler und Gewählte* (Berlin, 1957); Erich Peter Neumann and Elisabeth Noelle, *Antworten, Politik im Kraftfeld der öffentlichen Meinung* (Allensbach, 1954), and Otto Büsch and Peter Furth, *Rechtsradikalismus im Nachkriegsdeutschland* (Berlin, 1958).

The socioeconomic problems of the Second Republic are discussed in Edgar Salin, "Social Forces in Germany Today," *Foreign Affairs*, 28 (1950), pp. 265–77; Howard S. Ellis, *The Economics of Freedom* (New York, 1950), especially pp. 175–238; Sigmund Neumann, "The New Crisis Strata in German Society," in H. Morgenthau, ed., op. cit.; Howard Becker, "Changes in the Social Stratification of Contemporary Germany," *American Sociological Review*, 15 (1950), pp. 333–42; Eugen Lemberg and Lothar Krecker, eds., *Die Entstehung eines neuen Volkes aus Binnendeutschen und Ostvertriebenen* (Marburg, 1950). See also Dolf Sternberger, *Research in Germany on Pressing Social Problems* (Washington, D.C., 1951).

An outstanding study on recent economic developments is Henry C. Wallich, *Mainsprings of German Revival* (New Haven, 1955). See, also, Erich Reigrotzki, *Soziale Verflechtungen in der Bundesrepublik* (Tübingen, 1956), and die Europaischen Gespräche, esp. *Gewerkschaften und Parlament* (Köln-Deutz, 1956), and *Die Gesellschaft in der Wir leben* (Köln-Deutz, 1957). Thought-provoking analyses of the internal development of Germany as recorded by close observers of the scene are: Fritz René Allemann, *Bonn ist nicht Weimar* (Berlin, 1956); Horst Mönnich, *Das Land ohne Träume* (Braunschweig, 1954); Joachim Moras and Hans Paeschke, *Deutscher Geist zwischen Gestern und Morgen* (Stuttgart, 1954); and Helmut Schelsky, *Die skeptische Generation. Eine Soziologie der deutschen Jugend* (Düsseldorf, 1957).

The text of the constitution of the German Democratic Republic can be found in Karl Steinhoff, *Die Verfassung der Deutschen Demokratischen Republik* (Berlin, 1950), and E. R. Huber, *Quellen zum Staatsrecht der Neuzeit*, Vol. II, pp. 292–312. For an official exposition of Eastern German policies, see Walter Ulbricht, *Lehrbuch für den demokratischen Staats und Wirtschaftsaufbau* (Berlin, 1950); Otto Grotewohl, *Der Kampf um den Frieden und die Nationale Front des Demokratischen Deutschlands* (Berlin, 1950); Karl Polak, *Marxismus und Staatslehre* (Berlin, 1947), and *Beschlüsse und Dokumente des 3. Parteitages der SED* (1950); Wilhelm Pieck, *Reden und Aufsätze* (Berlin, 1950), Vol. II; see, also, the party organs *Die Einheit* and *Neue Justiz*. For an English text of the eastern constitution, see United States High Commissioner for Germany, *Soviet Zone Constitution and Electoral Law* (1951).

The information on the Eastern German Democratic Republic is limited indeed. For a remarkable analysis, in view of this limitation, see J. P. Nettl, *The Eastern Zone and Soviet Policy in Germany, 1945–50* (London and New York, 1951); cf. also Franz Neumann, "Soviet Policy in Germany," *Annals of the American Academy of Political and Social Science*, 263 (1949), pp. 165–79; and Otto Kirchheimer, "The Government of Eastern Germany," in H. Morgenthau, ed., op. cit. Among the recent publications, note particularly Horst Duhnke, *Stalinismus in Deutschland* (Köln, 1955); Carola Stern, *Porträt einer Bolschewistischen Partei* (Köln, 1957); M. G. Lange, *Totalitäre Erziehung, Das Erziehungssystem der Sowjetzone Deutschlands* (Frankfurt a.M., 1954); and Joachim Schultz, *Der Funktionär in der Einheitspartei* (Stuttgart, 1956). See also Ernst Richert, *Agitation und Propaganda* (Berlin, 1958), and *Macht ohne Mandat* (Köln, 1958).

A rich source of general information is offered by the annual *Deutschland Jahrbuch*, edited by Klaus Mehnert and Heinrich Schulte. See also Elisabeth Noelle and Erich Peter Neumann, *Jahrbuch der Öffentlichen Meinung, 1947–1955* (Institut für Demoskopie, Allensbach, 1956).

Among notable periodicals, the following cover major areas of public affairs: *Archiv des Öffentlichen Rechts, Aussenpolitik, Deutsche Verwaltung, Die Öffentliche Verwaltung, Europa Archiv, Frankfurter Hefte, Die Gegenwart, Deutsche Rundschau, Hochland, Kölner Zeitschrift für Soziologie, Der Monat, Neue Juristische Wochenschrift, Schmollers Jahrbücher, Soziale Welt, Die Welt als Geschichte, Weltwirtschaftliches Archiv, Zeitschrift für die Gesammte Staatswissenschaft, Viertel-*

jahrshefte für Zeitgeschichte, Zeitschrift für Politik, Politische Studien, and *Das Parlament.*

Representative newspapers of the Western Federal Republic are *Frankfurter Allgemeine Zeitung, Süddeutsche Zeitung, Die Welt, Deutsche Zeitung und Wirtschaftszeitung, Christ und Welt,* and *Die Zeit.* For the Eastern Democratic Republic, see *Neues Deutschland.*

For official information consult: *Verhandlungen des deutschen Bundestages, Sitzungen des Deutschen Bundesrates,* and *Entscheidungen des Bundesverfassungsgerichtes.*

PART FOUR

ITALY

———◆———

by Gerard J. Mangone

19

THE ITALIAN HERITAGE

1. TWO THOUSAND YEARS OF HISTORY

It has been said that Italians are sometimes overwhelmed by their history, for Italy is a land where, to the north, Etruscans built roads and bridges, used sewing needles and razors, long before Rome appeared in the records; a land where, in the south, Greek colonists erected colossal temples for the teeming cities of Agrigento and Selinunte, which predated Julius Caesar by as many centuries as the discovery of America predates Dwight D. Eisenhower. To contemplate the heritage of a country that has known the classical rule of republican and imperial Rome, the invasions of German tribes from the north and both Arabs and Normans in the south, and to understand the imprint of the Catholic Church upon this land are preliminary to any study of the Italian political process.

The very weakness of the late Roman Empire, first Byzantine then German, meant the ascendancy of papal authority upon the peninsula of Italy. Thus the presence of a powerful international church, combined with the intrigues of would-be emperors who dreamed of the classic past, blocked the kind of dynastic unification that occurred in England, France, and Spain. During the Renaissance, which breathed fire into commerce and politics no less than letters and art, princes, dukes, and oligarchical republics vied with each other to consolidate their petty states by fractious alliances with the Pope or foreign monarchs. With good reason the Italian Christopher Columbus sought the resourceful Spanish court of Ferdinand and Isabella to support his bold exploration, for in 1492 the Italian peninsula, about the size of California, was divided into twelve different states—one kingdom, four duchies, six republics, and the papal domain, itself fragmented by powerful families who ruled such towns as Bologna, Perugia, Rimini, and Urbino.

By failing to unite under any banner in the sixteenth century, Italy, with its wealth of land, handicrafts, commerce, and art, became an easy prey for foreign aggressions: Spain, Austria, and France fought with each other for the booty and, in turn, overran the Italian peoples, each conqueror leaving a special imprint upon the Italian society.

Between 1559 and 1713, Spain completely dominated the peninsula with the exception of the Republic of Venice in the northeast and the Duchy of Savoy in the northwest. Among the undesirable features of this long, alien rule were an irresponsible nobility, an arrogant bureaucracy, and a cumbersome and inefficient public administration. Above all, Spanish tutelage was notorious for a burdensome tax system that imposed upon the masses imposts, excises, duties, and donations of various kinds, while largely exempting the clergy and the aristocracy. Such an experience could not fail to leave some traces upon the modern Italian state. The succeeding eighteenth century, for Italian politics, was marked by the territorial changes resulting from the rivalries between the Spanish-French Bourbons and the Austrian Hapsburgs. Among these changes Lombardy in the north was settled within the Austrian Empire, while the Kingdom of the Two Sicilies, encompassing the southern peninsula and the island of Sicily, was made a possession of the Bourbons, who succeeded in misruling almost uninterruptedly until 1860.

The French Revolution swept across Italy in the conquests of Napoleon Bonaparte, not only toppling the old political orders to suit the revived imperial dream, but bringing fresh ideas on the rights of man and liberty to Italians. Republics, dukedoms, and papal states were consolidated into three great French dependencies and, while the land and its treasures were exploited for the emperor, the French began vigorous economic and administrative reforms as well as numerous public works to improve water supply, transport, and river navigation. While these projects were often too ambitious, they furnished a healthy shock to the Italian lethargy of the past. This blast from the north, however, was short-lived, and its effects hardly reached the southern provinces. Indeed, this experience with French rule and the various Austrian occupations in the north, especially in Lombardy, emphasizes a fundamental feature of the historical background of modern Italian politics, namely, the impact of special European cultural influences on the north, while the south remained in the traditional Mediterranean orbit of Greece, Spain, and North Africa. No small part of the difficulties through which the Italian people have passed in building their nation, particularly along democratic principles, can be attributed to the fact that for centuries the economic and social development of the north and the south differed.

After the defeat of Napoleon the great statesmen of Europe, at the Congress of Vienna, once again bartered with the Italian peninsula and redivided it into ten different pieces. Austria dominated the situation, directly annexing Lombardy and the Veneto in the north, controlling the duchies of Parma, Lucca, Modena, and Tuscany through family ties, restoring a grateful pope to his domains, and vigilantly supporting the autocracy of the Kingdom of the Two Sicilies in the south against revolutionary demands for a constitution. Thus Italy entered the mid-nineteenth century, as Prince Metternich had truly said, "only a geographical expression," and destined to be among the very last European states to achieve unity.

The Austrian rule, though dependent upon a strong police, was by standards of the day commendable for its efficiency and honesty, and it would be wrong to suppose that the Italian subjects thoroughly disliked the regime of the empire or the duchies linked to it. Moreover, the masses of the people, overwhelmingly illiterate and out of touch with events beyond their province, emphatically thought of themselves as Piedmontese, Milanese, Tuscan, Roman, Neapolitan, or Sicilian, rather than "Italian." But the cycle of centuries of foreign occupation in Italy was nearing its end, for nowhere outside of France itself had the revolution of 1789 produced such a great effect as in Italy. Napoleon had broken the boundaries of the past, humbled the old aristocracy, enlisted thousands of Italian soldiers in his triumphant armies, and transmitted the fiery slogans of equality, fraternity, and liberty—with hopes of constitutional government—to the peninsula.

A revolution in Naples in 1820, a conspiracy at Modena in 1831, and an uprising in Bologna against the papal officials were suppressed by Austria. Nevertheless, fertile seeds of the independence movement had been planted, and they were cultivated by such poets and playwrights as Ugo Foscolo, Silvio Pellico, and Alessandro Manzoni. Students, doctors, and lawyers strengthened the spearhead of the national cultural and political revival known as the *Risorgimento*. Long frustrated in the development of national consciousness by the partitions of foreign rulers and the anomolous position of the Pope at Rome, Italy at last made ready to respond to Niccolò Machiavelli's sixteenth-century plea to liberate Italy from the barbarians and to act upon Vittorio Alfieri's clanging, nationalistic verses:

> The day shall come, return it must,
> When spirited Italians boldly thrust
> Themselves in battle.[1]

The shining apostle of Italian nationalism was Giuseppe Mazzini, who dedicated his entire life to Italian freedom. At first a member of the secret Carbonari society, which had been working subversively throughout the peninsula since Napoleonic times, he later organized the dynamic *Giovine Italia* organization to enlist the idealism of youth for Italian liberty. Mazzini fervently believed that God had granted Italy natural boundaries in the Alps and the surrounding seas with their islands of Corsica, Sardinia, and Sicily, so that all Italy must be united under one government. Furthermore, he felt that the truest expression of God was the free will of men and that a republic would be the most desirable government for Italy. The personal influence of Mazzini was enormous, for he charged the Italian people with their moral duties as patriots to make sacrifices for their fatherland and to resort to revolutionary action. Another approach to Italian unity was offered by Vin-

---

[1] From *Il Misogallo* (*The French-hater*). Alfieri, born in Piedmont in 1749, like other Piedmontese aristocrats, spoke French and in his youth despised the Italians. But later he willfully de-gallicized himself, voluntarily left Piedmont for Tuscany, and became the most ardent literary herald of Italian nationalism.

THE ITALIAN REPUBLIC

0 — 100
SCALE OF MILES

SWITZERLAND

FRANCE

Innsbruck

AUSTRIA

Aosta

Como

Torino
(Turin)

LOMBARDY

Milano
(Milan)

Bolzano

Belluno

VENEZIA

Cuneo

PIEDMONT

Brescia

Verona

VENETO

Udine

Cremona

Venice

Trieste

Zagreb

LIGURIA

Genova
(Genoa)

EMILIA

Parma

Modena

Bologna

POR.

Fiume

YUGOSLAVIA

Spezia

Ravenna

LIGURIAN SEA

Pisa

Florence

ARNO

Livorno

TUSCANY

MARCHES

Pesaro

Ancona

ADRIATIC SEA

CORSE (CORSICA)
(France)

ELBA

Siena

Perugia

Macerata

Aleria

Grosseto

UMBRIA

Ajaccio

Terni

Viterbo

Teramo

TIBER

LATIUM

ABRUZZI

Chieti

SARDEGNA
(SARDINIA)

(Italy)

ROMA
(Rome)

Anzio

CAMPANIA

Foggia

Bari

STRAIT OF OTRANTO

Napoli
(Naples)

APULIA

Salerno

BASILICATA

TYRRHENIAN SEA

Taranto

GULF OF
TARANTO

MEDITERRANEAN

Cosenza

CALABRIA

LIPARI ISLANDS

Palermo

TUNISIA

Tunis

SICILIA
(SICILY)

Messina

Reggio

STRAIT OF MESSINA

IONIAN SEA

Catania

STRAIT OF

Ragusa

SEA

MALTA (GREAT BRITAIN)

cenzo Gioberti, a sensitive priest who doubted the stern theistic tones of Mazzini's program and its lack of compromise with the Catholic Church. He addressed himself to the then-prevalent opinion that a unitary state was not really desirable for Italy in view of the enduring local and regional sentiments, and argued that the principalities should be peacefully joined in a federal state, along the lines of the Swiss confederation, with the Pope at its head.

2. "HOW A PRINCE OUGHT TO COMPORT HIMSELF"

In the spectacular years that bridged the first war of Italian liberation in 1848 and the final surrender of the king of the Two Sicilies to nationalist forces at Gaeta in 1861, Italy might have been unified in different ways. The rooted institution of the papacy and its steadfast resistance to any subordination of the Church to a national government might possibly have led to a federation under the Pope. Even after Pius IX had denounced the first war of liberation, adherents of democratic federalism could appreciate the difficulties in uniting a peninsula of many diverse regions—where Turin and Milan had already felt the influences of the Industrial Revolution and liberalism, where Rome was a little theocratic state, where outside Naples and Palermo peasants still lived in feudalism dating from the Middle Ages. Meanwhile the republicans, constantly goaded by Mazzini, were kindling frequent revolts, were seizing power here and there, and, carried on by their zeal for representative government without the institution of monarchy, were always hoping for a mass uprising. In reality, no unification of Italy was possible as long as Austria garrisoned Lombardy-Veneto, the most populous and fertile area of the country, and stood ready to intervene in any rebellious part of the peninsula.

In 1831 Charles Albert had succeeded to the Piedmont-Sardinian throne and had embarked upon a series of remarkable reforms designed to strengthen his realm, which stretched from the French frontier to the Ticino River and which included the cities of Genoa and Turin as well as the rugged, underdeveloped island of Sardinia. The civil laws, in a chaotic condition, were pruned, clarified, and codified; a new, comprehensive criminal and procedural code soon followed. The army was reorganized, equipped, and trained, so that the state could count upon eighty thousand ready men—including a corps of light infantry known as the Bersaglieri. Agriculture was promoted, subventions were given by the state to industry, and commerce was encouraged by prudent tariffs. Though definitely opposed to any parliamentary institutions, Charles Albert instituted a Council of State, composed of distinguished men, to whom he submitted both legislative proposals and the budget for advice.

Europe was aflame in 1848 and, as early as January 12 of that year, Palermo revolted against the Bourbon troops of the Kingdom of the Two Sicilies; Naples soon followed, and within a month Ferdinand had granted a constitution to his people. At the beginning of February, therefore, Charles Albert appointed a Conference Council to advise him on the revolutionary turn of events, and it soon came to the regretful conclusion that a fundamental law, called the Statuto, must be promulgated. The Conference Council advised, "It is necessary to give it, not let it be imposed: to dictate the conditions, not receive them . . . the constitution is without doubt an evil, but we are brought to the point of choosing the lesser evil to avoid greater ones." [2] Thus there was proclaimed for the Kingdom of Piedmont-Sardinia a constitution under which the king would share legislative power with a parliament composed of two houses. The membership of the Senate would be unlimited in number and appointed by the king; the Chamber of Deputies would be limited in number and elected by men, at least twenty-five years old, literate, and paying direct taxes of a certain amount or, in the case of tradesmen and manufacturers, possessing property of a certain value. It was these legal codes and constitution that were adapted to the later Kingdom of Italy.

Charles Albert had led forty thousand Piedmontese troops across the Ticino River into Lombardy when Milan rebelled against Austria in 1848, but the first war of liberation failed disastrously, for the enthusiastic slogans of nationalism failed to produce soldiers. The other Italian states gave suspicious, halfhearted support.[3] Democrats and republicans fared no better against the might of Austria in Tuscany or Venice, nor could Mazzini's dictatorship in the Republic of Rome, supported by the courageous Giuseppe Garibaldi, long withstand thirty thousand French troops who intervened at the plea of the Pope. In the reaction of 1849–50, moreover, constitutional government was toppled everywhere in Italy except Piedmont, where the son of Charles Albert, Victor Emmanuel II, barely thirty years old, had upheld the Statuto. Inexorably patriots were drawn behind the banner of the House of Savoy, which offered the only Italian prince willing both to head a national unity movement and to maintain constitutional government.[4]

3. IN UNITY THERE SHOULD BE STRENGTH

If the seeds of rebellion had been sown and the symbol of national liberation virtually agreed upon, only an engineer, patient and astute, was needed to build the state. Camillo Benso di Cavour in November, 1852, at the age of forty-two, became prime minister of Piedmont. An eco-

[2] Taken from the original protocol (which was written in French), partly reproduced in Italo Pauli, *Leggi e lotte elettorali in Italia* (1953).

[3] Lombardy-Veneto raised 15,000 volunteers, Tuscany another 7,000, and the Pope was forced by public opinion to send 10,000, while 16,000 came from the Kingdom of the Two Sicilies. But neither the pontiff nor the princes broke relations with Austria, and they forbade their troops to go beyond the Po!

[4] In 1851 Gioberti abandoned all ideas of federalism and threw his support for unification under the House of Savoy; in 1853 a futile rebellion of the republicans permanently eclipsed the star of Mazzini.

nomic liberal, he encouraged foreign trade, lowered the grain tariff, modernized agricultural production, and especially promoted the infant textile industry. To improve railroad communications, he did not hesitate to float respectable public loans and, though a staunch Catholic, firmly held to the belief of a free church in a free state.[5] But his fame rests upon his foreign policy: he cultivated painstakingly the favor of Louis Napoleon at almost any price, raised the plight of a divided Italy into an international issue at the Congress of Paris in 1856, and intrigued France, with Piedmont at her side, into war against Austria in 1859.

Thus the goal of driving Austria out of Italy succeeded, but the travail of liberation left deep wounds in the body politic. Lombardy had been won, and the National Society had tirelessly prepared the way for the annexation of Tuscany and Emilia-Romagna to the new kingdom of Italy.[6] Yet national pride had been wounded in the sacrifice of Nice and Savoy to Napoleon III; and the invasion of the Papal States, which resulted in limiting the temporal power of the Pope to Rome and a small strip of the Latium coast, aligned the Roman Catholic Church vigorously against the new state.

Above all other problems towered that of the south. How could a third of the whole peninsula and the island of Sicily, with their poverty, ignorance, and corrupt governments, be integrated into the new Piedmontese-oriented polity? Garibaldi had swept away the molded crust of the Bourbon rule in his triumphant march from Marsala to Naples, while Cavour had been quick enough to urge Victor Emmanuel II on the scene to receive the plebiscite for union with Italy. But when the dizzy infatuation for Garibaldi had passed and the ardor for Victor Emmanuel II had cooled, the feudal extortions of the peasantry by the landowners remained, the bribery of local officials continued, the lack of roads and railroads still limited the markets, the malarial swamps still decimated the villages, while beggary and brigandage festered upon the people from Naples to Palermo.

The intense regional sentiment in Italy that had been restrained by the achievements of national unification, moreover, inevitably reacted against Piedmontese bureaucratic centralism and Piedmontese laws and customs. Before his untimely death in 1861 Cavour, consequently, had to steer a course for the new state between the demands of those at Turin who thought that Italy should be Piedmont written larger and the agitators for regional autonomy who might undo a decade of careful planning.

[5] Between 1848 and 1857 the silk trade doubled, the cotton trade quadrupled, and agricultural wages rose 25 per cent, while six hundred miles of railroad were put in operation in Piedmont. Each commune was required to support one elementary school and Cavour accepted a bill mildly regulating private (clerical) schools and further strengthening secondary public schools.

[6] The National Society was founded by men of vision who renounced republicanism: Giorgio Pallavicino, who spent fourteen years in an Austrian prison with Silvio Pellico; Daniele Manin, hero of the Venetian Republic of 1848; and Giuseppe La Farina, a former minister of Sicily. The Society prepared the way for unification by tireless propaganda and by winning public opinion for its slogan, "Italy and Victor Emmanuel." Giuseppe Garibaldi even joined as a vice-president, but not Mazzini.

The weakness of Italy was painfully revealed by the fact that she did not liberate herself. Unification of the north and central provinces had only been possible through French alliance. Where France paused, at the border of Venetia or in Rome, Italy went no further. Indeed, Venetia was added in 1866 only as a result of the victory of the Prussians over Austria and the mediation of France. Finally, although the 443 deputies of the first parliament of Italy at Turin, on February 18, 1861, had unanimously endorsed Cavour's dictum that Rome must be the capital of Italy, the government waited weakly for ten years, obstructed the bold moves of Mazzini and Garibaldi, first transferred its capital to Florence, and then ignominiously entered the Eternal City only after Napoleon III's troops had been withdrawn to defend France against Prussia in 1870.

4. TRASFORMISMO: HOW TO MANIPULATE MAJORITIES

The Statuto of Charles Albert served as the constitution of Italy from the inception of the kingdom in 1861 until the advent of Benito Mussolini, who, by 1925, had without abrogating the Statuto fundamentally altered the entire political structure. Though some observers are prone to divide the period of parliamentary "democracy" from that of fascist "dictatorship," the line between them was not so sharp as it might seem. In forty years the weaknesses of parliamentary government had been evident in Italy, so that the economic distress and moral disillusionment that followed World War I made many Italians willing witnesses to the sacrifice of their own civil liberties.

From the beginning the people had not "won" their rights; the nation had been liberated by foreign intervention, and the implementation of the Piedmontese constitution had rested largely in the hands of an elite. Poverty, particularly in the south, and an illiteracy rate ranging from 40 to 50 per cent of the Italian population in 1900 operated to limit greatly the political participation of the masses. From 1870 until 1913 less than 9.5 per cent of the legal residents were eligible to vote and, of these, some 30 to 40 per cent did not exercise the voting privilege. Parliamentary government thus rested on a narrow base. Furthermore, the broadening of the suffrage, although not lagging far behind the developments in other European democracies, was accomplished through the maneuvers of the parliamentarians, pressed by republicans and socialist deputies, rather than through popular agitation. When, finally, the suffrage was greatly enlarged in 1913, the government conducted one of the most violent campaigns in parliamentary history, and six years then elapsed before a still-inexperienced electorate was summoned in 1919 to judge from among the array of squabbling parties, functioning under a new proportional-representation system, in a tense setting of postwar unemployment, inflation, and social upheaval.

The following table will give some indication of the number of eligible voters and of popular participation in elections from 1870–1921:

FIG. VII

ITALIAN ELECTIONS FOR THE CHAMBER OF DEPUTIES, 1870–1921

ELECTION YEAR	ELIGIBLE VOTERS	PER CENT OF POPULATION	ACTUAL VOTERS	PER CENT OF ELECTORATE
1870	530,018	2.0	240,974	45.5
1874	571,939	2.1	318,517	55.7
1876	605,007	2.2	358,258	59.2
1880	621,896	2.2	369,624	59.4
1882	2,017,829	6.9	1,223,851	60.7
1886	2,420,327	8.1	1,415,801	58.5
1890	2,752,658	9.0	1,477,173	53.7
1892	2,934,445	9.4	1,639,298	55.9
1895	2,120,185	6.7	1,251,366	59.0
1897	2,120,909	6.6	1,241,486	58.5
1900	2,248,509	6.9	1,310,480	58.3
1904	2,541,327	7.5	1,593,886	62.7
1909	2,930,473	8.3	1,903,687	65.0
1913	8,443,205	23.2	5,100,615	60.4
1919	10,239,326	27.3	5,793,507	56.6
1921	11,477,210	28.7	6,701,496	58.4

The most serious problem of the decades between the unification of Italy and the rise of fascism, however, was the unhappy relationship between the Church and the state. The passive hostility of the papacy to the united kingdom, composed as it was of an overwhelmingly Catholic population, damaged the growth of responsible political parties and affected the Italian social order. Cavour, with his liberal belief of a free church in a free state, had come close to arranging a mutual agreement between Italy and the Holy See. But at the last moment Pius IX, unwisely counseled and still hoping for a foreign intervention to restore his temporal power, refused. Thus in 1871 the Italian Parliament passed its own Law of Papal Guarantees, which promised the Pope freedom in the exercise of his spiritual ministry, including inviolability of person and communications, the full possession of the Vatican and Lateran palaces as well as Castel Gandolfo, and an annual subsidy from the state of roughly $600,000.[7]

Pius IX and Leo XIII, the latter becoming Pope in 1878, adamantly refused to reconcile themselves to an Italian state that had seized papal territory, dissolved monasteries and various ecclesiastical foundations, and seemed to offer inadequate or insincere safeguards to the independence of the Church. The subsidies from the state were not accepted. Until 1905, moreover, Catholics were prohibited by the Pope from voting in any Italian parliamentary elections. Except for the staunchest

[7] The state relinquished the right to nominate bishops, gave acts of the Pope civil recognition, and denied appeal to civil courts in cases involving ecclesiastics charged with abuse of spiritual powers. It should be added that this generous spirit of the law was sometimes perverted by the state in practice. Only civil marriages, moreover, were legally recognized, and religious education was only permitted on request of the parents in public schools.

Catholic districts the admonition of the bishops to the electorate probably counted far less than the general ignorance, apathy, and disdain for politics as a cause of non-voting.[8] But the attitude of the Church *was* responsible for the lack of a genuine Catholic-oriented party that might effectively express the feelings of many inarticulate Italians and give to Parliament the kind of constructive opposition it badly needed. Only the rise of socialism at the end of the nineteenth century, coming as a specter more disturbing to the Church than the liberalism of Cavour, roused Pius X to permit Catholics to vote where a check to the extreme left was necessary.

The unsolved "Roman question" and the alienation of a strong conservative tradition from the parliamentary contests contributed to the weakness of programmatic parties in Italy between 1870 and 1913. A second factor was *"trasformismo"*—political transformation—carried on under the aegis of the Liberal Party.

Unification had been a triumph of Piedmontese statesmanship girded by principles of nineteenth-century liberalism: the agitation for republicanism and certain democratic innovations had either been checked or redirected through the exigencies of national solidarity. Entrusted with the leadership of the new nation, the Liberal successors of Cavour were loosely divided into a right and a left, often indistinguishable except as to their leadership. The Piedmontese Liberal policy had by 1876 resulted in the extension of heavy state debt to poorer regions, the dropping of tariff protection for the weaker handicraft industries of the south, the hasty sale of church and public lands obtained in the annexed provinces, and the levying of heavy taxes to bring the budget into balance. Discontent welled up, and the leaders of the Liberal right were defeated in 1878. The king selected Agostino Depretis, a mild, petty-minded leader of the Liberal left, to be his prime minister.

With brief interruptions in his eleven-year tenure Depretis saddled upon Italy some of those disillusioning practices of parliamentary life that brought it under the caustic analysis of such men as Gaetano Mosca and Vilfredo Pareto.[9] Once in office, most of the men of the left abandoned ideas of social-economic reform and consumed their energies in their quest for ministerial posts. Distinguished for his lack of any policy and never sure of his supporters, Depretis cajoled and rewarded deputies of the right or left who would ensure his tactical majority. The result was to blur all party distinctions. The lukewarm opposition was "transformed" or translated into a majority of the moment around a leader who was often incapable of crystallizing important issues for public de-

---

[8] Catholics could vote in local elections, but the percentage of abstention was almost as high as in the national elections.

[9] Gaetano Mosca (1858–1941) wrote *On the Theory of Governments and Parliamentary Government* (1884) and *Elements of Political Science* (1896, 1923) which is known in English as *The Ruling Class* (New York, 1939). Although he found both the doctrine and practice of fascism repugnant to his personal philosophy, his writings added support to the adherents of rule by elites. Vilfredo Pareto (1848–1923), mathematical economist and sociologist, had a contempt for democratic methods. His fame rests upon his *Treatise of General Sociology,* in 1916, translated as *The Mind and Society* in 1935. See also "The Parliamentary Regime in Italy," *Political Science Quarterly,* 3 (December, 1893), pp. 677–721.

bate and decision. Worst of all were the corruption of the bureaucracy and the mismanagement of elections. Piedmontese practice, borrowing from French administrative precedents, had fastened the French prefect upon Italy, thus giving the minister of the interior far-reaching control over local government and politics. The strength of the left stemmed from the south, where corrupt government had a long history. Neither Depretis nor his successor, Francesco Crispi, who was the "strong man" of Italian politics between 1887 and 1896, hesitated in using the prefects to intimidate, arrest, and dissolve opposition to the government-supported candidates. Meanwhile, many deputies, in the absence of effective party criticism, passed on to their constituents favors from the ministers, in the form of pensions, jobs in the civil service, state subsidies, or lush contracts.

During the years preceding World War I the practice of *trasformismo* reached its height under the parliamentary maneuvering of Giovanni Giolitti. Prime minister in 1892, again in 1903, again in 1906, again in 1911, and again in 1921, the shrewd Piedmontese Liberal balanced and combined with great dexterity the several groups in the Chamber to make majorities for the government and to ensure the proper amount of pressure within a constituency to get the favored deputy elected. He tamed the Radicals in 1904 by getting one of their members appointed president of the Chamber; he conciliated the Socialists in 1901 after their repression by the government and discouraged them from revolutionary action by inviting them to participate in the government while he proposed universal suffrage; he made a pact with the Catholics in 1913, giving various guarantees sought by the Vatican in exchange for electoral support of Liberal Conservative candidates. At times castigated by both Conservatives and Socialists, Giolitti sought to steer a nation of disparate regions, which was marked by the maldistribution of wealth and which was scarcely acquainted with the idea of self-government, through the perils of parliamentary crises and along the easier channels of mild reform. No credit is due for his use of prefects, troops, and ruffians to smash opposition meetings in the south, to harass or arrest speakers, and to administer beatings to recalcitrant electors. These practices fascism inherited and developed more terribly. Yet in many respects there was fostered during this period an environment that encouraged liberty, generally honest local governments and a relatively free press in the north, and criticism within the Chamber of Deputies of the government. The meaning of the whole period was brilliantly caught by the scholar and statesman Gaetano Salvemini when he wrote: "Italian democracy would have needed still another generation of trial and error before becoming not a 'perfect democracy,' but a 'less imperfect democracy.' " [1]

[1] Preface in Arcangelo William Salomone, *Italian Democracy in the Making* (1945).

5. THE RISE OF FASCISM

Some parties of principle managed to survive the practices of Depretis and Crispi: Mazzinian idealism continued to influence high-minded deputies who earnestly sought economic and social reforms, and a new, powerful Socialist doctrine began winning converts. In 1890, Republicans, Radicals, and Socialists pooled their limited resources in the Chamber to form the extreme left for united action against Crispi. From then until 1922, Italy felt the injection of new and earnest, but confused, ideological forces that inherited an unsavory political climate at home and were divided on questions of foreign policy. The table opposite will give some indication of the party composition of the Chamber of Deputies.

During this period many young Catholics, interpreting liberally the *Rerum Novarum* encyclical (1891) of Leo XIII and taking the message of Christian justice seriously, sought a middle ground between the ideological position of the Conservative Liberals and the anticlerical, economic determinism of the Socialists. In some areas they turned their attention to communal banks, provided implements and seeds through rural co-operatives, and encouraged Catholic trade and employer unions. A few modernists even verged on doctrinal reform and were scathingly rebuked by the Pope; others, like Don Luigi Sturzo, a Sicilian priest and mayor, worked to shape a democratic Catholic party that might independently mobilize votes for reform rather than barter them in the Chamber for occasional concessions to the Vatican.

Italy, moreover, provided no exception to the trials of socialism in other Western European countries. Marxist doctrine had captured many of the intellectuals and, at the opening of the twentieth century, legal recognition of trade unionism and universal manhood suffrage helped draw the proletariat into the political struggle. The main ideological schism among the Socialists centered around the question of revolution versus evolution. Men such as Leonida Bissolati, who had been elected to the Chamber in 1897, led the party toward gradualism and reform through parliamentary action. But the war against Turkey in 1911 to seize Tripoli, the World War, which found Italy at its beginning in a Triple Alliance with Germany and Austria, only to enter later on the side of the Allies, and, finally, the success of the Soviet revolution in Russia—all served to spread confusion among Socialist leaders and affected Socialist programs. While Bissolati tried to keep socialism within parliamentary bounds and gain improved legislation on sickness and old-age insurance, working conditions, reduction of military service, and progressive taxation, the radical Syndicalists, led by Arturo Labriola, preached the general strike to terrify the bourgeoisie.

The war with Turkey, clearly for imperialistic gain, sent the first major tremor through the Socialist leadership and, though he defended his position of parliamentary accommodation, Bissolati received a major rebuke from the congress of the party in 1911. Then at the congress in 1912 an ardent Socialist from Romagna, twenty-nine years old, de-

FIG. VIII

PARTY AFFILIATION: ITALIAN CHAMBER OF DEPUTIES

ELECTION YEAR	EXTREME LEFT						INDEPENDENTS	COMMUNISTS	CATHOLIC POPOLARI	NATIONAL FASCIST BLOC	DEMOCRATS LIBERALS OTHERS	TOTAL DEPUTIES
		SOCIALISTS	REPUBLICANS	RADICALS	REFORM SOCIALISTS	DEMOCRATIC SOCIALISTS						
1900	96										413	508
1904		29	24	37			8				436	508
1909		41	24	45							400	508
1913		52	8	62	19		8				347	508
1919		156	4	12		29			100		236	508
1921		123	6	—				14	108	43	212	535

N.B. Party affiliations cannot be fixed with complete accuracy. In the Chamber of 1921 there were no fewer than twelve political groupings. The National-Fascist bloc number is an estimate of the parliamentary strength of these two groups in July, 1922. The Senate, its membership unlimited and appointed by the king on the advice of the prime minister, was of minor political importance.

livered a blistering attack against reformist socialism and ridiculed bourgeois parliaments. On his motion the party expelled Bissolati. Shortly thereafter the young man, whose name was Benito Mussolini, was appointed editor of the leading Socialist newspaper, *Avanti!*

A second shake-up in the Socialist Party arose out of the struggle of World War I. Although the government pursued a neutral policy at the outbreak of hostilities, while still bound by its Triple Alliance with Austria and Germany, Prime Minister Antonio Salandra secretly negotiated a treaty to bring Italy into the war on the side of the Allies in exchange for territorial acquisitions in the Trentino, the Tyrol, Trieste and Istria, the Dalmatian coast, and possibly parts of the dismantled Turkish Empire and Africa. To the policy of neutralism the Socialists lent their traditional support, but Mussolini, chafing at any acceptance of the policies of a bourgeois government, hungry for revolutionary action and personal power, in the fall of 1914 cried out for intervention in the great conflict on the side of the Allies. Expelled by the party, he started the newspaper *Popolo d'Italia* and allied himself with Filippo Corridoni, a radical syndicalist and, like Mussolini, a man of action. With others they organized *Fasci di Combattimento* or *Fasci di Azione Revoluzionaria.*[2]

The furtive war policy of the government might have been resisted at this juncture by the majority of the deputies that Giolitti in the opposition could muster had it not been for the growing temper of the mobs in the streets, aroused by the furious agitation of men like Cesare Battisti, Corridoni, and Mussolini, and most dramatically by Gabriele D'Annunzio, a daredevil soldier, air pilot, and ecstatic poet. With the king and the Salandra government in collusion the fearful deputies voted to declare war on May 24, 1915, despite the appeal of Giolitti.

But the initial enthusiasm soon disappeared when the war dragged on bloodily on the eastern front against Austria. Desertions from the army mounted after the disaster at Caporetto in 1917, where some two hundred thousand Italians surrendered. At home defeatism was widespread in the ranks of both Socialists and Catholics. When the final victory of the Allies came in 1918, the peace conference was presented with the ambitious Italian claims by Sidney Sonnino, foreign minister from 1914 to 1919, who accompanied Vittorio Orlando in 1919 to Paris. Although Italy gained both the Trento and the Alto Adige, thereby bringing within her frontiers a quarter of a million Austrians, and although she pushed her boundary beyond Trieste to include all Istria, where, except for the port cities, Slavs outnumbered Italians, the cry of a "lost peace" echoed cynically throughout the peninsula.

Just when the effects of postwar inflation and unemployment were being coupled with the disillusionment of the peace terms to unsettle Italy, D'Annunzio gathered about him a rootless group of deserters, mobilized soldiers, and thrill-seeking youth. On September 12, 1919, he

---

[2] *"Fasci"* literally means "bundles." The term had been used on several occasions to describe small political groups: e.g., *Fasci Siciliani* had been formed in 1891 by Socialists among the peasants to further education, popular libraries, land reform, and co-operatives. They were severely repressed by the Crispi government.

defied the peace conference and brazenly challenged the government of Francesco Nitti when he landed with his nationalist group at Fiume and proclaimed the city Italian. Popular intoxication with the arrogant act meant a further decline in respect for authority. The base of responsible government was strained. To this troubled atmosphere the Socialists lent further confusion. After having scored a great electoral success in 1919, when they returned 156 deputies in the first election to be held in six years, they refused to meet the king in Parliament and incited or supported postal, railway, dock, and textile strikes that were frequently marked by violence. In the summer of 1920 certain factories in the north were occupied by the workers. Although the danger of any revolutionary action quickly faded, the fears of the property owners remained in view of the lack of decisiveness on the part of the government and of the revolutionary slogans of the extreme Socialists, who, hailing the glory of Lenin, founded the Communist Party in January, 1921.

Some blame for the ultimate collapse of responsible Italian government must also be laid upon the Catholic *Popolari,* who had succeeded remarkably in their first campaign for seats by sending 100 deputies to the Chamber in 1919. Many of their demands for economic-social reforms coincided with the program of the Socialists. But the Catholic Party, which also harbored many ultraconservative opinions, could not co-operate with a militant anticlerical group. Indeed, though the Socialist Party snubbed Nitti and his government, the *Popolari* jealously suspected him of favoring the Socialists and forced his resignation. A desperate appeal was made in 1920 to seventy-eight-year-old Giolitti, who showed his mastery in clearing Fiume of D'Annunzio and settling the boundary with Yugoslavia. But Giolitti could no longer transform a Chamber, elected by proportional representation, where one mass party, the Socialists, criticized and condemned without shouldering responsibility, while the other, the *Popolari,* was willing neither to be led by Giolitti nor to combine with other groups to provide leadership.

In this background of scares, disillusionment, mistrust, and ineffective government signs of reaction began to appear. From the beginning of 1919 Mussolini had attracted increasing numbers of the D'Annunzian nationalists, the demobilized officers, the disenchanted in search of fiery ideals, the passionate patriots, and the rootless unemployed. Step by step the Fascists became a tool of reaction for the industrialists, the petty bourgeoisie, the big landowners, and then the government itself. From the Nationalists (and D'Annunzio) came the trappings of the movement: the uniforms, the military formations, the Roman salute, the hysterical chorus of obedience to the leader, and fatuous worship of the nation. Indirectly or directly, however, the property owners, large and small, supported the efforts to harass trade unions and to oppose strikes and Socialist agitation. In the agrarian areas many landowners welcomed allies who would stop peasant reforms and restrict co-operatives fostered by either *Popolari* or Socialists. The final miscalculation came from Giolitti himself. Unable to manage a majority in the old manner, he called for new elections in the spring of 1921 and invited the Fascists[3] to join in a "bloc" comprising Liberal, agrarian, and nationalist candidates. It was clearly Giolitti's intention to win a victory for the "bloc," and then control the Fascist deputies in the Chamber through his skillful maneuvering.

The electoral campaign became a pitched battle. Little impeded by the Giolittian prefects or local police, Fascist action groups burned opposition newspaper offices, smashed the headquarters of trade unions or peasant organizations, and engaged in many acts of violence. Italy had known violence in the past electoral campaigns, mainly in the south, but never before had terror been so ruthlessly organized all over the nation and carried out with such disregard of law. Here and there the Socialists fought back and committed their own excesses. In the elections, despite the many intimidations, the voters again returned the Socialists and the *Popolari* as the two largest parties in the Chamber. Not only had Giolitti failed in gaining control of the Chamber—for the *Popolari* would not co-operate with him on any terms—but respect for law and the government had declined still further. Under comparable circumstances other peoples throughout history have sought a return to stability, authority, and national prestige through dictatorship.

From July, 1921 to the fall of 1922 successive Italian governments under, first, Ivanoe Bonomi and then Luigi Facta, drifted impotently with a Chamber in which the Socialists, ever divided among themselves, could not bring their deputies to share responsibility; a Chamber in which the *Popolari,* combining social reformers and clerical conservatives, gave only brittle support to the government on specific conditions; in which the Fascists, now a bloc of thirty-two seats, were increasingly determined to seize the state. Mussolini, with insatiable will to power, used his genius to accommodate opportunistically the Nationalists one day, the Church and monarch another, and even on occasion the Socialists (with whom he reached a temporary agreement in August, 1921). In the summer of 1922 the Socialists called a general strike, but the dispirited and disorganized trade unions failed to respond and shortly thereafter largely deserted the Socialist Party.

From October 26 to 28, 1922, several thousand Fascists began their "march on Rome," taking over communications centers and communal-provincial governments, while the authorities—apathetic, intimidated, or without instructions—yielded. When the gravity of the situation was finally realized, Premier Facta pressed the king to sign a decree proclaiming martial law. Whether the Fascist threat might easily have been stopped by firm military action or whether the army, penetrated itself by Fascists, might have divided and brought the nation into civil war is a moot question. In any case Victor Emmanuel III refused to sign the decree proclaiming martial law and the Fascists occupied Rome.

[3] Perhaps nothing illustrates better the political dynamism and rapid growth of fascism in these days than the fact that Mussolini had run as an independent in Milan just sixteen months before his "deal" with Giolitti and had obtained fewer than 5,000 votes out of 346,000. Nineteen months after his election in Giolitti's bloc he was not only prime minister of Italy, but well on his way toward becoming dictator.

Although the black-shirt party with its nationalist allies could muster only some forty-three votes in a Chamber of 535, the king summoned Mussolini to be prime minister of Italy.

6. DUCE! DUCE! DUCE!

For over twenty years prior to the advance of the Allied troops up the peninsula in World War II the Italian people lived under the Fascist dictatorship of Benito Mussolini. Fascism had no coherent program when it came to power. Indeed, it was hardly a political party, rather a "movement" led by a former socialist, infected by syndicalist ideas, charged with extreme nationalism, and willing by violence to sweep away a government incapable of resolving the economic and social problems faced by it. Only with difficulty did Mussolini persuade some leaders late in 1921 that the Fascist movement *ought* to become a political party. But Mussolini perceived that the fundamental revolution had only begun, that conquest of the government is not conquest of the state, and that the proper instrument of social surgery could not be the action squads. To institutionalize the mass revolution required a disciplined political party, and an efficient, well-organized hierarchy, headed at the top by a supreme and idealized leader, Mussolini himself.

The absolute identification of the Fascist Party and the state took several awkward years: it required first the enervation of Parliament by the destruction of organized political opposition; second, the weaving of Fascist control over state organs, then economic institutions, and finally social groups; third, incessant propaganda to reinforce the doctrine and symbols of fascism, particularly *Il Duce* (The Leader).

The Statuto, under which Italy was still formally governed after the Fascist conquest of the government, contained no provision for its own amendment. Decree law had been frequently used in the strained years before Mussolini, so that the first delegations of emergency powers to him by Parliament were not in themselves extraordinary acts. The revision of the electoral law in the summer of 1923, however, was a complete break with the past in so far as it provided that two thirds of all the seats of the Chamber would be awarded to the party that succeeded in obtaining a plurality of votes (provided that it be at least 25 per cent of the total) throughout the nation. While the Socialists opposed the law with determination, the *Popolari* were divided, and their final support of the government in the confidence vote opened the way to Mussolini's legal domination of the Chamber. The Fascist "national list," comprising distinguished non-party members as well as Fascists and supported by the violence of the Fascist "voluntary militia," won the elections handily, and received 374 of the 535 seats. But the imminent destruction of parliamentary government could no longer be obscured by the false appeal to national unity. When Giacomo Matteotti boldly criticized the governmental policy in the Chamber, he was murdered in 1924 by orders of Fascist leaders—and, though the conscience of the nation was appalled and the Fascist hierarchy shaken by this act, the opposition simply failed to coalesce around any alternative program or leader. Who would risk death for a return to the pre-Fascist period? Who would risk a beating to cheer for Giolitti, or Bonomi, or Salandra? Had Italian socialism ever matured enough to convince the people that it could reconcile liberty with authority?

The final, foolish gesture of the anti-Fascist deputies in withdrawing from the Chamber hardly balked a despot who brooked no opposition. By 1925, Mussolini, as head of the government and responsible only to the king, was already seeking a new basis of representation in the Chamber through which the Fascist Party not only might dominate but should become the exclusive party. After the adoption of the new electoral law in 1928 all nominations to the Chamber were made by national confederations of employers and workers, and by various cultural associations. Such nominations were forwarded to the Grand Council of the Fascist Party, consisting of about twenty-five of the highest-ranking Fascists with Mussolini as president, which was made a legal organ of the state at the same time. The Grand Council pruned the nominations into lists that were then submitted to the people for approval or rejection en bloc. Two elections were held under this system with the following results:

YEAR	YES	NO
1929	8,519,559	135,761
1934	10,025,513	15,265

In 1938 even the pretense of an elected Chamber was ended when the Senate and the Chamber of Deputies approved a bill substituting a Chamber of Fasces and Corporations for the Deputies. In the new lower house of Parliament members were selected on a "functional" basis rather than by territorial representation of the electorate: a majority of the members come from the National Council of Corporations to comprise the "corporative" representation, and other members came from Fascist political organizations. All trace of liberal, representative government was thereby eradicated and in its place was the will of the Fascist hierarchy, ultimately the will of Mussolini. Figure IX will indicate the general outlines of the governmental structure.

To ensure obedience to the Fascist will in government required the strangulation of local as well as national government. Neither police nor elections had ever been under the local control of the seventy-five provinces of pre-Fascist Italy, which were generally comparable to the French departments. The use of the centrally appointed prefect to enforce the government's will, even to assist in the election of its candidates, has already been noted. But until 1927 there were elective councils with limited powers over poor relief, asylums, education, and public works, all of which functions were now placed directly under the prefect and an advisory council appointed by him. Even greater changes were made in municipal government, for many communes had ancient traditions and genuine responsibility for local police, schools, charity, and notably public utilities. Again fascism tolerated no political institu-

FIG. IX

SCHEMATIC GOVERNMENT OF ITALY, 1929–1938

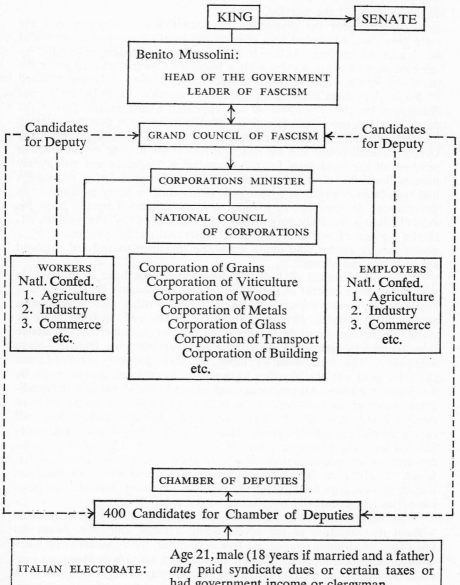

tion that might reflect opposition to the Duce and, after first terrorizing the communal administrations and ejecting many of the elected Socialist councilors, it forced through Parliament a bill conferring all municipal power upon a *podestà* who was completely subject to the prefect or the minister of the interior.

Year by year the distinction between the Fascist Party and the state grew less. Mussolini was at once the head of the government and the leader of fascism. Although the party's constitution originally resembled that of other parties with a National Council, elected from the members, and an administrative Directorate, in truth a Grand Council of the leaders soon decided all important matters. In 1926 the Grand Council of Fascism itself revised and approved a new constitution of the party in which the principle was specifically enunciated that the selected hierarchies shall receive their rules from above.[4] Two years later the Grand Council could not be distinguished from a state organ since it selected all the candidates for the Chamber of Deputies and completely monopolized the electoral process. What had begun as a movement had thus been changed at Mussolini's behest into a party to control the government. It represented, in sum, a force generated by the need for radical change in Italy, organized and militarized by the nationalists in the service of economic reaction, and continually galvanized by a power-hungry leader who made grandiose promises to Italy of a proud era at home and abroad.

The total control of Italian politics could not have been possible without a major control of the economy and the society. By denying any rights to employers' associations or trade unions other than government-sponsored syndicates, by outlawing both strikes and lockouts, and by using the myriad controls of the Fascist Party bureaucracy, collective labor contracts—including provisions for workingmen's benefits—were negotiated. The turbulence of labor disputes definitely declined, but the price paid was the freedom to organize, to criticize, and to resist by economic pressures. All employers and all workers did not join the syndicates; however, in industry, where pockets of resistance might be most easily formed, upwards of 85 per cent of the workers and at least half of the employers were in syndicates. Private enterprise prevailed under fascism until the economic crises of the early thirties impelled the government to establish the *Istituto per la Ricostruzione Italiana* (I.R.I.), which bolstered the banks by purchasing notes and stocks of insolvent industrial concerns held by them, thereby acquiring control over such industries and eventually over some banks themselves.

No dictatorship such as the Fascist one would have been possible without manipulation of the press. Being a rabid journalist, Mussolini knew best of all the power of the free newspaper. Systematically, by withholding licenses and other devices, he muzzled opinion contrary to Fascism. Similarly, the instruction in the schools was brought into line with Fascist dogma by textbooks glorifying the state and the leadership of Mus-

[4] Membership in the Fascist Party implicitly was limited to fewer than a million members during the twenties, and to about two million in the thirties. In addition there was a whole series of auxiliary organizations.

solini, while on the university level professors guarded their remarks.

Having neutralized the army by accepting its nationalism and also by creating an elite voluntary militia of the party, having destroyed the political parties and parliamentarism, having smashed the free labor movement and brought economic organization under its control, and having enslaved the press, fascism had only one possible center of major resistance in Italy, the Church. Yet in the early years of fascism the Church was more an ally than an enemy. The papacy had little but antipathy for the Liberal Kingdom of Italy, the Socialist Party, and some of the conceptions of government elected by the people. The idea of "corporations," moreover, widely used by the Fascist state, may have borrowed something from early Catholic socialism.[5] Mistakenly, too, the Catholic *Popolari,* under Don Luigi Sturzo, had flanked Mussolini's government until April, 1923, and the right wing of the party was not unsympathetic to fascism. In the heralded treaty and concordat of 1929, known as the Lateran Pact, Mussolini craftily settled with Pius XI the long-outstanding problem of Church-state relations in Italy. Thus Vatican City became an independent and sovereign state, while the supreme authority and inviolability of the Pope in carrying out his functions were recognized. Various basilicas, churches, and clerical institutions were given extraterritorial status or were exempted from expropriation and taxes as part of the Vatican's possessions, while the Italian government donated to the Church about $230,000,000 in bonds and over $17,000,-000 in cash as a complete settlement of all claims arising out of 1870. Religious instruction was introduced into the intermediate as well as the elementary schools, and the nullification of any Italian marriage was to be determined by ecclesiastical tribunals exclusively. Above all, the Roman Catholic religion was recognized as the only religion of the state.

Despite these compromises the Catholic religion could not be reconciled to the deification of the state under fascism nor the final, absolute loyalty that was demanded by the party; it could not accept the doctrines of racism, which were suddenly introduced after 1936 especially under the influence of Hitler's Germany, nor condone the creed of national egoism, which looked to struggle, combat, even war, for its fulfillment. Fascism, meanwhile, would not tolerate any of the manifold Catholic associations for youth, education, charities, and recreation unless most rigorously restricted to religious activities. By way of possible explanation for the Church's acquiescence in certain of the state controls and interference, the Pope knew that he could not reasonably live in Rome, protecting Catholic institutions, and guarding the spiritual destiny of Italy if the Church operated as an avowed and outspoken enemy of the regime.

[5] "Their economic panacea is a system of 'corporations' . . . with a common machinery for the settlement of disputes, but more often takes the fantastic form of a compulsory grouping into a close organization of all employers and workers in a trade, always with . . . Catholic propagandism, and sometimes with the strange political conception of parliaments representative not of localities, but of trades and professions." B. King and T. Okey, *Italy Today* (1901), p. 56. A preferable English translation of *corporazione* would have been "guild." Unfortunately the confusing word "corporation" has made its way into the political-science literature in English.

In comparing the dictatorship of Adolph Hitler or Joseph Stalin to that of Benito Mussolini one is compelled to observe that Italy never knew the ghastly concentration camps of Germany or the vast slave-labor projects of Russia; that the Church was permitted to exist as an institution parallel to, if circumscribed by, the state; that the regulation of the economy was partial and was left largely in private hands; that the numerous hard-working peasants in the long-depressed areas of the nation were hardly affected one way or another by fascism; and that the Italian, with his general skepticism of politics bred over the centuries, could sometimes rejoice in the color and pageantry of the movement, even while shrugging his shoulders at the government. Nevertheless, the traces of those long years of dictation from above, which sterilized individual liberties and killed off creative opposition, left a severe blight upon the development of democratic, responsible government in Italy.

The exaggerated nationalism of the Fascists inevitably led to an aggressive foreign policy. D'Annunzio and Mussolini had originally capitalized on the supposed Italian chagrin at not receiving colonies after World War I, allegedly due to the betrayal by France and Britain. Thus Mussolini's seizure of Ethiopia in 1936, despite the opposition of Britain and France and the League of Nations, represented for fascism a long-overdue claim for Italy's need of colonies and great-power status. Inexorably, as France had feared, Italy was increasingly drawn into an understanding with the rising power of Nazi Germany. In September, 1938, Mussolini himself drew the partition lines for those parts of Czechoslovakia handed over to Hitler at Munich by Britain and France, and in May, 1939, Italy and Germany signed a military alliance. But Italy, with its very limited economic resources and its lack of military potential, for all the boasts of fascism, was destined to be a subservient partner to the industrialized, disciplined Germany of Hitler during World War II. Jumping into the conflict when Germany had already vanquished France in June, 1940, Mussolini misjudged the intentions and capacity of Britain and the events that were to bring both the Soviet Union and the United States into the war against Italy.

Fascism went down to defeat as the Italian Army suffered a succession of reverses in Greece, in North Africa, and in the Mediterranean, despite the continued prodding and support of Germany. By July, 1943 the Allied troops had occupied Sicily and were already sending bombers over Rome. The defeat of Italy and the failure of Mussolini were irrefutable. On the afternoon of July 24 the Grand Council of Fascism met in an extraordinary, heated session. At the instigation of Galeazzo Ciano, Mussolini's son-in-law, Dino Grandi, and others, the Grand Council passed an order of the day inviting Mussolini to resign. The next day Mussolini requested an audience with the king. Arriving punctually at 4:00 P.M., the pallid *Duce* said that the action of the Grand Council had been illegal:

VICTOR EMMANUEL III (*objecting*): Why do you maintain this vote to be invalid? The Grand Council is an organ created

by you and approved by law in the Senate and Chamber
of Deputies. It functions therefore in full legality.

MUSSOLINI: But in that case I should have to resign . . .

VICTOR EMMANUEL III: . . . which I accept!

MUSSOLINI (*crushed*): Then my downfall is complete.[6]

Mussolini was arrested and the king designated Marshal Badoglio, who
had retired from the army in 1940, after fifty-three years of service, as
head of the government.

7. LIBERATION FOR WHAT?

The end of Fascist government did not lead to revolution in Italy or
signal an immediate reconstruction. The war had made a battleground
of the nation, not only adding to the burdens on the economy but increasing the political confusion left by the collapse of central authority.
Although Marshal Badoglio had signed an armistice with the Allied
forces on September 8, 1943, German troops moved down the peninsula
to contest vigorously the advance of the Anglo-American armies. In
consequence the "liberation" of Italy, again by a foreign army, was an
extremely difficult process. Between the end of the hostilities in Sicily
and the overthrow of Mussolini's puppet republic, which he had proclaimed at Salò after his escape from prison in 1943, there was an
interval of almost two years.

Thus the beginnings of Italian postwar reform were in the south.
The most articulate anti-Fascist groups in other parts of the country had
to operate for the time clandestinely, in great peril, and were unable to
make their opinions immediately effective. The monarchy, inescapably
compromised by fascism, still served as the source of authority for the
Badoglio government, which had moved first to the southern Adriatic
port of Bari, and then Salerno, after the armistice. The moderate anti-
Fascists[7] within the provisional Committee of National Liberation were
persuaded to defer raising the institutional question. Another significant development was the arrival from Moscow, in March, 1944, of
Palmiro Togliatti, secretary general of the Italian Communist Party, to
maintain that all anti-Fascist parties were entitled to ministries in the
Badoglio government, since the Communist Party was dedicated to the
elimination of fascism and nazism. By this stroke the Communists were
able to operate along with the militant republicans, who wanted no part
of the old regime, and the conservatives who wanted to proceed slowly
in governmental reorganization—a view favored by the British and
American governments. Togliatti's strategy had the important result of
entrenching Communists in the government—where they remained until

---

[6] Reconstructed from Pietro Badoglio, *Badoglio racconta* (1955).

[7] Among these were Enrico de Nicola, a president of the pre-fascist Chamber
of Deputies, later provisional president of the Italian Republic and then president of
the Constitutional Court; Carlo Sforza, minister of foreign affairs in 1920–21, who
later lived in exile, and who took charge of foreign relations in 1947; Benedetto
Croce, illustrious Neapolitan scholar, senator, and member of the Liberal Party.

the spring of 1947—and thereby of winning for the party a position in Southern Italy, where hitherto it had enjoyed little success.

While the liberation of the south, even Rome, was being achieved by the Allied armies, armed partisan groups had begun to operate in the north late in 1943. Soon local resistance committees were co-operating through the Committee of National Liberation for Northern Italy (C.N.L.A.I.). The leadership of the paramilitary units gradually fell into the hands of Feruccio Parri, for the Action Party, and Luigi Longo, for the Communists. Smaller groups operated under the leadership of Socialists and Christian Democrats, but the political weight of these underground forces, bitterly anti-Fascist, could not be fully exercised in the new provisional government under Ivanoe Bonomi, who had succeeded Badoglio in Rome after its occupation by Allied troops. Although Victor Emmanuel III had yielded to a regency under Prince Umberto, Bonomi still regarded his authority as stemming from the Crown. Both the Socialist and Action parties refused to support this position, but the Communists clung to the government. In sum, the Badoglio-Bonomi governments, with the co-operation of the Communists acting out of sheer opportunism, and supported by the Allied Military Command, continued to function under royal investiture throughout the southern half of the peninsula. The first anti-Fascist efforts to effectuate a radical change in the basis of the government and administration and a thorough purge of police rapidly faded under the direction of conservatives chiefly interested in both stability and continuity with the old pre-Fascist juridical order.

As the Allied armies had advanced north on the peninsula, the C.N.L.A.I. had grown bolder and stronger. To facilitate the overthrow of the German and Fascist forces, a military-economic liaison between the Allied Command and the partisans was effected, and it was agreed that the C.N.L.A.I. should govern provisionally any territories liberated by it until the arrival of the Allied troops. Between April 20–27, 1945, the cities of Northern Italy rose against the last retreating, demoralized Hitler-Mussolini troops while the Allied forces were still a few days distant. Immediately the C.N.L.A.I. assumed full powers of government and administration, proceeded to remove all Fascist prefects, chiefs of police, and mayors, vigorously disarmed and corralled in concentration camps Fascist or German sympathizers, established special courts for the trial of Fascist crimes, instituted sequestration commissions for firms that had collaborated with the Germans, and set up employer-worker boards to manage many factories. In this way Italy again suffered from another division between north and south, a south where the transition from Mussolini to liberation had hardly produced basic social or political changes and a north where fundamental changes had been made largely under the violent direction of the parties of the extreme left.

After liberation the Action, Socialist, and Communist parties sought to give their anti-Fascist revolutionary programs a broader base by demanding supreme, provisional power for the Committee of National Liberation in Rome. But to instant radical reforms the Labor Democrats under Bonomi, the Liberals, and, most tellingly, the Christian Democrats, led by Alcide de Gasperi, were strongly opposed. Nevertheless, the moderate parties were forced to accept the nomination of Feruccio Parri, head of the Action Party, as prime minister in 1945.

But during the six months of the government headed by Parri, from June to December, 1945, the revolutionary forces, which seemed to promise a fundamental upheaval in Italian life, were checked. The south, which had felt none of the Fascist brutality of the last months of the war, had accommodated itself to the Badoglio-Bonomi regimes, and separatist moves, especially in Sicily, had to be resisted by Parri. The impetus to radical change in the north also dissipated itself, especially in the face of the economic problems created by inflation. At the same time the obvious drop in production at the factories encouraged more moderate attitudes in the commissions of sequestration toward managers and technicians. Socialist and Communist parties were busily engaged in preparing for the forthcoming elections to the Constituent Assembly.[8]

The final factor contributing to abort radical change in Italy was the policy of the Allied governments, which, in these months, still held ultimate control over all Italy. The Christian Democrats, supported by the Church and symbolizing security after the turmoil of the past war, bided their time. Alcide de Gasperi, their leader, was the foreign minister of the Parri government, and with him the Allies treated. At the London Conference of September, 1945, to discuss the preliminaries of the peace treaty, De Gasperi represented Italy; Parri was not invited.

Early in December, 1945 the Christian Democrats withdrew their support from Parri's government, which collapsed. Having committed themselves to the early convocation of a Constituent Assembly and having taken a position in favor of a republic for Italy, they obtained the support of both the Socialists and the Communists for their leader, De Gasperi, as prime minister. Shortly thereafter the Allies turned over the administration of the northern provinces to the Italian government. De Gasperi proceeded at once to place old career officials in the posts of police chiefs and prefects, which the C.N.L.A.I. had filled with its partisans; the High Commission for the purge was abolished and the sentences of the popular courts of assize against Fascists or collaborators were made subject to appeal to the Court of Cassation, which had never been purged; the commissions of sequestration were ended and the factories returned to their owners; the project for the revaluation of the money was abandoned. One last opportunity for revolutionary reform would have remained had the Constituent Assembly retained power to legislate *ad interim,* but De Gasperi won from Nenni (still minister of the Constituent Assembly) the decree that finally limited its competence to the preparation of a constitution. At the same time it was

---

[8] Palmiro Togliatti, leader of the Communists, occupied the Ministry of Justice, and Pietro Nenni, leader of the Socialists, headed the High Commission for the purging of Fascists as well as the Ministry for the Constituent Assembly. Both men engaged in many party rallies during this period. Nenni's draft of a law for the purge was only promulgated during the last days of the Parri government.

agreed that the decision between a monarchy and republic should be left to a plebiscite.[9]

On June 2, 1946, therefore, the whole Italian electorate—including women—was called (a) to vote either for a monarchy or a republic, and (b) to elect deputies, by proportional representation, to the Constituent Assembly. In the voting 12,717,923 individuals expressed themselves as favoring a republic and 10,719,284 as favoring a monarchy. The following table will indicate the results of the elections for members of the Constituent Assembly and give some indication of the character of the party alignments:

FIG. X

ELECTIONS TO THE CONSTITUENT ASSEMBLY OF ITALY, 1946

PARTY	VOTES	PER CENT OF TOTAL
Christian Democrats	8,101,004	35.2
Socialists	4,758,129	20.7
Communists	4,356,686	19.0
Liberals	1,560,368	6.8
Qualunquists[1]	1,211,956	5.3
Republicans	1,003,007	4.4
Monarchists	637,328	2.8
Others	1,381,731	5.8

(Party Alignments by Deputies)

CENTER

Christian Democrats 207

LEFT	LEFTISH	RIGHTISH	RIGHT
Communists 104	Republicans 23	Liberals 41	Monarchists 16
Socialists 115	Action 7		Qualunquists 30
			Sicilian Ind. 4

Total *Left* of Center: 249   Total *Right* of Center: 91

The Constituent Assembly of Italy began its sessions in the summer of 1946 and on December 27, 1947, finished its work by ratifying a constitution of 139 articles and, in addition, some 18 transitional articles. The work of the Assembly of 556 deputies, organized through a committee of 75, was centered on three main problems of (a) rights and duties of citizens, (b) organization of the state, and (c) economic-social rights and duties. But during the long period while the Assembly was proceeding with its work the initiative for proposing and making laws was left entirely to the government. Although the Assembly estab-

[9] On June 25, 1944, the government decree had left in the hands of the future Constituent Assembly the power to determine the form of the state, but growing monarchist sentiment (encouraged by the Allied powers) rallied republicans around the decree of March 16, 1946, calling for a popular referendum.

[1] *Qualunque* means "ordinary fellow" or "man in the street." It was a skeptical movement of protest against a variety of things in the initial post-war period, rather than a political party, and quickly spent its strength after the elections to the Constituent Assembly.

lished committees, corresponding to the various ministries, to which decrees had to be submitted for "binding" advice, no urgent measure was subject to this procedure. The Italian electorate had already decided the question of monarchy versus republic for the Constituent Assembly, but compromises had to be worked out among the political parties on a number of other issues. Following the French model, a weak executive and an independent judiciary were agreed upon. While Communists, Socialists, and Liberals opposed regional autonomy, Christian Democrats and Republicans succeeded in providing for greater decentralization of government. The laic parties naturally opposed the inclusion of the Lateran Pact in the new constitution, but the Communists, with brazen opportunism, supported the Christian Democrats, thus continuing the Church-state relationship arranged by Mussolini. The Christian Democrats would have preferred an upper house of Parliament representing corporate interests, and the Communists would have preferred to abolish the Senate, but eventually provisions for an elective second chamber, with powers equal to those of the Chamber of Deputies, were drafted.

The Christian Democrat, De Gasperi, continued to hold the prime ministry. The efforts of the left failed in part through the inability of the Communists, who were pursuing throughout their opportunistic policies, under Soviet direction, to secure the continued support of a united Socialist Party. Divisions within the Socialist Party culminated in the withdrawal of Giuseppe Saragat and his followers from the party in 1947 in protest against any collaboration with the Communists. In the meantime De Gasperi, with Allied encouragement, excluded the Communists from the government coalition in May, 1947. Moving gradually more toward the right for support, De Gasperi first brought in the Liberals and, in December, 1947, the Republicans and Democratic Socialists. Essentially it has been this four-party coalition that has furnished the parliamentary support of the Italian government over most of the last ten years. The new Constitution of the Italian Republic, passed by a vote of 453 to 62, was promulgated by the provisional president of Italy, Enrico De Nicola, and went into effect on January 1, 1948.

Yet before beginning this new chapter of Italian history, with its promise of stable constitutional development, it should be noted that on February 7, 1948, De Gasperi obtained the consent of the anti-Fascist Republicans and Democratic Socialists to a decree that ended the purge of the Fascists in government administration and, in fact, opened the way to the rehabilitation of all except the most seriously implicated ex-Fascists in all ranks of the public service. Thus one might conclude that many important changes had taken place in Italy during the years since the republic had been born—the end of the monarchy, the extension of suffrage to women, the restoration of parliamentary government, and the rise of opposition political parties—but that much remained to be fulfilled in the way of democratic and economic-social reform and that the beginnings of a genuine revolution under pressures from the left in Italy had ended.

20

ITALIAN LIFE: CRUCIBLE OF POLITICS

1. THE RESOURCES OF THE LAND

It is no easy task to accommodate over forty-nine million Italians in an area no larger than the state of California. The United States of America was, before the inclusion of Alaska, almost exactly twenty-six times as large as Italy. The Italian population, almost equal in number to that of either Western Germany or the United Kingdom and greater than that of France, must confine itself to a narrow Mediterranean peninsula, divided by frequent hills and bare ridges, and the two rugged islands of Sicily and Sardinia. Of the total area of Italy almost 75 per cent can be classified as either sloping land, hilly, or mountainous. Of the land actually under cultivation only about 20 per cent is on level terrain.

Poverty can never be measured in purely economic terms, for the richness of Italian culture, the physical and spiritual splendor of her Church, and the vitality of her artistic life cannot be calculated in economic indices. But in respect to food production and sinews of modern industry Italy lags considerably behind Western Europe. Italy is forced to import wheat, the very base of Italian diet in *pasta* and bread. Nature has not supplied her kindly with other cereals: France produces several times as much rye, oats, and barley as Italy. Only rice is produced in surpluses large enough for export. The traditional export products of Italy, her olives, grapes, and citrus fruits, must today meet the strong competition of Spain, Greece, Yugoslavia, and France. But foodstuffs still comprise Italy's most important export items. Among the fibers only hemp is produced abundantly: cotton and wool must be imported for the Italian textile industry, rubber must be brought in for the fabrication of machines and transportation equipment, and wood pulp must be imported for the books, newspapers, posters, cartons, and bags that are manufactured.

As an industrial state, moreover, Italy hardly measures up to the standards of a great power. Water power has been the source of energy for nearly all her electricity, and this is chiefly concentrated in the north. In any case Italy falls behind the United Kingdom, Germany, and France in the production of electricity; on a per-capita basis an American has four times as much electrical energy at his disposal as an Italian. In recent years the use of Italian natural gas as a fuel has increased greatly, but 10 per cent of the nation's foreign exchange still goes for the purchase of coal from abroad. Italy imports about ninety per cent[1] of all the oil processed in her domestic refineries. Italy also sells to other nations her surplus of sulphur, mercury, pyrites, bauxite, salt, and marble, but she lacks tin and copper deposits. Italy is surpassed almost three times by France and four times by Germany in the production of steel.

How does Italy manage to pay for the many imports needed to maintain her large population? Thus far, out of her own production, she has not succeeded. Although she sells her foodstuffs, her textiles woven from raw materials, her ships, motorcycles, generators, chemicals, and processed rubber, leather, and paper products, and although she gains from such services as insurance, transportation, banking, and tourism, all this is not enough. Because her raw materials are costly, capital scarce, and labor not efficiently employed, Italy lags behind her vigorous European competitors, not to mention the United States, in her search for markets.

Since the end of World War II the deficits in the Italian balance of payments have largely been filled by United States dollars—either in the form of direct grants or indirect subsidies for purposes of reconstruction, loans, or mutual defense. In the immediate postwar period UNRRA and interim American gifts provided almost $600,000,000 in relief aid to Italy. By January 1, 1952, another $1,300,000,000 had gone to Italy under the European Recovery Program; in the three fiscal years 1953–55 Italy obtained another $137,000,000 under the Mutual Security Program. Apart from various development loans the United States placed contracts for aircraft, ammunition, vehicles, ships, electronics equipment, etc., with Italian industries that totaled $478,000,000 between 1952–54. Finally, annual private remittances of Italo-Americans run into many millions of dollars. No analysis of Italian politics can ignore this dependence upon American aid in past years. Any Italian government that seeks to expand the real income of the people must find a solution for the chronic disequilibrium of international trade. In 1954, the Italian deficit in foreign trade was $800,000,000; in 1955, it was $849,000,000; in 1956, $1,012,000,000; and in the first eight months of 1957 more than $730,000,000. Foreign grants or loans, United States military expenditures, emigrants' remittances, and invisible income, such as tourist travel in Italy, tend to balance the payments between Italy and other countries, but the foreign trade deficits exert a heavy pressure on these fluctuating credits.

[1] In December, 1954, the Gulf Oil Company began to extract oil from its wells at Ragusa, Sicily. Other oil strikes in Sicily and the Abruzzi are promising, but the total domestic production is a small percentage of the rapidly increasing demand for petroleum products in Italy.

2. THE PEOPLE AND THEIR ECONOMY

Almost one fourth of the entire Italian population lives in the north-western regions of Lombardy, Liguria (Genoa), and Piedmont, the historical nucleus of the nation. Flat, fertile Lombardy alone, with its dynamic business and cultural center of Milan, accounts for 14 per cent of the total inhabitants. Milan, together with Genoa and Turin, makes a triangle that contains the major part of Italian heavy industry and commerce. A second populous area is to be found in the south with its colorful city of Naples. Through this port, which today handles some 8,000 ships a year and whose province contains some 4,700 people per square mile, have come many of the Italian emigrants to the United States in the past. But the fastest-growing area of Italy, reflecting the centralization of government and the tremendous expansion of public administration, has been the capital city of Rome. The region of Latium has more than doubled its population of 1901. In the same period metropolitan Rome has grown from 766,000 to approximately 2,500,000 inhabitants. The geographical distribution of the Italian population helps to explain some of its attitudes and political orientation, for strong regional differences still prevail in language, economic organization, and both public and private *mores;* the Italian continues to identify himself as Sicilian or Tuscan or Milanese.

Although its surplus population, coupled with claimed needs for colonies and emigration, is marked off as a special Italian political problem, Italy, in fact, has a declining birth rate. While a hundred years ago the birth rate was 37 per thousand, in 1958 it was approximately 17 per thousand. About 26 per cent of the Italians are now in the age bracket 0–15 against 34 per cent one hundred years ago, and it is expected that within 20 years Italy's population will level out at about 53 million people. The real problem, however, is that the number of people of working age has been increasing in recent years much more rapidly than the number of new jobs available.

Of Italy's total working force about 40 per cent are employed in agriculture, forestry, hunting, and fishing; another 35 per cent work in industry; and 10 per cent in commerce. Services of public administration, transportation, and finance account for the balance. The hilly terrain, the aridity of the summers, and the dependence upon animals, oxen and horses, to till the soil do not make the lot of the Italian farmer an easy one. Some of the agricultural deficiencies are due to natural causes and some to human factors. Continued deforestation and soil exhaustion have been coupled with the concentration of good land into fewer and fewer hands, at least until quite recent years. The organization of Italian agriculture, however, is extremely complex, and generalizations about land reform, including the evil of the big landowners and the *latifondi*,[2] need careful scrutiny.

[2] Types of large farms usually encompassing land not intensively cultivated, sown fields alternately lying fallow, lacking farm buildings, and worked by a farm population living some distance from the fields.

Three main agricultural groups might be mentioned. There is, first, the petty landowner or renter who, even before World War II and the subsequent agrarian reforms, comprised the greatest number of peasants.[3] It is not necessarily his lack of any land, but the fragmentation of his holdings into tiny parcels, often poor in soil, in need of irrigation, tools, and easy access to markets, that prevents him from gaining an adequate income from his own soil and compels him to seek supplementary jobs. Second, Tuscany, Umbria, and the Marches in central Italy are notable for the *mezzadri,* the share farmers who contract with the landowner and who receive from him a house and the larger capital costs of farming and supply their own small tools, services, and labor. The owners and *mezzadri* split the yield. Not only has this contractual relationship, sanctioned by law, occasioned bitter political disputes, but the system breeds a hard, social stratification that leads to conflicts and it accounts in part for a large following in these areas of the extreme left—despite the generally higher standards of farm life in these regions than in the south. The third and most volatile group is the mass of low-paid *braccianti,* day and monthly farm laborers, who perhaps account for 20 per cent of the agricultural work.

Pressure for land reform by the left, aiming at greater security for the farmers, higher productivity, and a redistribution of agricultural income, after World War II became one of the most important political issues. The Sila Law and the Stralcio Law in 1950 led to expropriation acts against 2,805 landowners involving 1,446,390 acres; another 150,-000 acres in Sicily were expropriated under regional acts, and some 850,000 acres were voluntarily offered for sale. By the beginning of 1956 about 1,300,000 acres of land had been assigned to 99,357 peasant families with an average of 13 acres per family. But such fundamental reforms in agriculture, long overdue and still being implemented, do not entirely remove the agricultural problem as a political issue. The conservatives claim that the Christian Democratic government has essentially adopted the program of the Communists; on the other hand the Communists claim credit among the peasants for what they have already received, promise more for the future, and play upon the disappointments that maladministration, displacements, transfers, and still-inadequate farm income inevitably offer. Land distribution without adequate credit, tools, and market access can hardly succeed, so that the government has also embarked upon a substantial program of constructing farm roads, houses, and public works, while promoting cooperatives and extending credit.

Few economies professing to be free and democratic are more heavily

[3] A survey made in 1948 showed that 83.3 per cent of all privately held farms were less than 5 acres in size and that 53.9 per cent were less than 1.25 acres. About 26 per cent of the total farm area was held by 21,396 landowners out of the total of 9,512,242. See *Istituto Nazionale di Economia Agraria, La distribuzione della proprietà fondiaria in Italia, Relazione Generale* (Rome, 1948), p. 18. As a result of further surveys it was found that there are 10,000,000 firms and 12,400,000 persons who own farmland. Of the 12,400,000 persons about 6,000,000 own less than 2.5 acres. See *Istituto Nazionale di Economia Agraria, La distribuzione della proprietà fondiaria in Italia,* Giuseppe Medici, Vol. I (1956).

burdened with state ownership and state controls than the Italian economy. In agriculture the controls extend from the traditional monopolies of salt and tobacco to the regulation of wheat prices by the government's purchases as well as of the export of all rice through a public corporation. In industry and commerce government control is omnipresent, complicated, and confusing. Without delving into the incredible number of interlocking syndicates and corporations, it can be said that the state owns the railroads, telegraph, and radio, that the state administers three great banks as well as its own bank, that the state mines all the coal, produces three quarters of the natural gas, holds direct control over half the telephones, forges half the iron and steel, distributes one fourth of the electrical energy, supplies 40 per cent of the combustible liquids, and possesses one fifth of the merchant marine.

The new Italian Republic fell heir to a hodgepodge of devices for state intervention in the economy by fascism, an intervention prompted by the economic collapse of 1930–33 and then attuned to the war efforts of 1935–36 and 1939–43. State intervention was given a great impetus when the *Istituto per la Ricostruzione Industriale* (I.R.I.) was established in 1933 to help the banks. By acquiring the assets held by the banks I.R.I. gained control over the banks themselves, so that today the Italian Commercial Bank, the Bank of Rome, and the Italian Credit are under it. The stock of the National Bank of Labor is held directly by the minister of the Treasury. The mammoth, sprawling I.R.I. has four giant combines under it for the iron-steel industries, for shipping, for tools and armaments, and for electric power. But outside the companies controlled by the state through I.R.I. there are other holding companies such as the Public Domain, which includes steel mills and metal industries, the E.N.I., in which the various petroleum companies are grouped, and F.I.M., which embraces some armaments firms. Some of the dozens of companies in this maze are still stock companies in which private individuals own substantial shares; others are completely owned by the state. In his report on a study of government enterprise and holdings made to the Italian Senate on June 15, 1951, Ugo La Malfa, a leader of the Republican Party, said that he found one thousand instances of public ownership.

The permeation of government control over the economy may be further noted by the fact that I.R.I. employs over 200,000 workers. But in most instances, and this is a point of political issue, the management has not changed and the I.R.I. employees are not regarded as state employees. In providing these public services, it might be added, the acquisition of profits is not necessarily the primary objective. What policies should guide a holding company that looks like a private enterprise, maintains capital divisions in the form of shares, offers dividends, but is legally controlled by the state? Of what industries and enterprises should the state divest itself? To whom? And who should decide, in the whole range of policy questions, which services to the public warrant losses and which segments of the economy ought to be in private hands? The governments of Italy since World War II have lived uneasily with the corporate economic arrangements inherited from fascism. Since 1957 there has been a Minister of State Participations generally responsible for policy problems relative to the I.R.I. and E.N.I. There has been no haste to change the statute of the I.R.I., but firms within the organization are dropping their membership in *Confindustria,* the national federation of manufacturing and commercial associations. The left political opposition, meanwhile, harries the government by demanding outright nationalization on an extensive scale and a complete reorganization of management.

If the weakness in the Italian balance of payments is of continuous concern in the field of foreign relations, unemployment is a perennial political and economic problem on the domestic scene. Despite an increase in productivity in the years from 1948 to the present, which has been reflected in part in the form of new housing, a larger supply of consumer goods, and greater expenditures for transport and amusements, the number of unemployed workers remained almost static. A survey made a few years ago under parliamentary direction showed 1,300,000 people unemployed;[4] registered unemployment in recent years has fluctuated between 1,633,375 and 2,223,000 persons. The figures below illustrate the magnitude of the problem:

FIG. XI

ITALIAN UNEMPLOYMENT, 1954–56
(thousands)

	1954	1955	1956
Unemployed, formerly employed	1305	1303	1323
Seeking first employment	654	610	614
Housewives seeking employment	136	138	118
Retired persons seeking jobs	55	60	64
Employed, seeking change	47	50	52
TOTALS	2197	2161	2171

But the government statistics of these years further indicate that around a half million of those counted as "working" were actually employed less than twenty-four hours in a given week, so that underemployment, as well as unemployment, has been a curse of the Italian economy. This underemployment is particularly marked among the 1,500,000 day laborers on farms, where the average number of days worked has run to about 160 days per year, and among the masses of unskilled workers. The fact that only 10 per cent of the unemployed surveyed by the parliamentary commission received unemployment assistance reveals the hardship of those out of work.

Since 1948 the government has taken a number of steps to increase employment by organizing labor training centers and by subsidizing the housing program in order to stimulate the construction industry as

[4] See the summary and conclusions by Roberto Tremelloni, chairman of the parliamentary inquiry into unemployment in Italy, *International Labor Review,* LXVIII (September, 1953), pp. 256–78. For the stagnation of Italian employment see Paolo Sylos-Labini, "Sclerosi economica," *Il Mondo,* February 22, 1955, p. 3.

well as provide adequate homes. In 1950 the government initiated a twelve-year plan for the development of the south through the Fund for the South (*Cassa per il Mezzogiorno*), and in 1955 it launched the dramatic ten-year plan of Ezio Vanoni for economic development, which envisaged large-scale industrial investments with the object of creating about four million new jobs. It was the hope of Vanoni that a 5-per-cent increase of national income annually might be so channeled that one third went to investment and two thirds to consumption.

During the first four years of the "Plan," from 1955 to 1958, many developments in the Italian economy have been better than expected. The annual rate of growth of income, calculated in real terms, has been slightly higher than the 5 per cent prescribed by the "Plan." There has been an improvement in the balance of payments position of Italy and an absorption of labor into new jobs created by new investments, both of which were anticipated by the "Plan." Nevertheless, a major purpose of the "Plan" was to reduce the disparity of income between the north and the south by projecting a rate of income growth at 4 per cent for the north and 8.1 per cent for the south. To date, there is little sign that this ambitious goal will be realized. Moreover, the improvement in the balance of payments stems from large increases in receipts from invisible items while the balance of commodity trade remains weak. And the absorption of labor has been facilitated by more emigration than had been contemplated.

In any event the national income has been rising, above and beyond price inflation, but the gains have been spent somewhat more for consumer's goods than envisaged by the economic planners. In 1958 fixed investments actually decreased by 1 per cent from the level of 1957, whereas in 1957 they had increased by 7.6 per cent from 1956. In short, the eventual success of the Vanoni plan will depend upon a variety of wise fiscal policies, internal political stability, and continuous international co-operation.

The poverty of Italy is reflected in the low average of real income. Furthermore, there are wide differences in the real income of individual families. The most modern conveniences and the most luxurious villas are often located within a short distance of the quarters of those who may live three or four to a room, perhaps without any flooring, often without hot water, bath, and other conveniences. A parliamentary inquiry in 1952 into destitution in Italy revealed that, out of the 1,368,-000 families classified as having the lowest living conditions, almost a million lived in caves, shacks, and basements, or in quarters where two, three, and four people occupied a single room; that 650,000 consumed no meat, sugar, or wine; that 600,000 were wretchedly or poorly dressed. In another category of 1,345,000 families, which fell into the second-lowest standard of living, almost a million lived in "overcrowded" houses, about 150,000 consumed no sugar, meat, or wine, and 750,000 were dressed shabbily.[5] It is important to note that only 7.4 per cent of

[5] The study was carried out by a parliamentary commission of inquiry "to investigate the extent of poverty . . . and to examine the working of the social welfare institutions." Up to 1955 fourteen volumes of its report had been published. The

the families with the lowest living standard and 14 per cent of the families with the second lowest living standard reside in the north-central regions. The mass, crippling poverty is found primarily in the south, as the following table will indicate:

FIG. XII

GEOGRAPHICAL DISTRIBUTION OF LOW AND VERY LOW
LIVING STANDARDS, 1952–53

REGION	NUMBER OF FAMILIES	PERCENTAGE
North	314,000	11.6
Center	313,000	11.5
South	1,426,000	52.6
Islands	659,000	24.3
Italy	2,712,000	100.0

3. PROBLEM OF THE SOUTH

Statistics usually divide the Italian nation into four parts: the north, the center, the south, and the islands of Sardinia and Sicily. But in order to appreciate one of the most crucial problems of Italian politics it would be more appropriate to draw a line between the north and center, on the one side, and the south (*Mezzogiorno*), including the islands, on the other. As one moves from the north to the south and east of Rome, the economic-social organization of the Italian people begins to change rapidly. Forty-five miles south of Naples is Eboli, which Carlo Levi, in his book *Christ Stopped at Eboli,* took as a dividing line between the two Italies, between the progressive and vigorous Italy of the north, which is moored to a Western European economy, and the "other" Italy, the Italy of the *Mezzogiorno.* For example, while regions such as Liguria, Emilia-Romagna, and Tuscany in 1954 showed rates of infant deaths in their first year as less than 39 per thousand born living, the regions of the south and the islands averaged 66 per thousand. Since the beginning of the twentieth century, moreover, the nation as a whole has made rapid strides in reducing illiteracy. Leaving out the south, the index of absolute illiteracy in Italy is less than 3.7 per thousand. But in eight regions of Italy that include the south and the islands, 7.6 out of every *100 married persons* were unable in 1951 to write their own names.

In the provision of power, in the adequacy of the transportation network, in the facilities of communication, the south falls in the shadow of the active, business-conscious, industrialized regions of the north. No region of the south in 1954, including Campania with Naples, had more than seventeen telephones per thousand inhabitants, while in Basilicata

survey was based on a sample of 58,000 families representing all social classes, and of 2000 destitute families who were receiving government assistance in thirty-seven provincial capitals.

and Calabria there were fewer than five telephones for every thousand
inhabitants. The number and capitalization of stock companies supply
further indications of differences. Out of the 23,711 stock companies in
Italy in 1954 only 1,585 were located in the south, and of these the
province of Naples accounted for half of the total. More significant is the
fact that in 1953 around 93 per cent of the capital represented by
stock companies was accounted for by the north-central regions, a percentage that was not far different from that in 1897.

In overall figures the seven northern regions of Italy produce
more wheat and considerably more rye, corn, and rice than the seven
southern regions, including the islands. While the south leads in the
production of barley, oats, broad beans, peas, cabbages, cauliflowers,
and citrus fruits, the north is ahead in onions, asparagus, green beans,
and pears, apples, and peaches. Both Northern and Southern Italy
run close in the production of tomatoes and potatoes. What is noteworthy, however, is that Piedmont produces as much wheat as Sicily,
but needs only half the acreage for its production; Lombardy can get
two and a half times as much rye as Calabria for each acre under
cultivation; Emilia-Romagna harvests one and a half times as much
barley as Basilicata from an equal area planted.

Reasons of climate and soil play a large role in this disequilibrium
between northern and southern regions, but economic and social factors,
such as tariffs, public investment, taxation, expenditures for education
and health, all subject to political control, have in the past tended to
magnify the differences produced by history and nature. By laws of
1950 and 1952 the Italian government established the Fund for the
South, consisting of appropriations of $2,048,000,000 to be spent over a
period of twelve years for the economic and social development of the
south. Over one third of this sum is intended for land reclamation and
improvement, and about one quarter for watershed developments, aque-
ducts, and drainage. The balance will be allotted to agrarian reform
projects, roads, railroads, and tourist facilities. The Fund itself is primarily a financing organization, and actual work in the region is contracted
through local authorities, in co-operation with the national agencies for
agriculture, forestry, roads, etc. The achievements of the Fund, despite
initial difficulties, are impressive: by the beginning of 1957 thousands
of acres of swampland had been drained, arid wastes had been ir-
rigated, and treeless hills reforested; no fewer than thirty thousand farm
buildings and small houses had been constructed; and many thousands
of miles of farm and provincial roads had been improved. During the
first six months of operation the Fund for the South financed $537,000,-
000 of work—including $94,000,000 for loans to private enterprises in
the south and another $115,000,000 for land reform projects in the
area. The results of this large scale impetus to the economy, primarily
in land rehabilitation and communications, have already had an impact
upon the standard of living in the south. The number of motor buses
and tractors has doubled in the south since the inception of the Fund.
The number of automobiles, telephones, radios, as well as expenditures
for entertainment, have increased more rapidly *on a percentage basis*

in the south than in the north. Despite these trends, however, the real disparities between the two parts of Italy are still great.

In 1957 the government of Italy enacted a new law to encourage further investment in the south, particularly in industry. The law grants to firms a partial exemption of income tax on those profits, not to exceed 50 per cent of declared profits, which are invested in the south. Such tax-exempt profits cannot exceed 50 per cent of the total sum invested in the south. Moreover, the law also regulates the distribution of the investment of state-owned industrial enterprises by providing that not less than 40 per cent of their total gross investment shall be placed in the south. With the Fund and the investment incentive law Italy has boldly faced up to the problem of a divided economy which is likely to kindle political fires for many years.

4. POLITICAL PARTIES FROM SOCIAL FACTS

Italy is characterized by a multiparty system, due in part to its electoral system of proportional representation, but mainly to its historical heritage marked by the various institutional changes, to the ideology of Marxism and the religion of the Roman Catholic Church, as well as to the lack of social cohesion already noted. Out of its early history have come the Liberal and Republican parties; out of Marxism have come the Communists, the Socialists, and the Democratic Socialists; out of the Church has come Christian Democracy; out of its recent history have come the Monarchist parties; and, directly tied to the twenty-year Italian experience with fascism, is the present-day *Movimento Sociale Italiano* (M.S.I.). Since 1946 no party has been able to win a majority of the Italian vote. However, three parties—the Christian Democrats, the Socialists, and the Communists—have obtained upwards of 75 per cent of all the votes cast in national elections since 1946, leaving the other 25 per cent to six minor parties and a host of splinter groups. Figure XIII will provide certain details.

5. THE COMMUNIST PARTY

At the extreme left of the political spectrum is the Communist Party, which was constituted in Italy in January, 1921, by a very small band of revolutionary socialists inspired by the success of the Soviet Union. The Piedmontese branch led by Antonio Gramsci at Turin, whose chief support came from the metal-workers' union, eclipsed the southern wing in 1926, and when Gramsci went to prison some months later his chief lieutenant, Palmiro Togliatti, became the party's leader. Togliatti passed most of the Fascist years in Moscow, but hastened back to Italy in 1944 to proclaim the support of his party for the Badoglio government. In the successive governments of Bonomi, Parri, and De

FIG. XIII

POLITICAL PARTY STRENGTH IN ITALY, 1946–58

PARTY	1946	1948	1951–52	1953	1956	1958
Christian Democrats	8,101,004 (35.2%)	12,741,299 (48.5%)	8,006,923 (36.2%)	10,862,073 (40.1%)	9,233,450 (38.6%)	12,492,319 (42.4%)
Communists	4,356,686 (19.0%)			6,120,809 (22.7%)		6,704,454 (22.7%)
Communist-Socialists		8,151,529 (31.0%)	7,855,909 (35.5%)			
Socialists	4,758,129 (20.7%)			3,441,014 (12.7%)	8,341,932 (34.9%)	4,206,726 (14.3%)
Democratic Socialists		1,858,346 (7.1%)	1,702,906 (7.7%)	1,222,957 (4.5%)	1,792,769 (7.5%)	1,345,447 (4.6%)
Liberals	1,560,638 (6.8%)	1,004,889 (3.8%)	871,135 (3.9%)	815,929 (3.0%)	1,022,999 (4.3%)	1,047,081 (3.5%)
Republicans	1,003,007 (4.4%)	652,477 (2.5%)	560,562 (2.5%)	438,149 (1.6%)	342,596 (1.4%)	405,782 (1.4%)
Monarchists	637,328 (2.8%)	729,174 (2.8%)	800,476 (3.6%)	1,854,850 (6.9%)	1,253,091 (5.2%)	1,436,916 (4.8%)
Qualunquists	1,211,956 (5.3%)					
M.S.I.		526,670 (2.0%)	1,406,940 (6.4%)	1,582,154 (5.9%)	1,221,190 (5.1%)	1,406,140 (4.8%)
Minor Parties Mixed Lists	(5.8%)	(2.3%)	(4.2%)	(2.6%)	(3.0%)	(1.5%)

N.B. The figures representing the popular vote are for the elections to the Constituent Assembly in 1946, to the Chamber of Deputies in 1948, 1953, and 1958, to provincial councils in 1951–52, and 1956.

Gasperi the Communists obtained, first, the Ministry of Agriculture, then the ministries of Finance and Agriculture, then those of Justice, Finance, and Agriculture, and, finally, those of Justice, Agriculture, and Transportation just before they passed into the opposition in the summer of 1947.

With about 1,800,000 members, the Italian Communist Party is one of the largest Red parties outside the Soviet Union. The main source of Communist strength in Italy may be found in its active, intellectual leadership, dedicated to Marxist principles and loyal to the Soviet Union; in the trade unions; and in either the poverty of the peasant or the sullen discontent that arises out of rigid social stratification in many aspects of Italian life. The General Confederation of Labor (C.G.I.L.), Italy's largest confederation of trade unions, is controlled by the Communists. Prior to fascism the trade unions had, in the main, been linked to the policies of the Socialist Party, and during fascism all trade unions were controlled by the one-party government. At the end of World War II the national trade-union organization, taken over intact, was put in the charge of a political directorate of Communists, Socialists, Christian Democrats, and minor parties. The Communists, however, had been actively organizing among the ranks of workers even during the war and, by 1950, Giuseppe Di Vittorio, the Communist trade union leader, with the help of his Socialist colleague, was virtually dictating the policies of the confederation. Although the labor leaders who were loyal to the Christian Democrats and the Democratic Socialists seceded to form their own rival unions, the majority of organized labor still remains with the C.G.I.L. The Fourth Congress of the C.G.I.L. in 1956 elected a secretariat consisting of two Communist and two Socialist members of Parliament under a Communist Secretary General. No one would maintain that all the members of C.G.I.L. vote for either the Communists or the Socialists; indeed, the weakness of the leadership in calling purely political strikes in recent years betrays the limitations of the Communist-guided direction. The rival unions of the Christian Democrats and the Democratic Socialists, moreover, have been making vigorous inroads into the C.G.I.L. strength. Yet as a source of propaganda and funds, with its hierarchical organization penetrating the vitals of Italian industry, the C.G.I.L. is the very spine of the allied Communist-Socialist party organizations.

The most startling gains of the Communist Party in Italy since the end of World War II have come from the south where previously its strength had been negligible. A regional division of the Communist percentage of the vote indicates the party's penetration into an area noted for its impoverished peasantry rather than its urban proletariat or trade unions. See Figure XIV.

The Communist organization reaches the peasants partly through its national unions for field workers, agricultural office workers, share farmers, and direct cultivators, who are grouped in the National Confederation of Landworkers (*Confederterra*); partly through agricultural co-operatives and labor offices; and partly through direct agitation in local communities. Communist strength is greatest in the "red belt" of Emilia-Romagna, an amalgam of the historical duchies of Parma and Modena and a part of the Papal State, with its capital of Bologna. Agriculture is the mainstay of the region but is highly organized along capitalistic lines, with a rural proletariat. It is a mistake, moreover, to suppose that the poorest regions are the most communistic in Italy. The people of Tuscany are relatively well off, yet more than one third of them voted Communist in the national elections of 1958. They exhibited no special love for Russia and hardly any desire for the sovietization of the economy. The narrowness of employment opportunities, the inadequacies of the public service, the difficulties of the contractual relationships between share farmers and landowners in this region, and, perhaps, a characteristic Italian desire to protest against the government for *all* grievances may be the real explanations for this electoral behavior.

FIG. XIV

COMMUNIST PER CENT OF TOTAL VOTE BY REGIONS, 1946–58

	1946	1951–52	1953	1958
8 Northern Regions	22.4	19.8	21.2	20.8
4 Central Regions	24.6	27.3	28.2	28.3
5 Southern Regions	10.9	16.1	21.2	22.5
2 Islands	8.9	16.8	21.7	21.4

N.B. Figures for 1946, election to Constituent Assembly; 1951–52, provincial and regional councils; 1953 and 1958, Chamber of Deputies. In these elections the Communists ran on lists separate from the Socialists.

Under the leadership of Togliatti the Communist Party has provided the people a vent for many wraths and the party has exploited with skill a variety of political situations: it supported the Badoglio-Bonomi governments to win official influence from 1944 to 1947; it approved the Lateran Pacts in the constitution to attract or confuse liberal Catholic supporters; it rapidly penetrated the labor unions and won control over the national confederation, retaining its leadership, despite secessions, as the most articulate spokesman for the workingman; it played hard upon agrarian reform and obtained credit for government action among its increasing number of supporters in the south. All this was done with remarkable electoral results, despite the fact that the party's foreign policy has been slavishly bound to the Soviet Union and that its leadership was badly shaken by "de-Stalinization" in 1956, and despite the millions of dollars of economic aid that the United States has funneled through the Christian Democratic and coalition governments into Italy. In the elections for city councils in 1956 almost one Italian in every four voted for a Communist candidate. Above all, the party has masterfully kept the Socialist Party of Pietro Nenni in a Socialist-Communist alliance. At times they have presented separate electoral lists and at others popular bloc lists, but in any case they have been virtually united on domestic and foreign policies.

6. THE SOCIALIST PARTY

The perennial problem of the Italian Socialist Party has been its lack of unity. Through its confusion on strategy, its dogmatic schisms, and its personal divisions it has lost the primacy it once held among workers and intellectuals in Italy to the Communists, the Democratic Socialists, and the left wing of Christian Democracy. The party that Leonida Bissolati had nourished until 1912 upon a gradualist program, trading parliamentary co-operation for working-class reforms of universal suffrage, unemployment insurance, old-age pensions, etc., was a formidable one. Despite Bissolati's expulsion by Mussolini and Mussolini's own expulsion over the issue of intervention in World War I, the Socialist Party was by far the largest group in the Chamber of Deputies in 1919. But the party under Filippo Turati faltered between co-operation and nonco-operation with the bourgeois government, while the success of the Russian Revolution sharpened the doctrinal rifts between the reformists and the advocates of a maximum or revolutionary Marxian program. The Communist Party split off from the Socialists in 1921, and the Maximalists captured the party machinery late in 1922. Under fascism the unity of the Socialists with the Communists, confirmed in a pact at Paris in 1934, grew quite naturally out of the necessity of combining scattered exiled or underground forces in a common anti-fascist front. Similarly, in the violent months of 1945, Socialist and Communist partisans co-operated in dismantling the Fascist structure in the north. Almost immediately the question arose, therefore, as to whether the Socialist Party should fuse with the Communists, a proposal stoutly resisted by the followers of Giuseppe Saragat. Nevertheless the party, led by Pietro Nenni, signed a new pact of unity with the Communists in October, 1946, which called for a tight co-ordination of policies on every level.

It became increasingly obvious that unity with the Communists bound the Socialist Party, not only to a strict Marxian position in Italy, but also to solidarity with the Soviet Union as against the United States in the field of foreign affairs. In January, 1947, Saragat and some 40 per cent of the Socialist deputies seceded to form a new party, which, through various transformations and admixtures, is today known as the Democratic Socialist Party (*Partito Socialista Democratica Italiana*). But reformist socialism in Italy, involving collaboration with the government, as exemplified by the Democratic Socialists, no longer has the rationale that sustained it prior to World War I, when suffrage was an issue, when trade unions and the workingman had barely won legal rights and were seeking the most elementary social justice, when all the institutions of the state were in hostile, anti-socialist hands, and when no Soviet Union existed as an example of Socialist success. A comparison of the voting strengths of the two branches of the Socialists instantly reveals that a preponderant majority has remained loyal to the old Socialist Party, despite the latter's past subservience to the Communists:

FIG. XV

PERCENTAGE OF
COMMUNIST-SOCIALIST POPULAR VOTE IN ITALY, 1946–58

	1946	1948	1951–52	1953	1956	1958
Communists	19.0%		18.5%	22.7%		22.7%
Communists-Socialists		31.0%	35.5		34.9%	
Socialists	20.7		12.0	12.7		14.3
Democratic Socialists		7.1	7.7	4.5	7.5	4.6

N.B. 1946 figures are for the Constituent Assembly; 1948, 1953, and 1958 for the Chamber of Deputies; 1951–2, and 1956 for provincial councils.

Then why not complete fusion of the Socialists with the Communists? A deep respect for the historical autonomy of the party, which has played a significant role in Italian history, is one factor; the possibility of maneuver by Nenni for electoral gains and flexible tactics in an ever-changing political scene, coupled with an unwillingness to be completely compromised by Russian foreign policy may be others. In the summer of 1956 a meeting between Nenni and Saragat raised hopes of a union between the two Socialist parties, but Nenni could not adopt an active anti-Communist policy. On the other hand the Socialists abandoned their pact of unity with the Communists and ran on separate electoral lists in 1958. Fundamentally, the doctrines of the two parties of the extreme left are the same and it is helpful to add together their popular votes and members of Parliament to assess the force of the Communist-Socialist power in Italy.

7. THE CHRISTIAN DEMOCRATIC PARTY

The most powerful force in Italian politics today is Christian Democracy, cemented by the institution of the Church and almost completely responsible for the government of the nation since 1948. The Christian Democratic Party owes its origins to the Popular Party of Luigi Sturzo, the brilliant, energetic Sicilian priest who first injected a mass Christian party with a program of economic and social reform into Italian life after World War I. Against the Liberals, with their stern anticlericalism, their industrial-finance monopolists who sought centralization in a small, manageable group of political decision makers, and their baronial landowners, the Popular Party offered a program of equality between private and public schools, decentralization of governmental responsibilities to local authorities, and agrarian reform, including peasants' banks and co-operatives. Against the Socialists, who jealously guarded their exclusive control over the trade-union movement, the Popular Party offered its own trade unions and supported free associations and confederations of labor. In sum, the Popular Party offered a compromise between a Godless totalitarianism, considered by it to be inherent in Socialist ideas, and the exaggerated individualism of the Liberals, who in its eyes sanctified private property, narrowly construed the role of religion, and failed to relate political freedom to economic and social welfare. In the first election to which the Popular Party submitted lists of candidates in 1919, therefore, it immediately secured a mass base and obtained 20.5 per cent of the total votes.

Although originally inspired and guided by a priest, the Popular Party took great pains to present itself as a party inspired by Christian principles rather than as a Church party. It sought no special place for Roman Catholicism, but insisted that its reform program was a fundamental aspect of Christian life. Although the principles of the party were broad enough to embrace all men of good will, Sturzo could not sacrifice the democratic principles of his movement to combine with Giolitti, who epitomized the old Liberal state, despite the common menace of fascism in 1921. At the same time the only other hope of stopping fascism was an alliance between the Socialists and the Popular Party. Such an alliance was seriously considered by Alcide De Gasperi, who succeeded Don Sturzo as secretary general of the party in 1923, but the blunt repudiation of various feelers by the Vatican, horrified at the thought of pairing with Marxian socialists and perhaps hoping for better Church-state relationships through fascism, killed any chance of collaboration.

Like other parties the Popular Party was suppressed under fascism; Sturzo had been forced into exile, and De Gasperi, after a prison term, was employed as a librarian in Vatican City. But the Church itself soon turned against the total claims of fascism and managed to keep alive Catholic Action, non-political, indeed, but a nuclear non-Fascist organization easily transformed into a cadre for Christian Democracy as Mussolini fell. The new Christian Democratic Party, which appeared in July, 1943, with the free support of the capillary Church organization, immediately obtained a mass following. Sympathy for the Christian Democrats (in preference to the radical groups of Socialists and Communists) by the Allied forces, moreover strengthened the party's hand once the north had been liberated. From 1945 until the present every prime minister of Italy has been a Christian Democrat, the most outstanding being De Gasperi, who held that post for seven and a half years, to be followed by Giuseppe Pella in August, 1953, by Mario Scelba in February, 1954, by Antonio Segni in June, 1955, Adone Zoli in May, 1957, Amintore Fanfani in July, 1958, and Antonio Segni again in February, 1959.

The Christian Democratic Party reiterates that it is a movement guided by Christian principles, and that it is not a Church party; furthermore, it seeks economic and social justice on a popular basis, accepting substantial intervention by the state. It rejects the laicism of the Liberals, naturally, and condemns their narrow views of property; on the other hand, as a Christian party, it cannot accept the "mechanistic materialism" of socialism. In foreign policy, of course, the position of the Christian Democrats in adhering to the North Atlantic Treaty Alliance and Western union, as well as their close co-operation with the United States, has been opposite to that of the Communists and has been roundly condemned by the right-wing parties. In truth, the Christian Democratic Party is an uneasy coalition. Because it is such a mass party, capturing anywhere between 35 to 48 per cent of the total vote of the major elections between 1946 and 1958, it means many things to many men.

The party's primary support comes from the Catholic Church, fundamentally conservative, and its host of auxiliary organizations that permeate Italian life. Among these is the strong Catholic Action, the lay branch of the Church, and its various charitable, sports, educational, etc., groupings. Notable, for example, are the Catholic Association of Italian Workers (A.C.L.I.), which, while technically not a labor union, interests itself in the economic and social needs of its 800,000 members, and the Civic Committees, which provide electoral propaganda, as well as other social services, to bring out the Catholic vote against the threat of communism. Throughout the twentieth century, moreover, Italian women have always outnumbered men, and today there are at least one million more females in Italy than males. Responsive to the guidance of the Church and having achieved suffrage in 1946, women today play a crucial role for the Christian Democratic Party. No other party depends so much upon the female vote: in the national election of 1953 some 3,400,000 men, as compared to 7,500,000 women, cast their votes for the Christian Democrats. Finally, it should not be forgotten that in Italy about 3,600 hospitals and old-age or poorhouses, 3,700 schools, 16,500 religious homes, and 64,000 churches are in the keeping of the Roman Catholic faith. If Church brothers, sisters, teachers, and seminarians are included with the priests, the number of people in the electorate actively fulfilling the mission of the Church add up to about 230,000.

A second important source of Christian Democratic support comes from the Italian Confederation of Labor Unions (C.I.S.L.), the trade-union confederation, which split off from the Communist-dominated C.G.I.L. and which is led by Giulio Pastore. Both the Popular Party and its descendant, the Christian Democratic Party, have sought to free the trade unions from Socialist domination and, indeed, have made large inroads on that power. Yet the intimate relationships between the labor unions and the political parties in Italy tend to make the unions essentially internal pressure groups of the parties rather than large-scale forces in the general economy.[6] While C.I.S.L. has its branches for organized agriculture, which provide support for the Christian Democrats, the *Coltivatori Diretti,* pledged to the interests of small farm owners also taps the peasants of Italy. Though this latter organization is not officially connected with the party, its personnel and policies are very close to those of the Christian Democrats.

Not to be discounted in the ranks of the Christian Democrats are the liberal Catholics from the universities and the professions who are

[6] In addition to the C.G.I.L., oriented about the Communists and Socialists, the C.I.S.L., oriented about the Christian Democrats, there are the smaller *Unione Italiana de Lavoro* (U.I.L.), helpful to the Democratic Socialists, and the *Confederazione Italiana Sindicati Nazionali Lavoratori* (C.I.S.N.A.L.), headed by a *Movimento Sociale Italiano* deputy. All the unions claim to be non-party.

sincerely animated by their Christian faith to seek socio-economic progress at home and co-operation with democracy abroad. But to them
must also be added many businessmen and big landowners, bureaucrats
and petty politicians, and opportunists who are attracted to the party
that has controlled the government and its subsidies, contracts, and jobs
for more than ten years. Supported by these variegated elements, the
party is bound to reflect many internal differences.

The regional distribution of the Christian Democratic vote shows a
fairly even dispersal, with marked improvement recently in the South
where economic development has been fostered and comparative weakness in the "red belt" of Emilia-Romagna and the old papal state of
Umbria:

FIG. XVI

CHRISTIAN DEMOCRAT PER CENT OF TOTAL VOTE, BY REGIONS, 1946–58

	1946	1948	1951–52	1953	1956	1958
8 Northern Regions	37.3%	49.3%	40.7%	42.9%	42.1%	42.9%
4 Central Regions	29.9	44.5	30.4	36.1	34.2	37.2
5 Southern Regions	35.0	50.2	32.9	38.7	36.4	44.7
2 Islands	35.2	48.5	30.9	40.1	39.4	43.8

N.B. Figures for 1946 are for the Constituent Assembly; 1948, 1953, and 1958
the Chamber of Deputies; 1951–52 and 1956 provincial councils.

But the figures fail to reveal the spectrum of views within the Christian Democratic Party. The major faction of the party has been the
"Democratic Initiative," which supported Amintore Fanfani in working for a tightly knit party organization dedicated to a broad program of economic-social reform based on private property, but a corporate organization of the economy with state regulation. Another faction
has been the "Concentration," including such men as Guido Gonella
and Guiseppe Pella, who combine their zeal for conservatism in fiscal
policies with their desires for closer co-operation with the Church. A
third faction, oriented leftwards, follows President Giovanni Gronchi
and Giulio Pastore, head of the Catholic trade unions. And there are
other groups with special interests or leading personalities which make
the management of the Christian Democratic Party difficult.

De Gasperi was the great stabilizer of the party, holding the
centrifugal forces together with the weight of his personality at home
and his prestige abroad. De Gasperi turned from the left to the right,
and then back again, to find support for his governments. Indeed, his
very success in attracting members from the fringe parties aroused their
resentment and led to his fall in the summer of 1953. Yet, after De
Gasperi's resignation, Pella was chosen as prime minister by the president of the republic, Luigi Einaudi, without consultation with the Christian Democratic Party; Scelba and Fanfani's governments fell because
of dissidence among the Christian Democrats themselves; and Giovanni
Gronchi was elected president in April, 1955, due to disagreements within
the party and a strange combination of ultra-conservatives with leftists in
Parliament. That Christian Democracy is still the greatest force in Italian

politics goes without saying, but splits within its ranks will continue to be a serious problem for political stability in the government.

8. MINOR PARTIES

Two of the minor parties that have collaborated with the Christian Democratic Party in its government coalitions have been the Liberals and the Republicans, both shells of the Italian past when they played significant roles. It is difficult to classify the pre-World War I Liberals as a party, for they were really clusters of men, with various shades of opinion, in a small governing class that had supported the institution of a conservative, constitutional monarchy for Italy. Beyond that they were motivated by such principles as the separation of church from state and free enterprise in the economy. Prior to the rise of socialism and the introduction of universal manhood suffrage the battles between the right and left of the Liberal Party were fought on the parliamentary, tactical level rather than along broad ideological lines; after World War I, although there were three Liberal groups associated with Giolitti, Salandra, and Orlando respectively, the differences among them involved more the temperaments and methods of the leaders than differences in beliefs. Out of the rigid conservatism of the Liberals, supported by the industrialists and big landowners and still exercising considerable influence over the apparatus of the state, came the alliance with fascism with its anti-socialist base. Salandra looked favorably on the Fascists; Giolitti combined with them on a national electoral list; and nationalists like Enrico Corradini and Alberto Rocco, who played such important roles in fascism, originally were Liberals.

Not all the Liberals, however, were so shortsighted about fascism, and some moved to the opposition—after it was too late. Outstanding Liberals, with faith in the doctrine of liberty for the individual, property owner or not, were Benedetto Croce, the philosopher, and Luigi Einaudi, the eminent economist, who quietly maintained their beliefs and integrity despite the pressures of fascism. In 1943, Croce represented the Liberals on the six-party Committee of National Liberation, and in June, 1947, Einaudi joined the first non-Communist Christian Democratic government as vice-president of the Council of Ministers and minister of the budget. Einaudi received the crowning honor by being elected president of Italy in 1948. Similarly, the Liberal Party has contributed Gaetano Martino, the distinguished minister of foreign affairs in the cabinet of Prime Minister Segni (1956).

The electoral support for the Liberal Party is scant, however, and amounted in 1958 to around 3.5 per cent of the total Italian vote, mainly divided between its traditional home of Piedmont-Liguria and such agrarian areas as Abruzzi-Molise and Sicily, where the landowners command some following. Collaborating with the Christian Democrats, the Liberals have lost some of their opportunists to the chief government party, some of their conservatives to the Monarchists; and in December,

1955 they suffered a minor blow when the Piedmontese Bruno Villa-
bruna, in opposition to the party secretary, Giovanni Malagodi, led another faction from the Liberals to form the Radical Party. The Radical
Party seeks a return to the purer principles of liberalism in a united,
democratic, laic front. In 1958 it joined its small following to the Republican Party.

The Republican Party can trace its spirited origins directly back to
Mazzini and Garibaldi: the direct democracy for which the Republicans
had fought in the *Risorgimento* was compelled to yield to the Liberal
program of unification under the Savoian dynasty and of conservative
principles of government. Some of the irreconcilable Mazzinians were
suppressed; others either compromised their views and supported the
state that Cavour had successfully built or split into small left-center
groups. Reconstituted in 1895, the Republicans again raised their cry
against the monarchy as representative of the whole conservative state
and pushed radical democratic reforms by methods that aroused at
times the hostility of the Socialists as well as of the Liberals. Passionate
in their desire to liberate the Italians of Venezia Giulia and the Trento
from Austria, they fought in World War I with typical Garibaldian
spirit. With little coherent program other than the abolition of the
monarchy, no Republican deputy was elected in 1921. Three years later,
however, seven Republicans were returned to the terrorized Chamber
and they proved to be among the bravest anti-Fascists. Mussolini re-
taliated violently against the party, and forced its remnants underground
with the other parties.

In 1943 the small Republican Party immediately raised an un-
equivocal cry against the monarchy and in 1946 finally saw realized,
albeit with the help of Christian Democrats and Socialists, the century-
old platform of the party to make Italy a republic. Some of the leaders
of the former Action Party, the democratic partisans of the liberation
movement, passed into the ranks of the Republicans after 1945. Although the Republican Party received an insignificant 1.4 per cent of
the total vote in the national election of 1958, outstanding men like
Ugo La Malfa and Randolfo Pacciardi are still to be found in its ranks.

The Monarchists date their origins to the referendum of June,
1946, which, by a small majority, ended the Kingdom of Italy. But
there is more than a name involved, for the restoration of the monarchy
hardly serves alone as the basis of two political parties. The National
Monarchist Party obtained 6.9 per cent of the votes in the national
election of 1953. Five years later the Popular Monarchist Party and the
National Monarchist Party, with separate lists, polled a total of 4.8
per cent of the total votes. While there seems to be a wane of Monarchist
strength in Italy, nevertheless its attraction of voters after twelve years
of a republic is notable. How is this to be explained?

Every single region of the south had voted *in favor* of the monarchy
in the referendum of 1946—and in Campania (Naples) the vote ran
three to one against the institution of the republic. Thus the symbol of
the monarchy had a strong popular base, and many of the large property
owners of the south, reacting to the government's land-reform program,

found the National Monarchist Party a good political tool for their interests. At the same time ex-Fascists who did not want to be identified with the neo-Fascist Italian Social Movement (M.S.I.) were attracted by the conservative, anti-government policies of the Monarchists. The wealthy shipowner, Achille Lauro, former mayor of Naples and a benevolent demagogue, subsidized a small, new Popular Monarchist Party with an eye to *his* own interests, while the most conservative Liberals easily slipped into the Monarchists' ranks. Even any assumed link between the National Monarchist Party and Prince Umberto of Savoia was broken at the end of 1955, when the prince rebuked Alfredo Covelli, secretary-general of the party, by personally designating the leader of the Italian Monarchist Union to co-ordinate all monarchical elements.

The real significance of the Monarchist Party, however, has been its combination with the M.S.I. to provide the opposition in the past to the government from the right. The twelfth transitory article of the Constituent Assembly and an apposite law of December 23, 1947, had forbidden the reorganization of the Fascist Party in any form and denied the right to vote to all Fascist leaders for a period of five years. An early reaction to the Italian postwar collapse and to the alleged failure of the governments of the day to realize their programs had been the *Uomo Qualunque* movement, the man-in-the-street or the ordinary-fellow movement. This movement, with its cynical, antiparliamentary overtones, appeared in the south in 1946, but it rapidly died away for want of any program. The M.S.I. was founded in 1947 as a frankly neo-Fascist party, and in its first trial in the national election of 1948 obtained only 2.07 per cent of the vote. In the administrative elections of 1951–52, however, it tripled its vote over 1948. In June, 1952, the government became so alarmed over the potential of the M.S.I. that it passed a law penalizing public expression of Fascist ideas and tactics, especially by former leaders of that party. Despite these restrictions the M.S.I. obtained 5.9 per cent of the vote in the national elections of 1953 and 4.8 per cent in 1958.

FIG. XVII

PER CENT OF TOTAL VOTE BY REGIONS FOR MONARCHISTS
AND M.S.I., 1946–58

		1946	1948	1951–52	1953	1956	1958
North	Monarchists	0.9%	0.5%	0.5%	3.2%	5.6%	2.4%
	M.S.I.	—	0.9	3.4	3.5	—	3.4
Center	Monarchists	2.7	1.0	2.3	3.7	9.9	3.7
	M.S.I.	—	2.4	8.0	7.2	—	6.5
South	Monarchists	6.8	6.9	10.6	15.4	21.9	10.2
	M.S.I.	—	3.5	10.1	7.3	—	5.6
Islands	Monarchists	3.2	7.3	8.1	11.2	14.8	7.3
	M.S.I.	—	3.1	13.0	11.0	—	6.4

N.B. 1946 figures are for Constituent Assembly; 1948, 1953, and 1958 for the Chamber of Deputies; 1951–52 and 1956 for provincial councils; votes for two Monarchist parties and M.S.I. have been consolidated in 1956 figures.

The M.S.I. attacks the Christian Democrats, charging that they have appropriated Socialist policies in the domestic field and are subservient to the United States in the foreign field. The M.S.I. criticizes the weaknesses and confusion of the coalition government and the purpose and character of "socialist" reforms, all of which it contrasts with the order and idealism of fascism and the former dignity of Italy in world affairs.

The regional vote of the M.S.I. and the Monarchists in recent elections is indicated in Figure XVII.

In retrospect the Italian Republic has thus far failed to produce a mass party, other than the Christian Democrats, that is pledged to democratic, parliamentary government and that excludes either a Fascist or Communist orientation. The most likely opposition party to offer such an alternative to the electorate in the future would be the Socialists, but they are still divided among themselves, some intransigent against the Communists, others willing to co-operate with them, and still others frankly sympathetic with the big Red party. The Communist Party itself was badly shaken by deStalinization in Russia and the harsh repression of Hungary by the Soviet Union. Innumerable defections occurred in 1956 and 1957 among its intellectual leadership and serious tremors ran through its trade union control. Nevertheless, in the elections of 1958 the Communist Party secured the same percentage of the Italian vote as it had five years earlier, a continuous warning of the economic distress and social frustration which haunt the political system.

21

THE GOVERNMENT OF THE
ITALIAN REPUBLIC

1. THE CONSTITUTION

The old Piedmontese Statuto of 1848, under which Italy had been governed until the renovations of the Fascist order in the 1920's, was hardly more than a fundamental law defining the powers of king and Parliament, the religion of the state, and a few civic freedoms. It had been granted reluctantly by a sovereign to his people to forestall a revolution, and was a brief document containing no provision for formal amendment. The present constitution of the Italian Republic, in force since January 1, 1948, is by way of comparison a document of 139 articles and 18 transitional provisions worked out and approved by deputies in a Constituent Assembly elected through universal suffrage. The final preparation of the constitution, moreover, followed a period of war and military occupation from which Communists, Socialists, and Christian Democrats emerged as the parties commanding major popular support. Under these circumstances it is understandable that the document consists of two major parts. The first of these comprises 54 articles that deal with the democratic principles underlying the republic and the rights and duties of citizens, in their civic, ethical, social, economic, and political relationships; the second part deals in a detailed way with the organs of the state and places a stress upon the representation of the people in the national and local governments.

When the Constituent Assembly met, the voters had already decided by referendum that Italy was to be a republic, but, in enunciating the fundamental principles of the new state, the Constituent Assembly elaborated by calling Italy "a democratic Republic, based upon work" in which "sovereignty belongs to the people." Furthermore, the young republic was broadly obligated, in order to promote the welfare of the citizens: to remove obstacles of the economic and social order which in fact limit the liberty and equality of citizens; to recognize and promote the right to work; to recognize and promote local governments

504

and effect autonomy or decentralization adequately; to protect linguistic minorities; to promote the development of culture as well as scientific research; to repudiate war as a means of resolving international controversies; to recognize the rights of the family and to facilitate by economic and other means the formation of the family; to protect maternity, infancy, and youth; to protect health as a fundamental right of the citizen and guarantee free medical care to the poor; to promote the right to education through scholarships and family allowances; to care for labor in all its forms and applications, including guarantees of fair wages, paid holidays, and insurance against accident, illness, old age, or unemployment; to promote and favor co-operatives by suitable means; to recognize the right of labor to collaborate in the management of firms; and to encourage and protect savings. In addition to such broad economic and social norms for the republic, the citizen was guaranteed those freedoms of person, religion, speech, press, assembly, and legal defense that are associated with the French Declaration of Rights of Man and Citizen as well as with English and American guarantees and Bills of Rights.

Five years after the constitution was put into effect, however, an eminent Italian professor of political science at the Catholic University of Milan wrote that there had been "frightening constitutional omissions" on the part of the legislator, who had not enacted the laws necessary to implement the constitution; on the part of the government, which had not adopted suitable rules to make the legislative organs function as they should under the constitution; and on the part of the magistrates, who sought every pretext not to apply the new norms and showed themselves too ready to follow the will of the government. As late as 1955 a renowned scholar of jurisprudence commented that the years since the Constituent Assembly might be regarded, not only as a period of constitutional immobilism, but even as years of regression; while no *coup d'état* was threatened, he said, an erosion of the constitution had taken place that might, if continued, lead to its collapse.[1]

It has already been noted that the revolutionary fires from the north in 1945 had been checked by the stabilizing conservatism of Christian Democracy, and that the purge of Fascist sympathizers had first been laggard, then abandoned in both the bureaucracy and the magistracy. In place of a radical change in the political, economic, and social order to be *effected* immediately, the Christian Democrats, Communists, and Socialists essentially compromised on the *promise* of such changes in Italy through the new constitution. Thus it has been said by its sharpest critics that the constitution was born as a result of the original sin of delay, contained important provisions that were declaratory rather than mandatory, and left the implementation of important provisions to a period when the forces of the old state would have the opportunity to obstruct the projected democratic reforms.

In respect to implementing both major divisions of the constitution,

[1] See Balladore Pallieri, "La costituzione italiana nel decorso quinquennio," *Foro padano,* No. 2 (February, 1954); and Piero Calamandrei, "La costituzione e le leggi per attuaral," *Dieci anni dopo* (1955).

that is, (a) the one including the principles of the republic and the rights and duties of citizens, and (b) the one dealing with the organs of the state, the governments of Italy since 1947 have been slow, if not at times downright evasive. While the freedoms of the people are specifically guaranteed in the constitution, their limits are quite properly governed by laws or regulations that cannot permit the abuse of liberty. In this connection the Italian constitution occasionally notes that the exercise of a particular right is to be "according to the law." However, something of a denial in fact of the constitutional guarantees has arisen because the laws themselves sometimes date back to the Fascist period, or because the interpretation of the law by the magistracy or the police has been based upon long-standing norms that have not been brought into relationship with the spirit of the new constitution. In any case, there is need for statutory revision or enabling legislation to strengthen the declarations of the constitution. In addition there is some ambiguity and inconsistency in certain of the provisions of the constitution, which were inserted to satisfy several of the parties represented in the Constituent Assembly. For example, while the republic is pledged by Article 3 "to remove obstacles of an economic and social order which limit in fact the liberty and equality of citizens and impede the full development of the human personality," the prevailing law follows the somewhat inconsistent Article 30 in assuring "to all children born out of wedlock juridical and social protection compatible with the rights of the members of a legitimate family."

In the field of religion, moreover, the equivocations of the constitution raise many curious legal problems. On the one hand, Articles 8 and 19 of the Italian constitution categorically state that all confessional religions are equal before the law and that everyone has the right to profess his own religious faith, either in private or public—provided that the rites are not contrary to "morality." On the other hand, Article 7 of the constitution states that the Catholic Church and the state are each, in its own sphere, independent and sovereign and that their relations are to be regulated by the Lateran Pact of 1929. In juxtaposing the Lateran Pact and the Italian constitution it seems evident that Article 1 of the Pact, which proclaims the Roman Catholic religion as the "only" religion of Italy, has *de facto* been nullified. But it is also obvious that the Lateran Pact is still a binding treaty that cannot be altered unilaterally and that leaves the Roman Catholic Church in a unique position, demonstrable in view of the religious instruction carried on within the public schools and in the power of nullifying marriages which is vested in ecclesiastical courts.[2] While it

---

[2] The vigor of the Lateran Pact is easily attested. In June, 1955, for example, the Italian Court of Assize at Ferrara condemned a twenty-seven-year-old man to one year's imprisonment (suspended) for ridiculing a motion picture which showed the Pope at a religious ceremony. In February, 1958, the first arraignment of a bishop before a civil tribunal since the Lateran Pact took place. The bishop of Prato was charged with slander and libel for having denounced the civil marriage of two Italians as "the beginning of scandalous concubinage." Convicted by a trial court, the bishop was exonerated on appeal eight months later on a judgment that "he did not commit a crime."

can be maintained that Italy is not a "confessional" state in which the government confers a monopoly upon one church and actively and directly aids it in its work, nevertheless the state specifically recognizes the Roman Catholic ethic as an integral part of Italian life and subsidizes it.

To the fact that the magistracy and bureaucracy were never fully purged of Fascist sympathizers, to the fact that some laws of Italy have not yet been made consonant with the spirit of the constitution, to the fact that some of the provisions of the constitution were inconsistent and vague, there must be added the inescapable criticism that various governmental organs delineated in the constitution have either not been brought into being by Act of Parliament or have only recently been established. Among these were some of the very organs especially designed to strengthen democracy; namely, regions and regional assemblies to buttress local government: the Superior Council of the Magistracy, with its broad responsibility for appointments, promotions, transfers, and disciplining of judges, and designed in part to reduce political influences through the Ministry of Justice; the National Council of Economy and Labor, consisting of representatives from labor, industry, co-operatives, certain quasi-state corporations, and economic-social experts, to have consultative functions for both Parliament and the Government, including the examination or the suggestion of bills in the economic-social field; and, above all, the Constitutional Court which, with its original jurisdiction in cases concerning national or regional laws, or acts, in conflict with the constitution can check the excesses of an omnipotent Parliament and protect the autonomy guaranteed the regions.

Only four of the proposed nineteen regions have been constituted thus far. The Constitutional Court did not begin its work until 1956, eight years after the constitution had been in force. Neither the Superior Council of the Magistracy nor the National Council of Economy and Labor began to function actively before 1958.

But it should not be inferred that the constitution is a dead letter. In the main its provisions have been implemented. Today the citizen probably possesses a somewhat greater degree of freedom, including civil, economic, and social rights, then he ever experienced under the Statuto and a far greater degree than he had under fascism. But no nation can escape its history: the centuries of Spanish domination, with its extravagant formalism, the bureaucratic centralization of Piedmont, the blind idealization of the state and the enforced conformity to fascism, as well as the ever-gnawing poverty that has always compelled large numbers of citizens to think first of food and work rather than the niceties of personal freedom. The zealous urge to basic change and radical reconstruction, reflected in the original strength of the Communists and Socialists in the Constituent Assembly, has been tempered through time, the moderation of the Christian Democrats, and the role of various conservative groups on the Italian political scene since 1948.

In addition to including a long enumeration of principles and rights and provision for a Constitutional Court, an independent judiciary, and regional governments, the Italian constitution also and necessarily departed from the Statuto in providing for a president of the republic, who is elected by both houses of Parliament sitting together with a designated number of regional representatives. Following the Statuto, both the Chamber of Deputies and the Senate were revived as the lower and upper houses of Parliament, but with the Senate as an elective body rather than an appointive one. The principle of ministerial responsibility was written into the Statuto and the Savoian dynasty had quietly followed the practice of choosing ministers acceptable to the Chamber, although in times of crisis and party instability the king could exercise considerable discretion. Under the Italian constitution the president of the republic today appoints the president of the Council of Ministers (the "prime minister") and, on the recommendation of the prime minister, the other ministers. Within ten days after the formation of a new government the newly constituted government must obtain a vote of confidence by *both* houses of Parliament.

The constitution provides for a comparatively easy method of amendment by means of laws passed in each house of Parliament. The constitution requires that amendment laws be passed twice, with an interval of at least three months before the first and second passage, and that there must be an absolute majority of the members of each house in favor of the law at the second voting. A referendum of the people on constitutional revision, moreover, can be initiated by the petition of one fifth of the members of one house of Parliament, or 500,000 electors, or five regional councils; however, if the two houses of Parliament have passed the constitutional law by a two-thirds majority of their members, no referendum is possible. Finally, Italy seems to have cast out the monarchy forever under this constitution, despite the wishes of the Monarchist parties, for the republican form of government may not be a subject of constitutional revision.

2. THE PARLIAMENT

The Parliament of Italy consists of two houses, the Chamber of Deputies and the Senate, both of which are elected by the people. The Chamber, based upon one representative for each 80,000 inhabitants, consists of 596 deputies elected for five years on a party-list system of proportional representation that broadly reflects the popular vote in the nation.[3] In 1953 the Christian Democrats and their allies secured the passage after bitter debate of an amended electoral law under which parties might associate themselves in a group and, if any group obtained more than

---

[3] Party lists, upon which the voter may indicate a preference for three or four candidates, are presented within the thirty-one electoral districts. Each party receives a proportionate number of the seats assigned to the electoral district according to the total vote received by its list. Candidates are elected according to the preference vote they receive on the lists. The remainders of the vote not apportioned in each of the thirty-one districts are pooled nationally and further reallocated to parties.

one half of the total vote cast for all the party lists, it would automatically secure two thirds of the total, or 380 seats, in the Chamber. Clearly intended to give the Christian Democrats a commanding control over the Chamber of Deputies if they—with their allies—achieved a bare majority of the popular vote, and unhappily reminiscent to its critics of Mussolini's Acerbo Law of 1923, the law was called by these critics a "swindle." In the election of 1953, under this "Scelba Law," the Christian Democrat-center vote was 49.85 per cent of the total. About one and a half million votes, moreover, were spoiled for one reason or another, including defacement by lipstick, scratches, or other markings in a hotly-contested campaign. Although the Christian Democratic government needed only another 57,000 votes to secure two thirds of the Chamber's seats, it did not press further, sensing the lack of popular conviction for the electoral amendment, and in July, 1954, the law was abrogated.

The Senate is composed of 246 members,[4] elected for six years by regional constituencies (the regions for senatorial elections being different from those for Chamber elections). One seat is assigned for each 200,000 inhabitants within a region, subject to the limitation that no region may have fewer than six senators with the exception of tiny Valle D'Aosta. Senators may be elected directly if within a local electoral district they receive 65 per cent of the total vote. Otherwise a complicated form of the list system of proportional representation applies. Candidates for the Senate must be at least forty years old, and Italian citizens are eligible to vote in senatorial elections when they are twenty-five years of age. In contrast, candidates for the Chamber need be only twenty-five years of age and their electors twenty-one. It is notable that *at the time of their election* in 1953 some 63 senators (out of 243) were sixty-five years old and over, while only 37 Deputies (out of 590) were in those upper age brackets.

While the two houses of Parliament are legally equal, the Chamber has tended to acquire greater political power, in part because its membership contains a greater amount of talent and in part because its electorate is broader than that for the Senate. All of the presidents of the Council of Ministers (prime ministers), with the exception of Adone Zoli, have thus far been selected from the Chamber of Deputies, and the majority of the ministerial posts are assigned to deputies; nevertheless the Senate, including in its membership some eminent men and formally guaranteed equal legislative powers by the constitution, generally shares in the government. Out of the twenty-one ministers composing Antonio Segni's government in 1956 only three posts were held by senators, but two of those three were the Ministry of the Budget and

---

[4] The first Senate, from 1948 to 1953, included 87 senators (39 Communists) appointed by virtue of the transitional provision of the constitution, which made places for certain pre-Fascist and anti-Fascist leaders. At present only ex-presidents of the republic are senators by right. In addition the president of the republic may appoint five senators for life who are especially meritorious in the nation: e.g., the sculptor Pietro Canonica was appointed in 1950 and Don Luigi Sturzo was appointed in 1952. A bill to increase the number of senators appointed for life was defeated in March, 1958.

the Ministry of the Treasury.[5] In Zoli's and Fanfani's and Segni's second government, four ministers were chosen from the Senate. The difference in the terms of office of members of the Chamber and the Senate, five and six years respectively, may raise problems for a government that needs the confidence of both houses. In 1953 and 1958 the president, in accord with the prime minister, ordered the dissolution of the Senate, which could have remained in office another year, and thus brought about the election of members of both houses. But only future practice will confirm this action, which raised serious questions of constitutional interpretation. In 1957 the Council of Ministers approved the proposal of a bill that would have reduced the Senate term to five years and increased its membership to 324, but the Senate defeated the bill in 1958.

In 1948 the Christian Democrats benefited from an electoral land-slide and secured nearly an absolute majority of the popular vote and an absolute majority of seats in Parliament. Nevertheless, De Gasperi stead-fastly worked to hold together the coalition of center parties, Democratic Socialists, Liberals, and Republicans with the Christian Democrats—in part because a number of foreign-policy issues, such as the North Atlantic Treaty, needed the widest consensus; in part because the Democratic Socialists would strengthen the support for a government program of agrarian reform, development of the south, and tax revision; in part because De Gasperi sought to mitigate the clerical- versus secular-state issue; and in part because the 305 Christian Democratic deputies by no means represented men of a single conviction. From the beginning the coalition was under strain, for the Liberals and the Democratic Social-ists, by definition, hold opposing economic-social philosophies. In Janu-ary, 1950, the Liberals withdrew from the government, and in April, 1951, the Democratic Socialists gave up their portfolios, thus leaving the Christian Democrats flanked only by the tiny Republican Party. Neither of the ex-government parties, however, went into the opposition. In 1953 the four parties again rejoined their forces in the electoral group-ing previously mentioned. The percentage of Christian Democratic seats in the Chamber was cut from 53.6 per cent to 44.7 per cent, thus making coalition government not only desirable, but absolutely essential. Where could De Gasperi turn to form a government? The Monarchists and the Socialists had been the biggest gainers in the elections, but he would not yield to the right wing of his own party, which urged an alliance with reactionaries, nor could he yield to the Socialists, who still were closely aligned with the Communists. At this juncture Giuseppe Saragat, leader of the Democratic Socialists, stung by the loss of fourteen of his party's thirty-three seats in the Chamber, and in a gesture of independence from Christian Democratic policy orientation, announced his withdrawal from the government. De Gasperi's last hope was the Liberals and the few remaining Republicans, but they too inwardly resented the steady loss of their membership to the Christian Democratic Party and their declining influence. On July 28, 1953, the minor coalition parties took

[5] Upon the resignation of Silvo Gava from the Treasury and the death of Ezio Vanoni, minister of the budget, in February, 1956, two senators were chosen to fill these portfolios. In 1958 one of these ministries was held by a Senator.

their revenge against the man who had steered Italy through seven and a half difficult years. With only the Christian Democrats in favor, the right and left adamantly opposed, and the Republicans, Liberals, and Democratic Socialists abstaining, the government of Alcide De Gasperi went down to defeat by 263 to 282 votes in the Chamber of Deputies.

FIG. XVIII

PARLIAMENTARY SEATS HELD BY POLITICAL PARTIES,
1948, 1953, AND 1958

	CHAMBER OF DEPUTIES			SENATE		
	1948	1953	1958	1948	1953	1958
Left Opposition:						
Communists	131	143	140		49	59
Socialists	52	75	84		28	35
Others				72	10	3
TOTAL	183	218	224	72	87	97
Government Coalitions:						
Christian Democrats	305	261	273	131	116	123
Democratic Socialists	33	19	22	10	4	5
Liberals	19	14	17	9	3	4
Republican-Radicals	9	5	6	5		
Sardo-Action	1			1		
Valle D'Aosta Christian Democrats		1	1			
South Tyrol Christian Democrats	3	3	3	3	2	2
TOTAL	370	303	322	159	125	134
Right Opposition:						
Monarchists	14	40	25	3	16	7
Movimento Sociale Italiano	6	29	24	1	9	8
Others				2		
TOTAL	20	69	49	6	25	15
Others	1		1			
TOTAL OPPOSITION	203	287	273	78	112	112
TOTAL MEMBERSHIP	574	590	596	237	237	246

A subsequent attempt to form a center-party coalition around Attilio Piccioni by the Christian Democrats failed. At this point, nearly two months after the parliamentary elections, President Luigi Einaudi, apparently without consultation, called upon Guiseppe Pella of the conservative wing of the Christian Democrats to form a "technical" government. The Pella government, made up entirely of Christian Democrats, quickly received a vote of confidence to serve as a stopgap while Parliament recessed. But Pella plunged the country into an international crisis by taking a strong and popular stand on the burning Trieste issue, when he moved troops to that troubled frontier. He soon revealed his rightist leanings and made some overtures to secure the support of the Monarchists. The center and left factions of the Christian Democracy, never consulted in the nomination of Pella, angrily brought his ministry to an end in January, 1954. An effort by Amintore Fanfani to head a government at that time was short-lived.

The parliamentary problem in Italy today centers around the need of the Christian Democrats for support from the parties that are poised on both the right and left of the party as Figure XVIII indicates.

Internally the party, with its varied membership, must continually make compromises in order to maintain a semblance of outward unity, and these compromises often lead to vacillation. It is too early to say that *trasformismo* has returned to the Italian scene, but the prime minister has increasingly been faced by the need to mediate between competing groups in his own party and those on the fringes of it, to persuade the factions to subordinate their differences to the common goal of a parliamentary majority, and to balance the ministries, not only among the allied parties, but within his own party. Thus Mario Scelba's government was approved in March, 1954, by a narrow majority of seventeen votes provided by the revived coalition of the center parties, but within a few months Scelba was in difficulty. Not only had the coalition threatened to crack, but his own party pulled at the seams. On the one hand, there was the Democratic Initiative, oriented leftward, which had captured the party machinery at the Christian Democratic congress in June, 1954; on the other hand, there was a group of Christian Democratic dissidents, among them Giuseppe Pella, Guido Gonella, and Giulio Andreotti, who formed a Concentration faction; and in March, 1955, the Republican Party withdrew its support of the coalition. Finally, in April, 1955, to the chagrin of the Christian Democratic leadership, the Concentration group supported the left in the election of Giovanni Gronchi rather than Cesare Merzagora as president of the republic. Two months later, after failing to win the support of the Republicans or to gain the sympathy of the Concentration group, Scelba resigned, to be followed by the Sardinian professor of agrarian law, Antonio Segni. There were no substantial differences between the Scelba and Segni governments; rather, Segni sought compromises between factions within the Christian Democratic Party by including in the ministries, not only representatives of the Concentration group, but also some young reformers who provided the party with some crusading zeal. In order to win the favor of the Democratic Socialists in a coalition government and allay their fears of a clerical state, one of their members was placed in charge of public instruction. And during the months in office from July 18, 1955, to May 6, 1957, the government of Antonio Segni could point to several accomplishments: the entry of Italy into the United Nations; the beginning of the work of the Constitutional Court; the institution of the Superior Council of the Magistracy and the National Council of Economy and Labor; the enactment of laws on petroleum resources, public housing, and reorganization of the bureaucracy; an extension of the work of the Fund for the South; additional financing for the agrarian-reform program; some reduction in the national budgetary deficits; and the signing of the treaties for the European Common Market and Euratom. But the decision of the Democratic Socialists—long harassed by the tactics in the moves to reunite the Socialist Party—to leave the government forced the resignation of Prime Minister Segni.

On June 8, 1957, Senator Adone Zoli, a stalwart member of the Christian Democratic Party since its origin, began office as president of a Council of Ministers composed entirely of Christian Democrats. This arrangement was a temporary and precarious one, for the Christian Democrats alone could not muster a majority of votes in Parliament. Zoli, tacitly or otherwise, had to depend at times on the Monarchist-Fascist bloc for the continuance of his government. Both the Chamber of Deputies and the six-year Senate were dissolved by the President of the Republic in March, 1958 in preparation for the national elections held in May.

FIG. XIX

VOTES OF CONFIDENCE IN THE CHAMBER OF DEPUTIES

DATE	SUBJECT	FOR	VOTING AGAINST	ABSTAINED
March 10, 1954	Presentation of government by Mario Scelba	300	283	1
September 30, 1954	Reshuffling of ministries	294	264	7
October 19, 1954	Foreign affairs, budget	295	265	7
December 3, 1954	Law affecting whole bureacracy	263	215	2
		278	208	2
January 19, 1955	War pensions	281	256	
March 23, 1955	Motion to instruct government on Italian oil	278	211	5
July 18, 1955	Presentation of government by Antonio Segni	293	265	12
February 25, 1956	Appointment of new ministers	284	52	105
March 14, 1956	Revisions of electoral law	280	47	Socialist-Communists left the Chamber during the vote.
December 22, 1956	Regulation of electric utilities	282	220	4
February 28, 1957	Agrarian contracts	285	277	1
June 8, 1957	Presentation of government by Adone Zoli	305	255	11
July 26, 1958	Presentation of government by Amintore Fanfani	295	287	9
December 6, 1958	Surtax on gasoline	294	286	2
February 27, 1959	Presentation of government by Antonio Segni	333	248	1

In the words of one commentator, the vote throughout Italy in 1958 indicated "more left, less right, and the same old center." The Christian Democrats received 42.4 per cent of the total vote cast for the Chamber

ITALY

of Deputies and 41.2 per cent for the Senate. Although he had hoped to induce the Republicans to join the coalition, Amintore Fanfani presented a government of sixteen Christian Democrats and four Democratic Socialists to receive the confidence of Parliament in July, 1958, winning a bare majority of 8 votes with the Republicans abstaining. But Fanfani's government lasted little more than six months. Conservative members of the Christian Democracy were embittered by his apparent shift of policy toward the left, and some Democratic Socialists, led by minister of labor Ezio Vigorelli, decided to align themselves with the Socialists in opposition to the government. Left without a majority in Parliament, Fanfani resigned in January, 1959, but no Christian Democrat was able to put together a satisfactory coalition government.

In February, 1959, Antonio Segni was again chosen as prime minister, and headed a minority government composed exclusively of Christian Democrats, but initially supported also by the right-wing Liberals, Monarchists, and M.S.I. members. Combination still seems to be the order of Italian politics and a tabulation of the votes of confidence in the Chamber of Deputies indicates something of the difficulties which Italian governments must withstand. See Figure XIX.

3. PARLIAMENTARY LEGISLATION

According to the constitution, bills may be introduced in either house of Parliament by its members, by the government, by the regional councils, and by the National Council of Economy and Labor (another auxiliary organ of government that the Parliament was extremely slow in establishing). In the legislative sessions from 1948 to 1953 the government presented about 2,000 bills, the individual deputies and senators themselves about 1,000, and the Sicilian Regional Assembly a few. Of the government bills introduced around 98 per cent were enacted; of the bills presented on the initiative of members of Parliament, less than 30 per cent became law. From June, 1953, to May, 1956, Parliament enacted 960 laws, of which 743 were initiated by the government, 216 by members of Parliament, and one on the proposal of a region. A unique feature of the Italian parliamentary procedure is that bills are sent, according to their subject, to standing committees, where, unless they deal with constitutional matters, treaties, electoral provisions, or revenues and budget, they may be finally approved by the committee without ever coming before a plenary session.[6] However, a safeguard against arbitrary action is found in the composition of committees in proportion to their parliamentary party strength; in addition, one tenth of the members of the house in which the bill is under consideration or one fifth of those of the committee itself may demand at any time that the bill be placed before the whole house. When a bill is brought by a committee

[6] In 1955, 75 bills were approved in the Chamber and 59 in the Senate, while 169 bills were approved in the committees of the Chamber and 178 in the committees of the Senate.

before Parliament, there is usually a report (*relazione*), presenting various aspects of the bill and suggested modifications, made by a reporter (*relatore*) of the committee. There may be both a majority and minority reporter.

After passage of a bill by both houses of Parliament it is sent to the president of the republic, who may promulgate it within thirty days. The president may send the bill back for a second consideration along with his reasons, but, if the bill is passed again by the Parliament, he must promulgate it. Finally, a popular referendum on the law is possible, although no implementing legislation was yet available in 1958, if 500,000 electors or five regional councils request it, but no referendum may be held on laws dealing with taxes, budget, amnesty, or treaties.

The procedure of parliaments in Italy has been notoriously marked by unparliamentary conduct. The lively gesticulation of the face and hands, the emotion-charged voice, and the flashing response to wounded dignity in Italy have been ever present in the debates in the houses of Parliament. When heated by the debate on political issues, inflamed by the enmity that divides the ideological right from the ideological left, the deputies or senators can explode in violent sessions. From time to time one house or the other has rung out with invective, and every so often the floor has become a place for a push or a shove or even a brawl.[7] The normal parliamentary session, of course, goes along without incident. Questioning and interpellation of the government by deputies or senators are permitted: a "question" usually requires but a simple, single answer from a minister and may take either a written or an oral form; interpellation consists of a series of inquiries regarding the broad policies of the government and follows a more extended procedure of questions and answers.

Parliamentary practice in Italy had little chance to develop calmly or with dignity prior to World War I. Mussolini then stamped out all possibility for the maturation of parliamentary responsibility. In the present Italian Parliament, which harbors its sizable antiparliamentary groups, the daily strain on orderly procedures is still obvious.

[7] In March, 1955, for example, an unusual session of the Senate went like this: On the left the whole sector jumped to its feet, drowning out with their cries the voice of the M.S.I. leader. The bell of the president of the Senate rang and his words could no longer be heard. Members of the Socialist-Communist bloc came down from their benches and started to mass on the floor, while clerks and guards hastened to dam the rising tide.

COMMUNISTS: Get out! get out! traitors!
    M.S.I.: You're the traitors!
COMMUNISTS: Scoundrels! villains!
    M.S.I.: You stabbed our soldiers in the back!

On the government benches Martino ostentatiously leafed through a newspaper of sports while Marshal Messe, sitting at his usual center desk, continued to correct his notes. Meanwhile, the Communist Voccoli (seventy-eight years old!) punched an M.S.I. senator on the neck. Other senators joined the fray. Finally the president, in the midst of the confusion, succeeded in shrieking above the fray, "The session is suspended for one hour!"

Reconstructed from the Italian newspaper accounts of March 10, 1955.

4. THE PRESIDENCY

The president of the Italian Republic is elected for a term of seven years by the members of both houses of Parliament sitting together with three delegates from each region (except Valle D'Aosta, which has one delegate). A "weak" president was intended by the constitution, an official not dependent directly on the electoral power of the people and amply limited by Article 89, which provides that "No act of the President of the Republic is valid unless countersigned by the proposing minister who assumes responsibility for it." It is customary to think of a constitutional president, like a constitutional king, as a figurehead who furnishes an example of dignity and prestige, performs the ceremonial functions of state, and provides a symbol of unity for the people above the partisanship of politics. Such a picture, especially in respect to Italy, may be misleading. It is still early, however, to generalize about the office of the Italian president, for the first president of the new republic was in some ways an exceptional case, and the second president, Giovanni Gronchi, had only served half his term by the end of 1958.

The president, first of all, has certain important powers that he can exercise on his own discretion. He shares in the legislative power to a real extent by virtue of his authority to return bills to Parliament for reconsideration. Even without taking this unusual step he may hold up, on his own initiative, the promulgation of a law for as long as thirty days unless both houses of Parliament by an *absolute majority* specify a shorter time. Given uncertain parliamentary majorities and a highly controversial bill, the government would at least have to consult with the president in order to avoid possible political embarrassment. Much more important, in accordance with Article 88, "he can, having heard their presidents, dissolve the chambers, or one of them," except during the last six months of his term. A number of situations may arise out of no-confidence votes or resignations of governments, particularly in times of crises and of instability of coalitions, where the president can exercise a wide degree of discretion in the dissolution of both houses of Parliament in order to hold new elections, or, as noted above, the president may dissolve one house. In 1953, President Einaudi dissolved the Senate one year short of its official term in order to synchronize the elections for a new Parliament. President Gronchi did the same thing in 1958.

The requirement of ministerial countersignature "by the proposing minister," moreover, should not confuse anyone into believing that the *initiative* is always with the minister, for some acts, such as returning a bill to Parliament for reconsideration, may be on the initiative of the president. The president acts in a ministerial capacity in *formally* appointing certain officials, accrediting and receiving ambassadors, ratifying treaties, commanding the armed forces, etc., since these are political activities for which a government must be responsible to Parliament. However, the president, like Parliament, is also empowered to appoint five of the fifteen members of the highly important Constitutional Court.

Did the constitution intend to give to the ministers actual control over the nomination of both the parliamentary appointments and the presidential appointments to the Court? It seems highly unlikely, for otherwise why was a distinction made in the way the two types of officials were to be chosen? In this case, too, the president apparently can act on his own initiative, despite the formal requirement of a ministerial countersignature.

Finally, and most importantly, the president of the republic chooses the president of the Council of Ministers (prime minister) to head a new government. While this act of the president also must have a ministerial countersignature, it is obvious that the outgoing ministry will act in only a perfunctory fashion and that the new ministry cannot even be constituted until a prime minister has been designated by the president. In August, 1953, President Luigi Einaudi chose Pella as president of the Council of Ministers on his own initiative, when the Christian Democrats were unable to win parliamentary support for a new ministry and while the nation dragged along without a government. It need hardly be repeated that Pella's government had to obtain a vote of confidence by Parliament, but President Einaudi had made the initial selection independently and, through the weight of his prestige, thereby began a government that lasted for over four months.

The president of the republic, it might be added, is the presiding officer over such important institutions as the Supreme Council of Defense and the Superior Council of the Magistracy.

His power is by no means unlimited. No act of his is valid without the signature of *some* minister. Not being politically responsible himself, he must always be cognizant of and act in the light of actual political forces in the Parliament. In normal times, when one political party or a closely knit coalition has a working majority in the Chamber and Senate, the president's role is minor. But at other times when there may be shaky coalitions of parties in Parliament and when the strains between right and left are most in evidence, the degree of initiative potentially vested in him by the constitution may permit the Italian president to become much more than a figurehead.

President Giovanni Gronchi, was elected in April, 1955, after serving as president of the Chamber of Deputies. A man of political stature, a Christian Democrat of reformist tendencies with views to the left of his party's center, Gronchi brought, not only prestige to his role as chief of state, but intimations of political strength.[8] At the end of 1955, Don Luigi Sturzo himself interrogated the government on the appropriateness and political significance of Gronchi's meeting with newly appointed prefects and ambassadors. In 1956 Gronchi became the first Italian chief of State ever to visit the United States and Canada; he made significant

---

[8] Gronchi was a leading member of the *Popolari* party before the Fascist dictatorship and was at one time head of the Catholic trade-union organization; he served in the 1922 Mussolini cabinet and the 1944 Bonomi cabinet as Minister of Industry. The Socialists-Communists, who helped make the election of Gronchi to the presidency possible, have tried to read into his statements as much left-wing orientation as possible.

visits to the Middle East in 1957 and the United Kingdom in 1958. Through his formal messages to Parliament or his informal addresses and observations to organizations and the public at large, Gronchi has characterized his own role as president to be "a catalyst who, ever watchfully, thrusts and urges, yet without interfering with the responsibility of other organs of the State." The president of the Italian Republic has genuine constitutional powers, which, coupled to a liberal expression of views by an energetic leader, indicates an office of political significance and not merely ceremonial.

5. THE GOVERNMENT AND THE ADMINISTRATION

The president of the republic nominates the president of the Council of Ministers. He, in turn, proceeds to form a government of his own selection. The number of ministers varies slightly: twenty-one in Segni's governments, twenty-four in Fanfani's second government. The ministers are formally appointed by the president of the republic, and within ten days the government must receive a vote of confidence from both houses of Parliament. The constitution took pains to call the leading political figure in Italian government "the President of the Council of Ministers," rather than the "prime minister," in order to emphasize that he is one among equals in the Council, that he presides over a government rather than dictates to it, and that the government is collectively responsible. Nevertheless it is realistic to refer to the paramount role of the president of the Council of Ministers in the government when referring to men like De Gasperi, Scelba, Segni, or Fanfani, especially since the constitution specifically says that he directs the general policy of the government and is responsible for it, that he maintains the unity of political and administrative direction, and that he must sign those acts of the president of the republic that have the character of legislation.[9]

In addition to the ministers there are some thirty-one undersecretaries who are also political appointees. The undersecretaries are not mentioned in the constitution and legally do not form a part of the government; they have no authority to countersign the laws or acts of the Italian president, nor can they participate in the deliberations of the Council of Ministers except in an advisory capacity. In large measure they relieve the minister from the demands of the daily administration of his department in order that he may concentrate upon policy making and political problems of the government. To the undersecretaries should be added the three or four high commissioners who manage government boards for health, food, etc., which have usually been built around

[9] In this connection the government is expressly forbidden to govern by decree law, without delegation by Parliament, to avoid a recurrence of the dangerous practice of pre-Fascist ministers and the standard practice of dictators. Even in the event of emergency the government must present to Parliament its decrees for conversion into law on the very day of their promulgation or, if Parliament is recessed, call it into session within five days. Unless converted into law within sixty days, decrees lose all force whatsoever.

former units of the traditional ministries. Any citizen of Italy, it might be added, may be selected as president of the Council of Ministers, or minister, or undersecretary, but almost invariably deputies or senators have occupied these roles.

In early 1959, the government of Italy was constituted as follows:

FIG. XX

THE GOVERNMENT OF ITALY IN 1959

President of the Council of Ministers and Minister of Internal Affairs.

Vice-President of the Council and Minister of Defense

Minister without Portfolio for Government-Parliament Relations

Minister without Portfolio for Economic Development of Southern Italy and Depressed Areas

Minister without Portfolio for Administrative Reform

Minister without Portfolio for Tourism and Sport

Minister for Agriculture and Forests
Minister for the Budget-Treasury
Minister for Foreign Commerce
Minister for Finance
Minister for Pardons and Justice
Minister for Industry and Commerce
Minister for Foreign Affairs
Minister for Public Works
Minister for Labor and Social Welfare
Minister for the Merchant Marine
Minister for Posts and Telecommunication
Minister for Public Instruction
Minister for Health
Minister for Transport
Minister for State Participations

No "separation of powers" doctrine between legislative and executive branches of the Italian government exists, for the ministers are at once members of the government, which has the primary role in presenting bills to Parliament, and chiefs of executive departments with administrative responsibilities, as well as being deputies or senators. Furthermore, civil servants in Italy may also be members of Parliament, and it is notable that about 25 per cent of the members of Parliament receive some compensation, in addition to their salaries as deputies or senators, as employees of the national government, quasi-government boards, or local governments. A substantial number of these civil servants are schoolteachers and university professors. In general, public offices are filled by competitive examination, and promotions depend upon ratings, which stress seniority primarily but not exclusively.

As in all constitutional governments the ministers are held to strict account for the expenditures of public moneys. This function is performed in Italy by the Court of Accounts, which serves as a comptroller general, checking the payment of bills in accordance with the budget and the requirements of the law and reporting its findings directly to Parliament. While the Court of Accounts is not a new institution, it is for the first time based on constitutional provision rather than ordinary law, and its independence before the government is legally guaranteed.

The civil service of Italy is notoriously overstaffed and underpaid. The first complete count of the state employees in Italy in more than half a century yielded the following results as of November, 1954:

FIG. XXI

ITALIAN STATE EMPLOYEES IN 1954

	PERMANENT	TEMPORARY
Civil Service	178,737	50,103
Teachers	192,831	77,518
Magistrates	11,698	1
Subalterns	182,911	124,599
Officers	92,300	19,965
Non-commissioned Troops	77,548	93,529

The average monthly salary of certain of these employees in *lire* (with the official rate of exchange at approximately 625 *lire* to $1.00) was magistrates 150,000; university professors 119,000; civil servants 66,000; elementary teachers 52,000; officers 65,000; subalterns 46,000; and non-commissioned troops 42,000.

The Piedmontese government brought to the unification of Italy many of the worst practices of France in public administration—extreme centralization, rigid departmentalization, and wasteful procedures marked by great delay in the disposition of administrative problems. A further development of the bureaucracy took place under fascism, and the expansion of governmental activities in the more recent period has been unaccompanied by any adequate civil service reform. "Influence" plays a vital role in getting things done in Italy. Not to be overlooked is the lack of a public-service morale throughout the civil service. Underpaid, hopeful at best of slow promotions, and subject to the narrow supervision of their superiors, the public employees, particularly on the lower levels, often exhibit to the Italian citizen attitudes of apathy or even surliness. A basic reason for these attitudes is an economic one, but some weight can be placed on past traditions and the generally low prestige of public employment. Some ministries and government enterprises, of course, provide efficient services, but these are exceptional ones. In any event the issues created by the demands of the civil service, including pay rises, standardizations of rank and promotion, and the right to strike have been lively ones in Italy.

Some of the difficulties in reforming the Italian administration can be read in the financial deficits of each of the ten years after the end of World War II. The difficulties of adjusting expenditures to income in the immediate postwar period could be partially explained as a consequence of the drastic drop in productivity resulting from the destruction of capital equipment and general postwar maladjustments. The very genuine economic recovery that has taken place in Italy over the last years, reflecting the stimulation produced by American economic aid, coupled with the government's strenuous efforts to raise production levels, increase employment, and to improve conditions in the south, has resulted in substantially increased revenues for the Treasury. But the character of the economic-social reforms vigorously demanded of the people and often encouraged by political pressure groups, as well as the necessity of undertaking new public works and providing pay increases for the state employees, has caused expenditures to increase faster than revenues. In no year since 1948 have revenues and expenditures been balanced in the Italian budget. Deficits in current expenditures from current revenues have ranged anywhere from 175 billion *lire* to 500 billion *lire,* with a steady increase in the public debt.

The exertions of both private enterprise and government investment have caused substantial growth in national income: for example, during 1956 the gross national income at market prices rose 7.2 per cent in monetary terms and about 4 per cent in real terms. But with a continuously unfavorable balance of trade and national budgetary deficits the Italian economy is on trial to increase further its productivity and reduce unemployment. The pressure for increased government revenue, moreover, led Italy, for the first time in its history, to require annual income-tax declarations in 1951. Improved collections, in a country where evasions have been commonplace, resulted for the Treasury. But direct taxation still accounts for less than 20 per cent of the government's income. A large number of indirect taxes, ranging from sales to turnover taxes to taxes on stamps, license taxes, fees, etc., still provide the bulk of the state's revenue.

6. THE COURTS

Not only the Italian administrative system, but also the Italian court system, was modeled on the French example. The Statuto had dealt rather summarily with the courts, making the appointment of judges by the Crown permanent after three years of service, while the organization and procedure of the judiciary were left for legislative determination. But the Italian judiciary never enjoyed the prestige of the French. Not only did the system lack in tradition and its judges suffer from inadequate financial compensation, but the government often made political influence felt through the minister of justice, who, if he could not dismiss a judge, might transfer him to an undesirable bench. No constitution superior to the will of the king and Parliament in their ordinary law-making capacity existed, so that Italian judges could never declare a law unconstitutional. Fascism further subverted the courts to its own purposes, not only hamstringing the regular system of tribunals, but also creating special courts, such as the labor courts to settle industrial disputes, and permitting the removal of judges by the cabinet.

The present Italian constitution departed from the past in two ways. First, it envisaged an independent, practically self-perpetuating judiciary and, second, it contained provisions for a Constitutional Court, which might, in appropriate cases brought before it, hold laws or acts of Parliament to be unconstitutional or decide upon conflicts between the state and regions or among the regions.

At the end of November, 1955, Parliament finally completed the election of its own five out of the fifteen members of the Constitutional Court. The election of the judges was contested vigorously and ended in the selection of two Christian Democrats, one Liberal, one Socialist, and one independent favored by the Communists. Three days later the president of the republic appointed five other judges, all with a center-right orientation. These, added to the five already chosen by the Magistracy, completed the roster of the court.

In 1956 the fifteen-member Constitutional Court, whose members serve for twelve years, began its work. An entirely new institution, the Constitutional Court grafts upon the Italian-Continental system of justice some American practices. The Constitutional Court receives specific cases from the ordinary courts when a complaint is raised that a law, or an act having the force of law, of either the state or the regions is contrary to the Italian constitution. The question may be brought before the trial court by one of the parties, or by a government attorney. If the magistrate finds that the question of constitutionality is "not manifestly without grounds," he refers the case to the Constitutional Court. The Council of Ministers or a regional government, moreover, may have direct recourse to the Constitutional Court when either of them contends that an act of the other violates provisions of the constitution. In both these types of instances, that is, cases appealed to it from the ordinary courts or brought before it on the direct application of either the Italian or regional governments, the court may declare laws unconstitutional and thenceforth such laws cease to have effect. The Constitutional Court, with additional members, also tries impeachment charges brought by Parliament against the president of the republic, the president of the Council of Ministers, and the ministers.

The independence of the judiciary is to be assured by the role of a Superior Council of the Magistracy, whose members will include (a) the president of the republic, the chief justice of the Court of Cassation, and the chief prosecuting attorney ex officio, and (b) a number of lawyers who have had fifteen years of practice or are full professors of law, two thirds of whom will be elected for four years by the magistrates themselves and the other third by Parliament in joint session. All judges will be appointed by the Council after open competition, and the judiciary is regarded as providing career service carrying considerable prestige. However, the constitution did not reconcile adequately the powers granted to the minister of justice "to promote disciplinary action" in the court system and to be responsible for the "organization and services relative to justice," with other provisions designed to assure political independence of the judiciary. Is there adequate accountability of the judges to the politically responsible government when two thirds of the elected members of the Superior Council of the Magistracy will be completely independent of Parliament? How far can the minister of justice go in promoting disciplinary action? How responsible to Parliament can he be held for the organization and functioning of the courts? Whatever the answers, the failure to resolve them had held up the establishment of the Superior Council of the Magistracy until 1958.

Italy, like France, has codified both its criminal and civil law. The Codes of Piedmont, as previously indicated, were the basis of Italian law in the first generations of the kingdom, although many infusions of Lombardian and Tuscan practice took place. In 1889 and 1931, Italy adopted new criminal codes; in 1913 and 1931 new codes of criminal procedure were approved; the civil code and the code of civil procedure, dating from 1865, were not wholly replaced until 1942. Study of reforms in the code of criminal procedure was begun in 1945, and from 1949 to 1951 eight separate bills embodying reforms failed of passage in Parliament. Another bill died in Parliament in 1952, 1953, and 1954, but suddenly passed and was promulgated in July, 1955. While the judges of the Italian codified system do not follow the principle of *stare decisis* and seek only to "discover" the law for the case according to the code, in fact the historical interpretation of words and past precedents do carry weight in their decisions. Moreover, there is evidence of judicial "legislation" in the interpretations of the codes to meet new social situations. It is noteworthy, however, that the codes, now in force, largely date from the codification during the Fascist regime. While most of the provisions are the product of many years of juridical experience and are not controversial, the provisions on public security and criminal procedure have raised many constitutional questions. The ordinary Italian courts, which passed upon the constitutionality of laws pending the recent creation of the Constitutional Court, were limited by the fact that their judgments in individual cases had no general applicability. Furthermore, some of the provisions of the constitution were not self-executing and required implementation through Parliament for action. Where Parliament failed to pass such laws, the courts necessarily applied the old laws, whether Fascist or not in origin.

The Italian court system consists of the hierarchy of ordinary courts, which try civil and criminal cases, and the administrative courts, which are based upon the French model. On the lowest level of the Italian court structure for civil matters is a justice of the peace (*conciliatore*), an ordinary citizen paid from fees only, who tries to reconcile parties to disputes involving less than sixteen dollars. The lowest regular judges in the judicial hierarchy are the *pretori,* at least one of whom will be found in each of approximately one thousand judicial precincts in Italy. Sitting alone, the *pretore* may try civil cases involving sums up to $160 or, in criminal cases, punishments up to three years of imprisonment. Above the *pretore* is the Tribunal, composed of three judges, which has original jurisdiction over all civil controversies exceeding $160 in amount and criminal cases calling for penalties up to seven years. The Tribunal also hears appeals from the *pretore.* Finally, there are some twenty-three Courts of Appeal in Italy, each composed of five judges, from which there is no further appeal on the merits of the case. If a question of law should arise, however, the case may go to the Court of Cassation, where it is normally heard by a section composed of seven judges, which may quash the judgment or decision and send the case back for retrial. Very serious crimes are tried originally in the Courts of Assize, and here six laymen are chosen from a panel to sit with two judges. In

FIG. XXII

STRUCTURE OF THE ITALIAN COURTS
(Civil, Criminal, and Administrative Law)

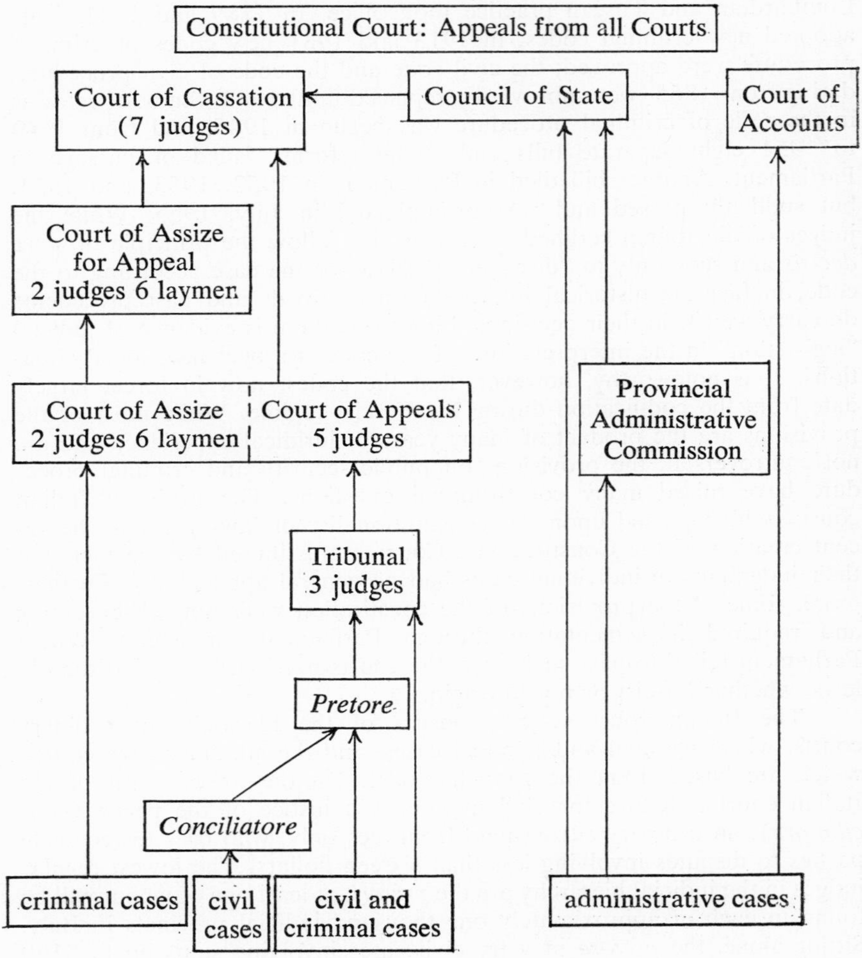

Constitutional Court: Appeals from all Courts

Court of Cassation (7 judges)

Council of State

Court of Accounts

Court of Assize for Appeal 2 judges 6 laymen

Court of Assize 2 judges 6 laymen | Court of Appeals 5 judges

Provincial Administrative Commission

Tribunal 3 judges

Pretore

Conciliatore

criminal cases | civil cases | civil and criminal cases

administrative cases

1951 there was established a new Court of Assize for Appeal, also composed of six laymen and two judges. Final appeal to the Court of Cassation is permitted only on points of law.

Where the interests of the individual are injured by acts of public administration, whether national or local, he may (1) have recourse to the Provincial Administrative Commission, which, in general, judges the *legitimacy* of an act of the public administration or (2), as is more frequently the case, have direct recourse to the Council of State. The Council of State, too, is primarily concerned with the legality of the act, and any damages resulting from such action must be recovered in the ordinary courts. Some sections of the Council of State serve as legal aids and administrative consultants to the ministers, while others act as an administrative court. The Court of Accounts also has a special section for judging the legitimacy of government acts in respect to finance.

As individuals some Italian lawyers and judges rank among the best in the world. Yet the courts are overcrowded, understaffed, and poorly equipped, so that the procedure is marked by its technicalities and delays. An ordinary civil lawsuit may require from eighteen to thirty months before a final judgment is reached. Warrants of arrest require judicial approval; the accused has the right to counsel and is innocent until proven guilty; there is no death penalty. Italy uses the investigating-judge system of prosecution, which subjects the suspect to a kind of pretrial to determine the sufficiency of evidence, and until 1955 a suspect could be held for periods ranging up to two years pending the outcome of the investigation. Italian prisons leave much to be desired. However, the full implementation of the constitutional provisions regarding the judiciary, and the inception of the Constitutional Court, should contribute to the improvement of the administration of Italian justice.

7. LOCAL GOVERNMENT

One of the goals of Don Luigi Sturzo, as a leader of the *Popolari* before fascism and elder statesman of the present Christian Democrats, has been administrative decentralization. As a Sicilian from an island that had fought for autonomy against the Bourbons no less than against the Savoians, he opposed vigorously the bureaucratic centralization he felt had taken place under Piedmontese tutelage; fascism brought this dependence upon the national government to its epitome by destroying all locally elected government, transferring municipal authority to a single, party-controlled *podestà,* and subjecting all local government to central dictation.

The first local elections of the postwar period were held in March, 1946, in 5,722 communes of Italy and provided the earliest concrete data on popular support for the political parties: candidates of the Christian Democrats won a majority of posts in 2,534 communes, while candidates of the Socialists-Communists were successful in 2,289 others. Meanwhile many Sicilians, liberated early from fascism and watching the turbulent Socialist-Communist strength in the north, raised their traditional cry for autonomy or even complete independence. The conservative interests on the island generally supported this demand. The first De Gasperi government, scarcely five months in office and completely provisional, hastily acted to still the agitation by granting Sicily the status of a region in May, 1946, and thereby instituting a new form of decentralized government in Italy that in some ways harked back to the federalism of Gioberti. The constitution of 1948 divides the Republic of Italy into regions, provinces, and communes for local government. Nineteen regions were to be created, but only four of these have thus far been actually constituted through special statutes. These are the regions of Sicily, Trentino-Alto Adige, Sardinia, and Valle D'Aosta.

Italy is not a federal state and the regions are not to be compared with American states, Swiss cantons, or even German *Laender*. Regions must be established by act of Parliament in implementing the constitutional provisions. Regional jurisdiction is recognized over such matters as the organization of regional offices, local police, charities, hospitalization, public works of regional interest, tourism, hunting, fishing, agriculture, etc., but the statutes are not identical in their provisions. A comparison of the statute for the Sicilian region, approved during the crisis of 1946, and the statutes for Sardinia, Trentino-Alto Adige, and Valle D'Aosta, enacted by Parliament in 1948, shows a considerably greater degree of autonomy granted to Sicily than to the other regions.[1] The regional council may be dissolved by the national government for violations of the constitution and the basic statute of the region, or for "serious legal violations," or "for reasons of national security." Nevertheless, once established, the region has a constitutionally recognized status, in contrast to the provinces and communes which are based upon the ordinary laws of Parliament. The constitutionality of laws or acts of the region, which are questioned by the State, may, as indicated, be judged by the Constitutional Court. Thus, while Italy is not a federal state, some local autonomy has been granted to the four regions which have been created.

Italy has 95 provinces and some 7,850 communes, the latter ranging in population from Clavières with little more than 100 to Rome with well over 1,500,000 inhabitants. Practically abolished by fascism, communal councils were reestablished and are now again elected by the people.[2] In the commune a mayor (*sindaco*) with a committee (*giunta*) of aldermen (*assessori*) are chosen from and by the council. Communal jurisdiction extends to such matters as regulation of traffic, licensing, zoning, urban police, etc., and may include the operation of municipally owned electricity, gas, and bus systems. The mayor acts, not only as the

[1] While the Christian Democrats were at first enthusiastic about regions, the possibility of Socialists-Communists getting control of certain regional governments has led to their opposition to new statutes since February, 1948.

[2] In the elections of 1956 the party that obtained the majority of votes obtained all the seats in communes with fewer than 10,000 inhabitants (in Sicily with fewer than 15,000 inhabitants); in all larger communes election to the councils was on a proportional basis.

head of the communal government, but also as a representative of the national government in maintaining the registries of births, deaths, and marriages, and the publication of laws and decrees. The provinces have little local responsibilities except over roads and asylums, although they too have an elected provincial council with a president and *giunta*. But the chief officer of the province is the prefect, the representative of the minister of the interior. The prefect and various associates comprise the Provincial Administrative Commission, which scrutinizes the discussions, ordinances, and finances of the communes and the provinces. Above all the prefect must harmonize national law with local practices. In emergencies, or where the public interest requires such action, he may even suspend the municipal or provincial councils.

The Italian Republic has reacted from the centralization of government under fascism, returning the election of local governments to the people and accepting an entirely new regional concept. At the same time the experiment with regionalism seems to have come to a standstill in the face of political obstacles, while the role of the prefect, representing and enforcing the will of the national government over local governments, is little changed from the past. The financial dependence of local governments upon the national government is crucial. To share political responsibility through further decentralized administration is a difficult challenge to the government in Rome, long accustomed to bureaucratic authority and ever worried by Socialist-Communist strength at the local level.

22

ITALY ON THE INTERNATIONAL HORIZON

1. THE END OF EMPIRE

The foreign policies of the young Italian Republic have been deeply influenced by the war claims that resulted from World War II and by the struggle for power between the Soviet Union and the Western Allies. Faced, on the one hand, by the largest Communist Party outside of Russia itself, the governments of De Gasperi and Scelba were often attacked by the left for following American leadership. On the other hand, the Monarchists and neo-Fascists, intensely nationalistic, bitterly criticized the government for its supine yielding to Western policy and deplored the lack of Italian prestige in world affairs. Despite these difficulties Italy, under the leadership of the Christian Democrats, has successfully maintained a political-economic orientation with the West.

Italy had colonized Somaliland and Eritrea in the nineteenth century, won Libya from Turkey in 1912, gained Istria, Fiume, parts of the Dalmatian coast, and various Aegean islands as an outcome of World War I. She conquered Ethiopia in 1936 and had virtual control over Albania prior to World War II. Hopes of even greater territorial acquisitions had been awakened by Mussolini during the war. All these territories were lost as a result of fascism's collaboration with Hitler. Bits of territory on the Italian western frontier, moreover, were ceded to France, while Trieste with its environs was detached from Italy, declared a free territory, and temporarily divided into Yugoslav and Anglo-American zones of occupation pending the appointment of a governor by the Security Council of the United Nations.

Under the peace treaty of 1947, furthermore, Italy was required to reduce her army to 250,000 and her air force to 25,000 men—and to pay reparations amounting to $360,000,000 to Albania, Ethiopia, Greece, Yugoslavia, and Russia. The negotiations of the peace treaty with Italy had revealed the divisions between the United States, the United Kingdom, and France, on the one side, and the Soviet Union, on the other. De Gasperi's Christian Democrats and his governments were soon regarded by the western Allies as potential friends. The western Allies took no reparations from Italy and, indeed, United Nations relief and rehabilitation aid had to be sent to Italy in 1946–47, to be followed by direct economic aid from the United States under the European Recovery Program.

With her immediate neighbors Italy had two major problems to settle. The border with Austria in the Alto Adige had been left unchanged by the Allied foreign ministers, who outlined the Italian peace terms. Here about one quarter of a million German-speaking people in Italy, who had been badly treated under fascism, still looked to Austria for hope. An agreement was reached between De Gasperi and Austria in 1946 by which regional status, with special tutelage of minorities, was guaranteed to Trentino-Alto Adige. But there is still friction between the Italians and the German-speaking population, particularly in the northern part of the province, and Austria has suggested a separate autonomous region for Bolzano. On the Yugoslav border the status of Trieste as a Free Territory was completely unsatisfactory to the Italians. The failure of the Security Council to appoint a governor left one small part of the territory in the hands of the Yugoslavs, while the other, with its overwhelmingly Italian city of Trieste, remained under the administration of the Anglo-Americans. In their wish to help the De Gasperi government the western Allies in March, 1948, had declared their willingness to see the whole territory returned to Italy, but three months later the break of Marshal Tito with the Soviet Union made Yugoslav interests a new concern of Western foreign policy. A long controversy ensued between Italy and Yugoslavia while the western Allies delayed in taking a decisive position, but the mobilization of Italian troops on the border during Pella's "caretaker" government in the fall of 1953 drove the Allies to announce their intention of abandoning their zone of occupation to Italy. The stormy reaction of Yugoslavia almost resulted in war, but moderation finally prevailed and in October, 1954, a Memorandum of Agreement was signed by Italy, Yugoslavia, the United States, and the United Kingdom. Under the terms of this agreement minor boundary adjustments between the two zones were made, the Italians were given the complete administration of the Anglo-American zone, and all Allied troops were withdrawn from the territory.

2. EUROPEAN UNITY

Never far in the background of the Trieste settlement for the Allies had been the larger schemes for the defense of Europe through the North Atlantic Treaty Organization and the further invigoration of the democratic states through the Council of Europe, the European Coal and Steel Community, and the European Defense Community. The first venture of republican Italy into a new international organization had been through her admission into the Organization for European Economic Cooperation in 1947, which had served in Europe as a planning and co-

ordinating agency for the European Recovery Program. Closely related
to the problem of the rehabilitation of the European economies was the
threat of Communist subversion, dramatized by the collapse of democratic Czechoslovakia under the internal and external pressure of the
Communists in February, 1948. Out of this pressure the North Atlantic
Treaty Organization (NATO) was born to promote collective security
by co-ordinated military action, and in 1949, despite bitter opposition
by the Communists, the Italian Republic joined NATO.

Thus, within two years of a peace treaty that compelled the Italians
to restrict their military establishment to a low level, the western Allies
and the government of Italy had agreed to a rebuilding of Italian security
forces. In truth, the Italian army was far below the limits imposed by
the peace treaty, but rearmament, with the aid of direct American
grants, American defense support moneys for Italian factories, and
American training personnel, was rapid. From an expenditure of 300
billion *lire* for defense in 1949, Italian appropriations rose to 521 billion in
1952, a sum representing almost 22 per cent of the entire budget. A re-
furbishing of communications lines, fuel supplies, and air facilities accompanied an expansion of the land and air forces of Italy. Headquarters of the Allied forces under NATO, moreover, were located in
Naples. The command of the Allied Forces for South Europe and the
command of the South European Air Forces are based at Naples, while
the Allied Territorial Forces for South Europe are at Verona. Despite
the considerable value of Italy to the North Atlantic Treaty Organization, the armed forces of the Italian Republic cannot be compared in
strength with those of any of the Great Powers, but the co-operation of
Italy as a strategically located base for NATO, including the availability
of missile launching sites, is vitally important to western defense.

During his visit to North America in 1956 President Gronchi particularly stressed the importance of Article 2 of the North Atlantic Treaty
"to promote conditions of stability and well-being" and encourage economic collaboration between the member states, thereby emphasizing
the Italian hope to supplement the military aspects of the Treaty with
broader co-operative arrangements in the future. With the mirage of
empire finally cleared from Italian eyes, the nation must face its secondary role among the powers with candid realism.

3. ITALY AMONG THE NATIONS

Italy, deprived of her colonies, remains more than ever a part of that
Europe which must pool its dwindling resources, utilize efficiently its
skills and its productive capacity, and expand its markets across traditional national barriers. Political co-operation, leading to both economic
improvements and social gains, crystallized in the Council of Europe in
1949, and in the Coal and Steel Community in 1951. Under the leadership of Count Sforza and De Gasperi, Italy lent wholehearted encouragement and support to these projects. The European Defense Community,

however, ran into a storm of criticism in the Italian Parliament. After the failure of France to ratify the pact, an action followed shortly by the Trieste settlement, the Italian government was able to win substantial support for the ratification of the Western European Union in March, 1955.[1] Late in July, 1957, the Italian Chamber of Deputies approved by decisive majorities the European Common Market and Euratom treaties. Only the Communists were united in their opposition.

The integration of Italy into these European organizations for the strengthening of democracy, however, did not entirely remove the sting of her colonial losses or the smart of her exclusion from the United Nations. The Allied foreign ministers, having failed to agree on the disposition of the Italian colonies, left to the General Assembly of the United Nations the ultimate decision. Prestige considerations and an outlet for her surplus population, rather than economic factors, motivated Italian interest in Eritrea, Somaliland, and Libya, mostly desert lands. Their strategic location, however, made them subjects for acrimonious discussion among the great powers, and at times it seemed that all of them might be returned to Italy under the UN trusteeship system. After many discussions by the member states in the General Assembly and after visiting missions had been sent to the territories themselves, agreement was reached to make Libya an independent state in 1952, after three years of tutelage under a UN commissioner. Somaliland was placed under the trusteeship system, with Italy as administering power for a period of ten years, and the territory has now become independent; and Eritrea was federated with Ethiopia. Although she was permitted to participate as a member of various United Nations specialized agencies and also in the work of the Trusteeship Council in consequence of her position in Somaliland, Italy was denied a place in the United Nations by Russia until 1955. Her admission to the United Nations marked the full return of Italy to international councils and helped remove the last stigma of her defeat in World War II.

At the same time Italy has renewed its interest in the Mediterranean and Middle Eastern areas, particularly through oil operations in Egypt and Persia. During the Suez crisis in 1956 Italy, which has important interests in the Egyptian National Oil Company and its subsidiary, the Oriental Oil Company, took a rather benign attitude toward Nasser. Some Italian leaders envisaged their country as the mediator between Western Europe and Egypt. In 1957, moreover, an agreement between the Italian national oil company (*Ente Nazionale Idrocarburi*) and the National Iranian Oil Company was signed with terms more favorable to Iran than those prevailing throughout the area between American companies and Middle Eastern countries. Not only has President Gronchi paid a number of personal visits to capital cities in the region, but Italy dramatically proposed an economic development program for the Middle East to be financed jointly by Western Europe and the United States, offering Naples as its headquarters. The idea of increasing Italian political influence in this area, however, is not shared by all leaders

[1] Approved in the Chamber by vote of 335 to 215 (December, 1954) and in the Senate by 139 to 82 (March, 1955).

of opinion, for many would argue that Italy must concentrate on the development of European unity to gain its greatest security and economic reward.

In view of her need to obtain a better balance of international trade Italy cannot fail to have overseas interests. Moreover, the employment of her citizens abroad on a temporary basis and the permanent emigration of her people continue to preoccupy the Italian government. About 3,800,000 Italian citizens live in foreign countries—in Europe, the Americas, Australia, Asia, and Africa. The "official" remittances of Italians abroad to their home country amount to no less than 150 million dollars annually.

For Italy, as with all modern states, foreign policy and domestic issues are inextricably mixed. Her emigration problems are related to her chronic lack of work at home; her unemployment is related to the availability of capital from foreign sources and productive investments; her productive investments are related to her international military commitments and the stewardship of her government; and her government, to promote the ideals of economic and social democracy, needs political stability with creative majority rule.

On the solution of these problems will depend the future direction of a nation which has made substantial economic and political progress since its experience with fascism. But Italian democracy is still imperfect, still finding its way through illiberal traditions, vested financial interests, clericalism, and unstable governments. The republic will have to face many hazards that lie ahead.

SELECTED BIBLIOGRAPHY

No book dealing both extensively and intensively with the politics and government of the Italian Republic has as yet been written in English. Three starting points for the general student, however, would be H. Stuart Hughes, *The United States and Italy* (Cambridge, 1953); Muriel Grindrod, *The Rebuilding of Italy* (London, 1955), which deals with the political and economic developments of Italy from 1945–55; and Margaret Carlyle, *Modern Italy* (London, 1957). For source material the student should be familiar with the *Annuario Statistico Italiano,* published yearly by the *Istituto Centrale di Statistica; Documenti di Vita Italiana,* published monthly by the Documentation Center, which is in the presidency of the Council of Ministers. The *Documenti* are published in English under the title of *Italian Affairs.* The Documentation Center also has issued *Italy Today* (Rome, 1955), a comprehensive collection of facts, figures, and pictures on all aspects of Italian life.

Both the Statuto and the constitution of Italy are conveniently available in English in Lionel H. Laing, *et al., Source Book in European Governments* (New York, 1950). Detailed analyses are given in P. Calamandrei and A. Levi, eds., *Il Commentario sistematico alla costituzione italiana* (Florence, 1950), two volumes of essays by various experts; pertinent laws are included in Ferruccio Pergolese, ed., *Codice costituzionale* (Bologna, 1954).

The *Atti parlamentari* of the Chamber of Deputies and the Senate have been published since 1848 and include the bills, other documents, and parliamentary debates. The decrees and laws are published in the *Gazzetta ufficiale.* Parliament publishes two very useful volumes, the *Annuario parlamentare,* a directory of offices and organizations in Italy, and the *Manuale parlamentare,* which contains the constitution, many basic laws, and a wealth of political information. *I Deputati e senatori del ——— parlamento* each year gives a biography of every legislator. Excellent summaries of current parliamentary developments can be found in the review *Resoconti parlamentari,* issued by the *Istituto di Studi Parlamentari,* Rome.

The decisions of the Court of Cassation are collected in *Massimari;* other judicial decisions are not systematically collected and must be found in the writings of various law reporters, in particular in the journals, *Giurisprudenza italiana, Giustizia penale, Il Foro italiano, Il Foro padano, Orientamenti della giurisprudenza del lavoro,* etc.

General historical references. Among the best background books dealing with Italian political history and pre-fascist government are Bolton King, *A History of Italian Unity* (New York, 1899), 2 vols.; Luigi Salvatorelli, *A Concise History of Italy* (New York, 1940); Benedetto Croce, *A History of Italy, 1871–1915* (Oxford, 1929); Cecil J. S. Sprigge, *The Development of Modern Italy* (New Haven, 1944); A. William Salomone, *Italian Democracy in the Making* (Philadelphia, 1945); Ivanoe Bonomi, *La Politica italiana da Porta Pia a Vittorio Veneto* (Turin, 1946); and Rene Albrecht-Carrié, *Italy from Napoleon to Mussolini* (New York, 1950). For a wider analysis of Italy and Italian life Leonardo Olschki, *The Genius of Italy* (New York, 1949); and Carlo Sforza, *Contemporary Italy* (New York, 1944), and *Italy and Italians* (New York, 1949) are worth reading. For studies centered on individual Italians see Edward Dicey, *Victor Emmanuel* (New York, 1886); G. M. Trevelyan, *Garibaldi and the Making of Italy* (New York, 1911, and *Memoirs of Francesco Crispi* (London, 1912–14), 3 vols.; and Giovanni Giolitti, *Memoirs of My Life* (London, 1923). Unparalleled literary insights to the pre-fascist Sicilian peasantry are to be found in the works of Giovanni Verga.

533

The Fascist period. Herman Finer, *Mussolini's Italy* (New York, 1935); H. W. Schneider, *The Fascist Government of Italy* (New York, 1936); and G. A. Borgese, *Goliath, the March of Fascism* (New York, 1937) are three good starting points of study. Other general texts are Max Ascoli and Arthur Feiler, *Fascism for Whom?* (New York, 1938); William Ebenstein, *Fascist Italy* (New York, 1939); H. A. Steiner, *Government in Fascist Italy* (New York, 1938); Henry Spencer's brief, but very useful, *Government and Politics of Italy* (Yonkers, 1932); and Luigi Salvatorelli and Giovanni Mira, *Storia d'Italia nel periodo fascista* (Turin, 1956).

For the ideology of fascism no writing is more significant than Mussolini's own article in Volume XIV of the *Enciclopedia italiana,* also available in translation as *The Political and Social Doctrine of Fascism* (New York, 1935). The fascist theories are examined by J. S. Barnes, *The Universal Aspects of Fascism* (London, 1927); William Y. Elliott, *The Pragmatic Revolt in Politics* (New York, 1928); and Mario Palmieri, *The Philosophy of Fascism* (Chicago, 1936). For Italian readers the writings of Giovanni Gentile, *Fascismo e cultura* (Milan, 1928), and *Origini e dottrina del Fascismo* (3rd ed., Rome, 1934); as well as Enrico Corradini, *Il Nazionalismo italiano* (Milan, 1914), and Giorgio A. Chiurco's detailed *Storia della rivoluzione fascista* (Florence, 1929), 5 vols., are important.

The transition from the parliamentary state to fascism can be traced in such works as Ivanoe Bonomi, *From Socialism to Fascism* (London, 1924); Curzio Malaparte, *Technique du coup d'état* (Paris, 1930); Gaetano Salvemini, *The Fascist Dictatorship in Italy* (New York, 1927); H. W. Schneider, *Making the Fascist State* (New York, 1928); Gaudens Megaro, *Mussolini in the Making* (New York, 1938); and A. Rossi (Angelo Tasca), *The Rise of Italian Fascism 1918–1922* (London, 1938). For the economy of the Fascist regime the most useful English studies are G. Lowell Field, *The Syndical and Corporative Institutions of Italian Fascism,* Columbia University Studies in History, Economics, and Public Law No. 433 (New York, 1938); Carl T. Schmidt, *The Plough and the Sword: Labor, Land, and Property in Fascist Italy* (New York, 1938); and William G. Welk, *Fascist Economic Policy* (Cambridge, Mass., 1938). Two volumes in French by Louis R. Franck are also recommended: *L'economie corporative fasciste en doctrine et en fait* (Paris, 1934) and *Les Etapes de l'economie fasciste italienne* (Paris, 1939). For educational and social policies, H. L. Childs, ed., *Propaganda and Dictatorship* (Princeton, 1936) is highly rewarding, while more particular studies are F. Gazzetti, *Social Welfare in Italy* (Rome, 1937), and D. S. Piccoli, *The Youth Movement in Italy* (Rome, 1936).

The thorny problem of church-state relations in Italy is examined in H. J. T. Johnson, *The Papacy and the Kingdom of Italy* (Dallas, 1934); F. A. Ridley, *The Papacy and Fascism* (London, 1937); B. Williamson, *The Treaty of the Lateran* (London, 1929); and two very good studies by S. W. Halperin, *The Separation of State in Italian Thought from Cavour to Mussolini* (Chicago, 1937) and *Italy and the Vatican at War* (Chicago, 1939). D. A. Binchy, *Church and State in Fascist Italy* (London, 1941), is worth consulting. Italian readers will profit from Arturo Carlo Jemolo, *Chiesa e stato negli ultimi cento anni di vita italiana* (Turin, 1949), and G. Spadolini, *L'opposizione cattolica* (Florence, 1954).

On the fall of fascism and the war period some of the best insights are provided by Pietro Badoglio, *Italy in the Second World War* (Oxford, 1948); Benito Mussolini, *Memoirs 1942–43* (London, 1949), edited by Raymond Klibansky, and also edited by Max Ascoli as *The Fall of Mussolini* (New York, 1948); and the diaries of Count Galeazzo Ciano, edited by Hugh Gibson, as *The Ciano Diaries* (New York, 1945) and *Ciano's Diplomatic Papers* (London, 1948), edited by Malcolm Muggeridge. The year between the fall of Mussolini and the liberation of Rome is covered in Benedetto Croce's memoirs, *Croce, the King, and the Allies* (New York, 1950), edited by Sylvia Sprigge. On the war itself and the conduct of military-political operations, Admiral Franco Maugeri, *From the Ashes of Disgrace* (New York, 1948); Admiral Raymond de Belot, *The Struggle for the Mediterranean 1939–45;* and General Mark W. Clark, *Calculated Risk* (New York, 1950) are useful studies. Important sections in the volumes by Robert Sherwood, *Roosevelt and Hopkins* (New York, 1948); Dwight D. Eisenhower, *Crusade in Europe* (New York, 1948); and Winston Churchill, *The Second World War* (Boston, 1948) deal with Italy. Recollections of the former Italian ambassador in Washington, Alberto Tarchiani, are *Dieci anni tra Roma e Washington* (Verona, 1955).

The resistance movement is covered by Max Salvadori, *Brief History of the Patriot Movement in Italy, 1943–45* (Chicago, 1954); Roberto Battaglia, *Storia della resistenza italiana* (Turin, 1953); and Franco Catalano, *Storia del C.L.N.A.I.* (Bari, 1956). W. Hilton-Young's *The Italian Left* (London, 1949) deals in part with the underground activity, and Aldo Garosci, *Storia dei fuorusciti* (Bari, 1953) follows the work of the exiles of fascism. Among the first books in English in the postwar period were Muriel Grindrod, *The New Italy: Transition from War to Peace* (London, 1947); Elizabeth Wiskemann, *Italy* (Oxford, 1947); and Ivor Thomas, *The Problem of Italy: An Economic Survey* (London, 1946). John Clarke Adam's section on Italy in *Foreign Governments and Their Backgrounds* (New York, 1950) gives a clear summary of the Italian constitution and immediate postwar government.

Documents on the Constituent Assembly and its work are the *Atti della assemblea costituente, discussioni* (Rome, n.d.), 11 vols.; *Commissione per la costituzione, discussioni, prima, seconda, e terza sottocommissioni* (Rome, n.d.); and *Progetto di costituzione, disegni di legge, relazioni, documenti* (Rome, n.d.), 2 vols. The Italian reader will also find most valuable V. Falzone, F. Palermo, and F. Cosentini, *La Costituzione della repubblica italiana illustrata con i lavori preparatori* (Rome, 1948), and Giuseppe Chiarelli, *La Costituzione italiana* (Rome, 1957). For English readers John Clarke Adams and Paolo Barile, "The Implementation of the Italian Constitution," *American Political Science Review*, 47 (1953), pp. 61–83, is a short, excellent analysis. Extremely interesting is the collection of essays, by Achille Battaglia and other leaders of the resistance, entitled *Dieci anni dopo, 1945–55: saggi sulla vita democratica italiana* (Bari, 1955), commenting on the implementation of the Italian constitution as well as other aspects of political life. Covering some of the same ground, though it is more apologetic, is Aldo Garosci and others, *Il Secondo risorgimento: nel decennale della resistenza e del ritorno alla democrazia, 1945–55* (Rome, 1955).

Parties and elections are dealt with in Mario Einaudi and François Goguel, *Christian Democracy in Italy and France* (Notre Dame, 1952), which contains an extensive bibliography by Eleanor Tananbaum; Mario Einaudi, Jean-Marie Domenach, and Aldo Garosci, *Communism in Western Europe* (Cornell, 1951); and Giovanni Conti, *I Partiti politici in Italia* (Rome, 1953). Antonio Gramsci, *Lettere dal carcere* (Turin, 1947), and Marcella and Maurizio Ferrare, *Conversando con Togliatti* (Rome, 1953), shed further light on the activities of the communists, while Giorgio Tupini, *I Democratici Cristiani: cronache di dieci anni* (Milan, 1954), follows the Christian Democrats in their work. The best single book for the figures on all Italian elections and the composition of the electorate is Giovanni Schepis, *Le Consultazioni popolari in Italia dal 1848 at 1957* (Empoli, 1958). For particular electoral studies, see Elio Carranti, *Sociologia e statistica delle elezioni italiane nel dopoguerra* (Rome, 1954); Francesco Compagna and Vittorio De Caprariis, "Geografia delle elezioni italiane dal 1946 al 1953," *Il Mulino* (Bologna, 1954); Ubaldo Prosparetti, *L'ettorato politico attivo* (Milan, 1954); and Giovanni Schepis, "Profilo della sociologia elettorale," *Amministrazione Civile*, 9 (1958), pp. 1–11.

Periodical articles on elections and parties in Italy of special interest have been written by Joseph LaPalombara, H. Stuart Hughes, Murray Edelman, Clifford A. L. Rich, Taylor Cole, and Mario Rossi in such journals as the *American Political Science Review*, the *Western Political Quarterly*, the *Midwest Journal of Political Science*, the *Journal of Politics*, and the *Virginia Quarterly Review*.

Two interesting books that treat problems of administration as well as government philosophy are Ezio Vigorelli, *L'Italiano è socialista e non lo sa* (Verona, 1952), written by a vigorous Democratic Socialist who headed the parliamentary inquiry into poverty in Italy; and Luigi Einaudi, *Il Buongoverno* (Bari, 1954), written by the first president of the republic. For a keen analysis of the Italian bureaucracy, Taylor Cole, "The Reform of the Italian Bureaucracy," *Public Administration Review*, 13 (1953), pp. 247–56, is highly rewarding. See also Silvano Spinetti, *Le Relazioni pubbliche nella pubblica amministrazione* (Rome, 1957); and the review,

La Tecnica della Organizzazione nella Pubblica Amministrazioni, published quarterly at Milan.

The *Banco di Roma* issues a bimonthly *Review of Economic Conditions in Italy* in English, as does the *Banco Nazionale del Lavoro* with its *Quarterly Review*. These volumes can be supplemented by the United Nations Economic Commission for Europe, *Economic Survey of Europe*, issued annually. *Atti della Commissione Parlamentare di Inchiesta sulla disoccupazione* (Milan-Rome, 1953), 5 vols., and *Atti della Commissione Parlamentare di Inchiesta sulla miseria in Italia e sui mezzi per combatterla* (Milan-Rome, 1953), 13 vols., are fundamental studies of unemployment and poverty. The United States Operations Mission to Italy, American Embassy, Rome, makes economic surveys from time to time. Other useful studies are Great Britain, Board of Trade, *Italy: Economic and Commercial Conditions in Italy* (London, 1955) and (*Banco di Roma*), *Review of Economic Conditions in Italy, 1947–1956* (Rome, 1957). Ernesto Rossi's *Lo Stato industriale* (Bari, 1953) has been abridged and included in the excellent volume of Mario Einaudi, Maurice Byé, and Ernesto Rossi, *Nationalization in France and Italy* (Cornell, 1955); while other provocative essays of Rossi on the economy are to be found in *Il Malgoverno* (Bari, 1954), and *Aria Fritta* (Bari, 1956). Of exceptional value is the *Economic Survey of Italy*, published biannually in English by the *Unione Italiana dell Camere di Commercio, Industria, e Agricoltura* at Rome.

For agrarian policy, Giuseppe Medici, *Politica agraria, 1945–1952* (Bologna, 1952); and Mario Bandini, *Politica agraria* (3rd ed., Bologna, 1953), are basic. Publications of the *Associazione per lo Sviluppo dell Industria nel Mezzogiorno*, the *Cassa per il Mezzogiorno*, and the various land-reform organizations are the best original sources on conditions in the south, particularly in respect to agrarian reform. One of the best books on the politics of the south is Francesco Compagna, *La Lotta political italiana nel secondo dopoguerra e il Mezzogiorno* (Bari, 1950). On agrarian problems and peasant conditions in the south, see Giovanni Russo, *Baroni e contadini* (Bari, 1955); as well as Jane and Andrew Carey, "The South of Italy and the Cassa per il Mezzogiorno," *Western Political Quarterly*, 8 (1955), pp. 569–88; and Mario Bandini, "Six Years of Italian Land Reform," *Quarterly Review* (*Banco Nazionale del Lavoro*, June, 1957).

On the labor unions, Humbert L. Gualtieri, *The Labor Movement in Italy* (New York, 1946) is a good introduction. Essays by leading Italian labor leaders are included in *I Sindicati in Italia* (Bari, 1955). John Norman, "Politics and Religion in the Italian Labor Movement," *Industrial and Labor Relations Review*, 5 (1951), pp. 73–91; Ferruccio Pergolesi, "The Place of Labor in the Constitution of the Italian Republic," *International Labor Review*, 61 (1950), pp. 118–42; John Clarke Adams, "Italy" in Walter Galenson, ed., *Comparative Labor Movements* (New York, 1952); and Joseph LaPalombara, *The Italian Labor Movement: Problems and Prospects* (Ithaca, 1957) are valuable studies. To be noted is Pietro Nenni, "The Italian Socialist Party and the Policy of the Unity of the Masses," *Labor Monthly*, 36 (1954), pp. 15–22. The Italian Ministry of the Budget, *Outline of Development of Income and Employment in Italy in the Ten-Year Period, 1955–1964* (Paris, 1955), published by the Organization for European Economic Cooperation, is extremely useful.

On the foreign policy of Italy the account of Maxwell H. H. Macartney, *Italy's Foreign and Colonial Policy, 1914–1937* (London, 1938), is very good. Also dealing with the same period, but with more hindsight, are the passages by H. Stuart Hughes and Felix Gilbert in *The Diplomats, 1919–1939* (Princeton, 1953), edited by Felix Gilbert and Gordon A. Craig; and Gaetano Salvemini, *Prelude to World War II* (London, 1953); as well as Elizabeth Wiskemann, *The Rome-Berlin Axis* (New York, 1949). Two important Italian works on postwar policy are Adstans (pseud.), *Alcide De Gasperi nella politica estera italiana, 1944–53* (Verona, 1953); and Carlo Sforza, *Cinque anni a Palazzo Chigi: la politica estera italiana dal 1947 al 1951* (Rome, 1952). See also Norman Kogan, *Italy and the Allies* (Cambridge, 1956). Pertinent documents, such as those on the declaration of war against Italy by the United States, the Italian military armistice, the treaty of peace with Italy, and the General Assembly of the United Nations' disposal of former Italian colonies, are conveniently abridged and collected in Francis O. Wilcox and Thorsten V. Kalijarvi,

Recent American Foreign Policy (New York, 1952). An Italian view of the peace treaty is Attilio Tamaro, *La Condanna dell'Italia nel trattato di pace* (Bologna, 1952); while an excellent study of the former Italian colonies and their disposition is Benjamin Rivlin, *The United Nations and the Italian Colonies* (New York, 1950). The definitive Italian work on Trieste is that of Diego De Castro, *Il Problema di Trieste; genesi e sviluppo della questione giuliana in relazione agli avvenimenti internazionali, 1943–1952* (Bologna, 1953). Short commentaries on Trieste are Gerard J. Mangone, "Renewed Struggle in Trieste," *Foreign Policy Bulletin,* 33 (1953), pp. 3–8; and Gerard J. Mangone and Stoyan Pribichevich, "What Can Be Done about Trieste?", *Foreign Policy Bulletin,* 33 (1953), pp. 4–6.

The periodicals *Esteri* (Rome) and *Relazioni internazionali* (Milan) deal extensively with foreign affairs, while *Il Ponte* (Florence) and *Il Mondo* (Rome) have challenging, generally antigovernment, anticlerical articles of high political and literary value. Since October, 1955 a new weekly, *L'Espresso,* has been publishing a wide variety of dynamic articles on political and cultural subjects. *Concretezza* (Milan) is a fortnightly political review directed by a leading Christian Democrat and containing a wealth of data on parliamentary life. The quality of Italian newspapers is very uneven, and practically all of the papers are highly partisan. Among the best are *Il Corriere della sera* (Milan), and *La Stampa* (Turin) which has a convenient index in English available from the U.S. Joint Publications Research Service, New York and Washington. English readers will also find that such periodicals as the (London) *Economist, Reporter, Commonweal,* and *Partisan Review* frequently contain substantial reports on Italy.

PART FIVE

THE SOVIET ORBIT: UNION OF SOVIET SOCIALIST REPUBLICS

by *Julian Towster*

CHAPTER

23

---◆---

THE CONDITIONING FACTORS

Among the many influences that have affected the evolution of government and politics in the Union of Soviet Socialist Republics (U.S.S.R.) three factors have played a primary conditioning role: the geography of the U.S.S.R., the heritage bequeathed by Russia's past, and the ideological setting in which the new regime had its inception and development.

1. GEOGRAPHY

The extent and character of the territory, population, and resources of the Soviet Union have had much to do with the nature of government in the Soviet state and with its position in the world system of states.

Area. The U.S.S.R. is a country of continental dimensions. Its vast expanse approximates 8,500,000 square miles, one sixth of the land surface of the globe. Embracing the northern third of Asia and the eastern half of Europe, the territory of the Soviet Union extends some 6,000 miles from west to east and between 1,800 and 2,800 miles from south to north. It stretches from the Baltic Sea, the Carpathians, and the Black Sea to the Pacific Ocean, from the deserts of Central Asia and the Tien Shan, Sayan, Altai, and Pamir mountains to the Arctic Ocean. With frontier lines (excluding those of countries occupied by the military forces) exceeding 37,500 miles in length, the U.S.S.R. borders on almost a dozen states in Europe and Asia, including Norway, Finland, Poland, Czechoslovakia, Hungary, Rumania, Turkey, Iran, Afghanistan, and China. In its Eurasian mass the Soviet Union exceeds in area the combined territories of the United States, together with those of the United

NOTE. In this section the titles of selections within Russian works have been rendered in English, although the titles of the works themselves are cited in Russian. This arrangement has been adopted for the convenience and understanding of the student and does not imply that English translations of the works exist.

541

Kingdom and India, the states of Western Europe, and the Near and Middle East. It is the largest single state in the world to occupy such an immense, continuous area.

Population.   In 1956 the population of the U.S.S.R. was officially declared to be 200,200,000. In January, 1946, one official Soviet estimate gave the figure as 193,000,000. By comparison with an expected population of around 215,000,000 by that date, this estimate would indicate a wartime population loss of around 22,000,000, i.e., an approximate birth deficit of 8,000,000 and war casualties of some 14,000,000 persons probably evenly divided between military personnel and civilians.[1] It may be noted that before the war, after the territorial accretions of 1939–40, the population likewise numbered 193,000,000.

The Soviet population has been growing rapidly, increasing from 134,000,000 in 1920 to 147,000,000 in 1926, and to 170,500,000 by January, 1939. Prior to the war the population was increasing at the rate of 3,000,000 a year, and since July, 1944, special incentives have been introduced to encourage large families. Sustained increases in the Soviet population are to be expected in the future, and by 1970 it may well reach a total of over a quarter of a billion.

Resources.   In natural resources the U.S.S.R. is one of the richest countries in the world, second only to the United States. It possesses vast reserves of a large variety of raw materials, including those that figure high among the components of state power.[2] The Soviet Union claims to have a higher percentage than any other state of certain of the world's known resources, i.e., water power (280 million kilowatts, or 28 per cent of the world's total); deposits of oil (8 billion tons, or 55 per cent); peat (151 billion tons, or probably 50 per cent); manganese (742.5 million tons, or 30 per cent); apatite (2,000 million tons, or 75 per cent); and others, including chrome ores, gold, and platinum. Second place among states has been claimed for its deposits of coal (1,654 billion tons, or 21 per cent) and of iron ore (10,900 million tons, or 23.5 per cent). Even if some of these estimates are unduly high, there is no doubt that the U.S.S.R. possesses these resources in abundance. It has also deposits of nickel, zinc, lead, copper, bauxite, vanadium, molybdenum, wolfram, and many other metals and minerals, but it lacks tin and natural rubber. It ranks high in the production of salt, potash, magnesite, asbestos, and aluminum. Though still far behind the United States in the production of steel, pig iron, coal, and oil, the Soviet Union is assuming second place

[1] Eugene M. Kulischer, "The Russian Population Enigma," *Foreign Affairs,* 27 (April, 1949), pp. 497–501. See also Theodore Shabad, *Geography of the USSR* (1951), pp. 39, 499.

[2] See *Bol'shaia Sovetskaia Entsiklopedia, Soiuz Sovetskikh Sotsialisticheskikh Respublik* (1947), pp. 243–72; Nicholas Mikhailov, *Land of the Soviets* (1939), pp. 20–25; George B. Cressey, *The Basis of Soviet Strength* (1945), *passim;* James S. Gregory and D. W. Shave, *The U.S.S.R.* (1944), pp. 600–6; Ernest J. Simmons, ed., *USSR: A Concise Handbook* (1947), pp. 28–29; Shabad, op. cit., pp. 33–38; Harry Schwarz, *Russia's Soviet Economy* (1950), pp. 14–26.

in the world's production of these vital elements of strength. No reliable information is available concerning its deposits of uranium, although there have been references in Soviet sources to the existence of such deposits in the Tajik and Kirghiz republics of central Asia, and the U.S.S.R. is known to be mining uranium and pitchblende in Czechoslovakia and Eastern Germany. As for food and timber resources, the U.S.S.R. possesses close to a quarter of a billion acres of black soil and two and a half billion acres, or one third, of the forest land of the globe.

The politico-military and economic value of these vast resources, the size of the Soviet territory, and its mass of manpower have never been lost sight of by the Soviet leaders. "Russia," said Stalin in 1920, "is an unbounded, huge country on the territory of which it is possible to hold out for a long time, retreating into the depth of the country in case of a failure, in order to pass again to the offensive after gaining strength." In addition to this advantage of maneuverability, he added, there is yet another permanent advantage, namely, Russia's "independence from abroad" in all forms of fuel, food, and raw materials.[3]

These geographic factors have made possible the rise of the Soviet Union to the status of a super-power in the short space of three decades. They have enabled the U.S.S.R. to establish new economic bases in Asiatic Russia and generally to attain a high degree of economic self-sufficiency. They were responsible in no small degree for the Soviet "defense in depth" in the recent war, which served again, as it did in the Napoleonic War of 1812, as the means of achieving ultimate victory, despite great intitial losses of territory and population. Although possible new elements of vulnerability will exist in future atomic warfare, waged across polar spaces, they do not detract from the present significance of the geographic factors in the political and economic plans and activities of the U.S.S.R.

The Geographic Configuration. Another factor of geography that strongly influenced the tsarist polity and is reflected in the government and politics of its successor is the configuration of the land: the Eurasian plain, the absence of secure outlets to the sea and of natural frontiers in the west, and the central geographic location of the U.S.S.R.

The Landlocked Plain. Probably the most important single geographic influence in Russian history is the great Eurasian plain. Five main lateral zones mark the highly diversified topography of the U.S.S.R. from north to south: 1) the treeless *tundra* belt along the Arctic Ocean, comprising 12–15 per cent of the Soviet land; 2) the *forest* zone, which merges into the tundra, embracing over 50 per cent of the territory of the Soviet Union and consisting of coniferous trees in the northern part (the taiga) and mixed forests of coniferous and deciduous trees in its southern belt; 3) the grassy, treeless *steppe,* extending from the western Ukraine to the Altai Mountains over some 964,000 square miles, or 12 per cent of the Soviet area, and including the rich belt of black soil; 4)

[3] Joseph Stalin, *Ob Oktiabr'skoi Revoliutsii* (1932), p. 22.

the *desert* and *semidesert* zone north of the Caspian Sea and including large areas of Central Asia, approximating 18 per cent of the territory of the Soviet Union; and 5) the *subtropical* zone, covering small areas along the Black Sea coast and in the far eastern regions of the Amur and southern Ussuri.

The vast plain embraces the forest, steppe, and desert zones, of which the steppe has been of particular significance. Together with the river system, the plain gives geographic unity to the land, since the great mountain chains are situated on the periphery, and the Urals—often referred to as the dividing line between European and Asiatic Russia— are not in fact high enough to constitute a physical barrier of consequence. Despite the fact that 80 per cent of the U.S.S.R. falls within the temperate zone, the climate prevailing over the plain is severe. It is characterized by inadequate rainfall and extremes of long, cold winters and hot summers because of the distance of the Soviet Union from the Atlantic, the barrier of the mountain ranges on the Pacific coast, and the open face of the country on the north along the Arctic Ocean. In the past the severity of the climate has not only affected Russia's agriculture but also has had a marked influence upon the character of the people.

Surrounded by mountain ranges on the east, south, and southwest, the plain is open on the west and extends into east Central Europe, without any sharp topographic demarcation such as large bodies of water, mountains, or other physicial barriers traditionally regarded as natural frontiers and bulwarks of defense. The U.S.S.R. has an extensive seacoast and is constructing a series of canals to connect its major rivers with its twelve seas, eight of which constitute direct outlets to the Arctic or Pacific Ocean. Yet the Soviet Union is properly considered landlocked, since most of its ports are not ice-free during the greater part of the year, whereas the outlets from the Baltic and Black seas (the Skagerrak and Kattegat and the Dardanelles straits) are controlled by the other powers.

The Waves of Invasion and Expansion.   These geographic features have contributed to a number of events in Russia's history that have left a deep imprint on the political physiognomy of the land. The steppe invited invasion from Asia. It served as the road of numerous migrations of Asiatic tribes into Europe, including the Mongol hordes that invaded Russia in the thirteenth century under descendants of Ghengis Khan and imposed their rule over the country for nearly two and a half centuries. The open western frontier was a beckoning gate for raids and annexations by border states, including such large-scale penetrations as the Polish occupation of Moscow in 1610, the Ukrainian operations of King Charles XII of Sweden at the opening of the eighteenth century, Napoleon's march into Russia in 1812, and the German invasions of the country in the course of the two world wars.

Paradoxically enough, these geographic features contributed greatly to Russia's own expansion. Once Mongol power had begun to disintegrate, Russian colonists and adventurers encountered little resistance in pushing eastward until they reached the Pacific, while the Russian rulers relentlessly sought to find natural frontiers in the west and to secure warm-water ports in every possible direction.[4] In this process of continuous expansion central Siberia was secured for Tsar Ivan the Terrible (1533–84) by the Cossack Yermak in 1582, and the Baltic countries of Estonia, Latvia, and Lithuania were annexed in the reigns of Peter the Great (1682–1725) and Catherine the Great (1762–96). Catherine also obtained the areas of south Russia, the Crimea, and the lands that are now called western Ukraine and western Byelorussia, as well as a large part of Poland proper during its three partitions in 1772, 1795, and 1796. Tsar Alexander I (1801–25) rounded out the empire's acquisitions in the Baltic by taking Finland from Sweden, and he continued his predecessors' encroachments on Turkish possessions by obtaining Bessarabia. Although the Russian drive for Constantinople and the Turkish Straits was stopped by the defeat of Nicholas I (1825–55) in the Crimean War of 1853–54, his son Alexander II (1855–81) succeeded in adding the Transcaspian region and Transcaucasia to the tsarist domain. He also acquired Turkestan, as well as the Maritime Provinces and Sakhalin, thus firmly establishing Russia's position in the Far East. This position was bolstered further by the acquisition of special rights in Manchuria at the end of the last century.

To be sure, some of these rights had to be yielded in 1905 to Japan, which also obtained the cession of southern Sakhalin; and, by the end of the civil war period in 1920, Soviet Russia had lost the Baltic States, Finland, Bessarabia, the western Ukraine, and western Byelorussia. Except for Finland—from which the U.S.S.R. received the Petsamo area and other strategic points—all of these territories, as well as Russia's former special rights in Manchuria, were recovered by the Soviet Union in the course of World War II. In addition the U.S.S.R. was ceded the Carpatho-Ukraine by treaty with Czechoslovakia, and also acquired the Kurile Islands from Japan and the Königsberg area in Eastern Germany under the terms of the Yalta and Potsdam agreements, respectively. It is estimated that, between the Crimean War and World War I, tsarist Russia gained over 971,000 square miles of territory. Up to the end of 1951 the latest territorial acquisitions during and since World War II have added close to 300,000 square miles to the former limits of the Soviet Union.

The recurring foreign invasions and Russia's expansionist drives have placed a premium on concentrated political authority to keep the sprawling empire and its scattered peoples together; with much justification historians have traced the roots of Russia's centralized and dictatorial system of rule, and of its population's predisposition for disciplined unity in crisis, to the enduring effect of these prolonged national experiences.

The Geocentric Position of the U.S.S.R. Lastly, cognizance should be taken of the central geographic location of the Soviet Union. The U.S.S.R. has been frequently referred to as a bridge between continents and as the "Eurasian Heartland" of the world. Whether or not one accepts the geopolitical theories of "land power versus sea power" in this age of air power, it remains true that, by its very position and size on the Eurasian continent, the U.S.S.R. is actually or potentially capable of exerting

[4] On this point see the writings of Robert J. Kerner, especially *The Urge to the Sea* (1942).

considerable influence upon neighboring areas in Europe as well as in the Near, Middle, and Far East. The nature and extent of this influence at any given time depend upon the shifting balance of power, the changing potential of the U.S.S.R., and the degree of concentration upon a particular area.

At the beginning of the Soviet regime there was a tendency to underestimate the significance of geographic factors, and Lenin could assert in 1919 that "the question of state boundaries is for an internationalist a second-rate if not a tenth-rate question." It was not long before the vital import of geography was fully acknowledged, and toward the end of the thirties the Soviet leaders were again freely using the concept of "sacred borders" in regard to the U.S.S.R.[5] The Soviet Union early exhibited an interest in the polar regions as avenues of communication and strategic air lanes. In more recent years it has demonstrated an interest in many military bases elsewhere and has shown in other ways its belief in the continued importance of geographic position and distance.

In sum, the elements of area, population, resources, and land configuration form the geographic background of Russia's traditional activities and of much Soviet political thought and action in the foreign as well as the domestic sphere.

2. HISTORICAL HERITAGE

Precedents and Parallels. Next in importance to the geographical factors, the heritage that the Soviet regime received from Russia's historical past has been a potent, if not always a conscious, influence in its political development.

In many respects this heritage created special problems of government. Thus the numerous nationalities absorbed by the tsarist empire in its process of expansion posed acute problems of ethnic friction and separatist sentiments. The general backwardness of Russian society, the underdeveloped state of its economy, and the lethargy and ignorance of its masses created difficult tasks of education, training, and organization that entailed a remolding of the life and attitudes of the entire populace.

At the same time this heritage simplified some serious problems of government for the new rulers. Although their purposes and motivations differed radically from those of their predecessors, there was much in the culture that they finally took over to facilitate the use of the tools and techniques of governance they came to employ. Centralized power and excessive utilization of propaganda and violence as instruments of government, the symbolization of an acclaimed highest leader, a popular predisposition for submission to authority, suspicion of foreign intentions, and alternating or converging tendencies toward isolationism and messianism—all these factors find precedents and parallels in the position and role of

[5] See Nikolai Lenin, *Sochinenia* [Works] (3rd ed., 1937), Vol. XXIX, pp. 645, 658. Also note Marshal Timoshenko's speech on the twenty-third anniversary of the revolution, *New York Times,* November 8, 1940.

the autocracy, church, and police under the old regime; in the peasants' faith in the infallibility and benevolence of the tsar; in the sporadic efforts at reform by the Moscow rulers; in Russia's periodic aloofness from Europe; and in the recurring missionary note in her Orthodoxy, Pan-Slavism, and other cultural currents, as well as in her foreign policy.

The Tradition of Autocracy and Centralism.   Autocracy and central-ism have a long tradition in Russia. Although the first Russian state was the Kiev principality, founded in 882, autocracy had its formal beginning in Russia when, following the fall of Constantinople (the "Second Rome") to the Turks in 1453, the grand duke of Muscovy, Ivan III, or "the Great" (1462–1505), assumed the Byzantine title of autocrat in 1472. He thus claimed succession to the last of the Eastern emperors and the role of defender of Orthodox Christendom, with Moscow becoming the "Third Rome." Ivan IV, or "the Terrible" (1533–84), followed up the claim by assuming the title of tsar (Caesar) in 1547, and Peter the Great in 1721 added the title of emperor.

By the Fundamental Laws of the empire the tsar was "an autocratic and unlimited monarch" to whom obedience "not only from fear but from conscience, God himself has commanded." Russian constitutionalists found hope in the omission of the word "unlimited" from this article in the 1906 version of the Fundamental Laws, following the imperial manifesto of February 20, which sought to quiet popular revolutionary moods born of the defeat in the Russo-Japanese War (1904–5) by establishing a state duma with powers of approval over legislation. In point of fact, however, another article of the same constitution specifically referred to the tsar as "unlimited autocrat," [6] and the autocracy found little difficulty in progressively emasculating the supposed constitutional limitations upon its rule.

The tsar exercised his absolute powers through his council of ministers at the center and his governors (*gubernatory*) in the provinces. He was assisted by the Imperial Council, which drafted legislation for his consideration and signature, by a senate, which served as the highest judicial and administrative organ, and by the Holy Synod and its procurator in religious affairs. Over all of these bodies the tsar had complete control, chiefly through his powers of appointment and removal.

In popular lore, as well, the autocracy was regarded as absolute, indispensable, and inevitable almost up to the eve of the revolution in 1917. "It is awe-inspiring, it is frightening, but we cannot do without a tsar," ran a Russian proverb. Other folk sayings emphasized the theme that "everything is in the power of God and the sovereign" and "the sovereign answers only to God," reflecting a reverent and fatalistic acceptance of the autocracy by the masses.

Proclivity for Conformity.   The Russian autocracy—its theory and practice molded by the triple impact of the Byzantine tradition, the long

---

[6] See N. I. Lazarevsky, *Russkoe Gosudarstvennoe Pravo* (1917), Vol. I, pp. 166–68.

Tartar domination, and the influence of German authoritarian ideas at the court—was one of the most despotic tyrannies in the world. Under the corrupt bureaucracy through which it ruled, the people endured endless suffering and injustice. Yet, with rare exceptions, they willingly supported the autocracy.

Here one encounters one of the main paradoxes of government in Russia. There was no innate love for authority among the Russian people. On the contrary, the peasant masses were imbued with a deep-seated negativism against all government and a particular hostility against the oppressive officials around them. The philosopher Berdyaev offers this summary: "Among a people who were anarchist in their fundamental bent, there existed a State that developed to a monstrous degree, and an all-powerful bureaucracy surrounding an autocratic tsar and separating him from the people. Such was the peculiarity of the Russian destiny." [7] There appears to be at least some support for the thesis that the Russian people submitted readily to authority because by their very character, influenced by climate and soil and historical experience, they were so much disposed toward anarchy and individualism as to require a strong hand from above to bind them to a common purpose.[8] Centrifugal and parochial tendencies were strong among the scattered communities of the vast land. But survival against the elements within and the enemy without dictated unity. And unity under an autocrat standing above law appeared to make combination easier. In any case, instead of voluntary compromise of individual differences, there was equal submission by all to the one supreme power.

On this foundation there emerged in the peasant mind the symbol of the tsar as the "Little Father"—the last resort and true protector of his people. If the people were suffering cruelties at the hands of the landlords and officials, it was not his fault, for "the tsar does not know what the scribe is doing." He was far away and "the sun cannot warm everybody, nor can the tsar please everybody." But someday he would save his people from their oppressors.

Meantime the imposition of unity from above was matched by pressure for conformity from below in the common faith and common service of God and tsar. Thus submission to authority and conformity became strong habits, deeply ingrained in the culture and life of the Russian people. On the residue of these habits the Communist leaders were able to build when they felt the need. As Berdyaev puts it: "The spirit of the people could very easily pass from one integrated faith to another integrated faith, from one orthodoxy to another orthodoxy, which embraced the whole of life." [9]

Consolation and Compulsion.   If the tsar could rely on a predominant spirit of loyalty in the people, which was born of fatalism and a sense

---

[7] Nicholas Berdyaev, *The Russian Idea* (1948), p. 144.

[8] This thesis, pervading the writings of Berdyaev, is most ably developed in Edward Crankshaw, *Russia and the Russians* (1948).

[9] Nicholas Berdyaev, *The Origin of Russian Communism,* as quoted in Sir John Maynard, *Russia in Flux* (1948), p. 431.

of collective necessity, he also had at his disposal two major tools to keep his subjects in line, namely, the church and the secret police.

Perhaps nowhere else in the world were the ties between church and state so close, the unity of accepted religion and civil rule, as symbolized in the "Orthodox Tsar," so complete. Russia's acceptance of Christianity from Byzantium is dated from the baptism of Grand Prince Vladimir of Kiev in 988, and his marriage to the Byzantine emperor's sister. From small beginnings, at first under Greek metropolitans appointed by the patriarch of Constantinople, the Russian Church grew into a strong national institution, ecclesiastically autonomous in relation to Constantinople and closely linked to the princes of Muscovy. It played an important role in the struggle against Tartar rule, and its spreading monasteries were a significant factor in Moscow's early territorial expansion.

The Russian church had decisively repudiated the attempted reunion of the Eastern and Western churches at the Council of Florence in 1439, and the only success of the papacy was the Brest-Litovsk Union in 1596, which won over a part of the Orthodox Church to a newly formed Uniat church under its jurisdiction. With the fall of Byzantium, followed by Moscow's claim to its succession, the status of the Orthodox Church reached a new high in "Holy Russia," and in 1589 the Moscow metropolitan assumed the title of patriarch. The influence of the church upon the throne was particularly strong about the time of the election of Mikhail Romanov, the son of Metropolitan Philaret (patriarch, 1619–33), as tsar of Russia in 1613 and during Nikon's occupancy of the Moscow patriarchate from 1652 to 1667. Economically the church prospered to the point where it became one of the largest landowners and serf owners. By the middle of the sixteenth century the monasteries were estimated to possess about one third of the land, and, at the time of Peter's ascendancy to the throne, about 14 per cent of the peasantry belonged to church lands.

It was the tsars' fear of this economic power, as well as the schism in the church that resulted from Nikon's reforms of the Orthodox ritual and liturgy in 1654, that led to restrictions on the power of the church and to its conversion into an obedient instrument of the autocracy. From the time of Ivan the Terrible, tax and service obligations were increased, and the secularization of church property was fostered. Peter the Great secured the political subordination of the church in 1721 by abolishing the patriarchate and by instituting in its place the tsar-appointed Holy Synod, which subsequently came to be dominated by its lay procurator. The higher clergy, inaccessible to the people and exercising disciplinary jurisdiction over the lower clergy, became the bulwark of the cult of absolutism and, from the time of Alexander I, the pillar of tsarist reaction. At the bottom of the hierarchy the village priests were "shepherds of the Crown" who helped to inculcate the virtues of humility, patience, and obedience in the neglected and maltreated masses. The parish priest, performing the required rites of marriage, birth, and death, and otherwise ministering to the religious needs of his simple flock, and the village church, with the beautiful and semi-mystical symbolism of its ceremonies, were virtually the sole sources of consolation to the peasant in his poverty and grief. And the autocracy did not hesitate to press even the village priests into police service by requiring them to divulge political secrets learned during the confidences of confession. In short, the institution of the church thus became a subordinate and trusted arm of the state.

As an instrument for consolation and persuasion the church provided a strong precedent for the propaganda departments established under Communist rule. In yet another way, it has been suggested, the church may have been an unconscious influence on practices of the present regime through its doctrine of *sobornost,* or "congregationalism." [1] The essence of this doctrine is that truth and love reside in the congregation as a whole, i.e., in the brotherhood of the faithful collectively and not in any of the brethren separately. The opinion of the congregation in its entirety, not that of its individual members, is the measure of truth, and the body of the congregation guards the orthodoxy of its adherents. Only by confessing and renouncing his errors can a deviating member rejoin the communion of the brethren. If the collectivity of the party in the present regime is substituted for that of the Orthodox congregation, the inference of an influence from the past upon the present is strong. [2]

The secret police is by no means a new phenomenon in Russian life. The *Oprichnina,* a separate armed force organized by Ivan the Terrible as his special instrument of control, was only the precursor of police rule in Russia, which grew in importance from the middle of the seventeenth century. Alexander I re-established the secret police organization, which existed under his father, and his successor, Nicholas I (1825–55), set up the dreaded Third Section in his personal chancery to supervise directly the work of a special secret police. Although the Third Section was abolished in 1880 toward the end of the reign of Alexander II, it was not long before the even more notorious *Okhrana* came into existence. Besides recourse to martial law and execution, this political police instituted the practice of infiltrating the labor unions and socialist parties with its own *agents provocateurs,* some of whom (Azev, Malinovsky, etc.) attained leading positions in the revolutionary movement. The Okhrana was among the first of the tsarist institutions to be abolished in 1917. But in less than a year the Cheka (Extraordinary Commission), with powers of summary arrest and execution, was brought into being by the new regime.

Reform from Above.   The outstanding characteristic of reform in Russia is that it has always been effected from above and that it has been piecemeal, inadequate, and too long delayed.

Over the stretch of the centuries a number of Russian rulers charted or experimented with social and political reforms. As early as 1550, Ivan the Terrible established the *Zemsky Sobor,* a representative assembly that played an important role during the great disturbances of the "Time of Troubles" (1584–1613). After the death of Ivan's son, Fedor, pretender followed pretender; the Poles seized and held the Russian throne from 1605 to 1610, when they were dispossessed in a popular rising under Kuzma Minin and Prince Pozharsky. It was this sobor that elected Fedor's father-in-law, Boris Godunov, in 1598, and Mikhail Romanov, the young

[1] See Sir John Maynard, *Russia in Flux,* pp. 51–52, 58–60, 299.
[2] Ibid., pp. 441–42.

founder of the Romanov dynasty, in 1613, as tsars of Russia. During the same troubled period the older assembly of the nobles, the Boyars' Duma, likewise asserted itself to a greater extent. Yet the Zemsky Sobor was merely an *ad hoc* body without clearly defined authority, and the Boyars' Duma was a class organ. Neither exercised much power in the face of a strong tsar. And both were discontinued by Peter the Great, whose revolutionary reforms augmented rather than diminished the power of the autocracy and were aimed chiefly at modernization in production and administration.

The Empress Anne (1730–40), Catherine the Great (1762–96), and Alexander I (1801–25) all initially displayed strong liberal ideas and intentions; particularly was this true of Alexander I, who thought of freeing the serfs and restricting the powers of the Crown. In each case the ideas found little if any implementation. Catherine established elective municipal *dumas* (councils) in the cities, but the greatest of all Russian evils—serfdom—actually expanded during her rule. Had the plans of Michael Speransky—drawn up at the special request of Tsar Alexander I— been carried out, Russia would have had a national representative duma, indirectly elected by the people through intermediate stages of local, county, and provincial dumas. Instead only one of his proposals, having no connection with representative government or the limitation of the tsar's prerogatives, was given effect in 1810; a co-ordinating administrative organ, the Imperial Council, was created at that time. The long reign of Alexander's successor, Nicholas I, was one of the darkest periods of reaction and tyrannical rule. Only during the reigns of Alexander II (1855– 81) and of the last tsar, Nicholas II (1894–1917), were a few beginnings made on the road to self-government in the *zemstvos* and dumas.

The liberal reforms inaugurated by Alexander II, the "Tsar Liberator," included changes in military service; the judicial legislation in 1864, which made the judges independent of administrative officials and introduced public trial by jury; and, most important, the abolition of serfdom by the imperial edict of March 3–17, 1861. Alexander II even signed a project to include elected representatives of the people in the government's legislative work. Yet so late was the hour in the eyes of the revolutionary wing of the intelligentsia that on the very eve of the intended promulgation of this project in 1881 the tsar was assassinated. This act put an end to all political reform for a quarter of a century.

Even the emancipation of the serfs, great as the achievement seemed, was tragically retarded and inadequate.[3] Serfdom finally had been legalized in Russia by the statute of 1649, when the tsars found it necessary to bind the peasants to the land in order to ensure the services of their landlords in military and administrative posts. And it was ultimately abolished when its usefulness to tsardom had ended and its demoralizing consequences had become obvious to the autocracy itself. Yet the reform did not satisfy the peasantry as a class. At the same time that it gave the serfs their personal freedom it enabled them to receive only half the land for

[3] For an excellent account of Russian agriculture and the peasantry see the pioneering study by Geroid T. Robinson, *Rural Russia under the Old Regime* (1932).

which the landlords were paid by the state, and required them to purchase this land in heavy installments over a forty-nine-year period. The surrendered land, far from sufficient in quantity for the needs of the liberated, became the property, not of the individual peasants, but of the mir, the village community, which through this reform was itself transformed into something like the lowest administrative unit. The mir was responsible for taxes and redemption payments and, consequently, for the peasants' movements, which it controlled by the old passport system.

The subsequent reforms enacted by Prime Minister Stolypin in November, 1906, enabled the peasants to claim their personal holdings (in one place rather than in scattered land strips) by a two-thirds majority vote to divide the village community property. These reforms appealed to an awakened peasant individualism and were potentially beneficial. Yet they did not increase substantially the total amount of land in the possession of the peasantry, which regarded itself as the rightful claimant to all the land. This deep discontent continued to the very eve of the revolution. The intervening years were hardly sufficient to erase the effects of the long serfdom. And on the eve of World War I, Lenin, in comparing the Russian and American emancipations, concluded that the former had been far less thorough than the latter, and that *"therefore now, half a century later, the Russians show many more marks of slavery than the Negroes."* [4]

Sprouts of Self-Government: Zemstvos and Dumas.   In the somber picture of tsarist political reality the zemstvos, created by Alexander II, and the State Duma, reluctantly conceded by Nicholas II, were among the brightest spots.

Prior to the establishment of the district and provincial zemstvos in 1864 the primitive village mir was virtually the only agency of self-government. The zemstvos were popularly elected bodies, with district councils choosing representatives to the provincial councils. Each zemstvo met only once a year but elected a standing executive committee to act in its place during the interim.

As organs of self-government the zemstvos suffered from several disabilities: elections were so arranged as to assure landlord control; as reaction set in under Alexander III (1881–94), their executive committees were subordinated to the provincial governors; and, above all, their jurisdiction was restricted to such non-political fields as health, highway maintenance, education, and agricultural experimentation. Nevertheless, so great was the need for some popular forum under the autocracy that even these timid bodies could not resist the temptation to speak out against oppression. Indeed, by 1902–04, the informal congress of zemstvo chairmen, meeting annually, felt bold enough to call for equal civil rights, a voice in legislation concerning the localities, and similar liberties.

The State Duma promised by the imperial manifesto of October, 1905, which Nicholas II published to meet the threat of revolution, was designed originally to give Russia a parliamentary government and a responsible executive. The popularly elected representative assembly was to have a real voice in legislation and public expenditure. Instead, the final

[4] Nikolai Lenin, *Sochinenia*, Vol. XVI, pp. 299–300.

product delivered by the autocracy appeared singularly shaped to frustrate the people's will. To begin with, a second chamber with equal powers was set up as a check upon the Duma; the Imperial Council was reorganized into the State Council, half of whose members were directly appointed by the tsar. Then, besides reserving certain crucial fields (such as those over fundamental laws and defense) within his exclusive competence, the tsar retained full powers to veto legislation, to dissolve the Duma, and to govern by ukase.

These powers he promptly used at the expense of the first Duma (May 10–July 21, 1906), and of the second Duma (March 5–June 16, 1907), whose liberal composition and bold efforts to discuss vital public matters were not to his taste. Disregarding all constitutional niceties, the autocracy then completely altered the election scheme to deny the vote to various areas and to allot 50 per cent of the representation to the big landowners alone. Packed with reactionaries and conservatives through these and other devices, the third Duma (1907–12) and the fourth Duma (1912–17) were permitted to serve out their terms. Even these dumas became increasingly critical of the inefficiency and corruption of the tsar's administration.

Thus, limited and unrepresentative as they were, the zemstvos and dumas afforded some opportunities for a public airing of accumulated grievances in the stifling atmosphere of the autocracy. Although they were unable to create a strong tradition of popular influence in national administration, they nonetheless offered the people a foretaste of the possibilities of participation in government.

The Legacy of Backwardness: Material Poverty.   On February 4, 1931, Stalin told a conference of Soviet industrial managers:

> The history of old Russia was one in which she was ceaselessly beaten for her backwardness. She was beaten by the Mongol khans. She was beaten by the Turkish beys. She was beaten by the Swedish feudal lords. She was beaten by the Polish-Lithuanian *pans*. She was beaten by the Japanese barons. All beat her because of her backwardness—for military backwardness, for cultural backwardness, for political backwardness. She was beaten because to beat her was profitable and went unpunished. . . . Do you wish our socialist Fatherland to be beaten . . . ? We are 50 or 100 years behind the advanced countries. We must make up this distance in ten years. Either we do it or we will be wiped out.[5]

A thousand times this cry has been echoed and repeated in official and semiofficial pronouncements, with the main emphasis invariably resting on the backward economy that the Soviet regime had inherited. Although the purpose of the Soviet leaders was to urge the people on to greater production, there was much truth in that plaint. Industrialism came late to Russia, and on the eve of World War I tsarist Russia still held fifth

[5] Joseph Stalin, *Voprosy Leninizma* (11th ed., 1945), pp. 328–29.

place in industrial production among the states of the world, despite her enormous resources; in certain specific fields, such as electrical energy, she was so far behind the other large states as to hold fifteenth place in world production. In 1913, Russia produced only about four million tons each of pig iron and steel, about nine million tons of oil, and less than thirty million tons of coal. Less than 2 per cent of her coal extraction and only about 6 per cent of her oil extraction were mechanized, and her huge territories were inadequately served by railway lines totaling less than 37,000 miles, while automotive traffic had barely begun.

Whatever the cost also in terms of military security, this economic backwardness spelled, first of all, material poverty for the great majority of Russia's populace. Before the revolution 65 per cent of the peasantry (which was Russia's largest class, constituting three fourths of the population) consisted of poor peasants, and another 20 per cent of middle peasants; only 15 per cent were relatively well-to-do. Of the total number of peasant households 30 per cent had no draft animals, 34 per cent had no agricultural equipment, and 15 per cent had no sowing lands. Tractors and combines were nonexistent. Plows and hoes constituted the main farm tools, and the 1910 census showed that a third of the plows were wooden and that close to eighteen million wooden harrows were in use. Productivity was extremely low, and the primitive nature of much of Russia's agriculture had its counterpart in the underdeveloped and inefficient state of many branches of industry. In the whole of Russia, for instance, only about 8,500,000 pairs of leather shoes were produced. Similar shortages existed in many other lines.[6]

Facts such as these could but contribute to the socio-political upheaval of 1917. And they continued to pose special problems for the new, Bolshevik rulers, who made initial use of them in attaining power.

Masses and Classes: Inertia and Ineptitude.   Along with widespread poverty went ignorance and inertia among the masses, irresponsibility and ineptitude among the ruling classes.

Features of Russian society before the revolution that account in no small measure for the lack of progress toward democratic government included the absence of a strong and stable middle class and the wide gulf that separated the upper class of nobles, landlords, higher bureaucracy, and clergy from the vast masses of the peasantry and peasant-derived city proletariat. Official Soviet figures give the percentage of the "bourgeoisie" in 1913—landlords, "big and petty urban bourgeoisie," merchants, and *kulaks*—as 15.9 per cent. In this figure kulaks alone, i.e., rich peasants, accounted for 12.3 per cent. "Workers and employees [i.e., intelligentsia]" comprised at that time 16.7 per cent of the population. Workers alone, who counted no more than a few million at the turn of the century, constituted approximately 14 per cent. It is obvious, then, that the educated urban middle class, traditional champion of constitutionalism and liberalism in government, was exceedingly small. Considerable sections of the similarly small workers' stratum, which was largely peasant in origin, continued to identify their interests with those of the peasantry. Other sections

[6] See *20 Let Sovetskoi Vlasti, Statisticheskii Sbornik* (1937), passim.

became increasingly attentive to programs offering radical socioeconomic and political solutions.

Even more fatal for the cause of free government in Russia was the fact that those at the pinnacle of the social hierarchy—the nobility and bureaucrats who surrounded the tsar and the governors and landlords who ruled in his name—were for the most part corrupt, reactionary, and inefficient. From fairly early days the *boyars* (landed aristocrats) appear to have believed that ordered freedom in a community of equal peers was an impossibility; consequently they preferred common subjection to a tsar. From the time that Ivan the Terrible curbed the unruly boyars and swelled their ranks by establishing the *dvoriane* (court gentry) and *pomeshchiki* (estate owners), all obligated to serve the state in compensation for the land grants they received, the nobility was an estate servile to the tsar. It enjoyed no independent, universally esteemed social position in the land. The table of ranks instituted by Peter the Great merely confirmed and regularized the service status of the nobility vis-à-vis the Crown. As this social stratum developed over the centuries, the nobility as a group, with rare exceptions, showed little vision, initiative, or responsibility; and as landlords and officials it came to be known rather for its abusive selfishness, venality, and marked ineptitude. To be sure, during the nineteenth century some of its members played a leading role in liberal and revolutionary groups. But by that time the tsarist nobility and its cohorts in the bureaucracy, army, and police were firmly identified in the popular mind with blind reaction and oppression.

The base and bulk of the social hierarchy was the huge, amorphous mass of the peasantry—illiterate, lethargic, cautious, and suspicious. It was collectively and individually possessed of an infinite capacity for patience and passivity, skepticism and procrastination, duality and flexibility, in meeting the hardships of nature and the demands and exactions of governors and landlords. Along with the effects of climate and the impact of serfdom, sheer ignorance has had a tremendous influence in shaping the peasant's basic attitudes and reactions. Around the turn of the century 27 per cent of the entire population of Russia (apart from that of her western periphery) was literate; in the rural areas only 23 per cent of the people could be so classified; in the backward regions inhabited by non-Russian nationalities the figure was as low as 13 per cent, and in some localities it was as low as 1 or 2 per cent. On the eve of World War I, despite the splendid efforts of the zemstvos, over 60 per cent, or more than half of Russia's population, was still illiterate. The whole of Russia had then no more than 222 clubs and reading rooms, and of these only 88 functioned in the countryside.

This state of the masses was probably the most difficult of all problems that confronted the Bolshevik rulers. In the light of the grandiose schemes of change proclaimed by them, the human material was inadequate. The biggest task they envisaged was to remold the character of the people, to shake off the age-old lethargy, and to stimulate enough of a desire for growth and initiative to make possible the modernization of Russia, while keeping individual and group aspirations within rigid bounds of political conformity.

Fear of the Foreigner: Isolationism and Messianism. Another legacy from the past was a well-nigh ingrained fear of the foreigner among the Russian people, despite their innate sociability and strong sense of curiosity. Suspicion of the stranger comes almost naturally to a backward peasant population long wary of its own governors. In this case fear and suspicion fed on memories of past invasions and conquests from east and west. Long before Nazi Germany sought *Lebensraum* in Russia, the Russian people had learned from bitter historical experience that their land was an alluring prize for their neighbors. Physically and spiritually the Russian reaction throughout the centuries has been a sort of dual urge for minimum and maximum security, sometimes seeking safety in retreat and sometimes in attack.

Minimum security lay in seclusion, at times enforced from outside, at other times willingly self-imposed. Mongol, Pole, Turk, Swede, and other peoples as well contributed to Russia's isolation long before the days of the *cordon sanitaire,* erected after World War I, and those of the cold war, which followed World War II. The Russian rulers themselves periodically found isolationism a military bulwark against outside threats. Moreover, spiritual withdrawal was a counterpart of "defense in depth." The unique and solitary position of Russia's Greek Orthodoxy in the world of religion, the calculated obscurantism of Russia's rulers, the cultural self-sufficiency preached by the Slavophiles and other groups in the nineteenth century combined to form a habit of aloofness and apartness that shut the Russian masses off from the cultural currents of the West, despite the "window in the wall" opened by Peter the Great.

Yet, alongside this apartness, there has always existed in Russian culture a strong strain of messianism, which in its more active phases took the form of territorial and ideological expansion. Moscow was "the Third Rome," possessed of "the true faith" in Christendom. As Berdyaev so penetratingly pointed out, there was a wide belief within the masses themselves in the mission of the Russian people to make social justice and the brotherhood of man a reality.[7] And the woes of the world constituted one of the most pronounced themes in the works of the Russian literati in the nineteenth century. Pan-Slavism and tsarist imperialism were merely facets of Russia's universalist messianism. One of its vital—though for the most part subconscious—underlying assumptions has apparently been that maximum security lies in advance, that is, in the ultimate total victory of Russian ideas.

Here, too, we find potent precedents or germs in the past for the practices of the present, for isolating the Soviet people from contact with the West, and for the minimum safety principle of "socialism in one country," as well as for the maximum security precept of ultimate victory for world communism.

Stirrings of Discontent: Rebels and Revolutionaries. Despite the Russian people's general submission to authority Russian history was not free from periodic outbursts of primitive wrath against the oppressive

[7] Berdyaev, *The Russian Idea,* passim.

conditions of serfdom, poverty, and maladministration. Besides palace revolutions and the seizure of the throne by impostors, violent peasant revolts occurred from time to time, the most noted of which were the rebellions of Bolotnikov (1606–7), Stenka Razin (1670–71), Bulavin (1707–8), and Pugachev (1773–75). But these large-scale uprisings, marked by extensive pillaging and bloodletting, were more basically social and economic than political in character. In the words of the Cossack Pugachev, they were directed "against the malefactor landowners and the bribetaking officials and judges," not against the autocracy. They failed because they were localized in scope, and the institution of tsardom remained intact.

Only in the revolt of the so-called Decembrists in the nineteenth century was the first assault made upon that institution itself. On December 26, 1825, a group of army officers—all members of the nobility who had contacted liberal political ideas during the Russian campaigns in the west—attempted a coup against the newly ascended Nicholas I and were mercilessly suppressed. This unsuccessful rising, the purposes of which were not even clearly or uniformly understood by the perpetrators themselves, became the prelude to the rise of the radical and revolutionary groups in the second half of the century.

The parent of these groups was the *Narodnik,* or Populist, movement, which sprang up among the students and literati in the sixties. The heart of its beliefs was that Russia, once freed of the autocracy, would attain its own brand of agrarian socialism without the evils of industrialism, and that her salvation lay in a non-capitalist peasant economy based on the communal mir of the village and on small handicraft. Placing their faith in the peasantry as the soul of the nation, the *Narodniki* felt that their purpose was "going to the people" (*Khozhdenie v narod*), living among the peasants, serving them as teachers, nurses, and craftsmen, and spreading the movement's teachings among them. Lack of response on the part of the confused peasantry and repressive measures by the government helped produce dissension over the future tactics of the Narodniki in the late seventies. One group began to pursue a program of terrorism against the autocracy that resulted in the assassination of Alexander II and many tsarist officials. Others continued to carry on underground propaganda work in the villages. Still others—among them Georgii Plekhanov, who formed the Emancipation of Labor group in 1883 and who came to be widely regarded as the father of Russian Marxism —lost faith in the possibility of Russia's salvation through the peasantry and turned to the more strictly Marxist program of reliance on the industrial proletariat. With the growth of industry, factory labor, and education, and with the increased incidence of sporadic strikes in the eighties and nineties, Marxist groups multiplied, until by the end of the century the Narodnik movement had completely disintegrated. To some extent, however, it was succeeded by the Social-Revolutionary party (established in 1901), which likewise centered its program on land and rights for the peasantry and which more than any other group inherited the tradition of individual acts of terrorism.

Other political groups that sought to organize themselves into parties were the Liberals and the Social Democrats. The first group, pursuing a liberal-democratic program, formed the Union of Liberation under the leadership of Paul Miliukov in 1903. It soon was known as the party of the Constitutional Democrats or Cadets, which played a prominent role in the dumas. The second group officially formed the Russian Social Democratic Labor Party (R.S.D.L.P.) at a small, abor- tive gathering in Minsk in 1898. This meeting was subsequently referred to as the first congress, but the party was actually organized at the second congress in Brussels and London in 1903. At this congress there occurred the momentous split of the newly formed party into majority (*bol'- shinstvo*) and minority (*men'shinstvo*) factions, which were thereafter called Bolsheviks (*Bol'sheviki*) and Mensheviks (*Men'sheviki*). This doctrinal schism was to have a profound effect on the destiny of Russia and on that of the rest of the world as well.

Design for Power: The Emergence of Bolshevism.   As a doctrine and political movement, bolshevism took shape in the writings and struggles of its leaders, not only against Populists, Liberals, and Social- Revolutionaries, but also against various currents in the Russian Social- Democratic movement itself. More than to any other man it owes its emergence to V. I. Ulianov—later known to the world as Nikolai Lenin —who entered upon his revolutionary Marxist career in 1887, follow- ing the execution of his brother for complicity in the attempt on the life of Alexander II. With gifted pen and relentless will power Lenin hammered away at all of the other parties: at the so-called Legal Marxists, who preached the possibility of gradual social progress without revolutionary violence and class struggle or the need for the withering away of the state; at the "Economists," who urged the party to forsake political pursuits and concentrate on securing economic benefits for the workers; and at the Mensheviks. The schism between the two factions of the R.S.D.L.P. in 1903 and their subsequent differences over the aims and consequences of the 1905 revolution and over the program to be followed led to a complete organizational break, which resulted in the formation of an independent Bolshevik party, the R.S.D.L.P. (B.), in 1912.

Initially the issue that divided Lenin from his coeditors of the Social Democratic paper *Iskra* (The Spark), L. Martov and Paul Axelrod (who became the leaders of the Menshevik wing and who were subsequently joined by the outstanding theoretician, Georgii Plekhanov), was the party organization. In *Iskra,* from 1900 to 1904, and later in *Vpered* (Forward) and in other journals and pamphlets, Lenin argued for molding the party into a militant, highly centralized, rigidly disciplined organization, composed of a select membership of professional revo- lutionaries who would be consciously bound by the party program and rules and who would operate under the strict guidance of the highest party leadership. He was against a federal structure for the party, which would recognize nationality differences and grant its ethnic components organizational autonomy; instead he insisted on constituting the party as a single organization rooted in the proletariat. The Mensheviks, led by

Martov, opposed these views, contending for a broadly based, de-centralized party that would embrace sympathizers no less than activists.

The essence of the rift, which distinguished the Bolsheviks not only from the Mensheviks but also from the Social-Revolutionaries and other groups, involved the central question of the fundamental nature and course of the Russian Revolution. Lenin believed that the proletariat must play a pivotal role in a bourgeois-democratic revolution in Russia, transforming it subsequently into a socialist revolution guided by a dictatorship of the proletariat in alliance with the peasantry. Rejecting individual terrorism as a means of struggle against the autocracy and opposing co-operation with the Liberals as vacillating and perfidious allies, the Bolsheviks urged the employment of the general strike and insurrection to achieve maximum aims in the 1905 revolution. From its failure they quickly drew lessons of a need for greater centralization and for better organized and timed insurrection in the future. With their primary goal of ultimate radical revolution in mind, the Bolsheviks began to take part in the Duma in order to discredit it. They generally combined legal and underground work; and during World War I they advocated conversion of the international armed conflict into internal civil wars and excoriated the "defensists" in the world socialist movement who partici-pated in the war efforts of their respective countries.

By contrast the Mensheviks did not consider the proletariat ready to play the leading role in securing radical change. Believing in social gradualism and in self-government, and visualizing a bourgeois-dem-ocratic revolution as the only possibility in Russia for many years ahead, they condemned the Bolshevik tactics in the 1905 revolution and sought to co-operate with the Liberals on a program to replace the autocracy by a constitutional regime that featured parliamentary democracy.

These basic differences determined the respective attitudes of the groups in the crucial period of March–November, 1917. When tsarism collapsed in March of that year under the dead weight of its rotten structure and its crippling wartime inefficiency, a coalition provisional government headed by representatives of the liberal bourgeoisie assumed authority in a sort of duality of power with the spontaneously established soviets, dominated by the Mensheviks and the Social-Revolutionaries. The battle cry of these parties became the convocation of a constituent assembly that would give formal expression to the democratic revolution. To the Bolsheviks, however, these events were merely a consummation of the bourgeois-democratic revolution, of the long-predicted first phase. After a short period of vacillation they came increasingly to be-lieve, under Lenin's relentless pressure following his return to Russia from abroad in April, in the need for transition to the second phase, the socialist revolution. Lenin charted a program of activity designed to exploit the popular discontent for the purpose of undermining the other parties and the government and to establish a republic of soviets in the name of a dictatorship of the proletariat. With the growing economic crisis and the war weariness of the masses making them singularly re-sponsive to the Bolshevik slogans of "land, peace, and bread," and with the winning of the majority in the soviets of the two capitals of Petrograd and Moscow by the end of the summer, the Bolsheviks seized power on November 6, 1917 (October 24, old calendar). On the following day the Second All-Russian Congress of Soviets proclaimed the establishment of Soviet rule.

Thus, if the experiences of the war proved the utter decay of the autocracy and the incompetence of the ruling classes, the legacy of backwardness they left behind, the weakness of the tradition of popular government or political compromise, and the weakness and vacillations of the other political groups made it relatively easy for the resolute group of Bolshevik leaders to step forth as spokesmen for the disaffected masses and to occupy the seat of power.

3. IDEOLOGICAL SETTING

Along with geography and history the teachings of Marxism embraced by the Bolsheviks and the lessons drawn by them from Russia's revolutionary experience provided a setting for the shaping of Soviet political institutions.

The Lessons of Revolutionary Experience. In the wake of the upheaval that followed Bloody Sunday in Russia—January 22, 1905, when a peaceful procession of workers, marching under Father Gapon to petition the tsar, was met by a hail of bullets at the Winter Palace— sporadic popular bodies informally elected in factories came into existence in a number of cities. These were the so-called soviets (councils) of workers' deputies. In October of that year the strikers of Petersburg elected a soviet of workers' deputies, which became the center of revolutionary activity. Although the experience of the soviets was brief, as the climax of the revolution was reached during the following month, Lenin at once assessed the soviets as embryonic organs of government. Later he described them as a suitable state form for "a revolutionary-democratic dictatorship of the proletariat and peasantry," which he then visualized as the goal for Russia.

In the revolution unleashed by the breakdown of the monarchy, in March, 1917, soviets of workers' and soldiers' deputies again sprang up, first in the capitals and later in the provinces and at army fronts. The most important of these was the soviet elected by the factories and military units of Petersburg (renamed Petrograd), which to all intents and purposes became a rival seat of power to the Provisional Government headed first by Prince Lvov, and, after the fiasco of the July offensive, by Alexander Kerensky. Gaining increasing influence among the populace and troops, the Petrograd Soviet convened the First All-Russian Congress of Soviets during June 3–24; the congress, in turn, elected a permanently functioning Central Executive Committee, thus providing a rudimentary framework of government in the soviets. Both in the Petrograd Soviet and in the All-Russian Congress of Soviets, the Social-Revolutionaries and the Mensheviks held a majority, the Bolsheviks comprising no more than 105 out of the 777 delegates from the different socialist groups at the congress. Nevertheless, convinced that the soviets constituted the best popular medium through which to control the further course of the revolution, Lenin formulated the slogan, "All Power to the Soviets." The consent of the Petrograd Soviet to the government's suppression of the largely spontaneous July 17 (July 4, old calendar) demonstration for the realization of this slogan convinced the Bolshevik leaders of the primary necessity of securing predominance in the soviets, at least in those of the capitals, as well as in the military committees. This task they pursued relentlessly and with much success throughout the following period. In September, Kerensky's reliance on the soviet as the main bulwark in meeting the revolt of the government's commander in chief, General Kornilov, disclosed clearly that controlling power had passed to the soviet, where the Bolsheviks were rapidly attaining a majority.

Earlier in August, 1917, Lenin had written that the soviets would constitute the Paris Commune type of governmental form, which Marx deemed appropriate for the period of transition to communism. Lenin saw in the soviets a proved form of mass organization, representing the poorer classes centrally through indirect elections from the local soviets and, like the model of the Paris Commune, "not a parliamentary institution, but a working one, legislating and executing the laws at the same time." [8] Thus the Second All-Russian Congress of Soviets, which convened on November 7, 1917, and in which the Bolsheviks had 390 out of a total of 649 delegates, became the natural instrument for the formal transition of power. The soviets became "the state form" of the dictatorship established by the Bolsheviks.

Organizational Principles: Prologue to Monolithism. Not only the form but the substance of Bolshevik rule was to be profoundly affected by the views and conceptions formed by its leaders before 1917. It can be argued with some justification that Lenin's steadfast insistence on the rightness of his own views concerning Russia's road to salvation and his unyielding pursuit of these views to the point of conscious separation from all other groups and factions, even in his own party during 1903–17, contained the germ of the future practice of a monopoly of legality in the Communist Party. In any case, there can be little doubt that another basic principle of power in the U.S.S.R., the concept of monolithism in the party, which was later applied to the whole of Soviet society, had its roots in the organizational principles expounded by Lenin in the years preceding the revolution.

Joseph Stalin accepted Lenin's conception of the party as a centralized and disciplined body of professional revolutionaries, the doctrine that led to the split in the R.S.D.L.P. in 1903.[9] While a young party organizer in Caucasia, he carried it even further by laying particular stress on the demand for unity of outlook in the ranks of the party. Stalin wrote in January, 1905, that the party, as a militant group of

[8] Nikolai Lenin, *Sochinenia,* Vol. XXI, pp. 401–2.
[9] See above, p. 558.

leaders of the proletariat, "cannot be an accidental agglomeration of individuals, but a coherent, centralized organization." There was no room in it for mere sympathizers. The world abounded in prattlers who would flock to any party, but "it would be a desecration of the holy of holies of the party to call such a prattler a party member." Only one who actively participated in one of the party's organizations, merging his personal interests in those of the party, could enter this "fortress, the doors of which will be opened solely for the tested." Above all, he said, "unity of views on programme, tactics, and organization forms the basis on which our party is being built. If the unity of views should crumble, the party will crumble too." [1] This was an early harbinger of a fateful thesis by the man who was to become the chief architect of monolithism in the Soviet state two decades later.

The Tenets of the Marxist Outlook. The fundamental tenets of the Marxist outlook constituted perhaps an influence even stronger than Russia's revolutionary experience on the early thinking of the framers of the Soviet polity. The tenets, which bear particularly on political development, can be somewhat arbitrarily limited to those covering dialectical materialism, class conflict, and the state.

Dialectical Materialism: Key to Historical Interpretation. The heart of Marx's doctrine is the idea that social life is in a perpetual flux, as social conditions are constantly changing, and that the basic factor in social life and social change is the material factor, i.e., the economic system of society and the mode of production and property relations that it entails. This material factor conditions all the other forms of social life: the legal, political, religious, cultural, and philosophical. As Marx phrased his thesis:

> In the social production of their means of existence men enter into definite, necessary relations which are independent of their will, productive relationships which correspond to a definite stage of development of their material productive forces. The aggregate of these productive relationships constitutes the economic structure of society, the real basis on which a juridical and political superstructure arises and to which definite forms of social consciousness correspond. The mode of production of the material means of existence conditions the whole process of social, political, and intellectual life.[2]

In sum, it is man's social existence that determines his consciousness and not vice versa.

The rhythm of history, the dynamics of social change, proceeds in the form of a dialectic, that is, from thesis to antithesis to synthesis. The prevailing conditions in a given period are the *thesis;* the con-

---

[1] Joseph Stalin, *Sochinenia* (1946), Vol. I, pp. 62–73.
[2] Karl Marx, "A Contribution to the Critique of Political Economy," in Emile Burns, ed., *A Handbook of Marxism* (1935), pp. 371–72.

tradictions and antagonisms called forth by these conditions are the *antithesis,* which works against the existing situation and ultimately brings about a new set of conditions—a *synthesis.* This synthesis in turn becomes the thesis—the positive force or framework—of the new society, and the whole process repeats itself. Concretely, Marx (and Engels) maintained that, at a certain point in their development in a particular epoch, the forces of production come into contradiction with the then-existing property relationships, which become fetters upon the further growth of the forces of production. The result is a social revolution. Thus each society itself hatched the conditions for the birth of a new society, and "the Asiatic, the ancient, the feudal, and the modern bourgeois modes of production" followed each other as successive epochs in the progress of the economic structure of society. The chief contradiction of modern society, said Marx, lies in the relations between the owners of the means of production and their wage-earning employees. This relationship he characterized as the appropriation of the "surplus value" of the employees' labor (assessed as the value of their work above the minimum subsistence wages they customarily received) by the owners, with the consequences of underconsumption by the workers, domestic crises of overproduction, and imperialistic strivings for markets abroad. Generally maintaining that "dialectical materialism" was a scientific key to the understanding of past and prospective social development, Marx concluded with the prediction that the "proletariat" or propertyless workers, who would become more and more geographically concentrated and increasingly conscious of their class purpose and strength, would be the instrument of a new social revolution and the creators of a new society.

Class and State: The Pattern of the Transition Period. This prediction by Marx is part and parcel of his teaching concerning class and state. "The history of all hitherto existing society," Marx stated in *The Communist Manifesto* (1848), "is the history of class struggles. Freeman and slave, patrician and plebeian, lord and serf, guildmaster and journeyman, in a word, oppressor and oppressed, stood in constant opposition to one another." It was this class conflict that constituted the motive power of historical change in successive epochs. The modern epoch, Marx continued, has simplified class antagonisms by splitting society more and more "into two great classes directly facing each other: bourgeoisie and proletariat."

In every epoch the class dominant in society has controlled the legal and political machinery. The state has not existed for all time. It emerged on the historical scene when antagonistic classes came into being, and it will disappear when such classes cease to exist.[3] The state is an instrument of class domination, and law the expression of the will of

[3] "We are now rapidly approaching a stage in the development of production at which the existence of these classes has not only ceased to be a necessity, but becomes a positive hindrance to production. They will fall as inevitably as they once arose. The state inevitably falls with them." Friedrich Engels, *The Origin of the Family, Private Property and the State* (1942), p. 158.

the dominant class. The essential role of the state is the employment of violence to guard the interests of the ruling class, which coerces or oppresses the other classes in the protection of its privileges.

Without offering any clear explanation as to why the dialectical process will cease to operate at a given time in the future, and despite his thesis of class conflict as a propeller of change, Marx maintained that the modern epoch is the last in which antagonistic forms will exist in the relations of production. The "socialist" epoch that will succeed it, he said, will usher in a "classless society," and with the end of classes the state as an institution will also come to an end. Marx's collaborator, Friedrich Engels, described this ultimate oblivion of the institution of the state in the following terms:

> As soon as there is no longer any class of society to be held in subjection, as soon as, along with class domination and the struggle for individual existence based on the former anarchy of production, the collisions and excesses arising from these have also been abolished, there is nothing more to be repressed, and a special repressive force, a state, is no longer necessary. . . . Government over persons is replaced by the administration of things and the direction of the processes of production. The state is not "abolished"; it withers away.[4]

Finally, in the most revolutionary part of his teachings, Marx argued that no class voluntarily yields its dominant position and that the proletariat, guided to class consciousness by the Communists, comprising its advanced guard, must seize state power, suppress the bourgeoisie, and establish a dictatorship of the proletariat during a period of transition to communism. Classlessness and, with it, statelessness are to be achieved during this period. In its initial stages citizens are to be rewarded in the measure of the work they perform. In a later or higher phase of Communist society, after labor has ceased to be a mere means of life and "has itself become the prime necessity of life," after the antithesis between mental and physical labor has vanished, and after the productive forces have increased and growing abundance is attained, the advent of communism will be signalized by realization of its principle: "from each according to his ability, to each according to his needs." [5]

The theory of the transition period was further elaborated by Lenin on the eve of the actual seizure of power in Russia by the Bolsheviks.[6] Conceding that, according to Marx, the proletariat "needs only a state that is withering away, i.e., a state that is so constituted that it begins to wither away immediately and cannot but wither away," Lenin contended that the exact moment of such future withering away could not be defined, "the more so as it must obviously be a rather lengthy process." After forcibly taking power the proletariat will need the state to

[4] Friedrich Engels, *Herr Eugen Dühring's Revolution in Science* (1939), pp. 306–7.

[5] Karl Marx, *Critique of the Gotha Programme* (1943), p. 14.

[6] See Nikolai Lenin, *State and Revolution* (1935).

break the resistance of the former ruling classes and suppress them and to guide the rest of the populace toward communism. Anxious to identify the dictatorship of the proletariat with the interests of the masses, and convinced that the functions of government had generally become such simple operations of registration, checking, or filing that "they will be quite within reach of every literate person," Lenin wrote that by that time the state—as the organ of "suppression of the minority of the exploiters by the majority of the exploited"—will have become "a transitional state, no longer a state in the usual sense." Armed workers organized in a people's militia would replace the old army and police; all civil servants would be paid no more than ordinary workers' wages; and the masses of the citizenry would learn more and more to perform tasks of public administration.

Progress toward the ultimate goal would be marked by two phases: first that of socialism and then that of communism. During the first phase the means of production would be socialized, and strict accounting and control would be maintained over labor output, consumption, and capital accumulation for the expansion of the means of production. At this stage, "bourgeois right" would continue to be the standard, for, while equality would seem to reign supreme, inequality would in fact persist because people differing in needs and capacities would still be remunerated on the same principle: "to each according to his toil." Only in the second phase, with the consummation of socialization, the attainment of classlessness, and the achievement of economic abundance, would the Communist principle of reward "according to his needs" be introduced. With material well-being the normal causes of crime would disappear, and the citizens themselves would deal with occasional individual transgressions. The people would learn habitually to observe the norms of the community without external compulsion, and the state would come to an end.[7]

Together the teachings of Marx and Lenin constituted a blueprint for the new rulers of Russia. As we shall presently see, however, these rulers departed from the blueprint on a number of crucial points.

[7] Under the condition of quiescence that the concepts of statelessness and classlessness seemed to imply, what was to happen to the struggle of opposites that the materialist dialectic regards as the perpetual source of progress? Lenin did not elaborate on the point, but in 1920 he made the vague comment that "antagonism and contradiction are not at all the same thing. The first will disappear, the second will remain under socialism." *Leninskii Sbornik* (2nd ed., 1931), Vol. XI, p. 357.

CHAPTER

24

THE SOCIAL ORDER

The social order in Russia under the new regime is acclaimed as a realization of Marxist ideas, knowledge of which is enjoined upon governors and governed alike. Yet, despite an obsessive faith in the scientific soundness of the principles of Marxist philosophy, the Soviet leaders have found it necessary or convenient for their purposes to modify a number of its postulates in governmental practice. Moreover, since the late thirties they have openly emphasized the thesis that "the Marxist-Leninist theory is not a dogma, but a guide to action" and that, as such, it may be revised or altered in application in accordance with changing conditions. Two of the chief modifications to date are in the conceptions of the nature of political power and of the class and nationality structures in the Soviet state.

1. POLITICAL THEORY

Constitutional Evolution: Three Constitutions. Adhering to Lenin's view that a constitution must express "the actual correlation of forces" in the social order, Soviet theoreticians maintain that the three constitutions that have followed each other in the U.S.S.R. reflect the evolution of Soviet society. The first, or R.S.F.S.R. (Russian Socialist Federated Soviet Republic), constitution, adopted on July 10, 1918, was essentially a proclamation of the goal of socialism as a state program. The second, or U.S.S.R. constitution, adopted on July 6, 1923, and definitively approved on January 31, 1924, signalized principally the establishment of a single federal union by the R.S.F.S.R., the Transcaucasian S.F.S.R. (comprising the Soviet republics of Azerbaijan, Armenia, and Georgia), the Ukrainian S.S.R., and the Byelorussian S.S.R. Drafted after the end of the civil war and the institution of the New Economic Policy, this Union constitution, in official views, reflected a social structure that—except for the landlords eliminated earlier in the regime—still comprised "capitalistic classes" in town and countryside.[1]

[1] Andrei Vyshinsky, ed., *Sovetskoe Gosudarstvennoe Pravo* (1938), p. 90.

Only the third (once called Stalin) constitution, put into effect by the last federal Congress of Soviets on December 5, 1936, is officially recognized as representing a completely transformed society.

The New Fundamental Law: The Mark of the Socialist Society. According to present Soviet theory, the dictatorship of the proletariat established by the Bolsheviks in Russia had progressed by the mid-thirties to the point of "socialism: the first phase of communism," thus necessitating the adoption of a new fundamental law of the land. This new 1936 constitution opens with the statement that the U.S.S.R. is a "socialist state," politically based on soviets of toilers' deputies, and resting upon a socialist system of economy, with public ownership of land, natural resources, and the means of production. The mark of the new society is set forth in Article 12: "The principle applied in the U.S.S.R. is that of socialism: 'From each according to his ability, to each according to his toil.'" And claims have since been made of strides toward the second phase—the goal of definitive communism, when the principle enunciated in Article 12 will be modified to read: "to each according to his need." It was thus that the suitability and applicability of some of the older Marxist conceptions of government came into question.

Political Conceptions: From "Withering" State to "Mightiest" of Governments. The Soviet leaders maintain that the political structure, which they set up in Russia in place of the tsarist regime, was an entirely new state, needed by the proletariat to establish its own primacy, to end the dominance of the "exploiting" classes, and to lead the populace toward "the complete liquidation of classes in general and the transition toward communism." While Lenin did not believe that this transition would be accomplished in short order, he tolerated much talk of the "withering away" of the state and frequently referred to it as a "semi-state," transitional in nature and "no longer a state in the usual sense." [2] Soviet publicists adopted and developed this trend of thought. For instance, one prominent jurist, Eugene Pashukanis, wrote that the proletariat cannot put any socialist content into such "bourgeois" forms of society as state, law, and ethics, and must take "a sober and critical attitude" as well toward its own state. Other jurists and administrators wanted to dispense with the village soviets when collectivization got under way, believing the newly formed *kolkhoz* (collective farm) to be a more suitable form of administration for the emerging period. Similar ideas were advanced in regard to courts, law, and other institutions, in line with the older Marxist theory of replacing "government over persons" by the "administration of things" in the withering-away process of political power.

All such reflections were terminated in 1937–39. Even before the definite emergence of the Nazi threat, Stalin gave the clue to a reversal of theory in a statement at the All-Union Party Congress in 1930:

[2] Nikolai Lenin, *State and Revolution* (1935), pp. 74–75.

We are for the withering away of the state. But at the same time we stand for a strengthening of the proletarian dictatorship, which constitutes the most powerful, the mightiest of all governing powers that have ever existed. The highest development of governmental power for the purpose of preparing the conditions *for* the withering away of governmental power, this is the Marxian formula. Is this "contradictory"? Yes, it is. But this contradiction is life, and it reflects completely the Marxian dialectic.[3]

In the following years he strongly emphasized this view, claiming in 1933 that increased governmental power was necessary to "put an end to remnants of the dying classes." By 1938 this increased power was deemed essential for the defense of the country, since the victory of socialism in the U.S.S.R. could not be considered final as long as it was surrounded by hostile states. In 1939 he answered the question of the future of the state under communism in the following words: "Will our state remain in the period of communism also? Yes, it will, unless the capitalist encirclement is liquidated . . . and a socialist encirclement takes its place."

The latest restatement of theory, made by Khrushchev at the 21st Party Congress in January, 1959, leaves the thesis of state retention intact, despite the fact that the concept of "capitalist encirclement" is abandoned. Although Khrushchev proclaimed officially that "capitalist encirclement" of the U.S.S.R. no longer exists, and that the victory of socialism there is now "final" because there are no forces in the world capable of re-establishing capitalism in the Soviet Union or of "crushing the camp of socialism," nevertheless he maintained that the Soviet state must remain, since "the functions of defending the Socialist Fatherland, now performed by the state, can wither away only when the danger of an imperialist attack on our country or on countries allied with us is completely removed." Even more important was his argument that "the question of withering away of the state is a question of evolution of the socialist state toward communist public self-government," which is a slow process. Asserting the belief that many functions performed by government agencies will *gradually* pass to public organizations, he warned that such transfer of "some functions" of state agencies should be carried out without undue haste, that it will not at all mean "weakening the role of the socialist state in the building of communism," and that the tasks of defense in the future call in fact for the further strengthening of the armed forces, the state security agencies, and similar organs. These theoretical reformulations leave little doubt as to the intentions of the Soviet leaders to postpone indefinitely the "withering away" of agencies exercising effective political power in the U.S.S.R.

The Change in the Concept of Law: From Nihilism to a Positive Attitude.   The cycle of thinking concerning the institution of the state was repeated with regard to law. Abandoning their initial conception of Soviet decrees as largely media of propaganda rather than enforceable

[3] Joseph Stalin, *Voprosy Leninizma* (1934), p. 427.

rules, the Soviet leaders early came to realize the need of law as an instrument of control and as a uniform regulator of social relations in the diverse localities of the land. Yet two factors worked against the entrenchment of law as a social institution. On the one hand, the Soviet leaders themselves—as administrators of a revolutionary regime bent upon radical transformation of society—sought to reserve for the courts a field of discretion outside formally enacted laws to enable them to meet the rapidly changing demands of governmental policy. This objective was achieved at various times by the employment of such formulas as "revolutionary legality," "revolutionary expedience," and "socialist concept of law." At the same time many legal authorities felt free to write of the "withering away" of law and to question its value and prospective usefulness in the U.S.S.R. Professor Stuchka, erstwhile dean of Soviet jurists, declared in 1927 that communism meant "not the victory of socialist law, but the victory of socialism over any law," since law will disappear when classes are abolished.

These views, not conducive at best to any high respect for law, required clarification by the late thirties, when it was officially stated that the Soviet Union had entered the phase of "completing" the establishment of a classless society. Such clarification came in 1937–38 through the medium of a thundering condemnation by Andrei Vyshinsky of all negative expressions concerning the form, content, or viability of Soviet law, which he denounced as legal nihilism, designed to undermine the might of the U.S.S.R. Vyshinsky, prosecutor in the purge trials who became the most trusted jurist of the regime, called for a positive interest in the study and development of law and for the complete mastery of its science and technique. Deprecating all predictions of the extinction of law in the foreseeable future, he instead urged its utmost strengthening. In so doing he invoked Stalin's statement, of December, 1936, declaring the need for "stability of laws" and explaining that such stability makes for "the durability of the state order, the durability of state discipline." [4] Also, in view of the now anticipated classlessness, Vyshinsky modified for the future the prevailing thesis that law in the U.S.S.R. was the will of the proletariat as the dominant class. "In such conditions," said he, "the place of the *class* is taken by the *people, the toilers.*" Consequently the present definition of Soviet law reads:

> Socialist law of the epoch of conclusion of socialist construction and the gradual transition from socialism to communism is a system of rules of conduct (norms) established in legislative order by the rule of the toilers and expressing their will, the will of the entire Soviet people, which is led by the working class headed by the Communist party (Bolsheviks), for the purpose of defending, strengthening, and developing socialistic relations and for the gradual construction of the Communist society.[5]

[4] Vyshinsky, op. cit., p. 54.
[5] Andrei Vyshinsky, "The XVIII Congress of the CPSU(B) and the Tasks of the Science of Socialist Law," *Sovetskoe Gosudarstvo i Pravo,* 3 (1939), pp. 9–10.

The revision of the concepts of state and law embraced also the "fundamental law"—the Soviet constitution. It is now held that the constitution will continue to exist in the U.S.S.R. even when communism is attained, as long as the state itself continues to exist. This reversal in theory is expected to enhance greatly the authority of public statutes in the Soviet social order. However, the Soviet leaders have never been willing to regard law—even the fundamental law—as an absolute category transcending the power of the government itself.

2. STRUCTURE OF SOCIETY

The Social Pattern. The social theory that prevailed in the U.S.S.R. during the first two decades was a theory of a society in conflict. The Bolsheviks proclaimed the political rule, which they established, a "dictatorship of the proletariat" designed to suppress and eliminate the formerly dominant classes and to lead the other social strata toward a "classless" society. To be sure, the Bolsheviks also called their government a "workers' and peasants' government." But that terminology, it was explained, was applicable only because the proletariat sought to associate the other toilers in its struggle to forge an "alliance" with the basic mass of the peasantry. Dictatorship of the proletariat could mean only "the rule of *one* class"—the proletariat—and with it the "conquest of the bourgeoisie" and the neutralization of the other classes. In the pursuit of this policy (according to official theory), after the early elimination of the landlords and the city capitalists, differential treatment was applied to the poor, "middle," and rich peasants (by associating the first outright with the regime, by gradually winning over the "middle" peasants, who became the great majority of the collectivized peasantry, and by liquidating the rich peasants, or kulaks, during 1928–34). Parts of the older intelligentsia were progressively drawn to the regime and merged with a newly created intelligentsia. By 1934–36 the class structure was considered so radically changed in official eyes as to make the then-existing social theory no longer suitable.

From Class Conflict to Class Peace. The new social theory—pronounced at that time—is a theory of a society in harmony. This theory does not state that all classes have already been abolished in the U.S.S.R. But it claims that "antagonistic" classes have been eliminated and that only two classes now remain, the workers and the peasants, who live in friendship among themselves and with the large stratum of the intelligentsia (which Marxist theory persistently refused to regard as a class). Although the new constitution expressly declares that the U.S.S.R. is "a socialist state of workers and peasants" (Article 1), it is still official theory that the dictatorship—defined as "state guidance of society"—continued. But the phrase now in official vogue is "dictatorship of the working class," rather than "dictatorship of the proletariat," because with public ownership of the means of production the Soviet workers are no longer a "proletariat."

Two points of emphasis stand out particularly in the present theory: that complete harmony prevails among the present social groups and that remaining class differences are vanishing and the community is in the process of becoming a unified "society of toilers." The cycle in theory thus represents a complex progression from class struggle through class differentiation to class peace, and on to prospective classlessness.

The Changing Social Strata: Workers, Peasants, Intelligentsia. Vast shifts have taken place in the Russian social structure in the period between the two world wars. With the socialization of land, industry, and trade the large estate holders and rich peasants in the country-side and the private industrialists and merchants in the cities, comprising about 16 per cent of the population, were entirely eliminated. The peasantry, comprising 77.4 per cent of the populace in 1913, was reduced to 46.4 per cent by 1939 and less than 40 per cent by 1956. As compared with 1913 the number of workers increased almost two and a half times by 1939, from around 14 per cent to 32.2 per cent—while "employees" or so-called intelligentsia (clerks, officials, managers, technicians, professionals, etc.) increased nearly sixfold to 17.5 per cent. In 1956 official figures gave the percentage of collectivized peasants and craftsmen in co-operatives as 41.2, non-collectivized peasants and independent craftsmen as one half per cent, and workers together with "employees" as 58.3 per cent—an 8.6 per cent increase over 1939 due largely to the growth of the intelligentsia.[6]

The program of industrializing the country, collectivizing agriculture, and mechanizing the processes of work, inaugurated on a large scale with the first Five Year Plan and still continuing, has called for further changes in the social structure. It calls for fewer peasants, more workers, and more people with technical and professional training.

One result of this program was the encouragement of migration from rural to urban areas, which contributed to altering the ratio between the village and city populations from 85 and 15 per cent respectively in 1914 to 67.2 and 32.8 per cent in 1939, 56.6 and 43.4 per cent by 1956.

Another consequence was the tremendous expansion of educational facilities. Universal compulsory education was introduced at the end of the first Five Year Plan, with particular attention given to the establishment of additional secondary and higher educational institutions. By 1954 the number of *tekhnikums,* or middle technical schools, was 4,000 with over 1,600,000 students in attendence, as compared with 295 such schools training 36,000 students in 1917. Between 1917 and 1941 the number of colleges and universities increased from 90 to 782, and the number of students attending them from 111,000 to 564,000. Although many of these schools were destroyed or ceased to operate during the war, official claims have been made that all higher educational institutions had been

[6] For a detailed discussion of the changes in the social structure see Julian Towster, *Political Power in the U.S.S.R., 1917–1947* (1948), pp. 28–49, 313–36.

restored by 1947–48 and that by 1955 the number of students reached the figure of 1,865,000 in 798 colleges and universities.

Still another by-product of the intensified industrialization program was the establishment of the system of labor reserves. On October 2, 1940, a decree was passed authorizing the annual drafting of from 800,000 to 1,000,000 young people between the ages of fourteen to seventeen, to be trained in factory and trade schools as semi-skilled and skilled laborers. On June 19, 1947, another decree raised to eighteen and nineteen the age limit for trainees in mining, oil, and certain other industries. The training period ranges from six months in factory schools for semi-skilled workers to two or three years for skilled laborers in trade and railroad schools. After graduation the draftees are assigned to work for four years at regular workers' wages in mines, mills, factories, etc. Although cities are required to provide annually determined quotas of trainees, the rural population contributes the bulk of the draftees, who are recruited on the basis of two youths for every hundred persons between the ages of fourteen and fifty-five. With huge losses of skilled and semi-skilled workers during the war, the labor reserve training system was given additional impetus in the postwar period. While the anticipated increase to 6,000 schools graduating yearly 1.5 million students has not materialized, the number of labor reserve schools grew from 2,700 to 3,152 by 1956, turning out annually 750,000 graduates. These schools have graduated a total of eight million workers. In addition millions of unskilled workers were receiving vocational training, while even greater numbers were required to improve their skills. Finally, in view of continuing shortages of skilled manpower, as well as the fact that higher educational institutions were able to accommodate only 450,000 freshmen yearly as against the 700,000 ten-year school graduates of 1957, a school reform was proposed by Soviet leader Khrushchev in 1958, which will subject pupils in secondary schools to regular vocational training as well as periods of compulsory work in factory or farm. These and other measures were intended to replenish the industrial labor force and to satisfy the pressure for its continuing expansion.

The requirements of the economic program inaugurated under the Five Year Plan suggested to the Soviet leaders the necessity of psycho-political readjustment. Hitherto the doctrine of "proletarian dictatorship" put the working class on a social pedestal and endowed it politically with a privileged status. This exclusive position was expressed in a sharp discrimination in favor of city dwellers as against rural voters in representation in the soviets, and in preferential treatment of workers in the party, the army, and other government institutions. Thus, although as late as 1939 workers and their families constituted no more than 32.2 per cent of the population, the percentage of workers reached 68.2 in the party and 71.2 at the Party Congress in 1930, rose to 47.6 per cent and 54.4 per cent respectively at the federal Central Executive Committee and Congress of Soviets by 1931, and comprised 45.8 per cent of the rank and file and 42.3 per cent of the officers of the army in 1933.

At the same time, the war waged by the regime against various sections of the peasantry for over a decade and a half was reflected in the restricted political participation by the peasants. The limited representation in political institutions of this large social stratum—which even after collectivization comprised almost half of the population—can be seen in the following comparative percentages for peasant members: in the party 20.4 per cent and in the Party Congress 6.7 per cent in 1930; in the federal Central Executive Committee and Congress of Soviets 16.3 per cent and 25.6 per cent respectively in 1931. By 1935 the percentages had fallen still lower. In the army, traditionally largely peasant in composition, the percentage of peasants among the rank and file was stated to have declined progressively from 71.3 per cent in 1926 to 42.5 per cent by 1933.

Although the intelligentsia, which by 1939 constituted 17.5 per cent of the population, was better represented in government than was the peasantry, it was treated with considerable distrust, and during the twenties its share of political participation likewise decreased quantitatively. Between 1923 and 1930, the percentage of members of the intelligentsia fell from 25.7 per cent to about 11.4 per cent in the party, and from 34.4 per cent to 22.1 per cent in the Party Congress. Between 1922 and 1931, it decreased from 40.4 per cent to 36.1 per cent in the Central Executive Committee, and from 28.8 per cent to 20.0 per cent in the Congress of Soviets.

If the much-needed professional and technical skills of the frequently persecuted intelligentsia were to be enlisted in the gigantic projects of industrialization, and if the kolkhoz peasantry—many of whose members were forcibly brought into the collectives—were to be pacified and induced to participate more willingly in the radically novel agricultural program, these groups of the population had to be placed, legally at least, on an equal footing with the working class.

In June, 1931, Stalin called not only for the training of a new "working-class intelligentsia," but for a more friendly attitude toward the old intelligentsia. Three years later the restrictions on education for children of the formerly dominant classes were abolished, and in 1936 the new constitution eliminated all suffrage and other inequalities between workers and peasants. The elections to the soviets in 1937, and all subsequent ones, have been officially conducted in the name of a "bloc of Communists and nonparty people," while the Party Congress in March, 1939, specifically equalized entrance into the party for workers, peasants, and the intelligentsia. This action was formally based on the new theory that "nonparty Bolsheviks," i.e., persons absolutely loyal to the party's cause, exist among all strata of the population.

In consequence of these and other measures the workers' share in government has decreased, while that of the intelligentsia has proportionately increased. The meager figures available for the thirties show a 10-per-cent increase in representation of the intelligentsia in the Central Executive Committee, the Congress of Soviets (1931–35), and the Party Congress (1930–34).[7] More recent data are provided by the elections to the soviets. Although the percentage of peasant representa-

---

[7] See Towster, op. cit., pp. 327–28.

tives in the village soviets elected in 1939 was 65.9 per cent, the intelligentsia predominated in the city soviets, where they constituted 55.6 per cent as against 38.9 per cent workers and 5.5 per cent peasants. In the regional soviets the intelligentsia also accounted for 44.9 per cent, the workers for 26.8 per cent, and the peasants for 28.3 per cent of the delegates. In the Supreme Soviet of the U.S.S.R., elected in 1937, the percentages stood as follows: workers 42 per cent; peasants 29.5 per cent; intelligentsia 28.5 per cent. In the 1946 elections to this body the respective percentages changed in favor of the intelligentsia in the following manner: workers 39 per cent; peasants 26 per cent; intelligentsia 35 per cent. The percentages in the Supreme Soviet elected in 1954 (computed from the absolute figures) were: workers 23.6 per cent; peasants 16.3 per cent; intelligentsia 60.1 per cent. These figures indicate a sharp rise for the last-named group.

In the eyes of the Soviet leaders the very considerations that necessitated greater political equalization dictated at the same time greater socioeconomic differentiation. This change in policy was heralded in the usual way by a pronouncement from Stalin. In a statement on June 23, 1931, he blamed the vast labor turnover, with its harmful effects on production, on "the 'Leftist' leveling in the sphere of wages," which had virtually wiped out all distinctions between skilled and unskilled labor. To make sure that skilled workers would stay at their jobs instead of moving around from place to place, he argued that it was necessary to raise their wage norms in order to reward their skills properly. This step, aside from all other benefits, would be designed "to open up a perspective before the unskilled workers and to give them a stimulus for moving upward, for moving into the category of the skilled."

The system of incentives instituted with this pronouncement entailed, not only a change to piece-rate wages, with prizes and bonuses for above-norm productivity, but also the extensive use of decorations, orders, and titles, and in some services, of uniforms and ranks. Millions of citizens were decorated with orders and medals during the war, and many thousands have since received titles carrying both economic privileges and social prestige. Aside from various war service decorations, ranks and uniforms were introduced in 1943 for diplomats, procurators, and railroad personnel, and in 1944 awards were established even for mothers of large families. Generally this system of incentives has been expanded in the postwar period, and it included additions of a number of awards for performance in agriculture, announced in April, 1949. In subsequent months there followed the introduction of ranks and uniforms for officials of the Ministry of State Control, for engineers, technicians, and officials in the Chief Administration of Geodetics and Cartography, and for many others.

These measures have resulted in considerable socioeconomic differences, felt particularly by the unskilled and lowest-paid workers because of the still-prevailing low standard of living and the perennial shortages of consumers' goods. The differences between high and low earnings have ranged widely, in some instances reaching ratios as great as thirty or forty to one, or even higher. From the standpoint of actual buying capacity, wages had decreased in the period of the first Five Year Plan, increased between 1935–38, and fallen drastically during the recent war, probably as much as 40 per cent. Although social services constitute a compensatory feature to some extent and living conditions have been improving in slow degrees in the postwar years, average earnings in terms of purchasing power remain exceedingly low by Western standards.

The range of material and social rewards and emoluments appears to point up the inferior condition of unskilled labor. Such factors as the inheritance laws, which permit the transmission of savings to heirs, and the October 2, 1940, decree (subsequently rescinded on June 6, 1956), which introduced fees for attendance in the higher grades of the secondary schools and in the colleges and universities, seemed to point in the same direction, since wage earners in the lower brackets would find it more difficult to give their children a higher education. The totality of these measures of socioeconomic differentiation led some observers to conclude that a stratified society of "caste" or "class" has emerged in the U.S.S.R., with the managerial groups of the intelligentsia as the new ruling class, seeking to freeze a hereditary privileged status for itself and to bar the road to higher education and positions of responsibility against workers and peasants.[8]

Although such a development is entirely possible, it is premature to conclude that it has already been consummated. To be sure, until Stalin's passing, membership turnover at the party's higher levels was limited, and at its summit—the Party Presidium and Secretariat—it was stationary for many years. But as the subsequent changes have shown the freezing of status was not conclusive. As far as the intelligentsia is concerned, it is more correct to state that it has been absorbed in large measure into the party and Soviet organs than that it has become the ruling class. As a social stratum it is predominantly new in composition—a product of the educational campaigns carried on since the thirties—and it is given such a broad definition that it includes factory foremen, accountants, nurses, record-breaking workers, and others without any intellectual attainments, though increasingly with technical schooling. Far from being permitted any independent political line, the intelligentsia is not only continuously indoctrinated but is pressed into the service of indoctrinating the rest of the populace, as the activities of the Society for the Dissemination of Political and Scientific Knowledge (formed in 1947 and now counting 40,000 active members and 20,000 alternates) amply demonstrate. Along with the factor of ideological conditioning, the economic differentials that exist within the ranks of the intelligentsia have so far evidently worked against any

[8] On this question compare the following expositions: G. Bienstock, S. M. Schwartz, and A. Yugow, *Management in Russian Industry and Agriculture* (1944), pp. 28–30, 111–12, 121–24; Nicholas S. Timasheff, *The Great Retreat* (1946), pp. 295–311, 389–90; Barrington Moore, Jr., *Soviet Politics—The Dilemma of Power* (1950), pp. 236–46, 407; Alex Inkeles, "Social Stratification and Mobility in the Soviet Union, 1940–1950," *American Sociological Review*, 15 (August, 1950).

marked consciousness of class solidarity within it. And despite the
fact that its services are greatly needed, past experience shows that
it is often expendable, that it can be purged, cajoled, and controlled
by party leaders. Actually, the standing of the members of this stratum
depends ultimately upon loyalty, skill, and performance, rather than
upon social origin.

Finally, several illuminating facts seem to militate against too
broad an interpretation of the consequences of socioeconomic differentiation at this stage. The evening secondary schools, established during the war to enable young people to complete their studies, which had
been interrupted by war service, have been made a permanent part of
the educational system. In 1946–47 there were in operation some 2,000
evening secondary schools for young workers, with around 375,000
pupils, and 5,000 such schools for young peasants, with 200,000 pupils.[9] It is estimated that during 1943–48 the schools of working youth
graduated 50,000 persons with a secondary-school education and 150,-
000 with a seven-year and primary education, while the schools of
rural youth graduated about 24,000 with a seven-year education and
over 75,000 with a primary education. Together with the network of
adult study courses and correspondence schools—which is being expanded further under the new school reform—and with the system of
scholarships for able students, these schools enable some working children of unskilled and lower-paid citizens to go on to institutions of
higher learning. Thus, although the opportunities for these groups to
pass into the ranks of the intelligentsia have substantially diminished,
they have not been eliminated altogether, and the ambitious, able, and
physically sturdy can still rise through extra effort and application.
Aptitude and loyalty to the regime are the chief criteria for recruitment. With the expanding activities of the state and the consequent
need for professional and technical personnel, it is hardly likely that
the ranks of the intelligentsia will be sealed off to newcomers from
the other strata in the near future.

Control over social mobility lies with the party direction. Even the
right of inheritance is no absolute guarantee of an ability to bequeath
to heirs such permanent advantages as a distinct social position. Outside
the constitutionally imposed duty to work, such developments as the
December 15, 1947, currency and price reform reveal a great deal concerning the Soviet government's powers—and intentions—with regard to
the social strata. With one sweep, through its deliberately unequal de-
valuation of different kinds of money, that reform wiped out the cash
hoards and large savings accumulated by collective farmers and others
during the war and distinctly favored the urban workers at the expense
of the peasants in regard to both savings and current income. The 1957
industrial reorganization was a body blow to numerous economic managers who lost their comfortable city berths. The educational reform
of 1958 (as well as the law against "anti-social and parasitic elements"
enacted in several republics) is directed in part against idling sons and

[9] See Nicolas Hans, "Recent Trends in Soviet Education," *Annals of the
American Academy of Political and Social Science,* 263 (May, 1949), pp. 118–19.

daughters of the managerial intelligentsia. Acts such as these, the strict labor discipline enforced upon the workers, and the consecrated service exacted from the managers—ultimately backed by sanctions that might include compulsory labor in the so-called correctional camps—serve as reminders that the destinies of all the social strata continue to be shaped by the small group of highest party leaders.

The Position of Women: Emphasis on Equality. Women in the U.S.S.R. are by the constitution guaranteed equal rights with men "in all spheres of economic, state, cultural, social, and political life" (Article 22). In contrast to their underprivileged position in old Russia a status of legal equality has been extended to them from the inception of the new regime. This fact, along with their numerical preponderance in the population, is responsible for their participation in many new fields of activity.

Though women are heavily underrepresented in government in proportion to their percentage of the populace, their participation in Soviet political life has gradually increased. At the Party Congress the percentage of women rose from 9.1 in 1939 to 12.3 in 1952 and 14.2 in 1956. In the central Soviet legislative bodies the percentage of women delegates increased from 3.5 per cent in the Congress of Soviets in 1922 to 21 per cent in 1936, and from 21 per cent in the Supreme Soviet in 1946 to 25.8 in 1954. In the local soviets the percentage of women members increased from a few per cent in the early twenties to 32.9 per cent in 1939. By 1955 there were over 540,000 women (35.2 per cent) in the local soviets, while 2,209 women were deputies of the supreme soviets of the union and autonomous republics. In the executive and administrative branches of the government women generally have scant representation. Only after 1956 was a woman (Furtseva) included in the all-important Party Presidium.

More notable than their share in politics has been the increased role of women in the professions and in the economic life of the country. Recent Soviet statistics list over a million women as teachers, about three million in scientific, cultural, and educational pursuits, and more than two million women in public health and physical culture work. Over one million women have been awarded orders and medals; 2,373 have received the titles Hero of Socialist Labor and Hero of the Soviet Union, and 746 hold Stalin prizes in science, literature, and art. In 1917 there were 940,000 women workers in industry; by 1937 this number had increased tenfold to 9,357,000, or nearly 35 per cent of all the workers and employees. Further increases in the number of women employed in various branches of the economy took place during the war, and this trend was not entirely reversed at the end of hostilities. In 1947 women constituted 47 per cent of the wage earners in all spheres of labor.

Since the beginning of the thirties women have in fact become one of the main reserves of the Soviet labor force in industry, agriculture, and transport. Soviet publicists stress the fact that women work together with men in all undertakings, including underground coal mining and similar heavy occupations. If such tasks underline the official emphasis on woman's equal status, they likewise bear witness to the less publicized equality of sacrifice increasingly borne by women in the U.S.S.R.

The Role of Young People: Stress on Service and Advancement. Since Soviet society is comparatively young in its age composition, the emphasis on youth has been strong in all fields in the U.S.S.R. The 1939 census showed that over three fifths of the people were under thirty, and, despite the losses of younger persons between 1939–45, more than half of the Soviet postwar population (according to an official statement of January, 1946), consisted of persons in their early thirties.

In their revolutionary transformation of society the Soviet leaders felt it necessary to capture and harness the zeal of the younger generation. During the first Five Year Plan hundreds of thousands of young people were trained for industrial, technical, and managerial tasks. In the aftermath of the 1936–38 purges, and during the recent war period, many of these young specialists stepped into positions of responsibility in industry, agriculture, administration, and the army. For these reasons most of the Soviet economic managers and generals were in their thirties and early forties at the time of the recent conflict.

The accent on youth has continued in the postwar period. In the constantly expanding network of labor reserve schools, secondary technical institutions, universities, and war colleges, millions of youths are undergoing intensive training. In the early stages of the economic plans strong reliance was placed on ideological-spiritual motives to induce voluntarism on the part of the youth. Since that time greater use has been made of material incentives, such as the prospects of good salaries, bonuses, and promotions. However, both types of motivation are utilized to extract the maximum in service and devotion from the younger citizens. Hundreds of thousands of those who won awards during and after the war years are relatively young persons.

In the post-Stalin period several hundred thousand young people have been induced to work and settle in Siberia and Kazakhstan in connection with the "virgin lands" program which has brought some additional 90 million acres of land under cultivation. And the educational reform proposed by Premier and First Secretary of the Party Khrushchev in April, 1958, with its emphasis on vocational training and actual work experience in industry and agriculture, is designed in part to meet the current problem of a labor shortage in connection with plans to establish another steel center and expand virgin lands cultivation in Siberia.

Long before it emerged in other fields of activity, the tendency to enlist and advance the youth was evidenced in the party organs and in the soviets, where persons under forty years of age have constituted the overwhelming majority of the members. Despite considerable postwar disillusionment among the citizenry and the evidence of so-called "unhealthy political attitudes" among youth, which came to the surface following the October-November, 1956, events in Poland and Hungary, the younger groups are regarded as a main prop of the regime, and the accent on youth is likely to continue.

The New Standing of the Family: The Return to Older Values. Closely related to the problem of the status of women and young people in Soviet society is that of the family. In few fields of Soviet life has the reversal of policy been greater, or the return to older values more complete, than in the field of family relations.

Until the mid-thirties official attitudes were anything but encouraging to the institution of the family. Basically they rested on Engels' view that, as an economic unit, the family will end with the socialization of the means of production, since housekeeping and the upbringing of children will then become public functions.[1] Engels also favored freedom of separation for the partners in marriage. Years later Lenin likewise thought that "it is impossible to be a socialist and a democrat without immediately demanding complete freedom of divorce." [2] Although neither Engels nor Lenin visualized the disappearance of monogamous marriage, and although Lenin even believed that freedom of divorce would make family relations more stable, Madame Alexandra Kollontay, later renowned as a Soviet diplomat, wrote in 1919 that "the family has ceased to be a necessity for both its members and the state." Other prominent old Bolsheviks held similar views, and the undisguised appeal to passion in Madame Kollontay's writings on the family under communism was echoed in many novels during the twenties. Even Soviet juridical writings of the period stressed the dissolubility of the marital ties and envisioned the ultimate end of the family as a source of rights and duties between spouses, parents, and children in the socialist state.

These attitudes both affected and reflected Soviet legislation on the subject. In 1917 civil marriage by act of simple registration with the civil authorities was substituted for religious marriage. The code enacted in 1926 made even mere de-facto marriage, without registration, the basis of all recognized rights of property and succession. A divorce could be secured with ease on the application of only one of the parties, without any statement of grounds. Children born out of wedlock enjoyed the same rights as those born in registered marriage vis-à-vis both parents. Neither in law nor in prevailing practice was much support given to parental responsibility or authority.

A reversal of attitude began in the mid-thirties. The responsibility of the parents for the acts of their children, which inevitably demanded greater parental authority, was decreed in 1935. In 1936 the performance of an abortion was made a crime, though the expectant mother's responsibility was abrogated in 1954. And minor restrictions were placed upon divorce. Then came the law of July 8, 1944, which radically altered the whole pattern of family relations. In accordance with its provisions and subsequent implementing legislation, only an officially

[1] See Friedrich Engels, *The Origin of the Family, Private Property and the State* (1942), pp. 61–73.
[2] Lenin, *Sochinenia*, Vol. XIX, p. 232.

registered marriage creates legal rights of spouses and parenthood. A child born of an unregistered marriage has no right to support or inheritance from the father or to the use of his name, though the unwed mother can receive a small state allowance for the child or can place it in a public institution. Only a court can entertain a petition for divorce. The court of first instance, the people's court, inquires into the reasons for the request and attempts to reconcile the parties; the next higher court considers the case and grants or refuses a divorce at its own discretion. Judges are enjoined to grant divorces only on the most serious grounds, as when the family relationship appears to have disintegrated beyond hope; moreover, divorce fees have been substantially raised.

In addition to these legal regulations vigorous propaganda in every form fosters the new attitude toward family relations. Early writings on free love, such as those by Madame Kollontay, are denounced as incitement to sexual license and hence as fraught with dire consequences for the Soviet social order. Early sex education was rejected as harmful and coeducation was partially abolished during the war, though it was again introduced in 1954. Popular literature and legal writings endlessly stress the theme that a lifelong union in marriage, resting on love and respect between parents and blessed with many children, is a fundamental Soviet ideal.

There were two principal reasons for this reversal of policy. The first was the Soviet desire to encourage an increase in population. A large part of the blame for the population deficit discovered in the mid-thirties (around thirteen millions in terms of expectations) was apparently laid by the Soviet leaders to the high abortion and divorce rates. The resulting drop in the birth rate was deemed a threat, in view of the mounting manpower needs of the state. In 1936 state aid for mothers was decreed on the birth of a seventh child. The law of 1944 went far beyond this, not only instituting payments on the birth of a third child, but also establishing the orders and medals Mother Hero, Mother's Glory, and Medal of Motherhood for mothers of large families. Distinct material benefits accompany these awards, and protective legislation for pregnant women workers and working mothers has also been extended. Recent figures indicate that under this program 4,500,000 women have received the Mother's Glory Order and the Medal of Motherhood, and 44,000 have received the honor title of Mother Heroine.[3]

The second and more important reason for the new policy was the belated realization on the part of the Soviet leaders that, even in a rigidly controlled society such as the U.S.S.R., the family is the foundation of the social order and the home the matrix of civic attitudes. Widespread hooliganism and waywardness in the thirties were painful reminders that sex laxness, filial disobedience, and the lack of firm attachments were poor foundations for labor discipline or for an attitude of respect for political authority, particularly in a society where disci-

[3] *Pravda* and *Izvestia*, March 5, 1955.

pline was the keystone of all civic relations. Order, self-control, and co-operation learned in the family circle carry over into the outer environment of workshop, club, and government. Hence, far from tolerating talk of the disappearance of the family, the official stand at present is that the state must take the greatest interest in strengthening and perfecting the institutions of marriage and the family.

Admitting the validity of Engels' statement that in a Communist society "the relations of the sexes will become a private matter that concerns only the interested parties and with which society will not interfere," Soviet writers now claim that Engels properly had in mind only the much later phase of the period of definitive communism. A recent Soviet commentator has declared that "one cannot speak of the life and fate of a single family as something personal, independent, or isolated." The Soviet family is a small part of the Soviet state, and their lives and fates are bound together. Since man "is not born brave or cowardly, labor-loving or an idler, patriot or traitor," the family inevitably plays a most important role in fostering desirable qualities and attitudes in the future citizens. In view of this role, it is currently emphasized, the state's right of intervention in family relations must remain paramount.[4]

Thus the present Soviet policy is a complex amalgam of lessons learned from the past coupled with the often contradictory demands of the present. Although further changes in legislation and official attitudes on particular aspects of the problem are not excluded, the basic return to the traditional values of family, motherhood, and parental authority seems destined to persist in the future.

The Status of the Church: Conditional Accommodation.   A change less far-reaching or stable in nature has likewise occurred in the policy of the Soviet government toward the church. The first two decades of Soviet rule were marked by an intermittent struggle against organized religion, in general, and against the once-powerful Russian Orthodox Church in particular. The intimate relationship between that church and tsardom,[5] the basic Marxist beliefs of the new rulers that "religion is the opium of the people" and a tool of the oppressing classes, and the fear of these rulers that religion would offer strong competition to the total claim of the regime's ideology upon the outlook and loyalty of the citizenry were all factors that probably made this struggle inevitable. But its immediate point of departure was the Soviet decree, in January, 1918 that disestablished the church and confiscated all church properties, and the proclamation of Patriarch Tikhon—newly elected by a sobor then in session—which declared anathema against the Soviet regime and called upon the faithful to oppose it. In the bitter conflict that ensued many members of the church supported the Whites, but the Soviet government resorted to violent repression, to the closing of churches, to relentless propaganda, and later, in 1923, to the encourage-

---

[4] See Z. Guseva, "Two Forms of the Family and Two Conceptions of Morality," *Oktiabr'*, No. 7 (July, 1949), pp. 158–76.
[5] See above, pp. 548–50.

ment of schismatic groups, such as the Living Church, to crush the resistance of organized religion and to undermine the faith of the believers. The government's attacks were particularly sharp in 1923–24, and again in 1928–29 during the collectivization drive in the countryside. Many clergymen were also apprehended in the purges of 1937–38, though on the whole the violence had subsided in the thirties.

The regime succeeded in breaking the power of the church, but religious faith survived in many sections of the country. From 1917 to 1941 the number of Orthodox churches was reduced from 46,457 to 4,225, the number of priests from 50,960 to 5,665, and the number of monasteries from 1,026 to 38. For all denominations there were only about 8,300 places of worship on the eve of the war. Yet the number of believers was estimated to exceed a hundred million, or more than half of the population in the early thirties, and must have been quite high in 1941.

These facts contributed to a somewhat milder policy on the part of the government, which was expressed particularly through the restoration of the franchise to the clergy in the 1936 constitution. At the same time, however, religious propaganda continued to be prohibited. Though the preceding federal constitution of 1923 did not cover the subject, the 1918 constitution provided in Article 13: "To insure for the toilers religious freedom, the church is separated from the state and the school from the church, and freedom of religious and antireligious propaganda is secured to all citizens." Until 1929, this provision was contained in the constitutions of all the union republics, but in that year the article was amended so as to eliminate the phrase "freedom of religious and antireligious propaganda" and to substitute the words "freedom of religious persuasion and antireligious propaganda." This phraseology was essentially that later embodied in the new constitution. In point of fact the church generally refrained from open propagation of the faith and attempted to live within the narrow limits of the law, which restricted it to mere practice of the cult. Although the government's antireligious propaganda continued, it slackened considerably in the thirties, and the membership of the League of Militant Atheists—established in 1925 to carry on this propaganda—dropped from some ten million in 1932 to around three million by 1940.

The coming of the war brought a notable change in the attitude of the government, which was anxious to gain the support of all groups of the populace in the armed conflict. The Orthodox Church, whose example was followed by the other denominations, rallied its adherents behind the government, collected over three hundred million rubles for the army, condemned collaboration with the invader, and pledged absolute loyalty to the regime, even going so far as to call Stalin publicly the "God-willed leader." On several occasions the church served as a vehicle of Soviet policy, acting particularly as an instrument of opposition to the Vatican and as an avenue of Soviet influence in the Slav world. On its side the government showed its conciliatory mood by a number of acts, more particularly by suspending the atheist publications in 1941 and by consenting to the re-establishment of the Holy Synod and the election of a patriarch in September, 1943. On the death of the latter the government even sent its official representative to the sobor in 1945, where Patriarch Alexei was elected in the presence of representatives of the Eastern patriarchates and Orthodox churches abroad. In October, 1943, and June, 1944, respectively, the Council for the Affairs of the Russian Orthodox Church and the Council for Affairs of the Religious Denominations were set up by the government for the purpose of regular liaison with the Orthodox and other churches.

This relationship has continued into the postwar period. The concessions made to the church have conciliated a large body of believers, and through its newly opened channels the re-established patriarchate has a measure of influence for the Soviet Union in Orthodox communities abroad, especially in the Balkans. The newly recognized standing of the Russian Orthodox Church made it easier for it to reinstitute its ecclesiastical authority over schismatic groups, the Uniates of western Ukraine and scattered Orthodox churches throughout the world. Essentially the church's gain lies in its greater ability to obtain physical facilities for worship and for training priests. Although permission was promised during the war to clergymen to give private instruction to groups of children, it does not appear that more than a limited application of this privilege has been granted. Nor does there seem to be any prospect for freedom of religious propaganda. An authoritative postwar statement makes it clear that "any kind of propagandizing, moralizing, and educational activity" beyond the bounds of a given community is not within the province of the church, which is "an association of believers created and existing solely for the conduct of religious worship." [6]

Thus, though the position of the church has improved, the changed relationship is not of such a nature as to amount to a permanent reconciliation between church and state. Soviet spokesmen openly point out that the party "never concealed and does not conceal its negative attitude toward religion" and that, together with the *Komsomol,* the schools, and other public institutions, it is dedicated to "the overcoming of religious prejudices." [7] Appeals have again appeared since the end of the war urging an intensification of the fight against religion. Elaborate theses are once more presented that religion has no roots in the Soviet social structure, that religious survivals play a harmful role, and that consequently it is the duty of the intelligentsia (the Soviet teacher, in particular), to be "an active *propagandist of Godlessness* among others, the bearer of ideas of militant proletarian atheism." [8]

The forces of communism and religion stand fundamentally opposed to each other in the U.S.S.R. Although the compromise between state and church arrived at during the war is likely to continue to be accepted, it permits only a conditional accommodation, since it rests,

[6] A. Kolosov, "Religion and Church in the USSR," *Bol'shaia Sovetskaia Entsiklopedia, Soiuz Sovetskikh Sotsialisticheskikh Respublik* (1947), pp. 1783–84.

[7] Ibid., pp. 1781–82.

[8] See F. Oleshchuk, "Religion—A Reactionary Ideology," *Uchitel'skaya Gazeta* (November 26, 1949), p. 2; "Religious Survivals and Ways of Overcoming Them," *Voprosy Filosofii,* No. 6 (1954), pp. 76–88.

basically, on the limited and subservient role devised for the church
and on the assumption of the Soviet leaders that the church's strength
will diminish rather than increase in the coming years.

The Ethnic Pattern: The Cycle in the Nationality Theory.   The
Soviet nationality theory is less a product of orthodox Marxist philosophy
than of a conceptual strategy evolved by the Soviet leaders to meet the
exigencies of a highly variegated multinational society.

The founders of Marxism were convinced internationalists and
strong opponents of nationalism. Believing that large industrialized economies are propellers of progress and steppingstones to world socialism
and that only large, centralized states are capable of organizing such
economies, they rejected both federalism and national self-determination
for small peoples as a matter of principle. Admitting some exceptions,
largely on tactical grounds, they held forth as the ideal state organization for the proletariat "the one and indivisible republic."

Following in their footsteps, Lenin and the other Bolshevik leaders
likewise favored maximum centralization of political power and, prior
to the revolution, rejected the idea of federation for Russia. But, unlike
Marx and Engels, they strongly advocated self-determination for small
nations, interpreting it after 1913 as a "right of secession and formation
of an independent state." This difference in approach did not rest on
any difference in attitude toward nationalism. Lenin adhered to the view
that Marxism and nationalism were irreconcilable, that "in place of
any nationalism Marxism proposes internationalism—the amalgamation
of all nations in a supreme unity." [9] But he vigorously sought and secured his party's support for the self-determination principle in the
double belief that it would contribute to the downfall of the tsarist empire and that, after such collapse, the separating nationalities would
voluntarily come together again under the impact of socialism in Russia.
At bottom his attitude on self-determination was also conditioned by his
conviction that of the two tendencies in the modern epoch—the sprouting
of nationalism and national states on the one hand, and the growth of
international intercourse, with the consequent breakdown of national
barriers on the other—the first was bound to continue strong, and national differences would remain in existence for a long time.

In tsarist Russia such differences were exacerbated by practices
that earned for the country the name of "the prison of nations." The
dominant slogans of tsarism—"One Tsar, One Religion, One Language," "Autocracy, Orthodoxy, Nationalism," "Russia One and Indivisible"—spelled political oppression, economic exploitation, and forcible
Russification for the ethnic minorities. *Divide et impera,* setting the nationalities against one another, was a standard political stratagem; and
the periphery peoples of the empire, particularly those of the east, were
kept in extreme backwardness. These practices left a heritage of enmity
and bitterness among the nationalities. Under the circumstances Lenin
thought that the Bolshevik slogan of self-determination to the point of

[9] Lenin, *Sochinenia,* Vol. XVII, p. 145.

secession would be politically useful. "We, on our part, do not want separation at all. We want as large a state as possible, as close a union as possible," he confessed in 1917. But in order to bring about such amalgamation voluntarily, he argued, recognition of freedom of secession was necessary. Six months before the seizure of power Lenin expressed this credo in the following terms: "the more decisively our republic recognizes freedom of secession for the non-Great Russian nations, the stronger will other nations be *attracted* toward union with us, the less friction will there be, the rarer will be the cases of actual secession, the shorter will be the period during which some of the nations will remain separated." [1] In short, although he warned that the interests of socialism take precedence over the right of nations to self-determination, he held high hopes that the Finns, Poles, Ukrainians, and other peoples would not want to secede from a socialist Russia.

The centrifugal pull unleashed by the revolution soon proved how exaggerated these expectations were. One after another of the border peoples began to break away and to proclaim their independence. The Bolsheviks quickly reversed their theoretical position on federalism, announcing the establishment of the Soviet federation as a suitable "transitional form" on the road to unity. After the brief period of "treaty relations" that, following the civil-war period, prevailed between the R.S.F.S.R. and the Ukrainian, Byelorussian, Georgian, Armenian, and Azerbaijanian republics, the U.S.S.R. was established at the end of December, 1922. The principle of the right of secession for the uniting republics was embodied in the Union constitution, but—as obviously intended—it has remained throughout a mere formal right. The schemes for dealing with the nationality problem have been accompanied by an evolution in theory, heavily emphasizing the singular monolithism of the entire Soviet people and the basic indivisibility of sovereignty in the U.S.S.R. This development in theory represents a complete cycle engendering once more a concept of state and ethnic structure in the U.S.S.R. that is "one and indivisible" in all fundamental aspects.

The Political Solution: Nationhood in a Soviet Federation. The problem of building a sense of solidarity among the Soviet peoples was complicated not only by the legacy of the past but by the extremely variegated character of the population. There were more than 175 different racial and ethnic groups in the U.S.S.R., speaking some 125 languages. Most of these were small groups, containing only a small percentage of the population. The three main Slav groups, totaling 132 million people, together constituted 78 per cent, or more than three fourths of the total population: the Russians (Great Russians) 58.5 per cent, or 99 million persons; the Ukrainians (Little Russians) 16.5 per cent, or 28 millions; and the Byelorussians (White Russians) 3 per cent, or over 5 millions. The remaining seven national groups, each of which comprised over 1 per cent of the populace, were: the Uzbeks—2.8 per cent, or 5 million people; the Tartars—2.5 per cent, or 4.5 millions; the Kazakhs and Jews—each 1.8 per cent, or 3 millions; and the Azerbaijanians, Geor-

[1] Ibid., Vol. XX, p. 325.

gians, and Armenians—each about 1.3 per cent, or 2 millions. All the other national minority groups together constituted less than 10 per cent of the population.

To keep this medley of nationalities together, a complex solution was devised along political, economic, and cultural lines. The political solution adopted was to grant to the nationalities various forms of separate political self-expression, while balancing these grants by arrangements securing the centralization of authority in practice.

There are three aspects to this solution. First, there is the recognition of equality for the nationalities. The first official pronouncement on the subject, the Declaration of Rights of the Peoples of Russia, on November 15, 1917, promised the nationalities equality and sovereignty; self-determination, including the right of secession; abolition of all national and national-religious privileges or restrictions; and free development for the national minorities and ethnic groups. Like the previous constitutions the 1936 constitution provides for the equality of citizens in all spheres of activity, irrespective of nationality or race (Article 123). The second aspect concerns representation for the national groups in the organs of the federal government. But the most important part of the political solution is its third aspect, the establishment of a network of territorial-administrative units built specifically on the nationality principle. In addition it includes the training of local personnel and staffing of party and government organs, trade unions, co-operatives, and economic enterprises in these national units primarily with their own nationals.

Thus the territorial-administrative structure of the Soviet Union comprises fifty-one distinct national units: fifteen constituent republics, called union republics, eighteen autonomous republics (A.S.S.R.), eight autonomous regions, and ten national areas. The union republics are the Russian Soviet Federated Socialist Republic (R.S.F.S.R.) and the Ukrainian, Byelorussian, Uzbek, Kazakh, Georgian, Azerbaijan, Lithuanian, Moldavian, Latvian, Kirghiz, Tajik, Armenian, Turkmen, and Estonian Soviet Socialist republics. The largest of these units is the R.S.F.S.R., which embraces more than three fourths of the entire territory and over three fifths of the population of the U.S.S.R. Of the eighteen autonomous republics fourteen are within the R.S.F.S.R., two in the Georgian, and one each in the Azerbaijan and Uzbek republics. Again, five of the autonomous regions, as well as all of the national areas, are in the territory of the R.S.F.S.R., while the Georgian, Azerbaijan, and Tajik republics contain an autonomous region each. There are no autonomous republics or autonomous regions in the remainder of the constituent republics, which (except for the Baltic States, which have no regional divisions) are divided into ordinary regions. The total number of such regions is 129, while in the R.S.F.S.R. there are six of the still-larger administrative divisions—the so-called territories. The basic lower links of this administrative-territorial ladder are the districts (*raion*), cities, and villages.

The national entities are represented in the Council of Nationalities of the federal Supreme Soviet (the second chamber specifically created as an organ that could reflect the national interests of the ethnic minorities) on the following basis: twenty-five deputies from each union republic, eleven from each autonomous republic, five from each autonomous region, and one from each national area. Moreover, each union republic is represented by one deputy chairman on the Presidium of the Supreme Soviet. From time to time other devices have been employed to assure the national groups that their specific interests will be represented.

Not only popular writers but Soviet jurists as well portray the national units in glowing terms of independence, self-governance, and mastery over their own destinies, though in practice these entities enjoy but limited autonomy, which frequently makes them hardly distinguishable from local administrative units of the central government. A union republic is defined as "a sovereign national Soviet socialist state," whose sovereignty is evidenced by the following features: a right of withdrawal from the Union; the unalterability of its territory without its consent; adoption of its own constitution; possession of separate legislative, executive-administrative, and judicial organs; the independent exercise of governmental power outside the sphere of jurisdiction reserved for the Union; its own republican citizenship, and the right to admit to this citizenship; representation in the federal Council of Nationalities, Council of Ministers, Supreme Court, and Presidium of the Supreme Soviet; the right to demand an extraordinary convocation of the federal Supreme Soviet or the holding of a national referendum; and, following the reform of February 1, 1944, the right to create its own military formations, as well as to enter into relations, conclude agreements, and exchange diplomatic and consular representatives with foreign states.[2] The last-named right was particularly emphasized in the early postwar period. The fact that the Ukrainian and Byelorussian constituent republics have achieved some international status through separate representation in the United Nations and other international bodies and conferences is also cited as an example of the high degree of national self-realization permissible within the Soviet federal framework.

A union republic has powers of supervision and control over the constitution, boundary changes, the formation of districts, economic plans and budgets of an autonomous republic within its territory, and it exercises similar powers with regard to autonomous regions and national areas. The decisions and orders of the council of ministers of an autonomous republic can be annulled by the Presidium of the Supreme Soviet and suspended by the council of ministers of the union republic above, which also exercises a general stewardship over economic and cultural development in the autonomous republic. Despite the existing realities present-day Soviet jurists call the autonomous republic a "state" possessed of "legislative autonomy" within the framework of the union republic of which it forms a part. This statehood is ascribed chiefly to the fact that an autonomous republic has its own constitution and governmental organs and is separately represented in the Council of Na-

[2] *Osnovy Sovetskogo Gosudarstva I Prava* (1947), pp. 139–43.

tionalities of the federal Supreme Soviet. In practice its autonomy is limited to administration of local economic enterprises and services, but even in regard to this autonomy it must be guided by general rules promulgated from above. For the most part its organs act as local agencies of the federal and union-republic authorities.

Even more limited is the "administrative autonomy" of the autonomous region, which operates on the basis of a statute confirmed by the union republic in which it is located. Nevertheless the autonomous region is authoritatively described as "a national state formation," a form of "Soviet national statehood" that secures for small peoples "all the conditions of free national development." [3]

Whatever the exaggerated degrees of autonomy claimed for the national entities at the various rungs of the territorial-administrative ladder, they are certainly amply balanced by the centralized aspects of the regime. In the first place, the scope of enumerated powers of the federal government listed in the new constitution (Article 14) is so wide as to restrict severely the residual powers theoretically left to the constituent republics. The jurisdiction exclusively allocated to the U.S.S.R. embraces: foreign trade; state security; supervision of constitutional observance; approval of boundary shifts and admission of new republics; the All-Union economic plan, budget, system of credit and money, insurance, and loans; administration of transport, communications, and All-Union economic enterprises; legislation on judicial organization, procedure, and codes, citizenship and rights of foreigners; determination of basic principles in the spheres of education, public health, labor, marriage, and the family; land tenure and the use of mineral wealth, forests, and waters; organization of a uniform system of economic statistics; and issuance of All-Union acts of amnesty. Moreover, while the union republics were formally given a voice in foreign affairs, the constitution still reserves for the Union, not only the right to organize the armed forces of the U.S.S.R., to decide on questions of war and peace, and to conclude, ratify, and denounce treaties, but also the right to establish the "directing principles" for the organization of the union republics' military formations, and "the general procedure governing establishment of relations of union republics with foreign states."

Between the time of the adoption of the two Union constitutions (1923–36), and subsequently, the jurisdiction of the federal Union has steadily grown. This increase is rationalized by Soviet political theorists as an index of the unity of the national entities, whose progress and security are directly related to the concentrated power of the U.S.S.R. The right of the federal Presidium to annul, and of the federal Council of Ministers to suspend, decisions of the union-republic councils of ministers, the fact that the procurator-general of the U.S.S.R. operates through his own representatives over the entire land with complete independence from any of the local authorities, the presence of representatives of the federal ministries on the councils of ministers of the union republics, the predominance of federal law over union-republic

[3] Ibid., pp. 145–46.

law in case of conflict between them (Constitution of 1936, Article 20) —these and similar arrangements are sinews of centralization.

Of similar import in securing local conformance with central objectives has been the concept of "Soviet patriotism," which emerged with the German threat in the thirties and has been given much public emphasis during and after the recent war. The Marxist thesis that "workers have no fatherland" has been cast aside, and a vigorous propaganda to instill a sentiment of love and service for the "Socialist Fatherland" in the Soviet citizens of all the nationalities has taken its place. For years the party leaders have fought so-called deviations toward "local nationalism" and "Great Russian chauvinism," i.e., on the one hand, a tendency among officials of the nationalities to stress national differences and foster particularistic sentiments and practices, and, on the other, an inclination on the part of Russian officials to pay little attention to national differences and to monopolize administrative positions. Although this policy has not been officially altered, a new view is publicly encouraged concerning the role of the Russians in the Soviet state. Apparently assuming that as the largest and most advanced nationality the Russians would play a crucial role in a future war, the Soviet leaders encouraged in the thirties a revival of the past traditions of the Russian nation, its history, culture, achievements, and language. This trend was likewise accelerated during the war and was accompanied by open admission of the large role played by Russians in the U.S.S.R. On May 24, 1945, Stalin acclaimed the Russian people as "the most outstanding of all nations of the Soviet Union" and "the leading force" among them. This statement gave an added impetus to the officially promulgated conception that the Russian nationality is the "first among equals" in the Soviet family of nations, helping the other peoples to material advancement and culture, and that "Soviet patriotism blends harmoniously the national traditions of the peoples and the common vital interests of all the working peoples of the Soviet Union." [4] In the name of this unifying concept adherence to some central purpose takes the highest precedence and has become in fact a condition for survival for the national entities.

The power to change the status of these entities is in practice a central prerogative. When the constitution of 1936 was in the process of adoption, Stalin laid down the following conditions for the upgrading of a national unit to the status of a union republic: 1) it must be a border republic, in order to be in a position logically to raise the question of secession; 2) it must contain a nationality group that constitutes a compact majority; and 3) it must have a population of at least one million people to be able to maintain its independent existence. These are at best purely formal criteria. Past practice suggests that political considerations, such as strengthening the allegiance or boosting the morale of a particular national group, curtailment of friction between nationalities, propagandizing peoples across the frontiers, etc., lie behind such elevation in status. During World War II the German Volga, Crimean, Chechen-Ingush, Kabardino-Balkar, and Kalmyk autonomous republics

[4] Joseph Stalin, *The Great Patriotic War of the Soviet Union* (1945), p. 135.

and Karachai Autonomous Region were dissolved for alleged collaborationist activities among their peoples. Groups of them were banished to other parts of the U.S.S.R., and their territories were reduced to the status of ordinary regions or were absorbed into other areas. Because the territory of an autonomous republic is "the national territory of the people of an autonomous republic," states a recent Soviet textbook, "the territory of the autonomous republic cannot be changed without its consent." Almost all of the changes did not become known until 1945 and 1946, and it is highly doubtful whether the republics involved consented even formally to their own territorial-administrative extinction. By a 1957 decree the above entities (except for the German Volga and Crimean) will be revived and their peoples returned.[5]

Of course the most important of all centralized aspects of the system of rule is the party itself. Whatever the temporary concessions to the federal principle, induced by the desire to arrest the disintegration of the multinational state, it was specifically resolved as early as March, 1919, at the Eighth Party Congress, that it was necessary "to have *one* centralized Communist party, with *one* central committee directing the entire work of the party . . . All decisions of the Russian Communist party and its leading institutions are unconditionally binding upon all parts of the party regardless of their national composition." The central committees of the Communist parties of the separate republics were given the standing of regional committees of the centralized, unitary party and "wholly subordinated to the Central Committee of the Russian Communist party." Renamed All-Union Communist Party (Bolsheviks) in 1925, the name was again changed in October, 1952, to Communist Party of the Soviet Union. Its all-pervading function of political control acts as a unitary lever throughout the Soviet federal system.

The Economic Solution: Material Progress on a Unified Plan. For the nationality problem the economic solution that the Soviet leaders evolved was to raise the material level of the backward peoples and areas through industrialization as well as through modernization of agriculture. However, this aim was to be accomplished on the basis of a Union-wide plan and unified patterns, both centrally determined and controlled.

The introduction of industries and advanced techniques into the backward localities was based on such considerations as: 1) the belief that equalization of economic patterns would minimize friction among the nationalities; 2) the aim to form a workers' stratum—usually deemed a political prop of the regime—among the once-pastoral or primarily agricultural peoples; 3) the need to utilize areas for the purposes of shifting industry eastward because of considerations of military security; and 4) the expectation that such an economic program would in the long run serve as a powerful unifying medium.

On the whole considerable success in terms of official objectives has attended this program. Modern technological processes, the mechani-

5 *Pravda* and *Izvestia,* February 12, 1957.

zation (along with collectivization) of agriculture, and new industries and means of communication were brought to regions with primitive economies. For the inhabitants of some of these regions the metamorphosis constituted a step—originally in many cases a highly involuntary one—toward more advanced forms of modern technology.

Whatever the long-range results of the economic program, the Soviet leaders have consistently insisted on keeping it under central control. The guiding thesis, formulated in 1920, was that "socialism aims to tie up all the regions, districts, and nationalities by the unity of the economic plan." In fact the Bolsheviks changed their earlier negative attitude toward federalism after the revolution only because they became convinced that federation would not bar the economic integration of the various parts of Russia. The agreements, concluded between the Russian and the bordering Soviet republics during the civil war and the so-called Treaty Relations Period (1920–22), provided for economic as well as military collaboration. But the Soviet leaders considered these agreements inadequate because, as Kalinin put it, they wanted each republic to contribute "not what it wants but what it can, according to a uniform economic plan" that embraced all the republics. Consequently the first Union constitution of 1923 placed vast economic powers in the federation. As augmented under the new constitution these powers gave central control over planning, budgets, taxes, and revenues of the union republics and smaller local units to the federal Union. The Union has used these powers freely to shape the economy and social structure over the entire country without any check or hindrance from the individual republics.

The Cultural Solution: Linguistic Autonomy in Ideological Uniformity. The formula for the cultural solution of the nationality problem was given by Stalin on May 18, 1925, in the following words: "Proletarian in content and national in form—such is the universal human culture toward which socialism is marching. Proletarian culture does not cancel national culture, but lends it content. National culture, on the other hand, does not cancel proletarian culture, but lends it form." [6] This formula was designed to provide an outlet for national self-expression by the nationalities, while they simultaneously absorbed common ideas and developed homogeneity of outlook.

This fundamental theoretical statement represented a change from the early position of the Bolshevik leaders. Fearing that any program for national cultural autonomy would separate the workers of different nationalities, and favoring an "international culture of the world-wide labor movement," Lenin in 1913 denounced the slogan of national culture as "a clerical and bourgeois fraud, regardless of whether the Great Russian, the Ukrainian, the Jewish, the Polish, the Georgian, or any other culture is meant." In the same year Stalin also opposed national cultural autonomy on the ground that, as compared with regional autonomy, "it shuts up the nations within their old shells." The effects of this

[6] Joseph Stalin, *Marxism and the National and Colonial Question* (n.d.), p. 210.

negativism after the Bolsheviks came to power were twofold: it failed to elicit any enthusiasm among the nationalities in Russia, and it encouraged Russian officials in the minority-inhabited regions to treat with indifference the cultural interests and aspirations of the national minorities. The resulting discontent brought about a reversal in theory in favor of national cultural autonomy and, with it, a policy of active promotion of cultural programs among the nationalities.

The germ of this change could be found prior to the revolution in the Bolshevik attitude on the question of a single state language. The Communist ideal was and remains a single language and a single culture for the peoples of the world; and the basic view generally has been that the assimilation of nations is a progressive development. However, Lenin opposed a single state language in Russia as impolitic in a multinational state; and Stalin wrote in 1913 that what particularly agitates a national minority is the lack of a right to use its native tongue: "Permit it to use its native language and the discontent will pass of itself." Since Stalin later became the chief architect of the Soviet nationality policy, he carried this concept into the change in party line on national cultural autonomy.

In pursuit of this cultural program schools, theaters, clubs, cinemas, newspapers, and periodicals, branches of the Academy of Sciences, and other cultural institutions were established in the national republics throughout the U.S.S.R. The native languages were given complete equality and their use was mandatory in certain institutions, such as the courts. Some sixty-seven written alphabets were created for such peoples as the Kazakh, Kirghiz, Nenets, and others, who had none before. The result of these measures was a tremendous growth of education and a cultural renaissance among various nationalities, particularly among the backward peoples of the eastern regions. Literacy, extremely low among these peoples up to the middle twenties, rose to about 70 per cent by the end of the thirties, according to official statistics. As compared with 1914 the number of pupils increased between three and eight times in the national republics, and in some of them many times higher (as in the Turkmen, Kirghiz, and Uzbek republics). The number of books published in the languages of the nationalities increased from 6.5 million in 1913 to nearly 133 million in 1936, the number of newspapers from eighty-four to about three thousand. Comparable increases took place in the development of national theaters, scholarly institutions, and literatures.

The Soviet leaders were satisfied that the fruit of this cultural activity in the native languages was political loyalty on the part of the nationalities toward the Soviet regime. Consequently they rebuked as "Great Russian chauvinism" all talk of the superiority of the Russian culture or language and all suggestions that it was time to eliminate the national entities and to amalgamate their separate cultures and languages. The dialectical thesis on the subject, propounded officially in 1930, was that, although the fusion of cultures and languages continues to be the ultimate goal, "the national cultures must be permitted to develop and expand and to reveal all their potential qualities, in order to create the conditions necessary for their fusion into a single, common culture with a single, common language."

Back of this thesis was the conviction that the continued use of a multiplicity of native languages mattered little, since through their own tongues and institutions the nationalities were learning the same principles and pursuing the same social, economic, and political practices, so that substantive uniformity would inevitably result in the end. At the same time the utility of the Russian language as an assimilating medium was not overlooked. Russian remained an official language for those who wished to use it; it was taught in the schools of the national localities, and its adoption was generally encouraged. Thus, partly in order to stimulate its study (though officially for the purpose of accelerating the spread of literacy), the alphabets composed for some of the nationalities were changed from the Latin to the Russian script in 1938–40.

The program for cultural uniformity was given a new impetus by the emergence of the concept of "Soviet patriotism." In the first place, the idea of a Soviet patriotism, having priority over the particular national attachments of the nationalities, made it possible to emphasize the culturally leveling and assimilating aspects of Soviet life. In the second place, it was accompanied by official admission that the Russians constitute the leading nationality among the Soviet peoples, the newer concept appearing to legitimize open praise and promotion of the Russian language.

These tendencies have become particularly pronounced since the end of World War II. There is ample evidence that the Russian language is looked upon as a potent integrating instrument for the future, and in the context of the world-wide ideological struggle recent Soviet statements have taken on increasingly chauvinistic overtones. The present aim appears to be the speeding up of the fusion of Soviet nationalities, and there is reason to believe that (outside of certain international considerations) this policy of intensified assimilation is at the root of the recent manifestations of anti-Semitism in the Soviet Union. The Soviet leaders expected that the Jewish minority—since it is not concentrated on any compact territory of its own in the U.S.S.R.—would be the first ethnically to dissolve. Evidence of lingering attachments within this group to the ethnic sentiments of its people has apparently induced a policy of extensive exclusion of members of this group from positions of responsibility and, in the latter part of Stalin's rule, was accompanied by a campaign of terror in the Soviet Union and its satellites to frighten the Jewish minority into ethnic self-extinction. This policy is a portent of the ultimate shape of things to come for all the nationalities in the U.S.S.R.

The latest restatement of Soviet theory is given in the following terms: a single world language is the ultimate Soviet ideal; such a universal language will not appear at one time, but will be established in several stages. Even when a "world dictatorship of the proletariat" is created, national languages will not wither away. Only during the second stage of that dictatorship, when "the single socialist world state" is formed, will a beginning be made in the formation of a common international language (though not yet of a single world language). There will probably be several common international languages, corresponding to the several zonal economic centers that will be set up for separate economic groupings of nations at that stage. Russian will be one of the zonal international languages, and its "world-historic influence" will grow steadily with the appearance of new socialist nations. When the zonal economic centers are united into "a single world center of socialist economy" and when socialism becomes rooted in the life of peoples, a common language for all nations will take shape. At that time, one of the international languages will be transformed gradually into "the sole world language." [7]

Significantly, this general formulation is currently accompanied by a distinct effort to expand the assimilating function of the Russian language in the U.S.S.R. What the Soviet leaders wish the nationalities to believe is evident from the following recent statement:

> The Russian language is great, rich, and mighty. It is the instrument of the most advanced culture in the world. From its inexhaustible treasures, the national languages of the U.S.S.R. draw a life-giving elixir; it is studied with love by all peoples of the great Soviet Union, who consider it a powerful tool for their cultural progress and socialist transformation.[8]

In the light of this conception earlier attempts by literati of the nationalities to borrow or adapt words from related languages across the Soviet frontiers are now denounced as "a policy of betrayal of national interests, a policy of cosmopolitanism," and efforts to invent or emphasize local variants of words are equally condemned as artificial attempts "to obstruct the penetration of Russian forms and words." This attitude on language is paralleled by claims of priority for Russian scientists in regard to numerous inventions and by a general positive emphasis on the cultural achievements of the Russian past.

In sum, the basic dogma stressed at present is that, although the development of the other national languages is entirely legitimate, the Russian language can and does serve as a source of enrichment for them, that it already plays a progressive international role for the Soviet nationalities, and that "the future belongs to the Russian language as the language of socialism." Lastly, it should be pointed out that the present concepts of language and culture—to which great political importance is attached—are merged in the dominant concept of Soviet patriotism, which is defined as "devotion to the Soviet Fatherland" and a sense of national pride, based on realization by all the Soviet peoples of the "great superiority" of the Soviet social order.

These conceptions entail a balance of loyalties that has at various

---

[7] T. P. Lomtev, "Stalin on Development of National Languages in the Epoch of Socialism," *Voprosy Filosofii*, No. 2 (1949), pp. 131–41; a condensed English translation appears in *Current Digest of the Soviet Press*, 2, No. 7 (April 1, 1950), pp. 3–6.

[8] Ibid.

times made the path of the nationalities a very difficult one in Soviet politics.

The Texture of Society. Soviet society has been essentially a pragmatically created society, molded and fashioned to a high degree by a psychopolitical strategy that counts on the sanctions of both the "carrot" and the "stick." In theory a society characterized by singular solidarity, it has in practice been marked by considerable tensions, engendered in part by abysmally low standards of living and by jealousies among groups or individuals of the perquisites and rewards enjoyed by others. But all groups are held in the grip of an iron discipline on a winding uphill road marked with signposts: "Climb or fall by the wayside."

The problems that the Soviet leaders considered paramount in the social field were fourfold: 1) to convince the Soviet people that an individual can rise to higher status in Soviet society through skillful and loyal performance; 2) to create a series of material and psychological incentives for the acquisition or perfection of skills and for productive achievement; 3) to demonstrate to the populace the continued existence of punitive force held in reserve for use against recalcitrants; and 4) to foster a feeling of unity among the different social strata.

These objectives have led to the abandonment of egalitarianism. Yet Soviet society is not at present one of "closed" social strata. Social climbing is still possible, though like everything in Soviet life it is controlled and permeated with a political purpose. This purpose is to satisfy the need for qualified, efficient, and loyal personnel for the expanding activities of the state, and to absorb in the process the more able and articulate of the citizens into the highly disciplined ranks of the public service. Social climbing is permitted because scientists, engineers, technicians, managers, and skilled workers are increasingly in demand and because the very existence of the U.S.S.R. is related to a manifold increase of productivity in every field of endeavor. The official expectation is that many peasants will become industrial workers and that considerable numbers of workers will pass into the broad ranks of the intelligentsia. The raised production norms that the performance of the record-breaking workers, the so-called "Stakhanovites," induces, coupled with their spectacular wages, frequently arouses bitter resentment on the part of the unskilled workers. However, the official belief apparently is that such resentment can be prevented from becoming socially explosive and that the majority of the unskilled will follow the example of the Stakhanovites.

The complex system of incentives is geared to these expectations. On the material side individual accomplishment is rewarded by increased wages, bonuses, better food or housing, and other economic benefits; on the psychological side compensations are orders, medals, ranks, titles, official publicity, and election to one of the soviets. Psychological considerations also appear to be implicit in a number of political and legal concepts relating to particular social groups. Thus, to stimulate emulation and technical attainment, the intelligentsia is now acclaimed as "the most advanced part of Soviet society." At the same time, to satisfy the sensitivities of the large and growing stratum of workers (especially since relatively few can become intellectuals, although more can reach the level of skilled workers), the regime is still called "the dictatorship of the working class." Some consideration for the sentiments of the peasantry is evidenced in the constitutional designation of the U.S.S.R. as a "state of workers and peasants" and in the continued public reference to the concept of an "alliance" between these two social groups. Again (and partly because a great expansion of the party membership is not deemed desirable), the concepts of "nonparty Bolsheviks" and a "bloc of party and nonparty people" in Soviet elections are apparently designed to offer a modicum of recognition to individuals and groups who, though not members of the party, are considered to perform loyally in their spheres of activity. And, as a sort of future millennium held up before the majority of the populace, the thesis is proclaimed that productivity by all citizens is the key to the progressive removal of the differences between physical and mental labor and will hasten the conversion of labor into "a source of joy and pleasure" and the "rounded development" of all members of Soviet society.

If these present or prospective material and psychological satisfactions constitute the "carrot" in the scheme of socio-political control, there is always in the background the "stick"—the powerful instrumentalities of institutionalized violence. Strict labor discipline, the rules of the agricultural collectives, and the responsibilities demanded of the managers are enforced, not only by public ridicule or reprimand and by the normal channels of judicial procedure, but also by the ultimate sanctions of political purges, confinement in the dreaded correctional labor camps, and even the death sentence. Although no official figures have been released concerning the number of inmates in these camps, estimates abroad have ranged from a few million to fifteen million persons, and even higher figures have been mentioned by some observers. The existence of these sanctions serves as a constant reminder to the members of all social groups of the wisdom of political conformity and compliance with established norms.

Lastly, the context for the use of concepts of social unity should be noted. Social strife, the ranging of class against class and group against group, is ever costly in blood and assets. The people of the U.S.S.R. have paid heavily for such strife in the past. Since the mid-thirties Marxist concepts of class struggle have given place to increasing emphasis on concepts of social solidarity in the Soviet Union, i.e., "friendly classes" (the workers and peasants), "popular sovereignty" residing in the "entire" people, and the monolithism of Soviet society. Whatever the rationalizations of official political theory, basic considerations behind this language of social unity are the realization of the probable political cost of further conflict between the social strata and the belief that the promulgation of concepts of unity will contribute to the promotion of actual unity in Soviet society.

The nationality aspect of Soviet society has been governed by considerations and calculations very similar to those which prevailed in the social field. The primary initial objective of the Soviet leaders was to

arrest the wave of separatism among the nationalities by impressing upon
them the idea that they would be treated as equals and that their national interests would be represented and advanced. Essentially its implementation entailed a triple problem: 1) to convince the remainder
of the populace that the Slavs would not be favored over the other nationalities; 2) to persuade the Slavs in the U.S.S.R. that the Russians
have abandoned the idea of dominating and forcibly "Russifying" them;
and 3) to assure the Russians that their national heritage was not being
frittered away, that their past was properly recognized, and that their
current contribution was specifically appreciated.

The nationality policies that have been mentioned were designed to
meet this problem; and again the method employed was that of the
carrot and stick, of material and psychological satisfactions in the economic, cultural, and political programs designed to foster a sense of national self-realization, and of periodic demands and caveats backed by
the ultimate sanction of force to keep the activities of the nationalities
within approved bounds. As indicated, psychological considerations are
particularly strong in the cultural program, and they lie at the base of a
number of important legal and political concepts used with regard to the
nationalities.

Certainly the sovereignty, independence, and right of secession of
the union republics and the statehood of the autonomous republics are
pure fiction. The representation of the nationalities in such organs as the
Supreme Soviet is not a fiction, but it means little in terms of actual
power in as much as Soviet assemblies are essentially public forums
rather than decision-making bodies. Still, from the standpoint of internal
morale, the nomenclature and paraphernalia of separate statehood yield
distinct advantages, since to the inarticulate masses of the nationalities
they represent visible signs of national identity and self-expression.
Again, because the Russians constitute about 60 per cent or more of
the membership of the federal Soviet organs and of responsible positions
in the military and diplomatic fields, the other nationalities cannot but be
aware of the predominant role of the Russians in Soviet political life.
Nevertheless the public emphasis on their role as "older brother," not
entailing any preferential status, is not without effect.

Deliberate gestures of deference, such as the periodic celebrations
or awards and honors for the institutions and leading personalities of
the national republics, are also part of the carrot treatment. The desire to
demonstrate to the minorities a major concern for their traditional interests has gone so far in recent internal propaganda as to portray the
U.S.S.R. in the role of guarantor of their true national aspirations. Thus
a recent text on the principles of the Soviet state and law contains the
following statement:

> The peoples of the U.S.S.R. have obtained the possibility of
> realizing their centuries-old national aspirations. Thus, the an-
> cient Ukrainian lands of the western Ukraine and Transcar-
> pathian Ukraine have become a part of a unified Ukrainian
> state for the first time in history. The unification of western

and eastern Byelorussia has been realized. Lithuania completed its national unification by adding to its composition the ancient capital of Vilna and the Baltic part of Klaipeda [Memel], torn from Lithuania by the militarist Poland of Pilsudski and Fascist Germany, which took advantage of the defenselessness of the small Lithuanian nation. . . . The unification of the Moldavian people on both sides of the Dniester was also realized. One must also note the return to the R.S.F.S.R. of the ancient Russian lands—South Sakhalin, the Kurile Islands, and Petsamo, and the inclusion in the U.S.S.R. of the Kaliningrad [Königsberg] region.[9]

If such statements leave a strong impression that nationalism and ethnocentrism revolving around national individuality are tolerated or encouraged in the separate nationalities, the realities of Soviet politics demonstrate conclusively that nothing could be further from the truth. Fine and often nebulous distinctions are drawn between permissible national pride and proscribed national haughtiness, between permissible appreciation of one's national traditions and proscribed nationalism, and between permissible "proletarian internationalism" and proscribed "cosmopolitanism." Since the ultimate fusion of nationalities, cultures, and languages is a basic objective, and since political centralism, ideological uniformity, social mingling, intermarriage, and cultural assimilation are expected to lead to this goal, responsible groups and individuals among the nationalities are required to sense the proper balance of loyalties and the inner meaning of changing emphasis in policy. In consequence the leaders of the Soviet nationalities, although predominantly party members and government officials, find that they must walk an ideological tightrope most of the time. Although the solution of the nationality problem has on the whole worked satisfactorily, particularly among the backward nationalities whose national awakening was begun or was encouraged under the Soviet regime, serious conflicts between the center and the national entities have occurred in the past and may recur again in the future. They stem from the fact that the rise of national cultures frequently stimulates a growth of national consciousness among the nationalities, with occasional demands for national self-assertion that exceed the centrally defined limits of the legitimate.

For those who fail to grasp the "dialectics" of the nationality policy there is the "stick" in reserve, as has been amply proved by the suppression of the nationalist parties and regimes in 1918–21; the liquidation of prominent leaders of the nationalities for "national deviations" at various times (particularly in the purges of 1937–38); the elimination of a number of national republics during the Soviet-German war; and the forcible removal of parts of the Baltic population in recent years.

As in the social field, so in the ethnic field the language of Soviet politics has been a language of unity with ample use of such phrases as "voluntary union," "mutual collaboration," "unity of aims of sov-

9 *Osnovy Sovetskogo Gosudarstva I Prava*, p. 132.

ereignty," "federation of nationalities," "multinational state," "fraternity of peoples," and "family of Soviet nations." The dominant consideration behind this vocabulary seems to be to prevent a resurgence of serious friction among the different nationalities or the use of ethnic minorities as targets and scapegoats in situations of social, economic, or political tension, although on the latter score some doubts have been raised by the recent anti-Semitic displays.

The key design for the future texture of Soviet society was laid down as early as January, 1918, in the following terms: "Unity in the fundamental, the cardinal, the essential is not violated, but is secured by *variation* in particulars, in local peculiarities, in modes of *approach* to the thing, in *methods* of effectuating control." [1] Whatever the advantages of particular social groups and whatever the concessions to the individuality of separate nationalities, however, uniformity in basic patterns and purposes and the effects of time are expected to forge a wholly unitary society.

3. TENOR OF CONSTITUTIONALISM

Basic to an understanding of the Soviet order is the tenor of Soviet constitutionalism, especially the nature of the rights granted and duties imposed by the constitution and their corresponding meaning in practice.

The Citizens' Rights: A Study in Futurities. The Soviet bill of rights includes in its written provisions most of the traditional rights and liberties embodied in certain of the great constitutional charters of the West (the United States Bill of Rights of 1791, the French Declaration of Rights of Man and Citizen of 1789), as well as a number of more recent and of more novel vintage. The relative emphasis in the arrangement of these rights shows a distinct scale of priorities. But most noteworthy is the fact that in practice these rights and freedoms guaranteed by the Soviet constitution are either sharply limited through interpretation or are entirely negated in application, constituting at best future possibilities rather than present realities.

The Soviet bill of rights begins with an enumeration of such relatively novel rights as the right to work, rest, leisure, "maintenance in old age and also in case of sickness or loss of capacity to work," and education (Arts. 118–21). The article on the right to work states that realization of this right in the U.S.S.R. is ensured by the socialist organization of economy, the steady growth of the productive forces, elimination of the possibility of economic crises, and the abolition of unemployment. For Soviet theoreticians the right to work "is the foundation of the entire system of rights of citizens, because it constitutes a necessary guarantee for the very physical existence of man." [2]

Paradoxical as it may seem, the right of personal property is

[1] Lenin, *Sochinenia*, Vol. XXII, p. 166.
[2] *Osnovy Sovetskogo Gosudarstva I Prava,* p. 196.

grouped with the above social rights in Soviet texts on law.[3] Considered in the context of the other constitutional provisions on property and ownership (Arts. 4–8), this right of personal property is narrowly defined and limited, as might be expected. In its opening chapters the constitution declares that "the socialist system of the economy and the socialist ownership of the instruments and means of production" form the economic foundation of the U.S.S.R. (Art. 4). Socialist property exists in two forms: state property and co-operative or collective-farm property (Art. 5). The land, mineral wealth, forests, mills, factories, mines, rail, water, and air transport, banks, communications, large state-organized agricultural enterprises, municipal enterprises, and the bulk of the dwelling houses in the cities and industrial localities are state property (Art. 6). The common enterprises of collective farms and of co-operative organizations, with their livestock, implements, products, and buildings are "the common, socialist property" of the collective farms and co-operatives (Art. 7), while the use of the land occupied by the collective farms is secured to them in perpetuity (Art. 8).

The right of personal property is covered by three constitutional provisions. The one on the kolkhoz and co-operative enterprises provides that, in addition to its basic income from the collective-farm enterprise, every household in a collective farm has for its own use a small plot of land attached to the dwelling. In addition individual property rights are recognized in the dwelling house, livestock, poultry, and minor agricultural implements in accordance with the statutes of the agricultural artel (Art. 7). Another article declares that, alongside the socialist system of economy, Soviet law permits the small private economy of individual peasants and handicraftsmen "based on their own labor and precluding the exploitation of the labor of others" (Art. 9). Finally, there is an article granting the citizens the right of personal property in their incomes, savings from work, dwellings and subsidiary household economy, household furniture and utensils, and articles of personal use, as well as the right to inherit personal property (Art. 10).

The constitution refers, after the social rights, to the equality of women with men in all spheres of activity (Arts. 122, 137) and the equal rights of citizens irrespective of nationality or race (Arts. 123, 135). These rights, together with the provisions permitting the use of one's own native language in judicial proceedings (Art. 110) and the application to all citizens of the right to be tried in court (except where otherwise provided by law) "with the participation of people's assessors" (Art. 103) and to be defended by counsel (Art. 111), make up the Soviet version of "equal protection of the laws."

Then come such familiar rights as "freedom of conscience" (Art. 124), freedom of speech, press, and assembly (Art. 125), and "the right to unite in public organizations—trade unions, co-operative associations, youth organizations, sport and defense organizations, cultural, technical, and scientific societies" (Art. 126). To these should be added the citizens' electoral rights (Arts. 134–40). Lastly, the constitution

[3] Ibid., p. 197.

contains guarantees of the inviolability of the person: "No person may be placed under arrest except by a decision of a court or with the sanction of a procurator" (Art. 127); and also of the inviolability of the homes of citizens and private correspondence (Art. 128).

The realities of Soviet life are such that many of these rights are as yet no more than paper guarantees. Probably the best implemented are the equality provisions, and the personal rights are least secure. The significance of the "freedom of conscience" provision as it relates to "freedom of religious worship" (Art. 124) and the guarantee of the right to education (Art. 121) were mentioned earlier.[4] The right to work carries no corollary right to strike against conditions of employment; and although collective agreements with union spokesmen representing the workers were restored in March, 1947, collective bargaining in the U.S.S.R. cannot override provisions regarding wages, rates, production norms, and standards of quality, which in all basic aspects are determined by the leaders of the party and government. Through the workbook and the labor-discipline laws the movements and activity of the worker are strictly controlled. Although the courts and boards of arbitration offer the worker some remedies against arbitrary decisions of management, these institutions, as well as the trade unions themselves, are in the last analysis auxiliary instruments of state policy rather than defenders of the worker's interest against such policy.

Much of the Soviet citizen's leisure time is planned, guided, and controlled for him. Although the acquisition, enjoyment, and bequest of personal property is now one of the most powerful incentives put forth by the government, and normal performance in an economic enterprise carries with it a certain degree of income security and welfare, the calculated consequences of the several currency devaluations of recent years are sufficient proof that the right of property is not an inalienable right in the U.S.S.R. and that it is ever subject to regulation or restriction in accordance with the dictates of party policy.

The bill of rights also contains articles that purportedly guarantee the implementation of the rights described. Thus the rights of free speech, press, and assembly and of freedom of street processions and demonstrations are to be ensured "by placing at the disposal of the working people and their organizations printing presses, stocks of paper, public buildings, streets, communications, facilities, and other material requisites for the exercise of these rights" (Art. 125). In point of fact no unauthorized street demonstrations have been permitted since the attempt made by the Left Opposition to organize such a demonstration on November 7, 1927. And the government's control over all the printing presses and media of communication, together with the entire system of official and unofficial censorship and the regulation and direction of every published statement and public utterance, has made the implementation of these rights entirely a government prerogative. The celebrated "criticism and self-criticism," officially urged so often on the Soviet public, means in fact party-guided discussion. It is designed to discover de-

[4] See above, pp. 571, 581–84.

ficiencies in the practical realization of party policy; it is not designed to permit one to criticize such policy, to attack the leaders of the party and the government, or to call in question the fundamental principles of the Soviet polity.

Likewise, the right to associate in public organizations was never understood as a right to form a political party in opposition to, or in competition with, the Communist Party. The presence of opposition as a fundamental and healthy element of government, expressive of an underlying spirit of political compromise and of "give and take" between conflicting groups and views, is totally alien to the Bolshevik conception of government. And it is not a mere coincidence that the article on the right to form public organizations contains the only reference in the constitution to the party, defining it as "the vanguard of the working people" and "the leading core of all organizations of the working people, both public and state." This all-pervading limitation of the right to unite in other public associations goes to the heart of the Soviet system of monopolized legality.

Lastly, the constitutional guarantees of the inviolability of the citizen's person, home, and correspondence (and the provisions of the Code on Criminal Procedure, which are supposed to implement these guarantees) have proved no bar in practice to the wholesale taking of human lives and to the deprivation of countless numbers of people of their basic freedoms. There appears to be no difficulty in securing the necessary authorization for the arrest, search, and seizure of citizens. Although Soviet law provides certain judicial avenues against wrongful detention, search, or seizure, there have existed from time to time practices that negated these remedies in fact. Special boards of the Ministry of Internal Affairs—which were abolished in 1953—were empowered by a 1934 law to condemn citizens to exile, forced labor, and even execution. Only the prosecutor general of the U.S.S.R. had the right to appeal from the decisions of the M.V.D. Boards to the Council of Ministers as the highest administrative body. There is no evidence to suggest any effective exercise of that right in the citizens' behalf. A 1956 decree rescinded this law, transferring all criminal cases to the regular courts. Whether the trial of cases by military tribunals of these courts will provide greater safeguards for the citizens' rights and liberties remains to be seen.

The Citizens' Duties.   Another limitation on the citizens' rights— consciously imposed as a necessary balance to the latter—are the duties that the Soviet constitution lists along with the rights. This particular constitutional feature has in Soviet Russia a theoretical origin that can be traced to Engels' dictum that true socialism must supplement the bourgeois-democratic guarantees of "equal rights," by adding the words "and *equal duties* of all," and rests on the basic Soviet conception that in the U.S.S.R. the rights and duties of citizens are inseparable.[5] The duties enumerated in the constitution are: the duty to work, described as "a matter of honor for every able-bodied citizen, in accordance with the principle: 'He who does not work, neither shall he eat' " (Art. 12); the

[5] Vyshinsky, *Sovetskoe Gosudarstvennoe Pravo*, pp. 573–74.

duty to abide by the constitution, observe the laws, maintain labor discipline, perform public duties honestly, and respect the rules of socialist intercourse (Art. 120); the duty "to safeguard and strengthen public, socialist property as the sacred and inviolable foundation of the Soviet system" (Art. 131); and the "sacred duty" of every citizen to give military service and defend the country (Arts. 132, 133).

The last two of the above duties, regarded as vital for the survival of the regime and given the highest emphasis in both theory and practice, inevitably bear heavily on the citizens' freedoms. The article on socialist property, supplemented and implemented by the severe provisions of the still-operative law of August 7, 1932, provides that "persons committing offenses against public, socialist property are enemies of the people" (Art. 131). Likewise the article on the duty to defend the country declares that "treason to the country—violation of the oath of allegiance, desertion to the enemy, impairing the military power of the state, espionage—is punishable with all the severity of the law as the most heinous of crimes" (Art. 133). It is the extremely broad definitions given the provisions of this article in practice and the vast range of what is considered public property in the U.S.S.R. that have often made these duties in reality grim limitations on the citizens' rights and liberties.

The Essence of Constitutionalism: Crises and Unbridled Power. One of the reasons for the restrictive and narrow interpretation of constitutional rights and liberties in the U.S.S.R. lies in the periodically advanced claim of a threat to the internal welfare or the external safety of the Soviet Union from enemies within or without. Constitutionalism ever takes a back seat—and the rights of individuals take on a sort of suspended or inanimate existence—when serious crises threatening the established system of government are invoked. The Soviet government has functioned under the actual or avowed impact of such threats through the greater part of its existence, and some of the most oppressive features of the regime can be traced to this fact.

Thus the law on treason to the fatherland of July 20, 1934, provided that, in case of the flight abroad of a member of the armed forces, members of his family who were of specified age were to be punished by deprivation of their liberty for five to ten years and by confiscation of their property, if they knew of, or aided in, the act of escape. All other members of his family who were living with him at the time of the crime and were of age were subject to loss of suffrage and deportation to Siberia for five years.[6] This law was only recently abolished.

The deterioration in the relations of the Soviet Union with the Western powers has been accompanied by such legislative developments as the decree of February 15, 1947 (annulled on December 1, 1953), which prohibited the marriage of Soviet citizens to foreigners; the law of June 8–9, 1947, on state secrets, enumerating, not only military, but economic, scientific, and other data of a non-military character as prohibited information, the disclosure or loss of which is subject to criminal

[6] William E. Rappard, ed., *Source Book on European Governments* (1937), Vol. V, pp. 169–70.

punishment; and the decree of January 12, 1950, restoring the death penalty (earlier abolished during peacetime by the decree of May 26, 1947, which replaced it with confinement to a correctional labor camp for twenty-five years) for "traitors to the motherland, spies, and subversive diversionists."

Whatever the justification officially advanced for such legislation and decrees, it adds to the enormous powers of life and death over the citizenry possessed by the Soviet rulers. Viewed over the span of the Soviet regime, the invocation of unlimited power for the dictatorship, justified from time to time in Soviet theory by the need to uproot "enemies of the people" or to overcome "survivals of capitalist consciousness" within the U.S.S.R., as well as to meet the threat of "capitalist encirclement" from without, has become a sort of *perpetuum mobile,* negating any likelihood of an early relaxation of political controls.

Party Fiat and Constitutionalism: The Law above the Law.   Probably the greatest limiting factor in Soviet constitutionalism is the fact that party fiat is regarded as the law above all laws.

The Soviet leaders have become increasingly cognizant of a deep inner urge among the Soviet people for greater stability in Soviet society. Accordingly there has been in recent years much public emphasis on law and legality and on the value of procedural safeguards against abuse of authority or maladministration by ignorant, stupid, or overzealous officials. There is a distinct effort afoot to convince the Soviet citizen that his interests will not suffer from lack of legality or stability in the framework of government. The constitution is referred to as the fundamental law of the land, the repository of governing principles, and the source of Soviet legislation. At the same time—and herein lies the core of the Soviet scheme of political authority—it is openly acknowledged that "the dictatorship of the proletariat is a power not limited by any laws," and that the directives of the party, which guide the dictatorship, are compelling for all the organs of government and for all public organizations.[7] In accordance with this all-important conception the constitution is not an absolute charter limiting the government to the constitutionally enumerated powers. Rather it is a convenient juridical instrument designed to serve and assist, not to bind and restrict, the highest political leadership.

The basic assumptions are that progress toward communism is the *sine qua non,* that in the period of transition toward communism untrammeled political power is needed, and that in the last analysis the party summit, i.e., the actual seat of power, must remain the ultimate judge of the limits, scope, and priorities of all rights and liberties during this period. These assumptions, together with the absence of strong traditions of constitutionalism in the country's past, leave the door open for much action exceeding or contravening the provisions of the constitution. The institution of tuition in 1940, the abolition of several autonomous republics during the war, and the raising of the age of candidates

---

[7] See Vyshinsky, *Sovetskoe Gosudarstvennoe Pravo,* p. 50; Towster, *Political Power in the U.S.S.R.,* pp. 20–21.

for election to the Supreme Soviet in 1945 are but a few of the many instances in which constitutional articles were altered by ordinance or decree long before they were formally amended. In the sphere of party life such instances have their counterpart in the disregard of a number of party rules, more particularly those on the convocation of the party conferences and congresses.

Such irregularities and numerous other practices are explained in terms of political expediency. Under the consciously fostered conception of an identity of interests between government, society, and individual, the party leadership itself becomes the arbiter of such expediency. The party sets the limits, tone, and temper of Soviet constitutionalism.

In sum, a dual strain marks the Soviet social order. On the one hand, in response to a deep popular yearning for stability in Soviet society, a series of concepts and practices have been brought into play over the past two decades that appears to portend a stabilization and conservation of social forms and forces. These include the concepts of class peace and ethnic harmony, the return to the value of the family and some of the traditions of Russia's past, the conditional accommodation with the church, the admission of a limited personal-property right and of the right of inheritance, and the reversal of theory on state and law, particularly the change from negation to acceptance of the institution of law.

On the other hand, there is the overriding conception that in Soviet society communism is the highest moral law and that the Communist leaders are the seers who alone are fit to interpret it and to adjust doctrine and practice in the interests of progress toward ultimate Communist goals—with all that this conception implies in the way of recurring alteration in Soviet social relations. Always in the background, this conception comes into play most forcefully when public urgency is invoked. As long as it prevails, the constitution and constitutionalism cannot function as absolute or controlling categories. Individual rights and liberties will remain basically conditional, and great flexibility will persist in all existing patterns in the U.S.S.R., whether social, ethnic, economic, or political. Although many aspects of Soviet life appear to have stabilized, social experimentation—albeit on a smaller scale than formerly—is still the prevailing practice and change, far more than stability, continues to mark the Soviet social order.

CHAPTER

25

THE POLITICAL STRUCTURE:
THE COMMUNIST PARTY

1. THEORY OF THE PARTY'S POSITION

The theory of the Communist Party's position in the U.S.S.R. is a theory of political leadership. Fundamentally it exhibits five facets, comprising the official explanations of the respective relationships of party and populace, party and working class, party and government, party and its rank and file, and party and its leaders.

Party and Populace: The Theory of the Fountainhead of Power. It is within the structure of the Communist Party that one finds the real seat of power in the U.S.S.R. In its widely ramified functions the party controls, directs, guides, and observes every kind of activity in Soviet society, either directly or through chosen agents and instrumentalities. As we have seen earlier, party fiat is the law above all laws in the Soviet state.[1]

Far from concealing this all-embracing role, official Soviet theory boastfully sanctions it. The 1936 constitution (Art. 126) terms the party "the leading core of all organizations of the working people, both public and state"; and the foremost theoretical organ, deprecating insufficient emphasis by Soviet authors on the controlling position of the party, declares: "Not to show the leading role of the leading force in Soviet society —the Communist Party—in a portrayal of Soviet actuality is to violate the most important requirement of socialist realism—faithfulness to actuality." [2]

The Communist Party is the only party permitted in the land. Within a period of less than nine months after their seizure of power the Bolsheviks proscribed the parties of the right or the center, such as the liberal Constitutional Democrats, and dispersed the lawfully elected constituent assembly (January, 1918). One by one they also eliminated the parties of the left, first the Menshevik Social Democrats and the

[1] See above, pp. 604–5.
[2] *Bolshevik,* No. 13 (July 1948), p. 48.

right and center Social-Revolutionaries, and then the left Social-Revolutionaries after the attempted incitement of a *coup d'état* by the latter in July, 1918. The official theory is that at the time "leadership passed over *wholly* and completely into the hands of *one* party," the Communist Party, which "does not share and cannot share the guidance of the state with any other party," and that this is what is actually meant by "the dictatorship of the proletariat." [3] The continued monopoly of power by a single party is formally justified by reference to the supposed absence of conflicting classes in the U.S.S.R. At the time of the adoption of the new constitution Stalin expostulated that "a party is a part of a class, its foremost part. Several parties, and consequently, freedom for parties, can exist only in a society in which there are antagonistic classes whose interests are mutually hostile and irreconcilable." Stalin contended that, since there were no longer any antagonistic classes in the U.S.S.R., there was no ground for the existence of several parties. "In the U.S.S.R.," he said, "there is ground only for one party, the Communist Party." This remains the official dogma to date.

Although the Bolsheviks seized the reins of government in the name of one class, the proletariat, and have been singularly free in both theory and practice from the competitive pressure of opposing parties, they have never lost sight of the political advantages of securing the broadest possible popular support. The objective before the seizure of power was to ensure at least the benevolent neutrality of the "nonproletarian toiling masses," and, after the seizure of power, to facilitate the consolidation and extension of Bolshevik rule. Hence, without abandoning the claim of a right to employ compulsion, and without actually recognizing any obligation to abide by public opinion, the Bolshevik theory of leadership lays considerable stress on the party's continuous need to gauge mass sentiment and "to convince the masses" of the rightness of its policies by the use of propaganda and agitation. [4] Apparently learning from bitter experience that stress on social struggle breeds strife and internal disruption, and determined to harness all forces in Soviet society to its economic and political program, the party reversed earlier formulas in the mid-thirties by publicly acclaiming nonmembers loyally serving the regime as "non-party Bolsheviks" and by conducting elections to the soviets under the slogan of a "bloc of party and non-party people." In his February, 1946, election speech Stalin stated that, although in the past party members were "rather distrustful of non-party people and non-partisans," the changes in the social system had wrought a change in attitude, and now "the non-party people are united with the Communists in one common collective body of people, the Soviet people." The newer tune of unity of the entire populace, endlessly repeated in recent years, has brought no change in the conception of the party's exclusive role. In Soviet theory the Communist Party continues to stand out before the populace as wielder of a monopoly of legality in the state or as the fountainhead of power and the

[3] Joseph Stalin, *Voprosy Leninizma* (1934), pp. 156–57, 182–83.
[4] For a discussion of this question see Alex Inkeles, *Public Opinion in Soviet Russia* (1950), Chapter II.

source of constant guidance on all values, programs, and relationships in Soviet society.

Party and Class: The Theory of Indispensable Tutelage.   One of the most remarkable paradoxes of Soviet theory is that the all-powerful Communist Party justifies its exclusive position by references to derivation from a class that the party at the same time claims the right to teach and direct.

The official conception is that the class of the proletariat took power in Russia singlehandedly and set up its own dictatorship, "the dictatorship of the proletariat"; that to consolidate its authority it entered into "a special kind of alliance" with the peasantry and other "toiling masses," retaining, however, its guiding role; and that the leader in this system of dictatorship (since 1936 referred to as "dictatorship of the working class") is the Communist Party, whose position was left intact by the new constitution. Regardless of the nationalities and ethnic groups composing its membership, the party is called the highest form of *class* organization, "the vanguard, the class-conscious detachment of the working class." Telling the Party Congress in 1925 that the dictatorship of the proletariat "is not carried out of its own accord," but primarily by the party forces under the party's direction, Stalin conceded that "without the direction of the party, the dictatorship of the proletariat" would have been impossible. In the following year, emphasizing even more strongly that not a single important political or organizational decision was taken in the U.S.S.R. without guiding direction from the party, Stalin concluded in somewhat guarded language—the implications of which, however, were clear enough—that "in *this sense* it could be said that the dictatorship of the proletariat is *in essence* the 'dictatorship' of its vanguard, the 'dictatorship' of its party, as the main guiding force of the proletariat." [5] The "sense" of this interpretation, in practice even more than in theory, has been that the party exercises a kind of tutelage over the class in whose name it rules, and that this tutelage can entail coercion no less than persuasion.

Prior to the 1917 revolution the need for such tutelage was argued on the ground that it would be sheer fantasy to expect that "the entire class, or almost the entire class, would be able to rise to the level of consciousness and activity of its vanguard." It was further argued that the masses of workers, although they might sense the proper direction, lacked the necessary class consciousness and organization to move consistently to ultimate, i.e., "revolutionary," goals, and that, consequently, their "spontaneous" movement tended either to be arrested midway by trade-union-sponsored reforms or to relapse altogether into spinelessness, disintegration, and "alternate moods of exaltation and dejection." [6] It

---

[5] Joseph Stalin, *Problems of Leninism* (1940), p. 135. It should be pointed out, however, that unlike the 1939 party rules, which called the party the "organized vanguard of the working class," the new rules adopted in October, 1952, define the party as "a voluntary militant union of Communists holding the same views, formed of people of the working class, the working peasantry, and the working intelligentsia." This definition is intended to emphasize the present theory of "equality" of all social groups; in reality it reflects the increased role of the intelligentsia.

[6] See Lenin, *Sochinenia,* Vol. VI, pp. 205–6; also Inkeles, loc. cit.

was the special task of the party, a numerically small group of militant professional revolutionaries, "to elevate spontaneity to consciousness," to provide the organizational leadership, and to inculcate the requisite sense of class aims and interests. After the seizure of power, when such clichés could no longer be utilized, new arguments were invented to the effect that the party was now even more indispensable to the proletariat, since the working masses, imbued with old habits and ideas and devoid of the knowledge of the techniques of governing, would have to go through a long period of schooling in the soviets. In this schooling the party would provide the theoretical orientation and practical training necessary to push them on to the road of definitive communism.

Possibly to make such pushing more palatable, Soviet theory insists in part that there is a mutually controlling relationship between party and class and that the party not only teaches but learns from the toilers. Thus from time to time the leaders are given an official warning against "an aristocratic attitude" that stems from a desire "to play the part of a mentor who tries to teach the masses from books, but who is averse to learning from the masses." [7] The basic emphasis, however, is on the party's role as teacher rather than learner and on the vanguard, as the leader, to point the way and to avoid the error of "tailism," that is, of falling behind the masses. The party must seek to convince the workers of the rightness of its policies. But if the latter fail to see the light, coercion is permissible—in theory, when urgency justifies it or when the majority of the workers approve its use against a minority; in practice, without much regard for such limitations.

Taken together, these conceptions comprise the theory of indispensable tutelage of the working class. As for the question of the duration of such tutelage, an early Comintern thesis (1920) stipulates that "the Communist party will become dissolved completely in the working class at the time when communism ceases to be the aim of the struggle and when the whole working class becomes Communist." However, as in the case of the institutions of state and law, current interpretations place the possibility of such a development in the distant future.

Party and Government: The Theory of Nuclear Authority. In order to reconcile the often-repeated claim that the soviets are the embodiment of popular government, with the reality of highly concentrated power in a party containing three and a half per cent of the population, the Soviet leaders have evolved what may be termed a nuclear theory of authority. According to this theory, the soviets have been and continue to be "the state power"; but the basic nucleus of this authority—"the core of state power"—is the party. Although the top layers of the party and the soviets have merged, the two hierarchies must not be considered identical: "the party . . . leads the soviets, with their national and local ramifications . . . but it cannot and should not replace them."

How is this leadership expressed? In September, 1927, Stalin an-

[7] Stalin, *Sochinenia,* Vol. VI, p. 61.

swered this question in an interview with an American labor delegation as follows:

> First of all, it is expressed in that the Communist party strives through the soviets and their congresses to secure the election to the principal posts in the government of its own candidates . . . Secondly, the party supervises the work of the administration, the work of the organs of power, it rectifies their errors and defects . . . and strives to secure for them the support of the masses. . . . Thirdly, when the plan of work is being drawn up by the various government departments, in industry or agriculture, in trade or in cultural work, the party gives general leading instructions, defining the character and direction of the work of these departments in the course of carrying out these plans.[8]

Official subsequent expatiation upon this frank statement makes it clear that, under the above theory of the relationship of party and government, the Soviet leaders reserve for the party primary responsibility for policy-making, for the enlistment of popular support behind policy decisions by means of the entire propaganda machinery and all the mass organizations, and for checking up on the implementation and execution of policy through a multiple system of controls by party and Soviet organs. The operation of these organs and mechanisms is discussed in later sections.

The Party and its Membership: The Theory of Maximized Unity. As an order of the dedicated, as the self-proclaimed elite or vanguard associating the advanced and select who perform the function of leadership in Soviet society, the party rests on three primary organizational principles. Its membership must be relatively small; it must be kept ideologically pure; and it must be based on absolute unity of will, outlook, and action. In vague outline these principles were suggested by Stalin as early as January 1, 1905, in the following terms: "The party of proletarians, in the first place, must be numerically much smaller than the class of proletarians; in the second place, it must stand higher than the class of proletarians in its consciousness and experience; and in the third place, it must represent a tightly knit organization." [9] Of these principles the last is by far the most important one by virtue of its bearing on the entire body politic.

One assumption of the theory of maximized unity has been that such unity is easier to achieve in a relatively small party than in a very large one. In terms of absolute numbers, the party's membership has increased tremendously in the four decades of Bolshevik rule: that is, from less than 24,000 members in 1917 to nearly 2.5 millions in 1939, 3.4 millions in 1940, 6 millions in 1946, 7.2 millions by 1956, 8.2 millions by 1959. As can be seen from these figures, the greatest increase, virtually

[8] Stalin, *Leninism* (1934), Vol. I, p. 365.
[9] Stalin, *Sochinenia,* Vol. I, p. 63.

doubling the previous membership, occurred during the recent war years, when the leaders threw the party gates open in order to replenish the great losses in membership suffered during the war and to admit Red Army officers and soldiers who were proving themselves in battle. Although the figure of 6–8 millions, around which the party membership has tended to hover in the postwar period, has given the party a larger base, this number is nevertheless small in proportion to the total population.

Whatever the efforts in the twenties to augment the number of industrial workers in the party, there has been no serious attempt since then to carry out the early (July, 1920) Comintern provision that "after the proletarian dictatorship will have deprived the bourgeoisie of such powerful weapons of effective influence" as the press, school, parliament, church, and administrative apparatus, "all, or practically all, the workmen" will gain admission into the ranks of the party. Skilled performance in any endeavor and loyalty to the regime have become the guiding criteria of selection for party membership; and these criteria are in no small degree responsible for the fact that the present-day membership is better educated and younger in age than that of the party's earlier periods.[1] Thus, as compared with the 1924 Party Congress, in which only 6.5 per cent of the regular delegates had a higher education, 31.5 per cent of the delegates in the 1939 Party Congress were college graduates. This figure reached 64.5 per cent at the Party Congress in 1956. Of the total party membership 2.4 million were without a secondary or higher education; 2.1 million had an incomplete high-school education; 1.6 million completed secondary or technical schools; 800,000 had an incomplete and 260,000 a complete university education. As for age, delegates below the age of fifty never constituted less than 66 per cent of the total number of participants at such Soviet conclaves as the Party Congress; and at the end of the war 63.6 per cent of the party's membership were under the age of thirty-five. The main principle of recruitment into the party appears to be the absorption of the skilled and the articulate—which often means the young and the educated—in order to give them a vested interest in the regime and, at the same time, to furnish the party leadership with a fund of information on organizing ability and productive talent in the U.S.S.R. Although this objective may necessitate additional enlargements of the membership in the future, there is little likelihood that such expansion will be permitted to reach unmanageable proportions or to alter greatly the existing ratio of party membership to populace.

The method of keeping the party membership within manageable limits quantitatively and attuned to ideological uniformity qualitatively is the system of controlled purges and admissions. On a mass scale such purges were carried out in 1921–22, 1928–29, and 1934–38. Mass enrollments were instituted on Lenin's death in 1924, on the tenth anniversary of the regime in 1927, and more recently in 1942–46. Lesser purges and membership campaigns are carried out from time to time.

[1] For details see Julian Towster, *Political Power in the U.S.S.R. 1917–1947* (1948), pp. 324–28, 332–36.

Although the conception, voiced by Stalin in 1924, that "the party becomes consolidated by purging itself of opportunist elements" still prevails, he himself admitted at the Eighteenth Party Congress that "grave mistakes" had been committed in the purge of 1934–38 and declared that there would be "no further need of resorting to the method of mass purge." In the first decade of the regime both purges and large-scale enrollments were distinctly related to the question of class purity of the "proletarian dictatorship." The party leaders made several endeavors to increase the number of workers (or children of workers) in the party and in important posts in all public institutions. Such attempts were abandoned in the early thirties when the party decided to bring under its wing persons with organizing talents and technical skills who, whatever their social origin, could help it to realize the new economic plans. The change found reflection in the social composition of the party and its organs and conclaves, where the percentage of members of the intelligentsia—professionals, officials, industrial managers, kolkhoz chairmen, engineers, technicians, foremen, clerks, and record-breaking workers in mine, factory, and field—has steadily risen. Basically this trend will probably continue despite demands at the Twentieth Party Congress to increase admission of "direct producers." While the mass purge of the thirties has not been repeated, and a number of survivors of the purge, as well as of the cultural purge of 1946–53, have been rehabilitated in the post-Stalin period, there is no reason to doubt that the policy of keeping members of the intelligentsia in the party ideologically steadfast will continue and that those falling short of required standards will be weeded out.

The established party rules provide the formal framework for this weeding-out process whereby errant members are first warned or placed on probation and then expelled altogether. An old party formula, restated authoritatively in 1937, was that "a member of the party is one who accepts the program of the party, pays membership dues, and works in one of its organizations." This formula did not speak about *mastering* the program, which became obligatory only in 1952. According to the party rules, which were amended in 1939 to remove preferential admission on the basis of working-class origin, an applicant for party membership must secure the recommendations of three party members of not less than three years standing. After admission he remains a candidate for a year. It is during this period that the candidate must both prove himself in practical work and demonstrate progress toward mastering the party's outlook and program. A vote by his primary organization (cell), confirmed by a higher party committee—usually the committee of the city or district—is necessary to raise his status to full membership. Even after such status has been gained by the party member, he remains under the constant surveillance of the party's organs and agents.

One of the principal objects of this surveillance is to ensure such uniformity of outlook and unity of action as will weld the entire membership into a solid, monolithic whole. Contrary to much recent interpretation, the principle of monolithism, or absolute unity, is not the invention of Stalin, although he gave it a magnified emphasis in actual application. Its original creator was Lenin, who, at the end of the civil war and intervention period, attributed the Bolshevik successes to the fact that "the authority of the party was able to unite all government departments and institutions . . . [and that] the slogans issued by the Central Committee were followed by tens, hundreds, thousands, and finally, millions of people as one man."

In theory the principle of "democratic centralism" still governs all party organizations. According to the party rules, this principle means: 1) that all directing bodies of the party from top to bottom shall be elected; 2) that party bodies shall give periodical accounts of their activities to respective party organizations; 3) that there shall be a strict party discipline and subordination of the minority to the majority; and 4) that all decisions of higher bodies shall be absolutely binding on lower bodies and on all party members.[2] In practice, however, the principle of democratic centralism has become wholly subordinated to the principle of monolithism. The decisive emphasis is on the "central-ism" rather than on the "democratic" part of the formula. Under Stalin co-optation virtually replaced election of the top party bodies, whose accounting became largely formal and infrequent. What effect present strictures against such practices will have remains to be seen. Organized minority groups are no longer permitted even to rise in the party.

On the other hand, the points concerning discipline and the bind-ing nature of upper-echelon decisions upon the lower echelons of the party are given the widest application. Current party literature endlessly reiterates Lenin's view, expressed in 1920, that in the present epoch the party can perform its duty "only if it is organized in the most centralized manner, only if iron discipline bordering on military discipline prevails in it." As a *raison d'état* it adds Stalin's claim that organization on the basis of democratic centralism—no doubt in the current meaning of that formula—enables the party "at any moment" to regroup its ranks and concentrate hundreds of thousands of its members on any task with-out creating confusion.[3]

These conceptions bear directly on the question of "intraparty democracy." In 1924, although insisting on the absolute need for iron discipline, Stalin claimed that such discipline did not preclude "the possibility of contests of opinion within the party" but that after a contest had been closed and a decision adopted "unity of will and unity of action of all party members are the necessary conditions with-out which neither party unity nor iron discipline in the party is con-ceivable." [4] It was not much later, however, that newer interpretations and different emphases in practice brought to an end any genuine contests of opinion on party policy among the party's rank and file and

[2] Commission of the Central Committee of the C.P.S.U.(B.), ed., *History of the Communist Party of the Soviet Union (Bolsheviks), Short Course* (1939), p. 198, cited hereafter as *Short History of C.P.S.U.(B.)*.

[3] *Pravda,* August 25, 1946.

[4] Stalin, *Problems of Leninism,* p. 89.

eliminated any possibility of appeals to the membership by holders of minority views in the highest organs of the party. Above all, the party leaders fear—and have rationalized this fear into a theory—that political factions or groupings in the party would lead to new parties or political centers in the country and cause the disintegration of the dictatorship; in consequence both must be proscribed. The Communist Party, so runs this theory, "cannot afford to be 'liberal' or to permit the formation of factions. The party represents unity of will, which precludes all factionalism and division of authority in the party." [5]

Such interpretations have made a mockery of the celebrated thesis that the party thrives on "criticism and self-criticism." The crucial question is criticism by whom, when, and how? As early as 1921, Lenin stated that "everyone who criticizes must see to it that the form of his criticism takes into account the position the party occupies in a ring of enemies" and must entail "practical efforts" by the critic to rectify the objectionable errors. Stalin made ample use of such qualifying definitions and the concept of monolithism to remove successively such former members of the highest leadership as Trotsky, Zinoviev, and Kamenev (Left Opposition), and Bukharin, Rykov, and Tomsky (Right Opposition). While the party rules provide that a party member has "the right and duty" to criticize other members and take part in discussions, the condition is that such participation must be a "businesslike discussion of practical questions of party policy." This "right" has in practice been restricted solely to criticism and discussion of the execution and implementation of policies already decided on by the leadership; as a rule, and especially in the case of more extended criticisms or discussions, they are initiated in the first place by the party leaders and are guided and controlled throughout toward such practical objectives as the fulfillment of plans, the combating of inefficiency, and the improvement of morale, standards, and skills. At no time are the criticisms permitted to touch on basic policies or strategies inaugurated by the highest party leadership.

The party member is made aware that he is a ward and consecrated servant of the party, whose interests and purposes are binding upon him. In his personal conduct, in his basic philosophy of life, in his attitudes on such questions as religion, and in his estimates of the party's internal and external policies and practices only one kind of outlook is possible for him, the outlook expressed in the party's writings and periodic interpretations. An individual course of action or thought running contrary to this outlook marks him as a transgressor against the sacrosanct principles of party unity and discipline, and, in extreme cases, even as "an enemy of the people," subject to all the sanctions of party and government. Such is the force of the concept of maximized unity in its actual application by the leaders of the party who stand at the pinnacle of power in the U.S.S.R.

The Party and Its Leadership: The Theory of an Infallible Elite. In 1937, Stalin once described the leading strata of the party as con-

---

[5] Ibid., pp. 81–82.

sisting of about 3,000 to 4,000 first-rank leaders, whom he called the party's "corps of generals"; 30,000 to 40,000 middle-rank leaders, designated as the party's "corps of officers"; and about 100,000 to 150,000 individuals of the "lower-ranks command staff," who were the party's "noncommissioned officers." [6] Since that time all these ranks have swollen in membership, but this growth has only contributed to the further concentration of decisive authority in the top stratum of the party's leadership, which comprised the members of the Politburo, Orgburo, and Secretariat until recently and now consists of the Presidium of the Central Committee of the party and the Secretariat.

Taken together, these conceptions of the party's relationship to populace, working class, government, and its own membership have produced an implicit, if not explicit, party law that the highest party leadership was endowed with attributes approaching omniscient wisdom and was incapable of serious error. Perhaps it could hardly be otherwise in a society that rests on a theory of universal progress, involving interpretations of past, present, and future, and requiring trained seers to explain and apply its "dialectical" formulas. For if the claim that this theory is a science were to retain a semblance of plausibility in the eyes of rank-and-file believers, the zigzags and changes in its application and the alterations and modifications in its postulates had to be interpreted with such skill and authoritativeness as to leave the reputation of its prophets untarnished. Only on that basis could fundamental continuity be claimed between the original gospel of Marx and Engels and its subsequent development by Lenin and Stalin. Thus arose the concept of infallibility of the highest leadership—now the Party Presidium, the "collective leadership" of the party.

In practice in the Soviet state the entrenchment of this concept has meant authoritarian rule by the small elite at the party summit. And increasingly theoretical justification for it has been offered, not only in terms of practical necessity, but also in terms of authoritative foundations in the party's past pronouncements. Thus, on the one hand, the equalitarian tradition of the party's ideology is still remembered too well to be totally disregarded. Party agencies, therefore, reiterate from time to time such theses as the party's readiness to discuss openly any of its shortcomings, in contrast to the practice of earlier revolutionary parties, which perished because they feared to speak of their weaknesses. Indeed, the *Short History of the C.P.S.U.(B.)*, published in 1938 as a guide for party members, went so far as to state that, to preserve the unity of its ranks, "the party must impose a common proletarian discipline, equally binding on all party members, both leaders and rank and file." [7] This remains the official conception of the party despite recent criticisms of the *Short History* at the Twentieth Party Congress (1956) and its impending revision. In the past the party writers used to recall for their readers such apparent justification of authoritarian practices as Lenin's statement in 1920 that "Soviet Socialist democracy is not contradictory to individual management and dictatorship in any

[6] Joseph Stalin, *Mastering Bolshevism* (1937), p. 36.
[7] *Short History of the C.P.S.U.(B.)*, p. 50.

way, that the will of a class may sometimes be carried out by a dictator, who at times may do more alone and who is frequently more necessary." Also Stalin's statement in 1924 that there were times in the history of the party "when the opinion of the majority or the momentary interests of the party conflicted with the fundamental interests of the proletariat" and the fact that on such occasions Lenin never hesitated to take a resolute stand "against the majority of the party" [8] are repeated. The party's *Short History* has frankly admitted that the agricultural collectivization and the industrialization drives were a revolution "accomplished from above," and discussions of the principle of democratic centralism described it shortly and, as far as practice was concerned, accurately as "combining iron discipline and the undisputed authority of the leaders of the party." The iteration of such views and rationalizations fostered a concept of infallible leadership with particular emphasis on the personality of Stalin. At present the emphasis on one-man leadership is denounced as "the cult of the individual" and the concept of "collective leadership" is promulgated in its place.

2. ORGANIZATION AND ROLE OF THE PARTY

The Organizational Hierarchy: The Ladder of Party Rule.   All power in the U.S.S.R. is hierarchical in nature. This applies in the first place to the Communist Party itself. The party structure resembles a ladder that is broad at the base and very narrow at the top. There are five basic rungs in this ladder of party authority. The lowest consists of the "primary party organizations," once called "cells." The second rung consists of the city and district (raion) party organizations. In large cities, which are divided into districts, the city district party organizations may be subordinate to the city party organization. The third rung consists of the regional (oblast') party organizations. Then come the territorial (krai) and union-republic party organizations, and, finally, the All-Union party bodies. In September, 1946, *Pravda* listed the units of this hierarchy as follows: 250,000 primary party organizations; 4,238 rural district, 514 city district, and 489 city party organizations; 11 area, 154 regional, 6 territorial, and 15 union-republic party organizations. The R.S.F.S.R. has no separate republican party organization. The above represents a considerable increase over 1939 in the number of party organizations at each level. Further increases in the number of party organizations were indicated at the Twentieth Party Congress, which was held in February, 1956. The number of primary units was reported to exceed 350,000. There were about 94,500 primary units in agriculture, over 43,000 in industry, and the remainder in other branches of the economy and administration.

[8] Nikolai Lenin, *Selected Works* (1943), Vol. VIII, p. 222; Stalin, *Sochinenia,* Vol. VI, pp. 58–59.

The Primary and Intermediate Party Organizations: Instruments of Party Control. The primary party organization is called "the foundation of the party." It is authoritatively described as the main link, which connects the masses of the workers, peasants, and intelligentsia with the leading party organs, and as a "school of Bolshevik training," where Communists learn to participate "in the struggle to achieve communism." Primary party organizations are established in factories, farms, mines, other economic enterprises, governmental institutions, units of the armed forces, offices, schools, etc. The setup of the primary party organization is determined largely by the size of its membership, which may range all the way from 3 members to 3,000 or more. In places of work where there are over 50 party members and candidates, such party units as shop, sectional, and departmental party organizations may be formed within the general primary party organization, subject to approval by a higher party committee. Within the shop, sectional, and departmental organizations, and within a primary party organization with fewer than 50 members and candidates, party groups may be formed in the brigades of machine units of the establishment. If a large enterprise, such as a factory, has over 300 party members and candidates, a factory committee may be established by decision of regional, territorial, and Republic Central Committees. In such an enterprise the shop party organizations are given the rights of primary party organizations. On the other hand, in a place of work with fewer than three party members, a candidate group or a joint Party-Komsomol group is set up under a party organizer appointed by the district or city party committee or, in the case of the armed forces, by a political department.

Primary party organizations are formed and confirmed by city and district party committees. The primary party organization itself, in a general meeting—which is designated as its highest body—decides on admitting candidates to full membership. Members and candidates pay monthly dues as follows: one-half per cent on a monthly income below 500 rubles, 1 per cent on an income above that sum but not exceeding 1,000 rubles, 1.5 per cent on earnings from 1,001 rubles to 1,500 rubles, 2 per cent on a sum from 1,501 to 2,000 rubles, and 3 per cent on monthly earnings above that sum. Non-payment of dues for three successive months is one of the grounds for expulsion from membership, an action that is likewise decided by the general meeting. However, both admission and expulsion decisions of a primary party organization require the endorsement of a district or city party committee.

A primary party organization comprising not fewer than fifteen members elects as its executive body for one year a bureau (of not more than eleven persons) to direct its current work. If its membership is fewer in number, it elects only a secretary. Shop party organizations with fifteen to a hundred members can likewise elect a bureau of three to five persons, and even up to seven persons if the membership is higher. As a rule party work is conducted on a voluntary part-time basis in a primary party organization with no more than a hundred members. Party secretaries are considered key people in their units, as is evidenced by the requirement that secretaries of primary and shop organizations must have a party standing of at least one year, and those of primary party organizations in the ministries must be endorsed by the Central Committee of the C.P.S.U.

As defined by the party rules, the functions of the primary party organizations are to conduct "agitational and organizational work"—both directly and by assisting the higher party committees—toward mobilizing the efforts of the masses in factories, farms, etc., for fulfillment of the economic plan, of labor discipline, and of socialist emulation in production; toward combating laxity and mismanagement in enterprises; toward improved cultural and living conditions; and toward active participation in the country's economic and political life. A distinction is made between a primary party organization in a productive enterprise and one in a governmental ministry. In the first, according to the party rules, a primary party organization has "the right of control over the work of the management." Since the specific conditions of work in a ministry are said to preclude such control by the primary party organization, the latter is authorized to note shortcomings in the operations of the ministry and its personnel and report such to the Central Committee of the C.P.S.U. and the heads of the ministry.

Concrete examples of work of the primary party organizations cited in the Soviet press as evidence of their growing economic and political role include the following: successful promotion of over-fulfillment of production plans through Stakhanovite methods in certain oil trusts and other enterprises; timely suggestions to the management of a kolkhoz that resulted in the creation of a permanent builders' brigade to overcome a lag in construction; organization of "Red corners" for reading, lectures, talks, and other "political work" by party groups operating in camps; work in a secondary school to "raise the ideological level of teaching" and promote better knowledge by the students, through such means as meetings with the other teachers, conducting discussions of current affairs with the school's non-teaching personnel, leading party-history study circles, and approving activity plans of the Komsomol and Pioneer groups of the school. Numerous other instances concerning every sphere of activity are related daily.

Judging by repeated official complaints, a good primary party organization in a ministry would not only look after the welfare arrangements, political education, and the raising of the professional skills of the employees, but would carefully observe whether efficiency and good order prevail in the functioning of the ministry. It would note particularly whether the collegium meets regularly; whether its decisions and the orders of the minister are clearly phrased and promptly released; whether subordinate institutions and enterprises are properly directed, and orders and directives of higher party and Soviet bodies executed without delay; whether workers' complaints are attended to, visitors politely received, state documents guarded, and bureaucracy, red tape, brawling, and officiousness steadily combated. And it would report all deficiencies to the leading party bodies. At the same time, however, primary party organizations in ministries are warned not to assume "functions of control" of administration. This results in a difficult problem of differentiation between control and surveillance by the primary party organizations in the ministries.

Both the criticisms and praise voiced in the newspapers suggest another dilemma facing all primary party organizations. It is obvious that what is wanted of these organizations is the distribution of their members and assignments in such a manner as to achieve maximum productivity in the given enterprise as well as to generate maximum enthusiasm for the party's pursuits. This is a difficult combination of objectives to attain because of the time and skill factors relating to the party members, on the one hand, and the frequent weariness and lack of receptivity to the party's propaganda work in the non-party personnel, on the other. Hence shortcomings are often charged in the party press.

Between the primary party organizations and the All-Union party organs lie the intermediate layers of the party agencies of cities, districts, regions, territories, and union republics. The party rules designate a party conference as the "highest organ" of each of these organizations, and in the case of the union republic a party congress. The larger city and district conferences and union-republic congresses are required to meet once in two years; congresses of union republics divided into regions (Ukraine, Byelorussia, Kazakh, Uzbek) every four years. Town or rural district conferences will apparently meet as needed. The greater frequency of conferences required by earlier rules was not observed in practice. While fifteen union-republic party congresses had been held between the early part of 1949 and the end of 1951, ten of these were again more than a year behind in convening as required. For the most part territorial and regional party conferences had likewise met at intervals longer than eighteen months.

The delegates to the city and district party conferences are elected by the primary party organizations, and those of the regional and territorial conferences and union-republic party congresses are elected by the city and district party conferences. Each of these conferences elects a party committee (the union-republic party congress elects a central committee), which is deemed the highest organ of the respective party organization during the interval between the conferences and congresses. Each conference and congress likewise elects an auditing commission for its respective party organization, and when an All-Union Party Congress is scheduled, it elects delegates to that congress.

Plenary meetings of the city and district party committees are required to convene once in three months, those of the regional and territorial party committees and the central committees of the union republics at least once every four months. For the performance of current work in the interim between these meetings each city and district committee elects as its executive body a bureau of seven to nine persons and several secretaries, and each regional and territorial committee and union-republic central committee appoints a bureau of not more than eleven persons including several secretaries. The importance of the secretaries is emphasized by the requirements that those of city and district committees must have a party standing of not less than three years and

be confirmed by the regional or territorial committee or the union-republic central committee; and secretaries of the regional and territorial
committees and the union-republic central committees must have at least
a five-year party status and be confirmed by the Central Committee of
the C.P.S.U., which sets the number for each committee.

The party rules provide that the party conferences and congresses,
in addition to appointing their respective committees, whose reports they
hear and act upon periodically, shall discuss questions of party, soviet,
economic, and trade-union work in their particular localities. The party
committees, which act in place of the conferences and congresses during
the interim periods, have such tasks as organizing and guiding party institutions; appointing the editorial boards of the party organs in the respective localities and controlling their work; establishing their own enterprises of general importance to the particular city, district, region,
territory, or union republic; distributing within their units the party personnel and resources; managing the party funds; and, most important,
directing the party groups in the non-party organizations.

The party committees and their bureaus carry on their work
through special administrative units. Under the revised party rules of
1939 the city and district committees maintained departments of propaganda and agitation, organization and instruction, and military affairs;
the regional and territorial committees and the union-republic central
committees had, in addition, departments concerned with cadres, agriculture, schools, transport, etc. The number and assignments of such
units have varied with time. The reorganization in 1948 has resulted in
the abolition of the cadre, military, and organization-instruction units,
and the distribution of most of their functions among new units corresponding to the principal mass organizations and the chief branches of
the economy. Thus most or all of the following departments exist in the
central committees of the union republics: party, trade-union, and
Komsomol organs; propaganda and agitation; agriculture; heavy industry; light industry; transport and communications; planning, finance, and
trade; and administration. Some have departments for work among
women, and occasionally among other special groups. The lower of
the intermediary party organizations have fewer departments. The party
rules adopted in 1952 omit the listing of departments on the ground that
frequent changes in the party apparatus make such enumeration in-
advisable.

Practice suggests that the party committees, especially at the city,
district, and regional levels, are the watchdogs, supervisors, and organizers of the party in their respective areas and play a crucial role in the
party's system of control. In serving the party's cause each committee is
bifocal in its surveillance: watching how party and government directives are being executed by the economic enterprises, Soviet organs,
and civil bodies, and, at the same time, observing whether the relevant
party organizations within the committee's jurisdiction are doing their
share to ensure the proper fulfillment of such directives by the non-
party organizations. In this supervisory task the party committee issues
instructions to the party organizations below, sending observers from

time to time, dispatching party instructors and party organizers to lagging units, training the secretaries of the primary party organizations, organizing special seminars and indoctrination schools for party personnel and lectures for non-party people, as well as selecting, placing, and removing personnel—especially for managerial positions—within its area. Typical points of criticism of intermediate party organizations (revealing what is chiefly wanted of them) are: weak contacts with, and poor assistance to, backward districts; the unsatisfactory selection, placement, and training of personnel; inability correctly to combine political work and guidance of the economy; and failure to exercise a day-to-day check on fulfillment of party and state orders.

A party committee of a region, district, or city is expected to step into the breach when things go wrong in some field of activity within its jurisdiction. Instances related in the Soviet press suggest that this becomes at times little short of a tightrope operation. Thus, when the Penza Region Party Committee thought that certain farms lacked the necessary expertise and required concrete guidance, it was criticized for "sending to collective farms all sorts of special representatives, who often substituted administrative for organizational work." [9] On another occasion a writer condemned the Kostroma Region Party Committee for *not* supplying "concrete leadership" and for relying instead on paper directives and telephone conversations.[1] The same party committee was later taken to task for the practice of "supplanting" the regular government of the region—the Kostroma Region Executive Committee of the Soviets—by encouraging the latter to seek parallel party resolutions for its decisions and by frequently attending directly to requests from the districts (for fuel, spare tractor parts, lumber, etc.).[2] Thus it is frequently no mean task for the intermediate party organizations to determine when substitution by them of direct personal guidance for supervision and intervention by directives ceases to be concrete leadership and results in a "supplanting" of the non-party institution or enterprise involved.

The line of command for the intermediate party organizations is laid down in the party rules. The city or district committee is subordinate to the regional committee, territorial committee, or union-republic central committee, reporting on its activities at the times and in the form prescribed by the All-Union Central Committee of the party. The same thing applies to area committees where areas exist. All of these party committees must "guide themselves in their activities by the decisions of the Communist party of the Soviet Union and its leading bodies."

This brings us to a consideration of the All-Union party organs.

The Congress and Central Committee: The Fiction of Delegated Power. Until October, 1952, the highest level of the party structure comprised the following central, or All-Union, organs: the Party Congress, Party Conference, Central Committee, Politburo, Orgburo, Secre-

[9] *Pravda,* December 28, 1949.
[1] Ibid., May 15, 1950.
[2] Ibid., August 4, 1951.

tariat, Central Auditing Commission, and Commission of Party Control. Changes introduced at that time by the Nineteenth Party Congress abolished the Party Conference and the Orgburo, replaced the Politburo by a Presidium of the Central Committee, and changed the Commission of Party Control into a Committee of Party Control.

The All-Union Party Congress is supposed to be the highest party body, "the sovereign organ of the party," which represents the rank-and-file membership. It is now supposed to convene every four years to hear and confirm reports of the Central Committee and other All-Union organs and to determine the tactical line of the party "on the principal questions of current policy." According to the party rules, the Central Committee, which is elected by the Party Congress and is responsible to it, stands in place of the congress in the interim between congress meetings. Although the Central Committee has essentially abdicated its once-powerful position to the Party Presidium, it has gained in importance in the post-Stalin period, as is evidenced by its role in the leadership struggle in 1956–57. Earlier, a Party Conference—composed of delegates sent by the union-republic, territorial, and regional party committees—was required to meet once a year in order to discuss questions of party policy. The Central Committee, according to the party rules, "directs the entire work of the party" during the interval between congresses, guiding all party institutions and publications, organizing important enterprises, allocating party personnel and finances, and directing "the work of the central soviet and public organizations through the party groups in them." In theory, then, there is a delegation of supreme authority, and the Central Committee, which consists of 133 members and 122 alternates (prior to February, 1956, it comprised 125 members and 111 alternates), is the highest seat of party power when the party Congress is not in session.

Until recently this formal description was contradicted on two scores. In the first place, the Party Congress met so rarely that it no longer played any significant role in policy-making. Having in any case grown unwieldy in membership (the membership of the Twentieth Congress numbered 1,436 delegates), the Party Congress has met no more than six times in the past thirty years, and only five times since 1930. The Nineteenth Party Congress was held in October, 1952, after an interval of thirteen and a half years.

At one time the Party Congress, which since the late twenties has become merely a body to ratify the decisions of the party leaders, played an important role in policy determination; the Party Conference, however, was always a subordinate body, since its decisions required ratification by the Central Committee. Moreover, the Party Conference, which was composed of 595 delegates and alternates when it last met, in February, 1941, has now been completely eliminated. Thus the Central Committee is the only one of the All-Union party assemblies that has actually operated in recent years. The new party rules provide for meetings of the Central Committee not less than once every six months, inferentially confirming the conclusion that the earlier provision for three meetings a year was not carried out.

But this supreme organ, theoretically the wielder of the powers of the Party Congress, has in practice become more and more an auxiliary of the Politburo—now the Party Presidium. Since the congress had not met for over thirteen years up to 1952, it certainly had not elected any members to vacancies in the Central Committee during that period. The Party Conference, which was empowered by party rules to select up to one fifth of the Central Committee membership, had not even met since 1941. The Central Committee, thus, had been co-opting its own membership, which in reality meant selection by the Orgburo and Secretariat and approval by the Politburo. The nature and number of Central Committee decisions, as compared with those of the Politburo, likewise left little doubt concerning the pre-eminence of the latter. Most decisions that were publicly announced as decisions of the Central Committee were in fact decisions of the Politburo, Orgburo, and Secretariat; and the "apparatus" of the Central Committee, discussed below, works directly under the supervision of the Secretariat.

The Presidium of the Central Committee and Secretariat: The Supreme Party Directorate. The Politburo and Orgburo were officially established at the Party Congress in March, 1919, although the Politburo actually had existed since October 23, 1917, when it was set up to prepare for the seizure of power. Along with these organs was created a Secretariat, which at an early date came to consist of a secretary-general and five, later four, secretaries. The original distribution of functions among these three bodies envisioned the making of political decisions by the Politburo, general guidance of organizational and personnel work by the Orgburo, and immediate handling of current questions of an organizational-executive nature by the Secretariat. But, under the impact of internal party struggles, changes in personnel throughout the mid-twenties, and other causes, these organs in practice have undergone a major transformation.

The Politburo, which numbered eleven members and one alternate before its recent abolition, had become the controlling organ of the party and, consequently, the nucleus of all power in the U.S.S.R. Called in party literature the "leading summit," "directing kernel," or "general staff" of the party, the Politburo made all important policy decisions on every aspect of Soviet life, whether political, economic, social, or cultural, and controlled all the other party, state, and public bodies. The Orgburo, which had eleven members and four alternates, and the Secretariat, which consisted of four secretaries besides the secretary-general, worked closely with the Politburo to give organizational effect to its decisions. The Secretariat met daily; the Politburo and Orgburo apparently held several sessions each week.

The Presidium of the Central Committee, which replaced the Politburo, consisted of twenty-five members and eleven candidates until March 6, 1953, and all ten members of the new Secretariat were simultaneously members of the Presidium. This enlargement of the party summit apparently aimed at introducing new blood into it, since half of its members were new to the power group. There was no doubt, however, that Stalin's closest colleagues would continue to exercise the strongest influence in the new organ and would form the hard core of leadership upon his passing. This was confirmed in the official announcement of Stalin's death, which was made on March 6, 1953. Disclosing for the first time the existence of a Bureau of the Presidium, which apparently consisted of these older colleagues, it declared the Bureau abolished and simply reduced the membership of the Party Presidium to fourteen (ten members and four candidates) on the ground that this action would "ensure more operative leadership."

As a result of a struggle over status and policies since Stalin's death the Presidium of the Central Committee has undergone the following alteration. Its total membership has increased and now stands at fourteen full members and ten candidates. The members are predominantly party bureaucrats (*apparatchiki*) and Khrushchev partisans. With the ouster of Molotov and Kaganovich—who had risen to power together with Stalin—and of Malenkov, who had long been an intimate collaborator of Stalin in the Party Secretariat, the old guard of the top leadership has been reduced to an insignificant few. The same fate has befallen the representation of the industrial-managerial elite, with the exclusion of Saburov from the Presidium of the Central Committee and demotion of Pervukhin to candidate status. All of the ousted leaders simultaneously lost their positions as deputy premiers or ministers in the Council of Ministers. The removal in November, 1957, of Marshal Georgii Zhukov from the highest leadership circle after a mere four months of tenure as full member of the Party Presidium, emphasizes further the concentration of the supreme power in the hands of professional party leaders. Along with the reorganization of the system of economic administration these changes spell a definite reassertion of the supremacy of the party leadership in the formulation as well as implementation of policy in all spheres of life.

As of the fall of 1958, the members of the Presidium of the Central Committee were A.B. Aristov, N.I. Belyayev, L.I. Brezhnev, N.S. Khrushchev, Ye. A. Furtseva, N.G. Ignatov, A.I. Kirichenko, F.R. Kozlov, O.W. Kuusinen, A.I. Mikoyan, N.A. Mukhitdinov, N.M. Shvernik, M.A. Suslov, and K. Ye. Voroshilov. The candidates were: P.N. Pospelov, D.S. Korotchenko, J.E. Kalnberzins, A.P. Kirilenko, A.N. Kosygin, K.T. Mazurov, V.P. Mzhavanadze, M.G. Pervukhin, N.V. Podgorny, and D.S. Poliansky. Until his ouster on September 5, 1958, Bulganin was also a member of the Presidium.[3] In 1953, Party Secretary Khrushchev alone of the Secretariat was also a member of the Party Presidium; in 1956, five members of the eight-man Secretariat were in the Presidium. After the "purge" of July, 1957, the entire Secretariat, consisting of Khrushchev, Aristov, Belyayev, Brezhnev, Pospelov, Suslov, Furtseva, and Kuusinen, was admitted into the Party Presidium in an apparent attempt to strengthen the professional party element in the highest ruling body of the C.P.S.U. In December, 1957, Presidium members A.I. Kirichenko, N.A. Mukhitdinov, and N.G. Ignatov were

[3] See *Pravda,* September 6, 1958.

added to the Secretariat, increasing its membership to eleven. While according to the party statutes the Secretariat is merely the organizational arm of the Central Committee, it is in fact becoming the most influential body of leaders around First Secretary Khrushchev in the policy-making summit.

The changes in membership in the Presidium and the Secretariat between 1952–58 are summarized in Figure XXIII on pages 626–27.

To prepare materials for the Presidium and to implement the execution of its decisions, there exist a number of high-level administrative units, generally referred to as the Central Committee departments of the Central Committee apparatus.[4] A reorganization of these departments in 1948, marking a partial abandonment of the functional arrangements adopted in 1939 and a return to the production-branch principle that existed in 1934, abolished altogether the cadres administration, as well as the unit that succeeded the Organization-Instruction Department. Apparently the following units still function: Department of Party, Trade-union, and Komsomol Organs; Department of Propaganda and Agitation; separate departments of Light Industry, Heavy Industry, Agriculture, and Transportation. Quite likely other departments, such as units corresponding to the economic ministries, a department for work among women, and a foreign department exist in the apparatus; and the Main Political Administration of the Armed Forces, always considered a department of the Central Committee, apparently continues in that status. The Department for Party, Trade-union, and Komsomol Organs supervises the lower levels of the party structure, the performance by the mass organizations, and the general execution of party decisions. The Propaganda and Agitation Department, operating through specific sections, checks on the guidance of the central and local press, publishing houses, films, radio, literature, art, cultural enlightenment, schools, science, party propaganda, and agitation. Apparently it also supervises the two highest schools of party leadership, the Higher Party School and the Academy of Social Sciences, both of which are attached to the Central Committee. The production-branch departments look after morale, personnel appointments, and actual performance in their respective fields through the supervision of party organs, which are supposed to exercise guidance or surveillance in those fields.

Besides this Central Committee apparatus, mention should be made here of the Central Auditing Commission and the Committee of Party Control. The first, which is supposed to be elected by the Party Congress, verifies the accounts of the central organs of the party. The Committee of Party Control, established by the Central Committee, works in close co-operation with the departments of the Central Committee and various ministries, especially the Commission of State Control, the Ministry of Internal Affairs (M.V.D.), and the Committee of State Security (K.G.B.),

---

[4] For an excellent description of these departments, see Louis Nemzer, "The Kremlin's Professional Staff: The 'Apparatus' of the Central Committee, Communist Party of the Soviet Union," *American Political Science Review,* 44 (March, 1950), pp. 64–85.

THE RULING BODIES OF THE COMMUNIST

POLITBURO	SECRETARIAT	ORGBURO	PRESIDIUM C.C.	SECRET. C.C.	PRESIDIUM C.C.
	SUMMER, 1952		OCTOBER 16, 1952		MARCH 6,
Stalin	Stalin (first secretary)	Stalin	Stalin	Stalin	
		Andrianov	Andrianov		
Andreyev			Aristov	Aristov	
Beria			Beria		Beria
Bulganin		Bulganin	Bulganin		Bulganin
Voroshilov			Voroshilov		Voroshilov
			Ignatiev	Ignatiev	
Kaganovich			Kaganovich		Kaganovich
Kosygin			Korotchenko		
		Kuznetsov	Kuznetsov		
			Kuusinen		
Malenkov	Malenkov	Malenkov	Malenkov	Malenkov	Malenkov
			Malyshev		
			Melnikov		
Mikoyan			Mikoyan		Mikoyan
		Mikhailov	Mikhailov	Mikhailov	
Molotov			Molotov		Molotov
			Pervukhin		Pervukhin
	Ponomarenko	Ponomarenko	Ponomarenko	Ponomarenko	
			Saburov		Saburov
	Suslov	Suslov	Suslov	Suslov	
Khrushchev	Khrushchev	Khrushchev	Khrushchev	Khrushchev	Khrushchev
			Chesnokov		
			Shvernik		
			Shkiriatov		
Candidate:			*Candidates:*		*Candidates:*
Shvernik					Shvernik
			Brezhnev	Brezhnev	Ponomarenko (until 1955)
			Vyshinsky		Melnikov (until June, 1953)
			Zverev		Bagirov (until 1953)
			Ignatov	Ignatov	Kirichenko (1954–55)
			Kabanov		
		Pospelov (?)	Kosygin		
		Patolichev	Patolichev		
			Pegov	Pegov	
			Puzanov		
			Tevosyan		
			Yudin		

PARTY OF THE SOVIET UNION, 1952–58

1953 SECRET. C.C.	FEBRUARY, 1956 PRESIDIUM C.C.	FEBRUARY, 1956 SECRET. C.C.	JULY, 1957 PRESIDIUM C.C.	JULY, 1957 SECRET. C.C.	1958 PRESIDIUM C.C.
		Aristov (since July 4, 1955)	Aristov	Aristov	
		Belyayev (since July 4, 1955)	Belyayev	Belyayev	
	Bulganin		Bulganin		Bulganin (removed Sept. 5, 1958)
			Brezhnev	Brezhnev	
	Voroshilov		Voroshilov		
Ignatiev (dropped 1954)			Ignatov	Ignatov (since Dec., 1957)	
	Kaganovich				
	Kirichenko (since July 4, 1955)		Kirichenko	Kirichenko (since Dec., 1957)	
			Kozlov		
			Kuusinen	Kuusinen	
Malenkov (March 6–14, 1953)	Malenkov				
	Mikoyan		Mikoyan		
	Molotov		Mukhitdinov (Dec., 1957)	Mukhitdinov (since Dec., 1957)	
	Pervukin				
	Saburov (since July 4, 1955)		Zhukov (until Nov., 1957)		
Suslov	Suslov	Suslov	Suslov	Suslov	
Khrushchev (first secretary on Sept. 7, 1953)	Khrushchev	Khrushchev (first secretary)	Khrushchev	Khrushchev (first secretary)	
			Shvernik		
			Furtseva	Furtseva	
	Candidates: Zhukov		*Candidates:* Mukhitdinov (until Dec., 1957)		*Candidates:*
	Shvernik Brezhnev		Pospelov Korotchenko Kalnberzins Kirilenko Kosygin	Pospelov	
	Mukhitdinov				
	Shepilov	Shepilov (since July 4, 1955)	Mazurov Mzhavanadze Pervukhin		
	Furtseva				
Pospelov Shatalin (until Feb., 1955?)	Kozlov (since Feb., 1957)	Pospelov			Added: Podgorny Poliansky

to check on violations of party discipline and to carry out periodic purges. Apparently to prevent the building of personal political machines, the 1952 party rule concerning the independent functioning of the Party Control Committee representatives in the localities was abolished in 1956.

The Presidium can overrule any decision of the other higher organs of the party. Although it is in theory accountable to the Central Committee, this accountability—as in the case of the Politburo earlier—is likely to be more nominal than real. The Presidium itself fashions the system of Soviet rule and makes basic Soviet policy. To ensure itself control even over policy-implementing decisions by the highest governmental organ, it assigns the vice-premierships in the Council of Ministers to Presidium members, and it also gives them certain direct administrative tasks, such as the supervision of vital or lagging ministries. In time of crisis it redistributes functions among its members in a manner that will secure further concentration of policy control in a smaller group, as in the case of the State Defense Committee (five, later eight, members), which functioned during the recent war. To make certain of obedience to its directives, it keeps a tight grip over the propaganda machine and the M.V.D.

As in the Politburo the dominant role in the Presidium was played by Joseph Stalin, who had emerged by the end of the twenties as "the Leader" of the party. As the party leaders revealed at the Twentieth Party Congress (1956), Stalin not only made many decisions on his own responsibility, but since the mid-thirties progressively usurped the functions of the Politburo. Available evidence points to fear or loyalty toward him on the part of the other members of the Politburo, whom he had personally co-opted into its membership; and the trinity of supreme organs—the Politburo, Orgburo, and Secretariat—operated in practice as a single directorate under him. The present directorate—the Presidium and Secretariat—has more of an aspect of collective leadership.

The Komsomol, Pioneers, and Octobrists: Junior Assistants of the Party. The Komsomol (Young Communist League), which is designated in the party rules as "an active assistant of the party in all state and economic work," was established in the autumn of 1918. Its membership consists of young people from fourteen to twenty-six years old. Members can stay on with consultative vote past the upper age limit, retaining voting privileges only if they are elected to leading organs. Admission to membership is effected at a general meeting of a local Komsomol organization on the basis of an application supported by two Komsomol members of not less than a year's standing, or, in the case of Pioneers, on the recommendation of a Pioneer brigade council. Such admission is subject to approval by a bureau of a city or district Komsomol committee, and expulsion from membership for non-payment of dues, inactivity, violations of regulations, etc., requires a similar endorsement.

The Komsomol is organized and operated on the model of the

party, with primary organizations in schools, institutions, and enterprises. Komsomol units of intermediate levels meet in conferences and congresses, each of which is guided by its respective committees, bureaus, and secretaries in areas, cities, districts, regions, territories, and republics. At the top of the pyramid are the central, All-Union organs. The All-Union Congress of the Komsomol—which, like the All-Union Party Congress, is officially called "the supreme organ" of the League—is supposed to convene not less than once every four years to hear and approve reports of the Komsomol Central Committee and the Komsomol Central Inspection Commission. The central committee, which represents the Komsomol in government offices and organizations and directs all its work in the interval between congresses, is required to hold at least one plenary meeting every six months. It elects a bureau to direct all Komsomol work between central committee plenums and appoints a secretariat for current work of an organizational-executive nature. In practice no Komsomol Congress met from 1936 until the spring of 1949, when the All-Union Congress of the Komsomol met for the first time in thirteen years, adopted amendments to its rules, and elected new central organs. In 1954 the central Komsomol hierarchy comprised a central committee of 103 members and 47 candidates, a central inspection commission of 31, a bureau of 13 members and 2 candidates, and a large secretariat headed by 7 responsible secretaries.[5]

The party's concern with, and control of, the Komsomol is openly admitted. The amended rules declare that the Komsomol "carries on all its work under the immediate direction of the All-Union Communist Party." The central committee of the Komsomol is directly subordinated to the Central Committee of the party, but "the work of the local Young Communist League organizations is guided and controlled by the corresponding region, territory, republic, city, and district party organizations." The party leaders have long followed the practice of delegating one of their number to supervise the Komsomol. In recent years N. A. Mikhailov, a member of the Orgburo, has served as first secretary of the Komsomol Central Committee and has, in fact, directed the central organs of the Komsomol. While Mikhailov was shifted to the Moscow Party Committee and Sergei P. Pavlov is now serving as first secretary of the Komsomol Central Committee, there is little doubt that another member of the Party Presidium is supervising Komsomol work. The Komsomol secretaries of cities, districts, and higher levels are required to be party members or candidates. Theoretically elected by their respective committees, these secretaries are actually appointed by the higher Komsomol hierarchy, and at the upper echelons no doubt on the basis of suggestions from the party summit.

The Komsomol thus serves as the arm of the party among the masses of youth. In the past it has helped the party in carrying out the Five Year plans for industry, agriculture, and transport, and has actively participated in the industrialization and collectivization drives, in training technicians and skilled personnel, and in military preparations. Cur-

[5] For a thorough recent survey of the Young Communist League see Merle Fainsod, *How Russia is Ruled* (1953), Chapter 9.

rently it is being asked to pioneer in new land and industry development. Generally its activites fall into five categories. In the political field the Komsomol is expected to master Marxist-Soviet theory, educate Soviet youth in communism, and help to propagate current policies. The number of Komsomol members studying Marxism-Leninism in political circles and schools has risen from four million in 1949 to five million by 1954. Many more were engaged in similar studies on their own. In 1954 ninety-three newspapers for youth and twenty for children had a total circulation of about eight million copies. Ten youth and twenty-two children's magazines had a total circulation of two million. This represents an increase of two and a half times over 1949. Komsomol members have traditionally been mobilized in connection with Soviet elections and every kind of propaganda campaign.

In the military field the Komsomol has deliberately been designated the "patron" of the armed forces, and its members have formed the core of the civilian auxiliaries of the army, navy, and air force. Komsomol members are supposed to set an example in both military preparation and actual warfare, and many of them were decorated during the recent war. In the social field the Komsomol member is called upon to fight against hooliganism, drunkenness, and caddishness; he must promote the new attitude with regard to the family by leading a model family life and follow the latest directives on the struggle against "the remains of religious prejudices." In the economic field the Komsomol is constantly enlisted in both seasonal campaigns and permanent undertakings to aid agriculture, transport, mining, and lagging sectors of industry through exemplary performance, perfection of skills, and promotion of productivity and labor discipline. In the cultural field the Komsomol is not only expected to serve as a vanguard for Soviet youth in acquiring scientific and technological knowledge but he is enjoined to make life for young people happier and more interesting by sponsoring glee clubs, sport societies, literary and theatrical groups, nature study circles, and similar recreations.

Along all of these lines the Komsomol has a direct responsibility to guide the still-younger party auxiliaries, the organizations of the Young Pioneers, for children from nine to fourteen, and the Little Octobrists, for children from eight to twelve. Since the Komsomol must in one way or another reach most of the Soviet youth, its membership was expected to be large. From some 22,000 members in 1918 it grew to 2 millions by 1928, 9 millions by 1939, and, reportedly, 15 millions by October, 1945. Even if the 1945 figure was too high, wartime losses and a general lowering of morale resulted in a sharp decline in membership, and at the Komsomol Congress in March, 1949, the membership figure given was 9,283,000. Strong measures to counteract what appeared to be a postwar apathy brought the membership up to over 12 millions by 1951 and over 18.8 million in 431,000 primary organizations by 1954.

The Pioneer organization, founded in 1922, is supposed to be both a character-building and ideological-conditioning instrument. It is called upon to develop self-reliance among school children, nine to four-

teen years of age, and to train them "in the spirit of Soviet patriotism
. . . love for knowledge, labor, discipline, accuracy, and respect for
elders." The Pioneers are organized into "troops" that can be broken
down into "detachments" and the latter in turn into "units." A troop or
detachment is led by a Komsomol member appointed by the city or
district committee of the Komsomol. The units are led by their own
elected leaders. For purposes of administration and supervision the
Pioneer hierarchy is organized in city or district organizations, subordinate to regional, territorial, or republic Pioneer organizations, which
in turn are subordinate to Komsomol committees of these levels. Octobrists form links of five members led by a Pioneer; five links constitute
a group under a Komsomol leader. Although both of the younger
organizations receive indoctrination, the instructional emphasis is on
sports, hobbies, rudimentary science and mechanics, preparatory military
training, theatrical activity, etc. Currently the Komsomol organizations
are being warned not to overload children with public and other extra-
curricular activities.

The Pioneer organization has grown from 5,000 members in 1923
to 11 millions by 1939, and 19 millions by 1953. At present the total
membership of the Komsomol, Pioneers, and Octobrists numbers in the
neighborhood of 40 millions or nearly one-fifth of the population.[6] Although in all probability only a fourth or a fifth of the membership of
these junior organizations can be considered to constitute a completely
devoted and reliable core, the party leaders look upon these organizations as a sufficient reserve from which to select and train leading cadres
for the party and state institutions.

[6] For the latest statutes and regulations on the Komsomol and Pioneers, see
Komsomol'skaia Pravda, March 30, and April 10, 1954.

26

THE POLITICAL STRUCTURE:
THE SOVIET GOVERNMENT

1. THEORY OF THE SOVIETS' POSITION

The theory of the soviets' position in the U.S.S.R. entails explanations, not only of the standing of the soviets vis-à-vis the Communist Party, but of their role in relation to the toilers and the populace as a whole. The soviets constitute the official governmental structure of the U.S.S.R., and their central organs represent the Soviet Union in dealings with foreign states. To the Soviet masses themselves the soviets are often depicted as institutions of popular rule, wielding sovereign power. When all the conceptions of the soviets are weighed in the balance, however, the theory of the soviets is essentially a theory of a subordinate instrument of government.

Soviets and Populace: The Theory of Mass Schooling in Administration. Both Communist ideology and the political expediency of the leaders of the U.S.S.R. have contributed to the elaboration of a conception of the soviets as a school of government for the masses. From the standpoint of ideology, in the words of Engels' dictum, if at the end of the march toward communism "government over persons is replaced by the administration of things and the direction of the processes of production," the training of many citizens in the rudiments of administration would then help to lay a basis for eventual processes of self-administration in a non-coercive social order. On the other hand, from the standpoint of political control, the mere belief on the part of masses of the populace that they are being schooled in the arts of administration would facilitate the immediate tasks of the Soviet leaders.

On the eve of the Bolshevik revolution and in the years following it Lenin, although admitting that "not every laborer or cook could at present undertake the administration of the state," argued that the soviets were re-educating the masses, bringing them to the forefront, and "turning them into legislators, and executives." Later Stalin and other Soviet leaders likewise maintained that the soviets were a "school of government for tens and hundreds of thousands of workers and peasants," binding the masses to the regime. This view is maintained to date, a recent official editorial reiterating the claim that the soviets are "the school of state administration in which millions of Soviet citizens receive their training for leadership." [1]

Soviets and Toiling Strata: The Theory of Popular Rule. In fact, the Soviet leaders appear to have become convinced that one of the best props for the maintenance of their own position in power is the repeated public assertion that the soviets are not only a "school" of administration but the actual embodiment of popular rule.

During 1917–19, the formative years of the regime, Lenin loudly claimed that the soviets were a "higher form" of democracy, "democracy for the vast majority of the people." He contended that in this new type of state there would be "no bureaucracy, no police, no standing army," that they would be replaced by popularly elected officials who earn ordinary workers' wages and are subject to recall at any time by their electors, and by "the universal arming of the people." Despite evidence in the years that followed of a growing conviction on their part that bureaucracy will characterize public administration in the U.S.S.R. for a long time, the Soviet leaders, realists though they claimed to be, repeatedly expressed themselves in favor of greater participation by the masses in government as the best antidote to red tape, evasiveness, irresponsibility, and other "bureaucratic distortions."

The semantics of democratic government and popular sovereignty lodged in the soviets continue to the present. Although Lenin's early ideas about equalizing officials' and workers' wages, abolishing the standing army, popular recall of officials, even of the higher levels, etc., have long since been abandoned, Molotov used the occasion of the twentieth anniversary of the revolution to reiterate the official claim that the basis of the soviet system is "the participation of the toiling masses in state administration"; and public statements of recent years likewise refer to the soviets as democratic "sovereign organs" that secure "the genuine and decisive participation of all toilers in the control of government." Soviet theoreticians suggest as examples of such participation and control, not only the soviets, but also such officially encouraged forms of "self-criticism" as letters to newspaper editors, especially the "letters of the workers to Stalin," pledging better quality or greater quantity in production, which fill the Soviet press.

Thus the semantics of mass participation in government through the soviets are given special connotations in theory. If practice falls far short of promise in this vital sphere, there are a number of distinct political considerations behind the continued employment of language of popular rule. They can be summarized in the following way. The Soviet leaders have always believed in the utility of maintaining and multiplying points of contact with the masses and regard the soviets— more particularly the local soviets—as one of the principal bridges between the party and the people, as good intelligence feelers or "barome-

[1] *Izvestia,* July 26, 1950.

ters," through which they can gauge changing popular moods. "Criticism and self-criticism" (*kritika i samokritika*)—since they are never permitted to touch basic policy, but are allowed only in regard to fulfillment of policy—serve the dual purpose of stimulating better execution of policy and canalizing popular discontent. Talking is a form of externalizing personal insecurity feelings. By "keeping them talking," criticism and self-criticism at sessions of the soviets or in letters to editors—never spontaneously directed against higher officials, but always aimed at lower-level bureaucrats—function as a cathartic device, as a harmless outlet for popular grievances that leaves the top leadership unscathed. To the extent that the operation of the local soviets yields some sense of participation in administration, it can induce mass identification with the regime, particularly if all official pronouncements and rationalizations propagate this sentiment to the utmost. In this way the theory of popular rule serves the highly utilitarian purpose of sustaining the authoritarian regime.

Soviets and Government: The Theory of Non-separation of Powers. To round out the theory of the role of the soviets in the system, we should point out that this theory never embodied the principle of separation of powers. The idea of setting up the legislative, executive, and judicial organs of the state as equal and co-ordinate branches of government, so that they may serve as checks and balances upon one another and prevent undue concentration of power, is totally alien to the Soviet conception of politics.

In the first place, the Soviet theoreticians regard the separation of the elements of power as an artificial arrangement, one of whose baneful consequences was the conversion of parliaments into "talking shops." The Paris Commune, they argue, showed the advantage of placing legislative and executive functions in the same hands. In view of this conception it is small wonder that, far from considering the extraordinarily large percentage of officials among the deputies of Soviet assemblies a vice, they consider it a virtue. In the second place, the Soviet leaders, little concerned lest individual freedoms would suffer from interference by the leviathan state, and primarily interested that their decisions should be given quick and effective application, sought and justified the concentration of government functions in the same organs on the ground that it made for speedy decisions, energetic mobilization of resources, and rapid execution of policy directives. Thus the Soviet organs that functioned under the older constitution (the Central Executive Committee, its Presidium, and the Council of People's Commissars) were frankly admitted to have been both legislative and executive in nature. It is true that under the new constitution the Supreme Soviet of the U.S.S.R. is called the sole legislative body and that the Council of Ministers is designated as an executive-administrative organ. Nevertheless, Soviet theory denies that these provisions imply a concession to the doctrine of separation of powers, which the leaders continue to reject as a matter of principle.

Aside from the fact that the above distribution of functions under the new constitution is in actuality a fiction, the reason for eschewing the doctrine of separation of powers seems clear enough. The party leaders look upon the entire network of soviets as tools and assistants, not as checks and balances upon their own power. The real seat of power, after all, is the party summit, while the soviets at the various levels are merely the vehicles for the implementation of the party's directives. Under these circumstances all talk of the separation of powers would be entirely superfluous.

2. ORGANIZATION AND ROLE OF THE SOVIETS

Election of the Soviet Hierarchy: The Vote without the Choice. Soviet elections are vast mass undertakings. In the elections held in recent years for the Supreme Soviet of the U.S.S.R. (March, 1954), for the supreme soviets of the union republics and the autonomous republics (February, 1955), and for local soviets (March, 1957), more than 120 million voters and many hundreds of thousands of candidates were involved. Numbers alone, however, are no guarantee of a democratic process. And this is particularly true in the case of Soviet elections, the characteristics of which differ fundamentally from those of the Western democratic polities.

Essentially Soviet elections are regarded as neither a means of changing rulers at stated intervals nor a club over them to induce greater responsibility and accountability during their tenure of office. Although the highest party leaders—in their own cases the sole judges and masters of personnel changes and responsibility—may formally use the elections to the soviets to achieve both ends at the lower echelons of the government bureaucracy, they possess and have frequently used other means for those purposes. Soviet elections are viewed primarily as a school of political education and ideological indoctrination, in official verbiage "a huge political school in which millions of working people deepen and extend their understanding of the party and governmental policy." They are conceived of as a device to build a consensus behind the regime, one of the mass activities designed to convey to the populace a sense of participation in politics. At the same time they are considered one of the principal occasions to whip up social pressure in behalf of increased productivity in every line of endeavor.

This conception is responsible for the extraordinary effort and fanfare that accompany the drive to bring out the vote. Several stages are envisaged: formation of electoral precincts, with their respective commissions; compilation of voters' lists; nomination and registration of candidates; preparations for election day; and tabulation of the results. An elaborate and sprawling electoral machinery is set up. Over the precinct and area electoral commissions stand those of the union republics and the autonomous republics; and the entire electoral machinery is topped by the Central Election Commission, which in 1954 was composed of twenty-seven members. In the 1958 federal elections to the

Supreme Soviet, electoral areas—which included special areas for the armed forces—yielded a total of 1,378 deputies: 738 in the Council of the Union and 640 in the Council of Nationalities. Electoral precincts were set up everywhere, even on passenger trains.

In part, no doubt, to sell the citizens on the idea that the elections are of significance, Party Presidium (Politburo) members stand for elections to the federal Supreme Soviet. While multiple honorary nominations of each Party Presidium member take place—and the number of such nominations constitutes a rough index to his standing in the Party summit—he can be an active candidate for election in only one district, apparently determined by the Presidium itself. The constitution provides that each citizen has the right to vote at the age of eighteen and to be elected to the Supreme Soviet at the age of twenty-three. It grants the right to nominate Supreme Soviet candidates to public organizations and societies of toilers, Communist Party organizations, trade unions, co-operatives, youth organizations, and cultural societies; and this right has been interpreted to include general meetings of various groups of citizens. Actual practice shows, however, that representatives of the party take part in and influence every meeting for the nomination of a candidate. As a result the one nominee for office is, in accordance with the prevailing custom of putting up only one candidate, the choice of the party as well as of the popular district. Always he is a person deemed loyal to the regime, regardless of whether he is formally a member of the party. And the area election commission, staffed predominantly with party members, would refuse to register him as a candidate if it had any doubts concerning his devotion to the party and its leaders or if higher party instances indicated dissatisfaction with his selection.

After the candidates have been nominated, the election preparations enter what the Soviet leaders regard as its most important stage, and a most intensive propaganda campaign is unleashed, despite the fact that to all intents and purposes the election of the registered candidates is assured. Operating from "agitation points" (centers) in election precincts, agitators appointed by the party organizations and aided by thousands of "activists" from such public organizations as trade unions and co-operatives, as well as from plain citizens' groups, use every type of special and general meeting and every medium of communication to reach even the smallest group of citizens in the city and countryside. In addition to discussing the qualities of the candidates the agitators concentrate on such local problems as schools, municipal utilities, working conditions, and on such broad questions as the Soviet socioeconomic structure and foreign policy, with the aim of convincing the citizens of the superiority of the Soviet order and of inducing "socialist competition" to facilitate its growth and military strength.

An illustration of the extent of this effort is offered by the propaganda drive that accompanied the elections to the local soviets in December, 1950. At the outset it was urged that the 7,700 newspapers of the country, with a circulation of 33 millions, should be used in the pre-election propaganda program. In the Moscow region alone the Moscow party organization was instrumental in organizing 25,000 meetings for the nomination of members of electoral commissions. Over 1.6 million voters participated, and 138,000 speakers addressed these meetings. To conduct the day-to-day propaganda work, 1,428 agitation centers were opened in the area and 282,000 agitators were selected for the purpose. More than 12,000 lectures and talks were given at these centers before 1,110,000 persons, while over 5 million citizens took part in group discussions held in apartment houses and dormitories. Campaigns of similar scope were conducted in other regions; even the small republic of Latvia was covered with a network of 1,900 agitation centers, from which 50,000 agitators carried on their operations.

These propaganda campaigns, along with general recognition that the party leaders—ultimately backed by the entire coercive machinery of the state—stand behind them, have led to phenomenal results in bringing the citizens to the polls. Out of a total of 133,836,325 registered voters for the federal Supreme Soviet elections in 1958, 133,796,091 actually voted. The 99.97 per cent participation in the voting for the federal elections of 1958 is an example of what is by now a standard and predictable result in the practice of elections in the U.S.S.R.

There are some lessons to be drawn from these and related election figures. If we compare the statistics for the 1937, 1950, and 1954 elections to the Supreme Soviet, we find, not only that the number of eligible voters has increased (which was to be expected in view of territorial accretions and population growth), but also that the percentage of those who voted rose by over 3 per cent by 1954. The percentage of party members in the Supreme Soviet, which had increased by 7.3 per cent in 1950, dropped by 5.5 per cent in 1954 and now stands at 77.9 per cent. At the same time the percentage of those who voted against the "bloc of Communists and non-party people" decreased from 1.8 per cent in 1937 to a fraction of 1 per cent by 1958. The number of invalidated ballots decreased from 636,000 (1937) to 1,487 (1950), and 680 (1954) in the elections for the Council of the Union, and from over 1,487,000 (1937) to 1,619 (1950) and 609 (1954) in the elections for the Council of the Nationalities. The conclusion is obvious that the purges of the thirties and mid-forties, the injection of larger numbers of party members into public bodies and all crucial positions of surveillance and control, and the relentless propaganda drives have had enough of an intimidating effect and have induced sufficient acceptance of the desired conception of elections to preclude the possibility of citizen use of the elections as a vehicle of opposition to the regime and its program.

In March, 1936, Stalin told Roy Howard that under the new constitution "elections will be lively; they will be conducted around numerous very acute problems, principally of a practical nature"; they will help to "tighten up all institutions and organizations and compel them to improve their work"; and they will serve as "a whip in the hands of the population against the organs of government that work badly." Soviet practice has given a singularly perverted connotation to this promise. The elections are indeed made "lively" as a vehicle of agitation to help in the attainment of industrial, agricultural, or military objectives. But the whip is in the hands of the leaders, and popular expressions of criticism of "organs of government that work badly" are invoked only at the instigation and within the bounds permitted by those leaders. They thus serve as a cathartic device, of which totalitarian states stand in the greatest need. They also meet a number of practical needs, among the most important (besides those already mentioned) being the provision of an additional sifting instrument to aid the party leaders in the course of the campaign to spot people with organizing or articulating skills for eventual recruitment in the service of the party. But, unlike elections in democratic states, they offer the citizen no contest of candidates and programs and no determining role in selecting and controlling his governors. All they grant him is a vote without choice.

The Soviets of the Localities: The Mass Tiers of the Government Structure.   Of all the mass organizations in the U.S.S.R. the Soviet leaders regard the local soviets as the most important. This is primarily because the very size and geographic expanse of the territorial-administrative network make these units of the official governmental structure particularly suitable for the kind of mass participation the leaders have in mind.

Below the fifteen union republics, as previously indicated, there are eighteen autonomous republics (fourteen in the R.S.F.S.R., two in the Georgian, one in the Uzbek, and one in the Azerbaijan S.S.S.R.); six territories (all in the R.S.F.S.R.), 129 regions, and eight autonomous regions (five in the R.S.F.S.R.), subordinated to the territories:[2] and ten national areas (all in the R.S.F.S.R., subordinated to the territory or region in which they are located). Within these territorial-administrative divisions—as of the end of 1956—there were in operation some 4,188 district soviets, 1,590 city soviets, and 505 borough (city district) soviets, 2,464 settlement soviets and 50,443 village soviets. Thus, throughout the union republics, the main tiers are the units of the regions and districts and the city and village soviets. The R.S.F.S.R., the only republic that also has territories and national areas, is the complicated exception. Altogether there are at present 59,335 local soviets with a total of 1,536,310 deputies in them.

In the eyes of the Soviet leaders these lower soviets are not only organs of local administration, increasingly utilized for more effective exploitation of local resources, but in view of the numbers of units and members involved, they also serve as outlets for popular criticism and for garnering support for the regime by securing participation in local tasks and objectives. One of the methods employed for that purpose is to attract citizens to work as volunteer activists in the standing committees (called permanent commissions) of the soviets. These committees are elected at sessions of the soviets from their regular membership. The majority of the local soviets have the following standing

---

[2] With the recent rehabilitation of four nationalities, the Kalmyk, Chechen-Ingush, and Kabardino-Balkar autonomous republics and the Karachai autonomous region, formerly in the R.S.F.S.R., have been restored.

committees: budget-finance, public education, public health, cultural-educational, agriculture and procurement, local industry, social insurance, trade and co-operatives, communal economy, and improvements and road building. Their main task is to assist the departments of the executive committees of the soviets in the implementation of their work plans. To make the standing committees serve as bridges between the local soviets and the populace, factories and institutions are urged to select some of their members, with the requisite skills or interests, for part-time work in these committees. In 1955 there were 245,000 standing committees in the U.S.S.R. comprising over one million deputies and more than 1.3 million activists. Most of these individuals were in the city and village soviets. In 1950 there were in the district soviets of the R.S.F.S.R. alone nearly 14,000 standing committees, with a total membership of over 140,000 persons about equally divided between regular Soviet deputies and activists. Some of the newer forms of participation encouraged in the postwar period are street and bloc committees, elected by general meetings of residents chiefly in order to assist the executive committees of the local soviets in the physical improvement of their residential areas.

Under the new constitution "soviets of toilers' deputies" exist at all levels of local government, including the districts and regions, where congresses of soviets functioned earlier. These soviets, elected for two-year terms, are supposed to meet with the frequency specified in the constitutions of the individual republics. These soviets are charged with the performance of the following functions: direction of the work of organs of administration subordinate to them, ensuring the maintenance of public order, observance of the laws, protection of the rights of citizens, direction of local economic and cultural affairs, and preparation of the local budget. The soviets of toilers' deputies elect as their "executive and administrative organs" executive committees composed of a chairman, vice-chairman, secretary, and members. In a small locality, such as the smaller settlements or villages, the chairman, vice-chairman, and secretary of the village soviet constitute the executive and administrative organ. On the principle of "dual subordination" these executive organs are accountable, not only to the soviets electing them, but also to the executive committee of the soviet higher in the hierarchy. Except in the case of the village the executive organs of the local soviets carry on their work through a number of administrative departments. Since the executive committees tend to usurp in practice whatever authority is given the soviets at the local level (in part, no doubt, because the sessions of the soviets of toilers' deputies are relatively brief and their required frequency of meeting is not always observed), special efforts have been made, particularly in recent years, to improve the quality of these local administrators. This is done by dispatching from time to time instructors from the district executive committees of the soviets to supervise local government activities in the smaller cities, villages, and settlements, and by holding regular monthly seminars for the chairmen and secretaries of these soviets for training in ideological matters and administrative efficiency.

Largely due to the consolidation of the collective farms, the village soviets—the lowest tier of the Soviet structure—decreased in number from the peak figure of some 74,500 in 1950 to 50,443 village soviets by 1956. The basis of representation in them differed in various localities. In some republics it was one deputy per 100–250 villagers; in others it was one per 100 villagers, etc. All village soviets are required to meet at least once a month. The following work plan illustrates the agenda of a village soviet, with the type of reports scheduled by administrators, deputies, standing-committee members, and activists:

FIG. XXIV

MEETINGS OF THE VILLAGE SOVIET EXECUTIVE COMMITTEE

July 4   Socialist competition among collective farmers and machine operators. Work of the village reading room. Work of nurseries in field brigades Nos. 1–3.

July 14   Results of financial plan fulfillment for first half of 1951.
          Progress of harvesting and grain deliveries.
          Receiving visitors and reviewing complaints and requests of working people (fulfilling region and district soviet executive committee resolutions).

Sessions of the Village Soviet

June 24   Budenny Collective Farm's preparedness for harvesting and grain deliveries.
          Fulfillment of voters' instructions. Report on work of standing committee on municipal improvement.

July 24   Results of socialist competition between Podgornoye and Arkhipovsk village soviets during first half of 1951.
          Improving the breed and raising the productivity of the collective farms' livestock.
          Report on work of the village soviet's standing committee on agriculture.

Organizational—Mass Work

June 27   Conference of leading agricultural workers on exchange of work experience.
          Conference of village soviet deputies on deputies' reports to the voters.*

* See "Work Plan of Podgornoye Village Soviet," *Izvestia,* June 29, 1951; a translation of this article appears in *Current Digest of the Soviet Press,* 3, No. 32 (September 22, 1951), pp. 7–11.

District soviets, which are supposed to meet a minimum of six times a year, are a key link in the Soviet structure, especially in the rural areas. Here too there were some differences in the bases of representation according to the different union-republic constitutions. The Bye-lorussian provided for one deputy per 500–1,000 citizens; the Turkmen specified one deputy per 1,000 for a district with a population of more than 25,000, and at least twenty-five deputies where the popula-tion is less. The executive committees of the district soviets have the primary responsibility for the transmission to the collective farms of the government's plans for agricultural production and deliveries and for the supervision of the organization of labor, sowing, harvesting, animal raising, and deliveries of the prescribed quotas of produce to the state. In addition to an organizational and instruction section, which operates directly under the chairman of the district executive committee and directs the instructors sent to the village soviets, each committee has a planning commission and usually the following departments: general, finance, trade, agriculture-education, health, social insurance, roads, and cultural-educational. With the approval of the region above them district executive committees may set up departments of local and communal industries, municipal services, and occasionally others called for by the special needs of the locality, i.e., the irrigation departments in the Turkmen S.S.R. Generally, following adoption of the sixth Five Year Plan, official statements have emphasized the need for more local initiative.

In the urban communities there are two types of soviets, the city soviets and the borough (city district) soviets, which may be formed in cities with more than 100,000 inhabitants. In 1956 there were 1,590 city soviets and 489 borough soviets. Again, the basis of representation in each varies to some extent. In the Ukraine, for example, one deputy is to be elected for every 350–900 persons, with 35 deputies for the soviets of cities with populations under 12,000. In city boroughs having more than 20,000 inhabitants one deputy is elected per 500 residents. Those with less than 20,000 citizens elect 35 deputies. The executive committees of the city soviets, which meet several times a month, have departments similar to those of the district. As a rule they maintain departments for local industry, communal economy, municipal services, and housing.

Mention should also be made of the settlement soviets, which numbered 2,464 in 1956. Where their size and nature take them out of the category of "small localities," as in the case of the urban type of mining communities, a settlement may have an executive committee, structurally patterned after that of a city soviet.

At the top of the hierarchy of local soviets stand the regional soviets, which are required to convene not less than four times a year. The differences in the norms of representation are illustrated by the follow-ing ratios: Byelorussia, one deputy per 2–3,000 persons; Turkmenia, one deputy per 4–5,000; the Ukraine, one deputy per 15–30,000 peo-ple. The executive committees of the regions maintain the same types of departments as the districts. In addition some have such departments as art, motion-picture industry, and irrigation. With the approval of the respective ministries they may set up departments or administrations of light industry, food, forest, fishing, meat and dairy, textiles, building construction industries, etc. Some federal ministries maintain separate administrations in the regions.

This vast array of local organs offers no assurance of any genuine autonomy in the local Soviet authorities. Aside from the all-pervading role of the party organizations, which now exist in telling numbers even in the rural localities, the principle of dual subordination, the budgetary and financial controls from the center, the supervision of All-Union operated industries and trusts, the omnipresence of agents of the security organs and various central agencies, and the operation of the federal prosecutors served in the past to curtail the role and initiative of the local authorities. Although the local planning commissions are formally elected by their respective soviets, they are also responsible to the federal *Gosplan* (State Planning Committee) and act as its agents. As a rule the local governments' expenditures are much greater than those of the republic in which they are located, although their revenues are much smaller. It is the federal government that allocates the revenues and expenditures to both, maintaining a firm check on them through an elaborate system of auditing and inspection. Each level of local authority can be overruled by the one above it, but all are subject to central directives and laws. Moreover, the government prosecutors can protest the decisions of the executive committees of the local soviets and, in case of non-compliance, can bring about their suspension. In sum, the local soviets are little more than agents of the federal government, subject to the ultimate guidance and control of the latter, not only in regard to questions of broader significance, but often even in respect to matters of purely local import.

The Soviets of the Republics: Mirrors of Central Patterns.   Above the soviets of the regions rises the tier of autonomous republics, which are considered one of the highest forms of political organization attainable by the ethnic groups; and above these republics stand the union republics, which officially represent the fruition of statehood for the Soviet nationalities.

The rationale of this conception is offered in terms of powers and rights. Whereas an autonomous republic, although called a "state," is conceded to be a dependent entity whose enactments can be suspended or annulled by the union republic in which it is located, a union republic is termed a "sovereign" state, restricted only by the powers constitutionally reserved for the U.S.S.R. and possessed of a right freely to secede from the Union (constitution of 1936, Arts. 15, 17). Other features furnishing alleged evidence of the political autonomy of a union republic are its possession of a separate constitution, the unalterability of its territory without its consent, and the rights granted it by the February, 1944, constitutional amendment to enter into direct diplomatic relations with foreign states and establish its own military formations (Arts. 16, 18, 18a, 18b).[3]

Despite these formal arrangements the powers of the Union are paramount, and neither in fundamental theory nor in actual constitu-

[3] See above, pp. 587–90.

tional practice has there been any significant retreat from centralism in the postwar period. The new constitution of the U.S.S.R. prescribes in marked detail the organs of government in the union republics (Arts. 57–63, 79–88, 102–17); and the powers reserved for the Union by Articles 14, 17, 19, and 20, representing a great increase in federal jurisdiction over that allowed by the 1924 constitution, ensure the supremacy of the U.S.S.R. over the union republics. A specific bill of particulars officially recognizing this supremacy has been provided in the following summary of powers of the Union:

(1) the competence of competence, i.e., the right to enlarge its (the Union's) competence by changing the constitution; (2) the right to issue laws and other normative acts within its field of competence which have equal force in the territories of all the Union Republics and are obligatory for them, especially for the legislative, executive-administrative and judicial organs of the Union Republics; (3) the priority of the Union laws over the laws of the Union Republics: in case of divergence between a Union Republic law and a Union law the latter prevails; (4) definition of the principles of the social and political order of the Union Republics in the Union constitution, and the right of control by the Union over [the enforcement of] conformance of the Union Republic constitutions with the U.S.S.R. constitution; (5) establishment of the general procedure governing the relations between the Union Republics and foreign states; (6) establishment of the directing principles for the organization of the military formations of the Union Republics; (7) confirmation of boundary changes between the Union Republics, as well as of the formation of new Autonomous Republics and Autonomous Regions within Union Republics; (8) the establishment of basic principles of legislation in a number of fields (education, public health, labour, marriage and the family, etc.).[4]

Although decisions of the union-republic supreme soviets (unlike decisions of the earlier congresses of soviets and central executive committees under the 1924 constitution) cannot be suspended or annulled by the federal Supreme Soviet Presidium, the latter has the explicit right to annul, and the federal Council of Ministers has the power to suspend, decisions of the union republic's council of ministers (Arts. 69, 49e). Likewise the procurator-general of the U.S.S.R., in exercising supervisory power over law observance by institutions and individuals, appoints and controls the procurator of the union republic, who in turn appoints all lower procurators and operates independently of all local authorities. The formal right of secession has always been hedged about with conditions and qualifications, even in theory, as implied in Lenin's dictum that "the interests of socialism stand higher than the interests and the right of nations to self-determination." Practice has demon-

4 "USSR" volume of *Bol'shaia Sovetskaia Entsiklopedia* (1947), p. 39.

strated repeatedly the wholly fictitious character of this right. Territorial changes have in fact been made without much regard for constitutional limitations. Other than the membership of the Ukraine and Byelorussia in the United Nations and a few minor initial agreements between Soviet border republics and satellites, there is still no evidence—fifteen years after the 1944 reform—of any separate diplomatic representation by the union republics or of any central intent to permit such representation. Indeed, an offer by Great Britain to establish relations with the Ukraine was never accepted. Nor is there any indication that the union republics have been allowed to set up their own national armies. If these and other facts make any discussion of the "sovereignty" of the union republics a meaningless exercise in semantics, Soviet jurists still rely on a reiteration of the formal rights and on rationalizations based on the existence of separate organs of government in the union republics to prove the genuine statehood of the latter.[5]

The supreme soviet of a union republic is formally designated as the "highest organ of state power" and the "sole legislative organ" of the republic. According to Article 60 of the constitution, this unicameral body is empowered to adopt and amend the union-republic constitution in conformity with the constitution of the U.S.S.R.; to confirm the constitutions and define the boundaries of the autonomous republics within its territory; to approve the national economic plan and budget of the republic; and to exercise the rights of amnesty and pardon in regard to citizens sentenced by the courts of the republic. Also, since 1944, it has been authorized to decide questions of "representation of the Union Republic in its international relations" and to determine "the manner of organizing" the republic's military formations. It also "elects" the members of the presidium of the supreme soviet, the council of ministers, and the supreme court of the republic (Arts. 61–63, 106).

In procedure and functions the supreme soviet of a union republic is virtually a facsimile of the federal Supreme Soviet. It meets twice a year, with special sessions convocative at the discretion of the presidium or on demand of one third of the deputies of the soviet. The items on its agenda include, as a rule, approval of the budget, interim presidium decrees, and appointments.

The formal budgetary procedure begins with a speech by the chairman of the council of ministers of the republic in which he discusses accomplishments and plans, confesses shortcomings, and exhorts the deputies to greater effort for the coming fiscal year. This is followed by a report on the budget by the minister of finance and a joint report by the chairman of the budget committee of the union-republic supreme soviet. Speeches by various deputies and ministers follow. Finally, the budget commission proposes adoption of the draft budget, perhaps with some minor amendments, and a unanimous vote of approval makes it the new budget law.

[5] For a more detailed discussion of these questions see Julian Towster, "Recent Trends and Strategies in Soviet Federalism," *Political Quarterly*, 23 (April-June, 1952), pp. 163–74, and "Soviet Policy on Nationalities," *Antioch Review*, 11 (Dec., 1951), pp. 437–48.

Past practice made it clear that this procedure spelled little union-republic initiative or control over its budget. Those parts of the national economic plan that relate to union republics are merely confirmed, with the addition of some few details, at the session of the union-republic supreme soviet. The U.S.S.R. budget comprises the budgets of the union republics and localities, and the discretion of the union republic is limited to those minor adjustments made possible by savings in expenditures or by finding new sources of income. A slight change was made, for example, at the 1951 session of the supreme soviet of the R.S.F.S.R., where the identical sum allocated to this republic by the U.S.S.R. budget, namely 54,136,000,000 rubles, was proposed by the R.S.F.S.R. council of ministers. The only alteration suggested by the budget committee of the R.S.F.S.R. supreme soviet regarding this item was a reduction in this sum to 54,132,900,000 rubles. Since the union republics have no power to levy taxes and merely act as tax collectors for the Union (their discretion being limited to adjusting rates within ranges set by the U.S.S.R.), taxes cannot serve as new sources of revenue for the republics. The lion's share of the most important single source of revenue, the turnover tax, goes to the federal government. Thus, although the R.S.F.S.R. in 1951 was to collect 171 billion rubles from the turnover tax, 160 billions of this sum was to be given to the central government for All-Union enterprises. Moreover, most of the republic's budget goes in fact for local governmental purposes. Over three fourths of the entire R.S.F.S.R. state budget for 1951 was allocated to the local governments.[6]

After adoption of the budget law the union-republic supreme soviet usually proceeds to the selection of a council of ministers, confirmation of decrees of the republic's supreme soviet presidium, election of a new presidium, and election of new members of the republic supreme court. One of the deputies of the supreme soviet (apparently at the instance of a steering committee called council of elders) proposes a list of members for the presidium, which includes as many vice-chairmen as there are autonomous republics within the union republic. This list is unanimously approved without discussion. Thus, in 1955, the supreme soviet of the R.S.F.S.R. elected a presidium consisting of a chairman, twelve vice-chairmen (representing the autonomous republics), a secretary, and thirteen additional members. Without discussion the republic supreme soviet also votes confirmation of interim decrees adopted by the union-republic presidium between supreme soviet sessions. Such decrees deal for the most part with administrative changes, appointment and removal of ministers, and reorganization of ministries.

The selection of the council of ministers of the union republic is usually preceded at the supreme soviet sessions by a resolution of confidence in the council of ministers, moved by one of the deputies and unanimously adopted. The same resolution charges the chairman of the council of ministers with the task of submitting recommendations con-

[6] For details of R.S.F.S.R. budget see *Pravda* and *Izvestia,* July 5 and 8, 1950.

cerning the composition of the council of ministers of the union-republic government, and the list suggested by him is always confirmed for the ensuing term. This republic government is responsible and accountable to the republic supreme soviet and to its presidium, and also to the U.S.S.R. Presidium and Council of Ministers.

The principle of political control remains in effect, even after the recent adoption of the law "On the Further Perfection of the Organization of Administration of Industry and Construction" aiming at the decentralization of the administrative apparatus of the economy.[7] This law ostensibly grants the councils of ministers of the union republics the right to establish economic-administrative districts headed by a Council of National Economy (*Sovnarkhoz*), which administers industry and agriculture in the district. A sovnarkhoz is subordinated to the council of ministers of the union republic in all of its activities. The council of ministers of the union republic in turn receives guidance from the Council of Ministers of the U.S.S.R. and from the State Planning Committee of the U.S.S.R. (Gosplan), the latter charged with ensuring the fulfillment of a "single centralized economic policy."

While economic policy-making thus remains centralized, operative control in other than selected branches of the economy has been decentralized. Previous to this decree these branches of the economy were directly administered by now-abolished All-Union ministries or co-ordinated union-republic ministries in Moscow and the republics.

Thus, for example, the following union-republic ministries in the R.S.F.S.R., along with corresponding ministries in Moscow, were abolished: urban and rural construction, light industry, meat and dairy products industry, food products industry, building materials industry, and fishing industry. To illustrate the composition of a republic council of ministers, the R.S.F.S.R. council of ministers, since May, 1957, consisted of a chairman, deputy chairmen, the chairman of the Union Republic Gosplan, the chairman of the Russian Republic State Scientific and Technical Committee, the chairman of the Russian Republic Committee for State Security, and the ministers of (a) the union-republic ministries of the R.S.F.S.R.: Internal Affairs, State Control, Public Health, Foreign Affairs, Culture, Defense, Communications, Agriculture, Trade, Finance, Grain Products, and (b) the republic ministries of the R.S.F.S.R.: Highway Transport and Highways, Paper and Wood Processing Industry, Communal Economy, Lumber Industry, Education, Inland Shipping, Social Security, Construction, and Justice. The union-republic ministries of the R.S.F.S.R. have federal counterparts and are responsible to these as well as to the higher organs of the republic. The republic ministries of the R.S.F.S.R. are local, i.e., they have no corresponding ministries in the central government and represent theoretically autonomous spheres of activity. There are some variations in this category of ministries in the separate republics. In addition, chairmen of *sovnarkhozi* can be appointed as ministers and enter the council of ministers of the union republics.

[7] *Pravda,* May 11, 1957.

It is to be noted that all fields of administration concerned with defense and chemical industries, basic transportation, and foreign trade are completely excluded from the union-republic category of ministries. All these matters fall directly or indirectly under the jurisidiction of All-Union ministries, or state committees, under the U.S.S.R. Council of Ministers. This results in exclusive central control of key sectors of the economy and national defense. Fundamentally there is little actual decentralization of policy-making in the economic field in the Soviet Union.

Even in the cultural field, where local control is supposed to be most in evidence, the union republics enjoy little autonomy. The federal Ministry of Higher Education, although of the "union-republic" type, appears to have no corresponding ministries in the union republics, whose ministries of education, although within the strictly "republic" category, are in fact subject to directives of the party and the central government. All higher schools are managed by federal ministries; and although the lower schools are supervised by agencies of the republics, the nature of the central directives is such that the entire educational system, from grade classification to textbooks, is singularly uniform. The same type of central-local relationship exists in such areas as social security and local industry.

Although the union republics were granted controlled administrative autonomy on an operative level in May, 1957, they do not enjoy sovereignty or political independence. It is to be seriously doubted whether the above "decentralizing" measures will result in a thoroughgoing retreat from centralism in practice.

The Federal Supreme Soviet: The Fiction of Exclusive Legislation. Of all the federal organs the Supreme Soviet of the U.S.S.R. is depicted in Soviet constitutional theory as the most important. The constitution calls it "the highest organ of state power in the U.S.S.R." and declares that it alone exercises the legislative power of the Union (Arts. 30, 32). Since the prerogatives of the Supreme Soviet are supposed to embrace all the powers assigned to the Union by Article 14 of the constitution, in so far as they do not fall within the specific jurisdiction of the federal Presidium, Council of Ministers, or ministries (Art. 31), the formal competence of the Supreme Soviet is indeed imposing. In practice, however, the role of the Supreme Soviet is quite different.

The Supreme Soviet is a bicameral body composed of two chambers: a Council of the Union, elected on the basis of one deputy per 300,000 people, and a Council of Nationalities, elected on the basis of twenty-five deputies from a union republic, eleven from an autonomous republic, five from an autonomous region, and one from a national area. Its regular term of office is four years. The Presidium of the Supreme Soviet, which convenes the Supreme Soviet twice a year, can call extraordinary sessions at its own discretion or on demand of a union republic. Also, in case of persistent disagreement between the chambers (a contingency that has never arisen and is very unlikely to occur), the Presidium is empowered to dissolve the Supreme Soviet and to order new elections. The two chambers are accorded equal powers. Their sessions begin and end simultaneously. Each elects a chairman and four vice-chairmen (prior to June, 1950, only two vice-chairmen), who are required to conduct the proceedings of the respective chambers, and the chairmen take turns in presiding over joint sittings. The passage of a law entails approval of both chambers by a simple majority vote in each. The same procedure is followed for constitutional amendments, except that a majority of not less than two thirds of the votes in each chamber is required for passage.

Like its predecessors under the earlier federal constitution the Congress of Soviets and the Central Executive Committee, the Supreme Soviet of the U.S.S.R. has always had a large membership.[8] From 1,143 deputies elected in 1937 its membership increased to 1,339 in 1946, declined slightly to 1,316 in 1950, and presently stands at 1,378 in the Supreme Soviet elected in 1958. But during the same period significant changes have occurred in the social composition of the Supreme Soviet. The percentage of workers among the deputies has fallen by 18.4 per cent—from 42 per cent in 1937 to 39 per cent in 1946, to 31.5 per cent in 1950, to 23.6 per cent in 1954. The percentage of peasant deputies has decreased respectively in the same years from 29.5 per cent to 26 per cent, to 20.5 per cent, to 16.3 per cent, i.e., by a total of 13.2 per cent. Members of the intelligentsia constituted 28.5 per cent of the deputies in 1937, 35 per cent in 1946, 48 per cent in 1950 and 60.1 per cent in 1954—a gain of 31.6 per cent in representation in the Supreme Soviet since 1937. In point of fact this gain is probably even greater than these percentage figures would indicate, if the actual current status and occupation are used as the primary criteria for classification. Thus, out of 238 deputies listed as "workers" in the Council of the Union of the 1950 Supreme Soviet, 169 were in fact engaged in party, Soviet, military, and other public work. Of 123 deputies listed as peasants 53 were similarly engaged while 63 were actually collective-farm chairmen. The intelligentsia clearly predominates now in both chambers; its strength in the Supreme Soviet— roughly reflecting its numerical weight in other organs of government— far exceeds its percentage in the population.

Another tendency, which reverses a prevalent trend in the changes in composition of federal assemblies up to the late thirties, is the progressive increase in party members. The percentage of Supreme Soviet deputies who were not party members has decreased from 23.9 in 1937 to 19 per cent in 1946, to 16.6 per cent in 1950. Only in 1954 did it rise to 22 per cent. The percentage of women deputies, which remained stabilized at 21 per cent until 1954, increased in that year to 25.9 per cent of the deputies. While the accent on youth is still strong, there is a growing tendency to elect somewhat older deputies. In both chambers today the age group of forty-one to fifty is the largest. In 1954, 210 out of 708 deputies in the Council of the Union and 170 out of 639 members in the Council of Nationalities were over fifty years of age.

[8] For composition of the present Supreme Soviet see *Pravda* and *Izvestia*, March 19, 1958.

The procedure of the Supreme Soviet has become quite standardized.[9] The first session of a newly elected Supreme Soviet differs from later sessions only in that it has the additional duties of electing a Presidium and Council of Ministers. Generally a session lasts about a week. As a rule the two chambers convene separately for the first meeting. In each council an opening speech by a veteran deputy is followed by the selection of the chairmen, approval of the procedure and agenda for the session, and election of a credentials commission and three standing commissions: a budget commission of twenty-six members, a legislative commission of nineteen members, and a foreign-affairs commission of eleven persons. The second meeting is a joint session of the two chambers, at which the minister of finance is called upon to report on the annual budget for the coming year (and every second year also on the fulfillment of the budget for the two preceding years). This meeting has become a special occasion, with the Party Presidium members in attendance and the government box filled with party dignitaries and members of the Supreme Soviet Presidium and Council of Ministers. At later meetings half of the Party Presidium members attend the sessions of the Council of the Union and the other half those of the Council of Nationalities.

The finance minister's report includes a statement of past and projected progress, sprinkled with references to the international position of the U.S.S.R. and denunciations of foreign opponents. The third meeting of the Supreme Soviet, when the report of the credentials commission is approved, is usually taken up with a "co-report" on the budget presented in each chamber by the chairman of its budget commission. As a rule this co-report proposes an increase in revenues through taxation, notes the petitions by various deputies for greater appropriations, and also criticizes some aspects of the work of different ministries. The following two or three meetings of the separate chambers are devoted to a discussion of the budget, which is one of the approved outlets for permissible types of criticism. Various deputies, probably instructed in advance, speak of progress as well as inadequacies in the fulfillment of plans in their respective areas, criticize some specific actions of ministries, and point out needed expenditures or sources of additional revenues. A number of ministers answer these criticisms, confess "defects," and promise improved performance in the future. At the end of the discussions the finance minister makes a virtually identical closing report in each chamber, accepting proposals for increasing the revenue and indicating that suggestions of individual members will subsequently be considered in detail by the ministries concerned. The brief report is followed by unanimous approval of the budget and an article-by-article vote on the budget law.

At one meeting the list of interim decrees issued by the Presidium of the Supreme Soviet is read. This list, which includes decrees involving changes in the ministries as well as appointment and removal of

[9] On the procedure of the Supreme Soviet note *Pravda* and *Izvestia,* June 12–24, 1950; March 7–15, 1951; March 5–11, 1952; April 21–28, 1954; February 6–13, 1957.

ministerial personnel, is presented by the secretary of the Presidium before each chamber and is unanimously approved without any discussion. If constitutional changes are proposed, the secretary submits a special bill embodying those changes. Separate laws, formally initiated for the first time in the Supreme Soviet, are presented infrequently and are passed without any serious debate.

The final meeting is a joint session of the two chambers that unanimously elects the federal Presidium by confirming the list suggested on behalf of the Council of Elders (steering committee) of each chamber and also "elects" the Council of Ministers by voting to approve its work and to instruct it to continue to discharge its duties. It also passes sundry resolutions, designed as a rule for specific internal or external propaganda purposes. In 1951 the joint final session of the chambers was devoted to the presentation of a "peace law" sponsored by the "World Congress of the Partisans of Peace." This was an obviously staged performance, highlighted by numerous speeches concerning the "peace efforts" of the Soviet Union and the "warmongering" of the Western democracies.

To summarize, the Supreme Soviet of the U.S.S.R. is not the powerful organ or source of authority that Soviet theory would make it. It is an assembly of notables, of persons whose membership in the Supreme Soviet is a reward for loyalty and proficiency and who, at most, serve as an added means of contact between localities and local interests and Moscow. The proceedings of the Supreme Soviet are largely perfunctory, and there is little evidence that its permanent commissions play more than a nominal role. The size of its membership and the manner of its election lend it the superficial appearance of a representative organ. As such it is used both as a formal ratifying body, which the regime can claim as an organ of "popular" rule, and as a sounding board for official propaganda. Since legal norms are produced in volume by the Presidium of the Supreme Soviet and by the Council of Ministers, and since interim Presidium decrees are not even debated prior to their approval by the Supreme Soviet, it is clear that the claim of "exclusive legislative powers" by the latter is mere fiction.

3. PRESIDIUM OF THE SUPREME SOVIET

Although first established by the new constitution, the Presidium of the Supreme Soviet, which began functioning in January, 1938, reflects in its operation the role performed earlier to a lesser degree by the Central Executive Committee and to a greater extent by the Executive Committee's Presidium. During the proceedings that led to adoption of the 1936 constitution an amendment was proposed that the chairman of the Presidium be elected by the people. Stalin objected to the proposal on the ground that an "individual president" elected by the entire population on an equal basis with the Supreme Soviet "might essay to stand out against the Supreme Soviet," and he concluded that the

U.S.S.R. must have a "collective" president chosen by the Supreme Soviet, namely, the Presidium of the Supreme Soviet. Thus the official conception to date is that the Presidium is the "collective president" of the Soviet Union. In practice, however, the chairman of the Presidium often acts as the titular head of the state in dealings with foreign countries, and consequently he has occasionally been referred to abroad as "the Soviet President."

Under the provisions of the constitution the Presidium is elected every four years at a joint sitting of the two chambers of the Supreme Soviet (Art. 48). During World War II, however, such election was delayed until 1946. The membership of the Presidium, which numbered forty-three persons earlier, was reduced to thirty-three by a law adopted on March 19, 1946—and later incorporated in the constitution —that prescribed the following composition: a chairman, fifteen vice-chairmen, a secretary, and sixteen members.[1] The present Presidium (including Secretary Georgadze as well as Chairman Voroshilov, who replaced former Chairman Nikolai M. Shvernik on March 6, 1953) was elected on March 27, 1958. In its structure and composition it reflects several established principles and customs. In as much as the Presidium is deemed to reflect, not only the interests of the entire populace, but the special interests of the separate nationalities, it has become customary to fill the posts of the vice-chairmen of the Presidium with the chairmen of the presidia of the fifteen union republics. It was also customary—in part, no doubt, for purposes of liaison, surveillance, and co-ordination—to have several members of the Politburo among the Presidium membership. This custom carries over to the newly created Party Presidium, seven of whose members and candidates are also on the Presidium of the Supreme Soviet. On the other hand, several practices that prevailed in the composition of the Presidium of the Central Executive Committee were not continued after 1936. For example, the inclusion of ministers in the membership of the Presidium is now considered improper on the ground that the new constitution has clearly delimited the respective functions of the Council of Ministers and the Presidium and has made the first body responsible and accountable to the second. Consequently, when Ponomarenko was appointed minister of procurements in 1951, he was released from membership in the Presidium.[2] The chairmen and vice-chairmen of the two chambers of the Supreme Soviet are not placed in the Presidium on the ground that these officers preside over the body to which the Presidium is constitutionally accountable. One or two members of the high command of the Soviet Army have also sat on the Presidium. Marshal Budenny, earlier a member of the Presidium of the Central Executive Committee, has been a member of the Presidium of the Supreme Soviet since its inception.

The Presidium is listed in the constitution as one of the "highest organs of state power," although it is at the same time declared answera-

[1] For election and composition of the present Presidium see *Pravda* and *Izvestia*, March 28, 1958.

[2] See *Pravda* and *Izvestia*, March 11, 1951.

ble for its acts to the other "highest organ," i.e., the Supreme Soviet (Art. 48). The Presidium has no veto power over Supreme Soviet legislation, and, except in the special case of disagreement between its two chambers, it has no authorization to dissolve the Supreme Soviet.

Nevertheless, the avowed primacy of the Supreme Soviet in the Soviet structure notwithstanding, the Presidium is vested by the constitution (Art. 49) with an impressive array of functions. These functions include executive duties, such as convening sessions of the Supreme Soviet, setting election dates, instituting and awarding decorations and medals, exercising the right of pardon, issuing decrees, and dissolving the Supreme Soviet in event of disagreement between its chambers. Executive functions of a military nature include the establishment of military titles, appointment and removal of the higher command of the armed forces, and proclamation of martial law and of general or partial mobilization. The Presidium is the chief Soviet organ for the conduct of foreign relations, as is evidenced by its powers to appoint and receive diplomatic representatives and to ratify and denounce treaties. Judicial functions are also assigned by the constitution to the Presidium; in particular, it interprets the laws of the U.S.S.R. in force and annuls decisions and ordinances of the Council of Ministers of the U.S.S.R. and of the councils of ministers of the union republics in case of non-conformance to law. Also, the Presidium acts for the Supreme Soviet in the period between sessions of the latter in the appointing and dismissal of members of the Council of Ministers, in proclaiming a state of war in event of armed attack, or in carrying out international treaty obligations. Finally, the Presidium may on its own initiative or upon the request of a union republic conduct referendums.

Of particular importance is the Presidium's decree-issuing power, since, despite the emphasis on the exclusive competence of the Supreme Soviet with regard to legislation, many of the Presidium's decrees are legislative in character and in fact become effective long before they are confirmed by the Supreme Soviet. In addition to decrees issued in pursuance of its functions under Article 49 of the constitution, the Presidium has issued decrees on subjects of U.S.S.R. jurisdiction not specifically assigned to it and on matters explicitly or implicitly within the competence of the Supreme Soviet, such as the alteration of union-republic boundaries and formation of new regions and autonomous republics. Recent examples of the types of decrees passed by the Presidium are found in the lists confirmed by the Supreme Soviet in 1956 that comprise enactments reorganizing governmental organs, including ministries; appointments and dismissals of ministers; constitutional amendments; approval of territorial-administrative changes, such as the conversion of the Karelo-Finnish Union Republic into the Karelian Autonomous Republic.[3] It may be remembered also that during World War II, when a State Defense Committee vested with "the full plenitude of power in the state" was created, the Presidium continued to issue decrees on many important matters. Presidium decrees, like

[3] See *Pravda* and *Izvestia,* July 15–17, 1956.

laws of the Supreme Soviet, are issued over the signatures of the chairman and secretary of the Presidium.

Unlike its predecessor under the old constitution the Presidium of the Supreme Soviet has no authority to annul or suspend decisions of the supreme soviets or presidia of the union republics. It is, however, the sole organ now vested by the constitution with the power to interpret laws, a power that under the earlier federal constitution was possessed, not only by the Presidium of the Central Executive Committee, but also by the Supreme Court of the U.S.S.R.

Thus the Presidium has operated as an organ for the conduct of foreign relations, performed duties of a titular executive, and served as a legislative body in the Soviet system. It would be a mistake, however, to conclude that the Presidium is an independent policy-determining organ. The Party Presidium, as earlier the Politburo, has many arms in both the party and the Soviet structures to carry out its will and to implement its decisions through particular methods and on different levels. The Presidium of the Supreme Soviet is merely one of them. Another such instrument is the Council of Ministers.

4. COUNCIL OF MINISTERS OF THE U.S.S.R.

The Council of Ministers was called the Council of People's Commissars, or *Sovnarkom,* until March 19, 1946. At that time the terms "commissar" and "commissariat" were abandoned in the U.S.S.R. and the union republics in favor of terms "minister" and "ministry." The earlier Sovnarkom dated from one of the first acts of the Bolshevik revolutionary regime, having been created by a decree of the Second Congress of Soviets on November 8, 1917.[4]

The official conception of the council's role was changed in the mid-thirties. The decree creating the Sovnarkom, with power to govern the country until the meeting of a constituent assembly (which convened but was dispersed by the Bolsheviks in January, 1918), declared that the "governmental power belongs to . . . the Council of People's Commissars." The constitution of 1918 made the council responsible and accountable to the Congress of Soviets and Central Executive Committee (Arts. 35–38, 40, 46). Likewise the Union constitution of 1924 designated the council as the "executive and administrative organ" of the Central Executive Committee and made it responsible to the committee and the Presidium (Arts. 37, 38, 40, 41). Yet, under each constitution, the council was vested with broad legislative powers, and in both constitutional theory and practice it was actually regarded as a legislative agency no less than an executive and administrative one.

Since the adoption of the 1936 constitution the legislative role of the council has been formally de-emphasized in consonance with the emphasis placed in theory upon the Supreme Soviet as *the* legislative

---

[4] For a more complete discussion of the evolution of the Council of Ministers see Julian Towster, *Political Power in the U.S.S.R., 1917–1947* (1948), pp. 272–76.

organ. Decisions and ordinances issued by the Council of Ministers, called the highest "executive and administrative" organ of state power, are said to be enacted solely "on the basis and in pursuance of the laws in operation" (Arts. 64–66). In practice, however, the role of the council as a legislative organ has not decreased. It takes an active part in the preparation of all legislation, including drafts of laws brought before the Supreme Soviet. And even though its decisions may be annulled or suspended by the Presidium, it is clear from the volume and range of its enactments that the Council of Ministers is actually the greater producer of compulsory and enforceable rules in the governmental system.

The council is endowed with broad powers by the constitution. According to Article 68, the council exercises the following functions: it co-ordinates and directs the work of the ministries and other institutions under its jurisdiction and directs the sovnarkhozi through the councils of ministers of the union republics; it adopts measures to implement the economic plan, budget, credit and monetary system, and to maintain public order and protect state interests and citizens' rights; it exercises general guidance in the sphere of foreign relations and directs the general organization of the armed forces; and whenever necessary it sets up special committees and central administrations for economic, cultural, and defense purposes. Moreover, it has the power to check on the execution of its decisions and orders; and with respect to branches of administration and economy under the jurisdiction of the U.S.S.R., the Council of Ministers may suspend decisions and orders of the union-republic councils of ministers and sovnarkhozi and annul orders and instructions of ministers of the U.S.S.R. (Art. 69).

As of March, 1959, the council consisted of its chairman, two first deputy chairmen, three deputy chairmen, the chairman of the State Planning Committee (who is one of the deputy chairmen), the ministers, and the chairmen of the following state committees: Labor and Wages, Construction Affairs, State Security, Foreign Economic Ties, Defense Technology, Aviation Technology, Shipbuilding Technology, Radio and Electronic Technology, Automation and Machine Building, Chemical Industry, Grain Products, and the Scientific-Technical Committee; and in addition the chairman of the Soviet Central Control Commission, the chairman of Administration of the State Bank, and the chief of the Central Statistical Administration. In addition the Council of Ministers includes the chairmen of the council of ministers of the fifteen union republics as members ex officio, and the chairman of the Council of Ministers of the U.S.S.R. may request the Supreme Soviet to appoint deputies of the chairman of Gosplan and chiefs of its basic branches as ministers within the council. These officials are voting members of the council, whose membership is formally "approved" by the Supreme Soviet for a term of approximately four years. The episode in 1938, when three names were dropped from the proposed list of ministers on the basis of criticisms voiced in the Supreme Soviet, was never repeated, and Supreme Soviet approval has become a matter of routine. Between sessions of the Supreme Soviet individual changes in the council's membership are made by a formal vote of the Presidium at the instance of the chairman of the council. Later they are placed before the Supreme Soviet for confirmation.

The extent to which the activities of the Council of Ministers pervade Soviet governmental life, placing this organ in a class by itself in the structure of the Soviets, can be seen from its composition. The post of chairman has always been filled by persons from the summit of the party hierarchy: Lenin until 1924, Rykov until 1930, Molotov until 1941, Stalin until March, 1953, Malenkov until February, 1955, Bulganin until 1958, and Khrushchev thereafter. The first deputy and deputy chairmen have always been party members of the highest standing. As of March, 1959, Frol R. Kozlov, Anastas I. Mikoyan, Alexei N. Kosygin, and Dmitrii F. Ustinov held the posts of first deputy and deputy chairmen in the Council of Ministers.[5] Shortly after Stalin's death on March 6, 1953, an official announcement proclaimed that two heretofore unidentified organs of the Council of Ministers, a "Presidium" (apparently consisting of the chairman and his deputies) and a "Bureau of the Presidium" (evidently composed of four or five of these individuals) had been replaced by one organ, "the Presidium of the U.S.S.R. Council of Ministers." The present Presidium of the Council of Ministers is presumably identical with the chairman and his deputies mentioned above.

The membership of the council has quadrupled since its inception. It has grown from thirteen voting members in 1917 to twenty-six in 1931, sixty-four in 1946, fifty-one in 1952, and sixty now. The decrease in the personnel of the Council of Ministers through the abolition of twenty-five ministries in May, 1957, was compensated for by introducing into the council the fifteen chairmen of the union-republic councils of ministers and the chairmen of the state committees. Further increases were effected when Gosplan officials were brought into the council. The development of the Soviet administrative machinery can also be seen below in the changes in the number of ministries until 1959:

FIG. XXV

MINISTRIES: 1924–59

	1924	1936	1947	1949	1952	1956	1957	1959
All-Union	5	8	36	28	30	23	7	6
Union Republic	5	10	23	20	21	29	12	10
Total	10	18	59	48	51	52	19	16

[5] Of the seven first deputy and deputy chairmen of the Council of Ministers prior to the shake-up of the top leadership at the Central Committee session of June 22–29, 1957 (Kaganovich, Malenkov, Mikoyan, Molotov, Pervukhin, Saburov, and Kuzmin, the last of whom had been appointed as first deputy in May, 1957, on assuming the chairmanship of Gosplan), the first six were members of the Party Presidium of the Central Committee. In that shake-up Kaganovich, Malenkov, and Molotov were ousted from both the Party Presidium and the Central Committee, and Saburov from the Party Presidium, while Pervukhin was demoted to candidacy in the Party Presidium. At the same time these five individuals were removed from the posts of first deputy and deputy chairmen of the Council of Ministers. Since the chairman, the first deputy and deputy chairmen make up the "Presidium," i.e., the actual governing body of the unwieldy Council of Ministers, that organ now includes only the six persons mentioned in the text above.

Figure XXV also shows that a distinction has always been made between two types of ministries. First, the "All-Union" ministries, which until 1957 administered their enterprises directly regardless of their location, now supervise the planning and the technical level of production of their enterprises through the sovnarkhozi, but non-industrial ministries (e.g., Foreign Trade, Merchant Marine), having relinquished all control over any productive enterprises to the sovnarkhozi, continue to administer their branches and institutions directly. Second, "union-republic" ministries of the U.S.S.R. operate through like-named ministries of the union republics. By February, 1959, the U.S.S.R. ministries (Arts. 77, 78 of the constitution as amended to date) were divided into All-Union ministries and union-republic ministries as follows:

FIG. XXVI

ALL-UNION MINISTRIES

1. Foreign Trade
2. Merchant Marine
3. Transportation
4. Medium Machine Building
5. Transport Construction
6. Power Plant Construction

FIG. XXVII

UNION-REPUBLIC MINISTRIES

1. Internal Affairs
2. Higher Education
3. Geology and Conservation of Mineral Resources
4. Public Health
5. Foreign Affairs
6. Culture
7. Defense
8. Communications
9. Agriculture
10. Finance

During 1956 a degree of decentralization had already been achieved by transferring several "All-Union" ministries dealing with industrial matters to "union-republic" jurisdiction. The 1957 decree further reduces the number of industrial "All-Union" ministries under the dual subordination of these ministries and the corresponding sovnarkhozi. Only the enterprises of two ministries (Medium Machine Building and Transport Construction) remain under the exclusive administrative control of the ministries—in the case of the former, headed by Ye. P. Slavsky, because the ministry presumably deals with matters related to the development of atomic energy. Only three non-industrial ministries (Foreign Trade, Merchant Marine, and Transportation) remain under exclusive All-Union control. By contrast, of the ten union-republic ministries, three deal with administrative-political, four with economic, and only three with socio-cultural matters. The relatively small number of socio-cultural ministries is merely a reflection of the party's concentrated interest in this field, since the party apparatus deals extensively with these matters.

On Malenkov's assumption of the premiership in 1953 the Council of Ministers was reduced to half its size in an obvious attempt to streamline administrative supervision. This was done by merging various related ministries and agencies. Between 1953 and 1956 the number of ministries had, however, proliferated again and assumed the proportions it had in 1952. After the 1957 reorganization decree and subsequent changes until March, 1959, the new Council of Ministers was composed as follows:

(A) PRESIDIUM

CHAIRMAN	Nikita S. Khrushchev
FIRST DEPUTY CHAIRMAN	Frol R. Kozlov
FIRST DEPUTY CHAIRMAN	Anastas I. Mikoyan
DEPUTY CHAIRMAN AND CHAIRMAN OF GOSPLAN	Alexei N. Kosygin
DEPUTY CHAIRMAN	Alexander F. Zasyadko
DEPUTY CHAIRMAN	Dmitrii F. Ustinov

(B) ALL-UNION MINISTRIES

MINISTER OF FOREIGN TRADE	Nikolai S. Patolichev
MINISTER OF MERCHANT MARINE	Viktor G. Bakayev
MINISTER OF TRANSPORTATION	Boris P. Beshchev
MINISTER OF TRANSPORT CONSTRUCTION	Yevgenii F. Kozhevnikov
MINISTER OF MEDIUM MACHINE BUILDING	Yefim P. Slavsky
MINISTER OF CONSTRUCTION OF POWER PLANTS	Ignatii T. Novikov

(C) UNION-REPUBLIC MINISTRIES

MINISTER OF INTERNAL AFFAIRS	Nikolai P. Dudorov
MINISTER OF HIGHER EDUCATION	Vyacheslav P. Yelyutin
MINISTER OF GEOLOGY AND CONSERVATION OF MINERAL RESOURCES	Piotr Ya. Antropov
MINISTER OF PUBLIC HEALTH	Sergei V. Kurachov
MINISTER OF FOREIGN AFFAIRS	Andrei A. Gromyko
MINISTER OF CULTURE	Nikolai A. Mikhailov
MINISTER OF DEFENSE	Rodion Ya. Malinovsky
MINISTER OF COMMUNICATIONS	Nikolai D. Psurtsev
MINISTER OF AGRICULTURE	Vladimir V. Matskevich
MINISTER OF FINANCE	Arsenii G. Zverev

(D) COMMITTEES, COMMISSIONS, AND ADMINISTRATIONS

CHAIRMAN OF SOVIET CONTROL COMMISSION	Georgii V. Yenyutin
CHAIRMAN OF STATE COMMITTEE ON LABOR AND WAGES	Alexander P. Volkov
CHAIRMAN OF STATE SCIENTIFIC AND TECHNICAL COMMITTEE	Iosif I. Kuzmin

CHAIRMAN OF STATE COMMITTEE ON AVIATION TECHNOLOGY	* Piotr V. Dementyev
CHAIRMAN OF STATE COMMITTEE ON DEFENSE TECHNOLOGY	* Konstantin N. Rudnev
CHAIRMAN OF STATE COMMITTEE ON AUTOMATION AND MACHINE BUILD-ING	* Anatolii I. Kostousov
CHAIRMAN OF STATE COMMITTEE ON RADIO AND ELECTRONIC TECHNOLOGY	* Valerii D. Kalmykov
CHAIRMAN OF STATE COMMITTEE ON SHIPBUILDING	* Boris Ye. Butoma
CHAIRMAN OF STATE CONSTRUCTION COMMITTEE	Vladimir A. Kucherenko
CHAIRMAN OF STATE COMMITTEE ON CHEMISTRY	Viktor S. Fyodorov
CHAIRMAN OF STATE COMMITTEE ON GRAIN PRODUCTS	* Leonid R. Korniyets
CHAIRMAN OF STATE COMMITTEE ON FOREIGN ECONOMIC TIES	Semyon A. Skachkov
CHAIRMAN OF STATE SECURITY COM-MITTEE	A. N. Shelepin
CHAIRMAN OF THE BOARD OF THE U.S.S.R. STATE BANK	Alexander K. Korovush-kin
DIRECTOR OF THE CENTRAL STATISTI-CAL ADMINISTRATION	Vladimir N. Starovsky

(E) DEPUTY CHAIRMEN AND CHIEFS OF BASIC DEPART-MENTS OF GOSPLAN

FIRST DEPUTY CHAIRMAN	* Georgii V. Perov
FIRST DEPUTY CHAIRMAN	* Mikhail A. Lesechko
DEPUTY CHAIRMAN	* Vasilii P. Zotov
DEPUTY CHAIRMAN	* Nikolai I. Strokin
DEPUTY CHAIRMAN	* Mikhail V. Khrunichev
DIRECTOR OF DEPARTMENT	* Grigorii S. Khlamov
DIRECTOR OF DEPARTMENT	* Alexander A. Ishkov
DIRECTOR OF DEPARTMENT	* Yefim S. Novoselov

(F) THE FIFTEEN CHAIRMEN OF THE UNION-REPUBLIC COUN-CILS OF MINISTERS, EX OFFICIO

* Chairmen and directors of the bodies listed under "D" and "E," who also carry the title "U.S.S.R. Minister."

On March 27, 1958, Bulganin resigned and First Secretary of the Party Nikita S. Khrushchev took his place as Chairman of the Council of Ministers (Premier). A few days later the Presidium of the Council was reorganized to include: First Deputy Chairmen—A. I. Mikoyan and Frol R. Kozlov; Deputy Chairmen—A. N. Kosygin, A. F. Zasyadko, I. I. Kuzmin, and D. F. Ustinov. In March, 1959, Kuzmin was dropped as Chairman of Gosplan and Deputy Chairman of the Council of Ministers, and Kosygin was appointed in his place. Generally the ministries have witnessed many changes in structure, size, and allocation of functions, and can be expected to experience further alterations in the future.

In addition to the ministries and such organs as the Bureau of Administrative Affairs and the Secretariat, which arrange the business of the council, a number of other agencies have been attached to the Council of Ministers from time to time.[6] These comprise: a) *chief administrations,* which are concerned with civil aviation, hydrometeorological services, the Northern Sea route, co-operatives, and the supply of the national economy with sundry fuels and gases; b) *committees* on physical culture, standards, weights and measures, broadcasting, architecture, and Lenin prizes; c) *commissions* on civil service, military deferments and exemptions; and d) *councils,* which deal with the affairs of the Orthodox Church and other religious denominations, and collective farms. A State Scientific and Economic Council was created in March, 1959. Also under the councils' aegis are such agencies as the State Arbitration Commission, the Academy of Sciences of the U.S.S.R., and the Telegraph Agency of the Soviet Union (T.A.S.S.). The Economic Council, which succeeded the important Council of Labor and Defense in 1937 and was designed to facilitate the operative supervision of the economic ministries and agencies, has apparently ceased to exist. The State Defense Committee, created at the beginning of World War II, was abolished when the war ended. Later mention will be made of Gosplan.

Within each ministry there is a collegium, consisting of the leading departmental officials and the minister, and a large council to serve as a liaison between the center and the field. The minister operates on the "one-man management principle," first advocated by Lenin but given fullest expression with the inauguration of the Five Year plans. To emphasize the minister's role the collegia were abolished in 1934, but they were restored in 1936 to serve as consulting bodies within the ministries. The minister's decisions are final, but in case of disagreement the collegium of his ministry has a formal right of appeal to the Council of Ministers and the party's Central Committee.

The Council of Ministers exercises control over each minister and on occasion has annulled departmental acts. In official theory the minister carries a dual responsibility. He is a "servant of the people"; consequently, both he and the Council of Ministers are responsible to the Supreme Soviet and must be ready to answer questions addressed to them by a Supreme Soviet deputy within a three-day period (Art. 71). The minister is also "a pupil of Lenin," deemed to owe supreme allegiance to the party and its highest leadership. Actually the second responsibility is by far the more important. And by virtue of the intimate relationship

[6] See I. I. Evitkhiev and A. A. Vlasov, *Administrativnoe Pravo* (1946), pp. 28–29.

between the Council of Ministers and party leadership the Council of Ministers is in fact the most powerful organ in the formal Soviet political hierarchy.

5. PUBLIC ADMINISTRATION IN THE SOVIET UNION

Public administration in the U.S.S.R. is unique in character.[7] Its over-all preoccupation, as in public administration of other countries, is to get things done in an efficient manner and at minimum cost, but the achievement of this objective is affected by many peculiar problems because all governmental activities in the U.S.S.R. are conditioned by requirements of theoretical dogma, on the one hand, and are subject to the shifting strategy of the party leaders, on the other.

Soviet administration has dealt with such customary problems as the proper division of labor and of liaison between the center and the localities, financial solvency, administrative efficiency, and training of reserves of skilled personnel. It has sought to meet the first of these through the graded territorial-administrative structure of the soviets, with its system of dual subordination of administrators at every level, and through the three grades of ministries: All-Union, Union-Republic, and Republic, the last of which has no counterpart on the Union level. Here is an administrative solution that fundamentally emphasizes centralized policy determination and control, occasionally permitting a measure of decentralized operative supervision. Financial solvency is supposed to be ensured by the work of the Ministry of Finance through its budget and bank-credit controls and its inspection machinery, and by the Commission of State Control through its periodic check on expenditures of state funds. The State Commission on the Civil Service seeks to promote administrative efficiency by preparing organizational charts, job classifications, suggestions for ceilings on personnel, and rationalized procedures in order to eliminate duplicated operations and to reduce surplus staffs. Although the Chief Administration of Labor Reserves trains the yearly contingents of recruits as skilled workers for Soviet economic enterprises, each sector of industry and administration maintains its own system of schools and institutes to train higher technical personnel and administrators. The combined efforts of these activities are obviously designed to produce a large pool of skilled personnel.

In addition public administration in the U.S.S.R. has been confronted with such unorthodox problems as the maintenance of the party's primacy in all spheres, the planning of all activities, the focusing of responsibility within each unit of administration, the periodic utilization of mass pressure devices over the lower bureaucracy, and the permanent guardianship of the political loyalty of all public employees. The activities of party organizations at all levels and those of the Gosplan provide Soviet solutions for the first two problems; the "one-man management"

[7] For a good discussion of Soviet public administration see Merle Fainsod, op. cit., pp. 327–53.

principle, the concentration of responsibility in the head of the administrative unit or enterprise, is designed to counteract the earlier tendency toward an escape from responsibility under the "collegial management" practice. The controlled practice of "criticism and self-criticism" is intended partly as an extra check against lethargy, nepotism, and ineffectiveness, and it is designed also as a "sop" to the populace. Finally, representatives of the security organs, operating within all branches of administration and the economy, are presumed to ensure the fealty of public service and the security of the regime.

Taken together, all these techniques and devices are designed to provide a comprehensive check on performance in the Soviet system of administration. Despite the multiplicity of controls, however, many bureaucratic features are in evidence. These characteristics of Soviet administration are rooted in the extraordinary scope of state activity and in the extreme degree of centralization that prevail in the U.S.S.R., conditions that are not likely to change appreciably in the foreseeable future.

27

ORGANS OF ENFORCEMENT AND DEFENSE

1. COURTS, PROSECUTORS, AND SECRET POLICE

The Soviet constitution of 1936 devotes a separate chapter (Arts. 102–17) to the courts and the procurator's office. Despite the federal character of the U.S.S.R. the constitution does not establish a double system of courts: that is, one set for the U.S.S.R. itself and separate parallel sets of courts in the constituent republics. Except for a limited number of special courts there exists only one "federal" court, the Supreme Court of the U.S.S.R.[1] The courts of the constituent republics enforce both state and federal laws and are subordinate to the federal Supreme Court. Criminal cases are tried by these general courts, by the special courts, and until September, 1953 by the Special Boards of the M.V.D. Civil cases may be tried by the general courts or by a special arbitral tribunal, the so-called State Board of Arbitration (*Gosarbitrazh*).[2] These state boards of arbitration adjudicate property and contract disputes between economic organs of different ministries; each of them is subordinate to the highest administrative body of the territorial unit in which it operates, i.e., the respective council of ministers or executive committee of a soviet. This administrative body appoints the members of the board of arbitration, supervises its activities, and may demand a retrial or reverse its decisions.

The Base of the System: People's Courts and "Comradely Courts." At the base of the judicial system stand the people's courts, established on a district (*raion*) basis and composed of popularly elected judges and people's assessors. The judges are chosen for a five-year term and are subject to recall by the electorate; the assessors are selected for an an-

---

[1] For a more extended discussion of the Soviet judiciary see Vladimir Gsovski, *Soviet Civil Law* (1948), 2 vols., *passim;* John N. Hazard and Harold L. Weisberg, *Cases and Readings on Soviet Law* (1950), *passim;* and Julian Towster, *Political Power in the U.S.S.R., 1917–1947* (1948), pp. 296–310.

[2] See Harold J. Berman, *Justice in Russia* (1950), pp. 63ff.

nual service of ten days. Although (contrary to the Judicature Act of 1938) no direct elections of people's judges and assessors were held until 1948, such elections took place at the end of that year and again in 1951 and 1954. The people's courts are courts of original jurisdiction over minor criminal cases and various types of civil cases.

Also at the base of the operative judicial system, but falling outside the regular court hierarchy, are the so-called "comradely courts." [3] These are informal *ad hoc* bodies, which may be organized in apartment houses, villages, factories, or other places of work to handle difficulties arising within such groups. A comradely court is usually elected by the workers of the particular enterprise, or it may be composed of all those present at the meeting. It can take cognizance of petty thefts, insults, rumormongering, or certain acts of hooliganism, and can impose reprimands and small fines. The people's courts exercise general supervision over the comradely courts and may annul their decisions if the latter violate law or wrongfully assume jurisdiction in a case.

The Courts of the Intermediate Rungs and the Republics: Instances of Dual Jurisdiction. Between the people's courts and the supreme courts of the union republics is a wide variety of courts organized in the territories, areas, regions, and autonomous regions and republics. For the most part there are three tiers in the republic system of courts: the supreme court of the union republic, the regional courts, and the people's courts. In the smaller union and autonomous republics, which are divided directly into districts, there is no tier of regional courts. The members of all these courts are elected for a term of five years by the corresponding soviet of the area or region involved, and they exercise appellate jurisdiction with respect to the people's courts and original jurisdiction in more important civil and criminal cases. In the criminal sphere, cases involving counterrevolutionary crimes, crimes against state administration, or theft of socialist property are a few examples where original jurisdiction is exercised by the area and regional courts. Their original civil jurisdiction extends to the important sphere of litigation between state and public institutions and enterprises. Cases on appeal are heard in these courts by a bench of three regular judges, and in such instances the decisions are final.

The highest judicial organ of a union republic is its supreme court, members of which are elected for a term of five years by the supreme soviet of the union republic. It has original jurisdiction in civil and criminal cases of major importance, such as crimes committed in office by highest union-republic officials and cases brought before it by the presidium of the union-republic supreme soviet and other agencies. The union-republic supreme court acts as an appellate court for the next lower court of original jurisdiction in the union republic, but in cases where the union-republic supreme court exercises original jurisdiction, its decisions are final. A supervisory function is also exercised by the union-republic supreme court when it acts in cases of protest by the procurator-general or chairman of the Supreme Court of the U.S.S.R.

[3] Ibid., pp. 266–69.

or by the corresponding officials of the union republics, against verdicts that have been rendered. As a result the verdict of any court of a union republic can be set aside by its supreme court.

The Supreme Court of the U.S.S.R.   According to the constitution, the Supreme Court is "the highest judicial organ" of the land. It is elected by the Supreme Soviet of the U.S.S.R. for a term of five years.

As reconstituted in February, 1957, the court consists of a chairman, two vice-chairmen, nine judges, and twenty people's assessors, in addition to the fifteen chairmen of the union-republic supreme courts as members ex officio—a total of twenty-seven regular judges and twenty people's assessors.[4]

The Supreme Court supervises the judicial work of the courts of the U.S.S.R. and union republics, and it can initiate legislation pertaining to the judicial system. It functions through a plenum, which is supposed to meet at least once in three months, and three collegia, or divisions: civil, criminal, and military. The prosecutor-general is obliged to be present at those sessions of the plenum, which examine protests by him or the court's chairman against decisions of union-republic courts that are not in conformity with All-Union laws or infringe upon the interests of other union republics. The plenum is also supposed to resolve conflicts between court decisions of the union republics. While the Supreme Court has never possessed any powers of judicial review over legislation, it can give the Supreme Soviet Presidium advisory opinions in the interpretation of U.S.S.R. laws.

The Supreme Court's civil and criminal collegia serve as courts of first instance in exceptionally important civil and criminal cases. They act as courts of review—on the basis of protests by the Supreme Court's chairman or the prosecutor-general—where verdicts of union-republic supreme courts contravene federal laws or violate the interests of other union republics. The military collegium deals with extraordinary cases of treason, espionage, and other high crimes against the state, and it examines appeals and protests against verdicts of district and fleet military tribunals. Where a collegium sits as a court of first instance, it consists of a judge (presiding) and two people's assessors. When it acts as a review court, all the members are regular judges.[5]

Recent changes have increased the competence of union-republic supreme courts at the expense of the U.S.S.R. Supreme Court, with the avowed aim of giving the latter more time "to generalize from judicial practice" and concentrate on offering guiding interpretations on the application of legislation to judicial proceedings. Although the Supreme Court is responsible to the U.S.S.R. Supreme Soviet and its Presidium, Soviet constitutional theory stresses the "independence" of the Supreme Court and of the judiciary as a whole, but "independence" does not signify a power of the judiciary to annul on legal grounds decisions of the higher administrative and executive organs of the state.

4 See *Pravda* and *Izvestia,* February 13, 1957.
5 See ibid.; *New York Times,* February 13, 1957.

Special Federal Tribunals. Additional U.S.S.R. courts, or special federal tribunals, are established by law from time to time. Until recently the network of such courts comprised special military tribunals, railroad-transport courts, and water-transport courts. The last two types of courts were subordinate to a separate Transport Collegium of the Supreme Court. The entire system of transport courts was abolished in 1957, coincident with the decentralization of the ministries in the transportation field. The grounds given for this change are that fewer violations of law have taken place in the transportation field in recent years and that the reduced number of cases can be effectively handled by the union-republic courts.

Military tribunals possess exceptional competence extending also to crimes committed by civilians, such as treason, espionage, subversive activity, etc. Between 1953 and 1956 a number of high-ranking Soviet officials were sentenced by the Supreme Court's Military Collegium. Sentences of lower military courts can be reviewed by the Supreme Court. Occasionally clemency appeals from the decisions of the military collegium of the Supreme Court were entertained by the Presidium of the Supreme Soviet.

Special Features: Lay Judges and Restricted Appeals. A special feature of the Soviet judicial system is the constitutional requirement (Art. 103) that all courts in which cases are to be tried are to include lay judges, the people's assessors, with certain exceptions permitted by law. People's assessors and regular judges are elected simultaneously in elections organized and conducted by the executive committees of the soviets. Voters receive two ballots, one for the regular judges and one for the people's assessors; the latter contain the names of fifty to seventy-five candidates formally nominated, as are the judges, by social organizations.

Panels of lay assessors are attached to each court. Assessors function only in original trials, not in instances of review. In trial cases two assessors sit with one judge, who acts as chairman. Decisions on all questions, whether of fact or of law, are taken by a majority vote.

Any citizen who is at least twenty-three years of age may be elected a judge or assessor, neither of whom needs to possess any legal training. However, there has been a distinct effort since the late thirties to propose candidates with some knowledge of law; and in the 1949 elections the great majority of judicial candidates in the Ukrainian Republic, for instance, were reported to be persons with experience and training in legal work.[6] In the preceding year a report by Minister of Justice Gorshenin complained of a generally low quality of work by the judiciary, and a decree was adopted designed to increase the responsibility of the judges.

Another special feature of the judicial system is the nature of appellate review. Appellate review is restricted to the next higher court in the judicial hierarchy, so that usually a case can only go before two

---

[6] See *Izvestia,* January 30, 1949, and *Pravda,* January 31, 1949.

courts unless a decision is protested by appropriate officials and is taken before a supreme court. Also, appellate review in the Soviet system is more comparable to the Continental practice of cassation (that is, review upon the record of the lower court) than to the practice in the United States, where appellate courts usually undertake some independent examination of evidence and issues.

The Courts and Politics: The Nature of the Soviet Judiciary. The operation of the Soviet court system is to be understood in terms of the Soviet-Marxist conception of law and of the judicial function. Although Soviet conceptions of law have varied considerably since the beginning of the revolutionary regime, in general law has not been conceived of as embodying or being based upon any abstract ideas of justice. Rather law is considered the expression of the will of the dominant class—in the U.S.S.R., at present, as the instrument of "the dictatorship of the working class" guided by the party. It is deemed an instrument for "strengthening social construction and defending the conquests of the October Socialist Revolution," as these matters are periodically reinterpreted by the leaders of the ruling party. In the Soviet conception the judiciary is merely an organ of state power, and consequently the "demand that the judiciary remain outside of politics is nowhere and under no circumstances realized." Under these circumstances court decisions can hardly serve to establish enduring judicial precedents.

The Procurator-General: Supreme Overseer of Soviet Legality. Closely associated with the Soviet judicial system is the procurator-general.[7] Under the constitution of 1936 he is elected for seven years by the Supreme Soviet and has broad powers to ensure the strict observance of the law by all ministries and their subordinate organs, as well as by officials and citizens of the U.S.S.R. in general (Art. 113).

The office of procurator-general dates from 1922, when Lenin announced that "legality" cannot be one thing "in Kaluga and another in Kazan," but must be uniform. At first the procurator-general was attached to the Supreme Court of the U.S.S.R. and did not have authority to oversee the activities of the procurators of the constituent republics. By 1936 the trend toward centralization of law-enforcement responsibilities had resulted in substantial evolution toward an independent office of procurator-general. The culmination of this trend may be read in the provisions of the constitution of 1936.

Current Soviet theory emphasizes that the procurator-general is not an agent of the executive power. The office of procurator-general, it is stated, is not a governmental department headed by a member of the Council of Ministers, and consequently "hierarchical influences" are not supposed to affect the office. In theory the procurator-general is accountable to the Supreme Soviet and its Presidium.

In order to perform his supervisory powers over the execution of the laws the procurator-general is vested with broad authority. He is

---

[7] See Towster, *Political Power,* pp. 305–10, and Berman, op. cit., pp. 168–73.

present at plenary sessions of the Supreme Court of the U.S.S.R., he may remove cases from any court in the U.S.S.R. to the Supreme Court, and he may lodge protests before courts in the republics. He has at his service a network of procurators, operating under his supervision and entirely free of local controls or influences.

An innovation introduced in February, 1959, is the institution of collegia in the offices of the procurators for purposes of consultation concerning problems of supervision over legality. While the procurator-general selects the collegium from the highest officials in his office, it must be confirmed by the Presidium of the Supreme Soviet. In case of serious differences between the procurator-general and his collegium, the decision of the former prevails, but the procurator-general has the duty and the collegium the right to report the differences to the Presidium of the Supreme Soviet. In the union republics, similar differences between the procurators and their collegia are supposed to be reported to the procurator-general of the U.S.S.R.

The Procuratorial Agents: Guardians of Local Conformance. The procurator-general appoints for five-year terms the procurators of the union republics, territories, regions, and autonomous regions and republics. Procurators in the lesser districts and areas are appointed subject to his approval. All of these officials, high and low, are agents of the procurator-general in checking on abuses of local administrators and on law observance. In this capacity they may be present at sessions of local soviets, they receive copies of orders and instructions issued by executive-administrative organs of the soviets, and they are formally empowered to guarantee the legality and correctness of actions of the secret police, organs of criminal investigation, and "corrective labor" camps. Orders and instructions deemed *ultra vires* or contrary to law may be protested by the procurators to higher administrative bodies; and generally the organs of the procuracy may institute civil suits, arrests, and criminal prosecution, and may appeal any court decision to the Supreme Court of the U.S.S.R. The major sources of such appeals are reports from lower procurators proceeding through channels to the Office of the Procurator-General. The latter also is charged with maintaining a section for letters of complaint by aggrieved parties in cases of wrongful arrest or conviction.

Needless to say, the procuratorial system, no less than the court system, serves as an arm of the political power center, and the nature and extent of the intervention by the procurators are by-products of the shifting strategies and changing theoretical postulates of the regime. The official conception of the procurators' role is embodied in Vyshinsky's statement that the "Soviet prosecuting officer is the watchman of socialist legality, the leader of the policy of the Communist Party and of Soviet authority, and champion of socialism."

The "Unsheathed Sword" of the Revolution: The Soviet Secret Police. Of fundamental importance in the network of Soviet enforcement agencies is the secret police, once called by Stalin "the unsheathed sword" of the revolution.[8] The secret police is not a Communist innovation; wide utilization of secret police was made by the tsarist regime. In fact during the earliest days of the revolution there was some opposition in the Communist Party, including Lenin himself, against terrorist methods. However, practically from 1917 to the present day, the secret police, variously known as *Cheka,* O.G.P.U., N.K.V.D., M.V.D., and M.G.B., or K.G.B., has played a conspicuous role in upholding the regime and in ferreting out opposition.

In 1943 the N.K.V.D. was divided into two commissariats, later renamed ministries: the Ministry of Internal Affairs (M.V.D.) and the Ministry of State Security (M.G.B.). The M.G.B. was performing the secret-police functions, including counterintelligence and foreign espionage; and the M.V.D. directed the internal-security troops, the frontier guards, the guards of industrial establishments, the convoy troops, the administration of the labor camps, and various local activities. On Stalin's death the two were merged in the M.V.D., but in 1954 a "Committee for State Security" (K.G.B.) was again set up under the Council of Ministers with the claim that this arrangement provides a more direct type of control by the leaders of the government over the security organs.

The change in status of this security organ was part of an overall effort in the post-Stalin period to tighten control over the secret police agencies by the government and the party. With the same end in view the Presidium of the Supreme Soviet established in April, 1956, a special division of the procurator-general's office to supervise investigation of state security organs. This division was empowered to check on the activities of security agencies, prison conditions, and civil and criminal proceedings.

The Scope of Police Surveillance: The M.V.D. and the K.G.B. While the precise delimitation of functions between the M.V.D. and K.G.B. is not clear, there is little doubt that between them these security organs carry out a vast job of continuing surveillance in the body politic.

The undercover activities of the M.V.D.-K.G.B. pervade the entire U.S.S.R. Internally the security organs have sections or agents in every functional branch of administration, including factories, collective farms, and mines. In addition there are security details at practically every territorial level of government. In the army there are so-called special sections of the K.G.B. attached to units down to the division; in the smaller military units there are K.G.B. representatives. Through its network of informers the secret police watches constantly for possible disaffection and dissension, and in the four decades of the regime it has demonstrated a ruthless capacity for repressive action. Agents of the security organs also operate abroad, not only in intelligence undertak-

---

[8] For details on the history, organization, and functions of the secret police see Gsovski, op. cit., Vol. I, pp. 234–40; Merle Fainsod, op. cit., Chapter 13; Barrington Moore, Jr., *Terror and Progress U.S.S.R.* (1954), Chapter 6; David Dallin, *The Changing World of Soviet Russia* (1956), pp. 127–68, 257–63; and B. D. Wolfe, *Khrushchev and Stalin's Ghost* (1957).

ings, but for purposes of surveillance over Soviet officials outside the U.S.S.R.

Until the latter part of 1953, M.V.D. agencies possessed quasi-judicial powers of an extraordinary nature, especially with regard to the arrest and sentencing of persons suspected of counterrevolutionary intentions or activities.[9] The secret police had the power to banish persons from certain areas of the U.S.S.R. or from the country, to sentence people to "correctional labor" camps for terms as high as twenty-five years, and even to impose and execute the death sentence without interference from the courts or—to judge by past practice—even from the procurator-general, who was supposed to exercise some control over it. In the exercise of these powers many thousands of Soviet citizens were executed and millions of people were deported to forced labor camps. During and after World War II various nationalities accused of collaboration with the nazis, such as the Volga Germans, the Crimean Tartars, Chechens, and Ingushes were transported to Central Asia and elsewhere. Mass deportations also took place from the Black Sea coastal areas and the Baltic republics.[1]

Since the autumn of 1953 the secret police has been deprived of many of its quasi-judicial powers, and the special M.V.D. boards that exercised them have been abolished. A decree passed in 1955 laid down the regulations that thereafter a prisoner was to be considered innocent until he has been proven guilty, and that the confession of an accused was not to be accepted any more as evidence of his guilt. The late Andrei Vyshinsky was castigated in official writings for developing the practice of trial by confession and using mere probability of guilt as a basis for conviction, and Soviet officials held out the promise that the abuses perpetrated by the secret police in the Stalin era—revealed in gruesome detail in Khrushchev's secret speech before the Twentieth Party Congress in February, 1956—will be eradicated from Soviet society.

The Economic Role of the Secret Police. The M.V.D. and its various predecessors have been credited, during the evolution of the Soviet regime, with building and operating a large number of enterprises through the use of forced labor.[2] Among them might be mentioned the Baltic-White Sea canal, the Moscow-Volga canal, the open-seam mines of Vorkuta, the copper mines of Karaganda, the Kolyma gold mines, the Pechora railroad, and numerous highways, railroads, and military installations. These projects were carried out by the inmates of the forced-labor camps—political prisoners, members of dispersed nationalities, rich and middle peasants who resisted collectivization, Soviet and foreign communists suspected of "deviations" at various times, prisoners

[9] See Gurian, op. cit., p. 149; an account of an M.V.D. trial is given in Berman, op. cit., pp. 86ff.

[1] Cf. Edward Crankshaw, *Cracks in the Kremlin Wall* (1951), p. 212, and Edmund Stevens, *This Is Russia Uncensored* (1950), p. 191.

[2] For a survey of the Soviet use of forced labor see Schwartz, op. cit., pp. 487ff.

of war, and many others accused of political hostility to the regime. Estimates of the number of these inmates in the past have ranged between three million and fifteen million or higher.

Under the supervision of the Chief Administration for Labor Camps, a division of the M.V.D., the camps supplied the labor force, not only for M.V.D. projects, but—on a "rental" basis—also for works of other ministries. Thus the secret police played a definite and by no means inconspicuous role in the Soviet economy.

However, in part for economic and in part for political reasons, this role has been rapidly declining in recent years.[3] Increased mechanization, the gradual drying up of unexploited sources of recruits for the camps, the high fatality rate, and low productivity of inmates may be causes for this decline. Another recent cause lies in the attempts of Stalin's successors to pacify the populace. As a result of the work of special commissions that were set up in 1953 to review old M.V.D. sentences, as well as of the 1953–55 amnesties for military and economic offenders, wartime collaborationists, and also some categories of political prisoners, thousands of forced-labor camp inmates were released from the camps. Many were allowed to return home. Others were permitted to bring their families and live as paid settlers working in the industries of the areas. This process was hastened by a series of violent strikes in the camps since 1953, and returned prisoners have testified to the abolition of a number of camps. In May, 1956, a Soviet spokesman even averred that the forced-labor camp system will be liquidated altogether within a period of several years.

Openly admitting that the individual rights and legal guarantees provided by the constitution have been brutally violated by the secret police for a number of years, the present Soviet leaders hope to convince the Soviet people that the recent deeds and promises detailed above mark a return to "Soviet legality," which will henceforth stand guard over citizens' rights. At the same time they stoutly maintain that during the existence of the present regime the secret police has played, and continues to play, a beneficial role in protecting the achievements of the revolution. The duality of this position holds out little promise for the Soviet citizen of any genuine freedom from police surveillance in the immediate future.

2. THE ARMY AND ITS AUXILIARIES

Conception, Composition, and Training: The Making of a Military Machine. The official conception of the Red Army, voiced by Stalin in 1928, is that it exhibits three facets: it is the army of "the emancipated workers and peasants" of the dictatorship; it is the army of the Soviet "fraternity of peoples"; and it is the army of those imbued with "the spirit of internationalism." Since the mid-thirties, and especially since the outbreak of World War II, increasing emphasis has been placed on

[3] Cf. Dallin, op. cit., p. 163ff.

the national rather than the international aspect of the army, and its name was changed from Red Army to Soviet Army in 1946.[4]

Although at the outset the Russian Army was overwhelmingly peasant in composition, theoretical considerations and practical fears of possible reactions to measures of agricultural collectivization combined to dictate to the Soviet leaders a policy of "proletarianizing" the armed forces. This policy gained impact under the industrialization program of the first Five Year Plan, and by 1933 over 40 per cent of the rank-and-file and officer corps in the army derived in social origin from the working class. Several years later, with the emergence of the nazi threat and the acclaimed changes in the Soviet social structure, however, this selective approach was abandoned. The new constitution in 1936 made universal military service the law of the land (Arts. 132, 133), and the various military schools were opened to the citizenry without regard to social origin.

These schools have grown steadily in number and fall into four main categories: schools functioning under the Suvorov system, officer-candidate schools, officer refresher schools, and military academies offering advanced specialized training.[5] The Suvorov schools, providing a military and general education for boys from the age of nine, admit almost exclusively war orphans and ex-partisans. The most numerous category is the officer-candidate schools, which prepare officers for every branch of service. The most advanced training schools are the military academies. These are supervised, not only by the Ministry of the Armed Forces, but also by the Ministry of Higher Education, since military sciences are placed on a par with all other branches of knowledge, and regular degrees, such as doctorates, are offered in them.

In contrast to those who receive this training in the special schools, the rank and file of the army consists of recruits, who are conscripted for a two-year period and given training that places a heavy emphasis on military indoctrination. There is thus a definite policy to create a vast reserve of highly trained officers. Although it may be too early to conclude that a caste system is emerging within the officer corps, the differentials in pay scales and living conditions between officers and men are far greater in the Soviet Army than in those of the Western states, and other factors point to a growing gap between commanding and enlisted personnel.[6]

From the standpoint of ethnic composition the Soviet Army is a multinational force. Although Great Russians predominate, especially in posts of command, members of the other nationalities have been permitted to rise to military positions of responsibility and prestige. As pointed out earlier, however, there is no present indication that the constitutional amendment of 1944 authorizing the creation of separate mili-

[4] For greater detail on the Soviet armed forces see D. Fedotoff White, *The Growth of the Red Army* (1944); Towster, *Political Power,* pp. 350–63; Louis B. Ely, *Red Army Today* (1949); Augustin Guillaume, *Soviet Arms and Soviet Power* (1949); and B. H. Liddell Hart, ed., *The Red Army* (1956).

[5] See Guillaume, op. cit., pp. 106ff.

[6] Cf. Ely, in Liddell Hart, op. cit., pp. 395ff.

tary formations in the union republics will be implemented. A number of such national units existed in their respective territories between 1923 and 1938, which were dissolved, ostensibly on other grounds, but actually because they were regarded as breeders of separatist sentiments. There is nothing to suggest any recent change in fundamental policy, regardless of later constitutional amendments. Consequently there is little likelihood that viable national armies will be permitted to form on a separate basis in the republics.

Political Indoctrination and Supervision: The Forging of an Obedient Instrument.   The Soviet Army is neither an independent political force nor an apolitical one. It is frankly regarded as an instrument of the dictatorship. There is considerable overlapping of membership between the army and the party. The percentage of party or party-affiliated members in the military rank and file has been steadily and purposely increased, reaching the 77 per cent mark by 1955. For the top-level command there was almost 100 per cent party membership at the outbreak of World War II. And, in the postwar period, the army has become the largest recruiting ground for party members.

According to the constitution of 1936 (Art. 138), members of the armed forces have the right to elect and to be elected on equal terms with all other citizens. Accordingly, army personnel have been elected to soviets, including the Supreme Soviet of the U.S.S.R. In general the army is more represented in the Soviet assemblies than in the higher party councils. But there seems to be a conscious effort to reward outstanding military officers with election to the Supreme Soviet, and in the postwar period use of military personnel for diplomatic and other political purposes has been made on a number of occasions.

Considerable care has been taken to ensure the maintenance of party control over the armed forces. Sundry measures have been adopted from time to time to guard against mass disaffection, as well as against "Bonapartism" among the officers or tendencies toward autonomy in the army as a whole. Of particular interest in this connection has been the institution of political commissars, thrice established between 1918 and 1942 as a device to secure party surveillance and control in the army, and finally abolished in the latter year, after two previous temporary abolitions, to re-establish unity of command. The disappearance of the commissar, however, has not meant the relaxation of party controls. At present the Main Political Administration of the Armed Forces, ranking also as a department of the Central Committee of the Communist Party, operates at all levels of the military hierarchy through its political officers, who have the status of "deputy commanders for political affairs" (*zampolit*) in every unit down to the regiment and battalion. There is no zampolit in a company, where the commander himself is called upon to conduct political work. He is assisted, however, by the *agit-prop* sections of the Military Political Administration, as well as by the party units, which are enjoined to offer every aid in maintaining discipline and morale, checking on loyalty and political inclinations, and generally setting examples of skill and devotion for the non-party members.

Additional eyes and ears for assisting in political controls over the military are the K.G.B. sections in divisions, corps, and armies, and the special agents of these sections in units below the division level. Following World War II, deliberate efforts were made to counterbalance the prestige of the military by stressing the role allegedly played by the party leaders—more particularly Stalin—in all matters of military organization, co-ordination, and strategy. While an effort has been made since Stalin's death to rehabilitate the names of military leaders fallen in the 1937–38 purges and rewrite the history of the war so as to recognize the merits of the marshals, the brief tenure of Zhukov in the party summit and the emphatic demands for a revival of "party spirit" in the army following Zhukov's ouster from the Party Presidium and the post of defense minister in November, 1957, as well as the renewed stress on the leading role of the party in the exploits and victories of the war, bear witness to the successful reassertion of the party's primacy in all spheres of life, including the military.

Osoaviakhim: The Mass Militarization of the Citizenry.   Operating alongside the army are a number of citizens' defense organizations. In 1927 several of these civilian organizations merged to form the *Osoaviakhim,* a voluntary society to assist in the development of military skills and defense techniques. Numbering around three million persons at the time of its formation, Osoaviakhim grew in membership to twenty million by 1939, of whom 30 per cent were women. By 1945 its membership had dropped to thirteen million, owing to the mass enlistment of its members in the regular combat forces. The services performed by Osoaviakhim included predraft military instruction for younger members and training of the bulk of its membership in air-raid protection, marksmanship, parachute jumping, skiing, gliding, and other skills of distinct military usefulness. During the war Osoaviakhim set up antiaircraft defenses, helped to organize partisan detachments, and formed instruction units on the regular army model in all of its organizations. Indeed, the scope of its activities, coupled with the extent of its membership, spelled little less than militarization of a large sector of the adult citizenry.

Dosaaf: The Present Auxiliary of the Armed Forces.   Apparently late in 1948 Osoaviakhim was split into three voluntary associations for co-operation respectively with the army (*Dosarm*), the air force (*Dosav*), and the navy (*Dosflot*). Each of these associations elected an All-Union Council, a central committee, and other organs in 1949 to direct its separate activities. But the history of other Soviet institutions was repeated, and this division according to branches was not to be permanent. In September, 1951, the three associations were integrated into a single organization, the All-Union Public Society for Co-operation with Armed Forces (*Dosaaf*).[7] This is the present citizen auxiliary of the Soviet Army.

7 See *Izvestia,* September 26, 1951.

Conclusion. Since March, 1946, several changes have taken place at the ministerial level in the administration of the army. At that time the Council of Ministers reorganized the armed forces and unified their command. Stalin was serving as minister and Bulganin as vice-minister of the armed forces. The Ministry of Armed Forces was divided into four parts: land, air, navy, and rear, each under a vice-minister. A year later Stalin resigned and was replaced by Bulganin. In March, 1949, Bulganin was succeeded by Marshal Vassilevsky, and in February, 1950, a separate All-Union Ministry of the Navy was re-established, only to be merged again with the Ministry of Defense in March, 1953, during the reorganization of the government after Stalin's death. At that time Bulganin was again appointed war minister of the U.S.S.R., with Marshals Vassilevsky and Zhukov serving as first deputies under him. Upon Bulganin's accession to the chairmanship of the Council of Ministers in February, 1955, Marshal Zhukov replaced him as minister of defense, with Marshal Vassilevsky continuing as first deputy. And on the return to the Soviet Union, in November, 1956, of Marshal Rokossovsky from Poland—where he held the post of minister of defense and head of the armed forces—he was made a deputy minister of defense of the U.S.S.R.

Despite evidence of large-scale surrender of Soviet troops during the German invasion of Russia early in World War II, and despite occasional defections in its occupation forces in Europe, the Soviet Army, on the whole, has been loyal to the regime. For the most part military personnel enjoys higher material benefits than the rest of the Soviet population. Moreover, indoctrination, organization, and discipline have contributed to make the armed forces a formidable military machine that, under firm party control, has been used repeatedly as an instrument of Soviet foreign policy in the postwar period.

Not only the army rank and file, but the officers of the highest echelons have demonstrated their loyalty to the party leadership in the post-Stalin period. The bloodless ouster of Beria in June, 1953, and of the so-called "anti-Party group" of Molotov, Malenkov, and Kaganovich in June, 1957, could hardly have been carried out without the backing of the army chiefs. At a special session devoted to the Beria case by the party *aktiv* of the Defense Ministry in mid-July, 1953, one marshal after another (Zhukov, Sokolovsky, Govorov, Peresypkin, etc.) rose to pledge full support to the Party Central Committee. Marshal Zhukov's backing is reported to have played a key role in Khrushchev's successful elimination of Molotov, Kaganovich, and Malenkov from the top leadership in the summer of 1957.

Generally the prestige of army chiefs has been consciously enhanced and a somewhat greater voice has been accorded them in the councils of government in the post-Stalin period. Marshal Zhukov, appointed deputy defense minister on Stalin's death in 1953, was not only promoted to the post of defense minister in February, 1955, but he was also elected to full membership in the party's Central Committee in the summer of 1953, then made a candidate member of the Presidium of the Central Committee in February, 1956, and finally—in June, 1957—designated a full-fledged member of that supreme policy-making body. His ouster from all these posts four months later, on the grounds that he was curtailing party control in the armed forces and was promoting a "cult" of himself in the army, emphasizes once more the perennial concern of the party leadership with the maintenance of the party's supremacy in the Soviet political system. The army has never played an independent role in Soviet politics, and, as the fate of Zhukov and earlier military leaders suggests, the party has always been able to assert its control over the armed forces. In all likelihood the army will continue to serve as an obedient instrument of the party leadership.

28

THE PLANNED ECONOMY

1. THE PLAN IN THEORY AND PRACTICE

Marx and Engels offered little in the way of a positive program for the socialist management of an economy. The *Communist Manifesto* of 1848 enumerated in the most general way some of their plans: the abolition of private property; the nationalization of industry, credit, communications, and transportation; a planned system of agriculture; etc. Although for Lenin, Marxism was fundamentally "an arsenal replete with the arms for revolution" rather than an "academy," his concentration on the staging and initial consolidation of the Russian Revolution did not cause him to neglect the importance of technological modernization, which he regarded in fact as the absolute prerequisite for survival. Said Lenin on December 22, 1920:

> Communism is the Soviet power plus electrification of the whole country. Otherwise the country will remain a small, peasant country, and that we must clearly realize. We are weaker than capitalism, not only on the world scale but within the country. Everyone knows that. We have realized it and we shall see to it that the economic basis is transformed from a small-peasant basis to a large-scale basis. Only when the country has been electrified, when industry, agriculture, and transport have been placed on a technical basis of modern large-scale industry, only then shall we finally be victorious.[1]

Yet in the few remaining years of his life Lenin was not able to elaborate in detail the theoretical or practical application of his generalizations.

Stalin and the Economic Plan: Establishment of a Principle. It was left to Stalin to draw up the concrete economic specifications for the vague Marxist blueprint. The result was his unique version of centralized

[1] *Selected Works* (1943), Vol. VIII, pp. 276–77.

676

economic planning. But Stalin's brand of "socialism in one country" was to be possible only through a permanent internal economic revolution that had fundamental non-economic consequences. Whether economic planning *per se* has been responsible for the sudden rise of the Soviet Union as a world power is highly debatable. But there is far less doubt concerning the intimate relationship between Soviet economic management and such non-economic aspects of the regime as the political monopoly and monolithism of the party, the emergence of Soviet nationalism and patriotism, and the revival of Soviet law. Just before the launching of the first Five Year Plan, Stalin, who had by that time established himself as the dominant party leader, described future Soviet society in the following terms:

> The anatomy of the Communist society may be described as follows: it is a society in which a) there will not be private ownership of the means of production but social collective ownership; b) there will be no classes or state but workers in industry and agriculture managing their economic affairs as a free association of toilers; c) national economy organized according to plan will be based on the highest technique in both industry and agriculture; d) there is no antagonism between city and country, between industrial and agricultural economy; the products will be distributed according to the principle of the old French Communists, "from each according to his ability, to each according to his needs." [2]

Thus planning is the basis of the promised millennium, and in the eyes of the Soviet leaders the above picture of the future is an anticipated consequence of "the application of reason" to society. In practice the implementation of the plan is attained by the use of the instruments of mass persuasion, with the existence of the security police still providing added incentive to the Soviet worker to maximize his productivity. In other words, what is propagated as a rational end is subverted by irrational means, with grim consequences for both citizen and society.

Institutionalization of the Plan: The Entrenchment of a Novel Practice. Article 11 of the Soviet constitution declares:

> The economic life of the U.S.S.R. is determined and directed by the state national economic plan, with the aim of increasing the public wealth, of steadily raising the material and cultural standards of the working people, of consolidating the independence of the U.S.S.R., and of strengthening its defensive capacity.

The pioneer organization of this type of planning was the *Goelro* (State Commission for Electrification of Russia), established in 1920. In Feb-

[2] "Interviews with American Labor Delegation," *Leninism* (1934), Vol. I, p. 387.

ruary, 1921, this body expanded its functions to become the *Gosplan* (State Planning Commission). Its newly assumed duties included the planning of special economic projects and the setting of production goals for various industries.

On October 1, 1928, the first Five Year Plan designed by the Gosplan was put into effect. Covering a period from 1928 to 1933, it gave priority to heavy industrial construction, to collectivization and mechanization of agriculture, and to the elimination of so-called "bourgeois residues" in the economy. The second Five Year Plan, from 1933 to 1937, sought to consolidate the gains made in the pursuit of these goals and was officially declared to have ushered in socialism. The third Five Year Plan, from 1938 to 1942, was to carry forward the transition from socialism to communism, concentrating on the chemical industries and on the industrialization and development of backward areas, particularly in the east. The aims of this plan were inspired to a large degree by Germany's aggressive intentions. The fourth Five Year Plan, from 1946 to 1950, was initiated for the purpose of rebuilding the war-torn economy and of raising production above the prewar level. What the aims of the subsequent plans were to be was broadly outlined in Stalin's pre-election speech on February 9, 1946:

> As regards long-term plans, our party intends to organize another powerful upswing of our national economy that will enable us to raise our industry to a level, say, three times as high as that of prewar industry. We must see to it that our industry [is] able to produce annually up to 50 million tons of pig iron, up to 60 million tons of steel, up to 500 million tons of coal, and up to 60 million tons of oil. Only when we succeed in doing this can we be sure that our Motherland will be insured against all contingencies.[3]

The fifth Five Year Plan, from 1952 to 1956, reiterated these aims and proclaimed as a primary objective the "surpassing" of the per-capita industrial output of the capitalist economies. The following, or sixth, Five Year Plan, approved by the Twentieth Party Congress in February, 1956, stressed the further development of all branches of the economy "to achieve a substantial rise in the material well-being and cultural standards of the Soviet people." By joint resolution of the Central Committee and Council of Ministers, published on September 26, 1957, the remaining years of the sixth Five Year Plan are to be integrated into a new—seven year—plan for the period from 1959–65 on the grounds that the industrial reorganization, the desirable exploitation of newly discovered raw materials and sources of power, as well as greater concentration on housing construction and increased farm output, necessitate longer-range planning of new industrial centers and enterprises. The revamped plan is an apparent answer to criticisms concerning alleged disproportions between the sixth Five Year Plan's targets and available resources, as well as an attempt on the part of Khrushchev and his asso-

[3] "Speech to Moscow Election District," *Pravda*, February 10, 1946.

ciates to demonstrate to the populace their conviction that "the building of a communist society in . . . the U.S.S.R. is no longer a remote goal but the immediate practical aim." [4]

Additional plans are drawn up for certain sectors of the economy requiring special attention. These plans may cut across the regular Five Year Plans, such as the afforestation program, which began in 1948, and the recent development of virgin-land agriculture. It should be remembered, however, that the Five Year Plans are devised with these special plans in mind.

By allocation of materials and manpower and the specification of methods the Soviet plan not only sets production goals but attempts to remove hindrances to the efficient production and distribution of essential goods. The plan deals with an all-inclusive variety of economic matters: construction, investment, industry, agriculture, transportation and communications, standard of living, quality and distribution of goods, labor, wages, and cultural activities.

On January 9, 1948, the State Planning Commission became the State Planning Committee (*Gosplan*), and a Committee for the Material-Technical Supply of the National Economy (*Gossnab*) was created. Gosplan was to concentrate on the planning of production and the ensuing financial arrangements. M. Z. Saburov replaced Voznesensky in 1949 as Gosplan chairman, and in the March, 1953, reorganization was in turn replaced by Kosyachenko. Saburov was again appointed Gosplan chairman in August, 1953. Gosplan was reorganized in May, 1955 and divided into the State Committee for Perspective Planning (Gosplan), headed by N. K. Baibakov, the State Committee for Current Planning (*Gosekonomkommissiya*), headed by Saburov and later by M. G. Pervukhin, and the State Committee on New Technology (*Gostekhnika*), headed until his death by V. A. Malyshev. The economic-administrative reorganization law of May 10, 1957, abolished Gosekonomkommissiya and Gostekhnika. In place of the latter a State Scientific-Technical Committee was created and charged with the study of foreign and domestic science, technology and advanced production techniques, the dissemination of this information, and the control over the development of new technology in the national economy. The scope of activities of the new State Planning Committee (Gosplan), headed by A. N. Kosygin has been greatly enlarged, and it was recognized as the "scientific planning-economic organ of the national economy." The chief functions of this elaborate organization are to work out current and long-range "perspective" plans, to carry out a single centralized policy for the development of the most important branches of the economy, to secure the proper allocation of productive forces for the balanced development of all branches of the economy, and, finally, to secure "control over the undeviating observance of state discipline in the realization of the tasks of industrial production." [5]

[4] Theses of Party Central Committee: "For the 40th Anniversary of the Great October Revolution (1917–57)," *Pravda*, September 15, 1957.

[5] "Law on the Further Perfection of the Organization of the Administration of Industry and Construction," *Pravda*, May 11, 1957.

The general production policy in the Soviet economy is laid down by the Party Presidium. This fact would seem to vitiate official Soviet claims that the masses participate in planning. The Presidium directives are based on the information collected by the State Planning Committee in co-operation with the Central Statistical Administration, a separate agency under the Council of Ministers. The plan is then formulated in accordance with these broad instructions. A day-to-day checkup on the fulfillment of the plan is of prime importance in order to discover and meet unplanned developments. Although it is emphasized that the plan is obligatory, its over-all significance is less that of an absolute and detailed blueprint than of a set of officially sanctioned objectives. It also serves the psychological purpose of dramatizing and concretizing a general economic plan, persistently related by propaganda to long-term expectations. In this sense the plan is characterized by a Marxist messianism brought down to earth for the benefit of the common citizen.

Official explanations concerning the operation of the State Planning Committee (Gosplan) since the May, 1957, reorganization, which created 105 economic-administrative regions (seventy in the R.S.F.S.R., eleven in the Ukraine, four in the Uzbek S.S.R., nine in the Kazakh S.S.R., and one in each of the remaining eleven union republics) and in them set up *sovnarkhozi* (councils of the national economy), furnish a general outline of its structure and functions.[6] The U.S.S.R. Gosplan comprises thirty-three units: nine general economic departments, twenty-three industrial departments, and one "council of technical and economic expertise." The industrial departments, which are supposed "to work out plans for the development of the given branch of the national economy by republics," are the following:

Industrial Departments:
1. Ferrous Metallurgy
2. Non-ferrous Metallurgy
3. Coal, Peat, and Shale Industry
4. Oil and Gas Industry
5. Electrification
6. Lumber, Paper, and Wood-processing Industry
7. Chemical Industry
8. General Machine Building
9. Heavy Machine Building
10. Automobile, Tractor, and Farm Machine Building
11. Electrical Equipment and Instrument Manufacturing Industry
12. Defense Industry
13. Building Materials Industry
14. Light Industry
15. Food Industry
16. Fishing Industry

[6] See the interview of G. V. Perov, Vice-Chairman of Gosplan, in *Trud*, July 2, 1957.

17. Agriculture and Procurements
18. Transportation and Communications
19. Construction Industry
20. Culture and Public Health
21. Geology
22/23. Others

The task of the general economic departments is stated to be "to work out in over-all fashion the separate aspects of the general state plan for the development of the national economy, as well as the over-all current and long-range plans for development of the national economy for each union republic and for the U.S.S.R. as a whole." These Gosplan units are listed as follows:

General Economic Departments:
1. Department of General Long-range Plans and the Development of the Union Republics
2. Department of Over-all Current Economic Plans of the Republics
3. Department of Labor and Wages
4. Department of Prices and Production Costs
5. Department of Material Balances and Over-all Distribution Plans
6. Department of Finance
7. Department of Commodity Turnover
8. Department of Capital Investments
9. Department of Foreign Economic Relations

The union-republic State Planning Commissions (Gosplan) are modeled after the U.S.S.R. Gosplan, but their structure is supposed to take into account the special characteristics of the economy of each union republic. The chief difference between the earlier and present structure of these commissions is the existence of new industrial departments. While the total planning procedure since the reorganization is still in the process of crystallization, the present practice of the planning channels is suggested in a general way. Draft plans of individual enterprises and construction projects are submitted to the sovnarkhozi and local Soviets. These two bodies in turn draft plans for the economy under their jurisdiction by separate economic branches, and submit the plans to the union-republic council of ministers, with copies for the union-republic state planning commission. These submissions serve as a basis for draft plans for the republic as a whole, including detailed plans for the individual branches of the economy and the separate administrative economic regions within the republic, which are presented for examination by the union-republic council of ministers. This last-mentioned body passes upon a composite plan for the union republic and submits an original of this plan to the U.S.S.R. Council of Ministers and a copy of it to the U.S.S.R. Gosplan. On the basis of the draft plans of the union republics, as well as of those of the U.S.S.R. ministries and agencies, the

U.S.S.R. Gosplan draws up a single state plan for the entire U.S.S.R. and submits it for approval to the U.S.S.R. Council of Ministers.

Continuing consultation and collaboration is supposed to mark the relationship between the U.S.S.R. Gosplan and the union-republic state planning commissions and sovnarkhozi. The U.S.S.R. Gosplan is said to base its planning largely on the activities of the union-republic Gosplans and sovnarkhozi, to organize the work jointly with them, and to check on the fulfillment of the plan by means of direct observation through periodic trips of officials from the central apparatus to the localities. The union-republic Gosplan is required to inform the U.S.S.R. Gosplan on the state of execution of the plan and, where problems of fulfillment arise, to make appropriate recommendations. On its part the U.S.S.R. Gosplan gives methodological aid to the sovnarkhozi and union-republic Gosplans in drawing up their plans. Generally the claim is made that the present planning procedure reflects an expansion of the powers of the union republics and an increased role for their planning commissions.

A recurrent problem of Soviet planning is how to decentralize operations sufficiently to decrease the rigidity of the economy and at the same time maintain a vigorous supervisory function. At present it does not appear as if constant reorganizations of Gosplan and the verbal emphasis on greater planning autonomy at the lower levels have adequately resolved the problems arising from comprehensive state planning for the entire U.S.S.R.

As in other sectors the K.G.B. and party units are on watch everywhere and the State Control Commission closely assists Gosplan in checking on fulfillment. This relationship draws the committee closer to the party, for the State Control Commission is an important adjunct to the Committee of Party Control.

2. MANAGEMENT OF THE ECONOMY

The Direction of Industry: Agencies, Managers, and Incentives. The basic industrial production unit in the U.S.S.R. is the enterprise, which is usually a single plant. Some of the more important enterprises are directly subordinate to the ministry involved; others—considered less vital—are under a chief administration, or *glavk,* which, as a sort of subministry, controls plants in a given area producing a particular type of product. Still others, together with similar or related plants, form trusts or combines, which in turn may be under either the glavk or the ministry. This organizational pattern exists in both the All-Union and union-republic ministries. Each enterprise operates on the basis of cost accounting with a given capital, in accordance with a financial plan that is geared to its production plan.

The enterprise has a working capital in the form of a planned allocation of materials and money. The money resources—of two kinds, turnover capital and planned credit—are supervised by the State Bank. Although the use of the turnover capital is unrestricted, the use of credit is carefully watched by the bank. Long-term credit for capital construction is controlled by special industrial banks. Capital investment in Soviet industry is heavily financed by the national budget, largely from the revenue provided by the turnover tax and, to a lesser degree, by taxes on profits and personal income. The profits of any enterprise are generally utilized in three ways: part of it is transferred to the state budget as taxation; a portion is left for the enterprise, to be used as turnover capital and as funds for capital investment; and a third share is paid into the special "director's fund," at a rate in the prewar period of 4 per cent of the total planned profit attained and 50 per cent of the profit above that planned.

Today one-man management rather than collective direction is the rule in all Soviet enterprises. The manager is all-powerful in matters concerning his enterprise, within, of course, the limits set by the law. Prior to 1937 an unofficial body known as the *troika* (triangle) existed within every enterprise. It consisted of the manager, a representative of the party, and a union representative, and was supposed to consider matters collectively and to arrive at a joint decision on all important managerial questions. Upon the personal intercession of Stalin the troika was replaced in 1937 by one-man management, with the avowed purpose of strengthening discipline and managerial responsibility.

A major problem of Soviet economic management is to raise labor productivity through a calculated system of incentives designed to apply, not only to the worker of an enterprise, but to the manager as well. The manager receives as a bonus a percentage of the decrease in the actual cost of production from the planned cost. In addition to this incentive, promotion within the Soviet hierarchy on the basis of loyalty and efficiency is expected to yield higher levels of performance by the managers. In turn the manager may use his so-called "director's fund" as a means of providing bonuses for his workers. Since 1940 management has taken a more active role in agitation for production among the workers, a role previously assumed almost entirely by the rank and file. A manager's social status and recognized ability are of distinct advantage in urging workers to higher goals or in criticizing them for poor work. Since the manager as agitator tended to widen the gulf between labor and management, however, both types of agitator, worker and manager, are now used.

In its efforts to raise labor productivity management has, of course, the constant and faithful assistance of both union and party. Labor decrees of 1938 and 1940 required the carrying of labor books and imposed strict penalties, from curtailment of holidays to correctional labor, for leaving a position without permission, excessive tardiness, and absence from work. The severity of these decrees was substantially modified by a decree of April 25, 1956, which replaced criminal liability with administrative disciplinary sanctions such as fines, dismissal, or action in "Comradely Courts" for unexcused absences. Voluntary change of employment is now possible but entails the loss of accrued bonuses and temporary loss of social security benefits.[7]

---

[7] *Vedomosti Verkhnovo Soveta SSSR*, No. 10 (May 8, 1956), pp. 246–48; *Institute for the Study of the USSR Bulletin*, Vol. III, No. 9, pp. 20–23.

In the attempts to increase output, piece-rate wages, the Stak-hanovite movement, and, more recently, the emphasis on the increase in "innovators" and "rationalizers" have played an important role. In 1935 the miner Stakhanov was reported to have produced 102 tons of coal in one shift, or fourteen times the norm. He was rewarded and decorated and his efforts were widely publicized by the party and govern-ment. "Stakhanovism" became the symbol of the drive for the over-fulfillment of production norms. Stakhanovites and innovators head a new labor aristocracy that officially belongs to the intelligentsia.

"Socialist competition" differs from Stakhanovism in that it is col-lective rather than individual. Over 90 per cent of the workers are now said to be engaged in socialist competition. This competition among areas, factories, and individuals raises the problem of maintaining a spirit of mass solidarity in view of the danger that the material rewards to the individual may lead to "bourgeois individualism." No final solution to this problem has as yet been found. In any event individualism bred by the use of a complex system of incentives is making a chimera of the ultimate goal "from each according to his ability, to each according to his needs."

The economy of the U.S.S.R. has made telling advances in a space of twenty-five years, if 1926–28 is taken as a beginning and the four war years are subtracted. As compared with the period before World War I the U.S.S.R. has risen in terms of industrial output from fifth among the nations of the world to second place, yielding only to the United States. Total gross industrial output today is claimed to be thirty-three times that of 1913. The increase, however, has not been proportionally distributed among the various sectors of the economy. In 1913 con-sumers' goods represented roughly two thirds, and capital goods one third, of the gross production. But by 1956 heavy industry accounted for 70 per cent of the total industrial output. In 1955 industrial output was four times greater than in 1940, whereas consumers' goods were only double the prewar amount. According to recent Soviet claims, steel out-put has increased eleven times, oil output nine times, coal output fifteen times, and electric power generated one hundred times over that of 1913.[8]

Industrial planning has thus concentrated on the economic sinews—capital goods, electricity, steel, oil, and coal—at the expense of con-sumers' goods and the standard of living. Clothing is extremely expensive: a ready-made man's suit costs approximately as much as the average worker's monthly wage. Rents are low, but housing for workers in the cities is very scarce, and most apartments are shared by two or more families; the average resident in Moscow has four to five square meters of housing floor space. Busses and streetcars are the chief means of transportation in the cities, for it has been estimated that only about four out of every ten thousand people can afford the cheapest car. The average Soviet consumer has thus paid a high price for the directives imposed from above upon Soviet industrial management.

[8] See Suslov, "39th Anniversary of the Great October Socialist Revolution," *Pravda*, November 7, 1956; cf. the excellent analysis by C. B. Hoover, *The Economy, Liberty and the State* (1959), Chapter 5.

Success in industrial management has been greatest in the basic industries, but not without the introduction of motivations deemed characteristic of non-Soviet societies, such as the profit motive and the inequality of awards and incomes. Production costs are still high, labor productivity is relatively low, and the goods are of mediocre quality. In addition distribution of goods has been one of the most unsatisfactory aspects of the Soviet economy. Continued shortages of consumers' goods have frequently undermined the work of the elaborate incentive system. Although repeated attempts have been made to reduce the red tape and to streamline the huge bureaucracy, the success of these efforts to date has been limited.

The Control of Agriculture: Instruments, Plans, and Realities. Land in the Soviet Union is farmed by individual peasants, by the state, and by collectives. Since 1946, when there were still over three million individual farms (largely in the territory annexed after 1939), a vigorous collectivization drive has reduced the number of individual holdings. Strictly socialistic agricultural institutions are the 5,400 *sovkhozes* (state farms) administered by the Ministry of State Farms. The sovkhozes are usually large; many of them contain over 5,000 acres, and they are worked by two million employees paid on a straight piecework basis. Some serve as model farms and agricultural experiment stations for the introduction of new methods of animal husbandry and agronomy.

Some 80,000 collective farms or *kolkhozes* are "voluntary associations" for the cultivation of land. As the legal offspring of the model charter of February 17, 1935, and Articles 7 and 8 of the 1936 constitution, they represent a stage midway between individual and socialist agriculture. Their objectives, as outlined in the charter, are to provide food for large industrial and urban areas, to mechanize farming, to eliminate the kulaks, and to strengthen the "alliance between worker and peasant." In theory it is assumed that the large-scale mechanization of farming will destroy the barrier between town and country, between mental and physical labor.

The collective farm is given the right to the permanent use of the land, which is owned by the state. Each peasant household in a kolkhoz is granted from one quarter to one hectare of land (depending on the locale) for its private use. The household is allowed a specified maximum of livestock on this tract, an individual dwelling, a few simple tools, etc. The size of the collective farms varies with regard to land and to the number of peasant households in the different regions: small in both respects in northern and central European Russia, a land of marshes, lakes, forests, and inferior soil; large in both respects on the treeless steppes of eastern and southern Russia.

The collective farm is supposed to be a democratic organization whose governing body is a general assembly of all members. It periodically elects a chairman, an executive board, and an auditing commission. The chairman of the kolkhoz may be an outsider and is hand-picked for the post by the Communist Party. The executive board, composed of from five to nine members, meets at least twice a month. The auditing commission, whose membership must be approved by the local soviet, supervises finances and economic measures. The farmers who give the major portion of their time to co-operative work are organized into brigades of from fifty to a hundred. These brigades are sometimes divided into smaller groups called "links," or *zvenos*. However, an earlier attempt to extend the link system was given up on the ground that it was reversing the trend toward the large-scale organization of agriculture.

A recent *Pravda* article expressed the hope that the annual report and election meetings would facilitate discussion and criticism of the work of the kolkhoz by the rank-and-file members.[9] At the same time it pointed out that the effectiveness of these meetings would depend on the participation of local party and Soviet agencies, and that it was the duty of the latter to ensure the timely preparation of the meetings and to focus public attention on them. It is significant today that, in contrast to the prewar period, these primary party organizations, acting in the interests of the regime, now exist in most of the kolkhozes. Thus, while in 1939 only some 8 per cent of the 240,000 kolkhozes then in existence had primary party organizations (cells), the consolidation of kolkhozes into larger units since 1950 and a vigorous drive to increase the number of primary party organizations in them brought the percentage of collectives with primary party units to about 92 per cent of the 92,000 kolkhozes in 1956.[1]

Heretofore the Machine Tractor Stations (M.T.S.), numbering about 8,500 at the beginning of 1958, constituted a vital part of the kolkhoz system.[2] As the name indicates, the M.T.S. have been centers of mechanized agricultural equipment, supplying to the kolkhozes machinery and operators for plowing, sowing, cultivation, and harvesting, and providing them also with technical assistance.[3] In addition the M.T.S. have played an extremely important role as political control points in the field of agriculture. The assistant director of an M.T.S., under the supervision of the local Communist Party organization, was responsible for the political activities of the farms; he kept close watch on morale, political opinion, and the loyalty of the peasants and assisted in their indoctrination.

However, on February 27, 1958, the party's Central Committee approved a reform in agriculture suggested by First Secretary Khrushchev, which would gradually abolish the M.T.S. in their present form. Under this reform their machinery would be sold to the collective farms. The kolkhozes would own and use the tractors, combines, and other machinery, while the M.T.S. would become mere repair and maintenance shops as well as sales depots for agricultural machinery. The official explanations offered were that the M.T.S. were no longer eco-

[9] *Pravda,* January 14, 1952.

[1] See T. H. Rigby, "Social Orientation of Recruitment and Distribution of Membership in the Communist Party of the Soviet Union," *American Slavic and East European Review,* 16 (October, 1957), esp. pp. 284–85.

[2] Before the recent amalgamation program there was an average of about thirty kolkhozes for each M.T.S.; in early 1958 the average was approximately ten for each M.T.S.

[3] *Kommunist,* No. 4 (March, 1956), pp. 44–57.

nomically justified, that they entailed a duplication of personnel and a conflict of interests with the kolkhozes, that they frequently reduced the initiative and incentive of the members of the kolkhozes, and that, with the recent strengthening of the party units of the amalgamated farms, they were no longer needed for purposes of political control. In all probability the most important single consideration behind the change is Khrushchev's expectation that it will be an indispensable step in a transition from the collective farm to the state farm system.

The quality and quantity of the work of each collective farmer is calculated by the number of workday units he performs and on the basis of which he is reimbursed. The workday unit is a measure of efficiency, there being nine different workday rates for different tasks and three crop/area categories. The output of a kolkhoz is generally allocated as follows: the major portion goes to the state to meet compulsory deliveries; a part is sold to the state at slightly higher prices on a contractual basis; a third portion is delivered for services rendered by the M.T.S., which receives its equivalent in money; the remainder is retained for kolkhoz consumption with a small surplus being sold on the free market. In an effort to provide incentives for greater productivity in agriculture, compulsory deliveries of farm produce to the state were abolished in June, 1958. Henceforth the state's acquisitions will be based on purchase and it appears that in the future collective farmers will receive regular cash remuneration for their work, rather than payment in kind calculated on the basis of workday units.

The party emphasizes that a sizable percentage of kolkhoz income, a so-called "undivided reserve," must be used to develop the kolkhoz communal economy rather than to augment the incomes of the members. It is the responsibility of the collective farm to see that these undivided reserves are used for the construction of livestock and production buildings, the acquisition of machines, and other types of improvement.

Direct responsibility for the technical operation and agricultural efficiency of the kolkhozes lies with the Ministry of Agriculture, acting largely through its chief M.T.S. Administration, the Chief Collective Farm Organizational Administration, and the Chief Agricultural Propaganda Administration. The latter agency, for example, aids in collective-farmer training and conducts farming and technical courses, which were attended by eight million collective farmers in 1950.[4] A decree of the Council of Ministers and the Central Committee of September 19, 1946, established a U.S.S.R. Government Council for Collective Farm Affairs, operating directly under the Council of Ministers through territorial-administrative representatives. It was particularly concerned with violations of collective-farm statutes, the proper functioning of the chairmen and executive boards, the frequency of general meetings, the accounting system, the use of the undivided reserves, the squandering of funds on items not related to the improvement of production, and the theft of collective-farm lands. Thus the controls over the kolkhozes, both political and technical, are numerous—through the local party organi-

[4] *Izvestia,* July 11, 1951.

zation, the district and village soviets (earlier the M.T.S.), the Ministry of
Agriculture and its various administrations, and the Council for Collective
Farm Affairs with its network of representatives.

A recent attempt at consolidating these controls was the launching
of an extensive amalgamation program. This program was spearheaded
by Politburo member Khrushchev in 1950. By October of that year
35,000 small farms had been eliminated, reducing the total of 254,000
kolkhozes at the beginning of the year to less than 220,000. Two years
later further amalgamation brought the number of kolkhozes down to
97,000. By 1956 the number had been reduced to 92,000, and it stands
today (1958) at less than 80,000. From the standpoint of political power
the program has been quite successful in tightening central control and
in concentrating party members on the farms.

In comparison with the forward strides of Soviet industry, agricultural production has lagged. Gross farm output is now no more than
one and a half times greater than it was in tsarist days. However, the
Soviets claim that grain production has more than doubled and that raw-
cotton production has increased sixfold. Sugar production is said to be
3.7 times greater than in 1917.[5] By 1953 there was less livestock in the
U.S.S.R. (56.6 million head) than in 1928 (66.8 million). This was due
less to wartime losses of cattle than to the inefficiency of Soviet agriculture, including livestock production. Only by 1958, as a result of
Khrushchev's launching of several crash programs (1954—virgin lands
cultivation, 1955—seven-fold increase of corn acreage to about 70 million acres) and the raising of farm prices, did the number of livestock
reach the 1928 figure.

Real wages declined between 1928 and the middle 1930's, rose
again at that time, and fell sharply once more between 1940 and 1945.
Although the over-all consumption level has risen and wages have climbed
upward since the end of the war, it is doubtful whether real wages had
regained the 1928 level by the mid-1950's.[6]

It is evident that the great effort in mechanizing Soviet agriculture
has not borne commensurable results in terms of the consumer's table.
The lack of experience and continued experimentation in large-scale
agricultural management, a governmental policy of guns instead of butter,
and the strong resistance of the peasantry have all contributed to this
situation. In consequence the agricultural situation in the U.S.S.R. continues to be the gravest economic problem for the Soviet leaders.

The Trade Unions: Labor Arm of the State.   Soviet trade unions
are organized by industries, rather than by crafts, in a hierarchical
structure embodying the principle of "democratic centralism," which, as
we have seen, applies also to the party and Soviet pyramids. The basic
unit is the enterprise or factory union, whose executive committee is
supposed to be elected every year at a general meeting of the workers

[5] *Pravda,* February 1, 1957.
[6] See *Statistical Handbook of the U.S.S.R.* (National Industrial Conference
Board, 1957), p. 76, and comments by Harry Schwartz in ibid., p. 25; cf. Hoover,
op. cit., pp. 138ff.

within the particular enterprise. At the discretion of factory or plant committees, shop committees may be set up in shops or enterprises that in turn may elect bureaus for a one-year term. The factory committee works through special commissions such as those for social insurance, wages, labor protection, and housing. It also participates in a "norms and conflicts commission," which consists of equal representation of labor and management (usually presided over by a representative of management) and which deals with complaints of both labor and management.

There are now over fifty million trade-union members in the Soviet Union out of a possible total of around fifty-five million workers. In 97 per cent of the trade-union primary organizations (405,000 in number) the work is done by the trade-union *aktiv*. Union members receive twice the sickness and disability benefits paid to non-members; they receive loans and grants from trade-union funds and obtain priorities for rest homes, sanatoria, recreational and cultural facilities. Membership is granted by the local membership committee, with approval of the shop or factory committee. Dues are proportioned to the wage, including overtime, and are paid monthly.

The factory unions send delegates to the district or city trade-union conferences, which convene every two years to elect an executive committee and an auditing commission. The committee elects a chairman, secretary, and presidium from its membership, holds regular plenary meetings, and acts for the conference between convocations. Above the district and city union organizations are the regional and territorial conferences, with their respective executive committees, and the union-republic conference, with its central committee. The Tenth All-Union Congress of Trade Unions established interunion conferences at the regional, territorial, and republic levels. The delegates to these conferences are elected by the different industrial unions at a given level at their separate conferences—for example, by the regional conferences of the Metallurgical Workers' Union and the Union of Workers in State Institutions—and also by individual enterprises within the region. The interunion conferences, convoked every two years to elect a trade-union council and an auditing commission, facilitate the co-ordination and liaison among the different industrial unions. Delegates are sent from the union-republic conferences to the All-Union Congress of Trade Unions.[7]

The highest organ of each trade union is the trade-union congress, which meets once every two years. Delegates are chosen according to the procedure established by the central committee of the trade union. The congress elects a central committee and an auditing commission and sends delegates to the All-Union Congress of Trade Unions.

The "supreme trade-union organization" of the Soviet Union is the Congress of the U.S.S.R. Trade Unions, according to the 1954 statutes and bylaws (Art. 20). It is supposed to meet not less than every four

[7] Statutes and bylaws of the Trade Unions of the U.S.S.R., approved by the Eleventh Congress of Trade Unions of the U.S.S.R. on June 15, 1954. *Trud,* June 19, 1954.

years, at which time it elects an auditing commission and the All-Union Central Council of Trade Unions, which in turn selects a presidium and secretariat. The Tenth All-Union Congress, convened in April, 1949, was the first to be held since 1932. Only 23.5 per cent of the delegates, representing sixty-seven unions, were rank-and-file workers; the remainder were largely trade-union officials. Of the total number of delegates 72 per cent were party members.[8] The Congress is given general responsibility for the planning of economic and welfare measures for the trade unions, though its actual role appears to be confined to hearing reports. The Central Council acts for the Congress in the intervals between its meetings; it "directs socialist competition," drafts labor legislation for government approval, administers social insurance, approves trade-union budgets, publishes the newspaper *Trud,* etc. It appears that the important power channel of the trade-union organization is from the Central Council, whose chairman, V. V. Grishin, is a member of the Party Central Committee, through the interunion councils at the republic, territorial, and regional levels, which in turn control the individual unions below.

In 1933, when the Commissariat of Labor was abolished, its funds and main functions were transferred to the trade unions, which were made responsible for the administration of social insurance through the Central Council's Department of Social Insurance and for the industrial safety of workers. The trade unions also look after the education, cultural needs, and welfare of the workers and institute various measures to improve their standard of living. In addition they serve to some extent as a check on management, and they are also agencies for feeling the public pulse for the regime. But by far the most important functions of the unions are to strengthen labor discipline and to increase production by fulfilling and exceeding the goals of the national plan. The right to strike, though not prohibited in the constitution of 1936, is not in fact recognized and is held incompatible with the principle of labor discipline and the theory that economic antagonisms are nonexistent in Soviet society.

"Collective bargaining," reinstituted in 1947 for the first time since it was abolished in 1933, is a unique method adopted by the regime to accelerate the production efforts of both labor and management. The collective agreement is signed by a ministry representing a particular industry and by the central committee of the union concerned. The terms of this agreement leave little of importance for "bargaining" between management and the union at the factory level. Thus collective bargaining in the U.S.S.R. functions largely as a psychological incentive, as a means of giving the worker an additional sense of participation in the productive process.

That every Soviet citizen is duty and honorbound to work and sacrifice is an iron law of a nation that strives to establish itself as a base for the world victory of communism. In this context any hint at a possible divergence of interests between the workers and the state,

8 See Deutscher, op. cit., pp. 128–29.

which employs them, is condemned as treason. The true nature of Soviet trade unionism can be assessed only in terms of a constant pursuit of a monolithic society, seeking to minimize or suppress antagonisms that might affect production and discipline, and with them the military potential and national morale. The actual, as distinguished from the theoretical, role of the trade unions is that of a trusted labor arm of the state.

The Co-operatives: Auxiliaries of the Planned Economy. Co-operatives have had a long and checkered history in Russia since the first retail society was founded in July, 1863. Under Soviet rule the retail consumers' co-operatives are the most important types, though the handicraft or producers' co-operatives have played a minor but noteworthy role in the Soviet economy. The handicraft co-operatives are "voluntary" associations of craftsmen and workers who pool their funds, equipment, and skills. They operate sawmills, chemical plants, fisheries, shops for the production of household goods, and provide a number of services such as carpentry, painting, and tailoring. In 1953 these co-operatives encompassed 126,000 enterprises and workshops employing 1,865,000 persons; by 1955 the number of workers had risen to 1,961,000.[9] Since 1932 they have been organized by the union republics under an All-Union Council of Handicraft Co-operative Societies. The council was abolished in 1941, and since 1946 general supervisory functions over co-operatives have been exercised by a chief administration for co-operatives under the U.S.S.R. Council of Ministers. Thus the independence of these handicraft societies is very doubtful. Not only must their operations conform to the plan, but the agencies of the republic ministries exercise strong control over them.

Consumers' co-operatives have had a particularly hectic history in the Soviet Union. In 1932, after the government had developed a network of retail shops, the urban consumers' co-operatives were abolished. The urban co-operative property was transferred to the state without payment to the members. A monopoly of rural retail trade, however, was given to the co-operatives. In November, 1946, consumers' co-operatives were reintroduced in urban areas in an effort to resuscitate the war-shattered economy. By 1947 the gross retail turnover of co-operative trade was double the 1945 level and about 22 per cent of the total trade turnover, and by 1954 accounted for 27 per cent of the total trade turnover. In August, 1949, a decree of the U.S.S.R. Council of Ministers again abolished the urban consumers' co-operatives and restricted co-operative trade to rural areas.

The Soviet consumers' co-operatives operate in a unique way. The dividends paid to the members are merely small returns on the consumers' initial investment and are not in proportion to his purchases. Evidently the co-operatives are primarily supply organizations, whose profit is shared among the consumers in the form of reduced prices on goods sold. Soviet consumers' co-operatives, according to the record,

[9] *Pravda,* August 26, 1953; *Large Soviet Encyclopedia* (1955), Vol. XXXV, p. 41.

may be liquidated without approval of or compensation to the stockholders. The fiat of the regime has thus completely transformed many of the traditional features of the co-operative movement.

The primary rural retail co-operative organization is the village co-operative (*selpo*). The majority of the members are collective farmers, but other members include workers on state farms, M.T.S. employees, and rural professional men. A small membership fee and subscription to the share capital of the co-operative in accordance to income are required. The selpo is governed by a general meeting, which is convened at least every three months. A management board and an auditing committee, the latter exercising general supervision over both management board and selpo, are elected for two years at the general meeting. The selpos are nationally organized in a manner similar to that of the trade unions. The district unions of co-operatives are key organizations, whose management boards are selected at meetings composed of delegates from local unions. Above these district unions are the regional, territorial, and republic unions of co-operatives. At the top of the hierarchy is the Council of the Central Union of Consumers' Co-operatives (*Tsentrosoyuz*), with a management board. The Fourth Congress of Representatives of U.S.S.R. Consumers' Co-operatives met in Moscow in July, 1954.

In general it may be assumed that Soviet co-operatives, both consumers' and producers', are a species distinct from Western co-operatives. They are tools in the hands of the Soviet leaders to be used as expediency and the exigencies of the economy dictate. In the economy as a whole they play only an auxiliary and circumscribed role, but, like the mass organizations in the other fields, they are intended to convey to their members a sense of more active participation in the shaping of the economic life of the country.

CHAPTER
29

SOVIET FOREIGN POLICY

1. GUIDING POSTULATES ON INTERNATIONAL RELATIONS

Soviet foreign policy is guided to a large extent by a hierarchy of postulates, the most basic of which emanate from the theory of "imperialism." It is this theory, more than any other, that determines the Soviet approach to war and peace, international law, international organization, and diplomacy.

"Imperialism": Key Concept of the Soviet Theory of the Present. Credit for developing the Soviet concept of imperialism is generally ascribed to Lenin. Rooting his ideas in Marx's theses on the nature of evolving capitalism and borrowing from the writings of J. A. Hobson and Rudolf Hilferding, Lenin presented this concept in its mature form in his *Imperialism—the Highest Stage of Capitalism,* first published in 1916. Its chief thesis is that at the beginning of the twentieth century capitalism had reached a new level of development, that of "monopoly." As compared with its earlier state it was characterized by predominance of finance rather than industrial capital, and by the existence of monopoly practices in place of free competition. Consequently gigantic trusts, cartels, and combines, controlling home markets and seeking markets, raw materials, and investment outlets in already-subjugated colonial and semi-colonial areas, engaged in devastating periodic conflicts for the "redistribution" of the world. As stated by Lenin in a frequently quoted paragraph:

> Imperialism is capitalism in that stage of development in which the domination of monopoly and finance capital has established itself; in which the export of capital has acquired pronounced importance; in which the division of the world among the international trusts has begun; and in which the

693

partition of all the territories of the globe among the great capitalist powers has been completed.[1]

This stage, he further maintained, was characterized by a number of inherent contradictions, since "the law of unequal development" of capitalism made for inequality in strength of states and for national antagonisms. The strife between mother countries and their colonies, together with the struggle for markets among the industrial powers, brought on colonial revolutions and rivalries, inevitably resulting in international wars, which undermined the mainstays of imperialism and lead to its collapse. Hence imperialism was the "last" or "moribund" stage of capitalism.

Disregarding all theories and practices that contradicted and negated Lenin's formulations, Stalin adopted them *in toto,* elaborating particularly the thesis that the "law of unequal development" produced a number of weaknesses in "the chain of the imperialist world." Some countries, such as Russia in 1917, were vulnerable to revolutionary socialism regardless of the extent of their industrialization. These views were embodied in the program of the Communist International, adopted in 1928, which proclaimed that "the dictatorship of finance capital is perishing, to give way to the dictatorship of the proletariat." [2]

"Just" and "Unjust" Wars: The Soviet Concept of Peace and War.   The compulsive and definitive mold in which the above formulations are cast render illusory any early expectation of a fundamental understanding between the Soviet and non-Soviet worlds on the nature and means for permanent eradication of war. In the Soviet view war is not a consequence of the continued imperfection of man or of the inadequacy of international organization; rather it is a result of economic processes. Echoing in part Clausewitz's views that "war is nothing but a continuation of policy by the use of other means," Lenin declared in 1916 that World War I was merely a continuation of the imperialist policies of the two opposing groups of powers. Under imperialism, he argued, peace can only be a temporary lull in the armed phase of the struggle, for peaceful coalitions and alliances are inevitably a mere truce between wars: "they prepare the ground for wars and in their turn grow out of wars." To hope for capitalism without wars would be sheer "utopia," and Social Democrats who dreamed of a peaceful advance toward socialism were guilty of rank "opportunism." [3] "Every 'peace program,' " said Lenin, "is a deception of the people and a piece of hypocrisy, unless its principal object is to explain to the masses the need for a revolution." Only the world-wide victory of communism, said he, will make wars impossible; only under universal communism will man's yearning for enduring peace finally be realized.

Thirty years later Stalin reiterated this basic thesis, despite the

---

[1] *Selected Works* (1943), Vol. V, p. 81.
[2] *Blueprint for World Conquest* (1946), pp. 164–65.
[3] *Collected Works* (1942), Vol. XIX, pp. 188–89, 363–64.

novel and, from the Marxist viewpoint, unorthodox experience of a wartime coalition between a "socialist" U.S.S.R. and the capitalist countries, Great Britain and the United States. It would be wrong to think, he stated in his February, 1946 election speech, that World War II broke out accidentally; rather it was "the inevitable result of the development of world economic and political forces on the basis of present-day monopolistic capitalism." Perhaps war could have been averted "if the possibility of periodic redistribution" of raw materials and markets by peaceful decisions had existed. But he declared this "impossible under the present capitalist development of world economy." [4]

The crowning conclusion drawn by Lenin—and subsequently accepted by Stalin and embodied in the statutes of the Communist International—was that, not only are armed collisions between "imperialist" states inescapable, but an ultimate military showdown between the Soviet and non-Soviet systems struggling for mastery of the world economy is inevitable. Later reference could thus be made to Lenin's comment in March, 1919:

> We are living not merely in a state but in *a system of states,* and the existence of the Soviet Republic side by side with imperialist states for a long time is unthinkable. One or the other must triumph in the end. And before that end supervenes, a series of frightful collisions between the Soviet republic and the bourgeois states will be inevitable.[5]

This set of doctrines conditioned the Soviet attitude toward peace and war. Since definitive peace was deemed possible only under communism, war was not looked upon by Communists as disaster but was gauged solely in terms of the degree of advancement toward their final goal. "We are not pacifists," Lenin proclaimed in 1917, "we have always declared it to be absurd for the revolutionary proletariat to renounce revolutionary wars that may prove necessary in the interests of socialism." From this they derived the theory of "just" and "unjust" wars, which was incorporated in the *Short History of the C.P.S.U.(B.).* Unjust wars were defined as wars of conquest "waged to conquer and enslave foreign countries and foreign nations." Just wars were not only wars of defense against foreign attack, but wars "to liberate the people from capitalist slavery" or "to liberate colonies and dependent countries from the yoke of imperialism." [6]

The operational leeway permitted by such a concept for Communist aggression and internal intervention in the affairs of other states is obvious. Consequently it becomes relevant to an examination of the

[4] *Pravda,* February 10, 1946. See also his last article, entitled "Economic Problems of Socialism in the USSR," in *Bol'shevik,* No. 18 (September, 1952); an English translation of it has been published in *Current Digest of the Soviet Press,* Special Supplement (October 18, 1952).

[5] *Selected Works,* Vol. VIII, p. 33.

[6] *History of the Communist Party of the Soviet Union (Bolsheviks), Short Course* (1939), pp. 167–68. See also Lenin, *Selected Works,* Vol. VI, p. 16; Vol. VII, p. 357.

whole question of the role of international law and organization in the present era.

International Law: The Concept of a Weapon in the Soviet Armory. Another derivative of the Soviet theory of imperialism is the Soviet conception of international law. Fundamentally speaking, the Soviet Union accepts only those principles of international law that will serve the expedience of particular strategies, tactics, and maneuvers in the foreign arena. Since all law is deemed to represent the interests of the dominant classes in a particular society, Soviet jurists have faced the difficulty of adjusting their definitions of international law to the needs of Soviet policy makers in certain periods to stress, and at other times to minimize, the discrepancies and conflicts between the Soviet and non-Soviet social systems. The gyrations and adjustments in evolution of the Soviet conception of international law fully reflect this difficulty.

In the mid-twenties, when the party held that in the field of foreign relations "there is a fortification and expansion of the 'breathing spell' which has been transformed into a whole period of so-called peaceful coexistence of the U.S.S.R. with the capitalist states," the prevailing conception of international law was that of Professor Eugene Korovin. During the "transitional period" from capitalism to communism it was a law based on two parallel systems, necessarily reflecting a compromise between them.[7] This conception was challenged and replaced in 1935 by that of Professor Pashukanis (later denounced as an "enemy of the people"), who characterized international law as an instrument of struggle among rival states, including those of different social and economic systems. However, by this date the Soviet Union had concluded a number of mutual-assistance pacts and had entered the League of Nations in pursuit of "collective security" against emerging threats from Germany and Japan, so that Pashukanis's emphasis on "struggle" was not in tune with the purposes of the Soviet policy makers. Accordingly, it was soon discarded after severe criticisms by Andrei Vyshinsky, who was emerging as the most trusted jurist of the regime.

In a statement to a congress of Soviet jurists in 1936, Vyshinsky suggested that in working out a new theory of international law they should keep in mind both "the fact of *the struggle and rivalry* between the socialist and capitalist systems, and also the ever increasing *co-operation* of the U.S.S.R. with certain capitalist countries." [8] The bifurcated "struggle-co-operation" concept has remained at the core of the official view on international law to date. Immediately prior to and during World War II the "struggle" part of this contradictory formula was not stressed, but since the end of the conflict it has been increasingly emphasized. The currently accepted definition, offered by Vyshinsky in 1948, characterized international law as "the aggregate of norms regulating relations between states in the process of their struggle and co-operation, which express the will of the dominant classes of the states,

---

[7] E. Korovin, *Mezhdunarodnoe Pravo Perekhodnogo Vremeni* (1924).
[8] Cited in L. B. Shapiro, "The Soviet Concept of International Law," *The Yearbook of World Affairs,* II (1948), p. 284. Italics mine.

and are guaranteed by coercion applied by the states individually or collectively." [9]

The light in which the Soviet Union regards these "norms" may be indicated by reference to the sources of international law. Soviet legal science recognizes such sources of international law as treaties, customs, courts' decisions, and writings of jurists, but accepts them only in the qualified and limited degree that considerations of expediency dictate. Some general principles of international law resting on custom, convention, etc., it accepts; others it questions and rejects; still others it seeks to reformulate in accordance with Marxist philosophy or Soviet needs and interests. Starting from the fundamental assumption that all international law must be based on the consent of sovereign states, it accepts treaties, especially bilateral treaties, as the *primary* source of international law. According to Vyshinsky, "the Soviet theory of international law regards treaties based on the sovereign equality of nations . . . as the basic source of international law," hence attaching "particular importance to the demand that treaties be fulfilled—*pacta servanda sunt.*" [1] If the practical consequence of this emphasis is to give the Soviet Union freedom of action in the foreign field without submission to universal legal principles except the few it chooses to accept, Soviet jurists are nevertheless told to continue their "contributions" to international law. Among these are listed, not only such earlier ones as the Soviet Union's definition of aggression (1933) or its winning of immunities for Soviet foreign-trade representatives, but also its "defense" —especially in the postwar period—of the principles of sovereignty, non-intervention, equality of states, national self-determination, and treaty observance. And the positions taken by the U.S.S.R. on such questions as the trusteeship system, German unity, the Marshall Plan, the Atlantic Pact, arms limitations, control of atomic weapons, warmongering, and the Korean conflict are cited as evidence that Soviet actions and interpretations have brought the concept of international law back to its original moorings to provide protection for the independence and national equality of all peoples against aggression and foreign intervention and to furnish a basis for the maintenance of international justice, peace, and security.

The facts of Soviet behavior obviously are not reconcilable with this statement of objectives: the territorial acquisitions of the U.S.S.R. since 1939; its provocation of war with Finland and interventions in the Baltic region (1939–40); its postwar ultimatums, coups, fifth columns, military and economic pressures in Eastern Europe; its persistent evasions with regard to agreements on Germany and Austria; its Azerbaijan venture (1946–47); its role in the Korean issue since 1950; its opposition to a system of sanctions for international organization and world law; its periodic cultural isolationism—these and many other data illustrate the inconsistency between Soviet theory and practice. But Soviet theorists are not disturbed by the obvious gap between words and action. In their various

[9] "International Law and International Organization," *Sovetskoe Gosudarstvo i Pravo,* No. 1 (1948), p. 22.
[1] Ibid.

ways these theories and practices are presumed to represent good "dialectics" and some advance toward the same goal—the entrenchment and expansion of Soviet power on the road to universal communism. Therefore, there is no conflict regarding international law, which is viewed by the Soviet leaders as but a tool in the struggle of the Communist camp to win the allegiance of mankind.

International Organization: The Concept of an Arena of Bipolar Conflict. Attitudes essentially similar to those concerning international law mark the Soviet approach toward international organization. It has long been a basic belief of the Soviet leaders that only international socialism (i.e., the Communist variety) can build a true international organization for world peace and security. Lenin declared in March, 1916, that future democratic peace must be sought, not "in a league of equal nations under capitalism," but in "the socialist revolution of the proletariat." [2] In the early years of the Soviet regime, when prospects for world revolution looked bright to the Bolshevik leaders, they denounced the League of Nations as an "alliance of world brigands" against the Soviet state and a "league also as of capitalists against the nations." [3] Even after the Soviet leaders, following recognition of the U.S.S.R. by most of the major powers in 1924–25 and the signing of neutrality and non-agression pacts with neighbor states, publicly conceded the fading of revolutionary opportunities and "the partial stabilization of capitalism," they continued to reject association with the League. Although the U.S.S.R. participated in the work of its disarmament commission, Stalin in 1927–28, called the League of Nations an instrument of "imperialist pacifism . . . masking preparations for war by pharisaical talk about peace." [4] Only the emergence of the Japanese threat in 1931 and the nazi menace in 1933 brought a reluctant U.S.S.R. into the League of Nations. On September 18, 1934, three years to the day after Japan's invasion of Manchuria, the Soviet Union became a member of the League. Stalin explained this change of attitude with the statement that perhaps for the very reason that Germany and Japan had resigned from it "the League [could] become an obstacle that might prevent or at least postpone war." When the intensive Soviet campaign in the League for "collective security"—of which the U.S.S.R. itself stood in great need—failed of accomplishment, Stalin told the Party Congress in 1939 that the League was a "weak international organization," although still useful to the friends of peace. Later that year, however, the Soviet Union was expelled from membership in the League of Nations for its aggressive attack upon Finland.

To the outside world a new page in the Soviet book appeared to have been opened during World War II. The Soviet leaders seemed to approve the formation of a strong, new international organization, as

[2] *Collected Works,* Vol. XIX, p. 67.

[3] See A. W. Davis, *The Soviet Union and the League of Nations,* "Geneva Special Studies," 5, No. 1 (1934); and C. D. Fuller, "Lenin's Attitude toward an International Organization for the Maintenance of Peace, 1914–1917," *Political Science Quarterly,* 64 (June, 1949), pp. 245–61.

[4] *Leninism* (1933), Vol. I, p. 401; Vol. II, p. 41.

for example in the Moscow Conference Declaration on General Security of October, 1943. And in a speech of November 6, 1944, Stalin went so far as to say that, to ensure the peace, the new international organization must have at its disposal "the minimum of armed forces necessary to prevent aggression" and must use these forces "without delay, in the event of necessity, to prevent or liquidate aggression and punish those responsible for it." [5] He added, however, a proviso that was in line with the Soviet position at the Dumbarton Oaks Conference during the preceding months: the projected international organization would be successful only if the Great Powers "continue to act in a spirit of unanimity and harmony." The same theme was repeated in March, 1946, when he told Associated Press correspondent Eddy Gilmore that he attributed great importance to the United Nations Organization, whose strength "is based on the principle of the equal rights of states and not on the principle of domination over others." And, in an interview with Elliott Roosevelt on December 21, 1946, he again emphasized that the fate of the United Nations as an organization depended "on a state of harmony being reached by these three powers, the U.S.S.R., Great Britain and the U.S." [6]

The meaning of these persistent statements became clear in time. Whatever the claims of Soviet theory and propaganda, the U.S.S.R. in practice differentiated between a formal equality of states and their power roles in international relations; and it has insisted that the Great Powers, which contributed the most to victory in war and which alone possess the means to preserve the peace, must play the greatest roles in world affairs. In reality "Big Three unity" was to ensure political gains for the U.S.S.R. on the basis of exclusive understandings among the Great Powers concerning territorial questions, spheres of influence, economic advantages, etc. Failing such understandings, the Soviet Union would fall back on the principle of Great Power unanimity—juridically embodied in the United Nations Security Council veto—as a shield against unwanted decisions affecting the interests of the U.S.S.R. Again the dominant consideration has been to guard Soviet postwar gains and retain for the U.S.S.R. maximum freedom of action.

From the latter part of 1946, Soviet spokesmen have referred to the deteriorating relations between the U.S.S.R. and the Western powers in terms of a struggle between two basic tendencies in the United Nations: one seeking to uphold peace and security and to strengthen the United Nations, the other to weaken its principles and undermine its foundations. In the following year Vyshinsky presented a bill of particulars when he associated Soviet Russia with the first tendency and accused the United States of spearheading the second by pursuing policies of "expansion and world dominion." The United Nations, he concluded, had become "the arena of a clash between these two contradictory trends in world relations." [7] This has remained the Soviet position to date.

[5] On the Great Patriotic War of the Soviet Union (4th ed., 1944), 172–73.
[6] Pravda, March 23, 1946.
[7] World Today, 4 (January, 1948), pp. 9–15.

These attitudes have conditioned all Soviet activity in the United Nations. The U.S.S.R. has abstained from participation in most specialized agencies (including, for example, the Postal Union and the Telecommunications Union), partly out of fear that such participation would involve disclosures of information about Soviet resources and conditions, and partly through lack of a desire to contribute to the recovery of sections of the world deemed potentially hostile. The latter consideration has also largely dominated the Soviet approach to the question of international economic co-operation. The Soviet Union has freely used its right of veto in the Security Council and general slow-down tactics in the Security Council to obstruct unpalatable United Nations decisions; and it has refused to abide by Assembly resolutions or to take part in their implementation through United Nations agencies whenever it regarded either action as prejudicial to its interests. It has also utilized the United Nations as a convenient observation post; and above all it has made use of the United Nations as a world forum from which to spread its propaganda in the world-wide battle of ideologies.

There is no indication whatever that the U.S.S.R. contemplated the possibility of the United Nations becoming a world government that would embrace all nations on the basis of a common citizenship. The reactions of the Soviet Union have likewise been entirely negative to every foreign plan for regional union. From 1915 to the present the Bolshevik leaders have consistently opposed all projects for a United States of Europe as false panaceas that would divert the masses from revolutionary struggle. And every recent non-Soviet suggestion for regional federations or world union has been ridiculed by them as an ill-concealed attempt at imperialist subjugation of the world by "the contemporary gravediggers of sovereignty." [8]

Basically the Soviet position on international organization rests on the assumption that the U.S.S.R. itself will lead humanity to world government, and ultimately to the millennium of statelessness, through a series of regional ties of its own making. In July, 1928, Stalin told the plenum of the Party Central Committee:

> In place of the slogan of a United States of Europe, the draft [of the Communist International] puts forward the slogan of a Federation of Soviet Republics of advanced countries and colonies which have broken away or are breaking away from the imperialist economic system, and which in its struggle for world socialism confronts the world capitalist system.

Earlier, in promulgating the first Union constitution, he proclaimed the association as "the Union of Soviet Socialist Republics, the prototype of the future World Soviet Socialist Republic." [9] There is nothing to indicate any fundamental change in these views and expectations.

[8] See Olga Gankin and H. H. Fisher, *The Bolsheviks and the World War* (1940), p. 423; also *Bolshevik,* No. 19 (1946), p. 28.

[9] *Leninism,* Vol. II, pp. 43–44; *Marxism and the National and Colonial Question* (n.d.), p. 130.

Diplomacy: The Concept of a Tactical Riveting Instrument.   The Soviet concept of diplomacy is in harmony with its conception of international law and organization. Diplomacy has always been regarded by the Soviet leaders, not as a medium for long-term accommodation in a world community permanently based on diverse systems and polities, but as a temporary auxiliary tool to be used with many others in the pursuit of a world victory for communism. Soviet writings accord diplomacy a significant role alongside other means for achieving national ends. "A good foreign policy," said Stalin in May, 1945, "sometimes counts for more than two or three armies at the front." [1]

A correct understanding of the relationship of diplomacy to foreign policy is considered particularly important. In the Soviet view diplomacy is primarily a tactical tool, standing in relation to foreign policy as means to a goal. Stalin once defined the task of political strategy to be the correct determination of the direction of the proletarian movement in a given country during a particular historical period; the role of tactics, however, was to decide on the basis of such strategy the forms and methods of struggle best suited to the concrete conditions of the moment. These definitions are involved in explaining the interrelationship of diplomacy and foreign policy:

> Foreign policy is the fundamental direction of the entire activity of the state in the sphere of external relations over an entire historical period. It comprises the determination of the basic aims of the state abroad as well as the general plan of disposition of all its means and forces: diplomatic, military, economic, etc. used to achieve those aims . . . in other words, foreign policy is the strategy of the foreign relations of the state.[2]

Diplomacy, on the other hand, consists of the procedures and methods of official activity of the government and its agencies involved in matters of foreign relations over much shorter spans of time. These techniques may change many times in the course of one historical period, since it is the purpose of diplomacy to correlate them correctly with other means in order to bring about successful realization of foreign-policy objectives. "Hence diplomacy is not only a method or means of foreign policy, but a special tactic of the foreign relations of the state subordinate to and serving its foreign policy." [3] Diplomacy is considered more an art than a science, although Soviet diplomats are told that they must evaluate scientifically all the facts in a situation and that in guiding themselves by Marxist theory they wield a scientific weapon possessed by none of their rivals. Finally, diplomacy is deemed to hold intimate (though "dialectical rather than mechanical") ties to international law, developing the latter by changing the concrete content of its institutions and norms.

[1] *Pravda,* May 25, 1945.
[2] D. B. Levin, "On the Question of the Concept of Diplomacy," *Sovetskoe Gosudarstvo i Pravo,* No. 9 (1948), p. 17.
[3] Ibid.

In line with all other political propaganda in the U.S.S.R., Soviet textbooks and writings on foreign policy abound in assertions that, as compared with the perfidy and amorality of "bourgeois diplomacy," the principles and practices of Soviet diplomacy are open, unselfish, and honest—marked by singular "fidelity to the given word." [4] However, the heritage of maxims handed down by Lenin and accepted by his disciples is thoroughly inconsistent with this propaganda line. Lenin drew a sharp distinction between fidelity to the core of the party's aims and the means for their realization, urging the utmost elasticity in the choice of means. "The strictest loyalty to the ideas of Communism must be combined with the ability to make all the necessary practical compromises, to 'tack,' to make agreements, zigzags, retreats and so on," wrote Lenin in 1920 in an essay that has become part of the Communist bible of politics.[5] If, for instance, the leaders of the Western European trade unions bar Communists, the latter should be able to agree to any sacrifice and if need be "resort to all sorts of stratagems, maneuvers, illegal methods, to evasions and subterfuges" in order to gain entrance into the unions and to carry on Communist work in them. Communists must know how to take advantage "of the antagonisms and contradictions existing among the imperialists," to gain a mass ally, "even though this ally be only temporary, vacillating, unstable, unreliable and conditional." Lenin cast scorn upon the left Communists in his own ranks who objected to the signing of the Brest-Litovsk treaty. "In war never tie your hands with considerations of formality. It is ridiculous not to know . . . that a treaty is a means of gaining strength." And he later excoriated the German Communists for urging refusal to sign the Versailles Treaty, in a statement that is acclaimed as a classic of Communist tactics:

> To tie one's hands beforehand, openly to tell the enemy, who is at present better armed than we are, whether and when we will fight him, is stupidity and not revolutionariness. To accept battle at a time when it is obviously advantageous to the enemy and not to us is a crime: and those political leaders of the revolutionary class who are unable to "tack, to maneuvre, to compromise" in order to avoid an obviously disadvantageous battle, are good for nothing.[6]

These maxims bear directly on the conduct of Soviet diplomacy. The goal is victory, not genuine compromise at the green table. But temporary retreats and compromises may be necessary to gain time and assemble strength. Ultimate victory can be realized through a succession of minor successes, provisional stalemates, and occasional retreats.

Stalin's concept of diplomacy in no way differed from Lenin's.

---

[4] Ibid., pp. 21–25; *Istoria Diplomatii* (1945), pp. 701–64; *Diplomaticheskii Slovar* (1948), Vol. I, pp. 570, 574, 588, 591–92.

[5] "Left-Wing Communism, an Infantile Disorder," *Selected Works* (1943), Vol. X, p. 138.

[6] Ibid., pp. 95–96, 112, 118–19.

In 1913 he characterized "bourgeois diplomacy" in the following words: "A diplomat's words must have no relation to action; otherwise what kind of diplomacy is it? Words are one thing, actions another. Good words are a mask for the concealment of bad deeds. Sincere diplomacy is no more possible than dry water or iron wood." [7] And in 1921 he berated Foreign Commissar Chicherin for not exploiting sufficiently the conflicts between foreign states "when the whole purpose of the existence of the People's Commissariat for Foreign Affairs is to take account of these contradictions, to use them as a basis and to maneuvre within these contradictions." [8]

In practice these attitudes have resulted in certain significant consequences. Far from encouraging an understanding of their countries by foreign diplomats, the leaders of the U.S.S.R. and other Communist states have obstructed the functioning of foreign representatives and progressively created more barriers to such understanding. Also, some of the traditional diplomatic skills, considered in the past to be essential for successful operation, have been little in evidence among Soviet diplomats. To a far greater extent than their colleagues from the opposite camp Soviet diplomats are subject to directives and control; and even the most reliable Marxists have little leeway in carrying out instructions. They come to the conference table under general orders to seek total victory, to delay the opponent's victory if such is inevitable, to leave as many avenues as possible for the subsequent reopening of the question in case of defeat, and to make maximum propaganda capital out of the negotiations. Hence the talents sought in Soviet diplomats are not the aptitude for conciliation, personal charm, or ability to make friends in order to facilitate agreement; rather they are knowledge of subject matter and procedural rules, capacity for argumentation, skill in concealment, and extraordinary tenacity in order to outlast, wear down, and outmaneuver the opponent.

The true nature of Soviet diplomacy as a relentless tactical riveting instrument was vividly described as early in the regime as 1924 in an interview given by a Soviet official to an American newspaperman:

> Our fixed resolve [is] that no matter interesting to Russia shall be, or can be, settled without our participation and approval. Outsiders may think our repeated insistence on these points stupid and monotonous. Nothing is more stupid and monotonous than drops of water falling, falling—but they wear away solid rock, and neither the Allies nor the League of Nations are solid rock.[9]

There appears little prospect of an early change in the basic features of Soviet diplomacy. The nature of the Soviet conceptions of diplomacy, as well as of peace and war, law of nations, and international organization, consequently evidences little faith on the part of the Soviet leaders

[7] *Sochinenia* (1946), Vol. II, p. 277.
[8] *Marxism and the National and Colonial Question*, pp. 105–6.
[9] Cited in Vera Micheles Dean, *The United States and Russia* (1947), p. 202.

in any community of nations in which Soviet and non-Soviet peoples would permanently exist side by side, harmoniously regulating their relations by common ethical precepts, legal principles, or institutional arrangements.

2. TOOLS AND RESERVES OF SOVIET COMMUNISM

In the pursuit of its world-wide aims Soviet communism resorts to various devices and disposes of a number of forces. In the metaphor of the military idiom favored by the Soviet leaders the Communist movement is likened to a great international army with shock troops, regular battalions, primary and secondary reserves. The U.S.S.R. is the base and the seat of the general staff, providing the core of the troops who, together with the Communist parties abroad, constitute the principal force. The foreign workers and colonial peoples, said Stalin on one occasion, are the direct reserves; the indirect reserves are the antagonisms within and between capitalist states. The following statement, made by Stalin in 1924, is taken as a guiding line:

> The main forces of the revolution: the dictatorship of the proletariat in one country [the U.S.S.R.], the revolutionary movement of the proletariat in all countries [i.e., the Communist parties and revolutionary workers]. Main reserves: the semi-proletarian and small-peasant masses in the developed countries, the liberation movement in the colonies and dependent countries.[1]

His plan for the disposition of forces (in addition to those for isolating the democratic and socialist parties) was to form an "alliance of the proletarian revolution with the liberation movement in the colonies and the dependent countries."

Other "reserves" mentioned from time to time included societies of women, young people, and professional and religious groups, which would serve as "front organizations" to win adherents and sympathizers for the Communist cause. All of these organizations and groups were regarded as assets in furthering Soviet foreign political aims; but the greatest weight was placed on the Communist parties.

Comintern-Cominform: National Communist Parties. The Communist International, or Comintern, was formed in Moscow during March, 1919. This Third International was brought into being as a legitimate heir to the Communist League (1847–50) and First International (1864–76) and as a successor to the existing Second, or Socialist, International, originally founded in 1889. From the time of the Kienthal and Zimmerwald conferences of antiwar Socialists in 1915 and 1916, Lenin had agitated for the creation of a Third International

[1] *Problems of Leninism* (1940), pp. 60–61; see also *Leninism* (1934), Vol. I, pp. 76–77.

to replace the Second, which he held to have betrayed its Marxist origins and revolutionary objectives by permitting its affiliated parties to support their governments during the war.

The Comintern was called "the centralized militant co-ordinating body" of a single, world-wide Communist Party, and at its first congress it proclaimed its mission to be "to unite the efforts of all genuinely revolutionary parties of the proletariat and thereby to facilitate and speed the victory of the Communist revolution in the entire world." [2] The congress also told the Communist parties to work within their respective countries for a resumption of trade and diplomatic relations with Soviet Russia, and for dispatching to Russia thousands of engineers, instructors, and skilled workers "in order to render the youthful Socialist republic real aid in the economic sphere." [3] The duality of the Comintern's role as an instrument for world revolution and as an agency for the succor and defense of the Soviet state was again and again evident in the resolutions of the congresses and other Comintern organs. As sections of the Comintern, Communist parties in other countries were directed to carry on work among young people, women, armed forces, trade unions, co-operatives, and other mass organizations in order to win over the masses and prepare the way for eventual seizure of power. And times without number the sections were told that the defense of the U.S.S.R. and its interests was their primary duty, because the Soviet Union was "the one and only fatherland" of the toilers of all countries, "the first and most important citadel of socialism and the international proletariat." [4]

The Comintern policy toward non-Communist Socialist parties was always dominated by tactical considerations, but for the most part it was one of bitter hostility. During the first years of the Comintern, Social Democrats were denounced as "social-patriots" and "social-traitors." In an effort to gain greater support among the masses after the failure of the short-lived Soviet republics in Munich and Hungary in 1919, the Communist parties during 1921–23 sought some reconciliation with rank-and-file Socialists through widespread use of such slogans as "United Front," "Labor Government," and "Workers-Peasants Government." Less of this type of effort was made after the defeat of the Communist uprising in Germany in 1923, when the Comintern ordered the "bolshevization" of its sections. Nevertheless one continued evidence of attempted co-operation at higher levels at that time was the formation of the Anglo-Russian Trade Union Committee, composed of trade-union leaders of both countries. With the breakdown of this committee and the collapse of the Communist-Kuomintang partnership in 1925–27 in China, however, Comintern pronouncements took a stronger revolutionary line, and, except for lip service to a "United Front from below," efforts at co-operation with the Socialists were abandoned.

[2] *Kommunisticheskii Internatsional v Dokumentakh* (1933), pp. 53–54, 57; cited hereafter as *K.I. v Dok.*
[3] Ibid., pp. 86–88.
[4] Ibid.

In 1933–35 the appearance of the nazi danger to the U.S.S.R. led the Comintern's Executive Committee to issue strenuous appeals to the Second International and its parties to form a united front against the common threat of fascism. The seventh congress of the Comintern in July–August, 1935 urgently and solemnly repeated these appeals. Yet, significantly enough, it proclaimed that unity of action cannot preclude the Communist parties from criticizing social democracy as an illusory ideology supporting "class collaboration" and "peaceful, legal methods" to achieve socialism. The Communist parties reserved full freedom to propagate communism among the Social Democratic workers. The Spanish Civil War was to provide a tragic test for Socialist-Communist collaboration throughout 1936–39 under the flag of the "Popular Front," formed in 1935.

Although Communists and Socialists participated jointly in the wartime resistance movement of a number of countries, the Western European Socialist parties—except for the Italian party under pro-Communist Pietro Nenni—have been wary about co-operating with the Communists since the war. The Eastern European Socialist parties have been swallowed by the Communist parties, with which they were forced to merge. A semblance of the Second International, which became defunct during the war, has reappeared in the International Socialist Conference. Since 1953 conferences or council meetings of this revived international have been held every year. While its attempts to expand the membership by securing the affiliation of large sections of the Asian Socialist movement have not met with success, it has steadfastly refused all proffers to join ranks with the Communist parties. The Communist International, formally dissolved in May, 1943, was revived as the Communist Information Bureau, or Cominform, in September, 1947. At that time the Cominform issued a pronouncement that underscored the abyss between Communist and Socialist organizations. Its first manifesto denounced the right Socialists (Atlee, Blum, Saragat, Schumacher, Renner) as "faithful toadies of the imperialists" and held them responsible for the dissension in the ranks of labor. However, the door to "united action" was not completely closed, as subsequent Communist efforts to enlist Socialists in "peace drives" and other tactical moves have clearly demonstrated. At the Twentieth Party Congress of the Communist Party of the Soviet Union in February, 1956, First Secretary Khrushchev went so far as to proclaim a number of doctrinal revisions—such as the thesis that there are many roads to socialism, including the parliamentary one—in order to induce the Socialists to join once more in forming a "United Front" with the Communists. This bid was rejected, however, by the General Council of the Socialist International, which met in Zurich the following month.

The Soviet leaders have used a number of occasions to deny that Communist parties take orders from Moscow. The official pronouncements of the Soviet government on this issue held that the Comintern, up to the time of its dissolution, was an independent body directed exclusively by its own organs. These were the World Congress, the executive committee (E.C.C.I.), the presidium, which was elected by the

E.C.C.I., a political secretariat, and an international control commission. However, quite outside the fact that the Communist Party of the Soviet Union provided the headquarters and, as the largest party, made the largest financial contributions, the records of the Soviet Party Congress and of Comintern organs leave no doubt that the Soviet leaders controlled all important appointments, purges, and policy shifts. Indeed, Stalin's leading role in the Comintern, particularly since the mid-twenties, has been admitted in Comintern sources in the most boastful terms.[5]

The Cominform, which succeeded the Communist International and established headquarters first in Belgrade and later (in 1948) in Bucharest, was equally a tool of Moscow, although of lesser significance. At the time of its establishment in 1947, it included representatives of the Communist parties of the U.S.S.R., Poland, Czechoslovakia, Rumania, Hungary, Bulgaria, and Yugoslavia, Italy, and France. In theory the Cominform was set up to "exchange experiences" and to co-ordinate the activities of the member parties. Actually it was launched mainly as an answer to the Marshall Plan and was intended as a warning that communism could again become internationally active and troublesome. In 1950 the membership of the Communist parties of the Cominform countries and China (not counting the Communist Party of the Soviet Union) was officially given as over 13,350,000, as compared with a prewar membership of less than 600,000. Early in 1956 the total membership of all the parties of the Cominform (including the C.P.S.U., with a membership of over 7,000,000) was estimated at close to thirty million.

In June, 1948, Yugoslavia was expelled from the Cominform after a break with the Kremlin, ostensibly because of errors in Yugoslavian peasant and party policies, actually because Yugoslavia rejected infiltration by Soviet military advisers and the extension of other types of Soviet control. Marshal Tito, it seems, had forgotten Stalin's injunction of 1927 that "an internationalist is he who, unreservedly, without hesitation, without conditions, is ready to defend the U.S.S.R." and its interests. Communist Yugoslavia put its national interests ahead of those of the U.S.S.R. and was excluded from the fold. In 1953, after Stalin's death, relations between the two countries progressively improved, and in September of that year the first Yugoslav ambassador since 1948 arrived in Moscow. A series of yearly trade agreements followed and, in their efforts to regain the confidence of the Yugoslavs, the Soviet leaders undertook to extend credits and construct a number of industrial enterprises in Yugoslavia. The most dramatic phase of this reversal of attitudes began with the arrival of Khrushchev and other Soviet leaders in Yugoslavia in May, 1955 to confess Stalin's injustices to the Yugoslav Communists and to re-establish party relations with the latter. Subsequent reciprocal visits between the Communist leaders of the two countries in June and September, 1956 sought to define further future

[5] See, for example, *Outline History of the Communist International* (1934), p. 51; and Wan Min's statement in *XVII S'ezd Vsesoiuznoi Kommunisticheskoi Partii (b)* (1934), p. 328.

relations. However, Tito's insistence on "the equality and sovereignty" of the separate Communist countries—though formally conceded by the Soviet leaders—could not be easily reconciled with the latter's insistence in practice on the hegemony of the U.S.S.R. in the Communist camp. And Tito's condemnation of Soviet intervention in the national Communist revolutions in Poland and especially in Hungary in October, 1956 led again to a cooling off of relations between Moscow and Belgrade.

There is little doubt, however, that, along with several other factors (such as the statements of Nehru and others at the Bandung conference, in April, 1955, that the Cominform is incompatible with "peaceful coexistence"), the desire of the post-Stalin Soviet leadership to conciliate Tito's Yugoslavia contributed to the dissolution of the Cominform on April 17, 1956. Such organizational dissolution, however, does not signify any absolute severance of ties between the Moscow-led Communist parties. On the contrary, the resolutions of the November, 1957 gathering of the leaders of the Communist parties in Moscow suggest continuing efforts at consolidation of the Communist camp.

Props of Soviet Foreign Policy: International Proletariat, Colonial Peoples, and "Front" Groups.   If the Communist parties constitute the outright tools or regular detachments in the service of Soviet foreign policy, other forces and groups that the Soviet leaders have sought to harness to their purposes are the "international proletariat," "colonial liberation" movements, and sundry "front" associations. On many occasions the Soviet leaders have deliberately told the world that any power daring to attack the U.S.S.R. will meet with disturbances and revolution at home and with uprisings in its dependent territories. Thus, at the 1930 Party Congress, Molotov boasted that "support of the U.S.S.R. on the part of the foreign proletariat" is one of the prime "factors which strengthen the international position of the U.S.S.R." On the same occasion Stalin uttered a typical threat:

> But intervention is a stick [usable] at both ends. Of this the bourgeoisie is fully aware. It is all right, it thinks, if intervention works out smoothly and ends in the defeat of the USSR. What, however, if it ends with the defeat of the capitalists? Wasn't there once an intervention which ended in collapse? If the first intervention—when the Bolsheviks were weak—ended in collapse, what guarantee is there that the second one will not end likewise in collapse? . . . What about the workers of the Capitalist countries who will block intervention in the USSR, fight against it, and if need be strike at the capitalists from the rear? [6]

The Comintern organs have also issued repeated warnings that a war against the Soviet Union would be converted into "a civil war" against the instigators, whose toilers will work for the victory of the Red Army.

[6] *XVI S'ezd Vsesoiuznoi Kommunisticheskoi Partii* (1931), pp. 7, 50–51, 732.

To ensure a sympathetic attitude toward the Soviet Union on the part of the international proletariat, several approaches, sometimes contradictory, were tried in dealing with foreign trade unions. At an early date the Comintern formed the Profintern, the Red Trade-union International, which, however, was never successful in attracting affiliates, except in France and Czechoslovakia. Efforts were also made from time to time to win good will for the Soviet Union among foreign trade unions through some form of collaboration between their leaders and those of the unions in the U.S.S.R. Such an objective will help explain the creation of the Anglo-Russian Trade Union Committee in 1925–27, the Anglo-Soviet Trade Union Committee in 1941, and the Franco-Soviet Trade Union Committee at a later date. In October, 1945, after repeated Soviet prodding, leaders of the British Trade Union Congress (T.U.C.) and the American Congress of Industrial Organizations (C.I.O.), together with Soviet trade-union leaders, formed the World Federation of Trade Unions (W.F.T.U.). The basic understanding was that the W.F.T.U. would devote itself strictly to trade-union problems. But shortly after the formation of the W.F.T.U. the Russians made their earlier intention clear and began to maneuver the W.F.T.U. into championing the U.S.S.R. and its satellites, attacking Marshall Plan aid, and denouncing the Western powers. The W.F.T.U. was also used as a vehicle for Communist infiltration and capture of trade unions in the Middle East, Latin America, Japan, Korea, and Southeast Asia. It thus became an aggressive political tool for supporting Soviet policy; and at the end of 1948 the T.U.C., the C.I.O., and other free trade unions withdrew from the W.F.T.U. A year later these trade unions, together with the American Federation of Labor (A.F. of L.), which had originally opposed the formation of the W.F.T.U., banded together to establish a new International Confederation of Free Trade Unions (I.C.F.T.U.), which promised a return to the principles of trade unionism.

The W.F.T.U., with headquarters moved successively from Paris to Vienna to Prague, claims a membership of around ninety-two million trade unionists in some fifty countries. Of this membership over eighty-four million are in Communist-bloc countries, the U.S.S.R. alone accounting for more than fifty million members, while Communist China follows with sixteen million members. Only a little over seven million belong to trade unions outside the Communist camp (primarily in France, Latin America, Southeast Asia, and the Middle East). The W.F.T.U. holds a consultative status with the International Labor Office (I.L.O.) and the Economic and Social Council of the United Nations (E.C.O.S.O.C.), and, to demonstrate its concern with traditional labor pursuits, it adopted in 1954 a "Charter of Working People's Trade Union Rights," which includes the right to strike. In practice its primary activity appears to center on the promotion of front organizations and propagation of Soviet conceptions and policies in the field of international relations. In this activity it has worked in close contact with such Communist-dominated front organizations as the: International Union of Youth, World Federation of Democratic Youth, Women's International Democratic Federation, World Federation of Scientific Workers, International Association of Democratic Lawyers, World Federation of Teachers Unions, International Federation of Resistance Fighters, World Peace Council, and others. And since the Geneva summit conference the W.F.T.U. has made repeated appeals for unity with the I.C.F.T.U. in order to reach non-Communist trade unionists.

The I.C.F.T.U. claims a membership of over fifty-four million trade unionists in eighty-one countries. Its declared program is to combat totalitarian ideas, defend the right of free trade unions to bargain collectively, help workers in underdeveloped areas to improve working conditions and achieve self-government and political freedom, strengthen the U.N. as an organization for collective security, and obtain proper representation in the latter and other international organizations. The I.C.F.T.U. does in fact hold a consultative status with the U.N. agencies and maintains regular relations with the Organization for European Economic Co-operation (O.E.E.C.), the Council of Europe, the European Coal and Steel Community and NATO. Ridiculing the reality of the avowed "right to strike" by trade unions in Communist countries, the I.C.F.T.U. has refused admission to Yugoslav trade unions, rejected all overtures for unity with the W.F.T.U., and has enjoined its own affiliates to sever all ties with the W.F.T.U. unions, wherever such existed. The I.C.F.T.U. has proclaimed as its main task a struggle against the W.F.T.U. for "the hearts, souls and minds" of the working people in the current world conflict between democracy and totalitarianism. Thus the issue has been clearly joined over one of the favorite props of Soviet policy abroad, the "international proletariat."

The challenge extends in fact to the other major prop, the colonial peoples. For theoretical, as well as "practical," political reasons, the strivings of the 750 million colonial peoples for independence have been a prominent topic in the writings of the Soviet leaders. The linking of these efforts to the "proletarian revolution" is now a basic element in the Communist doctrine of piercing "the chain of imperialism" at its weakest points. Colonial troubles, it is argued, keep the colonial powers preoccupied and away from the U.S.S.R. Moreover, in case of foreign attack on the U.S.S.R., the Communists expect "to cause uprisings . . . in colonial and semicolonial countries and to organize national-liberation wars against the imperialist enemies of the Soviet power." [7]

The Communists have relied upon three types of efforts among the colonial peoples: organizational work, intensive propaganda concerning the achievements of the Soviet regime, and—in recent years—stepped-up trade, cultural exchange, and outright economic and military aid. The extraordinary emphasis placed on propaganda is evidenced by Stalin's statement before the Party Congress in April, 1923:

> One of two things: either we inflame the deep rear of imperialism—the eastern colonial and semi-colonial countries, revolutionize them and thus hasten the fall of imperialism; or we shall botch things here and thereby strengthen imperial-

[7] *K.I. v Dok.*, p. 809.

ism and weaken our movement. This is how matters stand. The point is that the entire East regards our Union of Republics as an experimental field. Either we correctly decide and practically apply the national question within the framework of this Union . . . and then the entire East will see that in our Federation it possesses a banner of liberation, a vanguard in whose footsteps it should walk, and this will be the beginning of the collapse of world imperialism. Or we commit a mistake here, undermine the confidence of the formerly oppressed peoples in the proletariat of Russia, shear the Union of Republics of its power to attract the East, a power it now enjoys, in which event imperialism will gain and we shall lose.[8]

In fomenting independence movements the Communists are ready to "enter into a temporary alliance with bourgeois democracy in colonial and backward countries," at the same time retaining their own organization, at least in rudimentary form.[9] Once the colonial country has won its independence, its Communists are expected to make their own political conquests, always guided by the particular demands of Soviet foreign policy. Whatever its strategy, Soviet propaganda had made a deep impression in the colonial areas of Asia. And in the post-Stalin period it has been accompanied by intensive diplomatic maneuvering entailing: reciprocal visits with high officials of formerly dependent countries; exchange trips by cultural and parliamentary delegations; the conclusion of a series of friendship, trade, credit, and technical-assistance pacts; and feverish diplomatic activity ranging all the way from consultation and vigorous support vis-à-vis Western or pro-Western countries to the sale of arms and sundry forms of financial support and other aid, which have contributed to Communist penetration to positions of influence in a number of the newly independent states.

Lastly, there are the miscellaneous front organizations brought into being from time to time to further Soviet aims or Communist causes. Early in its history, by way of illustration, the Comintern formed a Peasant International (*Krestintern*) and Sports International (*Sportintern*) to attract peasants and sport lovers to organizations clearly identified as Communist. But such efforts failed to produce expected results, and there developed a reliance on front organizations, such as professional groups or societies for "friendship with Russia," to rally support for Soviet aims under innocuous or misleading labels. Examples of recent years are the "Stockholm peace petition" organization and the series of world congresses of Intellectuals for Peace held in Wroclaw, New York, Paris, and other places. Like such Communist-dominated organizations as the Women's International Democratic Federation and the World Federation of Democratic Youth, the World Peace Congress represents an effort to mobilize certain groups of individuals behind Soviet policies.

[8] *Sochinenia,* Vol. V, pp. 237–38.
[9] Lenin, *Selected Works,* Vol. X, p. 237.

3. THE FUNCTIONAL CONCEPTS OF SOVIET FOREIGN POLICY

When the numerous theorems, postulates, and teachings that shape Soviet foreign political conduct are reduced to essentials, they comprise a fundamental framework of perhaps no more than six concepts or ideas that appear to guide the Soviet policy makers at all times. The six concepts are: World Revolution, U.S.S.R. Survival, Provisional Coexistence, Continuing Competition, Balancing, and Flexibility.

World Revolution. The highest and ultimate aim of Soviet foreign policy is World Revolution—the victory of Communism on a world scale. Contrary to some wartime and immediate postwar interpretations, which asserted that the U.S.S.R. had become merely a Russian national state—and as such would forsake expansion and be satisfied with such traditional national interests of Russia as access to the world's seaways, trade, and raw materials—the Soviet Union proceeded to communize Eastern Europe and push far beyond such limited objectives in the years since the end of World War II. All Soviet foreign political activity issues from two basic assumptions: (1) that no permanent or absolute security is possible for the Soviet state until the "danger of an imperialist attack" on the U.S.S.R. or its allies is removed (Khrushchev), and (2) that the present era of "imperialism, the highest stage of capitalism," is the last for the non-Soviet order, which will reach its doom before the century is over. As the Soviet leaders read the historical clock, the victory of communism in large areas of the earth that followed the two world wars was substantiating proof of the Marxist thesis that the age of capitalism is coming to an end. To bring about this consummation and usher in the victory of communism all over the world remains the ultimate objective. It is the *maximum* goal they seek eventually to achieve.

U.S.S.R. Survival—The Minimum Goal. In the period between the two world wars Soviet theorists and propagandists never ceased to tell Communists everywhere that their first duty was the defense of the U.S.S.R., that the survival of the Soviet Union was an absolute prerequisite for Communist victory in their own individual countries. And after the war Duclos in France, Togliatti in Italy, and other Communist leaders had their parties declare that they will refuse to oppose the Red Army in a war with the U.S.S.R. Soviet writings leave no doubt that the Soviet leaders will stop at nothing to preserve the Soviet Union. U.S.S.R. survival is the absolute *minimum* objective of Soviet foreign policy. Thus these two objectives—*World Revolution* and *U.S.S.R. Survival*—are two poles, the two extreme ends of the range of Soviet foreign policy.

Provisional Coexistence. The term used in Soviet statements is "peaceful coexistence." The Soviet understanding of coexistence has been frequently misinterpreted abroad owing in large measure to contradictions in Soviet statements on the subject. In 1919, when hopes for world revolution were high among Soviet leaders, Lenin uttered the dictum:

> We are living, not merely in a state, but in a system of states, and the existence of the Soviet Republic side by side with imperialist states for a long time is unthinkable. One or the other must triumph in the end. And before that end supervenes, a series of frightful collisions between the Soviet Republic and the bourgeois states will be inevitable.

But by 1926–27, when Stalin decided that the prospects for world revolution were slim and that all efforts must be concentrated on industrializing Russia, he told the Soviet people that, since Western intervention in the Russian Revolution had failed and Communist revolution outside of Russia also had failed, a sort of equilibrium had arisen between capitalism and communism, a stage of "peaceful coexistence." Conscious of the Soviet need for credits and technical assistance as well as for a period of peace to launch the programs of industrialization and collectivization, Stalin reminded his countrymen about Lenin's warning to delay war with the capitalist countries until they either fight among themselves or are faced with domestic or colonial revolutions. Stalin concluded (1927): "Therefore, the maintenance of peaceful relations with capitalist countries is an obligatory task for us. The basis of our relations with capitalist countries consists in admitting the coexistence of two opposed systems."

Again at the end of World War II, Stalin stated to Harold Stassen, Elliott Roosevelt, visiting congressmen, and various journalists that "peaceful coexistence" between the U.S.S.R. and the U.S.A., between communism and capitalism is entirely possible.

Confounded by such contradictory pronouncements, foreign observers have been prone to interpret Soviet activity in terms of support for "coexistence" by some Soviet leaders and serious opposition by others. In reality, while there may be some divergences in emphasis, there is no essential difference between them with regard to the understanding of the concept of "peaceful coexistence." To the Soviet leaders the concept means simply recognition of the physical fact that in the prevailing balance of power in the world at present the two systems of communism and capitalism do exist on the same planet and may continue to coexist for a prolonged period. On no occasion have the Soviet leaders spoken of *permanent* coexistence, because that would undermine their first article of faith, that the capitalist system has reached a stage of decay and is bound eventually to collapse from its own iniquities and conflicts. Occasionally Soviet spokesmen use the term "long" or "prolonged" in regard to coexistence, and almost always "peaceful" but never "permanent." It is thus proper to designate it as the concept of "Provisional Coexistence." This concept has lent itself well to purposes of domestic and foreign propaganda, and will continue to be used in the future to the same purpose by the Soviet leaders.

Continuing Competition.   Every time a Soviet leader has made a pronouncement on coexistence, he used the occasion to speak at the same time of "peaceful competition." What the Soviet spokesmen mean is that the social and economic systems of capitalism and communism, and the two groups of states they comprise, stand in basic opposition to one another and compete for the adherence of the rest of mankind. In 1927, Stalin told a visiting American labor delegation:

> In the further progress and development of the international revolution, two world centers will be formed: the socialist center, attracting to itself all the countries gravitating toward socialism, and the capitalist center, attracting to itself all the countries gravitating toward capitalism. The fight between these two centers for the conquest of the world economy will decide the fate of Capitalism and Communism throughout the whole world, for the final defeat of world capitalism means the victory of socialism in the arena of world economy.

Twenty years later, echoing a statement made by another Soviet leader, Andrei Zhdanov, when the Cominform was established (1947), the publication *Trud* offered the latest version of the same theme:

> There exist now two diametrically opposed political lines. One, directed to bring down imperialism and strengthen democracy is followed by the USSR. The other, which is the policy of the United States of America and Britain, is directed to strengthen imperialism and stifle democracy . . . This has led to the formation of two camps in the postwar era. The aim of the imperialist and antidemocratic camp is to establish firmly the world domination of American capital. The aim of the anti-imperialist and democratic camp is to undermine imperialism, strengthen democracy and remove the remnants of fascism. The struggle between the two opposing camps is going on while the general crisis of capitalism is intensifying and the forces of socialism and democracy are strengthened.

This is the Soviet idea of "peaceful" competition, which is expected to continue throughout the period of coexistence of the two systems.

Balancing.   This concept means exploiting antagonisms and contradictions, every cleavage and conflict among non-Soviet states, as well as every weakness and division within non-Soviet states, to gain some advantage for the Soviet Union or its satellites. Here every possible technique and tool, legal and illegal, every legitimate instrument of the family of nations and every *sub-rosa* device of the Communist arsenal is utilized for the purpose. These include: diplomacy—to influence governments openly; propaganda—to influence peoples openly; trade—to influence peoples and governments; infiltration—to influence governments secretly; front organizations—to influence peoples secretly; and

Communist parties—for the recruitment of followers, political agitation, and, wherever deemed necessary, subversive activity.

Flexibility.   The concept of flexibility signifies a constant readiness to shift policies, strategy, and tactics in accordance with changing needs and opportunities to gain time, or win points of vantage for future exploitation. It means to hold no scruples about either advancing or retreating, biding time, zigzagging, maneuvering, compromising. Following the implications of this concept, the Soviet leaders found no difficulty in associating themselves in 1934 with the same League of Nations that they bitterly denounced earlier. In fact the Soviet spokesman in the League, Maxim Litvinov, became the strongest advocate of collective security in the succeeding five years. Thus it was also that in Soviet statements World War II was a "predatory, imperialist war" on the part of the Western democracies before the Soviet Union was attacked, but became a "war of liberation" by a coalition of "peace-loving nations" the day after the Soviet Union was invaded. Numerous additional examples of changes in practices, theories, and techniques to advance the principal objective of a given period, or extract other advantages from the changing equilibrium of forces, attest to the application of the flexibility concept in the pursuits of Soviet foreign policy.

Thus World Revolution, U.S.S.R. Survival, Provisional Coexistence, Continuing Competition, Balancing, and Flexibility constitute guiding concepts that have determined the static and dynamic aspects of Soviet foreign relations at all times, including the postwar period.[1]

4. RECENT POLICIES OF THE U.S.S.R.

The U.S.S.R. emerged from World War II in an international position never before experienced by any other power on the Eurasian Continent. The elimination of Germany and Japan, the serious weakening of Great Britain, and the decline of France and Italy to the rank of third-rate powers left the Soviet Union supreme on the continent. And, although in the eyes of prestige-conscious Soviet leaders this position was necessarily affected by America's priority in the development of the atom bomb, the U.S.S.R. had emerged to join the United States as the second super-power in the world. Essentially all Soviet activity in the international arena since the war's end has had a single purpose: to retain or to improve upon the U.S.S.R.'s advantageous position in the world balance of power.

This overriding purpose shaped Soviet policy in both Europe and Asia. In Eastern Europe, including the Balkans, the original postwar goal was to weld Czechoslovakia, Hungary, Rumania, Bulgaria, Albania, Yugoslavia, and eventually Greece into a solid block controlled by the U.S.S.R. Except for the defection of Tito's Yugoslavia and the

---

[1] For an earlier consideration of these concepts see Julian Towster, "Problems in Understanding Russia," *Forum,* 112 (October, 1949), pp. 200–4.

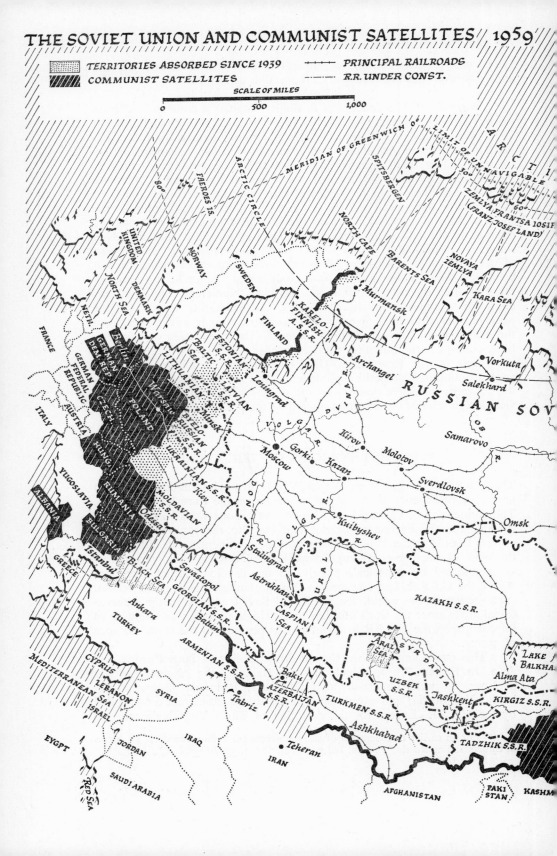

THE SOVIET UNION AND COMMUNIST SATELLITES 1959

TERRITORIES ABSORBED SINCE 1939   PRINCIPAL RAILROADS

COMMUNIST SATELLITES   R.R. UNDER CONST.

SCALE OF MILES

0   500   1,000

MERIDIAN OF GREENWICH 0°   LIMIT OF UNNAVIGABLE   A R C T I

SPITSBERGEN

ZEMLYA FRANTSA IOSIF (FRANZ JOSEF LAND)

FAEROES IS.

ARCTIC CIRCLE

NORTH CAPE

NOVAYA ZEMLYA

KARA SEA

UNITED KINGDOM

NORWAY

SWEDEN

FINLAND

BARENTS SEA

Murmansk

NORTH SEA

NETH.

DENMARK

Berlin

GERMAN DEM. REP.

GERMAN FEDERAL REPUBLIC

FRANCE

AUSTRIA

ITALY

CZECH.

POLAND

Warsaw

BALTIC SEA

ESTONIAN S.S.R.

LATVIAN S.S.R.

LITHUANIAN S.S.R.

Leningrad

KARELO-FINNISH A.S.S.R.

Archangel

RUSSIAN SOV

Vorkuta

Salekhard

BELO-RUSSIAN S.S.R.

Minsk

V O L G A

Moscow

Gorki

Kirov

Kazan

Molotov

Sverdlovsk

Samarovo

OB

D V I N A

DON R.

UKRAINIAN S.S.R.

Kiev

MOLDAVIAN S.S.R.

Odessa

HUNG.

RUMANIA

YUGOSLAVIA

ALBANIA

BULGARIA

GREECE

Istanbul

BLACK SEA

Sevastopol

GEORGIAN S.S.R.

Batum

Ankara

TURKEY

CYPRUS

LEBANON

MEDITERRANEAN SEA

SYRIA

ISRAEL

EGYPT

JORDAN

RED SEA

SAUDI ARABIA

IRAQ

ARMENIAN S.S.R.

Tabriz

Teheran

IRAN

Baku

AZERBAIJAN S.S.R.

Astrakhan

CASPIAN SEA

Stalingrad

U R A L R.

V O L G A R.

Kuibyshev

KAZAKH S.S.R.

Omsk

ARAL SEA

SYR DARIA

UZBEK S.S.R.

Tashkent

TURKMEN S.S.R.

Ashkhabad

AFGHANISTAN

TADZHIK S.S.R.

KIRGIZ S.S.R.

Alma Ata

LAKE BALKHA

PAKI STAN

KASHM

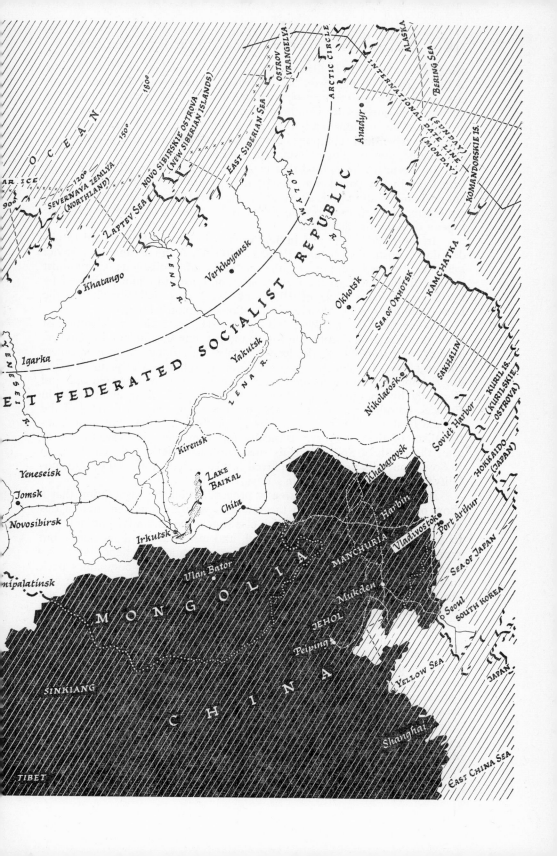

defeat of communism in Greece the U.S.S.R. has achieved its main aims in that area. This has been accomplished through various types of intervention, through military occupation, and through the domination of satellite governments by Communist parties. The U.S.S.R. has used the services of reparations and joint stock companies, and has devised a comprehensive and compulsory network of cultural pacts, economic agreements, and treaties of mutual assistance.

In Western Europe and that part of Central Europe still outside the Iron Curtain the Soviet aim has been to retard economic recovery and political stabilization and, above all, to prevent the participation of Western Germany, with its enormous industrial potential, in any Western European or Atlantic alignment.

In the Middle East and in Southeast Asia the U.S.S.R. aimed to undermine British, Dutch, and French colonialism and to increase Soviet influence through support of the activities of indigenous Communist groups. In the Far East the victory of communism in China, followed by the Soviet-Chinese pacts of 1950 and 1952, has radically altered the power equilibrium in that area in the Soviet Union's favor.

When the Marshall Plan and Truman Doctrine blocked Communist gains in Western Europe and Communist encroachments in Greece, Turkey, and Iran, the Soviet leaders evolved a strategy to meet the new circumstances. Its objectives were several: to retain Soviet gains in Eastern Europe and China; to retard the rearmament of Western Europe and Germany by stimulating the fear of German resurgence entertained in France and other nations; to arouse turmoil in the backward areas of the Middle East and Southeast Asia, by playing on the land hunger and nationalism of their peoples.[2] Basically this remained the Soviet strategy after the death of Stalin, but his successors have set a quickened tempo to Soviet pursuits and have displayed a vigor, tactical elasticity, and mobility quite unknown in Stalin's days.

In Eastern Europe, apparently proceeding on the assumption that a show of greater autonomy in the satellites would strengthen mutual ties and help to win prospective allies elsewhere, the U.S.S.R. not only extended the network of trade, cultural, and technical-aid agreements, but granted loans and credits, cancelled some reparations or debt claims, returned archives, transferred its shares of the joint stock companies back to Rumania, Hungary, and East Germany, and otherwise sought to create the appearance of a genuine partnership. However, as the de-Stalinization campaign gained momentum in Eastern Europe following Khrushchev's secret speech at the Twentieth Party Congress (February, 1956), Stalinist leaders were ousted (Chervenkov, Rakosi, Berman, etc.), earlier leaders executed for avowedly nationalist deviations were posthumously rehabilitated (Kostov, Rajk, etc.), and popular pressures mounted for greater independence from Moscow. Communist Poland's astute assertion of sovereignty under its new Premier Gomulka (released from prison in July) in October, 1956, and the bloody Hungarian

2 See Julian Towster, "Russia: Persistent Strategic Demands," *Current History* (Middle East issue), 21 (July, 1951), pp. 2–7; "The Soviet Union: Divide and Rule," ibid. (North Atlantic Community issue), 24 (February, 1953), pp. 66–71.

revolt, in October–November of that year, which was suppressed by Soviet troops, have compromised and to some extent weakened the Soviet position in Eastern Europe. Nevertheless the entrenchment of pro-Moscow regimes in Czechoslovakia, Bulgaria, Rumania, Eastern Germany, Albania, and again in Hungary, the right—reaffirmed in the November, 1956 Polish-Soviet agreement—to maintain Soviet troops in Poland (as elsewhere in the satellites), and other Soviet prerogatives under the unified command provisions of the Warsaw security pact, of May, 1955, guarantee the Soviet Union a grip on Eastern Europe. Present Soviet policies suggest the expectation that firmness coupled with concessions will succeed in pacifying the area and keep it bound to the U.S.S.R.

In Western Europe, Stalin's heirs continued their opposition to the growth of NATO and attempts to establish a European Defense Community with West Germany as a full participant. To dramatize this opposition, the U.S.S.R. abrogated in April, 1955, the treaties of friendship concluded during the war with Britain (1942) and France (1944). At the same time it used the methods of intensified trade, especially with the countries of Northern Europe and Finland, and exchange visits of parliamentary and other delegations, to demonstrate its peaceful pursuits. The high point in the easing of tensions in the post-Stalin period came in the summer of 1955 and early part of 1956, with the conclusion of the Austrian Peace Treaty, in May, 1955, and the holding of the four-power (U.S.S.R., U.S.A., England, and France) summit conference in Geneva in July of that year. The Soviet leaders apparently believed that the Austrian peace treaty, with its neutrality provisions, might set a pattern for a settlement of the German problem. They even established diplomatic relations with West Germany in the fall of 1955 and tied the question of German unity to a demand for the termination of West Germany's rearmament, in the hope of arresting the latter and securing an agreement on the neutralization of Germany. With the failure of these efforts, and the growing resentment in the West over Soviet policies in the Middle East and Soviet armed intervention in the Hungarian Revolution in October–November, 1956, relations between the U.S.S.R. and the Western powers have again deteriorated. The Soviet Union has voiced its objections to "Euratom," a common market, and other plans for greater integration of Western Europe, and it has warned of dire consequences in case of use of Western European and other bases for the launchings of missiles. The renewed challenge to the position of the West in Berlin is but the latest of a series of probing tactical moves designed to foster continued divisions in the Western camp and to exploit what the Soviet leaders believe to be present advantages in the Soviet military posture.

In the Middle East and Southeast Asia, Soviet policy centered on opposition to the Baghdad and SEATO pacts and on wooing the former colonial peoples. High dignitaries of the countries of these areas: the shah of Iran, President Kuwatly of Syria, Nehru of India, the prime ministers of Burma, Indonesia, and Afghanistan, and other leaders and officials visited Moscow in 1955 and 1956. On the Soviet side, Premier

Bulganin and First Secretary Khrushchev made a tour of Southeast Asia in November–December, 1955, and were later followed by First Deputy Premier Mikoyan, Marshals Zhukov and Voroshilov, and other officials, while the then-Foreign Minister Shepilov visited the Middle East in the summer of 1956. A whole network of trade agreements was established with the countries of these areas, and with some of them cultural and scientific-technical co-operation pacts were also concluded. While the Soviet Union reneged on its offer to Egypt to build the Aswan dam (July, 1956), it rendered the latter technical and other aid, sold Egypt and Syria arms, and gave Egypt complete diplomatic support in the crisis over Suez in 1956–57. Technical aid and credits were also extended to a number of South and Southeast Asian countries, and the U.S.S.R. sought to associate itself with the Afro-Asian block in U.N. activity and in Asian conferences. While the totality of these measures garnered for the Soviet Union considerable good will among the Asian nations, it was forfeited in part at least when segments of Asian public opinion reacted to the events in Poland and Hungary in the fall of 1956.

In the Far East the Soviet Union maintained its close relationship with China through trade and cultural co-operation agreements, the sending of specialists to render scientific and technical aid, and reciprocal visits by high party officials between Moscow and Peiping. It also assisted North Korea with a billion-ruble grant for industrial construction. The most noteworthy change in this area in the post-Stalin period was the termination of the state of war and re-establishment of normal diplomatic and trade relations with Japan in October, 1956.

The Soviet Union's attitudes in the U.N. invariably reflected its policies vis-à-vis the various countries and areas. In the first year after Stalin's death the Soviet Union joined a number of specialized agencies (UNESCO, ILO, UNICEF, etc.) and ratified the ILO conventions on forced labor and equal pay for men and women. It also displayed a willingness to co-operate in the "atoms for peace" program and shared sides with the U.S.A. in condemning the invasion of Egyptian territory in the fall of 1956. At the same time the stand of the U.S.S.R. against repeated U.N. General Assembly demands to remove Soviet troops from Hungary, and allow U.N. investigation of the situation in that country, ranged the Soviet Union against the United States and a majority of the Assembly. Again, while condemning the Eisenhower declaration with regard to the Middle East, the Soviet leaders, by-passing the U.N. and its disarmament machinery, continue to press for a U.S.S.R.-U.S.A. summit conference as an avowed means of settling the world's difficulties. There is little doubt that in the foreseeable future the Soviet position in the U.N. will continue to mirror the shifting strategy and tactics of Soviet global policy.

5. THE SOVIET POSITION AT MID-CENTURY

Many of the Soviet geopolitical pursuits bear marked resemblance to the policies of imperial Russia and have been interpreted, therefore, as a return to the traditional pattern of Russian nationalism. Although Soviet social and political institutions evidence some blending of Russian tradition and Marxist ideology, it is not Russian nationalism but the Communist world outlook that constitutes the primary source of Soviet conduct. Today Soviet aspirations reach far beyond the territorial aspirations, the quest for an ice-free port, and the other objectives of tsarist Russia.

In November, 1947, at a celebration of the thirtieth anniversary of the regime, Molotov stated: "The convulsive efforts of the imperialists under whose feet the ground is shaking will not save capitalism from its approaching doom. We are living in a century when all roads lead to Communism." This is not a mere avowal of faith; this is the key to Soviet policy at mid-century. The postwar Soviet estimate was that the world was moving toward a stage of parity in non-conventional weapons, when neither the Communist nor the Western nations would be able to afford all-out war. Barring the premature outbreak of such a war, the Soviet leaders expected to arrive at that stage of parity within ten to fifteen years, or possibly even earlier, upon the completion of projected Five Year plans and the consolidation of Communist power in Eastern Europe and China. Such achievement would signify the attainment of the minimum security goal. From there on, progress toward the maximum goal of universal communism was anticipated through the attraction that the U.S.S.R. would exert on the basis of the vast possibilities opened up by atomic power, and, in opposite vein, through the creeping malady of Communist-inspired unheavals in neighboring countries and backward areas. The common denominator in all Soviet postwar moves, consequently, was to gain time in order to arrive at that stage— which appears to have been reached by 1955.

Such is the challenge facing the Western world at mid-century. The balance of material power strongly favors the West, and the inherent strength of its democratic ideals are a great potential magnet if they are presented with courage and imagination. But the question of solidifying a unity of spirit and purpose remains the crucial problem of the West in the grim struggle for survival. The philosopher Schopenhauer once said that human beings are like porcupines out in the cold: they stick each other if they get close together and freeze to death if they get far apart. How to get together without sticking each other is the most vital question challenging the Western nations at mid-century.

SELECTED BIBLIOGRAPHY

The selection of a bibliography on the U.S.S.R. is of necessity conditioned by two factors: 1) the need to supplement official versions emanating from the party and the government by all available unofficial writings so as to obtain some sort of a balanced picture of Soviet developments, and 2) the extraordinary volume of secondary works and private accounts concerning the Soviet Union published over the past four decades, more particularly since the end of World War II. In the listing that follows, bibliographies, primary sources (chiefly documentary in nature), secondary general works, including a number of Soviet treatises, which must often be regarded as officially accepted interpretations propounded during certain periods (especially since the mid-thirties), biographies, and personal accounts are grouped under the major category of "General Sources." Other works bearing particularly on the separate subjects of the various sections are listed under groupings that correspond to the chapters on the U.S.S.R. Since they were selected primarily for their utility to students who are likely to use this text, no Russian-language titles have been included in these special groupings. This consideration, as well as space limitations, has dictated the exclusion of a number of otherwise excellent books and articles. The bibliography, as a whole, is offered merely as a general guide, in the preparation of which only limited reference could be made to periodical literature.

I. GENERAL SOURCES

1. Among the bibliographies on Soviet Russia mention might be made of the following: A.F.S.C. Committee on Russian-American Relations, *Suggestions for Reading and Study in Connection with the United States and the Soviet Union: Some Quaker Proposals for Peace* . . . (Philadelphia, 1949); Columbia University, *Report on Research and Publications, Sept. 1, 1948–Sept. 1, 1949* (New York, 1949); Philip Grierson, *Books on Soviet Russia, 1917–1942* . . . *a Bibliography and a Guide to Reading* (London, 1943); R. J. Kerner, *Slavic Europe: a Selected Bibliography in the Western European Languages, Comprising History, Languages, and Literatures* (Cambridge, Mass., 1918); W. L. Langer and H. F. Armstrong, *Foreign Affairs Bibliography: a Selected and Annotated List of Books on International Relations, 1919–1932* (New York, 1933); National Committee for a Free Europe, *Critical Bibliography of Communist Purges and Trials in the Soviet Union and in the People's Democracies since 1922* (New York, 1953); Nikolai N. Martianov, *Books Available in English by Russians and on Russia* (6th ed., New York, 1950); Nicholas N. Martianoff, ed., *Books Available in English by Russians and on Russia Published in the United States* (New York, 1945); Charles Morley, *Guide to Research in Russian History* (Syracuse, 1951); Harry Schwartz, *The Soviet Economy, a Selected Bibliography of Materials in English* (Syracuse, 1949); Witold S. Sworakowski, *The Hoover Library Collection on Russia* (Stanford, 1954); United States Department of State, *American Correspondents and Journalists in Moscow, 1917–1952, Bibliography of Their Books on U.S.S.R.* (Washington, 1953); United States Department of State, *Area Study Programs in American Universities* (Washington, 1954); United States Department of State, *Soviet Bibliography* (Fortnightly, discontinued); United States Department of State, *Unpublished Research on the U.S.S.R., Completed or in Progress, April, 1953* (Washington, 1953); United States Library of Congress, General Reference and Bibliography Division, *Biographical*

Sources for Foreign Countries, compiled by Helen Dudenbostel Jones (Washington, 1944), Vol. I; United States Library of Congress, European Affairs Division, *The European Press Today* (Washington, 1949); United States Library of Congress, General Reference and Bibliography Division, *Guide to Soviet Bibliographies: a Selected List of References,* compiled by John T. Dorosh (Washington, 1950); United States Library of Congress, European Affairs Division, *Introduction to Europe: a Selective Guide to Background Reading* (Washington, 1950); United States Library of Congress, Reference Department, "Soviet Union," *Russia: a Check List Preliminary to a Basic Bibliography of Materials in the Russian Language* (Washington, 1945), Part 9; United States Library of Congress, Reference Department, *Serial Publications of the Soviet Union, 1939–1951: a Preliminary Checklist* (Washington, 1951); United States Library of Congress, European Affairs Division, *The United States and Europe: a Bibliographical Examination of Thought Expressed in American Publications during 1949* (Washington, 1949); United States Library of Congress, European Affairs Division, *The United States and Postwar Europe: a Bibliographical Examination of Thought Expressed in American Publications during 1948* (Washington, 1948); United States National Archives, *Descriptive Guide to the USSR—Related Records, 1918–1945, among the Collections of the National Archives* (Washington, 1952); Robert Gale Woolbert, *Foreign Affairs Bibliography: a Selected and Annotated List of Books on International Relations 1932–1942* (New York, 1945).

2. Primary sources include: *Bol'shaia Sovetskaia Entsiklopedia,* "The Large Soviet Encyclopedia" (Moscow, 1926–48; 1949–); *Decisions of the Central Committee of the C.P.S.U.(B.) on Literature and Art; 1946–1948* (Moscow, 1951); *10 Let Verkhovnogo Suda Soiuza S.S.R., 1924–1934,* "Ten Years of the Supreme Court of the Union SSR., 1924–34" (Moscow, 1934); *20 Let Sovetskoi Vlasti, Statisticheskii Sbornik,* "Twenty Years of Soviet Power, a Collection of Statistics" (Moscow, 1937); *Entsiklopedia Gosudarstva i Prava,* "Encyclopedia of State and Law," (Moscow, 1925–27), 3 vols.; M. V. Frunze, *Izbrannye Proizvedeniia* (Moscow, 1950); *Istoria Sovetskoi Konstitutsii v Dekretakh i Postanovleniakh Sovetskogo Pravitel'stva 1917–1936,* "History of the Soviet Constitution in Decrees and Decisions of the Soviet Government, 1917–1936" (Moscow, 1936); *Kommunisticheskaia Partiia Sovetskovo soiuza v resoliutsiakh i resheniakh, S'esdov, Konferentsii i plenumov Ts. K., 1898–1954* (Moscow, 1954), 3 vols. Bela Kun, ed., *Kommunisticheskii Internatsional v documententakh: Reshenia, Tezisi i Vozvania Kongressov Kominterna i Plenumov IKKI 1919–1932,* "The Communist International in Documents: Decisions, Theses and Appeals of the Congresses of the Cominterns and of the Plenums of the E.C.C.I. for 1919–32" (Moscow, 1933); Nicolai Lenin, *Sochinenia,* "Works" (3rd ed., Leningrad, 1935–37), 30 vols.; *Lenin i Stalin o Sovetskoi Konstitutsii,* "Lenin and Stalin on the Soviet Constitution" (New York, 1937); *Krasnyi Arkhiv, Digest of the Krasnyi Arkhiv, Red Archives v. 31–106* (Ann Arbor, 1955), ed., A. Lobanov-Rostovsky; J. H. Meisel and E. S. Kozera, *Materials for the Study of the Soviet System* (Ann Arbor, 1950); V. M. Molotov, *Problems of Foreign Policy* (New York, 1949); *Narodnoye Khozyaistvo S.S.S.R.: Statistichesky Sbornik* (Moscow, 1956); *RSFSR: Vserossiskii Tsentral'nyi Ispolnitel'nyi Komitet. Sozyv . . . Stenograficheskii Otchet,* "R.S.F.S.R.: All-Russian Central Executive Committee, Convocation . . . Stenographic Report" (Moscow, 1918–23); *S'ezdy Sovetov RSFSR v Postanovleniakh i Rezoliutsiakh,* "The Congresses of Soviets of the R.S.F.S.R. in Decisions and Resolutions" (Moscow, 1939); *S'ezdy Sovetov RSFSR: Stenograficheskie Otchety,* "Congresses of Soviets of the R.S.F.S.R.: Verbatim Reports" (Petrograd, Leningrad, Moscow, 1918–1928), numerous volumes; *S'ezdy Sovetov SSSR v Postanovleniakh i Rezoliutsiakh,* "The Congresses of Soviets of the U.S.S.R. in Decisions and Resolutions" (Moscow, 1939); *S'ezdy Sovetov SSSR: Stenograficheskie Otchety,* "Congresses of Soviets of the U.S.S.R.: Verbatim Reports" (Moscow, 1923–35), numerous volumes; *Sistematicheskoe Sobranie Deistvuiushchikh Zakonov Soiuza Sovetskikh Sotsialisticheskikh Respublik,* "A Systematic Collection of the Laws of the U.S.S.R. in Force" (Moscow, 1927); *Sobranie Uzakonenii i Rasporiazhenii Rabochego i Krestianskogo Pravitel'stva R.S.F.S.R.,* "A Collection of Laws and Ordinances of the Workers and Peasants Government of

the R.S.F.S.R." (Moscow, 1917–38); *Sobranie Postanovlenii i Rasporiazhenii Pravitel'stva R.S.F.S.R.*, "A Collection of Decisions and Ordinances of the Government of the R.S.F.S.R." (Moscow, 1938); *Sobranie Zakonov i Rasporiazhenii Raboche-Krestianskogo Pravitel'stva SSSR,* "A Collection of Laws and Ordinances of the Worker-Peasant Government of the U.S.S.R." (Moscow, 1924–38); *Sobranie Postanovlenii i Rasporiazhenii Pravitel'stva SSSR,* "A Collection of Decisions and Ordinances of the Government of the U.S.S.R." (Moscow, 1938); *Soviet Foreign Policy during the Patriotic War: Documents and Materials, June 22, 1941–December 31, 1943,* Vol. I; *January 1, 1944–December 31, 1944,* Vol. II (London, 1946); Joseph Stalin, *Voprosy Leninizma* (11th ed., Moscow, 1945); Joseph Stalin, *Sochinenia,* "Works" (Moscow, 1946–49), 11 vols.; Joseph Stalin, *The Great Patriotic War of the Soviet Union* (New York, 1945); *Statistical Handbook of the U.S.S.R.* (National Industrial Conference Board, New York, 1957), annotated by Harry Schwartz; *Tsentral'nyi Ispolnitel'nyi Komitet. SSSR. Sozyv . . . Stenograficheskii Otchet,* "Central Executive Committee U.S.S.R. Convocation . . . Stenographic Report" (Moscow, 1923–37); *Verkhovnyi Sovet SSSR: Stenograficheskie Otchety,* "Supreme Soviet of the U.S.S.R.: Verbatim Reports" (Moscow, 1938); *Vsesoiuznaia Kommunisticheskaia Partia (B) v Rezoliutsiakh i Resheniakh S'ezdov, Konferentsii i Plenumov Ts. K., 1898–1939,* "The All-Union Communist Party (B) in Resolutions and Decisions of the Congresses, Conferences, and Plenums of the Central Committee, 1898–1939" (6th ed., Moscow, 1941), 2 vols. Also available are the resolutions and stenographic reports of various conferences and congresses of the party.

3. Some works of distinct relevance for an understanding of Soviet Russia are: Hannah Arendt, *The Origins of Totalitarianism* (2nd ed., New York, 1958); W. R. Batsell, *Soviet Rule in Russia* (New York, 1929); Zbigniew K. Brzezinski, *The Permanent Purge: Politics in Soviet Totalitarianism* (Cambridge, Mass., 1956); William H. Chamberlin, *The Russian Enigma* (New York, 1943); Edward Crankshaw, *Cracks in the Kremlin Wall* (New York, 1951), *Russia and the Russians* (New York, 1948); P. P. Kohler, ed. and trans., *Journey for Our Time* (New York, 1951); David J. Dallin, *The New Soviet Empire* (New Haven, 1951), *The Changing World of Soviet Russia* (New Haven, 1956); Isaac Deutscher, *Russia: What Next?* (New York, 1953); I. I. Evtikhiev and V. A. Vlasov, *Administrativnoe Pravo SSSR,* "The Administrative Law of the U.S.S.R." (Moscow, 1946); Merle Fainsod, *How Russia Is Ruled* (Cambridge, Mass., 1953); Michael T. Florinsky, *Towards an Understanding of the U.S.S.R.: a Study in Government, Politics, and Economic Planning* (New York, 1951); Carl J. Friedrich, ed., *Totalitarianism* (Cambridge, Mass., 1954); Carl J. Friedrich and Zbigniew K. Brzezinski, *Totalitarian Dictatorship and Autocracy* (Cambridge, Mass., 1956); Erich Fromm, *Escape from Freedom* (New York, 1941); René Fülop-Miller, *The Mind and Face of Bolshevism* (New York, 1929); Michel Gordey, *Visa to Moscow* (New York, 1952); Waldemar Gurian, *Bolshevism: Theory and Practice* (New York, 1932); Waldemar Gurian *et al.*, *The Soviet Union: Background, Ideology and Reality* (Notre Dame, 1951), a symposium; S. N. Harper and R. Thompson, *Government of the Soviet Union* (New York, 1949); John H. Hazard, *The Soviet System of Government* (Chicago, 1957); Eric Hoffer, *The True Believer* (New York, 1951); Walter Hildebrandt, *Die Sowjetunion—Macht und Krise* (Darmstadt, 1955); R. N. Carew Hunt, *The Theory and Practice of Communism: an Introduction* (New York, 1951); George B. de Huszar, ed., *Soviet Power and Policy* (New York, 1954); Arthur Koestler, *Darkness at Noon* (New York, 1941); Walter Kolarz, *How Russia Is Ruled* (London, 1953); N. V. Krylenko, *Osnovy Sudoustroistva S.S.S.R. i Soiuznykh Respublik,* "Principles of the Judicial Structure of the U.S.S.R. and Union Republics" (Moscow, 1947); Wladyslaw W. Kulski, *Soviet Regime; Communism in Practice* (Syracuse, 1954); Suzanne Labin, *Stalin's Russia* (London, 1950); Emil Lederer, *State of the Masses: the Threat of the Classless Society* (New York, 1940); John Maynard, *Russia in Flux,* edited and abridged by S. Haden Guest (New York, 1951); Anatole G. Mazour, *Russia Past and Present* (New York, 1951); Boris Meissner, *Sowjetrussland zwischen Revolution und Restauration* (Cologne, 1956); Czeslaw Milosz, *The Captive Mind* (New York, 1955); David Mitrany, *Marx against the Peasant* (Chapel Hill, 1951); Barrington Moore, Jr., *Soviet Politics—The Dilemma of Power* (Cambridge, Mass.,

1950), *Terror and Progress USSR* (Cambridge, Mass., 1954); Phillip E. Mosely, ed., "The Soviet Union Since World War II," *Annals of the American Academy of Political and Social Science*, 263 (May, 1949); Max Nomad, *Encyclopedia of World Communism, Socialism and other Radical Movements* (New York, 1952); George Orwell, *1984* (New York, 1949); *Osnovy Sovetskogo Gosudarstva i Prava* (Moscow, 1947); Georg von Rauch, *History of Soviet Russia* (New York, 1957); V. P. Potemkin, ed., *Istoria Diplomatii*, "History of Diplomacy," (Moscow, 1945), Vol. III; Geroid T. Robinson, *Rural Russia under the Old Regime* (London, 1932); Walt W. Rostow and Alfred Levin, *The Dynamics of Soviet Society* (New York, 1953); J. S. Roucek, ed., *Slavonic Encyclopedia* (New York, 1949); "Russia since Stalin," *Annals*, 303 (January, 1956); Rudolph Schlesinger, *The Spirit of Postwar Russia* (London, 1947); Rudolph Schlesinger, ed., *Changing Attitudes in Soviet Russia* (London, 1956); Frederick L. Schuman, *Soviet Politics at Home and Abroad* (New York, 1946), *Russia Since 1917* (New York, 1957); Ernest J. Simmons, ed., *U.S.S.R.: a Concise Handbook* (Ithaca, 1947); Sidney Post Simpson and Julius Stone, *Law, Totalitarianism and Democracy* (St. Paul, Minn., 1948–49), Vol. III; Walter B. Smith, *My Three Years in Moscow* (Philadelphia, 1950); Pitirim A. Sorokin, *Leaves from a Russian Diary—and Thirty Years After* (Boston, 1950); *Sovetskoe Administrativinoe Pravo*, "Soviet Administrative Law" (Moscow, 1950); "The Soviet Union," *Current History*, 25 (August, 1953); Fritz Sternberg, *The End of a Revolution: Soviet Russia—from Revolution to Reaction* (New York, 1953); Edmund Stevens, *Russia Is No Riddle* (New York, 1945), *This Is Russia: Uncensored* (New York, 1950); L. I. Strakhovsky, ed., *A Handbook of Slavic Studies* (Cambridge, 1949); N. S. Timasheff, *The Great Retreat* (New York, 1946); Julian Towster, *Political Power in the U.S.S.R., 1917–1947* (New York, 1948); Leon Trotsky, *The Revolution Betrayed* (London, 1937); Andrei Vyshinsky, ed., *Diplomaticheskii Slovar,* "Diplomatic Dictionary" (Moscow, 1940), 2 vols.; Andrei Vyshinsky, *The Law of the Soviet State* (Eng. ed., New York, 1948); Sidney and Beatrice Webb, *Soviet Communism: a New Civilization?* (New York, 1936), 2 vols.; Bertram D. Wolfe, *Khrushchev and Stalin's Ghost* (New York, 1957); Leonard Woolf and W. A. Robson, eds., "The Soviet Union," *Political Quarterly,* 23 (January–March, 1952).

4. Among the biographies the following deserve mention: Henri Barbusse, *Stalin* (New York, 1935); Nikolaus Basseches, *Stalin* (London, 1952); Isaiah Berlin, *Karl Marx, His Life and Environment* (2nd ed., London, 1948); George Bilainkin, *Maisky: Ten Years Ambassador* (London, 1944); Yves Delbars, *The Real Stalin* (London, 1953); Bulgarian Bibliographical Institute, *Georgi Dimitrov, 1882–1949* (Sofia, 1949); Isabel de Palencia, *Aleksandra Kollontay* (New York, 1947); Isaac Deutscher, *The Prophet Armed: Trotsky, 1879–1921* (New York, 1954), *Stalin, A Political Biography* (New York, 1949); Walter Duranty, *Stalin & Co.* (New York, 1949); Louis Fischer, *Gandhi and Stalin* (New York, 1947), *The Life and Death of Stalin* (New York, 1952); Ralph W. Fox, *Lenin: a Biography* (New York, 1934); Christopher Hill, *Lenin and the Russian Revolution* (New York, 1950); P. Kerzhentsev, *Life of Lenin* (New York, 1939); N. K. Krupskaya, *Memories of Lenin* (Eng. ed., New York, 1939), 2 vols.; Isaac Don Levine, *Stalin* (New York, 1931); G. M. Liubarov, *Felix Edmundovich Dzherzhinskii* (Moscow, 1950); Emil Ludwig, *Three Portraits: Hitler, Mussolini, Stalin* (New York, 1940); Ivan M. Maisky, *Before the Storm: Recollections* (Eng. ed., London, 1944); Valeriu Marcu, *Lenin* (New York, 1928); Marx-Engels-Lenin Institute, *Joseph Stalin: A Political Biography* (New York, 1949); Marx-Engels-Lenin Institute, *Vladimir Lenin: A Political Biography* (New York, 1944); Franz Mehring, *Karl Marx: the Story of His Life* (New York, 1935); Dmitrii Mirskii, *Lenin* (London, 1932); V. M. Molotov *et al., Stalin* (New York, 1940); J. T. Murphy, *Stalin, 1879–1944* (London, 1945); Anton Pannekoek, *Lenin as a Philosopher* (New York, 1948); Arthur Upham Pope, *Maxim Litvinov* (New York, 1943); Anna Rothe, ed., *Current Biography: Who's News and Why, 1940–51* (New York, 1940–51); Otto Rühle, *Karl Marx: His Life and Work* (Eng. ed., New York, 1929); Leopold Schwartzschild, *The Red Prussian* (London, 1948); David Shub, *Lenin: a Biography* (New York, 1948); Boris Souvarine, *Stalin* (New York, 1939); C. J. S. Sprigge, *Karl Marx* (London, 1938); Leon Trotsky, *The Case of Leon Trotsky* (New York, 1937), *Lenin* (New York, 1925),

My Life: an Attempt at an Autobiography (New York, 1930), and *Stalin* (New York, 1941); Alexander Uralov, *The Reign of Stalin* (London, 1953); George Vernadsky, *Lenin, Red Dictator* (New Haven, 1931); Bertram D. Wolfe, *Three Who Made a Revolution* (New York, 1948); Yemel'yau Y. Yaroslavski, *Landmarks in the Life of Stalin* (London, 1942); Klara Zetkin, *Reminiscences of Lenin* (New York, 1934).

5. Personal accounts provide valuable insights into certain phases of the Soviet system. Some of the best known are: Alexander Barmine, *One Who Survived* (New York, 1945); Louis Francis Budenz, *This Is My Story* (New York, 1947); Whittaker Chambers, *Witness* (New York, 1952); Anton Ciliga, *The Russian Enigma* (London, 1940); Sir Walter Citrine, *I Search for Truth in Russia* (New York, 1937), *In Russia Now* (London, 1942); Joseph E. Davies, *Mission to Moscow* (New York, 1941); Louis Fischer, ed., *Thirteen Who Fled* (New York, 1949); André Gide, *Afterthoughts on the U.S.S.R.* (New York, 1938), *Return from the USSR* (New York, 1937); Benjamin Gitlow, *I Confess* (New York, 1940); Valentin Gonzalez and J. Gorkin, *El Campesino—Life and Death in Soviet Russia* (New York, 1952); Igor Gouzenko, *The Iron Curtain* (New York, 1948); Anatoli Granovsky, *All Pity Choked: the Memoirs of a Soviet Secret Agent* (London, 1955); Samuel N. Harper, *The Russia I Believe In* (Chicago, 1945); Richard Hilton, *Military Attaché in Moscow* (Boston, 1951); Douglas Hyde, *I Believed* (London, 1951); Oksana Kasenkina, *Leap to Freedom* (Philadelphia, 1949); Lydia Kirk, *Post-Marked Moscow* (New York, 1952); Arthur Koestler *et al., The God That Failed* (New York, 1949); Mikhail Koriakov, *I'll Never Go Back* (New York, 1948); V. A. Kravchenko, *I Chose Freedom* (New York, 1946); W. G. Krivitsky, *In Stalin's Secret Service* (New York, 1939); Ivan Krylov, *Soviet Staff Officer* (Eng. ed., London, 1951); John D. Littlepage and Demaree Bess, *In Search of Soviet Gold* (London, 1939); S. M. Manton, *The Soviet Union Today: a Scientist's Impressions* (London, 1952); Nicholas Nyaradi, *My Ringside Seat in Moscow* (New York, 1952); Alexander Orlov, *The Secret History of Stalin's Crimes* (New York, 1953); Vladimir Orlov, *Underworld and Soviet* (New York, 1931); Vladimir and Evdokia Petrov, *Empire of Fear* (London, 1956); Herbert A. Philbrick, *I Led Three Lives: Citizen, "Communist," Counterspy* (New York, 1952); John Scott, *Behind the Urals* (Boston, 1942); Julien Steinberg, ed., *Verdict of Three Decades from the Literature of Individual Revolt against Soviet Communism 1917–1950* (New York, 1950); Z. Stypulkowski, *Invitation to Moscow* (London, 1951); Grigori A. Tokaev, *Stalin Means War* (London, 1951); Jan Valtin, *Out of the Night* (New York, 1941); William L. White, *Report on the Russians* (New York, 1945).

6. Periodicals and newspapers: *Bol'shevik* (Moscow); *Current Digest of the Soviet Press* (Washington); *For a Lasting Peace, for a People's Democracy* (Bucharest); *Izvestia* (Moscow); *Komsomol'skaia Pravda* (Moscow); *Krasnaia Zvezda* (Moscow); *Literaturnaia Gazeta* (Moscow); *New Times* (Moscow); *News from Behind the Iron Curtain* (New York); *Ost-Europa* (Stuttgart); *Partiinaia Zhizn'* (Moscow); *Planovoe Khoziaistvo* (Moscow); *Problems of Communism* (Washington); *Pravda* (Moscow); *Slaviane* (Moscow); *Sovetskoe Gosudarstvo i Pravo* (Moscow); *Soviet Literature* (Moscow); *Soviet Press Translations* (Seattle); *Soviet Studies* (London); *Trud* (Moscow); *Voprosy Ekonomiki* (Moscow); *Voprosy Filosofii* (Moscow); *Voprosy Istorii* (Moscow); *World News and Views* (London).

II. THE CONDITIONING COMPLEX

1. The geographic factor is discussed by S. S. Balzak, V. F. Vasyutin, and Ya. G. Feigin in Chauncey D. Harris, ed., *Economic Geography of the USSR* (New York, 1949); see also L. S. Berg, *The Natural Regions of the U.S.S.R.* (New York, 1950); George B. Cressey, *The Basis of Soviet Strength* (New York, 1945), *How Strong Is Russia? A Geographic Appraisal* (Syracuse, 1954); James S. Gregory and D. W.

Shave, *The U.S.S.R.* (London, 1944); H. Hassmann, *Oil in the Soviet Union* (Princeton, 1953); Georges Jorré, *The Soviet Union: the Land and Its People* (New York, 1950); Eugene M. Kulischer, "The Russian Population Enigma," *Foreign Affairs*, 27 (April, 1949), pp. 497–501; Werner Leimbach, *Die Sowjetunion: Natur, Volk und Wirtschaft* (Stuttgart, 1950); Frank Lorimer, *The Population of the Soviet Union: History and Prospects* (Geneva, 1946); N. N. Mikhailov, *Soviet Land and People* (London, 1945); Nicholas Tiho Mirov, *Geography of Russia* (New York, 1951); Frank W. Notestein *et al., The Future Population of Europe and the Soviet Union: Population Projections, 1940–1970* (Geneva, 1944); Theodore Shabad, *Geography of the U.S.S.R.* (New York, 1951); Dmitri B. Shimkin, *Minerals: A Key to Soviet Power* (Cambridge, Mass., 1953)); Erich Thiel, *The Soviet Far East* (New York, 1957).

2. On the historical heritage see: Crane Brinton, *The Anatomy of Revolution* (rev. ed., New York, 1952); D. W. Brogan, *The Price of Revolution* (New York, 1951); James Bunyan, ed., *Intervention, Civil War, and Communism in Russia, April–December, 1918* (Baltimore, 1936); James Bunyan and Harold H. Fisher, *The Bolshevik Revolution 1917–1918* (Stanford, 1934); Edward Hallett Carr, *A History of Soviet Russia. The Bolshevik Revolution, 1917–1923* (New York, 1951–58), 5 vols., and *The Romantic Exiles* (London, 1933); W. H. Chamberlin, *The Russian Revolution, 1917–1921* (New York, 1935), 2 vols.; Michael T. Florinsky, *The End of the Russian Empire* (New Haven, 1931); Olga Hess Gankin and Harold H. Fisher, *The Bolsheviks and the World War* (Stanford, 1940); Harold H. Fisher, *The Communist Revolution: An Outline of Strategy and Tactics* (Stanford, 1955); Michael T. Florinsky, *Russia: A History and an Interpretation* (New York, 1953); Valentin Gitermann, *Geschichte Russlands* (Zurich, 1944–49), 3 vols.; Sidney Harcave, *Russia a History* (Chicago, 1952); M. Karpovich, *Imperial Russia, 1801–1917* (New York, 1932); George F. Kennan, *Russia Leaves the War: Soviet-American Relations 1917–1920* (Princeton, 1956); Alexander Kerensky, *The Catastrophe* (New York, 1927), *The Crucifixion of Liberty* (New York, 1934); Robert J. Kerner, *The Urge to the Sea* (Berkeley, 1942); V. O. Kliuchevsky, *A History of Russia* (Eng. trans., New York, 1911–31), 5 vols.; Walter Kolarz, *Stalin and Eternal Russia* (London, 1944); Alexander Kornilov, *Modern Russian History* (rev. ed., New York, 1943); Joshua Kunitz, *Russia: The Giant That Came Last* (New York, 1947); Sidney Lens, *The Counterfeit Revolution* (Boston, 1952); Alfred Levin, *The Second Duma* (New Haven, 1940); Paul Miliukov *et al., Histoire de Russie* (Paris, 1932–33), 3 vols.; A. M. Pankratova, ed., *A History of the U.S.S.R.* (Moscow, 1947–48), 3 vols.; Sir Bernard Pares, *The Fall of the Russian Monarchy* (New York, 1939), *A History of Russia* (5th ed., New York, 1947); Henryk Paszkiewicz, *Origin of Russia* (New York, 1954); Richard Pipes, *Formation of the Soviet Union: Communism and Nationalism, 1917–1923* (Cambridge, Mass., 1954); Oliver Henry Radkey, *The Election to the Russian Constituent Assembly of 1917* (Cambridge, 1950); John S. Reshetar, Jr., *The Ukrainian Revolution: 1917–1920* (Princeton, 1952); Henry Rollin, *La Revolution russe* (Paris, 1931), 2 vols.; Arthur Rosenberg, *A History of Bolshevism* (London, 1939); Andrew Rothstein, *A History of the U.S.S.R.* (New York, 1950); Leonard Schapiro, *The Origin of the Communist Autocracy; Political Opposition in the Soviet State, First Phase, 1917–1922* (Cambridge, Mass., 1955); Hugh Seton-Watson, *The Decline of Imperial Russia* (New York, 1952); Ivar Spector, *Introduction to Russian History and Culture* (New York, 1949); Nikolai N. Sukhanov, *The Russian Revolution, 1917: A Personal Record* (New York, 1955); B. H. Sumner, *A Short History of Russia* (rev. ed., New York, 1949); Stuart Ramsay Tompkins, *Russia through the Ages: from the Scythians to the Soviets* (New York, 1940); Donald W. Treadgold, *Lenin and His Rivals: The Struggle for Russia's Future, 1898–1906* (New York, 1955); Leon Trotsky, *The History of the Russian Revolution* (New York, 1936), 3 vols.; George Vernadsky, *A History of Russia* (3rd rev. ed., New Haven, 1951).

3. For the ideological setting see: Michael Bakunin, *Marxism, Freedom and the State* (Eng. trans., London, 1950); Nicolas Berdyaev, *The Origin of Russian Communism* (Eng. ed., London, 1948), *The Russian Idea* (New York, 1948);

Eduard Bernstein, *Evolutionary Socialism* (Eng. trans., New York, 1909); Martin Buber, *Paths in Utopia* (London, 1949); Emile Burns, *A Handbook of Marxism* (New York, 1935); J. M. Cameron, *Scrutiny of Marxism* (London, 1948); E. H. Carr, *Studies in Revolution* (New York, 1950); Sherman Hsiao-Ming Chang, *The Marxian Theory of the State* (Philadelphia, 1931); G. D. H. Cole, *The Meaning of Marxism* (London, 1948), *What Marx Really Meant* (New York, 1937), *History of Socialist Thought* (New York, 1953–54), 2 vols.; Max Eastman, *Marxism. Is It a Science?* (London, 1941); Friedrich Engels, *Herr Eugen Dühring's Revolution in Science* (Eng. trans., New York, 1939), *The Housing Question* (London, 1942), and *The Origin of the Family, Private Property and the State* (London, 1946); Karl Federn, *The Materialist Conception of History* (London, 1939); Alexander Gray, *The Socialist Tradition from Moses to Lenin* (London, 1946); Leopold H. Haimson, *The Russian Marxists and the Origins of Bolshevism* (Cambridge, Mass., 1955); Richard Hare, *Pioneers of Russian Social Thought* (London, 1951); Sidney Hook, *From Hegel to Marx* (New York, 1936), *Towards the Understanding of Karl Marx* (London, 1933), *Marx and the Marxists; the Ambiguous Legacy* (Princeton, 1955); Karl Kautsky, *The Dictatorship of the Proletariat* (Manchester, 1919), *Terrorism and Communism* (London, 1920); Hans Kelsen, *The Political Theory of Bolshevism* (Berkeley, 1949); Hans Kohn, *Pan-Slavism: Its History and Ideology* (Notre Dame, 1953); E. Lampert, *Studies in Rebellion* (New York, 1957); Lucien Laurat, *Marxism and Democracy* (Eng. trans., London, 1940); Nathan Leites, *A Study of Bolshevism* (Glencoe, Ill., 1953); Alexander D. Lindsay, *Karl Marx's Capital: an Introductory Essay* (New York, 1947); Nikolay O. Lossky, *History of Russian Philosophy* (New York, 1951); Karl Marx, *Capital* (New York, 1933), *Critique of the Gotha Programme* (London, 1943), *Selected Works* (Moscow, 1935), 2 vols.; Karl Marx and Friedrich Engels, *The Communist Manifesto,* introduction by H. J. Laski (London, 1948); *The German Ideology, I and III,* edited with an introduction by R. Pascal (New York, 1939); *Selected Correspondence, 1846–1895,* translated and edited by Dona Torr (London, 1934); Herbert Marcuse, *Reason and Revolution* (New York, 1954); Thomas G. Masaryk, *The Spirit of Russia* (Eng. trans., London, 1919), 2 vols.; Alfred G. Meyer, *Marxism: The Unity of Theory and Practice* (Cambridge, Mass., 1954); Jules Monnerot, *Sociology and Psychology of Communism* (Boston, 1953); Michael Oakeshott, *Social and Political Doctrines of Contemporary Europe* (Cambridge, 1939); Henry Bamford Parkes, *Marxism: An Autopsy* (Boston, 1939); Roy Pascal, *Karl Marx: Political Foundations* (London, 1943); John Plamenatz, *What Is Communism?* (London, 1947), *German Marxism and Russian Communism* (New York, 1954); George V. Plekhanov, *In Defense of Materialism* (Eng. trans., London, 1947), *Essays in the History of Materialism* (Eng. trans., London, 1934), *Fundamental Problems of Marxism* (Eng. trans., New York, 1929); Karl R. Popper, *The Open Society and Its Enemies* (Princeton, 1950); George Holland Sabine, *A History of Political Theory* (rev. ed., New York, 1955); Eugene Pyziuk, *The Doctrine of Anarchism of Michael A. Bakunin* (Milwaukee, Wis., 1955); Emanuel Sarkisyanz, *Russland und der Messianismus des Orients* (Tuebingen, 1955); Rudolf Schlesinger, *Marx, His Time and Ours* (London, 1950); Joseph Alois Schumpeter, *Capitalism, Socialism and Democracy* (3rd ed., New York, 1950); M. Shirokov et al., *Textbook of Marxist Philosophy* (London, 1937); Ernest J. Simmons, ed., *Continuity and Change in Russian and Soviet Thought* (Cambridge, Mass., 1955); Paul M. Sweezy, *Socialism* (New York, 1949); Dinko A. Tomasic, *The Impact of Russian Culture on Soviet Communism* (Glencoe, Ill., 1953); Vernon Venable, *Human Nature, The Marxian View* (New York, 1945); Edmund Wilson, *To the Finland Station* (New York, 1940); Vasilii Zenkovskii, *A History of Russian Philosophy* (New York, 1953), 2 vols., *Russian Thinkers and Europe* (Washington, 1953).

III. THE SOCIAL ORDER

1. Out of the extensive list of materials on the political theory mention might be made of: Academy of Sciences of the U.S.S.R. and Academy of Medical Sciences

of the U.S.S.R., *Scientific Session on the Physiological Teachings of Academician I. P. Pavlov, June 28–July 4, 1950* (Moscow, 1951); G. F. Aleksandrov, *The Pattern of Soviet Democracy* (Washington, 1948), *A Soviet History of Philosophy* (Washington, 1950); Eric Ashby, *Scientist in Russia* (New York, 1947); Max Beer, *Fifty Years of International Socialism* (London, 1935); I. M. Bochenski, *Der Sowjetrussische Dialektische Materialismus* (Berne, 1950); Charles Boyer, *The Philosophy of Communism* (New York, 1952); Nikolai Bukharin, *Historical Materialism* (New York, 1925); Henri Chambre, *Le Marxisme en Union Soviétique: Idéologie et institutions, leur évolution de 1917 à nos jours* (Paris, 1955); Maurice H. Dobb, *Economic Theory and Socialism* (New York, 1955); Max Eastman, *Marx, Lenin and the Science of Revolution* (London, 1926), *Stalin's Russia and the Crisis of Socialism* (London, 1940); Mario Einaudi, "Western European Communism: A Profile," *American Political Science Review*, 45 (March, 1951), pp. 185–208; Feliks Gross, ed., *European Ideologies: a Survey of 20th Century Political Ideas* (New York, 1948); Historicus, "Stalin on Revolution," *Foreign Affairs*, 27 (January, 1949), pp. 175–214; Jakob Hommes, *Der technische Eros: Das Wesen der Materialistischen Geschichtsauffassung* (Freiburg, 1955); Leo Huberman, *The Truth about Socialism* (New York, 1950); P. S. Hudson and R. H. Richens, *New Genetics in the Soviet Union* (Cambridge, 1946); R. N. Carew Hunt, *Marxism, Past and Present* (New York, 1954); Julian S. Huxley, *Heredity East and West: Lysenko and World Science* (New York, 1949); Nikolai Lenin, *Collected Works* (New York, 1927–45), 23 vols., *Imperialism: the Highest Stage of Capitalism* (new rev. trans., New York, 1939), *Letters*, edited by Elizabeth Hill and Doris Mudie (New York, 1937), *Selected Works*, edited by J. Fineberg (New York, 1935–38), *The State and Revolution* (New York, 1935); *The Suppressed Testament of Lenin. The Complete Original Text with Two Explanatory Notes by L. Trotsky* (New York, 1935); A. Leontiev, *Political Economy* (New York, n.d.); Rosa Luxemburg, *Leninism or Marxism* (Glasgow, 1935); Trofim Lysenko, *The Science of Biology Today* (New York, 1948); Klaus Mehnert, *Stalin Versus Marx* (New York, 1952); John V. Murra et al., *The Soviet Linguistic Controversy* (New York, 1951); K. V. Ostrovityanov, *The Role of the State in the Socialist Transformation of the Economy of the U.S.S.R.* (Moscow, 1950), *Proceedings of the Lenin Academy of Agricultural Sciences of the U.S.S.R., July 31–August 7, 1948* (New York, 1949), "Complete Stenographic Report of Lysenko Controversy"; M. Rosenthal and P. Yudin, *Handbook of Philosophy*, edited by Howard Selsam (New York, 1949); Bertrand Russell, *The Practice and Theory of Bolshevism* (London, 1949); Massimo Salvadori, *The Rise of Modern Communism* (New York, 1952); Andrew M. Scott, *The Anatomy of Communism* (New York, 1951); Howard Selsam, *Socialism and Ethics* (2nd ed., New York, 1945), *The Situation in Biological Science: Verbatim Report of the Proceedings of the Lenin Academy of Agricultural Sciences of the U.S.S.R., July 31–August 7, 1948* (New York, 1949); John Somerville, *Soviet Philosophy* (New York, 1946); Joseph Stalin, *Anarchism or Socialism* (Moscow, 1950), *Concerning Marxism in Linguistics* (London, 1950), *Leninism: Selected Writings by Joseph Stalin* (New York, 1942), *Marxism and the National and Colonial Question* (New York, 1942); Leon Trotsky, *Lessons of October* (New York, 1937), *Our Revolution*, translated and edited by M. J. Olgin (New York, 1918), *The Real Situation in Russia* (New York, 1928), *Selected Works*, edited by Max Schachtman (New York, 1936), 7 vols., *Stalin's Falsification of History* (London, 1937); Gustav A. Wetter, *Der Dialektische Materialismus* (4th ed., Freiburg, 1958; Eng. trans., New York, 1958); P. F. Yudin, *The Prime Source of the Development of Soviet Society* (Moscow, 1950); Andrei A. Zhdanov, *Essays on Literature, Philosophy and Music* (New York, 1950); Conway Zirkle, *Death of a Science in Russia* (Philadelphia, 1949).

2. The structure of society is considered in: Paul B. Anderson, *People, Church and State in Modern Russia* (New York, 1944); John A. Armstrong, *Ukrainian Nationalism, 1939–1945* (New York, 1955); Vernon V. Aspaturian, "The Theory and Practice of Soviet Federalism," *Journal of Politics*, 12 (February, 1950), pp. 20–51; Frederick C. Barghoorn, *Soviet Russian Nationalism* (New York, 1956); J. B. Barron and H. M. Waddams, *Communism and the Churches: A Documentation* (London, 1950); E. S. Bates, *Soviet Asia: Progress and Problems* (London,

1941); Raymond A. Bauer, *The New Man in Soviet Psychology* (Cambridge, 1952); Raymond A. Bauer and Edward Wasiolek, *Nine Soviet Portraits* (Cambridge, Mass., 1955); Harold J. Berman, *Russians in Focus* (Boston, 1953); Olaf Caroe, *Soviet Empire: The Turks of Central Asia and Stalinism* (London, 1953); Robert P. Casey, *Religion in Russia* (New York, 1946); William H. Chamberlin, *Ukraine, a Submerged Nation* (New York, 1944); *Commentary* (special issue), "The New Red Anti-Semitism; a Symposium" (Boston, 1953); Lewis A. Coser, "Some Aspects of Soviet Family Policy," *American Journal of Sociology,* 56 (March, 1951), pp. 424–37; George S. Counts, *The Challenge of Soviet Education* (New York, 1957); George S. Counts and N. P. Lodge, *The Country of the Blind: The Soviet System of Mind Control* (Boston, 1949); John S. Curtiss, *The Russian Church and the Soviet State, 1917–1950* (Boston, 1953); Herbert S. Dinerstein and Leon Goure, *Communism and the Russian Peasant and Moscow in Crisis; Two Studies in Soviet Controls* (Glencoe, Ill., 1955); Milovan Djilas, *The New Class* (New York, 1957); Boris P. Esipov and N. K. Goncharov, *I Want to Be Like Stalin* (Eng. trans., New York, 1947); Stanley Evans, *The Churches in the U.S.S.R.* (London, 1943); Manya Gordon, *Workers before and after Lenin* (New York, 1941); Geoffrey Gorer and J. Rickman, *The People of Great Russia* (New York, 1950); G. D. B. Gray, *Soviet Land: The Country, Its People and Their Work* (London, 1947); Vladimir Gsovski, ed., *Church and State behind the Iron Curtain* (New York, 1955); Fannina W. Halle, *Women in the Soviet East* (New York, 1938); Eugenia Hanfmann and Jacob Getzels, *Interpersonal Attitudes of Former Soviet Citizens, as Studied by a Semi-projective Method* (Washington, 1955); J. F. Hecker, *Religion under the Soviets* (New York, 1927); M. Holdsworth, "Soviet Central Asia, 1917–1940: a Study in Colonial Policy," *Soviet Studies,* 3 (January, 1952), pp. 258–77; Charles W. Hostler, *Turkism and the Soviets* (New York, 1957); Alex Inkeles, "Social Stratification and Mobility in the Soviet Union, 1940–1950," *American Sociological Review,* 15 (August, 1950), pp. 465–79; P. G. Ionescu, *Kremlin and the Church* (Detroit, 1953); Oscar I. Janowsky, *Nationalities and National Minorities* (New York, 1945); William H. E. Johnson, *Russia's Educational Heritage* (New Brunswick, N.J., 1940); Beatrice King, *Russia Goes to School: A Guide to Soviet Education* (London, 1948); Susan M. Kingsbury and Mildred Fairchild, *Factory, Family and Woman in the Soviet Union* (New York, 1935); Hans Kohn, *Nationalism in the Soviet Union* (London, 1933); Walter J. Kolarz, *The Peoples of the Soviet Far East* (New York, 1954), *Russia and Her Colonies* (London, 1952); Ruth Korper, *Candlelight Kingdom; a Meeting with the Russian Church* (New York, 1955); Joshua Kunitz, *Dawn over Samarkand* (New York, 1935); Corliss Lamont, *The Peoples of the Soviet Union* (New York, 1946); Helen and Pierre Lazareff, *Soviet Union after Stalin* (London, 1955); Kurt London, *The Seven Soviet Arts* (Eng. trans., New Haven, 1938); R. S. Lynd, "Ideology and the Soviet Family," *American Slavic and East European Review,* 9 (December, 1950), pp. 268–78; Eugene Lyons, *Our Secret Allies: The Peoples of Russia* (Boston, 1953); Gary MacEóin, *The Communist War on Religion* (New York, 1951); Robert Magidoff, *The Kremlin vs. the People: The Story of the Cold Civil War in Stalin's Russia* (New York, 1953); William Mandel, *The Soviet Far East and Central Asia* (New York, 1944); Clarence A. Manning, *Twentieth Century Ukraine* (New York, 1951), *Ukraine under the Soviets* (New York, 1953); R. H. Markham, ed., *Communists Crush Churches in Eastern Europe* (Boston, 1950); Margaret Mead, *Soviet Attitudes Toward Authority* (London, 1955); W. H. Melish, *Religion Today in the U.S.S.R.* (New York, 1945); Moscow Patriarchate, *The Truth about Religion in Russia* (London, 1942); Boris I. Nicolaevsky, "The New Soviet Campaign against the Peasants," *Russian Review,* 10 (April, 1951), pp. 81–98; Gerhard Niemeyer and John S. Reshetar, Jr., *An Inquiry into Soviet Mentality* (New York, 1956); Olga P. Nogina, *Mother and Child Care in the U.S.S.R.* (Moscow, 1950); George Padmore, *How Russia Transformed Her Colonial Empire* (London, 1946); John S. Reshetar, *Problems of Analyzing and Predicting Soviet Behavior* (New York, 1955); George N. Shuster, *Religion behind the Iron Curtain* (New York, 1954); Solomon M. Schwarz, *The Jews in the Soviet Union* (Syracuse, 1951); Maurice Shore, *Soviet Education: Its Psychology and Philosophy* (New York, 1947); Henry E. Sigerist, *Medicine and Health in the Soviet Union* (New York, 1947); Kathleen M. Stahl, *British and Soviet Colonial Systems* (London,

1951); Jay W. Stein, "The Soviet Intelligentsia," *Russian Review,* 10 (October, 1951), pp. 283–92; Anna Louise Strong, *Peoples of the U.S.S.R.* (New York, 1944); Gleb Struve, *Soviet Russian Literature, 1917–1950* (Norman, 1951); N. S. Timasheff, "Religion in Russia, 1914–1950," in Waldemar Gurian, ed., *The Soviet Union* (Notre Dame, 1951), *Religion in Soviet Russia 1917–1942* (New York, 1942); Julian Towster, "The Soviet Federation," *Current History,* 16 (March, 1949), pp. 131–35, and "Soviet Policy on Nationalities," *Antioch Review,* 11 (December, 1951), pp. 437–48; United States Department of State, Office of Intelligence Research, *Soviet Union as Reported by Former Soviet Citizens. Interview Report No. 7, June 4, 1953* (Washington, 1953); N. A. Vinogradov, *Public Health in the Soviet Union* (Moscow, 1950); Edmund T. Weiant, *Sources of Modern Mass Atheism in Russia* (College Park, Md., 1953), *The Woman Question: Selections from the Writings of Karl Marx, Friedrich Engels, V. I. Lenin, and Joseph Stalin* (New York, 1951), *Women and Communism: Selections from the Writings of Marx, Engels, Lenin, and Stalin* (London, 1950); Nicholas Zernov, *The Russians and Their Church* (London, 1945); Klara Zetkin, *Lenin e la Questione Sessuale* (Rome, 1945).

3. The following sources contain materials and discussions on the tenor of constitutionalism: Hugh W. Babb, trans., *Soviet Legal Philosophy* (Cambridge, 1951); Harold J. Berman, *Justice in Russia: An Interpretation of Soviet Law* (Cambridge, Mass., 1950); Mary S. Callcott, *Russian Justice* (New York, 1935); Dudley Collard, *Soviet Justice, and the Trial of Radek and Others* (London, 1937); Arthur John Cummings, *The Moscow Trial* (London, 1933); John Dewey et al., *The Case of Leon Trotsky* (New York, 1937); *Not Guilty* (New York, 1938), report of the Commission of Inquiry into the charges made against Leon Trotsky in the Moscow trials; George C. Guins, *Soviet Law and Soviet Society* (The Hague, 1954); Vladimir Gsovski, *Soviet Civil Law* (Ann Arbor, 1948–49), 2 vols.; John N. Hazard and M. L. Weisberg, *Cases and Readings on Soviet Law* (mimeographed, New York, 1950); John N. Hazard, *Law and Social Change in the U.S.S.R.* (London, 1953); David H. Henry, *Legislative Restrictions on Freedom of Movement in the Union of Soviet Socialist Republics* (United States Foreign Service Institute, 1949), No. 3; Hans Kelsen, *The Communist Theory of Law* (New York, 1955); Boris A. Konstantinovsky, *Soviet Law in Action: The Recollected Cases of a Soviet Lawyer* (Cambridge, Mass., 1953); Nathan C. Leites and Elsa Bernaut, *Ritual of Liquidation; the Case of the Moscow Trials* (Glencoe, Ill., 1954); Reinhart Maurach, *Handbuch der Sowjetverfassung* (Munich, 1955); Rudolph Schlesinger, *Soviet Legal Theory* (London, 1946); Max Shachtman, *Behind the Moscow Trial* (New York, 1936); Iurii Starosolskyi, *The Principle of Analogy in Criminal Law; and Aspects of Soviet Legal Thinking* (New York, 1954); Alexander Weissberg, *The Accused* (New York, 1952); Judah Zelitch, *Soviet Administration of Criminal Law* (London, 1931).

IV. THE COMMUNIST PARTY

The theory of the party's position and the organization and role of the party hierarchy and its junior auxiliaries are considered in: L. Beria, *On the History of the Bolshevik Organisations in Transcaucasia* (Moscow, 1949); Walter Duranty, *Stalin & Co.* (New York, 1949); *The Fiftieth Anniversary of the Communist Party of the Soviet Union (1903–1953)* (New York, 1953); Raymond L. Garthoff, *The New Soviet Leadership* (Santa Monica, 1953); Sidney S. Harcave, *Structure and Functioning of the Lower Party Organization in the Soviet Union* (Maxwell Air Force Base, Ala., 1954), *History of the Communist Party of the Soviet Union (Bolsheviks) Short Course* (New York, 1939); Alex Inkeles, *Public Opinion in Soviet Russia* (Cambridge, Mass., 1950); Boris Meissner, *Das Ende des Stalin Mythos. Die Ergebnisse des 20. Parteikongresses der Kommunistischen Partei der Sowjetunion* (Frankfurt, 1956); Boris Meissner and John S. Reshetar, Jr., *The Communist Party of the Soviet Union* (New York, 1956); Louis Nemzer, "The Kremlin's Professional

Staff: The 'Apparatus' of the Central Committee, Communist Party of the Soviet Union," *American Political Science Review,* 44 (March, 1950), pp. 64–85; N. Popov, *Outline History of the Communist Party* (New York, 1934), 2 vols.; Virginia Rhine, trans., *Young Communists in the USSR* (Washington, 1950), a Soviet monograph describing the demands made upon members of the Komsomol organization; George K. Schueller, *The Politburo* (Stanford, 1951); "Der XX. Kongress der KPdSU," Sonderheft, *Ost-Europa,* 6, No. 3 (1956).

V. THE SOVIET GOVERNMENT

On the theory of the position of the soviets, elections to the soviets, the organization and role of the soviets of the localities and the republics, and the organs of the federal government, note: Henry Noel Brailsford, *How the Soviets Work* (New York, 1927); George Barr Carson, Jr., *Electoral Practices in the U.S.S.R.* (New York, 1955); John N. Hazard, "Soviet Public Administration and Federalism," *Political Quarterly,* 23 (January–March, 1952), pp. 4–14; Sir Ernest D. Simon *et al., Moscow in the Making* (London, 1937); Julian Towster, "Recent Trends and Strategies in Soviet Federalism," *Political Quarterly,* 23 (April–June, 1943), pp. 163–74; O. Utis, "Generalissimo Stalin and the Art of Government," *Foreign Affairs,* 30 (January, 1952), pp. 197–214.

VI. THE AGENCIES OF ENFORCEMENT AND DEFENSE

1. For the courts and prosecutors see entries under Section III. Discussions of the secret police are included in each of the following: Klaus Ackermann, *Das Land der Stummen Millionen* (Tübingen, 1951); American Federation of Labor, *Slave Labor in Russia* (Washington, 1949), the case presented by the A.F. of L. to the United Nations; Roger N. Baldwin, ed., *A New Slavery; Forced Labor: The Communist Betrayal of Human Rights* (New York, 1953); F. Beck and W. Godin, *Russian Purge and Extraction of Confession* (Eng. trans., New York, 1951); Margarete Buber, *Under Two Dictators* (New York, 1951); Joseph Czapski, *The Inhuman Land* (London, 1951); David J. Dallin, *Soviet Espionage* (New Haven, 1955); David Dallin and B. Nicolaevsky, *Forced Labor in Soviet Russia* (New Haven, 1950); Maurice Edelman, *G.P.U. Justice* (London, 1938); Jerzy Gliksman, *Tell the West* (New York, 1948); Harvard University Russian Research Center, *Prisoners of War Camps in Russia. The Account of a German Prisoner of War in Russia* (Cambridge, Mass., 1951); Otto Heilbrunn, *Soviet Secret Services* (London, 1956); Albert Conrad Herling, *The Soviet Slave Empire* (New York, 1951); Gustav Herling, *A World Apart* (Eng. trans., London, 1951); Walter Kotschnig, *Slaves Need No Leaders* (New York, 1943); Elinor Lipper, *Eleven Years in Soviet Prison Camps* (Eng. trans., Chicago, 1951); Vladimir Petrov, *Soviet Gold: My Life as a Slave Laborer in the Siberian Mines* (New York, 1949); David Rousset, ed., *International Commission against Forced Labor. Police State Methods in the Soviet Union* (Boston, 1953); Joseph Scholmer, *Vorkuta* (London, 1954); Vladimir V. Tchernavin, *I Speak for the Silent Prisoners of the Soviets* (New York, 1935); Simon Wolin and Robert E. Slusser, eds., *The Soviet Secret Police* (New York, 1957).

2. The armed forces and their civil auxiliaries are treated in: Armed Forces Information School, *The Soviet Military Organization: A Compilation of Articles from Army Information Digest* (Fort Slocum, 1951); Nikolaus Basseches, *The Unknown Army . . . the Nature and History of the Russian Military Forces* (Eng. trans., New York, 1943); Harold J. Berman and Miroslav Kerner, eds. and trans., *Documents on Soviet Military Law and Administration* (Cambridge, Mass., 1955), *Soviet Military Law and Administration* (Cambridge, Mass., 1955); Zbigniew

Brzezinski, ed., *Political Controls in the Soviet Army* (New York, 1954); Louis B. Ely, *The Red Army Today* (Harrisburg, 1951); I. Fomichenko, ed., *The Red Army* (London, 1945); George Fischer, *Soviet Opposition to Stalin* (Cambridge, Mass., 1952); Augustin Guillaume, *Soviet Arms and Soviet Power: the Secrets of Russia's Might* (Washington, 1949); Otto Heilbrunn and C. Aubrey Dixon, *Communist Guerilla Warfare* (New York, 1954); I. S. Isakov, *Red Fleet in the Second World War* (London, 1947); Walter B. Kerr, *The Russian Army* (New York, 1944); B. H. Liddell Hart, ed., *The Red Army* (New York, 1956); Asher Lee, *The Soviet Air Force* (New York, 1950); I. Mintz, *The Red Army* (New York, 1944); Mairin Mitchell, *The Maritime History of Russia 848–1948* (London, 1949); Mikhail Soloviev, *My Nine Lives in the Russian Army* (New York, 1955); Richard F. Stockwell, *Soviet Airpower* (New York, 1956); Frank Uhlig, Jr., "The Threat of the Soviet Navy," *Foreign Affairs,* 30 (April, 1952), pp. 444–54; D. Fedotoff White, *The Growth of the Red Army* (Princeton, 1944); E. Wollenberg, *The Red Army: A Study of the Growth of Soviet Imperialism* (Eng. trans., 2nd ed., London, 1940).

VII. THE PLANNED ECONOMY

For analyses and data on planning, on the management of industry and agriculture, and on the functions of trade unions and co-operatives, consult: A. Arakelian, *Industrial Management in the U.S.S.R.* (Eng. trans., Washington, 1950); George R. Barker, *Some Problems of Incentives and Labor Productivity in Soviet Industry* (London, 1956); Noah Barou, *Co-operation in the Soviet Union* (London, 1946); Alexander Baykov, *The Development of the Soviet Economic System* (Cambridge, 1948), "The Soviet Economic System," *Political Quarterly,* 23 (January–March, 1952), pp. 49–61; Fedor Belov, *The History of a Soviet Collective Farm* (New York, 1955); Abram Bergson, "The Fourth Five Year Plan: Heavy vs. Consumers' Goods Industries," *Political Science Quarterly,* 62 (June, 1947), pp. 195–227; Abram Bergson, ed., *Soviet Economic Growth; Conditions and Perspective* (Evanston, Ill., 1953), *The Structure of Soviet Wages* (Cambridge, 1944); Abram Bergson and Hans Heymann, Jr., *Soviet National Income and Product, 1940–1948* (New York, 1954); Gregory Bienstock, Solomon M. Schwartz, Aaron Yugow, *Management in Russian Industry and Agriculture* (New York, 1944); Isaac Deutscher, *Soviet Trade Unions: Their Place in Soviet Labour Policy* (London, 1950); Margaret Dewar, *Industrial Management in the U.S.S.R.: An Outline Study* (London, 1945), *Labour Policy in the USSR, 1917–1928* (London, 1956); Nicolas DeWitt, *Soviet Professional Manpower, Its Education, Training and Supply* (Washington, 1955); Maurice Dobb, *Soviet Economic Development since 1917* (London, 1948); Peter Francis, *I Worked in a Soviet Factory* (London, 1939); Walter Galenson, *Industrial Training in the Soviet Union* (Santa Monica, 1955), *Labor Productivity in Soviet and American Industry* (New York, 1955); David Granick, *Management of the Industrial Firm in the USSR; A Study in Soviet Economic Planning* (New York, 1954); Gregory Grossman, "Soviet Agriculture since Stalin," *Annals,* 303 (January, 1956); Donald R. Hodgman, *Soviet Industrial Production, 1928–1951* (Cambridge, Mass., 1954); D. Holzman, *Soviet Taxation: The Fiscal and Monetary Problems of a Planned Economy* (Cambridge, Mass., 1955); Franklyn Lucien Laurat, *Bilan de vingt-cinq ans de plans quinquennaux* (Paris, 1955); Naum Jasny, *Socialized Agriculture of the U.S.S.R.* (Stanford, 1949), *The Soviet Economy during the Plan Era* (Stanford, 1951), *The Soviet Price System* (Stanford, 1952); Joseph A. Kershaw, *The Economics of Soviet Agriculture* (Santa Monica, 1950), *Labour in the Land of Socialism: Stakhanovites in Conference* (Moscow, 1936); A. Lozovsky, *Handbook on the Soviet Trade Unions for Workers' Delegations* (Moscow, 1937); Peter I. Lyashchenko, *History of the National Economy of Russia* (New York, 1949); Nancy Nimitz, *The New Soviet Agricultural Decrees (September plenum, 1953)* (Santa Monica, 1954), *Statistics of Soviet Agriculture* (Santa Monica, 1954); Hans Raupach, *Die Agrarwirtschaft der Sowjetunion seit dem zweiten Weltkrieg* (Tuebingen, 1953); H. E. Ronimois, *Soviet Planning and Economic Theory* (Vancouver, 1950);

Andrew Rothstein, *Man and Plan in Soviet Economy* (Toronto, 1949); Otto Schiller, *Die Landwirtschaft der Sowjetunion, 1917–1953* (Tuebingen, 1954); Harry Schwartz, *Russia's Post-War Economy* (Syracuse, 1947), *Russia's Soviet Economy* (New York, 1954); Solomon M. Schwarz, *Labor in the Soviet Union* (New York, 1952); George Stec, *The Local Budget System of the USSR* (New York, 1955); Sergei P. Turin, *U.S.S.R.: An Economic and Social Survey* (3rd ed., Forest Hills, 1949); University of Birmingham, Department of Economics and Institutions of the U.S.S.R., *Bulletin on Soviet Economic Development* (Birmingham, England, 1949–51), Nos. 1–4; United States Bureau of Labor Statistics, *Labor Conditions in the Soviet Union* (Washington, 1955); United States Library of Congress, Legislative Reference Service, *Trends in Economic Growth, a Comparison of the Western Powers and the Soviet Bloc* (Washington, 1954); United States Office of Foreign Agricultural Relations, *Life of Soviet Collective Farmer* (Washington, 1951); Lazar Volin, *A Survey of Soviet Russian Agriculture* (Washington, 1951), "The Turn of the Screw in Soviet Agriculture," *Foreign Affairs,* 30 (January, 1952), pp. 277–89; Alexander Vucinich, *Soviet Economic Institutions* (Stanford, 1952); Nikolai Voznesenskii, *Economy of the U.S.S.R. during World War II* (Washington, 1948); T. Zavalani, *How Strong Is Russia?* (London, 1951).

VIII. FOREIGN POLICY

The wealth of literature, especially during the recent period, on Soviet foreign policy makes selection especially difficult. However, on major recent foreign policies and the international position of the U.S.S.R., see: *The Anti-Stalin Campaign and International Communism,* ed. by the Russian Institute, Columbia University (New York, 1956); Hamilton Fish Armstrong, *Tito and Goliath* (New York, 1951); Hanson W. Baldwin, *Power and Politics: the Price of Security in the Atomic Age* (Claremont, Calif., 1950); Frederick C. Barghoorn, *The Soviet Image of the United States: A Study in Distortion* (New York, 1950); Max Beloff, *Foreign Policy of Soviet Russia,* (New York, 1947–49), 2 vols., *Soviet Policy in the Far East, 1944–1951* (New York, 1953); R. R. Betts, ed., *Central and South East Europe, 1945–1948* (London, 1950); Michael Bialoguski, *The Case of Colonel Petrov* (New York, 1955); Donald G. Bishop, *Soviet Foreign Relations: A Book of Documents and Readings* (Syracuse, 1950); Franz Borkenau, *World Communism: A History of the Communist International* (New York, 1939), *European Communism* (New York, 1953); John Brown, *Who Next? The Lesson of Czechoslovakia* (London, 1951); Alfred Burmeister, *Dissolution and Aftermath of the Comintern; Experiences and Observation, 1937–1947* (New York, 1955); Jean J. Calvez, *Droit International et Souveraineté en URSS* (Paris, 1953); Ann Su Cardwell, *Poland and Russia: The Last Quarter Century* (New York, 1944); Edward H. Carr, *German-Soviet Relations between the Two World Wars, 1919–1939* (Baltimore, 1951), *The Soviet Impact on the Western World* (London, 1946); Georges Castellan, *D.D.R.—L'Allemagne de l'est* (Paris, 1955); David T. Cattell, *Communism and the Spanish Civil War* (Los Angeles, 1955); W. H. Chamberlin, ed., *Blueprint for World Conquest* (Washington, 1946); Lucius D. Clay, *Decision in Germany* (New York, 1950); William P. and Zelda K. Coates, *A History of Anglo-Soviet Relations* (London, 1944), *World Affairs and the U.S.S.R.* (London, 1939); Alexander Dallin and C. F. Latour, *The German Occupation of the USSR in World War II: A Bibliography* (Washington, 1955); David J. Dallin, *The Big Three* (New Haven, 1945), *The Rise of Russia in Asia* (New Haven, 1949), *The New Soviet Empire* (New Haven, 1951), *Russia and Post War Europe* (New Haven, 1943), *Soviet Russia and the Far East* (New Haven, 1948), *Soviet Russia's Foreign Policy, 1939–1942* (New Haven, 1942); Vera Micheles Dean, *Russia: Menace or Promise?* (New York, 1946), *The United States and Russia* (Cambridge, Mass., 1947); John Russell Deane, *The Strange Alliance* (New York, 1947); Jane Degras, ed., *Calendar of Soviet Documents on Foreign Policy, 1917–1941* (New York, 1948), *Soviet Documents on Foreign Policy, 1917–1941,* Vols. I–III (New York, 1951–53), *The Communist International, 1919–1943:*

Documents Vol. I, 1919–1922 (London, 1956); Raymond Dennett and J. E. Johnson, eds., *Negotiating with the Russians* (Boston, 1951); A. L. P. Dennis, *The Foreign Policies of Soviet Russia* (London, 1924); Ivo Duchacek, "The Strategy of Communist Infiltration: Czechoslovakia, 1944–1948," *World Politics,* 2 (April, 1950); Horst Duhnke, *Stalinismus in Deutschland* (Cologne, 1955); John F. Dulles, *War or Peace* (New York, 1950); W. Gordon East, "The New Frontiers of the Soviet Union," *Foreign Affairs,* 29 (July, 1951), pp. 591–607; Martin Ebon, *World Communism Today* (New York, 1948); George Fielding Eliot, *If Russia Strikes* (Indianapolis, 1949); Rupert Emerson and Inis L. Claude, Jr., "The Soviet Union and the United Nations: An Essay in Interpretation," *International Organization,* 6 (February, 1952), pp. 1–26; Merle Fainsod, *International Socialism and the World War* (Cambridge, Mass., 1935); François Fejtoe, *Histoire des démocraties populaires* (Paris, 1953); Louis Fischer, *The Soviets in World Affairs* (2nd ed., Princeton, 1951), 2 vols.; Ruth Fischer, *Stalin and German Communism* (Cambridge, Mass., 1948); Harold H. Fisher, *America and Russia in the World Community* (Claremont, Calif., 1946); Michael T. Florinsky, *World Revolution and the U.S.S.R.* (New York, 1933); J. Frankel, "The Soviet Union and the United Nations," in *Yearbook of World Affairs* (London, 1954); Gerard M. Friters, *Outer Mongolia and Its International Position* (Baltimore, 1949); Richard N. Frye, ed., *The Near East and the Great Powers* (Cambridge, Mass., 1951); J. F. C. Fuller, *Russia Is Not Invincible* (London, 1951); Alexander Gerschenkron, *Economic Relations with the U.S.S.R.* (New York, 1945); Kurt Glaser, *The Iron Curtain and American Policy* (Washington, 1953); Ygael Gluckstein, *Stalin's Satellites in Europe* (London, 1952); Waldemar Gurian *et al.,* eds., *Soviet Imperialism: Its Origins and Tactics, a Symposium* (Notre Dame, 1953); Charles G. Haines, *The Threat of Soviet Imperialism* (Baltimore, 1954); Verner von Harpe, *Die Sowjetunion, Finnland und Skandinavien, 1945 bis 1955* (Cologne, 1956); John N. Hazard, "The Soviet Union and International Law," *Soviet Studies,* 1 (January, 1950), pp. 189–99; Wilhelm Walter Hartlieb, *Das Politische Vertragssystem der Sowjetunion 1920–1935* (Leipzig, 1935); Friederich Hertz, *The Economic Problem of the Danubian States: A Study in Economic Nationalism* (London, 1947); Gustav Hilger and Alfred G. Meyer, *The Incompatible Allies; a Memoir-History of German-Soviet Relations, 1918–1941* (New York, 1953); George B. de Huszar, ed., *Soviet Power and Policy* (New York, 1955); George F. Kennan, *American Diplomacy, 1900–1950* (Chicago, 1951), "America and the Russian Future," *Foreign Affairs,* 29 (April, 1951), pp. 351–70, *Russia and the United States* (Stamford, Conn., 1950), "The Sources of Soviet Conduct," *Foreign Affairs,* 25 (July, 1947), pp. 566–82; Edward Kerstein, *Red Star over Poland: A Report from behind the Iron Curtain* (New York, 1947); William R. Kintner, *The Front Is Everywhere: Militant Communism in Action* (Norman, 1950); Peter Kleist, *Zwischen Hitler und Stalin* (Bonn, 1950); Lionel Kochan, *Russia and the Weimar Republic* (New York, 1954); Tadeusz Bor Komorowski, *The Secret Army* (London, 1951); S. Konovalov and F. Seeley, eds., *Russo-Polish Relations: An Historical Survey* (Princeton, 1945); Josef Korbel, *Tito's Communism* (Denver, 1951); W. W. Kulski, "Soviet Comments on International Law," *American Journal of International Law,* 45 (July, 1951), pp. 556–64, "The Soviet System of Collective Security Compared with the Western System," *American Journal of International Law,* 44 (July, 1950), pp. 453–76; Bornislaw Kusnierz, *Stalin and the Poles: An Indictment of the Soviet Leaders* (London, 1949); Arthur B. Lane, *I Saw Poland Betrayed* (Indianapolis, 1948); Melvin J. Lasky ed., *The Hungarian Revolution—A White Book* (New York, 1957); Nathan Leites, *The Operational Code of the Politburo* (New York, 1951); George Lenczowski, *The Middle East in World Affairs* (Ithaca, 1952), *Russia and the West in Iran, 1918–1948: A Study in Big-Power Rivalry* (Ithaca, 1949); A. Lobanov-Rostovsky, *Russia and Asia* (Ann Arbor, 1951); Joseph Mackiewicz, *The Katyn Wood Murders* (London, 1951); Reuben H. Markham, *Rumania under the Soviet Yoke* (Boston, 1949); Boris Meissner, *Das Ostpaktsystem; Documents* (Frankfurt, 1955), *Russland, die Westmaechte und Deutschland* (Hamburg, 1953), *Die Sowjetunion, die Baltischen Staaten und das Voelkerrecht* (Cologne, 1956); Dmitri E. Melnikov, *European Security; the Soviet Plan* (London, 1954); K. W. B. Middleton, *Britain and Russia: An Historical Essay* (London, 1947); Stanislaw Mikolajczyk, *The Rape of Poland: Pattern of Soviet Aggression* (New York,

1948); Pavel N. Miluikov, *La Politique extérieure des soviets* (2nd ed., Paris, 1936); Harriet Moore, *Soviet Far Eastern Policy, 1931–1945* (Princeton, 1945); Hans J. Morgenthau, *In Defense of the National Interest: A Critical Examination of American Foreign Policy* (New York, 1951); Philip E. Mosely, "Across the Green Table from Stalin," *Current History,* 15 (September, 1948), pp. 129–33; "Aspects of Russian Expansion," *The American Slavic and East European Review,* 7 (October, 1948), pp. 197–213; "Soviet Policy and the Revolutions in Asia," *Annals,* 276 (July, 1951), pp. 91–98; Ferenc Nagy, *Struggle behind the Iron Curtain* (London, 1949); J. P. Nettl, *The Eastern Zone and Soviet Policy in Germany, 1945–1950* (London, 1951); Robert Payne, *Red Storm over Asia* (New York, 1951); Harry E. Pierson, *The Asian Economic Empire of the Soviets the Chinese and the Mongols* (1951); Stefan T. Possony, *A Century of Conflict: Communist Techniques of World Revolution* (New York, 1953); Hubert Ripka, *Czechoslovakia Enslaved: The Story of the Communist Coup d'État* (New York, 1951); Henry L. Roberts, *Rumania: Political Problems of an Agrarian State* (New Haven, 1951), *Russia and America; Dangers and Prospects* (New York, 1956); A. Rossi, *The Russo-German Alliance, August, 1939–June 1941* (London, 1950); Andrew Rothstein, trans., *Soviet Foreign Policy during the Patriotic War: Documents and Materials* (London, 1946), 2 vols.; Joseph Roucek, *Balkan Politics: International Relations in No Man's Land* (Stanford, 1948); Royal Institute of International Affairs, *Soviet-Yugoslav Dispute* (New York, 1949), text of the published correspondence; "Russia's Foreign Policy," *Current History,* 28 (February, 1955); Benjamin I. Schwartz, *Chinese Communism and the Rise of Mao* (Cambridge, 1951); Hugh Seton-Watson, *The East European Revolution* (rev. ed., London, 1957), *From Lenin to Malenkov: The History of World Communism* (New York, 1953); Leonard Shapiro, ed., *Soviet Treaty Series, Vol. I, 1917–1928* (Washington, 1950), *Vol. II, 1929–1939* (Washington, 1955); James T. Shotwell and Max M. Laserson, *Poland and Russia, 1919–1945* (New York, 1945); John L. Snell, *The Meaning of Yalta* (Baton Rouge, La., 1956); Raymond James Sontag and James Stuart Beddie, eds., *Nazi-Soviet Relations, 1939–1941. Documents from the Archives of the German Foreign Office* (Washington, 1948), *Soviet-Polish Relations: A Collection of Official Documents and Press Extracts 1944–1946* (New York, 1946); Ivor Spector, *Soviet Strength and Strategy in Asia* (Seattle, 1950); Joseph Stalin, *A Selection of Stalin's Public Statements in the Post-war Period, 1945–1951* (Washington, 1952); Edward R. Stettinius, Jr., *Roosevelt and the Russians: the Yalta Conference,* Walter Johnson, ed. (Garden City, 1949); *Survey of International Affairs,* 1939–1946, "America, Britain, and Russia: Their Co-operation and Conflict, 1941–1946," by William H. McNeill (New York, 1953); T. A. Taracouzio, *The Soviet Union and International Law* (New York, 1953), *War and Peace in Soviet Diplomacy* (New York, 1940); G. A. Tokaev, *Soviet Imperialism* (New York, 1956); Pauline Tompkins, *American-Russian Relations in the Far East* (New York, 1949); Julian Towster, "The Framework of Soviet Foreign Policy," *California Monthly* (September, 1955); "Russia: Persistent Strategic Demands," *Current History,* 21 (July, 1951), pp. 2–7; Leon Trotsky, *The First Five Years of the Communist International* (New York, 1953), Vol. II, *Third International after Lenin* (New York, 1936); Adam B. Ulam, *Titoism and the Cominform* (Cambridge, 1952); United States Department of State, *A Decade of American Foreign Policy, 1941–1949* (Washington, 1950); United States Congress, House Committee on Foreign Affairs, *Background Information on the Soviet Union in International Relations* (81st Congress, 2nd sess., 1950), No. 3135; United States Library of Congress, *Economic Treaties and Agreements of the Soviet Bloc in Eastern Europe, 1945–1951* (Washington, 1952); United States Congress, Joint Committee on Atomic Energy, *Soviet Atomic Espionage, April, 1951* (82nd Congress, 1st sess., 1951); United States Congress, House Committee on Foreign Affairs, *The Strategy and Tactics of World Communism* (80th Congress, 2nd sess., 1948), No. 619; United States Department of State, *Trends in Russian Foreign Policy since World War I* (Washington, 1950), Vol. I; James P. Warburg, *How to Co-exist without Playing the Kremlin's Game* (Boston, 1952); Doreen Warriner, *Revolution in Eastern Europe* (London, 1950); Gerhard L. Weinberg, *Germany and the Soviet Union, 1939–1941* (Leiden, Holland, 1954); Leigh White, *Balkan Caesar: Tito vs. Stalin* (New York, 1951); Allen S. Whiting, *Soviet Policies in China, 1917–1924* (New York, 1954);

Chester Wilmot, *The Struggle for Europe* (London, 1952); Quincy Wright, "American Policy toward Russia," *World Politics,* 2 (July, 1950), pp. 463–81, *The Study of International Relations* (New York, 1955); Aitchen K. Wu, *China and the Soviet Union: A Study of Sino-Soviet Relations* (London, 1950); Victor A. Yakhontoff, *U.S.S.R.: Foreign Policy* (New York, 1945); Jan Yindrich, *Tito v. Stalin: The Battle of the Marshals* (London, 1950).

PART SIX

THE SOVIET ORBIT: THE PEOPLE'S DEMOCRACIES OF EASTERN EUROPE

———————————

by C. E. Black

and

R. L. Braham

30

STRUCTURE OF EASTERN EUROPEAN POLITICS

1. REGIONAL PERSONALITY

Introduction. The region comprising the countries treated in these chapters—Albania, Bulgaria, Czechoslovakia, Finland, Hungary, Poland, Rumania, and Yugoslavia—is characterized by so great a diversity of traditions, peoples, and problems, that at first glance it appears to possess little unity. Upon closer examination, however, it becomes clear that despite this diversity there are two general characteristics that the countries of Eastern Europe share and that fully justify consideration of them as a region with an integrated political personality. The first is the common desire of these peoples to raise their standard of living to a level comparable to that of the countries of Western Europe. The second is the belief that this improvement of living conditions cannot take place until the peoples have organized themselves as independent and sovereign states. The paradox of Eastern Europe is that the great efforts toward national unification and independence have been made largely at the expense of the improvement of living standards. The frustration caused by the apparent incompatibility of these two dominant trends explains much of the intensity of Eastern European politics.

Economic Problems. The economic backwardness of Eastern Europe may be explained by a number of factors. During the expansion of Europe, the key to political and economic power lay in the trade routes of the Mediterranean and Baltic seas and the Atlantic Ocean, and the peoples of Eastern Europe were able to participate in the economic benefits of this development only to a relatively slight degree. When the main emphasis of economic expansion shifted from commerce to industrialization, Eastern Europe again found itself at a disadvantage. Although important deposits of raw materials are located in the area now included in Poland, Czechoslovakia, Yugoslavia, and Rumania, the region as a whole possesses nothing resembling the natural wealth of England, France, and Germany.

For a time the lands of Eastern Europe supplied the industrialized Western states with foodstuffs, which the latter, now agriculturally dependent, began to import in increasing quantities. Even this economic function was largely lost for Eastern Europe, however, when non-European grain supplies began to compete successfully for the European market. During the period between the two world wars the major domestic concern of the new governments of Eastern Europe was to raise the standard of living through agricultural improvement and industrialization.

Political Problems.   To the natural obstacles in the way of the economic development of Eastern Europe were added very extensive political difficulties, for the peoples of this region lived in the border territories of the four great dynastic empires of the Hapsburgs, the Hohenzollerns, the Romanovs, and the Ottomans. The rivalries of these four dynasties, which occupied much of the diplomatic history of the nineteenth century and culminated in the disastrous events of World War I, affected profoundly the destinies of the peoples of Eastern Europe. The rivalry of the Russians and the Austrians over the legacy of the Ottoman Empire extended through the eighteenth and nineteenth centuries and gained in momentum until the reciprocal declarations of war in July, 1914. The struggle between the Hapsburgs and the Hohenzollerns for leadership in Germany ended with the victory of the latter in 1866, and the eastern provinces of both dynasties were active in trying to take advantage of this struggle to achieve independence. When Russia emerged at the end of the nineteenth century as a rival of Germany as well as of Austria-Hungary, the peoples of Eastern Europe again found themselves the focal point of this rivalry, and it was their lands that eventually became the battlefields of the imperial armies.

The time and the manner in which the various peoples of Eastern Europe began to realize that these destructive rivalries were being conducted to the detriment of their interests and largely at their expense differed in each case.

Even before the middle of the nineteenth century leaders of the minority peoples throughout Eastern Europe recognized that the great powers within whose frontiers they lived would in principle always tend to regard them as second-class citizens in an economic as well as a political sense. National independence therefore became increasingly their rallying cry, even though many realized that they derived distinct economic benefits from their participation in the large imperial trading areas. Yet the economic calculations of commercial interests could never win out over the exhortations of the nationalist leaders, for immediate evidence of oppression was always a more telling argument than were predictions as to the ultimate economic consequences of independence. Moreover, when the fighting became difficult on the Western front during World War I, the Western powers soon saw that they could embarrass their enemies by encouraging the minority peoples to revolt. For these and other reasons the goal of national independence was kept constantly before the peoples of Eastern Europe, and when it was finally

achieved in substance at the end of World War I its preservation came
to overshadow all other values.

2. ECONOMIC POSITION

The extent of economic backwardness in the countries of Eastern Europe
has always weighed heavily on their leaders, and the reasons for such
concern may readily be seen by comparing this region with Europe as a
whole. The relative position of Eastern Europe is illustrated by figures
that have been assembled under the supervision of the Economic,
Financial, and Transit Department of the League of Nations, on four key
problems: the proportion of the population engaged in agriculture; agricultural production per male engaged in agriculture and per hectare; net
production in agriculture, fishing, and forestry; and agricultural overpopulation.

Agricultural Population.   The predominantly agrarian character of
the countries of Eastern Europe is shown in Figure XXVIII. Of these
countries only Czechoslovakia may be considered primarily industrial,
although politically it has remained under strong agrarian influences.
A comparable dependence on agriculture also exists in the Baltic
States, which were absorbed by the U.S.S.R. in 1940, and in Ireland,
Spain, Portugal, Greece, and Italy. In the industrialized states of Western Europe, on the other hand, the proportion of the population dependent on agriculture is as low as 5 per cent in England and Wales
(1931), 15 per cent in Belgium (1930), and 20 per cent in Germany
(1933).[1] The U.S.S.R. remained primarily an agrarian country during

FIG. XXVIII

POPULATION DEPENDENT ON AGRICULTURE: EASTERN EUROPE *

COUNTRY	YEAR	PER CENT
Albania	1930	80
Bulgaria	1926	75
Czechoslovakia	1930	33
Finland	1930	57
Hungary	1930	51
Poland	1931	60
Rumania	1930	72
Yugoslavia	1931	76

* W. E. Moore, *Economic Demography of Eastern and Southern Europe*
(1945), p. 26.

the interwar period, although the proportion of the population dependent on agriculture declined approximately from 75 per cent in 1928 to 60

[1] W. E. Moore, *Economic Demography of Eastern and Southern Europe*
(1945), p. 26.

per cent in 1937 as a result of the intensive industrialization carried on under the Five-Year Plans.[2]

Agricultural Production. Another significant indication of the economic backwardness of the countries of Eastern Europe is contained in these figures on agricultural production:

FIG. XXIX

AGRICULTURAL PRODUCTION: EASTERN EUROPE: 1931–35 *
(INDEX NUMBERS: EUROPEAN AVERAGE, EXCL.
U.S.S.R. AND TURKEY = 100)

COUNTRY	PER MALE ENGAGED IN AGRICULTURE	PER HECTARE OF AGRICULTURAL LAND †
Albania	25	70
Bulgaria	55	80
Czechoslovakia	115	129
Finland	70	92
Hungary	75	87
Poland	56	75
Rumania	53	69
Yugoslavia	43	69

* Moore, op. cit., p. 35.
† One hectare equals 2.47 acres.

These figures stress the fact that, again with the exception of Czechoslovakia, the average of agricultural production in Eastern Europe is well below that of the Continent as a whole. In sharp contrast to this picture are the corresponding calculations on the agricultural production of such countries as Denmark (323 per male, 236 per hectare), England and Wales (240 per male, 181 per hectare), and Germany (191 per male, 181 per hectare). The index figure for agricultural production per male engaged in agriculture in the U.S.S.R. during the same period stood at 41, but no figure is available for production per hectare.[3]

Net Production. An even more accurate picture of the economic position of Eastern Europe with respect to the Continent as a whole is provided by the index figures of net production in agriculture, fishing, and forestry, i.e., figures of the gross value of output minus the production costs. These net production figures are listed in Figure XXX on page 745 and indicate that none of the countries of Eastern Europe equaled the average for Europe as a whole, although Czechoslovakia and Finland closely approximated it. The comparable index figure for the U.S.S.R. is 56.[4]

[2] A. Baykov, *The Development of the Soviet Economic System* (1947), p. 357.

[3] Moore, op. cit., p. 35.

[4] Ibid., p. 51.

FIG. XXX

NET PRODUCTION IN AGRICULTURE, FISHING, AND FORESTRY:
EASTERN EUROPE: 1931–35 *

COUNTRY	INDEX PER PERSON DEPENDENT ON AGRICULTURE (EUROPE = 100)
Albania	38
Bulgaria	66
Czechoslovakia	96
Finland	93
Hungary	76
Poland	50
Rumania	59
Yugoslavia	56

* Moore, op. cit., p. 51.

Overpopulation. As a final indication of the relative economic position of the countries of Eastern Europe, some estimates may be cited as to the extent of what the economists call agricultural overpopulation. This calculation is made by subtracting from the actual agrarian population in each country the number of persons that would be required to maintain existing production if per capita standards were equal to the European average. The resulting percentage indicates the proportion of the population dependent on agriculture that would be "surplus" if the standard of per-capita production were raised to the European average. See Figure XXXI, page 746.

The four tables cited do not in any sense present a balanced picture of the economic problems of the countries of Eastern Europe, for they omit such important elements as natural resources, industrial production, and foreign trade. Moreover, this material has reference only to the relatively brief interwar period for which adequate statistics are available. At the same time, these figures do not take into consideration the variations existing in each country, for almost all have a considerable diversity of economic conditions within their frontiers.[5] What these figures do illustrate, in relation to an estimated European average (excluding the U.S.S.R. and Turkey), is that the countries of Eastern Europe are in a very fundamental sense a backward area. They also indicate the considerable differences among the countries within the region and the extent to which Czechoslovakia, and to a lesser degree Finland and Hungary, approximate the European average in certain respects. Despite these differences the general picture of Eastern Europe remains one of a primarily agricultural region, where both production per unit and net production are on the whole well below the European average.

The agricultural overpopulation resulting from this situation has brought to the political struggles of the region a whole series of eco-

[5] Ibid., pp. 55–98; D. Warriner, *Economics of Peasant Farming* (1939), Chapters 5–7.

nomic and social problems. Although this material deals only with the 1930's, it is also indicative of the position of Eastern Europe before World War I. For the intellectual and political leaders of this region the great challenge has always been the improvement of its economic position and, concurrently, of its social and cultural conditions. How to achieve these objectives has been the subject of the stormy political controversies that have preoccupied the region during the past century.

FIG. XXXI

AGRICULTURAL OVERPOPULATION:
EASTERN EUROPE: CA. 1930 *

COUNTRY	PER CENT "SURPLUS" POPULATION
Albania	77.7
Bulgaria	53.0
Czechoslovakia	4.7
Finland	—
Hungary	22.4
Poland	51.3
Rumania	51.4
Yugoslavia	61.5

* Ibid., pp. 63–64.

3. TRADITIONS OF GOVERNMENT

Achievement of Independence. The ideas and example of the French Revolution were the principal influences to inspire the leaders of the Eastern European peoples in their struggle for national independence. The Poles and the minority peoples of the Hapsburg Empire felt the direct impact of these ideas during the Napoleonic Wars, and the peoples under Turkish rule received them indirectly through channels of propaganda and commerce. Revolutionary republicanism, which survived after 1815 in a modified form of constitutional monarchism, became the general rallying cry of the oppressed peoples of Eastern Europe. First political independence must be achieved through revolution, they believed; then order and prosperity would be assured under self-government.

These ideas were widely disseminated during the nineteenth century, but their implementation was beyond the strength and capacities of the individual peoples. Only with outside assistance could they hope to gain independence, and the Ottoman Empire was the one state not a member of the protective association of European rulers that dominated the affairs of the Continent during the greater part of the century. It was thus that the peoples of Southeastern Europe, in many respects the least prepared for self-government, gained their freedom before their neighbors to the north. Independence was granted first by the government at

Constantinople to the tiny province of Montenegro in 1799. Neighboring Serbia struck its initial blow for freedom in 1804, and received its first guarantee of autonomy in 1812. Greek independence came as a result of the long and bloody series of wars that started with the uprising in 1821; and the Danubian provinces, which were later to constitute the core of the Rumanian state, gained their first recognition of full autonomy under Russian protection in 1829. Bulgaria secured its independence in 1878 in the course of a diplomatic crisis in which all the European powers played an active role, and Albania declared its independence in 1912 under similar, if less dramatic, circumstances.

The other peoples of Eastern Europe made no comparable political gains during the nineteenth century. After a brief flurry of excitement at the time of the revolution of 1848, they settled down to a long period during which their aspirations for political and even for cultural independence were firmly restricted by the Hapsburg, Hohenzollern, and Romanov dynasties that ruled them. An exception to this pattern was formed by the Hungarians, who won a broad degree of autonomy from Vienna in 1867, and by the Croatians, who made a similar arrangement with Budapest in 1868. Under different circumstances, the Finns also succeeded toward the end of the century in implementing many of the rights that had been granted them in principle by the Russian government in 1809.

These were exceptional cases, however, and it was not until the Allied victory at the end of World War I that the minority peoples of Germany, Austria-Hungary, and Russia were able to organize independent states. In the south, the Croatians and Slovenes joined with the Serbians and Montenegrins to form the south Slav state that soon came to be known as Yugoslavia. To the east a greatly enlarged Rumania was formed by the annexation of Transylvania, Bucovina, and part of the Banat from Austria-Hungary, of southern Dobrudja from Bulgaria, and of Bessarabia from Russia. Hungary now emerged as a completely independent state, although greatly reduced in size, and the Czechs and Slovaks joined forces in the establishment of a new state that included the eastern province of Carpathian Ruthenia. The new Polish state faced the additional problem of welding into a single political unit territories that for over a century had been under German, Russian, and Austro-Hungarian rule. Finland, on the other hand, had the relatively simple task of converting an autonomous grand duchy into an independent republic without territorial changes, although the transition involved serious civil strife.

Reliance on Force.   Eastern Europe as a politically distinct region emerged clearly during the first postwar decade, and the traditions of government, which had been accumulating for over a century, gave it an integrated personality despite the very great differences of kind and of degree that existed within its limits. Of these common political traditions three deserve special emphasis. The first was the tendency to resort to violent political methods and the corresponding instability of the parliamentary system of government. None of these states gained independence except as a result of wars, and frequently wars of considerable proportions. Moreover, in Finland, Hungary, and Bulgaria, serious civil strife followed in the wake of World War I. The tradition of violence was also reflected in the frequent imprisonment and assassination of high officials in many of these countries, a tendency that was stimulated by the conspiratorial activities of Communist Russia during the 1920's and of Fascist Italy and Nazi Germany during the 1930's. Despite this tendency to rely on force the prospects of parliamentary democracy were considered to be good during the 1920's, and much was made of the benefits that the Allied victory over the Central Powers had brought to this region. The democratic aspirations of Eastern Europe were indeed genuine during this period, but in most cases experience in self-government was not adequate to meet the test of postwar adjustments. Thus the governments of Hungary (1921), Albania (1924), Poland (1926), and Yugoslavia (1929) all abandoned parliamentary methods in favor of varying degrees of authoritarianism during the first postwar decade. In Bulgaria (1934) and Rumania (1938) parliamentary institutions were also replaced by authoritarian forms under the stress of the world depression and its political repercussions. Only in Czechoslovakia and Finland did democratic government survive until World War II.

Influence of the Great Powers.   Another political tradition common to the states of Eastern Europe is their tendency to come under the guardianship of one or more of the great powers. This has been less a result of their size—for the Scandinavian and Lowland states and Switzerland have all retained a very considerable freedom from interference—than of the circumstances of their establishment. The Danubian provinces of Moldavia and Wallachia, for example, remained formally under a degree of Russian protection between 1774 and 1856. In the latter year they were placed under the joint guarantee of the European powers and they obtained recognition of their independence as the new state of Rumania only in 1878. Under somewhat different circumstances, Serbia came under the protection of Austria-Hungary between 1881 and 1903. Albania enjoyed a similar position with respect to Italy between 1927 and 1939.

In another sense, the newly established or enlarged states of Eastern Europe fell under the tutelage of the victorious Western Powers after World War I. Indicative of this status were the treaties that Poland, Yugoslavia, Czechoslovakia, and Rumania signed in 1919 with the Principal Allied and Associated Powers, in which they undertook to protect the rights of the minority peoples within their boundaries. The recognition of these new states was made contingent upon their acceptance of these obligations, and to this extent their sovereignty was limited. These obligations were placed under the guarantee of the League of Nations, however, and in practice were eventually allowed to lapse. Similar obligations with regard to their minorities were included in the peace treaty signed by Bulgaria in 1919 and in that signed by Hungary in 1920.

In a much more general sense the participation of the states of Eastern Europe in the alliance systems of the great powers may also be considered a form of tutelage. The alliances that France formed with Poland (1921), Czechoslovakia (1924), Rumania (1926), and Yugoslavia (1927), for instance, were indicative of the need of these states for additional assistance in preserving their security beyond that offered by the League of Nations. These alliances had the particular purpose of forming a "cordon sanitaire," or security zone, against possible Soviet aggression. When Soviet policy changed temporarily in the 1930's to one of "peaceful co-existence," Poland and Finland concluded nonaggression pacts with it in 1932, and Czechoslovakia signed a mutual-assistance treaty with it in 1935. As events developed further, the states of Eastern Europe that came under Axis influence formalized their position in treaties. Hungary and Rumania adhered to the Tri-partite Pact in November, 1940; and in the following March, Bulgaria and, for a brief interval, Yugoslavia likewise formally associated themselves with the Axis. When the victory of the United Nations led to a decisive strengthening of the position of the U.S.S.R., there resulted the formation of a new alliance system. The U.S.S.R. concluded mutual-assistance treaties with Czechoslovakia (December, 1943), Yugoslavia (April, 1945), and Poland (April, 1945), before the termination of hostilities with Germany, and in the spring of 1948, extended the network of alliances to Rumania, Hungary, Bulgaria, and Finland.

Predominance of Nationalism. A third tradition of government common to the states of Eastern Europe is the subordination of economic and social reform to national aims. The nineteenth-century doctrine of nationalism, as interpreted in Eastern Europe, regarded the achievement of national independence less as an end in itself than as a means of releasing the minority peoples from alien rule and, consequently, of enabling them to raise their own standard of living. As it turned out, however, the attainment and preservation of national independence required efforts of such magnitude that the economic and social goals were pushed into the background. The states of Southeastern Europe, for example, gained almost complete independence from the Ottoman Empire by 1878. They nevertheless continued to nurture internecine rivalries, which led to bitter controveries before the turn of the century and developed into almost uninterrupted warfare between 1913 and 1918. The peace treaties following World War I brought only a limited settlement of national differences to Eastern Europe. Hungary and Bulgaria, as defeated states, remained firmly unreconciled to their position, although Czechoslovakia and Poland covered a bitter rivalry over boundary issues with a transparent veil of friendly formal relations.

The efforts required to preserve national independence in Eastern Europe were almost as great as those expended in its attainment, and in both cases the cost was paid by a reduction in the standard of living. This tendency was reflected particularly in the field of domestic politics, where parties such as the Agrarians, the Socialists, and certain Liberal groups were frequently pushed aside by the militant nationalists when they proposed programs that subordinated frontier disputes to economic and social reform. It was in fact only when one or more of the great powers imposed their influence in Eastern Europe in an effort to maintain order that measures calculated to raise the standard of living tended to take precedence over the pursuit of nationalist aims.

4. NATIONALISM AND REGIONALISM

National Minorities. No sketch of the political personality of Eastern Europe would be complete without an analysis of the relationship between the divisive national objectives of the individual states and the interests common to the region as a whole. In the peace settlements following World War I the principles of national self-determination were carried out with considerable consistency. Yet it soon appeared that the national enthusiasms, which had contributed so greatly to the Allied victory, could become a profound source of disturbance if carried to the logical conclusion to which the doctrines of nationalism pointed. A glance at the situation of the minorities in Eastern Europe after World War I will convey an idea of the magnitude of the problem (Figure XXXII).

As a result of this overlapping of nationalities, numerous boundary disputes between the countries of Eastern Europe served to keep public opinion at a high pitch. Within the region, each state had disputes with all its neighbors over every boundary, with the exception of the short Rumanian-Czech and Rumanian-Polish frontiers. Of these intraregional controversies, the ones involving Hungary were the most acute, since that country never became reconciled to the territorial dispositions of the peace settlement. These disputes continued, throughout the interwar period, to be a serious obstacle to normal friendly relations among the states of Eastern Europe, and within each country, served as a constant source of inspiration to extremist nationalist groups that advocated violence and war as the only honorable solution.

Even more significant than these controversies within the region were the grievances of the minorities of the great powers bordering the region. Although the frontier issues of Albania and Bulgaria with Greece, of Yugoslavia with Italy and Austria, and of Finland with Sweden never became major international issues, the claims of Germany and the U.S.S.R. presented a different story. The large German minorities in Czechoslovakia and Poland never ceased to be a profound source of unrest, and in 1938 and 1939 they were used in connection with Hitler's expansionist aims as a pretext that was convincing to many besides the Germans themselves. Similarly, the Soviet Union, after adopting a conciliatory attitude during its years of weakness and reconstruction, made use of the sizable Ukrainian and Byelorussian minorities in eastern Poland and in the Rumanian province of Bessarabia in 1939 and 1940.

Economic Nationalism. The tendency toward extreme nationalism exhibited itself as much in the economic sphere as in the political after World War I. Desiring to strengthen the security—as they understood it—of the newly created states, the nationalist statesmen launched sharply competitive programs of protectionism, which brought their countries certain immediate benefits. It assured the peasants of high prices for their crops and freed the infant industries from the embarrassment of competition. During the prosperous years of the 1920's, this

FIG. XXXII

PRINCIPAL NATIONAL MINORITIES: EASTERN EUROPE: *
CA. 1930

COUNTRY	POPULATION	MINORITIES	
Albania (*ca.* 1930)	900,000	Greeks	50,000
Bulgaria (1926)	5,480,000	Turks	580,000
		Rumanians	70,000
		Armenians	27,000
		Greeks	10,000
Czechoslovakia (1930)	14,300,000	Germans	3,300,000
		Hungarians	700,000
		Ruthenians	550,000
		Poles	90,000
Finland (1930)	3,600,000	Swedes	396,000
		Russians	172,000
Hungary (1931)	8,949,000	Germans	478,000
		Slovaks	105,000
Poland (1931)	32,133,000	Ukrainians	4,800,000
		Byelorussians	1,500,000
		Germans	700,000
		Russians	100,000
		Lithuanians	50,000
		Czechs	30,000
Rumania (1930)	18,025,000	Hungarians	1,400,000
		Germans	720,000
		Ukrainians	500,000
		Bulgarians	360,000
Yugoslavia (1921)	12,017,000	Macedonians	600,000
		Germans	575,000
		Hungarians	468,000
		Albanians	442,000
		Rumanians	230,000
		Bulgarians	70,000

* Adapted from C. A. Macartney, *National States and National Minorities* (1934), pp. 510–34. Mohammedans, with the exception of Turks, and Jews, gypsies, and other non-national minorities, have been omitted.

pattern of economic nationalism met with considerable success, for the exports of these countries found ready markets outside the region and the guaranteed domestic price levels attracted foreign investments. When the world depression struck Eastern Europe in the early 1930's, however, the markets disappeared and the foreign capital took flight. The policies of economic nationalism now approached a doctrine of planned poverty, for the nationalists maintained that it was better to import nothing than to betray the mystic ideal of self-sufficiency. This contraction of trade reached such a point that by 1935 the total imports of the six Danubian states (Austria, Czechoslovakia, Hungary, Poland, Rumania, and Yugoslavia) were only 29 per cent of the 1928 level in value, while exports were 37 per cent of that level.[6] This relative stagnation could not be maintained indefinitely, and during the later 1930's these states fell easy prey to German economic penetration.

Regional Co-operation. Under these conditions, aggravated by political and economic nationalism, there was little incentive for any genuine regional co-operation. The major motive for political co-operation within the region that appealed to the nationalist statesmen was the protection of the victorious states against possible attempts at revenge by Hungary and Bulgaria. In this spirit the Little Entente, comprising Czechoslovakia, Yugoslavia, and Rumania, was created in 1920–21. As the years passed, the Little Entente came to play a more affirmative role in regional affairs, and its position in the councils of Europe was strengthened with the creation by its members, in 1933, of a permanent council and an economic council. The Entente, however, collapsed after the Munich crisis in 1938. In 1934 a Balkan Entente was created by Yugoslavia, Rumania, Greece, and Turkey after a series of semi-official Balkan conferences held between 1930 and 1934. The Balkan Entente was similarly motivated by a desire to guarantee the postwar frontiers, but it also made some efforts toward a larger regional co-operation before it disintegrated in 1940 under Nazi pressure. In the northern sector of Eastern Europe, negotiations were initiated in 1920 among Poland, Lithuania, Latvia, Estonia, and Finland to explore the possibilities of a Baltic federation. Lithuania soon dropped out of these discussions because of its enmity with Poland, and the final fruit of the effort was a convention for the pacific settlement of disputes concluded among the remaining four states in 1925.

[6] F. Hertz, *The Economic Problem of the Danubian States: a Study in Economic Nationalism* (1947), p. 81.

CHAPTER
31

POLITICAL PROGRAMS AND PARTIES

It is always difficult to classify political programs and parties. Consequently, the five general categories into which the national political organizations of Eastern Europe are somewhat arbitrarily divided in this chapter require numerous qualifications. In a region where personal leadership plays such an important role in politics, a classification based on political programs is bound to have many shortcomings. Moreover, in the course of time many prominent individuals and groups have migrated from one political program to another, thus defying precise identification. Despite the exceptions and reservations that must be made, however, these five categories represent the principal channels in which the political energies of Eastern Europe flowed before 1945 in the search for solutions to the complex problems that confronted countries of this region.

1. LIBERALISM

Program. The Liberals fell heir to the great national movements that culminated in the liberation of both the Balkan States in the nineteenth century and the northern countries at the end of World War I. Educated for the most part in France, and sometimes in Central Europe, the Liberal leaders were in the political tradition of European statesmanship of the early twentieth century. They favored the continental conception of parliamentary government and supported in general the political and civil liberties common to western nations. The process of liberation and unification had given them an acute sense of achievement, which led them to consider themselves the guardians of national honor and prestige. Their economic policy generally favored a degree of protectionism. The Liberals represented the small but important industrial and commercial interests and the larger landowners, although they were prepared if necessary to co-operate with the Agrarian and Socialist

753

parties. They did not take the initiative in land reform, nor did they oppose it in principle when pressure for it became sufficiently strong. As advocates of free enterprise and an active foreign trade, they were at the height of their influence during the prosperous 1920's. Few Liberal parties managed to preserve their power after the world depression, however, and only in Czechoslovakia and Finland did they successfully resist the pressures of the parties of the extreme left and right during the 1930's.

Triumphant Liberalism. Since the prestige of the Liberals was so closely associated with the national movements, they achieved their greatest successes in the states that emerged victorious after World War I. In Rumania, for instance, the National Liberal Party held power from 1922 to 1928, with a brief intermission in 1926–27, and some of its members were later associated with King Carol's regime from 1933 to 1937. The National Liberals inherited a tradition that had been influential in Rumanian politics since the middle of the nineteenth century. The smaller People's Party, the National Democratic Party, and the Young Liberals shared the general outlook of the National Liberals, although they technically remained political rivals.

In Czechoslovakia the groups supporting the program defined here as liberal were dominant at the end of World War I under the nonpartisan leadership of Thomas G. Masaryk, although in practice they shared political power throughout the interwar period with the Agrarians. In the complex pattern of Czechoslovak party politics the groups most readily indentified as liberal were the National Democratic Party, and the People's Socialist Party of Beneš. The latter party was originally associated with the Social Democrats, but it abandoned the conventional Marxist outlook before World War I. These parties played a dominant role in politics throughout the interwar period. Although the Agrarians held the premiership during the greater part of the time, the Liberals took the initiative in foreign policy and in economic matters other than agriculture. Beneš served as minister of foreign affairs from 1918 to 1935, under the presidency of Masaryk, and was himself president of the republic from 1935 to 1938.

In Poland and Yugoslavia the achievement of the political integration of these newly united territories, whose traditions were widely divergent, was the dominant issue after World War I. In both countries the Liberals held the initiative during the first postwar years, only to lose it before the end of the 1920's to authoritarian regimes. In Poland the National People's Party, a coalition group in which the National Democrats were the most important element, held power almost uninterruptedly until 1926. Its leaders served under nonpartisan premiers like the renowned musician, Ignace Paderewski, and shared political power during this period with the Christian Democratic Party and other groups.

Similarly, in Yugoslavia, the Serbian Radical Party did not long retain the undisputed prestige that it held at the end of the war. In association with the Democratic Party, the Independent Democratic Party, and the Slovene Clericals, the Radicals made a valiant effort to find a compromise with the Croats that would permit the Serbs to retain their dominant position. They failed in this undertaking, however, and the parliamentary system gave way to a royal dictatorship in 1929.

Minority Liberalism. In the remaining countries of Eastern Europe the Liberals never had the same opportunities for leadership that they enjoyed in Rumania, Czechoslovakia, Poland, and Yugoslavia. In Hungary there was no influential political party that could be classified as Liberal, although certain policies of the dominant National Union Party of Count Bethlen were akin to those pursued by Liberals in neighboring countries. Similarly in Albania there was no lasting Liberal group. In Bulgaria, on the other hand, the traditional Liberal groups such as the Democratic, Radical, and Democratic Entente parties might be included in this category. The Democratic Entente group held power during the transition period after the termination of the authoritarian regime of Tsankov in 1926, and the other Liberal parties joined in a coalition with the Agrarians between 1931 and 1934.

The National Progressive and the National Coalition parties formed the Liberal wing in Finnish politics. The Swedish People's Party, representing the interests of the Swedish minority, likewise belonged in this category. They held power intermittently in the twenties and thirties, co-operating with the Agrarians and the Social Democrats in numerous coalition cabinets.

2. SOCIALISM

Program. The Socialist parties in Eastern Europe were doctrinaire groups that struck deep roots in only a few countries, as in Finland. Their ideology was borrowed directly from the Social Democrats of Western Europe, and their leaders were mostly intellectuals with a Western education. Their membership was drawn from a relatively narrow circle of trade unionists and civil servants. The Socialists pursued a consistent policy and were frequently able to participate in coalitions by a skillful use of their parliamentary groups. They favored government control, if not ownership, of industry and public utilities, and they supported land reform. Their most fruitful efforts, however, were those directed toward the adoption of social security legislation.[1] The principal problem faced by the Socialists was the constant pressure of the Communists, who drew away important sectors of the trade-union membership by adopting a bolder program and by employing more dynamic methods. The hard core of convinced Socialists remained remarkably immune to such pressure, but many of their followers were won over once the Communists, after World War II, added blandishments and threats of political power to the arguments they had previously used.

[1] A full discussion of the ideology and political objectives of Marxian socialism will be found in Chapters 23–24 of this volume.

Socialist Politics.   The Social Democrats in Finland emerged from the trials of the civil war in 1918 without serious loss of prestige. Despite the defeat of the left-wing uprising by the White Guard, the Social Democrats became the largest party in the Finnish Diet during the interwar period, holding between fifty-three and eighty-three of the two hundred seats. The strength of the Finnish Social Democrats resided in the urban co-operative movement, in which their leader, Tanner, distinguished himself before he served as prime minister in 1926–27. The Social Democrats were members of numerous coalition cabinets during the interwar period and, with the Agrarians, played a leading political role.

In other Eastern European countries, the Social Democrats occupied a less prominent position. Weakened by the loss of the Communists who broke with them in 1919–20, as well as by the rise of the Agrarian parties, the most that the Socialists could hope for was participation as junior partners in coalition cabinets. In Poland, the several Socialist parties that existed at the end of the war exerted considerable influence during the early years of the republic. When dictatorial powers were assumed in 1926 by the former Socialist leader Pilsudski, however, the party went into permanent opposition. The Socialists in Hungary established a republic and stayed in power from November, 1918, to March, 1919, when they were overthrown by the Communists. They never completely recovered from their defeat, although they later became active again. In Czechoslovakia, Rumania, Yugoslavia, and Bulgaria, the Social Democrats played only a minor part in politics, but their leaders were generally able men who commanded wide respect as individuals.

3. AGRARIANISM

Program.   The one political trend that has been distinctive of Eastern Europe, apart from extreme and particularistic nationalism, is the growth of the Agrarian movement. The larger landed interests and certain sectors of the peasantry gave their support to other political movements, and not a few favored the various authoritarian regimes that came to power after the world depression; but in almost every country the bulk of the peasants voted for the parties advocating agrarian democracy.

The primary concern of agrarianism is to protect the interests of the small and medium peasant landholders, and to improve their economic and social position through political action.[2] In Eastern Europe, where agricultural overpopulation represents a serious problem, the challenge faced by such a movement is a powerful one. Peasant small-

---

[2] The Agrarian ideology is summarized in the "Program of the International Peasant Union," adopted in 1948, *International Peasant Union Bulletin,* 1 (January, 1950), pp. 30–34; the origins and background of agrarianism are discussed in Branko Pešelj, "Peasant Movements in Southeastern Europe" (Ph.D. dissertation, Georgetown University, 1950).

holders and landless peasants usually formed a majority of the population, but their ignorance and lack of organization left them helpless to oppose systematic exploitation by large landowners, by the urban middle class, and, more recently, by the urban proletariat. Emerging to political prominence only on the eve of World War I, the Agrarian leaders became important political figures during the interwar period in collaboration with the Liberal and Socialist parties. At the same time, their preoccupation with the problems of the peasantry brought them into sharp conflict with those authoritarian adherents who held that the welfare of peasant and city dweller alike should be sacrificed to national aims. It also provoked the Communists, who favored a vastly different approach to the problems of the peasant and whose chief rivals they became after World War II.

The doctrine of agrarianism is idealistic in a philosophical sense and is firmly rooted in the religious-cultural tradition and the family social pattern of the Eastern European peasantry. For the peasant, religion offers a sounder explanation of the forces of nature that determine his life than does the dialectic of Marx. That these religious convictions go deeper than dogma is illustrated by the fact that Agrarian leaders of the Eastern Orthodox, Roman Catholic, and Protestant faiths co-operate without serious friction. At the same time the family provides the framework for the peasant's social and economic life, since the isolated individual counts for little in an agrarian society. The structure of family organization varies considerably from one part of Eastern Europe to another, ranging in size from the Yugoslavian *zadruga* (clan or communal family) to the simple family in other countries, and forms the basic unit of agrarian production and consumption. Hence, great emphasis is placed by Agrarian doctrine on the sanctity of marriage and the home and on the equality of the sexes within the family. Living close to nature, the peasants tend to make use of biological analogies in thinking about dynamic social processes. Thus one school of Agrarian thought stresses biological materialism, or "biomaterialism," as a doctrine that emphasizes the importance of the instinct of self-preservation, considers man the supreme value of the social order, and advocates democracy and co-operative enterprise as the best means of preserving human values.[3] The Agrarian ideology provides a sharp contrast to that of communism, stressing co-operation in place of the class struggle, evolution in place of revolution, the supremacy of man in place of economic determinism, and parliamentary democracy in place of the dictatorship of the proletariat.

The economic program of agrarianism stems directly from this ideology. The Agrarians regard the traditional economic system of the peasant more as a way of life than as a form of agricultural production and favor private land tenure as the soundest means of guaranteeing the dignity of the individual. They recognize the inefficiency of peasant smallholdings as they have commonly existed in Eastern Europe and they propose to gain the advantages of large-scale agricultural produc-

[3] G. M. Dimitrov, "Agrarianism," in Feliks Gross, ed., *European Ideologies* (1948), pp. 396–452.

tion by the organization of non-compulsory co-operatives. These co-operatives would facilitate the mechanization of agriculture and the marketing of farm products and would be supplemented by government assistance in the form of price supports and other devices.

Radical Agrarianism. Agrarianism took its most extreme form among the Balkan Slavs, where the peasant organizations had been building a political structure since the end of the nineteenth century. In Bulgaria the National Agrarian Union, under the leadership of Stambolisky, became the dominant political party at the end of World War I. During Stambolisky's tenure of power, from 1919 to 1923, he introduced important changes in land tenure, passed a large body of social and educational legislation, and inaugurated a national labor service for young men to take the place of compulsory military service, which had been prohibited by the peace treaty.[4] At the same time he was responsible for the large number of new government employees brought in from the villages who used rather heavy-handed methods in implementing their ideas. This sudden accession to power gave many Agrarian leaders the impression that an era of permanent peasant rule had arrived, and, consequently, little care was taken to appease other parties. The extreme nationalists and the Macedonians exiled from their native province were particularly incensed at Stambolisky's policy of friendship with Yugoslavia at a time when the nationalist doctrine called for an attitude of studied hatred. In June, 1923, the nationalist parties united in a conspiracy to overthrow the Agrarians, and Stambolisky was assassinated. The Agrarian Union then went through a period of factionalism from which it did not recover until World War II, although a branch of the party under Gichev and Muraviev participated in a coalition government with the Liberals in 1931–34.

In Yugoslavia the Agrarian movement also took a radical turn. There the central role was played by the Croatian Peasant Party founded by Ante Radić, the leading theoretician of South Slav agrarianism, whose collected works fill nineteen volumes,[5] and led after World War I by his brother Stjepan. In addition to facing agrarian issues Stjepan Radić struggled against Serbian centralism to obtain a degree of autonomy for the province of Croatia. A temporary reconciliation was effected in 1925, but it came to an end three years later when Radić was assassinated, and there was no full reconciliation between the Serbians and the Croatians until the eve of World War II. Throughout this period the Peasant Party remained the dominant political force in Croatia, and its local co-operative organizations exercised a profound influence on peasant life. At the same time there was a smaller Serbian Agrarian Party, which was split by factional disputes and exercised relatively little influence.

---

[4] Stambolisky's principal doctrinal work is *Politicheski Partii ili Săslovni Organizatsii?* "Political Parties or Professional Organizations?" (1st ed., 1909; 2nd ed., 1920; 3rd ed., 1945); the standard biography is Nikola D. Petkov, *Aleksander Stambolisky: Lichnost i Idei* (1st ed., 1930; 2nd ed., 1946).

[5] *Sabrana Djela* (1936–38).

Moderate Agrarianism. In contrast to the peasant movement among the Balkan Slavs, which was acutely class-conscious during the interwar period, the Agrarian parties in the countries to the north adopted a more moderate attitude. In Czechoslovakia, for instance, the Czech and Slovak Agrarian parties participated in almost every cabinet between the two wars. Their leaders shared top governmental posts with the Liberals and carried through substantial land reforms and other measures. The Agrarians were able to compromise the differences that might have arisen between local Czech and Slovak interests and thus avoided the issues of federalism that had proved such a serious obstacle to the Agrarians in Yugoslavia. Moreover, Prague became a center of international Agrarian meetings and of agricultural co-operatives, and the Czechoslovak Agrarians were instrumental in European efforts to solve the agrarian crisis that resulted from the world depression.

Similarly in Finland, the Agrarian Party figured prominently in Finnish politics and government. The Agrarians and the Social Democrats together held a majority in the Diet during almost the entire interwar period. Moreover, co-operatives were well established in Finland, and this enabled the Agrarians there to move further toward their goal of peasant democracy than they did in other Eastern European countries.

The National Peasant Party of Rumania was not so successful in exerting political influence as the corresponding groups in Czechoslovakia and Finland. It was formed in 1926 by the fusion of two well-established parties, the Peasant Party and the National Party of the newly acquired province of Transylvania. Although the Rumanian Agrarians succeeded in overcoming the difficulties arising from the amalgamation of several new provinces in the enlarged Rumanian state, they refused to become reconciled to the strong position that King Carol wished to reserve for himself. As a result the National Peasant Party held power for only two brief periods, in 1929–31 and 1932–33, and during the rest of the interwar period it exerted political pressure only as an opposition party.

In Poland and Hungary the role of the Agrarians was even smaller. The Polish peasant movement was divided into a number of factions, of which the most important were the conservative Peasant Party and the more radical Liberation Party. The Peasant Party shared power in several cabinets with the nationalistic Liberal groups during the early 1920's, and again in 1926 when Pilsudski seized power. In 1931, the various Agrarian factions united as a single Peasant Party under the pressure of political events, but they remained in opposition to the government until World War II. Similarly, the Hungarian Smallholders Party could make little headway against the dominant nationalist trend. Although it occupied the Ministry of Agriculture under Count Bethlen between 1921 and 1924, it could win few concessions for the peasantry. In 1930, the peasant movement was revived as the Independent Smallholders Party, but was able to exert little pressure on the government. There was no Agrarian movement in Albania during the interwar period, but in 1949 the Balli Kombetar political movement was reorganized in exile as the Agrarian Democratic Party in association with the international peasant movement.

Agrarian Achievements. Despite the many blunders that they made as a result of inexperience and poor organization, the Agrarian parties made important contributions to the political life of Eastern Europe between the two wars. These lay chiefly in the two fields of agricultural improvement and regional co-operation.

The changes in land tenure that were effected in Eastern Europe after World War I cannot be attributed solely to the efforts of the Agrarian parties; nor were they always beneficial for the peasantry. They nevertheless represented an important step toward raising the living standards of the agricultural population, and the Agrarian parties were more responsible than any other single group for carrying out these reforms. In Finland, Czechoslovakia, Yugoslavia, and Bulgaria, an extensive redistribution of land was made. Less than 15 per cent of the peasants remained landless, and agricultural production was increased. In Rumania, where about one half of the farm land was affected by the reforms, the subdivision of the larger estates had the result of reducing agricultural production. In Poland, Hungary, and Albania, where the Agrarian movement was weak, only a beginning was made in land reform. In general, the subdivision of the larger estates was only one method, if the most spectacular, of improving the condition of the peasantry. The Agrarian movement also placed great importance on strengthening the agricultural co-operatives, on encouraging more intensive farming, and on government assistance to the peasants by such means as loans, price supports, and tariffs.

In some respects the greatest achievement of the Agrarians was the extent to which they were able to overcome the narrow-minded nationalism that dominated the thinking of their countrymen. Agrarian peoples tend to support emotional nationalism, and a number of the peasant leaders of Eastern Europe shared the nationalist spirit of the times; but as a regional movement the Agrarian parties were successful in promoting a peasant-class interest that surmounted national frontiers. The work of the International Agrarian Bureau, popularly known as the Green International, with headquarters at Prague, showed how far the Agrarian parties could go in reconciling national differences, even during the first difficult years after World War I.

The original international peasant organization, founded in 1921, included only Bulgaria, Czechoslovakia, and Poland. A larger organization came into existence in 1929, embracing eighteen national Agrarian movements, including the French, German, and Swiss, as well as those of the Eastern European countries. The course of international developments after the world depression was not conducive to the liberal and pacifist policies advocated by the International Agrarian Bureau, and it succumbed within a decade to the aggression of fascism. The international spirit of the peasant movement was not extinguished, however, for in 1942 representatives of seven Eastern European countries met in London and drew up a peasant program that reaffirmed the principles of agrarianism. After the consolidation of Communist power in Eastern Europe following World War II, this movement entered its most recent phase with the organization of the International Peasant Union in Washington, D. C., in 1947. By 1950 the union embraced eleven Agrarian parties, whose joint program it sponsored as a democratic alternative to the Communist regimes in Eastern Europe.

4. COMMUNISM

Program. The theoretical background of the Communist program is described elsewhere in this volume,[6] but certain aspects of Communist policy pertinent to the situation in Eastern Europe deserve emphasis. On the critical question of the position of the peasantry, for example, the Communists advocated a solution quite distinct from that of the Agrarians. They demanded the full nationalization of the land and the formation of collective farms under centralized government control. This was a bold position to adopt in countries where most peasants placed a high value on private tenure, and it formed a clear contrast to the program of agricultural co-operatives favored by the Agrarians.

The Communists also opposed the entire regional structure based on the peace treaties and on the framework of international relations created by the League of Nations. Instead they favored a federation of Communist regimes within which local autonomy was to be granted to dissatisfied minority peoples like the Macedonians. Although this approach ran counter to the prevailing spirit of nationalism, the Communists believed that conditions were so favorable to revolution in Eastern Europe at the end of World War I that the nationalist leaders would be swept away by popular discontent. The headquarters of the Communist International, which was founded in Moscow in 1919, therefore watched the development of communism in Eastern Europe with great concern, and after its initial failures made important changes in tactics.

Militant Communism. The first attempt by the Communists to seize power came in Finland, where they were organized as the left wing of the Social Democratic Party. They occupied the capital city of Helsinki in January, 1918, and a bloody civil war ensued, until the nationalist forces, led by General Mannerheim, finally recaptured Helsinki in May. Despite this defeat, the Communists continued to exercise a considerable influence in Finnish politics. In Hungary the Communist Party overthrew the Socialists in March, 1919, and remained in control of the government until the following August. This was the longest tenure of any Communist regime outside of the U.S.S.R. during this period, but it was doomed to failure because of the overwhelming strength of the anti-Communist governments in the countries surround-

6 See above, Chapters 23–24.

ing Hungary. It was also weakened internally by the inept methods and brutal policies of its leaders.

Only in Finland and Hungary did the Communists enjoy brief periods of political power. In Yugoslavia they called a general strike in June, 1919, but it was suppressed. In the 1920 elections, however, they exhibited their strength by winning fifty-eight of the 419 seats in the Yugoslavian National Assembly, but the party was outlawed at the end of the year and went underground. An equally unsuccessful attempt to call a general strike was made in Czechoslovakia in December, 1920. In Bulgaria, the Communists enjoyed a freer atmosphere for political activity during the relatively liberal rule of the Agrarians in 1919–23. Under the leadership of Georgi Dimitrov they organized a vigorous movement that was as much opposed to the peasant government of Stambolisky as to the nationalists. The Agrarians were overthrown in June, 1923, and the Communists stood aside in the hope of benefitting from the ensuing unrest. When they attempted to seize power in the following September, however, they were swiftly crushed by the nationalists. Another coup was attempted in April, 1925, by a group of Communists apparently acting without party authorization, but it likewise failed.

In contrast to these partially successful efforts to seize power during the period of postwar unrest, the Communists accomplished nothing substantial in Poland, Rumania, and Albania. Both Poland and Rumania had long regarded Russia as their national enemy, and no political movement with Russian connections could hope for much success in either country. In Albania, on the other hand, political conditions were still too primitive to provide fertile ground for communism.

5. AUTHORITARIANISM

Program. The term authoritarianism is used here in the dictionary sense of political movements "advocating the principle of obedience to authority as opposed to individual liberty." [7] The various regimes and movements grouped under this heading possessed none of the doctrinal consistency of other authoritarian parties, notably the Communist, but they shared the one common characteristic of favoring the use of forceful methods in times of crisis. The prevalence of authoritarianism in Eastern Europe may be attributed to certain conditions that characterized the region as a whole. One was the tradition of violence inherited from the dynastic regimes of the nineteenth century. This was particularly true of the provinces formerly under Russian and Turkish rule, where terrorist and conspiratorial organizations had played an important part in the struggle of the oppressed peoples for national liberation. Even under the relatively mild regime of the Hapsburg monarchy, experience in self-government was generally not adequate to prepare the minority

[7] *Webster's New International Dictionary of the English Language* (2nd ed., 1936).

peoples for the orderly handling of the many difficult problems that they faced after liberation.

Another condition conducive to strong-arm methods was the general political instability of the region at the end of World War I. The unification in new states of a variety of peoples and provinces, which were brought together for the first time, and the presence of violent political differences engendered by the war, created problems that were frequently too controversial to be capable of judicious settlement in parliamentary debate. Moreover, the political intrigues of Communist Russia in the east and of Fascist Italy, and later, Nazi Germany in the west stimulated the activity of many groups who felt that their countries would come under foreign rule or would dissolve into chaos if forceful methods were not applied.

Army Regimes. One of the characteristic forms of authoritarianism in Eastern Europe is that in which military leaders intervene in politics to establish order. Such interventions are generally made in a spirit of patriotism and are not necessarily accompanied by bloodshed. The character of these regimes is generally non-political, in the sense that their purpose is not that of aiding one or another of the traditional political parties, although they are generally conservative in character. The first army regime of this type in the interwar period was the Finnish White Guard movement led by General Mannerheim in 1918. Its purpose was to prevent the Red Guard, under Communist leadership and with Russian support, from establishing itself in power. After four months of bitter fighting this end was accomplished and the White Guards were dissolved. Nonetheless, in free parliamentary elections held within a year, the Social Democrats and the Communists won substantial successes.

In Bulgaria, under somewhat different circumstances, an organization known as the League of Reserve Officers joined with extremist Macedonians and other groups under the leadership of Professor Tsankov to overthrow Stambolisky's Agrarian government in June, 1923. This regime conducted a bloody purge of Agrarians and Communists, and three years later handed over power to a cabinet of Liberal politicians, who eventually restored a large measure of democratic government. Out of the Tsankov regime emerged an organization headed by certain leaders of the League of Reserve Officers. They organized the *Zveno* National Union, comprising reserve officers, businessmen, and intellectuals, who considered it their function to form a link (*zveno*) that would consolidate the traditional political parties. In May, 1934, they seized power in a bloodless coup and promptly instituted a series of reforms designed to make the administrative machinery more efficient. The republican tendencies of the *Zveno* National Union soon brought it into conflict with King Boris III, however, and within a year he ousted the military clique and instituted a personal regime.

A classic example of the army regime was that established in Poland by Marshal Pilsudski and his "colonels" in 1926. Combining the revolutionary zeal of a former Socialist and the temperament of a

MAJOR POLITICAL ORGANIZATIONS IN EASTERN EUROPE SINCE

	LIBERAL	SOCIALIST
Albania	Conservative Party (Zogu, Vrioni, Ypi), 1920–24 Democratic Party (Noli, Delvino, Kruja), 1920–21, 1924	
Bulgaria	Democratic Entente coalition (Lyapchev, Burov), 1926–31 Democratic Party (Malinov, Mushanov), 1931–34 Radical Party (Kosturkov)	Social Democratic Party (Sakazov, Pastukhov, Lulchev)
Czecho-slovakia	People's [or National] Socialist Party (Beneš, Zenkl), 1920–21, 1922–38 National Democratic Party (Kramář), 1921–38 People's Catholic Party (Šrámek)	Social Democratic Party (Tusar, Hampl), 1919–20
Finland	National Progressive Party (Cajander, Stahlberg, Ryti), 1919–23, 1927–46 National Coalition Party (Pennanen, Paasikivi), 1924–26, 1930–37, 1939–46 Swedish People's Party (Rettig, Born, Törngren), 1919–22; 1927–36, 1939–46, 1951–	Social Democratic Party (Tanner, Fagerholm, Skog), 1922–23, 1926–27, 1937–
Hungary	National Democratic [Liberal] Party (Rassay) Christian Social Party (Wolff, Zichy)	Social Democratic Party (Károlyi, Peyer, Szakasits, Kéthly), 1918–19, 1945–47
Poland	National People's Party (Glabinski, Grabski, Dmowski), 1919–26 Christian Democratic Party (Ponikowski, Korfanty)	Social Democratic Party (Daszynski, Arciszewski)
Rumania	National Liberal Party (C., I., and V. Brătiănu, Duca, Titulescu, Tătărescu), 1922–28, 1933–37, 1944–45 Young Liberal Party (G. Brătiănu) People's Party (Averescu), 1926–27 National Democratic Party (Iorga), 1931–32	Social Democratic Party (C. Dobrogeanu-Gherea, Bujor, Petrescu), 1944–45
Yugoslavia	Serbian Radical Party (Pašić, Ninčić, L. Marković), 1919–29 Democratic Party (Davidović, Grol), 1920–23 Independent Democratic Party (Pribičević, Kosanović), 1939–41 Slovene Clerical Party (Korošec, Krek) Bosnian Moslem Party (Spaho)	Social Democratic Party (Korać)

1919 (WITH PRINCIPAL LEADERS AND DATES OF TENURE OF OFFICE)

AGRARIAN	COMMUNIST	AUTHORITARIAN
Agrarian Democratic Party (Dosti)	Communist Party (Hoxha, Xoxe, Maleshova), 1944–	Republican dictatorship (Zogu, Kryeziu, Dibra), 1925–28 Royal dictatorship (King Zog, Kotta, Evangheli), 1928–39
National Agrarian Union (Stambolisky, Gichev, Muraviev, Petkov, G. M. Dimitrov), 1919–23, 1931–34, 1944–45	Workers' [Communist] Party (Blagoev, Georgi Dimitrov, Kostov, Chervenkov, Yugov), 1944–	Coalition dictatorship (Tsankov), 1923–26 Zveno National Union (Georgiev, Velchev), 1934–35 Royal dictatorship (King Boris III, Kiosseivanov, Filov), 1935–44 Internal Macedonian Revolutionary Organization (Alexandrov, Protogerov, Mihailov)
Agrarian Republican Party (Švehla, Malypetr, Hodža), 1922–38	Communist Party (Gottwald, Nosek, Slánský, Zápotocký, Siroky), 1945–	Slovak Autonomist Party (Hlinka, Tiso) Sudeten German Party (Henlein)
Agrarian Party (Kallio, Relander, Kekkonen), 1919–26, 1927–	Communist Party (O. and H. Kuusinen, Pessi, Aaltonen, Leino), 1945–48	White Guard (Mannerheim) Patriotic National [Lapua] Movement (Wallenius)
Smallholders Party (Nagyatády-Szabó) Independent Smallholders Party (Szijj, Tildy, F. Nagy, Varga, Kovács), 1945–47 Peasant Party (Witos, Mikolajczyk), 1926, 1945–47 Liberation Party (Róg, Thugutt)	Communist Party (Kun, Rákosi, Rajk, Gerő, I. Nagy, Kàdàr), 1919, 1945– Workers' Party [United Workers' Party, after 1948] (Bierut, Nowak, Gomulka), 1945—	National Union Party (Bethlen, Gömbös, Teleki, Kállay), 1920–44 Arrow Cross Party (Szálasi), 1944–45 Nonparty Union [National Unity Movement, after 1937] (Pilsudski, Smigly-Rydz, Koc, Beck), 1926–39
National Peasant Party (Maniu, Mihalache), 1929–31, 1932–33, 1944–45 Plowmen's Front (Groza)	Communist Party (A. Dobrogeanu-Gherea, Pătrăşcanu, Pauker, Gheorghiu-Dej), 1945–	Iron Guards (Codreanu, Sima) Front of National Rebirth (King Carol II, Călinescu), 1938–40 Nonparty regime (Antonescu), 1940–44
Croatian Peasant Party (A. and S. Radić, Maček, Šubašić), 1939–41 Serbian Peasant Party (J. Jovanović, Gavrilović, D. Jovanović), 1939–41	Communist Party (S. Marković, Djaković, Gorkić, Tito, Ranković), 1945–	National Party (King Alexander, Živković, Jevtić), 1929–35 Yugoslav Radical Union (Stojadinović, Cvetković), 1935–41 Croatian Ustaši Party (Pavelić)

gifted military leader, Pilsudski intervened in the national interest, as he saw it, in order to overcome the indecision of the warring politicians. With several close associates he dominated the government in coalition with leaders of the traditional parties. The appearances of parliamentary government were maintained until 1935 when, on the eve of Pilsudski's death, an authoritarian constitution was adopted in place of the relatively democratic constitution that had been drafted in 1921 and amended in 1926. It was this regime that faced the problems posed by the rise of Hitler and that fled into exile when Poland was overrun by the armies of Nazi Germany and Soviet Russia in 1939.

Royal Dictatorships. No less characteristic of Eastern European politics than the army regimes are the royal dictatorships that have been imposed from time to time in the Balkan States. These differed from the army regimes in that they represented a more orderly retreat from parliamentary government in times of trouble and generally had more popular support.

The first of these monarchical regimes, established in Hungary in 1920 under the regency of Admiral Horthy, was in many ways the least typical. Under Count Bethlen (1921–31), and later under a series of ministers who were increasingly influenced by Germany, the Hungarian regime ruled with a stern hand behind a thin veil of constitutionality. It differed from other regimes of this type, however, in that its support was more narrowly based on the larger landed interests and its political methods stemmed from the semifeudal practices of the Hapsburg dynasty in whose name the regency was theoretically maintained.

The regimes established in Albania by King Zog in 1928 and in Yugoslavia by King Alexander in 1929 were more characteristic examples of royal intervention during a period of political unrest. Zog remained in power until his country was absorbed by Italy in the spring of 1939. In Yugoslavia, Alexander made considerable progress in unifying his divided country before his assassination in October, 1934, when he was succeeded by his young son, Peter, under a regency headed by his brother, Prince Paul. Under both Alexander and Paul, the cabinets were made up predominantly of leaders of the Liberal parties.

In Bulgaria and Rumania royal intervention was provoked by the European depression and the resurgence of German power rather than by purely domestic issues. King Boris III of Bulgaria dissolved the *Zveno* regime in 1935 and established a form of personal government, which relied primarily on the efforts of nonpolitical specialists. He succeeded in maintaining a degree of stability under difficult circumstances until his death in 1943. The personal intervention of King Carol II in Rumania in 1938 came as a result of a weakening of the traditional parties in the face of the Iron Guard and other extremist groups. Carol rallied behind the new Front of National Rebirth the support of many former party leaders, and succeeded temporarily in maintaining control of his country. When combined German and Russian pressure became too strong in 1940, however, he went into exile and left his throne to his young son, Michael.

Extremist Movements.   The many extremist movements that flourished in Eastern Europe, particularly after the economic depression had undermined the position of the more moderate parties, may be divided roughly into two categories: the autonomists and the fascists.

Typical autonomist movements were the Croatian *Ustaši* (Rebels), and the Internal Macedonian Revolutionary Organization. Both movements aimed at the liberation of their provinces from Yugoslavia, and their terrorist activity reached its logical conclusion when they combined forces in October, 1934, to organize the assassination of King Alexander in Marseilles, France. They received Italian and Bulgarian support, and during World War II they enjoyed a brief period of influence under Axis patronage. Similar in spirit, though more circumspect in its methods, was the Slovak Autonomist movement. Upon the partition of Czechoslovakia in 1939 this movement sponsored, under Nazi auspices, a new Slovak state designated as a "Christian National Republic." In a like position was the Sudeten German Party, the demands of which for local rights served as the pretext for Hitler's decisive action against Czechoslovakia in 1938.

The Fascist groups deserve brief mention, for although they never had a mass following, they were at times able to exert considerable influence at critical junctures. Thus in Finland the Lapua movement, later to be known as the Patriotic National movement, was able in 1930–31 to capitalize on widespread Finnish apprehensions regarding the Communists. In Rumania the Iron Guard enjoyed a brief period of influence in the late thirties. Though its chief leaders were "shot while trying to escape" in 1938, they staged a comeback with the dismemberment of Rumania in 1940. During the Guardist uprisings in January, 1941, the Germans, needing order in the country, supported General Antonescu. In Hungary the Arrow Cross organization collaborated with the Nazis during World War II. After Admiral Horthy's unsuccessful attempt to extricate Hungary from the war against the Allies in October, 1944, the Arrow Cross Party assumed power. This regime lasted until the defeat of the Nazis in April, 1945.

32

COMMUNIST POLICIES IN EASTERN EUROPE

1. ESTABLISHMENT OF A SOVIET ORBIT

Soviet Policy. It is clear from the record that, both before and since the revolution, Russian statesmanship has been deeply concerned with the strategic importance of Eastern Europe. This territory is the buffer zone in which the Russian armies fought some of their greatest battles during the Napoleonic Wars and the two world wars. The zone has also been the scene of some of Russia's major diplomatic struggles since the days of Catherine II. At the end of World War I, as a result of its military weakness, Russia found it necessary to accept a frontier settlement in Eastern Europe less favorable than any it had known since the eighteenth century. During the interwar period the Soviet Union built up a system of treaty relations with its neighbors in Eastern Europe, but with the rise of Nazi Germany and the approach of World War II it became increasingly clear that the countries of this region were not disposed to co-operate with Russia in case of a general war.

The Soviet policy of establishing a formal sphere of influence in Eastern Europe was revealed in the negotiations during the summer of 1939, when the Russians insisted, with both the Western European states and Germany, on an extension of their influence over neighboring countries as the price of a treaty arrangement. This was a price that Germany could afford to pay more easily than the Western states, and the Nazi-Soviet pact of August, 1939, was thereupon concluded. The territorial gains that were made as a result of this arrangement are doubtless regarded by Soviet statesmen as an important factor in their successful defense against the German attack in 1941. Moreover, at the end of World War II, Soviet Russia exhibited a firm intention to assert a determining influence over all of the states of Eastern Europe from the Baltic to the Black Sea.

The difference between the type of influence exercised in this region by the Soviet Union and that which Russia exerted in the nineteenth century is that today no friendly relations with the states of this region are considered possible unless they conform to the Communist political pattern. Although the ultimate objective of establishing a sphere of interest in Eastern Europe resembles the traditional Russian policy, and in certain respects the policies of other great powers in comparable regions since World War II, it differs from them very strikingly in the means of its implementation. In the Soviet view the conversion of its neighbors to communism is a complex task that requires much skill and deliberation. The first step in this process is the seizure and consolidation of political control by the Communist Party in each country. The second is the creation of new political systems known as people's democracies, which ensure the exercise of Communist power during the period of transition to the full-fledged Soviet form of government. The substance of this transition, from the Soviet point of view, lies in the economic field, for only a state in which all the means of production are nationalized can be considered fully Sovietized and hence entirely friendly and reliable. A third aspect of the transition period is therefore the solution of the political problems involved in transferring to public ownership the industrial and agricultural resources of each country.

Soviet Political Initiative. The Soviet intention of establishing a sphere of influence in Eastern Europe after World War II was discernible during the war in its relations with the exiled governments of Czechoslovakia, Poland, and Yugoslavia. The fact that these governments in exile had their headquarters in London during the greater part of the war and that the British took considerable pains to keep the exiled statesmen under their own influence gave the Soviet Union occasion for concern.

Beneš, as head of the Czechoslovak government-in-exile, was acutely aware of the significance of his country's position as a state enjoying close ties with both Soviet Russia and the Western powers, but he had not forgotten the treatment given him by Great Britain and France in 1938. He therefore signed a twenty-year treaty of alliance with Russia in December, 1943, although he left no doubt of his determination to steer a middle course between Soviet and Western pressures.

With the other countries of Eastern Europe the Soviet Union had a more difficult time. Relations with the Polish government-in-exile, whose country the Russians had invaded in 1939, reached a crisis in the spring of 1943 when the Poles in London pressed for an impartial investigation of the "Katyn murders." The Soviet Union severed relations with the Polish government-in-exile and transferred its attentions to the Communist-controlled Union of Polish Patriots established on Russian soil. Russia maintained formal relations with the Yugoslav government-in-exile throughout the war; however, it also encouraged the National Liberation Front partisan movement, under the leadership of Tito, in occupied Yugoslavia. A similar movement in Albania also received Soviet encouragement. Bulgaria, although an Axis state, prudently refrained from declaring war on the Soviet Union, and diplomatic relations between the two countries were maintained until September,

1944. Rumania, on the other hand, participated as vigorously as it could in the Nazi invasion of Russia and for a period occupied a sizable portion of southern Ukraine, known as Transnistria, with Odessa as the seat of government.

The Baltic States were of particular concern to the Russians, both because of their accessibility to the Nazis by sea and because of their proximity to the key industrial city of Leningrad. Estonia, Latvia, and Lithuania permitted Russia to station armed forces on their territory under compulsory treaty arrangements in September and October, 1939, and were annexed by the Soviet Union in the following July. When Finland, however, refused to permit Russian troops on its territory, Russia launched a formal military attack on November 30, 1939. After a short but bitter war the Finns capitulated in March and were forced to yield certain strategic territories. Finland re-entered the war when the Germans attacked Russia in June, 1941.

Coalition Diplomacy.   The direct influence that the Soviet Union was able to exert over the governments of Eastern Europe during the war was greatly increased as a result of the course of its relations with Great Britain and the United States. In the treaty of alliance concluded with Great Britain, in May, 1942, Russia failed to obtain formal recognition of its territorial acquisitions in Eastern Europe in 1939 and 1940, that is, Estonia, Latvia, Lithuania, and parts of Finland, Poland, and Rumania. It succeeded, however, in diverting any plans of the Western Allies for an invasion of the Balkans, by insisting on the necessity for a second front in Western Europe. Moreover, as the war progressed, such tendencies as favored joint determination of policy by the Big Three gave way to a frank division of the various military zones into spheres of political influence, at least for the duration of the war. Thus, in October, 1944, Great Britain conceded to Russia a predominant influence in Rumania, Hungary, and Bulgaria, in return for a recognition of British interests in Greece and a fifty-fifty division of influence in Yugoslavia. This division was carried further in the armistice terms for Finland (September 10, 1944), Rumania (September 13, 1944), Bulgaria (October 28, 1944), and Hungary (January 20, 1945), which gave the Soviet Union almost unrestricted political and economic rights in these countries pending the signature of peace. The United States and Great Britain, on the other hand, enjoyed a similar position in Italy under the armistice terms (September 3, 1943), and British troops entered Greece at the request of the Greek government in October, 1944.

The wartime negotiations of the United Nations coalition with regard to Eastern Europe reached their final stage at the Yalta Conference of the Big Three in February, 1945. When this meeting took place, the Soviet Army was already occupying the greater part of Eastern Europe. The Western powers, on the other hand, were anticipating a transfer of their forces in the near future to the Pacific theater for the prosecution of the war against Japan and were eager for Russian participation in this effort. This disposition of forces gave the Soviet Union a marked advantage at Yalta, which was reflected in the terms of the agreements reached. As regards the difficult question of Poland, for instance, it was decided that the U.S.S.R. should annex a large portion of eastern Poland corresponding roughly to the territory that it had occupied in 1939 under the terms of the Nazi-Soviet pact. Poland was to be compensated with territories from eastern Germany. The Western powers agreed, moreover, to recognize the Communist regime that the Russians had established on Polish soil providing that representatives of the Polish government-in-exile be admitted. In the case of Yugoslavia it was agreed that Tito's Communist regime should form the nucleus of the new government, on condition that certain representatives of the non-Communist parties be included in it. In addition the Soviet Union enjoyed a preferential position in Czechoslovakia by virtue of an agreement concluded with the government-in-exile, in May, 1944, concerning the administration of territory liberated by the Soviet Army. In Albania, however, the Soviet position depended at this time entirely on the success of the Communist partisans.

In assessing the concessions made by the Western powers during the last year of the war to the Soviet position in Eastern Europe, it is important to note that they were intended to apply for a limited period only. The armistice terms, for instance, were to be superseded as soon as possible by peace treaties in which the preferential Soviet position would disappear. Moreover, the preferential position accorded to the Communists in Poland and Yugoslavia and the general position of Soviet influence in the other countries were counterbalanced by the statement of policy agreed upon at Yalta known as the Declaration of Liberated Europe. In this document the three great powers agreed to assist the new governments of Eastern Europe, among others, "to form interim governmental authorities broadly representative of all democratic elements in the population and pledged to the earliest possible establishment through free elections of governments responsible to the will of the people."

When World War II ended, the Soviet government thus found itself in a temporary position of great influence in Eastern Europe that had the recognition of the Western powers. At the same time the Soviet Union was committed to hold free elections in this region at the earliest possible time. It was under these conditions that Soviet policy embarked on the task of changing its position of temporary and conditional influence in Eastern Europe into a permanent political system.

2. UNITED FRONT AND PEOPLE'S FRONT

The Technique. In dealing with the countries of Eastern Europe, which Soviet armies overran in 1944–45, the Soviet statesmen possessed a subtle and tested technique. This was the co-ordinated use of the two methods of political collaboration and infiltration known as the united front and the people's front.

The united front was first adopted at the Third Congress of the

Communist International in 1921 and consisted of promoting co-operation between the Communist Party and other workers' parties, in particular the Social Democratic Party. Originally the united front was designed to win the rank and file of Socialists away from their party leaders and was therefore known in Communist terminology as the united front "from below." This technique met with little success in the 1920's, but it was revived in the 1930's when the rise of Hitlerism in Germany and of authoritarian movements elsewhere produced a split in the non-Communist ranks. In its new form, discussed and adopted at the Seventh Congress of the Communist International in 1935, the united front represented a policy of promoting formal political coalitions for electoral and propaganda purposes between the Communist and Socialist parties. Unlike the earlier united-front efforts, the new version was aimed at winning the collaboration of Socialist Party leaders and was therefore designated as the united front "from above."

At the same time the Comintern went a step further to authorize the broader type of political coalition known as the people's front. Unlike the united front, in which participation was limited to working-class parties, the people's front was intended to embrace political parties representing the interests of the peasants, the lower middle class, and the intellectuals. Georgi Dimitrov, secretary general of the Comintern at the time of its Seventh Congress, went to some lengths to point out the relationship of these two tactical maneuvers—the united front and the people's front—to the complex situation facing the Communist parties in Europe in the mid-thirties. In the countries of Western Europe where the Social Democratic parties occupied a strong position, Dimitrov explained, united fronts would have to be established first. Only when full co-operation with the Socialists had been achieved would the broader coalition stand any chance of success. In Eastern Europe, on the other hand, the key to the situation lay not with the workers but with the peasants. In these countries, as Dimitrov saw it, the Communists should start with a people's front embracing the Agrarian parties as well as the political organizations of the workers and the lower middle class. Only when the Communists had established this people's front were they to organize the narrower united front of Communists and Socialists, which would ultimately form the nucleus for the proletarian dictatorship.

That the purpose of both fronts was to bring the Communists to power was made about as clear as could have been expected under the circumstances. The final resolution on this subject, adopted by the Seventh Congress of the Communist International on August 20, 1935, stated explicitly: "The establishment of the united front of the working class is the decisive link in the preparation of the working people for the forthcoming great battles of the second round of proletarian revolutions." [1] What was not so explicitly stated was the precise

---

[1] See *VII Congress of the Communist International: Abridged Stenographic Report of Proceedings* (1939), pp. 570–86 for the Comintern resolution of August 20, 1935; for Dimitrov's two speeches explaining the "front" technique, see ibid., pp. 124–93, 356–85.

means by which the people's fronts and the united fronts would be turned to Communist ends. This technique was not fully revealed until the "second round" of revolutions was inaugurated in Eastern Europe in 1944.

The establishment of people's fronts in Eastern Europe at the end of World War II would not have been possible without the presence of the Soviet Army until 1947 and the conditional, but nevertheless effective, recognition given by the Western powers to the existence of a special Soviet orbit. The Soviet aim in the international field was to pacify the apprehensions of the Western powers and to win acceptance and recognition of Soviet-sponsored regimes on the part of the outside world. In the domestic field the objective of the people's fronts was to divide the opponents of Communist rule, giving a preferred position to Agrarian, Liberal, and Socialists groups while Communist power was being organized, and then liquidating their leaders one by one as occasion permitted. In some countries the Communists were able to adopt a dynamic approach, seizing the instruments of power almost immediately and eliminating or neutralizing all opposition elements in less than two years. In other countries serious obstacles were faced and a more cautious approach was adopted. How this control was consolidated can best be seen by reviewing the developments in the individual countries.

The Dynamic Approach. In four of the countries of Eastern Europe—Yugoslavia, Albania, Bulgaria, and Poland—the Communists were able to proceed with considerable dispatch. In Yugoslavia the Communist partisans under Tito outmaneuvered the royalist guerrillas of Mihailović in both a political and a military sense. By the summer of 1944, Tito had gained sufficient bargaining power to force King Peter in London to abandon his support of Mihailović and to consent to delay his return to Yugoslavia until a plebiscite had been held. As a price for these concessions, Tito agreed to form a coalition regime with members of the government-in-exile headed by Prime Minister Šubašić, a member of the Croatian Peasant Party. At Yalta the Big Three approved of this compromise and urged that it be implemented. This was accomplished on March 7, 1945, when the people's front regime in Yugoslavia, which was known as the National Liberation Front, established a provisional government. It was headed by Tito and included leading members of the Communist hierarchy, as well as representatives of the government-in-exile headed by Šubašić, who served as foreign minister. It was this cabinet that held office at the end of the war and that prepared the elections of November, 1945.

In Albania, first under Italian and later under German occupation, the Communist-dominated National Liberation Front, similarly succeeded in outmaneuvering the nationalist forces. Since there was no Albanian government-in-exile, the exiled King Zog and his followers not being recognized by either group of belligerents, the Communists faced a relatively simple task. When the Germans were forced to withdraw on November 29, 1944, as a result of military events to the north, they simply proclaimed their National Liberation Front (renamed the

Democratic Front in 1945), which included a few non-Communist members, as the government of Albania. Within a year they had consolidated their power and were ready to hold national elections.

As in Yugoslavia and Albania, the Communists in Bulgaria sponsored a people's front movement during the war and formed the Fatherland Front with Agrarian, Socialist, and Liberal leaders. When the Soviet Army approached, however, an independent group of Liberals and Agrarians formed a government on September 2, 1944, that attempted to negotiate an armistice with the Western powers before breaking off relations with the Germans. This obstacle was eliminated when the Russians, who had been at peace with Bulgaria until this time, declared war on the new government three days after its formation. The Fatherland Front leaders seized power on September 9 and negotiated for armistice terms under Soviet auspices. The new people's front regime in Bulgaria was more truly a coalition than those in Yugoslavia and Albania, and was headed by Georgiev, veteran of several authoritarian regimes and leader of the *Zveno* National Union. It also included a strong delegation of Agrarian ministers, headed by Petkov, and of Socialists and independent Liberals. The Communists had only two important ministries, Interior and Justice, but they exerted a determining influence from the start and within fourteen months had eliminated all rivals.

In the case of Poland a long process of negotiations was required to repair the breach between the U.S.S.R. and the Polish government-in-exile; this delay favored the Soviet Union since its army advanced steadily across Polish territory during the winter of 1944–45. In July, 1944, the Soviet government recognized the Communist-controlled Union of Polish Patriots as a formal Committee for National Liberation. This committee proclaimed itself the provisional government of Poland in the city of Lublin at the end of December, 1944. Most members of the Polish government-in-exile were unwilling to cede the eastern territories, which the Soviet government demanded as a price for its friendship, but the Big Three at Yalta nevertheless urged that it reach a compromise with the Soviet-sponsored provisional government. After prolonged negotiations a small group of exiled statesmen agreed to return to Poland, and on June 28, 1945, the creation of a new Provisional Government of National Unity was announced in Warsaw. Of its twenty-one members two thirds belonged to the Communist regime and held all the key positions. The remaining one third were led by Mikolajczyk, head of the Peasant Party.

The Cautious Approach.   Unable to seize such a vigorous initiative in Rumania, Hungary, Czechoslovakia, and Finland, the Communists had to content themselves for the time being with a less advantageous position in the people's front regimes. In Soviet-occupied Rumania and Hungary the weakness of the Communists was due to their lack of membership and organization, handicaps that they overcame as rapidly as possible once peace was established. In the Rumanian Government of National Unity, established in August, 1944, the National Peasant and Liberal parties played the predominant role. The Communists were unable to exercise greater influence until March, 1945, when the new National Democratic Front government was established under the pliable Groza. The Peasant and Liberal leaders were excluded from this regime after the first few months, and the key posts were held by prominent Communists. The party's position was still insecure, however, and its real leaders remained temporarily in the background.

Similarly in Hungary, the National Independence Front coalition, formed in December, 1944, was headed by the Independent Small-holders Party, and only two years later did the Communists gain a decisive lead. In Czechoslovakia the Communists occupied influential positions in the new government established after the return of Beneš in April, 1945. Both at home and abroad, however, the leadership of Beneš commanded decisive support, and it was three years before the Communists were able to seize power. Likewise in Finland, the Communists played a secondary role in the people's front regime established in November, 1944. The Agrarians and the Social Democrats controlled Finnish politics and neutralized most efforts to extend Communist influence.

3. CONFIRMATION OF COMMUNIST CONTROL

Liquidation of the Opposition. Once the people's front governments were established, the Communists worked steadily to reach a position of absolute power. Their strategy was to seize control of the police and the army, so that their position would be secure when Soviet occupation forces withdrew. They reduced the strength of their rivals by political pressure and by coercion. Many political leaders in Eastern Europe were convinced that there was no choice but to recognize the overwhelming strength of the Soviet Union and to collaborate with its agents. Thus certain well-known Liberals, Socialists, Agrarians, and independents with a predilection for authoritarianism became close collaborators with the Communists and contributed a great deal to their ultimate victory. In such cases, offers of political benefits were combined with direct or implicit threats to obtain obedience.

Where political pressure was not effective, force was used. Army officers, police officials, and political leaders who refused to co-operate with the Communists were eliminated. Occasionally they were formally tried as collaborators with Germany, in some instances on good evidence, but the majority were summarily executed. Once the Communists had the instruments of force under firm control, they proceeded to take action against their major political opponents. Almost always these were the Agrarian leaders, for their parties in general had the largest following. Agrarian leaders had been almost unanimously opposed to the Axis, unlike many adherents of the Liberal and authoritarian groups; and few were attracted to communism, unlike the Socialists who were relatively easy prey for Communist persuasion. As parties with mass membership but relatively poor discipline, the Agrarians had everything to gain from the exercise of civil liberties and free elections. As advocates of private ownership of the land the Agrarians had the support of the peasants against the collectivist aims of the Communists. The Agrarians were the principal group against which political pressure had little effect, and so they were attacked by brute force.

In Bulgaria the secretary-general of the Agrarian Union, G. M. Dimitrov,[2] was forced to resign his post as early as January, 1945, and went into exile eight months later. His colleague, Petkov, continued to defy the government and was finally arrested, tried for treason, and executed on September 23, 1947. Šubašić resigned from Tito's government in October, 1945, and Dragoljub Jovanović, a Serbian Agrarian who had long supported Tito, was tried and sentenced to nine years of hard labor on October 8, 1947. Kovács, secretary-general of the Independent Smallholders Party in Hungary, was arrested in Budapest by the Soviet police in February, 1947, and his colleagues Nagy, the prime minister, and Varga, president of the National Assembly, were forced into exile in the following June. In Rumania, Maniu and Mihalache were tried for treason and sentenced to life imprisonment on November 11, 1947. Finally, increasing personal threats forced Mikolajczyk to flee from Poland in October, 1947. Similar methods were used against the Social Democrats and the other participants in the people's fronts. As a final confirmation of Communist control, once power was securely in their hands, elections were held and new constitutions were drafted to legitimize the new regimes. By now the people's fronts had served their main purpose, but they were continued in name as part of the trappings of the transition period to full socialization.

FIG. XXXIV

PLEBISCITE ELECTIONS: EASTERN EUROPE

	DECISIVE COMMUNIST-CONTROLLED ELECTIONS	PEOPLE'S FRONT MAJORITY (PER CENT)
Yugoslavia	Nov. 11, 1945	89
Albania	Dec. 2, 1945	93
Bulgaria	Oct. 27, 1946	78
Rumania	Nov. 19, 1946	80
Poland	Jan. 19, 1947	90
Hungary	Aug. 31, 1947	60
Czechoslovakia	May 30, 1948	89

Czechoslovakia, Finland, and East Germany form an exception to the general pattern: the first because the Communists had to resort to

[2] It is always necessary to distinguish between the Bulgarian Agrarian leader, Georgi Mihov Dimitrov, popularly known by his initials "G.M.," and the veteran Communist leader Georgi Mihailov Dimitrov, of Leipzig Trial and Comintern fame, who died on July 2, 1949.

an open threat of force, the second because of the stubborn and success-ful resistance offered by the Finns to Communist pressure, and the third because it was only a fragment of a larger state and continued to be treated as an occupied territory. Figure XXXIV, page 776 lists the plebi-scite elections (generally not the first after World War II) by which the Communists confirmed their control of the Eastern European countries that became "people's democracies."

Czechoslovakia. The Communist seizure of power in Czecho-slovakia during February, 1948, deserves special consideration because of the methods that they found it necessary to use to defeat their opponents. The strong position gained by the Communists in the Czechoslovak elec-tions of May 26, 1946, when they won almost 38 per cent of the votes, declined markedly during 1947. Non-Communist leaders became in-creasingly aware of the nature of Soviet control, particularly after the pressure exerted on Czechoslovakia to reject the Marshall Plan, and there was good reason to believe that the Communists would lose heavily in the elections scheduled for 1948. In view of the increasing international tension an electoral setback in Czechoslovakia, which might be followed by a loss of their cabinet positions, would have been a severe blow to Communist prestige. They therefore made plans to seize power before the elections.

The strongholds of Communist power in Czechoslovakia were the ministries of Interior and Information, which controlled the police and radio facilities, and the "action committees" in government offices, business concerns, and labor organizations. These committees were composed of Communists, armed and trained to take over the organiza-tions to which they were attached. With these preparations the Com-munists proceeded to challenge the government by extending the con-trol of their party over the Prague police force against the orders of the cabinet. Unable to accept this affront, twelve ministers belonging to Liberal parties submitted their resignations on February 20, 1948. In the middle of this cabinet crisis President Beneš was confronted with large-scale demonstrations by armed members of action committees who had been brought to Prague to incite unrest. At the same time strikes developed in key industries and the state radio spread Communist propaganda. The non-Communist parties could offer no opposition to this show of force, and Beneš found himself constrained on February 25 to accept a Communist-controlled cabinet. Two weeks later Jan Masaryk died under tragic circumstances, and on September 3, Beneš himself passed away. In the meantime the Communists held elections on May 30, 1948, in which they won a majority of 89 per cent, and on June 9 they promulgated a new constitution.

Finland. In view of events elsewhere in Eastern Europe it is re-markable that Finland should have been able to maintain its freedom from Soviet control. There appear to be two reasons for this success. One is that Finland is not located in an area of primary strategic im-portance and in fact is flanked by the traditionally neutral Scandinavian states. Russian security is thus normally assured in this area, but the use of force in Finland might well provoke countermeasures from Norway or Sweden, which would ultimately weaken Russia's position. The other is the fact that the Finns and the Russians entertain no illusions regarding each other. The U.S.S.R. recognizes the Finns to be aware of Soviet designs and therefore treats them with a certain respect.

Under these conditions the Communists exerted only a modest influence on Finnish affairs. They won 25 per cent of the seats in the Diet elections of March, 1945, after joining with other left-wing elements to form a Democratic Union, which for three years participated in a coalition cabinet with the Social Democrats and the Agrarians. In the elections of July, 1948, the Democratic Union won only 19 per cent of the popular vote and was excluded from the Social Democrat cabinet. In the spring of 1948 the Communists engaged in a lengthy controversy with the government over their control of the Finnish Ministry of Interior, but the crisis passed without resort to force. A more critical test of strength came in August and September, 1949, when the Communists led strikes involving almost one half of Finland's organized labor. The ostensible purpose of these strikes was to force the government to share its power with the Communists, but Prime Minister Fagerholm stood his ground, and again the crisis passed.

While the electoral strength of the Communist-led Democratic Union has remained relatively stable, as reflected in the election of March, 1953, the position of the democratic parties has not again been seriously threatened. In accord with its new policy of co-existence the Soviet government agreed in September, 1955 to return its military base at Porkkala, and the return was effected the following January. Arrangements were also made to renew the Soviet-Finnish mutual defense treaty of 1948. Within the U.S.S.R. the Karelo-Finnish S.S.R., bordering on Finland, was demoted in July, 1956 to an autonomous republic of the Russian S.F.S.R. When the Karelo-Finnish S.S.R. was established in 1940, including territories recently annexed from Finland, it was generally regarded as a nucleus designed to serve as the basis for an eventual annexation of the whole of Finland to the U.S.S.R. Its change of status in 1956 may therefore be interpreted as a gesture of reconciliation.

East Germany. The Soviet zone of Germany became Communist as a result of military occupation, but unlike the rest of Eastern Europe it has continued to be occupied as enemy territory under the provisions of the inter-Allied agreements. Throughout the postwar period Soviet policies in this territory were based on its status as a fragment of Germany, and consequently were subordinated to the over-all requirements of Soviet policy on the German question. In this sense East Germany has had a different development in many respects from that of the people's democracies, and it is still formally occupied by some twenty Soviet divisions. Only in a superficial sense is it a people's democracy. It has a Communist Party, headed by a veteran Stalinist, Walter Ulbricht, which has a monopoly of such power as is left to it by the occupying authorities. It also has a centrally planned economy, and most of the constitutional and administrative trappings of a people's democracy.

The status of East Germany developed gradually as a result of the competition of the Soviet Union and the three Western powers, in their respective zones, for the control of a Germany that must ultimately be united. In the Soviet zone a German Democratic Republic was established in October, 1949, and the familiar policies of a Communist system were implemented. By 1953, industry had been largely socialized, and production was more than double the prewar level. After the Soviet authorities had drawn very substantial reparations from their zone, they greatly stimulated its industrial growth by assigning it the task of supplying the Soviet market with many specialized commodities. Also, many German technicians were offered positions in Soviet industry. Agricultural production did not follow the same upward trend, however, and has failed to attain the prewar level. By 1954 some 18 per cent of the agricultural land was socialized in collectives or in state farms.

The social pressures of this characteristically unbalanced economic development soon made themselves felt. The most spectacular sign of the growing unrest was a violent riot of workers in East Berlin in June, 1953, which was put down by Soviet troops. Efforts were now made to meet the crisis by reducing the rate of industrialization, but East Germany remained an area of low living standards in comparison with West Germany. Many thousands of Germans fled to the freer and vastly more prosperous Federal Republic, even though in Eastern Germany, as in the rest of Eastern Europe, there was some improvement in living standards after 1953. Khrushchev and Mikoyan spent a full week touring East Germany in August, 1957, and the marked lack of popular enthusiasm that greeted them everywhere confirmed the impression that Communist rule rests on Soviet arms alone.

4. PROBLEMS OF COMMUNIST CONTROL

Instrumentalities of Soviet Influence. The Russian armies that overran all the countries of Eastern Europe except Albania and Yugoslavia were the anvil on which the local Communists hammered out their people's-front regimes. The armies as such interfered relatively little in the administration of the occupied countries, except in Poland, but their presence neutralized the activity of local military organizations and other instruments of force that might otherwise have prevented the Communists from seizing power.

The political instrumentalities of Soviet influence are less apparent than the army, but hardly less effective. Important among these are the Communist parties in each country. The majority of their leaders had lived in Russia, some for many years, and with a few notable exceptions they could be trusted to understand and implement the broad lines of policy issuing from Moscow. A great many of them participated in the Spanish Civil War and were accustomed to disciplined international team work. Equally important are the representatives of the Communist Party of the Soviet Union in each country, along with agents of the Soviet Ministry of State Security. These keep a sharp eye on local developments, and occasionally intervene directly to make arrests or to supervise special operations. The regular Soviet diplomatic representatives, generally men of some distinction, handle the official business between the U.S.S.R. and the states of Eastern Europe, without normally intervening in domestic politics.

A more generalized form of control is exerted by the Soviet Union through its alliance system. To the mutual assistance treaties concluded during the war with Czechoslovakia (December, 1943), Yugoslavia (April, 1945), and Poland (April, 1945) were added in the spring of 1948 a new series of treaties with the remaining states of the region. These bilateral treaties between the U.S.S.R. and these countries pledge them to assist each other in case of aggression by Germany or "a third power," and are supplemented by a dozen or more bilateral agreements between the various people's democracies. This series of treaties was further strengthened by the conclusion of the Warsaw Pact in May, 1955. This pact created a unified command of the satellite armies under Soviet Marshal Konev.

Considerable influence for a period was also exerted by the Communist Information Bureau, commonly known as the Cominform, established on October 5, 1947. Unlike the Communist International (Comintern), which was disbanded on May 15, 1943, the Cominform did not ostensibly exercise a centralized control over the activities of the Communist parties of the member states. Instead it co-ordinated and publicized the work of the national parties, with a view to giving them an influence and sense of cohesion they would not otherwise have. It was not a successful venture, however, and its influence declined rapidly after the expulsion of Yugoslavia. Its dissolution was finally announced on April 13, 1956.

In the economic sphere a basic instrument of Soviet influence during the first postwar years was the collection of reparations from Rumania and Hungary, as well as from the Soviet zone in Germany and from Finland. An instrument of economic control of wider application was the establishment of binational joint stock companies in which the Soviet government invested German assets acquired under the peace settlement as its share. Through their control of these jointly owned companies, chiefly in the field of raw materials and transportation, the Russians obtained an important share in the business of these countries. These measures gave Russia a considerable profit, though one difficult to calculate, but they do not seem to have been based on an over-all plan. Similarly Soviet trade in Eastern Europe, which greatly exceeded that of the prewar period, was initially conducted on a rather haphazard basis. Plans for the economic integration of the region were finally announced on January 25, 1949, when the Council of Economic Mutual Assistance was established to include Bulgaria, Czechoslovakia, Hungary, Poland, and Rumania, as well as the U.S.S.R. This was the Soviet answer to the Marshall Plan, but it is difficult to judge whether as a formal council it bore any resemblance to the Organization for European Economic Co-operation. Whatever the formal instrumentalities, after 1949 the economies of the people's democracies were closely co-ordinated with the fifth Five-Year Plan (1950–55). The U.S.S.R. now gained a much more firm and systematic hold over the economies in its orbit, although the policies it pursued resulted before long in serious crises.

That Yugoslavia did not succumb was due in part to Tito's firm control over his party and country, and in part to the support he received from the West. The United States alone provided over half a billion dollars' worth of economic aid and almost double this amount in military aid. From Western Europe Tito received, not only a degree of economic assistance, but also considerable interest and sympathy for the alternative to Soviet methods that he evolved after 1950. This alternative, known as Titoism, soon gained prestige as a distinctive form of Communism. In domestic affairs Titoism means decentralization in the administrative and economic sphere. The administration of the country through local bodies, rather than by direct order from Belgrade, serves to adjust policies to local conditions and stimulates more ready compliance. Similarly, the system of economic planning was modified to take into consideration the requirements of supply and demand as reflected by the market. Forcible collectivization was terminated in 1950, and the number of collective farms was reduced from six thousand to eight hundred. Foreign observers question how much decentralization has actually taken place in Yugoslavia, but recognize that as a theory Titoism has been attractive to many Communist leaders in the other people's democracies. At the very least Titoism means to them the adaptation of Communism to the needs and circumstances of each individual country, and freedom from direct influence by Soviet officials on behalf of Soviet interests. In foreign affairs Titoism favors the neutralism of India, Burma, and Egypt, and refuses to make binding political alliances. Yugoslavia signed a pact of friendship and co-operation with Greece and Turkey in February, 1953, and followed this up in August, 1954 with a treaty of alliance and neutral aid; this agreement served temporarily to counterbalance the pressures of its Stalinist neighbors, but it did not involve Yugoslav participation in the NATO coalition. Titoism remains solidly founded on Marxism-Leninism and shares with it the beliefs in the inevitable trend of all peoples toward Communism. Where it differs from Stalinism is in methods rather than in ultimate goals.

The New Course. The strains resulting from the rapid and unbalanced pace of industrialization in the people's democracies finally forced a marked change in policy, which took effect shortly after Stalin's death in March, 1953. As the economic crisis had been apparent for some time, it seems likely that the Soviet government was unable to meet it until after the passing of the dictator. The heart of the crisis lay in the growing imbalance between industrial and agricultural production. Within industry there was a corresponding imbalance between producer and consumer goods. The countries of Eastern Europe had restored their economies by 1948, and in the next four years they embarked on an impetuous program of building up heavy industry. This program was essentially a reproduction of the Soviet pattern of the early Five-Year Plans, but it was stimulated further by a sharp increase in military expenditures after 1950. While statistics for this period tend to be inflated, it seems clear that by 1954 industrial production was well over double that of the prewar period. More significant from the political point of view, however, was the fact that the rate of increase in the production of producer goods was much more rapid than that of consumer goods. Indeed, during the period of rapid industrialization real wages remained static or declined somewhat. At the same time, while industrial production was more than doubling, the per-capita agricultural output increased by no more than 5 per cent.

This unbalanced economic development led to social and economic strains on the population that could not be ignored. The "new course" was formally inaugurated by Malenkov on August 8, 1953, although it was announced as early as July 4 in Hungary. The urgency of the crisis had already been emphasized in June by the extensive riots in East Germany and in Czechoslovakia, which had to be suppressed by force of arms. The purge of Beria in July, followed by his execution in the following December, drew attention to the uncertainty of the Soviet domestic situation. The widespread police network in Eastern Europe that Beria headed was now seriously demoralized, and before long signs of open divisions on policy appeared within the Communist parties of Hungary and Poland.

A series of economic measures calculated to meet this crisis was now put into effect. The rate of industrial expansion was decelerated, and the marked emphasis on producer goods was reduced. The average annual increase in industrial production in these countries declined from almost 25 per cent in the period 1949–52 to 7 per cent for 1954. This reduction in the rate of increase was particularly marked in Hungary. The pressure for agricultural collectivization was likewise reduced after 1953, but food production continued to fall well below the targets set by the planners. The government still persisted in refusing to offer adequate stimuli to agriculture through investment or the incentive of consumer goods, and after the fall of Beria it appeared to lack the brute police power to coerce agricultural deliveries at gun point.

The implementation of the "new course" was not uniform in the various people's democracies. In Czechoslovakia it was carried out gradually after the purge of Slansky in 1952. Owing to the more advanced stage of Czech industrialization, it was possible to make a relatively smooth transition to consumer goods and the standard of living of the workers was raised sufficiently to prevent violent outbreaks after 1953. In Hungary this policy was implemented in a much more extreme form by Nagy, who replaced Rákosi as prime minister in July, 1953 and held office until April, 1955. Drastic measures were taken to increase consumer production and to decollectivize agriculture, but only chaos resulted. There was no substantial improvement in the standard of living, and the extravagant resort to political and economic expediencies demoralized a Communist Party that was already weak. In Poland the new policy was applied in a very much more guarded fashion by Bierut, a veteran Stalinist, until his death in March, 1956. Not until after the "new course" had officially been superseded by more drastic policies did the anti-Stalinists win decisive influence among the Polish Communists. In Albania, Bulgaria, and Rumania the Stalinists remained in control throughout this period and made only modest efforts to alleviate economic pressures. In Yugoslavia, Tito pursued independently policies that somewhat resembled those of the "new course." Particularly in the field of consumer-goods production steps were taken after 1953 to restore a balance within the Yugoslav economy.

Different Roads to Socialism. By the end of the period of the "new course" it was clear that a considerable degree of initiative had passed from Soviet hands to those of the local Communist leaders, although no substantial improvement had been made in living conditions except in Czechoslovakia. The "new course," in so far as it had been implemented at all, had been in charge of Stalinists who still looked to Moscow for guidance. The gradual relaxation of Soviet political control, which was in no sense a part of the "new course," was the result of extraneous factors: the purge of Beria, the increasing discontent of native Communists, and the development of a struggle between Stalinists and anti-Stalinists within the Communist Party of the Soviet Union somewhat similar to that taking place in the people's democracies. Two alternatives now confronted the Soviet regime: it could either return to Stalinism, attempting once more the rapid development of heavy industry under a police-enforced policy that ignored popular discontent; or it could seek new policies that would leave local Communists sufficient initiative to take local problems and conditions into consideration. The first policy seemed to involve higher costs than the Kremlin was willing to pay. It would have to rely on sheer force, thus sacrificing the image of reasonable stability that the Kremlin wished to create for its orbit in the outside world. It also held out no hope of an end to the economic consequences of the old policy, which had resulted in such strains and popular discontent. Yet it appears that such a policy had strong support within the Kremlin from Molotov, Malenkov, Kaganovich, and Voroshilov. Indeed, it was not until the influence of Khrushchev and Bulganin came to the fore, the former continuing in the position of secretary of the party, which he had assumed in March, 1953, and the latter replacing Malenkov as prime minister in February, 1955, that the second, more lenient and experimental policy was put into effect.

The new policy was not long in making itself felt. In May, 1955, Khrushchev and Bulganin visited Tito and apologized at length for the expulsion of Yugoslavia from the Cominform. Tito returned the visit in June, 1956, and a policy statement was published in Moscow which asserted that "the roads of socialist development are different in different states." This statement summarized the shift in policy sponsored by

Khrushchev and Bulganin. In the meantime the new policy was formally announced at the Twentieth Congress of the Communist Party in February, 1956. The people's democracies did not have to follow identical economic policies, it was implied, as long as they associated themselves with the U.S.S.R. in the cold war. At the same time Moscow announced a program of aid and loans to Yugoslavia. This major concession by Moscow marked no substantial change in Yugoslavia's international position, but it promptly provoked widespread ferment within the Communist parties of Poland and Hungary.

In Poland the moderate, national wing of the party gradually gained the ascendancy. Extensive riots in Poznan in June, 1956, were the signal that the Polish workers could no longer tolerate their conditions of life. Even more striking was the relative moderation of the Poznan trials, in contrast to the earlier Stalinist ruthlessness. The two surviving Polish Stalinist leaders, Berman and Minc, were ousted from power and finally Gomulka was brought back in October as prime minister. At the same time Marshal Rokossovsky, Soviet commander of the Polish Army since 1949 and a member of the Politburo of the Polish Communist Party, was forced to resign. In a series of hasty meetings with Gomulka, Khrushchev was confronted by the necessity of making concessions or facing a full-fledged collapse of Communist influence in Poland. The difficulty of the Soviet decision, and of the task facing Gomulka, was that a great majority of the Poles were anti-Communist, and a majority of the Polish Communists were disillusioned with the outcome of their own policies in the postwar decade. For both Khrushchev and Gomulka the alternatives to a policy of moderate and national communism were bloody civil strife or a public recognition of Communist failure. Neither leader was willing to face these alternatives, and the Soviet government made the very extensive concessions necessary to keep Gomulka in power. The latter, in turn, headed a demoralized Communist Party and a country that had little faith in communism. To win the national elections in January, 1957, Gomulka had to remind the voters in substance that if he were not kept in power the alternative would be a reassertion of Soviet authority by Stalinist methods.

The implications of Gomulka's warning had been made clear to the Polish voters by the course of the revolution in Hungary. Here, as in Poland, hasty steps had been taken in the preceding summer to loosen Soviet controls, and on July 18 Rákosi, the leading Stalinist, was dropped from his post as first secretary of the party. The success of Gomulka stimulated the Hungarians to bolder measures. In the midst of public demonstrations in Budapest in favor of the developments in Poland, Nagy returned to office as prime minister on October 24, and on the following day Kádár replaced Gerö as first secretary of the Communist Party. From this point on, however, events took a different course in Hungary from that in Poland. Unlike Gomulka, Nagy was unable to retain control over the Communist Party, and the latter completely lost its influence in the country. A general revolt against Russia and communism took place, in which Hungarian workers, students, and soldiers played the leading role. Within a week the Russians were confronted by a different choice from that which they faced in Poland. An experiment with moderate, national communism was no longer possible in Hungary because the Communist Party did not have the authority to carry out such a policy. The Russians could either abandon Hungary to independence or restore a ruthless regime by force of arms. They chose the latter course, and on November 4, after feigning withdrawal, they reoccupied Budapest with an army of tanks after a bloody battle. Kádár was now made head of the government, but he could rule in his ruined capital only with the full support of the Soviet Army and police.

These events put the severest possible strain on Khrushchev's policy of "different roads to socialism" and it appears that in the winter of 1956–57 he had great difficulty in defending his policies in the Central Committee. It was not until July, 1957 that the opposition of Malenkov, Molotov, and Kaganovich was finally overcome, and Khrushchev's policies became the unquestioned general line of the Soviet government. In the meantime much had happened to take the initiative out of Soviet hands. The question of Russia's relationship to other "socialist" countries—those aspiring to the Soviet form of communism— was of concern outside Yugoslavia, Poland, and Hungary. The largest and most important people's democracy was China, where Mao Tse-tung had come to power in the heyday of Stalin's influence. Mao had relied heavily on Soviet assistance in these early days, especially during the Korean War, and he had been obliged to submit meekly to Stalin's guidance in matters of both theory and policy. Upon the announcement of Khrushchev's doctrine of "different roads to socialism" in 1956, Mao grasped the opportunity to assert China's interests.

In domestic affairs China was facing some of the same difficulties of overemphasis on heavy industry that confronted Poland and Hungary. In foreign relations China was ready to assert its position as an associate rather than a satellite of the U.S.S.R. It appears that as early as September, 1956, China assured Poland of support in its efforts to gain a degree of autonomy within the Soviet orbit. The victory of Gomulka was followed by an exchange of visits between Chinese and Polish party bosses, and a wide area of agreement was reached as to the degree of autonomy appropriate to "socialist" states. They could decide on their own pace of industrialization and collectivization, and could have independent relations with "capitalist" states. At home they must avoid the Hungarian error of letting the initiative pass to anti-Communist hands, and the unity of the Soviet orbit must be defended vis-à-vis the outside world. For home consumption Mao adopted the slogan: "Let a hundred flowers bloom, let a hundred schools of thought contend." There is good reason to believe that Khrushchev was worried lest this formulation stretch his doctrine of "different roads" to the breaking point, but he had to adapt himself as best he could to this fluid situation.

Tito was in a very different position from Gomulka and Mao, for he had been excommunicated from the Soviet orbit for nine years and still remained aloof from the Warsaw Pact and other binding commitments to Moscow. Like Mao, Tito favored Gomulka's efforts to win independence but felt that the Hungarians had overstepped legitimate bounds and that the Soviet action in crushing them had been necessary. Unlike Mao, however, Tito was publicly critical of the Soviet government for its entire conduct of relations with the people's democracies. In a powerful speech on November 15, 1956, Tito told the world that he had warned the Russians frequently on their errors, and that the crisis in Hungary was a result of their habit of making concession too little and too late. Tito's view was that the cause of world communism would best be served if all the people's democracies were as free as Yugoslavia from Soviet influence. This view was naturally rejected by Moscow, and Soviet-Yugoslav relations, which had seemed so warm in the summer of 1956, now became cool again. This relationship was closely affected by Khrushchev's struggle with his opponents within the Party Presidium, and only after his victory over opposition in July, 1957 did a change occur. Khrushchev and Tito met in Rumania in August and announced that they were in general agreement on policy. The Russians also agreed to restore the economic aid they had suspended nine months earlier. This reconciliation did not mark a profound change in Soviet-Yugoslav relations, however, for Yugoslavia in fact remained fully independent of Russia and carefully balanced between East and West.

The extent of Yugoslavia's isolation from the Soviet bloc was made apparent in the middle of November, 1957, when a conference of twelve Communist parties was held in Moscow without Yugoslav participation. Following as it did the consolidation of Khrushchev's position at home and the celebration of the fortieth anniversary of the Bolshevik Revolution, the conference served the purpose of reasserting the political and doctrinal leadership of the U.S.S.R. in the Communist world. In its final declaration, the conference warned against the "mechanical copying of the policies and tactics of the Communist parties of other countries," and recognized that "the diversity of forms and methods of building Socialism used in different countries are a collective contribution to the theory of Marxism-Leninism." At the same time, narrow limits were placed on this "diversity," and any straying beyond these limits was identified as opportunism, revisionism, dogmatism, and pedantry. There can be no question that the conference was pointing its finger at the absent Yugoslavs when it asserted that "a party that has locked itself up in sectarianism and that has lost contact with the broad masses can by no means bring victory to the cause of the working class."

As a result of these developments Yugoslavia retained its unique position of independence, and was not a model to which the other people's democracies were allowed to look for guidance. Poland, by contrast, was closely restricted by the Soviet insistence that a "friendly" Poland was a permanent Russian national interest. Poland was nevertheless sufficiently independent to solicit a loan of $98,000,000 from the United States, and to permit the free travel of foreign tourists within its borders. In domestic affairs the situation was in large measure reversed. In Poland there was very considerable freedom to criticize the government, and such a staunch representative of prewar Poland as Cardinal Wyszynski was able to express his opinions. In Yugoslavia, Milovan

Djilas, long a close associate of Tito's, was finally jailed for his out-spoken criticism of the regime. *The New Class,* Djilas' eloquent critique of the tyranny of communism, had to be published in New York and in English. Of the other people's democracies Albania, Bulgaria, and Rumania had changed little since the days of Stalin. Czechoslovakia, under the relatively mild rule of President Zapotocky and Prime Minister Siroky, after the death of Gottwald in March, 1953, underwent a gradual change. As the Communists inherited an industrialized country in 1948, Czechoslovakia did not undergo the severe economic strains that broke the unity of the party in Poland and Hungary. After the Pilsen riots in June, 1953, the government succeeded in raising the standard of living sufficiently to appease its critics. In foreign affairs Czechoslovakia re-mained a model satellite. Hungary was likewise a model satellite again, but under very changed circumstances. Much of the country's industrial capacity was no more than limping along, and the Communist regime of Kádár survived only because of the presence of Soviet troops.

5. CONCLUSION

At the end of its first decade Communist policy in Eastern Europe was in a state of general disorganization. From the start the mainstay of Communist power has been the Soviet Army and police. The strength of Communist policy, which won it significant adherents in the immedi-ate postwar period, was that it concerned itself with the central problem faced by this region: the transition from an agrarian to an industrialized society. Rapid progress had been made in this direction in the generation before World War I, but the interwar period was marked by many frustrations. Conflicts over national issues, inexperience in self-govern-ment, the world economic depression, and the instability of the European political system consequent to the great power rivalries—all these dis-turbances combined to discredit those who sought a middle road to industrialization.

Into this relative vacuum the Communists moved vigorously with the policies that Stalin had developed in and for the Soviet Union in the period after 1928. These policies were not widely understood, but as a verbal program they appeared to many to offer a dynamic solution to the needs of the region. These Soviet policies were introduced in 1944–45 with the tacit approval of the British and American governments. Liberal-minded political leaders in Eastern Europe—influenced by the division of the region into military zones at the end of the war, by the armistice terms, by the broadcasts of the BBC and the OWI, and by the day-to-day decisions of Western statesmen—had reason to believe that Soviet actions had the support of, and would in the last analysis be limited by, British and American policies. Only later did scholars discover, and Western statesmen admit, that what had the appearance of policy was in fact an absence of policy, a lack of foresight and planning.

Soviet policies, having been launched under these peculiar circumstances, did not fulfill the hopes either of the middle-of-the-road liberals or of the Communists themselves. Only in the fields of heavy industry and technological education was substantial progress made in the postwar decade, and the over-all achievements of communism have probably fallen a good deal short of what might have been expected of the prewar regimes if they had returned to power under postwar conditions. In Yugoslavia, Poland, and Hungary the failure of Stalinist policies speaks for itself. In Czechoslovakia, Rumania, Bulgaria, and Albania, where the Communists have met with no sharp reversals, it cannot be said that the younger generation or even the mature Communists themselves are particularly pleased with their achievements. If for no other reason than Soviet determination and military power, however, the people's democracies are likely to remain within the Soviet orbit for the time being. Western policy has shown itself to be rather sterile and unimaginative in relation to the people's democracies, and in the last analysis essentially disinterested. It is thus not a modicum of success on the part of Communist policies, but rather the outcome of the balance of power, that accounts for the continued subjection of Eastern Europe to the Soviet hegemony.

33

THE PEOPLE'S REPUBLICS

1. PEOPLE'S DEMOCRACY

Constitutional Theory. During the immediate postwar period Communist leaders in Eastern Europe concealed their real aims from the general public and even from their own followers. They permitted everyone to believe that the people's fronts represented an intermediate stage between Western and Soviet forms of democracy that might continue almost indefinitely, with the Communists remaining, if necessary, in their minority position merely to prevent the governments from deliberately pursuing anti-Soviet policies. It soon became clear, however, that the Communists planned to introduce full-fledged socialism of the kind that had been formalized in the Soviet constitution of 1936. Once they felt themselves to be securely in power, and especially after Tito's schism, they began to publicize these aims and to refer to the new states they had set up as "people's republics," and to the new form of government as "people's democracy." Whereas prior to the establishment of the new regimes emphasis had been laid upon the differences that prevailed between the Soviet system and those which had been established after the war within the Soviet orbit, the Communists now proclaimed their substantial identity.

The significant feature of the people's democracies is that they represent a form of proletarian dictatorship that differs only in form but not in essence from the Soviet model. According to the prevailing Soviet line on the theory of people's democracy, the people's republics are in the transitional period from capitalism to socialism and are being built in collaboration and friendship with the U.S.S.R.[1] The primary function of these governments is to provide political institutions suitable for transforming the countries of Eastern Europe from a system of relatively free enterprise to one of Soviet socialism. The constitutions

[1] H. Minc, "Some Problems of the People's Democracy in the Light of the Leninist-Stalinist Teachings on the Dictatorship of the Proletariat," *Political Affairs,* 29 (August, 1950), p. 96.

of these countries are thus different in significant respects from the Soviet constitution of 1936, which was not adopted until all sectors of the Russian economy had been fully nationalized. The constitutional structure of the people's democracies is comparable rather to that of the Soviet Union before 1936, when it also was going through the process of nationalizing its economy. This comparison is by no means complete, however, since the domestic and international conditions differ so greatly.

The people's democracies may be said to have come into existence when the Communists in each country secured the instruments of power and firmly controlled the people's front government.[2] This stage was signalized by general elections, which the Communist-sponsored coalition won by overwhelming majorities. These electoral victories were usually accompanied by the adoption of a new constitution establishing a people's republic.[3] The people's republics will presumably give way to Soviet republics when all sectors of the economy are fully nationalized, a process that may well take a number of years.

It now appears that before the establishment of a full-fledged Soviet regime the people's republics will have to go through three constitutional stages. The first stage was that of the early postwar period, when the role of the Communist Party was played down and, for the sake of appearance, some of the prewar constitutions were re-established (see Figure XXXV). The second stage is characterized by constitutions that were adopted after the regimes of people's democracy had been firmly established. In the interim the *de facto* political supremacy of the Communist Party had been recognized; the means of production, transportation and banking had been nationalized; the "socialist sector" of agriculture had been widened by the ever-growing influence of the state through the establishment of state farms and tractor stations; collectivization of the land had been consistently pursued through a policy aiming at the elimination of the "kulak elements" and at enlisting the support of the lower and middle class strata of the peasantry; the size, structure, and functions of the central and local governmental agencies and of the judiciary had been transformed along Soviet lines; the first economic plans had been inaugurated; the last remnants of the organized opposition had been eliminated, and the party rank and file had been purged of "unreliable" or "deviationist" elements. A Soviet-type constitution will presumably be adopted during the third stage, e.g., after

[2] The regime of people's democracy was first formally proclaimed in Albania on January 11, 1946; Poland was formally called a people's republic for the first time only on July 22, 1952, when the new constitution went into effect.

[3] See above, p. 776, for the dates of these elections; the best general guide to the political theory underlying the constitutions of the people's republics is N. P. Farberov, *Gosudarstvennoe Pravo Stran Narodnoi Demokratii,* "Constitutional Law of the People's Democracies" (1949), pp. 10–97; this material is summarized and related more closely to general Soviet legal theory in *Teoriya Gosudarstva i Prava,* "Theory of State and Law" (1949), pp. 454–92, a standard treatise published by the Institute of Law of the Soviet Academy of Science. See also: Michel-Henri Fabre, *Théorie des démocraties populaires* (1949), and Georges Vedel, *Les Démocraties marxistes* (1951).

the nationalization of industry and the collectivization of the land has
been completed.

FIG. XXXV

CONSTITUTIONAL DEVELOPMENT OF THE PEOPLE'S REPUBLICS

	FIRST STAGE	SECOND STAGE
Albania	Constitution of March 15, 1946	Constitution of July 4, 1950
Bulgaria	Tirnovo Constitution of 1879	Constitution of Dec. 4, 1947
Czechoslovakia	Constitution of 1920	Constitution of June 9, 1948
Hungary	Act I of 1946	Constitution of Aug. 20, 1949
Poland	Provisional Constitution of Feb., 1947	Constitution of July 22, 1952
Rumania	Constitution of 1923	Constitutions of Apr. 13, 1948, and of Sept. 24, 1952
Yugoslavia	Constitution of Jan. 31, 1946	Constitution of Jan. 13, 1953

The gradual approach to Sovietization, as an alternative to a more
immediate and complete seizure of power by the Communists, was
adopted for reasons of expediency. The Soviet Union was in no position
during the winter of 1944–45 to face the open break with the United
Nations coalition, which a more radical policy probably would have
involved; nor were the individual Communist parties in any of these
countries strong enough to take full political authority into their own
hands. Only in Finland did the people's front policy fail to bear fruit,[4]
and, since the liberal republican constitution of July 17, 1919, remains
in force, it is the only state in the Soviet orbit that has not become a
people's republic.

Role of the Party. As befits countries that are not yet fully
socialized, the Communist parties of all the people's republics except
those of Albania and Rumania do not enjoy the same exclusive role of
leadership under the new constitutions as that defined in the Soviet
constitution of 1936.[5] Instead they nominally share their power with
the leaders of a limited number of other parties, whose function it is to
represent the sectors of the national economy that have not yet been
nationalized. These modified people's front coalitions are variously known
as: the Socialist Alliance of Working People (formerly the National
Liberation Front) in Yugoslavia, the Democratic Front (formerly the

[4] See above, pp. 777–78, for a discussion of Finland's position.
[5] The Albanian constitution of 1950 (Art. 21) and the Rumanian constitution
of 1952 (Art. 86) copy almost verbatim the provisions incorporated in Article 126
of the Stalin constitution with regard to the exclusive role of the party in "guiding
the working people in their struggle to build a socialist [Communist] society."

National Liberation Front) in Albania, the Fatherland Front in Bulgaria, the National Democratic Front (formerly the Bloc of Democratic Parties) in Rumania, the Patriotic People's Front (formerly the People's Independence Front) in Hungary, the Front of National Unity in Poland, and the National Front in Czechoslovakia. Before 1948 these governments were all people's front coalitions in the conventional sense of the term, with the non-Communist members generally retaining some degree of bargaining power. By that year, however, all independent-minded Agrarian, Liberal, and Socialist leaders had been purged. Moreover, during 1948 the Socialists were absorbed by the Communist parties in most of the people's democracies to form, within the broader people's fronts, the united fronts of workers' parties that the Soviet theorists regard as the essential prerequisite for the eventual proletarian state (see Figure XXXIII).

It may well be asked why the Communists have bothered to retain these remnants of their former partners in the people's front regimes now that they have firmly entrenched themselves in power. One reason for this policy is undoubtedly doctrinal: according to the theory of people's democracy, the Communists should not assume exclusive political power until a nation is fully socialized. An equally valid reason, however, is that the remnants of the old parties are still able to fulfill a definite political function. In dealing with the as yet uncollectivized peasants, for instance, it is more efficacious to issue instructions in the name of a minister of agriculture who calls himself an Agrarian than in the name of an acknowledged Communist. One of the chief characteristics of the people's democracies is the Communists' use of innocuous labels to conceal their real intent, and in this stratagem their partners in the expurgated people's front governments play a useful role.

It is difficult to overestimate the extent to which the Communist parties have been able to concentrate all decision-making power in their own hands. The elaborate legislative-administrative structure provided in the constitutions is not meaningless, as it reveals the formal instrumentalities through which Communist power is exercised. The identification of the state and the party is illustrated by the fact that in almost every case highest state officials are members of the governing organs of the Communist parties. Like a nervous system, the Communist Party penetrates all political, social, cultural, and economic institutions. All decisions of the government are made on Communist Party initiative, and no individual may hold an official position or be a candidate for elective office without the approval of the party. In theory political power flows from the people through the elective assemblies to the executive branches of the government. In practice it flows from the party to the public, to the assemblies, and to the executive branches.

This decisive role of the Communist Party was at first played down for tactical reasons. But behind the façade of the people's fronts and the united fronts the Communist parties of Eastern Europe moved rapidly to gain full control, not only of such instruments of power as the army and the police, but also of all non-governmental organizations. Thus the trade unions, in which the Social Democrats were generally predominant, were among the first of these organizations to be taken over. The producers' and consumers' co-operative movement, which developed rapidly in Eastern Europe after World War I, was also an early target of the Communists, as were many professional, patriotic, athletic, youth, and other social organizations. The methods of achieving control generally involved threat of police or terrorist action to assure the election in these organizations of administrative officers subservient to Communist discipline.

Of all these organizations the churches presented the most difficult opposition for the Communists. The only church organization that the Communists could fit readily into the Soviet pattern was that of the Eastern Orthodox faith. The Orthodox Church has enjoyed close historical ties with the official Russian Orthodox Church, which was restored to favor in 1943, and its adherents include the great majority of the inhabitants of Rumania and Bulgaria, about one half the population of Yugoslavia, and an important minority in Albania. Here the Communists, by vigorous propaganda and direct pressure, have had considerable success in bringing the clergy under control without, for the time being, challenging them in the spiritual realm. The Roman Catholic and Protestant churches, by contrast, are bound to the West by powerful bonds of cultural tradition and ecclesiastical organization. The Catholic Church in particular represents a formidable obstacle to the Communists by virtue of the number of its adherents and its important traditional role in society. Its congregation includes a large majority of the peoples of Poland, Czechoslovakia, and Hungary, an important minority in Yugoslavia, and smaller minorities in Rumania, Bulgaria, and Albania. The Communists have used many pressure tactics to make the Catholic hierarchies subservient to government policy, and the Roman Catholic Church has been forced to make important concessions to the new regimes. Its hierarchies and adherents nevertheless continue actively to resist Communist policies in the spiritual and social spheres.

The important Protestant minorities in Hungary and Czechoslovakia have not been the object of such direct pressure as have the more powerful Catholic organizations, but they too have suffered seriously from restrictions on civil liberties. On the other hand, the small Protestant minority in Bulgaria was severely persecuted because of its religious ties with the West, and leading clergymen were tried and sentenced to prison as alleged agents of foreign enemies. Some Hebrew religious organizations continue to exist in Eastern Europe despite the ravages of Nazi terror and the Communist campaign against Zionism and cosmopolitanism, but a majority of their members have chosen to emigrate to Israel rather than remain under Communist rule. The Moslem majority in Albania and its minorities in Yugoslavia and Bulgaria represent less danger to the Communists and have not been so vigorously persecuted.

Republicanism.   Before four of the countries of Eastern Europe—Yugoslavia, Albania, Bulgaria, and Rumania—could proceed with their plans, it was necessary for them to abolish the monarchies, which at the end of World War II were still in existence. Although the Balkan kings were not so closely identified as their colleagues in Western Europe with vested landed interests and social hierarchies, since they were all of relatively recent origin, they nevertheless tended to symbolize the more extreme forms of the nationalist spirit that prevailed after World War I. Moreover, each dynasty had become involved to a greater or lesser degree in the authoritarian regimes that flourished on the eve of World War II and were completely identified with anti-Communist feeling.

In the case of Yugoslavia and Albania the kings were in exile at the end of World War II, and had also lost much of their appeal. Peter II of Yugoslavia had enjoyed a brief flurry of popularity in March, 1941, when a group of officers overthrew the pro-Axis government then in power and installed young Peter in the place of his uncle, Prince Paul. During the four years of exile, however, the young king's prestige was gradually reduced by the internecine struggles of his government-in-exile. When the Yugoslavian National Assembly proclaimed a republic on November 29, 1945, the king and his followers abroad issued a routine protest but were unable to obtain the rejection of Tito by the Big Three. Zog of Albania, a self-made king, commanded far less of a following than his Yugoslavian colleague. Even in exile he failed to win the support of the principal members of the United Nations, and when Hoxha proclaimed a republic in Tirana on January 12, 1946, it was recognized by the Western powers.

In the case of Bulgaria and Rumania the situation was more delicate, since both monarchs were still in residence in their respective capitals. In Bulgaria a people's front regency of three was provided in Septemer, 1944, for seven-year-old Simeon II, and the fiction of the monarchy was maintained until the Communists were firmly in control. When a plebiscite on the question of the monarchy was finally held on September 8, 1946, the vote went overwhelmingly in favor of a republic and the royal family was escorted politely but firmly into exile. Michael of Rumania, on the other hand, was a man of twenty-three at the end of the war and had already taken an active part in his country's affairs. Whatever his collaboration with the wartime regime of General Antonescu, his prestige had been increased by the coup he helped to execute on August 23, 1944—an act of heroism that was recognized even by the Russians when they bestowed upon him on July 19, 1945, their highest military decoration, the "Order of Victory." The king's popularity was cleverly exploited by the Communists for bringing about revolutionary changes in the country without risking the outbreak of open revolt. But as Soviet economic and political pressure increased and the dissatisfaction of the masses became increasingly apparent, he was more and more regarded as a symbol of unity and national independence. He continued to fulfill his ceremonial functions and to exert some influence until December 30, 1947, when he finally abdicated under pressure.

Sovereignty. Another important aspect of the people's democracies is that they are considered by Communist theory to represent a strengthening of the national sovereignty of the states of Eastern Europe. It is characteristic of Soviet legal writing that, although conventional conceptions of sovereignty are taken as a starting point, distinctions are made that alter the definition of this term as understood in Western political thought. One such distinction is that between formal or state sovereignty, on the one hand, and real or popular sovereignty, on the other. Capitalist states have only the formal sovereignty of the few, but socialist states enjoy the real sovereignty of the many, according to Soviet theorists. It is therefore possible for a Soviet commentator to write with regard to Hungary, for instance, after describing the liquidation of the investments of the Western powers and the organization in their place of Soviet-Hungarian stock companies and other instruments of Soviet economic influence: "In its relations with Hungary, as with the other small states, the Soviet Union is building on the principle of full respect for the national independence and sovereignty of this country." [6] This approach to the question of national sovereignty, which the Soviet theorists employ in regard to their own union republics as well as to the people's democracies, thus permits the Soviet Union to play an active role in their affairs while maintaining that it is in fact strengthening their independence and sovereignty. This differentiation between "state sovereignty" and "popular sovereignty" found legal crystallization in the Rumanian constitution of 1952. On the one hand, the Soviet Union is described as offering "selfless and brotherly support" to "ensure the independence, state sovereignty, development and flourishing of the Rumanian People's Republic"; while on the other, "The Armed Forces of the Rumanian People's Republic stand guard over the borders of the country, guard over the sovereignty and independence of the Rumanian people, their security and peace." [7]

Whatever conclusions one may draw regarding the national sovereignty of the people's republics as reflected in their relations with the great powers, the doctrine of the sovereignty of the people in domestic affairs is nominally adhered to. A typical constitution states, for instance, that "All authority . . . derives from the people and belongs to the people." [8] This theory of popular sovereignty is expressed through the organs of state authority, to use the terminology of these constitutions, which consist of elective bodies on the local and national level. Sharply distinguished from the state authority is the state administration, the executive branch of the government, of which the principal organ is the council of ministers. The importance attached to popular sovereignty, as understood in the people's democracies, is reflected in the explicit constitutional provisions for the control of state administration. At each level the elective bodies are given the right to annul administrative decisions made on the corresponding level and to recall officials who incur

[6] I. Laponogov, *Vengerskaya Demokraticheskaya Respublika Na Novom Etape,* "The Hungarian Democratic Republic at a New Stage" (1949), p. 31.

[7] Rumania: Pars. 4 and 5 of the introductory chapter. The constitutions will be referred to hereafter by an abbreviated citation of the country followed by the sections or articles in question; the texts of the constitutions may be found in Amos J. Peaslee, *Constitutions of Nations* (2nd ed., 1956), 3 vols.

[8] Yugo.: Art. 2; see also, Alb.: Art. 2; Bulg.: Art. 2; Czech.: Fundamental Art. 1, Para. 2; Hung.: Arts. 1–3; Pol.: Art. 1; Rum.: Arts. 1–2.

their disfavor. These provisions are the legal means by which the Communist parties and their front organizations, by controlling elections to local and national assemblies, impose their will on the entire administrative apparatus.

2. STATE AUTHORITY

People's Committees. Popular sovereignty is reflected in its broadest and most elementary aspect in the people's committees, or councils (soviets), which are formally elected by general, equal, and direct suffrage by secret ballot. Their function and jurisdiction are regulated in special laws identical in their fundamental provisions in all the people's democracies.[9] The people's committees, as described in the Rumanian constitution, direct the work of the organs of administration subordinate to them, direct local economic and cultural affairs, ensure the maintenance of public order, the observance of the laws and the protection of the rights of citizens, and draw up the local budget.[1] These committees thus represent the initiative of the people's-front oligarchy on the local level and permit it to supervise the implementation of directives by an officialdom that is to a large degree inherited from the old regimes.

The people's committees are organized in regions, districts, towns, and rural localities. They are built on the same hierarchical principle as the Communist Party, constituting a structural power pyramid. At the bottom of the pyramidal structure are the people's committees of the towns and rural localities, followed by those of the districts and regions. In Yugoslavia and Czechoslovakia, which are organized on a federal basis, elected assemblies also exist in the constituent republics or provinces. In Yugoslavia, moreover, the creation of workers' councils and management boards[2] has given the workers direct representation in the government. The district and town council are bicameral, being composed of the district and town council and of a producers' council representing the local producers.[3] While in this case the deputies to the district and town councils—the political representative bodies—are elected by the population as a whole, those to the council of producers are elected by the workers and employees actively employed in industry, transport, and trade only.

[9] See the following statutes: Albania, The Law on People's Councils of August 8, 1946; Bulgaria, The Law on People's Committees of February 17, 1948; Czechoslovakia, The Law on the Organization of the Local People's Committees of February 28, 1950; Hungary, Law I of 1950 on Local People's Committees; Poland, The Law on the Local Committees of March 20, 1950; Rumania, The Law on the Local People's Committees of January 13, 1949; Yugoslavia, The Law on People's Committees of April 1, 1952.

[1] Rum.: Art. 53, and Arts. 51–63; see also similar provisions in Alb.: Arts. 71–78; Bulg.: Arts. 47–55; Czech.: Secs. 123–33; Hung.: Arts. 29–35; Pol.: Arts. 34–45; Yugo.: Arts. 2–8.

[2] See *Službeni List* (Official Gazette) of the Federal People's Republic of Yugoslavia, No. 43, July 5, 1950.

[3] Yugo.: Art. 7.

National Assemblies.   The principal organ of government through which the people's front coalitions exercise their power is the national assembly, known under different names in the various people's democracies. The legislature is unicameral—except in Yugoslavia, where the federal structure requires two chambers—and is generally elected by universal suffrage. The term of the legislature is four years, and it usually meets twice a year.[4] Under the new Yugoslav constitution the federal people's assembly is composed of the federal council and the council of producers. The federal council is composed both of deputies popularly elected from the country as a whole and of deputies elected by the popularly chosen republican council of each people's republic (ten deputies each), the provincial council of the autonomous province (six deputies), and the region council of the autonomous region (four deputies).[5] On questions affecting the republics' status the latter group sits separately as a council of nationalities;[6] in all other cases the two types of deputies sit as a single body. The deputies to the council of producers are elected by the workers and employees of economic enterprises, by members of agricultural co-operatives, and by handicraft workers acting through organized guilds.[7] The council of producers has the same rights in the federal people's assembly as the federal council but also enjoys certain special privileges with respect to economic matters. In addition there are separate legislative organs in each of the eight territories comprising the federation.[8] The Czechoslovak constitution, by contrast, retains the unicameral assembly but gives recognition to the semi-autonomous status of Slovakia by providing for the Slovak National Council.[9]

In both the Yugoslavian and the Czechoslovak constitutions the line of jurisdiction between the national and provincial assemblies is carefully defined. In each instance the national assemblies are elected by universal suffrage under the terms of an electoral system defined in separate legislation. Unlike Soviet electoral procedure, as specified in the constitutions of 1918 and 1924, there are no disenfranchised classes in the people's republics. On the contrary, a full participation of the entire voting population is encouraged, and control of the results is exercised through the selection of candidates by the people's-front coalitions. National elections thus take on the dual character of plebiscite and propaganda campaign, and the full weight of the police apparatus is held in readiness for use against those who refuse to vote "yes" on the approved list of candidates. The national assemblies, like the people's committees, and in Yugoslavia and Czechoslovakia the provincial bodies, thus reflect the will of the people's front coalition and are entirely under its control. As the supreme organs of state power these assemblies are the sole legislative body and have the power to amend the constitution and to supervise the executive branch of the government known as the

[4] Alb.: Arts. 41–56; Bulg.: Arts. 15–33; Czech.: Secs. 39–62; Hung.: Arts. 10–19; Pol.: Arts. 15–24; Rum.: Arts. 22–35; Yugo.: Arts. 13–69.

[5] Yugo.: Arts. 25–27.

[6] Yugo.: Arts. 45–49.

[7] Yugo.: Arts. 28–29.

[8] Yugo.: Arts. 100–106 and 113.

[9] Czech.: Secs. 96–112.

state administration. The power that the people's front coalitions exercise through the national assemblies is best reflected in the attributes of the presidium, which is elected by the assembly.

Presidium. The presidium, an institution borrowed from Soviet constitutional law, is represented in its most complete form in the constitutions of Albania, Bulgaria, Hungary, and Rumania. Its membership ranges from fifteen (Albania) to between thirty and forty-five (Yugoslavia), including a president, several vice-presidents, and a secretary.[1] In Czechoslovakia the presidium is headed by a chairman and shares its powers with the president of the republic, who is elected by the assembly for a seven-year term.[2] In Poland the council of state, headed by the president of the republic, performs the functions of the presidium.[3] In Yugoslavia the federal executive council, whose chairman is the president of the republic, has wide decree powers—subject to disallowance by the assembly—and also performs guiding "political functions" in the executive branch of the government.[4] The president of the republic (Tito) is entrusted with extensive powers. He is commander in chief of the armed forces and general director of foreign affairs. He presides over the council of national defense and, subject to subsequent assembly approval, he may veto any act of the federal executive council. This represents a distinct departure from Soviet constitutional structure, in which the presidium acts for the assembly but with actual power wielded by the premier. In the other people's democracies the president of the presidium has the prerogatives of the head of a state, in so far as he receives the chiefs of foreign missions and performs other ceremonial functions. He is in no sense independent of the assembly, however, for the presidium may be recalled by a majority vote of the latter. The prerogatives of the presidium are extensive. It convenes the national assembly for ordinary and extraordinary sessions; it orders elections for the assembly; it proclaims laws and issues decrees; it interprets legislation; it appoints and recalls the members of the council of ministers and diplomatic representatives; and it has the right to grant pardons and to commute sentences.[5]

More significant than the mere enumeration of its prerogatives is the fact that the presidium exercises them when the assembly is not in session. It forms the apex of the structure of state authority in the people's republics and is a serviceable instrument of power in the hands of the people's front coalition. The presidium is less unwieldy than the full assembly and is, moreover, in permanent session. Its function of concealing the reality of Communist control, in so far as this is possible, is reflected in the fact that the members of the presidium and its president generally do not include leaders of the Communist Party. The presi-

[1] Alb.: Arts. 57–60; Bulg.: Arts. 34–37; Hung.: Arts. 19–21; Rum.: Arts. 35–41.
[2] Czech.: Secs. 63–79.
[3] Pol.: Arts. 24–28.
[4] Yugo.: Arts. 71–89.
[5] See, for instance, Rum.: Art. 37.

dent may even be a former Socialist, Liberal, or peasant leader who has cast his lot with the Communists and who lends his name and the prestige of his former party to the measures evolved by the Communists and enacted by the assembly and the presidium. There is no adequate evidence as to the actual workings of the presidiums in the people's republics, but from what is known they appear to perform their task efficiently. Such disputes as arise on the governmental level are based on disagreements within the Communist parties, and police control has thus far been adequate to assure that the national assemblies and their presidiums have reflected faithfully the views and policies of the dominant faction within the Communist parties.

3. STATE ADMINISTRATION

Council of Ministers. The implementation of the decisions of the national assembly and its presidium is entrusted to the council of ministers, which is appointed by and formally responsible to the legislative body. This council differs somewhat in structure from one country to another, but its principal characteristics do not vary greatly. It is headed by a president, generally referred to as the prime minister, and normally includes several vice-presidents and the heads of the state planning commission and other bodies of cabinet rank.[6] The vice-presidents of the council usually represent all of the parties in the people's-front coalition. They may be either heads of ministries or simply ministers without portfolio. In the latter case it is a purely formal post, carrying with it no administrative functions or staff, and is commonly used as a means of paying off persons who have been useful to the Communists. The number of ministries is not always listed in the constitution, but it tends to be large since a wide variety of economic functions is generally administered directly by cabinet officials in addition to the ministries traditional to Western government.[7]

In Yugoslavia, supreme executive power is vested in the federal executive council and the president of the republic. While these discharge only the "political side" of the executive branch of the government, the administrative functions are entrusted to the bodies of federal administration.[8] The separation of political and administrative powers within the executive branch is allegedly designed to safeguard against the "evils of

[6] Alb.: Arts. 61–70; Bulg.: Arts. 38–46; Czech.: Secs. 80–92; Hung.: Arts. 22–28; Pol.: Arts. 29–33; Rum.: Arts. 42–50.

[7] This trend seems to be reversed lately. During its March, 1957 session the newly elected Rumanian National Assembly, probably in an effort to tighten the party's hold over the nation and to cut down on the expenses involved in maintaining a large bureaucracy, resolved to reduce the number of ministries from thirty to sixteen. Furthermore, Khrushchev's economic reorganization of 1957, which replaced the industrial ministries with regional councils of national economy, was imitated by Bulgaria in 1959 and will doubtless be adopted by other people's democracies.

[8] Yugo.: Arts. 71–89 and 90–99.

the bureaucratic state capitalist system of the Soviet Union." There are only five federal state secretariats (ministries),[9] leaving the execution of functions formerly performed by ministries devoted to running specific industrial branches to other decentralized agencies. Those concerned with production have been allotted to the workers-management organs operating under the directives of the higher economic associations. Purely administrative matters have been delegated to the ministries of the constituent republics and the people's committees. Functions relating to co-ordination and over-all policies have been assigned to councils, committees, and boards consisting of officials appointed by both the federal and republic governments.

What is significant about the cabinet officers of the people's republics in general is less the organization of their ministries than the strict accountability to which they are held by the legislature. Not only are they appointed and recalled by that body, but they are held responsible under criminal law for illegal acts committed in the fulfillment of their functions. Since the interpretation of the law is in the hands of the presidium, the cabinet officers are entirely at the mercy of the organs of state authority.[1] In practice the public trial of ministers accused of treason or other abuse of their power has been one of the most common methods used by the dominant factions in the people's front coalitions to discipline their colleagues.

Federalism. In Yugoslavia and Czechoslovakia the provisions for federalism add complexity to the administrative system. The form of federalism that these states have adopted does not involve any weakening of the central political authority, but is conceived rather as a means of granting nominal recognition to minority groups so large that they might tend to demand political autonomy or even independence. As interpreted by one Soviet authority, it is Communist policy to "put forward federation as a means of holding the masses of the nationalities in the camp of the proletarian revolution, [and] as a way of strengthening the confidence between the toilers of all nationalities and of unifying their forces against common class enemies." [2]

The federal constitution of Yugoslavia makes provision for six republics: Serbia, Croatia, Slovenia, Bosnia-Herzegovina, Macedonia, and Montenegro. There are in addition one autonomous province (Vojvodina) and one autonomous region (Kosovo-Metohija), both within the republic of Serbia.[3] The relationship between the federal republic and the member republics—the new constitutional provisions notwithstanding—is closely modeled on that described in the Soviet constitution of 1936. There are federal state secretariats, including foreign

---

[9] These are the state secretariats for foreign affairs, national defense, internal affairs, national economy and budget, and state administration. Of these only the heads of the first two are members of the federal executive council.

[1] See, for instance, Rum.: Art. 37.

[2] Andrei Vyshinsky, *The Law of the Soviet State,* translated by H. W. Babb (1948), p. 224.

[3] Yugo.: Arts. 2, 9–13 of the 1946 constitution not affected by the provisions of Art. 115 of the new constitution, and Arts.: 100–14 of the 1953 constitution.

affairs, national defense, national economy, which administer their affairs for the entire territory of the federal republic. There are also republican executive councils, which administer their affairs through corresponding secretariats in the individual republics. Finally, there are independent republican secretariats established to handle certain unspecified branches of local administration. The administrative organ of the autonomous province of Vojvodina is a principal executive committee elected by the provincial assembly. Similarly the autonomous region of Kosovo-Metohija is provided with a regional executive committee. To what extent these complex constitutional provisions are carried out in full it is impossible to say. There can nevertheless be little doubt that these elaborate arrangements, accompanied as they are by linguistic and cultural rights, serve to temper somewhat the effect of the highly centralized administrative system.

The situation in Czechoslovakia is simpler since there is only one subordinate unit, the territory of Slovakia. Here the executive body, known as the board of commissioners, is appointed by the central government. It co-operates on the local level, however, with the Slovak National Council, which is elected. The Slovak board of commissioners is thus in the position of implementing the legislation of both the Czechoslovak National Assembly and the Slovak National Council. Only foreign affairs, national defense, and foreign trade are the exclusive province of the central government, according to the terms of the constitution. In addition to its administrative functions the board advises the central authorities with regard to the appointment of university professors, judges, and other civil servants in Slovakia.[4]

In Rumania, to assuage the feelings of the Hungarians, who constitute by far the largest minority group (numbering over 1,000,000), the new constitution provides for the establishment of a Magyar Autonomous Region[5] in the territories inhabited by compact Magyar and Szekely populations. It has an autonomous administrative body, elected by the population of the region, and possessing certain limited prerogatives.

Local Government. Relatively little is said in the constitutions of the people's republics regarding the organization of local government. The significant feature is that it represents a fusion of the representative and administrative institutions. However, Soviet constitutional theory emphasizes the distinction between the people's committees and their executive committees, depicting the former as "organs of state power," with directive functions, and the latter as mere executive and administrative organs of the committees. The executive committees usually consist of a chairman, one or more vice-chairmen, a secretary, and various members. The chairmen of the local people's committees, described in the previous section, serve as executive officers in certain categories of local affairs, and in this capacity are subordinate to both their local committees and the appropriate higher legislative bodies. At the same time, local representatives of the higher administrative organs are in turn

[4] Czech.: Secs. 93–122.
[5] Rum.: Arts. 19–21 and 57–58.

subordinated to the people's committee. Here again the constitutions do not go so far as to list the various local officials or to define the boundaries of their jurisdiction. The apparent purpose of these relationships, however, is to provide strict political supervision over local officials.[6] In Yugoslavia the people's committees were given a larger degree of autonomy. The dualism in the responsibility of the executive organs to the local and central authorities has been partially eliminated by virtue of the 1952 reorganization of the local self-government system. Organs directly subordinate to the central authorities can be established only by special law. This reduction in the degree of centralism, however, is more formal than real, since essentially the Yugoslav system is still a type of proletarian dictatorship differing primarily in its foreign but not in its basic internal aspects from the other people's republics.

4. PEOPLE'S JUSTICE

Judicial System. The organization of justice in the people's republics reflects clearly the Soviet interpretation of Marxism, which holds that "legal relationships (and, consequently, law itself) are rooted in the material conditions of life, and that law is merely the will of the dominant class, elevated into a statute." [7] In the people's republics, as yet not fully socialized, the dominant class is represented by the people's front coalition of the proletariat in alliance with certain elements of the lower middle class, the peasantry, and the "progressive intellectuals." Under these conditions the function of the judicial system is to make certain that persons charged with violating the laws passed by the national assembly are tried in accordance with the interests of the dominant class or coalition. The principles of "proletarian class justice" not embodied in the individual constitutions found legal expression in various decrees. Thus Decree No. 132, approved by the Rumanian Assembly on April 2, 1949, states that the function of the judiciary is the "defense of the socio-economic structure of the state . . ." (Art. 1), and that its aim is the "strengthening and furthering of popular democracy" (Art. 2).

Detailed provisions regarding the organization, competence, and procedure of the various courts have been specified in special statutes, while the general principles guiding their establishment were embodied in the individual constitutions.[8] The general supervision of the judicial system is entrusted to a supreme court, whose members are elected by

6 See above, p. 796.

7 Vyshinsky, *The Law of the Soviet State,* p. 13.

8 See the following statutes and their amendments: Albania, The Law on the Organization of the Courts of Aug. 13, 1946; Bulgaria, The Law on the People's Courts of Nov. 7, 1952; Czechoslovakia, The Law on the Democratization of Justice of Dec. 22, 1948; Hungary, Law XI of 1949, On the Organization of Justice; Poland, The Law on the Organization of the Courts, Uniform Text, of Aug. 16, 1950; Rumania, Decree on the Organization of Courts of June 5, 1952; Yugoslavia, The Law on the Organization of Courts of June 17, 1946.

the national assembly. The supreme court possesses sole competence with regard to certain cases; in addition it serves as a court of cassation for cases handled by the lower courts. Since Soviet theory of constitutional law rejects the idea of placing any power above that of the assembly, on the assumption that this body represents the will of the people, the supreme courts in the people's republics have been deprived of the right of interpreting the constitutionality of laws. As such they are more of an auxiliary than an independent branch of the government. The lower courts, generally known as people's courts, are headed by elected professional judges and people's assessors. The latter participate in judicial proceedings along with the judges, presumably to ascertain that the interests of the dominant class are adequately protected. Intermediate courts exist in certain cases, and provision is made for the establishment of courts with a specialized jurisdiction. The public prosecutor, known in some cases as the procurator, is elected by the national assembly and is independent of the state administration.[9]

Human Rights. The new constitutions of the people's republics follow the general lines of the Soviet constitution of 1936 in the matter of civil liberties. Although they differ in detail, these documents provide for civic equality, freedom of expression in all forms, inviolability of person and domicile, and a variety of social and economic rights.[1] As under the Soviet constitution, however, it is made clear that these rights are reserved only for those who support the government. Thus the Albanian constitution provides that "Citizens cannot use the rights given them by this constitution in order to change the constitutional regime of the People's Republic of Albania for anti-democratic purposes." [2] In a similar spirit the Czechoslovak constitution stipulates that "Statements and acts that constitute a threat to the independence, integrity, and unity of the State, the Constitution, the Republican form of government and the People's Democratic Order, are punishable according to law." [3] The substance of these limiting articles is that the constitutions nominally guarantee all human rights except the fundamental right of freedom of political opinion. A reflection of this attitude is seen in the fact that the people's republics that were members of the United Nations at the time joined with the Soviet Union on December 10, 1948, in abstaining on the vote in which the General Assembly adopted the Universal Declaration of Human Rights.

More important than the constitutional restrictions on human rights, however, are those provided for in special legislation, which generally goes so far as to impose capital punishment for certain broadly defined forms of opposition to the government. The Polish law concern-

[9] Alb.: Arts. 79–90; Bulg.: Arts. 56–64; Czech.: Secs. 134–45; Hung.: Arts. 36–44; Pol.: Arts. 46–56; Rum.: Arts. 64–76; Yugo.: Arts. 115–28 of the 1946 constitution, still in force.
[1] Alb.: Arts. 14–40; Bulg.: Arts. 71–94; Czech.: Secs. 1–38; Hung.: Arts. 45–61; Pol.: Arts. 57–79; Rum.: Arts. 77–92; Yugo.: Arts. 21–43 of the 1946 constitution.
[2] Alb.: Art. 38.
[3] Czech.: Sec. 37, para. 1.

ing "Offenses Particularly Dangerous during the Period of the Country's Reconstruction," for instance, provides the death penalty for "an offense against a group of the population because of nationality, religion or race, followed by death, or grave bodily injuries, or disturbance of, or danger to the public peace and order resulting from such offense." [4] Even Finland has adopted a "Decree Regarding Restrictions of Personal Freedom," which, however, does not include capital punishment among its sanctions.[5] The severity of the measures adopted by the people's democracies against the political opponents of communism was an important factor in alienating public opinion in Western Europe, especially when leading Protestant and Catholic clergymen were tried for treason under humiliating circumstances in Bulgaria and Hungary.

Minorities' Rights. In an attempt to win a larger place in the countries of Eastern Europe than they have traditionally enjoyed, the Communist parties have gone a long way toward encouraging national feeling and pride. At the same time, perhaps stimulated by Stalin's special personal interest in nationalities problems, the Communists have also gone out of their way to provide at least nominal constitutional protection for the minority peoples of Eastern Europe, who were usually the victims of this overinflated nationalism. As with the advocacy of federalism this concern on the part of the people's republics is less the result of any humanitarian interest than of the realization that the discontent of the minorities could be harnessed in the cause of communism. Many Communist Party leaders are, in fact, members of minority nationalities and religions.

The Rumanian constitution, for instance, makes the following provision:

> In the Rumanian People's Republic, the national minorities are guaranteed the free use of their own language, tuition of all categories in their own language, and books, newspapers and theatres in their own language. In districts inhabited also by populations of a nationality other than Rumanian, all organs and institutions shall use orally and in writing the language of the respective nationalities, and shall appoint officials from among the ranks of the respective nationality or of other local inhabitants conversant with the language and the way of life of the local population.[6]

Similar provisions, supplemented by special legislation,[7] appear in most of the other new constitutions. In Finland the Swedish-speaking

[4] Decree of June 13, 1946, Art. 32, published in the *Yearbook on Human Rights for 1946* (1947), p. 236.

[5] Decree of December 30, 1946, No. 899, in ibid., p. 104.

[6] Rum.: Art. 82.

[7] Alb.: Art. 15; Bulg.: Art. 71; Hung.: Art. 49; Pol.: Art. 69; Yugo.: Art. 13 of the 1946 constitution; the Czechoslovak constitution includes no general article on minorities beyond the special rights accorded to the territory of Slovakia.

minority has enjoyed liberal linguistic rights since 1919, under the protection of explicit provisions contained in the constitution of that year.[8] It should be noted that, apart from the federal system in Yugoslavia and Czechoslovakia and the provision for the Magyar Autonomous Region in Rumania, minority rights in the people's republics are limited to the linguistic and cultural field. These rights, in turn, may be exercised only within the framework of the Communist principles guiding the development of cultures, i.e., they may be national only in form but must be "socialist" in content.

[8] Fin.: Art. 14.

34

ECONOMIC AND SOCIAL STRUCTURE

1. TRANSITION TO SOCIALISM

Class and State. The period of transition to socialism, during which the people's democracies will in theory exercise control, presents the basic problem of the evolution of the class structure of the state. As long as private ownership of the means of production exists, according to Marxism, there will be exploitation of man by man and the resulting class struggle. The essence of the transition period is therefore the nationalization of all means of production. Only when this is accomplished will exploitation in the Marxian sense be eliminated and democracy and equality as understood by Soviet Marxism be fully achieved.

The nationalization of the means of production is not a simple matter, however, and at no time did the Communists expect to achieve it in the people's democracies by means of a mere decree. Such a procedure would have led to open revolt of the peasantry and to extensive disorganization in industry. The alternative adopted was that of extending nationalization only as rapidly as it could be accomplished without seriously impeding production. This was particularly necessary because of the vast destruction wrought by the war in most of this area. With the exception of Czechoslovakia and Bulgaria, Eastern Europe had been subjected to very extensive damage, and the task of reconstruction was recognized by all to take precedence over other objectives in the economic field. Moreover, these countries suffered from an overpopulation for the absorption of which both an expansion of industry and an increase of agricultural production were required. For these reasons the Communists envisaged a period of gradual nationalization during which state enterprise and private enterprise would coexist, with the former slowly replacing the latter.

Ownership of the Means of Production. The governments of the people's republics are profoundly aware of the problems raised by the transitional period, and a substantial section of each constitution is de-

voted to a definition of the relationship between public and private enterprise.[1] The provisions concerning this relationship assert that the
means of production may be owned by the state, by co-operative organizations, or by private physical or juridical persons. Certain sectors of
the economy are explicitly set aside for immediate nationalization. These
generally include natural resources and all transportation and communication systems, many of which had already been nationalized by the
Liberal and Agrarian regimes long before World War II.

More significant are the provisions for the expropriation of private
property when the state judges this to be in the public interest. The sole
assurance that expropriation will take place "only in accordance with
the law" is not greatly strengthened by the statement that the extent of
compensation "will be determined by law." [2] Private property and the
right of inheritance are nevertheless guaranteed, as long as they are employed within the framework established by the laws of the people's
republics. Cartels and monopolies are forbidden in industry, and in agriculture no landholdings are permitted beyond a maximum size determined by law. Small and medium-sized holdings are especially encouraged, however, and the principle that "the land belongs to those who till
it" is explicitly set forth. Co-operative organizations are similarly given
favorable mention in the constitutions of the people's republics, and
under this heading are presumably included both producers' and consumers' organizations.

The proper relationship of these three sectors of the economy—
public, private, and co-operative—is an important doctrinal issue in the
people's democracies. Many Communist leaders, including Gomulka in
Poland, Pătrăşcanu in Rumania, and, most notably, Tito in Yugoslavia,
were accused of having sought to establish a permanent equilibrium
among these three sectors that would give their countries an intermediate
position between the socialism of Britain and France and that of the
Soviet Union. They were soon informed by Soviet authorities in no uncertain terms that they had adopted an "incorrect formulation" of the
problem. Stalin's diatribe against the "Right deviationists" in 1929, in
which he stated that the idea of equilibrium between socialist production
and capitalist production was anti-Marxian, was presented in evidence.
"Either one way or the other, either *back* to capitalism or *forward* to
Socialism. There is no third way, nor can there be," Stalin argued.[3] It
was thus made quite clear to the Titoist heretics that small private landholdings and businesses could continue to exist only as a temporary expediency. As one Soviet authority has stated it:

> In the people's democracies there is no new or other road, than
> that by which the U.S.S.R. reached socialism. On the road to
> socialism these countries possess certain original traits in their
> methods, means, and rates of movement, only as these reflect

[1] Alb.: Arts. 7–13; Bulg.: Arts. 6–14; Czech.: Secs. 146–64; Hung.: Arts. 4–9;
Rum: Arts. 5–15; Yugo.: Arts. 14–20 of the 1946 constitution; Pol.: Arts. 7–14.
[2] Yugo.: Art. 18 of the 1946 constitution.
[3] J. Stalin, *Problems of Leninism* (11th ed., 1940), p. 309.

their diversity, but not their negation of the common road itself.[4]

State Planning. The method adopted by the people's democracies
for achieving the dual aim of increased production and systematic socialization is that of state planning. During the immediate postwar years
these plans were directed toward reconstruction, but today they are
chiefly concerned with long-term investments. Most significant is the decision of the people's democracies to rely primarily on industrialization
as a solution to the problem of agricultural overpopulation. Many informed critics, especially the Agrarians, are of the opinion that a heavier
proportional investment in agriculture would bring more immediate
benefits to the impoverished rural population. The Communists are more
interested in industrialization, however, since the independence of Eastern Europe from Western industry is vital to their purpose. This interest
is seen particularly in the concentration on heavy industry envisaged by
these plans, which will postpone for some time any significant increase
in real income.

The plans all cover a number of years and set specific objectives
that they hope to have attained by the end of the period. Within the
period, however, the rate of production is flexible. The periods for which
the plans were established in the early postwar years differed from the
point of view of their starting year and the number of years covered.
These early "reconstruction plans" were concluded between 1948
(Czechoslovakia, Bulgaria) and 1950 (Rumania). The first long-term
plans of development covering from four (Bulgaria) to six years (Yugoslavia) were scheduled to be completed between 1952 and 1955. These
plans, however, were substantially modified by the "new course" policies
introduced toward the end of 1953. It was subsequently decided to synchronize the planning periods so that in all the satellites, with the exception of Bulgaria,[5] a new planning period of five years would begin on
January 1, 1956, to coincide with the sixth Five-Year Plan of the Soviet
Union.[6] The various plans of reconstruction and development adopted
by the East European peoples' democracies are shown in Figure XXXVI,
while the annual rates of growth of national income envisaged by the
1956–60 plan are shown in Figure XXXVII on page 810.

2. ECONOMIC ACTIVITY

Expansion of Industry. The major efforts of the people's democracies in the economic realm have been directed toward increasing in-

---

[4] N. P. Farberov, *Gosudarstvennoe Pravo Stran Narodnoi Demokratii* (1949),
p. 33.

[5] The current economic plan of Bulgaria expired during the end of 1957 and
was to be followed by a Three-Year Plan extending from 1958 to 1960.

[6] In 1957, the Soviet Union announced its decision to scrap the sixth Five-Year
Plan and to begin a new Seven-Year Plan in 1959.

FIG. XXXVI

PLANS OF RECONSTRUCTION AND DEVELOPMENT, 1947–60 *

COUNTRY	PLANS OF RECONSTRUCTION				FIRST PLANS OF DEVELOPMENT			SECOND PLANS OF DEVELOPMENT	
	Period		Officially completed end of	Number of years	Period Jan. 1–Dec. 31	Officially completed end of	Number of years	Period Jan. 1–Dec. 31	Number of years
	First of Year	End of							
Czechoslovakia	1947	Jan. 1948 Dec.	1948	2	1949–1953	1953	5	1955–1960	5
Poland	1947	Jan. 1949 Dec.	1949	3	1950–1955	1955	5	1955–1960	5
Hungary	1947	Aug. 1950 July	1949	2¼	1950–1954	1954	5	1955–1960	5
Rumania	1949	Jan. 1950 Dec.	1950	2	1951–1955	1955	5	1955–1960	5
Bulgaria	1947	Apr. 1948 Mar.	1948	1¾	1949–1953	1952	4	1952–1957†	5
Yugoslavia	1947	Jan. ⟶			1951	1952	6	yearly plans	1

* Taken from Nicolas Spulber, *The Economics of Communist Eastern Europe* (1957), p. 280.

† A three-year plan, 1958–60, is to follow the Second Five-Year Plan.

FIG. XXXVII

NATIONAL INCOME AND INVESTMENT IN EASTERN EUROPE AND THE SOVIET UNION*

Country	NATIONAL INCOME Average Annual Percentage Rate of Growth				GROSS FIXED INVESTMENT Average Annual Percentage Growth		ACCUMULATION AS A PERCENTAGE OF NATIONAL INCOME		
	Preceding Plan			1955 to 1960	1955 to 1960	1951–56 to 1956–60	Annual Average for Preceding Plan Period	1955	Annual Average 1956 to 1960
	Period	Plan (1)	Actual (2)	Plan (3)	(4)	Plan (5)	Actual (6)	Actual (7)	Plan (8)
Albania	1951–55	15	11	9	..	5	..	..	..
Czechoslovakia	1949–53	11	9½	8	15	10	25	19	22
Eastern Germany	1951–55	10	10	8	18	13	12	12	18
Hungary	1950–54	18	8½	7	11	2	24	15	18
Poland	1950–55	13	11	8½	8	7	25	23	18
Rumania	1951–55	13	14	8½	13	11	25	24	25
U.S.S.R.	1951–55	10	11	10	10½	11	26	24	24

* Adapted from *Economic Survey of Europe in 1956* (1957), p. 2 of Chapter II, Table I.

dustrial production, and in this they have been able, after the initial period of reconstruction, to surpass the prewar level. The indices compiled by the Economic Commission for Europe probably provide the
most satisfactory estimate of the expansion of industrial production in
these countries during the first planning period:

FIG. XXXVIII

INDICES OF INDUSTRIAL PRODUCTION
EASTERN EUROPE AND CERTAIN OTHER COUNTRIES*
(BASE YEAR: 100)

COUNTRY	BASE YEAR	1947	1948	1949	1950
Bulgaria	1938	145	175	227	280
Czechoslovakia	1937	93	110	127	147
Hungary	1938	75	107	153	207
Poland	1938	104	143	175	213
Rumania	1938	55	83	117	160
Yugoslavia	1938	—	—	—	316
Finland	1938	117	133	142	145
Ireland	1938	122	134	143	161
Spain	1940	127	127	130	144
U.S.S.R.	1940	—	118	141	173
United Kingdom	1938	115	128	137	150
United States	1938	210	216	198	225

* Adapted from *Economic Survey of Europe in 1950* (1951), p. 30, Table 9;
the figures for the U.S.S.R. are from p. 40, and the Yugoslavian figure for 1950 is
from p. 37.

Several factors make it difficult to evaluate the significance of these
increases. In the case of Poland, for instance, the comparison is with
1938 in the prewar area—i.e., without the industrialized Silesian region
annexed in 1945—and is therefore relevant only to a limited degree. In
the case of both Poland and Yugoslavia some credit should be given
to the important contribution made by UNRRA in 1945–47. In Bulgaria and Yugoslavia, moreover, the level of industrial production in
absolute terms is so low that a high rate of increase means relatively
little. The comparisons suggested in the above table with three other
relatively underdeveloped countries and with the three more industrialized great powers provide a certain perspective to the figures on the
people's democracies.

These increases in industrial production were limited primarily to
producers' goods and were achieved in considerable measure at the expense of other sectors of the economy. Incomplete figures have been officially compiled on the total production (including agriculture, mining,
manufactures, building, transportation, and domestic trade) in Poland,
Czechoslovakia, Hungary, and Bulgaria. They indicate that the 1938

level of total production had scarcely been attained by 1948.[7] While great strides were made by 1955 in the development of capital-goods industries as compared with the prewar levels, the rate of increase of industrial and especially of agricultural production, as shown by Figure XXXIX is definitely on the decline.

FIG. XXXIX

CHANGE IN GROSS OUTPUT IN INDUSTRY AND AGRICULTURE IN EASTERN EUROPEAN COUNTRIES *

Country	Industrial Output				Agricultural Output			
	1955 Actual	1956 Plan	1956 Actual	1957 Plan	1955 Actual	1956 Plan	1956 Actual	1957 Plan
Albania	13	11	8	24	..	..	..	..
Bulgaria	10	12	16	8	30	18	— 5	32
Czecho-slovakia	11	9	10	8	12	9	3	7
East Germany	8	9	7	7	1	..	1	..
Hungary	8	6	—14	— 7	12	3	..	..
Poland	11	7	10	4	3	6	6	3
Rumania	14	..	11	4	25	..	—15	..
Yugoslavia	16	..	10					

Percentage Increases over Previous Year

* Adapted from *Economic Survey of Europe in 1956* (1957), p. 10, Table II; the figures for Yugoslavia are from p. 2 of Chapter III.

Agricultural Production. The problem of increasing agricultural production in Eastern Europe is partly political and partly technological. In the political field production depends on the peasants' assurance that the return for foodstuffs produced above their own requirements will be adequate and that taxes and other government policies will take their needs into consideration. The tendency in Eastern Europe during the past generation has been for the urban interests to dominate the rural, and the peasants are in principle suspicious of the government. Apart from periods of political control by the Agrarian parties, this difficulty was largely overcome only during the late thirties, when many of the governments were able to support agricultural prices as a result of their expanded trade with Germany. Since 1945 minimized trade with industrialized states and concentration on heavy industry at home have placed the governments of Eastern Europe in too poor a position to offer incentives to the peasants.

Technological improvements have also been slow in coming since 1945. UNRRA made notable contributions of expert advice and mechanical equipment in many of these countries during the immediate postwar years, but since its dissolution in 1947 the Eastern European peasant has received little direct assistance. An idea of the position of agriculture in six of these countries can be gained from Figures XXXIX and XL.

[7] Doreen Warriner, *Revolution in Eastern Europe* (1950), pp. 177–78, Table 3.

FIG. XL

INDICES OF AGRICULTURAL PRODUCTION: EASTERN EUROPE *
(1934–38 = 100)

COUNTRY	1946–47	1947–48	1948–49	1949–50
Bulgaria	72	70	87	—
Czechoslovakia	84	66	76	81
Hungary	60	64	98	94
Poland	—	62	65	71
Rumania	53	80	91	—
Yugoslavia	57	79	93	96
Total Europe (excl. U.S.S.R.)	81	80	91	93

* *Economic Survey of Europe in 1950*, p. 43, Table 14.

The accelerated program of industrialization, with the concomitant stress on mining and maufacturing at the expense of consumers' goods and agricultural production, led to the intensification of the tensions that began with the first attempts to collectivize the peasants. This, in turn, led to the inauguration of the "New Course" policy during the middle of 1953. This was characterized by the tendency to decrease the quotas for and to raise the prices of compulsory deliveries and to raise the level of consumption and agriculture by giving some concessions to private-enterprise incentives. It was soon obvious, however, that the "New Course" was not meant to be more than a transitory plan, and with the easing of tension during 1955 the drive for further collectivization and industrialization was resumed. Though the policies with regard to compulsory deliveries are being reconsidered everywhere, the basic lines of the "recourse" continue to be enforced in spite of the Polish and Hungarian events of 1956.

Foreign Trade. The new position of the countries of Eastern Europe has been sharply reflected in their trade relations. It is estimated that the total volume of foreign trade for the people's democracies in 1949 approximated the prewar level. Polish and Czechoslovak trade in 1949 was probably above the prewar level, but that of Bulgaria, Hungary, Rumania, and Yugoslavia was still below it.

The significant change in foreign trade since the war has been the shift from Western Europe to the Soviet Union and the intensification of trade within the area. In 1938 some 15 per cent of the trade of the Eastern European countries was with one another, and 1 per cent was with the Soviet Union. The remaining 84 per cent was with the rest of the world, and in large measure it represented the natural exchange of agricultural goods and few specialized industrial items for the vast array of machines and manufactured products available in the more industrialized countries to the west. By 1949 a great change had occurred in this pattern. Although the trade of the Eastern European countries with one another had increased to only 20 per cent of their total trade, the share of the Soviet Union had risen to 26 per cent of their exports and 32 per cent of their imports. The share of the rest of the world had declined correspondingly to 54 per cent of the exports and 48 per cent of the imports of the Eastern European countries. In 1954 the Soviet Union's share in the total trade of the countries considered represented from 30 to 45 per cent. This trend has not been uniform, however, among the six countries in question. Only in Bulgaria and Rumania did trade with the Soviet Union approximate one half of their foreign trade in 1949. Czechoslovakia, Hungary, and Poland still conducted more trade with the non-Communist world than with the Soviet Union and their smaller Communist neighbors combined. By 1954, however, satellite and Soviet intratrade represented 66 to 87 per cent. Yugoslavian trade with the non-Communist world rose from 46 per cent to over 80 per cent of its total trade between 1948 and 1949 as a result of the break with the Cominform.[8]

FIG. XLI

EASTERN EUROPE'S PATTERN OF TRADE BY AREAS *
1937, 1948, 1954 PERCENTAGES

	1937			1948			1954		
	U.S.S.R.	People's Democ- racies	Rest of World	U.S.S.R.	People's Democ- racies	Rest of World	U.S.S.R.	People's Democ- racies	Rest of World
East Germany	—	—	—	—75—		25	44	31	25
Czecho- slovakia	1	10	89	16	15	69	36	39	25
Poland	1	6	93	23	17	60	38	32	30
Hungary	—	13	87	17	17	66	30	36	34
Rumania	1	17	82	34	36	30	—72—		28
Bulgaria	—	12	88	56	27	17	45	42	13

* Nicolas Spulber, "Factors in Eastern Europe's Intratrade and Cooperation," *Journal of International Affairs,* 11 (1957), p. 23.

This decline in East-West trade may originally have been caused by the cold war, inasmuch as trade with the West held many advantages for people's democracies. Once the pattern was established, however, the production of the Eastern European states was deliberately adapted to the needs of the Soviet market. Although full economic integration of the people's democracies into the Soviet economic system has not been formally announced, it is significant that trade with these countries now accounts for about two thirds of all Soviet foreign trade. A major change in the mechanism of economic relations among the Communist states took place in June, 1957, when a multilateral clearing system was agreed upon. The agreement signed by the members of the Council for Mutual Economic Aid (Molotov Plan) will presumably eliminate the practice of trading on a year-to-year bilateral basis.

[8] The trade figures cited here are from *World Economic Report, 1949–50,* pp. 90–95; for further details see *Economic Survey of Europe in 1949,* pp. 89–94, *1950,* pp. 111–14, and *1955,* p. 111; also Margaret Dewar, *Soviet Trade with Eastern Europe, 1945–1949* (1951).

3. NATIONALIZATION

Industry and Trade. It has already been pointed out that nationalization of the means of production lies at the base of the economic program of the people's democracies and that any private ownership countenanced by the Communists is a temporary phenomenon. At the same time it should be noted that Eastern European industry was nationalized to a limited degree before World War II. In some of the countries state ownership of railroads, mines, and other basic elements of the economy dates back to the nineteenth century. Nationalization became most common, however, between the two world wars.

The principal reason for this trend toward state ownership before World War II was the desire to be independent of foreign control. Since there was little native capital, many of the larger enterprises in these countries were financed by foreign investments; in the course of time a number of important industries came to be owned by foreigners. The advantages of being able to draw on outside sources were not underestimated, but after the depression it was widely believed that if the various national economies relied too heavily on foreign capital the countries of Eastern Europe would become completely dependent on it. This feeling was increased by experience with Nazi Germany, which went to great lengths during the war to integrate and exploit the industrial resources of the countries it occupied. These developments created a widespread conviction, similar to that prevalent in Kemalist Turkey after World War I, that the presence of foreign capital was synonymous with foreign intervention. The trend toward state ownership was further stimulated after World War II, even in non-Communist circles, by the fact that the need for investments greatly surpassed the amount of foreign capital available at the time.

Although all these factors were present in 1945, they remained secondary to the doctrinal goal of carrying out the Communist program. Between 1945 and 1948 all of the people's democracies passed nationalization laws that were rapidly implemented in most cases with only nominal compensation for owners, whether native or foreign, whose property was confiscated. Priority was placed on establishments employing over fifty to one hundred workers, since the first aim of the governments was to gain the "commanding heights" of the economy. With the possible exception of Rumania over 90 per cent of industrial production in Eastern Europe was in the hands of state-owned enterprises by the end of 1948. Information regarding trade and banking is more difficult to obtain, but it may be assumed that any delay in their nationalization is due to expediency rather than to principle.[9]

Land Reform. Nationalization of land in Eastern Europe was a much more extensive task than the nationalization of industry and pre-

[9] Samuel L. Sharp and Laure Metzger, "Industry and Agriculture in Eastern Europe—I: Industry," *Foreign Policy Reports,* 26 (March 15, 1950), pp. 2–8.

sented far more serious difficulties from a political point of view. The private owners in industry had been either foreigners whose influence was now counterbalanced by that of the Soviet Union or members of the small, native business class who had lost their political power. The private owners of the land, however, were the millions of peasant farmers who were very much aware of their own interests and on whose efforts the welfare of each country depended. The question of how to handle the peasants was in fact so delicate that during the first years after World War II nationalization of land was scarcely mentioned in the public press. Instead emphasis was placed on land reform: the breaking up of the remaining large estates and the resettlement of landless peasants.

This measure had long been advocated by the Agrarian parties and was generally desired by the peasants. At the same time, land reform was in contradiction to Communist aims, since it involved creating additional small holdings and in a sense confirmed the principle of private ownership of land. In adopting a program of land reform the Communists were nevertheless following Lenin's policy of 1917, and for very similar reasons. The active enemies of communism at the start were not the peasants, despite the vigor of Agrarian leaders, but the urban political groups and the army and police force of the previous regimes. The Communists therefore adopted the stratagem of keeping the peasants contented by enouncing such principles as "the land belongs to those who till it," and by favoring land reform. Later, when they had the police and army well in hand, the Communists would turn their attention to the nationalization of the land.

Land reforms in the people's democracies, which were in most cases completed by 1948, were carried out in two stages. The first stage consisted of the expropriation of land belonging to former enemy minorities, such as the Germans in Poland, Czechoslovakia, and Yugoslavia, who had fled before the arrival of the Soviet Army. These lands were usually distributed to war veterans and to particularly needy peasants. The second stage involved dividing the estates of native landowners. From the incomplete information available it appears that only in Albania was as much as 50 per cent of the arable land (as distinct from forests and pastures) confiscated and turned over to the poorer peasants as a result of the land reform. The corresponding figure for Hungary, where no serious land reform was attempted after World War I, is about 28 per cent. In the remaining countries, where prewar land reforms had broken the back of the problem, a smaller proportion of land was redistributed: Czechoslovakia, about 20 per cent; Poland, Rumania, and Yugoslavia, about 15 per cent; and Bulgaria, no more than 2 or 3 per cent. In addition to the land distributed to the peasantry, between 5 and 10 per cent of all arable land was apparently taken over as state farms.[1]

[1] The best summaries of this complex problem are Irwin T. Sanders, "Changing Status of the Peasant in Eastern Europe," *Annals of the American Academy of Political and Social Science,* 271 (September, 1950), pp. 78–93; and James O. Howard, "Communist Formula for Land Reform," *Foreign Agriculture,* 15 (March, 1951), pp. 47–52. The fullest statement of the Communist interpretation is "Agrarnye

Collectives and Co-operatives. The land reforms were only a first and minor step in the Communist program. Once the period of dissimulation was over, the Communist leaders frankly admitted that the complete nationalization of the land was their goal. At the same time, however, they recognized that this measure would meet with great resistance if carried out without the proper preliminary preparations. Unlike the Russian peasants in the 1930's, those of Eastern Europe had behind them two generations of political activity. In the course of this experience they had developed a high sense of their own interests within the framework of the national economy, and a sound understanding of the bargaining power they possessed in their negotiations with the government. Moreover, the peasants of Eastern Europe were by no means so isolated from the outside world as the Russian peasants had been. In the relatively delicate balance that existed between East and West, especially after 1947, widespread and active discontent on the part of the peasantry would have seriously embarrassed Communist leaders. It was because of considerations such as these that the people's democracies decided to develop co-operatives rather than insist on collectivization.

Before long, however, it was clear that the co-operatives were being developed, not as an alternative to collectivization, but as a transitional stage that would serve to disarm opponents of the more extreme measure. As one Soviet commentator has analyzed the problem:

> Farm co-operatives are a unique first form of the socialist transformation of agriculture. They are a lower form than the collective-farm type of communalized collective production. . . . The struggle to overcome individualist, petty-ownership psychology is under way. The farm co-operatives create the conditions for introducing large-scale farming methods in agriculture, for establishing that material basis in agriculture without which the peasant's reeducation in the spirit of proletarian socialism is inconceivable. Herein is the significance of farm co-operatives.[2]

The significant feature of farm co-operatives is that the peasants retain ownership of their land. Moreover, members are required to make a capital investment in the co-operative, usually in the form of equipment and livestock. They are permitted to retain a limited amount of livestock as their private possession, although sometimes this arrangement is subject to the vote of all the members. Allocation of income in a co-operative is based partly on the amount of land and partly on the workdays contributed by a member. A certain proportion of the income is also set aside for reinvestment in the co-operative. In addition the co-operatives rely for their capital equipment on investments made

Reformy Poslevoennye" ("Postwar Agrarian Reforms"), *Bol'shaya Sovetskaya Entsiklopediya* (2nd ed., 1949), Vol. I, pp. 320–37. See also Irwin T. Sanders, ed., *Collectivization of Agriculture in Eastern Europe* (1958).

[2] V. Starodubrovskaya, "Formation of the Farm Labor Co-operatives in Bulgaria," *Current Digest of the Soviet Press,* 1 (October 11, 1949), p. 11, translated from *Sotsialisticheskoe Selskoe Khozyaistvo,* No. 8 (August, 1949), pp. 44–52.

by the state as part of the long-term plans. The most important item in the direct assistance of the state is usually the equipment of machine and tractor stations, modeled after the Soviet M.T.S., which serve as distributing centers for both farm equipment and technical advice. Co-operatives are thus distinguished from collectives both in the manner in which they are formed, which is nominally voluntary, and in the fact that the land remains the property of the member and is a source of income in the form of rent.

As a means of appeasing the opponents of collectivization the co-operative has several advantages. It accustoms the peasants to pooling their resources without, for the moment, questioning their ownership of the land. It provides a framework for the intensification of the class struggle between the poorer and richer peasants, by uniting the former in the co-operatives with government support and then turning them against the latter. Once a majority of the peasantry has been induced to join the co-operative movement, the government is able to increase its control through the machine and tractor stations. By the time the government is ready to decree nationalization of the land, the peasants have no bargaining power left.

FIG. XLII

THE CO-OPERATIVE SECTOR IN EASTERN EUROPEAN AGRICULTURE *

COUNTRY	YEAR AND MONTH	CO-OPERATIVE FARMS			
		Number	Incorporated Farms (Thousands)	Agricultural Land Thousands of Hectares	Percentage of Land
Albania	1956, 1 Jan.	318	15	..	15
	1956, 1 May	694	29	..	26
	1957, 1 Jan.	881	37	..	31
Bulgaria	1956, 1 Jan.	2,735	591	2,582	63
	1957, 1 Jan.	3,100	911	3,521	78
Czechoslovakia	1956, 1 Jan.	6,795	211	1,947	26
	1956, 1 Oct.	7,983	241	2,221	30
	1957, 1 Jan.	8,016	..	2,237	30
East Germany	1956, 1 Apr.	6,157	207	1,386	21.4
	1956, 1 July	6,273	219	1,463	22.6
	1956, 1 Oct.	6,287	221	1,488	23.0
	1957, 1 Jan.	6,281	..	1,582	23.2
Hungary	1956, 1 July	5,140	..	1,150	21
	1956, 15 Oct.	5,191	..	1,350	25
	1957, 15 Jan.	2,700	..	670	12
Poland	1956, 1 Jan.	9,963	200	1,800	8.8
	1956, 1 June	10,616	211	2,000	9.8
	1957, 1 Jan.	2–3,000	..	..	..
Rumania	1956, 1 Jan.	6,325	382	1,178	12.0
	1956, 1 July	9,436	577	..	..
	1957, 1 Jan.	10,709	684	1,696	17.5

* Adapted from *Economic Survey of Europe in 1956* (1957), p. 24 of Chapter I.

With the abandonment of the "New Course" the drive toward collectivization was begun anew, and the results in some countries were
impressive. As Figure XLII shows, while the share of co-operative farms
in the total agricultural area fell in Hungary from 21 per cent on July
1, 1956, to 12 per cent on January 15, 1957, and in Poland from
9.8 per cent on June 1, 1956, to about 3 per cent on January 1, 1957
—owing to the historical events of the fall of 1956—that of Bulgaria
rose from 63 per cent on January 1, 1956 to 78 per cent on January 1,
1957. The rate of collectivization was accelerated by lifting practically
all restrictions governing admission to co-operative farms, especially for
peasants with relatively large holdings. The disbanding of three quarters
of the existing co-operative farms in Poland, however, was attributed by
the chairman of the Council of Co-operative Farms to three main features
of collectivization policy:

> In the first place, co-operatives were created in a general
> atmosphere of coercion and illegality. Secondly, the establish-
> ment of the greatest number of co-operative farms was the
> only aim, disregarding basic economic conditions. Thirdly,
> while resources were dispersed lavishly to inefficient co-
> operative farms in order to assure their survival, the well-
> working co-operative farms were overburdened by taxes and
> deliveries almost as the private farmers were.[3]

Whatever concessions may have been made to the farmers, and
whatever the inducements to join the collectives, there can be no
doubt, however, that the co-operatives are not intended as an end in
themselves but merely as a means of preparing the peasantry for
nationalization.

4. SOCIAL WELFARE

Standard of Living. It is not particularly relevant to evaluate
the results of Communist rule in Eastern Europe in terms of an improvement in the standard of living, since the new regimes deliberately
emphasize the expansion of heavy industry at the expense of consumer
goods and agriculture. From the theoretical point of view the standard
of living is a secondary consideration during the period of transition to
socialism. For similar reasons it seems that until recently little improvement has taken place in the standard of living in the Soviet Union since
1917, as there also investments have continued to take precedence over
welfare.

From the fragmentary information available it appears that the prewar standard of living in Eastern Europe has not yet been attained. While
it is true that there has been a great increase in government spending for

[3] *Economic Survey of Europe in 1956* (1957), Chapter I, p. 25, as quoted from
Trybuna Ludu (November 20, 1956).

health and education, the pattern of private spending shows that a greater proportion of income is spent on food now than before World War II (see Figure XLIII), which can be taken as an index of a lowered standard of living. This is especially true in Hungary, where in 1936–38 only 40 per cent of the budget was spent on food as against the present 64 per cent.

FIG. XLIII

PER CENT OF FOOD IN BUDGET *

COUNTRY	1936–38	1953
Soviet Union	57	50
Poland	48	64
East Germany	38	39
Czechoslovakia	46	65
Hungary	40	64

* Adapted from *Trends in Economic Growth: a Comparison of the Western Powers and the Soviet Bloc. A Study Prepared for the Joint Committee on the Economic Report by the Legislative Reference Service of the Library of Congress* (1955), p. 73.

Future trends in the standard of living in the people's democracies will depend on both government policies and the more general influence of the Soviet economy. No over-all improvement can be expected until the people's democracies deliberately shift the weight of capital investments from heavy industry to agriculture and consumers' goods, and this change is not yet in sight. Moreover, the present trend is toward the gradual integration of these countries into the Soviet economy, where the standard of living only approximates that of the least developed of the Eastern European countries. Since tentative Soviet economic plans envisage a continued emphasis on heavy industry until 1965, substantial improvements in the standard of living in the Soviet Union and in its economic dependencies should not be expected before that date.

The Peasant and the State. There can thus be little doubt that the policies being pursued in the people's democracies will have the effect of holding down the standard of living for some time to come. Even if one accepts the general assumptions of Marxism regarding the evils of exploitation and the benefits of communal ownership of the means of production, there appears to be slight prospect for an improvement in the conditions of the peasantry of Eastern Europe. The policy of rapid industrialization without the help of foreign capital inevitably means that the cost must be assumed by the peasant. Even in a free enterprise system the agricultural population tends to bear a disproportionate share of investment unless special care is taken by the state to protect it. Under the system being elaborated by the people's democratic governments the tendency to extract a maximum profit from agriculture at the expense of the peasant is particularly strong, since the power of the state is theoretically unlimited and is harnessed to the aim of developing heavy industry as the key to prosperity.

Apart from Marxian considerations, the farm co-operatives in their present form and, more particularly, the collectives that will be introduced as soon as conditions permit will tend to reduce the bargaining power of the peasant in his relations with the state. In the past the peasant was able to get a satisfactory return for his efforts only by influencing government policy through the Agrarian parties or by threatening to boycott the cities. Under the people's democracies the trend is to reduce the bargaining power of the peasant, whether political or economic, and to leave him entirely at the mercy of state policy. In view of the extent to which Communist policy is concerned with urban interests, it appears likely that the peasant will in the future receive only the minimum consideration.

Industrial Labor. The status of industrial workers is somewhat different from that of the peasants, since the former have never possessed significant bargaining power in their relations with the state. The trade unions, which were brought under the influence of the Communist Party shortly after the war, have not generally been a source of opposition to the regime of the people's democracies. The trade unions themselves have lost whatever bargaining power they possessed, since the employer is now in almost every instance the state. The regulation of wages and conditions of labor is firmly controlled by the state, although the worker doubtless receives more favorable treatment than the peasant.

According to the theories under which the people's democracies operate, there can be no general conflict of interests between the worker and the state employer. Worker-employer relations are restricted to technical problems on the factory level. These problems are handled by bodies generally known as workers' councils, representing the workers in each factory, which have the function of collaborating with the management to improve the organization of production. The workers' councils help to elaborate details of the factory's production plan, to check on management policies, to supervise factory competitions and the distribution of bonuses, and in general to represent the dominant political party in factory affairs. They also supervise the administration of various social benefits and institutions connected with the factory. Since these councils have no share in determining the fundamental labor policies of the state, such as the level of wages, they do not serve in any sense to protect the larger interests of the workers. Within the framework of a system in which the state is considered to have the interests of the workers at heart, however, these councils may well give the workers a sense of participating in the management of production. They thus represent a sort of psychological substitute for the more decisive influence that labor is able to exert in the Western democracies.[4]

[4] J. deGivry, "Works Councils," *International Labour Review,* 59 (June, 1949), pp. 653–58; for an account of the organization of labor in a typical people's democracy see "Industrial Relations in Hungary," *International Labour Review,* 55 (March-April, 1947), pp. 247–60. See *Economic Survey of Europe in 1956* (1957), pp. 30–43, and *Economic Survey of Europe in 1957* (1958), pp. 37–43, for more recent developments in social policy and for the new wage and incentive systems.

SELECTED BIBLIOGRAPHY

I. BIBLIOGRAPHIES

Robert F. Byrnes, ed., *Bibliography of American Publications on East Central Europe, 1945–1957* (Bloomington, Ind., 1959).

Critical Bibliography of Communist Purges and Trials in the Soviet Union and the "People's Democracies" Since 1922 (New York, 1953).

Robert J. Kerner, ed., *Slavic Europe: A Selected Bibliography in Western European Languages* (Cambridge, Mass., 1918).

Library of Congress, *The Balkans: A Selected List of References* (5 vols.; Washington, 1945).

———, *East European Accessions List.* A monthly listing (since September, 1951) of monographs and periodicals currently received by the Library of Congress from the countries of Eastern Europe.

Léon Savadjian, *Bibliographie Balkanique, 1920–1938* (8 vols.; Paris, 1931–39).

Leonid I. Strakhovsky, ed., *A Handbook of Slavic Studies* (Cambridge, Mass., 1949).

Jirina Sztachova, comp., *Mid-Europe: A Selective Bibliography* (New York, 1953).

Fritz Valjavec, *Sudosteuropa—Bibliographie, Vol. I, 1945–50* (Munich, 1956).

II. GENERAL WORKS ON EASTERN EUROPE

1. Introductory surveys worth consulting for background on Eastern Europe would include:

Antonin Basch, *The Danube Basin and the German Economic Sphere* (New York, 1943). In dealing with German economic policy in the 1930's the author provides a comprehensive summary of regional problems.

Oscar Halecki, *Borderlands of Western Civilization: A History of East Central Europe* (New York, 1952). A masterful synthesis of the history of Eastern Europe.

Walter Kolarz, *Myths and Realities in Eastern Europe* (London, 1946). Insights into the heritage of the region.

Z. Lippai, *Borba Imperialistov v Dunaiskom Basseine* ("The Struggle of the Imperialists in the Danube Basin") (Moscow, 1939). A Soviet interpretation.

C. A. Macartney, *Problems of the Danube Basin* (Cambridge, 1942). A brief historical survey by a recognized authority.

Victor S. Mamatey, *The United States and East Central Europe, 1914–1918: A Study in Wilsonian Diplomacy and Propaganda* (Princeton, 1957).

David Mitrany, *The Effects of the War in Southeastern Europe* (New Haven, 1936). A valuable summary of the volumes of the *Economic and Social History of the World War* that deal with Southeastern Europe.

Leo Pasvolsky, *Economic Nationalism of the Danubian States* (London, 1928). An analysis of a fundamental problem.

F. N. Petrov, ed., *Balkanskie Strany* ("The Balkan Countries") (Moscow, 1946). A useful handbook of geographical and political information, prepared by the State Scientific Institute "Soviet Encyclopedia."

J. S. Roucek, ed., *Central-eastern Europe: Crucible of World Wars* (New York, 1946). An introduction to the problems of Eastern Europe.

822

Ferdinand Schevill, *A History of the Balkan Peninsula, from the Earliest Times to the Present Day* (rev. ed., New York, 1933). A standard text.

Rudolf Schlesinger, *Central European Democracy and Its Background: Economic and Political Group Organization* (London, 1953).

Hugh Seton-Watson, *Eastern Europe between the Wars, 1918–1941* (2nd ed., Cambridge, 1946). A valuable general introduction.

South-eastern Europe: A Political and Economic Survey (New York, 1939). A valuable handbook.

Georg Stadtmüller, *Geschichte Südosteuropas* (Munich, 1950). A history of South-eastern Europe to World War I.

L. S. Stavrianos, *The Balkans Since 1453* (Princeton, 1958). The latest full account, with an excellent bibliography.

Dinko Tomasic, *Personality and Culture in Eastern European Politics* (New York, 1948). A sociological interpretation.

Harriet Wanklyn, *The Eastern Marchlands of Europe* (New York, 1941). An indispensable geographical treatise.

2. For the developments since World War II see:

Hamilton Fish Armstrong, *Tito and Goliath* (New York, 1951). A well-informed study of Communist policies in Eastern Europe, with special emphasis on the growth of Titoism.

J. B. Barron, *Communism and the Churches: a Documentation* (London, 1950).

Tufton Beamish, *Must Night Fall?* (London, 1950). A description of Communist methods in Poland, Bulgaria, Rumania, and Hungary.

R. R. Betts, ed., *Central and South East Europe, 1945–1948* (London, 1950). A summary of developments by country, with primary emphasis on domestic affairs.

C. E. Black, ed., *Challenge in Eastern Europe* (New Brunswick, N.J., 1954).

———, ed., *Readings on Contemporary Europe* (New York, 1953). A useful collection of articles.

B. L. Borisov, *Mestnye organy gosudarstvennoi vlasti Evropeiskikh stran narodnoi demokratii* ("The local state organs in the European people's democracies") (Moscow, 1955).

Richard K. Carlton, ed., *Forced Labor in the "People's Democracies"* (New York, 1955). A documented account.

François Fejtö, *Histoire des Démocraties Populaires* (Paris, 1952). A general survey of the people's democracies.

P. George, *Les Démocraties populaires* (Paris, 1952).

Andrew Gyorgy, *Governments of Danubian Europe* (New York, 1949). A comprehensive account of political developments since World War II in Czechoslovakia, Rumania, Hungary, Yugoslavia, and Bulgaria.

John H. Hallowell, ed., *Soviet Satellite Nations: A Study of the New Imperialism* (Gainesville, Fla., 1958).

Denis Healey, ed., *The Curtain Falls: The Story of the Socialists in Eastern Europe* (London, 1951). Chapters on the defeat of the Socialist parties since World War II in Poland, Hungary, and Czechoslovakia, with a foreword by Aneurin Bevan denouncing Communist policy.

How Did the Satellites Happen? A Study of the Soviet Seizure of Europe, by a student of affairs (London, 1952).

E. Lemberg, *Osteuropa und die Sowjet-Union. Geschichte und Probleme der Welt hinter dem Eisernen Vorhang* (Salzburg, 1956). A general history of the countries behind the Iron Curtain.

V. P. Maksakovsy, *Stroiki sotsializma v evropeiskikh stranakh narodnoi demokratii* ("Construction of Socialism in the European People's Democracies") (Moscow, 1957). A Soviet view of socialism in the people's democracies.

R. H. Markham, ed., *Communists Crush Churches in Eastern Europe* (Boston, 1950). An account of the campaign against the Catholic and Protestant churches.

Mid-European Law Project (formerly *Digest-Index of East European Law*). The *Project* is financed by the National Committee for a Free Europe, Inc., and

conducted at the Law Library of Congress under the administrative supervision of Lawrence Keitt, law librarian, and the direction of Dr. Vladimir
Gsovski. The digest, translations, and studies, which will eventually cover the
principal changes in public and private law since 1944 in Bulgaria, Czechoslovakia, Estonia, Latvia, Lithuania, Poland, Rumania, and Yugoslavia, will be
published in serial form. The reports and index are currently available for
consultation at the Law Library. The Hungarian section was published in 1956.

Bernard S. Morris, "The Cominform: A Five-Year Perspective," *World Politics,* 5
(April, 1953), pp. 368–76.

"Die neuen Parteistatuten in den Ostblockstaaten," *Osteuropa,* 5 (Feb., 1955), pp.
52–63. On the party statutes in Eastern Europe.

Ithiel de Sola Pool, *Satellite Generals: A Study of Military Elites in the Soviet
Sphere* (Stanford, 1955). A social science approach to a study of the satellite
armies.

Henry L. Roberts, "The Future of Eastern Europe," *Journal of International Affairs,*
11, No. 1 (1957), pp. 72–77.

———, ed., "The Satellites in Eastern Europe," *Annals of the American Academy
of Political and Social Science,* 317 (May, 1958), pp. 1–163.

Joseph S. Roucek, ed., "Moscow's European Satellites," *Annals of the American
Academy of Political and Social Science,* 271 (Sept., 1950). A stimulating collection of articles.

Hugh Seton-Watson, *The East European Revolution* (London, 1950). A valuable
introduction to the people's democracies.

———, "Eastern Europe since Stalin," *Problems of Communism,* 3 (March-April,
1954), pp. 10–17.

George N. Shuster, *Religion behind the Iron Curtain* (New York, 1954).

Robert Tobias, *Communist-Christian Encounter in Eastern Europe* (Indianapolis,
1956).

Piotr S. Wandycz, "The Soviet System of Alliances in East Central Europe," *Journal
of Central European Affairs,* 16 (July, 1956), pp. 177–86.

Doreen Warriner, *Revolution in Eastern Europe* (London, 1950). A pro-Soviet account by a well-informed economist.

Robert Lee Wolff, *The Balkans in Our Time* (Cambridge, Mass., 1956). An authoritatively documented account of the Balkan countries.

Paul E. Zinner, *National Communism and Popular Revolt in Eastern Europe* (New
York, 1956). A collection of documents on events in Poland and Hungary,
February to November, 1956.

3. Writings in political theory include those on the significant problems of
agrarianism:

Agrarian Problems from the Baltic to the Aegean (London, 1944). A concise survey of the agricultural basis of Eastern European politics, with special reference to the program of the peasant parties.

W. B. Bizzell, *The Green Rising* (New York, 1926). A general history of agrarianism.

Georgi M. Dimitrov, "Agrarianism," in Feliks Gross, ed., *European Ideologies*
(New York, 1948).

Sigismund Gargas, *Die Grüne Internationale* (Halberstadt, 1927). A discussion of
the development of the international agrarian movement after World War I.

Rudolf Herceg and Stjepan Radić, *Die Ideologie der kroatischen Bauernbewegung*
(Zagreb, 1923).

David Mitrany, *Marx against the Peasant: A Study in Social Dogmatism* (Chapel
Hill, 1951). An indispensable introduction to agrarian problems in Eastern
Europe by a leading expert.

Branko M. Pešelj, "Peasant Ideology and Its Sources," *Bulletin of the International
Peasant Union,* II (Sept., 1951).

Ivo Sarinić, "Die Ideologie der kroatischen Bauernbewegung," *Slavische Rundschau,*
9 (1937), pp. 147–56.

4. On communism and people's democracy, note:

C. E. Black, "Constitutional Trends in Eastern Europe, 1945–48," *Review of Politics,* 11 (April, 1949), pp. 196–207.

Georgi Dimitrov, *Political Report Delivered to the V Congress of the Bulgarian Communist Party* (Sofia, 1948). One of the first authoritative views on the essence of a "people's democracy."

Milovan Djilas, *The New Class: An Analysis of the Communist System* (New York, 1957). A devastating criticism of Communism and of the Communist system by a former Titoist leader.

Michel-Henry Fabre, *Théorie des démocraties populaires. Contribution à l'étude de l'état socialiste* (Paris, 1949). A French political scientist's analysis of the theory of people's democracy.

N. P. Farberov, *Gosudarstvennoe Pravo Stran Narodnoi Demokratii* ("Constitutional Law of the People's Democracies") (Moscow, 1949). The principal Soviet study of the theory and law of people's democracy.

————, *Osnovnye Nachala Gosudarstvennogo Stroya Narodnykh Respublik Tsentral'noi i Yugo-Vostochnoi Evropy* ("Basic Principles of the Constitutional Structure of the People's Republics of Central and Southeastern Europe") (Moscow, 1950). A further contribution by a Soviet authority.

L. Figueres, "A Form of Socialist Democracy: People's Democratic Power," *Political Affairs,* 31 (Nov., 1952), pp. 46–57. A Communist view.

William Z. Foster, "People's Front and People's Democracy," *Political Affairs,* 29 (June, 1950), pp. 14–31. A Communist view.

T. Georgescu, "Political Foundations of the People's Democratic System," *For a Lasting Peace, for a People's Democracy,* 38, No. 11 (June 1, 1949), pp. 4–5.

G. A. Gmanaberov, "Problems of State and Law in the Countries of People's Democracy," *Current Digest of the Soviet Press,* 1 (Sept. 13, 1949), pp. 10–16.

F. T. Konstantinov, ed., *O Narodnoi Demokratii v Stranakh Evropy* ("Concerning People's Democracy in the European Countries") (Moscow, 1956).

B. S. Mankovsky, "The New Stage in Development of the People's Democracies as States of the Socialist Type," *Current Digest of the Soviet Press,* 2 (Oct. 14, 1950), pp. 3–8.

Hilary Minc, "Some Problems of the People's Democracy in the Light of the Leninist-Stalinist Teachings on the Dictatorship of the Proletariat," *Political Affairs,* 29 (July, 1950), pp. 87–96; (Aug., 1950), pp. 86–96. A Communist view.

B. Mirkine-Guetzevitch, *Les Constitutions européennes* (Paris, 1952), 2 vols. An authoritative discussion of general theory, with constitutional texts.

"Narodnaya Demokratiya" ("People's Democracy"), *Bolshaya Sovetskaya Entsiklopediya,* 2nd ed., Vol. XXIX, pp. 131–36.

Nekotorye Voprosy Gosudarstva i Prava Stran Narodnoi Demokratii Tsentral'noi i Yugo-Vostochnoi Evropy ("Some Problems of State and Law in the People's Democracies of Central and Southeastern Europe") (Moscow, 1951). A symposium of four chapters on problems of theory.

Robert G. Neumann, "Constitutional Documents of East-central Europe," in Arnold J. Zurcher, ed., *Constitutions and Constitutional Trends since World War II* (New York, 1951).

Amos J. Peaslee, *Constitutions of Nations* (2nd ed., The Hague, 1956), 3 vols. Contains the texts of all the new constitutions of the people's democracies.

Branko M. Pešelj, "Legal Trends in 'People's Democracies': The Satellite States," *George Washington Law Review,* 22 (April, 1954), pp. 513–53. A very useful article.

L. Rabcewicz-Zubkowski, "Traits caractéristiques des constitutions des 'Démocraties Populaires,'" *Revue de l'Université d'Ottawa,* 22 (July-Sept., 1952), pp. 339–53. A study of the constitutions of the people's democracies.

Jozsef Revai, "The Character of a People's Democracy," *Foreign Affairs,* 28 (Oct., 1949), pp. 143–52. A Communist view.

Ruth Amende Rosa, "The Soviet Theory of People's Democracy," *World Politics,* 1 (July, 1949), pp. 489–510.

A. Rossi, "Théorie des démocraties populaires," *Preuves*, 3 (May, 1953), pp. 61–68.

Samuel L. Sharp, *New Constitutions in the Soviet Sphere* (Washington, 1950). A useful commentary.

——, "People's Democracy: Evolution of a Concept," *Foreign Policy Reports*, 26 (Jan. 1, 1951), pp. 186–88.

Gordon A. Skilling, " 'People's Democracy' in Soviet Theory," *Soviet Studies*, 3 (July, 1951), pp. 16–33; 3 (Oct., 1951), pp. 131–49.

R. F. Staar, "Theory of the Polish People's Democracy," *Western Political Quarterly*, IX (Dec., 1956), pp. 835–49.

P. B. Steanu, "Constitutionalism in the Satellite States," *Journal of Central European Affairs*, 12 (April, 1952), pp. 56–69.

Teoriya Gosudarstva i Prava ("The Theory of State and Law") (Moscow, 1949). An authoritative treatise, prepared by the Institute of Law of the Soviet Academy of Science, which includes a chapter (pp. 454–92) relating the theory of people's democracy to general Soviet theory.

V. Tikhomirov, "Ukreplenie Soyuza Rabochikh i Trudyashchikhsya Krestyan v Stranakh Narodnoi Demokratii" ("The Strengthening of the Alliance between the Workers and the Toiling Peasantry in the People's Democracies"), *Bol'shevik*, 27 (April, 1950), pp. 41–8.

D. A. Tomasic, *National Communism and Soviet Strategy* (New York, 1957). On "Titoism" in Yugoslavia and the other Eastern European countries.

Georges Vedel, *Les Démocraties marxistes* (Paris, 1950–51), 2 vols. A French political scientist's analysis of the constitutional developments in the people's democracies.

Zakonodatel'stvo Stran Narodnoi Demokratii ("Leglislation of the People's Democracies") (Moscow, 1950). A series of small volumes, giving constitutions and selected legislative acts. Volumes on Albania, Bulgaria, Czechoslovakia, Poland, and Rumania have been issued.

5. For discussions of economic problems consult:

"Agrarnye Reformy Poslevoennye" ("The Postwar Agrarian Reforms"), *Bol'shaya Sovetskaya Entsiklopediya* (2nd ed., Moscow, 1949), Vol. I, pp. 320–37.

I. G. Alekseev, ed., *Plany razvitiya narodnogo khozyaistva stran narodnoi demokratii* ("Plans for the development of the national economies of the people's democracies") (Moscow, 1952).

B. G. Boldyrev, *Finansy Evropeiskikh Stran Narodnoi Demokratii* ("Finances of the European People's Democracies") (Moscow, 1951).

Jean Chardonnet, *Géographie économique de l'Europe Danubienne et de la Pologne* (Paris, 1949), 2 vols. A scholarly study of recent economic and social developments.

Jean De Givry, "Works Councils," *International Labour Review*, 59 (June, 1949), pp. 633–67.

Margaret Dewar, *Soviet Trade with Eastern Europe, 1945–1949* (London, 1951). A well-documented study.

Dorothy W. Douglas, *Transitional Economic Systems: the Polish-Czech Example* (London, 1953).

I. Dubinskii, "Ekonomicheskoe Sotrudnichestvo SSSR i Stran Narodnoi Demokratii" ("Economic Co-operation of the U.S.S.R. with the People's Democracies"), *Bol'shevik*, 26 (March, 1950), pp. 9–19.

Economic Survey of Europe in 1948 . . . 1957 (Geneva, 1949–58). Annual studies prepared by the Research and Planning Division of the Economic Commission for Europe, containing reasonably reliable statistics of the countries of Eastern Europe.

Economic Treaties and Agreements of the Soviet Bloc in Eastern Europe, 1945–1951 (New York, 1952).

Pierre George, *L'Economie de l'Europe Centrale Slave et Danubienne* (Paris, 1949). Agrarian problems and economic plans of the postwar regimes.

Kazimierz Gryzbowski, "Foreign Investment and Political Control in Eastern Europe," *Journal of Central European Affairs*, XIII (April, 1953), pp. 13–27.

J. Gutteridge, "Expropriation and Nationalization in Hungary, Bulgaria, and Rumania," *International and Comparative Law Quarterly*, 1 (Jan., 1952), pp. 14–28.

Frederick Hertz, *The Economic Problem of the Danubian States: A Study in Economic Nationalism* (London, 1947). A competent estimate of the difficulties faced by the new regimes.

N. I. Ivanov, *Khozyaistvennoe razvitie stran narodnoi demokratii* ("Economic development of the people's democracies") (Moscow, 1954). A Soviet interpretation.

Joint Committee on the Economic Report, *Trends in Economic Growth. A Comparison of the Western Powers and the Soviet Bloc* (Washington, 1955). A useful study.

G. Kemeny, "Eastern Europe: Developments in Social and Economic Structure," *World Politics*, 6 (Oct., 1953), pp. 67–83.

N. G. Klimko, *Ekonomicheskii stroi Evropeiskikh stran narodnoi demokratii* ("Economic structure of the European people's democracies") (Moscow, 1955).

V. Kolarov, "The World Agrarian Crisis and the Peasant Movement," *Communist International*, 8 (May 15, 1931), pp. 265–72.

Jan Marczewski, *Planification et croissance économique des démocraties populaires* (Paris, 1956). An extensive and scholarly study on postwar economic growth.

W. E. Moore, *Economic Demography of Eastern and Southern Europe* (Geneva, 1945). A fundamental study, prepared under the auspices of the Economic, Financial, and Transit Department of the League of Nations.

S. Ogurtsov, *Podyem blagosostoyaniya trudyashchikhsya v evropeiskikh stranakh narodnoi demokratii* ("Progress of the workers' welfare in the European people's democracies") (Moscow, 1954).

A. E. Pashertnik, *Trudovoe pravo stran narodnoi demokratii* ("Labor law in the people's democracies") (Moscow, 1955).

Branko M. Pešelj, *The Industrialization of Peasant Europe* (New York, 1953).

Norman Pounds and Nicolas Spulber, eds., *Resources and Planning in Eastern Europe* (Bloomington, Ind., 1957).

Irwin T. Sanders, "Changing Status of the Peasant in Eastern Europe," *Annals of the American Academy of Political and Social Science*, 271 (Sept., 1950), pp. 78–93.

————, ed., *Collectivization of Agriculture in Eastern Europe* (Lexington, Ky., 1958). A valuable collection of papers.

Nicolas Spulber, *The Economics of Communist Eastern Europe* (New York, 1957). An original and authoritative treatise.

U. S. Foreign Operations Administration, *Soviet Bloc Economic Activities in the Free World* (Washington, 1955).

Vneshnyaya torgovlya stran narodnoi demokratii ("Foreign trade of the people's democracies") (Moscow, 1955).

Jan Wszelaki, "The Rise of Industrial Middle Europe," *Foreign Affairs*, 30 (Oct., 1951), pp. 123–34.

Zakonodatel'stvo po Vneshnei Torgovle Stran Narodnoi Demokratii ("Legislation on Foreign Trade of the People's Democracies") (Moscow, 1952). A collection of laws and regulations, relating to foreign trade, for Albania, Bulgaria, Hungary, Poland, Rumania, and Czechoslovakia.

S. D. Zagoroff and others, *The Agricultural Economy of the Danubian Countries, 1935–1945* (New York, 1955).

A. Zauberman, *Economic Imperialism: The Lesson of Eastern Europe* (London, 1955).

6. Out of the great wealth of material on international relations, special mention may be made of the following:

C. E. Black, "Soviet Policy in Eastern Europe," *Annals of the American Academy of Political and Social Science*, 263 (May, 1949), pp. 152–64.

Zbigniew Brzezinski, "U.S. Foreign Policy in East Central Europe—A Study in Contradiction," *Journal of International Affairs*, 11, No. 1 (1957), pp. 60–71.

Robert F. Byrnes, "East Europe in Crisis," *Current History*, 32 (Feb., 1956), pp. 71–76.

J. C. Campbell, "Diplomacy on the Danube," *Foreign Affairs,* 27 (Jan., 1949), pp. 315–27.

Nicolas Clarion, *Le Glacis soviétique: théorie et pratique de la démocratie nouvelle* (Paris, 1948). A brief critical analysis of Soviet expansionist techniques in Europe and in the Near and Middle East.

Alexander Dallin, "Soviet Policy toward Eastern Europe," *Journal of International Affairs,* 11, No. 1 (1957), pp. 48–59.

Georgi Dimitrov, *The United Front: The Struggle against Fascism and War* (New York, 1938). A collection of speeches by the secretary-general of the Comintern.

Harry N. Howard, "The Soviet Alliance System, 1942–1948," *Documents and State Papers,* 1 (July, 1948), pp. 219–49; and "New Links in the Soviet Alliance System, 1948–1949," *Documents and State Papers,* 1 (March-April, 1949), pp. 12–13.

Informatsionnoe Soveshchanie Predstavitelei Nekotorykh Kompartii v Polshe v kontse Sentyabrya 1947 Goda ("Informatory Conference of the Representatives of Several Communist Parties Held in Poland in the Latter Part of September 1947") (Moscow, 1958). A collection of speeches and reports made at the meeting that established the Cominform, available in English in the early issues of *For a Lasting Peace, for a People's Democracy.*

Stephen D. Kertesz, ed., *The Fate of East Central Europe: Hopes and Failures of American Foreign Policy* (Notre Dame, 1957). An authoritative collective work.

———, "The Method of Soviet Penetration in Eastern Europe," in Waldemar Gurian, ed., *The Soviet Union: Background, Ideology, Reality* (Notre Dame, 1951), pp. 85–136.

W. W. Kulski, "The Soviet System of Collective Security Compared with the Western System," *American Journal of International Law,* 44 (July, 1950), pp. 453–76.

Kermit E. McKenzie, "The Soviet Union, the Comintern and World Revolution: 1935," *Political Science Quarterly,* 65 (June, 1950), pp. 214–37.

Philip E. Mosely, "Soviet Policy and Nationality Conflicts in East Central Europe," in Waldemar Gurian, ed., *The Soviet Union: Background, Ideology, Reality* (Notre Dame, 1951), pp. 67–84.

Robert G. Neumann, "U.S. Foreign Policy and the Soviet Satellites," *Review of Politics,* 11 (April, 1949), pp. 220–36.

The Strategy and Tactics of World Communism (Washington, 1948). A summary of Soviet policy, prepared for the Committee on Foreign Affairs of the House of Representatives, with many documents relating to the Soviet orbit in Eastern Europe.

Adam B. Ulam, "The Cominform and the People's Democracies," *World Politics,* 3 (Jan., 1951), pp. 200–17.

VII Congress of the Communist International: Abridged Stenographic Report of Proceedings (Moscow, 1939). This report contains the resolution of the Comintern relating to united fronts and people's fronts and the discussions in which these techniques were interpreted.

Sergius Yakobson, "The Soviet Concept of Satellite States," *Review of Politics,* 11 (April, 1949), pp. 184–95.

Paul E. Zinner, "Soviet Policies in Eastern Europe," *Annals of the American Academy of Political and Social Science,* 303 (Jan., 1956), pp. 152–65.

7. The following periodicals should also be consulted for authoritative current information on Eastern Europe:

Borba (daily). The official paper of the Yugoslav Communist Party.

Current Digest of the Soviet Press (weekly). Translations and summaries of important articles in the Soviet press, including much material on Soviet policy in Eastern Europe.

East Europe (monthly), superseding *News from behind the Iron Curtain.* A review of Eastern European affairs.

East Europe and Soviet Russia (weekly). Published in London by Countess Judith of Listowel and Col. J. Kowalewski.

For a Lasting Peace, for a People's Democracy (weekly). The official journal of the Cominform, containing a record of current trends and theories in the people's democracies as seen through Soviet eyes. Discontinued in 1956.

International Peasant Union Bulletin (monthly). A periodical representing the views of the exiled peasant leaders of Eastern Europe, published in Washington, D.C.

Journal of Central European Affairs (quarterly). A scholarly journal published at the University of Colorado.

Kommunist (bimonthly). The theoretical organ of the Central Committee of the Yugoslav Communist Party.

Lupta de Clasa (monthly). The theoretical journal of the Rumanian Communist Party.

Nepszabadsag (daily). The official organ of the Hungarian Communist Party. Supersedes *Szabad Nep*, which was suspended following the Hungarian Revolution of Oct.-Nov., 1956.

Ost-Europa (bimonthly). A German-language periodical dealing with satellite affairs.

Polish Affairs (monthly). A bulletin representing the views of the Polish Political Council in London.

Problems of Communism (bimonthly). Frequently carries material on Eastern Europe, although it is mainly devoted to reports on the Soviet Union and Communist China.

Rabotnichesko Delo (daily). The official organ of the Bulgarian Workers' (Communist) Party.

Review of International Affairs (biweekly). An English-language journal published in Belgrade, reflecting the views of the Yugoslav government.

Rudé Právo (daily). The official organ of the Czechoslovakian Communist Party.

Scinteia (daily). The official organ of the Rumanian Communist Party.

Tarsadalmi Szemle (monthly). The theoretical journal of the Hungarian Communist Party.

Trybuna Ludu (daily). The official organ of the United Workers' (Communist) Party of Poland.

III. WORKS BY COUNTRY

ALBANIA

1. Background:

Margaret Hasluck, *The Unwritten Law in Albania* (New York, 1954).

M. D. A. von Redlich, *Albania Yesterday and Today* (Worcester, 1936). A general survey.

Vandaleur Robinson, *Albania's Road to Freedom* (London, 1941). A description of Albania and King Zog under Italian influence.

Joseph Swire, *King Zog's Albania* (New York, 1937). A thorough account by a journalist.

Dalib Zavalani, *Die landwirtschaftlichen Verhältnisse Albaniens* (Berlin, 1938). A careful economic study.

2. World War II and after:

Julian Amery, *Sons of the Eagle: A Study in Guerrilla War* (New York, 1949). An account of the relations among the various resistance movements in Albania, by a member of a British mission.

Vladimir Dedijer, "Albania, Soviet Pawn," *Foreign Affairs,* 30 (Oct., 1951), pp. 103–11.

"History of the Albanian Communist Party," *News from behind the Iron Curtain,* 4 (Nov., 1955), pp. 3–10; 5 (Jan., 1956), pp. 22–30.

P. Manchkha, *Albaniya na Puti k Sotsializmu* ("Albania on the Road to Socialism") (Moscow, 1951). A Soviet account.

Daniel Norman, "Albania: A Communist Colony," *Problems of Communism,* 5 (March-April, 1956), pp. 34–41.

"La République populaire d'Albanie," *La Documentation française. Notes et études documentaires,* No. 1, 843 (March, 1954).

V. V. Shvets, *Stroitel'stvo ekonomicheskikh osnov sotsializma v Albanii* ("Construction of the economic bases of socialism in Albania") (Moscow, 1955). A Soviet study of economic development.

Stavro Skendi, ed., *Albania* (New York, 1956). A documented account.

BULGARIA

1. Background:

K. Dimitriev, *Bolgariya* (Moscow, 1941). A survey from the Soviet viewpoint.

Angel Dinev, *Političkite ubistva vo Bulgarija* ("Political assassinations in Bulgaria") (Skopje, 1951). The history of Bulgaria from a Titoist point of view.

Venelin Ganev, *Demokratsiya: Săshtnost i Osnovni Nachala* ("Democracy: Its Nature and Fundamental Principles") (Sofia, 1946). A declaration of faith by the Liberal leader and legal scholar who served as senior regent (1944–46) after World War II.

G. P. Genov, *Bulgaria and the Treaty of Neuilly* (Sofia, 1935). A semi-official nationalist account of Bulgarian grievances arising from the World War I peace settlement.

Vasil Kolarov, "The Tactics of the Bulgarian Communist Party," *Communist International,* No. 30 (Jan., 1924), pp. 11–44.

Nikola D. Petkov, *Alexander Stambolisky: Lichnost i Idei* ("Personality and Ideas") (Sofia, 1930). A biography of the Agrarian leader by a noted successor.

Alexander Stambolisky, *Politicheski Partii ili Săslovni Organizatsii?* ("Political Parties or Professional Organizations?") (3rd ed., Sofia, 1945). The principal theoretical work of the Bulgarian Agrarian leader.

James Swire, *Bulgarian Conspiracy* (London, 1939). A journalist's account of the political intrigues of the Internal Macedonian Revolutionary Organization.

T. Tchitchovsky, *The Socialist Movement in Bulgaria* (London, 1931). A brief summary.

Kosta Todorov, *Balkan Firebrand: The Autobiography of a Rebel, Soldier and Statesman* (Chicago, 1943). Memoirs of an Agrarian leader, valuable for its discussion of negotiations with the Communists after 1923.

2. World War II and after:

Y. I. Aizenshtat, *Gosudarstvennye Stroi Narodnoi Respublik Bolgarii* ("Constitutional Structure of the Bulgarian People's Republic") (Moscow, 1951). A Soviet view of the development of the new political system, with a background chapter.

L. A. D. Dellin, ed., *Bulgaria* (New York, 1957). A well-documented account of the Communist period.

Dimo Kazasov, *Burni Godini, 1918–1944* ("Stormy Years, 1918–1944") (Sofia, 1949). A pro-Communist interpretation of Bulgarian politics.

Dragomir Nenoff, ed., *Forced Labor Camps and Prisons in Bulgaria* (New York, 1952).

Michael Padev, *Dimitrov Wastes No Bullets* (London, 1948). A critical account of the Petkov trial.

Le Procès de Traitcho Kostov et de son groupe (Sofia, 1950). Official record of the trial of the Bulgarian Communist leader.

R. P. Rochlin, *Die Wirtschaft Bulgariens seit 1945* (Berlin, 1957). A Communist view of Bulgaria's economic development.

V. N. Starodubrovskaya, *Stroitel'stvo ekonomicheskogo fundamenta sotsializma v narodnoi respublike Bolgarii* ("Construction of the economic bases of socialism in the Bulgarian People's Republic") (Moscow, 1953). A Soviet view of Bulgaria's economic development.

E. O. Stillman and R. H. Bass, "Bulgaria: A Study in Satellite Non-Conformity," *Problems of Communism,* 4 (Nov.-Dec., 1955), pp. 26–33.

The Trial of Nikola D. Petkov: Record of the Judicial Proceedings, August 5–15, 1947 (Sofia, 1947).

L. B. Valev, *Iz Istorii Otechestvennogo Fronta Bolgarii* ("From the History of the Bulgarian Fatherland Front") (Moscow, 1950). A Soviet account of the origins of the Bulgarian people's front movement.

Orlin Vasilev, *Văorazhenata Săprotiva Sreshtu Fashizma v Bălgariya, 1923–1944: Ocherki i Dokumenti* ("The Armed Resistance against Fascism in Bulgaria, 1923–1944: Sketches and Documents") (Sofia, 1946). A Communist rewriting of history.

CZECHOSLOVAKIA

1. Background:

Edward B. Hitchcock, *"I Built a Temple for Peace": the Life of Eduard Beneš* (New York, 1940). An authorized biography.

Milan Hodža, *Federation in Central Europe: Reflections and Reminiscences* (London, 1942). The memoirs of the Slovak Agrarian leader.

Robert J. Kerner, ed., *Czechoslovakia* (Berkeley, 1949). The best general introduction.

Kamil Krofta, *A Short History of Czechoslovakia* (New York, 1934).

Thomas G. Masaryk, *The Making of a State: Memories and Observations, 1914–1918* (New York, 1927). Memoirs of the founder of the Czechoslovakian state.

Jaroslav Papousek, *Czechoslovakia, Soviet Russia and Germany* (Prague, 1936).

P. Reimann, *Dějiny Komunisticke Strany Československa* ("History of the Communist Party of Czechoslovakia") (Prague, 1931).

R. W. Seton-Watson, *History of the Czechs and Slovaks* (London, 1943). A general history.

Lucy E. Textor, *Land Reform in Czechoslovakia* (London, 1923). A standard work.

S. Harrison Thomson, *Czechoslovakia in European History* (2nd ed., Princeton, 1953). An excellent introductory history.

William Preston Warren, *Masaryk's Democracy* (Chapel Hill, 1941). A study of Masaryk's political thought.

2. World War II and after:

Vratislav Busek and Nicholas Spulber, eds., *Czechoslovakia* (New York, 1957). A documented account of the "People's Democratic era."

Ivo Duchacek, "Czechoslovakia: New Course or No Course?", *Problems of Communism*, 4 (Jan.-Feb., 1955), pp. 12–19.

———, "The Strategy of Communist Infiltration: Czechoslovakia, 1944–48," *World Politics*, 2 (April, 1950), pp. 345–72; and "The February Coup in Czechoslovakia," *World Politics*, 21 (July, 1950), pp. 511–32.

Otto Friedman, *The Break-up of Czech Democracy* (London, 1950). A comprehensive study based on firsthand information.

I. Gadourek, *The Political Control of Czechoslovakia* (Leiden, 1953).

Robert Bruce Lockhart, "The Czechoslovak Revolution," *Foreign Affairs,* 26 (July, 1948), pp. 632–44.

———, "Report on Czechoslovakia," *Foreign Affairs,* 33 (April, 1955), pp. 484–498.

A. I. Nedorezov, *Agrarnye preobrazovaniya v narodno-demokraticheskoi Chekhoslovakii* ("Agrarian reforms in the Czechoslovak People's Democracy") (Moscow, 1954). A Soviet study.

Purges in the Czechoslovak Communist Party (New York, 1952).

Hubert Ripka, *Czechoslovakia Enslaved: The Story of the Communist Coup d'État* (London, 1950). By the former minister of foreign trade, 1945–48.

Dana Adams Schmidt, *Anatomy of a Satellite* (Boston, 1952). A judicious appraisal of Communist policy in Czechoslovakia by an experienced American journalist.

Gordon A. Skilling, "People's Democracy, the Proletarian Dictatorship and the Czechoslovak Path to Socialism," *American Slavic and East European Review,* 10 (April, 1951), pp. 100–16.

The Slansky Trial; Verbatim Transcript of Court Proceedings and Minutes (New York, 1953).

Jan Stransky, *East Wind over Prague* (New York, 1951). An account of Communist rule by a former minister of education.

Edward Taborsky, "The Administration of Justice in a 'People's Democracy,'" *American Political Science Review,* 49 (June, 1955), pp. 402–15.

———, "Beneš and the Soviets," *Foreign Affairs,* 27 (Jan., 1949), pp. 302–14.

———, "Local Government in Czechoslovakia, 1918–1948," *American Slavic and East European Review,* 10 (Oct., 1951), pp. 202–15.

Harriet Wanklyn, *Czechoslovakia* (New York, 1954). A thorough survey, emphasizing the physical and economic geography of Czechoslovakia.

Paul Zinner, *Communist Strategy and Tactics in Czechoslovakia, 1945–1950* (Ph.D. dissertation, Harvard University, 1954).

———, "Marxism in Action: The Seizure of Power in Czechoslovakia," *Foreign Affairs,* 28 (July, 1950), pp. 644–58.

FINLAND

1. Background:

Tancred Borenius, *Field-Marshal Mannerheim* (London, 1940). A friendly biography of the Finnish national leader.

J. H. Jackson, *Finland* (New York, 1938). A useful introduction to modern Finland.

William Sommer, *Geschichte Finnlands* (Munich, 1938). A standard general history.

John H. Wuorinen, *Nationalism in Modern Finland* (New York, 1931). An indispensable study.

2. World War II and after:

Sigyn Alenius, *Finland between the Armistice and the Peace* (Helsingfors, 1947). A brief account.

Eric C. Bellquist, "Finland: Democracy in Travail," *Western Political Quarterly,* 2 (June, 1949), pp. 217–27.

Arvid Enckell, *Democratic Finland* (London, 1948). A sympathetic description of Finland's institutions since the war.

C. Leonard Lundin, *Finland in the Second World War* (Bloomington, Ind., 1956).

Anatole G. Mazour, *Finland: Between East and West* (Princeton, 1956).

Hugh Shearman, *Finland: The Adventures of a Small Power* (New York, 1950). A competent analysis of Finland's postwar position.

John H. Wuorinen, ed., *Finland and World War II, 1939–1944* (New York, 1948).

HUNGARY

1. Background:

Count Stephen Bethlen, *The Treaty of Trianon and European Peace* (New York, 1934). The nationalist case for the revision of the World War I peace settlement.

Ivan Boldizsar, *The Other Hungary* (Budapest, 1946). An account of the Hungarian resistance to the Nazis.

Nikolaus von Horthy, *Ein Leben für Ungarn* (Bonn, 1953). Memoirs of the former regent of Hungary (1919–44).

Nicholas Kallay, *Hungarian Premier: A Personal Account of a Nation's Struggle in the Second World War* (New York, 1954). The account of the former prime minister of Hungary (1942–44).

Domokos G. Kosary, *A History of Hungary* (New York, 1941). A standard general account.

C. A. Macartney, *A History of Hungary 1929–1945* (New York, 1956). A most authoritative study.

———, *Hungary and Her Successors: The Treaty of Trianon and Its Consequences, 1919–1937* (London, 1937). A noteworthy discussion of the political and economic problems of the extensive provinces ceded by Hungary to its neighbors in 1919.

T. Mende, *Hungary* (London, 1944). A summary account, in the Crossroads Series.

J. F. Montgomery, *Hungary: The Unwilling Satellite* (New York, 1947). A sympathetic account of the policies of the Horthy regime, by the American minister, 1933–41.

R. W. Seton-Watson, *Treaty Revision and the Hungarian Frontiers* (London, 1934). A rapid review of the controversial problems of revisionism by a distinguished British authority.

2. World War II and after:

Bela Fabian, *Cardinal Mindszenty* (New York, 1949). A statement of the Catholic case.

Ernst C. Helmreich, ed., *Hungary* (New York, 1958). A documented account of the postwar era.

Howard J. Hilton, Jr., "Hungary: A Case History of Soviet Economic Imperialism," *United States Department of State Bulletin,* 25 (Aug. 27, 1951), pp. 323–27.

Hungarian National Council, *Genocide by Deportation: An Appeal to the United Nations to Enforce the Law* (New York, 1951). Regarding the deportations in Hungary during 1950–51.

"Hungary: The Technique of the United Front," *Eastern Economist,* 19 (Sept., 1952), 399–400.

William Juhasz, *Blueprint for a Red Generation* (New York, 1952). On the educational system in Hungary.

Gyorgy Kemeny, *Economic Planning in Hungary, 1947–9* (New York, 1952). A former undersecretary for finance in the Hungarian coalition government gives a firsthand critical account of the Three-Year Plan of 1947–49.

Stephen Kertesz, "Church and State in Hungary. The Background of the Cardinal Mindszenty Trial," *Review of Politics,* 11 (April, 1949), pp. 208–19.

———, "The Expulsion of the Germans from Hungary: A Study in Post-War Diplomacy," *Review of Politics,* 15 (April, 1953), pp. 179–208.

———, "The Methods of Communist Conquest: Hungary, 1944–1947," *World Politics,* 3 (Oct., 1950), pp. 20–54.

I. Laponogov, *Vengerskaya Demokraticheskaya Respublika na Novom Etape* ("The Hungarian Democratic Republic at a New Stage") (Moscow, 1949). A summary of the Soviet viewpoint.

Melvin J. Lasky, ed., *The Hungarian Revolution: The Story of the October Uprising as Recorded in Documents, Dispatches, Eyewitness Accounts and World Wide Reactions* (New York, 1957).

Laszlo Rajk and His Accomplices before the People's Court (Budapest, 1949). The official record of the trial of the Communist deviationist.

V. N. Myshkov, *Vengriya: ekonomika i vneshnaya torgovlya* ("Hungary: economy and foreign trade") (Moscow, 1956).

Ferenc Nagy, *The Struggle behind the Iron Curtain* (New York, 1948). Memoirs of the leader of the Smallholders Party, with a detailed account of Communist tactics.

Nicholas Nyaradi, *My Ringside Seat in Moscow* (New York, 1952). Experiences of a Hungarian minister of finance on an economic mission to the U.S.S.R. in 1947.

The Organization and Strategy of the Hungarian Workers' (Communist) Party (New York, 1952).

Matyas Rakosi, *A bekeert es a szocializmus epiteseert* (Budapest, 1951). Rakosi's speeches and articles on peace and socialism.

K. C. O. Shann et al., *Report of the Special Committee on the Problem of Hungary* (New York, 1957). A United Nations report.

Charles I. Stastny, *The Hungarian Communist Party: A Study of Ideology and Operational Development* (Ph.D. dissertation, Harvard University, 1954).

The Trial of Josef Mindszenty (Budapest, 1949). The official record.

POLAND

1. Background:

Raymond Leslie Buell, *Poland: Key to Europe* (New York, 1939). A good introductory survey, stressing political problems.

Yvonne Delmas, *L'Evolution constitutionnelle de la Pologne depuis 1919* (Paris, 1936). A critical study of the Pilsudski regime.

Oscar Halecki, *The History of Poland* (London, 1942). A general history by a leading Polish historian.

William F. Reddaway *et al.*, eds., *The Cambridge History of Poland, 1697–1935* (New York, 1941).

William John Rose, *The Rise of Polish Democracy* (London, 1944). An evaluation of the social and economic background of Polish political institutions.

Bernadotte E. Schmitt, ed., *Poland* (Berkeley, 1945). A significant collection of chapters on the problems faced by Poland between the two world wars.

2. World War II and after:

Immanuel Birnbaum, "Warsaw and the Communist Bloc," *Problems of Communism,* 6 (May-June, 1957), pp. 30–35.

J. Ciechanowski, *Defeat in Victory* (New York, 1947). The story of Poland's wartime experience, as seen by the Polish ambassador to the United States.

P. I. Glushakov, *Polsha* ("Poland") (Moscow, 1949). A brief statement of the Soviet viewpoint.

Oscar Halecki, ed., *Poland* (New York, 1957). A documented account of the postwar era.

Ralph A. Jones, "Polish Local Government Reorganized on Soviet Model," *American Slavic and East European Review,* 10 (Feb., 1951), pp. 56–68.

Arthur Bliss Lane, *I Saw Poland Betrayed: An American Ambassador Reports to the American People* (Indianapolis, 1948). A critique of American policy in Eastern Europe by the United States ambassador to Poland, 1944–47.

Stanislaw Mikolajczyk, *The Rape of Poland: Pattern of Soviet Aggression* (New York, 1948). A full account of the Communist victory in Poland by the leader of the Peasant Party who served as prime minister of the government-in-exile, 1943–44, and deputy prime minister of the provisional government, 1945–47.

Dimitri T. Pronin, "Land Reform in Poland: 1920–1945," *Land Economics,* 25 (May, 1949), pp. 133–45.

William J. Rose, *Poland Old and New* (London, 1948). A mature discussion of Polish problems by a leading British authority.

Joseph B. Schechtman, "The Polish-Soviet Exchange of Populations," *Journal of Central European Affairs,* 9 (Oct., 1949), pp. 289–314.

Richard F. Staar, "The Central Committee of the United Polish Workers' Party (PZPR)," *Journal of Central European Affairs,* 16 (Jan., 1957), pp. 371–83.

————, "The Polish Communist Party, 1918–1948," *Polish Review,* 1 (Spring-Summer, 1956), pp. 41–58.

————, "The Secretariat of the United Polish Workers' Party (PZPR)," *Journal of Central European Affairs,* 15 (Oct., 1955), pp. 272–85.

W. J. Stankiewicz, "Socio-Economic Changes in Post-War Poland," *Political Science Quarterly,* 71 (Sept., 1956), pp. 387–406.

S. Strzetelski, "The Background of the October Events in Poland," *Polish Review,* 1 (Oct., 1956).

J. Taylor, *The Economic Development of Poland: 1919–1950* (Ithaca, 1952). A thorough monograph.

Adam B. Ulam, "The Crisis in the Polish Communist Party," *Review of Politics,* 12 (Jan., 1950), pp. 83–98.

Elizabeth Valkenier, "The Catholic Church in Communist Poland, 1945–1955," *Review of Politics,* 18 (July, 1956), pp. 305–26.

RUMANIA

1. Background:

Gheorghe Alexianu, *et al., Roumanie* (Paris, 1933). Authoritative chapters on Rumanian political and economic problems.

Alexander Cretzianu, "The Soviet Ultimatum to Rumania (26 June, 1940)," *Journal of Central European Affairs,* 9 (Jan., 1950), pp. 396–403.

V. Dembo, *Rumyniya* ("Rumania") (Moscow, 1937). A Soviet interpretation.

Mircea Djuvara, *Die neue rumänische Verfassung* (Berlin, 1940). A study of the authoritarian constitution of 1938.

Ion Gheorghe, *Rumaniens Weg zum Satellitenstaat* (Wels, Austria, 1952). A defense of the Antonescu regime in Rumania.

Matila Costiescu Ghyka, *A Documented Chronology of Rumanian History, from Prehistoric Times to the Present Day* (New York, 1942).

Andreas Hillgruber, *Hitler, König Carol und Marschall Antonescu. Die Deutsch-Rumanischen Beziehungen 1938–1944* (Wiesbaden, 1954).

Gheorghe Ionescu-Sisesti and N. Cornateanu, *La Réforme agraire en Roumanie et ses conséquences* (Bucharest, 1937). A factual summary.

Nicolae Iorga, *Istoria Romanilor* (Bucharest, 1937–38). A ten-volume history of Rumania by the late dean of Rumanian historians.

David Mitrany, *The Land and the Peasant in Rumania: The War and Agrarian Reform, 1917–21* (New Haven, 1930). A classic study by the leading authority.

Politics and Political Parties in Roumania (London, 1936). A compendium of useful information.

Mihail Roller, *Probleme de istorie, contributii la lupta pentru o istorie stiintifica in RPR* (Bucharest, 1951). Chapters of Rumanian history rewritten according to the Communist view.

R. W. Seton-Watson, *A History of the Roumanians* (New York, 1934). A full-length and authoritative history.

Friedrich E. Weinreich, *Die Verfassung von Rumanien von 1923* (Leipzig, 1933). A study of the Rumanian constitution of 1923.

2. World War II and after:

Randolph L. Braham, "The New Constitution of Rumania," *American Journal of Comparative Law,* 3 (July, 1954), pp. 418–27. An analysis of the constitution of 1952.

Alexander Cretzianu, ed., *Captive Rumania: A Decade of Soviet Rule* (New York, 1956).

Stephen Fisher-Galati, ed., *Rumania* (New York, 1957). A documented account of the postwar era.

Reuben H. Markham, *Rumania under the Soviet Yoke* (Boston, 1949). A detailed account based on personal observations by an experienced correspondent.

The Peter Groza Government and the Yalta Declaration (Bucharest, 1945). A pamphlet defending the Groza "people's front" regime.

Nicolae Pop, *Kirche unter Hammer und Sichel. Die Kirchenverfolgung in Rumanien, 1945–1951* (Berlin, 1953). Antireligious policies of the postwar regime.

Nicolae Radescu, *Forced Labor in Rumania* (New York, 1949). Brief exposé of Communist methods by a former prime minister, 1944–45.

G. M. Razi, "La Constitution de la République Populaire de la Romanie," *Revue Internationale de Droit Comparé* (April-June, 1951), pp. 262–98. An analysis of the 1948 constitution.

Henry L. Roberts, *Rumania: Political Problems of an Agrarian State* (New Haven, 1951). A study of outstanding value.

Pamfil Seicaru, *Rien que des cendres (Dotla)* (Paris, 1949). Deals with Rumania as a Nazi satellite and the process by which it was Bolshevized.

P. B. Steanu, "The Nationalization of Rumanian Industry," *Journal of Central European Affairs,* 11 (Jan.-April, 1951), pp. 47–56.

Alexandre Tilman-Timon, *Les Actes constitutionels en Roumanie de 1938 à 1944* (Bucharest, 1947). Study of Rumanian wartime constitutional developments.

The Trial of the Former National Peasant Party Leaders, Maniu, Mihalache, Penescu, Gr. Niculescu-Buzesti and Others (Bucharest, 1947). The official record.

YUGOSLAVIA

1. Background:

Charles A. Beard and George Radin, *The Balkan Pivot: Yugoslavia* (New York, 1929). A good introduction to the first decade following World War I.

Otto von Franges, *Die Sozialökonomische Struktur der Jugoslawischen Landwirt-schaft* (Berlin, 1937). A scholarly study.

Émile Haumant, *La Formation de la Yougoslavie* (Paris, 1930). Excellent general history.

Robert J. Kerner, ed., *Yugoslavia* (Berkeley, 1949). A collaborative work by out-standing authorities.

Déyan Loutzitch, *La Constitution du royaume de Yougoslavie du 3 Septembre 1931* (Paris, 1933). A study of the authoritarian constitution of King Alexander.

Stjepan Radić, *Sabrana Dela* ("Collected Works") (Zagreb, 1936–38), 19 vols. Writings of the theoretician of the Croat peasant movement.

Miloutine Yovanovitch, *La Réforme administrative en Yougoslavie* (Paris, 1932). Administrative changes introduced by King Alexander.

2. World War II and after:

Robert Bass and Elizabeth Marbury, eds., *The Soviet-Yugoslav Controversy, 1948–1958: A Documentary Record* (New York, 1959).

C. Brobowski, *La Yougoslavie socialiste* (Paris, 1956).

Robert F. Byrnes, ed., *Yugoslavia* (New York, 1957). An authoritative and compre-hensive handbook.

Stephen Clissold, *Whirlwind: An Account of Marshal Tito's Rise to Power* (London, 1949). By a member of the British Military Mission to the partisans.

Vladimir Dedijer, *Tito* (New York, 1953).

"The Disgrace of Djilas and Its Implications," *The World Today*, 10 (1954), pp. 98–105.

Milovan Djilas, *Lenin über die Beziehungen zwischen sozialistischen Staaten* (Bel-grade, 1950). An essay on Lenin's views on the relations among socialist states.

———, *The New Class: An Analysis of the Communist System* (New York, 1957).

———, "Yugoslav-Soviet Relations," *International Affairs*, 27 (April, 1951), pp. 167–75. An authoritative statement of the Yugoslav case.

Jovan Djordjević, "Constitutional Reform in Yugoslavia," *Review of International Affairs* (Belgrade), 3 (Dec. 16, 1952), pp. 15–17. A discussion of certain amendments adopted on Jan. 13, 1953.

Alex N. Dragnich, *Tito's Promised Land: Yugoslavia* (New Brunswick, N.J., 1954).

Constantine Fotitch, *The War We Lost* (New York, 1948). An account of Yugo-slavian affairs during World War II from the point of view of the government-in-exile, by the Yugoslavian ambassador to the United States, 1935–44.

Joseph Frankel, "Federalism in Yugoslavia," *American Political Science Review*, 49 (June, 1955), pp. 416–30.

Edvard Kardelj, *The Communist Party of Yugoslavia in the Struggle for New Yugo-slavia, for People's Authority and for Socialism* (Belgrade, 1948). Report by the Communist leader to the Fifth Congress of the Communist Party of Yugo-slavia.

Josef Korbel, *Tito's Communism* (Denver, 1951). Notes by a well-informed Czecho-slovak observer.

Richard Lowenthal, "Tito's Affair with Khrushchev," *New Leader*, 41 (Oct. 6, 1958), pp. 10–19. A well-informed account of Yugoslav-Soviet relations.

Fitzroy Maclean, *Eastern Approaches* (London, 1949). This volume of memoirs in-cludes an account of the relations between Tito and the Western Allies, by the head of the British Military Mission to the Yugoslav partisans, 1943–45.

———, *The Heretic: The Life and Times of Josip Broz-Tito* (New York, 1957).

Roy Macridis, "Stalinism and the Meaning of Titoism," *World Politics*, 4 (Jan., 1952), pp. 219–38.

R. H. Markham, *Tito's Imperial Communism* (Chapel Hill, 1947). A critical ac-count of Tito's regime by an experienced American journalist.

Charles P. McVicker, *Titoism: Pattern for International Communism* (New York, 1957).

Fred Warner Neal, *Titoism in Action* (Berkeley, 1958). An analysis of Titoism as an alternative form of Communism.

M. B. Petrovich, "The Central Government of Yugoslavia," *Political Science Quarterly*, 62 (Dec., 1947), pp. 504–30.

Eric L. Pridonoff, *Tito's Yugoslavia* (Washington, 1956).

Protiv Sovremennogo Revizionizma ("Against Contemporary Revisionism") (Moscow, 1958). A symposium setting forth the Soviet case against the Yugoslav Communist Party program of 1958.

Revizionizm—Glavnaya Opastnost ("Revisionism—The Principal Danger") (Moscow, 1958). A collection of articles by prominent Communist leaders directed in particular against Titoism.

Soviet-Yugoslav Dispute: Text of the Published Correspondence (London, 1948). A valuable collection of the exchange of diatribes between the Soviet and Yugoslavian Communist parties, providing the essential issues of the controversy.

Josip Broz Tito, *For Independence and Equality* (Belgrade, 1950).

Jozo Tomasevich, *Peasants, Politics, and Economic Change in Yugoslavia* (Stanford, 1955).

The Trial of Dragoljub-Draža Mihailović (Belgrade, 1946). The official record.

Adam B. Ulam, *Titoism and the Cominform* (Cambridge, 1952). A carefully documented study.

Yugoslavia's Way: Program of the League of the Yugoslav Communists (New York, 1958). A translation of the party program that sets forth the distinctive features of Titoism.

INDEX

Aaltonen, Aimo, 765

Abendroth, W., 409 (n. 4)

Ackermann, Anton, 413, 414 (n. 4)

Act of Settlement, 1701, England, 18, 59, 85

Act of Supremacy, 1534, England, 13

Act of Union, 1707, Great Britain, 61

Act of Union, 1800, Great Britain, 61

Acton, Lord, 14

Adams, John, 164

Adenauer, Dr. Konrad, 331, 397 (n. 3), 402, 403 (n. 7), 408, 414, 416, 417–19, 423–5, 426, 429, 440

administrative law and justice, Great Britain, 100–3, 115

administrative tribunals
 France: 237–8; Council of State, 229–30
 Great Britain, 102–3, 115
 Italy, 525

agrarianism
 Eastern Europe: 756–61; parties, Fig. XXXIII, 764–5
 France: 270–1; role of peasantry, 271–3

agriculture
 Eastern Europe: population, 743–4, 745–6; production, 744–6, 812–813; reform and collectivization, 815–19
 France, 271–3, 278
 Germany: 370, 387, 435; East Germany, 413 (n. 3)
 Great Britain, 129, 143
 Italy: 459, 482; postwar situation, 484–6, 490
 U.S.S.R.: 543–4; present organization, 685–8

Agricultural Marketing Acts, Great Britain, 129

Agricultural Wages Act, Great Britain, 140 (n. 4)

Agriculture Act, 1947, Great Britain, 102, 143

Agriculture Act, 1957, Great Britain, 143

Agriculture Act, 1958, Great Britain, 143

Air Corporations Act, 1949, Great Britain, 132

Alain (Emile A. Chartier), 194

Alaric, 328

Albania: independence, 747; Italian control, 766; King Zog's regime, 766; power seized by Communists, 773–4; see also Eastern Europe

Alexander, Edgar, 418 (n. 2)

Alexander I, Russia, 545, 549, 551

Alexander I, Yugoslavia, 765, 766, 767

Alexander II, Russia, 545, 550, 551, 552, 557, 558

Alexander III, Russia, 552

Alexandrov, Todor, 765

Alexei, Patriarch, 583

Alfieri, Count Vittorio, 457

Allemann, F. R., 420 (n. 4)

Amann, Max, 373, 382, 383

American Congress of Industrial Organizations, withdrawal from World Federation of Trade Unions, 709

American Federation of Labor, withdrawal from World Federation of Trade Unions, 709

Andreotti, Giulio, 512

Andreyev, A., 626

Andrianov, V. M., 626

Anglo-Russian Trade Union Committee, 705, 709

Anglo-Soviet Trade Union Committee, 709

Anne, empress of Russia, 551

Anselm, 19

Anson, Sir William, on the Crown, 83

Anthon, Carl G., 412 (n. 2)

anticlericalism
 France, 193, 261, 264–5, 281–3
 Italy, 463–4; see also Catholicism, Christian Democratic Party, Popular Party

anti-Semitism
 Germany, 379–80, 392

i

anti-Semitism (*continued*)
U.S.S.R., 593, 599
Antier, Paul, 273
Antonescu, Ion, 765, 767, 794
Antropov, Piotr, 657
Arciszewski, Tomasz, 764
Arendt, Hannah, 380 (n. 6)
Aris, R., 366 (n. 3)
Aristotle, 22, 25, 27
Aristov, A. B., 624, 626, 627
army
Eastern Europe: army regimes, 763–766
France: 198, 219 (n. 4), 311; Algerian crisis, 294–5
Germany: in Second Empire, 346–7; under Hitler, 388–90, 392–3; in East Germany, 412–13; rearmament, 440–1
Great Britain, 53, 98
Italy: after World War II, 528–30
U.S.S.R.: 670–5; in union republics, 588
Arndt, Adolf, 427
Arnold, Dr. Karl, 424
Aron, Raymond, 306
Asquith, Herbert, 35, 36, 97, 163
Atomic Energy Act, 1954, Great Britain, 133
Attlee, Lord (Clement), 28, 35, 36, 40 (n. 5), 42 (n. 9), 43, 62 (n. 6), 93, 146 (n. 5), 149, 706
Auriol, Vincent, 220
Austin, John, 8, 26
Australia: citizenship legislation, 176; federalism, 159–60; foreign policy problems, 174; labor movement, 165–6; as social laboratory, 155; *see also* Commonwealth of Nations
Austria: *Anschluss,* 390–1; in Eastern Europe, 747, 748–9; peace treaty of 1955, 719; and Prussia, 330–2; relations with Italy, 466, 468
authoritarianism: Eastern Europe, 747–748, 762–7; France, 189–90, 195–196, 205, 268; Germany, 336–8, 352–3, 377–9, 395–6; Great Britain, 18, 21, 23; Italy, 471–4, 476; Russia, 547–50
Auwi, Prince (Prince August Wilhelm von Hohenzollern), 382
Averescu, General Alexandru, 764
Axelrod, Paul, 558
Azev, Evno, 550

Bacon, Francis, 27
Baden, Prince Max von, 358, 362
Badoglio, Pietro, 477, 478
Bagehot, Walter, 48, 85, 86, 175, 353 (n. 8)
Bagirov, M., 626
Baibakov, N. K., 679
Bakayev, V. G., 657
Baldwin, Stanley, 11 (n. 8), 85, 129
Balfour, Lord (Arthur), 38 (n. 3), 42
Balkan Entente, 752
Balke, Siegfried, 403 (n. 7)
Baltic federation proposal, 752
Barker, Sir Ernest, 11, 27, 78 (n. 2), 127
Barlow report, 1940, 121, 130
Barton, G. B., 159 (n. 5)
Barton, Sir Edmund, 159 (n. 5)
Bate's Case, 1606, 16
Battisti, Cesare, 468
Bavarian Party, 421, 430
Bavarian People's Party, 360
Baykov, A., 744 (n. 2)
Beard, Charles A., 78 (n. 2)
Bebel, August, 351
Beck, Colonel Josef, 765
Beck, General Ludwig von, 392
Becket, Thomas à, 19
Beer, Samuel H., 45 (n. 3)
Beethoven, Ludwig van, 333
Bellamy, Edward, 156
Belyayev, N. I., 624, 627
Beneš, Eduard, 754, 764, 767, 775, 777
Bennigsen, Rudolf von, 351 (n. 6)
Bentham, Jeremy, 25–6, 46
Bentwich, Norman, 177 (n. 4)
Berdyaev, Nicholas, 548
Bergsträsser, Ludwig, 420 (n. 4)
Beria, L. P., 626
Berman, Harold J., 662 (n. 2), 666 (n. 7)
Berman, Jakub, 718, 734
Bernhard, G., 361 (n. 3)
Beschev, B. P., 657
Bethlen, István, 759, 765, 766
Bethmann, Moritz A. von, 338
Bethmann-Hollweg, Theobold von, 353, 354, 355
Bevan, Aneurin, 36, 40 (n. 5), 53, 65 (n. 2), 76, 117, 260
Beveridge, Lord, 47, 131
Bidault, Georges, 264, 304
Bienstock, G., 575 (n. 8)
Bierut, Boleslaw, 765, 783

Bill of Rights, 1689, Great Britain, 5, 18, 58, 114

Bismarck, Prince Otto von, 325, 330, 331, 333, 339, 340, 391; activities in Second Empire, 341–52 passim

Bissolati, Leonida, 466, 495

Blackstone, William, 78

Blageov, Dimiter, 765

Blank, Theodore, 403 (n. 7)

Blatchford, Robert, 156

Blind Persons Act, 1920, Great Britain, 130

Blöck der Heimatvertriebenen und Entrechteten (B.H.E.), 421, 430

Blomberg, General Werner von, 381

Blum, Leon, 199, 203, 261, 287, 706

Blumenthal, Werner M., 435 (n. 9)

Bodin, Jean, 8

Boeckler, Hans, 435

Bolotnikov, I. I., 557

Bolsheviks: from conflict with Mensheviks to seizure of power, 1917, 558–60; see also Communist Party

Bonapartism, in France, 189–90, 200

Bonar Law, Andrew, 38, 85

Bonn "Contractual Agreement," 1952, 397, 400

Bonn Republic, see Germany

Bonomi, Ivanoe, 470, 472, 478

Boris, Georges, 290–1

Boris III, Bulgaria, 763, 765, 766

Bormann, Martin, 373, 382

Born, Ernst von, 764

Bornkamm, Heinrich, 330 (n. 6)

Bosanquet, Bernard, 48

Botha, General Louis, 167

Bott, Hans, 417 (n. 1)

Böttger, Gerd, 415 (n. 5)

Bouhler, Philipp, 382

Boulanger, General Georges, 200, 266

Boulard, Abbé, 282 (n. 1)

Bourassa, Henri, 163

Bourgès-Maunoury, Premier, 227, 257

Boveri, Margaret, 417 (n. 1)

Boyen, General Hermann von, 338, 347

Bracton, Henry de, 16, 21

Bradley, F. H., 48

Brady, R. A., 384 (n. 8)

Brandt, Karl, 427

Brant, Stefan, 412 (n. 1)

Brătiănu, Constantine, 764

Brătiănu, Gheorghe, 764

Brătiănu, Ion, 764

Brătiănu, Vintila, 764

Brauchitsch, General Walther von, 381

Brauer, Theodor, 427

Braun, Otto, 365, 371

Braunias, Karl, 366 (n. 3)

Brecht, Arnold, 404 (n. 8), 407 (n. 2)

Bredow, General Ferdinand von, 389

Breitling, Rupert, 422 (n. 5)

Brentano, Heinrich von, 403 (n. 7)

Brest-Litovsk, treaty of, 356, 358, 702

Brest-Litovsk Union, 1596, 549

Brezhnev, L. I., 624, 626, 627

Briand, A., 441

Brickner, R. M., 376 (n. 3)

Bright, John, 90, 163

British Empire, see Commonwealth of Nations

Brockdorff-Rantzau, Count Ulrich von, 437 (n. 5)

Brogan, D. W., 97

Brown, Douglas Clifton, 69

Browne, Robert, 22

Bruck, Moeller van den, 437 (n. 5)

Brückner, Lieutenant Wilhelm, 383

Brüning, Heinrich, 368, 369 (n. 7), 370, 419

Bryce, Lord, 60, 63, 159

Buch, Walter, 382

Budenny, Marshal S. M., 651

Bujor, M. G., 764

Bukharin, N. I., 614

Bulavin, K., 557

Bulganin, Nikolai A., 624, 626, 627, 655, 658, 674, 720, 783, 784

Bulgaria: communism after World War I, 762; communist seizure of power after World War II, 774; independence, 747; see also Eastern Europe

Bülow, Bernhard von, 351, 353, 354

bureaucracy; see also cabinet, council of ministers, government corporations, planning

Commonwealth of Nations, 152

France: Third Republic, 196; Fourth Republic: administrative personnel, 227–8; Council of State, 229–30; decentralization, 233–4; Inspectorate General of Finances, 230–1; prefectoral corps, 231–2; reforms, 228–9

Germany: in Second Empire, 347–8; in Weimar Republic, 370–1

Great Britain: medieval, 12–13; mod-

bureaucracy (*continued*)
    ern civil service, 90–2; problems, 92–5, 100–3
    Italy, 519–21
    U.S.S.R., 660–1
Burgh, Hubert de, 13 (n. 4)
Burke, Edmund, 24, 33, 47–8, 78–9, 81, 84, 146, 163
Burns, Emile, 562 (n. 2)
Burns, James M., 44 (n. 1), 74 (n. 9)
Burov, A., 764
Business Party, Germany, 368
Butler, D. E., 37 (n. 9), 44 (n. 2), 65 (n. 2), 66, 145 (n. 3), 148 (n. 1)
Butler, R. A., 38
Butoma, Boris Y., 658
Byé, Maurice, 243

cabinet; *see also* chancellor, Council of Ministers, premier, prime minister
    France: of De Gaulle in Algerian crisis, 295–6; Fifth Republic, 298–300, 303–5; formation of, 214; Fourth Republic, and instability, 215–16, 226–7; size, 226–7; Third Republic, and instability, 199–200, 202–4
    Germany: in Bonn Republic, 403–6; list of members, 1959, 403 (n. 7); in Second Empire, 353–5; in Weimar Republic, 362–3; in World War I, 355–6
    Great Britain: "cabinet government," 74–7; relation to bureaucracy, 93–5; relation to monarch, 85; relation to Parliament, 58–60; relation to parties, 38–44; structure of, and ministry, 87–90; "Treasury control," 95; wartime, 97–9, 174
    Italy: in liberal monarchy, and *trasformismo*, 462–5; under Republic, 518–19
Cadets, *see* Constitutional Democratic Party
Caesar, Julius, 455
Cairns, Mary B., 135 (n. 2)
Cajander, Aino K., 764
Calamandrei, Piero, 505 (n. 1)
Călinescu, Armand, 765
Calvinism, in South Africa, 168
Cambridge University, 32 (n. 6), 92

Camphausen, Ludolf, 337
Camps, Miriam, 433 (n. 7)
Canada: citizenship legislation, 176; federalism, 157–8; special relations with Great Britain, 174; special relations with U.S., 173; *see also* Commonwealth of Nations
Canaris, Admiral Wilhelm, 392
Canberra Agreement, 1944, 174
Canonica, Pietro, 509 (n. 4)
Caprivi, General Leo von, 353
Carol II, Rumania, 754, 759, 765, 766
Carter, Mark Bonham, 36 (n. 7)
Catering Wages Act, 1943, Great Britain, 140 (n. 4)
Catherine the Great, Russia, 545, 551, 767
Catholic Association of Italian Workers (A.C.L.I.), 498
Catholicism
    Eastern Europe, 757, 793, 804
    France: 198, 264, 281–3; *see also* Popular Republic Movement
    Germany: 328–31; and Hitler, 393; in Bonn Republic, 423–4; *see also* Center Party, Christian Democratic Union
    Great Britain: 32, 77; and Tudors, 13, 22; church-state conflict, 18–20; of James II, 17–18
    Italy: under fascism, 475; in liberal monarchy, 463–4; and rise of fascism, 466, 469; after World War II, 496–9; *see also* Christian Democratic Party, Populist Party
Cavour, Count Camillo di, 460, 461, 463, 464
Center Party, Germany, 349 (n. 4), 351, 423; in Weimar Republic, 360, 368 (n. 6)
Ceylon, 113, 152, 172
Chamber of Fasces and Corporations, Italy, 472
Chamberlain, Arthur Neville, 35, 38 (n. 3), 42, 97, 391
Chamberlain, Austen, 38 (n. 3), 42
Chamberlain, Joseph, 34, 37–8
Chancellor, Germany: in Second Empire, 343–4, 345–6; in Weimar Republic, 362–3; in Bonn Republic, 404, 417–18
Chapman, Brian, 234 (n. 4)
Charlemagne, 327, 328

Charles, Prince, named Prince of Wales, 85

Charles I, England, 14, 17

Charles II, England, 17, 32

Charles XII, Sweden, 544

Charles Albert, Savoy, 459, 460

Charter of Liberties, 1100, England, 12 (n. 2)

chartism, 30

Chase, Eugene P., 98 (n. 3)

Cheka, see police, U.S.S.R.

Chervenkov, Vulko, 718, 765

Chesnokov, D. I., 626

Chicherin, G. V., 703

Children and Young Persons Act, 1933, Great Britain, 140 (n. 3)

China: and Great Britain, 47, 149; and U.S.S.R., 709, 718, 720, 721, 789

Chrimes, S. B., 12 (n. 3), 86 (n. 6)

Christian Democratic Party, Italy, 478–481, 496–500; parliamentary seats, postwar, 511

Christian Democratic Union, Germany, 423–5; in *Bundestag* elections, 421; leadership of Adenauer, 408, 417–419

Christian socialism, Great Britain, 27

Christian Socialist Union, Germany, 421, 423–5

Church of England, 13, 17, 22, 61

Churchill, Sir Winston, 4, 29, 35, 36, 38, 48, 62 (n. 6), 88 (n. 1), 97, 123, 125, 131, 145, 146; on party government, 29

Ciano, Count Galeazzo, 476

Cincinnatus, 97

citizenship: Commonwealth of Nations, 176–7; French Community, 303; French Union, 247; Great Britain, 176; U.S.S.R., 587

Citizenship Act, 1949, South Africa, 177

Civic Restaurants Act, 1947, Great Britain, 117

Civil Aviation Act, 1946, Great Britain, 132

civil liberties: Commonwealth of Nations, 154, 168, 169; Eastern Europe, 803–5; France, 189, 191, 212, 226; Germany, 360–1, 402 (n. 5), 431 (n. 5); Great Britain, 7–8, 9–10, 18, 114–15; Italy, 504–7; U.S.S.R., 599–602

civil service, *see* bureaucracy

Clausewitz, Karl von, 694

Clay, General Lucius B., 438

Clegg, H. A., 141 (n. 6), 142 (n. 7)

Clemenceau, Georges, 355

Clovis, 327

Cnut, England, 12 (n. 9)

Coal Act, 1930, Great Britain, 129–30

Coal Industry Nationalization Act, 1946, Great Britain, 133

Coke, Edward, 16, 78, 82

Colbert, Jean B., 239

Cole, G. D. H., 28, 51, 80–1, 126 (n. 1)

Cole, Taylor, 98 (n. 3), 404 (n. 8), 431 (n. 6), 434 (n. 8), 435 (n. 2)

Colombo Plan, 179

Colonial League, Germany, 348

colonialism, *see* Imperialism

colons, Algeria, 294, 305

Combination Acts, Great Britain, 127

Cominform: activities, 707–8; formation, 1947, 706; Tito expelled, 1948, 707

Comintern (Third International): activities, 705–6; dissolution, 1943, 706; formation, 1919, 704–5

Commissariat-général du plan (Monnet Commission), 288–9

Commission on Modernization of the Overseas Territories, France, 289

Committee of National Liberation, Italy, 477, 478

Committee of National Liberation for Northern Italy, 478

Commonwealth of Nations: British heritage, 153–5; citizenship legislation, 176–7; common bonds and institutions, 175–8; nationalism in, 176–8; parties and ideas, 163–71; politics in Asian members, 168–71; as an international entity, 151–3, 171–5; *see also* Australia, Canada, Ceylon, Ghana, India, Malaya, New Zealand, Pakistan, Union of South Africa, West Indies

communism: basic tenets, 560–5; in Commonwealth of Nations, 169; in Eastern Europe, 761–2; in France, 198, 258–60; in Germany, 368, 431; in East Germany, 409–411, 414–15; in Italy, 491–4; lack of strength in Britain, 27–8, 50, 76; *see also* Communist Party

Communist League, 1847–50, 704

Communist Manifesto, 351, 427, 563, 676

Communist Party

Eastern Europe: before World War II, 761–2; front techniques after World War II, 770–1, 771–5; seizure of power after World War II, 775–9; Soviet control, 779–87

France: constitutional program 1945–1946, 206–7, 209–12, 245–6; and labor, 274–6; leadership and organization, 258–9; and peasantry, 273; strength, 259–60

Germany: *Bundestag* elections, 1949–1955, 421; declared unconstitutional, 1956, 431; *Reichstag* elections, 1919–33, 368 (n. 6); in revolution of 1918, 359

East Germany: strength, and merger with Socialist Unity Party, 410, 411 (n. 8)

Great Britain: in election of 1955, 52 (n. 4)

Italy: constituent assembly, 1946, 480–1; election, 1921, 467; elections, 1948–58, 511; leadership, organization and popular strength, 491–4, 496; resistance during World War II, 478

U.S.S.R.: authority and power, 606–610; auxiliary organizations, 628–31; and class structure, 572–3; Congress and Central Committee, 621–3; higher organs, 621–8; leadership and elite, 614–16; members of Presidium (Politburo), Orgburo, Secretariat, Chart, 626–7; nature of membership, 610–16; organization and structure, 616–21; *see also* Bolsheviks

Companies Acts, 1844, 1855, Great Britain, 127

Conciliation Act, 1896, Great Britain, 141

Confederation of Small Business, France, 270

Confederation of the Rhine (*Rheinbund*), 341, 342

Conference on Devolution, 1920, Great Britain, 122

Congregationalists, England, 22

Congress of Paris, 1856, 461

Congress Party, India, 162, 169–70

conservatism: German Second Empire, 338–9; Great Britain, 47–50; *see also* Conservative parties

Conservative parties: Commonwealth of Nations, 164–5; Eastern Europe, 762–6; France, 265–8; Germany, 338–9, 349–52; Italy, 501–3

Conservative Party, Great Britain: beginnings, 32–3; conference of 1958, 53–4; leadership and organization, 38–40, 42–4; in nineteenth century, 33–5; principles and program, 47–50; in twentieth century, 35–7

Constant, Benjamin, 191

Constituent Assembly: France, 1945, 1946, 207–12; Italy, 1946, 479–81

constitutions

Commonwealth of Nations: democratic institutions, 153–7

Eastern Europe: adoption of since World War II, 791; provisions of, 796–805; theory of, 789–91

France: Fifth Republic, 296–303; Fourth Republic, 213–26, 245–248; of Petain, 204–5; Third Republic, 195–7

Germany: Bonn, 401–7; East Germany, 409–11; Second Empire, 341–6; Weimar, 359–67

Great Britain: constitutional conventions, 9–11; principles of, 5–11; sovereignty of Parliament, 5; unwritten nature of, 5, 9

India: 160–3

Italy: under Mussolini, 471–4; of 1948, 504–8; *Statuto,* 460, 462, 471, 504

Pakistan: 170–1

Russia: first (R.S.F.S.R.) constitution of 1918, 566; Fundamental Laws of 1905, 547, 552–3; second (Union) constitution of 1924, 566; Stalin Constitution of 1936, 567–70, 599–605

Constitutional Committee, Fourth Republic, France, 225–6, 301

Constitutional Council, Fifth Republic, France, 301

Constitutional Court, Italy, 521–2

Constitutional Democratic Party, Russia, 558

Consultative Assembly, 1944–45, France, 207
Convention on Relations with the Federal Republic of Germany, *see* Bonn "Contractual Agreement," 1952
Convention Parliament, 1689, England, 18
Cooperative Commonwealth Federation, Canada, 155–6
co-operatives: Eastern Europe, 757–8, 817–19; U.S.S.R., 691–2
Corn Laws, Great Britain, 34, 129
Corradini, Enrico, 500
Corridoni, Filippo, 468
Cotton Spinning Industry Act, 1936, Great Britain, 130
Coty, René, 295
Council for the Affairs of the Religious Denominations, U.S.S.R., 583
Council for the Affairs of the Russian Orthodox Church, U.S.S.R., 583
Council of Europe, 311–12, 441, 529
Council of Florence, 1439, 549
council of ministers
  Eastern Europe: 799–800
  U.S.S.R.: All-Union and Union Republic ministries, 655–6; attached agencies, 659; functions, 653–5, 659–60; membership, March, 1959, 654, 657–8; Presidium of, 655; in the Union republics, 646–7
Council of Mutual Economic Assistance (Molotov plan), 415, 780–781
Council of People's Commissars (*Sovnarkom*), U.S.S.R., 653
Council of People's Commissioners, Germany, 359
Council of State, France, 229–30; Italy, 525
Covelli, Alfredo, 502
Crankshaw, Edward, 548 (n. 8), 669 (n. 1)
Creighton, Bishop, 14
Cressy, George B., 542 (n. 2)
Crèvecoeur, Michel, 155
Cripps, Sir Stafford, 3, 81
Crisp, L. F., 166 (n. 1)
Crispi, Francesco, 465, 466
Croan, Melvin, 412 (n. 2)
Croce, Benedetto, 344 (n. 1), 477 (n. 7)
Cromwell, Oliver, 11, 17, 84

Crosland, C. A. R., 146, 147, 428 (n. 2)
Crossman, R. H. S., 50 (n. 2), 146, 147 (n. 9)
Crouch, Winston, 117 (n. 4)
Crown, British: in Commonwealth, 84, 151, 152–3, 175–6; historical development, 11–14; monarchy, 84–87; in parliamentary system, 58–60; powers and immunities, 96–7
Crown Proceedings Act, 1947, Great Britain, 96–7, 102 (n. 1)
Curtin, John, 166
Curzon, Lord, 85
Cvetković, Dragiša, 765
Cyprus, and Great Britain, 150
Czechoslovakia: alliances after World War I, 748–9; communism after World War I, 762; Communist coup of 1948, 775, 777; independence, 747; riots of 1953, 782; *see also* Eastern Europe

Dahlem, Franz, 413
Dallin, David, 668 (n. 8)
Dalton, Hugh, 132
D'Annunzio, Gabriele, 468, 469, 476
Danegeld, 12
Danton, Georges Jacques, 358
Darré, R. Walter, 373, 382
Darwin, Charles, 25
Daszynski, Ignacy, 764
Davidović, Lyubomir, 764
Davies, G., 25 (n. 5), 33 (n. 9)
Davis, A. W., 698 (n. 3)
Deakin, Alfred, 163, 166
Dean, Vera Micheles, 703 (n. 9)
Debré, Michel, 296, 301, 303, 304, 305
Decembrists, 557
Declaration of Liberated Europe, 771
Declaration of Rights of the Peoples of Russia, 1917, 586
Declaration of the Rights of Man, 1789, 189, 191, 226, 599
Defence of the Realm Acts (DORA), Great Britain, 98
Dehio, Ludwig, 334 (n. 1)
Dehler, Dr. Thomas, 430
Deist, Heinrich, 427
Delvino, Suleiman, 764
Dementyev, Piotr V., 658
Democratic and Socialist Union of the Resistance (U.D.S.R.), France, 263

Democratic Labor Party, Italy, 478–9
Democratic Socialist Party (Nenni), Italy, 491, 495, 496
Denmark, and Germany, 341, 343
Denning, Sir Alfred, 102 (n. 1)
Depretis, Agostino, 464, 466
Derby, Lord, 34
Deutsche Bund, see German Confederation
Deutscher, Isaac, 690 (n. 8)
Dewar, Margaret, 814 (n. 8)
Dialogus de Scaccario, 13
Dibra, Abdurrahman, 765
Dicey, A. V., 96, 114; on parliamentary sovereignty, 5, 26
Diebold, William, 436 (n. 3)
Dietrich, Otto, 373
Diggers, 25
Dilke, Sir Charles, 157
Dimitrov, Georgi Mihailov (Bulgarian Communist), 762, 765, 772, 776 (n. 2)
Dimitrov, Georgi Mihov (Bulgarian Agrarian leader), 757 (n. 3), 765, 776
Disraeli, Benjamin, 34, 50, 164; on Tory democracy, 48
Distribution of Industry Act, 1945, Great Britain, 121, 143 (n. 1)
Djaković, Djuro, 765
Djilas, Milovan, 787
Dmowski, Roman, 764
Dobrogeanu-Gherea, Alexandru, 765
Dobrogeanu-Gherea, Constantin, 764
Dock Workers Regulation of Employment Act, 1946, Great Britain, 140 (n. 4)
Doering, Wolfgang, 430
Donoughmore Committee, *Report . . . on Ministers' Powers,* 1932, Great Britain, 100, 103
Dosaaf, 673
Dosti, Hasan, 765
Doumergue, Gaston, 204
Drexler, Anton, 379
Dreyfus Affair, 198
Duca, Ion, 764
Duchet, M., 304
Dudorov, N. P., 657
Duhnke, Horst, 413 (n. 3)
Duma, Russia: Boyars', 551; State after 1905, 552–3, 559
Dumbarton Oaks Conference, Soviet position, 699

Dunkmann, Karl, 329 (n. 4)
Durham, Lord, 154
Duverger, Maurice, 290, 366 (n. 3)

Earle, E. M., 379 (n. 4)
Eastern Europe: abolition of monarchy, 793–4; army regimes, 763–6; churches, 793; collectives, 817–19; Communist fronts, 771–5; Communist seizure of power, 768–79; economic background, 741, 743–6; foreign trade, 813–14; governmental structure, 796–802; investment and industry, 808–13; labor, 821; land reforms, 815–16; local Communist parties, 761–2, 765; minorities, 750–1, 803–5; movements for independence, 746–7; peasantry, 757–61, 820–1; political ideologies and parties, 753–67; regional cooperation, 752; relations with great powers, 742, 748–9; royal dictators, 766; Soviet controls and policies, 779–88; standard of living, 819–20; state enterprise, 815; Titoism, 781; treaties with U.S.S.R., 779–81; *see also* Albania, Bulgaria, Czechoslovakia, Finland, Hungary, Poland, Rumania, Yugoslavia
Ebert, Friedrich, 358, 359, 361, 362
École Libre des Sciences Politiques, 228
Economic Council, France, 224–5
Eden, Sir Anthony, 36, 38, 42, 66 (n. 3); 87, 99; on British conservatism, 48–9
education
    France: and church schools, 198, 211, 264–5, 282–3
    Great Britain: background of higher civil servants, 92, of members of Parliament, 66; and Labour Party, 53; of lawyers, 114
    Italy: early public provisions, 461; illiteracy in the South, 489
    U.S.S.R.: expansion of facilities, 571–2; literacy, 555, 592; social consequences, 575–7
Education Act, 1944, Great Britain, 102
Edward I, England, 15, 82
Egbert, England, 84
Ehlers, Hermann, 406, 423
Ehrmann, Henry W., 45 (n. 3)
Einaudi, Luigi, 499, 511, 516, 517

Eire, 173
Eisenhower, Dwight D., 455
elections; *see also* electoral systems, suffrage
Eastern Europe: post World War Communist plebiscites, 776
France: constitutional referendums, 1946, 210–11, 212; of De Gaulle as President, 1958, 303; in Fourth Republic, 255–7; of National Assembly, 1958, 303–4; referendum on De Gaulle Constitution, 1958, 296–8
Germany: *Bundestag,* Bonn Republic, 421; in East Germany, 409–412; of November, 1932, 371–2; *Reichstag,* Second Empire, 394 (n. 4); *Reichstag,* Weimar Republic, 368 (n. 6)
Great Britain: by-elections, 68; 1867–1910, 34–5; 1918–1955, 35–6; party conferences of 1958 and impending general election, 52–5
India: 1951–1952, 170
Italy: Constituent Assembly, 1946, 480; under Mussolini, 1929, 1934, 472; 1900–1921, 467, 469–70; Parliament, 1948, 1953, 1958, 509, 510, 511, 513–14; postwar local elections, 525–6
U.S.S.R.: State Duma 1905 and after, 552–3; to Supreme Soviet and local soviets, 1954, 1955, 1957, 1958, 635–8
electoral systems; *see also* elections, suffrage
Eastern Europe, 796–8
France: Fifth Republic, 303–4; Fourth Republic, 253–5; Third Republic, 201–2
Germany: Bonn Republic, 422–3; East Germany, 409–10; Second Empire, 345–6; Weimar Republic, 365–7
Great Britain, 29–32, 37, 65–8
Italy: under fascism, 472; liberal monarchy, 460, 462–3; Republic, 508–9
U.S.S.R., 635–8
Electricity Act, 1947, Great Britain, 133
Electricity Act, 1957, Great Britain, 133
Elizabeth I, England, 16
Elizabeth II, Great Britain, 38, 84, 87 (n. 8)

Elliott, Baroness, 62
Ely, Louis B., 671 (nn. 4, 6)
Emancipation of Labor group, Russia, 557
Emergency Powers (Defence) Acts, Great Britain, 98
Employment of Women, Young Persons and Children Act, 1920, Great Britain, 140 (n. 3)
Enabling Act, 1933, Germany, 381
Engels, Friedrich, 563 (n. 3), 564, 579, 583, 615, 676
Epstein, Leon D., 74 (n. 9)
equalitarianism: in Commonwealth of Nations, 155; economic, in Britain, 148; in French tradition, 191, 194, 197, 202; in Soviet Union, 574–6, 577–8
Erhard, Dr. Ludwig, 403 (n. 7), 424, 426, 428, 432–4
Erler, Fritz, 427
Erzberger, Matthias, 368
Eschenburg, Theodor, 422 (n. 5)
Estonia, annexation by U.S.S.R., 545, 770
Ethiopia, and Italy, 476
Etzel, Franz, 403 (n. 7)
Europe: agricultural population, 743–4; agricultural production, 744–5; industrial production, 811
European Atomic Energy Community, 312, 439, 531, 719
European Coal and Steel Community, 310–11, 529
European Defense Community, 311, 529, 530–1, 719
European Economic Community, 312, 439, 441, 531, 719
European Recovery Program, *see* Marshall Plan
Evangheli, Pandeli, 765
Evitkhiev, I. I., 659 (n. 6)
Evola, Count, 334
Ex parte Yaffee, 1930, 100 (n. 6)
executive powers
France: decree laws, 203, 216–17; Fifth Republic, 299–300, 301; Fourth Republic, 214–16, 218–220; Third Republic, 197, 200–201, 203
Germany: Bonn Republic, 404–6; Second Empire, 343–4; Weimar Republic, 361–3, 364–5, 369

executive powers (*continued*)
Great Britain, 11–14, 85–6, 87, 94–5,
95–105
Italy: liberal monarchy, 460, 470–1;
Republic, 516–18

Fabians, Great Britain, 28, 146–9, 156,
166
Fabre, Michel-Henri, 790 (n. 3)
Facta, Luigi, 470
Factory Acts, Great Britain, 127, 140
(n. 3)
Fagerholm, Karl A., 764, 778
Fainsod, Merle, 629 (n. 5), 660 (n. 7),
668 (n. 8)
Fanfani, Amintore, 497, 499, 512, 514
Farberov, N. P., 790 (n. 3), 808 (n. 4)
fascism, Italy: comparison with nazism,
476; fall of Mussolini, 476–7; institutions of, 472–5; murder of Matteoti, 471–2; Mussolini appointed
premier, 470–1; purge of the fascists after World War II, 481; relations with the church, 475; rise
of Mussolini, 466–71
Fascist Grand Council, 472, 474; and
overthrow of Mussolini, 476–7
Fascist Party, Italy: Acerbo electoral
law, 471; growth of party, 469–70;
march on Rome, 1922, 470; organization of first fascist groups, 468;
party and state, 472, 474; post
World War I discontent in Italy,
469; *see also* fascism
Fatherland Front, Bulgaria, 774, 792
Faulhaber, Cardinal, 393
Faure, Edgar, 216, 256, 257, 263
Feder, Gottfried, 379
Federal Constitutional Court, Germany,
431
Federal Union of German Industry,
369
federalism: Commonwealth of Nations,
157–63; Eastern Europe, 800–1;
Germany, 344–5, 364–5, 402–4;
U.S.S.R., 585–90, 642–7; *see also*
French Community, French Union,
regionalism
Federation of Farmers' Unions, France,
273
Fedor I, Russia, 550
Ferdinand and Isabella, 455
Ferry, Jules, 199

feudalism: England, 11–12; Germany,
327, 329, 339–40; Russia, 554–5
Figgis, J. N., 48
Filov, Bogdan, 765
Finer, Herman, 363 (n. 6)
Finer, S. E., 45 (n. 3)
Finland: acquisition by Russia, 545;
civil war after World War I, 761,
763; independence, 747; relations
with U.S.S.R. after World War II,
775, 777–8; Swedish minority,
804–5; *see also* Eastern Europe
First Charter of Stephen, 1135, Eng-
land, 12 (n. 2)
First International, 1864–76, 704
Fischer, Fritz, 330 (n. 7)
Fisher, H. H., 700 (n. 8)
Fiume, 468–9
Five Year Plans, U.S.S.R., *see* planning,
U.S.S.R.
Food Estate Law, Third Reich, 387
"Flapper" Act, 1928, Great Britain, 31
Force Ouvrière, 259–60
Fortescue, Sir John, 21, 78
Foscolo, Ugo, 457
Fox, Charles James, 163
Fox, W. T. R., 395 (n. 1)
Fraenkel, Ernst, 385 (n. 2)
France: Algerian crisis, 1958, 293–5;
antidemocratic forces, 189–90;
church problem, 198, 281–2; collapse of 1940, 204–5; constitutional
reform, 202–4, 206–12, 295–6,
296–8, 298–303; economy, 284–92;
electoral reform, 201; equalitarian
tradition, 191, 194; freedom of
the press, 283–4; French Community, 297, 302–3; French Union,
243–51; governmental structure,
Fifth Republic, 298–305; governmental structure, Fourth Republic,
213–38; immigration, 281; international affairs, 307–13; libertarian
tradition, 191–2; nationalized industries, 238–43; political parties,
252–70; population problems, 280;
social and economic groups, 270–
278; social services, 274–6; taxation problems, 279–80; wealth and
income, 278–9; Western European
unity, 311–13
Franco-Soviet Trade Union Committee,
709
Franco-Soviet treaty, 309

Frankfurt Assembly, 1848, 337, 342, 360
Franks, Sir Oliver, 103
Franks Committee on Administrative Tribunals and Enquiries, Great Britain, 103
Frederick III, Germany, 352
Frederick the Great, 346
Frederick William IV, Prussia, 338, 352
Free Democratic Party (F.D.P.), Germany, 417, 421, 429–30
Free French movement, 205–6
Free German Trade Union League, 410
Free German Youth, 410
Free Peoples Party (F.V.P.), Germany, 421, 430
Freeman, E. A., 56 (n. 1)
Freikonservative, 338, 349 (n. 3)
French Confederation of Christian Workers (C.F.T.C.), 265
French Community, 297, 302–3
French National Railroad Corporation, 239
French Union, 243–51
Friedmann, W., 134
Friedrich, Carl J., 4, 5, 134, 363 (n. 6), 412 (n. 2)
Fritsch, General Werner von, 381, 392
Fuller, C. D., 698 (n. 3)
Funk, Walther, 373, 380, 386
Furtseva, Ye. A., 624, 627
Fyodorov, V. S., 658
fyrd, 12

Gablentz, Otto H. v.d., 332 (n. 9)
Gaillard, Félix, 249, 258, 294
Gaitskell, Hugh, 40n., 53, 148
Galen, Bishop, 393
Gandhi, Mohandas K., 169
Gankin, Olga, 700 (n. 8)
Gapon, Father, 560
Garibaldi, Giuseppe, 460, 461, 462, 501
Gas Act, 1948, Great Britain, 133
Gasperi, Alcide de, 479, 481, 497, 499, 530
Gaulle, Charles de, 218, 228, 232 (n. 2), 235, 240, 280; Algerian crisis and Fifth Republic, 295–306 *passim;* formation of French Union, 244–5; party politics, 253, 255, 265; foreign policy views, 308, 309, 310; leadership, World War II and reconstruction period, 205–12; R.P.F., 266–8

Gava, Silvo, 510 (n. 5)
Gavrilović, Milan, 765
Gelasius, Pope, 7
General Association of German Workers, 351
General Confederation of Agriculture (C.G.A.), France, 270
General Confederation of Labor (C.G.T.), France, 259–60, 274
Ghenghis Khan, 544
Georgadze, 651
George, Henry, 156
George III, Great Britain, 59
George V, Great Britain, 85
Georgiev, Kimon, 765
German Christian Church, 393
German Confederation, 342, 344
German Confederation of Trade Unions (D.G.B.), 434–5
German Democratic Party (D.D.P.), 360; *Reichstag* elections, 1919–1933, 368 (n. 6)
German Democratic Republic (D.D.R.), general description of, 408–15
German Farmers' Party (D.B.P.), 410
German Labor Front, 378, 384, 387
German Nationalist Party (D.N.V.P.), 368 (n. 6)
German Party (D.P.), 421, 430
German People's Party (D.V.P.), 368 (n. 6), 429
Germany: Austrian-Prussian conflict, 331–2; Bonn Republic, government under, 401–8, 416–32; colonial aspirations, 348; Counter Reformation, 330; *Daily Telegraph* Affair, 354; economic progress of Bonn Republic, 432–7; European unity, 438–9, 439–40; failure of the middle class, 335–6; industrialists, 348, 369–70, 385–7; inflation of 1923, 367; influence of French Revolution, 350; influence of geography, 324–5; influence of Holy Roman Empire, 325, 328, 332; influence of Revolution of 1848, 336–8; influence of Roman Empire, 327–8; *Junkers,* 338, 346, 370, 413 (n. 3); as *Land der Mitte,* 324–5; lateness of national unity, 334–5; Nazi Government, 375–94; Nazi "war on the world," 390–2; occupation after World War II, 396–401; particularism, 327–8; peasantry under

Germany (*continued*)
Third Reich, 387; problem of expellees in Bonn Republic, 409 (n. 3), 430–1, 436–7; proletariat in Third Reich, 387–8; Prussian militarism, 332–3, 346–7; *Reichswehr* and Hitler, 388–90; religious schism, 328–31; resistance to Hitler, 392–4; revolution of 1918, 356, 357–9; rise of Hitler, 371–4; Saar problem, 439; Second Empire, government of, 343–52; unification of Germany, 437–8, 439–40, 411; universalism, 327–8; Versailles Treaty, 358; Weimar Republic, government, 361–72; World War I dictatorship, 355–6

Gerö, Ernö, 765, 784

Gerstenmaier, Eugen, 406, 423

Gessler, 418

Ghana, 152

Gheorghiu-Dej, Gheorghe, 765

Gichev, Dimiter, 758, 765

Giles, F. T., 112 (n. 8)

Gilmore, Eddy, 699

Gioberti, Vincenzo, 459, 460 (n. 4)

Giolitti, Giovanni, 465, 468, 469, 470, 472, 497, 500

Givry, J. de., 821 (n. 4)

Glabinski, Stanislaw, 764

Gladstone, William E., 30, 35, 154, 163

Glanvil, Ranulf de, 21

Glickman, Harvey, 93 (n. 8)

Gneisenau, General August von, 338, 347

Gneist, Rudolf, 352

Godunov, Boris, 550

Godwin, William, 27

Goebbels, Paul Joseph, 373, 382, 394, 410

Goelro, see planning, U.S.S.R.

Goerdeler, Dr. Karl, 393, 418

Goering, Hermann, 373, 381, 382, 383

Goerlitz, Walter, 389 (n. 5)

Goethe, Johann Wolfgang von, 325, 333, 359

Goguel, François, 290

Goldsmith, Oliver, on Burke, 33

Gömbös, Gyula, 765

Gomulka, Wladislaw, 718, 765, 784, 785, 807

Gonella, Guido, 499, 512

Gooch, G. P., 17

Gorkić, Milan, 765

Gosarbitrazh, 662

Gosplan, *see* planning, U.S.S.R.

Gossnab, 678

Gottwald, Klement, 765, 787

government corporations: France, 238–43; Great Britain, 103–5, 131–4; Italy, 486–7; Soviet binational stock companies in Rumania, Hungary, East Germany, 718, 780; *see also* nationalization

Government of India Act, 1935, 160

Govorov, Marshal, 674

Grabski, Stanislaw, 764

Gramsci, Antonio, 491

Grand Remonstrance, 1641, England, 17

Grandi, Dino, 476

Great Britain: British political institutions, influence in other countries, 3, 106; British political thought, 18–28; cabinet government, 74–6; cabinet and ministry, 87–90; civil service, 90–4; common law, 106–7; Conservative Party principles, 47–50; courts, 107–13; crisis government, 97–9; Cromwell's Commonwealth, 17; Crown, components of, 83–4; delegated powers, 100–2; development of parties before 1832, 32–3; economic background, 125–30; economic planning, 142–4; external relations, 149–50; growth of suffrage, 29–32; historical development of the Crown, 11–14; historical development of Parliament, 14–18, 56–60; labor force, 139 (n. 9); labor relations, 139–42; Labour Party principles, 50–2; legal profession, 113–14; Liberal Party principles, 45–7; local government, 115–20; Loyal Opposition, 76–7; monarchy, 84–7; national budget, 73 (n. 4); National Health Service, 137–8; officers and committees of Parliament, 69–70; organization of House of Commons, 63–5; organization of House of Lords, 60–2; parliamentary bills and procedure, 71–2; parliamentary elections, 66–8; party conferences, 1958, 52–5; party organization, 37–45; parties in the nineteenth century, 33–5; parties since World War I, 35–7; powers of the executive, 95–7;

Great Britain (*continued*)

    principles of the Constitution, 5–11; redistribution of wealth, 143–4; reform of the House of Lords, 63–5; regionalism, Scotland, Wales, Northern Ireland, 122–4; revolution of the seventeenth century, 14–18; "rule of law," 114–15; social services, 136–8; theory and practice of representation, 77–82; theories and problems of the Welfare State, 145–9; Town and Country planning, 120–2; Welfare State and industry, 131–6

Greece: British interests, 770; independence, 745; war with Italy, 476

Green, T. H., 26–7, 46

Gregg, Pauline, 128 (n. 3)

Gregoire, Roger, 228, 229

Gregory, James S., 542 (n. 2)

Gregory VII, Pope, 19

Grévy, Jules, 197, 198

Griewant, Karl, 336 (n. 2)

Grimond, Jo, 37, 54

Grishin, V. V., 690

Groener, Wilhelm, 389

Grol, Milan, 764

Gromyko, Andrei A., 657

Gronchi, Giovanni, 499, 516, 517, 530

Gross, Feliks, 757 (n. 3)

Grotewohl, Otto, 410, (n. 6), 411

Groza, Petru, 765, 775

Gsovski, V., 662 (n. 1), 668 (n. 8)

Guillaume, Augustin, 671 (nn. 4, 5)

Guradze, Heinz, 397 (n. 3)

Gurian, Waldemar, 669 (n. 9)

Guseva, Z., 581 (n. 4)

Habeas Corpus Act, 1679, England, 18, 114

Haldane, Lord, 112–13

Halder, General Franz, 388 (n. 3)

Haller, Karl Ludwig von, 350

Haller, W., 25 (n. 5), 33 (n. 9)

Hammerstein, General Gunther von, 392

Hampl, Antonin, 764

Hans, Nicolas, 576 (n. 9)

Hansemann, David, 337

Hapsburgs: and Hohenzollerns, 331–2; and Italy, 456–7

Harden, Macmilian, 346

Hardenberg, Prince Karl von, 347 (n. 2)

Hardie, Keir, 156

Hare, Thomas, 80

Harrington, James, 25

Hart, Liddell, 388 (n. 3), 671 (nn. 4, 6)

Hassell, Ulrich von, 392, 393

Haubach, Theodor, 394

Hauptmann, Gerhard, 353

Haushofer, General Karl, 391, 437 (n. 5)

Haydn, Franz Joseph, 331

Hazard, John N., 662 (n. 1)

Heck, Dr. Bruno, 424

Hegel, Georg, 26, 27, 347

Heiden, Konrad, 379 (n. 5)

Hemmerle, Eduard, 344 (n. 1)

Henlein, Konrad, 765

Henry I, England, 13, 19

Henry II, England, 19

Henry IV, England, 58

Henry IV, Holy Roman Empire, 19

Henry VIII, England, 13, 16, 20, 22, 125

Herbert, Sir A. P., 72

Herder, Johann, 325, 333

Hermens, F. A., 365 (n. 3)

Herrfahrdt, H., 361 (n. 3)

Herriot, Édouard, 209, 262

Hertz, F., 752 (n. 6)

Hertzog, General James B., 167, 172

Hervé, Pierre, 259

Herz, John H., 404 (n. 8)

Hess, Rudolf, 373, 382, 383

Heuss, Theodor, 360, 389, 404, 416, 417, 429

Hewart, Lord, 100

Heydebrand, Ernst von, 348

Heydrich, Reinhard, 383

Heydte, F. A. von der, 420 (n. 4)

Hilferding, Rudolf, 693

Himmler, Heinrich, 373, 382, 383

Hindenburg, Paul von: 359, 362, 368, 369 (n. 7), 372, 389; death, 380; and *Junkers,* 370; and von Papen, 371

Hinduism, 168–70

Hitler, Adolf: 55, 98, 99, 144, 324, 327, 334, 341, 355, 371, 408, 420, 434, 476, 766; and generals, 388–390; and von Hindenburg, 362 (n. 4), 380, 389; July 20, 1944 attempt at assassination, 389, 393, 394; June purge, 1934, 380; Munich, 391; National Coalition, 363, 370; resistance, 392–4; rise to power, 358, 374, 379–81

Hlinka, Monsignor Andrej, 765

Hobbes, Thomas, 8, 23–4
Hobhouse, Leonard T., 46–7
Hobson, J. A., 693
Hodža, Milan, 765
Hoegner, Wilhelm, 427
Hogan, James, 78 (n. 2)
Hohenlohe, Prince Chlodwig, 353
Hohenzollerns, 331–2, 336, 742, 747
Holborn, Hajo, 328 (n. 2), 334 (n. 1), 395 (n. 1)
Holstein, Friedrich von, 354
Holy Alliance, 342
Holy Roman Empire, 13, 19–20, 325, 328–9, 332, 340
Home Rule Bill of 1886, Great Britain, 35
Homicide Act, 1957, Great Britain, 72
Hooker, Richard, 22–3
Horthy, Admiral Nicholas, 766, 767
Houphouet-Boigny, Félix, 249
House of Commons Disqualification Act, 1957, Great Britain, 67, 88, 89
House of Savoy: rejection in referendum of 1946, 480, 481; unification of Italy, 459–60
Howard, James O., 816 (n. 1)
Howard, Roy, 637–8
Hoxha, Enver, 765, 794
Huber, E., 365 (n. 1)
Hugenberg, Alfred, 370, 374, 380, 386
Huizinga, Johan, 335
Humboldt, Wilhelm von, 350
Hume, David, 46–7
Hungary: Communist regime after World War I, 705, 761–2; consolidation of Communist control after World War II, 770, 775, 776; Horthy regime, 766; independence, 747; revolt of 1956, 718–19, 720, 784–5, 787; ties with Nazi Germany, 749; World War II armistice, 770; see also Eastern Europe
Hyndman, Henry M., 27

Ignatiev, S. D., 626, 627
Ignatov, N. G., 624, 626
Ilbert, Sir Courtenay, 153
impeachment: in Britain, 17, 58–9; in Italian Republic, 522
Imperial Conference of 1926, 172, 173
imperialism: as the "highest stage" of capitalism (Lenin), 693–4; British, 34, 48–9, 127–8, 149–50, 151–2;

imperialism (continued)
French, 199, 243–5; German, 348; Italian, 466–7, 476, 528; Nazi, 379, 390–2; Russian, and Soviet, 544–5, 715–21
Independent Republican Party, France, 256, 165
Independent Socialist Party, Germany, 359 (n. 2), 368 (n. 6)
India: constitution and government, 160–3, 178; parties, 168–70; and Soviet foreign policy, 708, 719–20; see also Commonwealth of Nations
Industrial Courts Act, 1919, Great Britain, 141
Industrial Revolution: in Germany, 333; in Great Britain, 33–4, 126–7
industrialism: Eastern Europe, 741–2, 808–12; East Germany, 413–15; France, 284–8, 290–2; Germany, 339–40, 348, 369–70, 385–7, 432–6; Great Britain, 125–30; Italy, 482–3, 484, 486–8; U.S.S.R., 553–4, 684
Inkeles, Alex, 575 (n. 8), 607 (n. 4), 608 (n. 6)
Institutes of Justinian, 21
Intellectuals for Peace, 711
International Agrarian Bureau, 760
International Confederation of Free Trade Unions, 709–10
International Federation of Women, 711
international law, Soviet conception of, 696–8
International Peasant Union, 761
International Workers' Association, 351
investiture conflict, 19–20
Iorga, Nicolae, 764
Ipsen, H. P., 385 (n. 9), 402 (n. 5)
Iran: oil crisis, 150; Italian interest, 531–2; Soviet aims, 718
Irish Free State, 30, 61
Irish Nationalist Party, 35
Iron and Steel Act, 1949, Great Britain, 134
Iron and Steel Act, 1953, Great Britain, 134, 136
Iron Guard, Rumania, 765, 766, 767
Ishkov, A. A., 658
Islam, 168, 170–1
Italian Confederation of Labor Unions (C.I.S.L.), 498

Italian Democratic Socialist Party, 491, 495
Italian General Confederation of Labor (C.G.I.L.), 493
Italian Social Movement (M.S.I.), 491, 502–3
Italy: balance of payments, 483; cabinet and administration, 518–21; Church question, 463–4, 466, 475, 506–7; constitution of 1948, provisions, 504–8; courts, 521–5; economy, 484–9; European unity, 529–31; failure to become united, 455–6; fall of Fascism, 476–7; Fascist government, 471–7; foreign trade, 483; framing of 1948 constitution, 479–81; government under Liberal Monarchy, 462–5, 467; historical background and influences, 455–7; imperialism, 528–9; international affairs, 528–32; legislative procedure, 514–16; liberation from Fascism, 477–9; local government, 525–7; movement for unity, 457–8, 460–2; Napoleonic invasions, 456; parliamentary institutions, 508–14; parties and party systems, 491–503; Piedmont-Sardinia, 459–60; physical resources, 482–3; presidency, 516–18; problem of the South, 489–91; regions, 526; rise of Fascism, 466–71; standard of living, 488–9; unemployment, 487; unrest of early nineteenth century, 455
Ivan III (the Great), Russia, 547
Ivan IV (the Terrible), Russia, 545, 547, 550, 555

Jackson, R. M., 107 (n. 2), 113 (n. 2)
Jackson, W. Eric, 120 (n. 3)
James I, England, 16, 17, 23
James II, England, 17, 18 (n. 3), 32
Japan, 128; and Hitler's Germany, 392; and Russia, 545, 547, 696, 698, 709, 715, 720
Jaurès, Jean, 261
Jenkins, Roy, 148
Jennings, Sir Ivor, 76, 77, 86 (n. 6), 98, 161 (nn. 6, 7), 406
Jevtić, Bogoljub, 765
John of Salisbury, 19
Jouvenel, Robert de, 198–9, 227
Jovanović, Dragoljub, 765, 776
Jovanović, Jovan, 765

judicial review: absence of in Britain, 5, 107, 114; in Bonn Republic, 431; in Commonwealth of Nations, 158, 161–2, 177–8; in France, 225–6, 301; in Italy, 521–3
judicial system
Commonwealth of Nations, 158, 159, 161–2, 177–8
Eastern Europe, 802–3
France: administrative courts, 237–8; Constitutional Committee, Fourth Republic, 225–6; Constitutional Council, Fifth Republic, 301; Council of State, 229–30, 237–8; Court of Accounts, 231; Court of Cassation, 235–6; High Council of the Judiciary, 236; personnel, 236; special courts, 237
Germany: 347, 365; under Bonn, 431; special Nazi courts, 385
Great Britain: civil courts, 109–10; common law system, 106–7; court hierarchy, 107–9; criminal courts, 110–12; Judicial Committee of the Privy Council, 112–13; "law lords," 61, 63, 110; legal profession, 113–14
Italy: structure under Republic, 521–5
U.S.S.R.: lay judges, 665–6; Procurator General, 666–7; relation to politics, 666; structure and jurisdiction, 662–7
Jünger, Ernst, 379 (n. 4)
"just and unjust" wars, Soviet concepts, 694–6
justiciars, England, 13

Kabanov, I. G., 626
Kádár, János, 765, 784, 785, 787
Kaganovich, L. M., 624, 626, 627, 655 (n. 5), 674, 783, 785
Kaisenberg, G., 363 (n. 6)
Kaiser, Joseph, 422 (n. 5)
Kállay, Miklós, 765
Kallio, Kyösti, 765
Kalmykov, V. D., 658
Kalnberzins, J. E., 624, 627
Kamenev, L. B., 614
Kant, Immanuel, 26, 27, 350
Károlyi, Count Mihály, 764
Katyn murders, 769
Keitel, General Wilhelm, 381
Kekkonen, Urho, 765
Kelly, M. A., 434 (n. 8)

Kelsall, R. K., 94 (n. 9)
Kennan, George, 438
Keppler, Wilhelm, 386
Kerensky, Alexander, 560, 561
Kerner, Robert J., 545 (n. 4)
Kerr, Clark, 435 (n. 9)
Kéthly, Anna, 764
Keynes, John M., 144
Khlamov, G. S., 658
Khrunichev, M. V., 658
Khrushchev, Nikita S.: agriculture re-
    forms, 686–8; Communist party
    leadership, 624–7, 674; Communist
    policies in Eastern Europe, 707,
    779, 783, 784, 786, 799; Council
    of Ministers, 655–8; foreign policy,
    707, 720; speech to twentieth party
    Congress, 669
Kienthal conference, 1951, 704
Kiev principality, 549
King, B., 475 (n. 5)
King, William Lyon Mackenzie, 165,
    174
Kingsley, Charles, 27
Kingsley, J. D., 94
Kiosseivanov, Georgi, 765
Kirchheimer, Otto, 407 (n. 2)
Kirichenko, A. I., 624, 626
Kirilenko, A. P., 624
Knoeringen, Waldemar von, 427
Koc, Colonel Adam, 765
Koch-Weser, 418
Koehler, Bernhard, 386
Koerner, Paul, 386
Kohn, Hans, 334 (n. 1)
kolkhoz, 685–8
Kollontay, Madame Alexdranda, 579,
    580
Kolosov, A., 583 (n. 6)
Komsomol, 628–31
Konev, Marshal, 780
Korác, Vitomir, 764
Korfanty, Wojciech, 764
Kornilov, General L. G., 561
Korniyets, L. R., 658
Korniyets, S. R., 658
Korošec, Anton, 764
Korotchenko, D. S., 624, 626, 627
Korovin, Professor Eugene, 696
Korovushkin, A. K., 658
Kosanović, Sava, 764
Koslov, F. R., 627, 655, 657, 659
Kostousov, A. I., 658
Kostov, Traicho, Djunev, 718, 765

Kosturkov, Stoyan, 764
Kosyachenko, G., 679
Kosygin, A. N., 624, 626, 627, 655,
    657, 659, 679
Kotta, Constantin, 765
Kovács, Béla, 765, 776
Kozhevnikov, Y. F., 657
Kozlov, F. R., 624, 655, 657
Kramář, Karel, 764
Kreisau circle, 394
Krek, Miho, 764
Krestintern, 711
Kruja, Mustafa, 764
Krupp interests, 348
Kryeziu, Tsena, 765
Kucherenko, V. A., 658
Kulischer, Eugene M., 542 (n. 1)
Kulturkampf, 330, 340, 351
Kun, Béla, 765
Kurachov, S. V., 657
Kuusinen, Hertta, 765
Kuusinen, Otto, 624, 626, 627, 765
Kuzmin, I. I., 655 (n. 5), 657, 659
Kuznetsov, V. V., 626

labor
    Commonwealth of Nations, 156–7,
        165–7
    Eastern Europe: post World War II
        fronts, 772; prewar Socialist par-
        ties, 755–6; status of industrial
        workers, 821
    France: Catholic influences, 265;
        Communist influences, 258,
        259–60, 262; Conseils de prud'-
        hommes, 237; postwar gains,
        274–6; urban workers and labor
        force, 273–4
    Germany: beginnings of unioniza-
        tion, 351; Bismarcks' Socialisten-
        gesetzgebung, 340; in Bonn Re-
        public, 434–5; codetermination,
        428, 435; in East Germany, 410;
        under Hitler, 384, 387–8, 394;
        and revolution of 1848, 336–7;
        unemployment in Weimar Re-
        public, 373
    Great Britain: beginnings of union-
        ism, 127; enfranchisement of
        workers, 30, 34; labor relations,
        139–42; nationalized industries,
        133, 142; negotiating and dis-
        putes machinery, 141–2; rela-

labor (*continued*)
tion to Labour Party, 41–2, 43, 52, 128; trade unions, members, etc., 139, 140

Italy: Catholic influences, 466, 498–9; Communist influences, 493–4; under fascism, 469, 474, 521; labor force, 484; labor organization, 493, 498; unemployment, 487

U.S.S.R.: "collective bargaining," 690; constitutional rights and duties, 599, 601, 602–3; forced labor, 669–70; incentives, 574, 595–6; proportion of workers in pre- and postrevolutionary society, 554, 571–4; trade unions, membership, organization, functions, 688–91; workers in Supreme Soviet, 648

Labor parties, in Commonwealth of Nations, 165–7

Labour Party, Great Britain: beginnings, 35, 50–1, 128; organization, 40–2; party Conference of 1958, 52–5; party leadership, 42–5; principles and program, 27–8, 50–2; in twentieth century, 35–7; welfare state policies, and recent critiques, 125, 131, 146–9

Labour Representation Committee, Great Britain, 50

Lacoste, Robert, 293

La Farina, Giuseppe, 461 (n. 6)

Lamennais, F. de, 233

Lamine-Gueye, M., 249

Lammers, Karl-Heinrich, 388

Landauer, Karl, 435 (n. 1)

Lange, M. G., 415 (n. 5)

Lansbury, George, 40 (n. 4)

Laponogov, I., 795 (n. 6)

Laski, Harold, 28, 51, 142, 145

Lassalle, Ferdinand, 324, 351, 426

Lateran agreements, 475, 480, 506

Latvia, and U.S.S.R., 545, 770

Laurier, Sir Wilfred, 163

Lauro, Achille, 502

Laval, Pierre, 203, 205, 308 (n. 1)

Law for Liberation from National Socialism and Militarism, 1946, 400 (n. 4)

law of papal guarantees, 1871, Italy, 463

law on state secrets, 1947, U.S.S.R., 603

law on treason to the fatherland, 1934, U.S.S.R., 603

Lazarevsky, N. I., 547 (n. 6)

League of Militant Atheists, U.S.S.R., 582

League of Nations: and Italo-Ethiopian war, 476; and the Soviet Union, 698

Leber, Julius, 394

Lecoeur, Auguste, 259

Left Republican Rally (R.G.R.), France, 263

Legien-Stinnes understanding, 359

legislative bodies
Commonwealth of Nations, *see* Parliament
Eastern Europe: national assemblies, 797–8; people's committees, 796–7
France, *see* Parliament
Germany: *Bundesrat,* Bonn Republic, 403; *Bundesrat,* Second Empire, 344–5; *Bundestag,* Bonn Republic, 406–7; People's Chamber, East Germany, 409–10; Prussian, in Second Empire, 346; *Reichsrat,* Weimar, 364; *Reichstag,* Second Empire, 345–6, 353–4; *Reichstag* under Hitler, 381; *Reichstag,* Weimar, 365–7
Great Britain, *see* Parliament
Italy, *see* Parliament
U.S.S.R.: early Dumas, 551; State Council, 553; State Duma, 553–4; *Zemsky Sobor,* 550; *zemstvos,* 551, 552; *see also* soviets, Supreme Soviet

Leino, Yrjö Kaarle, 765

Lemmer, Ernst, 403 (n. 7)

Lenin, Nikolai, 169, 469, 611, 655, 659, 668; activities in revolution of 1917, 558–61; views and pronouncements on: diplomacy, 702, 711; divorce, 579; emancipation of serfs, 552; federation and nationalities, 584–5, 591, 592, 599; geography, 546; imperialism, 693–4; industrialization of Russia, 676; international organizations, 698; party, 561, 613–16; war and peace, 694–5, 713; withering away of the state, 564, 565, 567, 633

Lens, Sidney, 434 (n. 8)

Leo XIII, Pope, 463, 466

Leonard, Wolfgang, 415 (n. 5)
Leonhardt, H. H., 328 (n. 3)
Lerner, Daniel, 382 (n. 7)
Lesechko, M. A., 658
Lessing, Gotthold E., 333, 350
Leuschner, Wilhelm, 394
Levellers, 25, 33, 77
Levi, Carlo, 489
Levin, D. B., 701 (n. 2)
Lewis, H. O., 413 (n. 3)
Ley, Robert, 373
Liaquat Ali, 170
Liberal Democratic Party, East Germany, 410
Liberal parties: Commonwealth of Nations, 163–4; Eastern Europe, 753–5, 764; Germany, 349 (n. 5), 350, 368 (n. 6), 417, 429–30; Russia, 559
Liberal Party, Great Britain: antecedents, 32–3; conference of 1958, 54–5; decline, 35–7; in nineteenth century, 33–5; principles, 45–7
Liberal Party, Italy: constituent assembly, 1946, 480; in Liberal Monarchy, 463–5; in Republic, 500–1, 511
liberalism
    Commonwealth of Nations, 163–5, 168, 169, 170
    Eastern Europe, 753–5
    France: laissez faire, 202, 238, 262, 266, 291; libertarian tradition, 191, 194; middle classes, 276–7; postwar parties, 262–3, 266
    Germany, 336–8, 350, 360, 417, 429
    Great Britain: civil war of seventeenth century, 16–18; tenets, 23–4, 26–7, 45–7, 54, 80
    Italy: 500–1; economic situation, 485–6; in Liberal Monarchy, 464–5
    Russia: liberal tsars, 551–2
Libya, independence, 531
Liebermann, Max, 553
Liebknecht, Karl, 351, 361
Lilburne, John, 25 (n. 5)
Lindrath, Hermann, 403 (n. 7)
Lipset, S. M., 156 (n. 4)
Litchfield, E. H., 434 (n. 8)
Lithuania, and U.S.S.R., 545, 770
Little Entente, 752
Litvinov, Maxim, 715
Lloyd, Henry Demarest, 155

Lloyd George, David, 35, 36, 97, 355
local government
    Eastern Europe: people's committees, 796, 801–2
    France: influence of French Revolution, and Napoleon, 196; prefects, 231–2; problems of centralization, 233–4
    Germany: revival after World War II, 397 (n. 3); as school for political leaders, 418
    Great Britain: career service, 118; central government control, 119–20; finance, 119; local units, 115–16; medieval, 13; powers and services, 116–18
    Italy: communal councils, 526–7; local autonomy under Republic Constitution, 525–6
    U.S.S.R.: local soviets, 638–42; under tsars, 552–3
Local Government Act, 1888, Great Britain, 115
Local Government Act, 1894, Great Britain, 115
Local Government Act, 1948, Great Britain, 117, 119
Local Government Act, 1958, Great Britain, 115–16, 120
Locke, John, 23–4, 33, 45–6, 80, 81
Lomtev, T. P., 594 (n. 7)
Londonderry, Marquess of, 375
Longo, Luigi, 478
Lowell, A. Lawrence, 74
Lübke, Heinrich, 403 (n. 7)
Lücke, Paul, 403 (n. 7)
Luddites, 127
Ludendorff, General Erich von, 352, 355, 356
Ludwig of Bavaria, 343
Lueders, Marie-Elizabeth, 430
Luethy, Herbert, 290, 291
Lulchev, Kosta, 764
Luther, Martin, 329, 418
Lütkens, Gerhart, 406 (n. 9)
Lvov, Prince G., 560
Lyapchev, Andrei, 764

Macartney, C. A., 751
Macaulay, Thomas A., 34, 169
MacDonald, Sir John, 164
MacDonald, Ramsay, 28, 35 (n. 3), 40 (n. 4), 76

Maček, Vladko, 765
Machiavelli, Nicolo, 457
Mackenzie, K. R., 15 (n. 7)
Mackenzie, W. J. M., 92 (n. 5)
MacMahon, Marshal M., 197, 300
Macmillan, Harold, 52, 53, 87, 88, 89, 125; election as Conservative party leader, 38; on British conservatism, 50
McIlwain, C. H., 21 (n. 8), 57
McKenzie, R. T., 37 (n. 1), 43 (n. 2), 166 (n. 1)
Magna Carta, 5, 12
Maier, Reinhold, 430
Maine, Sir Henry Sumner, 48
Maitland, F. W., 21, 48
Malan, D. F., 168
Malaya, 113, 152, 175
Malenkov, F. M., 624, 626, 627, 655, 674, 782, 783, 785
Maleshova, Sejfulla, 765
Malfa, Ugo La, 486, 501
Malinov, Alexander, 764
Malinovsky, Rodian Y., 657
Malinovsky, Roman, 550
Malypetr, Jan, 765
Malyshev, V. A., 626, 679
Manin, Daniele, 461 (n. 6)
Maniu, Juliu, 765, 776
Mannerheim, General Carl Gustav, 761, 763, 765
Mansergh, Nicholas, 172 (n. 3)
Manteuffel, General Edward von, 338, 347
Manzoni, Alessandro, 457
Mao Tse-tung, 785, 786
Marat, Jean Paul, 358
Marković, Lazar, 764
Marković, Sima, 765
Marshall Plan, 309, 707, 718, 777
Marsiglio of Padua, 19 (n. 5)
Martin, Alfred von, 334 (n. 1)
Martino, Gaetano, 500
Martov, L., 558
Marty, André, 259
Marx, Karl: tenets of Marxism, 562–5, 584, 615, 676
Masaryk, Jan, 777
Masaryk, Tomás G., 754
Matrimonial Causes Act, 1937, Great Britain, 72
Matskevich, V. V., 657
Matteotti, Giacoma, 471
Maurice, F. D., 27

Maurras, Charles, 205
Maynard, Sir John, 548 (n. 9), 550 (n. 1)
Mazzini, Giuseppe, 457, 459, 460, 462, 501
Mazurov, K. T., 624, 627
Medici, Giuseppe, 48 (n. 3)
Meighen, Arthur, 165
Meinecke, Friedrich, 334 (n. 1)
Meissner, Erich, 329 (n. 5)
Melnikov, L. G., 626
Mende, Erich, 430
Mendès-France, Pierre, 256, 257, 263, 267, 281, 291, 295, 297, 312
Mensheviks, 558–60
Merchant Shipping Act, 1876, Great Britain, 72
Merkatz, Hans-Joachim von, 403 (n. 7)
Messe, Marshal, 515 (n. 7)
Metternich, Prince Klemens von, 336, 342, 456
Metzger, Laure, 815 (n. 9)
Michael, Rumania, 794
Michaelis, Georg, 356
Michels, Roberto, 426
Mihailov, Ivan, 765
Mihailović, Dragoljub, 773
Mihalache, Ion, 765, 776
Mikhailov, N. A., 626, 629, 657
Mikhailov, Nicholas, 542 (n. 2)
Mikolajczyk, Stanislaw, 765, 776
Mikoyan, A. I., 624, 626, 627, 655, 657, 659, 720, 779
militarism, Prussia, 332
Miliukov, Paul, 558
Mill, John Stuart, 26, 46–7, 80, 169
Millerand, Alexander, 200
Milne, R. S., 142
Milton, John, 33, 77
Minc, H., 784, 789 (n. 1)
Mines and Quarries Acts, Great Britain, 140 (n. 3)
Minin, Kuzma, 550
Ministerial Salaries Act, 1957, Great Britain, 88 (n. 2)
Ministers of the Crown Act, 1937, Great Britain, 87, 88
ministries and ministers
    Eastern Europe, 799–800
    France: experience of Fourth Republic, 226–7; innovations of De Gaulle Constitution, 299–300
    Germany: as of January 1, 1959, 403 (n. 7); in East Germany, 410–11

ministries and ministers (*continued*)
  Great Britain: posts in Macmillan government, 87–8, 89
  Italy: government posts as of 1959, 519
  U.S.S.R.: All-Union and Union-Republic ministries, 656; ministers as of March, 1959, 657–8; number of ministries, 1924–59, 655; in the union republics, 654–7
Miquel, Johannes von, 348, 351 (n. 6)
Mirza, General Iskander, 170
Mitterand, François, 263
Möbius, Walter, 413 (n. 3)
Model Parliament, 1295, England, 15, 57, 82
Mohler, Armin, 332 (n. 9)
Mollet, Guy, 227, 257, 267, 293, 296
Molotov Plan, *see* Council of Mutual Economic Assistance
Molotov, V. M., 624, 626, 627, 633, 655, 674, 708, 721, 783, 785; ouster from Presidium of party, 624
Moltke, Count Helmut von, 394
monarchist parties: in Eastern Europe, 765, 766; France, 197; in Italy, 501–2, 511
monarchy: British, 84–6; in the Commonwealth of Nations, 152–3; in Eastern Europe, 766, 793–4; France, 189–90, 195–6; Germany, Second Empire, 324–43; Italy, 460, 462, 476–7, 478, 480; in Russia, 547–8
Mongols, invasion of Russia, 544
Monnet, Jean, 288, 310
Montague, F. C., 21 (n. 7)
Montesquieu, Charles de, 191
Montfort, Simon de, 57
Moore, Barrington, Jr., 575 (n. 8), 668 (n. 8)
Moore, W. E., 743
More, Sir Thomas, 22, 27
Morris, William, 27, 156
Morris, William A., 15 (n. 6)
Morrison, Herbert, 40 (n. 5), 100, 131, 240
Mosca, Gaetano, 464
Moscow Conference, 1943, 698–9
Mouvement Républicain Populaire, see Popular Republican Movement, France
Movimento Sociale Italiano, see Italian Social Movement

Mozart, Wolfgang A., 332
Muir, Ramsay, 94–5
Mukhitdinov, N. A., 624, 627
Müller, Adam, 350
Müller, Hermann, 368
Municipal Corporations Act, 1835, Great Britain, 115
Muralt, Leonhart von, 344 (n. 1)
Muraviev, Konstantin, 758, 765
Mushanov, Nikola, 764
Muslim League, 170
Mussolini, Benito, 264, 334, 362 (n. 4), 382, 462, 495, 515; as *Duce,* 471–476; early career as Socialist, 467–468; fall of, 476–7; rise of fascism, 468–70
Mutiny Act, 1689, England, 18
Mzhavanadze, V. P., 624, 627

Nagy, Ferenc, 765
Nagy, Imre, 765, 776, 782, 784
Nagyatády-Szabó, István, 765
Naphtali, Fritz, 435 (n. 1)
Napoleon I, 195, 229, 327, 333, 456
Napoleon III, 190, 194, 266, 337, 461, 462
Narodnik movement, Russia, 557
National Congress of the Councils of Workers, Peasants, and Soldiers, Germany, 359
National Council of Corporations, Italy, 472
National Defence Committee, France, 219
National Democratic Party, East Germany, 410
National Harzburg Front, Germany, 363
National Health Service (Amendment) Act, 1949, Great Britain, 138
National Insurance Act, 1946, Great Britain, 102, 136–7
National Insurance (Industrial Injuries) Act, 1946, Great Britain, 136–7
National Liberal Party, Germany, 349 (n. 3), 350–1
National Liberal Party, Great Britain, 47 (n. 4)
national minorities
  Canada, 158
  Eastern Europe, 750, 751, 804–5
  Union of South Africa, 156, 167–8
  U.S.S.R.: cultural and linguistic pol-

national minorities (*continued*)
icy, 591–4; and federalistic structure, 585–8; "Soviet patriotism," 589; Soviet theories, 584–5

national socialism (Nazism), Germany: anti-Semitism, 385; appeals, 372–4; demagoguery, 378–9; expansionism, 379, 390–2; *Führerprinzip*, 381; monolithism, 388; one-party rule, 383–5; party and state, 385; position of army, 388–90; position of peasantry, industrialists, proletariat, 385–8; traits of authoritarianism, 377–8; Twenty Five Points, 379; resistance, 392–4

nationalism
Commonwealth of Nations, 163–4, 167–8, 176–8
Eastern Europe: autonomists, 767; economic, 750–2; independence movements, 747–50; Titoism, 781, 783–4, 785–7
France: in overseas territories, 244–245, 293–5, 302; and postwar foreign policy, 307–9
Germany: effect of Versailles, 358; and European unity, 438–41; industrialists and imperialism, 348, 369; lateness of national unity, 334–5; Nazi expansionism, 379, 390–2; postwar economic pressures, 435–6; problem of reunification, 437–9; World War I, 355
Great Britain: and imperialism, 34, 48–9, 127
Italy: background of fragmentation, 455–9; end of empire, 528–9; in World War I, 466–9; Mussolini's policies, 476
U.S.S.R.: expansion under tsars, 544–545; messianism, 556; resemblance of Soviet aims to tsarist goals, 720–1; Soviet patriotism, 593–4

Nationality Act, 1948, Great Britain, 176

nationalization
Commonwealth of Nations, 156–7, 166
Eastern Europe, 815
France: course of nationalization, 239–41; mixed corporations, 239; problems of controls, 242–243; statist, syndicalist, and au-

nationalization (*continued*)
tonomist formulas, 241–2
Germany: in East Germany, 413; Erhard's "social market economy," 432–4
Great Britain: historical background, 127–30; industries denationalized, 135–6; industries nationalized after World War II, 131–4; method, 134–5
Italy, 486–7

Naumann, Friedrich, 417

Nazi Party (N.S.D.A.P.), Germany: beginnings, 379; election of 1932, 371–2; Hitler becomes Chancellor, 380, 381; Hitler's lieutenants, 382–383; June purge, 1934, 380; mass support, 372–4; party and state, 381–2, 383–5; relations with army, 388–90, resistance, 392–4

Neesse, Gottfried, 385 (n. 9)
Nehru, 162, 170
Nemzer, Louis, 625 (n. 4)
Nenni, Pietro, 479, 494, 495, 496, 706
Nettl, J. P., 413 (n. 3)
Neumann, Franz L., 384 (n. 8)
Neumann, Sigmund, 332 (n. 9), 349 (n. 4), 350 (n. 5), 367 (n. 5), 375 (n. 2), 385 (n. 9), 407 (n. 2)
Neurath, Konstantin von, 381
New Towns Act, 1946, Great Britain, 121
New Zealand: citizenship legislation, 176; labor movements, 165–6; relations to Australia, 174; as social laboratory, 155; *see also* Commonwealth of Nations
Nicholas I, Russia, 545, 551
Nicholas II, Russia, 551, 552
Nicola, Enrico de, 477 (n. 7), 481
Niemoller, Pastor Martin, 330
Nietzsche, Friedrich W., 353, 383
Nikon, Patriarch, 549
Ninčić, Momčilo, 764
Nitti, Francesco, 469
Noli, Fan Stylian, 764
North Atlantic Treaty Organization (N.A.T.O.): and Commonwealth of Nations, 173; and Germany, 439, 440–1; and Great Britain, 149; and Italy, 529–30; and U.S.S.R., 719
North German Federation, 343
Northern Ireland, 123

Nosek, Vaclav, 765
Noske, Gustav, 359
Notverordnungsrecht, 344
Novalis (Friedrich von Hardenburg),
    333
Novikov, I. T., 657
Novosilov, Y. S., 658
Nowak, Zenon, 765

Oath of Salisbury, 1086, England, 12
Oberländer, Theodor, 403 (n. 7)
Occupation Statute, 1949, West Ger-
    many, 397, 400
Odoaker, 328
Oelssner, Fred, 411 (n. 8), 414 (n. 4)
O.G.P.U., *see* police, U.S.S.R.
Okhrana, see police, U.S.S.R.
Oldenburg-Januschau, Elard von, 370
Oleschuk, F., 583 (n. 8)
Ollenhauer, Erich, 426
Oprichnina, see police, U.S.S.R.
Orlando, Vittorio, 468, 500
Osborne Case, 1910, 81 (n. 7)
Osoaviakhim, 673
Oster, General Hans, 392
Otto the Great, 328 (n. 2)
Overacker, Louise, 166 (n. 1)
Overton, Richard, 25 (n. 5)
Owen, Robert, 27
Oxford University, 32 (n. 6), 92

Paasikivi, Juho K., 764
Pacciardi, Randolfo, 501
Paderewski, Ignace, 754
Pakistan, 113, 152, 170–1, 172, 175,
    178; *see also* Commonwealth of
    Nations
Pallavicino, Giorgio, 461 (n. 6)
Pallieri, Balladore, 505 (n. 1)
Pan-German League, 348
Pan-Slavism, 556
papal states, 456, 461, 462
Papen, Franz von, 338, 364, 365, 370,
    371, 374
Pareto, Vilfredo, 383, 464
Parliament
    Commonwealth of Nations, 153–5
    France: control of executive, 202–3,
        204, 217–18, 301; Council of the
        Republic, Fourth Republic, 222–
        224; dissolution, 200–1, 215–17,
        299; of Fifth Republic, 299–301;

Parliament (*continued*)
    National Assembly, Fourth Re-
        public, 220–1; in Third Republic,
        196–8
    Great Britain: historical develop-
        ment, 14–18, 56–60; House of
        Commons, 65–6; House of
        Lords, 60–2; parliamentary elec-
        tions, 66–8; parliamentary or-
        ganization and procedure, 68–
        74; reform of the House of
        Lords, 63–5; relations with exec-
        utive, 74–7, 100–5; representa-
        tive character, 77–82
    Italy: Chamber of Deputies, 508–9;
        under Liberal Monarchy, 460,
        462, 467; under Mussolini, 471–
        472; parliamentary legislation,
        514–15; Senate, 509–10
Parliament Act, 1911, Great Britain, 10,
    11 (n. 7), 60, 63, 64, 66, 71 (n. 1),
    72, 145
Parliament Act, 1949, Great Britain,
    60, 64, 134
Parri, Feruccio, 478, 479
Partito Nazionale Fascista, see Fascist
    party, Italy
Partito Popolare Italiano, see Populist
    Party, Italy
Pashukanis, Eugene, 567, 696
Pašić, Nikola, 764
Pastore, Giulio, 498, 499
Pastukhov, Krustyu, 764
Patolichev, N. S., 626, 657
Pătrăşcanu, Lucretiu, 765, 807
Pauker, Ana, 765
Paul, Prince, Yugoslavia, 794
Pavelić, Ante, 765
Peace of Augsburg, 1555, 330
Peasant Independents, France, 265–6
Peaslee, Amos V., 795 (n. 7)
Pegov, N. M., 626
Pella, Giuseppe, 497, 499, 511, 512, 517
Pellico, Silvio, 457, 461 (n. 6)
Pennanen, Pekka, 764
Peresypkin, Marshal, 674
Perov, G. V., 658
Pervukhin, M. G., 624, 626, 655 (n. 5),
    679
Pessi, Ville, 765
Pétain, Marshal Henri-Philippe, 204,
    205, 232 (n. 2), 274, 282
Peter II, Yugoslavia, 794

Peter the Great, Russia, 545, 549, 555, 556, 773
Peters, H., 407 (n. 1)
Petkov, Nikola D., 765, 774, 776
Petrescu, Constantin Titel, 764
Peyer, Károly, 764
Pflimlin, Pierre, 294–6
Philaret, Metropolitan, Russia, 549
Philip, André, 209, 210
Philip, Prince, Duke of Edinburgh, 84 (n. 4), 85
Piccioni, Attilio, 511
Pieck, Wilhelm, 411
Piedmont-Sardinia, kingdom, 459–62
Pilsudski, Jósef, 756, 759, 763, 765, 766
Pinay, Antoine, 266, 267, 304
Pitt, William, 59 (n. 9)
Pius IX, Pope, 459, 463
Pius X, Pope, 464
Pius XI, Pope, 475
planning
    Eastern Europe, 808
    France: national planning, 287–9; overseas planning, 289; problems, 290–2
    Germany: Erhard's social market economy, 432–4; five year plans in East Germany, 413–14
    Great Britain: 88, 142–4; Town and Country, 120–2
    Italy: 486–7; Southern Italy, 490–1
    U.S.S.R.: Five Year Plans, 678–9; Goelro, 677–8; Gosplan (State Planning Commission and related agencies), 679–82; management of agriculture, 685–8; management of industry, 682–5; position of labor and cooperatives, 688–92; results of plans, 684, 688; as solution to diversity of nationalities, 590–1
Plato, 27
Plekhanov, G., 557, 558
Pleven, Rene, 263
Plimsoll, Samuel, 72
Podgorny, N. W., 624, 627
Poetzsch-Heffter, F., 363 (n. 6)
Poincaré, Raymond, 200
Polak, K., 409 (n. 4), 410 (n. 5)
Poland: exile government after World War II, 769, 774; flight of Mikolajczyk, 776; independence, 747; Khrushchev's "different roads to socialism" policy, 783–7; Poznan

Poland (continued)
    riots, 1956 and Gomulka regime, 784–5, 786, 787, 807; see also Eastern Europe
Poliansky, D. S., 624, 627
police
    Germany: Gestapo, 378; in East Germany, 412
    U.S.S.R.: and army, 673; Cheka, 550, 668; and Communist party, 667–668; forced labor camps, 669–670; general organization and functions, 667–70; K.G.B. (Committee for State Security), 668; M.G.B., M.V.D., N.K.V.D., O.G.P.U., 668; Okhrana, 550; Oprichnina, 550; Third Section, 550
political parties, see also names of particular parties
    Commonwealth of Nations, 163–71
    Eastern Europe, 753–67
    France, 251–70
    Germany: Bonn Republic, 407–8, 420–32; in East Germany, 409–411; under Hitler, 382, 383–5; Second Empire, 348–52; Weimar Republic, 367–9
    Great Britain, 32–55; and cabinet government, 74–7
    Italy: Liberal Monarchy, 462–71; under Mussolini, 471–2; Republic, 491–503; revival after World War II, 477–81
    Russia: in revolutionary period, 559–562; under tsars, 556–9
Pollard, A. F., 56
Ponikowski, Antoni, 764
Ponomarenko, P. K., 626, 651
Poor Law, 1834, Great Britain, 127
Popular Republican Movement (M.R.P.), France: 254, 257 (n. 5), 263–5; in constituent assemblies after World War II, 208–12
Populist Party, Italy: and fascism, 469, 471, 475, 497; formation of, 466, 469; Popolari as antecedent of Christian Democrats, 496–7
Pospelov, P. N., 624, 626, 627
Postgate, Raymond, 126 (n. 1)
Poujade, Pierre, 254, 268–9, 297
Poujadism (Union for the Defense of Shopkeepers and Artisans), France, 268–9

Pozharsky, Prince D. M., 550

Prato, Bishop of, 506 (n. 2)

premier, France: and dissolution problem, Third and Fourth Republics, 200–1, 215–16; Fifth Republic, 299–300; office in Fourth Republic, 218–19

president
Eastern Europe, 798–9
France: Fourth Republic, 219–20; Fifth Republic, 298–300; French Community, 302–3; French Union, 247; Third Republic, 197–8, 200
Germany: Bonn Republic, 404, 416–417; East Germany, 411; Weimar Republic, 361–3, 380
India, 163
Italy, 516–18

Presidium of the Supreme Soviet, 650–653; chairman as titular head of state, 651; decree power, 650, 652–3; election by Supreme Soviet, 650; power to interpret laws, 652–653; and union-republic governments, 646

presidiums, Eastern Europe, 798–9

Preuss, Hugo, 360

Prévost-Paradol, Lucien-Anatole, 307

Pribičević, Svetozar, 764

Price, Arnold H., 407 (n. 2)

Price, G. Ward, 375 (n. 2)

prime minister
Great Britain: cabinet, 87–90; cabinet government, 58–9, 74–7; party leader, 38, 41, 42–3; relations with monarch, 85–6
Italy: under Liberal Monarchy and trasformismo, 464–5; in Republic, 511, 518

Privy Council, Great Britain: 90; Judicial Committee, appeals to, 90, 112–13, 177–8

Profintern, 709

Progressive parties, Germany, 349 (n. 3), 351

proportional representation: in France, 201–2, 253–5, 303–4; in Germany, 365–7, 422–3; in Great Britain, failure to adopt, 31, 54, 74, 75, 80–81; in Italy, 462, 508–9

Protestantism: in Eastern Europe, 757, 793, 804; in Germany, 328–31,

Protestantism (continued)
423–4; in Great Britain, 13, 18, 22–3, 85

Protogerov, Alexander, 765

Prussia: and Austria, 331–2; position in Second Empire, 343–5; role in German unification, 338–9, 342–3; traditions of government, 330, 332, 333, 336; in Weimar and ouster of Braun, 364–5

Pryor, Matthew, 62

Psurtsev, N. V., 657

Public Health Acts, Great Britain, 116, 140 (n. 3)

Pugachev, Emelian, 557

Puritans, 17, 22

Puttkamer, Robert von, 347

Puzanov, A. M., 626

qualunquismo, 502

Queuille, Henri, 263

Radić, Ante, 758, 765

Radić, Stjepan, 758, 765

Radical Socialist party, France, 201, 257 (n. 5), 262–3

Radowitz, Joseph Maria von, 338

Rajk, Laszló, 718, 765

Rákosi, Mátyás, 718, 765, 782

Rally of the French People (R.P.F.), 257 (n. 5), 267–8

Ramasswamy, M., 162 (n. 8)

Ranković, Aleksandar, 765

Rappard, William E., 603 (n. 6)

Rassay, Károly, 764

Rathenau, Walter, 437 (n. 5)

Razin, Stenka, 557

Reform Act, 1832, Great Britain, 11 (n. 7), 29–30, 33–4

Reform Act, 1867, Great Britain, 30, 34

Reformation, 22, 329, 330, 333

Regency Act, 1953, Great Britain, 85

regionalism: Eastern Europe, regional cooperation, 752; in France, 232 (n. 2); in Great Britain, 122–4; in Italy, 489–91, 525–6

Reichwein, Adolf, 394

Relander, Lauri Kristian, 765

Remer, General, O. E., 389

Renaissance, 333, 455

Renner, Karl, 706

Rent Act, 1957, Great Britain, 54

Report of the Machinery of Government Committee, 1918, Great Britain, 87

Representation of the People Act, 1884, Great Britain, 30

Representation of the People Act, 1918, Great Britain, 31

Representation of the People Act, 1948, Great Britain, 32

Republican Federation, France, 208

Republican Liberty Party, France, 265

Republican Party, Italy, 465, 480, 501, 511

republicanism: in Commonwealth of Nations, 152–3; in Eastern Europe, 793–4; in France, 195–7, 198; in Germany, 361–3; in Italy, 457, 461 (n. 6), 480

Rerum novarum, 1891, 466

Rettig, Erich von, 764

Reynaud, Paul, 216, 266, 291, 296, 299, 302, 304

Rheinbund, see Confederation of the Rhine

Rhondda, Viscountess, 62

Ribbentrop, Joachim von, 373, 381, 383

Richter, Eugen, 345

Richter, Werner, 352 (n. 7)

Richert, Ernst, 415 (n. 5)

Rigby, T. H., 686 (n. 1)

Rights of Entry Bill, 1954, Great Britain, 72

Ritter, Gerhard, 330 (n. 7), 334 (n. 1), 344 (n. 1)

Roberts, M., 168 (n. 2)

Robespierre, M., 191, 194, 206, 358

Robinson, Geroid T., 551 (n. 3)

Robson, W. A., 102 (n. 9)

Rocco, Alberto, 500

Roehm, Ernst, 379, 382, 383

Róg, Michal, 765

Rokossovsky, Marshal, 674, 684

Roman Empire, 327–8, 333, 455

Romanov, Mikhail, 549, 550

Rommel, Marshal Erwin, 388 (n. 3)

Roon, General Albrecht von, 347

Roosevelt, Elliott, 699, 713

Roosevelt, Franklin D., 226

Röpke, Wilhelm, 328 (n. 3)

Rosenberg, Alfred, 373

Rothfels, Hans, 344 (n. 1), 394 (n. 7)

Rousseau, Jean Jacques, 191, 194, 197, 206, 259

Rudnev, K. N., 658

Rumania: abdication of Michael, 1947, 794; independence, 747; interwar alliances, 749; minorities rights, 804; regime of Carol, 766; war against U.S.S.R., 770; *see also* Eastern Europe

Ruskin, John, 27

Rykov, A. I., 655

Ryti, Rysto H., 764

Saar question, 311, 439

Saburov, M. Z., 624, 626, 627, 655 (n. 5), 679

Sacherl, K., 420 (n. 4)

Sait, E. M., 78 (n. 2)

Sakazov, Yanko, 764

Salan, General Raoul, 294

Salandra, Antonio, 468, 472, 500

Salisbury, Lord, 38

Salomon, Ernst von, 400 (n. 4)

Salomone, Arcangelo Wm., 465 (n. 1)

Sanders, Irwin T., 816 (n. 1), 817 (n. 1)

Sandig, Helmut, 413 (n. 3)

Saragat, Giuseppe, 481, 496, 510, 706

Sauvy, Alfred, 290

Scelba, Mario, 497, 512

Schacht, Hjalmar, 374, 380, 386, 390

Schäffer, Fritz, 403 (n. 7)

Scharnhorst, General Gerhard von, 338, 347

Schaub, Julius, 383

Schauff, Johannes, 366 (n. 4)

Scheidemann, Philipp, 361

Schiller, Johann von, 325, 333, 359

Schirdewan, Karl, 411 (n. 8)

Schlegel, August W. von, 333

Schleicher, General Kurt von, 370, 371, 389

Schmertzing, Wolfgang P., 431 (n. 6)

Schmid, Carlo, 427

Schmitt, Bernadotte E., 332 (n. 8)

Schmitt, Carl, 363 (n. 5), 365 (n. 2)

Schmitt, Kurt, 386

Schnabel, Franz, 344 (n. 1)

Schoeps, Hans Joachim, 332 (n. 9)

Scholl, Hans and Sophie, 394

Schopenhauer, Arthur, 721

Schreck, Willi, 383

Schroder, Gerhard, 403 (n. 7)

Schueller, George K., 382 (n. 7)

Schultz, Joachim, 411 (n. 8)

Schultz, Theodore H., 436 (n. 3)

Schumacher, Kurt, 425, 426, 706

Schuman Plan, 310, 428
Schwartz, Bernard, 102
Schwartz, Harry, 542 (n. 2), 688 (n. 6)
Schwartz, S. M., 575 (n. 8)
Schwarz, Franz, 382
Schwerin-Krosigk, Count Lutz, 386
Scott report, 121, 130
Second International, 1889, formation, 704
Second Statute of Praemunire, 1393, England, 13 (n. 5)
Seddon, Richard, 163
Seebohm, Hans-Christoph, 403 (n. 7)
Seeckt, General Hans, 389, 437 (n. 5)
Segni, Antonio, 497, 509, 512, 513
Selbmann, Fritz, 411 (n. 8)
Seldte, Franz, 380, 386
Semichastny, V. E., 629
Senghor, Léopold, 249
separation of powers doctrine: in France, 195, 196, 197, 203, 214, 299; in Italy, 519; in Soviet theory, 634-5
serfdom, in Russia, 551-2
Sex Disqualification (Removal) Act, 1919, Great Britain, 62
Sforza, Carlo, 477 (n. 7), 530
Shabad, Theodore, 542 (n. 1)
Shapiro, L. B., 696 (n. 8)
Sharp, Samuel L., 815 (n. 9)
Shatalin, N. N., 627
Shave, D. W., 542 (n. 2)
Shaw, George Bernard, 28
Shelepin, A. N., 658
Shepard, Max A., 8 (n. 4)
Shepilov, D. T., 627, 720
Shkiriatov, M. F., 626
Shops Acts, Great Britain, 116, 140 (n. 3)
Shvernik, N. M., 624, 626, 651
Sicily, regional autonomy, 525, 526
Siegfried, Andre, 155
Sila Law, Italy, 485
Sima, Horia, 765
Simeon II, Bulgaria, 794
Simmons, Ernest J., 542
Sinn Fein, 37 (n. 2), 52 (n. 4)
Siroky, Viliam, 765, 787
Skog, Emil, 764
Slánský, Rudolf, 765
Slavsky, Y. P., 657
Smellie, K. B., 31
Smigly-Rydz, Marshal Edward, 765

Smith, Adam, 25, 46, 126
Smith, Goldwin, 159 (n. 5)
Smith, Sir Thomas, 22, 78
Smuts, Jan, 152-3, 167, 173
social contract: Bentham, 46; Burke, 24, 48; T. H. Green, 27, 46; Hobbes, 23-4; Locke, 23-4, 45-6, 81
Social Democratic Federation, Great Britain, 28, 50
Social Democratic Labor Party, Russia, 558, 561, 606
Social Democratic Party (S.P.D.), Germany: in Bonn Republic, 420, 425-9, 440; in East Germany, 410-11; resistance to Hitler, 394; in Second Empire, 349 (n. 3), 351, 355; in Weimar Republic, 358, 359, 360, 368
Social-Revolutionary Party, Russia, 557, 559
socialism: in Commonwealth of Nations, 156-7, 165-7, 169; in Eastern Europe, 755-6; in France, 260-2; in Germany, 351, 425-9; in Great Britain, 27-8, 50-2, 146-9; in Italy, 495-6; in U.S.S.R., 557-558; see also communism, specific socialist parties
Socialist parties, Eastern Europe, 755-756, 764
Socialist Party, France: Popular Front, 204; role in Constituent Assemblies, 1945-46, 208-12; postwar, 255-8, 260-2
Socialist Party, India, 169
Socialist Party (P.S.I.), Italy: and Mussolini, 468, 469, 470; murder of Matteoti, 471-2; and World War I, 466-8; post World War II, 480, 495-6, 511
Socialist Reich Party, Germany, declared unconstitutional, 431
Socialist Unity Party (S.E.D.), East Germany, 410, 411, 412
Society for the Dissemination of Political and Scientific Knowledge, U.S.S.R., 575
Sokolovsky, Marshal, 674
Sollmann, Friedrich, 371
Sonnino, Sidney, 468
Sorel, Georges, 358
Soulier, Auguste, 366 (n. 3)

Soustelle, Jacques, 294, 304
South Seas Regional Commission, 174
soviets, U.S.S.R.: elections to, 635–8;
    local, number, and functions, 638–
    642; party members in, 637; peas-
    ants, workers and intelligentia in,
    573–4; theory of their role, 632–
    635; union republic soviets, 642–7
Sovkhoz, 685
Sovnarkom, 653
Spaho, Mehmed, 764
Spanish Civil War, 390, 706
Speer, Albert, 385, 386, 394
Speidel, General Hans, 388 (n. 3)
Speier, Hans, 379 (n. 4)
Spencer, Herbert, 25 (n. 8), 46
Spengler, Oswald, 325
Speransky, Michael, 551
Sportintern, 711
Spiro, Herbert J., 435 (n. 9)
Spulber, Nicolas, 814
Šrámek, Monsignor Jan, 764
Srbik, Heinrich Ritter von, 344 (n. 1)
Stahl, Friedrich Julius, 343, 350
Stahlberg, Kaarlo Juho, 764
Stalin, Joseph: and anti-Semitism, 593;
    and army, 673; as chairman of the
    Council of Ministers, 655; and cult
    of the individual, 616; death, 624,
    655, 673, 674; de-emphasis of, 669;
    in Politburo, 626; party purges,
    612, 614
  views on: building up of Soviet
    strength, 553; capitalist encircle-
    ment, 568; diplomacy, 701; five
    year plans, 678; imperialism,
    695; international affairs, 694,
    698; intervention, 708; languages,
    589, 592, 593; and management
    of industry, 683; nationalities,
    591, 592; party organization,
    561, 562, 607, 608, 610, 613,
    615, 616; peaceful coexistence,
    713; League of Nations and
    United Nations, 698, 699, 700;
    roads to socialism, 807; secret
    police, 667, 668; socialism in one
    country, 677; withering away of
    the state, 568
Stambolisky, Alexander, 758, 765
Stammer, Otto, 414 (n. 4)
Starodubrovskaya, V., 817 (n. 2)
Starovsky, V. N., 658

Stassen, Harold, 713
Statute of the Provisors of Benefices,
    1351, England, 13 (n. 5)
Statute of Westminster, 1931, Great
    Britain, 85, 172, 176, 178
Statutory Instruments Act, 1946, Great
    Britain, 101
Statutory Orders Act, 1945, Great Brit-
    ain, 101
Stavisky scandal, 204
Stein, Freiherr Heinrich vom, 338, 347
    (n. 2)
Stein, Lorenz von, 353
Steinhoff, Karl, 409 (n. 4)
Steiniger, Alfons, 410 (n. 5)
Stennes, Walter, 379
Stephen, Sir James, 48
Stern, Carola, 411 (n. 7), 412 (n. 9)
Stern, Fritz, 419 (n. 3)
Sternberger, Dolf, 406 (n. 9)
Stevens, Edmund, 669 (n. 1)
Stojadinović, Milan, 765
Stolypin, P. A., 552
Stoph, Willy, 412 (n. 2)
Strachey, John, 145, 147, 375 (n. 1)
Stralcio law, 1950, Italy, 485
Strasser, Gregor, 373, 379
Strasser, Otto, 379
Strauss, Franz-Josef, 403 (n. 7)
Strauss, Johann, 332
Strayer, Joseph R., 15 (n. 6)
Stresemann, Gustav, 367, 368, 441
Strokin, N. I., 658
Strydom, J. G., 168
Stuchka, P., 569
Stücklen, Richard, 403 (n. 7)
Stumm interests, 348
Sturzo, Don Luigi, 466, 475, 496, 497,
    509 (n. 4), 517, 525
Šubašić, Ivan, 765, 773, 776
Suez crisis, 1956, 38, 150, 175, 531, 720
Suffrage: Commonwealth of Nations,
    156, 167–8, 170, 177; Eastern
    Europe, 797; France, 220, 250;
    Germany, 345, 365; Great Britain,
    29–32; Italy, 460, 462–3, 509;
    U.S.S.R., 573, 603, 637
Summerskill, Edith, 44 (n. 9)
Supplies and Services (Transitional
    Powers) Bill, Great Britain, 99
Supreme Soviet, U.S.S.R.: Council of
    Nationalities, 647–8; Council of
    the Union, 647–8; elections to,

635–8; party members in, 637, 649; procedure and functions, 649–650; social composition, 648

Suslov, M. A., 624, 626, 627, 684 (n. 8)

Švehla, Antonín, 765

Swansborough, Baroness of, 62

Sweden, 329, 341, 544, 778

Switzerland, 312, 337, 363

Sylos-Labini, Paolo, 487 (n. 4)

syndicalism, in France, and public enterprise, 242

Szakasits, Árpád, 764

Szálasi, Ferenc, 765

Szijj, Valentine, 765

Tacitus, 325, 327

Tanner, V. R., 16

Tanner, Väinö, 756, 764

Tătărescu, Gheorghe, 764

Tatarin-Tarnheyden, E., 361 (n. 3)

Tawney, R. H., 28, 126

taxation problems: France, 272, 278–280; in Great Britain, 143–4, 148; in Italy, 521

Taylor, A. J. P., 344 (n. 1)

Teleki, Pál, 765

Television Act, 1954, Great Britain, 132

Tevosyan, I. F., 626

Theodoric, 328

Third International, see Comintern

Thoma, R., 363 (n. 6)

Thorez, Maurice, 259

Thugutt, Stanislaw, 765

Thyssen interests, 348, 376

Tikhon, Patriarch, 581

Tildy, Zoltán, 765

Tillon, Charles, 259

Timasheff, Nicholas, 575

Timoshenko, Marshal S., 546

Tirpitz, Admiral Alfred von, 348

Tiso, Father Josef, 765

Tito, Marshal Josip Broz, 765, 769, 773, 787, 794, 798; Titoism, 312, 707–708, 785–6, 807

Titulescu, Nicolae, 764

Tocqueville, Alexis de, 191

Todt, Fritz, 385

Togliatti, Palmiro, 479 (n. 8), 491, 494

Tomsky (Michael P. Efremov), 614

Tories, Great Britain, 32, 33, 34

Törngren, Ralf J. G., 764

Touré, Sékou, 249, 297

Town and Country Planning Acts, Great Britain, 102, 120–2, 130

Towster, Julian, 571 (n. 6), 573 (n. 7), 611 (n. 1), 644 (n. 5), 653 (n. 4), 662 (n. 1), 666 (n. 7), 671 (n. 4), 715 (n. 1), 718 (n. 2)

Trade Disputes and Trade Unions Act, 1927, Great Britain, 139 (n. 9)

Trades Union Congress, Great Britain, 140

Transport Act, 1947, Great Britain, 131–2, 133

Transport Act, 1953, Great Britain, 133

Tremelloni, Roberto, 487 (n. 4)

Trevelyan-Northcote Report, 90–1

Triple Alliance, 466

Triple Entente, 355

Tribunals and Inquiries Act, 1958, Great Britain, 103, 109, 115

Troeltsch, Ernst, 329 (n. 4), 330 (n. 7)

Trollip, A. E. G., 168 (n. 2)

Trotsky, Leon, 614

Tsankov, Alexander, 763, 765

Turati, Filippo, 495

Turkey: and Eastern Europe, 742, 746, 752; and Italy, 466; and U.S.S.R., 541, 545, 718

Tusar, Vlastimir, 764

two-swords doctrine, 18–19

Ulbricht, Walter, 410 (n. 6), 411, 412, 413

Umberto, Prince, Italy, 478, 502

Union of Italian Labor, 498 (n. 6)

Union of South Africa: Afrikaans nationalism, 167–8; attack on liberalism, 168; citizenship legislation, 176–7; racial problems, 156, 168; see also Commonwealth of Nations

U.S.S.R.: area, population, resources, 541–6; army and auxiliaries, 670–675; attitudes toward international organizations and international law, 696–700; autocratic heritage, 546–50, 554–6; basic tenets of Marxism, 562–5; Bolsheviks, 558–560, 561–2; capitalist imperialism and wars, 693–6; Communist Party organization, 616–21; constitutions and constitutional theory and practice, 566–70, 599–605; Council of Ministers, 653–61; courts, 662–6; economic back-

U.S.S.R. (*continued*)
wardness, 553–4; economic planning, 676–82; educational policies, 571–6; elections to soviets, 635–8; elite position of Communist Party, 606–16; family, 579–81; foreign policy aims and techniques, 701–704, 712–15; fronts for Soviet foreign policy, 704–12; *Komsomol* and auxiliaries, 628–31; local soviets, 638–42; management of agriculture, 685–8; management of industry, 682–5; membership in Communist Party, 610–14; nationality and cultural policies, 584–90, 591–4, 598; Orthodox Church, 549–50, 581–4; party congress and central committee, 621–2; position of women, 577–8; Presidium (Politburo) or party, 623–8; Presidium of Supreme Soviet, 650–3; procurators, 666–7; recent foreign policy, 715–21; reforms under tsars, 550–553; revolution of 1917, 560–1; revolutionary movements under tsars, 556–8; role of soviets, 632–635; secret police, 667–71; social changes, 570–6, 595–8; soviets of the union-republics, 642–7; Supreme Soviet, 647–50; trade unions and corps, 688–92; youth, 578–9
United Nations: admission of Italy, 531; attitude of U.S.S.R., 698–700
United States: and Great Britain, 53, 149; influence in Commonwealth, 155, 156, 157–8, 159, 173–5, 179; relations with France, 308–13 *passim;* relations with Germany, 396–401, 437–41; relations with Italy, 483, 528–32; relations with Tito, 781; and U.S.S.R., 693–721 *passim;* World War II policies in Eastern Europe, 770–1
Universal Declaration of Human Rights, 803
Ustinov, D. F., 655, 657, 659
Uthwatt report, 1942, 121, 130
utilitarianism, British, 25–6, 28

Valjavec, Fritz, 350 (n. 5)
Vanoni, Ezio, 488, 510 (n. 5)
Varga, Béla, 765, 776
Vassilevsky, Marshal A., 674
Velchev, General Damyan, 765

Verwoerd, H. F., 168
Victor Emmanuel II, Italy, 460, 461, 476
Victor Emmanuel III, Italy, 362 (n. 4), 470, 476–7, 478
Victoria, Queen, Great Britain, 352
Vigorelli, Ezio, 514
Vittorio, Giuseppi di, 493
Vladimir, Grand Prince of Kiev, 549
Vlasov, A. A., 659 (n. 6)
Vogel, Walther, 407 (n. 1)
Volkov, A. P., 657
Volkskonservative, 338, 349 (n. 3)
Voroshilov, K. Y., 624, 626, 651, 783
Voznesensky, N. A., 679
Vrioni, Elias, 764
Vyshinsky, Andrei: party posts, 626; views on: Constitution of 1936, 566; dictatorship of the proletariat, 604; federation, 800; international law, 696, 697; rights and duties of U.S.S.R. citizens, 602; Soviet law and courts, 569, 667, 802

Wach, Joachim, 329 (n. 4)
Wages Councils Acts, Great Britain, 140 (n. 4)
Wagner, Joseph, 386
Waldersee, Count Alfred, 352
Wallenius, Kurt, 765
Wallich, Henry C., 433 (n. 7)
Walpole, Sir Robert, 59
Wan Min, 707 (n. 5)
Ward, Irene, 72
Warren, J. H., 117 (n. 4)
Warriner, D., 745 (n. 5), 812 (n. 7)
Wartenburg, Yorck von, 394
Webb, Beatrice, 28, 51, 80
Webb, Sidney (Lord Passfield), 28, 51, 80
Weber, Alfred, 334 (n. 1)
Weber, Max, 329 (n. 4), 358
Weber, Werner, 407 (n. 1)
Weisberg, Harold L., 662 (n. 1)
Welchert, H. H., 417 (n. 1)
Wensleydale, Lord, 63
Werner, Bruno E., 394 (n. 8)
West Indies, 157
Weymar, Paul, 418 (n. 2)
Wheare, K. C., 102 (n. 9), 172 (n. 3)
Wheeler-Bennett, John W., 358 (n. 1)
White, D. Fedotoff, 671 (n. 4)
Wiedemann, Carl, 383

William I (Conqueror), England, 12, 13, 14
William I, Germany, 339, 341, 352
William II, England, 13
William II, Germany, 324, 341, 343, 346, 352–5, 362, 382
William of Occam, 20
Williams, Philip, 221 (n. 5), 225 (n. 8)
Wilson, H. H., 93 (n. 8)
Wilson, Woodrow, Fourteen Points, 391
Windhorst, Ludwig, 330
Winstanley, Gerrard, 25 (n. 6), 27
Wirth, Joseph, 368
With Burning Sorrow, 1937, 393
Witos, Wincenty, 765
Wochenblattpartei, 338
Wolfe, B. D., 668 (n. 8)
Wolfe, D. M., 25 (n. 5)
Wolfers, Arnold, 396 (n. 2)
Wolff, Károly, 764
Wollweber, Ernst, 411 (n. 8)
World Congress of the Partisans of Peace, 650
World Federation of Democratic Youth, 709, 711
World Federation of Trade Unions (W.F.T.U.), 709, 710
World Peace Congress, 709, 711
Wuermeling, Franz-Josef, 403 (n. 7)
Wurm, Bishop, 393
Wyclif, John, 20, 21
Wyszynski, Cardinal, 786

Xoxe, Koci, 765

Yalta Conference, 308, 545, 770, 771, 773
Yelyutin, V. P., 657
Yenyutin, G. V., 657

Yermak, the Cossack, 545
York Tracts, 19
Young, C. M., 161 (n. 6)
Young, Desmond, 388 (n. 3)
Young Persons Employment Act, 1938, Great Britain, 140 (n. 3)
Young Plan, 363
Ypi, Djafer, 764
Yudin, P. F., 626
Yugoslavia: exile government in World War II, 769, 771, 773; independence, 747; interwar royalist regime, 766; overthrow of Peter II, 794; rise of Tito, 771, 773; Titoism, 781, 783–4, 785–7; Trieste question, 529; *see also* Eastern Europe
Yugov, Anton, 765
Yugow, A., 575 (n. 8)

Zápotocký, Antonin, 765, 787
Zasyadko, Alexander F., 657, 659
Zenkl, Petr, 764
Zentrum, see Center party, Germany
Zhadanov, Andrei, 714
Zhukov, Marshal Georgii, 624, 627, 673, 674, 675, 720
Zichy, János, 764
Zimmermann, Hartmut, 413 (n. 3)
Zimmerwald Conference, 704
Zink, Harold, 98 (n. 3), 397 (n. 3)
Zinn, Friedrich A., 427
Zinoviev, G. E., 614
Živković, Petar, 765
Zog, Albania, 765, 766, 773, 794
Zogu, 764, 765
Zoli, Adone, 497, 509, 513
Zotov, V. P., 658
Zotschew, Theodore, 436 (n. 3)
Zverev, A. G., 626, 657

A NOTE ON THE TYPE

The text of this book was set on the Linotype in a face called TIMES ROMAN, *designed by* STANLEY MORISON *for* The Times (*London*), *and first introduced by that newspaper in 1932.*

Among typographers and designers of the twentieth century, Stanley Morison has been a strong forming influence, as typographical adviser to the English Monotype Corporation, as a director of two distinguished English publishing houses, and as a writer of sensibility, erudition, and keen practical sense.

In 1930 Morison wrote: "Type design moves at the pace of the most conservative reader. The good type-designer therefore realises that, for a new fount to be successful, it has to be so good that only very few recognize its novelty. If readers do not notice the consummate reticence and rare discipline of a new type, it is probably a good letter." It is now generally recognized that in the creation of Times Roman *Morison successfully met the qualifications of this theoretical doctrine.*

Composed, printed, and bound by H. Wolff, New York. Paper manufactured by P. H. Glatfelter Company, Spring Grove, Pennsylvania.

DATE DUE

NOV 12 '70			
OCT 26 '72			
GAYLORD			PRINTED IN U.S A.